MM

canadian

marketing

thirteenth

management

edition

philip
KOTLER
NORTHWESTERN UNIVERSITY

kevin lane
KELLER
DARTMOUTH COLLEGE

peggy h.
CUNNINGHAM
DALHOUSIE UNIVERSITY

subramanian
SIVARAMAKRISHNAN
UNIVERSITY OF MANITOBA

MM

canadian
marketing
thirteenth
management
edition

Pearson Canada
Toronto

Library and Archives Canada Cataloguing in Publication

Marketing management/Philip Kotler . . . [et al.]—Canadian 13th ed.

Includes index.
ISBN 978-0-13-206397-5

1. Marketing—Management—Textbooks.   I. Kotler, Philip.

HF5415.13.K68 2009   658.8   C2008-903608-5

ISBN-13: 978-0-13-206397-5
ISBN-10:   0-13-206397-2

Vice-President, Editorial Director: Gary Bennett
Acquisitions Editor: Don Thompson
Marketing Manager: Leigh-Anne Graham
Developmental Editor: Michelle Harrington
Production Editor: Imee Salumbides
Copy Editor: Laura Neves
Proofreader: Michael Arkin
Production Coordinators: Patricia Ciardullo and Sarah Lukaweski
Compositor: Macmillan Publishing Solutions
Photo and Permissions Researcher: Lisa Brant
Art Director: Julia Hall
Cover and Interior Designer: Anthony Leung

1 2 3 4 5   12 11 10 09 08

Printed and bound in the United States of America.

ABOUT THE AUTHORS

Philip Kotler is one of the world's leading authorities on marketing. He is the S. C. Johnson & Son Distinguished Professor of International Marketing at the Kellogg School of Management, Northwestern University. He received his master's degree at the University of Chicago and his Ph.D. at MIT, both in economics. He did postdoctoral work in mathematics at Harvard University and in behavioral science at the University of Chicago.

Dr. Kotler is the co-author of *Principles of Marketing* and *Marketing: An Introduction*. His *Strategic Marketing for Nonprofit Organizations*, now in its sixth edition, is the best seller in that specialized area. Dr. Kotler's other books include *Marketing Models; The New Competition; Marketing Professional Services; Strategic Marketing for Educational Institutions; Marketing for Health Care Organizations; Marketing Congregations; High Visibility; Social Marketing; Marketing Places; The Marketing of Nations; Marketing for Hospitality and Tourism; Standing Room Only—Strategies for Marketing the Performing Arts; Museum Strategy and Marketing; Marketing Moves; Kotler on Marketing; Lateral Marketing: Ten Deadly Marketing Sins;* and *Corporate Social Responsibility.*

In addition, he has published more than one hundred articles in leading journals, including the *Harvard Business Review, Sloan Management Review, Business Horizons, California Management Review,* the *Journal of Marketing,* the *Journal of Marketing Research, Management Science,* the *Journal of Business Strategy,* and *Futurist.* He is the only three-time winner of the coveted Alpha Kappa Psi award for the best annual article published in the *Journal of Marketing.*

Professor Kotler was the first recipient of the American Marketing Association's (AMA) Distinguished Marketing Educator Award (1985). The European Association of Marketing Consultants and Sales Trainers awarded him their Prize for Marketing Excellence. He was chosen as the Leader in Marketing Thought by the Academic Members of the AMA in a 1975 survey. He also received the 1978 Paul Converse Award of the AMA, honoring his original contribution to marketing. In 1995, the Sales and Marketing Executives International (SMEI) named him Marketer of the Year. In 2002, Professor Kotler received the Distinguished Educator Award from The Academy of Marketing Science. He has received honorary doctoral degrees from Stockholm University, the University of Zurich, Athens University of Economics and Business, DePaul University, the Cracow School of Business and Economics, Groupe H.E.C. in Paris, the Budapest School of Economic Science and Public Administration, and the University of Economics and Business Administration in Vienna.

Professor Kotler has been a consultant to many major U.S. and foreign companies, including IBM, General Electric, AT&T, Honeywell, Bank of America, Merck, SAS Airlines, Michelin, and others in the areas of marketing strategy and planning, marketing organization, and international marketing.

He has been Chairman of the College of Marketing of the Institute of Management Sciences, a Director of the American Marketing Association, a Trustee of the Marketing Science Institute, a Director of the MAC Group, a member of the Yankelovich Advisory Board, and a member of the Copernicus Advisory Board. He was a member of the Board of Governors of the School of the Art Institute of Chicago and a member of the Advisory Board of the Drucker Foundation. He has traveled extensively throughout Europe, Asia, and South America, advising and lecturing to many companies about global marketing opportunities.

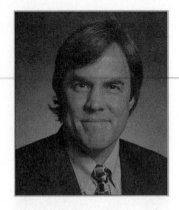

Kevin Lane Keller is the E. B. Osborn Professor of Marketing at the Tuck School of Business at Dartmouth College. Professor Keller has degrees from Cornell, Carnegie-Mellon, and Duke universities. At Dartmouth, he teaches an MBA elective on strategic brand management and lectures in executive programs on that topic. Previously, Professor Keller was on the faculty of the Graduate School of Business at Stanford University, where he also served as the head of the marketing group. Additionally, he has been on the marketing faculty at the University of California at Berkeley and the University of North Carolina at Chapel Hill, been a visiting professor at Duke University and the Australian Graduate School of Management, and has two years of industry experience as Marketing Consultant for Bank of America.

Professor Keller's general area of expertise is in consumer marketing. His specific research interest is in how understanding theories and concepts related to consumer behavior can improve marketing strategies. The research has been published in over fifty papers in three of the major marketing journals—the *Journal of Marketing*, the *Journal of Marketing Research*, and the *Journal of Consumer Research*. He also has served on the Editorial Review Boards of those journals. His research has been widely cited and has received numerous awards.

Professor Keller is acknowledged as one of the international leaders in the study of brands, branding, and strategic brand management. Actively involved with industry, he has worked on a host of different types of marketing projects. He has served as brand confidant to marketers for some of the world's most successful brands, including Accenture, American Express, Disney, Ford, Intel, Levi Strauss, Miller Brewing, Procter & Gamble, and Starbucks. He has done additional brand consulting with other top companies such as Allstate, Beiersdorf (Nivea), Blue Cross Blue Shield, Campbell Soup, General Mills, Goodyear, Kodak, The Mayo Clinic, Nordstrom, Shell Oil, Unilever, and Young & Rubicam. He is also an academic trustee for the Marketing Science Institute. A popular speaker, he has conducted marketing seminars and workshops with top executives in a variety of forums.

Professor Keller is currently conducting studies that address marketing strategies and tactics to build, measure, and manage brand equity. His textbook on those subjects, *Strategic Brand Management*, the second edition of which was published September 2002 by Prentice-Hall, has been heralded as the "bible of branding."

An avid sports, music, and film enthusiast, in his spare time, he helps to manage and market one of Australia's great rock and roll treasures, *The Church*. Professor Keller lives in New Hampshire with his wife, Punam (also a Tuck marketing professor), and his two daughters, Carolyn and Allison.

Peggy Cunningham is the R.A. Jodrey Chair, the Director of the School of Business Administration, and the Associate Dean of the Faculty of Management, Dalhousie University. She received her undergraduate degree from Queen's University, her MBA from the University of Calgary, and her Ph.D. from Texas A&M University. She was the founding Director of the Accelerated MBA program for business graduates (2001–2004). She previously was the Co-Chair of the E-Commerce Research Program (1998–2001), and she is currently one of the founding members of the Global Responsible Leadership Initiative (2004–present). She has considerable international experience and has been a visiting professor at universities and government training programs in France, Germany, China, the U.K., and the U.S. Her experience in industry and consulting helps her bring the perspective of the practitioner to the study of marketing. Her research interests centre on two related themes: marketing ethics and marketing partnerships (international strategic alliances and partnerships between for-profit and not-for-profit organizations). While these may seem like totally divergent areas of study, they are linked by their focus on the concepts of trust, integrity, and commitment which are the core elements to both ethical behaviour and successful partnership behaviour. She has received a number of awards for this work including the ANBAR citation award for her Strategic Alliances article written with Rajan Varadarajan and a nomination for the 2006 Accenture Award for her work in Social Alliances with Ida Berger and Meme Drumwright. Her research is published in a number of journals including the *Journal of the Academy of Marketing Science*, the *California Management Review*, and the *Journal of International Marketing*. She is a devoted teacher who tries to inspire her students to realize their full and unique potential. She currently teaches courses in marketing management and strategy, marketing ethics, and branding in the B.Comm., M.Sc., Ph.D., and Executive training programs. She is one of Queen's University's most acclaimed and awarded teaching professors. In 2004, she received the PricewaterhouseCoopers Leaders in Management Education award. She was named the Academy of Marketing Science's Outstanding Teacher in 2001. She has been nominated twice for the Frank Knox Award for Teaching Excellence, one of the most prestigious awards given at Queen's for undergraduate teaching. She won this award in 1993. Dr. Cunningham also does a considerable amount of research and writing to further educational practice. She has written over 40 cases that have been used in case competitions and have been published in a number of leading North American marketing textbooks.

Subramanian (Subbu) Sivaramakrishnan is Associate Professor of Marketing at the I. H. Asper School of Business, University of Manitoba. Subbu got his Ph.D. in Marketing from Penn State University, an MBA from Bharathiar University, India, and B.Sc. Mathematics from Madras Christian College, India.

Subbu has received several awards for teaching. He received the Associates Award for Teaching from the University of Manitoba. He was also honored with an Award for Innovative Teaching by the University of Arkansas and an Outstanding Teaching Award by Penn State University. Subbu has been teaching at the Universidad de Murcia in Spain as a Visiting Professor for the last 18 years.

Subbu's research concerns use of information in decision-making. His research interests extend to knowledge management by organizations and to online marketing. His recent publications have appeared in the *International Journal of Research in Marketing*, *Journal of Product & Brand Management*, *Journal of Interactive Marketing*, and *Journal of Strategic Marketing*. Subbu is the recipient of two large research grants from the *Social Sciences and Humanities Research Council of Canada*.

BRIEF CONTENTS

CONTENTS

WHAT IS MARKETING MANAGEMENT ALL ABOUT?

Marketing Management is the leading marketing text because its content and organization consistently reflect changes in marketing theory and practice. The very first edition of *Marketing Management*, published in 1967, introduced the concept that companies must be customer and market-driven. But there was no mention of what have become fundamental topics, such as segmentation, targeting, and positioning. Concepts such as brand equity, customer value analysis, database marketing, e-commerce, value networks, hybrid channels, supply chain management, and integrated marketing communications were not even part of the marketing vocabulary then. Firms now sell goods and services through a variety of direct and indirect channels. Mass advertising is not nearly as effective as it was. Companies are exploring new forms of communication, such as experiential, entertainment, and viral marketing. Customers are increasingly telling companies what types of product or services they want and when, where, and how they want to buy them.

In response, companies have shifted gears from managing product portfolios to managing customer portfolios, compiling databases on individual customers so they can understand them better, and constructing individualized offerings and messages. They are doing less product and service standardization and more customization. They are replacing monologues with customer dialogues. They are improving their methods of measuring customer profitability and customer lifetime value. They are intent on measuring the return on their marketing investment and its impact on shareholder value. They are also concerned with the ethical, social, and environmental implications of their marketing decisions.

As companies change, so does their marketing organization. Marketing is no longer a company department charged with a limited number of tasks—it is a company-wide undertaking. It drives the company's vision, mission, and strategic planning. Marketing includes decisions like who the company wants as its customers; which needs to satisfy; what products and services to offer; what prices to set; what communications to send and receive; what channels of distribution to use; and what partnerships to develop. Marketing succeeds only when all departments work together to achieve goals: when engineering designs the right products, finance furnishes the required funds, purchasing buys quality materials, production makes quality products on time, and accounting measures the profitability of different customers, products, and areas.

To address all these different shifts, good marketers are practicing holistic marketing.

Holistic marketing can be seen as the development, design, and implementation of marketing programs, processes, and activities that recognize the breadth and interdependencies involved in today's marketing environment. Holistic marketing recognizes that *everything matters* with marketing and that a broad, integrated perspective is often necessary. Holistic marketing has four key dimensions:

- *Internal marketing,* which means ensuring everyone in the organization embraces appropriate marketing principles, especially senior management.
- *Integrated marketing,* which means ensuring that multiple means of creating, delivering, and communicating value are employed and combined in the optimal manner.
- *Relationship marketing* and having rich, multifaceted relationships with customers, channel members, and other marketing partners.
- *Socially responsible marketing* in understanding the ethical, legal, environmental, and social effects of marketing.

These four dimensions are woven throughout the book and at times spelled out explicitly. The text specifically addresses the following tasks that constitute modern marketing management in the 21st century and is organized in eight parts to allow for maximum flexibility:

1. Understanding Marketing Management
2. Capturing Marketing Insights
3. Connecting with Customers

WHAT MAKES MARKETING MANAGEMENT THE MARKETING LEADER?

Marketing is of interest to everyone, whether they are marketing goods, services, properties, persons, places, events, information, ideas, or organizations. As the "ultimate authority" for students and educators, *Marketing Management* must be kept up-to-date and contemporary. Students (and instructors) should feel that the book is talking to them directly in terms of both content and delivery.

The success of *Marketing Management* can be attributed to its ability to maximize three dimensions that characterize the best marketing texts—depth, breadth, and relevance—as reflected by the following questions.

- *Depth.* Does the book have solid academic grounding? Does it contain important theoretical concepts, models, and frameworks? Does it provide conceptual guidance to solve practical problems?

- *Breadth.* Does the book cover all the right topics? Does it provide the proper amount of emphasis on those topics?

- *Relevance.* Does the book engage the reader? Is the book interesting to read? Does it have lots of compelling examples?

The thirteenth Canadian edition builds on the fundamental strengths of past editions:

- *Managerial Orientation.* The book focuses on the major decisions that marketing managers and top management face in their efforts to harmonize the organization's objectives, capabilities, and resources with marketplace needs and opportunities.

- *Analytical Approach.* This book presents conceptual tools and frameworks for analyzing recurrent problems in marketing management. Cases and examples illustrate effective marketing principles, strategies, and practices.

- *Multidisciplinary Perspective.* This book draws on the rich findings of various disciplines—ethics and corporate social responsibility, economics, behavioural science, management theory, information technology, and mathematics—for fundamental concepts and tools.

- *Universal Applications.* This book applies strategic thinking to the complete spectrum of marketing: products and services, consumer and business markets, profit and nonprofit organizations, domestic and foreign companies, small and large firms, manufacturing and intermediary businesses, and low- and high-tech industries.

- *Comprehensive and Balanced Coverage.* This book covers all the topics an informed marketing manager needs to understand to execute strategic, tactical, and administrative marketing

REVISION STRATEGY FOR THE THIRTEENTH EDITION

As marketing techniques and organizations have changed, so has this text. The thirteenth edition is designed not only to preserve the strengths of previous editions, but also to introduce new material and organization to further enhance learning. We retained the key theme of holistic marketing, and the recognition that 'everything matters' with marketing and that a broad, integrated perspective is often necessary. This theme is not developed so deeply, however, that it would restrict or inhibit an instructor's flexibility and teaching approach. To provide flexibility in the classroom, we also retained the new modular structure and eight parts corresponding to the eight key marketing management tasks. The thirteenth edition was changed to include the following:

- All chapters have new introductory vignettes that set the stage for the chapter material to follow. By covering topical brands or companies, the vignettes serve as great discussion starters.
- **Marketing Insight** boxes delve into important marketing topics, often highlighting current research findings. New and updated Marketing Insight boxes include such topics as "Eco-Friendly Marketing," "Understanding Brain Science," "Negative Emotional Appeals in Social Marketing," "Product Placements in Children's Entertainment," and "Country-of-Origin: To Communicate or Not?"
- **Marketing Memo** boxes offer practical advice and direction in dealing with various decisions at all stages of the marketing management process. New and updated Marketing Memo boxes include "Calculating Customer Lifetime Value," "Hey Marketer, Leave the Kids Alone," "Types of Illegal Pricing," "Maximizing Customer References," and "Segmenting Tech Users."
- About ten in-text boxes are included in each chapter, with roughly two-thirds new. These in-text boxes provide vivid illustrations of chapter concepts using actual companies and situations. The boxes cover a variety of products, services, and markets, and many have accompanying ads or products shots.
- Chapters are updated throughout, especially in terms of academic references and Canadian content.
- At the end of each chapter, the Marketing Applications section has two practical exercises to challenge students: **Marketing Debate** suggests opposing points of view on an important marketing topic from the chapter and asks students to take a side. **Marketing Discussion** identifies provocative marketing issues and allows for a personal point of view. **Breakthrough Marketing** boxes replace the Marketing Spotlight boxes from the twelfth edition. Each chapter has one box that highlights innovative and insightful marketing accomplishments by leading organizations.

NEW FOR THE THIRTEENTH EDITION: INTRODUCING PEARSON ONE AND GLOBAL CASES

Each title in this series is part of a collaborative global editorial development process that aligns the talent and expertise of Pearson's authors, editors, and production capabilities from around the world. Titles in the Pearson One Series offer students increased understanding of the global business environment through content and cases, with both local and global relevance.

Marketing Management, 13th edition, an international bestseller by Philip Kotler and Kevin Keller, has been translated into 26 different languages. It has been adapted into English language editions for the US, Asia, Canada, Europe, Africa, the Middle East and Australia. The current edition was simultaneously developed and produced to launch around the world through an innovative publishing model that brought our authors and editors together in a truly global endeavour.

Readers of the Canadian edition will benefit from these diverse perspectives and expertise through our international case studies, authored by our partners worldwide. These cases will be identified by a marginal note in each chapter linked to relevant content and available through links on our Companion Website.

NEW! GLOBAL CASES

The new edition of *Marketing Management* features global case studies based on the international versions of the book. The cases come from the US, India, China, Middle East, other parts of Asia, Europe, Africa, and Australia. Also included are Canadian cases. These cases give students insight into international business from the perspective of local authors. These cases are identified by a marginal note in each chapter linked to relevant content on our Companion Website.

CHAPTER BY CHAPTER CHANGES. This edition has been both streamlined and expanded to bring essentials and classic examples into sharper focus, while covering new concepts and ideas in depth. Some chapters received more extensive revisions than others. Here is an overview of the chapter changes:

- Chapter 1, *Defining Marketing for the Twenty-First Century,* now covers the role of Chief Marketing Officer (CMO) and information on what makes a great marketer. The chapter also includes material on internal marketing and effective marketing departments.

- Chapter 2, *Developing Marketing Strategies and Plans,* has new coverage on market sensing and becoming more market-driven as well as assigning resources to SBUs.

- Chapter 3, *Gathering Information and Scanning the Environment,* has new sections to reflect the move toward "green" marketing and the increasing use of technology by marketers. Moreover, demographic data throughout the chapter have been updated based on the 2006 Statistics Canada census and other recent reports.

- Chapter 4, *Conducting Marketing Research and Forecasting Demand,* has a feature on neuroscience, one of the latest developments in marketing research. It also has a new section on marketing metrics.

- Chapter 5, *Creating Customer Value, Satisfaction, and Loyalty,* introduces material on calculating Customer Lifetime Value and outlines the success and failure factors of Customer Relationship Management.

- Chapter 6, *Analyzing Consumer Markets,* includes a section on the legal aspects of advertising to children. Keeping up with the latest trends in consumer behaviour amongst university students, a discussion feature on online social networking (e.g., Facebook) has been provided.

- Chapter 7, *Analyzing Business Markets,* now contains a discussion feature on how B2B marketers are becoming increasingly eco-friendly. A section on the Dos and Don'ts of developing customer references has been added.

- Chapter 8, *Identifying Market Segments and Targets,* includes discussion of niche marketing and the 'long tail,' consumers trading up and down, and coverage of the brand funnel.

- Chapter 9, *Creating Brand Equity,* includes discussion of brand equity models, internal branding, brand valuation, and customer equity.

- Chapter 10, *Crafting the Brand Positioning,* discusses creating new markets and categories, and building a breakaway brand.

- Chapter 11, *Dealing with Competition,* discusses value innovation ('blue ocean thinking'), selecting customers, and competing with value-based rivals.

- Chapter 12, *Setting Product Strategy,* includes coverage of product returns, and product and product line simplification.

- Chapter 13, *Designing and Managing Services,* discusses customer empowerment, coproduction, customer interface systems, and service strategies for product companies.

- Chapter 14, *Developing Pricing Strategies and Programs,* presents the results of exciting research on the placebo effect of price discounts. In addition, it has a new section that discusses illegal pricing methods and an interesting feature on the strategic aspects of setting parking rates.

- Chapter 15, *Designing and Managing Integrated Marketing Channels,* discusses channel stewardship and e-marketing.

- Chapter 16, *Managing Retailing, Wholesaling, and Logistics,* includes coverage of the new retail environment, 'fast-forward' retailers, RFIDs, and private-label competition.

- Chapter 17, *Designing and Managing Integrated Marketing Communications,* has new sections on the use of negative appeals and sports celebrities in advertising. It also provides guidelines on how to specify a target market.

- Chapter 18, *Managing Mass Communications: Advertising, Sales Promotions, Events, and Public Relations,* now includes a feature on product placement directed at kids.

- Chapter 19, *Managing Personal Communications: Direct Marketing and Personal Selling,* introduces new material on segmenting technology users and mobile marketing. It also provides tips on how to identify good salespeople and discusses strategies for motivating the sales force.

- Chapter 20, *Introducing New Market Offerings,* includes a discussion on the success and failure factors of brand extensions. The chapter also provides guidelines on how to draw new product ideas from customers.
- Chapter 21, *Tapping into Global Markets,* now has an expanded feature on the standardization versus adaptation decision that international marketers have to make. A feature providing research highlights on the country-of-origin effect has been added.
- Chapter 22, *Managing a Holistic Marketing Organization,* features discussion of new developments in social responsibility, cause marketing guidelines, marketing metrics, and marketing creativity and discipline.

Additional concepts that have been added or explored in greater detail include customer relationship management, database marketing, customer equity, eco-friendly marketing, marketing to small businesses, questionnaire design, brand management principles, cause-related marketing, consumer decision heuristics, consumer involvement, consumer memory models, events and experiences, innovation and creativity, qualitative research techniques, marketing metrics, mental accounting, reference prices, and sponsorships.

THE TEACHING AND LEARNING PACKAGE

Marketing Management is an entire package of materials available to students and instructors. This edition includes a number of ancillaries designed to make the marketing management course an exciting, dynamic, and interactive experience.

INSTRUCTOR'S RESOURCE CD-ROM. One source for all of your supplement needs. The IRCD includes all the same supplements hosted at our online catalogue; however, the PowerPoint Media Rich set is provided only on this CD-ROM due to its larger file size and embedded video clips. The CD-ROM also contains many images from the textbook, which you may incorporate into your lectures.

INSTRUCTOR RESOURCES ON THE ONLINE CATALOGUE. The Pearson Education Canada online catalogue at http://vig.pearsoned.ca is where instructors can access our complete array of teaching materials. Simply go to the catalogue page for this text and click on the Instructor link to download the Instructor's Manual, TestGen, PowerPoint slides (Basic only), and more.

INSTRUCTOR'S RESOURCE MANUAL. The Instructor's Resource Manual includes chapter/ summary overviews, key teaching objectives, answers to end-of-chapter materials, Harvard Business School case suggestions, exercises, projects, and detailed lecture outlines. A new feature, "Professors on the Go!", was created with the busy professor in mind. It brings key material upfront, where an instructor who is short on time can find key points and assignments that can be incorporated into the lecture, without having to page through all the material provided for each chapter.

TESTGEN. The TestGen contains more than 3,000 multiple-choice, true-false, short-answer, and essay questions, with page reference and difficulty level provided for each question. *A new feature is an entire section of application questions.* These real-life situations take students beyond basic chapter concepts and vocabulary and ask them to apply marketing skills. The TestGen is available on the IRCD and from the online catalogue.

POWERPOINTS. When it comes to PowerPoints, Pearson Education Canada knows one size does not fit all. That's why *Marketing Management,* Canadian Thirteenth Edition, offers instructors more than one option.

- **PowerPoint BASIC.** This simple presentation includes only basic outlines and key points from each chapter. No animation or forms of rich media are integrated, which makes the total file size manageable and easier to share online or via email. BASIC was also designed for instructors who prefer to customize PowerPoints or want to avoid having to strip out animation, embedded files, or other media rich features.
- **PowerPoint MEDIA RICH.** This media-rich alternative includes basic outlines and key points from each chapter, plus advertisements and art from the text, images from outside the text,

discussion questions, weblinks, and embedded video snippets. It's the best option if you want a complete presentation solution. Instructors can further customize this presentation using the image library featured on the IRCD.

Aside from these two PowerPoint options, a select number of slides, based on the media-rich version, are also available as overhead transparencies.

CBC/PEARSON EDUCATION CANADA LIBRARY. This supplement features video segments and accompanying cases.

COMPANION WEBSITE. This site offers students valuable resources including quizzes, internet exercises and more at www.pearsoned.ca/kotler

MARKETING MANAGEMENT CASES. Prentice Hall Custom Business Resources can provide instructors and students with all of the cases and articles needed to enhance and maximize learning in a marketing course. Instructors can create Custom CoursePacks or Custom CaseBooks. Resources include top-tier cases from Darden, Harvard, Ivey, NACRA, and Thunderbird, plus full access to a database of articles. For details on how to order these value-priced packages, contact your local Pearson representative.

MARKETING PLAN: A HANDBOOK, THIRD EDITION, WITH MARKETING PLANPRO. Marketing PlanPro is a highly rated commercial software program that guides students through the entire marketing plan process. The software is totally interactive and features 10 sample marketing plans, step-by-step guides, and customizable charts. Customize your marketing plan to fit your marketing needs by following easy-to-use plan wizards. Follow the clearly outlined steps from strategy to implementation. Click to print, and your text, spreadsheet, and charts come together to create a powerful marketing plan. The new *Marketing Plan: A Handbook*, by Marian Burk Wood, supplements the in-text marketing plan material with an in-depth guide to what student marketers really need to know. A structured learning process leads to a complete and actionable marketing plan. Also included are timely, real-world examples that illustrate key points, sample marketing plans, and Internet resources. The Handbook and Marketing PlanPro software are available as value-pack items at a discounted price. Contact your local Pearson representative for more information.

ACKNOWLEDGMENTS

Without excellent students and exciting and productive colleagues, no instructor or author can stay vibrant and connected. I wish to thank the following colleagues at other schools who have reviewed past editions of this book including:

- Lilly Buchwitz, Brock University
- Sheldon Deitcher, McGill University
- Bill Lucas, Mohawk College
- John Milne, York University
- Doug Olsen, University of Alberta
- Charles Royce, McGill University
- David Smith, Lakehead University

This book is truly a team effort rather than the product of any single person's work. I also wish to thank the entire Pearson team who worked so hard to make this book a success: Michelle Harrington, Don Thompson, Imee Salumbides, Patricia Ciardullo, and John Polanszky. I am grateful for their hard work, patience, efficiency, and good humour. My overriding debt continues to be to my husband, Paul, who provides me with the love, time, support, and inspiration needed to prepare this edition. I also wish to thank my daughter, Krista, a former business student and marketing practitioner, who critiques my work with a user's vigilant eye.

Peggy H. Cunningham
Professor
Director, School of Business Administration
Associate Dean, Faculty of Management
R.A. Jodrey Chair
Dalhousie University, Halifax, Nova Scotia

I really appreciate the excellent research assistance provided by Jesse Finlay, Arun Iyer, Andrea Jasysyn, Shailos Levreault, Lauren MacKay, Lee Milne, Kathryn Patrick, Chelsea Peters, Blair Purvis, Gillian Purvis, and Esther Schultz. I could not have co-authored this book without their contribution. I am grateful to the Pearson team—Don Thompson, Michelle Harrington, Imee Salumbides, Duncan Mackinnon, and Laura Neves—for their outstanding professionalism, support, and patience throughout the publication process. Working with them was indeed a pleasure. I am indebted to Peggy Cunningham, who was my mentor during the writing process and generously shared her authoring expertise with me. I am very thankful to two close family members, L. V. V. Iyer and S. H. Sarma, who constantly encouraged me to write a book some day. Last, but not least, I thank my wife Kala and children Varsha and Varun for the sacrifices they made to give me time to write, and to my family in India for their support all along.

Subramanian (Subbu) Sivaramakrishnan
Associate Professor, Department of Marketing
I. H. Asper School of Business
University of Manitoba

A Great Way to Learn and Instruct Online

The Pearson Education Canada Companion Website is easy to navigate and is organized to correspond to the chapters in this textbook. Whether you are a student in the classroom or a distance learner you will discover helpful resources for in-depth study and research that empower you in your quest for greater knowledge and maximize your potential for success in the course.

[www.pearsoned.ca/kotler]

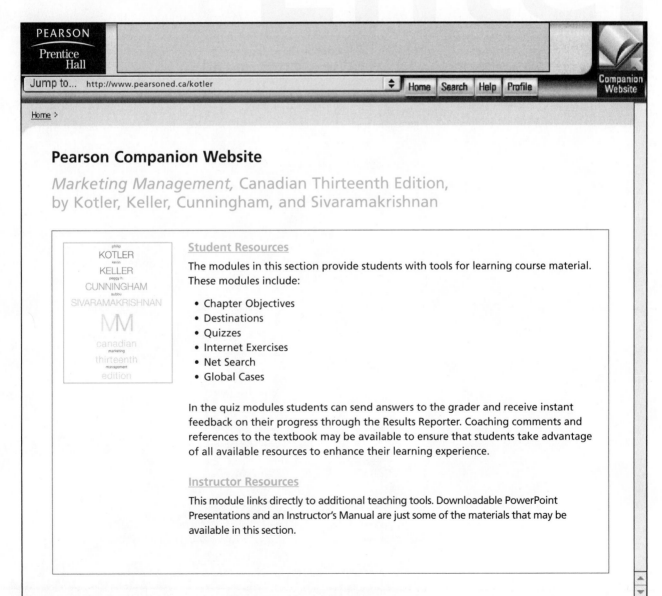

Pearson Companion Website

Marketing Management, Canadian Thirteenth Edition, by Kotler, Keller, Cunningham, and Sivaramakrishnan

Student Resources

The modules in this section provide students with tools for learning course material. These modules include:

- Chapter Objectives
- Destinations
- Quizzes
- Internet Exercises
- Net Search
- Global Cases

In the quiz modules students can send answers to the grader and receive instant feedback on their progress through the Results Reporter. Coaching comments and references to the textbook may be available to ensure that students take advantage of all available resources to enhance their learning experience.

Instructor Resources

This module links directly to additional teaching tools. Downloadable PowerPoint Presentations and an Instructor's Manual are just some of the materials that may be available in this section.

1 UNDERSTANDING MARKETING MANAGEMENT

IN THIS CHAPTER, WE WILL ADDRESS THE FOLLOWING QUESTIONS:

- Why is marketing important?

- What is the scope of marketing?

- What are some fundamental marketing concepts?

- How has marketing management changed?

- What are the tasks necessary for successful marketing management?

CHAPTER 1

DEFINING MARKETING FOR THE TWENTY-FIRST CENTURY

one

Marketing is everywhere. Formally or informally, people and organizations engage in a vast number of activities that could be called marketing. Good marketing has become an increasingly vital ingredient of business success, embedded in everything we do—from the clothes we wear, to the websites we visit, to the ads we see. Consider:

Two teenaged girls walk into their local Starbucks, which happens to be in Shanghai. One goes to the crowded counter and waits to hand the barista cards for two free peppermint lattes. The other sits at a table and opens her Lenovo ThinkPad R60 notebook computer. Within a few seconds she connects to the Internet, courtesy of Starbucks' deal with China Mobile to provide the café's customers with wireless access to hotspots on the China Mobile network. Once on the Net, the girl uses Baidu.com—the Chinese search-engine market leader—to search for information about the latest online game release from China's Shanda Interactive. In addition to links to various reviews, news sites, and fan pages, Baidu's search results feature a link to a chat room where hundreds of other gamers are discussing the game. The girl enters the chat room to ask whether people who have played the game recommend it. The response is overwhelmingly positive, so she clicks on a sponsored link from the results page, which generates a sliver of paid-search revenue for Baidu and takes her to Shanda's official site, where she sets up an account.

Now her friend has returned with lattes in hand. She's eager to show off her parents' New Year's gift to her: a BlackBerry Curve. She was the first of her friends to have the world-famous BlackBerry. It was only recently that Research In Motion, based in Waterloo, Ontario, was given approval by Chinese regulators to market the device in China. The two girls are admiring the slender wireless device when it receives an email message announcing that Shanda's latest game is available for mobile download. The girls chat excitedly as they gauge the buzz for the mobile version of the game.

Source: Sumner Lemon, "BlackBerry Goes to China," *ABC News*, October 24, 2007, http://abcnews.go.com/Technology/PCWorld/story?id=3769740 (viewed March 2008).

Good marketing is no accident, but a result of careful planning and execution. It is both an "art" and a "science"—there is constant tension between the formulistic side of marketing and the creative side. It is easier to learn the formulistic side, which will occupy most of our attention in this book; but we will also describe how real creativity and passion operate in many companies. This book will help to improve your understanding of marketing and your ability to make the right marketing decisions. In this chapter, we lay the foundation for our study by reviewing a number of important marketing concepts, tools, frameworks, and issues.

THE IMPORTANCE OF MARKETING

Financial success often depends on marketing ability. Finance, operations, accounting, and other business functions will not really matter if there is not demand for products and services sufficient for the company to make a profit. There must be a top line for there to be a bottom line. Many companies have now created a chief marketing officer (CMO) position to put marketing on an equal footing with other C-level executives, such as the chief executive officer (CEO) and chief financial officer (CFO). For example, in March 2007, Sears Canada Inc. issued a press release announcing the appointment of Pamela Griffith-Jones as Vice-President and Chief Marketing Officer. In addition to leading the company's marketing organization, she will be responsible for developing the Sears brand and private merchandise brand positioning in Canada.[1]

Organizations of all kinds—from consumer-goods makers to insurers, and from nonprofit organizations to industrial-product manufacturers—trumpet their latest marketing achievements with similar press releases, which can be found on their websites. In the business press, countless articles are devoted to marketing strategies and tactics.

In stating their business priorities, CEOs acknowledge the importance of marketing. A 2006 survey of the top ten challenges faced by CEOs around the world revealed that among the top five were both "sustained and steady top-line growth" and "customer loyalty/retention"—challenges whose achievement depends heavily on marketing.[2] CEOs also recognize the importance of marketing to building brands and a loyal customer base, intangible assets that make up a large percentage of the value of a firm.

Marketing is tricky, however, and it has been the Achilles' heel of many formerly prosperous companies. Large, well-known businesses such as Bell Canada, Canadian Tire, Loblaws, Nortel, Bombardier, and Zellers have confronted newly empowered customers and new competitors, and have had to rethink their business models. Even market leaders such as Microsoft, Wal-Mart, Intel, and Nike recognize that they cannot afford to relax. Jack Welch, GE's brilliant former CEO, repeatedly warned his company: "Change or die." Small companies must also pay close attention to how they market themselves and their products.

But making the right decisions is not always easy. Marketing managers must make major decisions such as what features to design into a new product, what prices to offer customers, where to sell products, and how much to spend on advertising or sales. They must also make more detailed decisions such as the exact wording or colour of new packaging. The companies at greatest risk are those that fail to carefully monitor their customers and competitors and to continuously improve their value offerings. They take a short-term, sales-driven view of their business and, ultimately, they fail to satisfy their stockholders, their employees, their suppliers, and their channel partners. Skillful marketing is a never-ending pursuit, as Big Rock Brewery has discovered:

Big Rock Brewery

Big Rock Brewery of Calgary (www.bigrockbeer.com), Canada's leading craft brewery, was the inspiration of one man, Ed McNally, who began the brewery in 1984. He founded his business on one guiding principle: "The marketplace will take notice of a superior product backed by superior service." He soon learned, however, that even high-quality products don't sell themselves. In 2005, he decided he needed to totally revamp his product packaging, and in order to get the attention of drinkers in Alberta's increasingly crowded premium-beer market, he launched the company's first multimedia advertising campaign in years. Paradoxically, the company looked back to its roots in order to move ahead. Using retro-marketing, it hopes to evoke westerners' nostalgia by using the best of the labels created two decades ago by local artist Dirk van Wyk. To reach the rest of the country, Big Rock uses a number of partnerships and sponsorships, such as the 4-year deal signed in 2007 that made the brewer the official sponsor of the Juno awards. Exceptional marketing and high-quality products have brought continued success. In 2007, two of the company's beers, Grasshopper and Jack Rabbit, received gold medals in the Canadian Brewing Awards.[3]

THE SCOPE OF MARKETING

To prepare to be a marketer, you need to understand what marketing is, how it works, what is marketed, and who does the marketing.

What Is Marketing?

Marketing deals with identifying and meeting human and social needs. One of the shortest definitions of marketing is "meeting needs profitably." When eBay, recognizing that people were unable to locate some of the items they desired most, created an online auction clearing house, and when IKEA, noticing that people want good furniture at a substantially lower price, created knock-down furniture, they demonstrated marketing savvy and turned a private or social need into a profitable business opportunity.

The American Marketing Association, the largest professional and academic marketing association in North America, offers the following formal definition of marketing: *Marketing is an organizational function and a set of processes for creating, communicating, and delivering value to customers and for managing customer relationships in ways that benefit the organization and its stakeholders.* Coping with these exchange processes calls for a considerable amount of work and skill. *Marketing management* takes place when at least one party to a potential exchange thinks about the means of achieving desired responses from other parties. Thus we see **marketing management** as *the art and science of choosing target markets and getting, keeping, and growing customers through creating, delivering, and communicating superior customer and stakeholder value.*

In designing its new labels, Big Rock went back to its roots.

We can distinguish between a social and a managerial definition of marketing. A social definition shows the role marketing plays in society. For example, one marketer said that marketing's role is to "deliver a higher standard of living." Here is a social definition that serves our purpose: *Marketing is a societal process by which individuals and groups obtain what they need and want through creating, offering, and freely exchanging products and services of value with others.*[4]

Managers sometimes think of marketing as "the art of selling products," and they are surprised when they hear that the most important part of marketing is not selling! Selling is only the tip of the marketing iceberg. Peter Drucker, a leading management theorist, puts it this way:

> There will always, one can assume, be a need for some selling. But the aim of marketing is to make selling superfluous. The aim of marketing is to know and understand the customer so well that the product or service fits him and sells itself. Ideally, marketing should result in a customer who is ready to buy. All that should be needed then is to make the product or service available.[5]

When Sony designed its PlayStation 3 game system, when Apple launched its iPod nano digital music player, and when Toyota introduced its Prius hybrid automobile, they were swamped with orders because they had designed the "right" product based on careful marketing homework.

What Is Marketed?

Marketing people are involved in marketing ten types of entities: goods, services, events, experiences, persons, places, properties, organizations, information, and ideas. Let's take a quick look at these categories.

GOODS Physical goods constitute the bulk of most countries' production and marketing efforts. For example, despite Canada's history as a resource-based economy, primary industries (agriculture, fishing, forestry, hunting, mining, and oil and gas extraction) constituted only 7.6 percent of the gross domestic product (GDP) in 2006 while manufacturing made up 16.3 percent of GDP.[6] Not only do companies market their goods, but thanks in part to the Internet, even individuals can effectively market goods. Take the case of Vancouver-based entrepreneurs Alix Cameron and Cindy Ball, founders and designers behind the up-and-coming lingerie brand and web store SayItWithUndies.com. Their goods are also sold at chic retailers across Canada and the U.S. Inspired to develop lingerie that was sassy, comfortable, sexy, and fun, and known for their comfortable thongs with the message "be a smart ass" on the back T-bar, they've grown to having their underwear grace the bottoms of celebrities like Jennifer Lopez and Tori Spelling.[7]

A successful new product is the result of careful marketing homework.

SERVICES   As economies advance, a growing proportion of their activities is focused on the production of services. Services have increased from just over half of Canada's GDP in 1961 to about 70 percent today. The service sector currently employs about three out of every four Canadians, and the sector creates about 80 percent of the new jobs in Canada.[8] According to Statistics Canada, between 1997 and 2006 the services sector grew by 38 percent while goods-producing industries grew by 26 percent. The top industries within the service sector are wholesale and retail trade; health care and social assistance; accommodation and food services; finance and insurance; professional, scientific, and technical services; and educational services.[9]

EVENTS   Marketers promote time-based events, such as major trade shows, artistic performances, and company anniversaries. Global sporting events, such as the Winter Olympics being held in Vancouver in 2010, are promoted aggressively to both companies and fans. There is a whole profession of meeting planners who work out the details of an event and make sure it comes off perfectly.

EXPERIENCES   By orchestrating several services and goods, a firm can create, stage, and market experiences. Walt Disney World's Magic Kingdom, where customers can visit a fairy kingdom, a pirate ship, or a haunted house, represents experiential marketing—and so does the Hard Rock Café, where

Goods marketers, like entrepreneurs Alix Cameron and Cindy Ball, can build their business using the Internet as well as traditional channels.

customers can enjoy a meal or see a band in a live concert. Skiing at Whistler and visiting the Toronto Zoo would also fall under experiential marketing. There is also a market for customized experiences, such as spending a week at a baseball camp playing with some retired baseball greats or climbing Mount Everest.[10]

PERSONS Celebrity marketing is a major business. Today, every major film star has an agent, a personal manager, and ties to a public-relations agency. Artists, musicians, CEOs, physicians, high-profile lawyers and financiers, and other professionals are also getting help from celebrity marketers.[11] Some people have done a masterful job of marketing themselves—think of Wayne Gretzky, Avril Lavigne, Sarah McLachlan, the Tragically Hip, and Oprah Winfrey. Management consultant Tom Peters, himself a master at self-branding, has advised each person to become a "brand."

PLACES Cities, provinces, regions, and whole nations compete actively to attract tourists, factories, company headquarters, and new residents. The Nova Scotia government has turned to high-profile online tools to help it win the hearts of fickle tourists. One tool, Google Earth, which features an online world map that meshes satellite photos with regular road maps, is being used to show prospective visitors 100 points of interest in Nova Scotia, including cycling the Cabot Trail and touring vineyards in the Annapolis Valley. Each point of interest is indicated by a tartan dot on the map. YouTube is another tool in Nova Scotia's new arsenal. A number of video clips of Celtic music, motorcycling, and surfing have been posted on YouTube as well as on Nova Scotia's Official Tourism website. The campaign to promote tourism also included print, TV, and online advertising. Len Goucher, Nova Scotia's Minister of Tourism, turned to online tools since the province's research showed 70 percent of tourists use the Internet for travel planning.[12]

PROPERTIES Properties are intangible rights of ownership of either real property (real estate) or financial property (stocks and bonds). Properties are bought and sold, and this requires marketing. Real estate agents work for property owners or sellers or buy residential or commercial real estate. Investment companies and banks are involved in marketing securities to both institutional and individual investors.

ORGANIZATIONS Organizations actively work to build a strong, favourable, and unique image in the minds of their target publics. In the United Kingdom, Tesco's "Every Little Bit Helps" marketing program reflects the food marketer's attention to detail in everything it does within the store as well as outside in the community and the environment. The campaign has vaulted Tesco to the top of the U.K. supermarket-chain industry. Universities, museums, performing-arts organizations, and not-for-profits all use marketing to boost their public images and to compete for audiences and funds. This is certainly the case with Philips's "Sense and Simplicity" campaign.

Royal Philips

In dozens of in-depth and quantitative interviews and focus groups, Philips researchers asked 1650 consumers and 180 customers what was most important to them in using technology. Respondents from the U.K., United States, France, Germany, the Netherlands, Hong Kong, China, and Brazil agreed on one thing: they wanted the benefits of technology without the hassles. With its "Sense and Simplicity" advertising campaign and focus, Philips believes "our brand now reflects our belief that simplicity can be a goal of technology. It just makes sense." The campaign consists of print, online, and television advertising directed by five experts from the worlds of health care, lifestyle, and technology whose role is to provide "additional outside perspectives on the journey to simplicity."[13]

INFORMATION Information can be produced and marketed as a product. This is essentially what schools and universities produce and distribute at a price to parents, students, and communities. Encyclopedias and most nonfiction books also market information. Magazines such as *Canadian Gardening,* winner of the Canadian Society of Magazine Editors' 2007 Editors' Choice Awards, provide a wealth of information about growing plants in Canada's different climate zones. The production, packaging, and distribution of information is one of our society's major industries.[14] Even companies that sell physical products attempt to add value through the use of information. For example, the CEO of Siemens Medical Systems, Tom McCausland, says "[our product] is not necessarily an X-ray or an MRI, but information. Our business is really health-care information technology, and our end product is really an electronic patient record: information on lab tests, pathology, and drugs as well as voice dictation."[15]

Organizations market ideas as well as products, as is done in this ad from the Government of Ontario.

Most children aren't shy about showing affection. Which makes them excellent spreaders of the flu.

Children are major spreaders of the flu. And young children 6 to 23 months of age are at high risk of flu-related complications. So make sure your children get their free flu shot. Talk to your doctor, pharmacist or local public health unit. Call 1-877-844-1944 (TTY 1-800-387-5559). Or visit www.health.gov.on.ca

The flu. It's not just about you.

Ontario

IDEAS Every market offering includes a basic idea. Charles Revson of Revlon observed: "In the factory, we make cosmetics; in the store we sell hope." Products and services are platforms for delivering some idea or benefit. Social marketers are busy promoting such ideas as "Friends Don't Let Friends Drive Drunk" and "A Mind Is a Terrible Thing to Waste." Seasonal public-health ads in Ontario urge people in the community to protect themselves against potentially harmful viruses such as influenza in the winter months and West Nile in the summer months.

Who Markets?

MARKETERS AND PROSPECTS A **marketer** is someone seeking a response (attention, a purchase, a vote, a donation) from another party called the **prospect**. If two parties are seeking to sell something to each other, we call them both marketers.

Marketers are skilled in stimulating demand for a company's products, but this is too limited a view of the tasks they perform. Just as production and logistics professionals are responsible for supply management, marketers are responsible for demand management. Marketing managers seek to influence the level, timing, and composition of demand to meet an organization's objectives. Eight demand states are possible:

1. *Negative demand*—Consumers dislike the product and may even pay a price to avoid it.
2. *Nonexistent demand*—Consumers may be unaware of or uninterested in the product.
3. *Latent demand*—Consumers may share a strong need that cannot be satisfied by an existing product.
4. *Declining demand*—Consumers begin to buy the product less frequently or not at all.
5. *Irregular demand*—Consumer purchases vary on a seasonal, monthly, weekly, daily, or even hourly basis.

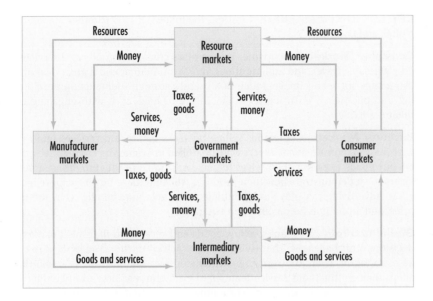

FIGURE 1.1

Structures of Flows in a Modern Exchange Economy

6. *Full demand*—Consumers are adequately buying all products put into the marketplace.

7. *Overfull demand*—More consumers than can be satisfied would like to buy the product.

8. *Unwholesome demand*—Consumers may be attracted to products that have undesirable social consequences.

In each case, marketers must identify the underlying cause(s) of the demand state and then determine a plan of action to shift the demand to a more desired state.

MARKETS Traditionally, a "market" was a physical place where buyers and sellers gathered to buy and sell goods. Economists describe a market as a collection of buyers and sellers who transact over a particular product or product class (e.g., the housing market or grain market). Modern economies abound in such markets.

Five basic markets and their connecting flows are shown in Figure 1.1. Manufacturers go to resource markets (raw-material markets, labour markets, money markets), buy resources and turn them into goods and services, and then sell finished products to intermediaries who sell them to consumers. Consumers sell their labour and receive money with which they pay for goods and services. The government collects tax revenues to buy goods from resource, manufacturer, and intermediary markets and uses these goods and services to provide public services. Each nation's economy and the global economy consist of complex, interacting sets of markets linked through exchange processes.

Marketers often use the term *market* to cover various groupings of customers. They view the sellers as constituting the industry and the buyers as constituting the market. They talk about need markets (the diet-seeking market), product markets (the shoe market), demographic markets (the youth market), and geographic markets (the Quebec market), or they extend the concept to cover other markets, such as voter markets, labour markets, and donor markets.

Figure 1.2 shows the relationship between the industry and the market. Sellers and buyers are connected by four flows. The sellers send goods and services and communications (ads, direct mail) to the market; in return, they receive money and information (attitudes, sales data). The inner loop shows an exchange of money for goods and services; the outer loop shows an exchange of information.

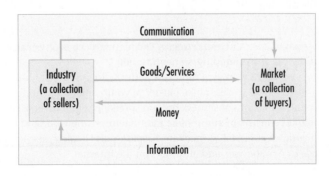

FIGURE 1.2

A Simple Marketing System

Consider the following key customer markets: consumer, business, global, and nonprofit.

Consumer Markets Companies selling mass consumer goods and services such as soft drinks, cosmetics, air travel, and athletic shoes and equipment spend a great deal of time trying to establish a superior brand image. Much of a brand's strength depends on developing a superior product and packaging, ensuring its availability, and backing it with engaging communications and reliable service.

Business Markets Companies selling business goods and services often face well-trained and well-informed professional buyers who are skilled in evaluating competitive offerings. Business buyers buy goods to enable themselves to make or resell a product to others at a profit. Business marketers must demonstrate how their products will help these buyers achieve higher revenue or lower costs. Advertising can play a role, but a stronger role may be played by the marketer's sales force, price, and reputation for reliability and quality.

Global Markets Companies selling goods and services in the global marketplace face additional decisions and challenges. They must decide which countries to enter; how to enter each country (as an exporter, licenser, joint-venture partner, contract manufacturer, or solo manufacturer); how to adapt their product and service features to each country; how to price their products in different countries; and how to adapt their communications to fit different cultures. These decisions must be made in the face of different requirements for buying, negotiating, owning, and disposing of property; different culture, language, and legal and political systems; and a currency that might fluctuate in value. Yet, the payoff for doing all this additional legwork can be huge according to forecasts by companies like Montreal-based Bombardier.

Bombardier Inc.

Jianwei Zhang is the soft-spoken engineer who spearheads Montreal-based Bombardier Inc.'s growth drive in China and the person who secured a crucial new partnership with China Aviation Industry Corp. (AVIC), one of China's biggest aviation manufacturers. Partnerships are essential for doing business in China and according to a recent report by trade publication *Defense News*, AVIC is a major partner with 240 000 employees (almost ten times more than Bombardier employs in its aerospace division worldwide) and 47 manufacturing facilities. According to Bombardier's forecasts, over the next 20 years China will need 1600 aircraft that seat up to 149 passengers. The demand for private jets is also expected to grow significantly. In betting so big on China, Bombardier is taking a huge risk, but there is also huge potential gain. Bombardier is betting that its edge as an innovator in design and advanced systems will help it beat its competitors in this emerging market.[16]

Nonprofit and Governmental Markets The government market in Canada is huge. For example, government-owned business enterprises (GBEs), public financial and non-financial corporations engaged in commercial operations involving the sale of goods and services to the public, are just one segment of this market. GBEs include the Bank of Canada at the federal level and lottery, gaming, and liquor enterprises at the provincial level. In 2006, federal and provincial GBEs generated more than $24 billion in profits and they purchased a vast array of goods and services.[17] Much government purchasing calls for bids, with the lowest bid being favoured in the absence of extenuating factors. Similarly, companies selling their goods to nonprofit organizations such as churches, universities, and charitable organizations need to price carefully because these organizations have limited purchasing power. Lower prices affect the features and quality that the seller can build into the offering.

Today we can distinguish between a *marketplace* and *marketspace*. The marketplace is physical, as in shopping in a store; marketspace is digital, as in shopping on the Internet.[18]

Mohan Sawhney, a professor at the Kellogg School of Management, has proposed the concept of a *metamarket* to describe a cluster of complementary products and services that are closely related in the minds of consumers but are spread across a diverse set of industries. The automobile metamarket consists of automobile manufacturers, new-car and used-car dealers, financing companies, insurance companies, mechanics, spare-parts dealers, service shops, auto magazines, classified auto ads in newspapers, and auto sites on the Internet.

In purchasing a car, a buyer will get involved in many parts of this metamarket, and this has created an opportunity for metamediaries to assist buyers in moving seamlessly through these clusters even though they are disconnected in physical space. One metamediary example is Edmund's (www.edmunds.com), a website where a car buyer can find the features and prices of different automobiles and easily click through to other sites to search for the lowest-price dealer, for financing, for car accessories, and for used cars at bargain prices. Metamediaries also serve other metamarkets such as the home-ownership market, the parenting and baby-care market, and the wedding market.[19]

Marketing in Practice

How is marketing done? Increasingly, marketing is *not* done only by the marketing department. Marketing needs to affect every aspect of the customer experience, which means that marketers must properly manage all possible touch points: store layouts, package designs, product functions, employee training, and shipping and logistics methods. Marketing must also be heavily involved in key general-management activities, such as product innovation and new-business development.

To create a strong marketing organization, marketers must think like executives in other departments, and executives in other departments must think more like marketers.[20] CMO and later CEO of WalMart.com, Carter Cast, noted that what surprised him most when he became CMO was "that I would interact so much with functions outside of marketing. I didn't realize it is a holistic assignment. Then I realized I really had to understand things like product supply, cost break-evens, and accounting."[21]

Companies generally establish a marketing department to be responsible for creating and delivering customer value, but as the late David Packard of Hewlett-Packard observed, "Marketing is far too important to leave to the marketing department." Companies now know that every employee has an impact on the customer and must see the customer as the source of the company's prosperity. So they're beginning to emphasize interdepartmental teamwork to manage key processes. They're also placing more emphasis on the smooth management of core business processes, such as new-product realization, customer acquisition and retention, and order fulfillment.

In practice, marketing follows a logical process. The marketing *planning* process consists of analyzing marketing opportunities, selecting target markets, designing marketing strategies, developing marketing programs, and managing the marketing effort. In highly competitive marketplaces, however, marketing planning is more fluid and is continually refreshed. Companies must always be moving forward with marketing programs, innovating products and services, staying in touch with customer needs, and seeking new advantages rather than relying on past strengths.

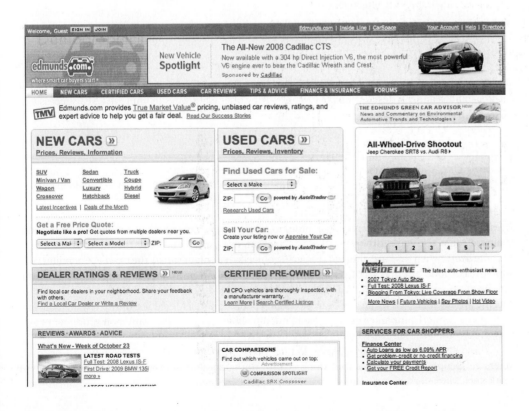

Edmund's is a metamediary website that helps prospective car buyers navigate the automobile metamarket online.

FIGURE 1.3

Improving CMO Success

Source: Gail McGovern and John A. Quelch, "The Fall and Rise of the CMO," *Strategy+Business,* Winter 2004. Reprinted by permission.

1. Make the mission and responsibilities clear. Be certain that the case for having a CMO is strong and the mission is well understood by leaders in the organization, particularly the CEO, the board, and line management. Without a clear need (real or perceived), the role will be rejected by the organization.

2. Fit the role to the marketing culture and structure. Avoid having a CMO in a marketing-led company that has many individual brands rather than a single corporate umbrella—unless the person appointed to the position is a well-connected insider.

3. Choose a CMO who is compatible with the CEO. Beware of the CEO who wants to hire a CMO but doesn't want to relinquish any marketing control. Find a CEO who recognizes his or her responsibility to be the cheerleader for marketing and the brand, but realizes the need to be guided and coached by a marketing specialist.

4. Remember that showpeople don't succeed. The CMO should work hard to ensure the CEO is successful at being the principal cheerleader for the brand.

5. Match the personality with the CMO type. Be certain that the chief marketer has the right skills and personality for whichever of the three CMO models he or she might fill (VP of Marketing Services, Classic CMO, or "Super" CMO). There is little tolerance for on-the-job training.

6. Make line managers marketing heroes. By stretching their marketing budgets, CMOs can improve a division's marketing productivity and help business unit leaders increase their top-line revenues.

7. Infiltrate the line organization. Have the CMO support the placement of marketing professionals from the corporate marketing department into divisional marketing roles. Provide input from the CMO into the annual reviews of line marketers.

8. Require right-brain and left-brain skills. The most successful CMO will have strong creative and technical marketing expertise, be politically savvy, and have the interpersonal skills to be a great leader and manager.

The changing marketing environment is putting considerable demands on marketing executives. Marketers must have diverse quantitative and qualitative skills, an entrepreneurial attitude, and a keen understanding of how marketing can create value within their organization,[22] and they must work in harmony with the sales function.

There are five key leadership functions for an organization's CMO:

1. Strengthening the brands.
2. Measuring marketing effectiveness.
3. Driving new-product development based on customer needs.
4. Gathering meaningful customer insights.
5. Utilizing new marketing technology.

Harvard's Gail McGovern and John Quelch note that there is tremendous variability in the responsibilities and job descriptions of CMOs.[23] They offer eight ways to improve CMO success (see Figure 1.3).

CORE CONCEPTS

To understand the marketing function, we need to understand the following set of core concepts.

Needs, Wants, and Demands

Needs are basic human requirements. In order to survive, people need air, water, food, clothing, and shelter. People also have strong needs for recreation, education, and entertainment. These needs become *wants* when they are directed to specific objects that might satisfy the need. A Canadian consumer needs food but may want pancakes and maple syrup. A person in Mauritius needs food but may want a mango, rice, lentils, and beans. Wants are shaped by one's society. *Demands* are wants for specific products backed by an ability to pay. Many people want a Mercedes; only a few are able and willing to buy one. Companies must measure not only how many people want their product but also how many would actually be willing and able to buy it.

These distinctions shed light on the frequent criticism that "marketers create needs" or "marketers get people to buy things they don't want." Marketers do not create needs: Needs pre-exist marketers. Marketers, along with other societal factors, influence wants. Marketers might promote the idea that a Mercedes would satisfy a person's need for social status. They do not, however, create the need for social status.

Understanding customer needs and wants is not always simple. Some customers have needs of which they are not fully conscious, or they cannot articulate these needs, or they use words that require some interpretation. What does it mean when the customer asks for a "powerful" lawnmower, a "fast" lathe, an "attractive" bathing suit, or a "restful" hotel? Consider the customer who says he wants an "inexpensive car." The marketer must probe further. We can distinguish among five types of needs:

1. Stated needs (the customer wants an inexpensive car).
2. Real needs (the customer wants a car whose operating cost, not its initial price, is low).
3. Unstated needs (the customer expects good service from the dealer).
4. Delight needs (the customer would like the dealer to include an onboard navigation system).
5. Secret needs (the customer wants to be seen by friends as a savvy consumer).

Responding only to the stated need may short-change the customer. Many consumers do not know what they want in a product. Consumers did not know much about cellular phones when they were first introduced. Nokia and Ericsson fought to shape consumer perceptions of cellular phones. Simply giving customers what they want isn't enough any more—to gain an edge, companies must help customers learn what they want.

Target Markets, Positioning, and Segmentation

A marketer can rarely satisfy everyone in a market. Not everyone likes the same cereal, hotel room, restaurant, automobile, university, or movie. Therefore, marketers start by dividing up the market into segments. They identify and profile distinct groups of buyers who might prefer or require varying product and service mixes by examining demographic, psychographic, and behavioural differences among buyers. The marketer then decides which segments present the greatest opportunity—which are its *target markets*.

M&M Meat Shops Ltd.

M&M Meat Shops Ltd., founded in 1980 in Kitchener, Ontario, by Mac and Mark (hence the name M&M) was based on a simple idea: create a place where people could purchase choice cuts of restaurant-quality meat and specialty food items at reasonable prices. Today, it is Canada's largest retail chain of specialty frozen-food stores with more than 400 locations coast to coast. Its growth is due to excellent products as well as to careful market research and targeting. It uses demographics, psychographics, census information, and information from a customer-loyalty program to gain insight into consumers in order to effectively market to them. For example, in early 2007, M&M launched a campaign targeting busy mothers. Using five humorous 30-second television spots, radio, and in-store advertising, the ads feature Julie, a working mother. Julie faces a different obstacle in each ad, such as getting her hair caught in a paper shredder or losing her car keys and eyeglasses in a mail chute. M&M shows that despite being pressed for time, Julie manages to prepare a meal for her family with the help of M&M. Chris Styan, director of marketing for M&M, noted "We went through a lot of research in the development of these ads, and the stories and scenarios that we speak about, although they're entertaining, definitely resonate with the target group." The tag line at the end of each spot reads "No matter what your day throws at you, you can have a great meal."[24]

For each chosen target market, the firm develops a *market offering*. The offering is *positioned* in the minds of the target buyers as delivering some central benefit(s). For example, Volvo develops its cars for buyers for whom automobile safety is a major concern. Volvo, therefore, positions its car as the safest a customer can buy. Companies do best when they choose their target market(s) carefully and prepare tailored marketing programs.

Offerings and Brands

Companies address needs by putting forth a **value proposition**, a set of benefits they offer to customers to satisfy their needs. The intangible value proposition is made physical by an *offering*, which can be a combination of products, services, information, and experiences.

Market research, insightful target marketing, and great products have contributed to M&M's success.

A *brand* is an offering from a known source. A brand name such as McDonald's carries many associations in the minds of people: hamburgers, fun, children, fast food, convenience, and Golden Arches. These associations make up the brand image. All companies strive to build brand strength—that is, a strong, favourable, and unique brand image.

Value and Satisfaction

An offering will be successful if it delivers value and satisfaction to the target buyer. The buyer chooses among different offerings on the basis of which offering is perceived to deliver the most value. *Value* reflects the perceived tangible and intangible benefits and costs to customers. Value can be seen as primarily a combination of quality, service, and price (qsp), called the customer value triad. Value increases with quality and service and it decreases with price, although other factors can also play an important role in our perceptions of value.

Value is a central marketing concept. Marketing can be seen as the identification, creation, communication, delivery, and monitoring of customer value. *Satisfaction* reflects a person's comparative judgments resulting from a product's perceived performance (or outcome) in relation to his or her expectations. If the performance falls short of expectations, the customer is dissatisfied and disappointed. If the performance matches the expectations, the customer is satisfied. If it exceeds them, the customer is delighted.

Marketing Channels

To reach a target market, the marketer uses three kinds of marketing channels. *Communication channels* deliver and receive messages from target buyers and include newspapers, magazines, radio, television, mail, email, telephone, billboards, posters, flyers, CDs, DVDs, and the Internet. Beyond these, communications are conveyed by facial expressions and clothing, the look of retail stores, and many other media. Marketers are increasingly adding dialogue channels (email and toll-free numbers) to counterbalance the more normal monologue channels (such as ads).

The marketer uses *distribution channels* to display, sell, and deliver the physical product(s) or service(s) to the buyer or user. These channels include distributors, wholesalers, retailers, and agents.

The marketer also uses *service channels* to carry out transactions with potential buyers. Service channels that facilitate transactions include warehouses, transportation companies, banks, and insurance companies. Marketers clearly face a design problem in choosing the best mix of communication, distribution, and service channels for their offerings.

Supply Chain

The supply chain is a long channel stretching from raw materials to components to final products that are carried to final buyers. The supply chain for women's purses starts with hides and moves through tanning operations, cutting operations, and manufacturing to the marketing channels that bring the purses to customers. The supply chain represents a value-delivery system. Each company in the chain captures only a certain percentage of the total value generated by the supply chain. When a company acquires competitors or moves upstream or downstream within the supply chain, its aim is to capture a higher percentage of supply-chain value.

Competition

Competition includes all the actual and potential rival offerings and substitutes that a buyer might consider. Suppose a company like Dofasco (www.dofasco.ca), a steel-maker based in Hamilton, Ontario, is hoping to sell steel to a car manufacturer. (Figure 1.4 shows several levels of competitors.) Algoma, Dofasco, and Stelco are all large, integrated steel companies and thus are close rivals. Together they produce three-fifths of Canada's steel. Clearly, Dofasco would be thinking of competition too narrowly if it thought only of other integrated steel companies. Canada also has ten smaller mills that use electric arc furnaces to produce specialized items such as carbon steel, bar and rod products, and specialty steels. However, since 90 percent of Canada's steel exports go to the United States, Dofasco cannot ignore its American rivals in this increasingly integrated market. Rivalry is further

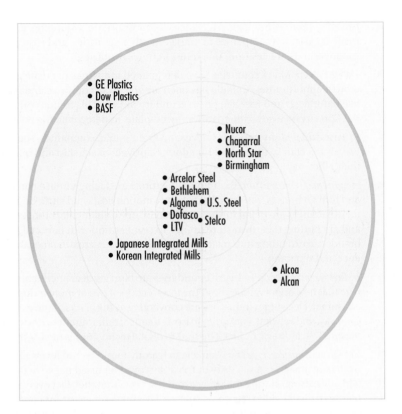

FIGURE 1.4

Dofasco Radar Screen

Source: Adapted from Adrian V. Slywotzky, *Value Migration* (Boston, MA: Harvard Business School Press, 1996), p. 99. Reprinted by permission of Harvard Business School Press.

increased by the fact that automobile manufacturers are replacing steel with other materials like plastic, aluminum, magnesium, and carbon fibre. In fact, Dofasco is more likely to be hurt in the long run by substitutes than by its immediate rivals. Thus, it may have to closely watch the moves of Alcan (www.alcan.com) since the aluminum manufacturer has been investing in research to develop components and parts that will lighten the weight of cars.

Marketing Environment

The marketing environment consists of the task environment and the broad environment. The *task environment* includes the immediate actors involved in producing, distributing, and promoting the offering. The main actors are the company, suppliers, distributors, dealers, and the target customers. Included in the supplier group are material suppliers and service suppliers such as marketing-research agencies, advertising agencies, banking and insurance companies, and transportation and telecommunications companies. Distributors and dealers include agents, brokers, manufacturer representatives, and others who facilitate finding and selling to customers.

The *broad environment* consists of six components: demographic environment, economic environment, natural environment, technological environment, political-legal environment, and social-cultural environment. These environments contain forces that can have a major impact on the actors in the task environment. Market actors must pay close attention to the trends and developments in these environments and make timely adjustments to their marketing strategies.

THE NEW MARKETING REALITIES

We can say with some confidence that "the marketplace isn't what it used to be." Marketers must attend and respond to a number of significant developments.

Major Societal Forces

Today, the marketplace is radically different as a result of major, and sometimes interlinking, societal forces that have created new behaviours, new opportunities, and new challenges:

■ *Network information technology.* The digital revolution has created an Information Age. The Industrial Age was characterized by mass production and mass consumption, stores stuffed with inventory, ads everywhere, and rampant discounting. The Information Age promises to lead to more accurate levels of production, more targeted communications, and more relevant pricing.

- *Globalization.* Technological advances in transportation, shipping, and communication have made it easier for companies to market in other countries, and easier for consumers to buy products and services from marketers in other countries.

- *Deregulation.* Many countries have deregulated industries to create greater competition and growth opportunities. Canada has been among these countries and has deregulated industries like natural gas and fees like post-secondary tuition. This trend is on-going and in April 2007, the Conservative government announced plans to deregulate the telephone market.

- *Privatization.* Many countries have converted public companies, such as British Airways and British Telecom in the United Kingdom, to private ownership and management to increase their efficiency.

- *Heightened competition.* Brand manufacturers are facing intense competition from domestic and foreign brands, resulting in rising promotion costs and shrinking profit margins. These manufacturers are being further buffeted by powerful retailers that control limited shelf space and are putting their own store brands in competition with national brands. Many strong brands are extending into related product categories, creating megabrands with much presence and reputation.

- *Industry convergence.* Industry boundaries are blurring at an incredible rate as companies recognize that new opportunities lie at the intersection of two or more industries. The computing and consumer-electronics industries are converging as the giants of the computer world such as Dell, Gateway, and Hewlett-Packard release a stream of entertainment devices from MP3 players to plasma TVs and camcorders. The shift to digital technology is fueling this massive convergence.[25]

- *Consumer resistance.* A 2004 Yankelovich study found record levels of marketing resistance from consumers.[26] A majority of those surveyed reported negative opinions about marketing and advertising, stating that they avoid products that they feel overmarket. The increased popularity of digital video recorders such as TiVo makes it easier for consumers to skip or "zap" TV commercials, in part reflecting consumers' desire for marketing avoidance.

- *Retail transformation.* Small retailers are succumbing to the growing power of giant retailers and "category killers." Store-based retailers face competition from catalogue houses; direct-mail firms; newspaper, magazine, and TV direct-to-customer ads; home-shopping TV; and e-commerce on the Internet. In response, entrepreneurial retailers are building entertainment into their stores with coffee bars, lectures, demonstrations, and performances—marketing an "experience" rather than a product assortment.

- *Disintermediation.* The amazing success of early online dot-coms (such as AOL, Amazon.com, Yahoo!, eBay, E*TRADE, and dozens of others), which created *disintermediation* in the delivery of products and services by intervening in the traditional flow of goods through distribution channels, struck terror into the hearts of many established manufacturers and retailers. In response, many traditional companies engaged in *reintermediation* and became "brick-and-click" retailers, adding online services to their existing offerings. Many brick-and-click competitors became stronger contenders than pure-click firms because they had both a larger pool of resources to work with and well-established brand names.

MAC Cosmetics Inc.

Originally established in 1984 in Toronto, MAC is now a division of cosmetics giant Estée Lauder. MAC Cosmetics is considered a significant reason for Lauder's 13 percent net increase in makeup sales in 2006. Yet MAC's 1000 stores worldwide don't simply sell Small Eye Shadow, Studio Fix, Lustreglass, and Pro Longwear Lipcolour. Instead, they rely on highly paid "artists" to bond with each customer during a free makeup consultation and application lesson. Although this tack is hardly new in the world of retail makeup, what's unique is that MAC's artists are not out there to bump up their commissions and load customers down with more products. Rather, they're trained to collaborate with customers so they'll leave the store with $50 or more of MAC products and the feeling that "I can definitely do this at home." The goal, says Matthew Waitesmith, MAC's head of "artist training and development," is for each customer to feel she's had an authentically artistic experience "that hopefully means they'll return to the place that makes them feel like an artist."[27]

The societal forces that spawned the Information Age have resulted in many new consumer and company capabilities.

New Consumer Capabilities

Customers today perceive fewer real product differences, show less brand loyalty, and in their search for value are becoming more sensitive to price and quality. Consider what consumers have today that they didn't have yesterday:

- *A substantial increase in buying power.* Buyers are only a click away from comparing competitor prices and product attributes on the Internet. They can even name their price for a hotel room, airline ticket, or mortgage. Business buyers can run a *reverse auction* in which sellers compete to capture their business. They can readily join with others to aggregate their purchases and achieve deeper volume discounts.

- *A greater variety of available goods and services.* Amazon.com quickly became the world's largest bookstore but has since branched into retail sales of music and movies, clothing and accessories, consumer electronics, health and beauty aids, and home and garden products. Buyers can order goods online from anywhere in the world, bypassing limited local offerings and realizing great savings by ordering from countries with lower prices.

- *A great amount of information about practically everything.* People can read almost any newspaper in any language from anywhere in the world. They can access online encyclopedias, dictionaries, medical information, movie ratings, consumer reports, and countless other information sources.

- *Greater ease in interacting and placing and receiving orders.* Today's buyers can place orders from home, the office, or a mobile phone 24 hours a day, seven days a week, and quickly receive goods at their home or office.

- *An ability to compare notes on products and services.* Social networking sites bring together buyers with common interests. At CarSpace.com, auto enthusiasts talk about chrome rims, the latest BMW model, and where to find a great mechanic in their local area. Marketers are eyeing the success of the site, given that 35 percent of young, first-time car buyers consider the Internet their most important shopping tool.[28]

- *An amplified voice to influence peer and public opinion.* The Internet fuels personal connections and user-generated content through social media such as MySpace and single-use social networks such as Flickr (photos), Del.icio.us (links), Digg (news stories), Wikipedia (encyclopedia articles), and YouTube (videos).[29] In late 2004, Kryptonite, a firm that makes high-priced bike locks, found itself in an awkward position when several blogs showed how the firm's U-shaped locks could be easily picked using only the plastic casing of a Bic pen.[30]

KFC, Converse, Wm. Wrigley Jr.

Although Chinese citizens are still prohibited from criticizing the government online, they have thousands of online forums for airing grievances about poor customer service, misleading ad campaigns, shoddy products, safety standards, and more. Chinese consumers are vocal and active, and when enough of them voice a complaint, companies listen. When a Chinese TV spot for Yum! Brand Inc.'s KFC Corp. depicted a hard-working student who didn't pass his exams and two carefree children who enjoyed KFC fried chicken and did, KFC received so many complaints for suggesting hard work doesn't pay that it changed the ad to show all three children doing well. Smart companies are enlisting their opinionated Internet consumers to offer input before a product is launched. Converse and Wm. Wrigley Jr. conducted a joint promotion encouraging Chinese consumers to come up with their own cool designs for Converse sneakers that featured Wrigley's Juicy Fruit logo.[31]

New Company Capabilities

Forces have also combined to generate a new set of capabilities for today's companies:

- Marketers can use the Internet as a powerful information and sales channel, augmenting their geographical reach to inform customers and promote businesses and products worldwide. By establishing one or more websites, they can list their products and services, history, business philosophy, job opportunities, and other information of interest to visitors.

- Researchers can collect fuller and richer information about markets, customers, prospects, and competitors. They can also conduct fresh marketing research by using the Internet to arrange focus groups, send out questionnaires, and gather primary data in several other ways.

- Managers can facilitate and speed internal communication among their employees by using the Internet to support a private intranet. Employees can query one another, seek advice, and download or upload needed information from and to the company's computer network.

- Companies can also facilitate and speed external communication among customers by creating online and offline "buzz" through brand advocates and user communities. To get media partners for a new Oxfam campaign, Canadian comedienne Mary Walsh donned her Marg Delahunty warrior regalia and paid visits to the heads of various advertising and media agencies. She sought their input, ideas, and support so that the charity would get the widest exposure possible. Videos of the ambushes were also posted on YouTube to generate extra buzz for the campaign. The result: 18 different agencies provided ideas to help raise Oxfam's profile in Canada and to get people to sign an online petition.[32]

- Target marketing and two-way communication are easier thanks to the proliferation of special-interest magazines, TV channels, and Internet newsgroups. Extranets linking suppliers and distributors let firms send and receive information, place orders, and make payments more efficiently. A company can also interact with individual customers by *personalizing* messages, services, and the relationship. In 2005, discount brokerage Charles Schwab spent 25 percent of its marketing-communication budget online to support its "Talk to Chuck" campaign, up from 8 percent in 2003.[33]

- Marketers can send ads, coupons, samples, and information to customers who have requested them or have given the company permission to send them. Companies can now assemble information about individual customers' purchases, preferences, demographics, and profitability. British supermarket giant Tesco is outpacing its rival, Sainsbury, by using its Clubcard data to personalize offers according to individual customer attributes.[34]

- Companies can reach consumers on the move with mobile marketing. Using GPS technology, for instance, consumers can download company logos so they can spot brands such as Tim Hortons and Baskin Robbins when they're on the road.[35] Firms can also advertise on video iPods and reach consumers on their cell phones through mobile marketing.[36] General Motors Corp. launched its Pontiac G6 with a promotion asking consumers use their camera phones to take photos of the sports sedan and send them to GM in return for a free classic punk-rock ringtone and a chance to win $1 million in cash. About 18 500 photos were sent, mostly from the G6 target market of young males under the age of 25.[37]

- Firms can produce individually differentiated goods, whether they're ordered in person, on the phone, or online, thanks to advances in factory customization, computers, the Internet, and marketing-database software. For a price, customers can buy M&M candies with their names on them, Wheaties boxes and Jones soda bottles with their pictures on the front, and Heinz ketchup bottles with customized messages.[38] BMW's technology now allows buyers to design their own models from among 350 variations, with 500 options, 90 exterior colours, and 170 trims. The company claims that 80 percent of the cars bought by individuals in Europe and up to 30 percent bought in North America are built to order.

- Managers can improve purchasing, recruiting, training, and internal and external communications. Companies as diverse as General Motors and McDonald's are embracing corporate blogging to communicate with the public, customers, and employees. Since aging is a touchy subject for many women, Toronto-based Medicis Aesthetics Canada launched a social networking community, www.defineyourself.ca, for women 35–55 to discuss their attitudes towards aging. The site wasn't product-focused and used no overt branding. "It's about market research and sponsoring a dialogue. . . . We wanted to capture the mind-set of women approaching these milestone ages."[39]

- Corporate buyers can achieve substantial savings by using the Internet to compare sellers' prices, purchase materials at auction, or post their own terms. Companies can improve logistics and operations to reap substantial cost savings and at the same time improve accuracy and service quality.

- Firms can also recruit new employees online, and many also prepare Internet training products for employees, dealers, and agents to download.

COMPANY ORIENTATION TOWARD THE MARKETPLACE

What philosophy should guide a company's marketing efforts? What relative weights should be given to the interests of the organization, the customers, and society? Very often these interests conflict. The competing orientations with which organizations have conducted marketing activities include the production concept, product concept, selling concept, marketing concept, and holistic marketing concept. Increasingly, marketers' operations are consistent with a holistic marketing concept.

The Production Concept

The production concept holds that consumers will prefer products that are widely available and inexpensive. Managers of production-oriented businesses concentrate on achieving high production efficiency, low costs, and mass distribution. This orientation makes sense in developing countries such as China where the largest PC manufacturer, Lenovo, and domestic appliances giant, Haier, take advantage of the country's huge inexpensive labour pool to dominate the market.[40] Marketers also use the production concept when a company wants to expand the market.

The Product Concept

The product concept holds that consumers will favour those products that offer the most quality, performance, or innovative features. Managers in these organizations focus on making superior products and improving them over time. However, these managers are sometimes caught up in a love affair with their products. They might accept the "better-mousetrap" fallacy, believing that a better mousetrap will lead people to beat a path to their door. A new or improved product will not necessarily be successful unless the product is priced, distributed, advertised, and sold properly.

The Selling Concept

The selling concept holds that consumers and businesses, if left alone, will ordinarily not buy enough of the organization's products. The organization must, therefore, undertake an aggressive selling and promotion effort. The selling concept is epitomized by the thinking of Sergio Zyman, Coca-Cola's former vice-president of marketing: The purpose of marketing is to sell more stuff to more people, more often, for more money, in order to make more profit.[41]

The selling concept is practised most aggressively with unsought goods: goods that buyers normally do not think of buying, such as insurance, encyclopedias, and funeral plots. Most firms practise the selling concept when they have overcapacity. Their aim is to sell what they make rather than make what the market wants. However, marketing based on hard selling carries high risks. It assumes that customers who are coaxed into buying a product will like it; and that if they do not, they will not return it or bad-mouth it or complain to consumer organizations and will buy it again.

The Marketing Concept

The marketing concept emerged in the mid-1950s.[42] Instead of a product-centred, "make-and-sell" philosophy, we shifted to a customer-centred, "sense-and-respond" philosophy. Instead of "hunting," marketing is "gardening." The job is not to find the right customers for your product, but the right products for your customers. Dell Computer doesn't prepare a perfect computer for its target market. Rather, it provides product platforms on which each person customizes the features he or she desires in the computer.

The marketing concept holds that the key to achieving organizational goals consists of the company being more effective than competitors in creating, delivering, and communicating superior customer value to its chosen target markets.

More and more companies can produce individually differentiated goods, even consumer products like these.

Theodore Levitt of Harvard drew a perceptive contrast between the selling and marketing concepts:

> Selling focuses on the needs of the seller; marketing on the needs of the buyer. Selling is preoccupied with the seller's need to convert his product into cash; marketing with the idea of satisfying the needs of the customer by means of the product and the whole cluster of things associated with creating, delivering, and finally consuming it.[43]

Several scholars have found that companies that embrace the marketing concept achieve superior performance.[44] This was first demonstrated by companies practising a *reactive market orientation:* understanding and meeting customers' expressed needs. Some critics say this means companies develop only low-level innovations. Narver and his colleagues argue that high-level innovation is possible if the focus is on customers' latent needs. He calls this a *proactive marketing orientation.*[45] Companies such as 3M, HP, and Motorola have made a practice of researching or imagining latent needs through a "probe-and-learn" process. Companies that practise both a reactive and proactive marketing orientation are implementing a *total market orientation* and are likely to be the most successful.

The Holistic Marketing Concept

To learn how Tata applied the marketing concept to deepen its understanding of customers in India, visit www.pearsoned.co.in/ marketingmanagementindia.

Without question, the trends and forces defining the twenty-first century are leading business firms to a new set of beliefs and practices. Today's best marketers recognize the need to have a more complete, cohesive approach that goes beyond traditional applications of the marketing concept. "Marketing Memo: Marketing Right and Wrong" suggests where companies go wrong—and how they can get it right—in their marketing.

The **holistic marketing** concept is based on the development, design, and implementation of marketing programs, processes, and activities that are broad in scope and interdependent. Holistic marketing recognizes that "everything matters" in marketing—and that a broad, integrated perspective is often necessary.

Holistic marketing is thus an approach that attempts to recognize and reconcile the scope and complexities of marketing activities. Figure 1.5 provides a schematic overview of four broad components characterizing holistic marketing: relationship marketing, integrated marketing, internal marketing, and socially responsible marketing. We'll examine these major themes throughout this book. Successful companies will be those that can keep their marketing changing with the changes in their marketplace—and marketspace. "Breakthrough Marketing: Nike," at the end of this chapter, describes how Nike has successfully changed—and thrived—over the years.

Relationship Marketing

Increasingly, a key goal of marketing is to develop deep, enduring relationships with all people or organizations that could directly or indirectly affect the success of the firm's marketing activities. **Relationship marketing** has the aim of building mutually satisfying long-term relations with key parties—customers, suppliers, distributors, and other marketing partners—in order to earn and retain their business.[46] Relationship marketing builds strong economic, technical, and social ties among the parties.

Four key constituents of relationship marketing are customers, employees, marketing partners (channels, suppliers, distributors, dealers, agencies), and members of the financial community (shareholders, investors, analysts). Marketers must also be cognizant of the intended and unintended impact their practices may have on other stakeholders. Marketers must respect the need to create prosperity among all these constituents and develop policies and strategies to balance the returns to all stakeholders. To develop strong relationships with these constituents requires an understanding of the company's capabilities and resources, as well as stakeholder needs, goals, and desires.

The ultimate outcome of relationship marketing is the building of a unique company asset called a marketing network. A **marketing network** consists of the company and its supporting stakeholders (customers, employees, suppliers, distributors, retailers, ad agencies, university scientists, and others) with whom it has built mutually profitable business relationships. Increasingly, competition is not between companies but between marketing networks, with the prize going to the company that has built the better network. The operating principle is simple: build an effective network of relationships with key stakeholders, and profits will follow.[47] Following this reasoning, more companies are choosing to own brands rather than physical assets. They are also increasingly subcontracting activities to outsourcing firms that can do them better and more cheaply, while retaining core activities.

MARKETING **MEMO** | MARKETING RIGHT AND WRONG

The Ten Deadly Sins of Marketing

1. The company is not sufficiently market focused and customer driven.
2. The company does not fully understand its target customers.
3. The company needs to better define and monitor its competitors.
4. The company has not properly managed its relationships with its stakeholders.
5. The company is not good at finding new opportunities.
6. The company's marketing plans and planning process are deficient.
7. The company's product and service policies need tightening.
8. The company's brand-building and communications skills are weak.
9. The company is not well organized to carry on effective and efficient marketing.
10. The company has not made maximum use of technology.

The Ten Commandments of Marketing

1. The company segments the market, chooses the best segments, and develops a strong position in each chosen segment.
2. The company maps its customers' needs, perceptions, preferences, and behaviour and motivates its stakeholders to obsess about serving and satisfying the customers.
3. The company knows its major competitors and their strengths and weaknesses.
4. The company builds partners out of its stakeholders and generously rewards them.
5. The company develops systems for identifying opportunities, ranking them, and choosing the best ones.
6. The company manages a marketing-planning system that leads to insightful long-term and short-term plans.
7. The company exercises strong control over its product and service mix.
8. The company builds strong brands by using the most cost-effective communication and promotion tools.
9. The company builds marketing leadership and a team spirit among its various departments.
10. The company constantly adds technology that gives it a competitive advantage in the marketplace.

Source: Adapted from Philip Kotler, *Ten Deadly Marketing Sins* (Hoboken, NJ: John Wiley & Sons, 2004).

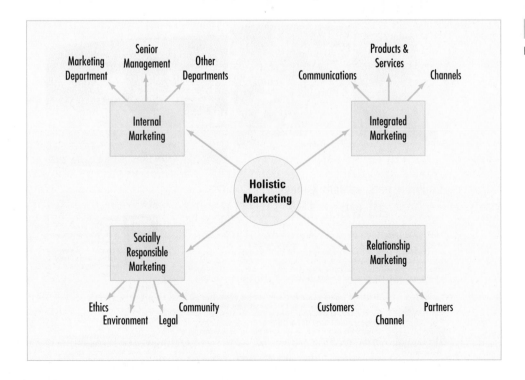

FIGURE 1.5

Holistic Marketing Dimensions

A growing number of today's companies are also shaping separate offers, services, and messages to *individual customers* based on information about past transactions, demographics, psychographics, and media and distribution preferences. By focusing on their most profitable customers, products, and channels, these firms hope to achieve profitable growth, capturing a larger share of each customer's expenditures by building high customer loyalty. They estimate individual customer lifetime value and design their market offerings and prices to make a profit over the customer's lifetime.

These activities fall under what Columbia Business School professor Larry Selden and his wife and business consulting partner, Yoko Sugiura Selden, call "customer centricity." They offer the Royal Bank of Canada as an example:

Royal Bank of Canada

In thinking of its business in terms of customer segments rather than product segments, Royal Bank of Canada (RBC) has tagged each of its roughly 11 million clients and put them into meaningful segments. Now it can focus on measuring and managing the customer profitability of these segments. In the process, RBC discovered a sizeable subsegment of customers hidden within its broader categories of "wealth preservers" and "wealth accumulators." Dubbed "snowbirds," these individuals spent a number of months each winter in Florida, where they were experiencing difficulties establishing credit as well as missing their Canadian communities, particularly the familiarity of the French-Canadian accent and fluency in French. In order to meet their unique needs, RBC created a Canadian banking experience in Florida.[48]

Another goal of relationship marketing is to place much more emphasis on customer retention. Attracting a new customer may cost five times as much as doing a job well enough to retain an existing one. A bank aims to increase its share of the customer's wallet; the supermarket aims to capture a larger share of the customer's "stomach." Companies build customer share by offering a larger variety of goods to existing customers. They train their employees in cross-selling and up-selling.

Marketing must skillfully conduct not only customer relationship management (CRM), but partner relationship management (PRM) as well. Companies are deepening their partnering arrangements

Terrapin Communications Inc. partners with OCM Manufacturing to ensure that its Safety Turtle product is manufactured offshore in a safe and reliable manner.

with key suppliers and distributors, thinking of these intermediaries not as customers but as partners in delivering value to final customers so everybody benefits. In the face of many product recalls over issues such as lead-tainted children's toys, forming such partnerships is becoming even more important. An Ottawa-based company, OCM Manufacturing Inc., is working with many clients, such as Terrapin Communications Inc. (also of Ottawa), to help them manage contracts with overseas suppliers. Terrapin's flagship product—a high-tech bracelet called Safety Turtle, which has an alarm that goes off if immersed in water and is designed for use by children, seniors, people who work near water hazards, and even pets—is manufactured in China by Baja Technology Inc. OCM maintains control over the entire Safety Turtle manufacturing process and inspects the contractor's premises and procedures. It prepared all the documentation of the manufacturing specifications and monitors the entire process so that things like substitute parts cannot be used.[49]

Integrated Marketing

The marketer's task is to devise marketing activities and assemble fully integrated marketing programs to create, communicate, and deliver value for consumers. Marketing activities come in all forms.[50] McCarthy classified these activities as *marketing-mix* tools of four broad kinds, which he called *the four Ps* of marketing: product, price, place, and promotion.[51]

The particular marketing variables under each P are shown in Figure 1.6. Marketers make marketing-mix decisions to influence their trade channels as well as their final consumers. Once they understand these groups, marketers make or customize an offering or solution, inform consumers—recognizing that many other sources of information also exist—set a price that offers real value, and choose places where the offering will be accessible.

The firm can change its price, sales force size, and advertising expenditures in the short run. It can develop new products and modify its distribution channels only in the long run. Thus, the firm typically makes fewer period-to-period marketing-mix changes in the short run than the number of marketing-mix decision variables might suggest.

The four Ps represent the sellers' view of the marketing tools available for influencing buyers. From a buyer's point of view, each marketing tool is designed to deliver a customer benefit. A complementary breakdown of marketing activities has been proposed that centres on customers. Its four dimensions (SIVA) and the corresponding customer questions these are designed to answer are:[52]

1. Solution: How can I solve my problem?
2. Information: Where can I learn more about it?
3. Value: What is my total sacrifice to get this solution?
4. Access: Where can I find it?

Winning companies satisfy customer needs and surpass their expectations economically and conveniently and with effective communication.

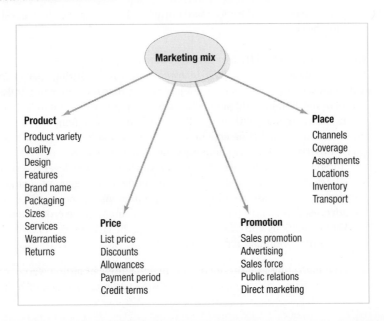

FIGURE 1.6

The Four P Components of the Marketing Mix

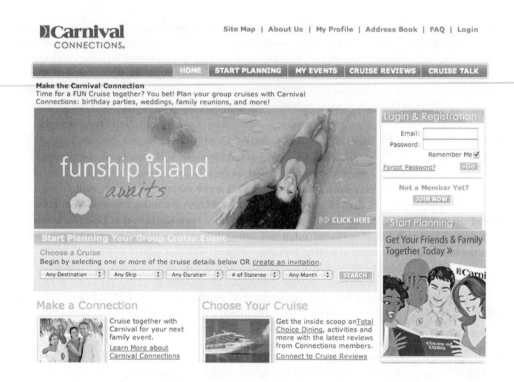

Carnival Connections' online marketing activities include an interactive site where cruise fans can compare notes. The site has generated about $1.6 million in bookings.

Two key themes of integrated marketing are that (1) many different marketing activities communicate and deliver value and (2) when coordinated, marketing activities maximize their joint effects. In other words, marketers should design and implement any one marketing activity with all other activities in mind.

For example, using an integrated communication strategy means choosing communication options that reinforce and complement each other. A marketer might selectively employ television, radio, and print advertising, public relations and events, and PR and website communications so that each contributes on its own as well as improving the effectiveness of the others. Each communication must also deliver a consistent brand image to customers at every brand contact. Applying an integrated channel strategy ensures that direct and indirect channels, such as online and retail sales, work together to maximize sales and brand equity.

Online marketing activities play an increasingly prominent role in building brands and selling products and services. Created for $300 000 and no additional promotional expense, online site Carnival Connections made it easy for cruise fans to compare notes on cruise destinations and onboard entertainment from casinos to conga lines. In a few short months, 2000 of the site's 13 000 registered users planned trips aboard Carnival's 22 ships, generating an estimated $1.6 million in revenue for the company.[53]

Internal Marketing

Holistic marketing incorporates *internal marketing*, ensuring that everyone in the organization, especially senior management, embraces appropriate marketing principles. Internal marketing is the task of hiring, training, and motivating able employees who want to serve customers well. Smart marketers recognize that marketing activities within the company can be as important, or even more important, than marketing activities directed outside the company. It makes no sense to promise excellent service before the company's staff is ready to provide it.

Internal marketing must take place on two levels. At one level, the various marketing functions—sales force, advertising, customer service, product management, marketing research—must work together. Too often, the sales force thinks product managers set prices or sale quotas "too high," or the advertising director and a brand manager cannot agree on an advertising campaign. All these marketing functions must be coordinated from the customer's point of view. The following example highlights the coordination problem:

The marketing vice-president of a major European airline wants to increase the airline's traffic share. His strategy is to build up customer satisfaction by providing better food, cleaner cabins, better-trained cabin crews, and lower fares, yet he has no authority in these matters. The catering department chooses food that keeps food costs down; the maintenance department uses cleaning services that keep cleaning costs down; the human-resources department hires people without regard to whether they are naturally friendly; and the finance department sets the fares. Because these departments generally take a cost or production point of view, the vice-president of marketing is stymied in his efforts to create an integrated marketing mix.

At the second level, other departments must embrace marketing; they must also "think customer." Marketing is not so much a department as a company orientation.[54] See Table 1.1.

| TABLE 1.1 | ASSESSING WHICH COMPANY DEPARTMENTS ARE CUSTOMER-MINDED |

R&D
- They spend time meeting customers and listening to their problems.
- They welcome the involvement of marketing, manufacturing, and other departments to each new project.
- They benchmark competitors' products and seek "best of class" solutions.
- They solicit customer reactions and suggestions as the project progresses.
- They continuously improve and refine the product on the basis of market feedback.

Purchasing
- They proactively search for the best suppliers.
- They build long-term relations with fewer but more reliable high-quality suppliers.
- They don't compromise quality for price savings.

Manufacturing
- They invite customers to visit and tour their plants.
- They visit customer plants.
- They willingly work overtime to meet promised delivery schedules.
- They continuously search for ways to produce goods faster and/or at lower cost.
- They continuously improve product quality, aiming for zero defects.
- They meet customer requirements for "customization" where possible.

Marketing
- They study customer needs and wants in well-defined market segments.
- They allocate marketing effort in relation to the long-run profit potential of the targeted segments.
- They develop winning offers for each target segment.
- They measure company image and customer satisfaction on a continuous basis.

- They continuously gather and evaluate ideas for new products, product improvements, and services.
- They urge all company departments and employees to be customer-centred.

Sales
- They have specialized knowledge of the customer's industry.
- They strive to give the customer "the best solution."
- They make only promises that they can keep.
- They feed back customers' needs and ideas to those in charge of product development.
- They serve the same customers for a long period of time.

Logistics
- They set a high standard for service delivery time and meet this standard consistently.
- They operate a knowledgeable and friendly customer service department that can answer questions, handle complaints, and resolve problems in a satisfactory and timely manner.

Accounting
- They prepare periodic "profitability" reports by product, market segment, geographic areas (regions, sales territories), order sizes, channels, and individual customers.
- They prepare invoices tailored to customer needs and answer customer queries courteously and quickly.

Finance
- They understand and support marketing expenditures (e.g., image advertising) that produce long-term customer preference and loyalty.
- They tailor the financial package to the customer's financial requirements.
- They make quick decisions on customer creditworthiness.

Public Relations
- They send out favourable news about the company and "damage control" unfavourable news.
- They act as an internal customer and public advocate for better company policies and practices.

Source: Philip Kotler, *Kotler on Marketing* (New York: Free Press, 1999), pp. 21–22. Reprinted with permission of The Free Press, a Division of Simon & Schuster Adult Publishing Group. Copyright © 1999 by Philip Kotler. All rights reserved.

FIGURE 1.7

Types of Marketing
Organizations (percent
of sample population in
parentheses)

*Source: Based on Booz Allen
Hamilton/Assn. of National
Advertisers Marketing Profiles,* in
conjunction with *Brandweek,* from
Constantine von Hoffman, "Armed
with Intelligence," *Brandweek,*
May 29, 2006, pp. 17–20.

Growth Champions (14.7%) emphasize growth-support functions, leading such general-management activities as product innovation and new-business development.

Marketing Masters (38.4%) oversee company-wide marketing efforts and the customer-focused side of new product and service launches but are typically not involved with strategic decisions.

Senior Counselors (16.9%) specialize in marketing strategy, advising the CEO and individual businesses, and may drive major communication programs, although not typically new product development.

Best Practices Advisors (8.9%) work with individual business units to improve their marketing effectiveness but are less likely to be linked with above-average growth than both the Growth Champions and the Marketing Masters.

Brand Builders (12.2%) support brands by providing marketing services like communications strategy, creative output, and campaign execution but exhibit little strategic leadership.

Service Providers (14.7%) coordinate marketing communications but often work in firms with lower revenue growth and profitability.

Internal marketing thus requires vertical alignment with senior management and horizontal alignment with other departments so that everyone understands, appreciates, and supports the marketing effort. As former Yahoo! CMO Cammie Dunaway states, "You want to be connecting at the very senior levels of the organization, and you also want to be connecting in with the engineers and scientists who are doing a lot of the work on the front lines." Dunaway also emphasizes the importance of integrated marketing, comparing her job to that of an orchestra conductor: "You have to figure out how to pull all those instruments together in a way that's delivering great marketing accountability and engaging marketing programs."[55]

A study conducted by Booz Allen Hamilton and the Association of National Advertisers, in conjunction with *Brandweek* magazine, asked 2000 executives to describe the marketing structure within their organizations and to detail the tasks they consider integral to their missions. The researchers identified six types of marketing organizations (see Figure 1.7 for a breakdown and descriptions). In the most successful type, Growth Champions, marketing heavily influenced all aspects of the organization. Growth Champions were 20 percent more likely to deliver revenue growth and profitability than were the other types of marketing organizations.

Performance Marketing

Holistic marketing incorporates *performance marketing* with an understanding of the returns to the business from marketing activities and programs and also addresses broader concerns and their legal, ethical, social, and environmental effects. Top management goes beyond sales revenue to examine the marketing scorecard and interpret what is happening to market share, customer-loss rate, customer satisfaction, product quality, and other measures.

FINANCIAL ACCOUNTABILITY Marketers are thus increasingly asked to justify their investments to senior management in financial and profitability terms, as well as in terms of building the brand and growing the customer base.[56] As a consequence, they employ a broader variety of financial measures to assess the direct and indirect value their marketing efforts create. They also recognize that much of their firms' market value comes from intangible assets, particularly their brands, customer base, employees, distributor and supplier relations, and intellectual capital.

SOCIAL-RESPONSIBILITY MARKETING The effects of marketing clearly extend beyond the company and the customer to society as a whole. Marketers must carefully consider their role in broader terms and the ethical, environmental, legal, and social context of their activities.[57] Increasingly, consumers demand such behaviour, as Starbucks Chair Howard Schultz has observed:[58]

> We see a fundamental change in the way consumers buy their products and services. . . . Consumers now commonly engage in a cultural audit of providers. People want to know your value and ethics demonstrated by how you treat employees, the community in which you operate. The implication for marketers is to strike the balance between profitability and social consciousness and sensitivity. . . . It is not a program or a quarterly promotion, but rather a way of life. You have to integrate this level of social responsibility into your operation.

TABLE 1.2	CORPORATE SOCIAL INITIATIVES	
Type	**Description**	**Example**
Corporate social marketing	Supporting behaviour-change campaigns	McDonald's promotion of the Public Health Agency of Canada's Stairway to Health, a fun and easy way to get employees active in the workplace.
Cause marketing	Promoting social issues through efforts such as sponsorships, licensing agreements, and advertising	McDonald's sponsorship of Forest (a gorilla) at Sydney's Zoo—a 10-year sponsorship commitment, aimed at preserving this endangered species.
Cause-related marketing	Donating a percentage of revenues to a specific cause based on the revenue occurring during the announced period of support	In 2007, McDonald's Restaurants of Canada celebrated its 15th McHappy Day. One dollar from the sale of every McMuffin, Big Mac, and Happy Meal on this day went to each restaurant's children's charity of choice. Proceeds from the sale of the Ronald McDonald Big Red Shoe (which could be purchased in-restaurant for $1) and the McHappy Day pin ($2) also went to local children's charities.
Corporate philanthropy	Making gifts of money, goods, or time to help nonprofit organizations, groups, or individuals	McDonald's contributions to Ronald McDonald House Charities.
Corporate community involvement	Providing in-kind or volunteer services in the community	McDonald's catering meals for firefighters in the December 1997 bushfires in Australia.
Socially responsible business practices	Adapting and conducting business practices that protect the environment and human and animal rights	McDonald's requirement that suppliers increase the amount of living space for laying hens on factory farms.

Sources: McDonald's Restaurants of Canada Community Commitment webpages, www.mcdonalds.ca/en/community/index.aspx; Philip Kotler and Nancy Lee, *Corporate Social Responsibility: Doing the Most Good for Your Company and Your Cause* (Hoboken, NJ: Wiley, 2004). Copyright © 2005 by Philip Kotler and Nancy Lee. Used by permission of John Wiley & Sons, Inc.

This realization calls for a new term that enlarges the marketing concept. We propose calling it the "societal marketing concept." The *societal marketing concept* holds that the organization's task is to determine the needs, wants, and interests of target markets and to deliver the desired satisfactions more effectively and efficiently than competitors in a way that preserves or enhances the consumer's and society's long-term well-being. Sustainability has become a major corporate concern in the face of challenging environmental forces. Firms such as Hewlett-Packard have introduced recyclable computers and printers and reduced greenhouse emissions; McDonald's strives for a "socially responsible supply system" encompassing everything from healthy fisheries to redesigned packaging.[59]

The societal marketing concept calls upon marketers to build social and ethical considerations into their marketing practices. They must balance and juggle the often conflicting criteria of company profits, consumer want satisfaction, and public interest. Table 1.2 displays some different types of corporate social initiatives illustrated by McDonald's.[60]

As goods become more commoditized and as consumers grow more socially conscious, some companies both small (like Rocky Mountain Soap, headquartered in Canmore, Alberta) and large (like oil and gas company Nexen, the Royal Bank, and Patagonia) are using social responsibility as a way to differentiate themselves from competitors, build consumer preference, and achieve notable sales and profit gains. These companies believe customers will increasingly look for signs of good corporate citizenship.

Ben & Jerry's

When they founded Ben & Jerry's, Ben Cohen and Jerry Greenfield embraced the performance marketing concept by dividing the traditional financial bottom line into a "double" bottom line which included a measurement of the environmental impact of their products and processes. That "double bottom line" later expanded into a "triple bottom line" to represent in objective terms the social impacts, both negative and positive, of the firm's entire range of business activities. Cohen and Greenfield informed their senior managers that they were going to be held accountable to maintain two bottom lines: "To improve the quality of life in the communities in which we operate, and to make a reasonable profit." Ben & Jerry's also recognized that just as companies require outside auditors to measure financial performance, they also require outside auditors to measure their performance along the environmental and social dimensions. As one of those outside auditors later recalled: "Measurement is a key tool to convince boards of directors and core executives that the socially responsible company is a sound business strategy. As companies make more data from their efforts available, the story becomes more compelling. . . . To advocate transparency in business and for all of us to ascribe to that—that's the ultimate acid test."[61]

MARKETING MANAGEMENT TASKS

With the holistic marketing philosophy as a backdrop, we can identify a specific set of tasks that make up successful marketing management and marketing leadership. We'll use the following situation to illustrate these tasks in the context of the plan of the book. ("Marketing Memo: Marketers' Frequently Asked Questions" is a good checklist for the questions marketing managers ask, all of which we examine in this book.)

Zeus, Inc. (name disguised) operates in several industries, including chemicals, cameras, and film. The company is organized into strategic business units (SBUs). Corporate management is considering what to do with its Atlas camera division. At present, Atlas produces a range of 35-mm and digital cameras. The market for cameras is intensely competitive. Although Zeus has a sizable market share and is producing much revenue for the company, the 35-mm market itself is growing very slowly and its market share is slipping. In the faster-growing digital-camera segment, Zeus is facing strong competition and has been slow to gain sales. Zeus's corporate management wants Atlas's marketing group to produce a strong turnaround plan for the division. Marketing management has to come up with a convincing marketing plan, sell corporate management on the plan, and then implement and control it.

MARKETING **MEMO** | MARKETERS' FREQUENTLY ASKED QUESTIONS

1. How can we spot and choose the right market segment(s)?

2. How can we differentiate our offerings?

3. How should we respond to customers who buy on price?

4. How can we compete against lower-cost, lower-price competitors?

5. How far can we go in customizing our offering for each customer?

6. How can we grow our business?

7. How can we build stronger brands?

8. How can we reduce the cost of customer acquisition?

9. How can we keep our customers loyal for longer?

10. How can we tell which customers are more important?

11. How can we measure the payback from advertising, sales promotion, and public relations?

12. How can we improve sales-force productivity?

13. How can we establish multiple channels and yet manage channel conflict?

14. How can we get the other company departments to be more customer-oriented?

Developing Marketing Strategies and Plans

The first task facing Atlas is to identify its potential long-run opportunities given its market experience and core competencies (see Chapter 2). Atlas can design its cameras with better features. It can also consider making a line of video cameras, or it can use its core competency in optics to design a line of binoculars and telescopes. Whichever direction it chooses, it must develop concrete marketing plans that specify the marketing strategy and tactics going forward.

Capturing Marketing Insights

Atlas needs a reliable marketing information system to closely monitor its marketing environment. Its microenvironment consists of all the players who affect its ability to produce and sell cameras: suppliers, marketing intermediaries, customers, and competitors. Its macroenvironment includes demographic, economic, natural, technological, political-legal, and social-cultural forces that affect sales and profits (see Chapter 3).

Atlas also needs a dependable marketing research system. To transform marketing strategy into marketing programs, marketing managers must measure market potential, forecast demand, and make basic decisions about marketing expenditures, marketing activities, and marketing allocation.[62] To make these allocations, marketing managers may use sales-response functions that show how the amount of money spent in each application will affect sales and profits (see Chapter 4).

Connecting with Customers

Atlas must consider how to best create value for its chosen target markets and develop strong, profitable, long-term relationships with customers (see Chapter 5). To do so, Atlas needs to understand consumer markets (see Chapter 6). Who buys cameras and why do they buy? What are they looking for in the way of features and prices? Where do they shop? Atlas also sells cameras to business markets, including large corporations, professional firms, retailers, and government agencies (see Chapter 7). Purchasing agents or buying committees make the decisions. Atlas needs to gain a full understanding of how organizational buyers buy. It needs a sales force that is well trained in presenting product benefits.

Atlas will not want to market to all possible customers. Modern marketing practice calls for dividing the market into major market segments, evaluating each segment, and targeting those market segments that the company can best serve (see Chapter 8).

Building Strong Brands

Atlas must understand the strengths and weaknesses of the Zeus brand with customers (see Chapter 9). Is its 35-mm film heritage a disadvantage in the digital-camera market? Suppose Atlas decides to focus on the consumer market and develop a positioning strategy (see Chapter 10). Should Atlas position its cameras as the "Cadillac" brand, offering superior cameras at a premium price with excellent service and strong advertising? Should it build a simple, low-priced camera aimed at more price-conscious consumers? Or something in between?

Atlas must also pay close attention to competitors (see Chapter 11), anticipating its competitors' moves and knowing how to react quickly and decisively. It may want to initiate some surprise moves, in which case it needs to anticipate how its competitors will respond.

Shaping the Market Offerings

At the heart of the marketing program is the product: the firm's tangible offering to the market, which includes the product quality, design, features, and packaging (see Chapter 12). To gain a competitive advantage, Atlas may provide various services, such as leasing, delivery, repair, and training (see Chapter 13). A critical marketing decision relates to price (see Chapter 14). Atlas has to decide on wholesale and retail prices, discounts, allowances, and credit terms. Its price should be commensurate with the offer's perceived value; otherwise, buyers will turn to competitors' products.

Delivering Value

Atlas must also determine how to properly deliver to the target market the value embodied by these products and services. Channel activities include the various activities the company undertakes to make the product accessible and available to target customers (see Chapter 15). Atlas must identify, recruit, and link various marketing facilitators to supply its products and services efficiently to the target market. It must understand the various types of retailers, wholesalers, and physical-distribution firms and how they make their decisions (see Chapter 16).

Communicating Value

Atlas must also adequately communicate to the target market the value embodied by its products and services. It will need an integrated marketing communication program that maximizes the individual and collective contribution of all communication activities (see Chapter 17). Atlas has to set up mass communication programs consisting of advertising, sales promotion, events, and public relations (see Chapter 18). It also has to set up more personal communications in the form of direct and interactive marketing and must also hire, train, and motivate salespeople (see Chapter 19).

Creating Long-Term Growth

Based on its product positioning, Atlas must initiate new-product development, testing, and launching (see Chapter 20). Strategy also will have to take into account changing global opportunities and challenges (see Chapter 21).

Finally, Atlas must build a marketing organization that is capable of implementing the marketing plan (see Chapter 22). Because of surprises and disappointments that can occur as marketing plans are implemented, Atlas will need feedback and control to understand the efficiency and effectiveness of marketing activities and how both could be improved.[63] Marketing evaluation and control processes are necessary to understand the efficiency and effectiveness of marketing activities and how both could be improved.

SUMMARY

1. From a managerial point of view, marketing is the process of planning and executing the conception, pricing, promotion, and distribution of ideas, goods, and services to create exchanges that satisfy individual and organizational goals. Marketing management is the art and science of choosing target markets and getting, keeping, and growing customers through creating, delivering, and communicating superior customer value.

2. Marketers are skilled at managing demand: they seek to influence the level, timing, and composition of demand. Marketers are involved in marketing many types of entities: goods, services, events, experiences, persons, places, properties, organizations, information, and ideas. They also operate in four different marketplaces: consumer, business, global, and nonprofit.

3. Marketing is not done only by the marketing department. Marketing needs to affect every aspect of the customer experience. To create a strong marketing organization, marketers must think like executives in other departments, and executives in other departments must think more like marketers.

4. Today's marketplace is fundamentally different due to major societal forces that have resulted in many new consumer and company capabilities. These forces have created new opportunities and challenges, and marketing management has changed significantly in recent years as companies seek new ways to achieve marketing excellence.

5. There are five competing concepts under which organizations can choose to conduct their business: the production concept, product concept, selling concept, marketing concept, and the holistic marketing concept. The first three are of limited use today.

6. The holistic marketing concept is based on the development, design, and implementation of marketing programs, processes, and activities that are broad in scope and are interdependent. Holistic marketing recognizes that in marketing "everything matters" and that a broad, integrated perspective is often necessary. Four components of holistic marketing are relationship marketing, integrated marketing, internal marketing, and socially responsible marketing.

7. The set of tasks necessary for successful marketing management includes developing marketing strategies and plans, capturing marketing insights, connecting with customers, building strong brands, shaping the market offerings, delivering and communicating value, and creating successful long-term growth.

APPLICATIONS

Marketing Debate: Does Marketing Create or Satisfy Needs?

Marketing has often been defined in terms of satisfying customers' needs and wants. Critics, however, maintain that marketing does much more than that and creates needs and wants that did not exist before. According to these critics, marketers encourage consumers to spend more money than they should on goods and services they really do not need.

Take a position: Marketing shapes consumer needs and wants *versus* Marketing merely reflects the needs and wants of consumers.

Marketing Discussion

Consider the broad shifts in marketing. Are there any themes that emerge in these shifts? Can they be related to major societal forces? Which force contributed to which shift?

Breakthrough Marketing: Nike

Nike hit the ground running in 1962. Originally known as Blue Ribbon Sports, the company focused on providing high-quality running shoes designed especially for athletes by athletes. Founder Philip Knight believed that high-tech shoes for runners could be manufactured at competitive prices if imported from abroad. The company's commitment to designing innovative footwear for serious athletes helped it build a cult following among consumers around the world.

Nike believed in a "pyramid of influence" whereby product and brand choices were influenced by the preferences and behaviour of a small percentage of top athletes. Therefore, from the start, Nike's marketing campaigns featured winning athletes as spokespeople. Nike's first spokesperson, runner Steve Prefontaine, had an irreverent attitude that matched the company's spirit.

In 1985, Nike signed up rookie guard Michael Jordan as a spokesperson. Jordan was still an up-and-comer, but he personified superior performance. Nike's bet paid off: The Air Jordan line of basketball shoes flew off the shelves with revenues of over US$100 million in the first year alone.

In 1988, Nike aired the first ads in its US$20 million "Just Do It" ad campaign. The campaign, which ultimately featured 12 TV spots in all, subtly challenged a generation of athletic enthusiasts to chase their goals; it was a natural manifestation of Nike's attitude of self-empowerment through sports.

As Nike began expanding overseas to Europe, however, it found that its U.S.-style ads were seen as too aggressive. Nike realized it had to "authenticate" its brand in Europe the way it had in the United States. That meant building credibility and relevance in European sports, especially soccer (known outside North America as football). Nike became actively involved as a sponsor of youth leagues, local clubs, and national teams.

Authenticity also required that consumers see athletes, especially athletes who win, using the product. The big break came in 1994, when the Brazilian team (the only national team for which Nike had any real sponsorships) won the World Cup. That victory in the world's most popular sport helped Nike succeed in other international markets such as China, where Nike came to command 10 percent of the shoe market. By 2003 overseas revenues surpassed U.S. revenues for the first time, and by 2006 international divisions generated nearly US$7.3 billion in revenue, compared to US$5.7 billion from the United States.

In addition to expanding overseas, Nike moved into new athletic footwear, apparel, and equipment product categories. These included the Nike Golf brand of footwear, apparel, and equipment, which was endorsed by megastar Tiger Woods. It wasn't all smooth sailing, however. Nike's foray into hockey, with its acquisition of Montreal-based Canstar Sports (makers of Bauer and Cooper hockey equipment), was a dismal failure. It put the division on the selling block in 2007. Analysts believe it made a number of mistakes that caused the downfall of the line, including dropping the iconic brand names and replacing them with its own, over-pricing some equipment (such as $899 skates), and picking the wrong endorsers (Eric Lindros never achieved the star status that was projected for him).

Despite this stumble, Nike dominates the athletic footwear market today. Swooshes abound on everything from wristwatches to golf clubs to swimming caps. As a result of its expansion across geographic markets and product categories, Nike is the top athletic apparel and footwear manufacturer in the world, with corporate fiscal 2007 revenues of nearly US$16 billion.

DISCUSSION QUESTIONS

1. Over its history, Nike took various orientations towards the marketplace. What orientations did it take and why were they successful or unsuccessful?

2. Why do you think Nike's foray into hockey failed? What does this tell you about where Nike is vulnerable?

3. What recommendations would you make to senior management at Nike to help it keep ahead of its very aggressive competitors?

Sources: Justin Ewers and Tim Smart, "A Designer Swooshes In," *U.S. News & World Report,* January 26, 2004, p. 12; "Corporate Media Executive of the Year," *Delaney Report,* January 12, 2004, p. 1; "10 Top Nontraditional Campaigns," *Advertising Age,* December 22, 2003, p. 24; Chris Zook and James Allen, "Growth Outside the Core," *Haravard Business Review,* 8 (December 2003): 66.

- How does marketing affect customer value?

- How is strategic planning carried out at different levels of the organization?

- What does a marketing plan include?

CHAPTER 2

DEVELOPING MARKETING STRATEGIES AND PLANS

two

A key ingredient of the marketing-management process is insightful, creative marketing strategies and plans that can guide marketing activities. Developing the right marketing strategy over time requires a blend of discipline and flexibility. Firms must stick to a strategy but must also find new ways to constantly improve it. Increasingly, marketing must also develop strategies for a range of products and services within the organization. As a highly successful service, Transat A.T. Inc., for instance, must continually design and implement marketing activities at many levels and for many units of the vertically integrated organization, including its airline operations and its vacation properties.

Transat A.T. Inc., has been described as an "octopus-like firm" with a tentacle in almost every aspect of the travel industry—it is a charter airline, tour packager, travel-magazine publisher, baggage handler, travel agency, property developer, and hotel operator. Transat has ridden the wave of increasing global travel and picked up early on the demand for all-inclusive holidays. It began by marketing to consumers interested in packages to sunny destinations and expanded the concept to more far-flung destinations. Air Transat's strategy has helped it overcome the seasonality of the travel business, which has sunk many other competitors. In the winter months it concentrates on holidays to the Caribbean and in the summer its focus switches to Europe. Over its 20-year history, Transat has grown through a series of acquisitions like the recent purchase of Thomas Cook's 190 Canadian branches to become the fifth-largest travel operator in the world. With 2.5 million passengers annually, it has a 50-percent market share of the Canadian travel business in much of the country.

No matter what part of the business you look at, you can see Transat A.T. creates value for its customers, suppliers, and social constituents while improving its own profitability. Take the promotion it ran one Christmas: working with the Children's Wish Foundation, it flew seriously ill kids north in search of Santa and distributed a wealth of fun and gifts when he was discovered. In early 2008, it renewed its program to provide financial support for sustainable tourism projects proposed by communities and not-for-profit organizations in any of the company's approximately 60 destination countries.

>>>   <<<

Described by one industry analyst as the "best-managed travel company in Canada," Transat A.T. must understand its market well and segment it carefully if it is going to create the value its diverse customers demand. For example, it knows Europeans prefer longer trips and travel far from home. Within this larger segment, however, are the French, who want culture served up with beach excursions. Canadians want culture when they visit Europe, but demand good value for money when seeking a sunny holiday.

Sources: John Lorinc, "Magic in the Air," *Report on Business*, March 2008, pp. 38–45; David Chilton, "Air Transat Magazine Takes Flight," *Marketing Daily*, March 6, 2006; Terry Poulton, "Air Transat Flies Kids—and Press—Northward to Search for Santa," *Strategy*, December 12, 2006; Air Transat website, www.transat.com/en/about/4.0.about.transat.asp.

This chapter begins by examining some of the strategic-marketing implications of creating customer value. It then provides several perspectives on planning and describes how to draw up a formal marketing plan.

MARKETING AND CUSTOMER VALUE

Marketing involves satisfying consumers' needs and wants. The task of any business is to deliver customer value at a profit. In a hypercompetitive economy with increasingly rational buyers faced with abundant choices, a company can win only by fine-tuning the value-delivery process and choosing, providing, and communicating superior value.

The Value-Delivery Process

The traditional view of marketing is that the firm makes something and then sells it. In this view, marketing takes place in the second half of the process. Companies that subscribe to this view have the best chance of succeeding in economies marked by goods shortages where consumers are not fussy about quality, features, or style—for example, with basic staple goods in developing markets.

The traditional view of the business process, however, will not work in economies where people face abundant choices. There, the "mass market" is actually splintering into numerous micro-markets, each with its own wants, perceptions, preferences, and buying criteria. The smart competitor must design and deliver offerings for well-defined target markets. This realization inspired a new view of business processes that places marketing at the *beginning* of planning. Instead of putting the emphasis on making and selling, companies now see themselves as part of a greater value-delivery process.

The sequence of value creation and delivery can be divided into three phases. The first phase, *choosing the value*, represents the "homework" marketing must do before any product exists. The marketing staff must segment the market, select the appropriate market target, and develop the offering's value positioning. The formula "segmentation, targeting, positioning" is the essence of strategic marketing. Once the business unit has chosen the value, the second phase is *providing the value*. Marketing must determine specific product features, prices, and distribution. The task in the third phase is *communicating the value* by utilizing the sales force, sales promotion, advertising, and other promotional tools to inform and promote the product. Each of these value phases has cost implications. The value-delivery process begins before there is a product and continues while it is being developed and after it becomes available.

Nike

Critics of Nike often complain that its shoes cost almost nothing to make yet cost the consumer so much. True, the raw materials and manufacturing involved in the making of a sneaker are relatively cheap, but selling the product to the consumer is expensive. Materials, labour, shipping, equipment, import duties, and suppliers' costs generally total less than $25 a pair. Compensating its sales team, its distributors, its administration, and its endorsers, as well as paying for advertising and R&D, adds $15 or so to the total. Nike sells its product to retailers to make a profit of US$7. The retailer therefore pays roughly $47 to put a pair of Nikes on the shelf. When the retailer's overhead (typically $30 covering personnel, lease, and equipment) is factored in along with a $10 profit, the shoe costs the consumer over $80.

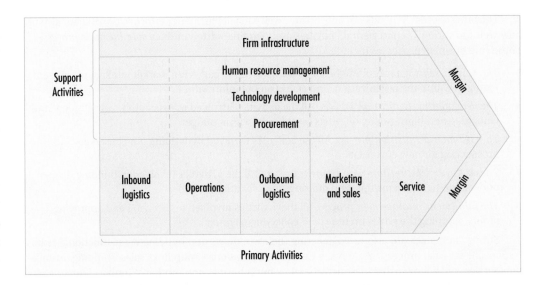

FIGURE 2.1

The Generic Value Chain

Source: Reprinted with the permission of the Free Press, an imprint of Simon & Schuster, from *Competitive Advantage: Creating and Sustaining Superior Performance*, by Michael E. Porter. Copyright © 1985 by Michael E. Porter.

London Business School's Nirmalya Kumar has put forth a "3 Vs" approach to marketing: (1) define the *value segment* or customers (and his or her needs); (2) define the *value proposition*; and (3) define the *value network* that will deliver the promised service.[1] Dartmouth's Frederick Webster views marketing in terms of (1) *value defining processes* (e.g., market research and company self-analysis), (2) *value developing processes* (e.g., new-product development, sourcing strategy, and vendor selection), and (3) *value delivering processes* (e.g., advertising and managing distribution).[2]

The Value Chain

Michael Porter of Harvard has proposed the **value chain** as a tool for identifying ways to create more customer value (see Figure 2.1).[3] According to this model, every firm is a synthesis of activities performed to design, produce, market, deliver, and support its product. The value chain identifies nine strategically relevant activities that create value and cost in a specific business. These nine value-creating activities consist of five primary activities and four support activities.

The *primary activities* cover the sequence of bringing materials into the business (inbound logistics), converting them into final products (operations), shipping out final products (outbound logistics), marketing them (marketing and sales), and servicing them (service). The *support activities*—procurement, technology development, human-resource management, and firm infrastructure—are handled in certain specialized departments, as well as elsewhere. Several departments, for example, may do procurement and hiring. The firm's infrastructure covers the costs of general management, planning, finance, accounting, legal, and government affairs.

The firm's task is to examine its costs and performance in each value-creating activity and to look for ways to improve it. The firm should estimate its competitors' costs and performances as *benchmarks* against which to compare its own costs and performance. It should go further and study the "best of class" practices of the world's best companies.[4]

Cisco Systems Inc.

Although Cisco Systems continues to grow, it is not growing at the breakneck speed of the 1990s, so its supply-base needs have changed. The company has reduced its number of suppliers and aligned itself more closely with the remaining suppliers for each of its product-based teams—from Application Specific Integrated Circuits (ASIC) to microprocessors and broadband chips. Steve Darendinger, Vice-President of Supply Chain Management for Cisco, says, "With ASIC we have gone from more than 20 suppliers to three suppliers," and "the three have a greater level of ASIC leverage." Involving suppliers in new-product development lets Cisco tap into its partners' expertise in improving the time it takes to reach high volumes in production, cutting costs, and improving supplier quality.[5]

The firm's success depends not only on how well each department performs its work, but also on how well the various departmental activities are coordinated to conduct *core business processes*.[6] These core business processes include:

- *The market-sensing process.* All the activities involved in gathering market intelligence, disseminating it within the organization, and acting on the information.
- *The new-offering-realization process.* All the activities involved in researching, developing, and launching new high-quality offerings quickly and within budget.
- *The customer-acquisition process.* All the activities involved in defining target markets and prospecting for new customers.
- *The customer-relationship-management process.* All the activities involved in building deeper understanding, relationships, and offerings to individual customers.
- *The fulfillment-management process.* All the activities involved in receiving and approving orders, shipping the goods on time, and collecting payment.

Strong companies are also re-engineering their workflows and building cross-functional teams responsible for each process.[7] At Xerox, a Customer Operations Group links sales, shipping, installation, service, and billing so that these activities flow smoothly into one another. Winning companies are those that excel at managing core business processes through cross-functional teams. AT&T, Polaroid, and Motorola have reorganized their employees into cross-functional teams; cross-functional teams are also found in nonprofits and government organizations. U.S. drugstore chain Rite Aid is using cross-functional teams to try to push its stores from third to first place in the drugstore hierarchy. The company has created teams to focus on sales and margin growth, operational excellence, market optimization, continued supply-chain improvements, and continued cost control.[8]

To be successful, a firm also needs to look for competitive advantages beyond its own operations into the value chains of suppliers, distributors, and customers. Many companies today have partnered with specific suppliers and distributors to create a superior **value-delivery network** (also called a **supply chain**).[9]

Lululemon Athletica Inc.

Lululemon, the Canadian-based yoga-apparel retail phenomenon, has learned the importance of an efficient and responsive supply chain the hard way. It has grown so fast in both Canada and the U.S. that supply can't keep up with demand, and its stores keep running out of products. Take the example of its new Chicago store where shelves were emptied of running outfits just when a big marathon was being held. What is even more worrisome is that the 59-stores-and-growing chain doesn't have the systems to track how much business it is losing due to inadequate inventory. These issues must be resolved before the company can successfully undertake the international expansion that is part of its strategy. New technology is being installed to help resolve the issues, and Lululemon has a plan to quickly airlift more merchandise from Asia in periods of heavy demand.[10]

Core Competencies

Traditionally, companies owned and controlled most of the resources that entered their businesses—labour power, materials, machines, information, and energy—but this situation is changing. Many companies today outsource less-critical resources if they can be obtained at better quality or lower cost. India has developed a reputation as a country that can provide ample outsourcing support.

The key is to own and nurture the resources and competencies that make up the essence of the business. Nike, for example, does not manufacture its own shoes because certain Asian manufacturers are more competent at this task; Nike nurtures its superiority in shoe design and shoe merchandising, its two core competencies. We can say that a **core competency** has three characteristics: (1) it is a source of competitive advantage in that it makes a significant contribution to perceived customer benefits, (2) it has applications in a wide variety of markets, and (3) it is difficult for competitors to imitate.[11]

Competitive advantage also accrues to companies that possess distinctive capabilities. Whereas core competencies tend to refer to areas of special technical and production expertise, *distinctive capabilities* tend to describe excellence in broader business processes. Consider the Hospital for Sick Children, located in Toronto.

Hospital for Sick Children

As Canada's most research-intensive hospital and the largest centre in the country dedicated to improving children's health, Sick Kids (as it is commonly called) is widely recognized as one of the best children's health-care and research institutions in the world. It is one of a handful of children's hospitals that are capable of developing and administering treatments for children with very severe and complex medical problems—children who would otherwise be untreatable. Its incredible reputation is based upon a set of unique and distinct capabilities that give Sick Kids its competitive advantage in the realm of children's hospitals. These capabilities include attracting and retaining world-class faculty and research trainees; creating state-of-the-art, high-quality, large-scale shared facilities; capitalizing on intellectual-property and technology-commercialization opportunities; maximizing opportunities for discovery and innovation; developing internationally competitive, cutting-edge infrastructure; and providing exceptional training and development opportunities. This set of capabilities has led to the development of many breakthrough treatments, helping Sick Kids maintain a level of public and private funding that is the envy of other hospitals.[12]

SickKids Foundation has leveraged the many distinctive capabilities of The Hospital for Sick Children so it can live its promise of being a world leader in children's health.

George Day, a Canadian academic who works at Wharton, sees market-driven organizations as excelling in three distinctive capabilities: market sensing, customer linking, and channel bonding.[13] With respect to market sensing, he believes that tremendous opportunities and threats often begin as "weak signals" from the "periphery" of a business. He offers a systematic process for developing peripheral vision, and practical tools and strategies for building "vigilant organizations" that attune themselves to changes in the environment by asking questions in three categories (see Table 2.1).

TABLE 2.1	BECOMING A VIGILANT ORGANIZATION

- Learning from the past
  - What have been our past blind spots?
  - What instructive analogies do other industries offer?
  - Who in the industry is skilled at picking up weak signals and acting on them?
- Evaluating the present
  - What important signals are we rationalizing away?
  - What are our mavericks, outliers, complainers, and defectors telling us?
  - What are our peripheral customers and competitors really thinking?
- Envisioning the future
  - What future surprises could really hurt or help us?
  - What emerging technologies could change the game?
  - Is there an unthinkable scenario that might disrupt our business?

Source: George S. Day and Paul J. H. Schoemaker, *Peripheral Vision: Detecting the Weak Signals That Will Make or Break Your Company* (Boston: Harvard Business School Press, 2006).

Competitive advantage ultimately derives from how well the company has fitted its core competencies and distinctive capabilities into tightly interlocking "activity systems." Companies such as Transat A.T., Dell, and IKEA are hard to imitate because their activity systems can't be copied by competitors.

Business realignment may be necessary to maximize core competencies. Realignment has three steps: (1) (re)defining the business concept or "big idea"; (2) (re)shaping the business scope; and (3) (re)positioning the company's brand identity. Consider what Kodak is doing to realign its business:

Kodak

With the advent of the digital era and consumers' new capacity to store, share, and print photos using their PCs, Kodak faces more competition than ever, both in-store and online. In 2004, after being bumped from the Dow Jones Industrial Average, where it had held a spot for more than 70 years, the company started the painful process of transformation. It started by expanding its line of digital cameras, printers, and other equipment, and it also set out to increase market share in the lucrative medical-imaging business. Making shifts is not without challenges, however. The company announced in the summer of 2006 that it would outsource the making of its digital cameras. Kodak eliminated almost 30 000 jobs between 2004 and 2007, and it spent money acquiring a string of companies for its graphics-communications unit. Not only must Kodak convince consumers to buy its digital cameras and home printers, but it also must become known as the most convenient and affordable way to process digital images. So far, the company faces steep competition from Sony, Canon, and Hewlett-Packard.[14]

A Holistic Marketing Orientation and Customer Value

A holistic marketing orientation, such as the one used by Transat A.T., can also help capture customer value. One view of holistic marketing is as "integrating the value exploration, value creation, and value delivery activities with the purpose of building long-term, mutually satisfying relationships and co-prosperity among key stakeholders."[15] According to this view, holistic marketers succeed by managing a superior value chain that delivers a high level of product quality, service, and speed. Holistic marketers achieve profitable growth by expanding customer share, building customer loyalty, and capturing customer lifetime value. Figure 2.2, the holistic-marketing framework, shows how the

FIGURE 2.2

A Holistic Marketing Framework

Source: P. Kotler, D.C. Jain, and S. Maesincee, "Formulating a Market Renewal Strategy," in *Marketing Moves* (Part 1), Fig. 1-1 (Boston: Harvard Business School Press, 2002), p. 29.

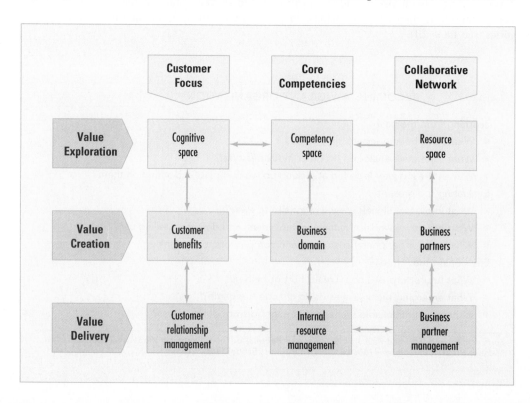

interaction between relevant actors (customers, company, and collaborators) and value-based activities (value exploration, value creation, and value delivery) helps to create, maintain, and renew customer value.

The holistic-marketing framework is designed to address three key management questions:

1. *Value exploration.* How can a company identify new value opportunities?
2. *Value creation.* How can a company efficiently create more promising new-value offerings?
3. *Value delivery.* How can a company use its capabilities and infrastructure to deliver the new-value offerings more efficiently?

Let's look at how marketers can answer these questions.

VALUE EXPLORATION Finding new value opportunities is a matter of understanding the relationships among three spaces: (1) the customer's cognitive space; (2) the company's competence space; and (3) the collaborator's resource space. The customer's *cognitive space* reflects existing and latent needs and includes dimensions such as the need for participation, stability, freedom, and change.[16] The company's *competency space* can be described in terms of breadth (broad versus focused scope of business) and depth (physical versus knowledge-based capabilities). The collaborator's *resource space* includes horizontal partnerships, with partners chosen for their ability to exploit related market opportunities, and vertical partnerships, with partners who can serve the firm's value creation.

VALUE CREATION Value-creation skills for marketers include identifying new customer benefits from the customer's view, utilizing core competencies from the company's business domain, and selecting and managing business partners from its collaborative networks. To create new customer benefits, marketers must understand what the customer thinks about, wants, does, and worries about. Marketers must also observe whom customers admire, whom they interact with, and who influences them.

VALUE DELIVERY Delivering value often means substantial investment in infrastructure and capabilities. The company must become proficient at customer relationship management, internal resource management, and business partnership management. *Customer relationship management* allows the company to discover who its customers are, how they behave, and what they need or want. It also enables the company to respond appropriately, coherently, and quickly to different customer opportunities. To respond effectively, the company requires *internal resource management* to integrate major business processes (e.g., order processing, general ledger, payroll, and production) within a single family of software modules. Finally, *business partnership management* allows the company to handle complex relationships with its trading partners in order to source, process, and deliver products.

The Central Role of Strategic Planning

Successful marketing thus requires having capabilities such as understanding customer value, creating customer value, delivering customer value, capturing customer value, and sustaining customer value. Only a handful of companies stand out as master marketers: Canadian Tire, Molson, Tim Hortons, Bombardier, Procter & Gamble, WestJet Airlines, Nike, Disney, Enterprise Rent-A-Car, Wal-Mart, McDonald's, and several Asian (Sony, Toyota, and Canon) and European (IKEA, Club Med, Bang & Olufsen, Nokia, Tesco, and Virgin) companies. "Breakthrough Marketing: Intel" at the end of this chapter describes how Intel created customer value and built a brand in a category for which most people thought branding impossible.

Ads like this were part of Intel's strategy for building a brand in a product area where no brand name had ever existed before: microprocessors.

A lighter-than-you-ever-imagined notebook? Everything is possible with me inside.

INTEL® CENTRINO® DUO PROCESSOR TECHNOLOGY. It's what drives your notebook's performance, wireless connectivity, and amazing battery life. It's the difference between a good computer and a great one. GREAT COMPUTING STARTS WITH INTEL INSIDE.

FIGURE 2.3

The Strategic-Planning,
Implementation, and Control
Processes

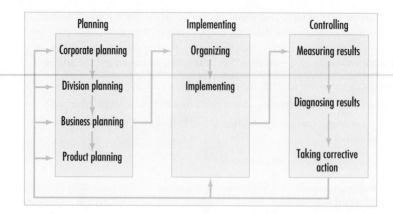

These companies focus on the customer and are organized to respond effectively to changing customer needs. They all have well-staffed marketing departments, and all their other departments—manufacturing, finance, research and development, personnel, purchasing—also accept the concept that the customer is king.

To ensure that the proper activities are selected and executed, strategic planning is paramount. Strategic planning calls for action in three key areas: The first is managing a company's businesses as an investment portfolio. The second involves assessing each business's strength by considering the market's growth rate and the company's position and fit in that market. The third is establishing a strategy. For each business, the company must develop a game plan for achieving long-run objectives.

To understand marketing management, we must understand strategic planning at different organizational levels. Most large companies consist of four organizational levels: the corporate level, the division level, the business-unit level, and the product level. Corporate headquarters is responsible for designing a corporate strategic plan to guide the whole enterprise; it makes decisions on the amount of resources to allocate to each division, as well as on which businesses to start or eliminate. Each division establishes a plan covering the allocation of funds to each business unit within the division. Each business unit develops a strategic plan to carry that business unit into a profitable future. Finally, each product level (product line, brand) within a business unit develops a marketing plan for achieving its objectives in its product market.

The **marketing plan** is the central instrument for directing and coordinating the marketing effort. The marketing plan operates at two levels: strategic and tactical. The **strategic marketing plan** lays out the target markets and the value proposition that will be offered, based on an analysis of the best market opportunities. The **tactical marketing plan** specifies the marketing tactics, including product features, promotion, merchandising, pricing, sales channels, and service.

Today, teams develop the marketing plan with inputs and sign-offs from every important function. Management then implements these plans at the appropriate levels of the organization, monitors results, and takes necessary corrective action. The complete planning, implementation, and control cycle is shown in Figure 2.3. We next consider planning at each of these four levels of the organization.

CORPORATE AND DIVISION STRATEGIC PLANNING

Some corporations give their business units a lot of freedom to set their own sales and profit goals and strategies. Others set goals for their business units but let them develop their own strategies. Still others set the goals and participate in developing individual business-unit strategies.[17]

All corporate headquarters undertake four planning activities:

1. Defining the corporate mission
2. Establishing strategic business units (SBUs)
3. Assigning resources to each SBU
4. Assessing growth opportunities

Defining the Corporate Mission

An organization exists to accomplish something: to make cars, lend money, provide a night's lodging, and so on. Its specific mission or purpose is usually clear when the business starts. Over time the mission may change to take advantage of new opportunities or respond to new market conditions. Amazon.com changed its mission from being the world's largest online bookstore to aspiring to become the world's largest online store. eBay changed its mission from running online auctions for collectors to running online auctions covering all kinds of goods.

To define its mission, the company should address Peter Drucker's classic questions:[18] What is our business? Who is the customer? What is of value to the customer? What will our business be? What should our business be? These simple-sounding questions are among the most difficult the company will ever have to answer. Successful companies continuously raise these questions and answer them thoughtfully and thoroughly.[19]

Organizations develop **mission statements** to share with managers, employees, and (in many cases) customers. A clear, thoughtful mission statement provides employees with a shared sense of purpose, direction, and opportunity. Mission statements are at their best when they are guided by a vision, an almost "impossible dream" that provides a direction for the company for the next 10 to 20 years. Fred Smith wanted to deliver mail anywhere in the United States before 10:30 a.m. the next day, so he created FedEx. Almost 30 years ago, Graeme McRae, founder of Bioniche, a bio-pharmaceutical company headquartered in Belleville, Ontario, wanted to improve the quality of life for both humans and animals through innovative research and therapeutics. Today, the company has developed a cattle vaccine that prevents the shedding of e-coli (which can contaminate water supplies) and a human bladder-cancer drug that is undergoing clinical trials. In 2007, it was recognized as one of the Top 10 Life Sciences Companies in Canada.[20] Table 2.2 lists three sample mission statements.

Good mission statements have three major characteristics. First, they focus on a limited number of goals. The statement "We want to produce the highest-quality products, offer the most service, achieve the widest distribution, and sell at the lowest prices" claims too much. Second, mission statements stress the company's major policies and values. They narrow the range of individual discretion so that employees act consistently on important issues. Third, they define the major competitive spheres within which the company will operate:

- *Industry.* The range of industries in which a company will operate. Some companies will operate in only one industry; some only in a set of related industries; some only in industrial goods, consumer goods, or services; and some in any industry. For example, DuPont prefers to operate in the industrial market, whereas Dow is willing to operate in the industrial and consumer markets.

- *Products and applications.* The range of products and applications a company will supply. Draxis Health Inc. of Mississauga, for example, is "focused on the development, production and distribution of radio-pharmaceutical products for diagnostic and therapeutic nuclear medicine plus contract manufacturing services for the pharmaceutical and biotechnology industries."[21]

- *Competence.* The range of technological and other core competencies that a company will master and leverage. Japan's NEC has built its core competencies in computing, communications, and components to support production of laptop computers, television receivers, and handheld telephones.

- *Market segment.* The type of market or customers a company will serve. For example, Aston Martin makes only high-performance sports cars. Gerber serves primarily the baby market.

- *Vertical.* The vertical sphere is the number of channel levels from raw material to final product and distribution in which a company will participate. At one extreme are companies with a large vertical scope; at one time, Ford owned its own rubber plantations, sheep farms, glass-manufacturing plants, and steel foundries. At the other extreme are "hollow corporations" or "pure marketing companies" consisting of a person with a phone, fax, computer, and desk who contracts out every service, including design, manufacture, marketing, and physical distribution.[22]

- *Geographical.* The range of regions, countries, or country groups in which a company will operate. At one extreme are companies that operate in a specific city. At the other are multi-nationals, such as Unilever and Caterpillar, which operate in almost every country in the world.

TABLE 2.2 | **SAMPLE MISSION STATEMENTS**

Corporate Express, Mississauga, Ontario

Corporate Express of Mississauga, Ontario was named One of the 50 Best Employers in Canada, 2008. It achieved this distinction by following its mission which states:

We will be the Number One Office Supplies Business in Canada by putting the Customer at the Heart of Everything we do.

We will be the premier supplier of office, technology products, furniture, facility supplies, and integrated essentials to companies and organizations that value innovative procurement solutions.

We will leverage our other business lines, as well as our electronic commerce and systems technology, distribution infrastructure, and logistics capabilities to reduce our customers' total procurement costs, while making it easy for them to do business with us.

We provide our customers with what they need, when and where they need it, and always with the best service they can possibly imagine.

We will measure our processes and train our employees to continuously improve the way we prepare the world for business.

Cara Operations Limited

Founded in 1883, Cara today is synonymous with food and travel in Canada. It is the country's largest operator of full-service restaurants (Swiss Chalet, Kelsey's, Milestones, Montana's, and Coza), as well as Harvey's fast-food restaurants and Cara Airline Solutions. Its vision is to be "Canada's leading branded restaurant and airline services company." It strives to be the leader in convenience and choice as well as a caring company, living by its values and supporting the communities where it operates. It accomplishes its aim through adherence to five principles: quality, responsibility, integrity, efficiency, and independence.

Mountain Equipment Co-op (MEC)

"We aspire to be the most viable, vibrant outdoor retail business in Canada. We want to bring about a future where Canadians of all ages, and especially our youth, play outdoors in self-propelled ways more often and in ever-increasing numbers; have access to a comprehensive, carefully nurtured network of parks, wilderness, and outdoor recreation areas; and have a connection to nature that is stronger than ever. We want MEC and our members to set examples that inspire other organizations and individuals towards environmental, social, and economic sustainability. In short, we want to leave the world better than we found it."

Its goals are to help people enjoy the benefits of "self-propelled wilderness-oriented recreation" through the sale of outdoor gear, clothing, and services." As a co-operative, MEC exists to serve the needs of its members, proclaiming its "products are built with purpose, people, and the planet in mind. . . . We match our members with gear that suits their needs. But we offer more than products. We offer passion. We love to share our expertise, experience, and enthusiasm." Following this mission, MEC has grown from six founding members to be Canada's largest retail co-operative with 2.6 million members.

Sources: Corporate Express website, www.corporateexpress.ca; Cara Operations Ltd. website, www.cara.com; Mountain Equipment Co-op website, www.mec.ca (all viewed March 7, 2008).

The fourth characteristic of mission statements is that they take a long-term view. They should be enduring; management should change the mission only when it ceases to be relevant. Finally, a good mission statement is as short, memorable, and meaningful as possible. Marketing consultant Guy Kawasaki even advocates developing short three- to four-word corporate mantras rather than mission statements, like "peace of mind" for Federal Express. Compare the rather vague mission statements on the left with Google's mission statement and philosophy on the right:

To build total brand value by innovating to deliver customer value and customer leadership faster, better, and more completely than our competition.

We build brands and make the world a little happier by bringing our best to you.

Google Mission:

To organize the world's information and make it universally accessible and useful.

Google Philosophy:

Never settle for the best.

1. Focus on the user and all else will follow.
2. It's best to do one thing really, really well.
3. Fast is better than slow.
4. Democracy on the Web works.
5. You don't need to be at your desk to need an answer.
6. You can make money without doing evil.
7. There is always more information out there.
8. The need for information crosses all borders.
9. You can be serious without a suit.
10. Great just isn't good enough.[23]

Establishing Strategic Business Units

Companies often define their businesses in terms of products: They are in the "auto business" or the "clothing business." But Harvard's famed marketing professor Ted Levitt argued that *market definitions* of a business are superior to product definitions. In other words, Levitt encouraged companies to redefine their businesses in terms of needs, not products.[24] A business must be viewed as a customer-satisfying process, not a goods-producing process. Products are transient; basic needs and customer groups endure forever. Transportation is a need: the horse and carriage, the automobile, the railroad, the airline, and the truck are products that meet that need.

Viewing businesses in terms of customer needs can suggest additional growth opportunities. IBM redefined itself from a hardware and software manufacturer to a "builder of networks." Table 2.3 gives several examples of companies that have moved from a product to a market definition of their business, highlighting the difference between a target-market definition and a strategic-market definition.

A *target-market definition* tends to focus on selling a product or service. Pepsi could define its target market as everyone who drinks a cola beverage, and competitors would therefore be other cola companies. A *strategic-market definition* could be everyone who might drink something to quench his or her thirst. Suddenly, Pepsi's competition would include noncola soft drinks, bottled water, fruit juices, tea, and coffee. To better compete, Pepsi might decide to sell additional beverages whose growth rate appears to be promising.

TABLE 2.3	PRODUCT-ORIENTED VERSUS MARKET-ORIENTED DEFINITIONS OF A BUSINESS	
Company	**Product Definition**	**Market Definition**
Via Rail	We run a railroad.	We are a people mover.
Xerox	We make copying equipment.	We help improve office productivity.
Imperial Oil	We sell gasoline.	We supply energy.
Salter Street Films	We make movies and television programs.	We market thoughtful entertainment.
Encyclopaedia Britannica	We sell encyclopedias.	We distribute information.
Carrier	We make air conditioners and furnaces.	We provide climate control in the home.

A business can be defined in terms of three dimensions: customer groups, customer needs, and technology.[25] Consider a small company that defines its business as designing incandescent lighting systems for television studios. Its customer group is television studios; the customer need is lighting; and the technology is incandescent lighting. The company might want to expand. It could make lighting for other customer groups, such as homes, factories, and offices; or it could supply other services needed by television studios, such as heating, ventilation, or air conditioning. It could design other lighting technologies for television studios, such as infrared or ultraviolet lighting.

Large companies normally manage quite different businesses, each requiring its own strategy. Bombardier has two core businesses: aerospace and transportation. It operates eight **strategic business units (SBUs)** under the aerospace umbrella and six units under transportation. An SBU has three characteristics:

1. It is a single business or collection of related businesses that can be planned separately from the rest of the company.
2. It has its own set of competitors.
3. It has a manager who is responsible for strategic planning and profit performance and who controls most of the factors affecting profit.

Assigning Resources to Each SBU[26]

Once it has defined SBUs, management must decide how to allocate corporate resources to each one. The 1970s saw several portfolio-planning models introduced to provide an analytical means for making investment decisions. The GE/McKinsey Matrix classifies each SBU according to the extent of its competitive advantage and the attractiveness of its industry. Management would want to grow, "harvest" or draw cash from, or hold on to the business. Another model, BCG's Growth-Share Matrix, uses relative market share and annual rate of market growth as criteria against which to make investment decisions.

Portfolio-planning models like these have fallen out of favour as oversimplified and subjective. More recent methods that firms use to make internal investment decisions are based on shareholder-value analysis and whether the market value of a company is greater with an SBU or without it (whether it is sold or spun off). These value calculations assess the potential of a business based on potential growth opportunities from global expansion, repositioning or retargeting, and strategic outsourcing.

Assessing Growth Opportunities

Assessing growth opportunities involves planning new businesses, downsizing, or terminating older businesses. If there is a gap between future desired sales and projected sales, corporate management will have to develop or acquire new businesses to fill it.

Figure 2.4 illustrates this strategic-planning gap for a major manufacturer of blank compact disks called Musicale (name disguised). The lowest curve projects the expected sales over the next five years from the current business portfolio. The highest curve describes desired sales over the same period. Evidently, the company wants to grow much faster than its current businesses will permit. How can it fill the strategic-planning gap?

FIGURE 2.4

The Strategic-Planning Gap

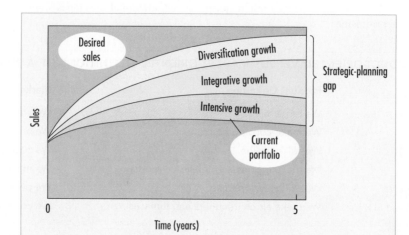

The first option is to identify opportunities to achieve further growth within current businesses (intensive opportunities). The second is to identify opportunities to build or acquire businesses that are related to current businesses (integrative opportunities). The third is to identify opportunities to add attractive businesses that are unrelated to current businesses (diversification opportunities).

INTENSIVE GROWTH   Corporate management's first course of action should be a review of opportunities for improving existing businesses. Ansoff proposed a useful framework for detecting new intensive growth opportunities, called a "product–market expansion grid" (Figure 2.5).[27]

The company first considers whether it could gain more market share with its current products in their current markets (market-penetration strategy). Next it considers whether it can find or develop new markets for its current products (market-development strategy). Then it considers whether it can develop new products of potential interest to its current markets (product-development strategy). Later it will also review opportunities to develop new products for new markets (diversification strategy).

Starbucks

Starbucks is a company that has achieved growth in many different ways. When Howard Schultz, Starbucks' CEO until 2000, came to the company in 1982, he recognized an unfilled niche for cafés serving gourmet coffee directly to customers. This became Starbucks' market-penetration strategy, and helped the company attain a loyal customer base in Seattle, Washington. The market-development strategy marked the next phase in Starbucks' growth: It applied the successful formula that had worked wonders in Seattle first to other cities in the Pacific Northwest, then throughout North America, and finally across the globe. Once the company established itself as a presence in thousands of cities internationally, Starbucks sought to increase the number of purchases by existing customers with a product-development strategy that led to new in-store merchandise, including compilation CDs, a Starbucks Duetto Visa card whose use allows customers to receive points toward Starbucks purchases, and high-speed wireless Internet access at thousands of Starbucks "HotSpots" through a deal with T-Mobile. Finally, Starbucks pursued diversification into grocery-store aisles with Frappuccino® bottled drinks, Starbucks-brand ice cream, and the purchase of tea retailer Tazo® Tea.[28]

How might Musicale use these three major intensive-growth strategies to increase its sales? Musicale could try to encourage its current customers to buy more by demonstrating the benefits of using compact disks for data storage in addition to recording music. Musicale could try to attract competitors' customers if it noticed major weaknesses in competitors' product or marketing programs. Finally, Musicale could try to convince nonusers of compact disks to start using them. How can Musicale use a product-development strategy? First, it might try to identify potential user groups in the current sales areas. If Musicale has been selling compact disks only to consumer markets, it might go after office and factory markets. Second, Musicale might seek additional distribution channels in its present locations. If it has been selling its disks only through stereo-equipment dealers, it might add mass-merchandising channels. Third, the company might consider selling in new locations in its home country or abroad. If Musicale sold only in North America, it could consider entering the European market.

Management should also consider new-product possibilities. Musicale could develop new features, such as additional data storage capabilities or greater durability. It could offer the CD at two or more quality levels, or it could research an alternative technology such as digital audiotape.

By examining these intensive growth strategies, management may discover several ways to grow. Still, that growth may not be enough. In that case, management must also look for integrative-growth opportunities.

INTEGRATIVE GROWTH A business's sales and profits may be increased through backward, forward, or horizontal integration within its industry. For example, drug company giant Merck has gone beyond just developing and selling ethical pharmaceuticals. It purchased Medco, a mail-order pharmaceutical distributor, in 1993, formed a joint venture with DuPont to establish more basic research, and formed another joint venture with Johnson & Johnson to bring some of its ethical products to the over-the-counter market.

Media companies have long reaped the benefits of integrative growth. Here is how one business writer explained the potential that NBC could reap from its merger with Vivendi Universal Entertainment to become NBC Universal. Admittedly, it's a far-fetched example, but it gets across the possibilities inherent in this growth strategy:[29]

> [When] the hit movie *Seabiscuit* (produced by Universal Pictures) comes to television, it would air on Bravo (owned by NBC) or USA Network (owned by Universal), followed by the inevitable bid to make the movie into a TV series (by Universal Television Group), with the pilot being picked up by NBC, which passes on the show, but it's then revived in the "Brilliant But Cancelled" series on cable channel Trio (owned by Universal) where its cult status leads to a Spanish version shown on Telemundo (owned by NBC) and the creation of a popular amusement-park attraction at Universal Studios.

How might Musicale achieve integrative growth? The company might acquire one or more of its suppliers (such as plastic-material producers) to gain more control or generate more profit (backward integration). It might acquire some wholesalers or retailers, especially if they are highly profitable (forward integration). Finally, Musicale might acquire one or more competitors, provided that the government does not bar this move (horizontal integration). However, these new sources may still not deliver the desired sales volume. In that case, the company must consider diversification.

DIVERSIFICATION GROWTH Diversification growth makes sense when good opportunities can be found outside the present businesses. A good opportunity is one in which the industry is highly attractive and the company has the right mix of business strengths to be successful. For example, from its origins as an animated film producer, Walt Disney Company has moved into licensing characters for merchandised goods, entered the broadcast industry with its own Disney Channel as well as ABC and ESPN acquisitions, and developed theme parks and vacation and resort properties.

Cisco Systems Inc.

Known for years as a mass producer of routers and switches, Cisco is attempting to diversify beyond these nuts-and-bolts products into the business of changing how consumers communicate and watch television. With its recent US$6.9 billion acquisition of Scientific-Atlanta Inc., widely recognized for its expertise in video delivery, Cisco hopes to enter consumers' living rooms with items such as home-networking equipment and wirelessly networked DVD players, and services such as video on demand. The diversification move is already paying off: Scientific-Atlanta produced 7 percent of Cisco's US$8 billion in revenue.[30]

Several types of diversification are possible for Musicale. First, the company could choose a concentric strategy and seek new products that have technological or marketing synergies with existing product lines, even though the new products themselves may appeal to a different group of customers. It might start a mini-disk manufacturing operation because it knows how to manufacture compact disks. Second, the company might use a horizontal strategy to search for new products that could appeal to current customers even though the new products are technologically unrelated to its current product line. Musicale might produce compact disk cases, even though producing them requires a different manufacturing process. Finally, the company might seek new businesses that have no relationship to its current technology, products, or markets (a conglomerate strategy).

DOWNSIZING AND DIVESTING OLDER BUSINESSES Weak businesses require a disproportionate amount of managerial attention. Companies must carefully prune, harvest, or divest themselves of tired old businesses in order to release needed resources to other uses and reduce costs. In 2004, Bombardier sold one of its "heritage assets," the recreational-products division, maker of its famous Sea-Doo personal watercraft and Ski-Doo snowmobiles. The sale took place as a recovery measure so the company could have the flexibility to focus on its rail-equipment and aerospace businesses.

Organization and Organizational Culture

Strategic planning is done within the context of the organization. A company's **organization** consists of its structures, policies, and corporate culture, all of which can become dysfunctional in a rapidly changing business environment. Whereas structures and policies can be changed (with difficulty), the company's culture is very hard to change. Yet changing a corporate culture is often the key to successfully implementing a new strategy.

What exactly is a **corporate culture**? Most businesspeople would be hard-pressed to find words to describe this elusive concept, which some define as "the shared experiences, stories, beliefs, and norms that characterize an organization." Yet, walk into any company and the first thing that strikes you is the corporate culture: the way people are dressed, how they talk to one another, the way they greet customers.

A customer-centric culture can affect all aspects of an organization. As one expert says,

> To me, being consumer-centric is more a principle—the driving value of a company—than a process. It's in a company's DNA, top to bottom. It means you recognize the diversity across the face of consumers, and that you are open to observations and opinions other than your own; this allows you to be an advocate for the consumer—whether you are a leading innovator or packing boxes in the warehouse.... The question is, do you see consumers as the driving life force of your company for as long as it exists, or do you see them as simply a hungry group of people that needs to be satisfied so your business will grow in the short term?[31]

Sometimes corporate culture develops organically and is transmitted directly from the CEO's personality and habits to company employees. Mike Lazaridis, president and co-CEO of BlackBerry producer Research In Motion (headquartered in Waterloo, Ontario), is a scientist in his own right, winning an Academy Award for technical achievement in film. He hosts a weekly, innovation-centred "Vision Series" at company headquarters to focus on new research and company goals. As he states, "I think we have a culture of innovation here, and [engineers] have absolute access to me. I live a life that tries to promote innovation."[32]

Research In Motion, the company that developed the BlackBerry wireless device, fosters a culture of innovation that CEO Mike Lazaridis carefully cultivates and values highly.

Marketing Innovation

Innovation in marketing is critical. The traditional view is that senior management hammers out the strategy and hands it down. Gary Hamel offers the contrasting view that imaginative ideas on strategy exist in many places within a company.[33] Senior management should identify and encourage fresh ideas from three groups who tend to be underrepresented in strategy making: employees with youthful perspectives; employees who are far removed from company headquarters; and employees who are new to the industry. Each group is capable of challenging company orthodoxy and stimulating new ideas. Jump Associates, an innovative strategy firm, offers five key strategies for managing change in an organization:[34]

1. Avoid the innovation title: Pick a name for the innovation team that won't alienate co-workers.
2. Use the buddy system: Find a like-minded collaborator within the organization.
3. Set the metrics in advance: Establish different sets of funding, testing, and performance criteria for incremental, experimental, and potentially disruptive innovations.
4. Aim for quick hits first: Start with easily implemented ideas that will work to demonstrate that things can get done, before quickly switching to bigger initiatives.
5. Get data to back up your gut: Use testing to get feedback and improve an idea.

"Marketing Insight: Different Approaches to Innovative Marketing" describes how some leading companies approach innovation.

Firms develop strategy by identifying and selecting among different views of the future. The Royal Dutch/Shell Group has pioneered scenario analysis. A scenario analysis develops plausible representations of a firm's possible future that make different assumptions about forces driving the market and include different uncertainties. Managers need to think through each scenario with the question: "What will we do if it happens?" They need to adopt one scenario as the most probable and watch for signposts that might confirm or contradict that scenario.[35]

BUSINESS-UNIT STRATEGIC PLANNING

The business-unit strategic-planning process consists of the steps shown in Figure 2.6. We examine each step in the sections that follow.

The Business Mission

Each business unit needs to define its specific mission within the broader company mission. Thus, a television studio–lighting-equipment company might define its mission as "The company aims to target major television studios and become their vendor of choice for lighting technologies that represent the most advanced and reliable studio-lighting arrangements." Notice that this mission does not attempt to win business from smaller television studios, win business by being lowest in price, or venture into nonlighting products.

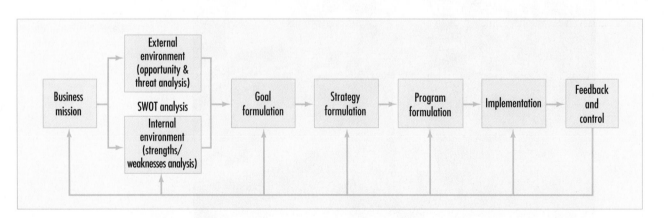

FIGURE 2.6

The Business-Unit Strategic-Planning Process

MARKETING INSIGHT | DIFFERENT APPROACHES TO INNOVATIVE MARKETING

When IBM surveyed top CEOs and government leaders about their agenda priorities, their answers about innovation were revealing. Business-model innovation and coming up with unique ways of doing things scored high. IBM's own drive for business-model innovation led to much collaboration, both within IBM itself and externally with companies, governments, and educational institutions. CEO Samuel Palmisano noted how the breakthrough Cell processor, based on the company's Power architecture, would not have happened without collaboration with Sony and Nintendo, as well as competitors Toshiba and Microsoft.

Procter & Gamble has similarly set a goal for 50 percent of the company's new products to come from outside P&G's labs—from inventors, scientists, and suppliers whose new-product ideas can be developed in-house.

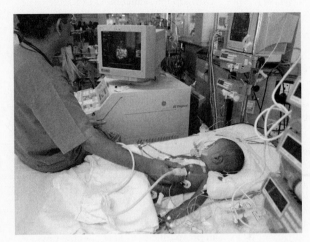

Low labour costs allow India's Narayana Hrudayalaya hospital to innovate through its pricing strategies.

Business guru Jim Collins' research emphasizes the importance of systematic, broad-based innovation: "Always looking for the one big breakthrough, the one big idea, is contrary to what we found: To build a truly great company, it's decision upon decision, action upon action, day upon day, month upon month.... It's cumulative momentum and no one decision defines a great company." He cites the success of Walt Disney with theme parks and Wal-Mart with retailing as examples of companies which were successful after having executed a big idea brilliantly over such a long period of time.

Northwestern's Mohan Sawhney and his colleagues outline 12 dimensions of business innovation that make up the "innovation radar" (see Table 2.4) and suggest that business innovation is about increasing customer *value*, not just creating new *things*; business innovation comes in many flavours and can take place on any dimension of a business system; and business innovation is systematic and requires careful consideration of all aspects of a business.

Business writer C. K. Prahalad believes much innovation in industries from financial and telecom services to health care and automobiles can come from developments in emerging markets such as India. Forced to do more with less, Indian companies and foreign competitors are finding new ways to maximize minimal resources and offer quality products and services at low prices. Consider Bangalore's Narayana Hrudayalaya hospital, which charges a flat fee of US$1 500 for heart-bypass surgery that would cost 50 times that much in the United States. The low cost is a result of the hospital's low labour and operating expenses and an assembly-line view of care that has specialists focus just on their own area. The approach works: the hospital's mortality rates are half those of U.S. hospitals. Narayana also operates on hundreds of infants for free and profitably insures 2.5 million poor Indians against serious illness for 11 cents a month.

Finally, to find breakthrough ideas, some companies find ways to immerse a range of employees in solving marketing problems. Samsung's Value Innovation Program (VIP) isolates product-development teams of engineers, designers, and planners with a timetable and end date in the company's centre just south of Seoul, Korea, while 50 specialists help guide their activities. To help make tough trade-offs, team members draw "value curves" that rank attributes such as a product's sound or picture quality on a scale from 1 to 5. To develop a new car, BMW similarly mobilizes specialists in engineering, design, production, marketing, purchasing, and finance at its Research and Innovation Center or Project House.

Sources: Steve Hamm, "Innovation: The View From the Top," *BusinessWeek*, April 3, 2006, pp. 52–53; Jena McGregor, "The World's Most Innovative Companies," *BusinessWeek*, April 24, 2006, pp. 63–74; Rich Karlgard, "Digital Rules," *Forbes*, March 13, 2006, p. 31; Jennifer Rooney and Jim Collins, "Being Great Is *Not* Just a Matter of Big Ideas," *Point*, June 2006, p. 20; Moon Ihlwan, "Camp Samsung," *BusinessWeek*, July 3, 2006, pp. 46–47; Mohanbir Sawhney, Robert C. Wolcott, and Inigo Arroniz, "The 12 Different Ways for Companies to Innovate," *MIT Sloan Management Review*, Spring 2006, pp. 75–85; Pete Engardio, "Business Prophet: How C.K. Prahalad Is Changing the Way CEO's Think," *BusinessWeek*, January 23, 2006, pp. 68–73.

TABLE 2.4	THE 12 DIMENSIONS OF BUSINESS INNOVATION	
Dimension	**Definition**	**Examples**
Offerings (WHAT)	Develop innovative new products or services.	▪ Gillette Mach3Turbo razor ▪ Apple iPod music player and iTunes music service
Platform	Use common components or building blocks to create derivative offerings.	▪ General Motors OnStar telematics platform ▪ Disney animated movies
Solutions	Create integrated and customized offerings that solve end-to-end customer problems.	▪ UPS logistics services Supply Chain Solutions ▪ DuPont Building Innovations for construction
Customers (WHO)	Discover unmet customer needs or identify underserved customer segments.	▪ Enterprise Rent-A-Car focus on replacement-car renters ▪ Bullfrog Power focus on "green power"
Customer Experience	Redesign customer interactions across all touch points and all moments of contact.	▪ ING Direct retail-banking concept ▪ Second Cup's "store as neighbourhood oasis" concept
Value Capture	Redefine how company gets paid or create innovative new revenue streams.	▪ Google paid search ▪ Blockbuster revenue sharing with movie distributors
Processes (HOW)	Redesign core operating processes to improve efficiency and effectiveness.	▪ Toyota Production System for operations ▪ General Electric Design for Six Sigma (DFSS)
Organization	Change form, function, or activity scope of the firm.	▪ Cisco partner-centric networked virtual organization ▪ Procter & Gamble front-back hybrid organization for customer focus
Supply Chain	Think differently about sourcing and fulfillment.	▪ Moen ProjectNet for collaborative design with suppliers ▪ General Motors Celta use of integrated supply and online sales
Presence (WHERE)	Create new distribution channels or innovative points of presence, including the places where offerings can be bought or used by customers.	▪ Starbucks music-CD sales in coffee stores ▪ Diebold RemoteTeller System for banking
Networking	Create network-centric intelligent and integrated offerings.	▪ Otis Remote Elevator Monitoring service ▪ U.S. Department of Defense Network-Centric Warfare
Brand	Leverage a brand into new domains.	▪ Virgin Group "branded venture capital" ▪ Yahoo! as a lifestyle brand

Source: Mohanbir Sawhney, Robert C. Wolcott, and Inigo Arroniz, "The 12 Different Ways for Companies to Innovate," *MIT Sloan Management Review*, Spring 2006, p. 78.

SWOT Analysis

The overall evaluation of a company's strengths, weaknesses, opportunities, and threats is called SWOT analysis. It's a way of monitoring the external and internal marketing environment.

EXTERNAL ENVIRONMENT (OPPORTUNITY AND THREAT) ANALYSIS A business unit has to monitor key *macroenvironment forces* (demographic-economic, natural, technological, political-legal, and social-cultural) and significant *microenvironment actors* (customers, competitors, suppliers, distributors, dealers) that affect its ability to earn profits. The business unit should set up a marketing-intelligence system to track trends and important developments. For each trend or development, management needs to identify the associated opportunities and threats.

Good marketing is the art of finding, developing, and profiting from opportunities.[36] A **marketing opportunity** is an area of buyer need and interest in which there is a high probability that a company can profitably satisfy that need. There are three main sources of market opportunities.[37] The first is to supply something in short supply. This requires little marketing talent, as the need is fairly obvious. The second is to supply an existing product or service in a new or superior way. There are several ways to uncover possible product or service improvements: by asking consumers for their suggestions (*problem-detection method*), by asking consumers to imagine an ideal version of the product or service (*ideal method*), and by asking consumers to chart their steps in acquiring, using, and disposing of a product (*consumption-chain method*). The third source often leads to a totally new product or service.

Opportunities can take many forms and marketers have to be good at spotting them. Consider the following:

- A company may benefit from converging industry trends and introduce hybrid products or services that are new to the market. Example: At least five major cell phone manufacturers released phones with digital-photo capabilities.

- A company may make a buying process more convenient or efficient. Example: Consumers can now use the Internet to find more books than ever and search for the lowest price with a few clicks.

- A company can meet the need for more information and advice. Example: Guru.com facilitates finding professional experts in a wide range of fields.

- A company can customize a product or service that was formerly offered only in a standard form. Example: P&G's Reflect.com website is capable of producing a customized skin-care or hair-care product to meet a customer's need.

- A company can introduce a new capability. Example: Consumers can now create and edit digital "iMovies" with the iMac and upload them to an Apple web server to share with friends around the world.

- A company may be able to deliver a product or a service faster. Example: FedEx discovered a way to deliver mail and packages much more quickly than the U.S. Post Office.

- A company may be able to offer a product at a much lower price. Example: Pharmaceutical firms have created generic versions of brand-name drugs.

To evaluate opportunities, companies can use **Market Opportunity Analysis (MOA)** to determine the attractiveness and probability of success, asking themselves:

1. Can the benefits involved in the opportunity be articulated convincingly to a defined target market(s)?

2. Can the target market(s) be located and reached with cost-effective media and trade channels?

3. Does the company possess or have access to the critical capabilities and resources needed to deliver the customer benefits?

4. Can the company deliver the benefits better than any actual or potential competitors?

5. Will the financial rate of return meet or exceed the company's required threshold for investment?

In the opportunity matrix in Figure 2.7(a), the best marketing opportunities facing the TV–lighting-equipment company are listed in the upper-left cell (#1). The opportunities in the lower-right cell (#4) are too minor to consider. The opportunities in the upper-right cell (#2) and lower-left cell (#3) should be monitored in the event that any improve in attractiveness and success probability.

An **environmental threat** is a challenge posed by an unfavourable trend or development that would lead, in the absence of defensive marketing action, to lower sales or profit. Threats should be classified according to seriousness and probability of occurrence. Figure 2.7(b) illustrates the threat matrix facing the TV–lighting-equipment company. The threats in the upper-left cell are major because they can seriously hurt the company and they have a high probability of occurrence. To deal with them, the company needs contingency plans that spell out changes it can make before or during the threat. The threats in the lower-right cell are very minor and can be ignored. The threats in the upper-right and lower-left cells need to be monitored carefully in the event that they grow more serious.

INTERNAL ENVIRONMENT (STRENGTHS/WEAKNESSES) ANALYSIS It is one thing to find attractive opportunities and another to be able to take advantage of them. Each business needs to evaluate its internal strengths and weaknesses relative to those of its competition. Loblaws, for example, when compared to Wal-Mart's new grocery business, has the advantage of great locations in the heart of most Canadian cities and strong private brands, but it is weaker when it comes to the management of inventory and suppliers. Businesses can evaluate their own strengths and weaknesses by using a form like the one shown in "Marketing Memo: Checklist for Strengths/Weaknesses Analysis."

FIGURE 2.7

Opportunity and Threat
Matrices

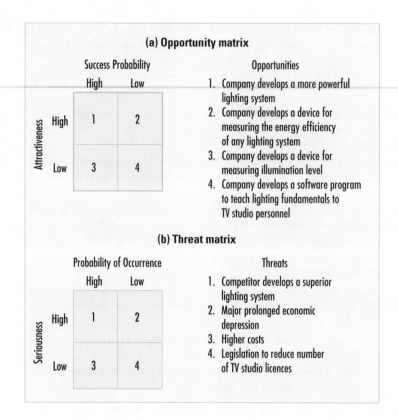

(a) Opportunity matrix

Success Probability			Opportunities

Attractiveness

	High	Low
High	1	2
Low	3	4

1. Company develops a more powerful lighting system
2. Company develops a device for measuring the energy efficiency of any lighting system
3. Company develops a device for measuring illumination level
4. Company develops a software program to teach lighting fundamentals to TV studio personnel

(b) Threat matrix

Probability of Occurrence

Seriousness

	High	Low
High	1	2
Low	3	4

Threats

1. Competitor develops a superior lighting system
2. Major prolonged economic depression
3. Higher costs
4. Legislation to reduce number of TV studio licences

Clearly, the business does not have to correct all its weaknesses, nor should it gloat about all its strengths. The big question is whether the business should limit itself to those opportunities where it possesses the required strengths or whether it should consider opportunities that mean it might have to acquire or develop certain strengths. For example, managers at Texas Instruments (TI) were split between those who wanted TI to stick to industrial electronics (where it has clear strength) and those who wanted the company to continue introducing consumer products (where it lacks some required marketing strengths).

Sometimes a business does poorly not because its people lack the required strengths, but because they do not work together as a team. In one major electronics company, the engineers look down on the salespeople as "engineers who couldn't make it," and the salespeople look down on the service people as "salespeople who couldn't make it." It is therefore critical to assess interdepartmental working relationships as part of the internal-environmental audit.

Goal Formulation

Once the company has performed a SWOT analysis, it can proceed to develop specific goals for the planning period. This stage of the process is called **goal formulation**. Managers use the term *goals* to describe objectives that are specific with respect to magnitude and time.

Most business units pursue a mix of objectives including profitability, sales growth, market-share improvement, risk containment, innovation, and reputation. The business unit sets these objectives and then manages by objectives (MBO). For an MBO system to work, the unit's objectives must meet four criteria:

1. *They must be arranged hierarchically, from the most to the least important.* For example, the business unit's key objective for the period may be to increase the rate of return on investment. Managers can increase profit by increasing revenue and reducing expenses. Revenue can be increased by increasing market share and prices.

2. *Objectives should be stated quantitatively whenever possible.* The objective "increase the return on investment (ROI)" is better stated as the goal "increase ROI to 15 percent within two years."

3. *Goals should be realistic.* They should arise from an analysis of the business unit's opportunities and strengths, not from wishful thinking.

4. *Objectives must be consistent.* It is not possible to maximize both sales and profits simultaneously.

| MARKETING MEMO | | | | | CHECKLIST FOR STRENGTHS/WEAKNESSES ANALYSIS | | | |

	Performance					Importance		
	Major Strength	Minor Strength	Neutral	Minor Weakness	Major Weakness	Hi	Med	Low
Marketing								
1. Company reputation	_____	_____	_____	_____	_____	_____	_____	_____
2. Market share	_____	_____	_____	_____	_____	_____	_____	_____
3. Customer satisfaction	_____	_____	_____	_____	_____	_____	_____	_____
4. Customer retention	_____	_____	_____	_____	_____	_____	_____	_____
5. Product quality	_____	_____	_____	_____	_____	_____	_____	_____
6. Service quality	_____	_____	_____	_____	_____	_____	_____	_____
7. Pricing effectiveness	_____	_____	_____	_____	_____	_____	_____	_____
8. Distribution effectiveness	_____	_____	_____	_____	_____	_____	_____	_____
9. Promotion effectiveness	_____	_____	_____	_____	_____	_____	_____	_____
10. Sales force effectiveness	_____	_____	_____	_____	_____	_____	_____	_____
11. Innovation effectiveness	_____	_____	_____	_____	_____	_____	_____	_____
12. Geographical coverage	_____	_____	_____	_____	_____	_____	_____	_____
Finance								
13. Cost or availability of capital	_____	_____	_____	_____	_____	_____	_____	_____
14. Cash flow	_____	_____	_____	_____	_____	_____	_____	_____
15. Financial stability	_____	_____	_____	_____	_____	_____	_____	_____
Manufacturing								
16. Facilities	_____	_____	_____	_____	_____	_____	_____	_____
17. Economies of scale	_____	_____	_____	_____	_____	_____	_____	_____
18. Capacity	_____	_____	_____	_____	_____	_____	_____	_____
19. Able, dedicated workforce	_____	_____	_____	_____	_____	_____	_____	_____
20. Ability to produce on time	_____	_____	_____	_____	_____	_____	_____	_____
21. Technical manufacturing skill	_____	_____	_____	_____	_____	_____	_____	_____
Organization								
22. Visionary, capable leadership	_____	_____	_____	_____	_____	_____	_____	_____
23. Dedicated employees	_____	_____	_____	_____	_____	_____	_____	_____
24. Entrepreneurial orientation	_____	_____	_____	_____	_____	_____	_____	_____
25. Flexible or responsive	_____	_____	_____	_____	_____	_____	_____	_____

Other important trade-offs include short-term profit versus long-term growth, deep penetration of existing markets versus development of new markets, profit goals versus nonprofit goals, and high growth versus low risk. Each choice in this set of trade-offs calls for a different marketing strategy.[38]

Many believe that adopting the goal of strong market-share growth may mean having to forgo strong short-term profits. For years, Compaq priced aggressively in order to build its market share in the computer market. Subsequently, Compaq decided to pursue profitability at the expense of growth. Yet Charan and Tichy believe that most businesses can be a growth business and can grow profitably.[39] They cite success stories such as GE Medical, Citibank, and GE Capital, all enjoying profitable growth. Some so-called trade-offs may not be trade-offs at all.

To understand the importance of staying focused in competitive marketing strategy and knowing exactly where to excel in terms of product and service differentiation, read about Singapore Airlines at www.pearsoned-asia.com/ marketingmanagementasia.

Strategic Formulation

Goals indicate what a business unit wants to achieve; **strategy** is a game plan for getting there. Every business must design a strategy for achieving its goals, consisting of a *marketing strategy*, and a compatible *technology strategy* and *sourcing strategy*.

PORTER'S GENERIC STRATEGIES   Michael Porter has proposed three generic strategies that provide a good starting point for strategic thinking: overall-cost leadership, differentiation, and focus.[40]

- *Overall-cost leadership.* Firms pursuing this strategy must be good at engineering, purchasing, manufacturing, and physical distribution. They need less skill in marketing. The problem with this strategy is that other firms will compete with still-lower costs and hurt the firm that rested its whole future on cost.

- *Differentiation.* The business concentrates on achieving superior performance in an important customer-benefit area valued by a large part of the market. Thus the firm seeking quality leadership, for example, must make products with the best components, put them together expertly, inspect them carefully, and effectively communicate their quality.

- *Focus.* The business focuses on one or more narrow market segments. The firm gets to know these segments intimately and pursues either cost leadership or differentiation within the target segment.

Belkin Corporation

For most people, a surge protector is a necessary item bought at a hardware store and hidden behind a PC within a jumble of dust bunnies and cable cords. Yet, one company decided to focus not on the utilitarian aspect of the surge protector but on its aesthetic aspect. An example of both focus and differentiation, Belkin Corporation's surge protectors organize consumers' workspaces and protect their equipment. Its Concealed Surge Protector organizes cables and keeps them out of view with a unique closing cover. By differentiating itself from the average surge protector, which costs about $15, Belkin can charge $50.[41]

The online air-travel industry provides a good example of these three strategies: Travelocity is pursuing a differentiation strategy by offering the most comprehensive range of services to the traveller. Lowestfare is pursuing a lowest-cost strategy; and Last Minute is pursuing a niche strategy in focusing on travellers who have the flexibility to travel on very short notice.

According to Porter, firms pursuing the same strategy directed to the same target market constitute a **strategic group**. The firm that carries out that strategy best will make the most profits. Firms that do not pursue a clear strategy and try to be good on all strategic dimensions do the worst. Eaton's fell upon hard times because it did not stand out in its industry as lowest in cost, highest in perceived value, or best in serving some market segment.

Porter draws a distinction between operational effectiveness and strategy.[42] Competitors can quickly copy an operationally effective company using benchmarking and other tools, thus diminishing the advantage of operational effectiveness. Porter defines strategy as "the creation of a unique and valuable position involving a different set of activities." A company can claim that it has a strategy when it "performs different activities from rivals or performs similar activities in different ways."

STRATEGIC ALLIANCES   Companies are also discovering that they need strategic partners if they hope to be effective. Even giant companies—AT&T, IBM, Philips, Siemens—often cannot achieve leadership, either nationally or globally, without forming alliances with domestic or multinational companies that complement or leverage their capabilities and resources.

Just doing business in another country may require the firm to license its product, form a joint venture with a local firm, or buy from local suppliers to meet "domestic content" requirements. As a result, many firms are rapidly developing global strategic networks, and victory is going to those who build the better global network. The Star Alliance, for example, joins Air Canada with 17 other airlines, including Lufthansa, United Airlines, Mexicana, Austrian Airlines, British Midland, Singapore Airlines, SAS, Thai Airways, Varig, Air New Zealand, and South African Airways, into a huge global partnership that allows travellers to make nearly seamless connections to hundreds of destinations.

Many strategic alliances take the form of marketing alliances. These fall into four major categories.

1. *Product or service alliances.* One company licenses another to produce its product, or two companies jointly market their complementary products or a new product. For instance, Bell Canada and Microsoft—two service businesses—have joined together in a marketing alliance, Sympatico/MSN.

2. *Promotional alliances.* One company agrees to carry a promotion for another company's product or service. For example, the Aeroplan rewards program promotes the products and services of its partners including Fairmont Hotels, Home Hardware, Avis Car Rental, Rogers Magazines, and Primus telephone and Internet service.[43]

3. *Logistics alliances.* One company offers logistical services for another company's product. For example, Abbott Laboratories warehouses and delivers all of 3M's medical and surgical products to hospitals across North America.

4. *Pricing collaborations.* One or more companies join in a special pricing collaboration. Hotel and rental car companies often offer mutual price discounts.

Companies need to give creative thought to finding partners that might complement their strengths and offset their weaknesses. Well-managed alliances allow companies to obtain a greater sales impact at less cost. To keep their strategic alliances thriving, corporations have begun to develop organizational structures to support them and have come to view the ability to form and manage partnerships as core skills (called **partner relationship management, PRM**).[44]

Both pharmaceutical and biotech companies are starting to make partnership a core competency. For example, Erbitux, a new drug to aid treatment of colorectal cancer, is the result of just such a partnership. The drug was originally discovered in biotech company ImClone Systems' clinical labs, but will be marketed via ImClone's partnership with pharmaceutical giant Bristol-Meyers Squibb.[45]

Program Formulation and Implementation

Even a great marketing strategy can be sabotaged by poor implementation. If the unit has decided to attain technological leadership, it must plan programs to strengthen its R&D department, gather technological intelligence, develop leading-edge products, train the technical sales force, and develop ads to communicate its technological leadership.

Once the marketing programs are formulated, the marketing people must estimate their costs. Questions arise: Is participating in a particular trade show worthwhile? Will a specific sales contest pay for itself? Will hiring another salesperson contribute to the bottom line? Activity-based cost (ABC) accounting should be applied to each marketing program to determine whether it is likely to produce results sufficient to justify the cost.[46]

Today's businesses are increasingly recognizing that unless they nurture other stakeholders—customers, employees, suppliers, distributors—the business may never earn sufficient profits for the shareholders. For example, it might aim to delight its customers, perform well for its employees, and deliver a threshold level of satisfaction to its suppliers. In setting these levels, a company must be careful not to violate the various stakeholder groups' sense of fairness about their relative treatment.[47]

There is a dynamic relationship connecting the stakeholder groups. A smart company creates a high level of employee satisfaction, which leads to higher effort, which leads to higher-quality products and services, which creates higher customer satisfaction, which leads to more repeat business, which leads to higher growth and profits, which leads to high shareholder satisfaction, which leads to more investment, and so on. This is the virtuous circle that spells profits and growth. "Marketing Insight: Marketing's Contribution to Shareholder Value" highlights the increasing importance of the proper bottom-line view to marketing expenditures.

According to McKinsey & Company, strategy is only one of seven elements in successful business practice (referred to as the seven Ss).[48] The first three elements—strategy, structure, and systems—are considered the "hardware" of success. The next four—style, skills, staff, and shared values—are the "software."

| MARKETING **INSIGHT** | MARKETING'S CONTRIBUTION TO SHAREHOLDER VALUE |

Companies normally focus on profit maximization rather than on shareholder-value maximization. Doyle, in his *Value-Based Marketing*, charges that profit maximization leads to short-term planning and underinvestment in marketing. It leads to a focus on building sales, market share, and current profits. It also leads to cost cutting and shedding assets to produce quick improvements in earnings and erodes a company's long-term competitiveness through neglect of investment in new market opportunities.

Companies normally measure their profit performance using ROI (return on investment, calculated by dividing profits by investment). This has two problems:

1. Profits are arbitrarily measured and subject to manipulation. Cash flow is more important. As someone observed: "Profits are a matter of opinion; cash is a fact."

2. Investment ignores the real value of the firm. More of a company's value resides in its intangible marketing assets—brands, market knowledge, customer relationships, and partner relationships—than in its balance sheet. These assets are the drivers of long-term profits.

Doyle argues that marketing will not mature as a profession until it can demonstrate the impact of marketing on shareholder value, the market value of a company minus its debt. The market value is the share price times the number of shares outstanding. The share price reflects what investors estimate is the present value of the future lifetime earnings of a company. When management is choosing a marketing strategy, Doyle wants it to apply shareholder-value analysis (SVA) to see which alternative course of action will maximize shareholder value.

If Doyle's arguments are accepted, marketing will finally get the attention it deserves in the boardroom. Instead of seeing marketing as a specific function concerned only with increasing sales or market share, senior management will see it as an integral part of the whole management process. It will judge marketing by how much it contributes to shareholder value.

Source: Peter Doyle, *Value-Based Marketing: Marketing Strategies for Corporate Growth and Shareholder Value* (Chichester, England: John Wiley & Sons, 2000).

The first "soft" element, *style,* means that company employees share a common way of thinking and behaving. Tim Hortons employees smile at the customer, and IBM employees are very professional in their customer dealings. The second element, *skills,* means that the employees have the skills needed to carry out the company's strategy. The third element, *staffing,* means that the company has hired able people, trained them well, and assigned them to the right jobs. The fourth element, *shared values,* means that employees share the same guiding values. When these elements are present, companies are usually more successful at strategy implementation.[49]

Another study of management practices found that superior performance over time depended on flawless execution, a company culture based on aiming high, a structure that is flexible and responsive, and a strategy that is clear and focused.[50]

Feedback and Control

A company's strategic fit with the environment will inevitably erode because the market environment changes faster than the company's seven Ss. Thus, a company might remain efficient while it loses effectiveness. Peter Drucker pointed out that it is more important to "do the right thing" (effectiveness) than "to do things right" (efficiency). The most successful companies excel at both.

Once an organization fails to respond to a changed environment, it becomes increasingly hard to recapture its lost position. Consider what happened to Lotus Development Corporation. Its Lotus 1-2-3 software was once the world's leading software program but now its market share in desktop software has slipped so low that analysts do not even bother to track it.

Organizations, especially large ones, are subject to inertia. It is difficult to change one part without adjusting everything else. Yet organizations can be changed through strong leadership, preferably in advance of a crisis. The key to organizational health is willingness to examine the changing environment and to adopt new goals and behaviours.

PRODUCT PLANNING: THE NATURE AND CONTENTS OF A MARKETING PLAN

Working within the plans set by the levels above them, product managers come up with marketing plans for individual products, lines, brands, channels, or customer groups. Each product level (product line, brand) must develop a marketing plan for achieving its goals. A **marketing plan** is a written document that summarizes what the marketer has learned about the marketplace and indicates how the firm plans to reach its marketing objectives.[51] It contains tactical guidelines for the marketing programs and financial allocations over the planning period.[52] It is one of the most important outputs of the marketing process.

Marketing plans are becoming more customer- and competitor-oriented, better reasoned, and more realistic than in the past. The plans draw more inputs from all the functions and are team-developed. Marketing executives increasingly see themselves as professional managers first and specialists second. Planning is becoming a continuous process to respond to rapidly changing market conditions.

Most marketing plans cover one year and can vary in length from under 5 to over 50 pages. The most frequently cited shortcomings of current marketing plans, according to marketing executives, are lack of realism, insufficient competitive analysis, and a short-run focus. (See "Marketing Memo: Marketing Plan Criteria" for some guideline questions to ask in developing marketing plans.)

What, then, does a marketing plan look like? What does it contain?

Contents of the Marketing Plan

- *Executive summary and table of contents.* The marketing plan should open with a brief summary of the main goals and recommendations. The executive summary permits senior management to grasp the plan's major thrust. The summary should be followed by a table of contents that outlines the rest of the plan and all the supporting rationale and operational detail.

- *Situation analysis.* This section presents relevant background data on sales, costs, the market, competitors, and the various forces in the macroenvironment. How is the market defined, how big is it, and how fast is it growing? What are the relevant trends affecting the market? What is the product offering and what are the critical issues facing the company? Pertinent historical information can be included to provide context. All this information is used to carry out a SWOT (strengths, weaknesses, opportunities, threats) analysis.

- *Marketing strategy.* Here the product manager defines the mission and marketing and financial objectives. The manager also defines those groups and needs that the market offerings are intended to satisfy. The manager then establishes the product line's competitive positioning, which will inform the "game plan" to accomplish the plan's objectives. All this is done with inputs from other organizational areas, such as purchasing, manufacturing, sales, finance, and human resources, to ensure that the company can provide proper support for effective implementation.

MARKETING MEMO   MARKETING PLAN CRITERIA

Here are some questions to ask in evaluating a marketing plan.

1. *Is the plan simple?* Is it easy to understand and act on? Does it communicate its content easily and practically?

2. *Is the plan specific?* Are its objectives concrete and measurable? Does it include specific actions and activities, each with specific dates of completion, specific persons responsible, and specific budgets?

3. *Is the plan realistic?* Are the sales goals, expense budgets, and milestone dates realistic? Has a frank and honest self-critique been conducted to raise possible concerns and objections?

4. *Is the plan complete?* Does it include all the necessary elements?

Source: Tim Berry and Doug Wilson, *On Target: The Book on Marketing Plans* (Eugene, OR: Palo Alto Software, 2000).

- *Financial projections.* Financial projections include a sales forecast, an expense forecast, and a break-even analysis. On the revenue side, the projections show the forecasted sales volume by month and product category. On the expense side, the projections show the expected costs of marketing broken down into finer categories. The break-even analysis shows how many units must be sold monthly to offset the monthly fixed costs and average per-unit variable costs.

- *Implementation controls.* The last section of the marketing plan outlines the controls for monitoring and adjusting implementation of the plan. Typically, the goals and budget are spelled out for each month or quarter so management can review each period's results and take corrective action as needed. A number of different internal and external measures will need to be taken to assess progress and suggest possible modifications. Some organizations include contingency plans outlining the steps management would take in response to specific environmental developments, such as price wars or strikes.

SAMPLE MARKETING PLAN: PEGASUS SPORTS INTERNATIONAL*

WWW.MPLANS.COM/SPV/3407/INDEX.CFM?AFFILIATE=MPLANS

1.0 EXECUTIVE SUMMARY

Pegasus Sports International is a start-up aftermarket inline skating-accessory manufacturer. In addition to its aftermarket products, Pegasus is developing SkateTours, a service that takes clients out, in conjunction with a local skate shop, and provides them with an afternoon of skating using inline skates and some of Pegasus' other accessories such as SkateSails. The aftermarket skate-accessory market has been largely ignored. Although there are several major manufacturers of the skates themselves, the accessory market has not been addressed. This provides Pegasus with an extraordinary opportunity for market growth. Skating is a booming sport. Currently most of the skating is recreational. There are, however, a growing number of skating competitions, including team-orientated competitions such as skate hockey, as well as individual competitions such as speed skate racing. Pegasus will work to grow these markets as well as develop the skate transportation market, a more utilitarian use of skating. Several of Pegasus' current products have patents pending and local market research indicates that there is great demand for these products. Pegasus will achieve fast, significant market penetration through a solid business model, long-range planning, and a strong management team that will be able to execute this exciting opportunity. The three principals on the management team have over 30 years of combined personal and industry experience. This extensive experience provides Pegasus with the empirical information as well as the passion to provide the skating market with much-needed aftermarket products. Pegasus will sell its products initially through its website. This "Dell" direct-to-the-consumer approach will allow Pegasus to achieve higher margins and maintain a close relationship with customers, which is essential for producing products that have true market demand. By the end of the year, Pegasus also will have developed relationships with different skate shops and will begin to sell some of its products through retailers.

1.1 TABLE OF CONTENTS

*Sample plan provided by and copyright Palo Alto Software, Inc. Find more complete sample marketing plans at www.mplans.com.

2.0 SITUATION ANALYSIS

Pegasus is entering its first year of operation. Its products have been well received, and marketing will be key to developing brand and product awareness and growing the customer base. Pegasus International offers several different aftermarket skating accessories, serving the growing inline skating industry.

2.1 MARKET SUMMARY

Pegasus possesses good information about the market and knows a great deal about the common attributes of the most-prized customer. This information will be leveraged to better understand who is served, what their specific needs are, and how Pegasus can better communicate with them.

Target Markets

- Recreational
- Fitness
- Speed
- Hockey
- Extreme

2.1.1 Market Demographics

The profile of the typical Pegasus customer includes the following geographic, demographic, and behaviour factors:

Geographics

- Pegasus has no set geographic target area. By leveraging the expansive reach of the Internet and multiple delivery services, Pegasus can serve both domestic and international customers.
- The total targeted population is 31 million users.

Demographics

- Male and female users, with an almost equal ratio between the two.
- Ages 13–46, with 48 percent clustering around the ages 23–34. The recreational users tend to cover the widest age range, including young users through active adults. The fitness users tend to be ages 20–40. The speed users tend to be in their late 20s and early 30s. The hockey players are generally in their teens through their early 20s, as are the extreme segment.
- Of the users who are over 20, 65 percent have an undergraduate degree or substantial undergraduate coursework.
- The adult users have a median personal income of $47 000.

Behaviour Factors

- Users enjoy fitness activities not as a means to a healthy life, but as an intrinsically enjoyable activity.
- Users spend money on gear, typically sports equipment.
- Users have active lifestyles that include some sort of recreation at least two to three times a week.

2.1.2 Market Needs

Pegasus is providing the skating community with a wide range of accessories for all variations of skating. Pegasus seeks to fulfill the following benefits that are important to its customers:

- *Quality craftsmanship.* The customers work hard for their money and do not enjoy spending it on disposable products that work only for a year or two.
- *Well–thought-out designs.* The skating market has not been addressed by well–thought-out products that serve skaters' needs. Pegasus' industry experience and personal dedication to the sport will provide Pegasus with the information needed to produce insightfully designed products.
- *Customer service.* Exemplary service is required to build a sustainable business that has a loyal customer base.

2.1.3 Market Trends

Pegasus will distinguish itself by marketing products not previously available to skaters. The emphasis in the past has been to sell skates and very few replacement parts. The number of skaters is not restricted to any one single country, continent, or age group, so there is a world market. Pegasus has products for virtually every group of skaters. The fastest-growing segment of this sport is the fitness skater. Therefore, the marketing is being directed to service this group. BladeBoots will enable users to enter establishments without having to remove their skates. BladeBoots will be aimed at the recreational skater, the largest segment. SkateAids, on the other hand, are great for everyone.

The sport of skating will also grow through SkateSailing. This sport is primarily for the medium-to-advanced skater. The growth potential for this sport is tremendous. The sails that Pegasus has manufactured have been sold in Europe, following a pattern similar to windsurfing. Windsurfing originated in Santa Monica, California, but did not take off until it had already grown big in Europe.

Another trend is group skating. More and more groups are getting together on skate excursions in cities all over the world. For example, San Francisco has night group-skating that numbers in the hundreds of people. The market trends are showing continued growth in all aspects of skating.

2.1.4 Market Growth

With the price of skates going down due to competition from so many skate companies, the market has had steady growth throughout the world, although sales have slowed down in some markets. Sales for 2009 are projected to be $31 million. Table 2.1 shows the projected growth rates over the next four years. Growth rates should be steady as more and more people are discovering—and in many cases rediscovering—the health benefits and fun of skating.

| TABLE 2.1 | TARGET-MARKET FORECAST | | | | | | |

		Target-Market Forecast					
Potential Customers	Growth	2009	2010	2011	2012	2013	CAGR*
Recreational	10%	19 142 500	21 056 750	23 162 425	25 478 668	28 026 535	10.00%
Fitness	15%	6 820 000	7 843 000	9 019 450	10 372 368	11 928 223	15.00%
Speed	10%	387 500	426 250	468 875	515 763	567 339	10.00%
Hockey	6%	2 480 000	2 628 800	2 786 528	2 953 720	3 130 943	6.00%
Extreme	4%	2 170 000	2 256 800	2 347 072	2 440 955	2 538 593	4.00%
Total	10.48%	31 000 000	34 211 600	37 784 350	41 761 474	46 191 633	10.48%

*Compound Annual Growth Rate

2.2 SWOT ANALYSIS

The following SWOT analysis captures the key strengths and weaknesses within the company and describes the opportunities and threats facing Pegasus.

2.2.1 Strengths

- In-depth industry experience and insight
- Creative yet practical product designers
- The use of a highly efficient, flexible business model utilizing direct customer sales and distribution

2.2.2 Weaknesses

- Reliance on outside capital necessary to grow the business
- Lack of retailers who can work face-to-face with customers to generate brand and product awareness
- Difficulty in developing brand awareness because it is a start-up company

2.2.3 Opportunities

- Participation within a growing industry
- Decreased product costs through economies of scale
- Ability to leverage other industry participants' marketing efforts to help grow the general market

2.2.4 Threats

- Future/potential competition from an already established market participant
- A slump in the economy that could have a negative effect on people's spending of discretionary income on fitness/recreational products
- The release of a study that questions the safety of skating or the inability to prevent major skating-induced traumas

2.3 COMPETITION

Pegasus Sports International is forming its own market. Although there are a few companies that do make sails and foils that a few skaters are using, Pegasus' are the only ones that are truly designed for and by skaters. The few competitors' sails on the market are not designed for skating, but for windsurfing or for skateboards. In the case of foils, storage and carrying are not practical. There are different indirect competitors which are manufacturers of the actual skates. After many years in the market, these companies have yet to become direct competitors by manufacturing accessories for the skates that they make.

2.4 PRODUCT OFFERING

Pegasus Sports International now offers several products:

- The first product that has been developed is BladeBoots, covers for the wheels and frame of inline skates that enable skaters to enter places that normally would not allow them in with skates on. BladeBoots come with a small pouch and belt that converts to a well-designed skate carrier.
- The second product is SkateSails. These sails are designed specifically for use while skating. Feedback that Pegasus has received from skaters indicates skatesailing could become a very popular sport. Trademarking this product is currently in progress.
- The third product, SkateAid, will be in production by the end of the year. Other ideas for products are under development, but will not be disclosed until Pegasus can protect them through pending patent applications.

2.5 KEYS TO SUCCESS

The keys to success are designing and producing products that meet market demand. In addition, Pegasus must ensure total customer satisfaction. If these keys to success are obtained, Pegasus will become a profitable, sustainable company.

2.6 CRITICAL ISSUES

As a start-up business, Pegasus is still in the early stages. The critical issues are for Pegasus to:

- Establish itself as the premier skating-accessory company.
- Pursue controlled growth with payroll expenses that never exceed the revenue base. This will help protect against recessions.
- Constantly monitor customer satisfaction, ensuring that the growth strategy will never compromise service and satisfaction levels.

3.0 MARKETING STRATEGY

The key to the marketing strategy is focusing on the speed, health and fitness, and recreational segments of skaters. Pegasus can cover about 80 percent of the skating market because it produces products geared toward each segment. Pegasus is able to address all of the different segments within the market because, although each segment is distinct in terms of its users and equipment, Pegasus' products are useful to all of the different segments.

3.1 MISSION

Pegasus Sports International's mission is to provide the customer with the finest skating accessories available. We exist to attract and maintain customers. With a strict adherence to this maxim, success will be ensured. Our services and products will exceed the expectations of the customers.

3.2 MARKETING OBJECTIVES

- Maintain positive, strong growth each quarter (notwithstanding seasonal sales patterns).
- Achieve a steady increase in market penetration.
- Decrease customer acquisition costs by 1.5 percent per quarter.

3.3 FINANCIAL OBJECTIVES

- Increase the profit margin by 1 percent per quarter through efficiency and economy-of-scale gains.
- Maintain a significant research and development budget (as a percentage relative to sales) to spur future product developments.
- A double- to triple-digit growth rate for the first three years.

3.4 TARGET MARKETS

With a world skating market that's over 31 million and steadily growing (statistics released by the Sporting Goods Manufacturers Association), the niche has been created. Pegasus' aim is to expand this market by promoting SkateSailing, a new sport that is popular in both Santa Monica and Venice Beach in California. The Sporting Goods Manufacturers Association survey indicates that skating now has more participation than football, softball, skiing, and snowboarding combined. The breakdown of participation of skating is as follows: 1+ percent speed (growing), 8 percent hockey (declining), 7 percent extreme/aggressive (declining), 22 percent fitness (nearly 7 million—the fastest growing), and 61 percent recreational (first-timers). Our products are targeting the fitness and recreational groups because they are the fastest growing. These groups are gearing themselves toward health and fitness, and combined, they can easily grow to 85 percent (or 26 million) of the market in the next five years.

3.5 POSITIONING

Pegasus will position itself as the premier aftermarket skating-accessory company. This positioning will be achieved by leveraging Pegasus' competitive edge: industry experience and passion. Pegasus is a skating company formed by skaters for skaters. Pegasus' management is able to use its vast experience and personal passion for the sport to develop innovative, useful accessories for a broad range of skaters.

3.6 STRATEGIES

The single objective is to position Pegasus as the premier skating-accessory manufacturer, serving both the domestic and international markets. The marketing strategy will seek first to create customer awareness of the offered products and services and then to develop the customer base. The message that Pegasus will seek to communicate is that Pegasus offers the best-designed, most useful skating accessories. This message will be communicated through a variety of methods. The first will be the Pegasus website. The website will provide a rich source of product information and offer consumers the opportunity to purchase products. A lot of time and money will be invested in the site to provide customers with a perception of total professionalism and the utility of Pegasus' products and services.

The second marketing method will be advertisements placed in numerous industry magazines. The skating industry is supported by several different glossy magazines designed to promote the industry as a whole. In addition, a number of smaller periodicals serve the smaller market segments within the skating industry. The last method of communication is the use of printed sales literature. The two previously mentioned marketing methods will create demand for the sales literature that will be sent to customers. The cost of the sales literature will be fairly minimal because it will use already-compiled information from the website.

3.7 MARKETING MIX

Pegasus' marketing is comprised of the following approaches to pricing, distribution, advertising and promotion, and customer service:

- *Pricing.* This will be based on a per-product retail price.
- *Distribution.* Initially, Pegasus will use a direct-to-consumer distribution model. Over time, Pegasus will use retailers as well.
- *Advertising and promotion.* Several different methods will be used for the advertising effort.
- *Customer service.* Pegasus will strive to achieve benchmarked levels of customer care.

3.8 MARKETING RESEARCH

Pegasus is blessed with the good fortune of being located in the centre of the skating world: Venice, California. Pegasus will be able to leverage this opportune location by working with many of the different skaters who live in the area. Pegasus was able to test all of its products not only with its principals, who are accomplished skaters, but also with the many other dedicated and "newbie" users located in Venice. The extensive product testing by a wide variety of users provided Pegasus with valuable product feedback and has led to several design improvements.

4.0 FINANCIALS

This section offers a financial overview of Pegasus related to marketing activities. It addresses break-even analysis, sales forecast, and expense forecast and indicates how these activities link to the marketing strategy.

4.1 BREAK-EVEN ANALYSIS

The break-even analysis (Table 4.1) indicates that $7 760 will be required in monthly sales revenue to reach the break-even point.

TABLE 4.1	BREAK-EVEN ANALYSIS	
Break-Even Analysis:		
Monthly Units Break-Even		62
Monthly Sales Break-Even		$ 7 760
Assumptions:		
Average Per-Unit Revenue		$125.62
Average Per-Unit Variable Cost		$ 22.61
Estimated Monthly Fixed Cost		$ 6 363

4.2 SALES FORECAST

Pegasus feels that the sales-forecast figures are conservative (Table 4.2). Pegasus will steadily increase sales as the advertising budget allows. Although the target-market forecast (Table 2.1) listed all of the potential customers divided into separate groups, the sales forecast groups customers into two categories: recreational and competitive. Reducing the number of categories allows the reader to quickly discern information, making the chart more functional.

Monthly-Sales Forecast

TABLE 4.2	SALES FORECAST		
	Sales Forecast		
Sales	**2009**	**2010**	**2011**
Recreational	$455 740	$598 877	$687 765
Competitive	$72 918	$95 820	$110 042
Total Sales	$528 658	$694 697	$797 807
Direct Cost of Sales	**2009**	**2010**	**2011**
Recreational	$82 033	$107 798	$123 798
Competitive	$13 125	$17 248	$19 808
Subtotal Cost of Sales	$95 159	$125 046	$143 605

4.3 EXPENSE FORECAST

The expense forecast (Table 4.3) will be used as a tool to keep the department on target and provide indicators when corrections/modifications are needed for the proper implementation of the marketing plan.

Monthly-Expense Budget

TABLE 4.3	MARKETING-EXPENSE BUDGET		
Marketing-Expense Budget	**2009**	**2010**	**2011**
Website	$25 000	$8 000	$10 000
Advertisements	$8 050	$15 000	$20 000
Printed Material	$1 725	$2 000	$3 000
Total Sales and Marketing Expenses	$34 775	$25 000	$33 000
Percent of Sales	6.58%	3.60%	4.14%
Contribution Margin	$398 725	$544 652	$621 202
Contribution Margin/Sales	75.42%	78.40%	77.86%

5.0 CONTROLS

The purpose of Pegasus' marketing plan is to serve as a guide for the organization. The following areas will be monitored to gauge performance:

- Revenue: monthly and annual
- Expenses: monthly and annual
- Customer satisfaction
- New product development

5.1 IMPLEMENTATION

The following milestones (Table 5.1) identify the key marketing programs. It is important to accomplish each one on time and on budget.

5.2 MARKETING ORGANIZATION

Stan Blade will be responsible for the marketing activities.

5.3 CONTINGENCY PLANNING

Difficulties and Risks

- Problems generating visibility, a function of being an Internet-based start-up organization.
- An entry into the market by an already established market competitor

Worst-Case Risks Include

- Determining that the business cannot support itself on an ongoing basis
- Having to liquidate equipment or intellectual capital to cover liabilities

Milestones

TABLE 5.1	MILESTONES					
Milestones		**Start Date**	**End Date**	**Plan Budget**	**Manager**	**Department**
Marketing-plan completion		1/1/09	2/1/09	$0	Stan	Marketing
Website completion		1/1/09	3/15/09	$20 400	outside firm	Marketing
Advertising campaign #1		1/1/09	6/30/09	$3 500	Stan	Marketing
Advertising campaign #2		3/1/09	12/30/09	$4 550	Stan	Marketing
Development of the retail channel		1/1/09	11/30/09	$0	Stan	Marketing
Totals				$28 450		

SUMMARY

1. The value-delivery process involves choosing (or identifying), providing (or delivering), and communicating superior value. The value chain is a tool for identifying key activities that create value and costs in a specific business.

2. Strong companies develop superior capabilities in managing core business processes such as new-product realization, inventory management, and customer acquisition and retention. Managing these core processes effectively means creating a marketing network in which the company works closely with all parties in the production and distribution chain, from suppliers of raw materials to retail distributors. Companies no longer compete—marketing networks do.

3. Holistic marketing maximizes value exploration by understanding the relationships among the customer's cognitive space, the company's competence space, and a collaborator's resource space. A company can maximize value creation by identifying new customer benefits

from the customer's cognitive space, utilizing core competencies from its business domain, and selecting and managing business partners from its collaborative networks. It can maximize value delivery by becoming proficient at customer relationship management, internal resource management, and business partnership management.

4. Market-oriented strategic planning is the managerial process of developing and maintaining a viable fit between an organization's objectives, skills, and resources and its changing market opportunities. The aim of strategic planning is to shape the company's businesses and products so that they yield target profits and growth. Strategic planning takes place at four levels: corporate, division, business unit, and product.

5. The corporate strategy establishes the framework within which the divisions and business units prepare their strategic plans. Setting a corporate strategy entails four activities: defining the corporate mission, establishing strategic business units (SBUs), assigning resources to each SBU based on its market attractiveness and business strength, and planning new businesses and assessing growth opportunities.

6. Strategic planning for individual businesses entails the following activities: defining the business mission, analyzing external opportunities and threats, analyzing internal strengths and weaknesses, formulating goals, formulating strategy, formulating supporting programs, implementing the programs, and gathering feedback and exercising control.

7. Each product level within a business unit must develop a marketing plan for achieving its goals. The marketing plan is one of the most important outputs of the marketing process.

APPLICATIONS

Marketing Debate: What Good Is a Mission Statement?

Virtually all firms have mission statements to help guide and inspire employees as well as signal what is important to the firm to those outside the firm. Mission statements are often the product of much deliberation and discussion. At the same time, some critics claim that mission statements sometimes lack "teeth" and specificity. Moreover, critics also maintain that in many cases, mission statements do not vary much from firm to firm and make the same empty promises.

Take a position: Mission statements are critical to a successful marketing organization *versus* Mission statements rarely provide useful marketing value.

Marketing Discussion

Consider Porter's value chain and the holistic-marketing model. What implications do they have for marketing planning? How would you structure a marketing plan to incorporate some of their concepts?

Breakthrough Marketing: Intel

Intel makes the microprocessors that are found in 80 percent of the world's personal computers. In the early days, Intel microprocessors were known simply by their engineering numbers, such as "80386" and "80486." Intel positioned its chips as the most advanced. The trouble was, as Intel soon learned, numbers can't be trademarked. Competitors came out with their own "486" chips and Intel had no way to distinguish itself from the competition. Worse, Intel's products were hidden from consumers, buried deep inside PCs. With a hidden,

untrademarked product, Intel had a hard time convincing consumers to pay more for its high-performance products.

Intel's response was a marketing campaign that created history. The company chose a trademarkable name—Pentium—and launched the "Intel Inside" marketing campaign to build awareness of the brand and get its name outside the PC and into the minds of consumers.

Intel used an innovative cooperative scheme to extend the reach of the campaign: It would help advertise the PCs of computer makers which used Intel processors, if the makers included the Intel logo in their ads. Intel also gave computer manufacturers a co-op reimbursement on Intel processors if they agreed to place an "Intel Inside" sticker on the outside of their PCs and laptops.

Intel continues its integrated ingredient campaigns to this day. For example, when launching its Centrino mobile microprocessor platform, Intel began with TV ads that aired in North America and ten other countries. These ads include the animated logo and now-familiar five-note signature melody of the brand. Print, online, and outdoor advertising followed shortly thereafter. Intel created eight-page inserts for major newspapers that urged the wired world not only to "unwire," but also to "Untangle. Unburden. Uncompromise. Unstress."

Intel even held a "One Unwired Day" event that took place in major cities such as New York, Chicago, San Francisco, and Toronto. In addition to allowing free trial Wi-Fi access, the company held festivals in each city that included live music, product demonstrations, and prize giveaways. In downtown Toronto, Intel of Canada erected a 24-foot-high notebook computer. It targeted GO Train (interregional public transit) and subway commuters with the Intel Mobile Technology Zone in the Royal Bank Plaza near Union Station.

The "Unwired" campaign was another Intel success in marketing. The $300-million total media effort for the Centrino mobile platform, which also included cooperative advertising with manufacturers, helped generate $2 billion in revenue for Intel during the first nine months of the campaign.

In 2006, Intel launched a new brand identity supported by a $2-billion global marketing campaign. The company introduced a new logo with a different font and updated look and also created a new slogan: "Leap Ahead." In addition to the new logo and slogan, Intel developed Viiv (rhymes with "five"), a new microprocessor platform aimed at home-entertainment enthusiasts. These moves were designed to create the impression of Intel as a "warm and fuzzy consumer company," with products that went beyond the PC. Intel remained one of the most valuable brands in the world, its $32-billion brand valuation earning it fifth place in the 2006 Interbrand/*BusinessWeek* ranking of the Best Global Brands.

DISCUSSION QUESTIONS

1. Over its history, Intel made two significant changes to its promotion strategy. Why were these changes essential?
2. Search the Intel company website. What is its corporate mission and values? Is it a good mission statement? Why or why not?
3. What are Intel's growth opportunities as it moves into the future?

Sources: Don Clark, "Intel to Overhaul Marketing in Bid to Go beyond PCs," *Wall Street Journal*, December 30, 2005; Cliff Edwards, "Intel Everywhere?" *BusinessWeek*, March 8, 2004, pp. 56–62; Scott Van Camp, "ReadMe.1st," *Brandweek*, February 23, 2004, p. 17; David Kirkpatrick, "At Intel, Speed Isn't Everything," *Fortune*, February 9, 2004, p. 34; "How to Become a Superbrand," *Marketing*, January 8, 2004, p. 15; Roger Slavens, "Pam Pollace, VP-Director, Corporate Marketing Group, Intel Corp," *B to B*, December 8, 2003, p. 19; Kenneth Hein, "Study: New Brand Names Not Making Their Mark," *Brandweek*, December 8, 2003, p. 12; Heather Clancy, "Intel Thinking Outside the Box," *Computer Reseller News*, November 24, 2003, p. 14; Cynthia L. Webb, "A Chip Off the Old Recovery?" Washingtonpost.com, October 15, 2003; "Intel Launches Second Phase of Centrino Ads," *Technology Advertising & Branding Report*, October 6, 2003; Michelle Warren, "Intel gets noticed outdoors," *Marketing Daily*, May 6, 2003.

2

CAPTURING MARKETING INSIGHTS

IN THIS CHAPTER, WE WILL ADDRESS THE FOLLOWING QUESTIONS:

- What are the components of a modern marketing information system?

- What are useful internal records?

- What is involved with a marketing intelligence system?

- What are the key methods for tracking and identifying opportunities in the macroenvironment?

- What are some important macroenvironment developments?

CHAPTER 3

GATHERING INFORMATION AND SCANNING THE ENVIRONMENT

three

Understanding the dynamics of the market environment is imperative for marketers. Trends in the consumer (and hence the business) marketplace are constant and unstoppable. As a result, the need to continuously and rigorously gather information about the market to detect trends in the firm's operating environments is crucial for success and sustainability. Consider how the environmental movement has impacted the way Canadian businesses operate.

A survey conducted by Environics Research Group in 2007 found that 75 percent of Canadians would be willing to switch their spending to companies that are committed to environmentally friendly policies, even if it meant paying a higher price for purchasing their products. This segment of the market was as high as 83 percent in British Columbia and 78 percent in Ontario. "We're seeing a fundamental shift in consumer behaviour that reflects the increased mainstreaming of environmental consciousness," said Michael Adams, founding president of Environics. "Canadians are very deliberately rewarding those companies who are taking action on the environment."

These changing consumer preferences have significant implications for many industries and can create both opportunities and threats for a business. Many astute marketers have been able to capitalize on the "Go Green" trend sweeping the country. Consider the case of Avalon Homes, based in Red Deer, Alberta. In 2002, Avalon was a new entrant in the booming and fiercely competitive Alberta housing market. In its quest for market share, it began marketing itself as a "green builder," focusing on building homes that fare better than those of competing developers in Alberta's Built Green program. Just a few years later, Avalon is one among a dozen builders across Canada to be recognized by the federal government as being one of the top environmentally conscious developers in the country. Despite its premium price, Avalon sold more new homes in 2007 than any other competitor in Red Deer.

Ozzie Jurock, president of Jurock Publishing Ltd., comments on the impact the environmental movement has had on the real estate industry: "The green real estate effect is already having an impact on everything from house sales to farmland, from condominiums to waterfront. We have seen some very interesting real estate reactions to the green philosophy, some of which were overdue and make good economic sense."

Victoria-based Chard Developments is another real estate developer with a green vision. In a slowing condominium market, Chard proposed an innovative incentive for new homebuyers. During presales for its high-rise Juliet tower-condo project, Chard offered to reduce the selling price by $25 000 for buyers willing to accept a bicycle locker and participation in a local car-sharing program in lieu of an underground parking space. The proposal was an instant hit with buyers and the discounted "green" condos were the first to sell. In addition, the project saved Chard money in parking-space expenditures and generated considerable positive publicity for the company.

Teknion Corporation, manufacturer of office systems and furniture products, has earned the recognition of the industry for its commitment to pursuing environmentally friendly methods of design, manufacturing, and business development. The firm formed a GreenWorks team within the organization to research its production and make improvements that would minimize its impact on the environment. Within four years, this national award-winning team reduced Teknion's waste generation by 56 percent, its natural gas consumption by 39 percent, and its electricity consumption by 26 percent. The electricity saved by the GreenWorks team could power nearly 7 000 homes for a month. Teknion states that sustainable development is a significant part of the company's culture and that employees are focused not only on creating a greener company, but a better one. Teknion's description of its culture and the implied connection between environmentally friendly policies and improved corporate performance highlights the growing perception that exists in Canadian business today that eco-friendliness and financial performance can co-exist.

Perhaps a more remarkable aspect of the environmental movement is the way it can affect industries that are seemingly quite impervious to environmental concerns. Take, for instance, the financial-services industry. Toronto-based Mercer Investment Consulting was recently recognized by GLOBE Foundation for its dedication to developing intellectual capital concerning the integration of environmental, social, and corporate governance considerations in investment-decision making. Its Responsible Investment business involves working with clients to develop socially and environmentally responsible investment policies, select investment managers, and monitor performance within this framework. It is based on the philosophy that responsible corporate behaviour has a positive influence on the financial performance of companies over the long term. This initiative was awarded the 2007 GLOBE Capital Markets Award for Sustainable Investment & Banking, as well as earning Mercer a consulting contract with the United Nations for the development of "Principles for Responsible Investment." As the GLOBE Foundation notes, "Financial markets are increasingly integrating environment factors into investment and banking decisions, and are placing more capital into sustainable technologies and ventures."

Environmental concerns have reached a level of importance where they are no longer simply a niche concept or a fad, but rather an integral facet of every business that is keen enough to recognize its value to consumers and the marketplace. Marketers cannot afford to ignore this trend while designing their strategies, as Yoplait recently learned the hard way. The company, in an attempt to create awareness for its new Yoptimal yogurt and help consumers recognize the container at the grocery store, launched a promotional campaign by distributing a plastic bag containing an empty yogurt container to homes across Canada. This led to numerous complaints from consumers and environmental groups that Yoplait was creating unnecessary waste that would end up in landfills. This caused considerable bad publicity for the company and made it look environmentally irresponsible.

Marketers must have comprehensive, up-to-date information if they are to develop insightful and inspirational marketing plans for serving their target audiences. As the preceding discussion shows, they must understand both the broad trends influencing their marketplace and the unique attitudes and habits of their buyers. In this chapter, we consider how firms can develop processes to track such trends. In Chapter 4 we will see how marketers conduct more customized research that addresses specific marketing problems or issues.

Sources: National poll conducted Feb 7–14, 2007 by the Environics Research Group for Bullfrog Power, ON. Survey data available at www.bullfrogpower.com/news/Survey_Data.pdf (viewed March 12, 2008); "Environmental Trend has Green Cash Potential," by Ozzie Jurock, published in *BC Real Estate News*, June 15, 2007, www2.jurock.com/articles/columnist.asp?id=7140 (viewed March 12, 2008); www.theglobeawards.ca/winners.cfm (viewed March 12, 2008); "Yogurt promo blitz hard to swallow," by Meghan Hurley, *Winnipeg Free Press*, March 13, 2008, p. B1.

COMPONENTS OF A MODERN MARKETING INFORMATION SYSTEM

The major responsibility for identifying significant marketplace changes falls to a company's marketers. More than any other group in the company, they must be the trend trackers and opportunity seekers. Although every manager in an organization needs to observe the outside environment, marketers have two advantages: they have disciplined methods for collecting information and they also spend more time interacting with customers and observing competition.

Some firms have developed marketing information systems that provide management with rich detail of buyer wants, preferences, and behaviour, as illustrated by the DuPont example below.

DuPont

DuPont commissioned marketing studies to uncover personal pillow behaviour for its Dacron Polyester unit, which supplies filling to pillow makers and sells its own Comforel brand. One challenge is that people don't give up their old pillows: 37 percent of one sample described their relationship with their pillow as like "an old married couple" and an additional 13 percent characterized it as like a "childhood friend." They found that people fell into distinct groups in terms of pillow behaviour: stackers (23 percent), plumpers (20 percent), rollers or folders (16 percent), cuddlers (16 percent), and smashers (10 percent), who pound their pillows into a more comfy shape. Women were more likely to plump, whereas men were more likely to fold. The prevalence of stackers led the company to sell more pillows packaged as pairs, as well as to market different levels of softness or firmness.[1]

Marketers also have extensive information about how consumption patterns vary across countries. On a per-capita basis within Western Europe, for example, the Swiss consume the most chocolate, the Greeks eat the most cheese, the Irish drink the most tea, and the Austrians smoke the most cigarettes.

Nevertheless, many business firms are not sophisticated about gathering information. Many do not have a marketing-research department. Others have a department that limits its work to routine forecasting, sales analysis, and occasional surveys. Many managers complain about not knowing where critical information is located in the company; getting too much information that they cannot use and too little that they really need; getting important information too late; and doubting the information's accuracy. Companies with superior information enjoy a competitive advantage. The company can choose its markets better, develop better offerings, and execute better marketing planning.

Every firm must organize and distribute a continuous flow of information to its marketing managers. Companies study their managers' information needs and design marketing information systems to meet these needs. A **marketing information system (MIS)** consists of people, equipment, and procedures to gather, sort, analyze, evaluate, and distribute needed, timely, and accurate information to marketing decision makers. A marketing information system is developed from internal

TABLE 3.1	INFORMATION-NEEDS PROBES

1. What decisions do you regularly make?
2. What information do you need to make these decisions?
3. What information do you regularly get?
4. What special studies do you periodically request?
5. What information would you want that you are not getting now?
6. What information would you want daily? Weekly? Monthly? Yearly?
7. What magazines and trade reports would you like to see on a regular basis?
8. What topics would you like to be kept informed of?
9. What data-analysis programs would you want?
10. What are the four most helpful improvements that could be made in the present marketing information system?

company records, marketing intelligence activities, and marketing research. The first two topics are discussed here; the latter topic is reviewed in the next chapter.

The company's marketing information system should be a cross between what managers think they need, what managers really need, and what is economically feasible. An internal MIS committee can interview a cross-section of marketing managers to discover their information needs. Table 3.1 displays some useful questions.

INTERNAL RECORDS AND MARKETING INTELLIGENCE

Marketing managers rely on internal reports on orders, sales, prices, costs, inventory levels, receivables, payables, and so on. By analyzing this information, they can spot important opportunities and problems.

The Order-to-Payment Cycle

The heart of the internal-records system is the order-to-payment cycle. Sales representatives, dealers, and customers send orders to the firm. The sales department prepares invoices and transmits copies to various departments. Out-of-stock items are back ordered. Shipped items are accompanied by shipping and billing documents that are sent to various departments.

Today's companies need to perform these steps quickly and accurately. Customers favour firms that can promise timely delivery. Customers and sales representatives fax or email their orders. Computerized warehouses quickly fill these orders. The billing department sends out invoices as quickly as possible. An increasing number of companies are using the Internet and extranets to improve the speed, accuracy, and efficiency of the order-to-payment cycle.

Sales Information Systems

Marketing managers need timely and accurate reports on current sales. Wal-Mart, for example, knows the sales of each product by store and total each evening. This enables it to transmit nightly orders to suppliers for new shipments of replacement stock. Wal-Mart shares its sales data with its larger suppliers such as Procter & Gamble (P&G) and expects P&G to re-supply Wal-Mart stores in a timely manner. Wal-Mart has entrusted P&G with the management of its inventory.[2]

Companies must carefully interpret the sales data so as not to get the wrong signals. Michael Dell gave this illustration: "If you have three yellow Mustangs sitting on a dealer's lot and a customer wants a red one, the salesman may be really good at figuring out how to sell the yellow Mustang. So the yellow Mustang gets sold, and a signal gets sent back to the factory that, hey, people want yellow Mustangs."

Technological gadgets are revolutionizing sales information systems and are allowing representatives from companies like insurance giant Clarica of Waterloo, Ontario, to have up-to-the-second information. Clarica's system allows agents to complete 90 percent of insurance applications electronically and enables the company to deliver policies to clients the day after they apply.[3]

Databases, Data Warehouses, and Data Mining

Today, companies organize their information in databases—customer databases, product databases, salesperson databases—and then combine data from the different databases. For example, the customer database will contain every customer's name, address, past transactions, and even demographics and psychographics (activities, interests, and opinions) in some instances. Instead of a company sending a mass "carpet bombing" mailing of a new offer to every customer in its database, it will score the different customers according to purchase recency, frequency, and monetary value. It will send the offer only to the highest-scoring customers. Besides saving on mailing expenses, this will often achieve a double-digit response rate.

Companies warehouse these data and make them easily accessible to decision makers. Furthermore, by hiring analysts skilled in sophisticated statistical methods, they can "mine" the data and garner fresh insights into neglected customer segments, recent customer trends, and other useful information. The customer information can be cross-tabbed with product and salesperson information to yield still deeper insights. To manage all the different databases efficiently and effectively, more firms are using business integration software (see "Marketing Insight: Getting the Most out of Customer Databases with CRM").

The Marketing Intelligence System

The internal-records system supplies *results* data, but the marketing intelligence system supplies *happenings* data. A **marketing intelligence system** is a set of procedures and sources that managers use to obtain everyday information about developments in the marketing environment. Marketing managers collect marketing intelligence by reading books, newspapers, and trade publications; talking to customers, suppliers, and distributors; and meeting with other company managers.

A company can take several steps to improve the quality of its marketing intelligence:

- *A company can train and motivate the sales force to spot and report new developments.* Sales representatives are positioned to pick up information missed by other means, yet they often fail to pass on that information. The company must "sell" its sales force on their importance as intelligence gatherers. Sales reps should know which types of information to send to which managers. For instance, the Pearson sales reps who sell this textbook let their editors know what is going on in each discipline, who is doing exciting research, and who plans to write cutting-edge textbooks.

- *A company can motivate distributors, retailers, and other intermediaries to pass along important intelligence.* Many companies hire specialists to gather marketing intelligence. Service providers often send mystery shoppers to their stores to assess how employees treat customers. Mystery shoppers for McDonald's discovered that only 46 percent of its restaurants met internal speed-of-service standards, forcing the company to rethink processes and training.[4] Retailers also use mystery shoppers. Neiman Marcus employs a professional shopper agency to shop at its stores. It finds stores that consistently score high on the service have the best sales. Typical questions their mystery shoppers report on are: How long before a sales associate greeted you? Did the sales associate act as if he or she wanted your business? Was the sales associate knowledgeable about products in stock?[5]

- *A company can network externally.* It can purchase competitors' products; attend open houses and trade shows; read competitors' published reports; attend shareholders' meetings; talk to employees, dealers, distributors, suppliers, and freight agents; collect competitors' ads; and look up news stories about competitors. Software developer Cognos created an internal website called Street Fighter where any of the firm's 3 000 workers can submit scoops about competitors and win prizes.[6] Competitive intelligence must be done legally and ethically, though. Procter & Gamble reportedly paid a multi–million-dollar settlement to Unilever when some external operatives hired as part of a P&G corporate-intelligence program to learn about Unilever's hair-care products were found to have engaged in such unethical behaviour as "dumpster diving."[7]

- *A company can set up a customer advisory panel.* Members might include representative customers, the company's largest customers, or its most outspoken or sophisticated customers. Many business schools have advisory panels made up of alumni and recruiters who provide valuable feedback on the curriculum.

- *A company can take advantage of government data resources.* The 2006 Canadian census performed by Statistics Canada provides an in-depth look at population growth and change, demographic groups, family structure, and many other useful facts about Canadians.

In today's fiercely competitive environment, finding and keeping customers is more critical than ever. Companies, realizing that the financial benefit of retaining existing customers is greater than that of finding new ones, are increasingly relying on data mining to keep their customers satisfied.

One of the hottest trends in data mining began during the nineties when formal and systematic Customer Relationship Management (CRM) came to the forefront. This new technology focused on building relationships with the firm's customers by analyzing their behaviour. CRM allowed companies to better utilize customer data they already possessed to uncover new-product opportunities, target customers more efficiently, and improve profitability. For instance, in some cases response rates to direct mail sent to customers reached 40 percent, far exceeding industry standards.

The system, however, has several drawbacks that management must consider prior to and during implementation. Two notable disadvantages are the considerable cost and the level of complexity. Forrester Research found that large companies could spend between US$15 million and US$30 million per year on CRM software. Similarly, the Meta Group estimates that, despite the heavy expenditure involved, 55 to 70 percent of CRM projects fail to meet their objectives. Implementing CRM can demand corporate reorganization and requires executives to wholeheartedly buy into the system prior to implementation. Such demands have led many companies to choose alternative routes to keep their customers satisfied.

That is not to say that many companies have not experienced significant success from their CRM systems. One such example is The Limited, the parent company of several brands including Victoria's Secret, Bath & Body Works, and La Senza. The Limited, upon investing in analytical CRM software, reported that increased cross-selling among its brands yielded a return on investment of 400 percent. Canadian companies such as Bank of Montreal and Royal Bank have also undertaken the expensive technological and conceptual changes that adoption of CRM requires and, although the process has been long and challenging, are finding the systems to be very beneficial. David Moxley, Vice-President of Customer Knowledge Management at the Bank of Montreal, estimates, "It's not unlikely our return on investment is in excess of 1 000 percent."

CRM is not just for large corporations—many small businesses have successfully implemented CRM and reaped its benefits. Martack Specialties Ltd. of Burlington, Ontario, manufacturer of products such as whiteboards and chalkboards, found that its productivity increased 50 percent and sales went up 15 percent within a year of implementing a CRM system. Similarly, Inortech Inc. in Terrebonne, Quebec, a supplier of paint, ink, and adhesives, experienced a boost in productivity and a reduction in outstanding-payment collection times following its adoption of CRM.

With the considerable success experienced by many companies that have implemented a CRM system, it comes as no surprise that many more continue to pursue CRM—although with varying success.

Sources: Viren Joshi and Richard Verity, "No Frills–CRM," *strategy+business Resilience Report*, July 29, 2004; Lesley Young, "Cutting Through All the Hype About CRM," *Marketing Direct*, February 12, 2001; "Marktack Specialties Ltd.: Organizational overhaul increases sales, productivity and customer service levels," www.maximizer.com/about/customers/max_martack.html (viewed March 16, 2008); "Inortech Optimizes Customer Loyalty with Sage CRM," crmadvantage.ca/casestudies.asp (viewed March 16, 2008).

- *A company can purchase information from outside suppliers.* Well-known data suppliers include A.C. Nielsen Canada and Information Resources, Inc. (see Table 3.2). These research firms gather consumer-panel data at a much lower cost than the company could manage on its own. Biz360 has partnerships with numerous information providers that give its clients access to millions of data sources through its wide network.[8]

- *A company can use online customer-feedback systems to collect competitive intelligence.* Online customer-feedback facilitates collection and dissemination of information on a global scale, usually at low cost. Through online customer review boards or forums, one customer's evaluation of a product or a supplier can be distributed to a large number of other potential buyers and, of course, to marketers seeking information on the competition. Currently existing channels for feedback include message boards; threaded discussion forums that allow users to post new threads and follow up on existing threads; discussion forums, which are more like bulletin boards; opinion forums, which feature more in-depth, lengthy reviews; and chat rooms. While chat rooms have the advantage of allowing users to share experiences and impressions, their unstructured nature makes it difficult for marketers to find relevant messages. To address this issue, various companies have adopted structured systems, such as customer discussion boards or customer reviews. See "Marketing Memo: Clicking on the Competition" on p. 75 for a summary of the major categories of structured, online feedback systems.[9]

TABLE 3.2	SECONDARY COMMERCIAL DATA SOURCES

- *Ipsos-Reid,*www.ipsos-reid.com. A weekly omnibus poll of more than 125 000 household and Internet panels, and syndicated studies such as *The Ipsos Trend Report Canada* and the *Inter@ctive Reid Report.*
- *NPD Group,* www.npd.com. Online panels that track purchasing behaviour in Canadian and world markets.
- *A.C. Nielsen Canada,* www.acnielsen.ca. Data on products and brands sold through retail outlets (Retail Index Services), supermarket scanner data (Scantrack), and others.
- *Information Resources, Inc.,* www.infores.com. Supermarket scanner data (InfoScan) and data on the impact of supermarket promotions (PromotioScan).
- *SAMI/Burke* (acquired by the PDI partnership—Promotion Decisions Inc. and Knowledge Networks). A range of research services, including the National Shopper Lab (a household panel of 10 million for consumer diagnostics) as well as controlled store testing and market mix modelling.
- *Experian Group,* www.experiangroup.com. Annual reports covering television markets, sporting goods, and proprietary drugs, with demographic data by sex, income, age, and brand preferences (selective markets and media reaching them).
- *NOP World* (includes Roper ASW). One of the world's largest market-research and business-information

companies, serving North America, Europe, and Asia. NOP offers an extensive range of both custom and syndicated research including media studies, industry-specific studies, and analytic CRM services.

- *Market Facts* (a subsidiary of Aegis Group Plc.). A leading global marketing-research and information company that provides services to many consumer–packaged-goods companies, as well as to the automotive, financial, telecommunications, pharmaceuticals, and government sectors.
- *Canadian Marketing Association,* www.the-cma.org. Publishes reports on a variety of topics of interest to professional marketers.
- *Retail Council of Canada,* www.retailcouncil.org. Publishes publicly accessible and proprietary reports for retailers.
- *ESOMAR,* www.esomar.org. The World Association of Opinion and Marketing Research Professionals, uniting over 4 000 members in 100 countries. Using its directory, marketers can locate member agencies that specialize in providing market research for specific markets and countries.
- Other commercial research houses selling data to subscribers include the Audit Bureau of Circulations, Arbitron, Dun & Bradstreet, and Starch.

Some companies circulate marketing intelligence. The staff scans the Internet and major publications, abstracts relevant news, and disseminates a news bulletin to marketing managers. It collects and files relevant information and assists managers in evaluating new information. See how Diagnosis combines data mining with artificial intelligence to improve efficiency.

Diagnosis Inc.

Headquartered in Brossard, Quebec, Diagnosis Inc. is taking data mining to the next level. Diagnosis has developed software tools that combine both data mining and artificial intelligence. With this new technology, companies can use intelligent computer software to identify patterns in large volumes of data and use those patterns to make predictions. These predictions, if made accurately, can result in significant revenue for a company. For example, this technology will be useful in mineral exploration, as geophysicists are currently collecting more data than they can use. The combination of data mining and artificial intelligence will allow mining companies to map out areas of land and determine high-probability zones with up to 80-percent accuracy, reducing the time and effort required in searching for minerals.[10]

ANALYZING THE MACROENVIRONMENT

Successful companies recognize and respond profitably to unmet needs and trends. Companies could make a fortune if they could produce any of these solutions: a cure for cancer; chemical cures for mental diseases; desalinization of seawater; nonfattening, tasty, nutritious food; practical electric cars; and affordable housing.

Needs and Trends

Enterprising individuals and companies manage to create new solutions to unmet needs. FedEx was created to meet the need for next-day mail delivery. Dockers was created to meet the needs of baby boomers who could no longer really wear—or fit into!—their jeans and wanted a physically and psychologically comfortable pair of pants. Amazon was created to offer more choice of, and information about, books and other products.

We can draw distinctions among fads, trends, and megatrends. A **fad** is "unpredictable, short-lived, and without social, economic, and political significance." A company can cash in on a fad such as Beanie Babies, Furbies, and Tickle Me Elmo dolls, but this is more a matter of luck and good timing than anything else.[11]

A **trend** is a direction or sequence of events that has some momentum and durability. Trends are more predictable and durable than fads. A trend reveals the shape of the future and provides many opportunities. For example, the percentage of people who value physical fitness and well-being has risen steadily. Yoga is experiencing a rebirth. Vancouver-based Lululemon was born to serve people following this trend, particularly upscale young women in the under-30 group. There is a growing trend toward buying organic foods. See how Safeway is responding to this trend with its O Organics line.

O Organics

In December 2006, Safeway introduced O Organics, its line of organic foods, after seeing the success its major competitor, Whole Foods Market, had obtained with its organic line. In order to compete effectively, Safeway priced the foods in the O Organics line to be competitive with the regular foods it offers. Since its launch, O Organics has grown to over 300 items, including milk, juices, eggs, bakery goods, chicken, and cereals. The line's sales reached over $300 million in 2007, up from $164 million in its first year. Originally, the O Organics was sold only in Safeway's network of 1 738 stores in the U.S. and western Canada. In December 2007, Safeway announced its plans to expand O Organics outside its store network in response to the growing consumer demand for organic food. This expansion includes forming partnerships to sell the line in Asia and South America, as well as an agreement with distribution giant Sysco Corp. to sell the product to the food service segment.[12]

Megatrends have been described as "large social, economic, political, and technological changes [that] are slow to form, and once in place, they influence us for some time—between seven and ten years, or longer."[13]

Trends and megatrends merit close attention. A new product or marketing program is likely to be more successful if it is in line with strong trends rather than opposed to them, but detecting a new market opportunity does not guarantee success, even if it is technically feasible. For example, today some companies sell portable electronic books but there may not be a sufficient number of people

Safeway has addressed the consumer shift toward natural foods with its O Organics product line.

MARKETING MEMO | CLICKING ON THE COMPETITION

There are four main ways marketers can find relevant online information on competitors' product strengths and weaknesses, as well as summary comments and overall performance-rating of a product, service, or supplier.

- *Independent customer goods-and-service review forums.* These forums include well-known websites such as Epinions.com and Bizrate.com. Epinions.com allows individuals to read and write reviews on a wide variety of goods and services, ranging from baby diapers to motorhomes. Writers give their overall rating of the product, what they consider to be pros and cons, and other details. The site also allows for price comparisons among competing stores. The average rating for a product is calculated based on the number of reviews. Bizrate.com combines consumer feedback from two sources: its 1.3 million online shoppers who have volunteered to provide ratings and feedback to assist other shoppers, and survey results on service quality collected from customers of stores listed in Bizrate. These sites have the advantage of being independent from the goods and service providers, which may reduce bias.

- *Distributor or sales-agent feedback sites.* These sites offer both positive and negative product or service reviews, but the stores or distributors have built the sites themselves. Chapters.Indigo.ca, for instance, offers an interactive feedback opportunity through which buyers, readers, editors, and others may review all products listed on the site, especially books. Elance.com is an online professional services provider that allows contractors to describe their level of satisfaction with subcontractors and provide details of their experiences.

- *Combo-sites offering customer reviews and expert opinions.* This type of site is concentrated in financial services and high-tech products that require professional knowledge. Zdnet.com, an online advisor on technology products, offers customer comments and evaluations based on ease of use, features, and stability, along with expert reviews. Zdnet summarizes the number of positive and negative evaluations and total download numbers within a certain period (commonly a week or a month) for each computer program. The advantage of this type of review site is that a product supplier can compare opinions of the experts with those of consumers.

- *Customer-complaint sites.* These forums are designed mainly for dissatisfied customers. Reviewers at most opinion sites tend to offer positive comments due to financial incentives and potential lawsuits for slanderous or libellous negative comments. In contrast, some websites offer a complaining forum with a moderator. For instance, Planetfeedback.com allows customers to voice unfavourable experiences with specific companies. Another site, Complaints.com, is devoted to customers who want to vent their frustrations with particular firms or their offerings.

Source: Adapted from Robin T. Peterson and Zhilin Yang, "Web Product Reviews Help Strategy," *Marketing News*, April 7, 2004, p. 18.

---

interested in reading a book on a computer screen or willing to pay the required price. This is why market research is necessary to determine an opportunity's profit potential.

To help marketers spot cultural shifts that might bring new opportunities or threats, several firms offer social-cultural forecasts. The Yankelovich Monitor interviews 2 500 people each year and has tracked 35 social trends since 1971, such as "anti-bigness," "mysticism," "living for today," "away from possessions," and "sensuousness." It describes the percentage of the population who share the attitude as well as the percentage who do not.

Identifying the Major Forces

Companies and their suppliers, marketing intermediaries, customers, competitors, and publics all operate in a macroenvironment of forces and trends that shape opportunities and pose threats. These forces represent "noncontrollables" that the company must monitor and respond to. In the economic arena, companies and consumers are increasingly affected by global forces (see Table 3.3).

The beginning of the new century brought a series of new challenges: the steep decline of the stock market, which affected savings, investment, and retirement funds; increasing unemployment; corporate scandals; and, of course, the rise of terrorism. These dramatic events were accompanied by the continuation of pre-existing, longer-term trends that have profoundly influenced the global landscape.

Within the rapidly changing global picture, firms must monitor six major forces: demographic, economic, social-cultural, natural, technological, and political-legal. Although these forces will be described separately, marketers must pay attention to their interactions, because these will lead to

TABLE 3.3	GLOBAL FORCES AFFECTING MARKETING

1. The substantial speedup of international transportation, communication, and financial transactions, leading to the rapid growth of world trade and investment, especially tripolar trade (North America, Western Europe, Asia).
2. The movement of manufacturing capacity and skills to lower-cost countries.
3. The rise of trade blocs such as the European Union and the NAFTA signatories.
4. The severe debt problems of a number of countries along with the increasing fragility of the international financial system.
5. The increasing use of barter and countertrade to support international transactions.
6. The move toward market economies in formerly socialist countries along with rapid privatization of publicly owned companies.
7. The rapid dissemination of global lifestyles.
8. The development of emerging markets, namely China, India, Eastern Europe, the Arab countries, and Latin America.
9. The increasing tendency of multinationals to transcend local and national characteristics and become transnational firms.
10. The increasing number of cross-border corporate strategic alliances—for example, airlines.
11. The increasing ethnic and religious conflicts in certain countries and regions.
12. The growth of global brands across a wide variety of industries such as automobiles, food, clothing, and electronics.

new opportunities and threats. For example, explosive population growth (demographic) leads to more resource depletion and pollution (natural), which leads consumers to call for more laws (political-legal), which stimulate new technological solutions and products (technological), which, if they are affordable (economic), may actually change attitudes and behaviour (social-cultural).

DEMOGRAPHIC ENVIRONMENT

Demographic trends are highly reliable for the short and intermediate run. There is little excuse for a company's being suddenly surprised by demographic developments. The Singer Company should have known for years that its sewing machine business would be hurt by smaller families and more working wives, yet it was slow in responding.

The main demographic force that marketers monitor is *population*, because people make up markets. Marketers are keenly interested in the size and growth rate of populations in cities, regions, and nations; age distribution and ethnic mix; educational levels; household patterns; and regional characteristics and movements.

Worldwide Population Growth

The world population is showing explosive growth: it totalled 6.65 billion in 2008 and will be nearly 8 billion by the year 2025.[14] In late 2007, Canada's population was estimated by Statistics Canada to be over 33 million people.[15] Canada's population growth exceeds that of many other developed nations; however, the population grew by only 5 percent in five years during the 2001 to 2006 census period. This is a remarkable decline, given the 13 to 14 percent growth Canada experienced during the late 1940s to 1950s.[16]

Here is an interesting picture:

If the world were a village of 1 000 people, it would consist of 520 women and 480 men, 330 children, 60 people over the age of 65, 10 college graduates, and 335 illiterate adults. The village would contain 52 North Americans, 55 Russians, 84 Latin Americans, 95 East and West Europeans, 124 Africans, and 584 Asians. Communication would be difficult because 165 people would speak Mandarin, 86 English, 83 Hindi/Urdu, 64 Spanish, 58 Russian, and 37 Arabic, and the rest would speak one of over 200 other languages. There would be 329 Christians, 178 Muslims, 132 Hindus, 62 Buddhists, 3 Jews, 167 nonreligious, 45 atheists, and 86 others.[17]

The population explosion has been a source of major concern. Unchecked population growth and consumption could eventually result in insufficient food supply, depletion of key minerals, overcrowding, pollution, and an overall deterioration in the quality of life. Moreover, population growth is highest in countries and communities that can least afford it. The less-developed regions of the world currently account for 82 percent of the world population and are growing at nearly 1.5 percent per year, whereas the population in the more-developed countries is growing at barely 0.3 percent per year.[18] In developing countries, the death rate has been falling as a result of modern medicine, but the birth rate has remained fairly stable. Feeding, clothing, and educating children, while also providing a rising standard of living, is nearly impossible in these countries.

Explosive population growth has major implications for business. A growing population does not mean growing markets unless these markets have sufficient purchasing power. Nonetheless, companies that carefully analyze their markets can find major opportunities. For example, to curb its skyrocketing population, the Chinese government has passed regulations limiting families to one child. One consequence of these regulations: These children are spoiled and fussed over as never before. Known in China as "little emperors," Chinese children are being showered with everything from candy to computers as a result of the "six-pocket syndrome." As many as six adults—parents, grandparents, great-grandparents, and aunts and uncles—may be indulging the whims of each child. This trend has encouraged toy companies, such as Japan's Bandai Company, Denmark's Lego Group, and the U.S.'s Hasbro and Mattel, to aggressively enter the Chinese market.[19]

Population Age Mix

National populations vary in their age mix. At one extreme is Mexico, a country with a very young population and rapid population growth. At the other extreme is Japan, a country with one of the world's oldest populations. Milk, diapers, school supplies, and toys would be important products in Mexico. Japan's population would consume many more adult products.

However, there is a global trend toward an aging population. In Canada in 2008, there were 3.4 million children below the age of 10 and twice that number of people who were 60 and over. From 1998 to 2008, the worldwide median age rose from 26 to 28 years. During the same period, Canada's median age went up from 36 to 40 years.[20] According to a survey in *The Economist*, more people will grow old in this century than ever before. It is the start of what the Japanese are calling the "Silver Century." The greying of the population is affected by another trend, the widespread fall in fertility rates. In most countries, women are not having enough babies to replace the people who die. The result will be fewer working people to replace those who retire. In a decade's time, many countries—Japan, the United States, Canada, and many European countries, for instance—will face the huge problem of having to support a vastly larger population of elderly people.[21]

A population can be subdivided into six age groups: preschool, school-aged children, teens, young adults aged 25 to 40, middle-aged adults aged 40 to 65, and older adults aged 65 and up. For marketers, the most populous age groups shape the marketing environment. Thus, baby boomers are one of the most powerful forces shaping the marketplace today.

Although there was a baby boom in both Canada and the United States, it is important for Canadian marketers to note that our baby boom was unique. It started later than the one in the United States (in 1947 versus 1946) and it lasted for a more prolonged period. (The American boom ended in 1964; the Canadian boom continued until 1966.) The boomer population comprises about a third of Canada's population.[22] Furthermore, the baby boom was not a worldwide phenomenon. No other developed countries, except for Australia and New Zealand, experienced the same expansion in the birth rate. In Europe, there was no baby boom, and in Japan, the birth rate declined during the baby-boom years.

A Mattel ad in Chinese for its Hot Wheels toy. The headline reads: "Hot Wheels Performance Tracks—Great Varieties, Great Challenges!"

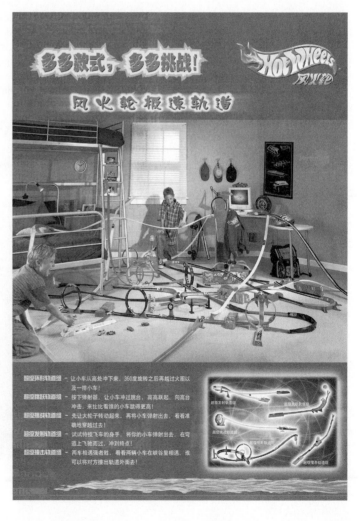

The age groups that will experience the most rapid growth in Canada in the coming decades will be older adults and teenagers—not good news for products aimed at other market segments. Consider what Canada Post did to respond to population-age shifts.

Canada Post

"Is mail going to die?" This is a critical question to which Canada Post would love to know the answer. The last ten years have seen a dramatic change in how we transmit messages between one another, in part because of email and social-networking websites. However, online retail business has created a new market for the courier industry, including Canada Post. It is estimated that online retail sales will top US$16 billion in Canada by the year 2009. Many online buyers are under the age of 30 and feel that they have no need for mail in the traditional sense. Canada Post has attempted to increase brand awareness with this segment by advertising in the virtual world, such as in Second Life (www.secondlife.com). This popular website has nearly 300 000 Canadians registered, many of whom were born after 1982. Canada Post feels that if it can get members to use its services in the virtual world, it may soon transfer into real-life usage.[23]

Baby boomers are fixated on their youth, not their age. Boomers grew up with TV advertising, so they are an easier market to reach than those born between 1965 and 1976, dubbed Generation X (and also the shadow generation and baby busters).[24] Generation Xers are typically cynical about hard-sell marketing pitches that promise more than they can deliver, but some marketers have been able to break through. Consider how Diet Pepsi used nostalgia to target older consumers.

Forever Young

Diet Pepsi, Canada's number-one-selling diet cola, has certainly gained considerable attention with its award-winning "Forever Young" advertising campaign created by BBDO Toronto. Launched in 1999, the campaign targets young-at-heart consumers. The commercials feature consumers doing embarrassingly youthful things. After realizing that the lifestyle they dream of may not quite fit their age group, they recognize that they still have Diet Pepsi to keep them feeling young. Diet Pepsi's popular "Make-out" commercial, which aired during the 2008 Super Bowl, depicts a young couple that wishes they could "make-out like they used to" when they were younger. The commercial shows the couple imagining themselves passionately kissing at socially inappropriate times and places, such as at the grocery store and at a parent–teacher interview, and ends humorously with the wife realizing that she would rather have a Diet Pepsi to keep her feeling young.[25]

Recognizing the need to communicate through new channels, Canada Post now targets the under-30 market through popular websites that young consumers frequent.

Both baby boomers and Generation Xers will be passing the torch to the latest demographic group: Generation Y or the echo boomers, born between 1977 and 1994. Totalling approximately 8.6 million Canadians, this group is almost equal in size to baby boomers. One distinguishing characteristic of this age group is their utter fluency and comfort with computer and Internet technology. Don Tapscott has christened them "Net-Gens" for this reason. He says: "To them, digital technology is no more intimidating than a VCR or a toaster."[26]

Ethnic and Other Markets

Countries also vary in ethnic and racial makeup. At one extreme is Japan, where almost everyone is Japanese; at the other extreme are Canada and the United States, whose populations are drawn from virtually all nations. Canada's population, which exceeded 33 million by the end of 2007, is becoming increasingly diverse. In addition to its founding nations (English, 6.6 million; French, 4.9 million; and Aboriginal peoples, 1.3 million), there is a rich mix of people from around the globe (e.g., Scottish, 4.7 million; German, 3.2 million; Italian, 1.4 million; Chinese, 1.3 million; Russian, 0.5 million; and Jamaican, 0.23 million).

Visible minorities (defined as non-Caucasian and non-Aboriginal) in Canada have grown substantially since 2001. In the 2006 census, visible ethnic minorities surpassed the five-million mark for the first time, now comprising 16.2 percent of the nation's population, up from 11.2 percent a decade earlier. Should current trends continue, Statistics Canada predicts one in five Canadians will be a visible minority within the next ten years. The largest groups of visible minorities currently include South Asian (25 percent), Chinese (24 percent), Black (15.4 percent), and Filipino (8 percent).

A vast majority of these minorities (95.9 percent) live in metropolitan areas, compared to only 68.1 percent of the total population. Visible minorities represent about 41 percent of the population in Toronto, 40.3 percent in Vancouver, 21 percent in Calgary, and 15.1 percent in Montreal. Toronto is Canada's most diverse city—in fact, the United Nations has proclaimed it as the most ethnically diverse city in the world. To understand where Toronto's population is headed, just consider the following statistics. Each year, over 250 000 landed immigrants enter Canada, of which nearly 50 percent settle in Toronto. As a result of this wave of immigration, 45 percent of Toronto's population will have a mother tongue and cultural background that is not English, French, or Aboriginal by the year 2011.[27]

Migration patterns are also changing. Whereas Chinese immigrants used to come mainly from Hong Kong, today they come from mainland China and so speak Mandarin instead of Cantonese. A second important trend is the growth in immigration from South Asia. Between the 2001 and 2006 censuses, the South Asian community in Canada grew by 38 percent. South Asians now account for a quarter of all ethnic minorities. The diversity of this community is witnessed by the range of languages spoken: Punjabi, Hindi, Urdu, Gujarati, Sinhalese, Tamil, Bengali, and, of course, English.

Marketing to new immigrants is both an opportunity and a challenge. It must be remembered that when people arrive in a new country, they often have no preconceptions of where to buy furniture or appliances, what car to buy, or even where to find personal-hygiene products. They are new consumers looking for information. Culturally sensitive firms have an opportunity to build relationships and develop brand loyalty.

Marketers must be careful not to overgeneralize about ethnic groups. Asian Canadians, for example, are not a homogeneous group. The identities and values of Filipinos, Sri Lankans, Chinese, and Koreans are as different from each other as they are from Canadians of European background. Bobby Siu, president of Infoworth Consulting, an agency specializing in ethnic markets, emphasizes that "each Asian ethnic group has its own identity, values, and lifestyle; yet they share common experiences as Asians in Canada."[28] Stereotypes must be avoided when approaching visible minorities, especially if they are second-generation Canadians. Research has shown that people become integrated into Canada's cultural mainstream in a single generation.

The needs of visible minorities are often underserved. Asian consumers, for example, often complain that the off-the-rack clothing found in most Canadian stores does not fit them well. Even the colours are wrong for Asian complexions. A more serious concern is that small Asian Canadians often find that they experience side effects when they take the recommended dosages of over-the-counter drugs.

Some firms are starting to listen to these voices. Until recently, many black women had to mix their own cosmetic shades to obtain the right tones, but now Revlon Canada offers a line of products specifically for black women. Neilson Dairy has launched Soy Delight, a product that is an alternative to milk for lactose-intolerant Asians. And when Nike, a global sponsor of the World Cup soccer tournament, wanted to promote its affiliation in Canada, it turned toward the Italian and Portuguese communities of Toronto. In Nike's view, they represented the most passionate devotees of the sport in Canada. As Jeff Spreit, Nike Canada's advertising manager, noted, "We ended up delivering a very relevant message to a very passionate consumer."[29]

The French-Canadian minority deserves special attention because of its large size and its dispersion through several provinces. Comprising 79 percent of Quebec households and 22 percent of Canadian households, this minority (6.8 million) cannot be ignored by national marketers.[30] Canada is officially a bicultural country, and Canadian marketers need to be sensitive to cultural differences between English and French Canadians. French Canadians have traditionally emphasized family, home, and church, but in recent decades, a growing secularism has weakened these ties in favour of materialism and nationalism.

The question of whether French-Canadian consumers are becoming more like other Canadians is debatable. But most marketers would agree that existing differences make it hazardous to employ a uniform promotional strategy across Canada. Differences in lifestyle, attitudes, and product usage make separate copy strategies and media decisions essential.

Diversity goes beyond ethnic markets. Persons with disabilities constitute almost 16 percent of Canada's population. The majority of these people are employed (65 percent of men, 50 percent of women). Since almost 60 percent of these people report mobility or agility problems, they are often a prime market for delivery and home-care services.[31]

Educational Groups

Canadian society (ages 25–64) falls into six educational groups: people with less than a high-school diploma (15 percent of the population); people with a high-school diploma (24 percent); people with a certificate from a trade school or community college (12 percent); people with a college or other non-university diploma (20 percent); people with a university certificate below a bachelor's level (5 percent); people with a university degree or diploma (23 percent). The 2006 census showed that the number of university graduates increased 24 percent since 2001. Young adults had a higher level of educational attainment than their older counterparts. About 29 percent of young adults aged 25 to 34 had a university degree in 2006, well above the proportion of 18 percent of adults aged 55 to 64. Also, fewer young adults were studying in trades than their parents. About 10 percent of young adults aged 25 to 34 had a trade certification in 2006, compared with 13 percent of the older adults aged 55 to 64. Of those aged 25 to 34, a much higher percentage of women than men (33 versus 25 percent) had a university degree. These percentages were higher than those observed for older adults aged 55 to 64, among whom 16 percent of women and 21 percent of men had university degrees.

Education and literacy are also highly correlated. Being able to read is a key skill in today's information-based society. It isn't surprising that people with literacy problems also have employment difficulties and tend to be low-income earners. According to Adult Literacy Canada, 22 percent of adult Canadians have serious problems dealing with any printed material, and an additional 24 percent of Canadians can deal only with simple reading tasks. It is not surprising that the 10 percent of the Canadian population with less than a Grade-9 education face most of the literacy challenges.[32]

Household Patterns

The "traditional household" consists of a husband, wife, and children (and sometimes grand parents). Yet, in Canada today household living arrangements are becoming more diverse. Of Canada's 12 437 470 households, couples with children still make up the largest proportion: 31.4 percent of the total. However, single-person households comprise the next-largest segment at 26.8 percent, couples with no children make up another 26.1 percent, and other family-household types comprise 15.8 percent. More people are divorcing or separating, choosing not to marry, marrying later, or marrying without the intention to have children. The number of common-law couples increased nearly 19 percent between 2001 and 2006, compared to only a 3.5 percent growth in married couples. Moreover, the nature of a couple is in itself changing, considering that the number of same-sex couples increased nearly 33 percent from 2001 to 2006, compared to only a 6 percent increase in opposite-sex couples during the same period. In some cases, these trends are even more pronounced within provincial boundaries. For example, in Quebec, the number of those who were never-married increased over 12 percent between 2001 and 2006. In Alberta, the number of single-parent households rose by over 12 percent during the same period; even more notable was the increase in male single-parent households of nearly 18 percent. Furthermore, the number of children people are having is declining. This, in combination with a growing number of single-parent homes, has resulted in a decline in the average family size from 3.7 persons in 1971 to 3.0 persons in 2006. Each household type has a distinctive set of needs and buying habits. For example, people in the SSWD group (single, separated, widowed, divorced) need smaller apartments; inexpensive and smaller appliances, furniture, and furnishings; and smaller-sized food packages. Marketers must increasingly consider the special needs of nontraditional households because they are now growing more rapidly than traditional households.

A study by Cava Research Group at the University of Leeds in the United Kingdom emphasized that single doesn't necessarily mean "alone." Researchers interviewed hundreds of people between the ages of 25 and 60 and concluded that "friends are the new family." They observed a growing trend for "neo tribes" of twenty-somethings to live communally. At the other end of the spectrum, older divorced people were seen centring their lives on their children and friends and keeping their romantic lives separate. This emphasis on friendship can influence marketers in everything from whom they target to how they craft their marketing messages. Travel with friends or with a group, for instance, now appeals to a wider swath of singles than college students on spring break or seniors going off to an elder hostel.[33] Online services are recognizing this trend, as the following example shows.

Facebook.com

Barely a few years after its launch, the social networking website Facebook has nearly 70 million people across the globe glued to their computers for several hours each day. First made available for public use in 2004 by Mark Zuckerberg, Facebook was created by the Harvard dropout in a dorm room as a way to meet up with his college friends. Now, anyone can sign up to be a member and view photos and videos of friends, have online conversations, write on users' "walls," or send a trivia quiz to their contacts. Facebook has grown so rapidly that, as of March 2008, 7 million Canadians (or about 15 percent of the country's population) are active users, and a quarter-million new users register worldwide each day. Many of these users are not casual users either: 60 percent of all members log onto the site daily. The high traffic that Facebook generates is drawing attention from marketers interested in online advertising. Marketers can create "sponsored groups" in which members can enter contests and receive other benefits, as Sony did to market its new PlayStation 3 and PSP gaming consoles. Another benefit of using Facebook for marketing is the endless research possibilities. For instance, marketers can view the results of member quizzes, determine popular music and favourite movies, and follow blog discussions to subsequently tailor their marketing campaigns to member groups based on those results.[34]

The gay market is thought to be a particularly lucrative segment. In 2003 and 2005, Statistics Canada conducted surveys that queried people on sexual orientation. Among Canadians aged 18 to 59, 1.9 percent identified themselves as gay, lesbian, or bisexual. The data showed that adult men were twice as likely to be gay than bisexual. Adult women, however, were more likely to be bisexual than lesbian.[35] However, the numbers from these surveys are thought to underestimate the actual gay and lesbian population, given, for example, that academics and marketing experts estimate that the gay and lesbian population ranges between 4 percent and 8 percent of the total North American population, with an even higher percentage in urban areas.[36] *Marketing Magazine* reported in 2004 that there are approximately 3.2 million gay and lesbian consumers in Canada. The statistics suggest that they are a market worth pursuing. For example, 46 percent describe themselves as trend-setters, 36 percent are usually the first people to buy new products, 57 percent are decision makers in either professional or management roles, and 94 percent would go out of their way to purchase products and services marketed directly to them. Furthermore, they report a much higher average income of $72 800 compared to the national average of $47 600. Moreover, 84 percent have no children, increasing the disposable portion of their income to well above that of the average family. In total, the gay and lesbian market in Canada is estimated to be worth a mind-blowing $100 billion.[37]

Geographical Shifts in Population

This is a period of great migratory movements between and within countries. Forward-looking companies and entrepreneurs are taking advantage of the growth in immigrant populations and marketing their wares specifically to these new members of the population.

Population movement also occurs nationally as people migrate from one region of the country to another. Each year, about 2.9 percent of Canadians have itchy feet and swap provinces. For the last few years, Alberta and Ontario have been the top two choices when it came to inter-provincial moves. Between the 2001 and 2006 censuses, Alberta experienced the highest population growth rate at 10.6 percent and Ontario gained 6.6 percent, while British Columbia's population rose 5.3 percent. The population of Northwest Territories increased 11 percent and that of Nunavut by 10.2 percent. During the same period, Newfoundland and Labrador's population went down by 1.5 percent and Saskatchewan's decreased by 1.1 percent.[38] Recent research has shown that inter-provincial moves and income are correlated. People who moved from one province to another tended to increase their earnings, especially if they moved away from a "have not" province. The effects were especially strong for men and younger people.[39]

Population movement also occurs as people migrate from rural to urban areas and then to suburban areas. This movement has been going on for more than half a century. According to the 2006 census, 80 percent of Canadians live in urban areas. Cities like Montreal, Toronto, and Vancouver are characterized by a faster pace of living, higher incomes, and a greater variety of goods, services, and cultural offerings than can be found in Canada's small towns and rural areas.

Some people are countering the trend toward urbanization and are moving out to the "country" or to small towns, away from apartment living and the hectic pace found in many cities. Kelowna, British Columbia, and its subdivision, Central Okanagan, is Canada's second-fastest-growing town. It has been the destination of choice for West Coasters fleeing Victoria and Vancouver. Such relocation makes a difference in goods and service preferences. Businesses with potential to cash in on the rural rebound might be those that cater to the growing SOHO (small office/home office) segment. See how FedEx Kinko's is doing just that:

FedEx Kinko's

Founded in the 1970s as a campus photocopying business, Kinko's is now reinventing itself as the well-appointed office outside the home. Where once there were copying machines, the nearly 1 900 Kinko's stores in Canada, the United States, and nine other countries now feature a mix of fax machines, ultra-fast colour printers, and networks of computers equipped with popular software and high-speed Internet connections. Kinko's, with annual revenues in excess of $2 billion, offers an unprecedented array of office services. People can come to a Kinko's store to do all their office jobs: copy, send and receive faxes, use various programs on the computer, go on the Internet, order stationery and other printed supplies, and even teleconference. And as more people work at home, Kinko's offers an escape from the isolation of the home office. Kinko's acquisition by FedEx in early 2004 resulted in further integration with the overnight delivery pioneer.[40]

To learn how Canadian Tire has overcome an increasingly changing macroenvironment to become a major retailing success in Canada, visit www.pearsoned.ca/marketingmanagementcanada.

OTHER MAJOR MACROENVIRONMENTS

Other macroenvironment forces profoundly affect the fortunes of marketers. Here we review developments in the economic, social-cultural, natural, technological, and political-legal environments.

Economic Environment

Markets require purchasing power as well as people. The available purchasing power in an economy depends on current income, prices, savings, debt, and credit availability. Marketers must pay careful attention to trends affecting purchasing power because they can have a strong impact on business, especially for companies whose products are geared to high-income and price-sensitive consumers.

INCOME DISTRIBUTION Nations vary greatly in level and distribution of income and industrial structure. There are four types of industrial structures: *subsistence economies* (few opportunities for marketers); *raw-material-exporting economies* like Zaire (copper) and Saudi Arabia (oil), with good markets for equipment, tools, supplies, and luxury goods for the rich; *industrializing economies*, like India, Egypt, and the Philippines, where a new rich class and a growing middle class demand new types of goods; and *industrial economies*, which are rich markets for all sorts of goods.

In a global economy, marketers need to pay attention to the shifting income-distribution in countries around the world, particularly countries where affluence levels are rising.

$2 500 Car

In early 2008, Tata Motors of India caught the attention of nearly every automaker when it announced its plans to release its $2 500 Nano car in India. Nicknamed the "People's Car," the affordability of the Nano made it seem like a natural fit for India. The company has kept costs down by including only the essentials, such as a dashboard that features little more than a speedometer, fuel gauge, and an oil light. The base model will be devoid of frills such as a radio, reclining seats, and power steering. The car will have a 650-cc engine that puts out a maximum of 70 horsepower but gives 20 to 25 kilometres per litre. Tata's real advantage may be in development costs. India has first-rate engineers but they are paid only about one-third of what Canadian or U.S. engineers earn. As well, factory workers in Mumbai, where the factory is located, earn just $1.20 per hour—less than wages even in China. Tata will also save with an innovative distribution strategy by which the company will supply kits to dealers who will do the final assembly. Tata will save approximately $900 per car by avoiding the restrictions it would face in the U.S., Europe, and Japan in the way of emission-control and safety standards.[41]

Marketers often distinguish countries with five different income-distribution patterns: (1) very low incomes; (2) mostly low incomes; (3) very low, very high incomes; (4) low, medium, high incomes; and (5) mostly medium incomes. Consider the market for Lamborghinis, an automobile costing more than US$150 000. The market would be very small in countries with type (1) or (2) income patterns. One of the largest single markets for Lamborghinis turns out to be Portugal (income pattern 3)—one of the poorer countries in Western Europe, but one with enough wealthy families to afford expensive cars.

Statistics Canada reports that the median income of full-year, full-time Canadian earners as of 2005 was $41 401. This represented little change from the corresponding figure of $40 443 in 2000. However, the same is not true for all income groups. Between 2000 and 2005, median earnings for the top one-fifth of families (in terms of wealth) increased 5.1 percent to $140 905. Median earnings for the bottom one-fifth of families declined 9.1 percent to $14 176 during the same time period. Earnings for this group have fallen steadily since 1980. In 2005, the top one-fifth of families were earning 9.9 times those of the bottom one-fifth. Therefore, for every $1 earned by the bottom 20 percent, the top 20 percent earned nearly $10.

Not surprisingly, the income of Canadian families is not consistent across provincial boundaries. The Northwest Territories has the highest median family income at $90 865. Furthermore, Ontario, Alberta, British Columbia, the Yukon, and the Northwest Territories are the only regions where the median family income is above the national median, whereas all other provinces and territories are below. Nunavut's median family income experienced the largest increase over the 2000s, growing over 19 percent to $62 592, while Ontario and British Columbia experienced the least income growth at 1.4 percent and 1.8 percent respectively ($72 734 and $65 787).[42]

Consider how Air Canada has segmented its market around income differences.

Air Canada

Montreal-based Air Canada, facing competition from discount airline WestJet, conducted marketing research to identify the different levels of price-sensitivity among consumers. Based on the segments its research discovered, Air Canada introduced à la carte pricing on its tickets. When consumers make a reservation, they can choose from four airfare levels: Tango, Tango Plus, Latitude, and Executive Class. Each level has a different combination of offerings such as frequent-flyer miles, reservation-change fees, and refund policies. For example, Tango has the least flexibility and offers the bare minimum for the traveller who is very price-sensitive whereas the Latitude fare offers much more in terms of "extras" for the less price-sensitive who are willing to pay more to get more. By having a different marketing mix for each market segment, Air Canada has reduced the risk of losing its price-conscious consumers to WestJet.

However, the spread of wealth may not be as useful to marketers as it once was. While it seems to be perfectly logical to segment markets along income boundaries, marketers are increasingly finding that income simply does not tell the whole story. More specifically, in Canada (and the broader North American market) the middle class is becoming increasingly rich in its tastes and, as a result,

AIR CANADA
Ticket Purchase
Achat de billets

Air Canada has been warding off threats from discount airlines with flexible pricing.

its purchases. According to experts, Canadians are increasingly seeking more expensive products, thus causing a major redefinition of the luxury customer. Consumers want to feel rich regardless of whether or not their income actually supports the notion. Retailers like Holt Renfrew are finding that their customer base is growing. The Liquor Control Board of Ontario is finding that it is selling increasing volumes of higher-priced wines. The trend even applies to some of the biggest-ticket items such as cars. Sales of luxury vehicles such as Jaguars, BMWs, and Mercedes-Benzes have grown substantially over the last several years.[43]

SAVINGS, DEBT, AND CREDIT AVAILABILITY   Consumer expenditures are affected by savings, debt, and credit availability. Over the past ten years in Canada, savings rates have been declining. In addition, with consistently lower interest rates over the 1990s and a more relaxed attitude toward consumer debt, the amount of household indebtedness is on the rise. This is consistent with the increasing availability of credit in Canada. The number of credit cards in circulation was over 55 million in 2005. Almost half of these credit cards have outstanding balances, and the size of those balances has increased in aggregate almost 16 percent since 1993. Even though that debt is on the rise and saving is down, overall household net worth in Canada has continued to increase. This means that while Canadians are saving less and spending more, their total assets still outpace their liabilities. This suggests that as long as net worth grows faster than liabilities, an increasing level of household debt is sustainable, providing the ability of households to service this debt remains stable.[44]

OUTSOURCING AND FREE TRADE   An economic issue of increasing importance is the migration of manufacturers and service jobs off-shore. Outsourcing is seen as a competitive necessity by many firms, but as a cause of unemployment by many domestic workers. For example, in December 2003, IBM decided to move the jobs of nearly 5 000 programmers to India and China. GE has moved much of its research and development overseas. Microsoft, Dell, American Express, and virtually every major multinational from Accenture to Yahoo! have already offshored work or are considering doing so.

The savings are dramatic, with companies cutting 20–70 percent of their labour costs, assuming the work is of comparable quality. However, beyond the short-term gain for employers and pain for displaced domestic white-collar employees is the scarier long-term prospect. The exodus of programming work, in particular, throws the future of North America's tech dominance into doubt. Many wonder whether the West can continue to lead the industry as computer programming spreads around the globe to countries such as India, China, and Brazil. In Hyderabad, India, for example, there are high-speed Internet access, a world-class university, and a venture capital industry—all the ingredients you need to spawn the next earthshaking technology innovation.[45]

Outside the labour market, advocates for and against free trade debate the merits of protective tariffs. Likewise, there is increasing awareness of unfair trade practices and consumers around the world are beginning to boycott products that are unfairly traded. The example below illustrates one such product.

Blood Diamonds

There has been growing global concern about the source of a significant proportion of the world's diamonds. Africa accounts for about 65 percent of the world's diamond production by value. In the 1990s, an estimated 15 percent of all diamonds on the market were "blood diamonds." Blood diamonds (also known as conflict diamonds) are mined in slave-like conditions in countries such as Sierra Leone and Angola, where workers are beaten and made to work long, hard hours. The revenues from these diamonds are allegedly used to fund rebel wars throughout Africa. Thanks to a certification system called the Kimberley Process begun in 2003, diamond-producing countries are now required to certify that their diamond revenues are not used to fund rebel armies. Partially due to these regulations, it is now estimated that 99 percent of the world's diamonds are conflict-free.[46]

Social-Cultural Environment

Purchasing power is directed toward certain goods and services and away from others according to people's tastes and preferences. Society shapes the beliefs, values, and norms that largely define these tastes and preferences. People absorb, almost unconsciously, a worldview that defines their relationships to themselves, to others, to organizations, to society, to nature, and to the universe.

To learn about challenges in conducting market research in China, visit www.pearsoned-asia.com/marketingmanagementchina.

- *Views of themselves.* People vary in the relative emphasis they place on self-gratification. During the 1960s and 1970s, "pleasure seekers" sought fun, change, and escape. Others sought "self-realization." People bought dream cars and dream vacations and spent more time in health activities (jogging, tennis), in introspection, and in arts and crafts. Today, some people are adopting more conservative behaviours and ambitions. Marketers must recognize that there are many different groups with different views of themselves.

- *Views of others.* People are concerned about the homeless, crime and victims, and other social problems. They would like to live in a more humane society. At the same time, people are seeking out their "own kind" and avoiding strangers. They hunger for serious and long-lasting relationships with a few others. These trends portend a growing market for social-support products and services that promote direct relations between human beings, such as health clubs, cruises, and religious activity. They also suggest a growing market for "social surrogates," things that allow people who are alone to feel that they are not, such as television, home video games, and chat rooms on the Internet.

- *Views of organizations.* People vary in their attitudes toward corporations, government agencies, trade unions, and other organizations. Most people are willing to work for these organizations, but there has been an overall decline in organizational loyalty. The massive wave of company downsizings and corporate-accounting scandals such as those at Nortel, Enron, WorldCom, and Tyco has bred cynicism and distrust.[47] Many people today see work not as a source of satisfaction, but as a chore required to earn money needed to enjoy their nonwork hours. This outlook has several marketing implications. Companies need to find new ways to win back consumer and employee confidence. They need to make sure that they are good corporate citizens and that their consumer messages are honest.

- *Views of society.* People vary in their attitudes toward their society. Some defend it (preservers), some run it (makers), some take what they can from it (takers), some want to change it (changers), some are looking for something deeper (seekers), and some want to leave it (escapers).[48] Consumption patterns often reflect social attitude. Makers tend to be high achievers who eat, dress, and live well. Changers usually live more frugally, drive smaller cars, and wear simpler clothes. Escapers and seekers are a major market for movies, music, surfing, and camping.

- *Views of nature.* People vary in their attitudes toward nature. Some feel subjugated by it, others feel in harmony with it, and still others seek mastery over it. A long-term trend has been humankind's growing mastery of nature through technology. More recently, however, people have awakened to nature's fragility and finite resources. They recognize that nature can be destroyed by human activities. Business has responded to increased interest in camping, hiking, boating, and fishing with hiking boots, tenting equipment, and other gear. Tour operators are packaging tours to wilderness areas and to places like Antarctica.

- *Views of the universe.* People vary in their beliefs about the origin of the universe and their place in it. Most North Americans are monotheistic, although religious conviction and practice have been waning through the years. Certain evangelical movements are reaching out to bring people back into organized religion. Some of the religious impulse has been redirected into an interest in Eastern religions, mysticism, the occult, and the human-potential movement.

As people lose their religious orientation, they seek self-fulfillment and immediate gratification. At the same time, every trend seems to breed a countertrend, as indicated by a worldwide rise in religious fundamentalism. Here are some other cultural characteristics of interest to marketers: the persistence of core cultural values, the existence of subcultures, and shifts of values through time.

HIGH PERSISTENCE OF CORE CULTURAL VALUES The people living in a particular society hold many *core beliefs* and have values that tend to persist. Core beliefs and values are passed on from parents to children and are reinforced by major social institutions: schools, churches, businesses, and governments. *Secondary beliefs* and values are more open to change. While marketers have little influence over core values, their efforts may result in the change of some secondary beliefs. For instance, the nonprofit organization Mothers Against Drunk Drivers (MADD) does not try to stop the sale of alcohol, but it does promote the idea of appointing a designated driver who will not drink that evening. It has undertaken some interesting partnerships to help further its responsible drinking agenda.

MADD Canada and Allstate

Allstate is the official sponsor of MADD Canada and the title sponsor of MADD Canada's Project Red Ribbon campaign. Each year, from the beginning of November to the first Monday in January, MADD Canada volunteers distribute red ribbons across the country and ask Canadians to display the ribbons on their cars, key chains, purses, backpacks, or other personal items. By doing so, they are making a personal commitment to driving sober. The red ribbon is a sign of respect for the thousands of Canadians who have lost their lives or been injured as a result of impaired driving. The red ribbon also reinforces the message to drive sober during the holiday season and throughout the year. MADD Canada hopes that the red ribbon will act as a reminder for people to call 911 if they suspect someone is driving impaired. Over 4 million such red ribbons were distributed throughout Canada during the 2007 campaign.[49]

Research has shown that Canadians and Americans, especially those who live along the border between the two countries, hold many values in common. Both believe in freedom, equality, and striving for happiness, mature love, self-respect, and true friendship. Canadian researcher and author Michael Adams notes, however, that Canadians operate with a set of social values fundamentally different than those of Americans, and marketers need to be sensitive to these differences:

For example, Americans are much more outer-directed, risk-taking, and yet are more concerned with maintaining social order and tradition. In contrast, Canadians are more inner-directed, more security-seeking, and yet are more socially liberal and tolerant of individual diversity. Americans celebrate those who have lived the American Dream—working hard, taking chances, and striking it rich—so visual markers of success such as expensive cars, homes, and vacations become important indicators of one's status in the social hierarchy. Canadians, on the other hand, believe in greater interdependence, achieving equitable balances, and the "fair" distribution of wealth.[50]

Canadians are also less trusting of business and are more skeptical of advertising. Canadians, therefore, seek to do business with companies perceived as being more ethical. Adams believes that this difference in social values results in more understated consumption. As Canadians, we focus less on what products and brands say about us and more on what the products do for us. In fact, Canadians are more likely to agree that a car is just an appliance for getting from A to B than that a car makes a statement about their personal style and image (57 percent versus 39 percent). Canadians, therefore, prefer smaller, more affordable, and more practical cars. It was for this reason that BMW chose to subtly change its slogan "The Ultimate Driving Machine" to "The Ultimate Driving Experience" for Canada.[51]

EXISTENCE OF SUBCULTURES   Each society contains **subcultures**, groups with shared values emerging from their special life experiences or circumstances. Members of subcultures share common beliefs, preferences, and behaviours. To the extent that subcultural groups exhibit different wants and consumption behaviour, marketers can choose particular subcultures as target markets.

Marketers sometimes reap unexpected rewards in targeting subcultures. Marketers have always loved teenagers because they are society's trendsetters in fashion, music, entertainment, ideas, and attitudes. Marketers also know that if they attract someone as a teen, there is a good chance they will keep the person as a customer later in life. Frito-Lay, which draws 15 percent of its sales from teens, said it saw a rise in chip-snacking by grown-ups. "We think it's because we brought them in as teenagers," said Frito-Lay's marketing director.[52]

SHIFTS OF SECONDARY CULTURAL VALUES THROUGH TIME   Although core values are fairly persistent, cultural swings do take place. In the 1960s, hippies, the Beatles, Elvis Presley, and other cultural phenomena had a major impact on young people's hairstyles, clothing, sexual norms, and life goals. Today's young people are influenced by new heroes and new activities: U2's Bono, golf's Tiger Woods, and extreme sports.

Natural Environment

The deterioration of the natural environment is a major global concern. In many world cities, air and water pollution have reached dangerous levels. There is great concern about greenhouse gases in the atmosphere due to the burning of fossil fuels, about the depletion of the ozone layer due to certain chemicals, and about growing shortages of water. In Western Europe, "green" parties have vigorously pressed for public action to reduce industrial pollution. In North America, experts have documented ecological deterioration, and watchdog groups such as the Sierra Club and Friends of the Earth carry these concerns into political and social action.

New regulations have hit certain industries very hard. Steel companies and public utilities have had to invest billions of dollars in pollution-control equipment and more environmentally friendly fuels. The auto industry has had to introduce expensive emission controls in cars. The soap industry has had to increase its products' biodegradability. The major hope is that companies will adopt practices that will protect the natural environment. Great opportunities await companies and marketers who can create new solutions that promise to reconcile prosperity with environmental protection.

Consumers often appear conflicted about the natural environment. One research study showed that although 80 percent of consumers stated that whether or not a product is safe for the environment influenced their decision to buy that product, only a little over half asserted that they bought recycled or environmentally safe products.[53] Young people especially were more likely to feel that nothing they did personally made a difference. Increasing the number of green products that are bought requires breaking consumers' loyalty habits, overcoming consumer skepticism about the motives behind the introduction of green products and their quality level, and changing consumer attitudes about the role they play in environmental protection. (See "Marketing Insight: Eco-Friendly Marketing.")

Marketers need to be aware of the threats and opportunities associated with four trends in the natural environment: the shortage of raw materials, especially water; the increased cost of energy; anti-pollution pressures; and the changing role of governments.

SHORTAGE OF RAW MATERIALS The earth's raw materials consist of the infinite, the finite renewable, and the finite nonrenewable. *Infinite resources*, such as air and water, are becoming a problem. Water shortages are already a political issue, and the danger is no longer long-term. *Finite renewable resources*, such as forests and food, must be used wisely. Forestry companies are required to reforest timberlands in order to protect the soil and to ensure sufficient wood to meet future demand. Because the amount of arable land is fixed and urban areas are constantly encroaching on farmland, food supply can also be a major problem. *Finite nonrenewable resources*—oil, coal, platinum, zinc, silver—will pose a serious problem as the point of depletion approaches. Firms making products that require these increasingly scarce minerals face substantial cost increases. Firms engaged in research and development have an excellent opportunity to develop substitute materials.

INCREASED ENERGY COSTS One finite nonrenewable resource, oil, has created serious problems for the world economy. Over the past few years, oil prices have shot up dramatically, surpassing US$140 per barrel in 2008,[54] reinforcing the need for alternative energy forms. Companies are searching for practical means to harness solar, nuclear, wind, and other forms of energy. In the solar-energy field alone, hundreds of firms introduced first-generation products to harness solar energy for heating homes and other uses. Other firms are engaged in building practical electric automobiles, with a potential prize of billions for the winner. Meanwhile, several automakers have come out with hybrid vehicles, such as the Toyota Prius, Toyota Camry Hybrid, Lexus Hybrid, Honda Civic Hybrid, Nissan Altima Hybrid, Ford Escape, and Chevy Malibu Hybrid, to name a few.

ANTI-POLLUTION PRESSURES Some industrial activity will inevitably damage the natural environment. Consider the dangerous mercury levels in the ocean, the quantity of DDT and other chemical pollutants in the soil and food supply, and the littering of the environment with bottles, plastics, and other packaging materials. Environment Canada is responsible for ensuring that Canadians, and Canadian companies in particular, comply with the Canadian Environmental Protection Act (CEPA) and "contribute to sustainable development through pollution prevention and to protect the environment, human life and health from the risks associated with toxic substances."[55] A survey conducted in 24 different countries found that Canadians are second on the list in terms of their concern about the environment. New Zealand tops the ranking. In fact, Canadians said protecting the environment was more important than promoting economic growth. Some companies are responding in a positive way to such concerns.[56]

MARKETING INSIGHT | ECO-FRIENDLY MARKETING

Nowadays, terms such as "climate change," "global warming," and "greenhouse-gas emissions" have become common lingo for most people around the world. In line with the growing number of issues concerning the environment is the growing ecological awareness of consumers. A recent survey of 20 countries by Synovate and BBC showed that over two-thirds (68 percent) of the world's population is concerned about climate change. In correlation with this, another survey found that 70 percent of Canadians are said to be buying more environmentally friendly products than they did even one year ago, with 77 percent agreeing that most companies do not pay enough attention to their own environmental responsibilities. However, recent changes in government regulation on greenhouse-gas emissions and environmental pressures from consumers have led companies to realize that they must put more emphasis on corporate and environmental responsibilities in order to turn a profit.

The necessity to adopt eco-friendly marketing has become so critical in today's marketplace that a number of companies are spending millions of dollars adopting eco-friendly practices. For instance, the world's largest company, Wal-Mart, known for its low-cost strategy, adopted a new sustainability strategy that would introduce a wide variety of environmentally friendly products, eliminate its own production of waste, and become 100% powered by renewable energy. In 2007, the company invested $5 million in sustainable store design and is on track to become the largest purchaser of green power in Canada.

In 2004, The Home Depot introduced into Canada a line of eco-friendly products under the Eco Options brand; it recently extended the line into the United States. In order to qualify for the label and accompanying benefits such as prominent shelf space and in-store signage, suppliers must qualify under at least one eco-friendly initiative such as energy efficiency, clean air, sustainable forestry, or water conservation.

There are drawbacks to expanding operations into this segment, and the grass isn't always greener on the other side. Many consumers are very suspicious and cynical about companies when they talk about the changes they have made that will lessen impact on the environment. An Ipsos Reid survey showed that 72 percent of consumers are at least somewhat skeptical about companies' claims of being environmentally conscious. This may stem from the vagueness of determining to what degree a company is indeed environmentally conscious and at what point it has done enough. It may also stem from the perception of an ulterior motive for the company whose primary goal is usually to maximize profits.

The automobile industry is one that has been under heavy pressure to become more environmentally friendly, as it is often targeted as the biggest contributor to global warming. General Motors has been exploring fuel alternatives such as ethanol, electricity, and diesel fuel. Although ethanol appears to be the "greenest" choice, the company faces several internal and external challenges such as inefficient methods of production and paucity of stations that sell ethanol. In attempts to further production of its ethanol-consuming automobiles, GM recently announced a partnership with Coskata, a company that makes ethanol from renewable sources including garbage, old tires, and plant waste, rather than from corn.

The road to successfully becoming and being viewed as an eco-friendly company may be an uphill one, but with consumers as environmentally conscious as they are today, it is expected that those who make the journey will reap the benefits.

Sources: Rebecca Harris, "Turning Green," *Marketing Magazine*, June 11, 2007, www.marketingmag.ca/magazine/current/feature/article.jsp?content=20070611_69764_69764 (viewed February 22, 2008); Paul Ferriss, "Green Means Go," *Marketing Magazine*, February 11, 2008, www.marketingmag.ca/magazine/current/feature/article.jsp?content=20080211_71056_71056 (viewed February 22, 2008); Michael Barbaro, "Wal-Mart Sets Agenda of Change," *The New York Times*, January 24, 2008, p. C3.

CHANGING ROLE OF GOVERNMENTS Governments vary in their concern and efforts to promote a clean environment. For example, the German government is vigorous in its pursuit of environmental quality, partly because of the strong green movement in Germany and partly because of the ecological devastation in former East Germany. Many poor nations are doing little about pollution, largely because they lack the funds or the political will. It is in the richer nations' interest to help the poorer nations control their pollution, but even the richer nations today lack the necessary funds.

Technological Environment

One of the most dramatic forces shaping people's lives is technology. Technology has released such wonders as penicillin, open-heart surgery, and the birth-control pill. It has released such horrors as the hydrogen bomb, nerve gas, and the submachine gun. It has also released such mixed blessings as the automobile and video games.

Every new technology is a force for "creative destruction." Transistors hurt the vacuum-tube industry, xerography hurt the carbon-paper business, autos hurt the railroads, and television hurt the newspapers. Instead of moving into the new technologies, many old industries fought or ignored them and their businesses declined. Yet, it is the essence of market capitalism to be dynamic and tolerate the creative destructiveness of technology as the price of progress.

Look out Dell, HP, and Microsoft: According to some seers, "smart" mobile phones will eventually eclipse the PC. Apple's iPhone may have already done so.

iPhone

The future has arrived for the cellular phone with the introduction of the Apple iPhone. When the iPhone hit U.S. retail stores in June 2007, it had so much demand that even many celebrities had difficulty getting one. The device is so powerful that some members of the media have dubbed it a "god machine." The iPhone has a touch screen that allows users to easily navigate through its various features, some of which include iPod music and video capabilities, PDA functions, BlackBerry-like email, full Internet access, and, of course, a cell phone with a Wi-Fi connection and Bluetooth. Apple CEO Steve Jobs claims that this product is far more revolutionary than a smartphone. The iPhone contains the OS X operating system, the same one used by Apple computers. In other words, the iPhone works like a portable computer. Because of high demand and problems finding a suitable cellular provider, the iPhone's Canadian release has been delayed for some time. Although the iPhone is just one brand of advanced phone, its launch speaks volumes about the future of the cellular telephone industry. Currently, there are over 3 billion cellular phones in the world; many of these have the processing power of a mid-1990s personal computer. The cellular revolution has occurred in only a few short years, and when the price of the futuristic phones comes down, most mobile phone users will own one such as the iPhone.[57]

The economy's growth rate is affected by how many major new technologies are discovered. Unfortunately, technological discoveries do not arise evenly through time—the railroad industry created a lot of investment, and then investment petered out until the auto industry emerged. Later, radio created a lot of investment, which then petered out until television appeared. In the time between major innovations, an economy can stagnate. In the meantime, minor innovations fill the gap: freeze-dried coffee, combination shampoo and conditioner, antiperspirants and deodorants, and the like. They involve less risk, but they also divert research effort away from major breakthroughs.

A recent Statistics Canada study revealed that more than 70 percent of successful new companies are high-tech in that they innovate, use advanced technologies, employ skilled workers, or emphasize training. They operate in all sectors of the economy, including publishing and farm services, not just in those industries usually thought of as high-tech, such as biotechnology and information technology. For example, the dairy-farming industry has adopted very high-tech processes. Technology is what helps the one or two farmers manage dozens or hundreds of highly productive dairy cattle. From computer-generated algorithms for designing feeding programs, to laboratory testing for determining the digestibility of feed ingredients, to computer chips and databases that track milk production, technology is used in all aspects of milk production.[58]

New technology also creates major long-run consequences that are not always foreseeable. The contraceptive pill, for example, led to smaller families, more working wives, and larger discretionary incomes—resulting in higher expenditures on vacation travel, durable goods, and luxury items.

The marketer should monitor the following trends in technology: the pace of change, the opportunities for innovation, varying R&D budgets, and increased regulation.

ACCELERATING PACE OF CHANGE Many of today's common products were not available 40 years ago. When your parents were your age, they did not have personal computers, MP3 players, DVD players, digital cameras, personal digital assistants, or the Internet; nor has the pace of technological change slowed down. The Human Genome project promises to usher in the Biological Century as biotech workers create new medical cures, new foods, and new materials. Electronic researchers are building smarter chips to make our cars, homes, and offices more responsive to changing conditions. The blending of personal computers, scanners, fax and copying machines, wireless phones, the Internet, and email has made it possible for people to *telecommute*—that is, work at home or on the road instead of travelling to an office. This trend may reduce auto pollution, bring the family closer together, and create more home-centred shopping and entertainment.

| MARKETING INSIGHT | THE CHANGING FACE OF THE MARKETPLACE DUE TO TECHNOLOGY |

Most people agree that they have never in their lifetime seen technology change as rapidly as it does nowadays. Although technology has always been an important aspect of the economy, over the past few decades it has considerably changed the marketplace and also the way we live our lives. Nowadays, it is rare for working professionals not to rely on email and cell phones for their business communication. Besides the obvious technological changes such as the Internet, there are several trends that are not as visible.

- **Adoption rates are much higher**. It has taken the Internet only 10 years and CD players only 12 years to be adopted by 50% of Canadian households. Compare that to the over 70 years it took for telephones and over 50 years for electricity.
- **New industries and new products**. The rapid growth in technology has led to new industries, such as biotechnology and e-commerce, and to new products, such as hybrid cars and laser eye-surgery.
- **Greater range in quality and prices.** Technological developments in design and manufacturing have brought down production times and costs. Increased online price comparison by consumers has forced marketers to lower their prices to stay competitive.
- **Rapid product obsolescence leading to technological stress.** Product life cycles are shrinking at an increasing rate, resulting in consumers finding themselves unable to keep up with the changes in technology and experiencing "upgrade fatigue."
- **Challenge to consumer protection.** Shortened technological cycles place great demands on the time available for consumer-protection regulators to ensure that human health and the environment are not compromised.
- **Environmental impact of electronic waste.** An estimated 140 000 tonnes of electronic waste in the form of computer equipment, phones, TVs, stereos, and small home appliances find their way to Canadian landfills each year. There is growing concern regarding toxic chemicals such as lead, cadmium, and mercury seeping into the earth from these items.

Source: Industry Canada "1.5: Key Macro-Economic Trends," *The Consumer Trends Report* Chapter 1, September 20, 2007, www.ic.gc.ca/epic/site/oca-bc.nsf/en/ca02093e.html#a15 (accessed March 10, 2008).

An increasing number of ideas are being worked on, and the time between the appearance of new ideas and their successful implementation is all but disappearing. So is the time between introduction and peak production. "Marketing Insight: The Changing Face of the Marketplace Due to Technology" discusses the impact of technology on consumers.

UNLIMITED OPPORTUNITIES FOR INNOVATION Scientists today are working on a startling range of new technologies that will revolutionize products and production processes. Some of the most exciting work is being done in biotechnology, computers, microelectronics, telecommunications, robotics, and designer materials. Researchers are working on AIDS cures, happiness pills, painkillers, totally safe contraceptives, and nonfattening foods. They are designing robots for fire-fighting, underwater exploration, and home nursing. In addition, scientists work on fantasy products, such as small flying cars, three-dimensional television, and space colonies. The challenge in each case is to develop affordable versions of these products. See how Banff is being innovative with its public transit system:

Banff Public Transit

The Town of Banff is planning to spend about $80 000 on transit fare-boxes for its new hybrid buses in a bid to increase the number of residents and visitors using public transit. Town officials say the new system has the technology to allow the municipality to track ridership, by way of coins or a special card, to help monitor the success of its new transit system. As well, they are in talks with various hotels to draw up financial contracts that would allow hotel guests to swipe their room cards when hopping on the bus. The new system will not issue change, but instead print out a voucher that can be taken to the town hall for correct change. Banff is also spending $95 000 to pilot a computer-based real-time passenger information service to provide bus riders with accurate bus-schedule information. The system operates with global positioning system (GPS) technology and advanced computer modelling. A GPS unit would be fitted to each of the transit buses, allowing the position of buses to be known in an instant via wireless communication. Knowing the stops, typical transit routes, bus speeds, and the location of buses, the computer software can accurately predict the length of time the bus will take to reach its next stop. Under the system, there would be LED displays at key transit stops indicating the expected time of bus arrival. These technologies are intended to increase bus ridership and encourage foreign tourists, who often do not have exact change, to take the bus.[59]

Companies are already harnessing the power of *virtual reality (VR)*, the combination of technologies that allows users to experience three-dimensional, computer-generated environments through sound, sight, and touch. Virtual reality has already been applied to gather consumer reactions to new automobile designs, kitchen layouts, exterior home designs, and other potential offerings.

VARYING R&D BUDGETS In 2002, Canada spent 1.8 percent of its gross domestic product (GDP) on R&D. Both business and government expenditures contribute to this effort. Canada, however, trails a number of other countries within the 30-member Organisation for Economic Co-operation and Development (OECD). For example, Sweden spends 4.2 percent of its domestic product on R&D, Japan spends just over 3 percent, and the United States spends 2.8 percent.[60] Because of the size of its GDP, the United States leads the world in annual R&D expenditures. The top five companies in terms of R&D expenditures in Canada are Nortel Networks, Magna International, Pratt & Whitney Canada, JDS Uniphase, and IBM Canada.[61]

INCREASED REGULATION OF TECHNOLOGICAL CHANGE As products become more complex, the public needs to be assured of their safety. Consequently, government agencies' powers to investigate and ban potentially unsafe products have been expanded. Canada has a complex web of legislation. Consider, for example, some of the legislation focused on food safety. Agriculture and Agri-Food Canada is responsible for the safety of food products, but Health Canada also has a food- and product-safety division. Health Canada also administers the nutrition labelling regulations for food products. To complicate matters further, the Department of Justice regulates the Food and Drug Act and the Hazardous Products Act. The Canadian Standards Association (www.csa.ca), a not-for-profit organization, also works with business, government,

Increased legislation, combined with consumer preference for eco-friendly alternatives, is resulting in more "green" products on the market.

and consumers to develop standards to enhance public safety and health. You will find its seal on products that have passed its safety tests and meet its rigorous standards. Marketers must be aware of these regulations when proposing, developing, and launching new products.

Political-Legal Environment

Marketing decisions are strongly affected by developments in the political and legal environment. This environment is composed of laws, government agencies, and pressure groups that influence and limit various organizations and individuals. Sometimes these laws also create new opportunities for business. For example, mandatory recycling laws have given the recycling industry a major boost and spurred the creation of dozens of new companies that make new products from recycled materials. Two major trends deal with the increase in business legislation and the growth of special-interest groups.

INCREASE IN BUSINESS LEGISLATION Business legislation has three main purposes: to protect companies from unfair competition, to protect consumers from unfair business practices, and to protect the interests of society from unbridled business behaviour. A major purpose of business legislation and enforcement is to charge businesses with the social costs created by their products or production processes. A central concern is this: At what point do the costs of regulation exceed the benefits? The laws are not always administered fairly; regulators and enforcers may be lax or overzealous. Although each new law may have a legitimate rationale, it may have the unintended effect of sapping initiative and retarding economic growth.

Legislation affecting business has increased steadily over the years. As noted earlier, Canada has a complex web of regulatory agencies. In addition to the federal departments already noted with regard to food safety, the Department of Transport governs road and vehicle safety, Environment Canada focuses on pollution prevention, and the Competition Act covers such diverse topics as mergers (Section 33), pricing (Sections 34 and 38), advertising (Section 37), and country-of-origin claims (Sections 52 and 74). Canadian business is also subject to provincial regulations and may come up against rulings by Canada's marketing boards. Regulations established in the North American Free Trade Agreement (NAFTA) also have to be respected. It is no wonder that most Canadian firms have large legal departments to help marketers stay within the law!

The European Commission has been active in establishing a new framework of laws covering competitive behaviour, product standards, product liability, and commercial transactions for the 25 member nations of the European Union. The United States has many laws on its books covering such issues as competition, product safety and liability, fair trade and credit practices, and packaging

More and more consumers are checking nutrition labels on the food products they purchase.

and labelling.[62] Several countries have gone further than the United States and Canada in passing strong consumer-protection legislation. Norway bans several forms of sales promotion—trading stamps, contests, premiums—as inappropriate or "unfair" instruments for promoting products. Thailand requires food processors selling national brands to market low-price brands also, so that low-income consumers can find economy brands. In India, food companies need special approval to launch brands that duplicate what already exists on the market, such as another cola drink or brand of rice.

Marketers must have a good working knowledge of the major laws protecting competition, consumers, and society. Companies generally establish legal-review procedures and promulgate ethical standards to guide their marketing managers, and as more business takes place in cyberspace, marketers must establish new parameters for doing electronic business ethically.

GROWTH OF SPECIAL-INTEREST GROUPS   The number and power of special-interest groups have increased over the past three decades. Political action committees (PACs) lobby government officials and pressure business executives to pay more attention to consumers' rights, women's rights, senior citizens' rights, minority rights, and gay rights.

Many companies have established public-affairs departments to deal with these groups and issues. An important force affecting business is the **consumerist movement:** an organized movement of citizens and government to strengthen the rights and powers of buyers in relation to sellers. Consumerists have advocated and won the right to know the true interest cost of a loan, the true cost per standard unit of competing brands (unit pricing), the basic ingredients in a product, the nutritional quality of food, the freshness of products, and the true benefits of a product.

With consumers increasingly willing to swap personal information for customized products from firms—as long as they can be trusted—privacy issues will continue to be a public-policy hot button.[63] Consumer concerns are that they will be robbed or cheated, that private information will be used against them, that someone will steal their identity, that they will be bombarded with solicitations, and that children will be targeted.[64] Several companies have established consumer-affairs departments to help formulate policies and respond to consumer complaints. Companies are careful to answer their email and to resolve and learn from any customer complaints.

Clearly, new laws and growing numbers of pressure groups have put more restraints on marketers. Marketers have to clear their plans with the company's legal, public-relations, public-affairs, and consumer-affairs departments. Insurance companies directly or indirectly affect the design of smoke detectors; scientific groups affect the design of spray products by condemning aerosols. In essence, many private marketing transactions have moved into the public domain.

SUMMARY

1. To carry out their analysis, planning, implementation, and control responsibilities, marketing managers need a marketing information system (MIS). The role of the MIS is to assess managers' information needs, develop the needed information, and distribute that information in a timely manner.

2. An MIS has three components: (a) an internal-records system, which includes information on the order-to-payment cycle and sales-reporting systems; (b) a marketing intelligence system, a set of procedures and sources used by managers to obtain everyday information about pertinent developments in the marketing environment; and (c) a marketing-research system that allows for the systematic design, collection, analysis, and reporting of data and findings relevant to a specific marketing situation.

3. Many opportunities are found by identifying trends (directions or sequences of events that have some momentum and durability) and megatrends (major

social, economic, political, and technological changes that have long-lasting influence).

4. Within the rapidly changing global picture, marketers must monitor six major environmental forces: demographic, economic, social-cultural, natural, technological, and political-legal.

5. In the demographic environment, marketers must be aware of worldwide population growth; changing mixes of age, ethnic composition, and educational levels; the rise of nontraditional families; large geographic shifts in population; and the move to micromarketing and away from mass marketing.

6. In the economic arena, marketers need to focus on income distribution and levels of savings, debt, and credit availability.

7. In the social-cultural arena, marketers must understand people's views of themselves, others, organizations,

society, nature, and the universe. They must market products that correspond to society's core and secondary values, and address the needs of different subcultures within a society.

8. In the natural environment, marketers need to be aware of raw-materials shortages, increased energy costs and pollution levels, and the changing role of governments in environmental protection.

9. In the technological arena, marketers should take account of the accelerating pace of technological change, opportunities for innovation, varying R&D budgets, and the increased governmental regulation brought about by technological change.

10. In the political-legal environment, marketers must work within the many laws regulating business practices and with various special-interest groups.

APPLICATIONS

Marketing Debate: Is Consumer Behaviour More a Function of a Person's Age or Generation?

One of the widely debated issues in developing marketing programs that target certain age groups is how much consumers change over time. Some marketers maintain that age differences are critical and that the needs and wants of a 25-year-old in 2005 are not that different from those of a 25-year-old in 1975. Others dispute that contention and argue that peer influence and generation effects are critical and that marketing programs must therefore suit the times.

Take a position: Age differences are fundamentally more important than peer-influence effects *versus* Peer-influence effects can dominate age differences.

Marketing Discussion

What brands and products do you feel successfully "speak to you" and effectively target your age group? Why? Which ones do not? What could they do better?

Breakthrough Marketing: Wal-Mart

Wal-Mart was founded by Sam Walton, with the first store opening in 1962 under the name Wal-Mart Discount City. Incorporated as Wal-Mart Stores, Inc. in 1969, today Wal-Mart is the world's largest public corporation with nearly US$375 billion in revenues; it employs more people worldwide than any other private employer. It has operations in the U.S., Canada, Mexico, the United Kingdom, Japan, Argentina, Brazil, and China, just to name a few. It is well known that Wal-Mart's phenomenal growth is due to its ability to offer to customers prices lower than its competitors', but what allows the company to achieve these low prices?

Wal-Mart's competitive advantage is its lower costs, particularly in inventory. The company has invested millions into inventory management in order to minimize the inventory it carries while effectively keeping shelves stocked and catering to seasonal trends. In addition, Wal-Mart has emphasized the minimization of supplier prices. Price negotiation with Wal-Mart is a strenuous process and finalized only when Wal-Mart representatives are confident that the product cannot be purchased at a lower price anywhere else. In order to do this, significant

time is put forward to meet vendors and understand their cost structure to ensure they are doing their best to cut down costs. Once a deal is complete, Wal-Mart believes in establishing long-term relationships with vendors and generally prefers local and regional vendors and suppliers.

Negotiation with vendors is only the tip of the iceberg when it comes to Wal-Mart's inventory management. In order to effectively track sales and merchandise inventories in its stores, Wal-Mart set up its own satellite communication system in 1983. This enabled senior management to walk into a room and instantly see what was happening in its many stores. They could also immediately see if there were any areas of concern that needed to be addressed.

Furthermore, the company is able to reduce unproductive inventory by allowing individual stores to manage their own stocks, rather than cutting inventories across the board. This provides greater responsiveness to the different customer needs and trends that may take place from store to store or city to city and reduces the overall inventory levels that each store has to maintain. To ensure timeliness of delivery, Wal-Mart has collaborated with major suppliers, such as Procter & Gamble, to build automated reordering systems. These systems allow Wal-Mart's computer systems to identify low product-inventory levels and send a signal to the supplier for restocking. These systems benefit both Wal-Mart and its vendors by enabling increased sales and cost savings due to better coordination and more efficient inventory management.

But how exactly does this system work? Wal-Mart's point-of-sale (POS) system monitors and tracks the merchandise sales and stock levels of the store shelves. Wal-Mart also uses a sophisticated system to determine the exact quantity of each item to be delivered to stores based on the current inventory in each store. Similarly, a centralized inventory-data system allows personnel at any store to find out the level of inventory and the location of each product at their own location or any other Wal-Mart store.

Bar-coding and radio-frequency technology have also been used to manage inventories. These technologies have been integral to directing goods to appropriate docks, efficient picking, receiving and proper inventory control, and made packing and physical counting of inventories considerably easier. The radio frequency identification (RFID) technology that

Wal-Mart has aggressively adopted allows for product information such as product type, manufacturer, and serial number to be transmitted to a scanner or data-collection system to ensure proper distribution takes place. This technology is also key in the point-of-sale system, where the bar codes or RFIDs tell scanners which items consumers are purchasing. These sales data are compared to quantities in stock, allowing management to keep track of sales trends and inventory levels, and even identify slow-moving products.

If joint systems are not in place, like the one previously mentioned with P&G, the computer software often makes recommendations or provides warnings to management when additional inventories are needed. These warnings, rather than automatic ordering systems, allow human decision making, which may be required to better evaluate the marketplace for factors that cannot be adequately addressed by a computer.

Much of the success that Wal-Mart has experienced can be attributed to the competitive advantage it has established by having such effective and efficient distribution systems and inventory management. Wal-Mart's diverse product offerings, which include perishable goods, has made the timeliness of shipments that much more important. Duplication of such a system will be difficult in the future, and due to the economies of scale and pressure that Wal-Mart can put on distributors, it can be expected that the retail giant's success will continue into the future.

DISCUSSION QUESTIONS

1. Identify and discuss how technological developments have helped Wal-Mart in its inventory management.

2. If technology and inventory management are largely responsible for Wal-Mart's lower costs, why aren't competitors able to duplicate Wal-Mart's lower cost structure? Discuss the challenges competitors must be facing.

3. Research RFID technology on the Internet. Analyze the pros and cons of using it in a retail environment.

4. Wal-Mart tries to carry minimum inventory. Examine the implications of this on its suppliers—particularly on their cost structure.

Sources: "Corporate Facts: Wal-Mart By the Numbers," www.walmartstores.com/media/factsheets/fs_2230.pdf (viewed March 29, 2008); "The Rise of Wal-Mart," *Frontline*, www.pbs.org/wgbh/pages/frontline/shows/walmart/transform/cron.html (viewed March 29, 2008); Tim Crosby, "How Inventory Management Systems Work," communication.howstuffworks.com/how-inventory-management-systems-work.htm/printable (viewed March 3, 2008); Mohan Chandran, "Wal-Mart's Supply Chain Management Practices," icmr.icfai.org/pdf/Operations%20Case%20Study%20-%20Wal-Marts%20Supply%20Chain%20Management%20Pr.pdf (viewed March 3, 2008); Jonathan Birchall, "Wal-Mart Profits Jump on Inventory Clean-up," *Financial Times*, May 17, 2006, p. 15.; Kris Hudson and Ann Zimmerman, "Wal-Mart Aims to Sharply Cut Its Inventory Costs," *Wall Street Journal*, April 20, 2006, p. B2.

IN THIS CHAPTER,
WE WILL ADDRESS
THE FOLLOWING
QUESTIONS:

- What constitutes good marketing research?

- What are good metrics for measuring marketing productivity?

- How can marketers assess the return on investment of their marketing expenditures?

- How can companies more accurately measure and forecast demand?

CONDUCTING MARKETING RESEARCH AND FORECASTING DEMAND

four

What are your expectations when you rent a room for a weekend stay at a three-star hotel? Would you expect to have a balcony with a nice view? Would you be disappointed if there were no in-room minibar? Do you expect fine linen and a pleasing décor, or would functional aspects like a desk and ironing board be more important to you? These are the questions that the Canada Select Accommodations Rating Council sought to understand about Canadian travellers in a marketing research study.

The council felt that consumer expectations may have changed in recent years, suggesting there may be a need to update the criteria that it currently uses to rate hotels, resorts, cottages, inns, and bed-and-breakfasts. The council commissioned a nationwide study aimed at finding out what factors are important to consumers in choosing these accommodations.

The results of the study confirmed that consumer expectations have indeed changed over the past decade. Expectations have risen, and what satisfied consumers a decade ago no longer meets the demands of the average Canadian traveller today. The study found that the average Canadian expects a three-star hotel to have, at the very minimum, a private bathroom with toiletries and a hair dryer, a mini-fridge, coffee machine, and bigger and better beds, among other things. Not surprisingly, there are new demands that customers have today that did not even exist a decade ago, such as the demand for a fitness centre, spa, and in-room Internet access. The council is using the results of the study to update the criteria it uses to evaluate hotels and other accommodations under its jurisdiction.

The Hilton Garden Inn, part of the Hilton Hotels chain, is a winner of several customer-service awards. How does the Hilton Garden Inn keep its customers satisfied? Each year, the hotel conducts an "Ask the Traveller" survey to learn what facilities and services hotel guests expect. For example, the survey showed that 22 percent of guests preferred being woken up by a personal wake-up call rather than an alarm clock or automated wake-up call. Similarly, the survey found that 54 percent of guests expected bottled water in the room whereas only 15 percent expected coffee. Using the results of the survey, Hilton Garden Inn tweaks its services so that its guests are kept satisfied.

In the previous chapters, we discussed the importance of marketers' keeping up with consumer needs and wants and satisfying them effectively. Research studies such as those conducted by Canada

>>>

Select Accommodations Rating Council and Hilton Garden Inn are examples of marketing research studies businesses conduct for that purpose. Without the information from marketing research, businesses would have little to base their judgments and decisions on, which could lead to catastrophic failures. Although using marketing research when making a marketing decision does not guarantee success, it greatly increases its chances.

Sources: Economic Growth Solutions Inc. and Corporate Research Association Inc., "Canada Select Accommodation Rating Program: 2003 Consumer Research Study—Final Report," May 2004; "Survey Reveals 22 Percent of Business Travelers Want to Be Tucked in by Carmen Electra and No Wake-Up Call at All," *Business Wire*, September 28, 2004, p.1.

In this chapter, we review the steps involved in the marketing-research process. We also consider how marketers can develop effective metrics for measuring marketing productivity. Finally, we outline how marketers can develop good sales forecasts.

THE MARKETING RESEARCH SYSTEM

Marketing managers often commission formal marketing studies of specific problems and opportunities. They may request a market survey, a product-preference test, a sales forecast by region, or an advertising evaluation. It is the job of the marketing researcher to produce insight into customers' attitudes and buying behaviour. We define **marketing research** as the systematic design, collection, analysis, and reporting of data and findings relevant to a specific marketing situation facing the company. Marketing research is now about a US$16.5-billion industry globally, according to ESOMAR, the World Association of Opinion and Market Research Professionals.

A company can obtain marketing research in a number of ways. Most large companies, such as Procter & Gamble (P&G) have their own marketing-research departments, which often play crucial roles within the organization.[1]

Procter & Gamble

P&G's large market-research function is called Consumer & Market Knowledge (CMK). Its goal is to bring consumer insight to decision making at all levels. Dedicated CMK groups work for P&G businesses around the world, including Global Business Units (GBUs), which focus on long-term brand equity and initiative development, and Market Development Organizations (MDOs), which focus on local-market expertise and retail partnerships. There is also a relatively smaller, centralized corporate CMK group, which focuses on three kinds of work: (1) proprietary research-methods development, (2) expert application of, and cross-business learning from, core research competencies, and (3) shared services and infrastructure. CMK leverages traditional research basics such as brand tracking. CMK also finds, invents, or co-develops leading-edge research approaches such as experiential consumer contacts, proprietary modelling methods, and scenario-planning or knowledge-synthesis events. CMK professionals connect market insights from all these sources to shape company strategies and decisions. They influence day-to-day operational choices, such as which product formulations are launched, as well as long-term plans, such as which corporate acquisitions best round out the product portfolio.

Yet, marketing research is not limited to large companies with big budgets and marketing-research departments. At much smaller companies, marketing research is often carried out by everyone in the company—and by customers too, as demonstrated by Karmaloop.

Karmaloop.com

Karmaloop bills itself as an online urban boutique, and it has built its reputation as a top shop for fashionistas because of its relentless tracking of trendsetters. The Boston company, founded in 1999, has made streetwear fashion a science by keeping tabs on young tastemakers' buying habits. In addition to its crew of moonlighting artists, DJs, and designers, Karmaloop recruits street-team members in their 20s to ferret out new trends and to spread the word about Karmaloop brands. The street team, which now boasts over 10 000 reps, passes out fliers and stickers at nightclubs, concerts, and on the street, and also reports on what trends they see at events. Fewer than 1 percent of Karmaloop's customers are reps, but their purchases and those they create account for 15 percent of sales. Karmaloop has an interesting marketing team: its customers. It gets new clothing design ideas not from formal marketing research, but from ideas submitted directly by its customers.[2]

Companies normally budget marketing research at 1 to 2 percent of company sales. A large percentage of that is spent on the services of outside firms. Marketing-research firms fall into three categories:

1. *Syndicated-service research firms.* These firms gather consumer and trade information, which they sell for a fee. Examples: Nielsen Media Research, Forrester, Market Facts, SAMI/Burke.

2. *Custom marketing-research firms.* These firms are hired to carry out specific projects. They design the study and report the findings.

3. *Specialty-line marketing-research firms.* These firms provide specialized research services. The best example is the field-service firm, which sells field-interviewing services to other firms.

Small companies can hire the services of a marketing-research firm or conduct research in creative and affordable ways, such as:

1. *Engaging students or professors to design and carry out projects.* One Boston University MBA project helped American Express develop a successful advertising campaign geared toward young professionals. The cost: US$15 000.

2. *Using the Internet.* A company can collect considerable information at very little cost by examining competitors' websites, monitoring chat rooms, and accessing published data.

3. *Checking out rivals.* Many small companies routinely visit their competitors. Tom Coohill, a chef who owns two Atlanta restaurants, gives managers a food allowance to dine out and bring back ideas. Atlanta jeweller Frank Maier Jr., who often visits out-of-town rivals, spotted and copied a dramatic way of lighting displays.[3]

Most companies, such as Fuji Photo Film, use a combination of marketing-research resources to study their industries, competitors, audiences, and channel strategies.

Fuji Photo Film

At the highest level, Fuji relies on data from market-research syndicate NDP Group to study the market for products ranging from digital cameras to ink-jet photo paper. Fuji also does custom research with a variety of research partners and it conducts internal research for projects requiring quick information, such as changes to package design. Regardless of how the marketing-research data are collected, it is a top priority for Fuji, which has had to adapt its film and digital-imaging products to a rapidly changing marketplace. "If you don't have market research to help you figure out what is changing and what the future will be, you will be left behind," says Fuji's director of category management and trade marketing.[4]

THE MARKETING RESEARCH PROCESS

Effective marketing research involves the six steps shown in Figure 4.1. We will illustrate these steps with the following situation:

Air Canada is constantly looking for new ways to serve its passengers; it was one of the first companies to install phone handsets. Now it is reviewing many new ideas, especially to cater to its first-class passengers on very long flights, many of whom are businesspeople whose high-priced tickets pay most of the freight. Among these ideas are: (1) to supply an Internet connection with limited access to webpages and email; (2) to offer 24 channels of satellite TV; and (3) to offer a 50-CD audio system that lets each passenger create a customized playlist of music and movies to enjoy during the flight. The marketing-research

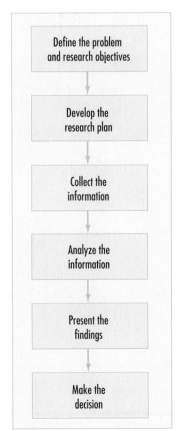

FIGURE 4.1

The Marketing-Research Process

Define the problem and research objectives

Develop the research plan

Collect the information

Analyze the information

Present the findings

Make the decision

manager was assigned to investigate how first-class passengers would rate these services and how much extra they would be willing to pay if a charge were made. He was asked to focus specifically on the Internet connection. One estimate says that airlines might realize revenues of $70 billion over the next decade from in-flight Internet access if enough first-class passengers would be willing to pay $25 for it. Air Canada could thus recover its costs in a reasonable time. Making the connection available would cost the airline $90 000 per plane.[5]

Step 1: Define the Problem, the Decision Alternatives, and the Research Objectives

Marketing management must be careful not to define the problem too broadly or too narrowly for the marketing researcher. A marketing manager who instructs the marketing researcher to "Find out everything you can about first-class air-travellers' needs" will collect a lot of unnecessary information. One who says "Find out if enough passengers aboard a B747 flying direct between Vancouver and Tokyo would be willing to pay $25 for an Internet connection so that Air Canada would break even in one year on the cost of offering this service" is taking too narrow a view of the problem. The marketing researcher might even raise this question: "Why does the Internet connection have to be priced at $25 as opposed to $10, $50, or some other price? Why does Air Canada have to break even on the cost of the service, especially if it attracts new users?"

In discussing the problem, Air Canada's managers discover another issue. If the new service were successful, how fast could other airlines copy it? Airline marketing research is replete with examples of new services that have been so quickly copied by competitors that no airline has gained a sustainable competitive advantage. How important is it to be first, and how long could the lead be sustained?

The marketing manager and marketing researcher agreed to define the problem as follows: "Will offering an in-flight Internet service create enough incremental preference and profit for Air Canada to justify its cost against other possible investments it might make?" To help in designing the research, management should first spell out the decisions it might face and then work backwards. Suppose management spells out these decisions: (1) Should Air Canada offer an Internet connection? (2) If so, should the service be offered to first-class only, or include business class, and possibly economy class? (3) What price(s) should be charged? (4) On what types of planes and lengths of trips should it be offered?

Now management and marketing researchers are ready to set specific research objectives: (1) What types of first-class passengers would respond most to using an in-flight Internet service? (2) How many first-class passengers are likely to use the Internet service at different price levels? (3) How many extra first-class passengers might choose Air Canada because of this new service? (4) How much long-term goodwill will this service add to the company's image? (5) How important is Internet service to first-class passengers relative to providing other services such as a power plug or enhanced entertainment?

Not all research projects can be this specific. Some research is exploratory: its goal is to shed light on the real nature of the problem and to suggest possible solutions or new ideas. Some research is descriptive: it seeks to ascertain certain magnitudes, such as how many first-class passengers would purchase in-flight Internet service at $25. Some research is causal: its purpose is to test a cause-and-effect relationship.

Step 2: Develop the Research Plan

The second stage of marketing research calls for developing the most efficient plan for gathering the needed information. The marketing manager needs to know the cost of the research plan before approving it. Suppose the company made a prior estimate that launching the in-flight Internet service would yield a long-term profit of $50 000. The manager believes that doing the research would lead to an improved pricing and promotional plan and a long-term profit of $90 000. In this case, the manager should be willing to spend up to $40 000 on this research. If the research would cost more than $40 000, it is not worth doing.[6] Designing a research plan calls for decisions on the data sources, research approaches, research instruments, sampling plan, and contact methods.

DATA SOURCES The researcher can gather secondary data, primary data, or both. *Secondary data* are data that were collected for another purpose and already exist somewhere. *Primary data* are data freshly gathered for a specific purpose or for a specific research project.

A focus group in session, with marketing people observing through a one-way mirror.

Researchers usually start their investigation by examining some of the rich variety of secondary data to see whether the problem can be partly or wholly solved without collecting costly primary data. Secondary data provide a starting point and offer the advantages of low cost and ready availability. When the needed data do not exist or are dated, inaccurate, incomplete, or unreliable, the researcher will have to collect primary data. Most marketing-research projects involve some primary-data collection. The normal procedure is to interview some people individually or in groups, to get a sense of how people feel about the topic in question, and then develop a formal research instrument, debug it, and carry it into the field.

RESEARCH APPROACHES   Primary data can be collected in five main ways: through observation, focus groups, surveys, behavioural data, and experiments.

Observational Research   Fresh data can be gathered by observing the relevant actors and settings.[7] Consumers can be unobtrusively observed as they shop or as they consume products. Ogilvy & Mather's Discovery Group creates documentary-style videos by sending researchers into consumers' homes with handheld video cameras. Hours of footage are edited to a 30-minute "highlight reel," which the group uses to analyze consumer behaviour. Other researchers equip consumers with pagers and instruct them to write down what they are doing whenever prompted, or hold more informal interview sessions at a café or bar. The Air Canada researchers might meander around first-class lounges to hear how travellers talk about the different carriers and their features. They can fly on competitors' planes to observe in-flight service.

Focus Group Research   A **focus group** is a gathering of six to ten people who are carefully selected based on certain demographic, psychographic, or other considerations and brought together to discuss at length various topics of interest. Participants are normally paid a small sum for attending. A professional research moderator provides questions and probes based on a discussion guide or agenda prepared by the responsible marketing managers to ensure that the right material gets covered.

Burger King

Burger King has recently developed a new product, called Apple Fries, aimed at children. Apple Fries are red apples peeled and cut julienne-style to look like french fries and served in containers similar to those for fries. This new product is part of Burger King's move toward offering healthy meal options for children and was one of about 20 products Burger King tested in focus groups as part of a product-excellence program. The focus group revealed that freshly cut apples was the product that appealed most to children and mothers alike. Burger King hopes that although Apple Fries are targeted at kids, they will be popular with adults, too.[8]

Focus groups led to the product idea for Burger King's new Apple Fries.

Moderators attempt to track down potentially useful insights as they try to discern the real motivations of consumers and why they are saying and doing certain things. The sessions are typically recorded in some fashion, and marketing managers often remain behind one-way mirrors in the next room. In the Air Canada research, the moderator might start with a broad question, such as "How do you feel about first-class air travel?" Questions then move to how people view the different airlines, different existing services, different proposed services, and specifically, Internet service. Although focus-group research has been shown to be a useful exploratory step, researchers must avoid generalizing the reported feelings of the focus-group participants to the whole market because the sample size is too small and the sample is not drawn randomly. "Marketing Insight: Conducting Informative Focus Groups" has some practical tips to improve the quality of focus groups.

Survey Research Companies undertake surveys to learn about people's knowledge, beliefs, preferences, and satisfaction, and to measure their magnitudes in the general population. A company such as Air Canada might prepare its own survey instrument to gather the information it needs, or it might add questions at a much lower cost to an omnibus survey that carries the questions of several companies. It can also put the questions to an ongoing consumer panel run by itself or another company. It may do a mall-intercept study by having researchers approach people in a shopping mall and ask questions. An increasing proportion of surveys are nowadays conducted on the Internet, as the following Home Depot example shows.

Home Depot

In an effort to improve its customer service, Home Depot has created a website devoted to collecting feedback from its customers. Upon entering the website, customers are invited to enter to win a Home Depot gift card simply by expressing their opinions about Home Depot and their recent experiences at the store. Following a purchase, the store receipt invites customers to participate in a survey and provides the website address where it can be found. The survey asks questions about different aspects of the interaction and questions that focus on how the customer feels about his or her relationship with Home Depot.[9]

Behavioural Data Customers leave traces of their purchasing behaviour in store-scanning data, catalogue purchases, and customer databases. Much can be learned by analyzing these data. Customers' actual purchases reflect preferences and often are more reliable than statements they offer to market researchers. People may report preferences for popular brands, and yet the data might show them actually buying other brands. For example, grocery-shopping data show that high-income people do not necessarily buy the more expensive brands, contrary to what they might state in interviews; and many low-income people buy some expensive brands. Clearly, Air Canada can learn many useful things about its passengers by analyzing ticket purchase records.

Experimental Research The most scientifically valid research is experimental research. The purpose of experimental research is to capture cause-and-effect relationships by eliminating competing explanations of the observed findings. To the extent that the design and execution of the experiment eliminate alternative hypotheses that might explain the results, research and marketing managers can have confidence in the conclusions.

Experiments call for selecting matched groups of subjects, subjecting them to different treatments, controlling extraneous variables, and checking whether observed response-differences are statistically significant. To the extent that extraneous factors are eliminated or controlled, the observed effects can be related to the variations in the treatments. Air Canada might introduce in-flight Internet service on one of its regular flights from Vancouver to Tokyo. It might charge $25 one week and charge only $15 the next week. If the plane carried approximately the same number of first-class passengers each week and the particular weeks made no difference, any significant difference in the number of passengers buying the service could be related to the different prices charged. The experimental design could be elaborated by trying other prices and including other air routes.

RESEARCH INSTRUMENTS Marketing researchers have a choice of three main research instruments in collecting primary data: questionnaires, qualitative measures, and mechanical devices.

| MARKETING INSIGHT | CONDUCTING INFORMATIVE FOCUS GROUPS |

Focus groups allow marketers to observe how and why consumers accept or reject concepts, ideas, or any specific notion. The key to using focus groups successfully is to *listen*. It is critical to eliminate biases as much as possible. Although many useful insights can emerge from thoughtfully run focus groups, there can be questions as to their validity, especially in today's marketing environment.

Some researchers believe that consumers have been so bombarded with ads, they unconsciously (or perhaps cynically) parrot back what they have already heard as compared to what they think. There is also always a concern that participants are just trying to maintain their self-image and public persona or have a need to identify with the other members of the group. Participants may not be willing to admit in public—or may not even recognize—their behaviour patterns and motivations. There is also always the "loudmouth" problem: one highly opinionated person drowns out the rest of the group. It may be expensive to recruit qualified subjects ($3 000 to $5 000 per group), but getting the right participants is crucial.

Even when multiple groups are involved, it may be difficult to generalize the results to a broader population. For example, focus-group findings often vary from region to region. One U.S. firm specializing in focus-group research claimed that the best city to conduct focus groups in was Minneapolis because it could get a fairly well-educated sample of people who were honest and forthcoming about their opinions. Many marketers interpret focus groups carefully in New York and other northeastern U.S. cities because the people in these areas tend to be highly critical and generally do not report that they like much. Too often, managers become comfortable with a particular focus-group format and apply it generally and automatically to every circumstance. Europeans typically need more time than North American marketers typically are willing to give—a focus group there rarely takes less than two hours and often more than four.[10]

Participants must feel as relaxed as possible and feel a strong obligation to "speak the truth." Physical surroundings can be crucial. Researchers at one agency knew they had a problem when a fight broke out between participants at one of their sessions. As one executive noted, "we wondered why people always seemed grumpy and negative—people were resistant to any idea we showed them." The problem was the room itself: cramped, stifling, forbidding: "It was a cross between a hospital room and a police interrogation room." To fix the problem, the agency gave the room a makeover. Other firms are adapting the look of the room to fit the theme of the topic—like designing the room to look like a playroom when speaking to children.

Although many firms are substituting observational research for focus groups, ethnographic research can be expensive and tricky: researchers have to be highly skilled, participants have to be on the level, and mounds of data have to be analyzed. The beauty of focus groups, as one marketing executive noted, is that "it's still the most cost-effective, quickest, dirtiest way to get information in rapid time on an idea." In analyzing the pros and cons, Wharton's Americus Reed might have said it best: "A focus group is like a chain saw. If you know what you're doing, it's very useful and effective. If you don't, you could lose a limb."

Sources: Sarah Stiansen, "How Focus Groups Can Go Astray," *Adweek*, December 5, 1988, pp. FK 4–6; Jeffrey Kasner, "Fistfights and Feng Shui," *Boston Globe*, July 21, 2001, pp. C1–C2; Leslie Kaufman, "Enough Talk," *Newsweek*, August 18, 1997, pp. 48–49; Linda Tischler, "Every Move You Make," *Fast Company*, April 2004, pp. 73–75; Alison Stein Wellner, "The New Science of Focus Groups," *American Demographics*, March 2003, pp. 29–33; Dennis Rook, "Out-of-Focus Groups," *Marketing Research*, Summer 2003, *15* (2), p. 11.

Questionnaires A questionnaire consists of a set of questions presented to respondents. Because of its flexibility, the questionnaire is by far the most common instrument used to collect primary data. Questionnaires need to be carefully developed, tested, and debugged before they are administered on a large scale. In preparing a questionnaire, the researcher carefully chooses the questions and their form, wording, and sequence. The form of the question can influence the response. Marketing researchers distinguish between closed-end and open-end questions. Closed-end questions specify all the possible answers and provide answers that are easier to interpret and tabulate. Open-end questions allow respondents to answer in their own words and often reveal more about how people think. Such questions are especially useful in exploratory research, where the researcher is looking for insight into how people think rather than a measure of the number of people that think a certain way. Table 4.1 provides examples of both types of questions. Also refer to "Marketing Memo: Questionnaire Dos and Don'ts."

TABLE 4.1 | TYPES OF QUESTIONS

Name	Description	Example
A. Closed-end Questions		
Dichotomous	A question with two possible answers.	In arranging this trip, did you personally phone Air Canada? Yes No
Multiple choice	A question with three or more answers.	With whom are you travelling on this flight? ☐ No one ☐ Children only ☐ Spouse ☐ Business associates/friends/relatives ☐ Spouse and children ☐ An organized tour group
Likert scale	A statement with which the respondent shows the amount of agreement/disagreement.	Small airlines generally give better service than large ones. Strongly disagree 1___ Disagree 2___ Neither agree nor disagree 3___ Agree 4___ Strongly agree 5___
Semantic differential	A scale connecting two bipolar words. The respondent selects the point that represents his or her opinion.	Air Canada Large --------------------Small Experienced --------------------Inexperienced Modern --------------------Old-fashioned
Importance scale	A scale that rates the importance of some attribute.	Airline food service to me is Extremely important 1___ Very important 2___ Somewhat important 3___ Not very important 4___ Not at all important 5___
Rating scale	A scale that rates some attribute from "poor" to "excellent."	Air Canada food service is Excellent 1___ Very Good 2___ Good 3___ Fair 4___ Poor 5___
Intention-to-buy scale	A scale that describes the respondent's intention to buy.	If an in-flight telephone were available on a long flight, I would Definitely buy 1___ Probably buy 2___ Not sure 3___ Probably not buy 4___ Definitely not buy 5___
B. Open-end Questions		
Completely unstructured	A question that respondents can answer in an almost unlimited number of ways.	What is your opinion of Air Canada?
Word association	Words are presented, one at a time, and respondents mention the first word that comes to mind.	What is the first word that comes to your mind when you hear the following? Airline _____ Air Canada _____ Travel _____
Sentence completion	An incomplete sentence is presented and respondents complete the sentence.	When I choose an airline, the most important consideration in my decision is _____.
Story completion	An incomplete story is presented, and respondents are asked to complete it.	"I flew Air Canada a few days ago. I noticed that the exterior and interior of the plane had very bright colours. This aroused in me the following thoughts and feelings. . . ." Now complete the story.
Picture	A picture of two characters is presented, with one making a statement. Respondents are asked to identify with the other and fill in the empty balloon.	WELL HERE'S THE FOOD.
Thematic Apperception Test (TAT)	A picture is presented and respondents are asked to make up a story about what they think is happening or may happen in the picture.	

MARKETING **MEMO** | QUESTIONNAIRE DOS AND DON'TS

---

1. *Consider respondent's ability and willingness to answer.* Most respondents would be unable to answer the question "How many litres of gas do you buy for your car each year?" and would be unwilling to answer the question "Do you have a communicable disease?"

2. *Ensure that questions are without bias.* The question "Do you agree that health care should be privatized?" is biased and leads the respondent into a positive answer.

3. *Avoid double-barreled questions.* Questions that include multiple ideas or two questions in one will confuse respondents.

4. *Steer clear of sophisticated and uncommon words, trade jargon, and acronyms.* Use only words found in common speech.

5. *Avoid ambiguous words.* Words such as "usually" and "frequently" have no specific meaning.

6. *Avoid questions with a negative in them.* It is better to say "Do you ever... ?" than "Do you never... ?"

7. *Avoid hypothetical questions.* It is difficult to answer questions about imaginary situations and answers cannot necessarily be trusted.

8. *Don't impose alternatives unless required.* "Do you usually pay by cash or by credit card?" assumes that credit cards are the only alternatives to cash and ignores other possible forms of payment.

9. *Don't assume the respondent is necessarily aware.* "To what extent do you think the recession in the U.S. will impact businesses in Canada?" should be preceded by a question to check if the respondent is aware of a recession in the U.S.

10. *Do not use words that could be misheard.* This is especially important when the interview is administered over the telephone. "What is your opinion of sects?" could yield interesting but not necessarily relevant answers.

11. *Desensitize questions by using response intervals.* For questions that ask people their age or companies their turnover, it is best to offer a range of response intervals.

12. *Ensure that fixed responses do not overlap.* Categories used in fixed-response questions should be sequential and not overlap.

13. *Allow for "other" in multiple-choice questions.* Multiple-choice questions should always allow for a response other than those listed.

Source: Adapted from Paul Hague and Peter Jackson, *Market Research: A Guide to Planning, Methodology, and Evaluation* (London: Kogan Page, 1999) and from Carl McDaniel and Roger Gates, *Marketing Research Essentials* (NJ: Wiley, 2008). See also Hans Baumgartner, Jan Benedict, and E. M. Steenkamp, "Response Styles in Marketing Research: A Cross-National Investigation," *Journal of Marketing Research*, May 2001, pp. 143–156.

Qualitative Measures Some marketers prefer more qualitative methods for gauging consumer opinion because consumer actions do not always match their answers to survey questions. *Qualitative research techniques* are relatively unstructured measurement approaches that permit a range of possible responses. Qualitative research techniques are a creative means of ascertaining consumer perceptions that may otherwise be difficult to uncover. The range of possible qualitative research techniques is limited only by the creativity of the marketing researcher. Here are seven techniques employed by design firm IDEO for understanding the customer experience:[11]

- *Shadowing:* observing people using products, shopping, going to hospitals, taking the train, using their cell phones.
- *Behaviour mapping:* photographing people within a space, such as a hospital waiting room, over two or three days.
- *Consumer journey:* keeping track of all the interactions a consumer has with a product, service, or space.
- *Camera journals:* asking consumers to keep visual diaries of their activities and impressions relating to a product.
- *Extreme user interviews:* talking to people who really know—or know nothing—about a product or service and evaluating their experience using it.
- *Storytelling:* prompting people to tell personal stories about their consumer experiences.
- *Unfocus groups:* interviewing a diverse group of people. To explore ideas about sandals, IDEO gathered an artist, a bodybuilder, a podiatrist, and a shoe fetishist.

| MARKETING INSIGHT | GETTING INTO CONSUMERS' HEADS WITH QUALITATIVE RESEARCH |

Here are some qualitative-research approaches commonly used to get inside consumers' minds and find out what they are thinking or feeling about brands and products:

1. *Word associations.* People can be asked what words come to mind when they hear the brand's name. "What does the Timex name mean to you? Tell me what comes to mind when you think of Timex watches." The primary purpose of free-association tasks is to identify the range of possible brand associations in consumers' minds. But these tasks may also provide some rough indication of the relative strength, "favourability," and uniqueness of brand associations.

2. *Projective techniques.* People are presented an incomplete stimulus and asked to complete it, or they are given an ambiguous stimulus that may not make sense in and of itself and are asked to make sense of it. The argument is that people will reveal their true beliefs and feelings. One such approach is "bubble exercises" based on cartoons or photos. Different people are depicted buying or using certain products or services. Empty bubbles, like those found in cartoons, are placed in the scenes to represent the thoughts, words, or actions of one or more of the participants. People are then asked to "fill in the bubble" by indicating what they believe is happening or being said. Another technique is comparison tasks. People are asked to convey their impressions by comparing brands to people, countries, animals, activities, fabrics, occupations, cars, magazines, vegetables, nationalities, or even other brands.

3. *Visualization.* People can be asked to create a collage from magazine photos or drawings to depict their perceptions. ZMET is a research technique that starts with a group of participants who are asked in advance to select a minimum of 12 images from their own sources (e.g., magazines, catalogues, and family photo albums) that represent their thoughts and feelings about the research topic. The participants bring these images to a personal one-on-one interview with a study administrator, who uses advanced interview techniques to explore the images with the participant and reveal hidden meanings. Finally, the participants use a computer program to create with these images a collage that communicates their subconscious thoughts and feelings about the topic. One ZMET study probed what women thought of pantyhose. Twenty hose-wearing women were asked to collect pictures that captured their feelings about wearing pantyhose. Some of the pictures showed fence posts encased in plastic wrap or steel bands strangling trees, suggesting that pantyhose are tight and inconvenient. Another picture showed tall flowers in a vase, suggesting that the product made a woman feel thin, tall, and sexy.

4. *Brand personification.* People can be asked to describe what kind of person they think of when the brand is mentioned: "If the brand were to come alive as a person, what would it be like, what would it do, where would it live, what would it wear, who would it talk to if it went to a party (and what would it talk about)?" For example, they may say that the John Deere brand makes them think of a rugged small-town male who is hardworking and trustworthy. The brand personality delivers a picture of the more human qualities of the brand.

5. *Laddering.* A series of increasingly more specific "why" questions can be used to gain insight into consumer motivation and consumers' deeper, more abstract goals. Ask why someone wants to buy a Nokia cellular phone. "They look well built" (attribute). Why is it important that the phone be well built?" "It suggests that the Nokia is reliable" (a functional benefit). "Why is reliability important?" "Because my colleagues or family can be sure to reach me" (an emotional benefit). "Why must you be available to them at all times?" "I can help them if they are in trouble" (brand essence). The brand makes this person feel like a Good Samaritan, ready to help others.

Sources: Allen Adamson, "Why Traditional Brand Positioning Can't Last," *Brandweek*, November 17, 2003, pp. 38–40; Todd Wasserman, "Sharpening the Focus," *Brandweek*, November 3, 2003, pp. 28–32; Linda Tischler, "Every Move You Make," *Fast Company*, April 2004, pp. 73–75; Gerald Zaltman, *How Customers Think: Essential Insights Into the Mind of the Market* (Boston: Harvard Business School Press, 2003).

Because of the freedom afforded both researchers in their probes and consumers in their responses, qualitative research can often be a useful first step in exploring consumers' brand and product perceptions. There are also drawbacks to qualitative research. The in-depth insights that emerge have to be tempered by the fact that the samples involved are often very small and may not necessarily generalize to broader populations. Moreover, given the qualitative nature of the data, there may also be questions of interpretation. Different researchers examining the same results from a qualitative research study may draw very different conclusions. "Marketing Insight: Getting into Consumers' Heads with Qualitative Research" describes some popular approaches.

MARKETING INSIGHT | UNDERSTANDING BRAIN SCIENCE

As an alternative to traditional consumer research, some researchers have begun to develop sophisticated techniques from neuroscience that monitor brain activity to better gauge consumer responses to marketing stimuli.

For example, a group of researchers at UCLA used functional magnetic-resonance imaging (fMRI) to measure how consumers' brains responded to 2006 Super Bowl advertisements. The research demonstrated how consumers' stated preferences often contradict their inner thoughts and emotions. The fMRI showed that the "I'm going to Disney World" ad featuring members of both teams rehearsing the famous line elicited the highest levels of positive brain activity, followed by a Sierra Mist commercial starring an airport security screener and a traveller. Yet in a consumer poll conducted independently, a Bud Light ad rated highest, despite not generating significant positive reaction in the fMRI tests.

Although it can be more effective in uncovering inner emotions than conventional techniques, neurological research is costly, running as much as $100 000 per project. One major finding to emerge from neurological consumer research is that many purchase decisions are characterized less by the logical weighing of variables than was previously assumed and more "as a largely unconscious habitual process, as distinct from the rational, conscious, information-processing model of economists and traditional marketing textbooks." Even basic decisions, such as the purchase of gasoline, are influenced by brain activity at the subrational level.

Neurological research can be used to measure the type of emotional response that consumers exhibit when presented with marketing stimuli. A group of researchers in England used an electroencephalograph (EEG) to monitor cognitive functions related to memory recall and attentiveness of 12 different regions of the brain as subjects were exposed to advertising. Brain-wave activity in different regions indicated different emotional responses. For example, heightened activity in the left prefrontal cortex is characteristic of an "approach" response to an ad and indicates an attraction to the stimulus. In contrast, a spike in brain activity in the right prefrontal cortex is indicative of a strong repulsion from the stimulus. In yet another part of the brain, the degree of memory-formation activity correlates with purchase intent. Other research has shown that people activate different regions of the brain in assessing the personality traits of people versus brands.

The term *neuromarketing* has been used to describe brain research on the effect of marketing stimuli. By adding neurological techniques to their research arsenal, marketers are trying to move toward a more complete picture of what goes on inside consumers' heads. Given the complexity of the human brain, however, many researchers caution that neurological research should not form the sole basis for marketing decisions. And these research activities have not been universally applauded: critics think that such research will lead only to more marketing manipulation by companies.

Sources: Carolyn Yoon, Angela H. Gutchess, Fred Feinberg, and Thad A. Polk, "A Functional Magnetic Resonance Imaging Study of Neural Dissociations between Brand and Person Judgments," *Journal of Consumer Research*, 33 (June 2006): 31–40; Daryl Travis, "Tap Buyers' Emotions for Marketing Success," *Marketing News*, February 1, 2006, pp. 21–22; Deborah L. Vence, "Pick Someone's Brain," *Marketing News*, May 1, 2006, pp. 11–13; Louise Witt, "Inside Intent," *American Demographics* (March 2004): 34–39; Samuel M. McClure, Jian Li, Damon Tomlin, Kim S. Cypert, Latané M. Montague, and P. Read Montague, "Neural Correlates of Behavioral Preference for Culturally Familiar Drinks," *Neuron*, 44, October 14, 2004, pp. 379–87; Melanie Wells, "In Search of the Buy Button," *Forbes*, September 1, 2003.

Mechanical Devices Mechanical devices are occasionally used in marketing research. For example, galvanometers can measure the interest or emotions aroused by exposure to a specific ad or picture. The tachistoscope flashes an ad to a subject with an exposure interval that may range from less than one hundredth of a second to several seconds. After each exposure, the respondent describes everything he or she recalls. Eye cameras study respondents' eye movements to see where their eyes land first, how long they linger on a given item, and so on. As one would expect, in recent years technology has advanced to such a degree that now devices like skin sensors, brain-wave scanners, and full-body scanners are being used to get consumer responses.[12] "Marketing Insight: Understanding Brain Science" provides a glimpse into some new marketing-research frontiers.

Technology has replaced the diaries that participants in media surveys used to have to keep. Audiometers can be attached to television sets in participating homes to record when the set is on and to which channel it is tuned. Electronic devices can record the number of radio programs a person is exposed to during the day or, using global positioning system (GPS) technology, how many billboards a person may walk by or drive by during a day. Consider how ASI Entertainment uses a device to measure audience response to TV shows.

ASI Entertainment

Television networks use marketing research to test their TV-pilot ideas. ASI, a leading media-research company, has all the major broadcast and cable TV networks among its clients. In a small screening room outfitted with one-way mirrors and video cameras, 48 voluntary subjects take their seats and watch pilots on twin TV sets at the front of the room. At each seat the subjects use a handset to register their reaction, turning the dial from a neutral position to a minus, double minus, plus, or double plus. If they think a show is really poor, they can hit a red button to indicate they would turn it off at home. Networks such as CBS and Fox pay as much as $20 000 per two-hour session to find their shows' weak points. Testing isn't perfect, however. Three shows that would have hit the cutting-room floor if marketers had listened to test results include *All in the Family, Seinfeld,* and *Lost.*[13]

SAMPLING PLAN After deciding on the research approach and instruments, the marketing researcher must design a sampling plan. This calls for three decisions:

1. *Sampling unit: Who is to be surveyed?* The marketing researcher must define the target population that will be sampled. In the Air Canada survey, should the sampling unit be only first-class business travellers, first-class vacation travellers, or both? Should travellers under the age of 18 be interviewed? Should all adults in the family be interviewed? Once the sampling unit is determined, a sampling frame must be developed so that everyone in the target population has an equal or known chance of being sampled.

2. *Sample size: How many people should be surveyed?* Large samples give more reliable results than small samples. However, it is not necessary to sample the entire target population or even a substantial portion to achieve reliable results. With a credible sampling procedure, samples of less than 1 percent of a population can often provide good reliability.

3. *Sampling procedure: How should the respondents be chosen?* To obtain a representative sample, a probability sample of the population should be drawn. Probability sampling allows the calculation of confidence limits for sampling error. Thus, one could conclude after the sample is taken that "the interval 5 to 7 trips per year has 95 chances in 100 of containing the true number of trips taken annually by first-class passengers flying between Vancouver and Tokyo." Three types of probability sampling are described in Table 4.2, part A. When the cost or time involved in probability sampling is too high, marketing researchers will take nonprobability samples. Table 4.2, part B, describes three types. Some marketing researchers feel that nonprobability samples are very useful in many circumstances, even though they do not allow sampling error to be measured.

CONTACT METHODS Once the sampling plan has been determined, the marketing researcher must decide how the subject should be contacted: mail, telephone, personal, or online interview.

Mail Questionnaire The *mail questionnaire* is the best way to reach people who would not give personal interviews or whose responses might be biased or distorted by the interviewers. Mail

TABLE 4.2	PROBABILITY AND NONPROBABILITY SAMPLES
A. Probability Sample	
Simple random sample	Every member of the population has an equal chance of selection.
Stratified random sample	The population is divided into mutually exclusive groups (such as age groups), and random samples are drawn from each group.
Cluster (area) sample	The population is divided into mutually exclusive groups (such as city blocks), and the researcher draws a sample of the groups to interview.
B. Nonprobability Sample	
Convenience sample	The researcher selects the most accessible population members.
Judgment sample	The researcher selects population members who are good prospects for accurate information.
Quota sample	The researcher finds and interviews a prescribed number of people in each of several categories.

questionnaires require simple and clearly worded questions. Unfortunately, the response rate is usually low or slow.

Telephone Interview *Telephone interviewing* is the best method for gathering information quickly; the interviewer is also able to clarify questions if respondents do not understand them. The response rate is typically higher than in the case of mailed questionnaires. The main drawback is that the interviews have to be short and not too personal. Telephone interviewing is getting more difficult because of consumers' growing antipathy toward telemarketers calling them in their homes and interrupting their lives.

Personal Interview *Personal interviewing* is the most versatile method. The interviewer can ask more questions and record additional observations about the respondent, such as dress and body language. At the same time, personal interviewing is the most expensive method and requires more administrative planning and supervision than the other three. It is also subject to interviewer bias or distortion. Personal interviewing takes two forms. In *arranged interviews,* respondents are contacted for an appointment, and often a small payment or incentive is offered. *Intercept interviews* involve stopping people at a shopping mall or busy street corner and requesting an interview. Intercept interviews can have the drawback of being nonprobability samples, and the interviews must not require too much time.

Online Interview Today, 70 percent of Canadian households and 95 percent of businesses are online. Furthermore, over 30 percent of Canadian households and businesses have broadband access. Therefore, it is not surprising that there is increased use of online research methods.[14] Online research in Canada grew by 800 percent from 1999 to 2007. Furthermore, online research was estimated to make up one-third of all survey-based research spending.[15]

An intercept interview at a mall.

There are so many ways to use the Internet to do research, as illustrated by the Dell example. A company can include a questionnaire on its website and offer an incentive to answer the questionnaire; or it can place a banner on some frequently visited site such as Yahoo!, inviting people to answer some questions and possibly win a prize. The company can sponsor a chat room or bulletin board and introduce questions from time to time, or host a real-time panel or virtual focus group. A company can learn about individuals who visit its site by following how they *clickstream* through the website and move to other sites. A company can post different prices, use different headlines, or offer different product features on different websites or at different times to learn the relative effectiveness of its offerings.

Dell

In February 2007, Dell launched IdeaStorm (www.ideastorm.com). This website was designed to allow people to make suggestions on improving Dell's products and services. Getting customer feedback is nothing new. What makes IdeaStorm interesting is that the community gets to vote on the ideas posted on the website, and if it makes sense to Dell, it will make the appropriate changes. For example, the Linux operating system was a popular topic when IdeaStorm first came out. Dell surveyed 100 000 customers and determined there was sufficient demand to offer Linux with certain computer systems. IdeaStorm is just one of the ways that Dell is trying to get closer to its customers and obtain ideas both for new products and for improving its customer service.[16]

Online product testing, in which companies float trial balloons for new products, is also growing and providing information much faster than traditional marketing-research techniques that were used to develop new products. For instance, marketers for Mattel's Hot Wheels toys rely heavily on the Web to interact with collectors to help develop new products, promotions, and licensed goods. Following one fan survey, marketing executives learned that they could expand licensed offerings to boys aged 11 to 16 to keep them interested in the brand franchise, resulting in extended partnerships with Bell Motorcycles and BMX bikes.[17]

Not everyone is on the Web, however, and online market researchers must find creative ways to reach certain population segments, such as older Canadians, French Canadians, and the disabled. One option is to combine offline sources with the online findings, as Ipsos-Reid has done.

Ipsos-Reid

The Vancouver-headquartered Ipsos-Reid Corporation, which started out as the Angus Reid Group almost 30 years ago in Winnipeg, Manitoba, is now a global heavyweight with operations around the world. It conducts surveys in more than 80 countries. To become a leader in the marketing-research field, Ipsos-Reid needed reliable techniques and representative samples. One way it has achieved these in Canada is through its Canadian Online Panel, the largest of its kind in Canada, composed of over 110 000 households. This panel can be divided into a number of subpanels, such as teens on the Web, online purchasers, small-office/home-office owners, Canadians who suffer from specific medical conditions, and affluent Canadians. To capture information from Canadians who may not be connected to the Web, Ipsos-Reid also utilizes its Canadian Consumer Panel, composed of 80 000 pre-selected households and over 150 000 individuals, to help companies better understand Canadian consumers. This pre-selected panel is also the biggest of its kind in Canada, allowing companies to gain information that would have been too difficult or expensive to obtain in the past. Together these two panels allow Ipsos-Reid's clients to do everything from concept, product, and ad testing to segmentation and forecasting studies.[18]

To learn how Nokia applied market research to develop a mobile handset especially suited to India, visit www.pearsoned.co.in/marketingmanagementindia.

While marketers are right to be infatuated with the possibilities of online research, it is important to remember that the field is still in its infancy and is constantly evolving to meet the needs of companies, advertising agencies, and consumers. "Marketing Memo: Pros and Cons of Online Research" outlines some of the advantages and disadvantages of online research thus far.

Step 3: Collect the Information

The data-collection phase of marketing research is generally the most expensive and the most prone to error. In the case of surveys, four major problems arise. Some respondents will not be at home and must be contacted again or replaced. Other respondents will refuse to cooperate. Still others will give biased or dishonest answers. Finally, some interviewers will be biased or dishonest. Getting the right respondents is critical. Conducting telephone surveys has also been affected by Canada's implementation of a Do Not Call List.

Do Not Call List

The landscape for telephone surveys in Canada has changed with the implementation of the Do Not Call List (DNCL) in September 2008. In July 2007, the Canadian Radio-television and Telecommunications Commission (CRTC) set out rules for a national registry for Canadians who do not wish to be bothered by unsolicited telemarketing calls. Individuals who violate the registry face fines of $1500; for companies it is $15 000.[19] While the designated List Operator, Bell Canada, is responsible for the ongoing management of the registry, the CRTC is responsible for investigating complaints and assessing penalties. According to a survey conducted by the Marketing Research and Intelligence Association, ironically enough by telephone, 63 percent of respondents said they would sign up for the registry. The registry may actually help the marketing-research industry because it will drastically reduce the number of telemarketing calls, which in turn is expected to improve the quality and response rate of telephone surveys being conducted by marketing researchers.[20]

Thanks to computers and telecommunications, data-collection methods are rapidly improving. Some research firms interview from a centralized location. Professional interviewers sit in booths and draw telephone numbers at random. When the phone is answered, the interviewer reads a set of questions from a monitor and types the respondent's answers into a computer. This procedure eliminates editing and coding, reduces errors, saves time, and produces all the required statistics. Other research firms have set up interactive terminals in shopping centres. Persons willing to be interviewed sit at a terminal, read the questions from the monitor, and type in their answers.

Consider what one Canadian research firm, Tangency, is doing with technology to improve the effectiveness of online focus groups while cutting costs at the same time.

MARKETING MEMO | PROS AND CONS OF ONLINE RESEARCH

Advantages

- *Online research is inexpensive.* The cost of gathering survey information electronically is much less than by traditional means. A typical email survey costs about half what a conventional survey costs, and return rates can be as high as 50 percent.[21] For instance, Virgin.net used online research to launch its broadband service in the United Kingdom in 2002. Now the company does all its research online. The brand has seen an increase in response rates from 17 percent with paper-based research to almost 72 percent, and costs have dropped 90 percent.[22]

- *Online research is faster.* Online surveys are faster to complete since the survey can automatically direct respondents to applicable questions and be sent electronically to the research supplier once finished. One estimate is that 75 to 80 percent of a survey's targeted response can be generated in 48 hours using online methods, as compared to a telephone survey that can take 70 days to obtain 150 interviews.[23]

- *People tend to be more honest online than they are in personal or telephone interviews.* Britain's online polling company YouGov.com took 500 people and surveyed half via intercom in a booth and the other half online, asking them politically correct questions such as "Should there be more aid to Africa?" Online answers were deemed much more honest. People may be more open about their opinions when they can respond to a survey privately and not to another person who they feel might be judging them, especially on sensitive topics.

- *Online research is more versatile.* The multimedia applications of online research are especially advantageous. For instance, virtual-reality software lets visitors inspect 3-D models of products such as cameras, cars, and medical equipment, and product characteristics can be easily manipulated online. Even at the most basic level, online surveys make answering a questionnaire easier and more fun than paper-and-pencil versions.

Disadvantages

- *Samples can be small and skewed.* Perhaps the largest criticism levelled against online research is that not everyone is online. Research subjects who respond to online surveys are more likely to be tech-savvy middle-class males. These people are likely to differ in socioeconomic and education levels from those who are not online. While marketers can be certain that more and more people will go online, it is important for online market researchers to find creative ways to reach certain population segments that are less likely to be online, such as older Canadians. One option is to combine offline sources with online findings. Providing temporary Internet access at locations such as malls and recreation centres is another strategy. Some research firms use statistical models to fill in the gaps in market research left by offline consumer segments.

- *Online market research is prone to technological problems and inconsistencies.* Because online research is a relatively new method, many market researchers have not gotten survey designs right. A common error is transferring a written survey to the screen. Others overuse technology, concentrating on the bells and whistles and graphics while ignoring basic survey-design guidelines. Problems also arise because browser software varies. The web designer's final product may be seen very differently depending on the computer hardware and software being used by the research subject to view the survey.

Sources: Catherine Arnold, "Not Done Net; New Opportunities Still Exist in Online Research," *Marketing News*, April 1, 2004, p. 17; Nima M. Ray and Sharon W. Tabor, "Contributing Factors: Several Issues Affect e-Research Validity," *Marketing News*, September 15, 2003, p. 50; Louella Miles, "Online, on Tap," *Marketing*, June 16, 2004, pp. 39–40.

Tangency

Toronto-based PR firm Tangency recently began an interactive market-research division after identifying a new market opportunity in data collection. Tangency believes that marketers are interested in online research, given the growth in broadband users, but they are uncomfortable with not having the research participants present. To address this, Tangency began a panellist-recruiting effort and gave each participant a webcam. As a result, its clients can view participants during online research efforts while also enjoying the benefits of being online. For example, focus-group members can be drawn from a large geographic area and clients can observe focus-group interaction from their offices, all without requiring any travel. Pressing queries can be answered almost immediately—and, of course, it is all more affordable. The one drawback of the system is that some technological knowledge is required, which may limit possible participants to younger, technologically savvy individuals.[24]

It is important to recognize that not everyone in the sample population will be online. (See "Marketing Insight: Global Online Market-Research Challenges.")

Step 4: Analyze the Information

The purpose of this step is to extract findings from the collected data. The researcher tabulates the data and develops frequency distributions. Averages and measures of dispersion are computed for the major variables. The researcher will also apply some advanced statistical techniques and decision models in the hope of discovering additional findings.

Step 5: Present the Findings

In the next-to-last step, the researcher presents the findings. The researcher should present findings that are relevant to the major marketing decisions facing management. The main survey findings for the Air Canada case show that:

1. The chief reasons for using in-flight Internet service are to pass the time surfing and to send and receive messages from colleagues and family. The charge would be put on passengers' charge accounts and paid by their companies.

2. About five first-class passengers out of every ten during a flight would use the Internet service at $25; about six would use it at $15. Thus, a charge of $15 would produce less revenue ($90 = 6 \times $15) than $25 ($125 = 5 \times $25). By charging $25, Air Canada would collect $125 per flight. Assuming that the same flight takes place 365 days a year, the company would collect $45 625 (= $125 \times 365) annually. Since the investment is $90 000, it will take approximately two years before Air Canada breaks even.

3. Offering in-flight service would strengthen the public's image of Air Canada as an innovative and progressive airline. It would gain some new passengers and customer goodwill.

Step 6: Make the Decision

The managers who commissioned the research need to weigh the evidence. If their confidence in the findings is low, they may decide against introducing the in-flight Internet service. If they are predisposed to launching the service, the findings support their inclination. They may even decide to study the issue further and do more research. The decision is theirs, but hopefully the research provided them with insight into the problem. (See Table 4.3.)[25]

A growing number of organizations are using a marketing decision-support system to help their marketing managers make better decisions. The Massachusetts Institute of Technology's John Little

TABLE 4.3	THE SEVEN CHARACTERISTICS OF GOOD MARKETING RESEARCH
1. Scientific method	Effective marketing research uses the principles of the scientific method: careful observation, formulation of hypotheses, prediction, and testing.
2. Research creativity	At its best, marketing research develops innovative ways to solve a problem: a clothing company catering to teenagers gave several young men video cameras, then used the resulting videos for focus groups held in restaurants and other places teens frequent.
3. Multiple methods	Marketing researchers shy away from overreliance on any one method. They also recognize the value of using two or three methods to increase confidence in results.
4. Interdependence of models and data	Marketing researchers recognize that data are interpreted from underlying models that guide the type of information sought.
5. Value and cost of information	Marketing researchers show concern for estimating the value of information against its cost. Costs are typically easy to determine, but the value of research is harder to quantify. It depends on the reliability and validity of the findings and management's willingness to accept and act on those findings.
6. Healthy skepticism	Marketing researchers show a healthy skepticism toward glib assumptions made by managers about how a market works. They are alert to the problems caused by "marketing myths."
7. Ethical marketing	Marketing research benefits both the sponsoring company and its customers. The misuse of marketing research can harm or annoy consumers, increasing resentment at what consumers regard as an invasion of their privacy or a disguised sales pitch.

When chipmaker Intel Research wanted to know how people in countries around the world use technology, it sent an anthropologist to find out. Dr. Genevieve Bell visited 100 households in 19 cities in 7 countries in Asia and the Pacific. She came back to Intel with 20 gigabytes of digital photos, 19 field notebooks, and insights about technology, culture, and design that would challenge company assumptions about digital technology.

It stands to reason that Intel—a global tech powerhouse—would want to know how technology is used in its international markets. Yet all companies have a stake in knowing how the rest of the world sees and uses what most Westerners take for granted: Internet technology. With online research becoming the fastest-growing market research tool, marketers with global ambitions need to know which countries are online and why they are or are not.

Internet penetration is low in most parts of Asia, Latin America, and Central and Eastern Europe. In Brazil, for example, only 7 percent of the population is online. While most people assume that the low penetration is due to economies that don't support an expensive technological infrastructure, there are other factors involved. There's climate, for one. In Malaysia, power surges caused by monsoons can fry computer motherboards. Government is also a powerful spur or barrier to Internet penetration. While the Chinese economy is zooming ahead, it's unlikely the authoritarian Chinese government will feel comfortable with market researchers gathering information from its citizens via the Internet. Contrast this with South Korea, where the government has made widespread broadband Internet access a priority and has provided incentives to PC makers to bring cheaper models to market.

Other significant factors that can keep computers and Wi-Fi and data ports from crossing the threshold are religion and culture. Dr. Bell found that values of humility and simplicity are deemed incompatible with Internet technology and make it less welcome in some Hindu homes in India and Muslim homes in Malaysia and Indonesia. She also noted that while North Americans have private space in the home for leisure activities, Japan's tighter quarters afford little privacy. This may explain the huge popularity of text messaging on mobile phones among Japan's young people.

Dr. Bell's findings on global responses to technology point out one of the biggest obstacles to conducting international research, whether online or not: a lack of consistency. Nan Martin, global accounts director for Synovate Inc., a market research firm with offices in 46 countries, says: "In global research, we have to adapt culturally to how, where, and with whom we are doing the research.... A simple research study conducted globally becomes much more complicated as a result of the cultural nuances, and it's necessary for us to be sensitive to those nuances in data collection and interpretation." For instance, suppose Internet penetration is equal. In Latin America, where consumers are uncomfortable with the impersonal nature of the Internet, researchers might need to incorporate interactive elements into a survey so participants feel they are talking to a real person. In Asia, focus groups are challenging because of the cultural tendency to conform. Online surveys may bring more honest responses and keep respondents from "losing face."

And what if a researcher collects data face-to-face in Mexico, but by Internet in the United States and Canada? Nan Martin says that "Not only are the subjects answering the question differently because of cultural difference, but the data is being collected by a different method. That can shake the underpinnings of how research scientists feel about collecting data: that every time you change a variable, you're making interpretation of the results more challenging. It is so challenging, in fact, that some say this is an area where global marketers are best served by hiring an expert—an outside research firm with expertise in acquiring and analyzing international data."

Sources: Arundhati Parmar, "Stumbling Blocks: Net Research Is Not Quite Global," *Marketing News*, March 3, 2003, p. 51; Catherine Arnold, "Global Perspective: Synovate Exec Discusses Future of International Research," *Marketing News*, May 15, 2004, p. 43; Michael Erard, "For Technology, No Small World After All," *New York Times*, May 6, 2004, p. G5; Deborah L. Vence, "Global Consistency: Leave It to the Experts," *Marketing News*, April 28, 2003, p. 37.

---

defines a **marketing decision-support system (MDSS)** as a coordinated collection of data, systems, tools, and techniques with supporting software and hardware with which an organization gathers and interprets relevant information from business and the environment and turns it into a basis for marketing action.[26]

A classic MDSS example is the CALLPLAN model, which helps salespeople determine the number of calls to make per period to each prospect and current client. The model takes into account travel time as well as selling time. When launched, the model was tested at United Airlines with an experimental group that managed to increase its sales over a matched control group by 8 percentage points.[27] Once a year, *Marketing News* lists hundreds of current marketing and sales computer programs that assist in designing marketing-research studies, segmenting markets, setting prices and advertising budgets, analyzing media, and planning sales-force activity.

Overcoming Barriers to the Use of Marketing Research

In spite of the rapid growth of marketing research, many companies still fail to use it sufficiently or correctly, for several reasons:[28]

- *A narrow conception of the research.* Many managers see marketing research as a fact-finding operation. They expect the researcher to design a questionnaire, choose a sample, conduct interviews, and report results, often without a careful definition of the problem or of the decisions facing management. When fact-finding fails to be useful, management's idea of the limited usefulness of marketing research is reinforced.

- *Uneven calibre of researchers.* Some managers view marketing research as little more than a clerical activity and treat it as such. As a result, less-competent marketing researchers are hired and their weak training and deficient creativity lead to unimpressive results. The disappointing results reinforce management's prejudice against marketing research. Management continues to pay low salaries to its market researchers, thus perpetuating the basic problem.

- *Poor framing of the problem.* In the famous case where Coca-Cola introduced New Coke after much research, the failure of New Coke was largely due to not setting up the research problem correctly from a marketing perspective. The issue was how consumers felt about Coca-Cola as a brand and not necessarily the taste in isolation.

- *Late and occasionally erroneous findings.* Managers want results that are accurate and conclusive. They may want the results tomorrow. Yet good marketing research takes time and money. Managers are disappointed when marketing research costs too much or takes too much time.

- *Personality and presentational differences.* Differences between the styles of line managers and marketing researchers often get in the way of productive relationships. To a manager who wants concreteness, simplicity, and certainty, a marketing researcher's report may seem abstract, complicated, and tentative. Yet in the more progressive companies, marketing researchers are being included as members of the product-management team and their influence on marketing strategy is growing.

Failure to properly conduct or use marketing research has led to numerous gaffes, including the following McDonald's example, one of the most expensive flops of all time.

McDonald's Arch Deluxe

In 1996, McDonald's introduced the Arch Deluxe burger, positioned as a sophisticated burger for adults. McDonald's hoped the burger, designed with the adult consumer in mind, would lead to an increase in its share of the adult fast-food market. An estimated $300 million was spent on the research, production, and marketing of the Arch Deluxe. However, adult customers found the price high and were unwilling to pay a premium for a burger that they did not see as being significantly different or better. Although marketing research showed that adult consumers loved the idea of having a burger designed specifically for them, the research ignored the fact that McDonald's is not where one would normally go to have a sophisticated burger. Moreover, the research was unable to detect adult consumers' negative perception of the Arch Deluxe's caloric content and price.[29]

MEASURING MARKETING PRODUCTIVITY

An important task of marketing research is to assess the efficiency and effectiveness of marketing activities. Marketers are increasingly being held accountable for their investments and must be able to justify marketing expenditures to senior management.[30] In a recent Accenture survey, 70 percent of marketing executives stated that they did not have a handle on the return of their marketing investments.[31] Another study revealed that 63 percent of senior management said they were dissatisfied with their marketing-performance measurement system and wanted marketing to supply prior and posterior estimates of the impact of marketing programs.[32] With marketing costs already high and continuing to rise, senior executives are tired of seeing what they consider to be wasteful marketing: failed new products and lavish ad campaigns, extensive sales calls, and expensive promotions that are unable to move the sales needle.

Marketing research can help address this increased need for accountability. Two complementary approaches to measuring marketing productivity are (1) marketing metrics to assess marketing

---

MARKETING INSIGHT | USING MARKETING METRICS TO MEASURE WHAT YOU ARE DOING

A 2000 survey by the Advertising Research Foundation found that "enhanced return on marketing investment" was one of the top priorities CEOs set for their marketing functions. Seven years later, a 2007 CMO Council survey found that measuring marketing performance and improving marketing efficiency rank as the top challenges faced by chief marketing officers. Findings from these studies highlight the importance of establishing measures to assess and evaluate marketing efforts. These measures, called marketing metrics, help management and marketers better evaluate whether marketing campaigns will meet or are meeting targeted goals. With the high number of products that fail to meet expectations, it is imperative that management have in place measurement systems that help them know when to continue pushing a product, change marketing tactics, or just cut their losses and end a project altogether.

It is not always easy to effectively measure marketing efforts, with many businesses spending money on marketing efforts such as sales forces, brochures, advertisements, and websites simultaneously, with no way of knowing the results of each expenditure. Considerable savings could be obtained if the company knew that one of the marketing efforts was bringing in 70 percent of the business. This knowledge would allow it to focus its efforts on expanding this one effort. A 2004 study by the CMO Council found that companies with formal marketing-measurement systems achieved 29 percent better sales, 32 percent more market share, and 37 percent more profit than companies without marketing metrics in place. However, the CMO Council's 2007 survey report showed that only a small percentage of companies have implemented a marketing-performance measurement system. It has been noted that management levels of dissatisfaction with marketing are at relatively high levels in today's workplace. The level of dissatisfaction has been shown to be lower in companies that have marketing metrics in place.

There are no simple metrics or performance measures that can apply to all companies, as the goals and objectives can be considerably different from one firm to the next. Finding the measures that correlate with the goals of the marketing strategy is important and these goals can be unique, but a few simple gauges will now be discussed.

The first goal of any marketing effort is to enable the organization to acquire customers. While marketing may not result in a purchase, marketing strategies move the customer through the buying process. Key performance indicators which address acquisition strategies include customer growth rates, share of preference, share of voice, and share of distribution.

A second goal of marketing is to keep existing customers and increase their overall value to the company. This is because it is cheaper to maintain repeat customers than to attract new customers. Measures for these goals include the frequency and recency of purchases, customer tenure, customer loyalty and advocacy, and share-of-wallet rates.

The last area of concern has to do with intangible assets such as intellectual property, customer value, goodwill, and other factors that ultimately have an effect on a company's value. Effective marketing tactics can increase this value by improving the rate of new-product acceptance or allowing for an increase in product price.

Regardless of the specific measures a company chooses to utilize, a continuous process must be established whereby the metrics are collected, analyzed, and reported on a regular basis. The metrics themselves can change over time as the market and company evolves, so the measures must be adjusted accordingly.

Although the process of establishing and maintaining metrics at first may seem fairly obvious, few firms properly install them. To work without metrics makes it extremely difficult to accurately judge whether a course of action is working or needs to be adjusted. The potential gains from marketing metrics far outweigh the drawbacks, as metrics can lead companies to expand market position, lower costs, and retain important customers.

Sources: Laura Patterson, "If You Don't Measure It, You Can't Manage It: The Best Metrics for Managing Marketing Performance," *Management First*, July/Aug 2005, pp. 2–3; Laura Patterson, "Taking on the Metrics Challenge," *Journal of Targeting, Measurement and Analysis for Marketing*, September 2007, 15(4), pp. 270–276; "Marketing Outlook 2007," *CMO Council*, p. 6, www.cmocouncil.org/resources (viewed May 12, 2008).

---

effects and (2) marketing-mix modelling to estimate causal relationships and how marketing activity affects outcomes.

Marketing Metrics

Marketers employ a wide variety of measures to assess marketing effects. **Marketing metrics** is the set of measures that help firms to quantify, compare, and interpret their marketing performance. Marketing metrics can be used by brand managers to design marketing programs and by senior management to decide on financial allocations. When marketers can estimate the dollar contribution of marketing activities, they are better able to justify the value of marketing investments to senior management.[33] See "Marketing Insight: Using Marketing Metrics to Measure What You are Doing" for a discussion of the types of marketing metrics.

TABLE 4.4	SAMPLE MARKETING METRICS	
I. External		**II. Internal**
Awareness		Awareness of goals
Market share (volume or value)		Commitment to goals
Relative price (market share value/volume)		Active innovation support
Number of complaints (level of dissatisfaction)		Resource adequacy
Consumer satisfaction		Staffing/skill levels
Distribution/availability		Desire to learn
Total number of customers		Willingness to change
Perceived quality/esteem		Freedom to fail
Loyalty/retention		Autonomy
Relative perceived quality		Relative employee satisfaction

Source: Tim Ambler, "What Does Marketing Success Look Like?" *Marketing Management*, Spring 2001, pp. 13–18.

Many marketing metrics relate to customer-level concerns such as their attitudes and behaviour; others relate to brand-level concerns such as market share, relative price premium, and profitability.[34] Companies can also monitor an extensive set of metrics internal to the company. One important set of measures relates to a firm's innovativeness. For example, 3M tracks the proportion of sales resulting from its recent innovations. Another key set relates to employees. Table 4.4 summarizes a list of popular internal and external marketing metrics from a survey in the United Kingdom.[35]

Amazon.com is a firm renowned for constantly monitoring its marketing activities. CEO Jeff Bezos wants to know average customer contacts per order, average time per contact, the breakdown of email versus telephone contacts, and the total cost to the company of each. The man in charge of Amazon's customer service and its warehouse and distribution operations looks at about 300 charts a week for his division.[36]

Firms are also employing organizational processes and systems to make sure that the value of all these different metrics is maximized by the firm. A summary set of relevant internal and external measures can be assembled in a *marketing dashboard* for synthesis and interpretation. Some companies are also appointing marketing controllers to review budget items and expenses. Increasingly, these controllers are using business-intelligence software to create digital versions of marketing dashboards that aggregate data from disparate internal and external sources.

Keystone Industries

Montreal-based Keystone Industries, maker of the French Dressing Jeans clothing line, implemented marketing-dashboard software technology called C-Trak in 2004. The software was developed by Unisys and Calgary-based marketing firm Venture Communications. The software works by having the user set goals and then measure quantitative objectives. For example, Keystone wanted to acquire 400 new accounts. To acquire new accounts, Keystone's marketing strategy involved using prospective customer lists and making trade-show appearances. The C-Trak software allows Keystone to directly attribute any new customer acquisitions to a particular activity through user-friendly software-generated reports. This helps Keystone understand how effective its lists and trade-show appearances actually are.

Information generated by the software led the company to make a significant change to the business. Historically, the company had marketed only to its channel partners such as retail stores. The software demonstrated that Keystone should be putting more emphasis on its consumer accounts. As a result, for the first time in the company's history, it began advertising directly to consumers.[37]

As input to the marketing dashboard, companies can prepare two market-based scorecards that reflect performance and provide possible early warning signals. A **customer-performance scorecard** records how well the company is doing year after year on such customer-based measures as shown in Table 4.5. Norms should be set for each measure and management should take action when results get out of bounds.

TABLE 4.5 | SAMPLE CUSTOMER-PERFORMANCE SCORECARD MEASURES

- Percentage of new customers to average number of customers.
- Percentage of lost customers to average number of customers.
- Percentage of win-back customers to average number of customers.
- Percentage of customers falling into very dissatisfied, dissatisfied, neutral, satisfied, and very satisfied categories.
- Percentage of customers who say they would repurchase the product.
- Percentage of customers who say they would recommend the product to others.
- Percentage of target-market customers who have brand awareness or recall.
- Percentage of customers who say that the company's product is the most preferred in its category.
- Percentage of customers who correctly identify the brand's intended positioning and differentiation.
- Average perception of company's product quality relative to chief competitor.
- Average perception of company's service quality relative to chief competitor.

The second measure is called a **stakeholder-performance scorecard**. Companies need to track the satisfaction of various constituencies who have a critical interest in and impact on the company's performance: employees, suppliers, banks, distributors, retailers, and shareholders. Again, norms should be set for each group and management should take action when one or more groups register increased levels of dissatisfaction.[38]

Measuring Marketing-Plan Performance

Marketers today have better marketing metrics for measuring the performance of marketing plans.[39] They can use four tools to check on plan performance: sales analysis, market-share analysis, marketing expense-to-sales analysis, and financial analysis.

SALES ANALYSIS **Sales analysis** consists of measuring and evaluating actual sales in relation to goals. Two specific tools are used in sales analysis.

Sales-variance analysis measures the relative contribution of different factors to a gap in sales performance. Suppose the annual plan called for selling 4000 widgets in the first quarter at $1 per widget, for total revenue of $4000. At quarter's end, only 3000 widgets were sold at $0.80 per widget, for total revenue of $2400. How much of the sales performance is due to the price decline and how much to the volume decline? The following calculation answers this question:

$$\textit{Variance due to price decline} = (\$1.00 - \$0.80)(3\,000) = \$\ \ 600 \quad 37.5\%$$
$$\underline{\textit{Variance due to volume decline} = (\$1.00)(4\,000 - 3\,000) = \$1\,000 \quad 62.5\%}$$
$$\$1\,600 \quad 100.0\%$$

Almost two-thirds of the variance is due to failure to achieve the volume target. The company should look closely at why it failed to achieve expected sales volume.

Microsales analysis looks at specific products, territories, and so forth that failed to produce expected sales. Suppose the company sells in three territories and expected sales were 1 500 units, 500 units, and 2 000 units, respectively. The actual sales volume was 1 400 units, 525 units, and 1 075 units, respectively. Thus, territory 1 showed a 7 percent shortfall in terms of expected sales; territory 2, a 5 percent improvement over expectations; and territory 3, a 46 percent shortfall! Territory 3 is causing most of the trouble. The sales vice-president needs to check into territory 3: maybe territory 3's sales rep is underperforming, a major competitor has entered this territory, or business is in a recession in this territory.

MARKET-SHARE ANALYSIS Company sales do not reveal how well the company is performing relative to competitors. For this purpose, management needs to track its market share.

Market share can be measured in three ways: **Overall market share** is the company's sales expressed as a percentage of total market sales. **Served market share** is its sales expressed as a percentage of the total sales to its served market. Its **served market** is all the buyers who are able and willing to buy its product. Served market share is always larger than overall market share. A company could capture 100 percent of its served market and yet have a relatively small share of the total market. **Relative market share** can be expressed as market share in relation to its largest competitor. A relative market share over 100 percent indicates a market leader. A relative market share of exactly 100 percent means that the company is tied for the lead. A rise in relative market share means a company is gaining on its leading competitor.

Conclusions from market-share analysis, however, are subject to certain qualifications:

■ *The assumption that outside forces affect all companies in the same way is often not true.* Health Canada's ad campaign on the harmful consequences of cigarette smoking caused total cigarette sales to falter, but not equally for all companies.

■ *The assumption that a company's performance should be judged against the average performance of all companies is not always valid.* A company's performance should be judged against the performance of its closest competitors.

■ *If a new firm enters the industry, then every existing firm's market share might fall.* A decline in market share might not mean that the company is performing any worse than other companies. Share loss depends on the degree to which the new firm hits the company's specific markets.

■ *Sometimes a market-share decline is deliberately engineered to improve profits.* For example, management might drop unprofitable customers or products.

■ *Market share can fluctuate for many minor reasons.* For example, it can be affected by whether a large sale occurs on the last day of the month or at the beginning of the next month. Not all shifts in market share have marketing significance.[40]

A useful way to analyze market-share movements is in terms of four components:

$$
\begin{array}{c}
\text{Overall} \\ \text{market} \\ \text{share}
\end{array}
=
\begin{array}{c}
\text{Customer} \\ \text{penetration}
\end{array}
\times
\begin{array}{c}
\text{Customer} \\ \text{loyalty}
\end{array}
\times
\begin{array}{c}
\text{Customer} \\ \text{selectivity}
\end{array}
\times
\begin{array}{c}
\text{Price} \\ \text{selectivity}
\end{array}
$$

where:

Customer penetration is the percentage of all customers who buy from the company.

Customer loyalty is the purchases from the company by its customers expressed as a percentage of their total purchases from all suppliers of the same products.

Customer selectivity is the size of the average customer purchase from the company expressed as a percentage of the size of the average customer purchase from an average company.

Price selectivity is the average price charged by the company expressed as a percentage of the average price charged by all companies.

Now suppose the company's dollar market share falls during the period. The overall market-share equation provides four possible explanations: The company lost some of its customers (lower customer penetration); existing customers are buying less from the company (lower customer loyalty); the company's remaining customers are smaller in size (lower customer selectivity); or the company's price has slipped relative to competition (lower price selectivity).

MARKETING EXPENSE-TO-SALES ANALYSIS Annual-plan control requires making sure that the company is not overspending to achieve sales goals. The key ratio to watch is *marketing expense to sales.* In one company, this ratio was 30 percent and consisted of five component expense-to-sales ratios: sales force-to-sales (15 percent); advertising-to-sales (5 percent); sales promotion-to-sales (6 percent); marketing research-to-sales (1 percent); and sales administration-to-sales (3 percent).

Management needs to monitor these ratios. Fluctuations outside the normal ranges are cause for concern. The period-to-period fluctuations of each ratio can be tracked on a *control chart* (see Figure 4.2). This chart shows that the advertising expense-to-sales ratio normally fluctuates between 8 percent and 12 percent, say 99 out of 100 times. In the fifteenth period, however, the ratio exceeded the upper control limit. One of two hypotheses can explain this occurrence: (1) The company still has good expense control and this situation represents a rare chance event. (2) The company has lost control over this expense and should find the cause. If no investigation is made, the risk is that some real change might have occurred and the company will fall behind. If the environment is investigated, the risk is that the investigation will uncover nothing and be a waste of time and effort.

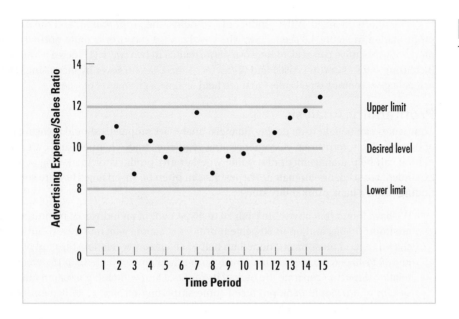

FIGURE 4.2

The Control-Chart Model

The behaviour of successive observations even within the upper and lower control limits should be watched. Note in Figure 4.2 that the level of the expense-to-sales ratio rose steadily from the ninth period onward. The probability of encountering six successive increases in what should be independent events is only 1 in 64.[41] This unusual pattern should have led to an investigation sometime before the fifteenth observation.

FINANCIAL ANALYSIS The expense-to-sales ratios should be analyzed in an overall financial framework to determine how and where the company is making its money. Marketers are increasingly using financial analysis to find profitable strategies beyond sales building.

Management uses financial analysis to identify the factors that affect the company's *rate of return on net worth*.[42] The main factors are shown in Figure 4.3, along with illustrative numbers for a large chain-store retailer. The retailer is earning a 12.5 percent return on net worth. The return on net worth is the product of two ratios, the company's *return on assets* and its *financial leverage*. To improve its return on net worth, the company must increase its ratio of net profits to its assets or increase the ratio of its assets to its net worth. The company should analyze the composition of its assets (i.e., cash, accounts receivable, inventory, and plant and equipment) and see if it can improve its asset management.

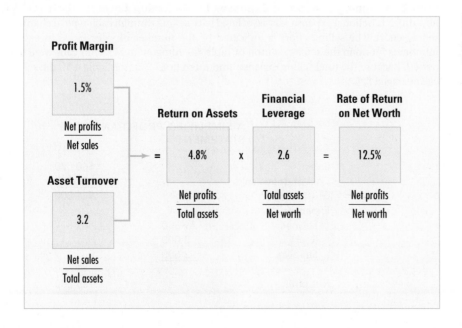

FIGURE 4.3

Financial Model of Return on Net Worth

The return on assets is the product of two ratios, the *profit margin* and the *asset turnover*. The profit margin in Figure 4.3 seems low, whereas the asset turnover is more normal for retailing. The marketing executive can seek to improve performance in two ways: (1) Increase the profit margin by increasing sales or cutting costs; and (2) increase the asset turnover by increasing sales or reducing assets (e.g., inventory, receivables) that are held against a given level of sales.[43]

Profitability Analysis

Companies can benefit from deeper financial analysis. Companies should measure the profitability of their products, territories, customer groups, segments, trade channels, and order sizes. This information can help management determine whether any products or marketing activities should be expanded, reduced, or eliminated. The results can often be surprising. Here are some disconcerting findings from a bank profitability study:

> We have found that anywhere from 20 to 40 percent of an individual institution's products are unprofitable, and up to 60 percent of their accounts generate losses. Our research has shown that, in most firms, more than half of all customer relationships are not profitable, and 30 to 40 percent are only marginally so. It is frequently a mere 10 to 15 percent of a firm's relationships that generate the bulk of its profits. Our profitability research into the branch system of a regional bank produced some surprising results . . . 30 percent of the bank's branches were unprofitable.[44]

MARKETING-PROFITABILITY ANALYSIS   We will illustrate the steps in marketing-profitability analysis with the following example:

The marketing vice-president of a lawnmower company wants to determine the profitability of selling its lawnmower through three types of retail channels: hardware stores, garden-supply shops, and department stores. The company's profit-and-loss statement is shown in Table 4.6.

Step 1: Identifying Functional Expenses   Assume that the expenses listed in Table 4.6 are incurred to sell the product, advertise it, pack and deliver it, and bill and collect for it. The first task is to measure how much of each expense was incurred in each activity.

Suppose that most of the salary expense went to sales representatives and the rest went to an advertising manager, packing and delivery help, and an office accountant. Let the breakdown of the $9 300 be $5 100, $1 200, $1 400, and $1 600, respectively. Table 4.7 shows the allocation of the salary expense to these four activities.

Table 4.7 also shows the rent account of $3 000 allocated to the four activities. Because the sales reps work away from the office, none of the building's rent expense is assigned to selling. Most of the expenses for floor space and rented equipment are for packing and delivery. The supplies account covers promotional materials, packing materials, fuel purchases for delivery, and home-office stationery. The $3 500 in this account is reassigned to the functional uses made of the supplies.

Step 2: Assigning Functional Expenses to Marketing Entities   The next task is to measure how much functional expense was associated with selling through each type of channel. Consider the selling effort. The selling effort is indicated by the number of sales made in each channel. This number is found in the selling column of Table 4.8. Altogether, 275 sales calls were made during the period. Because the total selling expense amounted to $5 500 (see Table 4.8), the selling expense per call averaged $20.

TABLE 4.6	A SIMPLIFIED PROFIT-AND-LOSS STATEMENT	
Sales		$60 000
Cost of goods sold		39 000
Gross margin		$21 000
Expenses		
Salaries	$9 300	
Rent	3 000	
Supplies	3 500	
		15 800
Net profit		$5 200

TABLE 4.7 | MAPPING NATURAL EXPENSES INTO FUNCTIONAL EXPENSES

Natural Accounts	Total	Selling	Advertising	Packing and Delivery	Billing and Collecting
Salaries	$9 300	$5 100	$1 200	$1 400	$1 600
Rent	3 000	—	400	2 000	600
Supplies	3 500	400	1 500	1 400	200
	$15 800	$5 500	$3 100	$4 800	$2 400

TABLE 4.8 | BASES FOR ALLOCATING FUNCTIONAL EXPENSES TO CHANNELS

Channel Type	Selling	Advertising	Packing and Delivery	Billing and Collecting
Hardware	200	50	50	50
Garden supply	65	20	21	21
Department stores	10	30	9	9
	275	100	80	80
Functional expense	$5 500	$3 100	$4 800	$2 400
÷ No. of Units	275	100	80	80
Equals	$ 20	$ 31	$ 60	$ 30

Advertising expense can be allocated according to the number of ads addressed to different channels. Because there were 100 ads altogether, the average ad cost was $31.

The packing and delivery expense is allocated according to the number of orders placed by each type of channel. This same basis was used for allocating billing and collection expense.

Step 3: Preparing a Profit-and-Loss Statement for Each Marketing Entity A profit-and-loss statement can now be prepared for each type of channel (see Table 4.9). Because hardware stores accounted for half of total sales ($30 000 out of $60 000), this channel is charged with half the cost of goods sold ($19 500 out of $39 000). This leaves a gross margin from hardware stores of $10 500. From this must be deducted the proportions of the functional expenses hardware stores consumed.

According to Table 4.8, hardware stores received 200 out of 275 total sales calls. At a value of $20 a call, hardware stores have to be charged with a $4 000 selling expense. Table 4.8 also shows that hardware stores were the target of 50 ads. At $31 an ad, the hardware stores are charged with $1 550

TABLE 4.9 | PROFIT-AND-LOSS STATEMENTS FOR CHANNELS

	Hardware	Garden Supply	Dept. Stores	Whole Company
Sales	$30 000	$10 000	$20 000	$60 000
Cost of goods sold	19 500	6 500	13 000	39 000
Gross margin	$10 500	$ 3 500	$ 7 000	$21 000
Expenses				
Selling ($20 per call)	$ 4 000	$ 1 300	$ 200	$ 5 500
Advertising ($31 per advertisement)	1 550	620	930	3 100
Packing and delivery ($60 per order)	3 000	1 260	540	4 800
Billing ($30 per order)	1 500	630	270	2 400
Total Expenses	$10 050	$3 810	$1 940	$15 800
Net profit or loss	$450	$(310)	$5 060	$5 200

of advertising. The same reasoning applies in computing the share of the other functional expenses to charge to hardware stores. The result is that hardware stores gave rise to $10 050 of the total expenses. Subtracting this from the gross margin, the profit of selling through hardware stores is only $450.

This analysis is repeated for the other channels. The company is losing money in selling through garden-supply shops and makes virtually all of its profits through department stores. Notice that gross sales is not a reliable indicator of the net profits for each channel.

DETERMINING CORRECTIVE ACTION It would be naïve to conclude that the company should drop garden-supply shops and possibly hardware stores so that it can concentrate on department stores. The following questions need to be answered first:

- To what extent do buyers buy on the basis of type of retail outlet versus brand?
- What are the trends with respect to the importance of these three channels?
- How good are the company marketing strategies directed at the three channels?

On the basis of the answers, marketing management can evaluate five alternatives:

1. Establish a special charge for handling smaller orders.
2. Give more promotional aid to garden-supply shops and hardware stores.
3. Reduce the number of sales calls and the amount of advertising going to garden-supply shops and hardware stores.
4. Do not abandon any channel entirely, but only the weakest retail units in each channel.
5. Do nothing.

In general, marketing-profitability analysis indicates the relative profitability of different channels, products, territories, or other marketing entities. It does not prove that the best course of action is to drop the unprofitable marketing entities, nor does it capture the likely profit improvement if these marginal marketing entities are dropped.

DIRECT VERSUS FULL COSTING Like all information tools, marketing-profitability analysis can lead or mislead marketing executives, depending on how well they understand its methods and limitations. The lawnmower company showed some arbitrariness in its choice of bases for allocating the functional expenses to its marketing entities. "Number of sales calls" was used to allocate selling expenses, when in principle "number of sales working hours" is a more accurate indicator of cost. The former base was used because it involves less record keeping and computation.

Far more serious is another judgmental element affecting profitability analysis. The issue is whether to allocate full costs or only direct and traceable costs in evaluating a marketing entity's performance. The lawnmower company sidestepped this problem by assuming only simple costs that fit in with marketing activities, but the question cannot be avoided in real-world analyses of profitability. Three types of costs have to be distinguished:

1. *Direct costs.* These are costs that can be assigned directly to the proper marketing entities. Sales commissions are a direct cost in a profitability analysis of sales territories, sales representatives, or customers. Advertising expenditures are a direct cost in a profitability analysis of products to the extent that each advertisement promotes only one product. Other direct costs for specific purposes are sales-force salaries and travelling expenses.
2. *Traceable common costs.* These are costs that can be assigned only indirectly, but on a plausible basis, to the marketing entities. In the example, rent was analyzed this way.
3. *Nontraceable common costs.* These are common costs whose allocation to the marketing entities is highly arbitrary. To allocate "corporate image" expenditures equally to all products would be arbitrary, because all products do not benefit equally. To allocate them proportionately to the sales of the various products would be arbitrary because relative product sales reflect many factors besides corporate image making. Other examples are top-management salaries, taxes, interest, and other overhead.

No one disputes including direct costs in marketing-cost analysis. There is a small amount of controversy about including traceable common costs, which lump together costs that would change with the scale of marketing activity and costs that would not change. If the lawnmower company drops garden-supply shops, it would probably continue to pay the same rent. In this event, its profits would not rise immediately by the amount of the present loss in selling to garden-supply shops ($310).

The major controversy concerns whether the nontraceable common costs should be allocated to the marketing entities. Such allocation is called the *full-cost approach*, and its advocates argue that all costs must ultimately be imputed in order to determine true profitability. However, this argument confuses the use of accounting for financial reporting with its use for managerial decision making. Full costing has three major weaknesses:

1. The relative profitability of different marketing entities can shift radically when one arbitrary way to allocate nontraceable common costs is replaced by another.
2. The arbitrariness demoralizes managers, who feel that their performance is judged adversely.
3. The inclusion of nontraceable common costs could weaken efforts at real cost control.

Operating management is most effective in controlling direct costs and traceable common costs. Arbitrary assignments of nontraceable common costs can lead managers to spend their time fighting arbitrary cost allocations rather than managing controllable costs well.

Companies are showing a growing interest in using marketing-profitability analysis or its broader version, activity-based cost accounting (ABC), to quantify the true profitability of different activities.[45] To improve profitability, managers can then examine ways to reduce the resources required to perform various activities, or make the resources more productive or acquire them at lower cost. Alternatively, management may raise prices on products that consume heavy amounts of support resources. The contribution of ABC is to refocus management's attention away from using only labour or material standard costs to allocate full cost, and toward capturing the actual costs of supporting individual products, customers, and other entities.

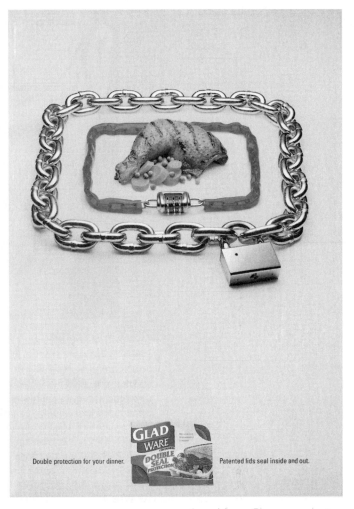

An ad for a Clorox product: Gladware. Clorox is one of the companies that use marketing-mix modelling to test the effectiveness of advertising.

Marketing-Mix Modelling

Marketing accountability also means that marketers can more precisely estimate the effects of different marketing investments. *Marketing-mix models* analyze data from a variety of sources, such as retailer scanner data, company shipment data, pricing, and media and promotion spending data, to understand more precisely the effects of specific marketing activities. To deepen understanding, multivariate analyses are conducted to sort through how each marketing element influences marketing outcomes of interest such as brand sales or market share.[46]

Especially popular with packaged goods marketers such as Procter & Gamble, Clorox, and Colgate, the findings from marketing-mix modelling are used to allocate or reallocate expenditures. Analyses explore which part of ad budgets are wasted, what optimal spending levels are, and what minimum investment levels should be.[47] Although marketing-mix modelling helps to isolate effects, it is less effective at assessing how different marketing elements work in combination.

FORECASTING AND DEMAND MEASUREMENT

One major reason for undertaking marketing research is to identify market opportunities. Once the research is complete, the company must measure and forecast the size, growth, and profit potential of each market opportunity. Sales forecasts are used by finance to raise the cash needed for investment and operations; by the manufacturing department to establish capacity and output levels; by purchasing to acquire the right amount of supplies; and by human resources to hire the needed number of workers. Marketing is responsible for preparing the sales forecasts. If its forecast is far off the mark, the company will be saddled with excess inventory or have inadequate inventory. Sales forecasts are based on estimates of demand. Managers need to define what they mean by market demand. Here is a good example of the importance of defining the market correctly:

Forecasting demand for
products, including building
materials such as Tyvek, is
part of the job of marketing.

Red Bull

When the Austrian company Red Bull began to sell its brand of energy drinks in North
America, it took a very distinctive approach to its marketing strategy. Rather than focus on
the entire soda-drinking market, like Coke and Pepsi had traditionally done, Red Bull adopted a different strategy. Red Bull focused its marketing efforts on a much smaller segment,
males who are in their teens and early twenties, where it felt demand would be the greatest. Red Bull is now the largest seller of energy drinks in North America.[48]

The Measures of Market Demand

Companies can prepare as many as 90 different types of demand estimates (see Figure 4.4).
Demand can be measured for six different product levels, five different space levels, and three different time levels.

Each demand measure serves a specific purpose. A company might forecast short-run demand
for a particular product for the purpose of ordering raw materials, planning production, and

FIGURE 4.4

Ninety Types of Demand
Measurement (6 × 5 × 3)

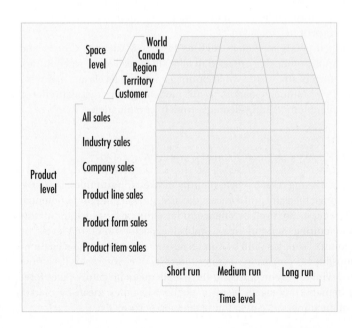

borrowing cash. It might forecast regional demand for its major product line to decide whether to set up regional distribution.

Forecasts also depend on which type of market is being considered. The size of a market hinges on the number of buyers who might exist for a particular market offer. But there are many productive ways to break down the market:

- The **potential market** is the set of consumers who profess a sufficient level of interest in a market offer. However, consumer interest is not enough to define a market. Potential consumers must have enough income and must have access to the product offer.

- The **available market** is the set of consumers who have interest, income, and access to a particular offer. For some market offers, the company or government may restrict sales to certain groups. For example, a particular province might ban motorcycle sales to anyone under 21 years of age. The eligible adults constitute the *qualified available market*—the set of consumers who have interest, income, access, and qualifications for the particular market offer.

- The **target market** is the part of the qualified available market the company decides to pursue. The company might decide to concentrate its marketing and distribution effort on the east coast. The company will end up selling to a certain number of buyers in its target market.

- The **penetrated market** is the set of consumers who are buying the company's product.

These definitions are useful tools for market planning. If the company is not satisfied with its current sales, it can take a number of actions. It can try to attract a larger percentage of buyers from its target market. It can lower the qualifications of potential buyers. It can expand its available market by opening distribution elsewhere or lowering its price; or it can reposition itself in the minds of its customers. Consider the case of the Loblaw Companies:

Loblaw Companies

Loblaw Companies Limited, Canada's largest food distributor, has recently come into hard times due to competition from rival chains. The company posted a $219-million loss in 2006. To combat the downslide, Galen Weston Jr. was named Executive Chairman and given the task of turning around the struggling grocery franchise. In 2007, Weston Jr. became spokesperson for the President's Choice (PC) brand and launched a new campaign in an effort to reposition the brand and the organization as a whole. The repositioning strategy included adopting a more customer-focused approach to doing business as well as focusing on social issues. The brand has implemented this strategy by introducing products such as 99-cent reusable shopping bags to help limit waste and creating the Blue Menu brand that specializes in healthier food choices. PC has also begun to cater more to ethnic groups and focus heavily on fair-trade products, all in an effort to better meet the needs of its customers. The recent transformation of Loblaws is exemplified by the $330-million profit posted in 2007 and the return of the beloved 1980s slogan "Worth switching supermarkets for," which is exactly what Loblaw Companies would like consumers to do in the coming years.[49]

Under the leadership of Galen Weston Jr., Loblaws stores have been repositioned as environmentally concerned and health conscious, in part through their reusable shopping bags and Blue Menu products.

A Vocabulary for Demand Measurement

The major concepts in demand measurement are market demand and company demand. Within each, we distinguish among a demand function, a sales forecast, and a potential.

MARKET DEMAND As we have seen, the marketer's first step in evaluating marketing opportunities is to estimate total market demand. **Market demand** for a product is the total volume that would be bought by a defined customer group in a defined geographical area in a defined time period in a defined marketing environment under a defined marketing program.

Market demand is not a fixed number, but rather a function of the stated conditions. For this reason, it can be called the *market demand function*. The dependence of total market demand on underlying conditions is illustrated in Figure 4.5(a). The horizontal axis shows different possible levels of industry marketing expenditure in a given time period. The vertical axis shows the resulting demand level. The curve represents

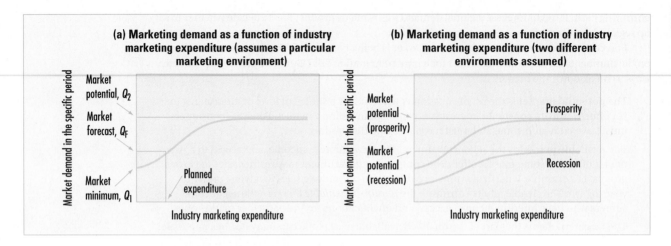

FIGURE 4.5

Market Demand Functions

the estimated market demand associated with varying levels of industry marketing expenditure. The analysis can be further refined if marketers consider responses to marketing expenditures under different economic conditions, such as prosperity or recession, as illustrated in Figure 4.5(b).

Some base sales (called the *market minimum*, labelled Q_1 in the figure) would take place without any demand-stimulating expenditures. Higher levels of industry marketing expenditures would yield higher levels of demand, first at an increasing rate, then at a decreasing rate. Marketing expenditures beyond a certain level would not stimulate much further demand, thus suggesting an upper limit to market demand called the *market potential* (labelled Q_2 in the figure).

The distance between the market minimum and the market potential shows the overall *marketing sensitivity of demand*. We can think of two extreme types of markets, the expansible and the nonexpansible. An *expansible market*, such as the market for racquetball playing, is very much affected in its total size by the level of industry marketing expenditures. In terms of Figure 4.5(a), the distance between Q_1 and Q_2 is relatively large. A *nonexpansible market*—for example, the market for opera—is not much affected by the level of marketing expenditures; the distance between Q_1 and Q_2 is relatively small. Organizations selling in a nonexpansible market must accept the market's size (the level of *primary demand* for the product class) and direct their efforts to winning a larger **market share** for their product (the level of selective demand for the company's product).

It pays to compare the current level of market demand to the potential demand level. The result is called the **market penetration index.** A low market penetration index indicates substantial growth potential for all the firms. A high market penetration index suggests that there will be increased costs in attracting the few remaining prospects. Generally, price competition increases and margins fall when the market penetration index is already high.

A company should also compare its current market share to its potential market share. The result is called the company's **share penetration index**. A low share penetration index indicates that the company can greatly expand its share. The underlying factors holding it back could be many: low brand awareness, low brand availability, benefit deficiencies, or too high a price. A firm should calculate the share penetration increases that would occur with investments to remove each deficiency in order to see which investments would produce the greatest improvement in share penetration.[50]

It is important to remember that the market demand function is not a picture of market demand over time. Rather, the curve shows alternative current forecasts of market demand associated with alternative possible levels of industry marketing effort in the current period.

Market Forecast   Only one level of industry marketing expenditure will actually occur. The market demand corresponding to this level is called the **market forecast**.

Market Potential   The market forecast shows expected market demand, not maximum market demand. For the latter, we have to visualize the level of market demand resulting from a "very high" level of industry marketing expenditure, where further increases in marketing effort would have little effect in stimulating further demand. **Market potential** is the limit approached by market demand as industry marketing expenditures approach infinity for a given marketing environment.

The phrase "for a given market environment" is crucial. Consider the market potential for automobiles in a period of recession versus a period of prosperity. The market potential is higher during prosperity. The dependence of market potential on the environment is illustrated in Figure 4.5(b). Market analysts distinguish between the position of the market demand function and movement along it. Companies cannot do anything about the position of the market demand function, which is determined by the marketing environment. However, companies influence their particular location on the function when they decide how much to spend on marketing.

Companies interested in market potential have a special interest in the **product penetration percentage**, which is the percentage of ownership or use of a product or service in a population. For example, a recent Ipsos-Reid poll revealed how Canadians feel about fixed-rate versus floating-rate mortgages. The survey found that 68 percent of those who own a home and carry a mortgage are in a fixed interest rate product, while only 22 percent of homeowners hold a flexible, variable-rate mortgage.[51]

COMPANY DEMAND We are now ready to define company demand: **Company demand** is the company's estimated share of market demand at alternative levels of company marketing effort in a given time period. The company's share of market demand depends on how its goods, services, prices, communications, and so on are perceived relative to the competitors'. If other things are equal, the company's market share would depend on the size and effectiveness of its market expenditures relative to competitors. Marketing model builders have developed sales-response functions to measure how a company's sales are affected by its marketing expenditure level, marketing mix, and marketing effectiveness.[52]

Company Sales Forecast Once marketers have estimated company demand, their next task is to choose a level of marketing effort. The chosen level will produce an expected level of sales. The **company sales forecast** is the expected level of company sales based on a chosen marketing plan and an assumed marketing environment.

The company sales forecast is represented graphically with company sales on the vertical axis and company marketing effort on the horizontal axis, as shown earlier in Figure 4.5. Too often the sequential relationship between the company forecast and the company marketing plan is confused. One frequently hears that the company should develop its marketing plan on the basis of its sales forecast. This forecast-to-plan sequence is valid if "forecast" means an estimate of national economic activity or if company demand is nonexpansible. The sequence is not valid, however, where market demand is expansible or where "forecast" means an estimate of company sales. The company sales forecast does not establish a basis for deciding what to spend on marketing. On the contrary, the sales forecast is the result of an assumed marketing expenditure plan.

Two other concepts are worth mentioning in relation to the company sales forecast. A **sales quota** is the sales goal set for a product line, company division, or sales representative. It is primarily a managerial device for defining and stimulating sales effort. Management sets sales quotas on the basis of the company sales forecast and the psychology of stimulating its achievement. Generally, sales quotas are set slightly higher than estimated sales to stretch the sales force's effort.

A **sales budget** is a conservative estimate of the expected volume of sales and is used primarily for making current purchasing, production, and cash-flow decisions. The sales budget is based on the sales forecast and the need to avoid excessive risk. Sales budgets are generally set slightly lower than the sales forecast.

Company Sales Potential Company sales potential is the sales limit approached by company demand as company marketing effort increases relative to that of competitors. The absolute limit of company demand is, of course, the market potential. The two would be equal if the company got 100 percent of the market. In most cases, company sales potential is less than the market potential, even when company marketing expenditures increase considerably, relative to competitors. The reason is that each competitor has a core of loyal buyers who are not very responsive to other companies' efforts to woo them.

Estimating Current Demand

We are now ready to examine practical methods for estimating current market demand. Marketing executives want to estimate total market potential, area market potential, and total industry sales and market shares.

TOTAL MARKET POTENTIAL Total market potential is the maximum amount of sales that might be available to all the firms in an industry during a given period, under a given level of industry marketing effort and environmental conditions. A common way to estimate total market potential is as follows: estimate the potential number of buyers times the average quantity purchased by a buyer times the price.

If 12 million Canadians buy books each year, the average book buyer buys three books a year, and the average price of a book is $20, then the total market potential for books is $720 million (12 million × 3 × $20). The most difficult component to estimate is the number of buyers for the specific product or market. One can always start with the total population in the nation, say, 32 million people. The next step is to eliminate groups that obviously would not buy the product. Let us assume that illiterate people and children under 12 do not buy books, and they constitute 20 percent of the population.

This means that only 80 percent of the population, or approximately 25.6 million people, would be in the suspect pool. We might do further research and find that people of low income and low education do not buy books, and they constitute over 30 percent of the suspect pool. Eliminating them, we arrive at a prospect pool of approximately 17.9 million book buyers. We would use this number of potential buyers to calculate total market potential.

A variation on this method is the *chain-ratio method*. It involves multiplying a base number by several adjusting percentages. Suppose a brewery is interested in estimating the market potential for a new light beer. An estimate can be made by the following calculation:

Demand for the new light beer = Population × personal discretionary income per capita × average percentage of discretionary income spent on food × average percentage of amount spent on food that is spent on beverages × average percentage of amount spent on beverages that is spent on alcoholic beverages × average percentage of amount spent on alcoholic beverages that is spent on beer × expected percentage of amount spent on beer that will be spent on light beer.

AREA MARKET POTENTIAL Companies face the problem of selecting the best territories and allocating their marketing budget optimally among these territories. Therefore, they need to estimate the market potential of different cities, provinces, regions, and nations. Two major methods of assessing area market potential are available: the market-buildup method, which is used primarily by business marketers, and the multiple-factor index method, which is used primarily by consumer marketers.

Market-Buildup Method   The **market-buildup method** calls for identifying all the potential buyers in each market and estimating their potential purchases. This method produces accurate results if we have a list of all potential buyers and a good estimate of what each will buy. Unfortunately, this information is not always easy to gather.

Consider a machine-tool company that wants to estimate the area market potential for its wood lathe in the Montreal area. Its first step is to identify all potential buyers of wood lathes in the area. The buyers consist primarily of manufacturing establishments that have to shape or ream wood as part of their operation, so the company could compile a list from a directory of all manufacturing establishments in the Montreal area. Then it could estimate the number of lathes each industry might purchase based on the number of lathes per thousand employees or per $1 million of sales in that industry.

An efficient method of estimating area market potentials makes use of the *North American Industry Classification System (NAICS)*, developed by the U.S., Canadian, and Mexican governments.[53] The NAICS classifies all manufacturing into 20 major industry sectors. Each sector is further broken into a six-digit, hierarchical structure as follows (illustrated with paging).

51	Industry Sector (Information)
513	Industry Subsector (Broadcasting and telecommunications)
5133	Industry Group (Telecommunications)
51332	Industry (Wireless telecommunications carriers, except satellite)
513321	Industry (Paging) North America

For each six-digit NAICS number, a company can purchase CD-ROMs of business directories that provide complete company profiles of millions of establishments, subclassified by location, number of employees, annual sales, and net worth.

To use the NAICS, the manufacturer of pagers must first determine the six-digit NAICS codes that represent products whose manufacturers are likely to require pagers. To get a full picture of all six-digit NAICS industries that might use pagers, the company can (1) determine past customers' NAICS codes; (2) go through the NAICS manual and check off all the six-digit industries that might have an interest in pagers; (3) mail questionnaires to a wide range of companies inquiring about their interest in pagers.

The company's next task is to determine an appropriate base for estimating the number of pagers that will be used in each industry. Suppose customer industry sales are the most appropriate base. Once the company estimates the rate of pager ownership relative to the customer industry's sales, it can compute the market potential.

Multiple-Factor Index Method Like business marketers, consumer companies also have to estimate area market potentials, but the customers of consumer companies are too numerous to be listed. The method most commonly used in consumer markets is a straightforward index method. A drug manufacturer, for example, might assume that the market potential for drugs is directly related to population size. If the province of British Columbia has 13.04 percent of the Canadian population, the company might assume that B.C. will be a market for 13.04 percent of total drugs sold in Canada.

A single factor, however, is rarely a complete indicator of sales opportunity. Regional drug sales are also influenced by per-capita income and the number of physicians per 10 000 people. Thus it makes sense to develop a multiple-factor index, with each factor assigned a specific weight. The numbers are the weights attached to each variable. For example, suppose B.C. has 12.79 percent of the Canadian disposable personal income, 11.71 percent of Canadian retail sales, and 13.04 percent of Canadian population, and the respective weights are 0.5, 0.3, and 0.2. The buying-power index for B.C. would be 12.52 [= 0.5(12.79) + 0.3(11.71) + 0.2(13.04)]. Thus, 12.52 percent of the nation's drug sales might be expected to take place in B.C.

The weights used in the buying-power index are somewhat arbitrary. Other weights can be assigned if appropriate. Furthermore, a manufacturer would want to adjust the market potential for additional factors, such as competitors' presence in that market, local promotional costs, seasonal factors, and local market idiosyncrasies.

Many companies compute other area indexes as a guide to allocating marketing resources. Suppose the drug company is reviewing the six cities listed in Table 4.10. The first two columns show its percentage of brand and category sales in these six cities. The third column shows the **brand development index (BDI)**, which is the index of brand sales to category sales. Montreal, for example, has a BDI of 114 because the brand is relatively more developed than the category in Montreal. Toronto has a BDI of 65, which means that the brand in Toronto is relatively underdeveloped. Normally, the lower the BDI, the higher the market opportunity, in that there is room to grow the brand. However, other marketers would argue the opposite, that marketing funds should go into the brand's strongest markets—where it might be important to reinforce loyalty or more easily capture additional brand share.[54]

After the company decides on the city-by-city allocation of its budget, it can refine each city allocation down to census tracts or postal-code centres. *Census tracts* are small, locally defined statistical areas in metropolitan areas and some other counties. They generally have stable boundaries and a population of about 4000. Postal-code centres are a little larger than neighbourhoods. Data on population size, median family income, and other characteristics are available for these geographical units. Marketers have found these data extremely useful for identifying high-potential retail areas within large cities and for buying mailing lists to use in direct-mail campaigns (see Chapter 19).

TABLE 4.10	CALCULATING THE BRAND DEVELOPMENT INDEX		
	(a) % of Brand Sales	(b) % of Category Sales	BDI (a ÷ b) × 100
Montreal	3.09	2.71	114
Toronto	6.74	10.41	65
Vancouver	3.49	3.85	91
Halifax	0.97	0.81	120
Winnipeg	1.13	0.81	140
Calgary	3.12	3.00	104

INDUSTRY SALES AND MARKET SHARES   Besides estimating total potential and area potential, a company needs to know the actual industry sales taking place in its market. This means identifying competitors and estimating their sales.

The industry trade association will often collect and publish total industry sales, although it usually does not list individual company sales separately. With this information, each company can evaluate its performance against the whole industry. Suppose a company's sales are increasing by 5 percent a year, and industry sales are increasing by 10 percent. This company is actually losing its relative standing in the industry.

Another way to estimate sales is to buy reports from a marketing-research firm that audits total sales and brand sales. Nielsen Media Research audits retail sales in various product categories in supermarkets and drugstores and sells this information to interested companies. These audits can give a company valuable information about its total product-category sales as well as brand sales. It can compare its performance to the total industry or any particular competitor to see whether it is gaining or losing share.

Business-goods marketers typically have a harder time estimating industry sales and market shares. Business marketers have no Nielsens to rely on. Distributors typically will not supply information about how much of the competitors' products they are selling. Business-goods marketers, therefore, operate with less knowledge of their market-share results.

Estimating Future Demand

Very few products or services lend themselves to easy forecasting; those that do generally involve a product whose absolute level or trend is fairly constant and where competition is nonexistent (public utilities) or stable (pure oligopolies). In most markets, total demand and company demand are not stable. Good forecasting becomes a key factor in company success. The more unstable the demand is, the more critical forecast accuracy is, and the more elaborate forecasting procedure is.

Companies commonly use a three-stage procedure to prepare a sales forecast. They prepare a macroeconomic forecast first, followed by an industry forecast, followed by a company sales forecast. The macroeconomic forecast projects inflation, unemployment, interest rates, consumer spending, business investment, government expenditures, net exports, and other variables. The end result is a forecast of gross national product, which is then used, along with other environmental indicators, to forecast industry sales. The company derives its sales forecast by assuming that it will win a certain market share.

How do firms develop their forecasts? Firms may do it internally or buy forecasts from outside sources such as marketing-research firms, which develop a forecast by interviewing customers, distributors, and other knowledgeable parties. Specialized forecasting firms produce long-range forecasts of particular macroenvironmental components, such as population, natural resources, and technology. Some examples are Global Insight (a merger of Data Resources and Wharton Econometric Forecasting Associates), Forrester Research, and the Gartner Group. The Economic Services Group of the Conference Board of Canada specializes in developing economic and forecasting models for Canadian companies. Canada's banks also perform economic forecasts, many of which are placed online. (For example, see TD Bank's Economic Group forecast at www.td.com/economics.)

The Conference Board of Canada, Economic Services Branch, specializes in developing economic and forecasting models for Canadian companies.

All forecasts are built on one of three information bases: what people say, what people do, or what people have done. The first basis—what people say—involves surveying the opinions of buyers or those close to them, such as salespeople or outside experts. It includes three methods: surveys of buyers' intentions, composites of sales-force opinions, and expert opinion. Building a forecast on what people do involves another method: putting the product into a test market to measure buyer response. The final basis—what people have done—involves analyzing records of past buying behaviour or using time-series analysis or statistical demand analysis.

SURVEY OF BUYERS' INTENTIONS **Forecasting** is the art of anticipating what buyers are likely to do under a given set of conditions. Because buyer behaviour is so important, buyers should be surveyed. For major consumer durables (for example, major appliances), several research organizations conduct periodic surveys of consumer-buying intentions. These organizations ask questions like the following:

Do you intend to buy an automobile within the next six months?

0.00	0.20	0.40	0.60	0.80	1.00
No chance	Slight possibility	Fair possibility	Good possibility	High possibility	Certain

This is called a **purchase probability scale**. The various surveys also inquire into consumers' present and future personal finances and their expectations about the economy. The various bits of information are then combined into a consumer-confidence (Conference Board) or consumer-sentiment measure (Survey Research Center of the University of Michigan). Consumer durable-goods producers subscribe to these indexes in the hope of anticipating major shifts in buying intentions so they can adjust production and marketing plans accordingly.

For business buying, research firms can carry out buyer-intention surveys regarding plants, equipment, and materials. Their estimates tend to fall within a 10-percent error band of the actual outcomes. Buyer-intention surveys are particularly useful in estimating demand for industrial products, consumer durables, product purchases where advanced planning is required, and new products. The value of a buyer-intention survey increases to the extent that the cost of reaching buyers is small, the buyers are few, they have clear intentions, they implement their intentions, and they willingly disclose their intentions.

COMPOSITE OF SALES-FORCE OPINIONS When buyer interviewing is impractical, the company may ask its sales representatives to estimate their future sales. Each sales representative estimates how much each current and prospective customer will buy of each of the company's products.

Few companies use sales-force estimates without making some adjustments. Sales representatives might be pessimistic or optimistic, or they might go from one extreme to another because of a recent setback or success. Furthermore, they are often unaware of larger economic developments and do not know how their company's marketing plans will influence future sales in their territory. They might deliberately underestimate demand so that the company will set a low sales quota, or they might lack the time to prepare careful estimates or might not consider the effort worthwhile. To encourage better estimating, the company could offer certain aids or incentives. For example, sales reps might receive a record of their past forecasts compared with actual sales and also a description of company assumptions on the business outlook, competitor behaviour, and marketing plans.

Involving the sales force in forecasting brings a number of benefits. Sales reps might have better insight into developing trends than any other single group. After participating in the forecasting process, reps might have greater confidence in their sales quotas and more incentive to achieve them. Also, a "grassroots" forecasting procedure provides detailed estimates broken down by product, territory, customer, and sales rep.

EXPERT OPINION Companies can also obtain forecasts from experts, including dealers, distributors, suppliers, marketing consultants, and trade associations. Large appliance companies periodically survey dealers for their forecasts of short-term demand, as do car companies. Dealer estimates are subject to the same strengths and weaknesses as sales-force estimates. Many companies buy economic and industry forecasts from well-known economic-forecasting firms. These specialists are able to prepare better economic forecasts than the company because they have more data available and more forecasting expertise.

Occasionally, companies will invite a group of experts to prepare a forecast. The experts exchange views and produce a group estimate (*group-discussion method*); or the experts supply their estimates individually, and an analyst combines them into a single estimate (*pooling of individual estimates*). Alternatively, the experts supply individual estimates and assumptions that are reviewed by the company, and are then revised. Further rounds of estimating and refining follow (this is the Delphi method).[55]

PAST-SALES ANALYSIS   Sales forecasts can be developed on the basis of past sales. *Time-series analysis* consists of breaking down past time series into four components (trend, cycle, seasonal, and erratic) and projecting these components into the future. *Exponential smoothing* consists of projecting the next period's sales by combining an average of past sales and the most recent sales, giving more weight to the latter. *Statistical demand analysis* consists of measuring the impact of each of a set of causal factors (e.g., income, marketing expenditures, price) on the sales level. Finally, *econometric analysis* consists of building sets of equations that describe a system and proceeding to fit the parameters statistically.

MARKET-TEST METHOD   When buyers do not plan their purchases carefully or experts are not available or reliable, a direct-market test is desirable. A direct-market test is especially desirable in forecasting new-product sales or established-product sales in a new distribution channel or territory. (We discuss market testing in detail in Chapter 20.)

SUMMARY

1. Companies can conduct their own marketing research or hire other companies to do it for them. Good marketing research is characterized by the scientific method, creativity, multiple research methods, accurate model building, cost-benefit analysis, healthy skepticism, and an ethical focus.

2. The marketing-research process consists of defining the problem and research objective, developing the research plan, collecting the information, analyzing the information, presenting the findings to management, and making the decision.

3. In conducting research, firms must decide whether to collect their own data or use data that already exist. They must also decide which research approach (observational, focus-group, survey, behavioural data, or experimental) and which research instruments (questionnaire, qualitative measures, or mechanical devices) to use. In addition, they must decide on a sampling plan and contact methods.

4. Analysis should ensure that the company achieves the sales, profits, and other goals established in its annual plan. The main tools are sales analysis, market-share analysis, marketing expense-to-sales analysis, and financial analysis of the marketing plan.

5. Profitability analysis seeks to measure and control the profitability of various products, territories, customer groups, trade channels, and order sizes. An important part of controlling for profitability is assigning costs and generating profit-and-loss statements.

6. There are two types of demand: market demand and company demand. To estimate current demand, companies attempt to determine total market potential, area market potential, industry sales, and market share. To estimate future demand, companies survey buyers' intentions, solicit their sales-force's input, gather expert opinions, analyze past sales, or engage in market testing. Mathematical models, advanced statistical techniques, and computerized data-collection procedures are essential to all types of demand and sales forecasting.

APPLICATIONS

Marketing Debate: What Is the Best Type of Marketing Research?

Many market researchers have their favourite research approaches or techniques, although different researchers often have different preferences. Some researchers maintain that the only way to really learn about consumers or brands is through in-depth, qualitative research. Others contend that the only legitimate and defensible form of marketing research involves quantitative measures.

Take a position: Marketing research should be quantitative *versus* Marketing research should be qualitative.

Marketing Discussion

When was the last time you participated in a survey? How helpful do you think the information you provided was? How could the research have been done differently to make it more effective?

Breakthrough Marketing: Enquiro Research: "Don't Guess. Know!"

Enquiro Research is a leading search-engine marketing firm based in Kelowna, B.C. Founded in 1999 when the industry of search-engine optimization was still in its infancy, Enquiro has quickly become a recognized leader in the industry and was ranked in *PROFIT* magazine's 2005 list of Canada's Fastest-Growing Companies. From 2002 to 2007, the company has grown nearly 1300 percent and has expanded its client base to include several Fortune 500 companies.

Enquiro's tagline "Don't Guess. Know!" speaks to the philosophy that is at the heart of the company's business: knowing its customers. Enquiro recognizes the key role that research plays in understanding how people use search engines and navigate websites, and the impact that these activities have on buying decisions. According to Enquiro, "[Research] allows us to glimpse inside the mind of the consumer at the time they're interacting with a site, or even using a search engine to get there in the first place—enabling us to improve pages and listings based on the expectations and intent of the user."

The company's research studies and understanding of consumer search habits has enabled Enquiro to help its clients build more effective websites that lead to higher traffic and greater conversion rates. For example, use of Enquiro's search-engine research led to Siemens enjoying a 38-percent increase in referrals it received from search engines. Similarly, Enquiro helped Contiki, a travel tour-operator, increase the click-through rate of its online advertisements by 47 percent in just one month. These are just some of the success stories that Enquiro can boast of. It has helped an array of clients increase the effectiveness of their websites and online advertisements through careful analysis of their customers' online browsing and clicking behaviour.

One of Enquiro's signature services is eye-tracking. It uses a combination of sophisticated equipment and software to intimately study users' behaviour when viewing Web search pages. Enquiro uses a Tobii 1750 eye-tracking monitor and ClearView software to detect where the users focus their attention on a webpage. The eye tracker has no visible or moving devices that might affect the subject, and minimal restrictions to head movement allow viewers to behave naturally, as they would in front of any regular computer screen. The system is linked to software that records and analyzes the eye-tracking data. To facilitate more valuable results, the software combines the collection and analysis of the eye-tracking data with numerous other data sources, including the keyboard (for key strokes), external devices, video recordings, and web-browser activity.

Enquiro researchers conducted a series of focus groups to study user search patterns and identified four types of web searchers, which the researchers labelled Scan and Clickers, Two-Step Scanners, Deliberate Researchers, and "1,2,3 Searchers." On the results page of a Web search-engine (such as Google), Scan and Clickers, who tend to be male, will scan the top three or four listings, ignore sponsored images, click top listings without reading the description, and will never go to the second webpage of the search results. Two-Step Scanners, who also tend to be male, will scan up and down the search-results page, pay attention to sponsored images, and read titles and descriptions more thoroughly during a second scan of the webpage. Deliberate Researchers, split between males and females, read through all the search-results listings on the first page, read both titles and descriptions carefully, check the URLs to make sure they are reliable sites before clicking on them, are quite likely to go the second page of search results, and will rarely go back to the search-results page once they click through to a site. Lastly, the group Enquiro calls 1,2,3 Searchers, who tend to be predominantly female, go through the search results in the order they appear, read titles and descriptions and click an interesting link without looking at the links appearing below it, and will go back to the results page if a site is not satisfactory. Enquiro found that the category of searcher the user belonged to affected the parts of the search-results page seen, the time taken to decide on a site, the types of sites clicked on, and the likelihood of conversion once a prospect visited a site.

DISCUSSION QUESTIONS

1. How can companies utilize the research conducted by companies such as Enquiro to improve their marketing strategies?

2. A typical eye-tracking study by Enquiro costs the client upwards of $10 000. After receiving the results of such a study, how would a company determine whether it was money well spent?

3. Clearly, technology plays a major role in Enquiro's business. Can you foresee any other technological developments in marketing research over the next few years?

Sources: www.enquiroresearch.com; Gord Hotchkiss, "Into the Mind of the Searcher," Enquiro Search Solutions Inc., pp. 26–28; www.enquiro.com/b2b-challenges/Siemens.asp; www.enquiro.com/b2b-challenges/contiki.asp; Kim Shiffman, "PROFIT 100 Overview: The only thing that matters," *PROFIT, 24*(3), June 2005, pp. 28–33.

PART THREE

3

CONNECTING WITH CUSTOMERS

IN THIS CHAPTER, WE WILL ADDRESS THE FOLLOWING QUESTIONS:

- What are customer value, satisfaction, and loyalty, and how can companies deliver them?

- What is the lifetime value of customers?

- How can companies both attract and retain customers?

- How can companies cultivate strong customer relationships?

- How can companies deliver total quality?

- What is database marketing?

CHAPTER 5

CREATING CUSTOMER VALUE, SATISFACTION, AND LOYALTY

five

In a market in which any difference in the quality of gasoline is barely noticeable, would you drive three kilometres to fill up at your favourite gas station? If you do, chances are it has to do with more than just price, according to a study conducted by the University of California. With fuel prices continuously rising and competition becoming intense, gas distributors across Canada are making every effort to retain their customers. To remain competitive and to prevent consumers from switching suppliers in such a highly competitive market, gas distributors must create a unique program that will build customer loyalty to their brand. Prices are relatively comparable within each geographic area; therefore, it is important for a brand of gasoline to have a loyalty program that is attractive and provides added value to its consumers.

Petro-Canada recognized that building long-term customer relationships is the way to create a sustainable competitive advantage in the cutthroat industry of fuel and convenience retailing. Petro-Canada's loyalty program has similarities with programs offered by other brands of gasoline, which include discounts at the pump, partnerships with credit-card companies, quick-payment options, and points programs. However, Petro-Canada has taken its loyalty program further by offering additional benefits that create more value for customers.

Besides having a points program, Petro-Canada has partnered with several other organizations such as Sears, Amazon.ca, and Cathay Pacific to make it even easier to accumulate points and to increase the variety of products and services available to customers. Petro-Canada card members who also have a Sears card can transfer points toward purchases at either business. This relationship gives consumers incentive to collect points in an effort to grow their accounts towards a larger purchase. In addition, Petro-Canada recently announced a partnership with itravel2000, one of Canada's major online travel retailers, to offer its members points when they purchase vacation packages, cruises, flights, hotels, and other travel services. "Members can now earn Petro-Points faster and put them towards purchases with itravel2000, a company known for providing Canadians with great selection, value and customer service," says Phil Churton, Vice-President of Marketing at Petro-Canada. Another unique aspect of the Petro-Points program is its partnership with the Canadian Cancer Society, which allows customers to donate points to the Canadian Cancer Society. Through this partnership, Petro-Points members have donated 282 million points to the cause over the past six years.

Petro-Canada recognizes that consumers often form brand loyalties early in life. To build loyalty among younger consumers, Petro-Canada allows minors to hold Petro-Points cards with a guardian's consent. The hope is that establishing a relationship with younger Canadians will result in brand loyalty further down the road.

Although it may take quite some time to accumulate enough points for a big-ticket purchase, most consumers purchase gas regularly enough for it to be worth being loyal to a particular brand of gas station. Petro-Canada's loyalty program is one of many techniques used to build customer loyalty in such a competitive industry. As the actual gas itself is almost the same from one gas station to another, a well-established loyalty program can help build sales and retain customers. As long as there are automobiles on the road, Petro-Canada needs to ensure its loyalty program is among the best, because as gas prices increase, consumers will be shopping around for the supplier that offers the best value for their money.

Other brands such as Shell, Esso, and Husky are strong competitors in the Canadian gasoline-distribution market and have loyalty programs of their own. Thus, it is easy to see why a loyalty program needs to be tailored to consumer needs and lifestyles to be successful. Petro-Canada's loyalty program has evolved to encompass a wide range of benefits, allowing consumers to build and redeem points in a way that best suits their lifestyle. Petro-Canada's Petro-Points program, launched in 1995, now boasts 8 million members, with 95 percent of enrollments occurring on-site. Thanks to the loyalty program, Petro-Canada now averages 800 000 transactions a day.

Sources: Market Wire, "Earn Petro-Points with itravel2000," http://retail.petro-canada.ca/en/petropoints/174.aspx, February 26, 2008 (viewed May 17, 2008); Petro-Canada, "Let's Make Cancer History," http://retail.petro-canada.ca/en/petropoints/174.aspx, (viewed May 20, 2008); Petro-Canada Terms and Conditions, http://retail.petro-canada.ca/en/independent/636.aspx, (viewed May 14, 2008); "Gas up—and start packing," *National Post*, April 10, 2008; Sharon Adams, "Oil and Gas Programs Fuel Loyalty," *Calgary Herald*, September 21, 2007; Jennifer R. Thompson, "Brand Loyalty and Gasoline Pricing in Sacramento," Giannini Foundation of Agricultural Economics, University of California, August 2007, pp. 9–11.

Today, companies face their toughest competition ever. Moving from a product and sales philosophy to a marketing philosophy, however, gives a company a better chance of outperforming its competition. And the cornerstone of a well-conceived marketing orientation is strong customer relationships. Marketers must connect with customers—informing, engaging, and maybe even energizing them in the process. John Chambers, CEO of Cisco Systems, put it well: "Make your customer the centre of your culture." Customer-centred companies are adept at building customers, not just products; they are skilled in market engineering, not just product engineering.

As the Petro-Canada experience shows, successful marketers are those that deliver value to their customers. In this chapter, we spell out in detail how companies can go about winning customers and beating competitors. The answer lies largely in doing a better job of meeting or exceeding customer expectations.

BUILDING CUSTOMER VALUE, SATISFACTION, AND LOYALTY

Managers who believe the customer is the company's only true "profit centre" consider the traditional organization chart in Figure 5.1(a)—a pyramid with the president at the top, management in the middle, and front-line people and customers at the bottom—obsolete. Successful marketing companies invert the chart (Figure 5.1b). At the top are customers; next in importance are front-line people who meet, serve, and satisfy customers; under them are the middle managers, whose job is to support the front-line people so they can serve customers well; and at the base is top management, whose job is to hire and support good middle managers. We have added customers along the sides of Figure 5.1(b) to indicate that managers at every level must be personally involved in knowing, meeting, and serving customers.

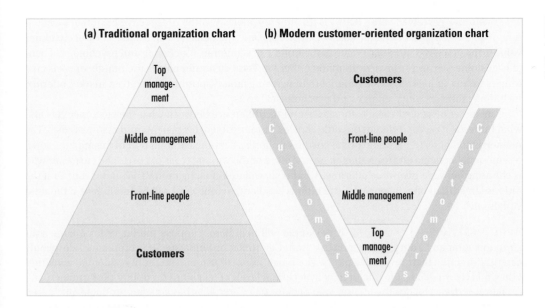

FIGURE 5.1

Traditional Organization versus Modern Customer-Oriented Organization

Some companies have been founded with the customer-on-top business model and have had customer advocacy as their strategy—and competitive advantage—all along. Online auction giant eBay Inc. epitomizes this New World Order:

eBay

At the end of March 2008, eBay's website boasted that it serves nearly 84 million active users in 39 countries, that it helps people sell goods in more than 50 000 categories, and that each and every day it hosts 115 million auctions worldwide, with over 6.9 million listings added per day. In fact, eBay sells US$2040 worth of goods on the site every second! Consumer trust is the key element of eBay's success, enabling the company to support commerce among millions of anonymous buyers and sellers. To establish trust, eBay tracks and publishes the reputations of both buyers and sellers on the basis of feedback from each transaction, and eBay's millions of passionate users have come to demand a voice in all major decisions the company makes. To date, eBay users have left over 7 billion feedback comments for one another regarding their transactions.[1]

Listening, adapting, and enabling are what eBay sees as its main roles. This is clear in one of eBay's most cherished institutions: the Voice of the Customer program. Every few months, eBay brings in as many as a dozen sellers and buyers and asks them questions about how they work and what else eBay needs to do. At least twice a week the company holds hour-long teleconferences to poll users on almost every new feature or policy. The result is that users (eBay's customers) feel like owners, and they have taken the initiative to expand the company into ever-new territory.[2]

With the rise of digital technologies like the Internet, today's increasingly informed consumers expect companies to do more than connect with them, more than satisfy them, and even more than delight them. For instance, customers now have a quick and easy means of doing comparison-shopping through sites like BizRate.com, Shopping.com, and Pricegrabber.com. The Internet also facilitates communication among customers. Websites like Epinions.com and Amazon.ca enable customers to share information about their experiences using various products and services.

Customer Perceived Value

Consumers are more educated and informed than ever, and they have the tools to verify companies' claims and seek out superior alternatives.[3] How, then, do they ultimately make choices? Customers tend to be value-maximizers, within the bounds of search costs and limited knowledge, mobility, and income. Customers estimate which offer will deliver the most perceived value and act on it (Figure 5.2). Whether or not the offer lives up to expectation affects customer satisfaction and the probability that the customer will purchase the product again.

FIGURE 5.2

Determinants of Customer-Delivered Value

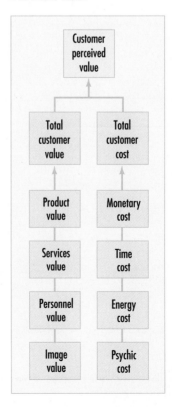

Customer perceived value (CPV) is the difference between the prospective customer's evaluation of all the benefits and all the costs of an offering and the perceived alternatives. **Total customer value** is the perceived monetary value of the bundle of economic, functional, and psychological benefits customers expect from a given market offering. **Total customer cost** is the bundle of costs customers expect to incur in evaluating, obtaining, using, and disposing of the given market offering, including monetary, time, energy, and psychological costs.

Customer perceived value is thus based on the difference between what the customer gets and what he or she gives for different possible choices. The customer gets benefits and assumes costs. The marketer can increase the value of the customer offering by some combination of raising functional or emotional benefits and/or reducing one or more of the various types of costs. The customer who is choosing between two value offerings, V1 and V2, will examine the ratio V1:V2 and favour V1 if the ratio is larger than one, favour V2 if the ratio is smaller than one, and will be indifferent if the ratio equals one.

APPLYING VALUE CONCEPTS An example will help here. Suppose the buyer for a large construction company wants to buy a tractor from Caterpillar or Komatsu. The competing salespeople carefully describe their respective offers. The buyer wants to use the tractor in residential construction work. He would like the tractor to deliver certain levels of reliability, durability, performance, and resale value. He evaluates the tractors and decides that Caterpillar has a higher product value based on perceptions of those attributes. He also perceives differences in the accompanying services—delivery, training, and maintenance—and decides that Caterpillar provides better service and more knowledgeable and responsive personnel. Finally, he places higher value on Caterpillar's corporate image. He adds up all the values from these four sources—product, services, personnel, and image—and perceives Caterpillar as delivering greater customer value.

Does he buy the Caterpillar tractor? Not necessarily. He also examines his total cost of transacting with Caterpillar versus Komatsu, which consists of more than the money. As Adam Smith observed over two centuries ago, "The real price of anything is the toil and trouble of acquiring it." Total customer cost includes the buyer's time, energy, and psychological costs. The buyer evaluates these elements together with the monetary cost to form a total customer cost. Then the buyer considers whether Caterpillar's total customer cost is too high in relation to the total customer value Caterpillar delivers. If it is, the buyer might choose the Komatsu tractor. The buyer will choose whichever source he thinks delivers the highest perceived customer value.

Now let us use this decision-making theory to help Caterpillar succeed in selling to this buyer. Caterpillar can improve its offer in three ways. First, it can increase total customer value by improving product, services, personnel, and/or image benefits. Second, it can reduce the buyer's nonmonetary costs by reducing the time, energy, and psychological costs. Third, it can reduce its product's monetary cost to the buyer.

Suppose Caterpillar concludes that the buyer sees its offer as worth $20 000. Further, suppose Caterpillar's cost of producing the tractor is $14 000. This means that Caterpillar's offer potentially generates $6 000 over the company's cost, so Caterpillar needs to charge a price between $14 000 and $20 000. If it charges less than $14 000, it won't cover its costs; if it charges more than $20 000, it will price itself out of the market.

The price Caterpillar charges will determine how much value will be delivered to the buyer and how much will flow to Caterpillar. For example, if Caterpillar charges $19 000, it is creating $1 000 of customer perceived value and keeping $5 000 for itself. The lower Caterpillar sets its price, the higher the customer perceived value and, therefore, the higher the customer's incentive to purchase. To win the sale, Caterpillar must offer more customer perceived value than Komatsu does.[4]

CHOICES AND IMPLICATIONS Some marketers might argue that the process we have described is too rational. Suppose the customer chose the Komatsu tractor. How can we explain this choice? Here are three possibilities:

1. *The buyer might be under orders to buy at the lowest price.* The Caterpillar salesperson's task is to convince the buyer's manager that buying on price alone will result in lower long-term profits.

2. *The buyer will retire before the company realizes that the Komatsu tractor is more expensive to operate.* The buyer will look good in the short run; he is maximizing personal benefit. The Caterpillar salesperson's task is to convince other people in the customer's company that Caterpillar delivers greater customer value.

3. *The buyer enjoys a long-term friendship with the Komatsu salesperson.* In this case, Caterpillar's salesperson needs to show the buyer that the Komatsu tractor will draw complaints from the tractor operators when they discover its high fuel cost and need for frequent repairs.

The point of these examples is clear: Buyers operate under various constraints and occasionally make choices that give more weight to their personal benefit than to the company's benefit.

Customer perceived value is a useful framework that applies to many situations and yields rich insights. Here are its implications: First, the seller must assess the total customer value and total customer cost associated with each competitor's offer in order to know how his or her offer rates in the buyer's mind. Second, the seller who is at a customer-perceived value disadvantage has two alternatives: increase total customer value or decrease total customer cost. The former calls for strengthening or augmenting the offer's product, services, personnel, and image benefits. The latter calls for reducing the buyer's costs by reducing the price, simplifying the ordering and delivery process, or absorbing some buyer risk by offering a warranty.[5]

DELIVERING HIGH CUSTOMER VALUE Consumers have varying degrees of loyalty to specific brands, stores, and companies. Oliver defines **loyalty** as "A deeply held commitment to re-buy or re-patronize a preferred product or service in the future despite situational influences and marketing efforts having the potential to cause switching behaviour."[6]

The key to generating high customer loyalty is to deliver high customer value. According to Michael Lanning, in his *Delivering Profitable Value*, a company must design a competitively superior value proposition aimed at a specific market segment, backed by a superior value-delivery system.[7]

The **value proposition** consists of the whole cluster of benefits the company promises to deliver; it is more than the core positioning of the offering. For example, Volvo's core positioning has been "safety," but the buyer is promised more than just a safe car; other benefits include a long-lasting car, good service, and a long warranty period. Basically, the value proposition is a statement about the experience customers will gain from the company's market offering and from their relationship with the supplier. The brand must represent a promise about the total experience customers can expect. Whether the promise is kept depends on the company's ability to manage its value-delivery system. The **value-delivery system** includes all the experiences the customer will have along the way to obtaining and using the offering. British Airways knows this all too well.

British Airways

British Airways and American Airlines may use the same kind of aircraft to fly executives first-class between New York and London, but British Airways (BA) beats American Airlines by meeting customers' needs for convenience and rest at every step of the journey. BA's value-delivery system includes separate first-class express check-in and security clearance, and a pre-flight express meal service in the first-class lounge so that time-pressed executives can maximize sleep time on the plane without the distraction of in-flight meals. BA was the first to install in its first-class section seats that recline into perfectly flat beds, and in the United Kingdom a fast-track customs area speeds busy executives on their way.[8]

A similar theme is emphasized by Simon Knox and Stan Maklan in their *Competing on Value.*[9] Too many companies create a value gap by failing to align brand value with customer value. Brand marketers try to distinguish their brand from others with a slogan ("washes whiter") or a unique selling proposition ("A Mars a day helps you work, rest, and play"), or by augmenting the basic offering with added services ("Our hotel will provide a computer upon request"). Yet, they are less successful in delivering distinctive customer value, primarily because their marketing people focus on the brand image and not enough on actual product or service performance. Whether customers will actually receive the promised value proposition will depend on the marketer's ability to influence various core business processes. Knox and Maklan want company marketers to spend as much time influencing the company's core processes as they do designing the brand profile. Here is an example of a company that is a master at delivering customer value.

WestJet

In the competitive industry of air travel, WestJet has employed various techniques to improve customer service and gain an edge over its competitors. WestJet was the first North American airline to launch electronic check-in on a user-friendly website where passengers can choose a seat and print their own boarding pass from home. Besides offering low fares to popular destinations, WestJet also has one of the newest fleets of airplanes with increased legroom, leather seats, and seat-back satellite television. While most North American airlines allow on domestic flights only one piece of checked baggage weighing 23 kilograms, WestJet permits two pieces weighing 27 kilograms each. The new WestJet slogan "Why do WestJetters care so much? Because we're also WestJet owners" exemplifies its commitment to delivering value to its customers. Over 80 percent of WestJet employees have an ownership stake in the company, giving the staff added incentive to make the customer experience that much more enjoyable.[10]

Total Customer Satisfaction

Whether the buyer is satisfied after purchase depends on the offer's performance in relation to the buyer's expectations. In general, **satisfaction** is a person's feelings of pleasure or disappointment resulting from comparing a product's perceived performance (or outcome) to his or her expectations. If the performance falls short of expectations, the customer is dissatisfied. If the performance matches the expectations, the customer is satisfied. If the performance exceeds expectations, the customer is highly satisfied or delighted.[11]

Although the customer-centred firm seeks to create high customer satisfaction, that is not its ultimate goal. If the company increases customer satisfaction by lowering its price or increasing its services, the result may be lower profits. The company might be able to increase its profitability by means other than increased satisfaction (for example, by improving manufacturing processes or investing more in R&D). Also, the company has many stakeholders, including employees, dealers, suppliers, and shareholders. Spending more to increase customer satisfaction might divert funds from increasing the satisfaction of other "partners." Ultimately, the company must divide its total resources such that it is able to deliver a high level of customer satisfaction while also delivering acceptable levels of satisfaction to the other stakeholders.

CUSTOMER EXPECTATIONS How do buyers form their expectations? From past buying experience, friends' and associates' advice, and marketers' and competitors' information and promises. If marketers raise expectations too high, the buyer is likely to be disappointed. However, if the company sets expectations too low, it won't attract enough buyers (although it will satisfy those who do buy).[12] Some of today's most successful companies are raising expectations and delivering performances to match. When General Motors launched the Saturn car division, it changed the whole buyer–seller relationship with a new deal for car buyers: There would be a fixed price (none of the traditional haggling); a 30-day guarantee or money back; and salespeople on salary, not on commission (none of the traditional hard sell).[13] Look at what high satisfaction can do:

Enterprise Rent-A-Car

Enterprise Rent-A-Car has significantly raised expectations of what a discount vehicle-rental service should do for customers. Enterprise is committed to strong customer service and creating added value for its customers. It is no wonder that J.D. Power and Associates and

Saturn has redefined the otherwise stressful car-shopping experience—no haggling over price, a 30-day money-back guarantee, and friendly salespeople on salary, not commission.

Market Metrix have repeatedly ranked Enterprise Rent-A-Car number one in customer satisfaction in the car-rental industry. Enterprise is now the largest vehicle-rental company in North America, with earnings over US$9.5 billion in 2007. To measure customer satisfaction, Enterprise created the Enterprise Service Quality index (ESQi), for which branches across the country call hundreds of thousands of customers every month to see if they were completely satisfied. In an effort to improve customer satisfaction, Enterprise goes the extra mile. For example, Enterprise will pick up customers at their homes and drive them to the nearest Enterprise location at no extra cost, hence the slogan "We'll pick you up." Enterprise encourages employees to go beyond their job description to get the whole job done right. Management even helps wash cars that are about to be rented out to help further satisfy customers. This team spirit is reflected in what Enterprise states on its website: "We are an extended family of more than 65 000 . . . But our goal has never been to be the biggest; we simply work hard to be the best."[14]

A customer's decision to be loyal or to defect is the sum of many small encounters with the company. Consulting firm Forum Corporation says that in order for all these small encounters to add up to customer loyalty, companies need to create a "branded customer experience." See what TD Canada Trust did to ensure ongoing customer satisfaction during one of the largest mergers in Canadian banking history:

TD Canada Trust

Mergers between two firms often drive customer satisfaction ratings to an all-time low. In fact, research has shown that during bank mergers, customers often flee at rates as high as 10 percent, since neither bank's customers like the products or services offered by the new entity. No one would have been surprised if this occurred in 2001 when Toronto Dominion Bank (TD) acquired Canada Trust—the big surprise was that customers did not make tracks!

Canada Trust was known for its high levels of customer service, while TD was valued for its extensive product offerings. To do the impossible and retain customers, TD Canada Trust knew it had to keep the best parts of both companies. Instead of beginning by marketing its new brand identity, TD Canada Trust started with an internal marketing campaign. "Our driving philosophy has always been, 'What does the customer want?' This knowledge is then translated into building favourable customer experiences," says Chuck Hounsell, senior VP, e-bank, TD Canada Trust. Each of the 1 300 branches and the 19 000 employees received information packages outlining the conversion and stressing the need to make customers feel that they belonged in the new entity. The employee-evaluation process was also changed to reward the creation of customer satisfaction. As one executive noted, "Employee marketing is where it starts." Continuous measurement was another key to success. Each and every day, the bank called 1 000 customers to inquire about their experience with the bank that day.

The efforts certainly paid off. Not only did TD Canada Trust gain market share, it ranked number one in customer satisfaction according to the annual survey conducted by Toronto's Market Facts.[15]

Measuring Satisfaction

Many companies are systematically measuring customer satisfaction and the factors shaping it. For example, IBM tracks how satisfied customers are with each IBM salesperson they encounter, and makes this a factor in each salesperson's compensation.

A company would be wise to measure customer satisfaction regularly because one key to customer retention is customer satisfaction. A highly satisfied customer generally stays loyal longer, buys more as the company introduces new products and upgrades existing products, talks favourably about the company and its products, pays less attention to competing brands and is less sensitive to price, offers product or service ideas to the company, and costs less to serve than new customers because transactions are routine.

The link between customer satisfaction and customer loyalty, however, is not proportional. Suppose customer satisfaction is rated on a scale from one to five. At a very low level of customer satisfaction (level one), customers are likely to abandon the company and even bad-mouth it. At levels two to four, customers are fairly satisfied but still find it easy to switch when a better offer comes along. At level five, the customer is very likely to repurchase and even spread good word-of-mouth about the company. High satisfaction or delight creates an emotional bond with the brand or company, not just a rational preference. Xerox's senior management found out that its "completely satisfied" customers are six times more likely to repurchase Xerox products over the following 18 months than its "very satisfied" customers.[16]

When customers rate their satisfaction with an element of the company's performance—say, delivery—the company needs to recognize that customers vary in how they define good delivery. It could mean early delivery, on-time delivery, order completeness, and so on. The company must also realize that two customers can report being "highly satisfied" for different reasons. One may be easily satisfied most of the time and the other might be hard to please but was pleased on this occasion.[17]

A number of methods exist to measure customer satisfaction. *Periodic surveys* can track customer satisfaction directly. Respondents can also be asked additional questions to measure repurchase intention and the likelihood or willingness to recommend the company and brand to others. Paramount attributes the success of its five theme parks to the thousands of web-based guest surveys it sends to customers who have agreed to be contacted. In 2003, the company conducted more than 55 web-based surveys and netted 100 000 individual responses that described guest satisfaction on topics including rides, dining, shopping, games, and shows.[18]

Companies can monitor the *customer loss rate* and contact customers who have stopped buying or who have switched to another supplier to learn why this happened. Finally, companies can hire *mystery shoppers* to pose as potential buyers and report on strong and weak points experienced in buying the company's and competitors' products. Managers themselves can enter company and competitor sales situations where they are unknown and experience firsthand the treatment they receive, or phone their own company with questions and complaints to see how the calls are handled.

For customer-satisfaction surveys, it's important that companies ask the right questions. Frederick Reichheld suggests that perhaps only one question really matters: "Would you recommend this product or service to a friend?" He maintains that marketing departments typically focus surveys on the areas they can control, such as brand image, pricing, and product features. According to

During its 2001 merger, TD Canada Trust did the impossible—it kept customer satisfaction high.

Reichheld, a customer's willingness to recommend to a friend results from how well the customer is treated by front-line employees, which in turn is determined by all the functional areas that contribute to a customer's experience.[19]

In addition to tracking customer-value expectations and satisfaction, companies need to monitor their competitors' performance in these areas. One company was pleased to find that 80 percent of its customers said they were satisfied. Then the CEO found out that its leading competitor had a 90-percent customer-satisfaction score. He was further dismayed when he learned that this competitor was aiming for a 95-percent satisfaction score.

For customer-centred companies, customer satisfaction is both a goal and a marketing tool. Companies need to be especially concerned today with their customer-satisfaction level because the Internet provides a tool for consumers to spread bad word-of-mouth—as well as good word-of-mouth—to the rest of the world. On websites like troublebenz.com and lemonmb.com, angry Mercedes-Benz owners have been airing their complaints about everything from faulty key fobs and leaky sunroofs to balky electronics that leave drivers and their passengers stranded.[20]

Companies that do achieve high customer-satisfaction ratings make sure their target market knows it. When J. D. Power began to rate national home-mortgage leaders, Countrywide was quick to advertise its number-one ranking in customer satisfaction. Dell Computer's meteoric growth in the computer-systems industry can be partly attributed to achieving and advertising its number-one rank in customer satisfaction.

A survey conducted by *Canadian Business* magazine found that some of the best and worst customer-satisfaction levels were found within the same industries, illustrating just how effective customer satisfaction can be as tool for differentiating against competitors. In financial services, credit unions were found to have 82-percent satisfaction, while the range of satisfaction for the big five banks was between 38 and 47 percent. The biggest gap was in the Canadian airline industry, where Air Canada fetched a rating of 16-percent satisfaction (the lowest in the survey, scoring even lower than the Canada Revenue Agency), while WestJet came in at 89 percent (the highest rating in the survey).[21]

Product and Service Quality

Satisfaction will also depend on product and service quality. What exactly is quality? Various experts have defined it as "fitness for use," "conformance to requirements," "freedom from variation," and so on.[22] We will use the American Society for Quality Control's definition: **Quality** is the totality of features and characteristics of a product or service that bear on its ability to satisfy stated or implied needs.[23] This is clearly a customer-centred definition. We can say that the seller has delivered quality whenever the seller's product or service meets or exceeds the customers' expectations. A company that satisfies most of its customers' needs most of the time is called a quality company, but it is important to distinguish between *conformance* quality and *performance* quality (or grade). A Lexus provides

"HIGHEST IN CUSTOMER SATISFACTION WITH INTERIOR PAINTS" FROM J.D. POWER AND ASSOCIATES.

J.D. Power's customer-satisfaction ratings make powerful advertising copy for customer-centred firms.

higher performance quality than a Hyundai: the Lexus rides more smoothly, goes faster, and lasts longer. Yet both a Lexus and a Hyundai can be said to deliver the same conformance quality if all the units are built to their design specifications (i.e., they produce the horsepower the engineers specified for the car, they consume the stated amount of fuel per 100 kilometres, etc.).

Total quality is the key to value creation and customer satisfaction and, as such, is the responsibility of every functional department in an organization. This idea was expressed well by Daniel Beckham:

> Marketers who don't learn the language of quality improvement, manufacturing, and operations will become as obsolete as buggy whips. The days of functional marketing are gone. We can no longer afford to think of ourselves as market researchers, advertising people, direct marketers, strategists—we have to think of ourselves as customer satisfiers—customer advocates focused on whole processes.[24]

Marketing managers have two responsibilities in a quality-centred company. First, they must participate in formulating strategies and policies to help the company win through total quality excellence. Second, they must deliver marketing quality alongside production quality. Each marketing activity—marketing research, sales training, advertising, customer service, and so on—must be performed to high standards.

Total Quality Management

The quest to maximize customer satisfaction led some firms to adopt principles of total quality management. **Total quality management (TQM)** is an organization-wide approach to continuously improving the quality of all the organization's processes, products, and services.

According to GE's former chairman, John F. Welch Jr., "Quality is our best assurance of customer allegiance, our strongest defense against foreign competition, and the only path to sustained growth and earnings."[25] The drive in world markets to produce superior goods has led some countries—and groups of countries—to recognize or award prizes (e.g., the Deming Prize in Japan, the Malcolm Baldrige National Quality Award in the United States, the European Quality Award, and the K. C. Irving Quality Award in Canada) to companies that exemplify the best quality practices.

Product and service quality, customer satisfaction, and company profitability are intimately connected. Higher levels of quality result in higher levels of customer satisfaction, which support higher prices and (often) lower costs. Studies have shown a high correlation between relative product quality and company profitability.[26]

In practising TQM, however, some firms ran into implementation problems as they became overly focused—perhaps even obsessed—with processes and *how* they were doing business. They lost sight of the needs and wants of customers and *why* they were doing business. In some cases, companies were able to achieve benchmarks against top quality standards, but only by incurring prohibitive increases in costs. For example, scientific-equipment maker Varian embraced TQM principles but found itself so rushed to meet production schedules and deadlines that managers now feel it may not have been that important to their customers to begin with.

In a reaction to this somewhat myopic behaviour, some companies now concentrate their efforts on "return on quality" or ROQ. ROQ adherents advocate improving quality only on those dimensions that produce tangible customer benefits, lower costs, or increased sales. This bottom-line orientation forces companies to make sure that the quality of the product offerings is in fact the quality consumers actually want.[27]

Rust, Moorman, and Dickson studied managers seeking to increase their financial returns from quality improvements.[28] They found that firms that adopted primarily a revenue-expansion emphasis (externally focusing on growing demand through catering to and increasing consumers' preferences for quality) performed better than firms that adopted primarily a cost-reduction emphasis (internally focusing on improving the efficiency of internal processes) or firms that attempted to adopt both emphases simultaneously.

Marketers play several roles in helping their companies define and deliver high-quality goods and services to target customers. First, they bear the major responsibility for correctly identifying the customers' needs and requirements. Second, they must communicate customer expectations properly to product designers. Third, they must make sure that customers' orders are filled correctly and on time. Fourth, they must check that customers have received proper instructions, training, and technical assistance in the use of the product. Fifth, they must stay in touch with customers after the sale to ensure that they are satisfied and remain satisfied. Sixth, they must gather customer ideas for product and service improvements and convey them to the appropriate departments. When marketers do all this, they are making substantial contributions to total quality management and customer satisfaction, as well as to customer and company profitability.

MAXIMIZING CUSTOMER LIFETIME VALUE

Ultimately, marketing is the art of attracting and keeping profitable customers. According to James V. Putten of American Express, the best customers outspend others by ratios of 16 to 1 in retailing, 13 to 1 in the restaurant business, 12 to 1 in the airline business, and 5 to 1 in the hotel and motel industry.[29] Yet every company loses money on some of its customers. The well-known 20–80 rule says that the top 20 percent of the customers may generate as much as 80 percent of the company's profits. Sherden suggested amending the rule to read 20–80–30, to reflect the idea that the top 20 percent of customers generate 80 percent of the company's profits, half of which are lost serving the bottom 30 percent of unprofitable customers.[30] The implication is that a company could improve its profits by "firing" its worst customers.

Furthermore, it is not necessarily the company's largest customers who yield the most profit. The largest customers demand considerable service and receive the deepest discounts. The smallest customers pay full price and receive minimal service, but the costs of transacting with small customers reduce their profitability. The midsized customers receive good service and pay nearly full price and are often the most profitable. This fact helps explain why many large firms are now invading the middle market. Major air-express carriers, for instance, are finding that it does not pay to ignore small and midsized international shippers. Programs geared towards smaller customers provide a network of drop boxes, which allow for substantial discounts over letters and packages picked up at the shipper's place of business. United Parcel Service (UPS) conducts seminars to instruct exporters in the finer points of shipping overseas.[31]

Customer Profitability

What makes a customer profitable? A **profitable customer** is a person, household, or company that over time yields a revenue stream that exceeds by an acceptable amount the company's cost stream for attracting, selling, and serving that customer. Note that the emphasis is on the lifetime stream of revenue and cost, not on the profit from a particular transaction.[32] Customer profitability can be assessed individually, by market segment, or by channel.

Although many companies measure customer satisfaction, most companies fail to measure individual-customer profitability. Banks claim that this is a difficult task because a customer uses different banking services and the transactions are logged in different departments. However, banks that have succeeded in linking customer transactions have been appalled by the number of unprofitable customers in their customer base. Some banks report losing money on over 45 percent of their retail customers. There are only two solutions to handling unprofitable customers: raise fees or reduce service support.[33]

CUSTOMER-PROFITABILITY ANALYSIS A useful type of profitability analysis is shown in Figure 5.3. Customers are arrayed along the columns and products along the rows. Each cell contains a symbol for the profitability of selling that product to that customer. Customer 1 is very profitable; he buys three profit-making products (P_1, P_2, and P_4). Customer 2 yields a picture of mixed profitability; she buys one profitable product and one unprofitable product. Customer 3 is a losing customer because he buys one profitable product and two unprofitable products.

What can the company do about customers 2 and 3? (1) It can raise the price of its less-profitable products or eliminate them, or (2) it can try to sell customers 2 and 3 its profit-making products. Unprofitable customers who defect should not concern the company. In fact, the company should encourage these customers to switch to competitors.

FIGURE 5.3

Customer–Product Profitability
Analysis

Sources: Thomas M. Petro,
"Profitability: The Fifth 'P' of
Marketing," *Bank Marketing*
(September 1990): 48–52; "Who
Are Your Best Customers?" *Bank
Marketing* (October 1990): 48–52.

	Customers			
	C_1	C_2	C_3	
P_1	+	+	+	Highly profitable product
P_2	+			Profitable product
P_3		−	−	Losing product
P_4	+		−	Mixed-bag product
Products	High-profit customer	Mixed-bag customer	Losing customer	

Customer-profitability analysis (CPA) is best conducted with an accounting technique called activity-based costing (ABC). The company estimates all revenue coming from the customer, less all costs. The costs should include not only the cost of making and distributing the goods and services, but also such costs as taking phone calls from the customer, travelling to visit the customer, entertainment, and gifts—all the company's resources that went into serving that customer. When this is done for each customer, it is possible to classify customers into different profit tiers: platinum customers (most profitable), gold customers (profitable), iron customers (low profitability but desirable), and lead customers (unprofitable and undesirable).

The company's job is to move iron customers into the gold tier and gold customers into the platinum tier, while dropping the lead customers or making them profitable by raising their prices or lowering the cost of serving them. More generally, marketers must segment customers into those worth pursuing versus those potentially less-lucrative customers who should receive less attention, if any at all. See how Royal Bank segments its customers to serve them better:

RBC Investments

Ultimately, "what we want to understand is what value propositions make sense to which customers," says Jay Slade, manager of client intelligence and analysis at RBC Investments in Toronto. RBC has discovered through customer-profitability analysis that some clients are very experienced investors and therefore do not require an advisor. While it would make sense for these customers to be using RBC's self-directed brokerage, that is not always the case. RBC has found through dissecting its customer information that its clients are not always aligned with the appropriate products and services. To protect the long-term retention and lifetime profitability of its clients, it sometimes makes sense to tell a customer he or she is not using the right service, even if that service generates more revenue in the short term. According to Slade, RBC's return on investment from this kind of customer analysis has been "in the millions of dollars—probably the tens of millions."[34]

Dhar and Glazer make an interesting analogy between the individuals who make up the firm's customer portfolio and the stocks that make up an investment portfolio.[35] Just as with the latter, it is important to calculate the beta, or risk–reward value, of each customer and diversify the customer portfolio accordingly. Firms should assemble portfolios of negatively correlated individuals so that the financial contributions of one offset the deficits of another to maximize the portfolio's risk-adjusted lifetime value.

COMPETITIVE ADVANTAGE Companies must be able to create not only high absolute value, but also high value relative to competitors at a sufficiently low cost. **Competitive advantage** is a company's ability to perform in one or more ways that competitors cannot or will not match. Michael Porter urged companies to build a sustainable competitive advantage.[36] But few competitive advantages are sustainable. At best, they may be leverageable. A *leverageable advantage* is one that a company can use as a springboard to new advantages, much as Microsoft has leveraged its operating system to Microsoft Office and then to networking applications. In general, a company that hopes to endure must be in the business of continuously inventing new advantages.

Any competitive advantage must be seen by customers as a *customer advantage*. For example, if a company delivers faster than its competitors, this will not be a customer advantage if customers do not value speed. Companies must focus on building customer advantages. Then they will deliver high customer value and satisfaction, which leads to high repeat purchases and ultimately to high company profitability.

Measuring Customer Lifetime Value

The case for maximizing long-term customer profitability is captured in the concept of customer lifetime value. **Customer lifetime value (CLV)** describes the net present value of the stream of future profits expected over the customer's lifetime purchases. The company must subtract from the expected revenues the expected costs of attracting, selling, and serving that customer, and apply the appropriate discount rate (e.g., 10–20 percent, depending on cost of capital and risk attitudes). Various CLV estimates have been made for different products and services:

- Carl Sewell, in *Customers for Life* (with Paul Brown), estimated that a customer entering his car dealership for the first time represents a potential lifetime value of over US$300 000.[37] If the satisfied customer brings in other customers, the figure would be higher. Similarly, General Motors estimates its lifetime customers to be worth US$276 000 on average. These six-figure values are a graphic illustration of the importance of keeping the customer satisfied for the life of the automobile to better the chances of a repeat purchase.[38]

- Even though tacos may cost less than a dollar each, executives at Taco Bell have determined that a repeat customer is worth as much as US$11 000. By sharing such estimates of customer lifetime value with its employees, Taco Bell's managers help employees understand the value of keeping customers satisfied.[39]

- Mark Grainer, former chairman of the Technical Assistance Research Programs Institute (TARP), estimated that a loyal supermarket customer is worth US$3 800 annually.[40]

We can work out an example of estimating CLV. Suppose a company analyzes its new-customer acquisition cost:

- Cost of average sales call (including salary, commission, benefits, and expenses): $300
- Average number of sales calls to convert an average prospect into a customer: 4
- Cost of attracting a new customer: $1 200

This is an underestimate because we are omitting the cost of advertising and promotion, plus the fact that only a fraction of all pursued prospects end up being converted into customers.

Now suppose the company estimates average customer lifetime value as follows:

- Annual customer revenue: $500
- Average number of loyal years: 20
- Company profit margin: 0.10
- Customer lifetime value: $1 000

A customer shops for a car at a GM showroom. For long-term profitability, he has to be satisfied enough so that he chooses GM over other brands each time he needs a car.

This company is spending more to attract new customers than they are worth. Unless the company can sign up customers with fewer sales calls, spend less per sales call, stimulate higher new-customer annual spending, retain customers longer, or sell them higher-profit products, it is headed for bankruptcy. Of course, in addition to an average customer estimate, a company needs a way of estimating CLV for each individual customer to decide how much to invest in each customer.

CLV calculations provide a formal quantitative framework for planning customer investment and help marketers to adopt a long-term perspective. One challenge in applying CLV concepts, however, is to arrive at reliable cost and revenue estimates. Marketers who use CLV concepts must also be careful to not forget the importance of short-term, brand-building marketing activities that will help to increase customer loyalty. Although calculation of CLV is often done for the company's current customers, it does not have to be limited to them. "Marketing Memo: Calculating Customer Lifetime Value" discusses how to calculate the CLV for a not-yet-acquired customer.

Customer Equity

Canadian marketing consultant Ian Gordon defines relationship marketing as:

> The ongoing process of identifying and creating new value with individual customers and then sharing the benefits from this over a lifetime of association. It involves the understanding, focusing, and management of ongoing collaboration between suppliers and

---

| MARKETING MEMO | CALCULATING CUSTOMER LIFETIME VALUE |

Researchers and practitioners have used many different approaches for modelling and estimating customer lifetime value (CLV). Columbia's Don Lehmann and Harvard's Sunil Gupta recommend the following formula to estimate the CLV for a not-yet-acquired customer:

$$CLV = \sum_{t=0}^{T} \frac{(p_t - c_t)r_t}{(1+i)^t} - AC$$

where, p_t = price paid by a consumer at time t,
c_t = direct cost of servicing the customer at time t,
i = discount rate or cost of capital for the firm,
r_t = probability of customer repeal buying or being "alive" at time t,
AC = acquisition cost,
T = time horizon for estimating *CLV*.

A key decision is what time horizon to use for estimating CLV. Typically, three to five years is reasonable. With this information and estimates of other variables, we can calculate CLV using spreadsheet analysis.

Gupta and Lehmann illustrate their approach by calculating the CLV of 100 customers over a 10-year period (see Table 5.1). In this example, the firm acquires 100 customers with an acquisition cost per customer of $40. Therefore, in year 0, it spends $4000. Some of these customers defect each year. The present value of profits from this cohort of customers over 10 years is $13 286.52. The net CLV (after deducting acquisition costs) is $9286.52 or $92.87 per customer.

Using an infinite time horizon avoids using an arbitrary time horizon for calculating CLV. In the case of an infinite time horizon, researchers have shown that if margins (price minus cost) and retention rates stay constant over time, then the future of CLV of an existing customer simplifies to the following:

$$CLV = \sum_{t=1}^{\infty} \frac{mr^t}{(1+i)^t} = m \frac{r}{(1+i-r)}$$

In other words, CLV simply becomes margin (m) times a margin multiple [$r/(1 + i -r)$].

Table 5.2 shows the margin multiple for various combinations of r and i. This table shows a simple way to estimate CLV of a customer. For example, when retention rate is 80 percent and discount rate is 12 percent, the margin multiple is about 2.5. Therefore, the future CLV of an existing customer in this scenario is simply his or her annual margin multiplied by 2.5.

Sources: Sunil Gupta and Donald R. Lehmann, "Models of Customer Value," in *Handboook of Marketing Decision Models*, ed. Berend Wierenga (Berlin, Germany: Springer Science and Business Media, 2007); Sunil Gupta and Donald R. Lehman, "Customers as Assets," *Journal of Interactive Marketing, 17*, no. 1 (Winter 2006): 9–24; Sunil Gupta and Donald R. Lehman, *Managing Customers as Investments* (Upper Saddle River, NJ: Wharton School Publishing, 2005); Peter Fader, Bruce Hardie, and Ka Lee, "RFM and CLV: Using Iso-Value Curves for Customer Base Analysis," *Journal of Marketing Research, 42*, no. 4 (November 2005): 415–30; Sunil Gupta, Donald R. Lehmann, and Jennifer Ames Stuart, "Valuing Customers," *Journal of Marketing Research, 41*, no. 1 (February 2004): 7–18; Werner J. Reinartz and V. Kumar, "On the Profitablility of Long-Life Customers in a Noncontractual Setting: An Empirical Investigation and Implications for Marketing," *Journal of Marketing, 64* (October 2000): 17–35.

TABLE 5.1	A HYPOTHETICAL EXAMPLE TO ILLUSTRATE CLV CALCULATIONS

	Year 0	Year 1	Year 2	Year 3	Year 4	Year 5	Year 6	Year 7	Year 8	Year 9	Year 10
Number of Customers	100	90	80	72	60	48	34	23	12	6	2
Revenue per Customer		100	110	120	125	130	135	140	142	143	145
Variable Cost per Customer		70	72	75	76	78	79	80	81	82	83
Margin per Customer		30	38	45	49	52	56	60	61	61	62
Acquisition Cost per Customer	40										
Total Cost or Profit	−4 000	2 700	3 040	3 240	2 940	2 496	1 904	1 380	732	366	124
Present Value	−4 000	2 454.55	2 512.40	2 434.26	2 008.06	1 549.82	1 074.7	708.16	341.48	155.22	47.81

TABLE 5.2	MARGIN MULTIPLE $\dfrac{r}{1+i-r}$

Retention Rate	Discount Rate			
	10%	12%	14%	16%
60%	1.20	1.5	1.11	1.07
70%	1.75	1.67	1.59	1.52
80%	2.67	2.50	2.35	2.22
90%	4.50	4.09	3.75	3.46

selected customers for mutual value creation and sharing through interdependence and organizational alignment.[41]

Toronto-based Bayer Canada, for example, works with Canadian firms to help them assess how they are spending their health-care dollars within their employer benefit programs and finds ways to save them money.

The aim of customer relationship management (CRM) is to produce high customer equity. **Customer equity** is the total of the discounted lifetime values of all of the firm's customers.[42] Clearly, the more loyal the customers, the higher the customer equity. Rust, Zeithaml, and Lemon distinguish three drivers of customer equity: value equity, brand equity, and relationship equity:[43]

- *Value equity* is the customer's perceptions of benefits relative to costs. The sub-drivers of value equity are quality, price, and convenience. These sub-drivers are industry specific. An airline passenger, for example, might define quality as seat width; a hotel guest might define quality as check-in speed. Value equity makes the biggest contribution to customer equity when products are differentiated and when they are more complex and need to be evaluated. Value equity drives customer equity especially in business markets.

- *Brand equity* is the customer's subjective and intangible assessment of the brand, above and beyond its objectively perceived value. The sub-drivers of brand equity are customer brand awareness, customer attitude toward the brand, and customer perception of brand ethics. Companies use advertising, public relations, and other communication tools to affect these sub-drivers. Brand equity is more important than the other drivers of customer equity where products are less differentiated and have more emotional impact. We consider brand equity in detail in Chapter 9.

- *Relationship equity* is the customer's tendency to stick with the brand, above and beyond objective and subjective assessments of its worth. Sub-drivers of relationship equity include loyalty programs, special recognition and treatment programs, community-building programs, and knowledge-building programs. Relationship equity is especially important where personal relationships count for a lot and where customers tend to continue with suppliers out of habit or inertia.

This formulation integrates *value management, brand management,* and *relationship management* within a customer-centred focus. Companies can decide which driver(s) to strengthen for the best payoff. The Bank of Montreal, for example, has been busy analyzing the 100 million transactions that take place through its multiple channels each month to better understand customer attitudes and behaviour so that it can build better relationships with its customers.

Customer equity represents a promising approach to marketing management. "Marketing Insight: Shift from Brand Equity to Customer Equity" highlights some recent thinking on the subject. Note, too, that customer-equity notions can be extended. Mohan Sawhney defines the **relational equity** of the firm as the cumulative value of the firm's network of relationships with its customers, partners, suppliers, employees, and investors.[44] Relational equity depends on the company's ability to attract and retain talent, customers, investors, and partners.

CULTIVATING CUSTOMER RELATIONSHIPS

Maximizing customer value means cultivating long-term customer relationships. In past centuries, producers customized their offerings to each customer: The tailor fitted a suit and a cobbler made shoes for each individual. The Industrial Revolution ushered in an era of mass production. To maximize economies of scale, companies made standard goods in advance of orders and left it to individuals to fit into whatever was available. Producers moved from *built-to-order* marketing to *built-to-stock* marketing.

Companies are moving away from wasteful mass marketing to more precision marketing designed to build strong customer relationships.[45] Today's economy is supported by information businesses. Information has the advantages of being easy to differentiate, customize, personalize, and dispatch over networks at incredible speed.

As companies have grown proficient at gathering information about individual customers and business partners (suppliers, distributors, retailers), and as their factories are designed more flexibly, they have increased their ability to individualize market offerings, messages, and media. **Mass customization** is the ability of a company to meet each customer's requirements—to prepare on a mass basis individually designed products, services, programs, and communications.[46] While Levi's and Lands' End were among the first clothing manufacturers to introduce custom jeans, now there are many players in the mass-customization market. Consider how BMW has been employing mass customization with its Mini brand:

BMW Mini

One of the main criticisms levied against BMW in the early 1990s was that all BMW cars looked alike. This was one of the reasons BMW introduced its customization program later that decade. BMW understood that, as a maker of luxury cars, it had to offer extra value to customers to be able to make an impact on the market. Today, BMW offers customers the ability to personalize their car to an extent most other automakers couldn't imagine. For example, for its Mini Cooper model, the buyer can select even the colour of the roof and choose from eight different upholsteries. This differs from traditional automobile customization, in which customers can choose only from a limited number of options. BMW has enhanced its customization program by allowing customers to walk out of the showroom and change their minds later. The company recognizes that people often have second thoughts and thus lets people make as many changes as they want up until six days before the car goes into production.[47]

Customer Relationship Management (CRM)

In addition to working with partners—called **partner relationship management (PRM)**—many companies are intent on developing stronger bonds with their customers—called **customer relationship management (CRM)**. This is the process of managing detailed information about individual customers and carefully managing all customer "touch points" to maximize customer loyalty. A

| MARKETING INSIGHT | SHIFT FROM BRAND EQUITY TO CUSTOMER EQUITY |

The marketplace has changed a great deal over time, with the economy becoming more service-based and experiencing a shift from a product focus towards a customer focus. This has resulted in greater awareness of the customer as being at the centre of the firm's marketing and a lower emphasis on just transactions.

Nevertheless, even with this shift taking place, many company marketing metrics have remained product-focused, with brand equity being the most commonly used measure of success for brands and companies alike. This focus on brand building and other product-centred programs has left many companies only pretending to be customer-centred, with marketing efforts and marketing standards not truly reflecting this goal.

According to Nick Wreden, author of *Fusion Branding: How to Forge Your Brand for the Future*, the concept of brand equity has numerous problems and pursuing it can warp executive decision making, resulting in lost profits and opportunities. The first problem is that there is no common definition of brand equity. As a result, there can be no universal measurement tool. Similarly, it is impossible to compare brands across different industries or perspectives, so there can be no valid benchmark for executive decision making. Another issue is that brand equity does not indicate market or financial success. Many companies that have established brand equity have disappeared or face financial difficulties. Lastly, brand equity is irrelevant to customers. Customers buy on value, service, or some other attribute, but rarely make a purchase decision based on brand equity. So, why should companies focus on this?

The new approach is that of customer equity. This concept combines customer-value management, brand management, and relationship/retention management into one all-encompassing idea.

If marketers consider all three forms of equity—value equity, brand equity, and retention equity—they can determine which aspects are most important to driving customer equity for their specific industry and/or firm, as well as the financial benefit from improving one or more of the drivers. Furthermore, unlike brand equity, customer equity can be calculated consistently using data that all companies regularly record, such as revenue, customer acquisition or marketing expenses, costs of goods/services, and retention rates. Customer equity can then be calculated by adding up revenues (or profits), subtracting relevant costs, and incorporating retention rates. This provides the current and future profitability of every customer. This information is relatively straightforward, in that employees at all levels can understand it and its implications.

Other advantages of customer equity include the ability to make direct links between marketing programs and increases (or decreases) in customer equity. It also enables segmentation of customers into highly profitable, moderately profitable, and unprofitable groups, allowing for more focused efforts to retain those customers who are most valuable to the company.

Nicke Wreden commented, "Do brands have value? Absolutely. But attempting to measure this value provides little benefit and distracts a company away from the critical task of retaining profitable customers. Ultimately, it is these customers—not a fallible calculation of a dated concept—who are responsible for brand value and long-term corporate success."

Sources: Nick Wreden, *FusionBranding: How to Forge your Brand for the Future*, Atlanta: Accountability Press, 2002, pp. 88–102; PR Web Newswire Press Release, "Brand Equity v. Customer Equity: The Best Way to Determine Brand Value," January 13, 2004, www.prweb.com/releases/2004/1/prweb98161.htm (viewed March 14, 2008); Kevin J. Clancy, "Customer Equity—A Fix for Modern Marketing," Copernicus Marketing Consulting Newsletter, February 20, 2001; Roland Rust, Valerie Zeithaml, and Katherine Lemon, *Driving Customer Equity: How Customer Lifetime Value is Reshaping Corporate Strategy* (New York: The Free Press, 2000), pp. 87–93.

---

customer touch point is any occasion on which a customer encounters the brand and product—from actual experience to personal or mass communications to casual observation. For a hotel, the touch points include reservations, check-in and checkout, frequent-stay programs, room service, business services, exercise facilities, laundry service, restaurants, and bars. For instance, the Four Seasons relies on personal touches, such as a staff who always addresses guests by name, high-powered employees who understand the needs of sophisticated business travellers, and at least one best-in-region facility, such as a premier restaurant or spa.[48]

Customer relationship management enables companies such as Harry Rosen to provide excellent real-time customer service through the effective use of individual account information. Based on what they know about each valued customer, companies can customize market offerings, services, programs, messages, and media. CRM is important because a major driver of company profitability is the aggregate value of the company's customer base.[49]

Harry Rosen

Harry Rosen, a nationwide retailer of menswear, has been recognized as an industry leader in customer service for almost 50 years. It has long been a goal of Harry Rosen to have personalized service that makes customers feel comfortable when buying menswear. This strategy has proved to be very successful over the years. Harry Rosen began as a single store in 1952 and has grown to 16 locations across Canada, now accounting for more than 35 percent of the high-end menswear market in Canada. To improve the personal service even more, Harry Rosen now uses web-based CRM software called SalesLogix. This software is designed to provide a detailed view of each customer and his individual preferences, allowing the company to tailor seasonal offerings and make recommendations for each customer, rather than lumping them into broad categories. The staff at the 16 locations can view detailed information on the over 500 000 Harry Rosen customers, including how often each shops, average purchase price, and most-purchased brands. This detailed information helps the staff to make product recommendations based on what each individual customer will most likely buy. This personalized approach to customer service is the next closest thing to having your neighbourhood tailor stitch a suit for you.[50]

Some of the groundwork for customer relationship management was laid by Don Peppers and Martha Rogers in a series of books.[51] Peppers and Rogers outline a four-step framework for one-to-one marketing that can be adapted to CRM marketing as follows:

- *Identify your prospects and customers.* Do not go after everyone. Build, maintain, and mine a rich customer database with information derived from all channels and customer touch points.

- *Differentiate customers in terms of (1) their needs and (2) their value to your company.* Spend proportionately more effort on the most valuable customers (MVCs). Apply activity-based costing and calculate customer lifetime value. Estimate net present value of all future profits coming from purchases, margin levels, and referrals, less customer-specific servicing costs.

- *Interact with individual customers to improve your knowledge about their individual needs and to build stronger relationships.* Formulate customized offerings that are communicated in a personalized way.

- *Customize products, services, and messages to each customer.* Facilitate customer/company interaction through the company contact centre and website.

Table 5.3 lists the main differences between mass marketing and one-to-one marketing.

Harry Rosen uses customer information to build relationship equity.

TABLE 5.3	MASS MARKETING VERSUS ONE-TO-ONE MARKETING
Mass Marketing	**One-to-One Marketing**
Average customer	Individual customer
Customer anonymity	Customer profile
Standard product	Customized market offering
Mass production	Customized production
Mass distribution	Individualized distribution
Mass advertising	Individualized message
Mass promotion	Individualized incentives
One-way message	Two-way messages
Economies of scale	Economies of scope
Share of market	Share of customer
All customers	Profitable customers
Customer attraction	Customer retention

Sources: Adapted from Don Peppers and Martha Rogers, *The One-to-One Future* (New York: Doubleday/ Currency, 1993); 1to1 Media website, www.1to1media.com.

A key driver of shareholder value is the aggregate value of the customer base. Winning companies improve the value of their customer base by excelling at strategies such as the following:

- *Reducing the rate of customer defection.* Whole Foods Market, the world's largest retailer of natural and organic foods (with stores in Toronto and Oakville, Ontario), woos customers with a commitment to marketing the best foods and a team concept for employees. Selecting and training employees to be knowledgeable and friendly increases the likelihood that the inevitable shopping questions from customers will be answered satisfactorily.

- *Increasing the longevity of the customer relationship.* The more involved a customer is with the company, the more likely he or she is to stick around. Some companies treat their customers as partners—especially in business-to-business markets—soliciting their help in the design of new products or improving their customer service. Instant Web Companies (IWCO), a direct-mail printer, launched a monthly Customer Spotlight program whereby guest companies provide an overview of their business and direct-mail programs and comment on IWCO practices, products, and services. IWCO's staff not only gains exposure to customers, but also develops a broader perspective on customers' business and marketing objectives and learns how to add value and identify options that help meet customers' goals.[52]

- *Enhancing the growth potential of each customer through "share-of-wallet," cross-selling, and up-selling.*[53] Harley-Davidson, Inc., capped off its 100th anniversary year by announcing record sales and a 21-percent rise in profits. Harley has enjoyed 18 consecutive years of growth. Harley-Davidson sells more than motorcycles and riding supplements (such as gloves, leather jackets, helmets, and sunglasses). Harley dealerships sell more than 3000 items of clothing— some even have their own fitting rooms. Licensed goods sold by others range from the predictable (shot glasses, cue balls, and Zippo cigarette lighters) to the more surprising items (cologne, dolls, and cell phones). The 2003 100th-anniversary model year also saw strong sales of apparel and collectibles tied to the anniversary.

- *Making low-profit customers more profitable or terminating them.* To avoid the direct need for termination, unprofitable customers can be made to buy more or in larger quantities, forgo certain features or services, or pay higher amounts or fees. Banks, phone companies, and travel agencies are all charging for once-free services to ensure minimum customer revenue levels.

- *Focusing disproportionate effort on high-value customers.* The most valuable customers can be treated in a special way. Thoughtful gestures such as birthday greetings, small gifts, or invitations to special sports or arts events can send a strong signal to the customer.

To read how Tesco built, maintains, and mines a richer customer database in the United Kingdom, visit www.pearsoned.co.uk/ marketingmanagementeurope.

Attracting, Retaining, and Growing Customers

Customers are becoming harder to please. They are smarter, more price conscious, more demanding, less forgiving, and they are approached by many more competitors with equal or better offers. The challenge, according to Jeffrey Gitomer, is not necessarily to produce satisfied customers; several competitors can do this. The challenge is to produce delighted and loyal customers.[54]

Companies seeking to expand their profits and sales have to spend considerable time and resources searching for new customers. To generate leads, the company develops ads and places them in media that will reach new prospects; it sends direct mail and makes phone calls to possible new prospects; its salespeople participate in trade shows where they might find new leads; it purchases names from list brokers; and so on. All this activity produces a list of suspects. *Suspects* are people or organizations which might conceivably have an interest in buying the company's product or service, but may not have the means or real intention to buy. The next task is to identify which suspects are really good *prospects*—customers with the motivation, ability, and opportunity to make a purchase—by interviewing them, checking on their financial standing, and so on. Then it is time to send out the salespeople.

It is not enough, however, to attract new customers; the company must keep them and increase their business. Too many companies suffer from high **customer churn**: high customer defection. It is like adding water to a leaking bucket. Cellular carriers, for example, are plagued with "spinners," customers who switch carriers at least three times a year looking for the best deal. Many lose 25 percent of their subscribers each year at an estimated cost of US$2 billion to US$4 billion. Unfortunately, much marketing theory and practice centres on the art of attracting new customers, rather than on retaining and cultivating existing ones. The emphasis traditionally has been on making sales rather than on building relationships; on pre-selling and selling rather than on caring for the customer afterwards.

There are two main ways to strengthen customer retention. One is to erect high switching barriers. Customers are less inclined to switch to another supplier when this would involve high capital costs, high search costs, or the loss of loyal-customer discounts. The better approach is to deliver high customer satisfaction. This makes it harder for competitors to offer lower prices or inducements to switch.

Some companies think they are getting a sense of customer satisfaction by tallying complaints, but 96 percent of dissatisfied customers don't complain; they just stop buying.[55] The best thing a company can do is to make it easy for the customer to complain. Suggestion forms, toll-free numbers, websites, and email addresses allow for quick, two-way communication. 3M Company claims that over two-thirds of its product-improvement ideas come from listening to customer complaints.

Listening is not enough, however. The company must respond quickly and constructively to any complaint. Of the customers who register a complaint, between 54 and 70 percent will do business with the organization again if their complaint is resolved. The figure goes up to a staggering 95 percent if the customer feels that the complaint was resolved quickly. Customers who have complained to an organization and had their complaints satisfactorily resolved tell an average of five people about the good treatment they received.[56]

Dell Computer Corp. quickly yanked its corporate PC tech support out of India and to a domestic call centre when its U.S.-based customers complained about the quality of help they received: rigid, "by the book" technicians who wasted their time wading through fixes they had already tried, problems with poor phone connections, and strongly accented English that was hard to understand.[57]

More companies now recognize the importance of satisfying and retaining customers. Satisfied customers constitute the company's *customer relationship capital*. If the company were to be sold, the acquiring company would have to pay not only for the plant and equipment and the brand name, but also for the delivered *customer base*, the number and value of the customers who would do business with the new firm. Here are some interesting facts bearing on customer retention:[58]

1. Acquiring new customers can cost five times more than the costs involved in satisfying and retaining current customers. It requires a great deal of effort to induce satisfied customers to switch away from their current suppliers.

2. The average company loses 10 percent of its customers each year.

3. A 5-percent reduction in the customer defection rate can increase profits by 25 percent to 85 percent, depending on the industry.

4. The customer profit rate tends to increase over the life of the retained customer.

Figure 5.4 shows the main steps in the process of attracting and keeping customers. The starting point is everyone who might conceivably buy the product or service (*suspects*). From these the

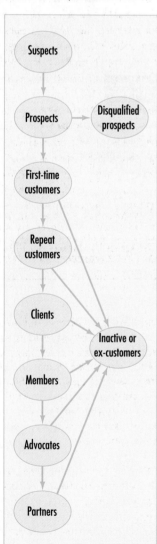

FIGURE 5.4

The Customer Development Process

Source: See Jill Griffin, *Customer Loyalty: How to Earn It, How to Keep It* (New York: Lexington Books, 1995), p. 36. See also Murray Raphel and Neil Raphel, *Up the Loyalty Ladder: Turning Sometime Customers into Full-Time Advocates of Your Business* (New York: HarperBusiness, 1995).

company determines the most likely *prospects*, which it hopes to convert into *first-time customers*, and then into *repeat customers*, and then into *clients*—people whom the company treats very specially and knowledgeably. The next challenge is to turn clients into *members* by starting a membership program that offers benefits to customers who join, and then into *advocates*, customers who enthusiastically recommend the company and its products and services to others. The ultimate challenge is to turn advocates into *partners*.

Markets can be characterized by their long-term buying dynamics and how easily and often customers can enter and leave.[59]

1. *Permanent capture markets*. Once a customer, always a customer (e.g., nursing homes and trust funds).
2. *Simple retention markets*. Customers can permanently be lost after each period (e.g., telecom, cable, financial services, other services, subscriptions).
3. *Customer migration markets*. Customers can leave and come back (e.g., catalogues, consumer products, retail, and airlines).

Some customers inevitably become inactive or drop out. The challenge is to reactivate dissatisfied customers through win-back strategies. It is often easier to re-attract ex-customers (because the company knows their names and histories) than to find new ones. The key is to analyze the causes of customer defection through exit interviews and lost-customer surveys. The aim is to win back only those customers who have strong profit potential.

Building Loyalty

How should a company invest in building loyalty so that the costs do not exceed the gains? We need to distinguish five different levels of investment in customer-relationship building:

1. *Basic marketing*. The salesperson simply sells the product.
2. *Reactive marketing*. The salesperson sells the product and encourages the customer to call if he or she has questions, comments, or complaints.
3. *Accountable marketing*. The salesperson phones the customer to check whether the product is meeting expectations. The salesperson also asks the customer for any product or service improvement suggestions and any specific disappointments.
4. *Proactive marketing*. The salesperson contacts the customer from time to time with suggestions about improved product uses or new products.
5. *Partnership marketing*. The company works continuously with its large customers to help improve the performance of the customer organizations. (General Electric, for example, has stationed engineers at large utilities to help them produce more power.)

Most companies practise only basic marketing when their markets contain many customers and their unit profit margins are small. Whirlpool is not going to phone each washing-machine buyer to express appreciation. It may set up a customer hotline. In markets with few customers and high profit margins, most sellers will move toward partnership marketing. Boeing, for example, works closely with American Airlines to design airplanes that fully satisfy American's requirements. As Figure 5.5 shows, the likely level of relationship marketing depends on the number of customers and the profit-margin level.

An increasingly essential ingredient for the best relationship marketing today is the right technology. Table 5.4 highlights five imperatives of CRM and where technology fits in. GE Plastics could not

	High Margin	Medium Margin	Low Margin
Many customers/ distributors	Accountable	Reactive	Basic or reactive
Medium number of customers/ distributors	Proactive	Accountable	Reactive
Few customers/ distributors	Partnership	Proactive	Accountable

FIGURE 5.5

Levels of Relationship Marketing

TABLE 5.4	BREAKING DOWN CUSTOMER RELATIONSHIP MANAGEMENT: WHAT CUSTOMER RELATIONSHIP MANAGEMENT REALLY COMPRISES				
	CRM Imperative				
	Acquiring the right customer	Crafting the right value proposition	Instituting the best processes	Motivating employees	Learning to retain customers
	You Get It When . . .				
	▪ You've identified your most valuable customers. ▪ You've calculated your share of their wallet for your goods and services.	▪ You've studied what products or services your customers need today and will need tomorrow. ▪ You've surveyed what products or services your competitors offer today and will offer tomorrow. ▪ You've spotted what products or services you should be offering.	▪ You've researched the best way to deliver your products or services to customers, including the alliances you need to strike, the technologies you need to invest in, and the service capabilities you need to develop or acquire.	▪ You know what tools your employees need to foster customer relationships. ▪ You've identified the HR systems you need to institute in order to boost employee loyalty.	▪ You've learned why customers defect and how to win them back. ▪ You've analyzed what your competitors are doing to win your high-value customers. ▪ Your senior management monitors customer-defection metrics.
	CRM Technology Can Help . . .				
	▪ Analyze customer revenue and cost data to identify current and future high-value customers. ▪ Better target your direct-marketing efforts.	▪ Capture relevant product/service consumption behaviour data. ▪ Create new distribution channels. ▪ Develop new pricing models. ▪ Build communities.	▪ Process transactions faster. ▪ Provide better information to the front line. ▪ Manage logistics and the supply chain more efficiently. ▪ Catalyze collaborative commerce.	▪ Align incentives and metrics. ▪ Deploy knowledge management systems.	▪ Track customer-defection and retention levels. ▪ Track customer-service satisfaction levels.

Source: Darrell K. Rigby, Frederick F. Reichheld, and Phil Schefter, *Harvard Business Review* (February 2002): 106. Reprinted by permission of Harvard Business Review.

effectively target its email to different customers if it were not for advances in database software. Dell Computer could not customize computer ordering for its global corporate customers without advances in web technology. Companies are using email, websites, call centres, databases, and database software to foster continuous contact between company and customer. The following example shows how General Motors used technology to build customer value.

OnStar by GM

General Motors has taken the concept of roadside assistance to the next level with the introduction of OnStar, the world most comprehensive in-vehicle security, communications, and diagnostics system. OnStar uses a simple three-button system that activates hands-free calling, emergency assistance, and direct contact to expert advisors, 24/7. OnStar also offers a service whereby critical vehicle features like the engine, airbags, and anti-lock brakes are checked once a month when customers drive. A detailed report that outlines any problems or areas that need attention is then automatically emailed directly to the customer. In addition to these features, OnStar provides a turn-by-turn voice-guided navigation system. OnStar is currently offered on more than 50 GM vehicles. When customers buy a GM vehicle with OnStar, they are not only buying a car, they are buying peace of mind.[60]

GM's OnStar utilizes technology to build customer value.

At the same time, companies need to make sure their attempts to create relationships with customers don't backfire, as when customers are bombarded by computer-generated recommendations that consistently miss the mark. Buy a lot of baby gifts on Amazon, and your personalized recommendations suddenly don't look so personal. E-tailers need to recognize the limitations of online personalization at the same time that they work harder to find technology and processes that really work.[61]

Companies are also recognizing the importance of the personal component to CRM and what happens once customers make actual contact. As Stanford's business guru Jeffrey Pfeffer puts it, "The best companies build cultures in which front-line people are empowered to do what's needed to take care of the customer." He cites examples of firms like SAS, the Scandinavian airline, which engineered a turnaround in part based on the insight that a customer's impressions of a company are formed through a myriad of small interactions: checking in, boarding the plane, eating a meal, and so on.[62]

Reducing Customer Defection

There are five main steps a company can take to reduce the defection rate. First, the company must define and measure its retention rate. For a magazine, the renewal rate is a good measure of retention. For a university or college, it could be the first- to second-year retention rate, or the class graduation rate.

Second, the company must distinguish the causes of customer attrition and identify those that can be managed better. (See "Marketing Memo: Asking Questions When Customers Leave.") The Forum Corporation analyzed the customers lost by 14 major companies for reasons other than leaving the region or going out of business: 15 percent switched because they found a better product; another 15 percent found a cheaper product; and 70 percent left because of poor or little attention from the supplier. Not much can be done about customers who leave the region or go out of business, but much can be done about those who leave because of poor service, shoddy products, or high prices.[63]

Third, the company needs to estimate how much profit it loses when it loses customers. In the case of an individual customer, the lost profit is equal to the customer's lifetime value—that is, the present value of the profit stream that the company would have realized if the customer had not defected prematurely—based on some of the calculations outlined above.

Fourth, the company needs to figure out how much it would cost to reduce the defection rate. As long as the cost is less than the lost profit, the company should spend the money. And finally, nothing beats listening to customers. Some companies have created an ongoing mechanism that keeps senior managers permanently plugged in to front-line customer feedback. MBNA, the credit-card giant, asks every executive to listen in on telephone conversations in the customer-service area or customer-recovery units. Deere & Company, which makes John Deere tractors and has a superb record of customer loyalty—nearly 98-percent annual retention in some product areas—uses retired employees to interview defectors and customers.[64]

MARKETING MEMO | ASKING QUESTIONS WHEN CUSTOMERS LEAVE

To create effective retention programs, marketing managers need to identify customer-defection patterns. This analysis should start with internal records, such as sales logs, pricing records, and customer-survey results. The next step is extending defection research to outside sources, such as benchmarking studies and statistics from trade associations. Some key questions to ask:

1. Do customers defect at different rates during the year?
2. Does retention vary by office, region, sales representative, or distributor?
3. What is the relationship between retention rates and changes in prices?
4. What happens to lost customers and where do they usually go?
5. What are the retention norms for your industry?
6. Which company in your industry retains customers the longest?

Source: Reprinted from William A. Sherden, "When Customers Leave," *Small Business Reports* (November 1994): 45.

Forming Strong Customer Bonds

"Marketing Memo: Building Strong Customer Bonds" offers some tips on connecting with customers. Berry and Parasuraman have identified three retention-building approaches: adding financial benefits, adding social benefits, and adding structural ties.[65]

ADDING FINANCIAL BENEFITS Two financial benefits that companies can offer are frequency programs and club-marketing programs. **Frequency programs (FPs)** are designed to provide rewards to customers who buy frequently and in substantial amounts.[66] Frequency marketing is an acknowledgment of the fact that 20 percent of a company's customers might account for 80 percent of its business. Frequency programs are seen as a way to build long-term loyalty with these customers, potentially creating cross-selling opportunities in the process.

American Airlines was one of the first companies to pioneer a frequency program when it decided in the early 1980s to offer free mileage credit to its customers. Hotels next adopted FPs, with Marriott taking the lead with its Honored Guest Program, followed by car rental firms. Then credit-card companies began to offer points based on card-usage levels.

In Canada alone there are many widely-recognized reward programs, such as the Shoppers Optimum card, which allows users to accumulate points to apply toward free goods at Shoppers Drug Mart; the CIBC Aerogold Visa, which allows users to accumulate Aeroplan points for Air Canada and Star Alliance flights; the President's Choice Financial Master Card, which allows users to accumulate points to purchase groceries at Loblaws stores; and the HBC Rewards card, which allows users to accumulate points with purchases from The Bay, Zellers, and other retailers. The list goes on and on. According to a 2002 Ipsos-Reid survey, of all Canadian adult credit-card holders (80 percent of all adults), 68 percent belong to at least one retail-store reward program, and between 40 and 60 percent of such users have redeemed points for rewards. And according to J. C. Williams Group, the average Canadian belongs to 4.5 different loyalty programs.[67]

Typically, the first company to introduce an FP gains the most benefit, especially if competitors are slow to respond. After competitors respond, FPs can become a financial burden to all the offering companies, but some companies are more efficient and creative in managing an FP. For example, airlines run tiered loyalty programs in which they offer different levels of rewards to different travellers (e.g., Aeroplan Prestige, Aeroplan Elite, Aeroplan Super-Elite). They may offer to occasional travellers one frequent-flyer mile for every mile flown and to top customers two frequent-flyer miles for every mile flown.

Many companies have created club-membership programs. Club membership can be open to everyone who purchases a product or service, or it can be limited to an affinity group or to those willing to pay a small fee. Although open clubs are good for building a database and snagging customers from competitors, limited-membership clubs are more powerful long-term loyalty builders since fees and membership conditions prevent those with only a fleeting interest in a company's products from

---

| MARKETING MEMO | BUILDING STRONG CUSTOMER BONDS |

Companies that want to form strong customer bonds need to attend to the following basics:

- Get cross-departmental participation in planning and managing the customer satisfaction and retention process.
- Integrate the "Voice of the Customer" to capture their stated and unstated needs or requirements in all business decisions.
- Create superior products, services, and experiences for the target market.
- Organize and make accessible a database of information on individual customer needs, preferences, contacts, purchase frequency, and satisfaction.
- Make it easy for customers to reach appropriate company personnel and express their needs, perceptions, and complaints.
- Run award programs recognizing outstanding employees.

---

joining. These clubs attract and keep those customers who are responsible for the largest portion of business. Etsy and Hallmark are examples of highly successful clubs.

Etsy

Etsy is an online marketplace for buying and selling all things handmade. Etsy encourages its customers to join Etsy Teams. Etsy Teams are groups of organized Etsy members who network, share skills, promote their shops, and "Etsy" together. A team forms around a shared location, crafting medium, or another mutual interest. Since Etsy's opening in 2005, over 170 Etsy Teams have formed across the world. Visiting Etsy's website and following the Community link helps a customer find a nearby Etsy Team.[68]

Hallmark

In 1994, Hallmark started the first consumer-loyalty program in the greeting-card industry. Today, Hallmark's Crown Rewards loyalty program has grown to include more than 12 million active members. Membership in the Crown Rewards program is free and customers earn points for every dollar they spend. These points can later be redeemed for store merchandise. Customers earn bonus points for every greeting card they buy and receive members-only offers every day. To encourage customers to spend more in its stores, Hallmark offers different member levels with each subsequent level offering better rewards. Customers can advance to higher levels by surpassing certain purchase amounts in Hallmark stores.[69]

Hallmark has been successful in retaining customers through an attractive loyalty rewards program.

ADDING SOCIAL BENEFITS   Company personnel work on cementing social bonds with customers by individualizing and personalizing customer relationships. In essence, thoughtful companies turn their customers into clients. Donnelly, Berry, and Thompson draw this distinction:

> Customers may be nameless to the institution; clients cannot be nameless. Customers are served as part of the mass or as part of larger segments; clients are served on an individual basis. Customers are served by anyone who happens to be available; clients are served by the professional assigned to them.[70]

E-commerce companies looking to attract and retain customers are discovering that personalization goes beyond creating customized information.[71] For example, the Lands' End Live website offers visitors the opportunity to talk with a customer-service representative. Nordstrom takes a similar approach with its website to ensure that online buyers are as satisfied with the company's customer service as are its in-store visitors; and, with the click of a button, Eddie Bauer's e-commerce site connects shoppers to customer-service representatives with a text-based chat feature.

A 2006 survey of 1058 web shoppers by JupiterResearch found that 33 percent of online shoppers who had a poor experience on a website abandoned the site completely, while 75 percent were likely never to shop at that site again.[72] Forrester Research reports that two-thirds of web shoppers abandon shopping carts during the online shopping process.[73] Worse, only 1.8 percent of visits to online retailers lead to sales, compared with 5 percent of visits to department stores. Analysts attribute this behaviour partly to a general absence of interactive customer service in e-commerce. Customers looking for help are often sent to a text help-file rather than a live sales representative. In response, companies such as Veseys are trying to add a personal touch to their websites.

Veseys

Based in Prince Edward Island, Veseys has over 60 years of experience providing goods, services, and advice to Canadian gardeners. To ensure that its customers will receive seeds and plants that will flourish in Canada's harsh conditions and short growing season, Veseys' flower and vegetable seed varieties undergo extensive trial gardening at the Veseys Research Farm. Today's operation has long outgrown the one room of his home Arthur Vesey used to start his seed business. Now customers can order products through its catalogues, by calling its toll-free number, or by ordering from its website. Veseys works to personalize its web offerings by showing photos of the service team that stands behind the company's products and by clearly posting contact information with which customers can reach a Veseys service person should they need a more personal touch.[74]

Not all customer-service features involve live personnel. Both Macys.com and gap.com offer prerecorded customer-service information. Gap's website includes a "zoom" feature that shoppers can use to get a close look at every detail of a garment, from elastic waistbands to fabric prints. Lands' End Live allows customers to "try on" clothes online using virtual models based on measurements supplied by customers.

ADDING STRUCTURAL TIES   The company may supply customers with special equipment or computer links that help customers manage orders, payroll, and inventory. A good example is McKesson Corporation, a leading pharmaceutical wholesaler, which invested millions of dollars in Electronic Data Interchange (EDI) capabilities to help independent pharmacies manage inventory, order-entry processes, and shelf space. Another example is Milliken & Company, which provides proprietary software programs, marketing research, sales training, and sales leads to loyal customers.

Lester Wunderman, an astute observer of contemporary marketing, thinks talk about "loyalizing" customers misses the point.[75] People can be loyal to country, family, and beliefs, but less so to their toothpaste, detergent, or even beer. The marketer's aim should be to increase the consumer's *proclivity to repurchase* the company's brand. Here are his suggestions for creating structural ties with the customer:

1. *Create long-term contracts.* A newspaper subscription replaces the need to buy a newspaper each day. A 20-year mortgage replaces the need to re-borrow the money each year. A home-heating-oil agreement assures continuous delivery without renewing the order.

2. *Charge a lower price to consumers who buy larger supplies.* Offer lower prices to people who agree to be supplied regularly with a certain brand of toothpaste, detergent, or beer.

3. *Turn the product into a long-term service.* DaimlerChrysler is considering selling miles of reliable transportation instead of cars, with the consumer able to order different cars at different times, such as a station wagon for shopping and a convertible for the weekend. Gaines, the dog food company, could offer a pet-care service that includes kennels, insurance, and veterinary care along with food.

CUSTOMER DATABASES AND DATABASE MARKETING

Marketers must know their customers. And in order to know the customer, the company must collect information, store it in a database, and do database marketing. A **customer database** is an organized collection of comprehensive information about individual customers or prospects that is current, accessible, and actionable for such marketing purposes as lead generation, lead qualification, sale of a product or service, and maintenance of customer relationships. **Database marketing** is the process of building, maintaining, and using customer databases and other databases (products, suppliers, resellers) for the purpose of contacting, transacting, and building customer relationships, as Suzy Shier does.

Suzy Shier

Suzy Shier has a three-pronged database-marketing strategy: gathering information about customers in stores, through its Prestige loyalty program, and via its website. In the stores, "join us today" cards invite customers to sign up, information about Prestige is on display, and staff ask customers if they are interested in participating. The website offers 20 percent off on the first purchase to customers who "join the Suzy Shier community" online. Prestige members constitute approximately 20 percent of customers in Suzy Shier's database. For a fee, customers can become Prestige members and receive 10 percent off all purchases year-long, as well as invitations to special shopping parties.[76]

Customer Databases

As the former chief marketing officer of Amazon liked to point out, when you walk through the door of a department store, the retailer has no idea who you are. When you log on to Amazon, however, you are greeted by name, presented a customized set of product-purchase suggestions based on your past purchase choices, and offered an accompanying series of frank customer reviews. As you log off the site, you are also asked permission to be emailed special offers.[77]

Many companies confuse a customer mailing list with a customer database. A **customer mailing list** is simply a set of names, addresses, and telephone numbers. A customer database contains much more information, accumulated through customer transactions, registration information, telephone queries, website cookies, and every customer contact.

Ideally, a customer database contains the consumer's past purchases, demographics (age, income, family members, birthdays), psychographics (activities, interests, and opinions), mediagraphics (preferred media), and other useful information. The catalogue company Fingerhut possesses some 1400 pieces of information about each of the 30 million households in its massive customer database. And the Royal Bank of Canada has individual data on its 9 million customers and is able to model the lifetime value of individual customers, their potential interest in different offerings, and their vulnerability to attrition.

Ideally, a **business database** would contain business customers' past purchases; past volumes, prices, and profits; buyer team-member names (and ages, birthdays, hobbies, and favourite foods); status of current contracts; an estimate of the supplier's share of the customer's business; competitive suppliers; assessment of competitive strengths and weaknesses in selling and servicing the account; and relevant buying practices, patterns, and policies. For example, a Latin American unit of the Swiss pharmaceutical firm Novartis keeps data on 100 000 of Argentina's farmers, knows their crop-protection chemical purchases, groups them by value, and treats each group differently.

Figure 5.6 displays a method for selectively gaining greater share of a customer's business, based on the presumption that the firm has gained a deep understanding of the customer.

FIGURE 5.6

Increasing Customer Share-of-Requirements

Source: James C. Anderson and James A. Narus, *MIT Sloan Management Review* (Spring 2003): 45.

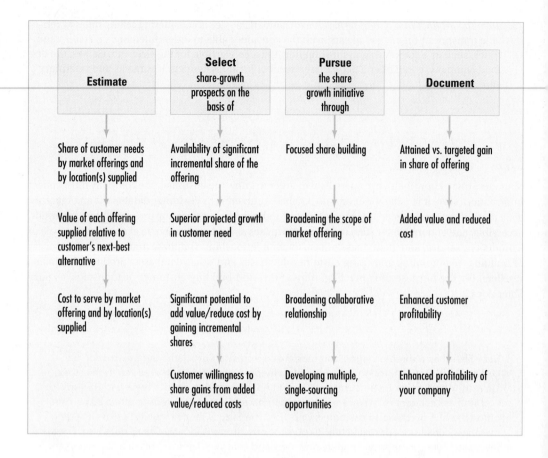

Estimate	Select share-growth prospects on the basis of	Pursue the share growth initiative through	Document
Share of customer needs by market offerings and by location(s) supplied	Availability of significant incremental share of the offering	Focused share building	Attained vs. targeted gain in share of offering
Value of each offering supplied relative to customer's next-best alternative	Superior projected growth in customer need	Broadening the scope of market offering	Added value and reduced cost
Cost to serve by market offering and by location(s) supplied	Significant potential to add value/reduce cost by gaining incremental shares	Broadening collaborative relationship	Enhanced customer profitability
	Customer willingness to share gains from added value/reduced costs	Developing multiple, single-sourcing opportunities	Enhanced profitability of your company

Data Warehouses and Datamining[78]

Savvy companies are capturing information every time a customer comes into contact with any of its departments. Touch points include a customer purchase, a customer-requested service call, an online query, and a mail-in rebate card. Banks and credit-card companies, telephone companies, catalogue marketers, and many other companies have a great deal of information about their customers, including not only addresses and phone numbers, but also their transactions and enhanced data on age, family size, income, and other demographics.

These data are collected by the company's contact centre and organized into a **data warehouse**. Company personnel can capture, query, and analyze the data. Inferences can be drawn about an individual customer's needs and responses. Telemarketers can respond to customer inquiries based on a total picture of the customer relationship.

Through **datamining**, marketing statisticians can extract from the mass of data useful information about individuals, trends, and segments. Datamining involves the use of sophisticated statistical and mathematical techniques such as cluster analysis, automatic interaction detection, predictive modelling, and neural networking.[79] Some observers believe that a proprietary database can provide a company with a significant competitive advantage. As such, a company that wants to learn the most from its database needs to engage the services of a person or company skilled in datamining. (See Figure 5.7 for examples of companies that use datamining.)

USING THE DATABASE In general, companies can use their databases in five ways:

1. *To identify prospects.* Many companies generate sales leads by advertising their product or service. The ads generally contain a response feature, such as a business reply card or toll-free phone number. The database is built from these responses. The company sorts through the database to identify the best prospects and then contacts them by mail, phone, or personal call in an attempt to convert them into customers.

2. *To decide which customers should receive a particular offer.* Companies are interested in selling, up-selling, and cross-selling their products and services. Companies set up criteria describing the ideal target customer for a particular offer. Then they search their customer databases for those who most closely resemble the ideal type.

Foster Parents Plan of Canada   Toronto-based Foster Parents Plan of Canada (FPP) recently began combining market research with information from its own database to help it predict whether a foster parent will continue his or her support of the organization. Having this information not only allows the nonprofit organization to better understand the financial risks it faces, it also enables it to take the appropriate actions to try to retain donors. To build predictive profiles that differentiate between committed versus uncommitted people required analysis of a large sample of over 5000 people. The analysis, however, revealed key predictors of commitment and allowed FPP to tag people in its database accordingly.

Royal Caribbean   Royal Caribbean uses its database to offer spur-of-the-moment cruise packages to fill all the berths on its ships. It focuses on retired people and single people because they are more able to make quick commitments. Fewer empty berths mean maximized profits for the cruise line.

Mars   Mars is a market leader not only in candy, but also in pet food. In Germany, Mars has compiled the names of virtually every cat-owning German family by contacting veterinarians and also advertising a free booklet titled "How to Take Care of Your Cat." Those who request the booklet fill out a questionnaire, so Mars knows the cat's name, age, and birthday. Mars now sends a birthday card to each cat each year, along with a cat food sample or money-saving coupons for Mars brands. Do the cat owners appreciate this? You bet!

American Express   It is no wonder that, at its secret location in Phoenix, security guards watch over American Express's 500 billion bytes of data on how its customers have used the company's 35 million green, gold, and platinum charge cards. Amex uses the database to include precisely targeted offers in its monthly mailing of millions of customer bills.

Qwest   Twice a year Qwest sifts through its customer list looking for customers that have the potential to be more profitable. The company's database contains as many as 200 observations about each customer's calling patterns. By looking at demographic profiles, plus the mix of local versus long-distance calls or whether a consumer has voice mail, Qwest can estimate potential spending. Next, the company determines how much of the customer's likely telecom budget is already coming its way. Armed with that knowledge, Qwest sets a cut-off point for how much to spend marketing to this customer.

FIGURE 5.7

Examples of Datamining

3. *To deepen customer loyalty.* Companies can build interest and enthusiasm by remembering customer preferences and by sending appropriate gifts, discount coupons, and interesting reading material.

4. *To reactivate customer purchases.* Companies can install automatic mailing programs (automatic marketing) that send out birthday or anniversary cards, Christmas shopping reminders, or off-season promotions. The database can help the company make attractive or timely offers.

5. *To avoid serious customer mistakes.* A major bank confessed to a number of mistakes that it had made by not using its customer database well. In one case, the bank charged a customer a penalty for late payment of his mortgage, failing to note that he headed a company that was a major depositor in this bank. He quit the bank. In a second case, two different staff members of the bank phoned the same mortgage customer offering a home-equity loan at different prices. Neither knew that the other had made the call. In a third case, a bank gave a premium customer only standard service in another country.

The Downside of Database Marketing and CRM

Five problems can deter a firm from effectively using CRM. The first is that building and maintaining a customer database requires a large investment in computer hardware, database software, analytical programs, communication links, and skilled personnel. It is difficult to collect the right data, especially to capture all the occasions of company interaction with individual customers. Building a customer database would not be worthwhile in the following cases: (1) where the product is a once-in-a-lifetime purchase (e.g., a grand piano), (2) where customers show little loyalty to a brand (i.e., there is lots of customer churn), (3) where the unit sale is very small (e.g., a chocolate bar), and (4) where the cost of gathering information is too high.

The second problem is the difficulty of getting everyone in the company to be customer-oriented and to use the available information. Employees find it far easier to carry on traditional transaction marketing than to practise customer relationship marketing. Effective database marketing requires managing and training employees as well as dealers and suppliers.

The third problem is that not all customers want a relationship with the company, and they may resent knowing that the company has collected that much personal information about them. Marketers must be concerned about customer attitudes towards privacy and security. American Express, long regarded as a leader on privacy issues, does not sell information on specific customer transactions.

However, American Express found itself the target of consumer outrage when it announced a partnership with KnowledgeBase Marketing, Inc., that would have made data on 175 million people available to any merchant that accepted American Express cards. American Express killed the partnership. AOL, also targeted by privacy advocates, junked a plan to sell subscribers' telephone numbers.

Online companies would be smart to explain their privacy policies and to give consumers the right not to have their information stored in a database. RBC Financial Group, Canada's largest financial institution, has been a forerunner in this regard; it implemented a privacy code in 1987.

Around the world, privacy legislation has gone in a number of different directions. European countries, for example, do not look favourably upon database marketing. In 1995, the European Union issued a Directive on the Protection of Personal Data that lays down strict guidelines about what information can be collected and how it can be used and transferred. Predictably, the United States and Canada have responded to the privacy issue very differently. While the United States opted for industry self-regulation, Canadian federal and provincial governments believed more controls were needed. Until recently, Quebec was the only province with legislation dealing with the privacy of personal information. Then, on January 1, 2001, the Personal Information Protection and Electronic Documents Act (PIPEDA) came into effect and companies had until January 1, 2004, to comply (see the Office of the Privacy Commissioner of Canada website at www.privcom.gc.ca). The act is based on four key principles:

- *Consumer knowledge and consent.* Consumers must know that information about them is being gathered, and they must provide consent before firms can collect, use, or disclose consumers' personal information.

- *Limitations.* Firms can collect and use only information appropriate to the transaction being undertaken. For example, if a firm needs to mail you something, it can ask for your home address, but it may not request additional information unrelated to this task.

- *Accuracy.* Firms must be sure that the information they gather is recorded accurately. Firms must appoint a privacy officer to be responsible for this task. For example, to comply with this portion of the legislation, Peter Cullen was designated as the corporate privacy officer at the Royal Bank of Canada.

- *Right to access.* Finally, individuals have the right to know what information about them is being held. They can also demand that errors in their personal information be corrected, and they may request that their personal information be withdrawn from a firm's database.

A fourth problem is that the assumptions behind CRM may not always hold true.[80] For example, it may not be the case that it costs less to serve more loyal customers. High-volume customers often know their value to a company and can leverage it to extract premium service and/or price discounts. Loyal customers may expect and demand more from the firm and resent any attempt by the firm to receive full or higher prices. They may also be jealous of attention lavished on other customers. When eBay began to chase big corporate customers such as IBM, Disney, and Sears, some small mom-and-pop businesses which helped to build the brand felt abandoned.[81] Loyal customers may not necessarily be the best ambassadors for the brand. One study found that customers who scored high on behavioural loyalty and bought a lot of a company's products were less active word-of-mouth marketers to others than customers who scored high on attitudinal loyalty and expressed greater commitment to the firm.

The benefits of database marketing do not come without heavy costs, not only in collecting the original customer data, but also in maintaining and mining them. Yet, when it works, a data warehouse yields more than it costs. A 2003 survey of 150 firms by the Gartner Group found that 61 percent of the firms realized improved efficiency due to CRM and 35 percent felt it gave them a competitive advantage.

Despite these apparent benefits, a fifth drawback of CRM is that its return on investment is often difficult to calculate. A 2004 study by the Gartner Group estimates that although 71 percent of companies calculate the cost of their CRM, only 22 percent calculate its return-on-investment (ROI).[82] Although in most cases a CRM would have a positive ROI, consider the following case where database marketing went awry:

British Columbia Telecom

British Columbia Telecom decided to invite 100 of its best customers to a Vancouver Grizzlies basketball game and selected customers who were heavy 900-number users. The invitations were already at the printer when the marketing staff discovered that heavy users of 900-numbers included sex-line enthusiasts. They quickly added other criteria to search for a revised list of guests. It turns out that database marketing is not for everyone.

Database marketing is most frequently used by business marketers and service providers (hotels, banks, airlines, insurance companies, credit-card firms, and telephone companies) that normally and easily collect a lot of customer data. Other types of companies that are in the best position to invest in CRM are companies that do a lot of cross-selling and up-selling (e.g., GE and Amazon) or companies whose customers have highly differentiated needs and are of highly differentiated value to the company. It is used less often by packaged-goods retailers and consumer packaged-goods companies, though some companies (Kraft, Quaker Oats, Ralston Purina, and Nabisco) have built databases for certain brands. Businesses where the CLV is low, that have high churn, and where there is no direct contact between the seller and ultimate buyer may not benefit as much from CRM. Some businesses cited as CRM successes include Enterprise Rent-A-Car, Fidelity Investments, Lexus, and Capital One.[83]

Deloitte Consulting reported in 1999 that 70 percent of firms found little or no improvement through CRM implementation. The reasons are many: the system was poorly designed, it became too expensive, users didn't make much use of it or report much benefit, and collaborators ignored the system. One set of business commentators suggested the following as the four main perils of CRM:[84]

1. Implementing CRM before creating a customer strategy.
2. Rolling out CRM before changing the organization to match.
3. Assuming more CRM technology is better.
4. Stalking, not wooing, customers.

All of this points to the need for each company to determine how much to invest in building and using database marketing to conduct its customer relationships. "Marketing Insight: Making CRM Work" provides some best-practice guidelines.

This Enterprise Rent-A-Car ad focuses on CRM: "There's a place where the number one priority is you."

MARKETING **INSIGHT**   MAKING CRM WORK

Customer Relationship Management (CRM) refers to the systems and tools that help businesses manage customer relationships in an organized way. These include processes that help identify and target the best customers, generate sales leads, assist in the planning and implementation of marketing campaigns, help form relationships with customers, and provide employees with information they need to know to serve customers better. However, generating the information needed to build useful databases can be a challenge.

Initially establishing a relationship with a customer can be a difficult task. Ask customers if they would like a "relationship" with their hotel, gas station, or telephone company, and odds are they will decline. However, ask them if they would like preferential, customized service, discounted pricing and special offers, and other potential benefits, the vast majority would gladly accept. Similarly, many individuals will reject responding to a survey questionnaire because they don't want companies knowing their personal details, yet expect certain companies, such as banks and airlines, to know all about them. Establishing your company as one that the customer trusts is a difficult task, but if achieved can lead to positive long-term benefits for both parties.

What makes a CRM system succeed or fail? Researchers have identified the critical success factors that determine whether a CRM system will result in profits for the organization or in a wasted investment:

1. Top-management support of CRM system
2. Communication of CRM strategy to all employees
3. Knowledge-management capabilities within the organization
4. Willingness to share data among departments within the organization
5. Willingness among employees to change processes to adapt to CRM system

6. Technological readiness of the organization

7. Culture of customer-orientation in the organization

8. Process change and systems-integration capabilities of the organization

A study of 700 firms identified the following as the prime reasons for failure of a CRM system:

1. Lack of organizational change

2. Company inertia and CRM-unfriendly policies

3. Little understanding of CRM among employees

4. Lack of CRM skills within the organization

An analysis of the above factors affecting success and failure reveals three categories of factors: human factors, processes, and technology. Clearly, an organization needs to manage all three. Studies have shown that unless all three categories are managed well, the CRM system is bound to fail; simply focusing on one or even two categories just won't do it.

Sources: Stephen F. King and Thomas F. Burgess, "Understanding Success and Failure in Customer Relationship Management," *Industrial Marketing Management, 37* (2008), pp. 421–431; Luiz E. Mendoza, Alejandro Marius, María Pérez, and Anna C. Grimán, "Critical Success Factors for a Customer Relationship Management Strategy," *Information and Software Technology, 49* (2007), pp. 913–945; Marcus Evans, "You Don't Know Me At All," *Marketing Magazine, 111*, 20 (June 5, 2006), p. 21.

SUMMARY

1. Customers are value-maximizers. They form an expectation of value and act on it. Buyers will buy from the firm that they perceive to offer the highest customer-delivered value, defined as the difference between total customer value and total customer cost.

2. A buyer's satisfaction is a function of the product's perceived performance and the buyer's expectations. Recognizing that high satisfaction leads to high customer loyalty, many companies today are aiming for TCS: total customer satisfaction. For such companies, customer satisfaction is both a goal and a marketing tool.

3. Losing profitable customers can dramatically affect a firm's profits. The cost of attracting a new customer is estimated to be five times the cost of keeping a current customer happy. The key to retaining customers is relationship marketing.

4. Quality is the totality of features and characteristics of a product or service that bear on its ability to satisfy stated or implied needs. Today's companies have no choice but to implement total-quality-management programs if they are to remain solvent and profitable.

5. Marketing managers have two responsibilities in a quality-centred company. First, they must participate in formulating strategies and policies designed to help the company win through total quality excellence. Second, they must deliver marketing quality alongside production quality.

6. Companies are also becoming skilled in customer relationship management (CRM), which focuses on meeting the individual needs of valued customers. The skill requires building a customer database and datamining to detect trends, segments, and individual needs.

APPLICATIONS

Marketing Debate: Online versus Offline Privacy?

As more and more firms practise relationship marketing and develop customer databases, privacy issues are emerging as an important topic. Consumers and public interest groups are scrutinizing—and sometimes criticizing—the privacy policies of firms; concerns are also being raised about potential theft of online credit-card information or other potentially sensitive or confidential financial information. Others maintain that online privacy fears are unfounded and that security issues are every bit as much a concern in the offline world; they argue that the opportunity to steal information exists virtually everywhere and that it is up to the consumer to protect his or her interests.

Take a position: (1) Privacy is a bigger issue in the online world than the offline world *versus* Privacy is no different online than offline. (2) Consumers on the whole receive more benefit than risk from marketers knowing their personal information.

Marketing Discussion

Consider the lifetime value of customers (CLV). Choose a business and show how you would go about developing a quantitative formulation that captures the concept. How would organizations change if they totally embraced the customer-equity concept and maximized CLV?

BREAKTHROUGH MARKETING: Tell Us About Us Inc.

In May 2008, Winnipeg-based Tell Us About Us Inc. launched an innovative customer-feedback program tailored specifically for small-business owners. Already a leader in its industry, Tell Us About Us capitalized on its experience in using sophisticated information-technology systems to deliver integrated solutions for large, multi-locale clients such as Dairy Queen, Ben & Jerry's, TravelCenters of America, and Culligan International, and used its expertise to tailor a system to suit the unique needs of smaller organizations.

The company's new product, Service Fundamentals Customer Feedback and Issue Resolution Program, is designed with the small-business owner's needs in mind. User-friendly and cost-effective, it aims to obtain actionable customer feedback by creating a dialogue with the customer. Administered on a point-of-sale receipt or through customer-feedback cards, the program also includes a resolution service that allows users to manage their customers' experiences.

The online portal and reporting structure provides clients with immediate access to valuable customer feedback. A unique feature of the system is the issue-resolution technology, which allows managers to follow up with customers to address concerns and service issues. The system also provides operational measures and ensures customer-service issues are highlighted and brought to the attention of management.

Essentially, a key focus at Tell Us About Us is the importance of managing customers' experiences. Explains Scott Griffith, Vice-President of Business Development, "In today's marketplace, companies that quantify the customer experience use the insight to make strategic decisions that not only increase customer loyalty, but positively impact their bottom line. As CEM [customer experience management] awareness grows, more companies are placing importance on the specific metrics that achieve business goals."

Unlike traditional customer-feedback programs that focus on a single mystery-shopper score or customer-satisfaction survey, Tell Us About Us combines best practices in customer surveying, mystery shopping, and live-agent support to offer a full suite of tools for customer-experience management. Another recent innovation, its online Knowledge Management Console (KMC), utilizes voice-recognition technology to analyze a consumer's voice, providing the client greater insight into the customer's experience. Tyler Gompf, CEO and co-founder of Tell Us About Us, comments on the innovation behind the KMC tool: "Over the past 18 months, Tell Us About Us took a page from our own notes by listening to our customers, understanding their requests, and taking action to meet their collective needs. This new version is very intelligent, and is the brainchild of our ten-years' experience in the CEM space."

KMC is only one tool in the company's new platform of CEM solutions. By bundling various product features, each with distinct benefits and capabilities, the company is able to provide its clients with a deeper understanding of how their customers are experiencing their brand.

The innovation of Tell Us About Us has earned the company exponential growth. Founded in 1997 by Tyler Gompf, a disgruntled customer dissatisfied with the service he was getting at a stereo store, and Kirby Gompf, his brother and co-founder, Tell Us About Us has expanded operations to include offices in Toronto and New York, and serves clients at over 30 000 locations throughout North America. CEO Tyler Gompf was a finalist for Ernst & Young's Entrepreneur of the Year award in 2006 and was recently chosen as one of 40 participants in the elite KPMG and Richard Ivey School of Business 2007 Quantum Shift Program, an exclusive, invitation-only leadership-development program.

DISCUSSION QUESTIONS

1. Discuss the role of technology in keeping customers satisfied and in developing customer loyalty. Is technology necessary for enabling customer satisfaction and loyalty?

2. What is the additional value provided by Tell Us About Us to its clients?

3. If a firm uses a service such as that provided by Tell Us About Us, how can the firm measure the benefit obtained?

Sources: "Young entrepreneur turns customer service idea into international success," *Manitoba Spirited Energy Newsletter*, www.spiritedenergy.ca/spirited_energy_newsletter_10.php (viewed May 21, 2008); Robert Price, "Creating a Positive Customer Experience," *Retailers Guide*, Retail Council of Canada, 3, no. 4, 2008; Tell Us About Us website, www.tellusaboutus.com (viewed May 21, 2008).

CHAPTER 6

ANALYZING CONSUMER MARKETS

six

Age, social status, income level, culture, and lifestyle—while designing its marketing strategy, Gap Inc., a major clothing retailer, takes into account all of these dimensions that influence consumers and their outfit preferences throughout their lifetime. Connecting with consumers at different levels allows Gap Inc. to tailor its products to varying consumer tastes and direct its marketing at multiple market segments. It is a major accomplishment for a company to effectively reach consumers in so many different groups with very different shopping expectations, finances, and lifestyles. Many clothing retailers restrict themselves to one target market. However, Gap Inc. has chosen to go after multiple consumer markets by varying its offerings in terms of retail stores and the product lines they carry.

Gap Inc. has four main retail chains, each targeting a different consumer segment. Each store has its own slogan to portray its sales intention. Gap ("Iconic American Style"), Banana Republic ("Accessible Luxury"), Old Navy ("Great Fashion, Great Prices"), and Piperlime ("A Fresh Online Shoe Shop"). Each store targets a unique consumer group: the style conscious, the luxury seeker, the price watcher, and the shoe lover. Although all of Gap Inc.'s stores are stylish and modern, they are targeted at different levels of price-consciousness, as reflected in the prices of the products at each store. More specifically, none of these stores is aimed primarily at one gender or age—they all have a wide variety of styles for both men and women. In addition, Gap chains include GapBody, GapMaternity, babyGap, and GapKids, with the latter two offering stylish and classy clothes for babies and children, something that is quite unique to Gap Inc. stores.

Not only does Gap Inc. offer a wide range of attire for the entire family, it also serves customers all over the world; as of May 2008, it had stores in Canada (185 stores), the U.S. (2684), the U.K. (138), France (38), and Japan (132). By opening stores on an international scale, Gap Inc. is reaching customers from several different cultures.

Expanding internationally can be very challenging for businesses no matter what industry they are in, and Gap Inc. has addressed this challenge by creating an international division focused on making the international shopping experience a good one. Managing its overseas operations, the international division of the company has two Presidents, one focused on Japan and the other on the European stores. This set-up allows Gap Inc. to create more focused strategies that are specific to the diverse needs of consumers and businesses in different parts of the world.

One of Gap Inc.'s most recent innovations is the online collaboration of all four of its stores. This allows consumers to conveniently shop online at four very different stores and put all of their purchases in one "cart." On average, people are now working more than ever and Gap Inc. is changing its marketing strategies to coincide with busy lifestyles. "We're thrilled to offer our customers the ease and convenience of shopping our four amazing brands online with only one check-out," says Toby Lenk, President of Gap Inc. Direct, the company's online retail division. "Universality allows us to leverage the strength of our iconic brands and still maintain each brand's identity."

Clearly, Gap Inc. works hard to find ways to connect with its current and potential customers by creating a unique shopping experience and environment at each of its distinctive stores. Over time, Gap Inc. has evolved to take into account a majority of the various factors that influence consumer behaviour. To minimize cannibalization among its four store chains, Gap Inc. distinguishes the stores from one another by carrying distinctly different product lines at each store. The different offerings, combined with the unique names of the four store chains, make it difficult for consumers to recognize that the stores are all part of the same parent company.

Gap Inc. periodically conducts extensive marketing research to understand the consumer behaviour of its target segments and uses this knowledge to serve its customers better. This effort has helped the company experience rapid growth, making it one of the leading clothing retailers in the world. It is little wonder that Gap Inc. now operates over 3100 stores worldwide, covering nearly 40-million square feet. The company's sales revenues in 2007 were US$15.8 billion, a long way from the US$1 billion it had just two decades ago.

Sources: Gap Inc., www.gapinc.com/public/OurBrands/brands.shtml (viewed May 28, 2008); "Gap Inc. Unveils New Online Feature, Offering Customers Four Brands In One Shopping Bag, One Check-out And One Low Shipping Rate," Gap Inc. Press Release, gapinc.com/public/Media/Press_Releases/med_pr_GIDuniversality052708.shtml, May 27, 2008 (viewed May 30, 2008); Gap Inc., "Leadership," www.gapinc.com/public/About/abt_leader.shtml (viewed May 31, 2008); Gap Inc., "Fact Sheet," www.gapinc.com/public/About/abt_fact_sheet.shtml (viewed May 30, 2008); Gap Inc., "Milestones," www.gapinc.com/public/About/abt_milestones.shtml (viewed May 30, 2008); Gap Inc., "Real Estate," www.gapinc.com/public/Investors/inv_re.shtml (viewed May 28, 2008).

The aim of marketing is to meet and satisfy target customers' needs and wants better than competitors. **Consumer behaviour** is the study of how individuals, groups, and organizations select, buy, use, and dispose of goods, services, ideas, or experiences to satisfy their needs and wants. Studying consumers provides clues for improving or introducing products or services, setting prices, devising channels, crafting messages, and developing other marketing activities. Marketers are always looking for emerging trends that suggest new marketing opportunities. The metrosexual is one:

> In the summer of 2003, some marketing pundits proclaimed the existence of a new male market—the "metrosexual"—which was defined as straight urban men who enjoy such things as shopping and using grooming products and services. English soccer star David Beckham, with his carefully crafted fashion look, has been touted as the quintessential metrosexual icon. He's not afraid to wear either nail polish or sarongs (off the field, that is). One researcher estimated that 30 to 35 percent of young North American men exhibited metrosexual tendencies, as evidenced in part by their purchase of products such as skin-care cream and fragrances. Another study found "an emerging wave of men who chafe against the restrictions of traditional male roles and do what they want, buy what they want, enjoy what they want—regardless of whether some people might consider them unmanly." The emergence of this market has been a boon for men's grooming products, fuelling the success of brands such as Unilever's Axe, a fragrant all-over body spray, The Body Shop's "For Men" line, and U.K. drugstore chain Boots' newly opened Men's Zones.[1]

Successful marketing requires that companies fully connect with their customers. Adopting a holistic marketing orientation means understanding consumers: gaining a 360-degree view of both their daily lives and the changes that occur during their lifetimes. Gaining a thorough, in-depth

consumer understanding helps to make sure that the right products are marketed to the right consumers in the right way. This chapter explores individual-consumer buying dynamics; the next chapter explores the buying dynamics of business buyers.

WHAT INFLUENCES CONSUMER BEHAVIOUR?

Marketers must fully understand both the theory and reality of consumer behaviour. Table 6.1 includes some interesting facts about Canadian consumption expenditures, and "Marketing Insight: A Maturing Market" describes the maturing marketplace in Canada and potential implications for marketing.

A consumer's buying behaviour is influenced by cultural, social, and personal factors. Cultural factors exert the broadest and deepest influence.

Cultural Factors

Culture, subculture, and social class are particularly important influences on consumer buying behaviour. **Culture** is the fundamental determinant of a person's wants and behaviour. The growing child acquires a set of values, perceptions, preferences, and behaviours through his or her family and other key institutions. A child growing up in Canada is exposed to the following values: respect for diversity, respect for basic human rights and individual freedoms (e.g., freedom of speech, freedom of religion, and the right to be equal before and under the law), love of the outdoors and nature, achievement and success, activity, efficiency and practicality, progress, material comfort and external comfort, humanitarianism, and youthfulness.[2]

The culturally based, shared understanding of certain symbols can provide marketers with powerful communication tools. Savvy marketers are using such Canadian icons as the Canadian flag, Canadian wildlife, and Mounties to help tie their products to the sense of pride many Canadians take in their country and its products. Companies such as Roots, Petro-Canada, Molson, Tim Hortons, and Air Canada follow this practice.[3]

Each culture consists of smaller **subcultures** that provide more specific identification and socialization for their members. Subcultures include nationalities, religions, racial groups, and geographic regions. When subcultures grow large and affluent enough, companies often design specialized marketing programs to serve them. *Multicultural marketing* grew out of careful marketing research, which revealed that different ethnic and demographic niches did not always respond favourably to mass-market advertising. Companies have capitalized on well-thought-out multicultural marketing strategies in recent years (see "Marketing Insight: Marketing to Quebec

TABLE 6.1	CANADIAN CONSUMPTION STATISTICS

Based on an estimated 12.4 million Canadian households, total average annual expenditures were reported to be $67 736 in 2006, broken down into the following categories:

Personal income taxes	$13 634
Shelter	$12 986
Transportation	$9240
Food	$7046
Recreation	$3975
Personal insurance payments and pension contributions	$3832
Household operation	$3251
Clothing	$2870
Household furnishings and equipment	$2131
Health care	$1867
Tobacco products and alcoholic beverages	$1475
Gifts of money and contributions	$1505
Education	$1157
Miscellaneous	$1087
Personal care	$1158
Games of chance (net amount)	$258
Reading materials and other printed matter	$264

Source: Statistics Canada, "Average Household Expenditures, by Province and Territory," *2006 Census Data*, CANSIM Table 203-0001, last modified May 23, 2008.

MARKETING **INSIGHT** | A MATURING MARKET

The median age in Canada is higher than ever before (median age is defined as the point at which exactly one-half of the population is older, and the other half is younger). The most recent (2006) census data on age and sex show the median age of Canada's population as 39.5 years, an increase of 1.9 years from 2001 and 4.2 years from 1996. To see how rapidly the Canadian population has aged, it is interesting to note that the median age in Canada in 1966 (the year when the last of the baby boomers was born) was 25.4 years. Today, Canada's working-age population is dominated by older individuals, but there are regional variations. Nova Scotia, Newfoundland and Labrador, and New Brunswick have the oldest populations with median ages exceeding 41 years. Among the provinces, Alberta is the youngest with a median age of 36.0, although this looks rather old in comparison with Nunavut, which has a median age of just 23.1 years.

The greying of Canada means that companies will have to do more than pay lip service to the idea of marketing to older people. Yet, businesses are not suddenly going to lose all interest in the younger demographic. Instead, companies will have to learn to establish brands that attract older consumers without alienating younger ones. One example: a recent Oreo-cookies commercial features NFL celebrity brothers Eli and Peyton Manning having an Oreo-licking contest. Other versions of the commercial show two police officers engaging in a similar contest and a grandmother competing with her granddaughter. Oreo, which has traditionally targeted kids, is now showing more adults than kids in its advertising.

As the populace gets older, the concept of "old" is also changing. People aren't considered "over the hill" at 50 any more. Smart marketers will capitalize on changing perceptions and create an image of an ageless society where people define themselves by the activities they are involved in rather than by their age. For instance, university students can be 20, 30, or 60 years old.

Sources: Alison Stein Wellner, "The Next 25 Years," *American Demographics* (April 2003): 24–27; Statistics Canada, "Portait of the Canadian Population in 2006, by Age and Sex, 2006 Census," Catalogue no. 97-551-XIE.

and French-Canadian Consumers"). Consider the tactics The Bay is using to attract Toronto's South Asian community:

FUSIA Boutique

With the majority of Canada's new immigrants settling in Toronto, it has become one of the most diverse cities in the world. Mainstream retailers are realizing that they must respond to this growing diversity if they want to compete. In May 2007, The Bay introduced a new line of South Asian fashions called Fusia in its downtown-Toronto store. The South Asian community is one of the fastest growing in Toronto. Two designers, Anokhi and Alia Khan, are responsible for the launch of the Fusia line. The ANOKHI label offers very trendy, but moderately priced, clothing that has eastern embroidery on western constructions. With a slightly different approach, the Alia Khan label is a moderate- to high-end, formal collection offering eastern fabrics and embellishment, combined with the designer's signature cuts in a western format. The two designers are confident that the Fusia line will offer something for everyone.[4]

Virtually all human societies exhibit *social stratification*. Stratification sometimes takes the form of a caste system in which the members of different castes are reared for certain roles and cannot change their caste membership. More frequently, it takes the form of **social classes**, relatively homogeneous and enduring divisions in a society, which are hierarchically ordered and whose members share similar values, interests, and behaviour.

Social classes have several characteristics. First, those within each class tend to behave more alike than persons from two different social classes. Social classes differ in dress, speech patterns, recreational preferences, and many other characteristics. Second, persons are perceived as occupying inferior or superior positions according to social class. Third, social class is indicated by a cluster of variables—for example, occupation, income, wealth, education, and value orientation—rather than by any single variable. Fourth, individuals can move up or down the social-class ladder during their lifetimes. The extent of this mobility varies according to how rigid the social stratification is in a given society.

Social classes show distinct product and brand preferences in many areas, including clothing, home furnishings, leisure activities, and automobiles. Social classes differ in media preferences, with upper-class consumers often preferring magazines and books and lower-class consumers often preferring television. Even within a media category such as TV, upper-class consumers tend to prefer news and drama, and lower-class consumers tend to prefer soap operas and sports programs. There are also language differences among the social classes. Advertising copy and dialogue must ring true to the targeted social class.

REGIONALISM   Canada is an increasingly regionalized country and the way people think, act, and buy varies greatly from one region to the next. The sheer size of the country and its varied geographic features and climate have certainly shaped regional character and personality. For example, Atlantic Canada is largely defined by its proximity to and historical relationship with the sea. Equally, the isolation imposed by the mountain barrier, along with the abundance and grandeur of British Columbia's natural environment, has shaped the outlook of that region's residents. Immigration has also had a differential effect on the different regions within Canada. The economy of each region furthers these differences. The rise and decline of such tradable commodities as fish, timber, wheat,

The Bank of Montreal's "Profitez" tagline conveyed to Quebecers meanings associated with the enjoyment of life.

| MARKETING INSIGHT | MARKETING TO QUEBEC AND FRENCH-CANADIAN CONSUMERS |

Quebec has long prided itself on being a "distinct society." Marketers must be aware of Quebec's uniqueness if they are to be successful in the province. Quebec is characterized by unique laws, a different mix of indigenous and national businesses and industries, and attitudes and values distinct from those in the rest of Canada. According to the 2006 census data, 5 877 660 (79 percent) of the 7 435 900 people who make up Quebec's population claim French as their mother tongue. In contrast, 575 560 (7.7 percent) claim English as their native language, with the remaining 13.3 percent having a different native tongue or a combination of French and English.

Known for their "joie de vivre," the majority of Quebec's population (49 percent, or 3.6 million people) lived in the Montreal area in 2006. Montreal has a large number of high-tech industries, is the second largest metropolitan area in Canada (behind Toronto), and is the second largest French-speaking city in the world. However, one must not assume that the population of the Montreal region is homogeneous and made up only of French Canadians. Bilingualism is very common and the population is quite diverse as a result of immigration. According to the 2006 census, 20.6 percent of Montrealers are immigrants.

As a means of perpetuating its French culture and affirming the province's French-speaking identity, Quebec governments have passed legislation to ensure the use of French in various areas of public life. This is most evident in the education system, where the majority of schools are French speaking, although a few English schools are available.

Marketers who want to appeal to Quebec consumers need to do more than communicate in French using dictionary translations of words. Take a successful campaign by the Bank of Montreal that used the tagline "Profitez." You wouldn't fully understand the campaign if you used only a dictionary-based interpretation of the word. You'd find translations that said *profitez* means "profit from," "to profit," "to earn," or "something profitable." However, for Quebec consumers the meaning is more nuanced. They translate it as "make the most of it," "enjoy," or "take advantage," and the expression is strongly associated with the enjoyment of life—meanings that make the campaign more powerful and rich. Language and the meanings derived from it are very cultural and context-based. Furthermore, research has revealed differences in the activities, interests, opinions, and consumption habits of French-Canadian and English-Canadian consumers. French Canadians value their European roots, their rich and diverse cultural venues, gourmet food, and fine wines. As a result, Montreal is known as one of the trendiest centres in the world. Additionally, French-Canadian women are more family-oriented and fashion-conscious than women in the rest of Canada. Such differences are partly derived from their Latin cultural roots.

Demographic and socioeconomic differences also exist: education and income are both lower in Quebec than in Ontario. The legal environment is also different for marketers in Quebec. Besides strict language laws, there are stronger restrictions on advertising to children, with Quebec having some of the strictest regulations in the country. To be successful in French Canada, marketers must develop appeals that take these differences into account. For example, while many marketers use national symbols to appeal to their customers, Quebec's separatist sentiments make this practice unwise.

Research conducted by S. C. Johnson revealed that even attitudes toward cleaning vary between English and French Canada. While English Canadians just want to get the job done and see cleaning as a necessary evil, people in Quebec get a sense of pride and accomplishment after they clean. Using this research, S. C. Johnson designed a highly successful campaign for its cleaning products that centred on the distinctly Quebecois custom of moving day: July 1, the date on which renters move from one apartment to another because leases in Quebec traditionally expire on June 30. Similarly, English and French Canadians differ in their attitudes towards cooking: 70 percent of English-speaking populations consider themselves "comfort cooks," that is, they cook to feed the family and to get the food on the table. On the other hand, 70 percent of Quebecers consider themselves creative cooks and are proud of their skills.

Quebec also has a distinct business and retail climate. Lavo Group, for example, is a packaged-goods manufacturer whose products rival those of Procter & Gamble and Colgate in the province. Many Québécois buy such Lavo products as La Parisienne laundry detergent and fabric softener instead of Tide and Downy, Hertel liquid cleanser instead of Mr. Clean, and Old Dutch powdered cleanser instead of Comet.

The financial-services industry is also very different in Quebec than in the rest of Canada. Two players that are almost nonexistent in English Canada, the Mouvement Desjardins (the federation of Quebec credit unions) and the National Bank, account for over 70 percent of the province's financial-services marketplace. Both use integrated and Quebec-specific communications campaigns.

Quebec-based hardware chains Réno-Depot and RONA have many loyal customers in the province. When Home Depot entered Quebec in 2000, it had to compete with these companies—a set of competitors completely different from those it had confronted in the rest of Canada. To help Home Depot gain acceptance, Montreal-based Cossette Communications developed an advertising campaign that appealed to the unique sense of humour of the Québécois. Rather than creating ads with rational appeals that proclaimed Home Depot's high-quality service, Cossette conducted qualitative research to uncover examples of realistic and believable bad shopping experiences of Quebec consumers. The campaign that resulted from this research features one commercial that shows a clerk literally running away from a client. In another commercial, a group of clerks chant, "It is not my department" despite customers' looks of dismay. The campaign not only created awareness of Home Depot, but was listed among Montrealers' favourite commercials at that time.

For a long time, Quebec lagged behind the rest of Canada in terms of Internet adoption and usage. Today, however, more than 65 percent of Quebec adults are online. There is a growing number of French sites and online services such as La Toile du Québec (www.toile.com), Canoë (http://fr.canoe.ca/), and PetitMonde (www.petitmonde.com), as well as the French versions of popular portals like Sympatico, Yahoo!, and MSN. Marketers have been quick to leverage this new interconnectivity. Volkswagen, Avon, L'Oréal, and La Senza are some of the Quebec-based companies that have jumped on the bandwagon. Not only are they building French versions of their company websites, they have intensified their email marketing campaigns in the province. The race is on to build databases to further this effort. Sympatico.ca, for example, has an opt-in email database of 700 000 French Canadians, comprising adults aged 25 to 49, most with families.

If marketers respect Quebec's unique laws with regard to contests and sweepstakes, they can utilize these tools to help build their databases. Sympatico.ca experienced phenomenal results when it ran a contest to meet Bryan Adams in Scotland. People had to register online and Sympatico amassed 20 000 new Quebec subscribers as a result of this campaign. As their marketing manager noted, "French-speaking people love to play. And because they love to play, they tend to give their personal information freely—and by that I mean their postal code, age, and gender." However, marketers have to tread softly. Quebecers still like to be wooed, especially when it comes to developing a one-to-one relationship. People from Quebec prefer more face-to-face interactions and personal contact than do people from the rest of the country.

Marketers must also be aware that Quebec has its own icons and unique media personalities. For example, Bell Canada's long-running Monsieur B campaign, which originated in 1992, is almost unknown in the rest of Canada. However, it has approached legendary status in the province, the way other advertising icons like the Green Giant, Aunt Jemima, and the lonely Maytag repairman have done in the rest of Canada. Jean-François Richard, vice-president of marketing communications at Bell in Montreal, notes, "I don't know of any creative platform (anywhere) that has lasted so long and generated such results for so long for any advertiser!"

Because of all these differences, many advertisers develop unique campaigns designed just for the Quebec marketplace. Take the case of Pepsi, for example. Five different young actors are featured in its spots. They walk around wearing T-shirts with the letters that spell the word Pepsi, while celebrating such cultural expressions as poutine and the fact that Quebecers say "icit," not "ici." Other firms, like Calgary-based Telus Mobility, use standardized themes, but heavily tailor them to better communicate with the Quebec audience. Says Anne-Marie LaBerge, director of communications (Quebec), for Telus Mobility, "We have one brand, and we don't create a separate campaign for Quebec. . . . We take the national campaign and work with Taxi to adapt it. The message is the same and we give it a Quebec flavour."

Regardless of the specific approach a company takes, one thing is clear: It is extremely important for the company to understand the culture and language of Quebecers. This goes further than knowing the subtleties of the French language—it requires having a deep understanding of Québécois consumers, including key insights into their culture, lifestyle, motivations, and attitudes.

Sources: Samson Okalow, "Vive la Difference: Does That Mean I Have to Have a Separate Campaign?" *Strategy* (October 15, 2004): p. 31; Nicolette Flemming, "The True Meaning of 'Profitez'," *Marketing* (June 10, 2002): p. 31; Samson Okalow, "Quebec Success: Weather Network and Dairy Farmers of Canada Hit the Right Formula," *Strategy* (October 15, 2004): p. 32; Bernadette Johnson, "E-mail Marketing Begins to Flourish in La Belle Province," *Strategy: The Canadian Marketing Report* (May 20, 2002): p. D10; Helena Katz, "Johnson Sharpens Its Quebec Strategy," *Marketing* (October 12, 1998): p. 3; Shawna Steinberg, "Only in English Canada, You Say?," *Marketing* (November 12, 1998): p. 10; Danny Kucharsky, "Monsieur B's Family," *Marketing Magazine Online* (June 11, 2001), www.marketingmag.ca; Nathalie Fortier, "Building Success: How Cossette Poked Fun at Bad Customer Service to Give Home Depot a Firm Foundation in Quebec," *Marketing Magazine Online* (September 24, 2001), www.marketingmag.ca; Tracey Arial, "Taking Aim at the Giants," *Marketing Magazine Online* (June 11, 2001), www.marketingmag.ca; Government of Quebec, www.gouv.qc.ca (viewed June 5, 2002); Sarah Dobson, "McCormick Adds Spice to Quebec." *Marketing, 108,* 9 (March 10, 2003): p. 2.

minerals, and petroleum have affected the mindsets and buying behaviour of people living within Canada's different regions. In particular, regional inequalities that resulted from fluctuating resource economies contributed to the rise of regional grievances, stereotypes, and dependencies that became part of each region's identity. However, many analysts today disagree with the view that regional disparities in outlook and behaviour are a simple byproduct of economics and geography. Instead they argue that these marked regional differences result from social relationships. In particular, disparities in political power have driven increased regionalism. The emergence of a new social class in Quebec—a new middle class of educated francophone professionals whose aspirations were blocked by the lack of opportunities for their skills within the old Quebec, with its backward state, its outdated, Church-administered social programs, and its Anglo-dominated business sector—is credited with giving birth to this trend. However, Quebec is not alone. In Alberta, a more regional identity has also emerged as the province has strived to become more politically assertive and pro-business. Alberta also focuses on a set of issues centred on energy and taxation policies that are quite different from those at the top of the political agenda in the other provinces.[5]

Social Factors

In addition to cultural factors, a consumer's behaviour is influenced by such social factors as reference groups, family, and social roles and statuses.

REFERENCE GROUPS A person's **reference groups** consist of all the groups that have a direct (face-to-face) or indirect influence on his or her attitudes or behaviour. Groups having a direct influence on a person are called **membership groups**. Some membership groups are **primary groups**, such as family, friends, neighbours, and co-workers, those with whom the person interacts fairly continuously and informally. People also belong to **secondary groups**, such as religious, professional, and trade-union groups, which tend to be more formal and require less continuous interaction.

People are significantly influenced by their reference groups in at least three ways. Reference groups expose an individual to new behaviours and lifestyles, they influence attitudes and self-concept, and they create pressures for conformity that may affect actual product and brand choices. People are also influenced by groups to which they do not belong. **Aspirational groups** are those a person hopes to join; **dissociative groups** are those whose values or behaviour an individual rejects. Teens, for example, often wish to dissociate themselves from their parents.

Manufacturers of products and brands for which group influence is strong must determine how to reach and influence opinion leaders in these reference groups. An **opinion leader** is the person in informal, product-related communications who offers advice or information about a specific product or product category, such as which of several brands is best or how a particular product may be used.[6] Marketers try to reach opinion leaders by identifying demographic and psychographic characteristics associated with opinion leadership, identifying the media read by opinion leaders, and directing messages at opinion leaders. The Influencers is an association that helps marketers find and reach opinion leaders.

TheInfluencers.ca

The Influencers is the first and only Canadian community committed to helping start and spread word-of-mouth conversations among Canada's opinion leaders. The people involved in this community—called the Influencers—are some of the most connected, informed, involved, and influential people in Canada. The Influencers are introduced to new, innovative, insider, or breakthrough products and opportunities. They are then encouraged to spread the word to others in their social networks. By participating in word-of-mouth activities, the Influencers collect Influence points. These points can later be redeemed for prizes or donations to worthy charities.[7]

In Japan, high-school girls have often been credited with creating the buzz that makes products such as Shiseido's Neuve nail polish a big hit.[8]

FAMILY The family is the most important consumer-buying organization in society, and family members constitute the most influential primary reference group.[9] We can distinguish between two families in the buyer's life. The **family of orientation** consists of parents and siblings. From parents a person acquires an orientation toward religion, politics, and economics, and a sense of personal ambition, self-worth, and love.[10] Even if the buyer no longer interacts very much with his or her parents, their influence on behaviour can be significant. In countries where parents live with grown children, their influence can be substantial. A more direct influence on everyday buying behaviour is the **family of procreation**—namely, one's spouse and children.

Marketers are interested in the roles and relative influence of family members in the purchase of a large variety of products and services. In North America, husband–wife involvement has traditionally varied widely by product category. The wife has usually acted as the family's main purchasing agent, especially for food, sundries, and staple-clothing items, while husbands were targeted for more infrequent, big-ticket items such as electronics and cars. Now traditional purchasing roles are changing, and marketers would be wise to see both men and women as possible targets. For example, in 1978 only 10 percent of males were classified as primary shoppers, but in 1998 the figure had risen to 17 percent. *Canadian Grocer* magazine estimates that 25 to 30 percent of men now shop for groceries. Some males are forced into the role of shopper by demographic and lifestyle changes such as late marriage and high divorce rates, but most take on the role as a result of being part of a time-pressed, two-income household.[11]

With expensive products and services like cars, vacations, and housing, the vast majority of husbands and wives engage in more joint decision making.[12] Given women's increasing wealth and income-generating ability, financial service firms such as Citigroup, Charles Schwab, and Merrill Lynch have expanded their efforts to attract women investors and business owners.[13] Upscale leisure activities are also being targeted more and more at women. For example, the golf club at the Whistler resort in British Columbia offers women-only golf lessons. And marketers are realizing that men aren't the main buyers of high-tech gizmos and gadgets these days. Women actually buy more technology than men do, but consumer-electronics stores have been slow to catch on to this fact. Some savvy electronics stores are starting to heed women's complaints of being ignored, patronized, or offended by salespeople. RadioShack Corp., a 7000-store chain, began actively recruiting female store managers so that now a woman manages about one out of every seven stores.[14]

Marketers are focusing more closely on women and their needs: This Dutch Boy "Twist and Pour" ad, which features a new, easy-to-use paint container, is targeted specifically at women.

Nevertheless, men and women may respond differently to marketing messages.[15] One study showed that women valued connections and relationships with family and friends and placed a high priority on people. Men, on the other hand, related more to competition and placed a high priority on action. Marketers are taking more direct aim at women with new products such as Quaker's Nutrition for Women cereals and Crest Rejuvenating Effects toothpaste. Gillette Co. researched psychological issues specific to women and came out with an ergonomically designed razor, Venus, that fit more easily in a woman's hand. Sherwin-Williams recently designed a Dutch Boy easy-to-use "Twist and Pour" paint can targeted specifically at women.

Canadian Tire is another organization that is actively pursuing the women's market.

Canadian Tire

Canadian Tire is one of Canada's most well-known and successful retailers, with over 450 locations all across the nation. Canadian Tire offers customers a large selection of national and retail brands through three "stores" under one roof: automotive, sports and leisure, and home products. The home-products department has received added focus of late, particularly in how it promotes itself to female consumers, and for good reason. Analysts estimate that 85 percent of all retail purchases are either directly or indirectly influenced by women. With this idea in mind, Canadian Tire, which previously had a hardware-store image, underwent a transformation in order to become more "women friendly." The transformation plan included incorporating many new design features, such as wider aisles, brighter lighting, and more "touch and feel" displays in newly built and renovated concept stores in order to attract more female-shoppers' dollars. In an attempt to sell more female-oriented products, Canadian Tire introduced the Debbie Travis brand of products, which specifically targets female shoppers.[16]

Another shift in buying patterns is an increase in the amount of money spent by, and the direct and indirect influence wielded by, children and teens.[17] Direct influence describes children's "pester power": their hints, requests, and demands (e.g., "I want to go to McDonald's"). Research by Toronto-based Corus Entertainment indicates that kids currently influence some $20 million in household spending in Canada each year and have memorized between 300 and 400 brand names by the age of ten. The study also suggests that time-pressed, guilt-ridden parents respond favourably to 75 percent of kids' requests. It's not surprising, therefore, that industry spending on advertising to children has exploded in the past decade, increasing from a mere $100 million in 1990 to more than $2 billion by the year 2000.[18] Indirect influence means that parents know the brands, product choices, and preferences of their children without hints or outright requests. One research study showed that teenagers

Canadian Tire has been moving away from its previous "hardware store" image that appeals more to men to a more "woman-friendly" one.

were playing a more active role than before in helping parents choose a car, audio/video equipment, or a vacation spot.[19] See how Hummer is trying to get kids interested in its brand early on:

Hummerkids.com

Hummer, a brand of rugged-looking SUVs sold by General Motors, has recognized the influence that children have on the vehicle-purchase decisions made by their parents. Hummer has created a website targeted at children, hummerkids.com, that contains games, downloads, and activities meant to attract children to the Hummer brand. Among other things, children can play See the World, a game modelled after the popular children's game Hangman, colour pictures of Hummers, download Hummer wallpaper for their rooms, and even customize their own Hummer and print it out to show their friends. Each game, download, and activity, of course, incorporates reminders of the Hummer brand, and is intended to teach children about the joys of travelling in a Hummer.[20]

Marketers use every possible channel of communication to reach kids, especially such popular media as television's Nickelodeon, the Cartoon Network, and the Disney Channel, and magazines such as *Nickelodeon*, *Sports Illustrated for Kids*, and *Disney Adventures*. Corus Entertainment offers Canadian advertisers a host of products they can use to reach young consumers, including YTV, Teletoon, and Discovery Kids.

YTV

YTV prides itself on being Canada's leading youth network. Its programs, aimed at audiences from 2 to 17 years of age and their families, reach over a million young viewers every week. The network broadcasts 15 of the top 20 children's shows in Canada. YTV is also Canada's number-one channel for tweens aged 9 to 14. It segments its programming by time of day. It has a daytime preschool block, *The Zone* is Canada's most popular after-school block, and *Crunch* is a Saturday-morning animation-fest. Sunday evenings, called *ZAPX* (pronounced Zap-Pics), are dedicated to showing blockbuster movies. YTV's offerings go far beyond television. It has bragging rights as the number-one Canadian kids' website; it has its own travelling road show, *Weird on Wheels*; and it publishes *YTV Whoa!*, a magazine. YTV also takes to heart its role as a responsible children's programmer. It is a founding member of Canadian Cable in the Classroom, it encourages media literacy awareness through *TV & Me*, and it has partnered with the Kids Help Phone.[21]

The Hannah Montana juggernaut demonstrates how powerful television can be in reaching children, and marketers are using television to target children at younger ages than ever before. By the time children are around two years old, they often can recognize characters, logos, and specific brands. Marketers are tapping into that audience with product tie-ins, placed at a child's eye level, on just about everything—from Scooby Doo vitamins to Elmo juice and cookies.[22]

The Canadian Marketing Association makes it clear that special care must be taken by marketers seeking to target the children's market. However, marketing to children is not new. Consider what many large cell-phone providers have done with regard to marketing their products to children:

Kids' Cell Phones

To tap the relatively untouched market of tweens (kids aged 8–12), numerous companies such as Mattel have begun to market cell phones to this demographic. The goal is both to generate revenue and to build brand loyalty early. Mattel licensed the "My Scene" brand name, which is aimed at the preteen market. Similarly, Firefly mobile has released a simple five-button phone aimed at kids aged 8–12, and in some cases, geared to kids as young as five. This new trend of marketing cellular phones to children is expected to yield huge dividends for these firms. In fact, according to IDC, a technology-research firm in Massachusetts, an estimated 31 million new young users will have joined the market by 2010 in the United States alone. However, this relatively new trend is not without controversy. Jovenes Verdes, an environmental advocacy group for young people, argues that "the mobile telephone industry is acting like the tobacco industry by designing products that addict the very young." Health Canada has also released a statement that warns consumers to limit cell phone use, especially by children.[23]

| MARKETING MEMO | HEY, MARKETER, LEAVE THE KIDS ALONE! |

There is no denying that children influence the purchases of their elders. So, it is no surprise that marketers try to use this influence to promote their products. Between 1992 and 1997, there was an explosion in advertising expenditures towards kids because of what marketers termed "kidfluence," the ability of children to influence an estimated $20 billion in purchases per year. As a result, the social issue of marketing to children has been put under the microscope, both by consumers and policy makers.

The targeting of kids by marketers has led to numerous new regulations to control advertising to kids. Only two countries (Sweden and Norway) and one province (Quebec) have outright bans on television advertising targeted at kids. That is not to say that other areas of the world don't take interest, as most countries have some form of regulation on advertising to children. But these regulations generally come in the form of statutory guidelines, self-regulatory guidelines, or specific restrictions rather than bans. Some of the Canadian Radio-television and Telecommunications Commission (CRTC) regulations on advertising to children (defined as below the age of 12 years) include:

- Maximum of eight minutes of commercials per hour of TV programming
- No repetition of commercials in the half-hour duration of a children's program
- No direct urging to act, such as "call now"
- No mail or telephone orders permitted
- No endorsement by any celebrity person or character (including cartoons) unless created by the advertiser
- No attempt to play down price with words such as "great deal," "bargain," "just," or "only" in price
- No advertising of drugs or vitamins
- No advertising comparing competing brands
- No portrayal of children or adults in unsafe acts or situations
- Most importantly, quite unlike advertisements directed at adults, the advertisement must not imply that possession or use of the product will make the owner superior or that without it the child will be open to ridicule or contempt

Due to the lack of concrete evidence against marketing campaigns aimed at children, it does not appear other Canadian provinces will follow the lead of Quebec. Moreover, children are still exposed to cross-border TV programming from the U.S., making a ban on advertising to children in English-speaking provinces ineffective. However, this does not mean that Quebec's efforts at curtailing advertising to children have failed, as a study published in the *Journal of Marketing Research* found that English-speaking children in Montreal who watched cross-border TV programming from the U.S. recognized more toys and consumed more boxed cereal than did French-speaking kids who did not watch American programs and so were not exposed to commercials.

Sources: Margaret Hastings, "Empower the Children," *Marketing*, 11, 31 (September 26, 2005): p. 16; Danny Kucharsky, "Targeting kids," *Marketing*, *109*, 24 (July 12–19, 2004): p. 6; Marvin Goldberg, "A Quasi-Experiment Assessing the Effectiveness of TV Advertising Directed to Children," *Journal of Marketing Research*, 27,4 (November 1990): pp. 445–454.

Today companies are also likely to use the Internet to show products to children and solicit marketing information from them. Millions of kids under the age of 17 are online. Marketers have jumped online with them, offering freebies in exchange for personal information. Many have come under fire for this practice and for not clearly differentiating ads from games or entertainment. The Canadian Marketing Association has taken a strong stand on marketing to children. See "Marketing Memo: Hey, Marketer, Leave the Kids Alone!"

ROLES AND STATUSES   A person participates in many groups: family, clubs, organizations. The person's position in each group can be defined in terms of role and status. A **role** consists of the activities a person is expected to perform. Each role carries a **status**. A senior vice-president of marketing has more status than a sales manager, and a sales manager has more status than an office clerk. People choose products that reflect and communicate their role and actual or desired status in society. Company presidents often drive Mercedes, wear expensive suits, and drink Chivas Regal scotch. Marketers must be aware of the status-symbol potential of products and brands.

Personal Factors

A buyer's decisions are also influenced by personal characteristics. These include the buyer's age and stage in the life cycle, occupation and economic circumstances, personality and self-concept, and lifestyle and values. Because many of these characteristics have a very direct impact on consumer behaviour, it is important for marketers to follow them closely.

AGE AND STAGE IN THE LIFE CYCLE People buy different goods and services over a lifetime. Taste in food, clothes, furniture, and recreation is often age-related. Consumption is also shaped by the *family life cycle* and the number, age, and gender of people in the household at any point in time. North American households are increasingly fragmented—the traditional family of four with a husband, wife, and two kids makes up a much smaller percentage of total households than it once did. In addition, *psychological* life-cycle stages may matter. Adults experience certain "passages" or "transformations" as they go through life.

Marketers should also consider *critical life events or transitions*—marriage, childbirth, illness, relocation, divorce, career change, widowhood—as giving rise to new needs. These should alert service providers—banks; lawyers; and marriage, employment, and bereavement counsellors—to ways they can help.[24]

OCCUPATION AND ECONOMIC CIRCUMSTANCES Occupation may also influence consumption patterns, but caution has to be used not to make stereotypical decisions. A blue-collar worker will buy work clothes, work shoes, and lunchboxes, but may also belong to the local yacht club. A company president will buy dress suits and air travel, but may also play in the local men's hockey league. Marketers try to identify the occupational groups that have above-average interest in their products and services. A company can even tailor its products for certain occupational groups: computer-software companies, for example, design different products for brand managers, engineers, lawyers, and physicians.

Product choice is greatly affected by economic circumstances: spendable income (level, stability, and time pattern), savings and assets (including the percentage that is liquid), debts, borrowing power, and attitudes towards spending and saving. Luxury goods makers such as Gucci, Prada, and Burberry can be vulnerable to an economic downturn. If economic indicators point to a recession, marketers can take steps to redesign, reposition, and reprice their products or they can introduce or increase the emphasis on discount brands so that they can continue to offer value to target customers.

PERSONALITY AND SELF-CONCEPT Each person has personality characteristics that influence his or her buying behaviour. By **personality**, we mean a set of distinguishing human psychological traits that lead to relatively consistent and enduring responses to environmental stimuli. Personality is often described in terms of such traits as self-confidence, dominance, autonomy, deference, sociability, defensiveness, and adaptability.[25] Personality can be a useful variable in analyzing consumer brand choices. The idea is that brands also have personalities, and consumers are likely to choose brands whose personalities match their own. We define **brand personality** as the specific mix of human traits that may be attributed to a particular brand.

Stanford's Jennifer Aaker conducted research into brand personalities and identified the following five traits:[26]

1. Sincerity (down-to-earth, honest, wholesome, and cheerful)
2. Excitement (daring, spirited, imaginative, and up-to-date)
3. Competence (reliable, intelligent, and successful)
4. Sophistication (upper-class and charming)
5. Ruggedness (outdoorsy and tough)

She proceeded to analyze some well-known brands and found that a number of them tended to be strong on one particular trait: Levi's with "ruggedness"; MTV with "excitement"; CNN with "competence"; and Campbell's with "sincerity." The implication is that these brands will attract persons who score high on the same personality traits. A brand personality may have several attributes: Levi's suggests a personality that is also youthful, rebellious, and authentic. The company utilizes product features, services, and image making to transmit the product's personality.

Consumers often choose and use brands that have a brand personality consistent with their own *actual self-concept* (how one views oneself), although in some cases the match may be based on a consumer's *ideal self-concept* (how one would like to view oneself) or even *others' self-concept* (how

A Levi's ad expresses the brand personality: youthful, rebellious, and authentic.

one thinks others see one) rather than actual self-image.[27] These effects may also be more pronounced for publicly consumed products than for privately consumed goods.[28] On the other hand, consumers who are high "self-monitors"—that is, sensitive to how others see them—are more likely to choose brands whose personalities fit the consumption situation.[29]

LIFESTYLE AND VALUES People from the same subculture, social class, and occupation may lead quite different lifestyles. A **lifestyle** is a person's pattern of living in the world as expressed in activities, interests, and opinions. Lifestyle portrays the "whole person" interacting with his or her environment. Marketers search for relationships between their products and lifestyle groups. For example, a computer manufacturer might find that most computer buyers are achievement-oriented. The marketer may then aim the brand more clearly at the achiever lifestyle. Marketers are always uncovering new trends in consumer lifestyles. Here's an example of one of the latest lifestyle trends businesses are currently targeting:

LOHAS

Consumers who worry about the environment, want products to be produced in a sustainable way, and spend money to advance their personal development and potential have been named "LOHAS." The name is an acronym standing for *lifestyles of health and sustainability*. The market for LOHAS products encompasses things like organic foods, energy-efficient appliances and solar panels, alternative medicine, yoga tapes, and eco-tourism. Rather than looking at discrete product categories like cars or organic foods, it is more important to look at the common factors linking these product groups—for example, at cars, energy, and household products that are perceived as better for the environment and society. Companies like Loblaws serve this emerging segment by offering alternative products such as organic foods and reusable cloth shopping bags. It is estimated that the market for LOHAS products well exceeds US$200 billion. It is also estimated that about 20 percent of adult consumers in the U.S. are LOHAS consumers.[30]

Lifestyles are shaped partly by whether consumers are *money-constrained* or *time-constrained*. Companies aiming to serve money-constrained consumers will create lower-cost products and services. By appealing to the money-constrained, Wal-Mart has become the largest company in the world. Its "everyday low prices" have wrung tens of billions of dollars out of the retail supply chain, passing the larger part of savings along to shoppers with rock-bottom bargain prices.[31]

Consumers who experience time famine are prone to **multitasking**, that is, doing two or more things at the same time. They will phone or eat while driving, or bicycle to work to get exercise. They will also pay others to perform tasks because time is more important than money. They may prefer bagels to breakfast cereals because they are quicker. Companies aiming to serve them will create convenient products and services for this group. Much of the wireless revolution is fuelled by the multitasking trend. Research In Motion (RIM), based in Waterloo, Ontario, is widely regarded as an industry leader in wireless solutions and handheld devices that provide seamless access to time-sensitive information from sources including email, phone, SMS messaging, Internet, and intranet-based applications.

In some categories, notably food processing, companies targeting time-constrained consumers need to be aware that these very same consumers seek the illusion that they are not operating within time constraints. The food processing industry has a name for those who seek both convenience and some involvement in the cooking process: the "convenience involvement segment"[32]—a market that Kraft Dinner has included as a target.

Kraft Dinner

Kraft Foods has specialized in developing easy meal solutions for over 100 years. However, few product releases have had the same success as Kraft Dinner. With a package of Kraft Dinner, some milk, and butter, a tasty meal is less than 15-minutes away. With an estimated 44 percent of evening meals prepared in under 30 minutes, and strong competition from fast food drive-through windows, restaurant deliveries, and precooked grocery store dishes, Kraft Dinner's days of prosperity might seem numbered. Market researchers found, however, that some consumers do not necessarily want the fastest microwavable meal solution possible—they also want to feel good about how they prepare a meal. In fact, on average, they would prefer to use at least one pot or pan and 15 minutes of time. To remain attractive to the segment that want to spend less time in the kitchen without totally abandoning their traditional roles as family meal-makers, marketers of Kraft Dinner are always introducing new flavours to tap into the latest consumer taste trends. In fact, Kraft even has recipes on its website in which Kraft Dinner is combined with other ingredients to make a wide variety of meals.[33]

Consumer decisions are also influenced by **core values**, the belief systems that underlie consumer attitudes and behaviours. Core values go much deeper than behaviour or attitude, and determine, at a basic level, people's choices and desires over the long term. Marketers who target consumers on the basis of their values believe that by appealing to people's inner selves, it is possible to influence their outer selves—their purchase behaviour.

KEY PSYCHOLOGICAL PROCESSES

The starting point for understanding consumer behaviour is the stimulus-response model shown in Figure 6.1. A set of psychological processes combines with environmental stimuli and certain consumer characteristics, ultimately resulting in purchase decisions. The marketer's task is to understand what happens in the consumer's consciousness between the arrival of the outside marketing stimuli and the ultimate purchase decisions. Four key psychological processes—motivation, perception, learning, and memory—fundamentally influence consumer responses to the various marketing stimuli.

Motivation: Freud, Maslow, Herzberg

A person has many needs at any given time. Some needs are *biogenic:* they arise from physiological states of tension such as hunger, thirst, and discomfort. Other needs are *psychogenic:* they arise from psychological states of tension such as the need for recognition, esteem, and belonging. A need becomes a motive when it is aroused to a sufficient level of intensity. A **motive** is a need that is sufficiently pressing to drive the person to act.

Three of the best-known theories of human motivation—those of Sigmund Freud, Abraham Maslow, and Frederick Herzberg—carry quite different implications for consumer analysis and marketing strategy.

FREUD'S THEORY Sigmund Freud assumed that the psychological forces shaping people's behaviour are largely unconscious and that a person cannot fully understand his or her own motivations.

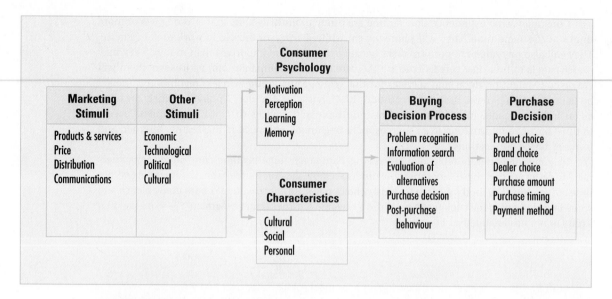

FIGURE 6.1

Model of Consumer Behaviour

When a person examines specific brands, he or she will react not only to their stated capabilities, but also to other, less conscious cues. Shape, size, weight, material, colour, and brand name can all trigger certain associations and emotions. A technique called *laddering* can be used to trace a person's motivations from the stated instrumental ones to the more terminal ones. Then the marketer can decide at what level to develop the message and appeal.[34]

Motivation researchers often collect "in-depth interviews" with a few dozen consumers to uncover deeper motives triggered by a product. They use various *projective techniques* such as word association, sentence completion, picture interpretation, and role playing. Many of these techniques were pioneered by Ernest Dichter, a Viennese psychologist who settled in the United States.[35]

Today, motivational researchers continue the tradition of Freudian interpretation. Jan Callebaut identifies different motives a product can satisfy. For example, whisky can meet the need for social relaxation, status, or fun. Different whisky brands need to be motivationally positioned in one of these three appeals.[36] Another motivation researcher, Clotaire Rapaille, works on breaking the "code" behind a lot of product behaviour. Research analyzing paper towels, according to Rapaille, revealed that its appeal to mothers is in how cleanliness plays into their instinctive desire to have their genes survive. "You are not just cleaning the table. You are saving the whole family," asserts the researcher.[37]

MASLOW'S THEORY   Abraham Maslow sought to explain why people are driven by particular needs at particular times.[38] Why does one person spend considerable time and energy on personal safety and another on pursuing the high opinion of others? Maslow's answer is that human needs are arranged in a hierarchy, from the most pressing to the least pressing. In order of importance, they are physiological needs, safety needs, social needs, esteem needs, and self-actualization needs (see Figure 6.2). People will try to satisfy their most important needs first. When a person succeeds in satisfying an important need, he or she will then try to satisfy the next-most-important need. For example, a starving man (need 1) will not take an interest in the latest happenings in the art world (need 5), nor in how he is viewed by others (need 3 or 4), nor even in whether he is breathing clean air (need 2); but when he has enough food and water, the next-most-important need will become salient.

Maslow's theory helps marketers understand how various products fit into the plans, goals, and lives of consumers.

HERZBERG'S THEORY   Frederick Herzberg developed a two-factor theory that distinguishes *dissatisfiers* (factors that cause dissatisfaction) and *satisfiers* (factors that cause satisfaction).[39] The absence of dissatisfiers is not enough; satisfiers must be present to motivate a purchase. For example, a computer that does not come with a warranty would be a dissatisfier. Yet the presence of a product warranty would not act as a satisfier or motivator of a purchase, because it is not a source of intrinsic satisfaction. Ease of use would be a satisfier.

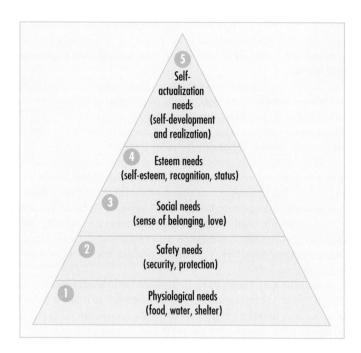

FIGURE 6.2

Maslow's Hierarchy of Needs

Source: *Motivation and Personality*, 2nd ed., by A. H. Maslow, 1970. Reprinted by permission of Prentice Hall, Inc., Upper Saddle River, New Jersey.

Herzberg's theory has two implications. First, sellers should do their best to avoid dissatisfiers (e.g., a poor training manual or a poor service policy). Although these things will not sell a product, they might easily "unsell" it. Second, the seller should identify the major satisfiers or motivators of purchase in the market and then supply them. These satisfiers will be the major determinant of which brand the customer buys.

Perception

A motivated person is ready to act. How the motivated person actually acts is influenced by his or her view or perception of the situation. **Perception** is the process by which an individual selects, organizes, and interprets information inputs to create a meaningful picture of the world.[40] Perception depends not only on the physical stimuli, but also on the stimuli's relation to the surrounding field and on conditions within the individual. The key point is that perceptions can vary widely among individuals exposed to the same reality. One person might perceive a fast-talking salesperson as aggressive and insincere; another, as intelligent and helpful. Each will respond differently to the salesperson.

In marketing, perceptions are more important than the reality, as it is perceptions that will affect consumers' actual behaviour. People can emerge with different perceptions of the same object because of three perceptual processes: selective attention, selective distortion, and selective retention.

SELECTIVE ATTENTION It has been estimated that the average person may be exposed to over 1500 ads or brand communications a day. Because a person cannot possibly attend to all of these, most stimuli will be screened out—a process called **selective attention**. Selective attention means that marketers have to work hard to attract consumers' notice. The real challenge is to explain which stimuli people will notice. Here are some findings:

1. *People are more likely to notice stimuli that relate to a current need.* A person who is motivated to buy a computer will notice computer ads; he or she will be less likely to notice DVD ads.

2. *People are more likely to notice stimuli that they anticipate.* You are more likely to notice computers than radios in a computer store because you do not expect the store to carry radios.

3. *People are more likely to notice stimuli whose deviations are large in relation to the normal size of the stimuli.* You are more likely to notice an ad offering $100 off the list price of a computer than one offering $5 off.

Although people screen out much of the surrounding stimuli, they are influenced by unexpected stimuli, such as sudden offers in the mail, over the phone, or from a salesperson. Marketers may attempt to promote their offers intrusively to bypass selective attention filters.

SELECTIVE DISTORTION   Even noticed stimuli do not always come across in the way the senders intended. **Selective distortion** is the tendency to interpret information in a way that will fit our pre-conceptions. Consumers will often distort information to be consistent with prior brand and product beliefs.[41]

A stark demonstration of the power of consumer brand beliefs is the typical result of product-sampling tests. In "blind" taste tests, one group of consumers samples a product without knowing which brand it is, whereas another group of consumers samples the product knowing which brand it is. Invariably, differences arise in the opinions of the two groups despite the fact that the two groups are *literally consuming exactly the same product*!

When consumers report different opinions between branded and unbranded versions of identical products, it must be the case that their brand and product beliefs, created by whatever means (e.g., past experiences, marketing activity for the brand), have somehow changed their product perceptions. Examples of branded differences can be found with virtually every type of product. For example, one study found that consumers were equally split in their preference for Diet Coke over Diet Pepsi when tasting both on a blind basis.[42] When tasting the branded versions, however, consumers preferred Diet Coke by 65 percent and Diet Pepsi by only 23 percent (with the remainder seeing no difference).

Selective distortion can work to the advantage of marketers with strong brands when consumers distort neutral or ambiguous brand information to make it more positive. In other words, beer may seem to taste better, a car may seem to drive more smoothly, the wait in a bank line may seem shorter, and so on, depending on the particular brands involved.

SELECTIVE RETENTION   People will fail to register much information to which they are exposed in memory, but will tend to retain information that supports their attitudes and beliefs. Because of **selective retention**, we are likely to remember good points about a product we like and forget good points about competing products. Selective retention again works to the advantage of strong brands. It also explains why marketers need to use repetition in sending messages to their target market: to make sure their message is not overlooked.

SUBLIMINAL PERCEPTION   The selective perception mechanisms require active engagement and thought by consumers. A topic that has fascinated armchair marketers for ages is **subliminal perception**. The argument is that marketers embed covert, subliminal messages in ads or packages. Consumers are not consciously aware of these messages, yet they affect consumers' behaviour.

A Pepsi Challenge taste test in New York's Central Park. Companies like Pepsi often conduct taste tests of their products against other branded products to see if brand really makes a difference in customer preferences.

Although it is clear many subtle subconscious effects can exist with consumer processing,[43] no evidence supports the notion that marketers can systematically control consumers at the subconscious level.[44]

Learning

When people act, they learn. **Learning** involves changes in an individual's behaviour arising from experience. Most human behaviour is learned. Learning theorists believe that learning is produced through the interplay of drives, stimuli, cues, responses, and reinforcement.

A **drive** is a strong internal stimulus impelling action. **Cues** are minor stimuli that determine when, where, and how a person responds. Suppose you buy a Dell computer. If your experience is rewarding, your response to computers and Dell will be positively reinforced. Later on, when you want to buy a printer, you may assume that because Dell makes good computers, Dell also makes good printers. In other words, you *generalize* your response to similar stimuli. The opposite of generalization is discrimination. **Discrimination** means that the person has learned to recognize differences in sets of similar stimuli and can adjust responses accordingly.

Learning theory teaches marketers that they can build demand for a product by associating it with strong drives, using motivating cues, and providing positive reinforcement. A new company can enter the market by appealing to the same drives that competitors use and by providing similar cue configurations, because buyers are more likely to transfer loyalty to similar brands (generalization); or the company might design its brand to appeal to a different set of drives and offer strong cue inducements to switch (discrimination).

Memory

All the information and experiences individuals encounter as they go through life can end up in their long-term memory. Cognitive psychologists distinguish between **short-term memory (STM)**—a temporary repository of information—and **long-term memory (LTM)**—a more permanent repository.

Most widely accepted views of long-term memory structure involve some kind of associative model formulation.[45] For example, the **associative network memory model** views LTM as consisting of a set of nodes and links. *Nodes* are stored information connected by *links* that vary in strength. Any type of information can be stored in the memory network, including information that is verbal, visual, abstract, or contextual. A spreading activation process from node to node determines the extent of retrieval and what information can actually be recalled in any given situation. When a node becomes activated because external information is being encoded (e.g., when a person reads or hears a word or phrase) or internal information is retrieved from LTM (e.g., when a person thinks about some concept), other nodes are also activated if they are sufficiently strongly associated with that node.

Consistent with the associative network memory model, consumer brand knowledge in memory can be conceptualized as consisting of a brand node in memory with a variety of linked associations. The strength and organization of these associations will be important determinants of the information that can be recalled about the brand. **Brand associations** consist of all brand-related thoughts, feelings, perceptions, images, experiences, beliefs, attitudes, and so on that become linked to the brand node.

Marketing can be seen as making sure that consumers have the right types of product and service experiences such that the right brand knowledge structures are created and maintained in memory. MasterCard has been successful in getting consumers to identify emotionally with its brand.

MasterCard

MasterCard has achieved success by positioning its brand on an emotional platform rather than on the rational platform that Visa uses. MasterCard uses the famous advertising campaign, "There are some things money can't buy. For everything else there's MasterCard." In 1996, when the campaign was launched, MasterCard faced sliding sales and competition from Visa was slowly pushing MasterCard out of people's minds. The "priceless" campaign was aimed at differentiating the brand on the basis of intangibles, that is, emotions. Through advertising, MasterCard has convinced people that using MasterCard can help them experience the "priceless" moments in life. The aim is to strengthen consumers' connections between MasterCard and the experiences they desire and will remember for a long time. The campaign has been very successful for MasterCard, increasing the company's international profile and heightening its appeal worldwide.[46]

FIGURE 6.3

Hypothetical Dole Mental Map

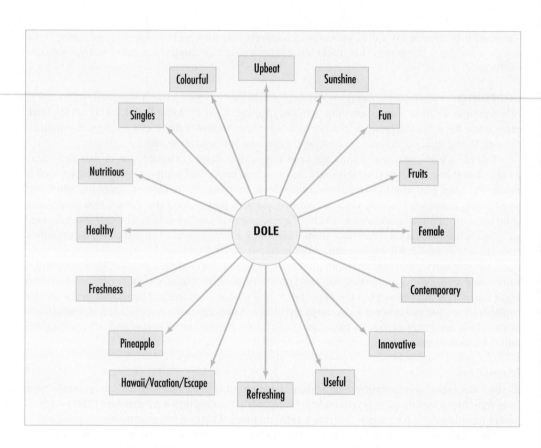

Companies such as Procter & Gamble like to create mental maps that depict brand associations that are likely to be triggered in a marketing setting, and their relative strength, favourability, and uniqueness to consumers. Figure 6.3 displays a very simple mental map highlighting brand beliefs for a hypothetical consumer for the Dole brand.

MEMORY PROCESSES: ENCODING **Memory encoding** refers to how and where information gets into memory. Memory encoding can be characterized according to the amount or quantity of processing that information receives at encoding (i.e., how much a person thinks about the information) and the nature or quality of processing that information receives at encoding (i.e., the manner in which a person thinks about the information). The quantity and quality of processing will be an important determinant of the strength of an association.[47]

In general, the more attention given to the meaning of information during encoding, the stronger the resulting associations in memory will be.[48] When a consumer actively thinks about and "elaborates" on the significance of product or service information, stronger associations are created in memory. Another key determinant of the strength of a newly formed association will be the content, organization, and strength of existing brand associations in memory. It will be easier for consumers to create an association to new information when extensive, relevant knowledge structures already exist in memory. One reason why personal experiences create such strong brand associations is that information about the product is likely to be related to existing knowledge.

Consider the brand associations that might be created by a new TV ad campaign employing a popular Canadian sports figure designed to create a new benefit association for a well-known brand. For example, consider the case when Olympic speed skater and gold-medallist Catriona Le May Doan appeared in a commercial for Nestlé PowerBar. Viewers might process the ad in very different ways:

1. Some consumers may barely notice the ads so that the amount of processing devoted to the ads is extremely low, resulting in weak to nonexistent brand associations.

2. The ads may catch the attention of other consumers, resulting in sufficient processing, but these consumers may devote most of the time during the ads thinking about the Olympics and wondering how they can get their children to this level of athletic excellence.

3. Another group of consumers may not only notice the ads but also think of how they had a wrong impression of PowerBars. The ad may cause them to think in a different way about the product. For example, women may have perceived that this is a "men's only" product and may now realize it is also aimed at their needs.

In addition to depending on congruency or consistency with existing knowledge, the ease with which new information can be integrated into established knowledge structures clearly depends on the nature of that information—characteristics such as simplicity, vividness, and concreteness.

Repeated exposures to information provide greater opportunity for processing and thus the potential for stronger associations. Recent advertising research in a field setting, however, suggests that qualitative considerations and the manner or style of consumer processing engendered by an ad are generally more important than the cumulative total of ad exposures.[49] In other words, high levels of repetition for an un-involving, unpersuasive ad is unlikely to have as much sales impact as lower levels of repetition for an involving, persuasive ad.

MEMORY PROCESSES: RETRIEVAL **Memory retrieval** refers to how information gets out of memory. According to the associative network memory model, the strength of a brand association increases both the likelihood that that information will be accessible and the ease with which it can be recalled by "spreading activation." Successful recall of brand information by consumers does not depend only on the initial strength of that information in memory. Three factors are particularly important.

First, the presence of *other* product information in memory can produce interference effects. It may cause the information to be either overlooked or confused. One challenge in a category crowded with many competitors—such as airlines, financial services, and insurance companies—is that consumers may mix up brands.

Second, the time at encoding since exposure to information affects the strength of a new association: the longer the time delay, the weaker the association. The time elapsed since the last exposure opportunity, however, has been shown generally to produce only gradual decay. Cognitive psychologists believe that memory is extremely durable, so that once information becomes stored in memory, its strength of association decays very slowly.[50]

Third, information may be "available" in memory (i.e., potentially recallable) but may not be "accessible" (i.e., unable to be recalled) without the proper retrieval cues or reminders. The particular associations for a brand that "comes to mind" depend on the context in which the brand is considered. The more cues linked to a piece of information, however, the greater the likelihood that the information can be recalled. The effectiveness of retrieval cues is one reason why marketing *inside* a supermarket or other retail store—the actual product packaging, the use of in-store mini-billboard displays, and so on—is so critical. The information contained and the reminders provided of advertising or other information already conveyed outside the store will be prime determinants of consumer decision making.

THE BUYING-DECISION PROCESS: THE FIVE-STAGE MODEL

These basic psychological processes play an important role in understanding how consumers actually make their buying decisions. Marketers must understand every facet of consumer behaviour. Table 6.2 provides a list of some key consumer-behaviour questions in terms of "who, what, when, where, how, and why." Smart companies try to fully understand the customers' buying-decision process: all their experiences in learning about, choosing, using, and even disposing of a product.[51]

Honda engineers took videos of shoppers loading groceries into car trunks to observe their frustrations and generate possible design solutions. Intuit, the maker of Quicken financial software, watched first-time buyers try to learn Quicken to sense their problems in learning how to use the product. Bissell developed its Steam 'n Clean vacuum cleaner based on the product-trial experiences of a local PTA group near its corporate headquarters. The result was a name change, colour-coded attachments, and an infomercial highlighting the cleaner's special features.[52]

Marketing scholars have developed a "stage model" of the buying decision process (see Figure 6.4). The consumer passes through five stages: problem recognition, information search, evaluation of

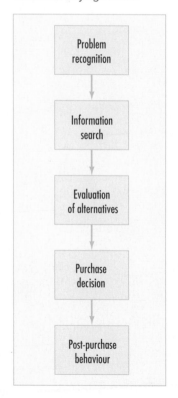

FIGURE 6.4

Five-Stage Model of the Consumer Buying Process

Problem recognition

Information search

Evaluation of alternatives

Purchase decision

Post-purchase behaviour

TABLE 6.2	UNDERSTANDING CONSUMER BEHAVIOUR

- Who buys our product or service?
- Who makes the decision to buy the product?
- Who influences the decision to buy the product?
- How is the purchase decision made? Who assumes what role?
- What does the customer buy? What needs must be satisfied?
- Why do customers buy a particular brand?
- Where do they go or look to buy the product or service?
- When do they buy? Any seasonality factors?
- How is our product perceived by customers?
- What are customers' attitudes toward our product?
- What social factors might influence the purchase decision?
- Do customers' lifestyles influence their decisions?
- How do personal or demographic factors influence the purchase decision?

Source: Based on list from George Belch and Michael Belch, *Advertising and Communication Management*, 6th ed. (Homewood, IL: Irwin, 2003).

alternatives, purchase decision, and post-purchase behaviour. Clearly, the buying process starts long before the actual purchase and has consequences long afterward.[53]

But consumers do not always pass through all five stages in buying a product. They may skip or reverse some stages. A woman buying her regular brand of toothpaste goes directly from the need for toothpaste to the purchase decision, skipping information search and evaluation. The model in Figure 6.4 provides a good frame of reference, however, because it captures the full range of considerations that arise when a consumer faces a highly involving new purchase.[54]

Problem Recognition

The buying process starts when the buyer recognizes a problem or need. The need can be triggered by internal or external stimuli. With an internal stimulus, one of the person's normal needs—hunger, thirst, sex—rises to a threshold level and becomes a drive; with an external stimulus, a need can be aroused. A person may admire a neighbour's new car or see a television ad for a Hawaiian vacation and this triggers thoughts about the possibility of making a purchase. A believer in "retail theatre," Krispy Kreme lights a neon "HOT NOW" sign to get attention—and purchase interest—each time a new batch of doughnuts is baked.

Marketers need to identify the circumstances that trigger a particular need by gathering information from a number of consumers. They can then develop marketing strategies that trigger consumer interest. This is particularly important with discretionary purchases such as luxury goods, vacation packages, and entertainment options. Consumer motivation may need to be increased so that a potential purchase is even given serious consideration.

Information Search

An aroused consumer will be inclined to search for more information. We can distinguish between two levels of arousal. The milder search state is called *heightened attention*. At this level a person simply becomes more receptive to information about a product. At the next level, the person may enter an *active information search:* looking for reading material, phoning friends, going online, and visiting stores to learn about the product.

Of key interest to the marketer are the major information sources to which the consumer will turn and the relative influence each will have on the subsequent purchase decision. These information sources fall into four groups:

- *Personal.* Family, friends, neighbours, acquaintances.
- *Commercial.* Advertising, websites, salespersons, dealers, packaging, displays.
- *Public.* Mass media, consumer-rating organizations.
- *Experiential.* Handling, examining, using the product.

The relative amount and influence of these sources vary with the product category and the buyer's characteristics. Generally speaking, the consumer receives the most information about a product from commercial sources—that is, marketer-dominated sources. However, the most effective information often comes from personal sources or public sources that are independent authorities. More than 40 percent of all car shoppers consult *Consumer Reports,* making it the biggest single source of information.[55] Each information source performs a different function in influencing the buying decision. Commercial information normally performs an information function, whereas personal sources perform a legitimizing or evaluation function. For example, physicians often learn of new drugs from commercial sources but turn to other doctors for evaluations.

The Internet has changed how people search for information. Today's marketplace is made up of traditional consumers (who do not shop online), cyber-consumers (who shop mostly online), and hybrid consumers (who do both).[56] Most consumers are hybrid: They shop in grocery stores but occasionally order from Grocery Gateway; they shop for books in Chapters Indigo bookstores but also sometimes order books from Chapters.Indigo.ca. People still like to squeeze the tomatoes, touch the fabric, smell the perfume, and interact with salespeople. They are motivated by more than shopping efficiency. Most companies will need a presence both offline and online to cater to these hybrid consumers. *Maclean's,* a popular Canadian magazine, has been doing this effectively.

Maclean's

Maclean's is Canada's only national weekly current-affairs magazine, focusing on politics, international affairs, business, culture, and a number of other topics. *Maclean's* currently has about 2.8 million readers, and has successfully made the jump online (www.macleans.ca). The *Maclean's* website contains many unique features that cannot be offered by a regular "paper-based" publication. These features include various forms of multimedia, blogs, and a search option to find archived material. Like many other magazines that have created an online presence, *Maclean's* must recognize the need to ensure online quality, but at the same time not cannibalize its magazine sales. This is a difficult balance that few publications have been able to achieve. Pricing is also a big issue, and magazines that have gone online have struggled to increase revenues, wondering if there should be a subscription fee to access online content. *Maclean's* has chosen to address this problem by having an advertisement-driven website that is free to the general public. Many of the advertisements on the *Maclean's* website have to do with subscribing to the magazine version of the publication. However, *Maclean's* also offers what it calls "subscriber services," whereby subscribers to the magazine can access material that is not accessible to the public. Some of this extra material includes a digital edition, back issues, and a comprehensive university guide. Only the future can tell if having a significant online presence will help or harm the hard-copy version of *Maclean's* magazine.[57]

Through gathering information, the consumer learns about competing brands and their features. The first box in Figure 6.5 shows the *total set* of brands available to the consumer. The individual consumer will come to know only a subset of these brands (*awareness set*). Some brands will meet initial buying criteria (*consideration set*). As the consumer gathers more information, only a few will remain as strong contenders (*choice set*). The consumer makes a final choice from this set.[58]

Figure 6.5 makes it clear that a company must strategize to get its brand into the prospect's awareness set, consideration set, and choice set. Food companies might work with supermarkets, for instance, in changing the way they display products. If a store owner arranges yogurt first by brand (like Dannon and Yoplait) and then by flavour within each brand, consumers will tend to select their flavours from the same brand. However, if the products had been displayed with all the strawberry yogurts together, then all the vanilla yogurts, and so forth, consumers would probably choose which flavours they wanted first, and then choose which brand name they would most like for that particular flavour. Australian supermarkets arrange meats by the way they might be cooked, and stores use more descriptive labels, like "a 10-minute herbed beef roast." The result is that Australians buy a greater variety of meats than North Americans, who choose from meats laid out by type: beef, chicken, pork, and so on.[59]

Successive Sets Involved in
Consumer Decision Making

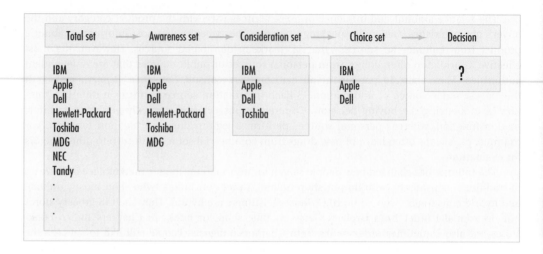

The company must also identify the other brands in the consumer's choice set so that it can plan the appropriate competitive appeals. In addition, the company should identify the consumer's information sources and evaluate their relative importance. Consumers should be asked how they first heard about the brand, what information came later, and the relative importance of the different sources. The answers will help the company prepare effective communications for the target market.

Evaluation of Alternatives

How does the consumer process competitive brand information and make a final value judgment? No single process is used by all consumers or by one consumer in all buying situations. There are several processes, the most current models of which see the process as cognitively oriented. That is, the consumer is seen as forming judgments largely on a conscious and rational basis.

Some basic concepts will help us understand consumer evaluation processes: First, the consumer is trying to satisfy a need. Second, the consumer is looking for certain benefits from the product solution. Third, the consumer sees each product as a bundle of attributes with varying abilities for delivering the benefits sought to satisfy this need. The attributes of interest to buyers vary by product; for example:

1. *Cameras.* Picture sharpness, camera speeds, camera size, price.
2. *Hotels.* Location, cleanliness, atmosphere, price.
3. *Mouthwash.* Colour, effectiveness, germ-killing capacity, price, taste/flavour.
4. *Tires.* Safety, tread life, ride quality, price.

Consumers will pay the most attention to attributes that deliver the sought-after benefits. The market for a product can often be segmented according to attributes that are important to different consumer groups.

BELIEFS AND ATTITUDES Evaluations often reflect beliefs and attitudes. Through experience and learning, people acquire beliefs and attitudes. These in turn influence buying behaviour. A **belief** is a descriptive thought that a person holds about something. People's beliefs about the attributes and benefits of a product or brand influence their buying decisions. Just as important as beliefs are attitudes. An **attitude** is a person's enduring favourable or unfavourable evaluation, emotional feeling, and action tendencies toward some object or idea.[60] People have attitudes towards almost everything: religion, politics, clothes, music, and food.

Attitudes put people into a frame of mind: liking or disliking an object, moving towards or away from it. Attitudes lead people to behave in a fairly consistent way towards similar objects. Because attitudes economize on energy and thought, they can be very difficult to change. A company is well advised to fit its product into existing attitudes rather than to try to change attitudes. Of course, there are exceptions for which the cost of trying to change attitudes might pay off, especially if you are trying to market a controversial product or idea.

Council for Biotechnology Information (CBI)

The Council for Biotechnology Information began a new transit-shelter campaign in Toronto to coincide with the BIO 2002 conference. The advertising was aimed at the 15 000 visitors expected to attend the conference, as well as at city residents. A series of three ads posed "teaser questions" and referred viewers to the council's website (www.whybiotech.com) to find answers. The copy read, "How can a canola plant save energy?" "How does Canada regulate biotech corn?" and "How can a cotton plant resist pests?" Since biotechnology is controversial and since it's neither a brand nor a product, generating awareness and encouraging people to get accurate information has been the focus of the council's advertising and communications efforts.[61]

EXPECTANCY-VALUE MODEL The consumer arrives at attitudes (judgments, preferences) towards various brands through an attribute-evaluation procedure.[62] He or she develops a set of beliefs about where each brand stands on each attribute. The **expectancy-value model** of attitude formation posits that consumers evaluate products and services by combining their brand beliefs—the positives and negatives—according to importance.

Suppose Linda Brown has narrowed her choice set to four laptop computers: A, B, C, and D. Assume that she is interested in four attributes: memory capacity, graphics capability, size and weight, and price. Table 6.3 shows her beliefs about how each brand rates on the four attributes. If one computer dominated the others on all the criteria, we could predict that Linda would choose it. But, as is often the case, her choice set consists of brands that vary in their appeal. If Linda wants the best memory capacity, she should buy A; if she wants the best graphics capability, she should buy B; and so on.

Most buyers consider several attributes in their purchase decision. If we knew the weights that Linda Brown attaches to the four attributes, we could more reliably predict her computer choice. Suppose Linda assigned 40 percent of the importance to the computer's memory capacity, 30 percent to graphics capability, 20 percent to size and weight, and 10 percent to price. To find Linda's perceived value for each computer, according to the expectancy-value model, we multiply her weights by her beliefs about each computer's attributes. This computation leads to the following perceived values:

Computer A = 0.4(10) + 0.3(8) + 0.2(6) + 0.1(4) = 8.0
Computer B = 0.4(8) + 0.3(9) + 0.2(8) + 0.1(3) = 7.8
Computer C = 0.4(6) + 0.3(8) + 0.2(10) + 0.1(5) = 7.3
Computer D = 0.4(4) + 0.3(3) + 0.2(7) + 0.1(8) = 4.7

To learn how the High-Tech Computer (HTC) from Taiwan has successfully connected with Asian consumers for touch-screen phones, visit www.pearsoned-asia.com/marketingmanagementasia.

Changing attitudes is difficult, but with good information, such as that presented by the Biotechnology Council's website, it can be accomplished.

TABLE 6.3	A CONSUMER'S BRAND BELIEFS ABOUT COMPUTERS			
	Memory Capacity	Graphics Capability	Size and Weight	Price
A	10	8	6	4
B	8	9	8	3
C	6	8	10	5
D	4	3	7	8

Note: Each attribute is rated from 0 to 10, where 10 represents the highest level of that attribute. Price, however, is indexed in a reverse manner, with a 10 representing the lowest price, because a consumer prefers a low price to a high price.

An expectancy-model formulation would predict that Linda will favour computer A, which (at 8.0) has the highest perceived value.[63]

Suppose most computer buyers form their preferences the same way. Knowing this, a computer manufacturer can do a number of things to influence buyer decisions. The marketer of computer B, for example, could apply the following strategies to stimulate greater interest in brand B:

- *Redesign the computer.* This technique is called real repositioning.
- *Alter beliefs about the brand.* Attempting to alter beliefs about the brand is called psychological repositioning.
- *Alter beliefs about competitors' brands.* This strategy, called competitive depositioning, makes sense when buyers mistakenly believe a competitor's brand has more quality than it actually has.
- *Alter the importance weights.* The marketer could try to persuade buyers to attach more importance to the attributes in which the brand excels.
- *Call attention to neglected attributes.* The marketer could draw buyers' attention to neglected attributes, such as styling or processing speed.
- *Shift the buyer's ideals.* The marketer could try to persuade buyers to change their ideal levels of one or more attributes.[64]

"Marketing Memo: Applying Customer Value Analysis" describes a cost–benefit technique that provides additional insight into consumer decision making in a competitive setting.

Purchase Decisions

In the evaluation stage, the consumer forms preferences among the brands in the choice set. The consumer may also form an intention to buy the most preferred brand. In executing a purchase intention, the consumer may make up to five sub-decisions: *brand* (brand A), *dealer* (dealer 2), *quantity* (one computer), *timing* (weekend), and *payment method* (credit card). Purchases of everyday products involve fewer decisions and less deliberation. For example, in buying sugar, a consumer gives little thought to vendor or payment method.

In some cases, consumers may decide not to formally evaluate each and every brand; in other cases, intervening factors may affect the final decision.

NONCOMPENSATORY MODELS OF CONSUMER CHOICE The expectancy-value model is a compensatory model in that perceived good about a product can help to overcome perceived bad. But consumers may not want to invest much time and energy to evaluate brands. They often take "mental shortcuts" that involve various simplifying *choice heuristics*.

With **noncompensatory models** of consumer choice, positive and negative attribute considerations do not necessarily net out. Evaluating attributes more in isolation makes decision making easier for a consumer, but also increases the likelihood that the person would have made a different choice if he or she had deliberated in greater detail. We highlight three such choice heuristics here:

1. With the **conjunctive heuristic**, the consumer sets a minimum acceptable cutoff level for each attribute and chooses the first alternative that meets the minimum standard for all attributes. For example, if Linda Brown decided that all attributes had to be rated at least a 7, she would choose computer B.

MARKETING MEMO | APPLYING CUSTOMER VALUE ANALYSIS

A useful technique to gain consumer insight is customer value analysis. *Customer value analysis* assumes that customers choose among competitive brand offerings on the basis of which delivers the most customer value. Customer value is calculated as:

Customer value = Customer benefits – Customer costs

Customer benefits include *product benefits, service benefits, personnel benefits,* and *image benefits.* Assume customers can judge the relative benefit level or worth of different brands. Suppose a customer is considering three brands, A, B, and C, and judges the customer benefits to be worth $150, $140, and $135, respectively. If the customer costs are the same, the customer would clearly choose brand A.

However, the costs are rarely the same. In addition to *purchase price,* costs include *acquisition costs, usage costs, maintenance costs, ownership costs,* and *disposal costs.* Often a customer will buy a more expensive brand because that particular brand will impose lower costs than the other kinds. Consider Table 6.4. A, the highest-priced brand, also involves a lower total cost than lower-priced brands B and C. Clearly, supplier A has done a good job of reducing customers' other costs. Now we can compare the customer value of the three brands:

TABLE 6.4	CUSTOMER COSTS OF THREE BRANDS		
	A	B	C
Price	$100	$90	$ 80
Acquisition costs	15	25	30
Usage costs	4	7	10
Maintenance costs	2	3	7
Ownership costs	3	3	5
Disposal costs	6	5	8
Total Cost	$130	$135	$140

Customer value of A = $150 – $130 = $20
Customer value of B = $140 – $135 = $5
Customer value of C = $135 – $140 = –$5

The customer will prefer brand A because the benefit level is higher and the customer costs are lower, but this does not have to be the case. Suppose A decided to charge $120 instead of $100 to take advantage of its higher perceived-benefit level. Then A's customer cost would be $150 instead of $130 and just offset its higher perceived benefit. Brand A, because of its greed, would lose the sale to brand B.

Very often, managers conduct a **customer value analysis** to reveal the company's strengths and weaknesses relative to various competitors. The major steps in such an analysis are:

1. *Identify the major attributes customers value.* Customers are asked what attributes and performance levels they look for in choosing a product and vendors.
2. *Assess the quantitative importance of the different attributes.* Customers are asked to rate the importance of the different attributes. If the customers diverge too much in their ratings, they should be clustered into different segments.
3. *Assess the company's and competitors' performances on the different customer values against their rated importance.* Customers are asked to describe the company's and competitors' performances on each attribute.
4. *Examine how customers in a specific segment rate the company's performance against a specific major competitor on an attribute-by-attribute basis.* If the company's offer exceeds the competitor's offer on all important attributes, the company can charge a higher price (thereby earning higher profits), or it can charge the same price and gain more market share.
5. *Monitor customer values over time.* The company must periodically redo its studies of customer values and competitors' standings as the economy, technology, and features change.

---

2. With the **lexicographic heuristic**, the consumer chooses the best brand on the basis of its perceived most important attribute. With this decision rule, Linda Brown would choose computer C.
3. With the **elimination-by-aspects heuristic**, the consumer compares brands on an attribute selected probabilistically—whereby the probability of choosing an attribute is positively related to its importance—and brands are eliminated if they do not meet minimum acceptable cutoff levels.

Characteristics of the person (e.g., brand or product knowledge), the purchase-decision task and setting (e.g., number and similarity of brand choices and time-pressure involved), and social context (e.g., need for justification to a peer or boss) all may affect if and how choice heuristics are used.[65]

Consumers do not necessarily adopt only one type of choice rule in making purchase decisions. In some cases, they adopt a phased decision strategy that combines two or more decision rules. For example, they might use a noncompensatory decision rule such as the conjunctive heuristic to reduce the number of brand choices to a more manageable number and then evaluate the remaining brands. Understanding if and how consumers screen brands can be critical. One reason for the runaway success of the Intel Inside campaign in the 1990s was that it made the brand the first cutoff for many consumers—they would buy only a PC that had an Intel microprocessor. PC-makers such as IBM and Dell had no choice but to support Intel's marketing efforts.

INTERVENING FACTORS Even if consumers form brand evaluations, two general factors can intervene between the purchase intention and the purchase decision (Figure 6.6).[66] The first factor is the *attitudes of others*. The extent to which another person's attitude reduces the preference for an alternative depends on two things: (1) the intensity of the other person's negative attitude toward the consumer's preferred alternative and (2) the consumer's motivation to comply with the other person's wishes.[67] The more intense the other person's negativism and the closer the other person is to the consumer, the more the consumer will adjust his or her purchase intention. The converse is also true: A buyer's preference for a brand will increase if someone he or she respects favours the same brand strongly.

Related to the attitudes of others is the role played by infomediaries who publish their evaluations. Examples include *Consumer Reports*, which provides unbiased expert reviews of all types of products and services; J. D. Power, which provides consumer-based ratings of cars, financial services, and travel products and services; professional movie, book, and music reviewers; customer reviews of books and music on Chapters.Indigo.ca; and the increasing number of chat rooms where people discuss goods, services, and companies. Consumers are undoubtedly influenced by these evaluations, as evidenced by the success of a small-budget movie like *My Big Fat Greek Wedding* by Canadian actor and screen-writer Nia Vardalos, which received a slew of favourable reviews by moviegoers on many websites.

The second factor is *unanticipated situational factors* that may erupt to change the purchase intention. Linda Brown might lose her job, some other purchase might become more urgent, or a store salesperson may turn her off. Preferences and even purchase intentions are not completely reliable predictors of purchase behaviour.

A consumer's decision to modify, postpone, or avoid a purchase decision is heavily influenced by *perceived risk*.[68] There are many different types of risks that consumers may perceive in buying and consuming a product:

1. *Functional risk*—the product does not perform to expectations.
2. *Physical risk*—the product poses a threat to the physical well-being or health of the user or others.
3. *Financial risk*—the product is not worth the price paid.
4. *Social risk*—the product results in embarrassment in front of others.
5. *Psychological risk*—the product affects the mental well-being of the user.
6. *Time risk*—the failure of the product results in the opportunity cost of finding a satisfactory replacement.

The amount of perceived risk varies with the amount of money at stake, the amount of attribute uncertainty, and the amount of consumer self-confidence. Consumers develop routines for reducing

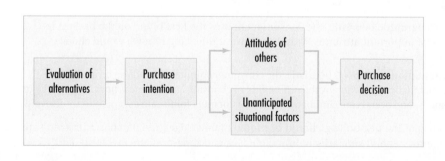

FIGURE 6.6

Steps between Evaluation of Alternatives and a Purchase Decision risk, such as decision avoidance, information gathering from friends, and preference for national brand names and warranties. Marketers must understand the factors that provoke a feeling of risk in consumers and provide information and support to reduce perceived risk.

Post-purchase Behaviour

After the purchase, the consumer might experience dissonance that stems from noticing certain disquieting features or hearing favourable things about other brands, and will be alert to information that supports his or her decision. Marketing communications should supply beliefs and evaluations that reinforce the consumer's choice and help him or her feel good about the brand.

The marketer's job therefore does not end with the purchase. Marketers must monitor post-purchase satisfaction, post-purchase actions, and post-purchase product uses.

POST-PURCHASE SATISFACTION What determines customer satisfaction with a purchase? Satisfaction is a function of the closeness between expectations and the product's perceived performance.[69] If performance falls short of expectations, the consumer is *disappointed*; if it meets expectations, the consumer is *satisfied*; if it exceeds expectations, the consumer is *delighted*. These feelings make a difference in whether the customer buys the product again and talks favourably or unfavourably about it to others.

Consumers form their expectations on the basis of messages received from sellers, friends, and other information sources. The larger the gap between expectations and performance, the greater the dissatisfaction. Here the consumer's coping style comes into play. Some consumers magnify the gap when the product is not perfect, and they are highly dissatisfied; others minimize the gap and are less dissatisfied.[70]

The importance of post-purchase satisfaction suggests that product claims must truthfully represent the product's likely performance. Some sellers might even understate performance levels so that consumers experience higher-than-expected satisfaction with the product.

POST-PURCHASE ACTIONS Satisfaction or dissatisfaction with the product will influence subsequent behaviour. If the consumer is satisfied, he or she will exhibit a higher probability of purchasing the product again. For example, data on automobile brand choice show a high correlation between being highly satisfied with the last brand bought and intention to buy the brand again. One survey showed that 75 percent of Toyota buyers were highly satisfied and about 75 percent intended to buy a Toyota again; 35 percent of Chevrolet buyers were highly satisfied and about 35 percent intended to buy a Chevrolet again. The satisfied customer will also tend to say good things about the brand to others. Marketers say: "Our best advertisement is a satisfied customer."[71]

Dissatisfied consumers may abandon or return the product. They may seek information that confirms its high value. They may take public action by complaining to the company, going to a lawyer, or complaining to other groups (such as business, private, or government agencies). Private actions include making a decision to stop buying the product (*exit option*) and warning friends (*voice option*).[72] In all these cases, the seller has done a poor job of satisfying the customer.[73]

Chapter 3 described CRM programs designed to build long-term brand loyalty. Post-purchase communications to buyers have been shown to result in fewer product returns and order cancellations.[74] Computer companies, for example, can send a letter to new owners congratulating them on having selected a fine computer. They can place ads showing satisfied brand owners. They can solicit customer suggestions for improvements and list the location of available services. They can write intelligible instruction booklets. They can send owners a magazine containing articles describing new computer applications. In addition, they can provide good channels for speedy redress of customer grievances.

POST-PURCHASE USE AND DISPOSAL Marketers should also monitor how buyers use and dispose of their product (Figure 6.7). A key driver of sales frequency is product consumption rate—the more quickly buyers consume a product, the sooner they may be back in the market to repurchase it.

One potential opportunity to increase frequency of product use is when consumer's perceptions of their usage differ from the reality. Consumers may fail to replace products with relatively short life spans in a timely manner because of a tendency to overestimate product life.[75] One strategy to speed up replacement is to tie the act of replacing the product to a certain holiday, event, or time of year.

FIGURE 6.7

How Customers Use or
Dispose of Products

Source: Jacob Jacoby, Carol K.
Berning, and Thomas Dietvorst,
"What about Disposition?" *Journal
of Marketing* (July 1977): 23.
Reprinted with permission of the
American Marketing Association.

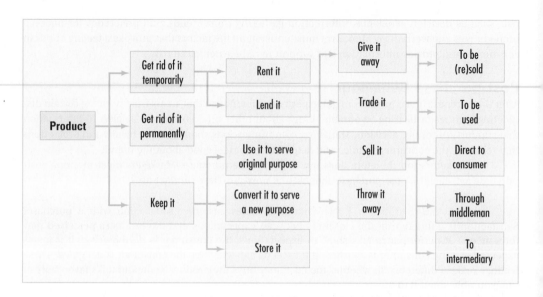

For example, several brands (e.g., Oral-B toothbrushes) have run promotions tied in with the springtime switch to daylight saving time. Another strategy might be to provide consumers with better information as to either (1) when the product was first used or would need to be replaced or (2) the current level of performance. For example, batteries offer built-in gauges that show how much power they have left, toothbrushes have colour indicators on their bristles to indicate when they are too worn, and so on. Perhaps the best time to increase usage is when actual usage of a product is less than optimal or recommended. In this case, consumers must be persuaded of the merits of more regular usage, and potential hurdles to increased usage must be overcome.

If consumers throw the product away, the marketer needs to know how they dispose of it, especially if it can damage the environment (as in the case with batteries, beverage containers, and disposable diapers). Increased public awareness of recycling and ecological concerns as well as consumer complaints about having to throw away beautiful bottles led French perfume maker Rochas to think about introducing a refillable fragrance line.

OTHER THEORIES OF CONSUMER DECISION MAKING

The consumer decision process may not always develop in a carefully planned fashion. It is important to understand other theories and approaches to how consumers make decisions and when they might apply.

Level of Consumer Involvement

The expectancy-value model assumes a high level of involvement on the part of the consumer. **Consumer involvement** can be defined in terms of the level of engagement and active processing undertaken by the consumer in responding to a marketing stimulus (e.g., in viewing an ad or evaluating a product or service).

ELABORATION LIKELIHOOD MODEL   An influential model of attitude formation and change, Richard Petty and John Cacioppo's *elaboration likelihood model*, describes how consumers make evaluations in both low- and high-involvement circumstances.[76] There are two means of persuasion in their model: the central route, whereby attitude formation or change involves much thought and is based on a diligent, rational consideration of the most important product or service information; and the peripheral route, whereby attitude formation or change involves comparatively much less thought and is a consequence of the association of a brand with either positive or negative peripheral cues. Examples of peripheral cues for consumers might be a celebrity endorsement, a credible source, or any object that engendered positive feelings.

Consumers follow the central route only if they possess sufficient *motivation*, *ability*, and *opportunity*. In other words, consumers must want to evaluate a brand in detail, must have the necessary brand and product or service knowledge in memory, and must be given sufficient time and the proper setting to actually do so. If any one of these three factors is lacking, consumers will tend to follow the peripheral route and consider less central, more extrinsic factors in their decisions.

LOW-INVOLVEMENT MARKETING STRATEGIES   Many products are bought under conditions of low involvement and the absence of significant brand differences. Consider salt. Consumers have little involvement in this product category. They go to the store and reach for the brand. If they keep reaching for the same brand, it is out of habit, not strong brand loyalty. There is good evidence that consumers have low involvement with most low-cost, frequently purchased products.

Marketers use four techniques to try to convert a low-involvement product into one of higher involvement. First, they can link the product to some involving issue, as when Crest toothpaste is linked to avoiding cavities. Second, they can link the product to some involving personal situation—for example, fruit juices began to include vitamins and calcium to fortify their drinks. Third, they might design advertising to trigger strong emotions related to personal values or ego defence, as when cereal makers began to advertise to adults cereals' heart-healthy nature and the importance of living a long time in order to enjoy family life. Fourth, they might add an important feature—for example, when GE light bulbs introduced "Soft White" versions. These strategies at best raise consumer involvement from a low to a moderate level; they do not necessarily propel the consumer into highly involved buying behaviour.

If, regardless of what the marketer can do, consumers have low involvement with a purchase decision, they are likely to follow the peripheral route. Marketers must pay special attention to giving consumers one or more positive cues that they can use to justify their brand choice. Brand familiarity can be important if consumers decide just to buy the brand about which they have heard or seen the most. Frequent ad repetition, visible sponsorships, and vigorous PR are all ways to enhance brand familiarity. Other peripheral cues can also be used. A beloved celebrity endorser, attractive packaging, and an appealing promotion all might tip the balance in favour of the brand.[77]

VARIETY-SEEKING BUYING BEHAVIOUR   Some buying situations are characterized by low involvement but significant brand differences. Here, consumers often do a lot of brand switching. Think about cookies. The consumer has some beliefs about cookies, chooses a brand of cookies without much evaluation, and evaluates the product during consumption. Next time, the consumer may reach for another brand out of a wish for a different taste. Brand switching occurs for the sake of variety rather than dissatisfaction.

The market leader and the minor brands in this product category have different marketing strategies. The market leader will try to encourage habitual buying behaviour by dominating the shelf space with a variety of related but different product versions, avoiding out-of-stock conditions, and sponsoring frequent reminder advertising. Challenger firms will encourage variety-seeking by offering lower prices, deals, coupons, free samples, and advertising that tries to break the consumer's purchase and consumption cycle and presents reasons for trying something new.

Decision Heuristics and Biases

As the low involvement and noncompensatory model discussions suggest, consumers do not always process information or make decisions in a deliberate, rational manner. Behavioural decision theory is a thriving area in consumer research. Behavioural decision theorists have identified many different heuristics and biases in everyday consumer decision making. **Heuristics** are rules of thumb or mental shortcuts in the decision process.

Heuristics can come into play when consumers forecast the likelihood of future outcomes or events.[78]

1. The **availability heuristic**: Consumers base their predictions on the quickness and ease with which a particular example of an outcome comes to mind. If an example comes to mind too easily, consumers might overestimate the likelihood of the outcome or event happening. For example, a recent product failure may lead a consumer to inflate the likelihood of a future product failure and make him or her more inclined to purchase a product warranty.

2. The **representativeness heuristic**: Consumers base their predictions on how representative or similar the outcome is to other examples. One reason why package appearances may be so similar for different brands in the same product category is that they want to be seen as representative of the category as a whole.

MARKETING **MEMO** | DECISION TRAPS

In *Decision Traps*, Jay Russo and Paul Schoemaker reveal the ten most common mistakes managers make in their decisions.

1. *Plunging in.* Beginning to gather information and reach conclusions without taking a few minutes to think about the crux of the issue you're facing or to think through how you believe decisions like this one should be made.

2. *Frame blindness.* Setting out to solve the wrong problem because you've created a mental framework for your decision, with little thought, that causes you to overlook the best options or lose sight of important objectives.

3. *Lack of frame control.* Failing to consciously define the problem in more ways than one or being unduly influenced by the frames of others.

4. *Overconfidence in your judgment.* Failing to collect key factual information because you are too sure of your assumptions and opinions.

5. *Shortsighted shortcuts.* Relying inappropriately on "rules of thumb" such as implicitly trusting the most readily available information or anchoring too much on convenient facts.

6. *Shooting from the hip.* Believing you can keep straight in your head all the information you've discovered, and therefore "winging it" rather than following a systematic procedure when making the final choice.

7. *Group failure.* Assuming that with many smart people involved good choices will follow automatically, and therefore failing to manage the group decision-making process.

8. *Fooling yourself about feedback.* Failing to interpret the evidence from past outcomes for what it really says, either because you are protecting your ego or because you are tricked by hindsight effects.

9. *Not keeping track.* Assuming that experience will make its lessons available automatically, and therefore failing to keep systematic records to track the results of your decisions and failing to analyze these results in ways that reveal their key lessons.

10. *Failure to audit your decision process.* Failing to create an organized approach to understanding your own decision making, so you remain constantly exposed to all the other nine decision traps.

Sources: J. Edward Russo and Paul J. H. Schoemaker, *Decision Traps: Ten Barriers to Brilliant Decision-Making and How to Overcome Them* (New York: Doubleday, 1990); see also J. Edward Russo and Paul J. H. Schoemaker, *Winning Decisions: Getting It Right the First Time* (New York: Doubleday, 2001).

---

3. The **anchoring and adjustment heuristic**: Consumers arrive at an initial judgment and then make adjustments of that first impression based on additional information. For services marketers, it is critical to make a strong first impression to establish a favourable anchor so that subsequent experiences are interpreted in a favourable light.

Note that marketing managers also may use heuristics and be subject to biases in their decision making. "Marketing Memo: Decision Traps" reveals ten common mistakes managers make in their decisions.

Mental Accounting

Researchers have found that consumers use mental accounting when they handle their money.[79] **Mental accounting** refers to the manner in which consumers code, categorize, and evaluate financial outcomes of choices. Formally, it has been defined in terms of "The tendency to categorize funds or items of value even though there is no logical basis for the categorization, e.g., individuals often segregate their savings into separate accounts to meet different goals even though funds from any of the accounts can be applied to any of the goals."[80]

For example, assume you spend $50 to buy a ticket to see a concert.[81] As you arrive at the show, you realize you've lost your ticket. You may be unsure about purchasing another ticket for $50. Assume, on the other hand, that you realized you had lost $50 on the way to buy the ticket. You might be much more likely to go ahead and buy the ticket anyway. Although the amount lost in each case was the same—$50—the reactions were very different. In the first case, you may have mentally allocated $50 for going to a concert. Buying another ticket would therefore exceed your mental concert budget. In the second case, the money that was lost did not belong to any account, so the mental concert budget had not yet been exceeded.

According to Richard Thaler, mental accounting is based on a set of key core principles:

1. Consumers tend to *segregate gains*. When a seller has a product with more than one positive dimension, it is desirable to have each dimension evaluated separately. Listing multiple benefits of a large industrial product, for example, can make the sum of the parts seem greater than the whole.

2. Consumers tend to *integrate losses*. Marketers have a distinct advantage in selling something if its cost can be added to another large purchase. House buyers are more inclined to view additional expenditures favourably given the high price of buying a house.

3. Consumers tend to *integrate smaller losses with larger gains*. The "cancellation" principle might explain why withholding taxes taken from monthly paycheques are less aversive than large lump-sum tax payments—they are more likely to be absorbed by the larger pay amount.

4. Consumers tend to *segregate small gains from large losses*. The "silver lining" principle might explain the popularity of rebates on big-ticket purchases such as cars.

The principles of mental accounting are derived in part from prospect theory. **Prospect theory** maintains that consumers frame decision alternatives in terms of gains and losses according to a value function. Consumers are generally loss averse. Consumers tend to overweight very low probabilities and underweight very high probabilities.

Profiling the Customer Buying Decision Process

How can marketers learn about the stages in the buying process for their product? They can think about how they themselves would act (*introspective method*). They can interview a small number of recent purchasers, asking them to recall the events leading to their purchase (*retrospective method*). They can locate consumers who plan to buy the product and ask them to think out loud about going through the buying process (*prospective method*); or they can ask consumers to describe the ideal way to buy the product (*prescriptive method*). Each method yields a picture of the steps in the process.

Trying to understand the customer's behaviour in connection with a product has been called mapping the customer's *consumption system*,[82] *customer activity cycle*,[83] or *customer scenario*.[84] This can be done for such activity clusters as doing laundry, preparing for a wedding, and buying a car. Buying a car, for example, involves a whole cluster of activities, including choosing the car, financing the purchase, buying insurance, buying accessories, and so on.

SUMMARY

1. Consumer behaviour is influenced by three factors: cultural (culture, subculture, and social class), social (reference groups, family, and social roles and statuses), and personal (age, stage in the life cycle, occupation, economic circumstances, personality, self-concept, and lifestyle). Research into all of these factors can provide marketers with clues to reach and serve consumers more effectively.

2. Four main psychological processes affect consumer behaviour: motivation, perception, learning, and memory.

3. To understand how consumers actually make buying decisions, marketers must identify the person who makes the decision to buy the product, the person who actually buys the product, and the people who influence the decision to buy the product.

4. The typical buying process consists of the following sequence: problem recognition, information search, evaluation of alternatives, purchase decision, and post-purchase behaviour. The marketer's job is to understand behaviour at each stage. The attitudes of others, unanticipated situational factors, and perceived risk may all affect the decision to buy, as will consumers' levels of post-purchase satisfaction and post-purchase actions on the part of the company.

APPLICATIONS

Marketing Debate: Is Target Marketing Ever Bad?

As marketers increasingly develop marketing programs tailored to certain target market segments, some critics denounce these efforts as exploitative. For example, the preponderance in low-income areas of billboards advertising lotteries, alcohol, video gaming machines, and other vices is seen as taking advantage of a vulnerable market segment. Critics can be especially harsh in evaluating marketing programs that target minority groups, claiming that they often employ clichéd stereotypes and inappropriate depictions. Others counter that targeting and positioning is critical to marketing and that these marketing programs are an attempt to be relevant to a particular consumer group.

Take a position: Targeting minorities is exploitative *versus* Targeting minorities is a sound business practice.

Marketing Discussion: What Are Your Mental Accounts?

What mental accounts do you have for purchasing products or services? Do you employ any rules in spending money? Are they different from what other people do? Do you follow Thaler's four principles in reacting to gains and losses?

Breakthrough Marketing: Online Social Networking

Toronto-based Solutions Research Group (SRG) has been tracking consumer behaviour and attitudes in media, technology, entertainment, leisure, food and beverage, and retail sectors for over a decade. In addition to conducting specialized research studies that focus on understanding consumer behaviours and trends, the company uses the insight it has gained to provide consulting services and custom client-specific services.

One study SRG conducted focused on the overwhelming and sudden popularity of social-networking websites such as Facebook and MySpace. A social-networking site is one in which communities of people who share interests and activities build an online social network. The popularity of social-networking websites has been skyrocketing over the last few years. For example, the Facebook social media platform, which was created in 2004 and opened to the general public in 2006, has undergone tremendous growth, boasting membership of 67 million users worldwide. Canada is third in the Facebook ranks, behind the United Kingdom and the U.S., with 7.8 million Canadian memberships in 2007—an astounding 760 percent growth rate from 900 000 in 2006.

The tremendous popularity of social networking has not gone unnoticed by advertisers and investors alike. Launched from a university student's dorm room in 2004, Facebook has quickly grown to generate millions in revenue from advertisers keen to take advantage of the powerful influence Facebook has on today's younger generations. Many companies find social-networking sites useful for other than opportunities to advertise. Although some companies have banned the use of social-networking websites at the workplace via firewalls and IT controls, other firms such as Accenture, a global technology-services firm, and Youthography, a Toronto-based advertising agency, are embracing them as a valuable recruitment and networking tool. To recruit new talent, global consulting firm Ernst & Young created a Facebook group showcasing videos, Q&As, and discussion forums. Facebook application Jobster, which sends users alerts about job opportunities, has secured the membership of many large employers including Nike, KPMG, General Electric, Merrill Lynch, and Boeing.

Social-networking websites are especially attractive to online marketers, considering that more than 95 percent of frequent visitors to social networks also visit retail websites, compared with 80 percent of all Internet users, according to a study by comScore, an Internet information provider. Clothing retailers are among the primary beneficiaries. The study found that nearly 25 percent of visitors to apparel-retailer websites were heavy social networkers.

Social-networking sites such as Facebook and MySpace are only one of many channels Canadians are using to stay connected. Services such as online chats, text messaging, online photo and video sharing, and products such as BlackBerry and iPhone smartphones are all allowing people to stay on top of current happenings in their social and work environments.

Many psychologists, sociologists, and marketing researchers ponder the roots and psychosocial implications of the social-media frenzy. Dr. Sherry Turkle, professor of the social studies of science and technology at MIT, has suggested that this rampant communication may be linked to an inability of people to be alone without experiencing loneliness. "One of the gold standards of thinking about a fully developed individual is an ability to enjoy one's solitude. I wonder if we are part of a generation that is not able to be alone," she says.

In the spring of 2008, SRG, which tracks Facebook user trends, published the results of its study "Age of Disconnect Anxiety: And Four Reasons Why It's Difficult to Stay Off the Grid." The study focuses on a modern-day affliction described as "disconnect anxiety": the feelings of nervousness and disorientation associated with the absence of virtual communication. SRG interviewed 3000 Canadians and found over half of them exhibit above-average levels of disconnect anxiety, with participants using words such as "panic," "loss of freedom," "inadequate," and "empty" to express their feelings of being without modern connectivity. The study concluded several factors contribute to this, including fear of missing important information at work, missing vital gossip, and a general feeling of disorientation and nervousness.

In response to some critics who are forecasting "Facebook Fatigue," SRG analyst Kaan Yigit states:

"Everything in our research points to this as being long term. Will there be another social-media platform? Sure. But I think the fundamentals of social media—staying connected to friends and family and, in some cases, work life—that's here to stay."

DISCUSSION QUESTIONS

1. Discuss the role that the three main factors influencing consumer behaviour (cultural, social, personal) play in the social-networking phenomenon discussed above.

2. At which stage(s) of the consumer buying decision process are marketers most likely to find social-networking websites to be an effective medium to reach consumers? Why?

3. From your understanding of the elaboration likelihood model, discuss how the consumer's level of involvement while visiting a social-networking website, such as Facebook, can affect which aspects of the website influence the consumer.

Sources: Solutions Research Group, "Age of Disconnect Anxiety and Four Reasons Why It's Difficult to Stay Off the Grid," March 2008; Craig Offman, "Connection Problems; 59% of Canadians Feel Anxious Without the Net," *National Post*, March 10, 2008, p. A1; Elisabeth A. Sullivan, "Be Sociable," *Marketing News, 42*, no. 1 (January 15, 2008): p. 12; "Facebook Analysis," *FastForward Quarterly*, December 2007, Solutions Research Group; Chris Sorensen, "Has Facebook Fatigue Arrived?," *Toronto Star*, March 7, 2008, p. B1; "MySpace and Isobar Debut First Comprehensive Research Study on Social Networks and Marketing," WebKnowHow Press Release, April 23, 2007, www.webknowhow.net/news/press/070423SocialNetworkingStudy.html (viewed June 2, 2008); Dana Flavelle, "Worries Follow Rise of Facebook: Employers Not Happy with Time Spent on Web Site," *Toronto Star*, May 4, 2007, p. F1; Roberto Rocha, "Facebook Used to Recruit Employees," *CanWest News*, August 31, 2007, p. 1; Facebook website, www.facebook.com/ernstandyoungcareers?ref=s (viewed June 2, 2008).

IN THIS CHAPTER, WE WILL ADDRESS THE FOLLOWING QUESTIONS:

- What is the business market, and how does it differ from the consumer market?

- What buying situations do organizational buyers face?

- Who participates in the business-to-business buying process?

- How do business buyers make their decisions?

- How can companies build strong relationships with business customers?

- How do institutional buyers and government agencies do their buying?

CHAPTER 7

ANALYZING BUSINESS MARKETS

seven

Rogers Communications Inc., a diversified communications service provider and media company, has thrived since Ted Rogers, Sr., founded it in 1925. The company has seen significant growth over the years and currently offers services in wireless, telephone, Internet, cable television, and media, serving both businesses and residential consumers coast-to-coast. With 2007 revenues in excess of $10 billion, Rogers is Canada's largest communications service provider.

Communication is essential to any successful business relationship, and companies such as Rogers offer business solutions to satisfy that need. Rogers serves small, medium, and large organizations with the services that residential consumers also use, but tailors them to meet the differing needs that businesses have. Rogers strives to be reliable, flexible, and cost effective, all of which are important qualities that appeal to its current and potential business customers.

As a business itself, Rogers knows what is important for organizational success and stays on top of the changing needs that its business clients have. Through its many services, Rogers has been able to address all of these needs and offer communication solutions that allow businesses to be productive anywhere, anytime. Rogers is making it much easier for business people to stay connected, even when they are not in the office. Besides being one of Canada's service providers for the BlackBerry, Rogers offers a host of other services such as Conference Anywhere (wireless conferencing), Internet-based faxing, mforms (to process orders and invoices more quickly), mFleet (a fleet-management solution), and eOffice (which connects a user's BlackBerry to his or her desktop computer), all allowing businesses to communicate more efficiently and increase productivity. Data integrity and information security are also factors that businesses take seriously. Rogers has developed Data Secure BackupT, a system that continually backs up files to secure a client's databases in the event its computer crashes or is hacked. Information maintenance is incredibly important to businesses, and services such as the backup system and Rogers' All-in-One Security Suite add value to the overall communications package that Rogers has to offer. Cost management and customer service are also addressed by Rogers' businesses solutions. With ongoing promotions and cost-cutting solutions such as audio conferencing, Rogers addresses the needs of its business customers of all sizes.

Like residential consumers, businesses also have needs differing from one another. Rogers recognizes this and has created solutions that are specific to various industry sectors such as consumer goods, manufacturing, oil and gas, and services. It truly appears that Rogers takes pride in creating solutions that are suitable for each business type. In addition to an incredible number of services, Rogers offers a support-services team that is dedicated to helping businesses.

As with most products and services, Rogers is not the sole provider of communication services to businesses in Canada. Thus, Rogers needs to constantly review its marketing strategies to ensure it meets business consumers' changing needs and remains ahead of the competition. Business customers can account for a considerable portion of a firm's revenues and profitability, and Rogers knows well that a business-to-business arm allows it to diversify its offerings, rather than risk putting all its eggs into the residential-consumer basket. With 2007 revenues up 15 percent and a healthy shareholder return of 31 percent, Rogers Communications Inc. is clearly going in the right direction.

Sources: Rogers Communications Inc. website, "History of Rogers," "Improve Your Customer Services," "Manage Your Business Expenses," "Secure Your E-mail and Data," "Why Choose Rogers for Your Business," "Industry Solutions," and "2007 Annual Report," www.rogers.com (all viewed May 31, 2008).

Business organizations do not only sell. They also buy vast quantities of raw materials, manufactured components, plant and equipment, supplies, and business services. There are over 14 million buying organizations in North America alone. To create and capture value, sellers need to understand these organizations' needs, resources, policies, and buying procedures—something that Accenture knows very well.

Accenture

Accenture, a global management consulting, technology services, and outsourcing company, has become a leading seller in the business market with net revenues surpassing $19 billion for the fiscal year ended August 31, 2007. Accenture boasts a client list that includes several governments and two-thirds of the *Fortune Global 500* companies. It strengthens and extends its relationships through its commitment to client satisfaction. All of Accenture's top 100 clients in fiscal year 2007, based on revenue, had been clients for at least five years, and 85 had been clients for at least ten years.[1]

Some of the world's most valuable brands belong to business marketers: Magna International, Research In Motion, Caterpillar, DuPont, FedEx, GE, Alcan, IBM, Intel, and Bombardier. Much of basic marketing also applies to business marketers. They need to embrace holistic marketing principles, such as building strong relationships with their customers, just like any marketer. Consider the case of Dofasco. It is Canada's most successful steel producer and one of North America's most progressive and profitable steel-makers. And it has achieved its success not only by providing high-quality flat-rolled and tubular steel to customers throughout North America, but also by practising a customer-focused "Solutions in Steel™" strategy. This breakthrough strategy has transformed Dofasco from a manufacturer of steel to a producer of innovative, value-added steel products designed to solve the immediate and future needs of its customers. But there are some unique considerations in selling to other businesses.[2] In this chapter, we will highlight some of the crucial differences for marketing in business markets.

WHAT IS ORGANIZATIONAL BUYING?

Webster and Wind define **organizational buying** as the decision-making process by which formal organizations establish the need for purchased products and services and identify, evaluate, and choose among alternative brands and suppliers.[3]

The Business Market versus the Consumer Market

The **business market** consists of all the organizations that acquire goods and services used in the production of other goods or services that are sold, rented, or supplied to others. The major industries making up the business market are agriculture, forestry, and fisheries; mining; manufacturing; construction; transportation; communication; public utilities; banking, finance, and insurance; distribution; and services.

More dollars and items are involved in sales to business buyers than to consumers. Consider the process of producing and selling a simple pair of shoes. Hide dealers must sell hides to tanners, who sell leather to shoe manufacturers, who sell shoes to wholesalers, who sell shoes to retailers, who finally sell them to consumers. Each party in the supply chain also has to buy many other goods and services.

Business markets have several characteristics that contrast sharply with those of consumer markets:

- *Fewer, larger buyers.* The business marketer normally deals with far fewer, much larger buyers than the consumer marketer does. The fate of Goodyear Tire Company and other automotive-part suppliers depends on getting contracts from a few major automakers. A few large buyers do most of the purchasing in such industries as aircraft engines and defence weapons. A slowing economy can put a stranglehold on large corporations' purchasing departments, offering suppliers new opportunities to market to small and midsized businesses instead.[4] See "Marketing Memo: Guidelines for Selling to Small Business" for more on how to access this sometimes-ignored business-to-business (B2B) market.

- *Close supplier–customer relationship.* Because of the smaller customer base and the importance and power of the larger customers, suppliers are frequently expected to customize their offerings to individual business-customer needs. Business buyers often select suppliers that also buy from them. An example is a paper manufacturer that buys chemicals from a chemical company that buys a considerable amount of its paper.

- *Professional purchasing.* Business goods are often purchased by trained purchasing agents, who must follow their organization's purchasing policies, constraints, and requirements. Many of the buying instruments—for example, requests for quotations, proposals, and purchase contracts—are not typically found in consumer buying. Professional buyers spend their careers learning how to buy better. Many belong to the Purchasing Managers Association of Canada (PMAC), which seeks to improve professional buyers' effectiveness and status. This means that business marketers have to provide greater technical data about their product and its advantages over competitors' products.

- *Several buying influences.* Typically, more people influence business buying decisions. Buying committees consisting of technical experts and even senior management are common in the purchase of major goods. Business marketers have to send well-trained sales representatives and sales teams to deal with the well-trained buyers.

- *Multiple sales calls.* Because more people are involved in the selling process, it takes multiple sales calls to win most business orders, and some sales cycles can take years. A study by McGraw-Hill found that it takes four to four and a half calls to close an average industrial sale. In the case of capital-equipment sales for large projects, it may take multiple attempts to fund a project, and the sales cycle—between quoting a job and delivering the product—is often measured in years.[5]

- *Derived demand.* The demand for business goods is ultimately derived from the demand for consumer goods. For this reason, the business marketer must closely monitor the buying patterns of ultimate consumers. For instance, aging of the Canadian population has been leading to an increased demand for condominiums, which in turn has been leading to an increased demand for construction material. Business buyers must also pay close attention to current and expected economic factors, such as the level of production, investment, consumer spending, and the interest rate. In a recession, business buyers reduce their investment in plant, equipment, and inventories. Business marketers can do little to stimulate total demand in this environment. They can only fight harder to increase or maintain their share of demand.

- *Inelastic demand.* The total demand for many business goods and services is inelastic—that is, not much affected by price changes. Shoe manufacturers are not going to buy much more leather if the price of leather falls, nor will they buy much less leather if the price rises, unless they can find satisfactory substitutes. Demand is especially inelastic in the short run

MARKETING **MEMO**	GUIDELINES FOR SELLING TO SMALL BUSINESS

Small businesses—defined as those with fewer than 100 employees—are responsible for employing over 5 million Canadians, or 48 percent of the private-sector labour force. According to Industry Canada, as of June 2007 there were over 2.4 million small businesses in Canada, with about 135 000 starting up each year. All these new businesses need capital equipment, technology, supplies, and services. Look beyond Canada to small businesses around the world and you have a huge and growing B2B market. Here's how some companies are reaching it:

- With its new suite of run-your-business software, Microsoft is counting on sales to 45 million small to midsized businesses worldwide to add $10 billion to annual revenue by 2010. Yet even Microsoft can't afford to send reps to all its customers. Instead, the company is unleashing an army of 24 000 independent computer-consulting companies and adding 300 sales managers to support resellers and customers.

- IBM counts small to midsized customers as 20 percent of its business and has launched Express, a line of hardware, software services, and financing, for this market. IBM sells through regional reps as well as independent software vendors and resellers, and it supports its small/midsized push with millions of dollars in annual advertising.

- American Express has been steadily adding new features to its credit card for small business, which some small companies use to cover hundreds of thousands of dollars a month in cash needs. It has also created a small business network called OPEN (www.openamericanexpress.com) to bring together various services, web tools, and discount programs with other giants such as Dell, FedEx, and Staples. With OPEN, American Express not only allows customers to save money on common expenses, it also encourages them to do much of their recordkeeping on its website.

Small businesses present a huge opportunity and huge challenges. The market is large and fragmented by industry, size, and number of years in operation. Small-business owners are notably averse to long-range planning and have an "I'll buy it when I need it" decision-making style. Here are some guidelines for selling to small businesses:

- *Don't lump small and midsized business together.* There's a big gap between $1 million in revenue and $50 million and between a start-up with ten employees and a more mature business with 100. IBM customizes its small and midsized business portal (www.ibm.com/businesscenter/us) with call-me or text-chat buttons that are connected to products for different market segments.

- *Don't waste their time.* That means no cold calls, entertaining sales shows, or sales pitches over long boozy lunches.

- *Do keep it simple.* This could be a corollary to "don't waste their time." Simplicity means one point of contact with a supplier for all service problems or one single bill for all services and products. Telus Corporation bundles phone, wireless, data management, networking, conferencing, and other services all into a convenient, single package called TELUS Business One Bundle for this market.

- *Do use the Internet.* In its research on buying patterns of small-business owners, Hewlett-Packard found that these time-strapped decision makers prefer to buy, or at least research, products and services online. To that end, HP has designed a site targeted to small and midsized businesses and pulls business owners to the site through extensive advertising, direct mail, email campaigns, catalogues, and events. IBM prospects via eBay by selling refurbished and phased-out equipment on its new B2B site. About 80 percent of IBM's equipment is sold to small businesses that are new to IBM—half of which have agreed to receive calls with other offers.

- *Don't forget about direct contact.* Even if a small-business owner's first point of contact is via the Internet, you still need to offer phone or face time. TD Canada Trust has Small Business Advisors who meet with small-business owners and help them with their financial-management needs.

- *Do provide support after the sale.* Small businesses want partners, not pitchmen. When the DeWitt Company, a 100-employee landscaping-products business, purchased a large piece of machinery from Moeller, a German company, the company's president paid DeWitt's CEO a personal visit and stayed until the machine was up and running properly.

- *Do your homework.* The realities of small and midsized business management are different from those at a large corporation. Microsoft created a small fictional executive-research firm, Southridge, and baseball-style trading cards of its key decision makers in order to help Microsoft employees tie sales strategies to small-business realities.

Sources: Industry Canada, "Key Small Business Statistics—January 2008," *Small Business Research and Policy*, www.ic.gc.ca/epic/site/sbrp-rppe. nsf/en/h_rd02243e.html (viewed June 8, 2008); Barnaby J. Feder, "When Goliath Comes Knocking on David's Door," *New York Times*, May 6, 2003, p. G13; Jay Greene, "Small Biz: Microsoft's Next Big Thing?" *Business Week*, April 21, 2003, pp. 72–73; Jennifer Gilbert, "Small but Mighty," *Sales & Marketing Management*, January 2004, pp. 30–35; Verne Kopytoff, "Businesses Click on eBay," *San Francisco Chronicle*, July 28, 2003, p. E1; TD Canada Trust website, www.tdcanadatrust.com/smallbusiness/advisor/index.jsp (viewed June 8, 2008).

because producers cannot make quick changes in production methods. Demand is also inelastic for business goods that represent a small percentage of the item's total cost, such as shoelaces.

- *Fluctuating demand.* The demand for business goods and services tends to be more volatile than the demand for consumer goods and services. A given percentage increase in consumer demand can lead to a much larger percentage increase in the demand for plant and equipment necessary to produce the additional output. Economists refer to this as the *acceleration effect.* Sometimes a rise of only 10 percent in consumer demand can cause as much as a 200-percent rise in business demand for products in the next period; a 10-percent fall in consumer demand may cause a complete collapse in business demand.

- *Geographically concentrated buyers.* About 58 percent of all Canadian businesses are located in Ontario and Quebec, concentrated in the metropolitan areas between Windsor and Quebec City. Thirty-five percent of Canada's businesses are in the Western provinces, and 6 percent are located in the Atlantic provinces.[6] The provinces of Ontario and Quebec are home to the country's auto industry, and Canada's high-tech firms are clustered in Ottawa, Montreal, and Toronto. The petroleum industry calls Calgary and Edmonton home, while New Brunswick attracts the telemarketing industry and is the location of many companies' call centres. Most agricultural output comes from relatively few provinces.

- *Direct purchasing.* Business buyers often buy directly from manufacturers rather than through intermediaries, especially items that are technically complex or expensive (such as mainframes or aircraft).

Buying Situations

The business buyer faces many decisions in making a purchase. The number of decisions depends on the buying situation: complexity of the problem being solved, newness of the buying requirement, number of people involved, and time required. Patrick Robinson and others distinguish three types of buying situations: the straight rebuy, modified rebuy, and new task.[7]

STRAIGHT REBUY The purchasing department reorders on a routine basis (e.g., office supplies, bulk chemicals) and chooses from suppliers on an "approved list." The suppliers make an effort to maintain product and service quality and often propose automatic reordering systems to save time. "Out-suppliers" attempt to offer something new or to exploit dissatisfaction with a current supplier. Out-suppliers try to get a small order and then enlarge their purchase share over time.

MODIFIED REBUY The buyer wants to modify product specifications, prices, delivery requirements, or other terms. The modified rebuy usually involves additional participants on both sides. The in-suppliers become nervous and have to protect the account. The out-suppliers see an opportunity to propose a better offer to gain some business.

NEW TASK A purchaser buys a product or service for the first time (e.g., office building, new security system). The greater the cost or risk, the larger the number of participants and the greater their information gathering—and therefore the longer the time to reach a decision.[8]

The business buyer makes the fewest decisions in the straight rebuy situation and the most in the new-task situation. Over time, new-buy situations become straight rebuys and routine purchase behaviour. New-task buying passes through several stages: awareness, interest, evaluation, trial, and adoption.[9] The effectiveness of communication tools varies at each stage. Mass media are most important during the initial awareness stage; salespeople have their greatest impact at the interest stage; and technical sources are the most important during the evaluation stage.

In the new-task situation, the buyer has to determine product specifications, price limits, delivery terms and times, service terms, payment terms, order quantities, acceptable suppliers, and the selected supplier. Different participants influence each decision, and the order in which these decisions are made varies. This situation is the marketer's greatest opportunity and challenge. Because of the complicated selling involved, many companies use a *missionary sales force* consisting of their most effective salespeople. The brand promise and the manufacturer's brand-name recognition will be important in establishing trust and in the customer's willingness to consider change. The marketer also tries to reach as many key participants as possible and provide helpful information and assistance.

Once a customer is acquired, in-suppliers are continually seeking ways to add value to their market offer to facilitate rebuys. Often they do this by giving customers customized solutions:

Magna International

Magna International, based in Aurora, Ontario, is the most diversified automotive-parts supplier in the world. As of March 2008, Magna had 241 production and 62 engineering and R&D centres in 23 countries across 5 continents. Magna International's success comes from supplying automobile parts to virtually every major automobile manufacturer such as GM, Ford, Toyota, Volkswagen, and BMW. Magna has a history and culture of offering innovation and customization as a key supplier in the automobile industry. For example, thanks to its flexible manufacturing strategy and the MAGNA STEYR Production System (MSPS), Magna now offers complete-vehicle assembly. Magna can act as the general contractor: a one-stop shop from the idea to the complete vehicle, as Magna did with the BMW X3 which was forwarded by BMW to Magna for serial development and production. In 2007, Magna reported over $25 billion in worldwide sales and a 19-percent compound average growth rate in sales since 1996.[10]

Customers considering dropping six or seven figures on one transaction for big-ticket goods and services want all the information they can get. One way to entice new buyers is to create a customer-reference program in which satisfied existing customers act in concert with the company's sales and marketing department by agreeing to serve as references. Companies that have such programs include Siebel Systems, PeopleSoft, and Sun Microsystems. "Marketing Memo: Maximizing Customer References" provides some tips for developing activities and programs with impact.

Sun Microsystems

Since its inception in 1982, Sun Microsystems, a company that provides a cornucopia of software, systems, services, and microelectronics, has achieved tremendous success with a 2007 ranking of 187 on the *Fortune 500* and with customers in more than 100 countries around the globe. Part of Sun's remarkable success can be attributed to its customer reference program. The company asks its customers to share their success stories by allowing Sun to publish one-page summaries that highlight the customers' organizations and their Sun solutions along with realized benefits. In addition to sharing their success stories, customers can publish quotes about their experiences with Sun, speak at Sun events, talk with press and analysts, develop video and audio clips, and talk with potential Sun customers. Customers benefit from participating in Sun's customer reference program because it brings their companies publicity and allows them to keep abreast of the ever-changing IT landscape.[11]

Specialized B2B marketers such as Magna International provide customized solutions to their customers. Magna developed an automated roof rack specifically designed for the Hummer H2.

Many firms depend on the opinions and experiences of others in evaluating a new business proposal from a new company. Here is some industry wisdom as to what works and doesn't work when developing customer-information and customer-reference programs to respond to these demands.

Five Common Mistakes in Developing Customer-Reference Stories

1. *Failing to state the customer's need and its implications with specificity.* Clearly state why customers had a need and how the company's products resolved it. Such detailed information can better allow salespeople to assess whether a prospect has similar needs and could obtain similar payoffs.

2. *Failing to quantify your customer's results.* Although outside companies may seem reluctant to share too much hard data, their reluctance may just reflect the fact that they don't have the information readily accessible. Assist them in getting it.

3. *Failing to describe business benefits of any kind (quantified or not).* Don't focus on your expertise in various technologies and industries without telling how it specifically helped customers to enter or grow markets. Make an obvious cause-and-effect link between the solution provided and the claims for your product.

4. *Failing to differentiate your offerings from competition.* Make it clear why it was the case that not just any company's products or services could have led to the same solution.

5. *Failing to provide a concise, accessible summary of the story.* Make sure you package the customer-reference story in a way that a prospect can easily and quickly understand. Here are seven ways to do so:

Seven Keys to Successfully Developing Customer-Reference Stories

1. State the customer's needs in compelling terms.
2. Emphasize the barriers to satisfying customer needs.
3. Describe your company's solution in terms of value.
4. List quantified results, especially those that affect ROI.
5. Differentiate your offering from those of competitors.
6. Provide a brief, comprehensive summary.
7. Include numerous customer quotes.

Source: Based on the white paper by Bill Lee, "Success Stories: The Top 5 Mistakes," www.lee-communications.com.

Systems Buying and Selling

Many business buyers prefer to buy a total solution to a problem from one seller. Called *systems buying*, this practice originated with government purchases of major weapons and communications systems. The government would solicit bids from *prime contractors*, which assembled the package or system. The contractor that was awarded the contract would be responsible for bidding out and assembling the system's subcomponents from *second-tier contractors*. The prime contractor would thus provide a turnkey solution, so-called because the buyer simply had to turn one key to get the job done. Companies such as Ford are finding this kind of buying to be more cost-effective.

Ford

Ford has transformed itself from being mainly a car manufacturer to being mainly a car assembler. Ford relies primarily on a few major systems-suppliers to provide seating systems, braking systems, door systems, and other major assemblies. In designing a new automobile, Ford works closely with (say) its seat manufacturer and creates a *black box specification* of the basic seat dimensions and performance that it needs, and then waits for the seat supplier to propose the most cost-effective design. When they agree, the seat supplier subcontracts with parts suppliers to produce and deliver the needed components.

Ford assembly line in action: Worker assembling autos at Ford Motor Company's St. Thomas auto plant in Ontario.

Sellers have increasingly recognized that buyers like to purchase in this way, and many have adopted systems selling as a marketing tool. One variant of systems selling is *systems contracting*, whereby a single supplier provides the buyer with its entire requirement of MRO (maintenance, repair, and operating) supplies. During the contract period, the supplier manages the customer's inventory. For example, Shell Oil manages the oil inventory of many of its business customers and knows when they require replenishment. The customer benefits from reduced procurement and management costs and from price protection over the term of the contract. The seller benefits from lower operating costs because of a steady demand and reduced paperwork.

Systems selling is a key industrial marketing strategy in bidding to build large-scale industrial projects, such as dams, steel factories, irrigation systems, sanitation systems, pipelines, utilities, and even new towns. Project-engineering firms must compete on price, quality, reliability, and other attributes to win contracts. Consider the following example:

Japan and Indonesia

The Indonesian government requested bids to build a cement factory near Jakarta. A U.S. firm made a proposal that included choosing the site, designing the cement factory, hiring the construction crews, assembling the materials and equipment, and turning over the finished factory to the Indonesian government. A Japanese firm, in outlining its proposal, included all of these services, plus hiring and training the workers to run the factory, exporting the cement through its trading companies, and using the cement to build roads and new office buildings in Jakarta. Although the Japanese proposal involved more money, it won the contract. Clearly, the Japanese viewed the problem not just as one of building a cement factory (the narrow view of systems selling) but as one of contributing to Indonesia's economic development. They took the broadest view of the customer's needs. This is true systems selling.

PARTICIPANTS IN THE BUSINESS BUYING PROCESS

Who buys the trillions of dollars' worth of goods and services needed by business organizations? Purchasing agents are influential in straight-rebuy and modified-rebuy situations, whereas the personnel of other departments are more influential in new-buy situations. Engineering personnel usually have a major influence in selecting product components, and purchasing agents dominate in selecting suppliers.[12]

The Buying Centre

Webster and Wind call the decision-making unit of a buying organization the *buying centre*. It is composed of "all those individuals and groups who participate in the purchasing decision-making process, who share some common goals and the risks arising from the decisions."[13] The buying centre includes all members of the organization who play any of seven roles in the purchase decision process:[14]

1. *Initiators*. Those who request that something be purchased. They may be users or others in the organization.

2. *Users*. Those who will use the product or service. In many cases, the users initiate the buying proposal and help define the product requirements.

3. *Influencers*. People who influence the buying decision. They often help define specifications and also provide information for evaluating alternatives. Technical personnel are particularly important influencers.

4. *Deciders*. People who decide on product requirements or on suppliers.

5. *Approvers*. People who authorize the proposed actions of deciders or buyers.

6. *Buyers*. People who have formal authority to select the supplier and arrange the purchase terms. Buyers may help shape product specifications, but their major role is selecting vendors and negotiating. In more complex purchases, the buyers might include high-level managers.

7. *Gatekeepers*. People who have the power to prevent sellers or information from reaching members of the buying centre. For example, purchasing agents, receptionists, and telephone operators may prevent salespersons from contacting users or deciders.

Several individuals can occupy a given role (e.g., there may be many users or influencers), and the individual may occupy multiple roles.[15] A purchasing manager, for example, often occupies simultaneously the roles of buyer, influencer, and gatekeeper: he or she can determine which sales reps may call on other people in the organization, what budget and other constraints to place on the purchase, and which firm will actually get the business, even though others (deciders) might select two or more potential vendors who can meet the company's requirements.

The typical buying centre has a minimum of five or six members and often dozens. The buying centre may include people outside the target customer organization, such as government officials, consultants, technical advisors, and other members of the marketing channel.

Buying-Centre Influences

Buying centres usually include several participants with differing interests, authority, status, and persuasiveness. Each member of the buying centre is likely to give priority to very different decision criteria. For example, engineering personnel may be concerned primarily with maximizing the actual performance of the product, production personnel may be concerned mainly with ease of use and reliability of supply, financial personnel may focus on the economics of the purchase, purchasing may be concerned with operating and replacement costs, union officials may emphasize safety issues, and so on.

Business buyers also respond to many influences when they make their decisions. Each buyer has personal motivations, perceptions, and preferences, which are influenced by the buyer's age, income, education, job position, personality, attitudes toward risk, and culture. Buyers definitely exhibit different buying styles. There are "keep it simple" buyers, "own expert" buyers, "want the best" buyers, and "want everything done" buyers. Some younger, highly educated buyers are computer experts who conduct rigorous analyses of competitive proposals before choosing a supplier. Other buyers are "toughies" from the old school and pit competing sellers against one another, or simply fire those suppliers that fail to meet specifications.

General Motors

Every year Bo Andersson, vice-president of global purchasing at General Motors, is charged with knocking a whopping $2 billion from GM's purchasing bill. A former Swedish army officer, Andersson is a hands-on individual who buys US$85 billion worth of wheels, axles, seats, bolts, and other parts in a purchasing bill topped only by the U.S. military. Yet, he is not focused as much on squeezing suppliers as he is on squeezing inefficiencies out of the system, such as getting GM's vehicles to share more parts. (GM currently makes 26 versions of seat frames, whereas Toyota makes two.) Still, Andersson does not suffer inefficiency from suppliers. If they don't meet his standards, he will drop them even if it means forcing them into bankruptcy. In 2006, for instance, he decided to jettison 3200 suppliers. Perhaps that's why GM ranks last in an annual supplier-satisfaction survey![16]

Webster cautions that ultimately individuals, not organizations, make purchasing decisions.[17] Individuals are motivated by their own needs and perceptions in an attempt to maximize the rewards (pay, advancement, recognition, and feelings of achievement) offered by the organization. Personal needs "motivate" the behaviour of individuals, but organizational needs "legitimize" the buying-decision process and its outcomes. People are not buying "products." They are buying solutions to two problems: the organization's economic and strategic problem and their own personal "problem" of obtaining individual achievement and reward. In this sense, industrial buying decisions are both "rational" and "emotional," as they serve both the organization's and the individual's needs.[18]

Buying-Centre Targeting

To target their efforts properly, business marketers have to figure out: Who are the major decision participants? What decisions do they influence? What is their level of influence? What evaluation criteria do they use? Consider the following example:

A company sells nonwoven disposable surgical gowns to hospitals. The hospital personnel who participate in this buying decision include the vice-president of purchasing, the operating-room administrator, and the surgeons. The vice-president of purchasing analyzes whether the hospital should buy disposable gowns or reusable gowns. If the findings favour disposable gowns, then the operating-room administrator compares various competitors' products and prices and makes a choice. This administrator considers absorbency, antiseptic quality, design, and cost, and normally buys the brand that meets the functional requirements at the lowest cost. Surgeons influence the decision retroactively by reporting their satisfaction with the particular brand.

The business marketer is not likely to know exactly what kind of group dynamics take place during the decision process, although whatever information he or she can discover about personalities and interpersonal factors is useful.

Small sellers concentrate on reaching the *key buying influencers*. Larger sellers, such as CN Rail, go for *multilevel in-depth selling* to reach as many participants as possible; their salespeople virtually live with high-volume customers. Companies have to rely more heavily on their communications program to reach hidden buying influences and keep current customers informed.[19]

Canadian National Railway Company

In April 2004, CN undertook a major reorganization of its sales organization, principally by separating it from the marketing function and creating a whole new sales department, complete with a new vice-president of sales. Under the new structure, the sales department effectively has two tiers: national accounts and regional accounts. National-account sales are managed across customer product lines, while regional-account sales are managed across geographical boundaries. This structure allows CN to establish clear objectives for its sales organization and prioritize more important accounts. For example, a national-sales manager in the forest-products division can focus exclusively on developing and cultivating relationships with large national forestry-products producers, whereas a regional-sales manager for the Alberta region will focus on smaller accounts within that region in any particular industry requiring rail-transport services. By having separately managed national accounts, CN can dedicate significant resources to understanding and delivering on the customer needs of high-value, national clients.[20]

Business marketers must periodically review their assumptions about buying-centre participants. For years, Kodak sold X-ray film to hospital lab technicians. Kodak research indicated that professional administrators were increasingly making purchasing decisions. As a result, Kodak revised its marketing strategy and developed new advertising to reach out to these decision makers.

Major business marketers like the Canadian National Railway Company have developed unique sales-force structures to ensure customer needs are met appropriately.

In defining target segments, four types of business customers can often be identified, with corresponding marketing implications:

1. *Price-oriented customers* (transactional selling). Price is everything.

2. *Solution-oriented customers* (consultative selling). They want low prices but will respond to arguments about lower total cost or more dependable supply or service.

3. *Gold-standard customers* (quality selling). They want the best performance in terms of product quality, assistance, reliable delivery, and so on.

4. *Strategic-value customers* (enterprise selling). They want a fairly permanent sole-supplier relationship with your company.

Some companies are willing to handle price-oriented buyers by setting a lower price, but establishing restrictive conditions: (1) limiting the quantity that can be purchased; (2) no refunds; (3) no adjustments; and (4) no services.[21]

Risk and gain sharing can be used to offset requested price reductions from customers. For example, say Medline, a hospital supplier, signs an agreement with Highland Park Hospital promising $350 000 in savings over the first 18 months in exchange for a tenfold increase in the hospital's share of supplies. If Medline achieves less than this promised savings, it will make up the difference. If Medline achieves substantially more than this promise, it participates in the extra savings. To make such arrangements work, the supplier must be willing to assist the customer in building a historical database, reaching an agreement for measuring benefits and costs, and devising a dispute-resolution mechanism.

Solution selling can also alleviate price pressure and comes in different forms. Here are three examples:[22]

▪ *Solutions to enhance customer revenues.* Hendrix Voeders used its sales consultants to help farmers deliver an incremental animal weight gain of 5 to 10 percent over competitors' gains.

▪ *Solutions to decrease customer risks.* ICI Explosives formulated a safer way to ship explosives for quarries.

▪ *Solutions to reduce customer costs.* W. W. Grainger employees work at the facilities of large customers to reduce materials-management costs.

THE PURCHASING/PROCUREMENT PROCESS

Every organization has specific purchasing objectives, policies, procedures, organizational structures, and systems. In principle, business buyers seek to obtain the highest benefit package (economic, technical, service, and social) in relation to a market offering's costs. A business buyer's incentive to purchase will increase as the ratio of perceived benefits to costs improves. The marketer's task is to construct a profitable offering that delivers superior customer value to the target buyers.

Purchasing Orientations

In the past, purchasing departments occupied a low position in the management hierarchy, in spite of often managing more than half the company's costs. Recent competitive pressures have led many companies to upgrade their purchasing departments and elevate administrators to vice-presidential rank. Today's purchasing departments are staffed with MBAs who aspire to be CEOs—like Thomas Stallkamp, Chrysler's former executive vice-president of procurement and supply, who cut costs and streamlined the automaker's manufacturing processes.[23]

These new, more strategically oriented purchasing departments have a mission to seek the best value from fewer and better suppliers. Some multinationals have even elevated them to "strategic supply departments" with responsibility for global sourcing and partnering. At Caterpillar, for example, purchasing, inventory control, production scheduling, and traffic have been combined into one department. Quality Foods is another firm that has improved its business buying practices.

Quality Foods

Quality Foods is a privately held, independent food company located on Vancouver Island which operates nine retail food stores. Quality Foods is known throughout the industry as a leader in supply-chain innovation. The company has been instrumental in introducing a standards-based technology solution within its supply chain. By implementing technology solutions that follow items from time of purchase to the customer's door, the retailer has improved organizational effectiveness and sales, and has also achieved savings in cost and time. In 2006, thanks in part to these supply-chain innovations, Quality Foods was awarded the GS1 Canada Supply Chain Efficiency Award. This award, which is given by the Canadian Federation of Independent Grocers, recognizes members which have successfully introduced a standards-based technology solution within their organization's supply chain. In 2007, Quality Foods was listed among Canada's 50 Best Managed Companies.[24]

The upgrading of purchasing means that business marketers must upgrade their sales personnel to match the higher calibre of the business buyers. Formally, we can distinguish three company purchasing orientations:[25]

- *Buying orientation.* The purchaser's focus is short-term and tactical. Buyers are rewarded on their ability to obtain the lowest price from suppliers for the given level of quality and availability. Buyers use two tactics: *commoditization*, whereby they imply that the product is a commodity and care only about price; and *multisourcing*, whereby they use several sources and make them compete for shares of the company's purchases.

- *Procurement orientation.* Here buyers simultaneously seek quality improvements and cost reductions. Buyers develop collaborative relationships with major suppliers and seek savings through better management of acquisition, conversion, and disposal costs. They encourage early supplier involvement in materials handling, inventory levels, just-in-time management, and even product design. They negotiate long-term contracts with major suppliers to ensure the timely flow of materials. They work closely with their manufacturing group on materials requirement planning (MRP) to make sure supplies arrive on time.

- *Supply-chain management orientation.* Here purchasing's role is further broadened to become a more strategic, value-adding operation. Purchasing executives at the firm work with marketing and other company executives to build a seamless supply-chain management system, from the purchase of raw materials to the on-time arrival of finished goods to the end users.

Types of Purchasing Processes

Marketers need to understand how business purchasing departments work. These departments purchase many types of products, and the purchasing process will vary depending on the types of products involved. Peter Kraljic distinguished four product-related purchasing processes:[26]

1. *Routine products.* These products have low value and cost to the customer and involve little risk (e.g., office supplies). Customers will seek the lowest price and emphasize routine ordering. Suppliers will offer to standardize and consolidate orders with blanket contracts and facilities management.

2. *Leverage products.* These products have high value and cost to the customer but involve little risk of supply (e.g., engine pistons) because many companies make them. The supplier knows that the customer will compare market offerings and costs, and it needs to show that its offering minimizes the customer's total cost.

3. *Strategic products.* These products have high value and cost to the customer and also involve high risk (e.g., computer servers). The customer will want a well-known and trusted supplier and will be willing to pay more than the average price. The supplier should seek strategic alliances that take the form of early supplier involvement, co-development programs, and co-investment.

4. *Bottleneck products.* These products have low value and cost to the customer but they involve some risk (e.g., spare parts). The customer will want a supplier which can guarantee a steady supply of reliable products. The supplier should propose standard parts and offer a tracking system, delivery on demand, and a help desk.

Purchasing Organization and Administration

Most purchasing professionals describe their jobs as more strategic, technical, team-oriented, and involving more responsibility than ever before. "Purchasing is doing more cross-functional work than it did in the past," says David Duprey, a buyer for Anaren Microwave, Inc. Sixty-one percent of buyers surveyed said the buying group was more involved in new-product design and development than it was five years ago; and more than half of the buyers participate in cross-functional teams, with suppliers well represented.[27]

In multidivisional companies, most purchasing is carried out by separate divisions. Some companies, however, have started to centralize purchasing. Headquarters identifies materials purchased by several divisions and buys them centrally, thereby gaining more purchasing clout. The individual divisions can buy from another source if they can get a better deal, but in general, centralized purchasing produces substantial savings. For the business marketer, this development means dealing with fewer and higher-level buyers and using a national-account sales group to deal with large corporate buyers.

At the same time, companies are decentralizing some purchasing operations by empowering employees to purchase small-ticket items such as special binders, coffeemakers, and Christmas trees. This has come about through the availability of corporate purchasing cards issued by credit-card organizations. Companies distribute the cards to supervisors, clerks, and secretaries; the cards incorporate codes that set credit limits and restrict where they can be used. National Semiconductor's purchasing chief has noted that the cards have cut processing costs from US$30 an order to a few cents. An additional benefit is that buyers and suppliers now spend less time on paperwork.

STAGES IN THE BUYING PROCESS

At this point we are ready to describe the general stages in the business buying-decision process. Robinson and associates have identified eight stages and called them *buyphases.*[28] The stages are shown in Table 7.1. This model is called the *buygrid* framework.

Table 7.1 describes the buying stages involved in a new-task buying situation. In modified-rebuy or straight-rebuy situations, some stages are compressed or bypassed. For example, in a straight-rebuy situation, the buyer normally has a favourite supplier or a ranked list of suppliers. Thus, the supplier search and proposal solicitation stages would be skipped.

The eight-stage buyphase model describes the major steps in the business buying process. Tracing out a buyflow map can provide many clues to the business marketer. A buyflow map for the purchase of a packaging machine in Japan is shown in Figure 7.1. The numbers within the icons are defined to the right. The italicized numbers between icons show the flow of events. Over 20 people in

TABLE 7.1	BUYGRID FRAMEWORK: MAJOR STAGES (BUYPHASES) OF THE INDUSTRIAL BUYING PROCESS IN BUYCLASSES

		BUYCLASSES		
		New Task	Modified Rebuy	Straight Rebuy
BUYPHASES	1. Problem recognition	Yes	Maybe	No
	2. General-need description	Yes	Maybe	No
	3. Product specification	Yes	Yes	Yes
	4. Supplier search	Yes	Maybe	No
	5. Proposal solicitation	Yes	Maybe	No
	6. Supplier selection	Yes	Maybe	No
	7. Order-routine specification	Yes	Maybe	No
	8. Performance review	Yes	Yes	Yes

FIGURE 7.1

Organizational Buying Behaviour in Japan: Packaging-Machine Purchasing Process

Source: "Japanese Firms Use Unique Buying Behavior," *The Japan Economic Journal*, December 23, 1980, p. 29. Reprinted by permission.

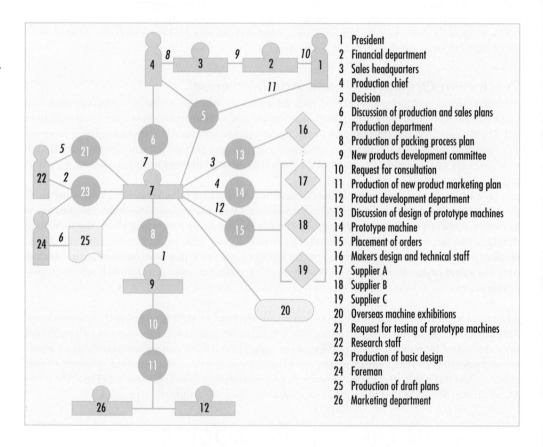

1 President
2 Financial department
3 Sales headquarters
4 Production chief
5 Decision
6 Discussion of production and sales plans
7 Production department
8 Production of packing process plan
9 New products development committee
10 Request for consultation
11 Production of new product marketing plan
12 Product development department
13 Discussion of design of prototype machines
14 Prototype machine
15 Placement of orders
16 Makers design and technical staff
17 Supplier A
18 Supplier B
19 Supplier C
20 Overseas machine exhibitions
21 Request for testing of prototype machines
22 Research staff
23 Production of basic design
24 Foreman
25 Production of draft plans
26 Marketing department

the purchasing company were involved, including the production manager and staff, new-product committee, company laboratory, marketing department, and the department for market development. The entire decision-making process took 121 days. There are important considerations in each of the eight stages.

Problem Recognition

The buying process begins when someone in the company recognizes a problem or need that can be met by acquiring a good or service. The recognition can be triggered by internal or external stimuli. Internally, some common events lead to problem recognition: The company decides to develop a new product and needs new equipment and materials. A machine breaks down and requires new parts. Purchased material turns out to be unsatisfactory and the company searches for another supplier.

A purchasing manager senses an opportunity to obtain lower prices or better quality. Externally, the buyer may get new ideas at a trade show, see an ad, or receive a call from a sales representative who offers a better product or a lower price. Business marketers can stimulate problem recognition by direct mail, telemarketing, and calling on prospects.

General-Need Description and Product Specification

Next, the buyer determines the needed item's general characteristics and required quantity. For standard items, this is simple. For complex items, the buyer will work with others—engineers, users—to define characteristics like reliability, durability, or price. Business marketers can help by describing how their products meet or even exceed the buyer's needs. While many people believe that only feature/function-based messaging appeals to today's sophisticated purchasers, Ceridian Canada has discovered that powerful B2B brand messages with an emotional dimension can also help to win over business clients.

Ceridian Canada Ltd.

Ceridian Canada Ltd., headquartered in Winnipeg, Manitoba, provides payroll management and related services to large and small businesses across Canada. It is the country's leading payroll-services provider, with offices from coast to coast, serving 40 000 businesses and paying more than 2.6 million Canadians. In 2002, Ceridian launched a new multifaceted campaign based on the platform "The freedom to succeed." The advertisements are full of images associated with success and freedom, but they also provide information on cost savings and employee satisfaction. "This brand strategy allows Ceridian to communicate the benefits of their services at an emotional level, aligning their product with core audience goals such as success, creativity, freedom, focus, and confidence," said Rick Denomme, the CEO of Ceridian's marketing and communications agency, HBS.[29]

The buying organization now develops the item's technical specifications. Often, the company will assign a product-value-analysis engineering team to the project. *Product value analysis* (PVA) is an approach to cost reduction in which components are studied to determine if they can be redesigned or standardized or made by cheaper methods of production. The PVA team will examine the high-cost components of a given product. The team will also identify overdesigned components that last longer than the product itself. Tightly written specifications will allow the buyer to refuse components that are too expensive or that fail to meet specified standards. Suppliers can use product value analysis as a tool for positioning themselves to win an account.

Supplier Search

The buyer next tries to identify the most appropriate suppliers through trade directories, contacts with other companies, trade advertisements, and trade shows. Business marketers also put products, prices, and other information on the Internet. While B2B electronic commerce has not delivered on its early promise, it still outstrips B2C (business-to-consumer) commerce. In 2005, according to Industry Canada, 62.4 percent ($24.5 billion) of Canadian e-commerce sales were B2B compared to 37.6 percent ($11.9 billion) for B2C. The total value of Canadian e-commerce sales in 2005 was estimated at $39.2 billion, compared to $28.3 billion just a year earlier. However, only 7 percent of Canadian firms used the Internet to sell their goods or services, although this number is on the rise.[30] The move to Internet purchasing has far-reaching implications for suppliers and will change the shape of purchasing for years to come.

E-PROCUREMENT   Websites are organized around two types of e-hubs: *vertical hubs* centred on industries (plastics, steel, chemicals, paper) and *functional hubs* (logistics, media buying, advertising, energy management). In addition to using these websites, companies can carry out e-procurement in other ways:

- *Direct extranet links to major suppliers.* A company can set up extranet links to its major suppliers. For example, it can set up a direct e-procurement account at Dell or Office Depot, and its employees can make their purchases this way.

- *Buying alliances.* Coca-Cola, Sara Lee, Kraft, PepsiCo, Gillette, P&G, and several other companies joined forces to form a buying alliance called Transora to use their combined leverage to obtain lower prices for raw materials. Transora members also share data on less expensive ways to ship products and track inventory. Several auto companies (GM, Ford, DaimlerChrysler) formed Covisint for the same reason. They believe they can save as much as US$1200 per car through this buying alliance.

- *Company buying sites.* Bombardier Aerospace posts lists of approved suppliers, its quality specifications, and requests for proposals (RFPs) on the suppliers' section of its website (www.bombardier.com).

Moving into e-procurement involves more than acquiring software; it requires changing purchasing strategy and structure. However, the benefits are many: aggregating purchasing across multiple departments gains larger, centrally-negotiated volume discounts; there is less buying of substandard goods from outside the approved list of suppliers; and a smaller purchasing staff is required. Consider how Royal Bank has benefited from e-procurement:

Royal Bank of Canada

Royal Bank of Canada (RBC) provides on a global basis personal and commercial banking, wealth-management services, insurance, and corporate, investment banking, and transaction-processing services. RBC uses a secure enterprise-wide e-procurement system called Ariba Buyer to efficiently manage the purchase of goods and services of all the companies of RBC Financial Group. Ariba, maker of Ariba Buyer, is one of the world's leading vendors of secure electronic-marketplace technologies. RBC uses the Ariba Supplier Network, a system by which buyers and sellers are connected securely via the Internet. RBC expects that e-procurement will greatly increase supply-chain efficiencies, reduce costs, centralize supplier information, and speed payment of invoices. For example, the network provides fast transmission, order tracking, and efficient processing of orders and payments. This means that RBC will no longer have to worry about issues such as lost paper trails, which are common in paper-based procurement.[31]

The supplier's task is to get listed in major online catalogues or services, develop a strong advertising and promotion program, and build a good reputation in the marketplace. This often means creating a well-designed and easy-to-use website, such as that of Staples.

Staples

In 2005, Staples.com was featured in *BtoB* magazine as one of the top ten business-to-business websites due to its fast-loading, user-friendly design. In order to achieve these results, Staples conducted extensive usability studies and subsequently created seven different personas. For example, research by Staples discovered that more than 50 percent of its online customers fell into two categories based on their shopping behaviour. This analysis has helped Staples improve its website design to make ordering and reordering easier. For instance, the site now has an Order by Item Number feature that lets customers input product numbers without scanning through product menus. In addition, it provides an Easy Reorder option, which brings up a list of previously ordered items that users can search and select. Staples.com has also improved product-menu pages by adding photos for shoppers who drill down into menus. This helps shoppers sort through the over 30 000 different products Staples offers through its website.[32]

Suppliers who lack the required production capacity or suffer from a poor reputation will be rejected. Those who qualify may be visited by the buyer's agents, who will examine the suppliers' manufacturing facilities and meet their personnel. After evaluating each company, the buyer will end up with a short list of qualified suppliers. Many professional buyers have forced suppliers to change their marketing to increase their likelihood of making the cut.

Proposal Solicitation

The buyer invites qualified suppliers to submit proposals. If the item is complex or expensive, the buyer will require a detailed written proposal from each qualified supplier. After evaluating the proposals, the buyer will invite a few suppliers to make formal presentations.

Business marketers must be skilled in researching, writing, and presenting proposals. Written proposals should be marketing documents that describe value and benefits in customer terms. Oral presentations should inspire confidence and position the company's capabilities and resources so that they stand out from the competition.

Consider the hurdles that Xerox has set up in qualifying suppliers:

Xerox

Xerox qualifies only suppliers who meet the ISO 9000 quality standards, but to win the company's top award—certification status—a supplier must first complete the Xerox Multinational Supplier Quality Survey. The survey requires the supplier to issue a quality-assurance manual, to adhere to continuous-improvement principles, and to demonstrate effective systems implementation. Once qualified, a supplier must participate in Xerox's Continuous Supplier Involvement process: the two companies work together to create specifications for quality, cost, delivery times, and process capability. The final step towards certification requires a supplier to undergo additional, rigorous quality training and an evaluation based on the same criteria as for the Malcolm Baldrige National Quality Award. Not surprisingly, only 176 suppliers worldwide have achieved the 95-percent rating required for certification as a Xerox supplier.[33]

Supplier Selection

Before selecting a supplier, the buying centre will specify desired supplier attributes and indicate their relative importance. To rate and identify the most attractive suppliers, buying centres often use a supplier-evaluation model such as the one shown in Table 7.2.

To develop compelling value propositions, business marketers need to better understand how business buyers arrive at their valuations.[34] Researchers studying how business marketers assess customer value found eight different *customer value assessment (CVA)* methods. Companies tended to use the simpler methods, although the more sophisticated ones promise to produce a more accurate picture of customer-perceived value. (See "Marketing Insight: Developing Compelling Customer Value Propositions.")

The choice and importance of different attributes vary with the type of buying situation.[35] Delivery reliability, price, and supplier reputation are important for routine-order products. For procedural-problem products, such as a copying machine, the three most important attributes are technical service, supplier flexibility, and product reliability. For political-problem products that stir

| TABLE 7.2 | AN EXAMPLE OF VENDOR ANALYSIS |

Attributes		Rating Scale			
	Importance Weights	Poor (1)	Fair (2)	Good (3)	Excellent (4)
Price	0.30				x
Supplier reputation	0.20			x	
Product reliability	0.30				x
Service reliability	0.10		x		
Supplier flexibility	0.10			x	
Total score: 0.30(4) + 0.20(3) + 0.30(4) + 0.10(2) + 0.10(3) = 3.5					

rivalries in the organization (such as the choice of a computer system), the most important attributes are price, supplier reputation, product reliability, service reliability, and supplier flexibility. Firms may use yet other attributes while selecting suppliers, as the following example illustrates.

Procter & Gamble

Supplier diversity is a fundamental business strategy at Procter & Gamble (P&G). In 2005, P&G was inducted into the Billion Dollar Round Table, a forum that was created in 2001 to recognize and celebrate corporations that achieved spending of at least US$1 billion with ethnic minority- and women-owned supplier firms. P&G's goal is to reach US$2.5 billion in annual spending with ethnic minority- and women-owned businesses by 2010. Management at P&G strongly believes that a diverse organization will out-think, out-perform, and out-innovate a homogeneous organization. In the U.S., the company requires that all prospective minority- or women-owned suppliers be certified by the National Minority Supplier Development Council, the Women's Business Enterprise National Council, the federal government's Central Contractor Registration System, or other government agencies.[36]

The buying centre may attempt to negotiate with preferred suppliers for better prices and terms before making the final selection. Despite moves toward strategic sourcing, partnering, and participation in cross-functional teams, buyers still spend a large chunk of their time haggling with suppliers on price. In 1998, 92 percent of buyers responding to a *Purchasing* magazine survey cited negotiating price as one of their top responsibilities. Nearly as many respondents said price remains a key criterion they use to select suppliers.[37]

Marketers can counter the request for a lower price in a number of ways. They may be able to show evidence that the "total cost of ownership"—that is, the "life-cycle cost" of using their product—is lower than that of competitors' products. They can also cite the value of the services the buyer now receives, especially if those services are superior to those offered by competitors.

Cutting costs is crucial to a firm's ability to have at least some flexibility in setting prices. Consider how Ariba helps companies lower their procurement costs:

Ariba

As the leading provider of "Spend Management" solutions, Ariba helps companies analyze, understand, and manage their corporate spending to achieve increased cost savings and business-process efficiency. Ariba delivers sourcing, procurement, and commodity expertise that helps companies improve their purchasing processes and supplier relationships. Included in the Spend Management solutions offered by Ariba is an extensive array of supplier-management solutions. These solutions allow companies to connect and transact reliably with their entire global supplier base. Ariba applications operate on over four million desktops around the world. Colgate-Palmolive, Heinz, Nestlé, and Toyota are among the companies that put their trust in Ariba solutions.[38]

As part of the buyer-selection process, buying centres must decide how many suppliers to use. Companies are increasingly reducing the number of suppliers. Ford, Motorola, and Honeywell have cut the number of suppliers by anywhere from 20 to 80 percent. These companies want their chosen

---

| MARKETING INSIGHT | DEVELOPING COMPELLING CUSTOMER VALUE PROPOSITIONS |

To command price premiums in competitive B2B markets, firms must create compelling customer value propositions. Here are a number of productive research methods:

1. *Internal engineering assessment.* Company engineers use laboratory tests to estimate the product's performance characteristics. Weakness: Ignores the fact that in different applications, the product will have different economic value.

2. *Field value-in-use assessment.* Customers are interviewed about cost elements associated with using the new-product offering compared to an incumbent product. The task is to assess how much each element is worth to the buyer.

3. *Focus-group value assessment.* Customers in a focus group are asked what value they would put on potential market offerings.

4. *Direct survey questions.* Customers are asked to place a direct dollar value on one or more changes in the market offering.

5. *Conjoint analysis.* Customers are asked to rank their preference for alternative market offerings or concepts. Statistical analysis is used to estimate the implicit value placed on each attribute.

6. *Benchmarks.* Customers are shown a "benchmark" offering and then a new market offering. They are asked how much more they would pay for the new offering or how much less they would pay if certain features were removed from the benchmark offering.

7. *Compositional approach.* Customers are asked to attach a monetary value to each of three alternative levels of a given attribute. This is repeated for other attributes. The values are then added together for any offer configuration.

8. *Importance ratings.* Customers are asked to rate the importance of different attributes and the supplier-firms' performance on these attributes.

Having done this research, you can specify the customer value proposition, following a number of important principles. First, clearly substantiate value claims by concretely specifying the differences between your offerings and those of competitors on the dimensions that matter most to the customer. For example, Rockwell Automation determined the cost savings customers would realize from purchasing its pump solution instead of a competitor's by using industry-standard metrics of functionality and performance: kilowatt-hours spent, number of operating hours per year, and dollars per kilowatt-hour. Also, make the financial implications obvious.

Second, document the value delivered by creating written accounts of costs savings or added value that existing customers have actually captured by using your offerings. Chemical producer Akzo Nobel conducted a two-week pilot on a production reactor at a prospective customer's facility to document points-of-parity and points-of-difference of its high-purity metal organics product.

Finally, make sure the customer value proposition is well implemented within the company, and train and reward employees for developing a compelling one. Quaker Chemical conducts training programs for its managers that include a competition to develop the best proposals.

Source: James C. Anderson, James A. Narus, and Wouter van Rossum, "Customer Value Propositions in Business Markets," *Harvard Business Review* (March 2006): 2–10; James C. Anderson and James A. Narus, "Business Marketing: Understanding What Customers Value," *Harvard Business Review* (November 1998): 53–65; James C. Anderson and James A. Narus, "Capturing the Value of Supplementary Services," *Harvard Business Review* (January 1995): 75–83; James C. Anderson, Dipak C. Jain, and Pradeep K. Chintagunta, "A Customer Value Assessment in Business Markets: A State-of-Practice Study," *Journal of Business-to-Business Marketing,* 1, no. 1 (January 1993): 3–29.

---

suppliers to be responsible for a larger component system; they want them to achieve continuous quality and performance improvement while at the same time lowering the supply price each year by a given percentage. These companies expect their suppliers to work closely with them during product development, and they value their suggestions. There is even a trend towards single sourcing.

Companies that use multiple sources often cite the threat of a labour strike as the biggest deterrent to single sourcing. Another reason companies may be reluctant to use a single source is that they fear they will become too comfortable in the relationship and lose their competitive edge.

Order-Routine Specification

After selecting suppliers, the buyer negotiates the final order, listing the technical specifications, the quantity needed, the expected time of delivery, return policies, warranties, and so on. Many industrial buyers lease heavy equipment like machinery and trucks. The lessee gains a number of advantages: conserving capital, getting the latest products, receiving better service, and some tax advantages. The lessor often ends up with a larger net income and the chance to sell to customers who could not afford outright purchase.

In the case of maintenance, repair, and operating items, buyers are moving toward blanket contracts rather than periodic purchase orders. A blanket contract establishes a long-term relationship in which the supplier promises to resupply the buyer as needed, at agreed-upon prices, over a specified period of time. Because the stock is held by the seller, blanket contracts are sometimes called *stockless purchase plans*. The buyer's computer automatically sends an order to the seller when stock is needed. This system locks suppliers in tighter with the buyer and makes it difficult for out-suppliers to break in unless the buyer becomes dissatisfied with the in-supplier's prices, quality, or service.

Companies that fear a shortage of key materials are willing to buy and hold large inventories. They will sign long-term contracts with suppliers to ensure a steady flow of materials. For example, General Motors wants to buy from fewer suppliers which are willing to locate close to its plants and produce high-quality components. In addition, business marketers are using the Internet to set up extranets with important customers to facilitate and lower the cost of transactions. The customers enter orders on their computers and these orders are automatically transmitted to the supplier. Some companies go further and shift the ordering responsibility to their suppliers in systems called *vendor-managed inventory*. These suppliers are privy to the customer's inventory levels and take responsibility to replenish inventory automatically through *continuous replenishment programs*.

"OTIFNE" is a term that summarizes three desirable outcomes of a B2B transaction:

- OT—deliver on time
- IF—in full
- NE—no error

All three matter. If a supplier achieves on-time compliance of only 80 percent, in-full compliance of 90 percent, and no error compliance of 70 percent, overall performance computes at 80% × 90% × 70%—only 50%!

Performance Review

The buyer periodically reviews the performance of the chosen supplier(s). Three methods are commonly used. The buyer may contact the end users and ask for their evaluations; the buyer may rate the supplier on several criteria using a weighted-score method; or the buyer might aggregate the cost of poor performance to come up with adjusted costs of purchase, including price. The performance review may lead the buyer to continue, modify, or end a supplier relationship.

Many companies have set up incentive systems to reward purchasing managers for good buying performance, in much the same way that sales personnel receive bonuses for good selling performance. These systems are leading purchasing managers to increase pressure on sellers for the best terms.

MANAGING BUSINESS-TO-BUSINESS CUSTOMER RELATIONSHIPS

To improve effectiveness and efficiency, business suppliers and customers are exploring different ways to manage their relationships. Closer relationships are driven in part by trends related to supply-chain management, early supplier involvement, purchasing alliances, and so on.[39] Cultivating the right relationships with business is paramount to a holistic marketing program.

The Benefits of Vertical Coordination

Much research has advocated greater vertical coordination between buying partners and sellers so that they transcend mere transactions to engage in activities that create more value for both parties. Building trust between parties is often seen as one prerequisite to healthy long-term relationships.[40] "Marketing Insight: Establishing Corporate Trust and Credibility" identifies some key dimensions of those concepts. Consider the mutual benefits from the following arrangement:

Motoman Inc. and Stillwater Technologies

Motoman Inc., a leading supplier of industry robotic systems, and Stillwater Technologies, a contract tooling and machinery company and a key supplier to Motoman, are tightly integrated. Not only do they occupy office and manufacturing space in the same facility, but their telephone and computer systems are linked, and they share a common lobby, conference room, and employee cafeteria. Philip V. Morrison, chair and CEO of Motoman, says it is like "a joint venture without the paperwork." Short delivery distances are just one benefit of the unusual partnership. Also key is the fact that employees of both companies have ready access to one another and can share ideas on improving quality and reducing costs. This close relationship has opened the door to new opportunities. Both companies had been doing work for Honda Motor Company, and Honda suggested that they work together on systems projects. The integration makes the two bigger than they are individually.[41]

One historical study of four very different business-to-business relationships found that several factors, by affecting partner interdependence and/or environmental uncertainty, influenced the development of a relationship between business partners.[42] The relationship between advertising agencies and clients illustrates these findings:

- *In the relationship formation stage, one partner experienced substantial market growth.* Manufacturers capitalizing on mass-production techniques developed national brands, which increased the importance and amount of mass-media advertising.

- *There was sufficient information asymmetry that the clients would generate more profits from a partnership with the agency than they would if they attempted to perform the agency's function themselves.* Advertising agencies had specialized knowledge that their clients would have had difficulty obtaining.

- *At least one partner had high barriers to entry that would prevent the other partner from entering the business.* Advertising agencies could not easily become national manufacturers, and for years, manufacturers were not eligible to receive media commissions.

MARKETING INSIGHT | ESTABLISHING CORPORATE TRUST AND CREDIBILITY

Strong bonds and relationships between firms depend on their perceived credibility. *Corporate credibility* refers to the extent to which customers believe that a firm can design and deliver goods and services that satisfy their needs and wants. Corporate credibility relates to the reputation that a firm has achieved in the marketplace and is the foundation for a strong relationship. It is difficult for a firm to develop strong ties with another firm unless it is seen as highly credible.

Corporate credibility, in turn, depends on three factors:

- *Corporate expertise:* the extent to which a company is seen as able to make and sell products or conduct services.

- *Corporate trustworthiness:* the extent to which a company is seen as motivated to be honest, dependable, and sensitive to customer needs.

- *Corporate likability:* the extent to which a company is seen as likable, attractive, prestigious, dynamic, and so on.

In other words, a credible firm is seen as being good at what it does, keeps its customers' best interests in mind, and is enjoyable to work with.

Trust is a particularly important determinant of credibility and a firm's relationships with other firms. Trust is reflected in the willingness and confidence of a firm to rely on a business partner. A number of interpersonal and interorganizational factors affect trust in a business-to-business relationship, such as the perceived competence, integrity, honesty, and benevolence of the firm. Trust will be affected by personal interactions among employees of a firm as well as opinions about the company as a whole, and perceptions of trust will evolve with more experience with a company.

Trust can be especially tricky in online settings, and firms often impose more stringent requirements on their online business partners. Business buyers worry that they won't get products of the right quality delivered to the right place at the right time. Sellers worry about getting paid on time—or at all—and how much credit they should extend. Some firms, such as transportation and supply-chain management company Ryder System, are using tools such as automated credit-checking applications and online trust services to help determine the credibility of trading partners.

Sources: Robert M. Morgan and Shelby D. Hunt, "The Commitment-Trust Theory of Relationship Marketing," *Journal of Marketing, 58,* no. 3 (1994): 20–38; Christine Moorman, Rohit Deshpande, and Gerald Zaltman, "Factors Affecting Trust in Market Research Relationships," *Journal of Marketing, 57* (January 1993): 81–101; Kevin Lane Keller and David A. Aaker, "Corporate-Level Marketing: The Impact of Credibility on a Company's Brand Extensions," *Corporate Reputation Review, 1* (August 1998): 356–378; Bob Violino, "Building B2B Trust," *Computerworld,* June 17, 2002, p. 32; Richard E. Plank, David A. Reid, and Ellen Bolman Pullins, "Perceived Trust in Business-to-Business Sales: A New Measure," *Journal of Personal Selling and Sales Management, 19,* no. 3 (Summer 1999): 61–72.

- *Dependence asymmetry existed such that one partner was more able to control or influence the other's conduct.* Advertising agencies had control over media access.
- *One partner benefited from economies of scale related to the relationship.* Ad agencies gained by providing the same market information to multiple clients.

Cannon and Perreault found that buyer–supplier relationships differed according to four factors: availability of alternatives, importance of supply, complexity of supply, and supply market dynamism. Based on these four factors, they classified buyer–supplier relationships into eight different categories:[43]

1. *Basic buying and selling:* relatively simple, routine exchanges with moderately high levels of cooperation and information exchange.
2. *Bare bones:* similar to basic buying and selling but more adaptation by the seller and less cooperation and information exchange.
3. *Contractual transaction:* generally low levels of trust, cooperation, and interaction; exchange is defined by formal contract.
4. *Customer supply:* traditional custom supply situation where competition, rather than cooperation, is the dominant form of governance.
5. *Cooperative systems:* although coupled closely in operational ways, neither party demonstrates structural commitment through legal means or adaptation approaches.
6. *Collaborative:* much trust and commitment leading to true partnership.
7. *Mutually adaptive:* much relationship-specific adaptation for buyer and seller, but without necessarily strong trust or cooperation.
8. *Customer is king:* although bonded by a close, cooperative relationship, the seller adapts to meet the customer's needs without expecting much adaptation or change on the part of the customer in exchange.

Some firms find that their needs can be satisfied with fairly basic supplier performance. They do not want or require a close relationship with a supplier. Alternatively, some suppliers may not find it worth their while to invest in customers with limited growth potential. One study found that the closest relationships between customer and suppliers arose when the supply was important to the customer and when there were procurement obstacles such as complex purchase requirements and few alternative suppliers.[44] Another study suggested that greater vertical coordination between buyer and seller through information exchange and planning is usually necessary only when high environmental uncertainty exists and specific investments are modest.[45]

Business Relationships: Risks and Opportunism

To understand how Dome Coffee worked its business relationships to grow its operations from an Australian to an international presence, visit www.pearsoned.com.au/ marketingmanagementaustralia.

Buvik and John note that in establishing a customer–supplier relationship, there is tension between safeguarding and adaptation. Vertical coordination can facilitate stronger customer–seller ties but at the same time may increase the risk to the customer's and supplier's specific investments. *Specific investments* are those expenditures tailored to a particular company and value-chain partner (e.g., investments in company-specific training, equipment, and operating procedures or systems).[46] Specific investments help firms grow profits and achieve their positioning.[47] For example, Xerox worked closely with its suppliers to develop customized processes and components that reduced its copier-manufacturing costs by 30 to 40 percent. In return, suppliers received sales and volume guarantees, an enhanced understanding of their customer needs, and a strong position with Xerox for future sales.[48]

Specific investments, however, also entail considerable risk to both customer and supplier. Transaction theory from economics maintains that because these investments are partially sunk, they lock the firms that make the investments into a particular relationship. Sensitive cost and process information may need to be exchanged. A buyer may be vulnerable to hold-up because of switching costs; a supplier may be more vulnerable to hold-up in future contracts because of dedicated assets and/or expropriation of technology/knowledge. In terms of the latter risk, consider the following example:[49]

An automobile-component manufacturer wins a contract to supply an under-hood component to an original equipment manufacturer. A one-year, sole-source contract safeguards the supplier's OEM-specific investments in a dedicated production line. However, the supplier may also be obliged to work (noncontractually) as a partner with the OEM's internal engineering staff (using linked computing facilities) to exchange detailed engineering information and coordinate frequent design and manufacturing changes over the term of the contract. These interactions could reduce costs and/or increase quality by improving the firm's responsiveness to marketplace changes. Such interactions could also potentially magnify the threat to the supplier's intellectual property.

When buyers cannot easily monitor supplier performance, the supplier might shirk or cheat and not deliver the expected value. *Opportunism* can be thought of as "some form of cheating or undersupply relative to an implicit or explicit contract."[50] It may involve blatant self-interest and deliberate misrepresentation that violates contractual agreements. In creating the 1996 version of the Ford Taurus, Ford Corporation chose to outsource the whole process to one supplier, Lear Corporation. Lear committed to a contract that, for various reasons, it knew it was unable to fulfill. According to Ford, Lear missed deadlines, failed to meet weight and price objectives, and furnished parts that did not work.[51] A more passive form of opportunism might involve a refusal or unwillingness to adapt to changing circumstances.

Opportunism is a concern because firms must devote resources to control and monitoring that otherwise could be allocated to more productive purposes. Contracts may become inadequate to govern supplier transactions when supplier opportunism becomes difficult to detect; as firms make specific investments in assets that cannot be used elsewhere; and as contingencies are harder to anticipate. Customers and suppliers are more likely to form a joint venture (versus a simple contract) when the supplier's degree of asset specificity is high, monitoring the supplier's behaviour is difficult, and the supplier has a poor reputation.[52] When a supplier has a good reputation, for example, it is more likely to avoid opportunism to protect this valuable intangible asset.

The presence of a significant future time horizon and/or strong solidarity norms so that customers and suppliers are willing to strive for joint benefits can cause a shift in the effect of specific investments, from expropriation (increased opportunism on the receiver's part) to bonding (reduced opportunism).[53]

INSTITUTIONAL AND GOVERNMENT MARKETS

Our discussion has concentrated largely on the buying behaviour of profit-seeking companies. Much of what we have said also applies to the buying practices of institutional and government organizations. However, we want to highlight certain special features of these markets.

The **institutional market** consists of schools, hospitals, nursing homes, prisons, and other institutions that must provide goods and services to people in their care. Many of these organizations are characterized by low budgets and captive clienteles. For example, hospitals have to decide what quality of food to buy for patients. The buying objective here is not profit, because the food is provided as part of the total service package; nor is cost minimization the sole objective, because poor food will cause patients to complain and hurt the hospital's reputation. The hospital purchasing agent has to search for institutional-food vendors whose quality meets or exceeds a certain minimum standard and whose prices are low. In fact, many food vendors set up a separate division to sell to institutional buyers because of these buyers' special needs and characteristics. Heinz produces, packages, and prices its ketchup differently to meet the requirements of hospitals, colleges, and prisons.

Governments—federal, provincial, and municipal—are major purchasers of goods and services. The Canadian government buys approximately $13-billion worth of goods and services every year from thousands of suppliers. There are over 85 departments, agencies, Crown corporations, and special operating agencies. Public Works and Government Services Canada (PWGSC) is the government's largest purchasing organization, averaging 33 000 contracts totalling $10 billion annually. While PWGSC buys goods for most departments of the federal government, the departments buy most services themselves.[54]

Government organizations typically require suppliers to submit bids, and normally they award the contract to the lowest bidder. In some cases, the government unit will make allowance for the supplier's superior quality or reputation for completing contracts on time. Governments will also buy on a negotiated-contract basis, primarily in the case of complex projects involving major R&D costs and risks and in cases where there is little competition. Government organizations tend to favour domestic suppliers. A major complaint of multinationals operating in Europe was that each country showed favouritism toward its nationals in spite of superior offers available from foreign firms. The European Union is removing this bias.

Like consumer and business buyers, government buyers are affected by environmental, organizational, interpersonal, and individual factors. One unique aspect of government buying is that it is carefully watched by outside publics, from Parliament to various private groups interested in how the government spends taxpayers' money. Because their spending decisions are subject to public review, government organizations require considerable documentation from suppliers, which often complain about excessive paperwork, bureaucracy, regulations, decision-making delays, and frequent shifts in procurement personnel.

Many firms complain about selling to governments because of the red tape they perceive to be involved in making a sale. Federal, provincial, and municipal governments are now posting a great deal of information online to help businesses better understand their purchasing processes, supplier-selection criteria, and sales opportunities. For example, on the federal government's

Business Access Canada site (http://contractscanada.gc.ca), you can find a wealth of information with only a click of the mouse on such links as "How does the Government buy goods and services?" and "Government Electronic Tendering Service," which posts opportunities to bid to supply government services. You can also access information about how to become a registered government supplier. Canada Business: Services for Entrepreneurs (www.cbsc.org) is another site established by the government to help Canadian businesses. The site is a goldmine of information on topics as varied as training, importing, and taxation. It features online workshops for small businesses as well as a comprehensive database of government services and programs. The federal government also issues a weekly bulletin, *Government Business Opportunities*, to alert prospective suppliers to the government's plans to purchase products and services.

If anyone knows how to market to institutional and government clients, it is Microsoft, with its years of experience providing solutions to the federal, provincial, and municipal governments in Canada.

Microsoft

Microsoft has worked extensively with the federal, provincial, and municipal governments in Canada to develop solutions that will enable them to effectively serve Canadians as one coherent enterprise. In 2007, the Government of Alberta turned to Microsoft when faced with a need to enhance information-technology security and decrease the amount of time required to get computers up and running. The Government of Alberta decided to upgrade some of its server computers to the Windows Server 2008 Standard operating system. After the system was deployed, the Government of Alberta saw benefits such as enhanced security, reduced downtime, and improved IT efficiency.[55]

There are a number of reasons many companies that sell to the government have not used a marketing orientation. The government's procurement policies have traditionally emphasized price, leading suppliers to invest considerable effort in bringing down costs. Where product characteristics are carefully specified, product differentiation is not a marketing factor nor are advertising and personal selling of much consequence in winning bids. Some companies have pursued government business by establishing separate government-marketing departments.

Companies such as Dell Canada, Kodak, and Goodyear anticipate government needs and projects, participate in the product-specification phase, gather competitive intelligence, prepare bids carefully, and produce strong communications to describe and enhance their companies' reputations.

SUMMARY

1. Organizational buying is the decision-making process by which formal organizations establish the need for purchased products and services, then identify, evaluate, and choose among alternative brands and suppliers. The business market consists of all the organizations that acquire goods and services used in the production of other products or services that are sold, rented, or supplied to others.

2. Compared to consumer markets, business markets generally have fewer and larger buyers, a closer customer–supplier relationship, and more geographically concentrated buyers. Demand in the business market is derived from demand in the consumer market and fluctuates with the business cycle. Nonetheless, the total demand for many business goods and services is quite price-inelastic. Business marketers need to be aware of the role of professional purchasers and their influencers, the need for multiple sales calls, and the importance of direct purchasing, reciprocity, and leasing.

3. The buying centre is the decision-making unit of a buying organization. It consists of initiators, users,

influencers, deciders, approvers, buyers, and gatekeepers. To influence these parties, marketers must be aware of environmental, organizational, interpersonal, and individual factors.

4. The buying process consists of eight stages called buyphases: (1) problem recognition, (2) general-need description, (3) product specification, (4) supplier search, (5) proposal solicitation, (6) supplier selection, (7) order-routine specification, and (8) performance review.

5. Business marketers must form strong bonds and relationships with their customers and provide them added value. Some customers, however, may prefer more of a transactional relationship.

6. The institutional market consists of schools, hospitals, nursing homes, prisons, and other institutions that provide goods and services to people in their care. Buyers for government organizations tend to require a great deal of paperwork from their vendors and often favour open bidding and domestic companies. Suppliers must be prepared to adapt their offers to the special needs and procedures found in institutional and government markets.

APPLICATIONS

Marketing Debate: How Different Is Business-to-Business Marketing?

Many business-to-business marketing executives lament the challenges of business-to-business marketing, maintaining that many traditional marketing concepts and principles do not apply. For a number of reasons, they assert that selling products and services to a company is fundamentally different from selling to individuals. Others disagree, claiming that marketing theory is still valid and involves only some adaptation in the marketing tactics.

Take a position: Business-to-business marketing requires a special, unique set of marketing concepts and principles *versus* Business-to-business marketing is really not that different and the basic marketing concepts and principles apply.

Marketing Discussion

Consider some of the consumer-behaviour topics from Chapter 6. How might you apply them to business-to-business settings? For example, how might non-compensatory models of choice work?

Breakthrough Marketing: Go Green or Go In The Red

While environmentally friendly practices have always had their place in the business world, increasing eco-consumerism and the escalating concern about climate change has made going green the newest trend. Now, in order to win contracts from businesses, suppliers must focus not only on their core products, but also on the environmental impacts of production, packaging, and delivery. Wal-Mart suppliers have been told to cut back on unnecessary packaging and to use environmentally friendly materials in order to keep their contracts. The retailer has begun using a packaging scorecard to rate its suppliers and identify where changes can be made in order to save packaging and cut costs. By January 2008, over 97 000 products had been rated, all as part of Wal-Mart's goal to become more green. With an investment of US$500 million annually toward this goal, Wal-Mart hopes to reduce packaging by 5 percent in

five years and has been working with its 60 000 suppliers to help them make eco-friendly changes throughout their supply chains. Besides reducing their environmental impact, this initiative has helped numerous suppliers improve their profitability by eliminating unnecessary product packaging and becoming more energy-efficient in their operations.

For example, in 2005, NatureWorks LLC began supplying Wal-Mart with corn-based plastic containers for packaging fresh produce—a change that is expected to save the equivalent of 3 million litres of gasoline and eliminate more than 5000 tons of greenhouse-gas emissions each year. To win the Wal-Mart contract, executives from NatureWorks worked for almost a year to smooth out the deal, which replaced with NatureWorks' materials the packaging for four products amounting to over 100 million containers per year. One of the major attractions of the new packaging, which is an order-winner for NatureWorks, is that it is relatively price-stable compared to plastic containers that use oil in the manufacturing process.

Consumer perception has begun to drive companies to seek environmentally friendly solutions of their own. This trend creates ripples that can be felt throughout the supply chain, as changing to smaller, biodegradable packaging, like that required by Wal-Mart, is not easy for many manufacturers. Suppliers do see cost savings in smaller packaging, but can lose money since their products may be less visible on retail shelves. This is where having a good customer–supplier relationship is necessary. After asking Unilever to reduce the size of its detergent container, Wal-Mart compensated by moving the detergent to a more visible shelf location, which actually increased sales of the product, making it a win-win situation.

The trend of environmentally friendly practices has begun to take off in recent years, and with rising concerns over oil prices, energy supply, and the environment in general, businesses must examine their operations closely if they want to remain competitive in their markets. Switching to eco-friendly production and practices can help reduce environmental impact and at the same time improve the bottom line, as many of Wal-Mart's suppliers have discovered.

DISCUSSION QUESTIONS

1. Consider the stages in the buying process. At which stage must an organization specify its expectations from the supplier, both in terms of economics and environmental friendliness?

2. How can a relatively hard-to-measure factor such as environmental friendliness be built into the performance review of suppliers?

3. What is the role played by "power" in a business-to-business relationship? If Wal-Mart threatened a firm such as Procter & Gamble to use eco-friendly packaging or risk losing Wal-Mart's business, what would be the outcome?

Sources: Tom Stundza, "Wal-Mart Goes Green BIG TIME," *Purchasing*, 135, no. 16 (November 2, 2006); Mindy Fetterman, "Wal-Mart Goes 'Green.'" *USA Today*, September 24, 2006, www.usatoday.com/money/industries/retail/2006-09-24-wal-mart-cover-usat_x.htm (viewed June 2, 2008); Jennifer Paxinos and Ann Tucker, "SAM'S CLUB Partners with NatureWorks PLA to Help the Environment," Wal-Mart Press Release, October 21, 2005, WalMartstores.com/FactsNews/NewsRoom/5412.aspx (viewed June 2, 2008); Linda Rano, "Wal-Mart, ASDA Adopt More Sustainable Packaging Schemes," *MeatProcess.com*, February 8, 2008, www.meatprocess.com/news/printNewsBis.asp?id=83133 (viewed June 2, 2008).

IN THIS CHAPTER, WE WILL ADDRESS THE FOLLOWING QUESTIONS:

- What are the different levels of market segmentation?

- How can a company divide a market into segments?

- How should a company choose the most attractive target markets?

- What are the requirements for effective segmentation?

CHAPTER 8

IDENTIFYING MARKET SEGMENTS AND TARGETS

eight

Markets are not homogeneous. A company cannot connect with all customers in large, broad, or diverse markets; but it can divide such markets into groups of consumers or segments with distinct needs and wants. It then needs to identify which market segments it can serve effectively. Such decisions require a keen understanding of consumer behaviour and careful strategic thinking. To develop the best marketing plans, managers need to understand what makes each segment unique.

One lucrative market segment is the baby boomers, the group that University of Toronto demographer and economist David Foot defines as anyone living in Canada (including immigrants) born from 1947 to 1966. According to Statistics Canada, boomers make up a bit more than 30 percent of the population. Many own their homes and, having purchased them before prices skyrocketed, many represent wealthy targets. Nonetheless, marketers often overlook baby boomers. For example, in network-television circles, viewers over 50 are referred to as "undesirables," because advertisers are interested primarily in 18- to 49-year-olds. Some marketers have come to their senses. Take the beauty industry, where older women such as 53-year-old Christie Brinkley are gracing many ads for Cover Girl, 61-year-old Diane Keaton for L'Oréal, and 66-year-old Raquel Welch for M.A.C.

Boomers view themselves as ambitious, but not materialistic, and many regard their kids as their best friends. Almost 50 percent state they have a better relationship with their kids than they ever had with their parents. All is not rosy for the group, however. Diabetes and obesity rates are rising. While they claim to exercise a lot, government statistics suggest many are couch potatoes. They are generally an optimistic group, but many worry about having enough savings to fund their retirement. Thus, it is not surprising that many plan to work past 65.

According to a recent poll, most boomers don't think of themselves as old. In fact, almost half of the group regard themselves as younger than they are, and 10 percent claim they still feel like they are in their 20s. As they search for the fountain of youth, sales of hair-replacement and hair-colouring aids, health-club memberships, home-gym equipment, skin-tightening creams, nutritional supplements, and organic foods have all soared. Furthermore, contrary to the conventional

>>>

marketing wisdom that the brand preferences of consumers over 50 are fixed, one study found that 52 percent of boomers are willing to change brands, in line with the total population.

Sources: Louise Lee, "Love Those Boomers," *Business Week*, October 24, 2005, p. 94; Bob Moos, "Last of Boomers Turn 40," *Dallas Morning News*, January 1, 2005; Linda Tischler, "Where the Buck Are," *Fast Company*, March 2004, pp. 71–77; Michale J. Weiss, "Chasing Youth," *American Demographics*, October 2002, pp. 35–40; Becky Ebenkamp, "When They're 64," *Brandweek*, October 7, 2002, pp. 22–25; Andy Hoffman, "Mirror, mirror," *The Globe and Mail*, June 24, 2006; Tralee Pearce, "by definition: Boom, bust, X and why," *The Globe and Mail*, June 24, 2006; Clara Young, "Baby boomers: Hotter than ever!" *Elle Canada*, www.ellecanada.com/Beauty/face/Baby%20boomers:%20Hotter%20than%20ever!-n238846p1.html (viewed March 2008).

To compete more effectively, many companies are now embracing target marketing. Instead of scattering their marketing effort (a "shotgun" approach), they focus on those consumers they have the greatest chance of satisfying (a "rifle" approach).

Effective target marketing requires that marketers:

1. Identify and profile distinct groups of buyers who differ in their needs and preferences (market segmentation).

2. Select one or more market segments to enter (market targeting).

3. For each target segment, establish and communicate the distinctive benefit(s) of the company's market offering (market positioning).

This chapter focuses on the first two steps. Chapters 9 and 10 will discuss brand and market positioning.

LEVELS OF MARKET SEGMENTATION

The starting point for discussing segmentation is **mass marketing**. In mass marketing, the seller engages in the mass production, mass distribution, and mass promotion of one product for all buyers. Henry Ford epitomized this strategy when he offered the Model-T Ford in one colour, black. Coca-Cola also practised mass marketing when it sold only one kind of Coke in one size of bottle.

The argument for mass marketing is that it creates the largest potential market, which leads to the lowest costs, which in turn can lead to lower prices or higher margins. However, many critics point to the increasing splintering of the market, which makes mass marketing more difficult. The proliferation of advertising media and distribution channels is making it difficult and increasingly expensive to reach a mass audience. Some claim that mass marketing is dying. Most companies are turning to *micro-marketing* at one of four levels: segments, niches, local areas, or individuals.

Segment Marketing

A market segment consists of a group of customers who share a similar set of needs and wants and who are likely to respond to a marketing campaign in a similar way. Rather than creating the segments, the marketer's task is to identify the segments and decide which one(s) to target. Segment marketing offers key benefits over mass marketing. The company can presumably better design, price, communicate, and deliver the product or service to satisfy the target market. The company also can fine-tune the marketing program and activities to better respond to competitors' marketing aimed at the same or similar segments.

However, even a segment is partly a fiction, in that not everyone wants exactly the same thing. Anderson and Narus have urged marketers to present flexible market offerings to all members of a segment.[1] A **flexible market offering** consists of two parts: a *naked solution* containing the product and service elements that all segment members value, and *discretionary options* that some segment members value. Each option might carry an additional charge. For example, Air Canada offers all economy passengers a seat and soft drinks, and charges extra for alcoholic beverages, snacks, and meals. Siemens Electrical Apparatus Division sells metal-clad boxes to small manufacturers whose price includes free delivery and a warranty, but also offers installation, tests, and communication peripherals as extra-cost options.

Market segments can be defined in many different ways. One way to carve up a market is to identify *preference segments*. **Homogeneous preferences** exist when all consumers have roughly the same preferences; the market shows no natural segments. At the other extreme are consumers with **diffused preferences**. If several brands are in the market, they are likely to position themselves throughout the space and show real differences to match differences in consumer preference. Finally, **clustered preferences** result when natural market segments emerge from groups of consumers with shared preferences.

Niche Marketing

A niche is a more narrowly defined customer group seeking a distinctive mix of benefits. Marketers usually identify niches by dividing a segment into subsegments. For example, whereas Hertz, Avis, Budget, and others specialize in airport rental cars for business and leisure travellers, Enterprise has attacked the low-budget, insurance-replacement market by renting primarily to customers whose cars have been wrecked or stolen. By creating unique associations to low cost and convenience in an overlooked niche market, Enterprise has been highly profitable. Niche markets can also be international. A classic Canadian-made aircraft, the Twin Otter, is being reborn as the result of demand from a niche market. Production was halted in 1988, but demand for the rugged aircraft from niche markets in Asia, Africa, and the Middle East has given the plane a second life.[2]

What does an attractive niche look like? The customers in the niche have a distinct set of needs; they will pay a premium to the firm that best satisfies their needs; the niche is fairly small but has size, profit, and growth potential and is unlikely to attract many other competitors; and the "nicher" gains certain economies through specialization. Larger companies, such as IBM, have lost pieces of their market to nichers. This confrontation has been labelled "guerrillas against gorillas."[3] This is happening in the online social networking market, where MySpace and Facebook are becoming mature service providers.

MySpace, Facebook

A drop in traffic numbers has made headlines for the nation's biggest social-networking sites, MySpace and Facebook. The sites, with 130 million and 12 million users respectively, rely on advertising revenue to survive and risk losing out by trying to be all things to all people. A host of upstart social-networking nichers hope to capitalize on the tendency of individuals to want to congregate with others who share their own particular passions, however arcane. For instance, there is now 1Up.com, a content-heavy social site where online-gaming fanatics can trade tips, stories, opinions, and gossip. Gather.com is a social network for the so-called NPR crowd: people in the prime of their careers who, unlike students, have disposable income to burn. Then there's Dogster, an ultra-niche site that has 3500 active communities for dog owners and is already attracting scads of advertisers.[4]

Even some large companies have turned to niche marketing. Hallmark commands over half of the global greeting-card market by rigorously segmenting its greeting-card business. In addition to popular sub-branded card lines like the humorous Shoebox Greetings, Hallmark has introduced lines targeting specific market segments. Fresh Ink targets 18- to 39-year-old women. Hallmark Warm

Hallmark targets several market segments including young women, people of African descent, Hispanics, and Jews. It also promotes targeted product lines including Warm Wishes (inexpensive greeting cards) and Shoebox Greetings (humorous cards).

Wishes offers hundreds of 99-cent cards. Hallmark's three ethnic lines—Mahogany, Sinceramente Hallmark, and Tree of Life—target African American, Hispanic, and Jewish consumers respectively.

Marketers can aim at local niches or niches in the worldwide marketplace. The latter is where Toronto's Brunico Communications plays.

Brunico Communications

Entrepreneur Jim Shenkman founded Brunico Communications in 1986 around a single product: a trade publication called *Playback*, aimed at Canadian film and TV producers and broadcasters. Three years later, he launched *Strategy* as a rival to *Marketing Magazine*. Today, Brunico publishes five trade magazines that appeal to different niche markets. Three have an international readership and over half the company's revenues come from outside of the country. *RealScreen* has become the leading publication in the world for documentary filmmakers and broadcasters, while *KidScreen* is the world leader for producers, broadcasters, and consumer marketers interested in reaching children through entertainment.[5]

Niche marketers presumably understand their customers' needs so well that the customers willingly pay a premium. Fairmont Hotels, like the Banff Springs and the Royal York, cater to the personal preferences of their President's Club members so well that members return again and again despite the chain's premium pricing.

As marketing efficiency increases, niches that were seemingly too small may become more profitable.[6] The low cost of setting up shop on the Internet has led to many small-business start-ups aimed at niches. The recipe for Internet niching success: choose a hard-to-find product that customers don't need to see and touch. The example that follows and "Marketing Insight: Chasing the Long Tail" outline how provocative the implications of Internet niching are.

Internet Niching

The experience of Dan Myrick, director of *The Blair Witch Project*, illustrates what can happen when you move away from targeting the mass market. In 1999, just two years out of film school, Myrick spent eight days in the woods of Maryland shooting *The Blair Witch Project*. The crudely made film netted nearly US$250 million on a US$35 000 production budget, largely from audiences drawn to the movie through Myrick's website. Myrick has also used the web to distribute *The Strand*, a series of "webisodes" set in Venice Beach, California. He says "The great thing about the Internet is it opens up this realm of micromarkets and I don't need an 8 or 9 or 10 Nielsen share to be a success. NBC will cancel a show if it didn't get 3 million viewers."[7]

To emphasize its new drive towards "three-mile marketing" with a heavily local concentration, Baskin-Robbins stopped advertising on TV.

Local Marketing

Target marketing is leading to marketing programs tailored to the needs and wants of local customer groups (trading areas, neighbourhoods, even individual stores). Canada's credit unions provide different mixes of banking services in their branches, depending on neighbourhood demographics. Curves, an exercise chain aimed at middle-aged women, places paper bags in local businesses such as ice-cream shops, pizza parlors, and other places where guilt can strike. In 2004, Baskin-Robbins dropped all TV advertising for its ice-cream specialty stores for the first time in 17 years to focus on "three-mile marketing" with more emphasis on local events and promotions, remodelled stores with vibrant new colours, and improved customer service achieved through greater employee training.

Local marketing reflects a growing trend called *grassroots marketing*. Marketing activities concentrate on getting as close and personally relevant to individual customers as possible. Much of Nike's initial success has been attributed to its ability to engage target consumers through grassroots marketing such as sponsorship of local school teams, expert-conducted clinics, and provision of shoes, clothing, and equipment. "Breakthrough Marketing: HSBC" (at the end of this chapter) profiles another success story.

Those who favour localized marketing see national advertising as wasteful because it is too "arm's length" and fails to address local needs. Those against local

The advent of online commerce, made possible by technology and epitomized by Amazon.ca, iTunes, and Netflix, has led to a shift in consumer buying patterns, according to Chris Anderson, editor-in-chief of *Wired* magazine and author of *The Long Tail.*

In most markets, the distribution of product sales conforms to a curve weighted heavily to one side—the "head"—where the bulk of sales are generated by a few products. The curve falls rapidly toward zero and hovers just above it far along the x-axis—the "long tail"—where the vast majority of products generate very little sales. The mass market traditionally focused on generating "hit" products that occupy the head, disdaining the low-revenue market niches comprising the tail.

Anderson asserts that as a result of consumers' embrace of the Internet as a shopping medium, the long tail harbours significantly more value than before. In fact, Anderson argues, the Internet has directly contributed to the shifting of demand "down the tail, from hits to niches" in a number of product categories, including music, books, clothing, and movies.

New consumer buying patterns, including Internet use, are highlighting the revenue potential of "the long tail" of the market where many seemingly-niche products can find broader success. My Chemical Romance is an example of a hit band that emerged from this "long tail."

On his blog, Anderson boils down his argument as follows: "The Long Tail equation is simple: (1) The lower the cost of distribution, the more you can economically offer without having to predict demand. (2) The more you can offer, the greater the chance that you will be able to tap latent demand for minority tastes that was unreachable through traditional retail. (3) Aggregate enough minority taste and you'll often find a big new market."

Anderson identifies two aspects of Internet shopping that contribute to this shift. First, greater choice is permitted by increased inventory and variety. Given a choice among ten hit products, consumers are forced to select one of the ten. If, however, the choice set is expanded to 1000, then the top ten hits will be chosen less frequently. Second, the "search costs" of finding relevant new products are lowered due to the wealth of information-sources available online, the filtering of product recommendations based on user preferences that vendors can provide, and the word-of-mouth network of Internet users.

Anderson sees the long-tail effect as particularly pronounced in media, a category that's historically hit-driven but that benefits enormously from these two aspects of online shopping. He points to the success of niche media properties such as the book *Touching the Void*, the band My Chemical Romance, and the documentary film *Capturing the Friedmans*, which all benefited from the choice and information-organization aspects of Internet shopping to achieve greater success than was expected.

The long-tail thesis was also supported by researchers Erik Brynjolfsson and Yu "Jeffrey" Hu at MIT and Michael D. Smith at Carnegie Mellon, who conducted two studies to measure the tail in online and offline book-selling and clothing retail. The book-selling study concluded that the increased product variety offered by online bookstores increased consumer welfare by US$731 million to US$1.03 billion in 2000. In the case of online clothing retail, the study found that consumers who used both online and catalogue channels of a midsized retailer purchased a more even distribution of products than those who purchased through the catalogue alone.

The same companies that compete in the business of creating hits are beginning to develop ways to evolve niche successes in the long tail. For example, in 2006 the Universal Music Group released 3000 out-of-print European recordings in download-only digital format on the Internet. The release generated 250 000 individual downloads of the songs, and after this encouraging start Universal planned to eventually release more than 100 000 out-of-print recordings. In a press release, Universal stated that "Overall, these results lend weight to author Chris Anderson's The Long Tail theory."

Yet companies like Universal may soon face additional competition from unconventional sources. Anderson predicts that as a result of the proliferation of free user-generated content, the variety popularized by YouTube, the end of the long tail where this content resides will be a "nonmonetary economy."

Others have countered that, especially in entertainment, the "head" where the hits are concentrated is valuable to consumers and not only to the content creators. An article in *The Economist* argued that "most hits are popular because they are of high quality," and a critique in the *New Yorker* notes that the majority of products and services making up the long tail originate from a small concentration of "long-tail aggregators": sites such as Amazon.ca, eBay, iTunes, and Netflix. This observation challenges the premise that old business paradigms have changed as much as Anderson suggests.

Sources: Chris Anderson, *The Long Tail* (New York: Hyperion, 2006); "Reading the Tail," interview with Chris Anderson, *Wired*, July 8, 2006, p. 30; "Wag the Dog: What the Long Tail Will Do," *The Economist*, July 8, 2006, p. 77; Erik Brynjolfsson, Yu "Jeffrey" Hu, and Michael D. Smith, "From Niches to Riches: Anatomy of a Long Tail," *MIT Sloan Management Review* (Summer 2006): 67; John Cassidy, "Going Long," *New Yorker*, July 10, 2006; www.longtail.com.

marketing argue that it drives up manufacturing and marketing costs by reducing economies of scale. Logistical problems are magnified. A brand's overall image might be diluted if the product and message are different in different localities.

Individual Marketing

The ultimate level of segmentation leads to "segments of one," "customized marketing," or "one-to-one marketing."[8] Today, customers are taking more individual initiative in determining what and how to buy. They log onto the Internet; look up information and evaluations of product and service offers; dialogue with suppliers, users, and product critics; and in many cases, design the product they want.

Wind and Rangaswamy see a movement toward "customerizing" the firm.[9] **Customerization** combines operationally-driven mass customization with customized marketing in a way that empowers consumers to design the product and service offering of their choice. The firm no longer requires prior information about the customer, nor does the firm need to own manufacturing. The firm provides a platform and tools and "rents" out to customers the means to design their own products. A company is customerized when it is able to respond to individual customers by customizing its goods, services, and messages on a one-to-one basis.[10]

Customization is certainly not for every company.[11] It may be very difficult to implement for complex products such as automobiles. Customization can raise the cost of goods by more than the customer is willing to pay. Some customers do not know what they want until they see actual products. Customers cannot cancel the order after the company has started to work on the product. The product may be hard to repair and have little resale value. In spite of this, customization has worked well for some products, such as those sold by Cervélo Cycles and Guru Bicycles.

Cervélo Cycles Inc., Guru Bicycles

"Custom bikes are on the rise, and we're nowhere near the saturation point," said Megan Tompkins, editor of *Bicycle Retailer and Industry News*. As if to prove her point, two Canadian manufacturers have made their mark in two very different market segments. The first is Cervélo Cycles Inc., a company committed to performance through design. Its target customer is the professional cyclist or hard-core amateur who is willing to pay between $2000 and $11 000 for a bike. Cervélo gained international recognition when its cycles were purchased by teams and individual riders competing in the Tour de France. Gerard Vroomen, founder of the Toronto-based company, noted that it was the firm's ability to be a specialized manufacturer that insulated the firm from offshore competition: "Manufacturing in Canada will always be more expensive than manufacturing in China," especially when it comes to something as basic as an ordinary bicycle. "So you have to figure out the best way to compete. In our case, it's pushing the envelope [of] bicycle design," said Vroomen.

The other market for custom-made bikes is made up of wealthy, aging baby boomers with worn-out knees who have embraced cycling as a low-impact, aerobic alternative to basketball, tennis, or running. When they come to these tiny shops seeking custom-made bikes, they face a detailed interview process similar to an adoption proceeding. They may buy a $9000 brushed-silver titanium custom bike made by Guru Bicycles, headquartered near Montreal, whose bikes are known throughout North America for their high performance, ultralight strength, and lifetime durability.[12]

BASES FOR SEGMENTING CONSUMER MARKETS

Two broad groups of variables are used to segment consumer markets. Some researchers try to form segments by looking at descriptive characteristics: geographic, demographic, and psychographic. Then they examine whether these customer segments exhibit different needs or product responses. For example, they might examine the differing attitudes of "professionals," "blue collars," and other groups towards, say, "safety" as a car benefit.

Other researchers try to form segments by looking at "behavioural" considerations, such as consumer responses to benefits, use occasions, or brands. Once the segments are formed, the researcher sees whether different characteristics are associated with each consumer-response segment. For example, the researcher might examine whether people who want "quality" rather than "low price" when buying an automobile differ in their geographic, demographic, and psychographic makeup.

Regardless of which type of segmentation scheme is employed, the key is that the marketing program can be profitably adjusted to recognize customer differences. The major segmentation variables—geographic, demographic, psychographic, and behavioural segmentation—are summarized in Table 8.1.

To learn how BMW studies changing consumer lifestyles to match product development to segmentation, visit www.pearsoned.co.uk/ marketingmanagementeurope.

Geographic Segmentation

Geographic segmentation calls for dividing the market into different geographical units such as nations, provinces, regions, counties, cities, and neighbourhoods. The company can operate in one or a few areas, or operate in all but pay attention to local variations. For example, Coast Hotels and Resorts offers full-service hotels with locations in Alberta, British Columbia, and the Northwest Territories. Major retailers such as The Bay, Zellers, Shoppers Drug Mart, and Bed Bath & Beyond allow managers to stock products that suit the local community.

Bed Bath & Beyond

Home-furnishing retailer Bed Bath & Beyond's ability to cater to local tastes has fuelled its phenomenal growth. The firm's managers pick 70 percent of their own merchandise, and this fierce local focus has helped the chain evolve from bed linens to the "beyond" part: products from picture frames and pot holders to imported olive oil and designer door mats. In some downtown stores, for instance, managers are beginning to stock wall paint. You won't find paint in suburban stores, where customers can go to Home Depot. One manager says that several customers have been surprised to find out the store is part of a national chain and not a mom-and-pop operation. That's the ultimate compliment.[13]

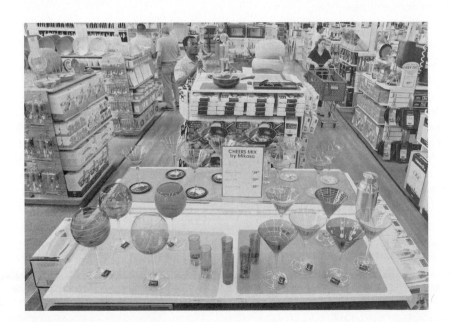

Local Bed Bath & Beyond managers choose most of their own merchandise, allowing stores separated by only a few kilometres to address the different taste preferences of city and suburbia with unique product mixes for each.

TABLE 8.1	MAJOR SEGMENTATION VARIABLES FOR CONSUMER MARKETS
Geographic	
Region	Atlantic Provinces, Quebec, Central Provinces, Western Provinces, Northern Territories
City or metro size	Under 5000; 5001–20 000; 20 001–50 000; 50 001–100 000; 100 001–250 000; 250 001–500 000; 500 001–1 000 000; 1 000 001–4 000 000; 4 000 001 or over
Density	Urban, suburban, rural
Climate	Far north, near north, mountain, maritime, prairie, Great Lakes
Demographic	
Age	Under 6, 6–11, 12–19, 20–34, 35–49, 50–64, 65+
Family size	1–2, 3–4, 5+
Family life cycle	Young, single; young, married, no children; young, married, youngest child under 6; young, married, youngest child 6 or over; older, married, with children; older, married, no children under 18; older, single; other
Gender	Male, female
Income	Under $10 000; $10 001–$15 000; $15 001–$20 000; $20 001–$30 000; $30 001–$50 000; $50 001–$100 000; $100 001 and over
Occupation	Professional and technical; managers, officials, and proprietors; clerical; sales; craftspeople; supervisors; operatives; farmers; retired; students; homemakers; unemployed
Education	Grade school or less, some high school, high-school graduate, some community college, community-college graduate, some university, university graduate, graduate degree
Religion	Catholic, Protestant, Jewish, Muslim, Hindu, other
Race	White, Black, Asian, Native Canadian
Generation	Baby boomers, Gen-Xers
Nationality	English, French, German, Italian, Japanese, Middle Eastern
Social class	Lower lowers, upper lowers, working class, middle class, upper middles, lower uppers, upper uppers
Psychographic	
Lifestyle	Culture-oriented, sports-oriented, outdoor-oriented
Personality	Compulsive, gregarious, authoritarian, ambitious
Behavioural	
Occasions	Regular occasion, special occasion
Benefits	Quality, service, economy, speed
User status	Nonuser, ex-user, potential user, first-time user, regular user
Usage rate	Light user, medium user, heavy user
Loyalty status	None, medium, strong, absolute
Readiness stage	Unaware, aware, informed, interested, desirous, intending to buy
Attitude toward product	Enthusiastic, positive, indifferent, negative, hostile

More and more, regional marketing means marketing right down to a specific neighbourhood. Many companies use mapping software to show the geographic locations of their customers. The software may show a retailer that most of his customers are within only a 10-kilometre radius of his store, and further concentrated within a certain area. By mapping the densest areas, the retailer can resort to *customer cloning*, assuming that the best prospects live where most of his customers come from.

Some approaches combine geographic data with demographic data to yield even richer descriptions of consumers, as was discovered by the publishers of *Unlimited*.

Unlimited

Unlimited is a new magazine being launched by Venture Publishing Inc., publisher of the business magazine *Alberta Venture*. Combining geographic and demographic segmentation variables, it has been designed to target young, technology-savvy people in business

aged 20 to 35. In contrast to the buttoned-down approach of conventional business magazines, *Unlimited* reflects how young people view work in the context of their lives. As Joyce Byrne, associate publisher at *Alberta Venture*, notes, "*Alberta Venture* really holds down the niche for business leaders and owners, but we saw a gap for the younger demographic. Work is changing so radically, and this demographic is really shaping that. They think about work in different ways, so we wanted to create something that reflects those attitudes."[14]

Environics recently launched PRIZM$_{CE}$, a new consumer segmentation system that classifies all 55 000 Canadian neighbourhoods into one of 66 lifestyle types, with names like Cosmopolitan Elite, Electric Avenues, Les Chics, and Lunch at Tim's. The inhabitants in a cluster tend to lead similar lives, drive similar cars, have similar jobs, and read similar magazines. These categories are based on the most important drivers of consumer behaviour: demographics, lifestyles, and values. The groupings also take into consideration 39 factors in five broad categories: (1) education and affluence, (2) family life cycle, (3) urbanization, (4) race and ethnicity, and (5) mobility. Using a cluster analysis of 2001 Census demographics combined with geodemographics, psychographics, and social-values data from Environics Research, the system can be used to understand product preferences and explain consumer behaviour. With PRIZM$_{CE}$'s ability to link every neighbourhood and postal code to one of 66 segments, the system offers new possibilities with regard to customer profiling and acquisition, cross-selling, site selection, strategic planning, and media buying, and can be used by Canadian marketers from a wide range of industries including financial services, packaged goods, retail, telecommunications, government agencies, and automotive.[15]

Here are several examples of PRIZM$_{CE}$ clusters:[16]

Young Digerati: These young, well-off urban trendsetters are made up of couples or single-headed households living in fashionable in-town neighbourhoods which are typified by high-rise apartments and expensive condos, home offices, casual restaurants, and fitness clubs and which are located in a handful of big cities like Vancouver and Toronto. Affluent, highly educated, and tech-savvy, this group tends to be ethnically mixed. They have deep pockets and like to shop for the latest styles; however, many are also socially conscious consumers who support many causes including environmental groups.

Mini Van & Vin Rouge: These young Quebec families live in comfort in exurban areas beyond the boundaries of Quebec's big cities. Well-educated white-collar professionals with young children, they engage in kid-centred lifestyles like ice skating and boating. They make a point of sitting down to a family dinner every night. When picking media, they favour comedy shows like "Les Simpson" and current-affairs programs.

Lunch at Tim's: These are old and young working-class people living in industrial towns and cities located across southern Ontario. These communities are closely knit and residents like to socialize at local eateries from doughnut shops to pizza parlours to Chinese restaurants. They relax by watching TV, playing video games, or occasionally visiting a casino. They may also be big snowboarding enthusiasts.

Marketing to micro-segments has become accessible even to small organizations as database costs decline, PCs proliferate, software becomes easier to use, data integration increases, and the Internet grows.[17]

Demographic Segmentation

In demographic segmentation, the market is divided into groups on the basis of variables such as age, family size, family life cycle, gender, income, occupation, education, religion, race, generation, nationality, and social class. One reason demographic variables are so popular with marketers is that they're often associated with consumer needs, wants, usage rates, and product and brand preferences. Another is that demographic variables are easier to measure. Even when the target market is described in non-demographic terms (say, a personality type), the link back to demographic characteristics is needed in order to estimate the size of the market and the media that should be used to reach it efficiently.

Here is how certain demographic variables have been used to segment markets:

AGE AND LIFE-CYCLE STAGE Consumer wants and abilities change with age. Toothpaste brands such as Crest and Colgate offer three main lines of products to target kids, adults, and older consumers. Age segmentation can be even more refined. Pampers divides its market into prenatal, newborn (0–1 month), infant (2–5 months), cruiser (6–12 months), toddler (13–18 months), explorer (19–23 months), and preschooler (24 months+).

Nevertheless, age and life cycle can be tricky variables.[18] In some cases, the target market for products may be the psychologically young. For example, Honda tried to target 21-year-olds with its boxy Element, which company officials described as a "dorm room on wheels." So many baby boomers were attracted to the car's ads depicting sexy college kids partying near the car at a beach,

To market the new Fit model, Honda used what it had learned from the launch of the Element: that baby boomers hanging on to their youthful image were just as interested in the stylish new cars as the original target audience, 21-year-old drivers.

however, that the average age of buyers turned out to be 42! With baby boomers seeking to stay young, Honda decided that the lines between age groups were getting blurred. When it was ready to launch a new subcompact called the Fit, Honda deliberately targeted Gen Y buyers as well as their empty-nest parents.[19]

LIFE STAGE   Persons in the same part of the life cycle may differ in their life stage. **Life stage** defines a person's major concern, such as going through a divorce, going into a second marriage, taking care of an older parent, deciding to cohabit with another person, deciding to buy a new home, and so on. These life stages present opportunities for marketers who can help people cope with their major concerns. Just take the expenses associated with a Canadian wedding and you will see how powerful life-stage marketing can be.

The Wedding Industry

Each year, 150 000 brides will walk down the aisle in Canada, and they happily spend an average of $25 883 on their weddings. The price of the gown alone ranges from $1000 to $9000 and up, cakes can cost anywhere from $900 to $12 000, and the reception will set the happy couple back at least $50 per person. All this expense for the "perfect day" translates into a $3.8-billion market. It's not surprising that there are huge trade shows like Canada's Bridal Show and the Total Wedding Show catering to brides and wedding planners. It is estimated that couples spend 250 hours planning their wedding, thus wedding planners have become a big service industry.[20] But marketing opportunities don't end when couples say "I do."

GENDER   As Canadian academics Robert Fisher and Laurette Dube noted, men and women tend to have different attitudinal and behavioural orientations, based partly on genetic makeup and partly on socialization.For example, women tend to be more communal-minded and men tend to be more self-expressive and goal-directed; women tend to take in more of the data in their immediate environment; men tend to focus on the part of the environment that helps them achieve a goal. A research study examining how men and women shop found that men often need to be invited to touch a product, while women are likely to pick it up without prompting. Men often like to read product information; women may relate to a product on a more personal level.[21]

Some studies suggest that women control or influence over 80 percent of consumer goods and services, make 75 percent of the decisions about buying new homes, and purchase 60 percent of new cars outright. Gender differentiation has long been applied in clothing, hairstyling, cosmetics, and magazines. Some products have been positioned as more masculine or feminine. Gillette's Venus is the most successful female shaving line ever, with over 50 percent of the market, and has product design, packaging, and advertising cues appropriate to reinforcement of a female image.[22]

But it's not enough to tout a product as masculine or feminine. Hypersegmentation is now occurring within both male and female personal-care segments. To expand beyond the metrosexual market, Unilever's Axe brand includes "Snake Eel Shower Scrub with Desert Minerals + Cactus Oil," the ingredients of which sound more rugged than "exfoliating liquid soap with plant oils."[23] And Unilever earned kudos by targeting women who don't look like (or aspire to look like) fashion models with its award-winning "Dove Campaign for Real Beauty," led largely by its Canadian operation.

Dove

Dove's Campaign for Real Beauty featured women of all shapes, sizes, and colours posing proudly in their underwear. The company claims that the ad series, developed by Ogilvy & Mather, was not just a vehicle to sell more soap but "aim[ed] to change the status quo and offer in its place a broader, healthier, more democratic view of beauty." The springboard was a global study sponsored by Dove that researched women's attitudes toward themselves and beauty. Only 2 percent of women in the study considered themselves beautiful, so not only women, but everyone, took notice when the pictures of beaming full-figured and average-looking women began appearing in Dove's ads. Even the National Organization for Women (NOW), not known for approving of depictions of women in advertising, called the campaign "a step forward for the advertising industry."[24]

Media have emerged to make gender targeting easier. Marketers can reach women more easily on Bravo, the Food Network, and HGTV television channels and through scores of women's magazines. To respond to differences in online behaviour, Yahoo! Canada launched a new lifestyle website aimed at women aged 24 to 54. Full of Canadian content, the site is organized into five categories that appeal to many women: Home and Garden, Fashion and Beauty, Health and Fitness, Family and Relationships, and Food and Entertaining. Men are more likely to be reached via Rogers Sportsnet, The Score, and Spike TV channels, and through magazines such as *Maxim* and *Men's Health*.[25]

Some traditionally more male-oriented markets, such as the automobile industry, are beginning to recognize gender segmentation and are changing the way they design and sell cars.[26] Women shop differently for cars than do men; they are more interested in environmental impact, care more about interior than exterior styling, and view safety in terms of features that help survive an accident rather than handling to avoid an accident.[27]

Armed with research suggesting that 80 percent of home-improvement projects are now initiated by women, Lowe's designed its stores with wider aisles—to make it easier for shopping carts to get around—and to include more big-ticket appliances and high-margin home furnishings. Half its clientele is now female, forcing its more traditional competitor, Home Depot, to introduce "Ladies' Night at the Depot" to appeal to women.[28] Another hot retail trend is athletic stores and boutiques that target women, such as Lucy, Paiva, and NikeWomen.

INCOME Income segmentation is a long-standing practice in such product and service categories as automobiles, clothing, cosmetics, travel, and financial services.[29] See how BMO InvestorLine uses this tactic.

BMO InvestorLine

To attract wealthy executives aged 40 to 55 and encourage them to buy investment products during a recent RRSP season, BMO scored with its online Ultimate Golf Getaway contest. Contestants had to play a virtual round of golf to qualify for the chance to win golf vacations. The goal of the innovative campaign was to increase market share by retaining existing clients and acquiring new ones. BMO shunned traditional methods in striving towards this goal. With its agency, Tribal, it developed a Flash-based golf game that challenged players to sink a putt or drive down the fairway while learning about InvestorLine products. The campaign was a huge success. Participation in the promotion increased 165 percent over what was achieved in previous years, and 15 percent of the people who took part in the promotion opened up new accounts with InvestorLine.[30]

However, income does not always predict the best customers for a given product. Blue-collar workers were among the first purchasers of colour-television sets; it was cheaper for them to buy these sets than to go to movies and restaurants.

Many marketers are deliberately going after lower-income groups, in some cases discovering fewer competitive pressures or greater consumer loyalty.[31] Casual Male created a big-and-tall brand aimed at the lower-income market. Procter & Gamble launched two discount-priced brand extensions: Bounty Basic and Charmin Basic. Prepaid debit cards and wireless-service accounts are the fastest-growing sub-segments in the low-income segment.

Yet, at the same time, other marketers are finding success with premium-priced products. When Whirlpool launched the pricey Duet washer line, sales doubled forecasts in a weak economy, due primarily to middle-class shoppers who traded up.

Increasingly, companies are finding that their markets are "hourglass-shaped" as middle-market consumers migrate toward more premium products.[32] If companies miss out on this new market, they risk being "trapped in the middle" and seeing their market share steadily decline. General Motors was caught in the middle, between highly engineered German imports in the luxury market and high-value Japanese and Korean models in the economy class, and has seen its market share continually slide.[33] "Marketing Insight: Trading Up (and Down): The New Consumer" describes the factors contributing to this trend and what it means to marketers.

GENERATION Each generation is profoundly influenced by the times in which it grows up—by the music, movies, politics, and defining events of its period. Demographers call these groups *cohorts*. Members of a cohort share the same major cultural, political, and economic experiences. They have

| MARKETING INSIGHT | TRADING UP (AND DOWN): THE NEW CONSUMER |

A new pattern in consumer behaviour has emerged in recent years, according to Michael Silverstein and Neil Fiske, the authors of *Trading Up*. In unprecedented numbers, middle-market consumers are periodically trading up to what Silverstein and Fiske call "New Luxury" products and services "that possess higher levels of quality, taste, and aspiration than other goods in the category but are not so expensive as to be out of reach." For example, these consumers might trade up to an imported French wine, use a premium skin cream, or stay in a luxury hotel for a few nights on vacation, depending on the emotional benefits gained in the trade. In 2003, 96 percent of consumers said they were willing to pay a premium for at least one type of product.

The authors identify a number of broad demographic and cultural explanations for the trend. In general, people have more money to spend than in years past. Average household income has risen in the past 30 years, with growth highest for the top 20 percent of households. In Canada, median family income exceeds $50 000 in all cities across the country and may reach as high as $70 000 in some cities. Individuals earning an annual income of $89 000 qualify for membership in the exclusive club that includes the top 5 percent of Canada's top earners. Furthermore, more women are entering the workforce and commanding higher salaries than before. They feel entitled to spend the money they earn: women account for about 75 percent of discretionary spending. And, since baby boomers are now finding themselves with empty nests and adults continue to marry later and divorce more often, the typical consumer has fewer mouths to feed. Finally, consumers today are better educated and more comfortable analyzing and satisfying their emotional needs, which New Luxury goods often target. As a result, the authors assert, the typical consumer has been transformed into "a sophisticated and discerning consumer with high aspirations and substantial buying power and clout."

Thanks to the trading-up trend, New Luxury goods sell at higher volumes than traditional luxury goods, although they are priced higher than conventional mid-market items. The authors identify three main types of New Luxury products:

- *Accessible superpremium products*, such as Victoria's Secret underwear and Kettle gourmet potato chips, carry a significant premium over middle-market brands, yet consumers can readily trade up to them because they are relatively low-ticket items in affordable categories.

- *Old Luxury brand extensions* extend historically high-priced brands down-market while retaining their cachet, such as the Mercedes-Benz C-class and the American Express Blue card.

- *Masstige goods*, such as Kiehl's skin care and Kendall-Jackson wines, are priced between average middle-market brands and superpremium Old Luxury brands. They are "always based on emotions, and consumers have a much stronger emotional engagement with them than with other goods."

The authors note that in order to trade up to the brands that offered these emotional benefits, consumers often "trade down" by shopping at discounters such as Wal-Mart and Costco for staple items or goods that confer no emotional benefit but still deliver quality and functionality. In a subsequent book entitled *Treasure Hunt*, Michael Silverstein notes that 82 percent of consumers trade down in five or more categories (what he calls "treasure hunting"), whereas 62 percent focus on trading up in the two categories that provide the most emotional benefits. This makes the new consumer "part martyr and part hedonist," willingly sacrificing on a number of purchases in order to experience enhanced benefits from a handful of others.

Silverstein reasons that with the trading-up segment of the market expected to rise from US$605 billion in 2005 to US$1 trillion in 2010, and the trading-down segment predicted to grow from US$1.1 trillion to US$1.5 trillion in the same period, the firms that succeed will offer one of two kinds of value: New Luxury or Treasure Hunting. The remaining firms, which occupy the middle market, will continue to see their market share shrink as they get "trapped in the middle." Traditional grocers and department stores are already suffering, having experienced market share declines of 30 percent and 50 percent, respectively. Silverstein argues that most middle-market companies do not offer the economic, functional, and emotional value that modern consumers are searching for. Brands that offer opportunities to trade up, such as Coach, Holt Renfrew, Boss, Victoria's Secret, and Bath & Body Works, or to trade down, such as Best Value Inn, Great Canadian Dollar Store, and IKEA, are optimally positioned to deliver the value that modern consumers seek.

Sources: Michael J. Silverstein, *Treasure Hunt: Inside the Mind of the New Consumer* (New York: Portfolio, 2006); Jeff Cioletti, "Movin' on Up," *BeverageWorld* (June 2006): p. 20; Michael J. Silverstein and Neil Fiske, *Trading Up: The New American Luxury* (New York: Portfolio, 2003); News Staff, "Canada's top earners make $89K or More: StatsCan," *CTV.ca*, September 24, 2007, www.ctv.ca/servlet/ArticleNews/story/CTVNews/20070924/statscan_earners_070924?s_name=&no_ads= (viewed March 2008); Statistics Canada, "Median Family Income Highest in Ottawa-Hull, Oshawa," undated, www12.statcan.ca/english/census01/products/analytic/companion/inc/subprovs.cfm (viewed March 2008).

So-called New Luxury products and services, including premium hotels, personal-care products, and Kendall-Jackson wines, are riding a number of demographic and cultural trends that allow consumers to "trade up" their purchase decisions.

Jess Jackson, Upper Hawkeye Mountain Estate, Alexander Valley

Terroir can be defined as that mystical melding of light, water, soil, air and human touch. It is a definition I often use. The simple fact is, you must have a world-class grape in order to make a world-class wine. And when it comes to grapes, their source, the land is what matters.

Precious few places exist on this Earth that will produce grapes of this caliber. We have been fortunate to find several of those places in California's cool coastal mountains, hillsides, ridges and benchlands. It is some of the best land in California. And why you will see the Jackson Estates Grown designation proudly displayed on our labels.

My family and I have made it our life's work to seek out these special places, have the knowledge and respect to work in concert with Mother Nature, then commit to the hard work, expense and patience to steward the wine into the bottle. It is a commitment many in our industry are either unwilling or unable to make. But we are convinced you can and will taste the difference because, ultimately, the wine's distinct personality will reflect its source, the special terroir.

I understand that many of you enjoy the taste of our wines but you aren't sure why. My goal is to help with **A Taste of the Truth.**

kj.com/truth
©2007 Kendall-Jackson Wine Estates

similar outlooks and values. Marketers often advertise to a cohort by using the icons and images prominent in their experiences. "Marketing Insight: A Guide to Generation Y" provides insight into one key age cohort and "Marketing Memo: Cheat Sheet for 20-Somethings" looks at a key segment of Gen Y.

Yet, while distinctions can be made among different cohorts, generational cohorts also influence each other. For instance, because so many members of Generation Y—"Echo Boomers"—are living with their boomer parents, the parents are being influenced and are exhibiting what demographers are calling a "boom-boom effect." The same products that appeal to 21-year-olds are appealing to youth-obsessed baby boomers. Boomer parents watched MTV's *The Osbournes*, the reality show based on heavy-metal rocker Ozzy Osbourne and his family, right alongside their children. This is what writer and corporate consultant Christopher Noxon has called the "rejuvenile" mindset. Here are two examples of the rejuvenilization phenomenon:

- Adult gadgets, such as cell phones, automobiles, and even housewares have been transformed from purely utilitarian to toy-like. Vacuums come in candy-apple red and baby blue, and Target sells a Michael Graves version of a toaster shaped like a fluffy cartoon cloud. Cars such as lemon-yellow Mini Coopers look like they're designed for the toddler set.

- Half the adults who visit Disney World every day do so without kids, and Noxon found that Disney enthusiasts return to the Magic Kingdom to recapture the safety and serenity of childhood.[34]

SOCIAL CLASS Social class has a strong influence on preference in cars, clothing, home furnishings, leisure activities, reading habits, and retailers. Many companies design products and services for specific social classes. The tastes of social classes change with the years. The 1990s were about greed and ostentation for the upper classes. Affluent tastes now run more to the conservative, although luxury goods makers such as Coach, Tiffany, Burberry, TAG Heuer, and Louis Vuitton still successfully sell to those seeking the good life.[35]

MARKETING INSIGHT | A GUIDE TO GENERATION Y

They're dubbed "Echo Boomers" or "Generation Y." David Foot, a Toronto-based demographer and author of the *Boom, Bust & Echo* series of books, says members of the echo generation—those born between 1980 and 1995—are a generation marked by racial diversity, and they may be the first truly "colour-blind" generation. They have the ability to "jump around tasks" at breakneck speed. They've been "wired" almost from birth—playing computer games, navigating the web, downloading music, and connecting with friends via instant messaging, mobile phones, and the BlackBerry. These tools enhance their productivity and efficiency. But David Foot notes that while the group's greater ability to multitask can be an advantage, it has a downside too: an inability to concentrate over long periods of time on a single task.

This is a generation that has grown up amid economic abundance. Douglas Coupland, another Canadian demographer, notes that Gen-Yers were raised in a more nurturing environment that inspired more confidence and hopefulness than found in the generation that preceded them. They want lives that are creative, challenging, and collaborative, and they come to new jobs after post-secondary graduation with a lot of high expectations. They have a sense of entitlement and abundance from growing up during the economic boom and being pampered by their boomer parents. They are selective, confident, and impatient. They want what they want when they want it—and they often get it by using plastic. The average 21-year-old carries almost $3000 in credit-card debt. Generation Y's spending power is growing and if you factor in career growth and household and family formation, and multiply by another 53 years of life expectancy, you're looking at a significant market.

It's not surprising, then, that market researchers and advertisers are racing to get a bead on Gen Y's buying behaviour. Because its members are often turned off by overt branding practices and a "hard sell," marketers have tried many different approaches to reach and persuade them.

1. *Online buzz:* Rock band Foo Fighters created a digital street team that sends targeted e-mail blasts to members who "get the latest news, exclusive audio/video sneak previews, tons of chances to win great Foo Fighters prizes, and become part of the Foo Fighters Family."

2. *Student ambassadors:* Red Bull enlists college students as Red Bull Student Brand Managers to distribute samples, research drinking trends, design on-campus marketing initiatives, and write stories for student newspapers.

3. *Unconventional sports:* Dodge automobiles sponsors the World Dodgeball Association, which is taking the sport "to a new level by emphasizing teamwork, strategy, and skill."

4. *Cool events:* Molson Canadian sponsors concerts and tours by various groups under its Molson Rocks banner. In 2008, Capital One Canada built awareness of its services among anglers when it sponsored the first annual Canadian Open of Fishing. Pam Girardo, director of communications for Capital One Canada, exclaimed "We know Canadians are passionate about the great outdoors, and they're passionate about sports. And a great combination of the two is sport fishing."

5. *Computer games:* Product placement is not restricted to movies or TV. Mountain Dew, Oakley, and Harley-Davidson all made deals to put logos on Tony Hawk's Pro Skater 3 video game from Activision.

6. *Videos:* Burton Snowboards ensures that its boards and riders are clearly visible in any videos that are shot.

7. *Street teams:* As part of its 2008 "Full of Potential" campaign for the launch of its redesigned Matrix, Toyota Canada used street teams with video cameras strapped to their backs to entice a young, hip demographic to test drive the vehicle.

Sources: "Gen Y and the Future of Mall Retailing," *American Demographics* (December 2002–January 2003): J1–J4; Michael J. Weiss, "To Be about to Be," *American Demographics* (September 2003): 28–36; John Leo, "The Good-News Generation," *U.S. News & World Report*, November 3, 2003, p. 60; Kelly Pate, "Not 'X,' but 'Y' Marks the Spot: Young Generation a Marketing Target," *Denver Post*, August 17, 2003; Bruce Horovitz, "Gen Y: A Tough Crowd to Sell," *USA Today*, April 22, 2002; Bruce Horovitz, "Marketers Revel with Spring Breakers," *USA Today*, March 12, 2002; Martha Irvine, "Labels Don't Fit Us, Gen Y Insists," *Denver Post*, April 19, 2001; J. M. Lawrence, "Trends: X-ed Out: Gen Y Takes Over," *Boston Herald*, February 2, 1999; Erin Pooley, Generation Y: How Twentysometings are Changing the Workplace," *Canadian Business*, June 2005; Matt Semansky, "Capital One and Shimano Lure Fishing Event Sponsorship," *Marketing* June 25, 2008; Russ Martin, "Ridonculous' Matrix Campaign Targets Youth," *Marketing*, June 5, 2008.

Psychographic Segmentation

Psychographics is the science of using psychology and demographics to better understand consumers. In *psychographic segmentation*, buyers are divided into different groups on the basis of lifestyle or personality or values. People within the same demographic group can exhibit very different psychographic profiles.

MARKETING **MEMO** | CHEAT SHEET FOR 20-SOMETHINGS

There are approximately five million North Americans who are 21 years of age. Here are some facts you need to know about them:

- 41 percent currently live with mom and/or dad
- 60 percent of college students plan to move back home after graduation
- 1 in 5 was raised by a single parent
- 78 percent are concerned with national and international issues
- 4 out of 5 supported a charitable cause in 2006
- most are employed in either a full- or part-time job—they are experiencing the highest employment rates of their age group to date; it's forecast that by 2015, there won't be enough qualified Canadians to fill available jobs
- they plan to stay in their jobs only for three to five years and then they will move on
- 70 percent have begun a savings plan
- they have received about 23 million ad impressions to date
- the average 21-year-old will spend $2 241 141 before the end of his or her life
- the average 21-year-old man will marry for the first time in 5.8 years
- the average 21-year-old will buy his or her first vacation home in 10 years
- 43 percent of 21-year-olds have a tattoo or a body piercing

Sources: "Population by Sex and Age Group," Statistics Canada, CANSIM Table 051-0001; CNW Group, "Myspace/Youthography Survey Reveals Gen-Y'ers are Committed to Social Causes—If Only Someone Would Notice," *CNW Group*, December 4, 2007, www.newswire.ca/en/releases/archive/December2007/04/c7190.html (viewed March 2008); John Fetto, "Cheat Sheet for 21 Year-olds" in "Twenty-One, and Counting...," *American Demographics*, September 2003, p. 48. Reprinted with permission of Primedia BMMG. Copyright © 2003. All rights reserved.

One of the most popular commercially available classification systems based on psychographic measurements is SRI Consulting Business Intelligence's (SRIC-BI) VALS™ framework. VALS classifies all adults into eight primary groups based on personality traits and key demographics. The segmentation system is based on responses to a questionnaire featuring four demographic and 35 attitudinal questions. The VALS system is continually updated with new data from more than 80 000 surveys per year (see Figure 8.1).[36] You can find out which VALS type you are by going to SRIC-BI's website (www.sric-bi.com).

The main dimensions of the VALS segmentation framework are consumer motivation (the horizontal dimension) and consumer resources (the vertical dimension). Consumers are inspired by one of three primary motivations: ideals, achievement, or self-expression. Those primarily motivated by ideals are guided by knowledge and principles. Those motivated by achievement look for products and services that demonstrate success to their peers. Consumers whose motivation is self-expression desire social or physical activity, variety, and risk. Personality traits such as energy, self-confidence, intellectualism, novelty seeking, innovativeness, impulsiveness, leadership, and vanity—in conjunction with key demographics—determine an individual's resources. Different levels of resources enhance or constrain a person's expression of his or her primary motivation.

The major tendencies of the four groups with high resources are:

1. *Innovators.* Successful, sophisticated, active, "take-charge" people with high self-esteem. Purchases often reflect cultivated tastes for relatively upscale, niche-oriented products and services.

2. *Thinkers.* Mature, satisfied, and reflective people who are motivated by ideals and value order, knowledge, and responsibility. In products they favour durability, functionality, and value.

3. *Achievers.* Successful career- and work-oriented people who value consensus and stability, and favour established, prestige products that demonstrate success to their peers.

4. *Experiencers.* Young, enthusiastic, impulsive people who seek variety and excitement, and spend a comparatively high proportion of income on fashion, entertainment, and socializing.

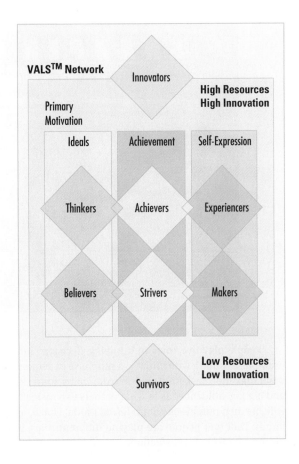

FIGURE 8.1

The VALS Segmentation System: An Eight-Part Typology

Source: VALS™ ©, SRI Consulting Business Intelligence. Used with permission.

The major tendencies of the four groups with low resources are:

1. *Believers.* Conservative, conventional, and traditional people with concrete beliefs. They prefer familiar products and are loyal to established brands.
2. *Strivers.* Trendy and fun-loving people who seek the approval of **others** but are resource-constrained. They favour stylish products that emulate the purchases of those with greater material wealth.
3. *Makers.* Practical, self-sufficient, traditional, and family-oriented people who focus on their work and home context. They favour basic products with a practical or functional purpose.
4. *Survivors.* Elderly, passive people who are concerned about change. They are loyal to their favourite brands.

Marketers can apply their understanding of VALS segments to marketing planning. For example, Transport Canada, the agency that operated major Canadian airports, found that Actualizers, who desire to express independence and taste, made up a disproportionate percentage of air travellers. Given that segment's profile, stores such as Sharper Image and Nature Company were expected to do well in airports.

Psychographic segmentation schemes are often customized by culture. The Japanese version of VALS divides society into ten segments on the basis of two key consumer attributes: life orientation (traditional ways, occupations, innovation, and self-expression) and attitudes to social change (sustaining, pragmatic, adapting, and innovating).

Behavioural Segmentation

In behavioural segmentation, buyers are divided into groups on the basis of their knowledge of, attitude towards, use of, or response to a product.

DECISION ROLES It is easy to identify the buyer for many products. In North America, men normally choose their shaving equipment, and women choose their cosmetics; but even here marketers must be careful in making their targeting decisions because buying roles change. When ICI, the giant British chemical company, discovered that women made 60 percent of the decisions on which brand of household paint to use, it decided to advertise its DuLux brand to women.

People play five roles in a buying decision: *initiator, influencer, decider, buyer,* and *user.* For example, assume a wife initiates a purchase by requesting a new treadmill for her birthday. The husband may then seek information from many sources, including his best friend who has a treadmill and is a key influencer as to what models to consider. After presenting the alternative choices to his wife, he then purchases her preferred model which, as it turns out, ends up being used by the entire family. Different people are playing different roles, but all are crucial in the decision process and ultimate consumer satisfaction.

BEHAVIOURAL VARIABLES Many marketers believe that behavioural variables—occasions, benefits, user status, usage rate, buyer-readiness stage, loyalty status, and attitude—are the best starting points for constructing market segments.

Occasions Occasions can be defined in terms of the time of day, week, month, or year, or in terms of other well-defined temporal aspects of a consumer's life. Buyers can be distinguished according to the occasions when they develop a need, purchase a product, or use a product. For example, Canadian chocolate makers Purdy's and Gagnon know that sales skyrocket on special days like Valentine's Day and birthdays. Air travel is triggered by occasions related to business, vacation, or family. Occasion segmentation can help firms expand product usage. During the 1960s and 1970s, Ocean Spray Cranberries, Inc., a grower cooperative, produced what was essentially a single-purpose, single-usage product: consumption of cranberries was almost entirely confined to the serving of cranberry sauce at Thanksgiving and Christmas holiday dinners. After a pesticide scare one Thanksgiving drastically cut sales and almost put growers out of business, the cooperative embarked on a program to diversify and create a year-round market by producing cranberry-based juice drinks and other products.[37]

Marketers also can try to extend activities associated with certain holidays to other times of the year. For instance, while Christmas, Mother's Day, and Valentine's Day are the three major gift-giving holidays, these and other holidays account for just over half of the gifters' budgets. That leaves the rest available throughout the year for occasion-driven gift-giving: birthdays, weddings, anniversaries, housewarmings, and new babies.[38]

Benefits Buyers can be classified according to the benefits they seek. Not everyone who buys a product wants the same benefits from it. A marketer of wines identified six different benefit segments in the premium wine market.[39]

- *Enthusiast* (12 percent of the market). Skewing female, their average income is about US$76 000 a year. About 3 percent of this segment are "luxury enthusiasts," and men with a higher income make up a larger proportion of this sub-segment.
- *Image Seekers* (20 percent). Predominantly male, this segment has an average age of 35. They use wine basically as a badge to say who they are, and they're willing to pay more to make sure they're getting the right bottle.

- *Savvy Shoppers* (15 percent). They love to shop and believe they don't have to spend a lot to get a good bottle of wine. They are happy to use the bargain bin.

- *Traditionalist* (16 percent). With very traditional values, they like to buy brands they've heard of and from wineries that have been around a long time. Their average age is 50 and 68 percent are female.

- *Satisfied Sippers* (14 percent). Not knowing much about wine, they tend to buy the same brands. About half of what they drink is white zinfandel.

- *Overwhelmed* (23 percent). A potentially attractive target market, they find purchasing wine confusing.

User Status Every product and service has its nonusers, ex-users, potential users, first-time users, and regular users. Blood banks cannot rely only on regular donors to supply blood; they must also recruit new first-time donors and contact ex-donors. Each will require a different marketing strategy. The key to attracting potential users, and possibly even nonusers, is understanding the reasons they are not using. Do they have deeply held attitudes, beliefs, or behaviours, or do they just lack knowledge of the product, brand benefits, and usage?

Included in the potential-user group are consumers who will become users in connection with some life stage or life event. Mothers-to-be are potential users who will turn into heavy users. Producers of infant products and services learn their names and shower them with products and ads to capture a share of their future purchases. Market-share leaders tend to focus on attracting potential users because they have the most to gain. Smaller firms focus on trying to attract current users away from the market leader.

Usage Rate Markets can be segmented into light, medium, and heavy users. Heavy users are often a small percentage of the market but account for a high percentage of total consumption. For example, heavy beer drinkers account for 87 percent of the beer consumed—almost seven times as much as the light beer drinkers. Marketers would rather attract one heavy user than several light users. A potential problem, however, is that heavy users are often either extremely loyal to one brand or never stay loyal to a brand and are always looking for the lowest price.

Buyer-Readiness Stage Some people are unaware of a product, some are aware, some are informed, some are interested, some desire the product, and some intend to buy. To help characterize how many people are at different stages and how well they have converted people from one stage to another, some marketers employ a marketing funnel. Figure 8.2 displays a funnel for two hypothetical brands, A and B. Compared to Brand B, Brand A performs poorly at converting one-time users to more recent users: Brand A converts only 46 percent; Brand B converts 61 percent.

The relative numbers of consumers likely to adopt a product and the most effective media to influence them are key factors in designing the marketing program. For example, in 2007, word-of-mouth communication (sometimes called buzz) edged out television as the most useful medium for introducing new products, according to BrandSpark's survey of 10 000 Canadians. The survey also revealed that four out of five Canadians look at weekly grocery flyers. Such information is very useful

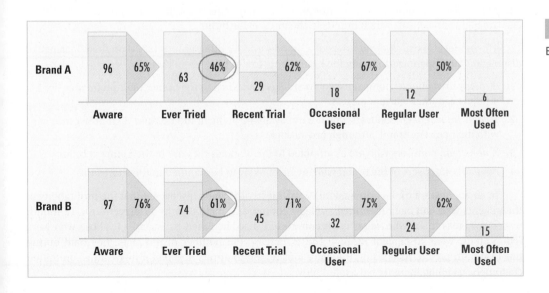

FIGURE 8.2

Brand Funnel

information for companies when they launch new products, like Dempster's award-winning Ancient Grains bread. Dempster's needed to use awareness-building advertising and a simple message. It chose to promote the healthy benefits of the Ancient Grains bread since healthiness is one of the top criteria consumers consider when choosing food products. Consumers don't seek wheat germ, but they do want the perceived health benefit.[40]

Loyalty Status Buyers can be divided into four groups according to brand-loyalty status:

1. *Hard-core loyals:* Consumers who buy only one brand all the time.
2. *Split loyals:* Consumers who are loyal to two or three brands.
3. *Shifting loyals:* Consumers who shift loyalty from one brand to another.
4. *Switchers:* Consumers who show no loyalty to any brand.[41]

A company can learn a great deal by analyzing the degrees of brand loyalty: (1) By studying its hard-core loyals, the company can identify its products' strengths. (2) By studying its split loyals, the company can pinpoint which brands are most competitive with its own. (3) By looking at customers who are shifting away from its brand, the company can learn about its marketing weaknesses and attempt to correct them. One caution: what appear to be brand-loyal purchase patterns may reflect habit, indifference, a low price, a high switching cost, or the unavailability of other brands.

Attitude Five attitude groups can be found in a market: enthusiastic, positive, indifferent, negative, and hostile. Door-to-door workers in a political campaign use voter attitude to determine how much time to spend with that voter. They thank enthusiastic voters and remind them to vote; they reinforce those who are positively disposed; they try to win the votes of indifferent voters; they spend no time trying to change the attitudes of negative and hostile voters.

Combining different behavioural bases can help to provide a more comprehensive and cohesive view of a market and its segments. Figure 8.3 depicts one possible way to break down a target market by various behavioural segmentation bases.

THE CONVERSION MODEL The Conversion Model has been developed to measure the strength of the psychological commitment to brands and openness to change.[42] To determine the ease with which a consumer can be converted to another choice, the model assesses commitment based on factors such as consumer attitudes towards, and satisfaction with, current brand choices in a category and the importance of the decision to select a brand in the category.[43]

The model segments *users* of a brand into four groups based on strength of commitment, from low to high, as follows:

1. *Convertible:* users who are most likely to defect.
2. *Shallow:* consumers who are uncommitted to the brand and could switch; some are actively considering alternatives.
3. *Average:* consumers who are committed to the brand they are using, but not as strongly as Entrenched users; they are unlikely to switch brands in the short term.
4. *Entrenched:* consumers who are strongly committed to the brand they are currently using; they are highly unlikely to switch brands in the foreseeable future.

The model also classifies *nonusers* of a brand into four other groups based on their "balance of disposition" and openness to trying the brand, from low to high, as follows:

1. *Strongly unavailable:* nonusers who are unlikely to switch to the brand; their preference lies strongly with their current brands.
2. *Weakly unavailable:* nonusers who are not available to the brand because their preference lies with their current brand, although not strongly.
3. *Ambivalent:* nonusers who are as attracted to the brand as they are to their current brands.
4. *Available:* nonusers of the brand who are most likely to be acquired in the short run.

In an application of the Conversion Model, Lloyds TSB bank discovered that the profitability of their clients who had been identified as "least committed" had fallen by 14 percent in a 12-month period, whereas those who were "most committed" had increased by 9 percent. Those who were "committed" were 20-percent more likely to increase the number of products they held during the 12-month period. As a result, the bank took action to attract and retain high-value committed customers, resulting in increased profitability.

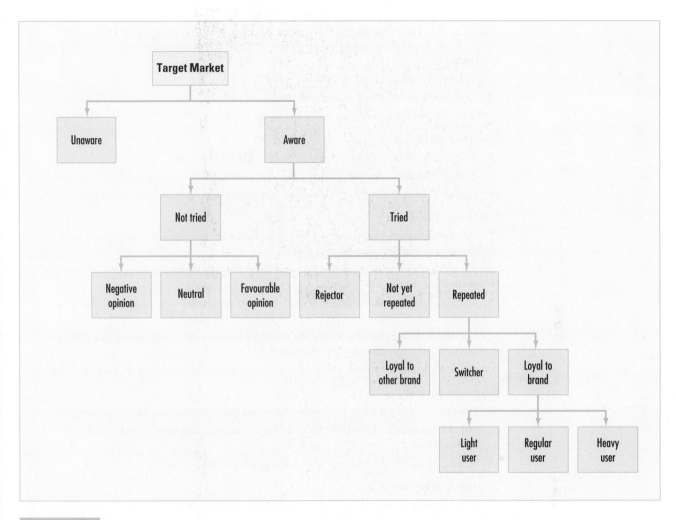

FIGURE 8.3

Behavioural-Segmentation Breakdown

Finally, a related method of behavioural segmentation has recently been proposed that looks more at the expectations a consumer brings to a particular kind of transaction and locates those expectations on a "Gravity-of-Decision Spectrum." On the shallow end of the spectrum, consumers seek products and services, such as toiletries and snacks, they think will save them time, effort, and money. Segmentation for these items would tend to measure consumers' price sensitivity, habits, and impulsiveness. At the other end of the spectrum, the deep end, are those decisions in which consumers' emotional investment is greatest and their core values most engaged, such as deciding on a health-care facility for an aging relative or buying a new home. Here the marketer would seek to determine the core values and beliefs related to the buying decision. As the model suggests, focusing on consumers' relationships and involvement with products and product categories can often reveal where and how the firm should market to consumers.[44]

BASES FOR SEGMENTING BUSINESS MARKETS

Business markets can be segmented with some of the same variables used in consumer market segmentation, such as geography, benefits sought, and usage rate, but business marketers also use other variables. Table 8.2 shows one set of variables for segmentation of the business market. The demographic variables are the most important, followed by the operating variables—down to the personal characteristics of the buyer.

The table lists major questions that business marketers should ask in determining which segments and customers to serve. A rubber-tire company should first decide which industries it wants

| TABLE 8.2 | MAJOR SEGMENTATION VARIABLES FOR BUSINESS MARKETS |

Demographic

1. *Industry:* Which industries should we serve?

2. *Company size:* What size companies should we serve?

3. *Location:* What geographical areas should we serve?

Operating Variables

4. *Technology:* What customer technologies should we focus on?

5. *User or nonuser status:* Should we serve heavy users, medium users, light users, or nonusers?

6. *Customer capabilities:* Should we serve customers needing many or few services?

Purchasing Approaches

7. *Purchasing-function organization:* Should we serve companies with highly centralized or decentralized purchasing organizations?

8. *Power structure:* Should we serve companies that are engineering dominated, financially dominated, and so on?

9. *Nature of existing relationships:* Should we serve companies with which we have strong relationships or simply go after the most desirable companies?

10. *General purchase policies:* Should we serve companies that prefer leasing? Service contracts? Systems purchases? Sealed bidding?

11. *Purchasing criteria:* Should we serve companies that are seeking quality? Service? Price?

Situational Factors

12. *Urgency:* Should we serve companies that need quick and sudden delivery or service?

13. *Specific application:* Should we focus on certain applications of our product rather than all applications?

14. *Size of order:* Should we focus on large or small orders?

Personal Characteristics

15. *Buyer–seller similarity:* Should we serve companies whose people and values are similar to ours?

16. *Attitudes toward risk:* Should we serve risk-taking or risk-avoiding customers?

17. *Loyalty:* Should we serve companies that show high loyalty to their suppliers?

Source: Adapted from Thomas V. Bonoma and Benson P. Shapiro, *Segmenting the Industrial Market* (Lexington, MA: Lexington Books, 1983).

to serve. It can sell tires to manufacturers of automobiles, trucks, farm tractors, forklift trucks, or aircraft. Within a chosen target industry, a company can further segment by company size. The company might set up separate operations for selling to large and small customers.

Small businesses, in particular, have become a Holy Grail for business marketers.[45] In Canada, small businesses are responsible for roughly 25 percent of the gross domestic product according to Industry Canada. Here is an example of a consumer-focused company that also is striving to serve small businesses:

Costco Wholesale Corp. (Vancouver)

Big-box stores such as Costco have been strictly a suburban phenomenon, but this is beginning to change. Costco Wholesale Corp. unveiled a 147 000 square-foot store in the vicinity of GM Place in downtown Vancouver. One of its objectives is to get closer to small businesses such as convenience stores. To accomplish this aim, it designated a segment marketing group that will be responsible for building relationships and integrating with the business community.[46]

Within a given target industry and customer size, a company can segment by purchase criteria. For example, government laboratories need low prices and service contracts for scientific equipment;

university laboratories need equipment that requires little service; and industrial laboratories need equipment that is highly reliable and accurate.

Business marketers generally identify segments through a sequential process. Consider an aluminum company: The company first undertook macro-segmentation. It looked at which end-use market to serve: automobile, residential, or beverage containers. It chose the residential market, and needed to determine the most attractive product application: semi-finished material, building components, or aluminum mobile homes. Deciding to focus on building components, it considered the best customer size and chose large customers. The second stage consisted of micro-segmentation. The company distinguished among customers buying on price, service, and quality. Because the aluminum company had a high-service profile, it decided to concentrate on the service-motivated segment of the market.

MARKET TARGETING

There are many statistical techniques for developing market segments.[47] Once the firm has identified its market-segment opportunities, it has to decide how many and which ones to target. Marketers are increasingly combining several variables in an effort to identify smaller, better-defined target groups. Thus, a bank may identify not only a group of wealthy retired adults, but within that group distinguish between several segments depending on current income, assets, savings, and risk preferences. This has led some market researchers to advocate a *needs-based market segmentation approach*. Roger Best proposed the seven-step approach shown in Table 8.3.

Effective Segmentation Criteria

Not all segmentation schemes are useful. For example, table-salt buyers could be divided into blond and brunette customers, but hair colour is undoubtedly irrelevant to the purchase of salt. Furthermore, if all salt buyers buy the same amount of salt each month, believe all salt is the same, and would pay only one price for salt, this market would be minimally segmentable from a marketing point of view.

To be useful, market segments must rate favourably on five key criteria:

- *Measurable.* The size, purchasing power, and characteristics of the segments can be measured.

- *Substantial.* The segments are large and profitable enough to serve. A segment should be the largest possible homogeneous group worth going after with a tailored marketing program. It would not pay, for example, for an automobile manufacturer to develop cars for people who are 120-cm tall.

- *Accessible.* The segments can be effectively reached and served.

TABLE 8.3	STEPS IN THE SEGMENTATION PROCESS	
1. Needs-Based Segmentation	Group customers into segments based on similar needs and benefits sought by customer in solving a particular consumption problem.
2. Segment Identification	For each needs-based segment, determine which demographics, lifestyles, and usage behaviours make the segment distinct and identifiable (actionable).
3. Segment Attractiveness	Using predetermined segment-attractiveness criteria (such as market growth, competitive intensity, and market access), determine the overall attractiveness of each segment.
4. Segment Profitability	Determine segment profitability.
5. Segment Positioning	For each segment, create a "value proposition" and product-price positioning strategy based on that segment's unique customer needs and characteristics.
6. Segment "Acid Test"	Create "segment storyboards" to test the attractiveness of each segment's positioning strategy.
7. Marketing-Mix Strategy	Expand segment positioning strategy to include all aspects of the marketing mix: product, price, promotion, and place.

Source: Adapted from Robert J. Best, *Market-Based Management* (Upper Saddle River, NJ: Prentice Hall, 2000).

Single-segment concentration

M₁ M₂ M₃

P₁
P₂
P₃

Selective specialization

M₁ M₂ M₃

P₁
P₂
P₃

Product specialization

M₁ M₂ M₃

P₁
P₂
P₃

Market specialization

M₁ M₂ M₃

P₁
P₂
P₃

Full market coverage

M₁ M₂ M₃

P₁
P₂
P₃

P = Product   M = Market

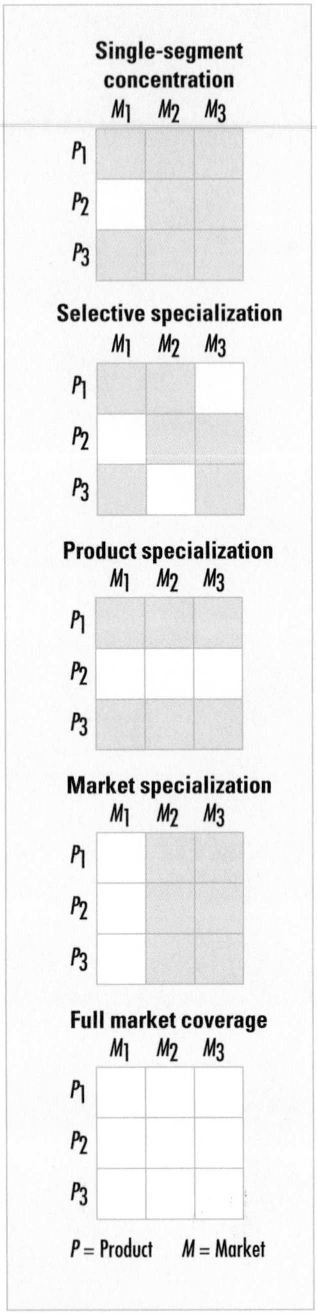

FIGURE 8.4

Five Patterns of Target-Market Selection

Source: Adapted from Derek F. Abell, *Defining the Business: The Starting Point of Strategic Planning* (Upper Saddle River, NJ: Prentice Hall, 1980), pp. 192–196.

- *Differentiable.* The segments are conceptually distinguishable and respond differently to different marketing-mix elements and programs. If married and unmarried women respond similarly to a sale on perfume, they do not constitute separate segments.
- *Actionable.* Effective programs can be formulated for attracting and serving the segments.

Evaluating and Selecting the Market Segments

In evaluating different market segments, the firm must look at two factors: the segment's overall attractiveness and the company's objectives and resources. How well does a potential segment score on the five criteria? Does a potential segment have characteristics, such as size, growth, profitability, scale economies, and low risk, that make it generally attractive? Does investing in the segment make sense given the firm's objectives, competencies, and resources? Some attractive segments may not mesh with the company's long-run objectives, or the company may lack one or more competencies necessary to offer superior value.

After evaluating different segments, the company can consider five patterns of target-market selection, as shown in Figure 8.4.

SINGLE-SEGMENT CONCENTRATION Volkswagen concentrates on the small-car market and Porsche on the sports-car market. Through concentrated marketing, the firm gains a strong knowledge of the segment's needs and achieves a strong market presence. Furthermore, the firm enjoys operating economies through specializing its production, distribution, and promotion. If it captures segment leadership, the firm can earn a high return on its investment.

However, there are risks. A particular market segment can turn sour or a competitor may invade the segment: when digital-camera technology took off, Polaroid's earnings fell sharply. For these reasons, many companies prefer to operate in more than one segment. If deciding to serve more than one segment, the company should pay close attention to the interrelationships of segment costs, performance, and technology. A company carrying fixed costs (sales force, store outlets) can add products to absorb and share some costs. The sales force will sell additional products, and a fast-food outlet will offer additional menu items. Economies of scope can be just as important as economies of scale.

Companies can try to operate in super-segments rather than in isolated segments. A **super-segment** is a set of segments sharing some exploitable similarity. For example, many symphony orchestras target people who have broad cultural interests, rather than only those who regularly attend concerts.

SELECTIVE SPECIALIZATION The firm selects a number of segments, each objectively attractive and appropriate. There may be little or no synergy among the segments, but each promises to be a moneymaker. This multi-segment strategy has the advantage of diversifying the firm's risk. When Procter & Gamble launched Crest Whitestrips, initial target segments included newly engaged women and brides-to-be as well as gay males.

PRODUCT SPECIALIZATION The firm makes a certain product that it sells to several different market segments. An example is a microscope manufacturer that sells to university, government, and commercial laboratories. The firm makes different microscopes for the different customer groups and builds a strong reputation in the specific product area. The downside risk is that the product may be supplanted by an entirely new technology.

MARKET SPECIALIZATION The firm concentrates on serving many needs of a particular customer group. An example is a firm that sells an assortment of products only to university laboratories. The firm gains a strong reputation in serving this customer group and becomes a channel for additional products the customer group can use. The downside risk is that the customer group may suffer budget cuts or shrink in size.

FULL MARKET COVERAGE The firm attempts to serve all customer groups with all the products they might need. Only very large firms such as IBM (computer market), General Motors (vehicle market), and Coca-Cola (nonalcoholic-beverage market) can undertake a full-market-coverage strategy. Large firms can cover a whole market in two broad ways: through undifferentiated marketing or differentiated marketing.

In *undifferentiated marketing,* the firm ignores segment differences and goes after the whole market with one offer. It designs a product and a marketing program that will appeal to the broadest number of buyers. It relies on mass distribution and advertising. It aims to endow the product with a superior image. Undifferentiated marketing is "the marketing counterpart to standardization and mass production in manufacturing."[48] The narrow product line keeps down costs of research and development, production, inventory, transportation, marketing research, advertising, and product management. The undifferentiated advertising program keeps down advertising costs. Presumably, the company can turn its lower costs into lower prices to win the price-sensitive segment of the market.

In *differentiated marketing*, the firm operates in several market segments and designs different products for each segment. Cosmetics firm Estée Lauder markets brands that appeal to women (and men) of different tastes: The flagship brand, the original Estée Lauder, appeals to older consumers; Clinique caters to middle-aged women; M.A.C. to youthful hipsters; Aveda to aromatherapy enthusiasts; and Origins to eco-conscious consumers who want cosmetics made from natural ingredients.[49] See how Starwood Hotels and Resorts differentiated itself:

Starwood Hotels and Resorts

In its rebranding attempt to go "beyond beds," Starwood Hotels & Resorts has differentiated its hotels along emotional, experiential lines. In order to quickly provide distinctive definitions for each Starwood brand, the company took an innovative co-branding approach, creating alliances for each brand that helped telegraph that brand's particular identity. At upscale Westin Hotels, the key definition became "renewal." Not only are guests welcomed with herbal drinks, candles, and soft music, but each room features Westin's own "Heavenly Beds," sold exclusively online through the Westin Store, thus enhancing the brand's upscale image. Somewhat less upscale, Sheraton's core value centres on "connections," an image aided by the hotel's alliance with Yahoo!, which co-founded the Yahoo! Link@Sheraton lobby kiosks and cybercafés. Four Points by Sheraton is a more value-oriented Sheraton chain that uses "comfort" as its watchword and promises all "the comforts of home."[50]

Multi-segment strategies work well for products like Crest Whitestrips that appeal equally to several attractive but separate markets.

Differentiated marketing typically creates more total sales than undifferentiated marketing. However, it also increases the costs of doing business. Because differentiated marketing leads to both higher sales and higher costs, nothing general can be said regarding this strategy's profitability. Companies should be cautious about oversegmenting their market. If this happens, they may want to turn to *countersegmentation* to broaden the customer base. For example, Johnson & Johnson broadened its target market for its baby shampoo to include adults. SmithKline Beecham launched its Aquafresh toothpaste to attract three benefit-segments simultaneously: those seeking fresh breath, whiter teeth, and cavity protection.

Additional Considerations

Two other considerations must be taken into account in evaluating and selecting segments: segment-by-segment invasion plans and ethical choice of market targets.

SEGMENT-BY-SEGMENT INVASION PLANS A company would be wise to enter one segment at a time. Competitors must not know to what segment(s) the firm will move next. Segment-by-segment invasion plans are illustrated in Figure 8.5. Three firms, A, B, and C, have specialized in adapting computer systems to the needs of airlines, railroads, and trucking companies. Company A meets all the computer needs of airlines. Company B sells large computer systems to all three transportation sectors. Company C sells personal computers to trucking companies.

Where should company C move next? Arrows have been added to the chart to show the planned sequence of segment invasions. Company C will next offer mid-sized computers to trucking companies. Then, to allay company B's concern about losing some large-computer business with trucking companies, C's next move will be to sell personal computers to railroads. Later, C will offer mid-sized computers to railroads. Finally, it may launch a full-scale attack on company B's large-computer position in trucking companies. Of course, C's hidden planned moves are provisional, in that much depends on competitors' segment moves and responses.

Unfortunately, too many companies fail to develop a long-term invasion plan. PepsiCo is an exception. It first attacked Coca-Cola in the grocery market, then in the vending-machine market, then in the fast-food market, and so on. Japanese firms also plot their invasion sequence. They first gain a foothold in a market and then enter new segments with products. Toyota began by introducing small cars (Tercel, Corolla), then expanded into midsized cars (Camry, Avalon), and finally into luxury cars (Lexus).

A company's invasion plans can be thwarted when it confronts blocked markets. The invader must then figure out a way to break in. The problem of entering blocked markets calls for a mega-marketing approach. **Megamarketing** is the strategic coordination of economic, psychological, political, and public-relations skills to gain the cooperation of a number of parties in order to enter or operate in a given market. Pepsi used megamarketing to enter the Indian market.

FIGURE 8.5

Segment-by-Segment Invasion Plan

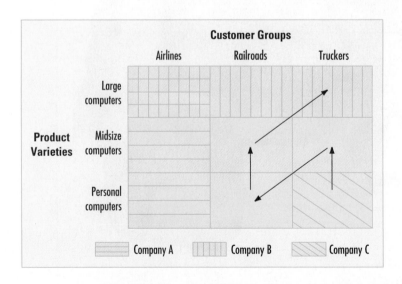

PepsiCo

After Coca-Cola left India, Pepsi worked with an Indian business group to gain government approval for its entry, over the objections of domestic soft-drink companies and anti-multinational legislators. Pepsi offered to help India export some agricultural products in a volume that would more than cover the cost of importing soft-drink concentrate. Pepsi also promised to help rural areas in their economic development. It further offered to transfer food-processing, packaging, and water-treatment technology to India. Pepsi's bundle of benefits won the support of various Indian interest groups.

ETHICAL CHOICE OF MARKET TARGETS Marketers must target segments carefully to avoid consumer backlash. Some consumers may resist being labelled. Singles may reject single-serving food packaging because they don't want to be reminded they are eating alone. Elderly consumers who don't feel their age may not appreciate products that identify them as "old."

Market targeting sometimes generates public controversy.[51] The public is concerned when marketers take unfair advantage of vulnerable groups (such as children) or disadvantaged groups (such as the urban poor), or promote potentially harmful products. McDonald's and other chains have drawn criticism for pitching their high-fat, salt-laden fare. The cereal industry has been heavily criticized for marketing efforts directed towards children. Critics worry that high-powered appeals presented through the mouths of lovable animated characters will overwhelm children's defences and lead them to want sugared cereals or poorly balanced breakfasts. Even though it is illegal to use celebrity endorsers and licensed product characters (such as Mickey Mouse and Buzz Lightyear) to promote products to Canadian children, cereal marketers can still use their own proprietary characters (e.g., Tony the Tiger). Citing concerns with rising childhood obesity rates, in early 2008 Dr. David McKeown, Toronto's Medical Officer of Health, damned such marketing and called for a total ban on "all commercial advertising of food and beverages" to children under 13. He claimed most foods advertised to children "are dominated by those that are calorie-dense and nutrient-poor."[52] Toy marketers have been similarly criticized. Not all attempts to target children, minorities, or other special segments draw criticism, as illustrated by the following RBC example.

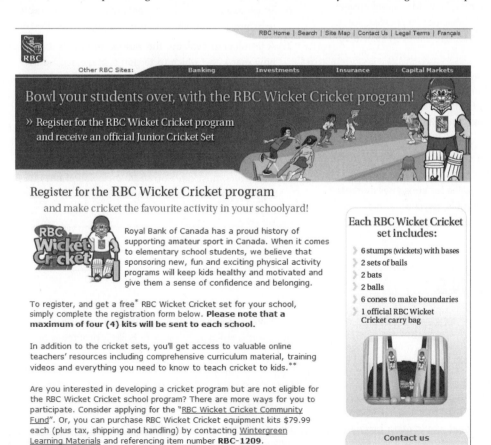

As part of its commitment to multicultural communities, RBC launched its Wicket Cricket program in 2008.

RBC

RBC recently announced its sponsorship of the Wicket Cricket program. Aimed at physical-education teachers and community-recreation leaders, the program introduces the basics of cricket to kids in grades two to six. Participants in the program can register for the program at www.rbc.com/cricket. They receive a free kit that includes youth-sized bats, balls, wickets, and a DVD resource guide that outlines the rules of the game and practice drills. The site also provides coaching tips and information on establishing a house league and tournament play. The program is one manifestation of RBC's commitment to multicultural communities. Mark Whitmell, director, cultural markets, notes "When somebody is new to Canada they're looking for things that are common, that are familiar, that even bring a sense of home." Many immigrants love cricket and appreciate companies that can help them play the game in Canada, he adds. "They've told us that they're looking for an organization that respects culture."[53]

Thus, the issue is not who is targeted, but rather, how and for what. Socially responsible marketing calls for targeting that serves not only the company's interests, but also the interests of those targeted.

SUMMARY

1. Target marketing involves three activities: market segmentation, market targeting, and market positioning.

2. Markets can be targeted at four levels: segments, niches, local areas, and individuals. Market segments are large identifiable groups within a market. A niche is a more narrowly defined group. Marketers appeal to local markets through grassroots marketing for trading areas, neighbourhoods, and even individual stores.

3. More companies now practise individual and mass customization. The future is likely to see more self-marketing, a form of individual marketing in which individual consumers take the initiative in designing products and brands.

4. There are two bases for segmenting consumer markets: consumer characteristics and consumer responses. The major segmentation variables for consumer markets are geographic, demographic, psychographic, and behavioural. These variables can be used singly or in combination.

5. Business marketers use all these variables along with operating variables, purchasing approaches, and situational factors.

6. To be useful, market segments must be measurable, substantial, accessible, differentiable, and actionable.

7. A firm has to evaluate the various segments and decide how many and which to target: a single segment, several segments, a specific product, a specific market, or the full market. If it serves the full market, it must choose between differentiated and undifferentiated marketing. Firms must also monitor segment relationships and seek economies of scope and the potential for marketing to super-segments.

8. Marketers must develop segment-by-segment invasion plans and choose target markets in a socially responsible manner.

APPLICATIONS

Marketing Debate: Is Mass Marketing Dead?

With marketers increasingly adopting more and more refined market-segmentation schemes—fuelled by the Internet and other customization efforts—some critics claim that mass marketing is dead. Others counter that there will always be room for large brands that employ marketing programs targeting the mass market.

Take a position: Mass marketing is dead *versus* Mass marketing is still a viable way to build a profitable brand.

Marketing Discussion: Descriptive versus Behavioural Market-Segmentation Schemes

Think of various product categories. How would you classify yourself in terms of the various segmentation schemes? How would marketing be more or less effective for you depending on the segment involved? How would you contrast demographic and behavioural segment schemes? Which do you think would be most effective for marketers trying to sell to you?

Breakthrough Marketing: HSBC

HSBC wants to be known as the "world's local bank." This tagline reflects HSBC's positioning as a globe-spanning financial institution with a unique focus on serving local markets. Originally the Hong Kong and Shanghai Banking Corporation Limited, HSBC was established in 1865 to finance the growing trade between China and the United Kingdom. It's now the second-largest bank in the world. Despite serving over 100 million customers through 9500 branches in 79 countries, the bank works hard to maintain a local presence and local knowledge in each area. Its fundamental operating strategy is to remain close to its customers. As HSBC chairman Sir John Bond said, "Our position as the world's local bank enables us to approach each country uniquely, blending local knowledge with a worldwide operating platform."

Ads for the "world's local bank" campaigns have long been built on how different cultures and people view things. A global print execution juxtaposes a baby and computer, alternating the headings "work" and "play." One of three Canadian ads features hockey and curling images, and the headings "exciting" and "boring." In a spot for radio, "Hockey Song," the distinctive music used to pump up crowds at NHL games, asked listeners whether they hear a rally cry or just four simple notes.

About 13 000-kilometres away, HSBC undertook a two-part "Support Hong Kong" campaign to revitalize the local economy, which was hit hard by the 2003 SARS outbreak. First, HSBC delayed interest payments for personal-loan customers who worked in industries most affected by SARS (cinemas, hotels, restaurants, and travel agencies). Second, the bank offered discounts and rebates to HSBC credit-card users when they shopped and dined out. More than 1500 local merchants participated in the promotion.

HSBC also targets consumer niches with unique products and services. For example, it found a little-known product area growing at 125-percent a year: pet insurance. The bank now sells pet insurance to its depositors through its HSBC Insurance agency. In Malaysia, HSBC offered a "smart card" and no-frills credit cards to the underserved student segment and targeted high-value customers with special "Premium Centers" bank branches.

The bank pulls its worldwide businesses together under a single global brand with the "world's local bank" slogan. The aim is to link its international size with close relationships in each of the countries in which it operates. HSBC spends US$600 million annually on global marketing, which it consolidated in 2004 under the WPP group of agencies. In the future, it will be seeking to leverage its position as "the world's local bank" to improve upon its US$13.5-billion brand value, which placed it 23rd on the 2007 Interbrand/*BusinessWeek* global brand rankings, up five spots from its 2006 ranking.

DISCUSSION QUESTIONS

1. How has segmentation helped HSBC become successful?
2. What bases has it used to segment its markets?
3. What are the strengths and weaknesses of its segmentation efforts?

Sources: Carrick Mollenkamp, "HSBC Stumbles in Bid to Become Global Deal Maker," *Wall Street Journal*, October 5, 2006; Kate Nicholson, "HSBC Aims to Appear Global Yet Approachable," *Campaign*, December 2, 2005, p. 15; Deborah Orr, "New Ledger," *Forbes*, March 1, 2004, pp. 72–73; "HSBC's Global Marketing Head Explains Review Decision," *Adweek*, January 19, 2004; "Now Your Customers Can Afford to Take Fido to the Vet," *Bank Marketing* (December 2003): 47; Kenneth Hein, "HSBC Bank Rides the Coattails of Chatty Cabbies," *Brandweek*, December 1, 2003, p. 30; Sir John Bond and Stephen Green, "HSBC Strategic Overview," presentation to investors, November 27, 2003; "Lafferty Retail Banking Awards 2003," *Retail Banker International*, November 27, 2003, pp. 4–5; "Ideas that Work," *Bank Marketing* (November 2003): 10; "HSBC Enters the Global Branding Big League," *Bank Marketing International* (August 2003): 1–2; Normandy Madden, "HSBC Rolls out Post-SARS Effort," *Advertising Age*, June 16, 2003, p. 12; www.hsbc.com; Annette Bourdeau, "HSBC: groundbreaker or cliché?" *Strategy Magazine*, February 2006, p. 23.

PART FOUR

4

BUILDING STRONG BRANDS

IN THIS CHAPTER, WE WILL ADDRESS THE FOLLOWING QUESTIONS:

- What is a brand and how does branding work?

- What is brand equity?

- How is brand equity built, measured, and managed?

- What are the important decisions in developing a branding strategy?

CHAPTER 9

CREATING BRAND EQUITY

nine

Bell Canada is the nation's largest telecommunications company, providing consumers with solutions to all their communications needs, including telephone services, wireless voice and data, digital television, voice over IP, and Internet access. It also has one of the most recognized and trusted brands in the country.

The basis of brand trust is multi-faceted, as was revealed in the results of a 2007 international survey. The survey found that Canadian consumers trust Bell Canada more than any other brand, including those of multinational firms like Procter & Gamble, IBM, and Amazon, when it comes to protecting privacy. Bell's trust ratings also beat out Canada's major banks'. Bank of Montreal and Royal Bank of Canada ranked second and third, respectively, in the survey.

Brands that performed well in the survey shared certain characteristics, such as the level of respect shown when communicating with customers and the fact that the firms regarded privacy as a key part of building their brands. Bell has also risen to prominence because the brand represents quality, on-going innovation, real benefits, and strong customer relationships. Furthermore, these qualities have been effectively communicated to consumers. Bell has used two animated beavers, Frank and Gordon, as its spokespersons for several years and advertising using these characters has dominated the Canadian advertising landscape. According to a recent survey, the campaign achieved the highest rankings in terms of top-of-mind awareness. Of those survey respondents who could recall any advertising at all, an average of 12.2 percent remembered Bell. While this may not seem high, compare it to the next most-noticed advertiser, Capital One, which achieved only 4-percent awareness.

Bell retired Frank and Gordon in August 2008. In an attempt to re-brand itself, it launched a new campaign where everything is better. Only time will tell if the new campaign positions the giant telecommunications provider as a company whose services are easier, better, and faster than those of its competitors.

Sources: Matt Semansky, "Bell Tops List of Trusted Brands in Privacy Survey," *Marketing Daily*, August 23, 2007; Dave Scholz, "The Year of the Beavers," *Marketing*, January 15, 2007; Mary Maddever, "Do You Have a Real Brand?" *Strategy*, March 2008, p. 4.

Marketers of successful twenty-first-century brands like Bell must excel at the strategic brand management process. **Strategic brand management** combines the design and implementation of marketing activities and programs to build, measure, and manage brands to maximize their value. The strategic brand management process has four main steps:

- Identifying and establishing brand positioning
- Planning and implementing brand marketing
- Measuring and interpreting brand performance
- Growing and sustaining brand value

Chapter 10 deals with brand positioning. The remaining topics are discussed in this chapter.[1] Chapter 11 reviews important concepts for dealing with competition.

WHAT IS BRAND EQUITY?

Perhaps the most distinctive skill of professional marketers is their ability to create, maintain, enhance, and protect brands. Successful brands such as Bell, Dove, Sony, and Nike command a price premium and elicit much loyalty. New brands such as Google, Porter Airlines, and Lululemon capture the imagination of consumers and the financial community alike.

The American Marketing Association defines a **brand** as "a name, term, sign, symbol, or design, or a combination of them, intended to identify the goods or services of one seller or group of sellers and to differentiate them from those of competitors." A brand is thus a product or service with added dimensions that differentiate it in some way from other products or services designed to satisfy the same need. These differences may be functional, rational, or tangible—related to product performance of the brand. They may also be more symbolic, emotional, or intangible—related to what the brand represents.

Branding has been around for centuries as a means to distinguish the goods of one producer from those of another.[2] The earliest signs of branding in Europe were the medieval guilds' requirement that craftspeople put trademarks on their products to protect themselves and consumers against inferior quality. In the fine arts, branding began with artists signing their works. Brands today play a number of important roles that improve consumers' lives and enhance the financial value of firms.

The Role of Brands

Brands identify the source or maker of a product and allow consumers—either individuals or organizations—to assign responsibility to a particular manufacturer or distributor. Consumers may evaluate the identical product differently depending on how it is branded. Consumers learn about brands through past experiences with the product and its marketing program. They find out which brands satisfy their needs and which ones do not. As consumers' lives become more complicated, rushed, and time-starved, the ability of a brand to simplify decision making and reduce risk is invaluable.[3]

Brands also perform valuable functions for firms.[4] First, they simplify product handling or tracing. Brands help to organize inventory and accounting records. A brand also offers the firm legal protection for unique features or aspects of the product.[5] The brand name can be protected through registered trademarks, manufacturing processes can be protected through patents, and packaging can be protected through copyrights and designs. These intellectual-property rights ensure that the firm can safely invest in the brand and reap the benefits of a valuable asset.

Brands can signal a certain level of quality so that satisfied buyers can easily choose the product again.[6] Brand loyalty provides predictability and security of demand for the firm and creates barriers to entry that make it difficult for other firms to enter the market. Loyalty also can translate into a willingness to pay a higher price—often 20- to 25-percent more.[7] Although competitors may easily duplicate manufacturing processes and product designs, they cannot easily match lasting impressions in the minds of individuals and organizations from years of marketing activity and product experience. In this sense, branding can be seen as a powerful means to secure a competitive advantage.[8]

To firms, brands thus represent enormously valuable pieces of legal property that can influence consumer behaviour, be bought and sold, and provide the security of sustained future revenues to their owner. Large earning multiples have been paid for brands in mergers and acquisitions, the premium price often justified on the basis of the extra profits that could be extracted and sustained from the brands, as well as the tremendous difficulty and expense of creating similar brands from scratch. The financial industry believes that strong brands result in better earnings and profit performance for firms, which, in turn, create greater value for shareholders.[9] One of the master marketers at creating brands is Procter & Gamble, as described in "Breakthrough Marketing: Procter & Gamble" at the end of this chapter.

The Scope of Branding

How, then, do you "brand" a product? Although firms provide the impetus to brand creation through marketing programs and other activities, ultimately a brand is something that resides in the minds of consumers. A brand is a perceptual entity that is rooted in reality but reflects the perceptions and perhaps even the idiosyncrasies of consumers.

BRANDING is endowing products and services with the power of a brand. Branding is all about creating differences. To brand a product, it is necessary to teach consumers "who" the product is—by giving it a name and using other brand elements to help identify it—as well as "what" the product does and "why" consumers should care. Branding involves creating mental structures and helping consumers organize their knowledge about products and services in a way that clarifies their decision making and, in the process, provides value to the firm.

For branding strategies to be successful and for brand value to be created, consumers must be convinced that there are meaningful differences among brands in the product or service category. Brand differences often are related to attributes or benefits of the product itself. Gillette, Merck, Sony, 3M, and others have been leaders in their product categories for decades due, in part, to continual innovation. Other brands create competitive advantages through non–product-related means. Gucci, Louis Vuitton, and others have become leaders in their product categories by understanding consumer motivations and desires and creating relevant and appealing images of their products.

Marketers can apply branding virtually anywhere a consumer has a choice. It is possible to brand a physical good (Campbell's Gardennay Mediterranean Herbed Tomato soup or Molson's Canadian beer), a service (Air Canada travel, Bank of Nova Scotia banking, or Great-West Life insurance), a store (Foot Locker's specialty store or Sobey's supermarket), a person (Margaret Atwood, Shania Twain, or Wayne Gretzky), a place (the city of Sydney, province of Newfoundland and Labrador, or country of Spain), an organization (UNICEF, Canadian Automobile Association, or CARE), or an idea (abortion rights, free trade, or freedom of speech).[10] Becel and the Heart and Stroke Foundation formed a long-lived partnership to market an idea and position the Becel brand.

To convey the idea that Becel is a heart healthy choice, every tub of Becel margarine displays the Heart and Stroke Foundation's Health Check symbol.

Becel and the Heart and Stroke Foundation

In early 2008, Becel margarine joined forces with the Heart and Stroke Foundation to brand an idea: that heart health is a women's issue. The educational marketing campaign "The Heart Truth" used 30-second television commercials, print ads, in-store promotions, packaging, public relations, and the website www.loveyourheart.ca to convey an important message to women. Despite the fact that heart disease and stroke kill one in three Canadian women, only one woman in eight knows it's their most serious health concern. Becel gave away a "Heart Truth Bracelet," a black beaded bracelet with a red dress charm, to make the brand more tangible. The campaign's logo was also placed inside two-pound packages of Becel margarine along with heart-health information. The website acts as the cornerstone of the campaign. It provides tools to help women embrace a heart-healthy lifestyle; these tools include an activity calculator and the Heart Age tool: a quiz that measures users' heart age relative to their actual age.[11]

MARKETING **INSIGHT** | BRAND COOKING WITH JAMIE OLIVER

Jamie Oliver got his start as a chef at London's River Café. In 1997, when he was prominently featured in a TV documentary about the restaurant, his engaging personality led five different TV-production companies to contact him the next day. His resulting television show on cooking, "The Naked Chef," became a worldwide hit, and a celebrity chef was born. Oliver has since leveraged his cooking fame and reputation to launch a number of successful new products:

Jamie Oliver has skillfully managed his career as a brand.

- Seven books published internationally in 26 languages with over 14 million sold worldwide
- Eleven different television series with over 123 episodes shown in over 60 countries
- Eleven DVDs distributed in 25 countries
- Two U.K.-based newspaper columns syndicated in five countries
- Jamie Oliver Professional Series of pots and pans, bakeware, and kitchen accessories, licensed by Tefal (North American spelling is T-Fal) and sold in department stores in 15 countries
- Porcelain tableware and serveware licensed by Royal Worcester
- New products such as the Flavour Shaker, traditional Italian pasta sauces, antipasti, olive oils, and vinegars
- A website, www.jamieoliver.com, that logs 250 000 unique visitors per month

An endorser for U.K. supermarket giant Sainsbury since 2000, Jamie Oliver is also credited with helping the chain's "Recipe for Success" campaign deliver a staggering £1.12 billion of incremental revenue. The company believes the campaign has been 65-percent more effective than any of its other campaigns.

Besides these commercial ventures, Oliver is involved in philanthropy. For instance, he created the Fifteen Foundation whose mission is to "inspire young people." An important activity was the introduction of the Fifteen restaurant, in London in 2002, that trains 15 disadvantaged young people to work in the hospitality industry. Additional restaurants in Amsterdam, Melbourne, and Cornwall have followed. Oliver next turned his sights on a high-profile campaign "to ban the junk in schools and get kids eating fresh, tasty, nutritious food instead." Dialogue, publicity, and new school-food standards have resulted.

Jamie Oliver clearly has a strong brand and benefits from all its advantages. And like any strong brand, his has a well-defined brand image and appealing brand promise. Figure 9.1 displays a Brand Print assembled to help his marketing brand trust to better understand and explain its brand. Oliver's success in brand building is reflected in the profitable financial performance of the company he created to manage his businesses, Sweet as Candy Limited.

Source: Tessa Graham, Sweet as Candy Limited.

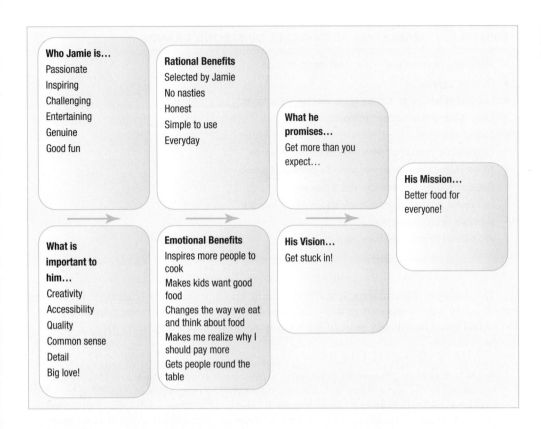

FIGURE 9.1

The Jamie Oliver Brand Print

Defining Brand Equity

Brand equity is the added value endowed to goods and services. This value may be reflected in how consumers think, feel, and act with respect to the brand, as well as in the prices, market share, and profitability that the brand commands for the firm. Marketing Insight: "Brand Cooking with Jamie Oliver" shows how this chef and television personality has built his own brand equity. Marketers and researchers use various perspectives to study brand equity.[12] Customer-based approaches view brand equity from the perspective of the consumer—either an individual or an organization.[13] The premise of customer-based brand-equity models is that the power of a brand lies in what customers have seen, read, heard, learned, thought, and felt about the brand over time.[14]

Customer-based brand equity can be defined as the differential effect that brand knowledge has on consumer response to the marketing of that brand.[15] A brand is said to have positive customer-based brand equity when consumers react more favourably to a product and the way it is marketed when the brand is identified than when it is not. A brand is said to have negative customer-based brand equity if consumers react less favourably to marketing activity for the brand under the same circumstances.

There are three key ingredients of this definition. First, brand equity arises from differences in consumer response. If no differences occur, then the brand-name product can essentially be classified as a commodity or generic version of the product.[16] Competition would then probably be based on price.

Second, these differences in response are a result of consumers' knowledge about the brand. **Brand knowledge** consists of all the thoughts, feelings, images, experiences, beliefs, and so on that become associated with the brand. In particular, brands must create strong, favourable, and unique brand associations with customers, as has been the case with Volvo (*safety*), Hallmark (*caring*), and Harley-Davidson (*adventure*).

Third, the differential response by consumers that makes up the brand equity is reflected in perceptions, preferences, and behaviour related to all aspects of the marketing of a brand. Stronger brands lead to greater revenue.[17] Table 9.1 summarizes some of these key benefits of brand equity.

TABLE 9.1	MARKETING ADVANTAGES OF STRONG BRANDS

- Improved perceptions of product performance
- Greater loyalty
- Less vulnerability to competitive marketing actions
- Less vulnerability to marketing crises
- Larger margins
- Less elastic consumer response to price increases
- More elastic consumer response to price decreases
- Greater trade cooperation and support
- Increased marketing-communications effectiveness
- Possible licensing opportunities
- Additional brand-extension opportunities

The challenge for marketers in building a strong brand, therefore, is ensuring that customers have the right type of experiences with goods and services and their marketing programs to create the desired brand knowledge. See how Apple Computer has accomplished this task:

Apple Computer

Apple Computer is recognized as a master at building a strong brand that resonates with customers across generations and national boundaries. Apple achieves incredible brand loyalty largely by delivering on its mission as defined by CEO Steven Jobs: "To create great things that change people's lives." The company has created an army of Apple evangelists, not just because it produces great advertising but also because it focuses on the consumer in everything it does. Apple's innovative products combine superior design functionality and style, and many cite the wildly successful iPod music player and the MacBook Air—the world's thinnest notebook, introduced in Canada in January 2008—as prime examples. Apple has also created 150 retail stores worldwide to fuel excitement for the brand. The rationale behind the move to retail was that the more people that can see and touch Apple products—and see what Apple can do for them—the more likely Apple will be to increase its market share. Apple has also picked up on consumers' concern with environmental issues and is therefore committed to being a responsible environmental citizen. To ensure its electronic equipment is properly disposed of at the end of its useful life, Apple offers free computer and iPod recycling programs in Canada and the US.[18]

Consumer knowledge is what drives the differences that manifest themselves in brand equity. In an abstract sense, brand equity can be seen as providing marketers with a vital strategic "bridge" from their past to their future.[19]

Brand Equity as a Bridge

From the perspective of brand equity, all the marketing dollars spent each year on goods and services should be thought of as investments in consumer brand knowledge. The *quality* of the investment in brand building is the critical factor, not necessarily the *quantity*, beyond some minimal threshold amount.

It is actually possible to "overspend" on brand building if money is not spent wisely. In the beverage category, brands such as Labatt Blue and 7Up saw sales decline in the early 1990s despite sizable marketing support, arguably because of poorly targeted and delivered marketing campaigns. At the same time, the brand knowledge created by these marketing investments dictates appropriate future directions for the brand. Consumers will decide, based on what they think and feel about the brand, where (and how) they believe the brand should go and grant permission (or not) to any marketing action or program. New products such as Crystal Pepsi, Levi's Tailored Classic suits, Fruit of the Loom laundry detergent, and Roots Air failed because consumers found them inappropriate extensions of the brand.

A brand is essentially a marketer's promise to deliver predictable product or service performance. A **brand promise** is the marketer's vision of what the brand must be and do for consumers. At the end of the day, the true value and future prospects of a brand rest with consumers, their knowledge about the brand, and their likely response to marketing activity as a result of this knowledge. Understanding consumer brand knowledge—all the different things that become linked to the brand in the minds of consumers—is thus of paramount importance because it is the foundation of brand equity.

Oxford University's Douglas Holt believes that for companies to build iconic, leadership brands, they must assemble cultural knowledge, strategize according to cultural-branding principles, and hire and train cultural experts.[20] Even Procter & Gamble, a company that has long orchestrated how shoppers perceive its products, has started on what its chief executive, A. G. Lafley, calls "a learning journey" with the consumer. "Consumers are beginning in a very real sense to own our brands and participate in their creation," he said. "We need to learn to begin to let go." One company that has let go is Burger King.

Burger King

"If you have a global brand promise, 'Have It Your Way'," says Russ Klein, Burger King's president for global marketing, strategy, and innovation. "It's about putting the customer in charge," even if he or she says "bad things" about the brand. In competing against McDonald's, with its family-friendly image, "it's more important for us to be provocative than pleasant," adds Klein, especially when appealing to a market of mainly teenaged boys. Burger King's brash ad campaigns—featuring its creepy bobble-headed king and talking chicken—appear on social-networking sites such as YouTube.com and MySpace, so that the company can take advantage of what Klein calls "social connectivity" as consumers react to the ads. Burger King encourages customers to build online communities around their favourite company icons and products. The mascot King even has his own site on MySpace. "If you'd like to be the King's friend, he's totally down with that," his page introduction says.[21]

Brand Equity Models

Although there is agreement about basic principles, a number of models of brand equity offer some different perspectives. Here we briefly highlight four of the more established ones.

BRAND ASSET VALUATOR Advertising agency Young and Rubicam (Y&R) developed a model of brand equity called Brand Asset Valuator (BAV). Based on research with almost 500 000 consumers in 44 countries, BAV provides comparative measures of the brand equity of thousands of brands across hundreds of different categories. There are five key components—or pillars—of brand equity according to BAV:

- *Differentiation* measures the degree to which a brand is seen as different from others.
- *Energy* measures the brand's sense of momentum.
- *Relevance* measures the breadth of a brand's appeal.
- *Esteem* measures how well a brand is regarded and respected.
- *Knowledge* measures how familiar and intimate consumers are with a brand.

Staples Business Depot/Bureau en Gros has mastered these five elements to increase its market share and profitability:

Staples Business Depot/Bureau en Gros

Today, when people think about Staples Business Depot (Bureau en Gros in Quebec) the office-supplies store, chances are they think of the "easy button." To build this strong point of differentiation as the basis for its brand, the company employed strong brand discipline: consistently delivering the "that was easy" experience and message at every customer touchpoint. But this wasn't always the case. As recently as 2001, Staples played second fiddle to Office Depot. Staples discovered, however, that their most profitable customers weren't the masses they'd been pursuing with a low-price, big-box strategy, but harried small-business owners with a narrow set of needs. These people would pay a price premium if Staples could deliver an easy shopping experience. So Staples invested heavily to live up to this brand promise. It ditched ceiling-scraping shelves and the dizzying array of products. It improved its in-store service and customers are always asked "did you find everything you were looking for today?" It made the website easy to navigate and shop and provided free next-day delivery on orders of $50 or more. Building a unique, clear brand position has enabled Staples Business Depot to become Canada's largest supplier of office supplies, business machines, office furniture, and business services to small-business and home-office customers. The chain now operates almost 300 stores across Canada, sales and profits have skyrocketed, and its stock price has more than tripled.[22]

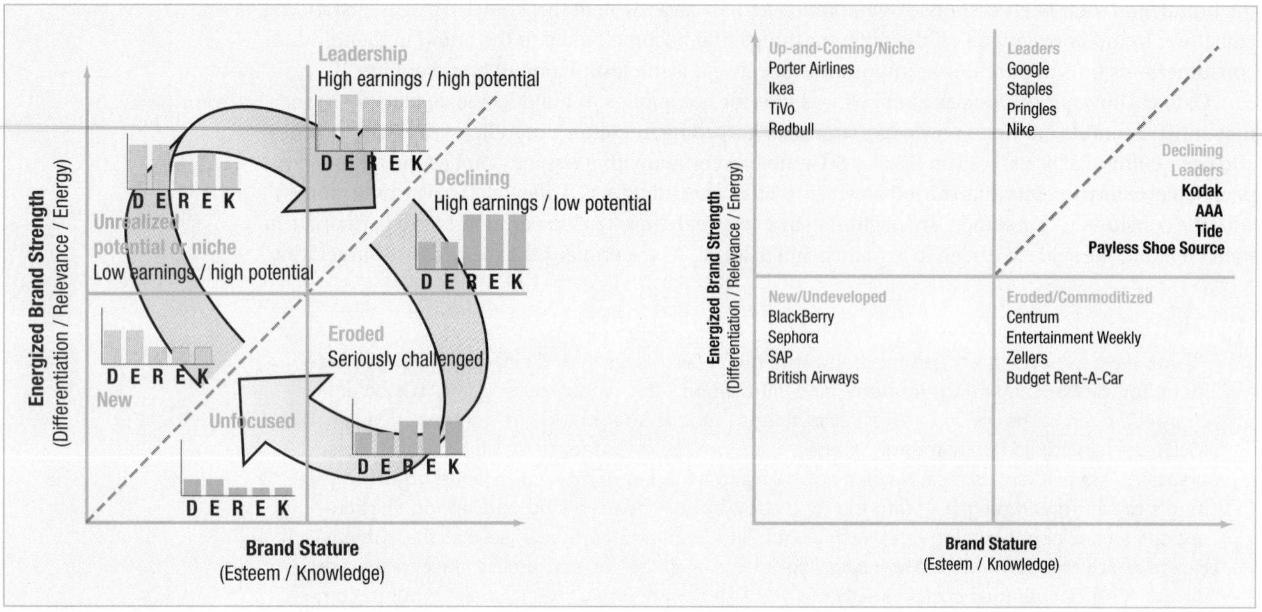

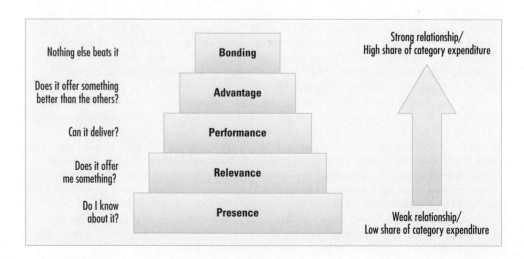

FIGURE 9.2

BAV Power Grid

Differentiation and Relevance combine to determine *Brand Strength*. These two pillars indicate the brand's future value, rather than just its past. Esteem and Knowledge together create *Brand Stature*, which is more of a "report card" on past performance.

Examining the relationships among these four dimensions—a brand's "pillar pattern"—reveals much about the brand's current and future status. Brand Strength and Brand Stature can be combined to form a power grid that depicts the stages in the cycle of brand development—each with its characteristic pillar patterns—in successive quadrants (see Figure 9.2). Strong new brands show higher levels of Differentiation and Energy than Relevance, whereas both Esteem and Knowledge are lower still. Leadership brands show high levels on all pillars. Finally, declining brands show high Knowledge—evidence of past performance—a lower level of Esteem, and even lower Relevance, Energy, and Differentiation.

BRANDZ Marketing research consultants Millward Brown and WPP have developed the BRANDZ model of brand strength, at the heart of which is the BrandDynamics pyramid. According to this model, brand building follows a sequential series of steps, each contingent upon successfully accomplishing the preceding one (see Figure 9.3).

"Bonded" consumers, those at the top of the pyramid, build stronger relationships with the brand and spend more on it than those at lower levels. More consumers, however, will be found at the

FIGURE 9.3

BrandDynamics™ Pyramid

Source: BrandDynamics™ Pyramid. Reprinted by permission of MillwardBrown.

lower levels. The challenge for marketers is to develop activities and programs that help consumers move up the pyramid.

AAKER MODEL Former UC-Berkeley marketing professor David Aaker views brand equity as a set of five categories of brand assets and liabilities linked to a brand that add to or subtract from the value provided by a product or service.[23] According to Aaker, brand management starts with developing a *brand identity:* the unique set of brand associations that represent what the brand stands for and promises to customers—an aspirational brand image.[24] Brand identity is typically 8 to 12 elements that represent concepts such as product scope, product attributes, quality/value, uses, users, country of origin, organizational attributes, brand personality, and symbols. The most important of these, which will drive brand-building programs, are the *core identity elements.* The others, *extended identity elements*, add texture and guidance. In addition, a *brand essence* can communicate the brand identity in a compact and inspiring way.

For example, according to Aaker, Ajax, a large industrial service company, has a brand essence of "Commitment to Excellence—Anytime, Anywhere, Whatever It Takes"; a core identity of "Spirit of Excellence," "Team Solutions," and "Technology That Fits"; and an extended identity of "Worldly But Informal," "Confident and Competent," "Open Communicator," "Global Network of Local Experts," and a "Supporter of World Health." The "Team Solutions" core identity was aspirational for a firm that consisted of several autonomous divisions, but necessary to support its strategy going forward.

Aaker maintains that the identity should be differentiating on some dimensions, suggest parity on others, resonate with customers, drive brand-building programs, reflect the culture and strategy of the business, and be credible. Credibility can be based on proof points such as current assets, programs, strategic initiatives, or investments in new or revitalized assets or programs.

BRAND RESONANCE The brand-resonance model also views brand building as an ascending, sequential series of steps, from bottom to top: (1) ensuring customers' identification with the brand and an association of the brand in customers' minds with a specific product class or customer need; (2) firmly establishing the totality of brand meaning in the minds of customers by strategically linking a host of tangible and intangible brand associations; (3) eliciting the proper customer responses in terms of brand-related judgment and feelings; and (4) converting brand response to create an intense, active loyalty relationship between customers and the brand.

According to this model, following the four steps involves establishing six "brand building blocks" with customers. These brand building blocks can be assembled into a brand pyramid, as illustrated in Figure 9.4. The model emphasizes the duality of brands—the rational route to brand building is the left-hand side of the pyramid, whereas the emotional route is the right-hand side.[25]

MasterCard is an example of a brand with duality, as it emphasizes both the rational advantage of the credit card, through its acceptance at establishments worldwide, and the emotional advantage through its award-winning "priceless" advertising campaign, which shows people buying items to reach a certain goal. The goal itself—a feeling, an accomplishment, or other intangible—is "priceless" ("There are some things money can't buy. For everything else, there's MasterCard").

MasterCard appeals to "the head and the heart" in its long-running Priceless campaign.

Creating significant brand equity involves reaching the top or pinnacle of the brand pyramid and will occur only if the right building blocks are put into place.

- *Brand salience* relates to how often and easily the brand is evoked under various purchase or consumption situations.

- *Brand performance* relates to how the product or service meets customers' functional needs.

- *Brand imagery* deals with the extrinsic properties of the product or service, including the ways in which the brand attempts to meet customers' psychological or social needs.

- *Brand judgments* focus on customers' own opinions and evaluations.

- *Brand feelings* are customers' emotional responses and reactions with respect to the brand.

- *Brand resonance* refers to the nature of the relationship that customers have with the brand and the extent to which customers feel that they are "in sync" with the brand.

FIGURE 9.4

Brand Resonance Pyramid

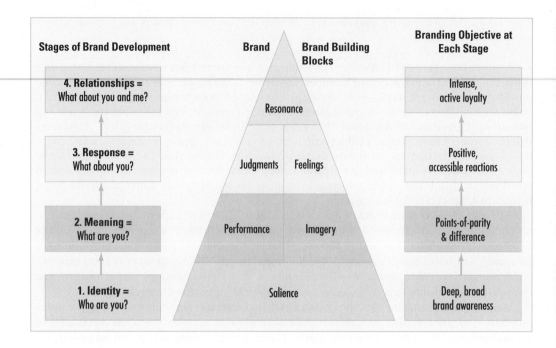

Resonance is characterized in terms of the intensity or depth of the psychological bond customers have with the brand, as well as the level of activity engendered by this loyalty.[26] Brands with high resonance include Harley-Davidson, Apple, and eBay.

Harley-Davidson, Inc.

In an outdoor campaign created for the Quebec market in early 2008, Harley-Davidson, Inc. increased its brand resonance by giving riders a number of new reasons to hit the road. The campaign consisted of 40 different messages on 85 billboards located throughout the province. The billboards featured headlines (in French) such as "138 reasons to see the Stadium, which your taxes paid for, in Montreal," "116 reasons to live in the boring suburbs," and "132 reasons to see a hole in a rock in Percé." The numbers in the messages corresponded to the highway or road where the billboard was located, and the message made reference to "in-jokes" designed to grab the attention of locals.[27]

Harley-Davidson, Inc., increased its brand resonance with Quebec consumers with its recent billboard campaign.

BUILDING BRAND EQUITY

Marketers build brand equity by creating the right brand-knowledge structures with the right consumers. This process depends on *all* brand-related contacts—whether marketer-initiated or not. From a marketing-management perspective, however, there are three main sets of *brand-equity drivers*:

1. *The initial choices for the brand elements or identities making up the brand* (e.g., brand names, URLs, logos, symbols, characters, spokespeople, slogans, jingles, packages, and signage). Concrobium, a Canadian company that produces mold-control products, carefully chose the blue and green colours (blue for cleanliness, green for environmental friendliness) that characterize both its products and website. Its website also features clean-looking lettering and an uncluttered design. Unlike bleach, which can damage the environment when it goes down the drain, Concrobium is a non-toxic, all natural product approved by Health Canada.[28]

2. *The product and service and all accompanying marketing activities and supporting marketing programs.* Liz Claiborne's fastest-growing label is Juicy Couture, whose edgy, contemporary sportswear and accessories have a strong lifestyle appeal to women, men, and kids. Positioned as an affordable luxury, the brand creates its exclusive cachet via limited distribution and a somewhat risqué name and rebellious attitude.[29]

3. *Other associations indirectly transferred to the brand by linking it to some other entity (e.g., a person, place, or thing).* The brand name of New Zealand vodka 42 Below refers to both a latitude that runs through New Zealand and the percentage of its alcohol content. All the packaging and other visual cues are designed to leverage the perceived purity of the country to communicate the positioning for the brand.[30]

Choosing Brand Elements

Brand elements are those trademarkable devices that serve to identify and differentiate the brand. Most strong brands employ multiple brand elements. Nike has the distinctive "swoosh" logo, the empowering "Just Do It" slogan, and the mythological "Nike" name based on the winged goddess of victory.

Marketers should choose brand elements to build as much brand equity as possible. The test of the brand-building ability of these elements is what consumers would think or feel about the product if they knew only about the brand element. A brand element that provides a positive contribution to brand equity, for example, would be one whereby consumers assumed or inferred certain valued associations or responses. Based on its name alone, a consumer might expect ColorStay lipsticks to be long-lasting and SnackWell to be healthful snack foods.

CRITERIA FOR BRAND-ELEMENT CHOICE There are six main criteria for choosing brand elements. The first three (memorable, meaningful, and likable) can be characterized as "brand

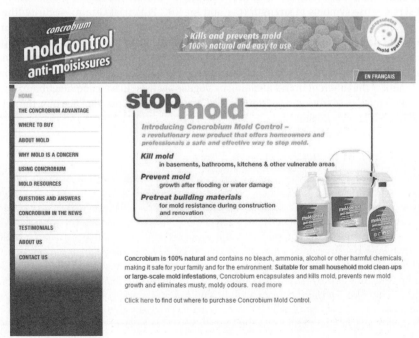

Concrobium carefully chose its brand elements—the colours, lettering, packaging, and label design—when launching its mold-control product.

To learn how Lee Kum Kee is meeting the challenges of developing and preserving traditional Asian brands in Hong Kong, visit www.pearsoned-asia.com/marketingmanagementasia.

building" in terms of how brand equity can be built through the judicious choice of a brand element. The latter three (transferable, adaptable, and protectable) are more "defensive" and are concerned with how the brand equity contained within a brand element can be leveraged and preserved in the face of different opportunities and constraints.

1. *Memorable.* How easily is the brand element recalled? How easily recognized? Is this true at both purchase and consumption? Short brand names such as Tide, WestJet, and Shell can help.

2. *Meaningful.* To what extent is the brand element credible and suggestive of the corresponding category? Does it suggest something about a product ingredient or the type of person who might use the brand? Consider the inherent meaning in names such as Mastercraft tools sold by Canadian Tire, Mop & Glo floor wax, and Lean Cuisine low-calorie frozen entrées.

3. *Likable.* How aesthetically appealing do consumers find the brand element? Is it inherently likable—visually, verbally, and in other ways? Concrete brand names such as Sunkist, Apple MacBook Air, and the BlackBerry Curve evoke much imagery.

4. *Transferable.* Can the brand element be used to introduce new products in the same or different categories? To what extent does the brand element add to brand equity across geographic boundaries and market segments? Although initially an online book seller, Amazon.com was smart enough not to call itself "Books 'R' Us." The Amazon is famous as the world's biggest river, and the name suggests the wide variety of goods that could be shipped, an important descriptor of the diverse range of products the company now sells.

5. *Adaptable.* How adaptable and updatable is the brand element? Betty Crocker has received over eight makeovers through the years—although she is over 75 years old, she doesn't look a day over 35!

6. *Protectable.* How legally protectable is the brand element? How competitively protectable? Can it be easily copied? It is important that names that become synonymous with product categories—such as Kleenex, Kitty Litter, Jell-O, Scotch Tape, Xerox, and Rollerblade—retain their trademark rights and do not become generic.

DEVELOPING BRAND ELEMENTS Brand elements can play a number of brand-building roles.[31] If consumers do not examine much information in making their product decisions, brand elements should be easily recognized and recalled and inherently descriptive and persuasive. Memorable or meaningful brand elements can reduce the burden on marketing communications to build awareness and link brand associations. The different associations that arise from the likability and appeal of brand elements may also play a critical role in the equity of a brand.[32] Bell's two beavers, Frank and Gordon, evoke strong responses in consumers who either love or hate the spokescharacters. Brand names are not the only important brand element. Often, the less concrete brand benefits are, the more important it is that they capture the brand's intangible characteristics. Many financial services use symbols of strength (the lion for RBC Financial Group), security (the key for Great-West Life), or symbols of their Canadian roots (the stylized maple leaf used by London Life).

Like brand names, slogans are an extremely efficient means to build brand equity. Slogans can function as useful "hooks" or "handles" to help consumers grasp what the brand is and what makes it special. They are an indispensable means of summarizing and translating the intent of a marketing program. Think of the inherent brand meaning in slogans such as "like a good neighbour, State Farm is there," "like a rock" (GM trucks), and "Rona—the Canadian how-to people." See how the Avis Group developed its well-known slogan:

Avis Group Holdings Inc.

A classic case of a company using a slogan to build brand equity is that of Avis's "We Try Harder" ad campaign. In 1963, when the campaign was developed, Avis was losing money and was widely considered the number-two car rental company next to market-leader Hertz. When account executives from DDB ad agency met with Avis managers, they asked: "What can you do that we can say you do better than your competitors?" An Avis manager replied "We try harder because we have to." Someone at DDB wrote this down and it became the heart of the campaign. Avis was hesitant to air the campaign because of its blunt, break-the-rules honesty, but also because the company had to deliver on that promise. Yet, by creating buy-in on "We Try Harder" from all Avis employees, especially its front-line employees at the rental desks, the company was able to create a company culture and brand image out of an advertising slogan that lives to this day.[33]

But choosing a name with inherent meaning creates less flexibility, making it harder to add a different meaning or update the positioning.[34]

Designing Holistic Marketing Activities

Brands are not built by advertising. Customers come to know a brand through a range of contacts and touch points: personal observation and use, word of mouth, interactions with company personnel, online or telephone experiences, and payment transactions. A **brand contact** can be defined as any information-bearing experience a customer or prospect has with the brand, the product category, or the market that relates to the marketer's product or service.[35] Any of these experiences can be positive or negative. The company must put as much effort into managing these experiences as it puts into producing its ads.[36]

The strategy and tactics behind marketing programs have changed dramatically in recent years.[37] Marketers are creating brand contacts and building brand equity through many avenues, such as clubs and consumer communities, trade shows, event marketing, sponsorships, factory visits, public relations and press releases, and social-cause marketing. Ted Matthews is the founding partner of a company called Instinct and labels himself as a "Brand Coach." He compared two very different situations to bring home the importance of customer experience and emotional connection in building brand associations:

> The National Ballet of Canada. Soft, gracious and caring, right? Maybe not. Our friend paid $1500 for season tickets, but after two months of waiting and no contact other than the charge to his Visa card, he sent an e-mail to the National Ballet to express his frustration. The subject line: "National Ballet, where are you??" The response: a curt form-letter saying that the tickets would arrive in due course. Compare this with STIHL, the chainsaw maker, a brand that managed to out-love a ballet company! The same friend recently bought a $400 chain saw at Home Hardware. He was given a full demonstration outside the store while his little daughter was given a toy STIHL chainsaw to play with! He was presented with a generous trade-in allowance, a free storage case, and entry to a draw for a new Harley. He was also invited to bring his saw back for free winterizing and storage on-site. Three weeks later, he received a wonderful thank you letter signed by both the Home Hardware dealer and the president of STIHL, promising their future support, and was assured that the warranty had been duly registered.[38]

Regardless of the particular tools or approaches they choose, holistic marketers emphasize three important new themes in designing brand-building marketing programs: personalization, integration, and internalization.

PERSONALIZATION   The rapid expansion of the Internet has created opportunities to personalize marketing.[39] Marketers are increasingly abandoning the mass-market practices that built brand powerhouses in the 1950s, 1960s, and 1970s for new approaches that are in fact a throwback to marketing practices from a century ago, when merchants literally knew their customers by name. *Personalizing marketing* is about making sure the brand and its marketing are as relevant as possible to as many customers as possible—a challenge, given that no two customers are identical. Fairmont Hotels keeps extensive profiles of all its President's Club members, noting everything—like their preferences for pillows, room location, bed size, and gym gear—so that they can welcome and personalize the experience for their regular guests.

To adapt to the increased consumer desire for personalization, marketers have embraced concepts such as experiential marketing, one-to-one marketing, and permission marketing. From a branding point of view, these different concepts are about getting consumers more actively involved with a brand.

Permission marketing, the practice of marketing to consumers only after gaining their express permission, is based on the premise that marketers can no longer use "interruption marketing" via mass-media campaigns. According to Seth Godin, a pioneer in the technique, marketers can develop stronger consumer relationships by respecting consumers' wishes and sending messages only when they express a willingness to become more involved with the brand.[40] Godin believes permission marketing works because it is "anticipated, personal, and relevant."

Permission marketing, like other personalization concepts, does presume consumers know what they want. But in many cases, consumers have undefined, ambiguous, or conflicting preferences. "Participatory marketing" may be a more appropriate concept than permission marketing, because marketers and consumers need to work together to find out how the firm can best satisfy consumers.

INTEGRATION One implication of these new marketing approaches is that the traditional "marketing mix" concept and the notion of the "four Ps" may not adequately describe modern marketing programs. **Integrating marketing** is about mixing and matching marketing activities to maximize their individual and collective effects.[41] As part of integrated marketing, marketers need a variety of different marketing activities that reinforce the brand promise, as CCM did in its 2008 campaign for the U+ skate.

Reebok-CCM Hockey

In a new campaign designed to reveal the DNA of its new U+ skate, Montreal-based Reebok-CCM Hockey developed a 30-second commercial that demonstrated how the U+ skate is an extension of the athlete. The commercial starts at a molecular stage of the body's inner workings: cells merge with other cells, morphing into tissue and bone to eventually form the U+ skate. The tag line used at the end of the commercial, "Built to be a part of you," brings home the powerful message. The television ads rolled out in the "Original Six" hockey markets—Montreal, Toronto, Boston, Detroit, Chicago, and New York—during NHL games. Print ads in hockey magazines across North America supported the television advertising. The campaign also included merchandising and in-store displays featuring the same muscle-morphing images. This was followed by a summer "Guts and Glory Tour." Hosted by CCM, power-skating and stick-handling tutorials were held in 30 major hockey markets across North America.[42]

We can evaluate all integrated marketing activities in terms of the effectiveness and efficiency with which they affect brand awareness and create, maintain, or strengthen brand image.

Let's distinguish between brand identity and image. *Identity* is the way a company aims to identify or position itself or its product. *Image* is the way the public actually perceives it. For the right image to be established in the minds of consumers, the marketer must convey brand identity through every available communication vehicle and brand contact.

Powerful imagery and an integrated marketing campaign have helped to build a strong brand identity for CCM's U+ skate.

Identity should be diffused in ads, annual reports, brochures, catalogues, packaging, company stationery, and business cards. If "IBM means service," this message must be expressed in symbols, colours and slogans, atmosphere, events, and employee behaviour. Although it's fast becoming an economic powerhouse, China is late in the game when it comes to developing these aspects of branding—both image and identity—but some Chinese companies, like Haier, are learning fast.

BUILT TO BE A PART OF YOU.

CCMSPORTS.COM

Haier

If one company can subvert China's old reputation for producing low-cost but shoddy products, it's the appliance manufacturer Haier (pronounced *higher*). Adopting the strategy of successful Japanese and Korean companies, Haier concentrated on building a big market at home and then going on the offensive overseas. Since entering the North American market in 1999, it has become the top-selling brand of compact refrigerators, the kind in college dorm rooms. Yet, the company had to rely on innovation to get past a reputation for producing "me-too" products. The product that really got Haier noticed was a free-standing home wine cooler—a more convenient way of storing wine for the growing number of wine aficionados. Another way Haier is going for a more premium image is by producing a line of eco-friendly, technology-rich appliances priced at US$600–$1500, compared with the US$200–$300 range of its other appliances. Its Genesis top-loading washing machine and a dishwasher with a particle sensor to detect when plates are clean and an automatic shutoff to save energy are among its newest offerings.[43]

Different marketing activities have different strengths and can accomplish different objectives. Marketers should therefore engage in a mixture of activities, each of which plays a specific role in building or maintaining brand equity. Although Michelin may invest in R&D and engage in advertising, promotions, and other communications to reinforce its "safety" brand association, it may also choose to sponsor events to make sure it is seen as contemporary and up-to-date. Marketing programs should be put together so that the whole is greater than the sum of the parts. In other words, the effects of any one option should be enhanced or complemented by the presence of another.

INTERNALIZATION Marketers must now "walk the walk" to deliver the brand promise. They must adopt an *internal* perspective to consider what steps to take to be sure employees and marketing partners appreciate and understand basic branding notions, and how they can help—or hurt—brand equity.[44] **Internal branding** is activities and processes that help to inform and inspire employees.[45] It is critical for service companies and retailers that all employees have an up-to-date, deep understanding of the brand and its promise. Holistic marketers must go even further and train and encourage distributors and dealers to serve their customers well. Poorly trained dealers can ruin the best efforts to build a strong brand image.

Brand bonding occurs when customers experience the company as delivering on its brand promise. All of the customers' contacts with company employees and company communications must be positive.[46] *The brand promise will not be delivered unless everyone in the company lives the brand.* Eli Lilly knows that one of the most potent influences on brand perception is the experience customers have with company personnel.

Eli Lilly

In 2000, Eli Lilly launched a new brand-building initiative with the slogan, "Answers That Matter." The aim was to establish Eli Lilly as a pharmaceutical firm that could give doctors, patients, hospitals, HMOs, and governments trustworthy answers to questions of concern to them. To make sure everyone at Eli Lilly could deliver the right answers, the company developed a comprehensive Brand-to-Action training program. These sessions educated and engaged employees in the role of the corporate brand, Lilly's intended positioning, and how employees' behaviour affected the customer experience and key touch points. Lilly also set up a brand-governance structure, began to measure its corporate brand image, and developed a communications plan for the corporate branding effort.[47]

When employees care about and believe in the brand, they're motivated to work harder and feel greater loyalty to the firm. Some important principles for internal branding are:[48]

1. *Choose the right moment*—Turning points are ideal opportunities to capture employees' attention and imagination. BP found that after it ran an internal branding campaign to accompany its external repositioning, "Beyond petroleum," most employees were positive about the new brand and thought the company was going in the right direction.

2. *Link internal and external marketing*—Internal and external messages must match. IBM's e-business campaign not only helped to change public perceptions of the company in the marketplace, it also sent a signal to employees that IBM was determined to be a leader in the use of Internet technology.

3. *Bring the brand alive for employees*—A professional branding campaign should be based on marketing research and supervised by the marketing department. Internal communications should be informative and energizing. In Alberta's hot economy, internal marketing to employees is an increasingly important element of marketing strategies. Many of the firms that sponsor the famous Calgary Stampede are tying employee programs to their sponsorships to increase motivation and passion. For example, WestJet treated its employees to breakfast and a private bull-riding demonstration, and TransAlta Utilities gave more than 3000 employees a sneak peek at the grandstand show the night before the official opening. Joel Thompson, TransAlta's director of communications, says engaging employees is not only a big part of his company's corporate culture, "it also has important strategic value in a tightening labour market."[49]

Leveraging Secondary Associations

The third and final way to build brand equity is, in effect, to "borrow" it. That is, create brand equity by linking the brand to other information in memory that conveys meaning to consumers (see Figure 9.5).

FIGURE 9.5

Secondary Sources of Brand
Knowledge

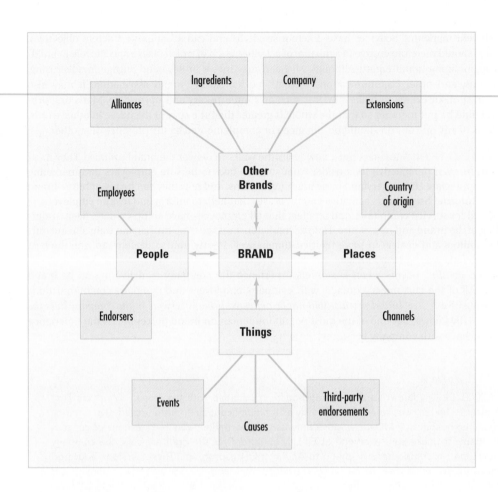

These "secondary" brand associations can link the brand to sources such as the company itself (through branding strategies), countries or other geographical regions (through identification of product origin), and channels of distribution (through channel strategy), as well as to other brands (through ingredient or co-branding), characters (through licensing), spokespeople (through endorsements), sporting or cultural events (through sponsorship), or some other third-party sources (through awards or reviews).

For example, assume Burton—makers of snowboards as well as ski boots, bindings, clothing, and outerwear—decided to introduce a new surfboard called "The Dominator." Burton has over a third of the snowboard market by closely aligning itself with top professional riders and creating a strong amateur-snowboarder community. In creating the marketing program to support the new Dominator surfboard, Burton could attempt to leverage secondary brand knowledge in a number of different ways:

- Burton could leverage associations to the corporate brand by "sub-branding" the product, calling it "Dominator by Burton." Consumers' evaluations of the new product would be influenced by how they felt about Burton and how they felt that such knowledge predicted the quality of a Burton surfboard.

- Burton could try to rely on its rural New England origins, but such a geographical location would seem to have little relevance to surfing.

- Burton could also try to sell through popular surf shops in the hope that their credibility would "rub off" on the Dominator brand.

- Burton could attempt to co-brand by identifying a strong ingredient brand for its foam or fibreglass materials (as Wilson did by incorporating Goodyear tire rubber on the soles of its ProStaff Classic tennis shoes).

- Burton could attempt to find one or more top professional surfers to endorse the surfboard or choose to become a sponsor of a surfing competition or even the entire Association of Surfing Professionals (ASP) World Tour.

- Burton could attempt to secure and publicize favourable ratings from third-party sources like *Surfer* and *Surfing* magazine.

Thus, independent of the associations created by the surfboard itself, its brand name, or any other aspects of the marketing program, Burton may be able to build equity by linking the brand to these other entities.

MEASURING BRAND EQUITY

Given that the power of a brand resides in the minds of consumers and how it changes their response to marketing, there are two basic approaches to measuring brand equity. An *indirect* approach assesses potential sources of brand equity by identifying and tracking consumer brand-knowledge structures.[50] A *direct* approach assesses the actual impact of brand knowledge on consumer response to different aspects of the marketing. "Marketing Insight: The Brand Value Chain" shows how the two measurement approaches can be linked.[51]

The two general approaches are complementary, and marketers can employ both. In other words, for brand equity to perform a useful strategic function and guide marketing decisions, it is important for marketers to fully understand (1) the sources of brand equity and how they affect outcomes of interest, as well as (2) how these sources and outcomes change, if at all, over time. Brand audits are important for the former; brand tracking is important for the latter.

A **brand audit** is a consumer-focused exercise that involves a series of procedures to assess the health of the brand, uncover its sources of brand equity, and suggest ways to improve and leverage its equity. Marketers should conduct a brand audit whenever they consider important shifts in strategic

---

MARKETING **INSIGHT** | THE BRAND VALUE CHAIN

The **brand value chain** is a structured approach to assessing the sources and outcomes of brand equity and the manner in which marketing activities create brand value. The brand value chain is based on several basic premises.

The brand value creation process begins when the firm invests in a marketing program targeting actual or potential customers. Any marketing program investment that can be attributed to brand-value development, either intentional or not, falls into this category: product research, development, and design; trade or intermediary support; and marketing communications.

The marketing activity associated with the program affects the customer "mindset" with respect to the brand. The issue is "In what ways have customers been changed as a result of the marketing program?" This mindset, across a broad group of customers, then results in certain outcomes for the brand in terms of how it performs in the marketplace. This is the collective impact of individual customer actions regarding how much and when they purchase, the price that they pay, and so on. Finally, the investment community considers market performance and other factors such as replacement cost and purchase price in acquisitions to arrive at an assessment of shareholder value in general and the value of a brand in particular.

The model also assumes that a number of linking factors intervene between these stages and determine the extent to which value created at one stage transfers to the next stage. Three sets of multipliers moderate the transfer between the marketing program and the subsequent three value stages: the program multiplier, the customer multiplier, and the market multiplier. The *program multiplier* determines the ability of the marketing program to affect the customer mindset and is a function of the quality of the program investment. The *customer multiplier* determines the extent to which value created in the minds of customers affects market performance. This result depends on contextual factors external to the customer. Three such factors are competitive superiority (how effective is the quantity and quality of the marketing investment of other competing brands), channel and other intermediary support (how much brand reinforcement and selling effort is being put forth by various marketing partners), and customer size and profile (how many and what types of customers, profitable or not, are attracted to the brand). The *market multiplier* determines the extent to which the value shown by the market performance of a brand is manifested in shareholder value. It depends, in part, on the actions of financial analysts and investors.

Sources: Kevin Lane Keller and Don Lehmann, "How Do Brands Create Value," *Marketing Management* (May/June 2003): 27–31. See also Rajendra K. Srivastava, Tasadduq A. Shervani, and Liam Fahey, "Market-Based Assets and Shareholder Value," *Journal of Marketing*, 62, no. 1 (1998): 2–18; M. J. Epstein and R. A. Westbrook, "Linking Actions to Profits in Strategic Decision Making," *MIT Sloan Management Review* (Spring 2001): 39–49. For related empirical insights, see Manoj K. Agrawal and Vithala Rao, "An Empirical Comparison of Consumer-Based Measures of Brand Equity," *Marketing Letters*, 7, no. 3 (1996): 237–247; Walfried Lassar, Banwari Mittal, and Arun Sharma, "Measuring Customer-Based Brand Equity," *Journal of Consumer Marketing*, 12, no. 4 (1995): 11–19.

TABLE 9.2	THE WORLD'S TEN MOST VALUABLE BRANDS IN 2007	
Rank	**Brand**	**2007 Brand Value (Billions of US$)**
1	Coca-Cola	65.32
2	Microsoft	58.71
3	IBM	57.09
4	GE	51.57
5	Nokia	33.70
6	Toyota	32.07
7	Intel	30.95
8	McDonald's	29.40
9	Disney	29.21
10	Mercedes-Benz	23.57

Source: "The Best Global Brands," *BusinessWeek*, August 6, 2007.

direction. Conducting brand audits on a regular basis (e.g., annually) allows marketers to keep their fingers on the pulse of their brands so that they can manage them more proactively and responsively. Audits are particularly useful background for managers as they set up their marketing plans.

Brand-tracking studies collect quantitative data from consumers on a routine basis over time to provide marketers with consistent, baseline information about how their brands and marketing programs are performing on key dimensions. Tracking studies are a means of understanding where, how much, and in what ways brand value is being created, to facilitate day-to-day decision making.

Brand Valuation

Brand equity needs to be distinguished from **brand valuation**, which is the job of estimating the total financial value of the brand. Table 9.2 displays the world's most valuable brands in 2007 according to one ranking.[52] With these well-known companies, brand value is typically over one-half of the total company market capitalization. John Stuart, co-founder of Quaker Oats, said: "If this business were split up, I would give you the land and bricks and mortar, and I would take the brands and trade marks, and I would fare better than you." North American companies do not list brand equity on their balance sheets because of the arbitrariness of the estimate. However, brand equity is given a value by some companies in the United Kingdom, Hong Kong, and Australia. "Marketing Insight: What Is a Brand Worth?" reviews one popular valuation approach.

MANAGING BRAND EQUITY

Effective brand management requires a long-term view of marketing decisions. Because consumer responses to marketing activity depend on what they know and remember about a brand, short-term marketing actions (by changing brand knowledge) necessarily increase or decrease the success of future marketing actions.

Brand Reinforcement

As the company's major enduring asset, a brand needs to be carefully managed so that its value does not depreciate.[53] Many brand leaders of 70 years ago are still today's brand leaders—Wrigley's, Canadian Tire, Coca-Cola, Heinz, and Campbell Soup—but only by constantly striving to improve their goods, services, and marketing. Brand equity is reinforced by marketing actions that consistently convey the meaning of the brand to consumers in terms of (1) what products the brand represents, what core benefits it supplies, and what needs it satisfies, as well as (2) how the brand makes those products superior and which strong, favourable, and unique brand associations should exist in the minds of consumers.[54] Nivea, one of Europe's strongest brands, has expanded its meaning from a skin-cream brand to a skin-care and personal-care brand through carefully designed and

---

| MARKETING INSIGHT | WHAT IS A BRAND WORTH? |

Top brand valuation firm Interbrand has developed a model to formally estimate the dollar value of a brand. Interbrand defines brand value as the net present value of the earnings a brand is expected to generate in the future and believes both marketing and financial analyses are equally important in determining the value of a brand. Its process follows the following five steps (see Figure 9.6 for a schematic overview):

1. **Market Segmentation** The first step in the brand valuation process is to divide the market(s) in which the brand is sold into mutually exclusive segments of customers that help to determine the variances in the brand's economic value.

2. **Financial Analysis** Interbrand assesses purchase price, volume, and frequency to help calculate accurate forecasts of future brand sales and revenues. Specifically, Interbrand performs a detailed review of the brand's equities, industry and customer trends, and historic financial performance across each segment. Once it has established branded revenues, it deducts all associated operating costs to derive earnings before interest and tax (EBIT). It also deducts the appropriate taxes and a charge for the capital employed to operate the underlying business, leaving intangible earnings, that is, the earnings attributed to the intangible assets of the business.

3. **Role of Branding** Interbrand next attributes a proportion of intangible earnings to the brand in each market segment, by first identifying the various drivers of demand, then determining the degree to which the brand directly influences each. The Role of Branding assessment is based on market research, client workshops, and interviews, and represents the percentage of intangible earnings the brand generates. Multiplying the role of branding by intangible earnings yields brand earnings.

4. **Brand Strength** Interbrand then assesses the brand's strength profile to determine the likelihood that the brand will realize forecast earnings. This step relies on competitive benchmarking and a structured evaluation of the brand's market, stability, leadership position, growth trend, support, geographic footprint, and ability to be legally protected. For each segment, Interbrand applies industry and brand-equity metrics to determine a risk premium for the brand. The company's analysts derive the overall brand discount rate by adding a brand-risk premium to the risk-free rate, represented by the yield on government bonds. The brand discount rate, applied to the brand earnings forecast, yields the net present value of the brand earnings. The stronger the brand, the lower the discount rate, and vice versa.

5. **Brand Value Calculation** Brand value is the net present value (NPV) of the forecast brand earnings, discounted by the brand discount rate. The NPV calculation comprises both the forecast period and the period beyond, reflecting the ability of brands to continue generating future earnings.

Increasingly, Interbrand uses brand value assessments as a dynamic, strategic tool to identify and maximize return on brand investment across a whole host of areas.

Source: Interbrand, the Interbrand Brand Glossary, and Jeff Swystun.

---

implemented brand extensions reinforcing the Nivea brand promise of "mild," "gentle," and "caring" in a broader arena.

Reinforcing brand equity requires innovation and relevance throughout the marketing program. Marketers must introduce new products and conduct new marketing activities that truly satisfy their target market. The brand must always be moving forward—but moving forward in the right direction with new and compelling offerings and ways to market them. Brands that fail to do so—such as Kmart, Levi-Strauss, Eaton's, Oldsmobile, and Polaroid—find that their market leadership dwindles or even disappears.

An important consideration in reinforcing brands is the consistency of the marketing support the brand receives, in terms of both amount and kind. Consistency does not mean uniformity and no changes: many tactical changes may be necessary to maintain the strategic thrust and direction of the brand. Unless there is some change in the marketing environment, however, there is little need to deviate from a successful positioning. When change *is* necessary, marketers should vigorously preserve and defend sources of brand equity, as Volvo has discovered over the last few years.

FIGURE 9.6

Interbrand Brand Valuation
Method

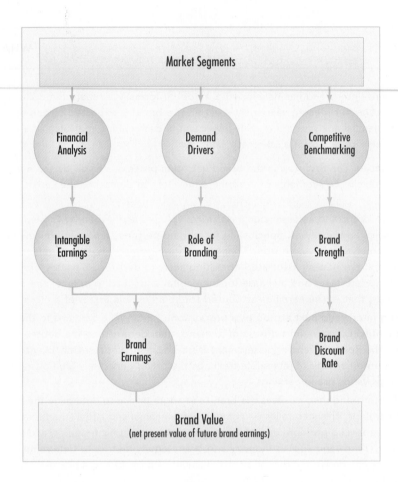

Volvo

In an attempt to woo a different audience, Volvo drifted away from its heritage of safety in the late 1990s to push driving fun, speed, and performance. Purchased by Ford in 1999, the company dropped its ReVOLVOlution-themed ad campaign for the brand and went back to its roots in an attempt to revive sagging sales. Volvo's positioning was updated, however, to convey "active safety" and transcend the brand's boxy, sturdy, "passive safety" image. With product introductions that maximized safety but that still encompassed style, performance, and luxury, Volvo set new records in sales.[55]

In managing brand equity, it is important to recognize the trade-offs between those marketing activities that fortify the brand and reinforce its meaning, such as a well-received new product improvement or a creatively designed ad campaign, and those that attempt to leverage or borrow from existing brand equity to reap some financial benefit, such as a short-term promotional discount that just emphasizes a lower price.[56] At some point, failure to reinforce the brand will diminish brand awareness and weaken brand image.

Brand Revitalization

Changes in consumer tastes and preferences, the emergence of new competitors or new technology, and any new development in the marketing environment could potentially affect the fortunes of a brand. In virtually every product category, there are examples of once prominent and admired brands—such as Eaton's, Smith Corona, Zenith, and Canadian Airlines—that have fallen on hard times or, in some cases, disappeared.[57] Nevertheless, a number of these brands have managed to make impressive comebacks in recent years, as marketers have breathed new life into their customer franchises. Volkswagen, Dr. Scholl's, and Hyperion Solutions have all seen their brand fortunes successfully turned around to varying degrees.

Often, the first place to look in turning around the fortunes of a brand is to understand what the sources of brand equity were to begin with. Are positive associations losing their strength or uniqueness?

Have negative associations become linked to the brand? Decisions must then be made as to whether or not to retain the same positioning or create a new positioning and, if so, which positioning to adopt. Sometimes the positioning is still appropriate and it's the actual marketing program that is the source of the problem because it is failing to deliver on the brand promise. In such instances, a "back to basics" strategy may make sense, as was the case with Harley-Davidson.

Harley-Davidson

Founded in 1903 in Milwaukee, Wisconsin, Harley-Davidson has twice narrowly escaped bankruptcy but is today one of the most-recognized motor-vehicle brands in the world. In dire financial straits in the 1980s, it desperately licensed its name to such ill-advised ventures as Harley-Davidson cigarettes and wine coolers. Although consumers loved the brand, sales were depressed by product-quality problems. Harley's return to greatness began by improving manufacturing processes. Harley also developed a strong brand community in the form of an owners' club, called the Harley Owners Group (HOG), which sponsors bike rallies, charity rides, and other motorcycle events. Harley-Davidson has continued to promote its brand with grassroots marketing efforts and finds itself in the enviable position of having consumer demand exceed what it can supply.[58]

In other cases, however, the old positioning is just no longer viable and a "reinvention" strategy is necessary. Mountain Dew completely overhauled its brand image to become a soft-drink powerhouse. As its history reveals, it is often easiest to revive a brand that is still around but has more or less been forgotten.

Mountain Dew

Introduced in 1969, Pepsi initially marketed Mountain Dew with the countrified tagline "Yahoo Mountain Dew! It'll tickle your innards." By the 1990s, the brand was languishing on store shelves despite an attempt to evolve the image with outdoor-action scenes. To turn the brand around, Mountain Dew updated the packaging and launched ads featuring a group of anonymous young males—the "Dew Dudes"—participating in extreme sports such as bungee jumping, skydiving, and snowboarding while consuming Mountain Dew. The brand slogan became "Do the Dew." The brand's successful pursuit of young soda drinkers led to Mountain Dew challenging Diet Coke to become the number-three-selling soft drink in terms of market share by 2005.

There is obviously a continuum involved with revitalization strategies, with pure "back to basics" at one end and pure "reinvention" at the other end, and many combinations in between. Brand

Harley recovered from a brush with bankruptcy and revitalized its brand with a renewed commitment to quality and to grassroots marketing efforts that appeal to its image-conscious customers.

revitalizations of almost every kind start with the product. General Motors' turnaround with its fading Cadillac brand was fuelled by new model designs that redefined the Cadillac look and styling, such as with the CTS sedan, XLR roadster, and ESV sport utility vehicle.[59]

DEVISING A BRANDING STRATEGY

A firm's **branding strategy** reflects the number and nature of common and distinctive brand elements applied to the different products sold by the firm.

Deciding how to brand new products is especially critical. When a firm introduces a new product, it has three main choices:

1. It can develop new brand elements for the new product.
2. It can apply some of its existing brand elements.
3. It can use a combination of new and existing brand elements.

A firm's use of an established brand to introduce a new product is called **brand extension**. When a new brand is combined with an existing brand, the brand extension can also be called a **sub-brand**, as with Hershey Kisses candy, Adobe Acrobat software, the Toyota Camry automobile, and the CIBC Aerogold Visa. An existing brand that gives birth to a brand extension is referred to as the **parent brand**. If the parent brand is already associated with multiple products through brand extensions, then it may also be called a **family brand**.

Brand extensions can be broadly classified into two general categories:[60] In a **line extension**, the parent brand is used to brand a new product that targets a new market segment within a product category currently served by the parent brand (e.g., through new flavours, forms, colours, added ingredients, and package sizes). Dannon has introduced several types of Dannon yogurt line extensions through the years: Fruit on the Bottom, All Natural, and Fruit Blends. In a **category extension**, the parent brand is used to enter a product category different from that currently served by the parent brand (e.g., Swiss Army watches). Honda has used its company name to cover such different products as automobiles, motorcycles, snowblowers, lawnmowers, marine engines, and snowmobiles. This allows Honda to advertise that it can fit "six Hondas in a two-car garage."

A **brand line** consists of all products—original as well as line and category extensions—sold under a particular brand. A **brand mix** (or brand assortment) is the set of all brand lines that a particular seller makes available to buyers. Many companies are now introducing **branded variants**, which are specific brand lines supplied to specific retailers or distribution channels. They result from the pressure retailers put on manufacturers to provide distinctive offerings. A camera company may supply its low-end cameras to mass merchandisers while limiting its higher-priced items to specialty camera shops. Valentino may design and supply different lines of suits and jackets to different department stores.[61]

A **licensed product** is one whose brand name has been licensed to other manufacturers which actually make the product. Corporations have seized on licensing to push their company name and image across a wide range of products—from bedding to shoes—making it a US$35-billion business.[62] Jeep's licensing program, which now has 600 products and 150 licensees, includes everything from strollers (built for a father's longer arms) to apparel (with Teflon in the denim)—as long they fit the brand's positioning of "Life without Limits." Licensing revenue rose by 20 percent from 2004 to 2006.[63]

Branding Decisions

The first branding-strategy decision is whether to develop a brand name for a product. Today, branding is such a strong force that hardly anything goes unbranded.

Assuming a firm decides to brand its products or services, it must then choose which brand names to use. Four general strategies are often used:

1. *Individual names.* This policy is followed by General Mills (Bisquick, Gold Medal flour, Nature Valley granola bars, Old El Paso Mexican foods, Pop Secret popcorn, Wheaties cereal, and Yoplait yogurt). A major advantage of an individual-names strategy is that the company does not tie its reputation to the product's. If the product fails or appears to have low quality, the company's name or image is not hurt. Companies often use different brand names for different quality lines within the same product class. For example, when Air Canada experimented with low-cost fares, it introduced its Tango service. UTC Technologies also relies on individual names.

UTC Technologies

UTC's brand portfolio includes Otis Elevators, Carrier air conditioners, Sikorsky helicopters, and Pratt & Whitney jet engines. Most of its brands are the names of the individuals who invented the product or created the company decades ago—they have more power and are more recognizable in the business buying marketplace. The parent brand, UTC, is advertised only to small but influential audiences: the financial community and opinion leaders in New York, Toronto, Ottawa, and Washington, D.C. After all, the parent trademark dates to 1972, and employees are loyal to the individual companies owned by UTC. "My philosophy has always been to use the power of the trademarks of the subsidiaries to improve the recognition and brand acceptance, awareness, and respect for the parent company itself," said UTC CEO George David.[64]

2. *Blanket family names.* Many firms, such as Heinz and General Electric, use their corporate brand across their range of products.[65] Development cost is less because there is no need for "name" research or heavy advertising expenditures to create brand-name recognition. Campbell's introduces new soups under its brand name with extreme simplicity and achieves instant recognition. Sales of the new product are likely to be strong if the manufacturer's name is good. Corporate-image associations of innovativeness, expertise, and trustworthiness have been shown to directly influence consumer evaluations.[66] Finally, a corporate branding strategy can lead to greater intangible value for the firm.[67]

3. *Separate family names for all products.* This policy is followed by Sears (Kenmore for appliances, Craftsman for tools, and Homart for major home installations). If a company produces quite different products, it is not desirable to use one blanket family name. Mars, for example, has separate names for its confectionary products such as Snickers, M&Ms, and Mars and its petcare lines: Whiskas, Pedigree, and Cesar.

4. *Corporate name combined with individual product names.* This sub-branding policy is followed by Kellogg (Kellogg's Rice Krispies, Kellogg's Raisin Bran, and Kellogg's Corn Flakes), as well as Honda, Sony, and Hewlett-Packard. The company name legitimizes, and the individual name individualizes, the new product.

Individual names and blanket family names are sometimes referred to as a "house of brands" and a "branded house," respectively, and can be seen as representing two ends of a brand-relationship continuum. Separate family names come in between the two, and corporate-plus-individual names combine them. Not every company follows one strategy. For instance, when FedEx acquired copier chain Kinko's, the branding decision was trickier. Named Kinko's for founder Paul Orfalea's kinky red hair, the copying service had enough brand equity that FedEx didn't want to throw out the name. After numerous focus groups, FedEx decided to co-brand the chain. Hence, the name "FedEx Kinko's."

So, although firms rarely adopt a pure version of any of the four strategies, deciding which general strategy to emphasize depends on several factors, as suggested by Table 9.3.

TABLE 9.3	SELECTING A POSITION IN THE BRAND-RELATIONSHIP SPECTRUM
Towards a Branded House	**Towards a House of Brands**
Does the parent brand contribute to the offering by adding. . .	Is there a compelling need for a separate brand because it will. . .
■ Associations enhancing the value proposition?	■ Create and own an association?
■ Credibility through organizational associations?	■ Represent a new, different offering?
■ Visibility?	■ Retain/capture a customer/brand bond?
■ Communication efficiencies?	■ Deal with channel conflict?
Will the master brand be strengthened by associating with the new offering?	Will the business support a new brand name?

Source: Adapted from David A. Aaker and Erich Joachimsthaler, *Brand Leadership* (New York: Free Press, 2000), Figure 4–6, p. 120.

Two key components of virtually any branding strategy are brand extensions and brand portfolios.

Brand Extensions

Recognizing that one of their most valuable assets is their brands, many firms have decided to leverage that asset by introducing a host of new products under some of their strongest brand names. Most new products are in fact line extensions—typically 80 to 90 percent in any one year. For example, winners of the 2008 Best New Product Awards (which recognize the best food, personal care, and household products launched in Canada based on a survey of 10 000 Canadian consumers) included Ocean Spray 100% Juice Blend Cranberry & Pomegranate, Dove Ultimate Clear antiperspirant, and Charmin Ultra Soft bathroom tissue.[68] Nevertheless, many new products are introduced each year as new brands, such as the mood stabilizer drug Zyprexa, TiVo digital video recorders, and the Mini Cooper automobile.

ADVANTAGES OF BRAND EXTENSIONS Two main advantages of brand extensions are that they can facilitate new product acceptance and provide positive feedback to the parent brand and company.

Improved Odds of New Product Success Consumers can make inferences and form expectations as to the likely composition and performance of a new product based on what they already know about the parent brand itself and the extent to which they feel this information is relevant to the new product.[69] For example, when Sony introduced Vaio, a new personal computer tailored to multimedia applications, consumers may have been more likely to feel comfortable with its anticipated performance because of their experience with and knowledge of other Sony products.

By setting up positive expectations, extensions reduce risk.[70] Because of the potentially increased consumer demand resulting from introducing a new product as an extension, it also may be easier to convince retailers to stock and promote a brand extension. From a marketing communications perspective, an introductory campaign for an extension does not have to create awareness of both the brand and the new product, but instead can concentrate on the new product itself.[71]

Extensions can thus result in reduced costs for the introductory launch campaign, important given that establishing a new brand name in the North American marketplace for a mass-consumer-packaged good can cost over $100 million! They also can avoid the difficulty—and expense—of coming up with a new name. Extensions allow for packaging and labelling efficiencies. Similar or virtually identical packages and labels for extensions can result in lower production costs and, if coordinated properly, more prominence in the retail store by creating a "billboard" effect. For example, Stouffer's offers a variety of frozen entrées with identical orange packaging that increases their visibility when they are stocked together in the freezer. By offering consumers a portfolio of brand variants within a product category, consumers who need a change—because of boredom, satiation, or whatever—can switch to a different product type without having to leave the brand family. Business-to-business companies are even finding that brand extensions are a powerful way to enter consumer markets, as these two name-brand rubber companies discovered.

Groupe Michelin, Goodyear

Both Groupe Michelin and Goodyear, known primarily for their rubber tires, have launched a number of brand extensions in recent years. Although Michelin's extensions have been mainly in the auto-accessories area—from inflation- and pressure-monitoring goods to automotive floor mats—its sports and leisure category now has the potential to overtake its auto-accessories line. So far its brand extensions fall into three categories: (1) automotive and cycle-related products, (2) footwear, apparel, accessories, and equipment for work, sports, and leisure, and (3) personal accessories—gifts and collectibles promoting Michelin culture and heritage featuring Bibendum, the trademark "Michelin Man." Like Michelin, Goodyear has a category of products closely aligned to the automotive industry, such as jack stands and auto-repair tools, but it, too, has branched out into consumer areas. The company is selling its own line of cleaning wipes for windows and upholstery, mechanics' gloves, and garden-hose nozzles, among other products, at Home Depot stores.[72]

Positive Feedback Effects Besides facilitating acceptance of new products, brand extensions can also provide feedback benefits.[73] They can help to clarify the meaning of a brand and its core brand values or improve consumer perceptions of the credibility of the company behind the extension.[74] Thus, through brand extensions, Crayola means "colourful crafts for kids," Aunt Jemima means "breakfast foods," and Weight Watchers means "weight loss and maintenance."

Line extensions can renew interest and liking for the brand and benefit the parent brand by expanding market coverage. Kimberly-Clark's Kleenex unit has a goal of getting facial tissue in every room of the home. This philosophy has led to a wide variety of Kleenex facial tissues and packaging, including scented, ultra-soft, and lotion-infused tissues; boxes with drawings of dinosaurs and dogs for children's rooms and colourful, stylish designs to match room décor; and a "man-sized" box with tissues 50-percent larger than regular Kleenex.

One benefit of a successful extension is that it may also serve as the basis for subsequent extensions.[75] During the 1970s and 1980s, Billabong established its brand credibility with the young surfing community as a designer and producer of quality surf apparel. This success permitted it to extend into other youth-oriented areas, such as snowboarding and skateboarding.

DISADVANTAGES OF BRAND EXTENSIONS On the downside, line extensions may cause the brand name to not be as strongly identified with any one product.[76] Ries and Trout call this the "line-extension trap."[77] By linking its brand to mainstream food products such as mashed potatoes, dried milk, soups, and beverages, Cadbury ran the risk of losing its more specific meaning as a chocolates and candy brand.[78] **Brand dilution** occurs when consumers no longer associate a brand with a specific product or highly similar products and start thinking less of the brand.

If a firm launches extensions consumers deem inappropriate, they may question the integrity and competence of the brand. Different varieties of line extensions may confuse and perhaps even frustrate consumers: Which version of the product is the "right one" for them? Retailers have to reject many new products and brands because they do not have the shelf or display space for them. And the firm itself may become overwhelmed. When Lego decided to become a lifestyle brand and launch its own lines of clothes, watches, and video games, as well as design programs to attract more girls into the brand franchise, it neglected its core market of five- to nine-year-old boys. When plunging profits led to layoffs of almost half its employees in 2004, the firm streamlined its brand portfolio to emphasize its core businesses.[79]

The worst possible scenario with an extension is that not only does it fail, but it harms the parent brand image in the process. Fortunately, such events are rare. "Marketing failures," where insufficient consumers were attracted to a brand, are typically much less damaging than "product failures," where the brand fundamentally fails to live up to its promise. Even then, product failures dilute brand equity only when the extension is seen as very similar to the parent brand. The Audi 5000 car suffered from a tidal wave of negative publicity and word of mouth in the mid-1980s when it was alleged to have a "sudden acceleration" problem. The adverse publicity also spilled over to the 4000 model. But the Quattro was relatively more insulated from negative repercussions, because it was distanced from the 5000 by its more distinct branding and advertising strategy.[80]

Even if sales of a brand extension are high and meet targets, it is possible that this revenue may have resulted from consumers switching to the extension from existing product offerings of the parent brand—in effect *cannibalizing* the parent brand. Intrabrand shifts in sales may not necessarily be so undesirable, as they can be thought of as a form of *pre-emptive cannibalization*. In other words, consumers might have switched to a competing brand instead of the line extension if it had not been introduced into the category. Tide laundry detergent maintains the same market share now as it did 50 years ago because of the sales contributions of the various line extensions (scented and unscented powder, tablet, liquid, and other forms).

One easily overlooked disadvantage to brand extensions is that by introducing a new product as a brand extension, the firm forgoes the chance to create a new brand with its own unique image and equity. Consider the advantages to Disney of having introduced more adult-oriented Touchstone films, to Levi's of having introduced casual Dockers pants, and to Black and Decker of having introduced high-end DeWalt power tools.

SUCCESS CHARACTERISTICS A potential new product extension for a brand must be judged by how effectively it leverages existing brand equity from the parent brand to the new product, as well as how effectively the extension, in turn, contributes to the equity of the parent brand.[81] Crest Whitestrips leveraged Crest's strong dental-care reputation to provide reassurance in the teeth-whitening arena, while also reinforcing its dental-authority image. The most important consideration with extensions is that there is "fit" in the minds of the consumer. Consumers may see a basis for the fit of an extension in its common physical attributes, usage situations, or user types—amongst other characteristics.

"Marketing Memo: Research Insights on Brand Extensions" lists a number of academic research findings on brand extensions.[82] One major mistake in evaluating extension opportunities is failing to take *all* consumers' brand knowledge structures into account and focusing instead on one or perhaps a few brand associations as a potential basis of fit. See what happened when Bic forgot this rule!

Bic

The French company Societé Bic, by emphasizing inexpensive, disposable products, was able to create markets for nonrefillable ballpoint pens in the late 1950s, disposable cigarette lighters in the early 1970s, and disposable razors in the early 1980s. It unsuccessfully tried the same strategy in marketing Bic perfumes in the United States and Europe in 1989. The perfumes—two for women ("Nuit" and "Jour") and two for men ("Bic for Men" and "Bic Sport for Men")—were packaged in quarter-ounce glass spray bottles that looked like fat cigarette lighters and sold for about $5 each. The products were displayed on racks at checkout counters throughout Bic's extensive distribution channels. At the time, a Bic spokeswoman described the new products as extensions of the Bic heritage—"high quality at affordable prices, convenient to purchase, and convenient to use." The brand extension was launched with a US$20-million advertising and promotion campaign containing images of stylish people enjoying themselves with the perfume and using the tagline "Paris in Your Pocket." Nevertheless, Bic was unable to overcome its lack of cachet and negative image associations, and the extension was a failure.[83]

Brand Portfolios

All brands have boundaries—a brand can be stretched only so far. Multiple brands are often necessary to pursue multiple market segments. Any one brand is not viewed equally favourably by all the different market segments that the firm would like to target. Some other reasons for introducing multiple brands in a category include:[84]

1. To increase shelf presence and retailer dependence in the store.
2. To attract consumers seeking variety who may otherwise have switched to another brand.
3. To increase internal competition within the firm.
4. To yield economies of scale in advertising, sales, merchandising, and physical distribution.

The **brand portfolio** (like the Armani brand portfolio described below) is the set of all brands and brand lines a particular firm offers for sale to buyers in a particular category or market segment.

Armani

Armani has set out to create a product line differentiated by style, luxury, customization, and price to compete in three distinct price tiers. In the most expensive Tier I, it sells Giorgio Armani and Giorgio Armani Privé, which are custom-made runway couture products that sell for thousands of dollars. In the more moderately priced Tier II, it offers Emporio Armani, young and modern with more affordable prices, as well as the informal Armani jeans that focus on technology and ecology. In the lower-priced Tier III, the firm sells the more youthful and street-savvy translation of Armani style, AX Armani Exchange, at retail locations in cities and suburban malls.

The hallmark of an optimal brand portfolio is the ability of each brand in it to maximize equity in combination with all other brands in the portfolio. Marketers generally need to trade off market coverage and these other considerations with costs and profitability. A portfolio is too big if profits can be increased by dropping brands; a portfolio is not big enough if profits can be increased by adding brands. The basic principle in designing a brand portfolio is to *maximize market coverage* so that no potential customers are being ignored, but to *minimize brand overlap* so that brands are not competing to gain customer approval. Each brand should be clearly differentiated and appeal to a marketing segment sizable enough to justify its marketing and production costs.[85]

Brand portfolios need to be carefully monitored over time to identify weak brands and kill unprofitable ones.[86] Brand lines with poorly differentiated brands are likely to be characterized by much cannibalization and require pruning.[87] Kellogg's Eggo frozen waffles come in over two dozen flavours. Investors can choose among thousands of mutual funds. Students can choose among hundreds of business schools. For the seller, this spells hypercompetition. For the buyer, it may mean too much choice.

Brands can also play a number of specific roles as part of a portfolio.

FLANKERS   Flanker or "fighter" brands are positioned with respect to competitors' brands so that more important (and more profitable) *flagship brands* can retain their desired positioning. Procter & Gamble markets Luvs diapers in a way to flank the more premium-positioned Pampers. In designing these fighter brands, marketers must walk a fine line. Fighter brands must not be so attractive that they take sales away from their higher-priced comparison brands or referents. At the same time, if fighter brands are seen as connected to other brands in the portfolio in any way (e.g., by virtue of a common branding strategy), then fighter brands must not be designed so cheaply that they reflect poorly on these other brands.

CASH COWS   Some brands may be kept around despite dwindling sales because they still manage to hold on to a sufficient number of customers and maintain their profitability with virtually no marketing support. These "cash cow" brands can be effectively "milked" by capitalizing on their reservoir of existing brand equity. For example, despite the fact that technological advances have moved much of its market to the newer Mach III and Fusion brands of razors, Gillette still sells the older Trac II, Atra, and Sensor brands. Because withdrawing these brands may not necessarily result in customers switching to another Gillette brand, it may be more profitable for Gillette to keep them in its brand portfolio for razor blades.

LOW-END ENTRY-LEVEL   The role of a relatively low-priced brand in the brand portfolio often may be one of attracting customers to the brand franchise. Retailers like to feature these "traffic builders" because they are able to "trade up" customers to a higher-priced brand. For example, BMW introduced certain models into its 3-series automobiles in part as a means of bringing new customers into the brand franchise with the hope of later "moving them up" to higher-priced models when customers decided to trade in their cars.

HIGH-END PRESTIGE   The role of a relatively high-priced brand in the brand family often is to add prestige and credibility to the entire portfolio. For example, one analyst argued that the real value to Chevrolet of its Corvette high-performance sports car was "its ability to lure curious customers into showrooms and at the same time help improve the image of other Chevrolet cars. It does not mean a hell of a lot for GM profitability, but there is no question that it is a traffic builder."[88] Corvette's technological image and prestige were meant to cast a halo over the entire Chevrolet line.

Armani's line of luxury clothing is differentiated to appeal to three distinct price tiers, each with different styles and levels of luxury and customization.

| MARKETING MEMO | RESEARCH INSIGHTS ON BRAND EXTENSIONS |

Academics have studied brand extensions closely. Here is a summary of some of their key research findings.

- Successful brand extensions occur when the parent brand is seen as having favourable associations and there is a perception of fit between the parent brand and the extension product.
- There are many bases of fit: product-related attributes and benefits, as well as non–product-related attributes and benefits related to common usage situations or user types.
- Depending on consumer knowledge of the categories, perceptions of fit may be based on technical or manufacturing commonalties or on more superficial considerations such as whether the extension is related to the needs or situations associated with the parent brand.
- High-quality brands stretch farther than average-quality brands, although both types of brands have boundaries.
- A brand that is seen as prototypical of a product category can be difficult to extend outside the category.
- Concrete attribute associations tend to be more difficult to extend than abstract benefit associations.
- Consumers may transfer associations that are positive in the original product class but become negative in the extension context.
- Consumers may infer negative associations about an extension, perhaps even based on other inferred positive associations.
- It can be difficult to extend into a product class that is seen as easy to make.
- A successful extension can contribute not only to the parent brand image but also enable a brand to be extended even farther.
- An unsuccessful extension hurts the parent brand only when there is a strong basis of fit between the two.
- An unsuccessful extension does not prevent a firm from "backtracking" and introducing a more similar extension.
- Vertical extensions can be difficult and often require sub-branding strategies.
- The most effective advertising strategy for an extension emphasizes information about the extension (rather than reminders about the parent brand).

Source: Kevin Lane Keller, *Strategic Brand Management*, 2nd ed. (Upper Saddle River, NJ: Prentice-Hall, 2003).

CUSTOMER EQUITY

Brand equity should be a top priority of any organization. "Marketing Memo: Twenty-First-Century Branding" offers some contemporary perspectives on enduring brand leadership.

Finally, we can relate brand equity to one other important marketing concept: customer equity. The aim of customer relationship management (CRM) is to produce high customer equity.[89] Although we can calculate it in different ways, one definition of customer equity is "the sum of lifetime values of all customers."[90] As Chapter 5 reviewed, customer lifetime value is affected by revenue and cost considerations related to customer acquisition, retention, and cross-selling.[91]

- *Acquisition* is affected by the number of prospects, the acquisition probability of a prospect, and acquisition spending per prospect.
- *Retention* is influenced by the retention rate and retention spending level.
- *Add-on spending* is a function of the efficiency of add-on selling, the number of add-on selling offers given to existing customers, and the rate of response to new offers.

The brand-equity and customer-equity perspectives certainly share many common themes.[92] Both emphasize the importance of customer loyalty and the notion that value is created by having as many customers as possible pay as high a price as possible.

As they've been put into practice, however, the two perspectives emphasize different things. The customer-equity perspective focuses on bottom-line financial value. It's clear benefit is its quantifiable measures of financial performance. But it offers limited guidance for go-to-market strategies. It largely ignores some of the important advantages of creating a strong brand, such as the ability to

<table>
<tr><td colspan="2">

MARKETING MEMO | TWENTY-FIRST-CENTURY BRANDING

One of the most successful marketers of the past fifteen years, Scott Bedbury played a key role in the rise of both Nike and Starbucks. In his insightful book *A New Brand World,* he offers the following branding principles:

1. *Relying on brand awareness has become marketing fool's gold*—Smart brands are more concerned with brand relevance and brand resonance.
2. *You have to know it before you can grow it*—Most brands don't know who they are, where they've been, and where they're going.
3. *Always remember the Spandex rule of brand expansion*—Just because you can, doesn't mean you should.
4. *Great brands establish enduring customer relationships*—They have more to do with emotions and trust than with footwear cushioning or the way a coffee bean is roasted.
5. *Everything matters*—Even your washroom.
6. *All brands need good parents*—Unfortunately, most brands come from troubled homes.
7. *Big is no excuse for being bad*—Truly great brands use their superhuman powers for good and place people and principles before profits.
8. *Relevance, simplicity, and humanity*—Rather than technology, these will distinguish brands in the future.

Source: Scott Bedbury, *A New Brand World* (New York: Viking Press, 2002). Copyright © 2001 by Scott Bedbury. Used by permission of Viking Penguin, a division of Penguin Group (USA) Inc.
</td></tr>
</table>

attract higher-quality employees, elicit stronger support from channel and supply-chain partners, and create growth opportunities through line and category extensions and licensing. The customer-equity approach can overlook the "option value" of brands and their potential to affect future revenues and costs. It does not always fully account for competitive moves and countermoves, or for social-network effects, word of mouth, and customer-to-customer recommendations.

Brand equity, on the other hand, tends to emphasize strategic issues in managing brands and creating and leveraging brand awareness and image with customers. It provides much practical guidance for specific marketing activities. With a focus on brands, however, managers don't always develop detailed customer analyses in terms of the brand equity they achieve or the resulting long-term profitability they create.[93] Brand-equity approaches could benefit from sharper segmentation schemes afforded by customer-level analyses and more consideration of how to develop personalized, customized marketing programs for individual customers—whether individuals or organizations such as retailers. There are generally fewer financial considerations put into play with brand equity than with customer equity.

Nevertheless, both brand equity and customer equity matter. There are no brands without customers and no customers without brands. Brands serve as the "bait" that retailers and other channel intermediaries use to attract customers from whom they extract value. Customers serve as the tangible profit engine for brands to monetize their brand value.

SUMMARY

1. A brand is a name, term, sign, symbol, or design, or some combination of these elements, intended to identify the goods and services of one seller or group of sellers and to differentiate them from those of competitors. The different components of a brand—brand names, logos, symbols, package designs, and so on—are brand elements.

2. Brands offer a number of benefits to customers and firms. Brands are valuable intangible assets that need to be managed carefully. The key to branding is that consumers perceive differences among brands in a product category.

3. Brand equity should be defined in terms of marketing effects uniquely attributable to a brand. That is: how do

the results of product or service marketing differ with and without brand identification?

4. Building brand equity depends on three main factors: (1) the initial choices for the brand elements or identities making up the brand; (2) the way the brand is integrated into the supporting marketing program; and (3) the associations indirectly transferred to the brand by linking the brand to some other entity (e.g., the company, country of origin, channel of distribution, or another brand).

5. Brand equity needs to be measured in order to be managed well. Brand audits measure "where the brand has been," and tracking studies measure "where the brand is now" and whether marketing programs are having the intended effects.

6. A branding strategy for a firm identifies which brand elements a firm chooses to apply across the various

products it sells. In a brand extension, a firm uses an established brand name to introduce a new product. Potential extensions must be judged by how effectively they leverage existing brand equity to a new product, as well as how effectively the extension, in turn, contributes to the equity of the existing parent brand.

7. Brands can play a number of different roles within the brand portfolio. Brands may expand coverage, provide protection, extend an image, or fulfill a variety of other roles for a firm. Each brand-name product must have well-defined positioning so that brands can maximize coverage and minimize overlap and thus optimize the portfolio.

8. Customer equity is a concept complementary to brand equity that reflects the sum of lifetime values of all customers for a brand.

APPLICATIONS

Marketing Debate: Are Line Extensions Good or Bad?

Some critics vigorously denounce the practice of brand extensions as they feel that too often companies lose focus and consumers become confused. Other experts maintain that brand extensions are a critical growth strategy and source of revenue for firms.

Take a position: Brand extensions can endanger brands *versus* Brand extensions are an important brand-growth strategy.

Marketing Discussion

How can you relate the different models of brand equity presented in this chapter? How are they similar? How are they different? Can you construct a brand-equity model that incorporates the best aspects of each model?

Breakthrough Marketing: Procter & Gamble

Procter & Gamble (P&G) successfully markets nearly 300 brands in 160 countries, including Canada. Its Canadian headquarters is in Toronto, it has manufacturing plants in Belleville and Brockville, and its regional sales offices are in Montreal and Calgary. In 2007, it was named one of the Top Employers in Canada.

P&G is one of the most skillful marketers of consumer packaged goods and is known for its focus on quality, innovation, and unmatched brand-management and extension strategies. The company's scope and accomplishments are staggering. It employs 138 000 people in more than 180 countries; is a global leader in the majority of the 22 different product categories in which it competes; has 23 billion-dollar

global brands; spends more than US$5 million a day on R&D; and has total worldwide sales of more than US$76 billion a year. Its sustained market leadership depends on a number of different capabilities and philosophies:

- Customer knowledge: P&G studies its customers—both end consumers and trade partners—through continuous marketing research and intelligence gathering. It spends more than US$100 million annually on more than 10 000 formal consumer research projects and generates more than 3 million consumer contacts via its email and phone centre. It also puts more emphasis on getting its marketers and researchers out into the field, where they can interact with consumers and retailers in their natural environment.

- Long-term outlook: P&G takes the time to analyze each opportunity carefully and prepare the best product before it commits itself to making this product a success. It struggled with Pringles potato chips for almost a decade before achieving market success.

- Product innovation: P&G is an active product innovator, devoting US$1.8 billion (3.5% of sales) to research and development, an impressively high amount for a packaged-goods company. It employs more science PhDs than Harvard, Queen's, UBC, and MIT combined, and applies for roughly 3000 patents each year. Part of its innovation process is developing brands that offer new consumer benefits. Recent examples include Febreze, an odour-eliminating fabric spray; Swiffer, a cleaning system that more effectively removes dust, dirt, and hair from floors and other hard surfaces; and Mr. Clean Magic Eraser, an innovative cleaning sponge that contains a specialty chemical compound developed by BASF.

- Quality strategy: P&G designs products of above-average quality and continuously improves them. When P&G says "new and improved," it means it. Recent examples include Pantene Ice Shine shampoo, conditioner, and styling gel, and Pampers BabyDry with Caterpillar Flex, a diaper designed to prevent leaks when babies' stomachs shrink at night.

- Brand extension strategy: P&G produces its brands in several sizes and forms. This strategy gains more shelf space and prevents competitors from moving in to satisfy unmet market needs. P&G also uses its strong brand names to launch new products with instant recognition and much less advertising outlay. The Mr. Clean brand has been extended from household cleaner to bathroom cleaner, and even to a car-wash system. Old Spice was successfully extended from men's fragrances to deodorant.

- Multibrand strategy: P&G markets several brands in the same product category, such as Luvs and Pampers diapers and Oral-B and Crest toothbrushes. Each brand meets a different consumer want and competes against specific competitors' brands. At the same time, P&G is careful not to sell too many brands and has begun to reduce its vast array of products, sizes, flavours, and varieties in recent years to assemble a stronger brand portfolio.

- Communication pioneer: With its acquisition of Gillette, P&G became North America's largest advertiser, spending over US$5 billion a year on advertising. A pioneer in using the power of television to create strong consumer awareness and preference, P&G is now taking a leading role in building its brands on the web. It is also infusing stronger emotional appeals into its communications to create deeper consumer connections.

- Aggressive sales force: P&G's sales force has been named one of the top 25 sales forces by *Sales & Marketing Management* magazine. A key to its success is the close ties its sales force forms with retailers, notably Wal-Mart. The 150-person team that serves the retail giant works closely with Wal-Mart to improve both the products that go to the stores and the process by which they get there.

- Manufacturing efficiency and cost cutting: P&G's reputation as a great marketing company is matched by its excellence as a manufacturing company. P&G spends large sums developing and improving production operations to keep its costs among the lowest in the industry, allowing it to reduce the premium prices at which some of its goods sell.

- Brand-management system: P&G originated the brand-management system, in which one executive is responsible for each brand. The system has been copied by many competitors but not often with P&G's success. Recently, P&G modified its general management structure so that each brand category is now run by a category manager with volume and profit responsibility. Although this new organization does not replace the brand-management system, it helps to sharpen strategic focus on key consumer needs and competition in the category.

It's easy to see that P&G's success is based not on doing one thing well, but on successfully orchestrating the myriad factors that contribute to market leadership.

DISCUSSION QUESTIONS

1. Choose one Procter & Gamble brand you have used. What brand elements has P&G used for this product? Rate the brand elements using the Brand Element Choice Criteria.

2. Has the brand been extended? If not, why? If it has, what advantages has the extension created for P&G?

Sources: Robert Berner, "Detergent Can Be So Much More," *BusinessWeek*, May 1, 2006, pp. 66–68; "A Post-Modern Proctoid," *The Economist*, April 15, 2006, p. 68; *P&G Fact Sheet* (December 2006); John Galvin, "The World on a String," *Point* (February 2005): 13–24; Jack Neff, "P&G Kisses Up to the Boss: Consumers," *Advertising Age*, May 2, 2005, p. 18; www.pg.com/en_CA/company/who_we_are/regional_ops.jhtml.

CRAFTING THE BRAND POSITIONING

ten

No company can win if its products and services resemble every other product and offering. As part of the strategic brand-management process, each offering must represent a compelling, distinctive, big idea in the mind of the target market.

Victoria's Secret, purchased by Limited Brands in 1982, has become one of the most identifiable brands in retailing through skillful marketing of women's clothing, lingerie, and beauty products. Most North American women a generation ago did their underwear shopping in department stores and owned few items that could be considered "lingerie." After witnessing women buying expensive lingerie as fashion items from small boutiques in Europe, Limited Brands founder Leslie Wexner felt a similar store model could work on a mass scale on this side of the Atlantic, although it was unlike anything the average shopper would have encountered amid the bland racks at department stores. Wexner, however, had reason to believe that North American women would relish the opportunity to have a European-style lingerie shopping experience. "Women need underwear, but women want lingerie," he observed. Wexner's assumption proved correct: A little more than a decade after he bought the business, Victoria's Secret's average customer bought eight to ten bras per year, compared with the national average of two. To enhance its upscale reputation and glamorous appeal, the brand is endorsed by high-profile supermodels in ads and fashion shows. Since 1985, Victoria's Secret has delivered 25-percent annual sales growth, selling through its stores, catalogues, and company website. Despite its past success, business results were disappointing in early 2008, and CEO Sharen Turney decided it was time to reposition the brand and go back to its roots. Believing the identity of the firm has become too sexy, Turney notes that Victoria's Secret was launched with the idea that Victoria was manor-born and lived in London. "We've so much gotten off our heritage . . . too sexy, and we use the word sexy a lot and really have forgotten the ultra feminine." Thus, the brand is being repositioned and working to become much more relevant to its customers.

Sources: Michael J. Silverstein and Neil Fiske, *Trading Up: The New American Luxury* (New York: Portfolio, 2003); Dylan Machan, "Sharing Victoria's Secret," *Forbes*, June 5, 1995, p. 132.

As the Victoria's Secret case demonstrates, a company can reap the benefits of carving out a unique position in the marketplace. But circumstances often dictate that companies reformulate their marketing strategies and offerings several times. Economic conditions change, competitors launch new assaults, and products pass through new stages of buyer interest and requirements. Marketers must develop strategies for each stage in a product's life cycle. This chapter explores specific ways a company can effectively position and differentiate its offerings to achieve a competitive advantage throughout the life cycle of a product or an offering.

DEVELOPING AND COMMUNICATING A POSITIONING STRATEGY

To learn how Procter & Gamble regained market share in China for Tide from a local competitor by adjusting its brand strategy, visit www.pearsoned-asia.com/ marketingmanagementchina.

All marketing strategy is built on STP—*segmentation*, *targeting*, and *positioning*. A company discovers different needs and groups in the marketplace, targets those needs and groups that it can satisfy in a superior way, and then positions its offering so that the target market recognizes the company's distinctive offering and image. If a company does a poor job of positioning, the market will be confused. This happened when National Car Rental and Alamo Rent-a-Car were combined by their former parent, ANC Rental Corp.

National Car Rental and Alamo Rent-a-Car

Premium brand National traditionally catered to business travellers, whereas Alamo Rent-a-Car received 90 percent of its business from leisure travellers. After the two merged, the dual Alamo/National logos were plastered on everything from airport shuttle buses to workers' polo shirts. Customers of both Alamo and National had problems distinguishing between the brands, even though National's cars typically rented for 10 to 20 percent more than Alamo's. After all, the customers had to stand in the same line in front of the same airport counter, received service from the same rental agents, rode the same shuttle buses, and drove cars from the same fleet. National was most hurt by the lack of differentiation at these key touch points, and its market share fell 5 to 10 percent. Interestingly, after the consolidation of the brands, shuttle-bus frequency improved 38 percent and business travellers were given even more options to bypass the rental counter entirely. Still, in surveys, National renters perceived the buses to be slower, the lines longer, and customer service poorer. The clear implication was that in order for the two brands to maintain their integrity and their positioning with their respective market segments, they needed to be separated.[1]

Positioning is the act of designing the company's offering and image to occupy a distinctive place in the mind of the target market.[2] The goal is to locate the brand in the minds of consumers to maximize the potential benefit to the firm. A good brand positioning helps guide marketing strategy by clarifying the brand's essence, what goals it helps the consumer achieve, and how it does so in a unique way. Everyone in the organization should understand the brand positioning and use it as context for making decisions.

The result of positioning is the successful creation of a *customer-focused value proposition*, a cogent reason why the target market should buy the product. Table 10.1 shows how three companies—Perdue, Volvo, and Domino's—have defined their value proposition given their target customers, benefits, and prices.

Positioning requires that similarities and differences among brands be defined and communicated. Specifically, deciding on a positioning requires determining a frame of reference by identifying the target market and the competition, and identifying the ideal points-of-parity and points-of-difference brand associations. "Breakthrough Marketing: UPS," at the end of this chapter, chronicles how UPS has successfully positioned itself against a formidable opponent, FedEx.

Competitive Frame of Reference

A starting point in defining a competitive frame of reference for a brand positioning is to determine **category membership**—the products or sets of products with which a brand competes and which function as close substitutes. As we discuss in Chapter 11, competitive analysis will consider a whole host of factors—including the resources, capabilities, and likely intentions of various other firms—in choosing those markets where consumers can be profitably served.

TABLE 10.1	EXAMPLES OF VALUE PROPOSITIONS, DEMAND STATES, AND MARKETING TASKS			
Company and Product	**Target Customers**	**Benefits**	**Price**	**Value Proposition**
Butterball (turkey)	Inexperienced or time-pressured cooks	Juicy turkey guaranteed	10% premium	Risk- and hassle-free cooking for anyone lacking time or confidence in preparing a weekday or holiday meal
Volvo (station wagon)	Safety-conscious "upscale" families	Durability and safety	20% premium	The safest, most durable wagon in which your family can ride
Domino's (pizza)	Convenience-minded pizza lovers	Delivery speed and good quality	15% premium	A good pizza, delivered to your door within 30 minutes of ordering, at a moderate price

Deciding to target a certain type of consumer can define the nature of competition because certain firms have decided to target that segment in the past (or plan to do so in the future), or consumers in that segment already may look to certain brands in their purchase decisions. Determining the proper competitive frame of reference requires understanding consumer behaviour and the consideration-sets consumers use in making brand choices. In the United Kingdom, for example, the Automobile Association has positioned itself as the fourth "emergency service"—along with police, fire, and ambulance—to convey greater credibility and urgency. And look at how the City of Victoria has worked to re-position itself:

The City of Victoria

The City of Victoria has long had an image of being an old-fashioned place with a strong British heritage where people still sip afternoon tea. This image wasn't effective in attracting more adventurous travellers, so, for the first time in a decade, Victoria began a campaign to re-position itself, investing $3 million in the process. The familiar shots of gardens, teas, and horse-drawn carriages still hover in the background, but distinct ads were aimed at different audiences. Victoria ranks fourth after Vancouver, Toronto, and Montreal as a gay- and lesbian-friendly destination, and has the second-highest number of restaurants per capita in North America, after San Francisco. Thus, one ad targets the gay and lesbian market with the headline: "Time to experience that tingling sensation," and another states "Meet Victoria. Beautiful, talented, and dead sexy." The most controversial ad, which promotes the city's dining experiences and appears only in culinary magazines is: "Your search for the perfect orgasm is over." Melissa McLean, senior vice-president of marketing and communications at Tourism Victoria, says "Instead of casting off those beloved traditional icons, we wanted to add to them." Research revealed that it was risky to tinker with long-standing perceptions, but there was also a danger that the city's image might become stale without changes. "So in part the brand promise reads that Victoria is a place where old-world traditions meet new-world experiences."[3]

Points-of-Parity and Points-of-Difference

Once the competitive frame of reference for positioning has been fixed by defining the customer target market and nature of competition, marketers can define the appropriate points-of-difference and points-of-parity associations.[4]

POINTS-OF-DIFFERENCE Points-of-difference (PODs) are attributes or benefits consumers strongly associate with a brand, positively evaluate, and believe that they could not find to the same extent with a competitive brand. Strong, favourable, and unique brand associations that make up PODs may be based on virtually any type of attribute or benefit. Examples are Apple (*design*), Nike (*performance*), and Lexus (*quality*). Creating strong, favourable, and unique associations as PODs is a real challenge, but essential in terms of competitive brand positioning. See what Cascades is doing:

Cities, like products, sometimes have to find a more relevant position to attract consumers. This is what the City of Victoria did with its new marketing campaign.

Cascades

Normally quiet Cascades Inc., headquartered in Kingsey Falls, Quebec, wants to shout out to its customers its unique point of difference—that its products are the "real thing" and truly good for the environment. This change in strategy was brought about by an investigation conducted by an Ottawa-based consulting firm that found that 1018 consumer products sold in North America made unsupportable environmental claims. Only paper towels made by Cascades were found to present truly accurate information. Cascades' towels are really made from 100-percent recycled material, and they are biodegradable and compostable. Up until now, Cascades' consumer products—paper towels, toilet paper, and napkins—have been marketed as private-label brands. But given growing environmental concerns by consumers, Cascades decided to flaunt its green credentials in a nationwide television advertising campaign that launched just ahead of Earth Day in April 2008. Cascades has been in the recycling business since its founding in the 1960s. Currently, 77 percent of the material going into its products is recycled fibre. Cascades has deep green credentials. Its mills recycle water, thereby using far less water than most paper makers. One of its mills gets most of its heat from a nearby biogas facility. Cascades has chopped its greenhouse gas emissions by 18 percent in the past three years.[5]

POINTS-OF-PARITY Points-of-parity (POPs), on the other hand, are associations that are not necessarily unique to the brand but may in fact be shared with other brands.[6] These types of associations come in two basic forms: category and competitive.

Category POPs are associations consumers view as essential to be a legitimate and credible offering within a certain product or service category. In other words, they represent necessary—but not necessarily sufficient—conditions for brand choice. Consumers might not consider a travel agency truly a travel agency unless it is able to make air and hotel reservations, provide advice about leisure packages, and offer various ticket-payment and delivery options. Category POPs may change over time due to technological advances, legal developments, or consumer trends, but they are the "greens fees" to play the marketing game.

Competitive POPs are associations designed to negate competitors' PODs. If, in the eyes of consumers, a brand can "break even" in those areas where the competitors are trying to find an advantage *and* can achieve advantages in other areas, the brand should be in a strong—and perhaps unbeatable—competitive position. See how Moores Clothing for Men uses both points-of-parity and points-of-difference.

Cascades is communicating its significant point of difference: that it makes from recycled materials products that are truly green, unlike the "greenwashed" products of other firms.

Moores Clothing for Men

Moores Clothing for Men has grown from one family-owned, Mississauga-based store to be the leading menswear retailer in Canada employing over 1200 people in over 100 stores. From the outset, the founders made the commitment to offer the largest selection of quality menswear (its point-of-parity) at the lowest possible prices (its point-of-difference). Unlike other low-priced retailers, however, Moores' other point of difference is its devotion to customer satisfaction and service. For example, if you want alterations made to purchases at other men's retailers, you may have to wait for a week, while at Moores they offer "while-you-wait hemming." Moores has a clear picture of who its customers are. "He's an average guy on the street, with a house and a mortgage, two kids and a dog. He has a great sense of humour, and he doesn't like to shop, but he likes to look good." High levels of service are made possible because Moores is also an employee-centred company where people have a sense of pride in being a Moores employee. Satisfied employees translate into satisfied customers.[7]

POINTS-OF-PARITY VERSUS POINTS-OF-DIFFERENCE To achieve a point-of-parity (POP) on a particular attribute or benefit, a sufficient number of consumers must believe that the brand is "good enough" on that dimension. There is a "zone" or "range of tolerance or acceptance" with POPs. The brand does not literally have to be seen as equal to competitors, but consumers must feel that the brand does well enough on that particular attribute or benefit. If consumers feel that way, they may be willing to base their evaluations and decisions on other factors potentially more favourable to the brand. A light beer presumably would never taste as good as a full-strength beer, but it would have to taste close enough to be able to effectively compete. With PODs, however, the brand must demonstrate clear superiority. Consumers must be convinced that Louis Vuitton has the most stylish handbags, Energizer is the longest-lasting battery, and Merrill Lynch offers the best financial advice and planning. Often, the key to positioning is not so much in achieving a POD as in achieving POPs!

Visa's POD in the credit-card category is that it is the most widely accepted card, which underscores the category's main benefit of convenience. American Express, on the other hand, has built the equity of its brand by highlighting the prestige associated with the use of its card. Having established their PODs, Visa and American Express now compete by attempting to blunt each other's advantage to create POPs. Visa offers gold and platinum cards to enhance the prestige of its brand and advertises "It's Everywhere You Want to Be" in settings that reinforce exclusivity and acceptability. American Express has substantially increased the number of vendors that accept its cards and created other value enhancements.

Establishing Category Membership

Target customers are aware that Maybelline is a leading brand of cosmetics, Cheerios is a leading brand of cereal, Accenture is a leading consulting firm, and so on. Often, however, marketers must inform consumers of a brand's category membership. Perhaps the most obvious situation is the introduction of new products, especially when the category membership is not apparent.

Category membership can be a special problem for high-tech products. There are also situations where consumers know a brand's category membership, but may not be convinced that the brand is a valid member of the category. When GO Corporation created the first pen-based tablet computer in the early 1990s, analysts and the media responded enthusiastically to the concept, but consumer interest never materialized. GO was eventually purchased by AT&T for use in a pen-computer venture that folded in 1994. With the current development of tablet PCs, however, the pen-computing idea has achieved new life.[8]

There are also situations where consumers know a brand's category membership, but may not be convinced that the brand is a valid member of the category. For example, consumers may be aware that Hewlett-Packard produces digital cameras, but they may not be certain whether Hewlett-Packard cameras are in the same class as those of Sony, Olympus, Kodak, and Nikon. In this instance, HP might find it useful to reinforce category membership.

Brands are sometimes affiliated with categories in which they do not hold membership. This approach is one way to highlight a brand's POD, providing that consumers know the brand's actual membership. With this approach, however, it is important that consumers understand what the brand stands for, and not just what it is *not*. It is important not to be trapped between categories. The Konica e-mini M digital camera and MP3 player was marketed as the "four-in-one entertainment solution" but suffered from functional deficiencies in each of its product applications and languished in the marketplace.[9]

The typical approach to positioning is to inform consumers of a brand's membership before stating its POD. Presumably, consumers need to know what a product is and what function it serves before deciding whether it dominates the brands against which it competes. For new products, initial advertising often concentrates on creating brand awareness and subsequent advertising attempts to craft the brand image.

Occasionally, a company will try to straddle two frames of reference:

BMW

When BMW first made a strong competitive push into the North American market in the early 1980s, it positioned the brand as being the only automobile that offered both luxury *and* performance. At that time, American luxury cars were seen by many as lacking performance, and American performance cars were seen as lacking luxury. By relying on the design of its cars, its German heritage, and other aspects of a well-conceived marketing program, BMW was able to simultaneously achieve (1) a POD on luxury and a POP on performance with respect to performance cars, and (2) a POD on performance and a POP on luxury with respect to luxury cars. The clever slogan "The Ultimate Driving Machine" effectively captured the newly created umbrella category—luxury performance cars.

Although a straddle positioning often is attractive as a means of reconciling potentially conflicting consumer goals, it also carries an extra burden. If the POPs and PODs with respect to both categories are not credible, the brand may not be viewed as a legitimate player in either category. Many early PDAs that unsuccessfully tried to straddle categories ranging from pagers to laptop computers provide a vivid illustration of this risk.

COMMUNICATING CATEGORY MEMBERSHIP There are three main ways to convey a brand's category membership:

1. *Announcing category benefits.* To reassure consumers that a brand will deliver on the fundamental reason for using a category, benefits are frequently used to announce category membership. Thus, industrial tools might claim to have durability and antacids might announce their efficacy. A brownie mix might attain membership in the baked-desserts category by claiming the benefit of great taste and support this benefit claim by possessing high-quality ingredients (performance) or by showing users delighting in its consumption (imagery).

2. *Comparing to exemplars.* Well-known, noteworthy brands in a category can also be used to specify category membership. When Tommy Hilfiger was an unknown, advertising announced his membership as a great American designer by associating him with Geoffrey Beene, Stanley Blacker, Calvin Klein, and Perry Ellis, who were recognized members of that category.

3. *Relying on the product descriptor.* The product descriptor that follows the brand name is often a concise means of conveying category origin. Ford Motor Co. invested more than US$1 billion in a radical new 2004 model named the X-Trainer, which combines the attributes of an SUV, a minivan, and a station wagon. To communicate its unique position—and to avoid association with its Explorer (SUV) and older Country Squire (station wagon) models—the vehicle was designated a "sports wagon."[10]

BMW has achieved market success in the U.S. with a straddle-positioning strategy that emphasizes both luxury and performance.

Prom King   Science Club President

Introducing the most powerful BMW 3 Series Coupe ever. It's a balance of breathtaking design on the outside and endorphin-producing technology on the inside. The Coupe's 300-hp inline six-cylinder, twin-turbo engine is more powerful yet fuel-efficient. Without adding incremental weight, the new high tech steel body improves both handling and agility. Its advanced automatic transmission shifts in milliseconds for a smoother ride. And with Run-flat tires come the confidence and convenience of driving up to 150 miles on a flat. As an independent company, we make sure great ideas live on to become ultimate driving machines.

MARKETING **MEMO** | WRITING A POSITIONING STATEMENT

To communicate a company or brand positioning, marketing plans often include a *positioning statement*. The statement should follow the form: To *(target group and need)*, our *(brand)* is *(the concept)* that *(what the point-of-difference is or does)*. For example: "To *busy professionals who need to stay organized, Palm Pilot* is *an electronic organizer* that *allows backing-up files on a PC more easily and reliably than does competitive products.*" Sometimes the positioning statement is more detailed:

Mountain Dew: To young, active soft-drink consumers who have little time for sleep, Mountain Dew is the soft drink that gives more energy than any other brand because it has the highest level of caffeine. With Mountain Dew, you can stay alert and keep going even when you haven't been able to get a good night's sleep.

Note that the positioning first states the product's membership in a category (Mountain Dew is a soft drink) and then shows its point-of-difference from other members of the group (it has more caffeine). The product's membership in the category suggests the points-of-parity that it might have with other products in the category, but the case for the product rests on its points-of-difference. Sometimes the marketer will put the product in a surprisingly different category before indicating the points of difference.

Sources: Bobby J. Calder and Steven J. Reagan, "Brand Design," in *Kellogg on Marketing*, ed. Dawn Iacobucci (New York: John Wiley & Sons, 2001), p. 61; Alice M. Tybout and Brian Sternthal, "Brand Positioning," in *Kellogg on Marketing*, ed. Dawn Iacobucci (New York: John Wiley & Sons, 2001), p. 54.

Choosing POPs and PODs

Points-of-parity are driven by the needs of category membership (to create category POPs) and the necessity of negating competitors' PODs (to create competitive POPs). In choosing points-of-difference, two important considerations are that consumers find the POD desirable and that the firm has the capabilities to deliver on the POD. As Table 10.2 shows, three criteria can be used to judge both desirability and deliverability.

Marketers must decide at which level(s) to anchor the brand's points-of-differences. At the lowest level are the *brand attributes*, at the next level are the *brand's benefits*, and at the top are the *brand's values*. Thus marketers of Dove soap can talk about its attribute of one-quarter moisturizing cream, or its benefit of softer skin, or its value of being more attractive. Attributes are typically the least desirable level to position. First, the buyer is more interested in benefits. Second, competitors can easily copy attributes. Third, the current attributes may become less desirable.

Research has shown, however, that brands can sometimes be successfully differentiated on seemingly irrelevant attributes *if* consumers infer the proper benefit.[11] Procter & Gamble differentiates its Folger's instant coffee with its "flaked coffee crystals" created through a "unique patented process." In reality, the coffee particle's shape is irrelevant because the crystal immediately dissolves in the hot water. Saying that a brand of coffee is "mountain grown" is irrelevant because most coffee is mountain grown. "Marketing Memo: Writing a Positioning Statement" outlines how positioning can be expressed formally.

Creating POPs and PODs

One common difficulty in creating a strong competitive brand positioning is that many of the attributes or benefits that make up the POPs and PODs are negatively correlated. For example, it might be difficult to position a brand as "inexpensive" and at the same time assert that it is "of the highest quality." Con-Agra must convince consumers that Healthy Choice frozen foods are good for you and taste good. Table 10.3 displays some other examples of negatively correlated attributes and benefits. Moreover, individual attributes and benefits often have positive *and* negative aspects. For example, consider a long-lived brand such as La-Z-Boy recliners. The brand's heritage could suggest comfort, wisdom, and expertise. On the other hand, it could also easily be seen as a negative: it might imply being old-fashioned and not up to date.[12] See how Burberry avoided this pitfall.

Burberry Ltd.

In recent years the trademark Burberry plaid has become one of the world's most recognizable patterns. From its staid place on Burberry raincoats, the plaid began showing up on dog collars, taffeta dresses, bikinis, on gear worn by British soccer hooligans, and, unfortunately, on an increasing number of counterfeit goods. This integral part of Burberry's heritage, called "the check" by those in the fashion industry, had suddenly become a liability due to over-exposure. Consequently, Burberry's sales are sluggish and its CEO, Angela Ahrendt, is attempting to jump-start sales growth in numerous ways. For one, she has studied Burberry's 150-year history to create new brand symbols, such as an equestrian-knight logo that was trademarked by the company in 1901. Handbags will allude to the brand's tradition as a trench-coat maker by featuring leather belt buckles or the quilt pattern that lined Burberry's outerwear. The other tactic Ms. Ahrendt is pushing is to invest aggressively in selling Burberry accessories—handbags, shoes, scarves, and belts—rather than apparel, which now accounts for 75 percent of the company's sales. Not only do these accessories have higher profit margins, but they are also less exposed than clothing to changes in fashion.[13]

TABLE 10.2   JUDGING DESIRABILITY AND DELIVERABILITY FOR POINTS-OF-DIFFERENCE

Desirability Criteria

Relevance

Target consumers must find the POD personally relevant and important.

- The Westin Stamford hotel in Singapore advertised that it was the world's tallest hotel, but a hotel's height is not important to many tourists.

Distinctiveness

Target consumers must find the POD distinctive and superior.

- Splenda sugar substitute overtook Equal and Sweet'N Low to become the leader in its category in 2003 by differentiating itself on its authenticity as a product derived from sugar, without any of the associated drawbacks.[14]

Believability

Target consumers must find the POD believable and credible. A brand must offer a compelling reason for choosing it over the other options.

- Mountain Dew may argue that it is more energizing than other soft drinks and support this claim by noting that it has a higher level of caffeine.
- Chanel No. 5 perfume may claim to be the quintessential elegant French perfume and support this claim by noting the long association between Chanel and haute couture.

Deliverability Criteria

Feasibility

The product design and marketing offering must support the desired association. Does communicating the desired association require real changes to the product itself, or just perceptual shifts in the way the consumer thinks of the product or brand? The latter is typically easier.

- General Motors has had to work to overcome public perceptions that Cadillac is not a youthful, contemporary brand.

Communicability

Consumers must be given a compelling reason and understandable rationale as to why the brand can deliver the desired benefit. What factual, verifiable evidence or "proof points" can ensure consumers will actually believe in the brand and its desired associations?

- Substantiators often come in the form of patented, branded ingredients, such as Nivea Wrinkle Control Crème with Q10 co-enzyme and Herbal Essences hair conditioner with Hawafena.

Sustainability

The firm must be sufficiently committed and willing to devote enough resources to create an enduring positioning. Is the positioning preemptive, defensible, and difficult to attack? Can the favourability of a brand association be reinforced and strengthened over time?

- It is generally easier for market leaders such as ADM, Visa, and SAP, whose positioning is based in part on demonstrable product or service performance, to sustain their positioning than for market leaders such as Fendi, Prada, and Hermes, whose positioning is based on fashion and is thus subject to the whims of a more fickle market.

TABLE 10.3   EXAMPLES OF NEGATIVELY CORRELATED ATTRIBUTES AND BENEFITS

Low price vs. High quality	Powerful vs. Safe
Taste vs. Low calories	Strong vs. Refined
Nutritious vs. Good tasting	Ubiquitous vs. Exclusive
Efficacious vs. Mild	Varied vs. Simple

A straddle brand positioning can help convince customers that the product can accomplish two or more seemingly conflicting benefits, such as Gore-Tex's promise to deliver both breathability and water protection.

Porter Airlines strongly differentiates itself from rivals by providing convenient, fast, high-quality service, along with a number of unexpected amenities.

Unfortunately, consumers typically want to maximize *both* attributes and benefits. Much of the art and science of marketing is dealing with trade-offs, and positioning is no different. The best approach clearly is to develop a product or service that performs well on both dimensions. BMW was able to establish its "luxury and performance" straddle positioning due in large part to product design and the fact that the car was seen as both luxurious and high-performance. Gore-Tex was able to overcome the seemingly conflicting product image of "breathable" and "waterproof" through technological advances.

Some marketers have adopted other approaches to address attribute or benefit trade-offs: launching two different marketing campaigns, each one devoted to a different brand attribute or benefit, linking themselves to any kind of entity (person, place, or thing) that possesses the right kind of equity as a means to establish an attribute or benefit as a POP or POD, and even attempting to convince consumers that the negative relationship between attributes and benefits, if they consider it differently, is in fact positive.

DIFFERENTIATION STRATEGIES

To avoid the commodity trap, marketers must start with the belief that you can differentiate anything. (See "Marketing Memo: How to Derive Fresh Consumer Insights to Differentiate Products and Services.") Brands can be differentiated on the basis of many variables. See what Canada's newest airline, Porter Airlines, has done:

Porter Airlines

porter
flying refined

Porter's food, drink and wireless cost the same as our good manners: nothing.

www.flyporter.com

Billing itself as the airline that "does it right," Porter started flying out of the Toronto City Centre Airport in 2006, specializing in short-haul flights to cities like Ottawa, Montreal, Quebec City, and New York. Using a stylized raccoon as its mascot, Porter promised to "change the way people fly," offering new planes, upscale amenities, a refreshing approach to customer service, speed, and convenience. Customers could reach the island airport from downtown Toronto with a short cab ride, public transit or Porter's complimentary shuttle bus. It is much easier to reach than Pearson International airport, which is located in a suburb, far from downtown. Porter also promised exceptional service, something almost unbelievable for passengers more accustomed to flying Air Canada. Passenger reviews reveal that the new airline has lived up to its promise. One passenger exclaimed, "This is how flying should be—great service on the ground, in the air with a smile, on time departure and arrival." Another stressed, "I would travel with Porter again without hesitation."[15]

MARKETING **MEMO** | HOW TO DERIVE FRESH CONSUMER INSIGHTS TO DIFFERENTIATE PRODUCTS AND SERVICES

In "Discovering New Points of Differentiation," Ian C. MacMillan and Rita Gunther McGrath argue that if companies examine customers' entire experience with a product or service—the consumption chain—they can uncover opportunities to position their offerings in ways that neither they nor their competitors thought possible. MacMillan and McGrath list a set of questions marketers can use to help them identify new, consumer-based points of differentiation:

- How do people become aware of their need for your product and service?
- How do consumers find your offering?
- How do consumers make their final selection?
- How do consumers order and purchase your product or service?
- What happens when your product or service is delivered?
- How is your product installed?
- How is your product or service paid for?
- How is your product stored?
- How is your product moved around?
- What is the consumer really using your product for?
- What do consumers need help with when they use your product?
- What about returns or exchanges?
- How is your product repaired or serviced?
- What happens when your product is disposed of or no longer used?

Source: Ian C. MacMillan and Rita Gunther McGrath, "Discovering New Points of Differentiation," *Harvard Business Review* (July–August 1997): 133–145.

Competitive advantage is a company's ability to perform in one or more ways that competitors cannot or will not match. Michael Porter urged companies to build a sustainable competitive advantage.[16] But few competitive advantages are sustainable. At best, they may be leverageable. A *leverageable advantage* is one that a company can use to lever itself to new advantages, much as Microsoft has leveraged its operating system to Microsoft Office and then to networking applications. In general, a company that hopes to endure must be in the business of continuously inventing new advantages.

Customers must see any competitive advantage as a *customer advantage.* For example, if a company delivers more quickly than its competitors, it won't be a customer advantage if customers don't value speed. Select Comfort has made a splash in the mattress industry with its Sleep Number beds, which allow consumers to adjust the support and fit of the mattress for optimal comfort with a simple numbering index.[17] Companies must also focus on building customer advantages.[18] Then they will deliver high customer value and satisfaction, which leads to high repeat purchases and ultimately to high company profitability.

The obvious means of differentiation, and the means often most compelling to consumers, relate to aspects of the product and service (reviewed in Chapters 12 and 13). Swatch offers colourful, fashionable watches. Subway differentiates itself with healthy sandwiches as an alternative to fast food. In competitive markets, however, firms may need to go beyond these. Consider these other dimensions, among the many that a company can use to differentiate its market offerings:

- *Personnel differentiation.* Companies can have better-trained employees. Porter and Singapore Airlines are well regarded in large part because of their flight attendants. The sales forces of such companies as General Electric, Cisco, Frito-Lay, and Pfizer enjoy an excellent reputation.[19]

- *Channel differentiation.* Companies can more effectively and efficiently design their distribution channels' coverage, expertise, and performance. Back in 1946, pet food was cheap, not too nutritious, and sold exclusively in supermarkets and the occasional feed store. Iams found success selling premium pet food through regional veterinarians, breeders, and pet stores.

- *Image differentiation.* Companies can craft powerful, compelling images. Dove has made its name synonymous with "real beauty," which struck a chord with many women and enabled the product line to build incredible market share. Wine and liquor companies also work hard to develop distinctive images for their brands. Even a seller's physical space can be a powerful image generator. Hyatt Regency developed a distinctive image through its atrium hotel lobbies.

PRODUCT LIFE-CYCLE MARKETING STRATEGIES

A company's positioning and differentiation strategy must change as the product, market, and competitors change over the *product life cycle* (PLC). To say that a product has a life cycle is to assert four things:

1. Products have a limited life.
2. Product sales pass through distinct stages, each presenting different challenges, opportunities, and problems to the seller.
3. Profits rise and fall at different stages of the product life cycle.
4. Products require different marketing, financial, manufacturing, purchasing, and human-resource strategies in each life-cycle stage.

Product Life Cycles

Most product life-cycle curves are portrayed as bell-shaped (see Figure 10.1). This curve is typically divided into four stages: introduction, growth, maturity, and decline.[20]

1. *Introduction.* A period of slow sales growth as the product is introduced to the market. Profits are nonexistent because of the heavy expenses of product introduction.
2. *Growth.* A period of rapid market acceptance and substantial profit improvement.
3. *Maturity.* A slowdown in sales growth because the product has achieved acceptance by most potential buyers. Profits stabilize or decline because of increased competition.
4. *Decline.* Sales show a downward drift and profits erode.

The PLC concept can be used to analyze a product category (liquor), a product form (white liquor), a product (vodka), or a brand (Smirnoff). Not all products exhibit a bell-shaped PLC.[21] Three common alternative patterns are shown in Figure 10.2.

Figure 10.2(a) shows a *growth-slump-maturity pattern*, often characteristic of small kitchen appliances such as handheld mixers and bread makers. Sales grow rapidly when the product is first introduced and then fall to a "petrified" level that is sustained by late adopters buying the product for the first time and early adopters replacing the product.

The *cycle-recycle pattern* in Figure 10.2(b) often describes the sales of new drugs. The pharmaceutical company aggressively promotes its new drug, and this produces the first cycle. Later, sales

FIGURE 10.1

Sales and Profit Life Cycles

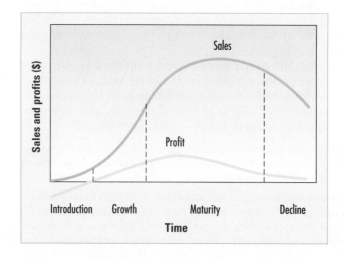

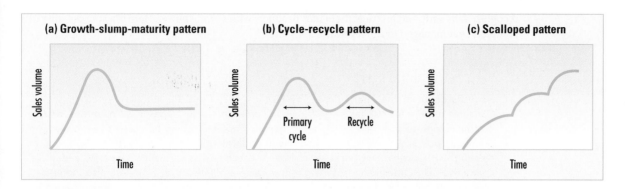

FIGURE 10.2

Common Product Life-Cycle Patterns

start declining and the company gives the drug another promotion push, which produces a second cycle (usually of smaller magnitude and duration).[22]

Another common pattern is the *scalloped PLC* in Figure 10.2(c). Here, sales pass through a succession of life cycles based on the discovery of new product characteristics, uses, or users. Sales of nylon, for example, show a scalloped pattern because of the many new uses for the product—parachutes, hosiery, shirts, carpeting, boat sails, automobile tires—that continue to be discovered over time.[23]

Style, Fashion, and Fad Life Cycles

We need to distinguish three special categories of product life cycles—styles, fashions, and fads (Figure 10.3). A style is a basic and distinctive mode of expression appearing in a field of human endeavour. Styles appear in homes (colonial, ranch, Cape Cod), clothing (formal, casual, funky), and art (realistic, surrealistic, abstract). A style can last for generations, and go in and out of vogue. A fashion is a currently accepted or popular style in a given field. Fashions pass through four stages: distinctiveness, emulation, mass fashion, and decline.[24]

The length of a fashion cycle is hard to predict. One point of view is that fashions end because they represent a purchase compromise, and consumers start looking for missing attributes.[25] For example, as automobiles become smaller, they become less comfortable, and then a growing number of buyers start wanting larger cars. Another explanation is that too many consumers adopt the fashion, thus turning others away. Still another observation is that the length of a particular fashion cycle depends on the extent to which the fashion meets a genuine need, is consistent with other trends in the society, satisfies societal norms and values, and does not exceed technological limits as it develops.[26]

Fads are fashions that come quickly into public view, are adopted with great zeal, peak early, and decline very fast. Their acceptance cycle is short, and they tend to attract only a limited following of those who are searching for excitement or want to distinguish themselves from others. Fads do not survive because they do not normally satisfy a strong need. The marketing winners are those who

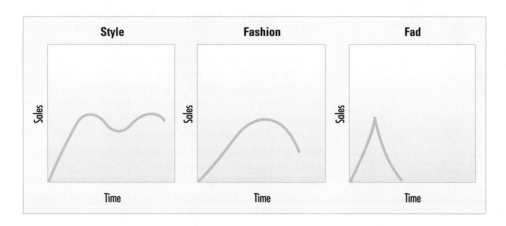

FIGURE 10.3

Style, Fashion, and Fad Life Cycles

recognize fads early and leverage them into products with staying power. Here is a success story of a company that managed to extend a fad's life span:

Trivial Pursuit

Since its debut at the International Toy Fair in 1982, Trivial Pursuit (developed by two Canadian entrepreneurs) has sold 80 million copies in 18 languages in 32 countries, and it remains one of the best-selling adult games. Parker Brothers has kept the product's popularity going by making a new game with updated questions every year. It also keeps creating offshoots—travel packs, a children's version, Trivial Pursuit Genus IV, and an interactive CD-ROM version from Virgin Entertainment Interactive. There are also themed versions of the game that tap into niches tied to various sports, movies, and decades. The game is available in a variety of platforms: an interactive CD-ROM from Virgin Entertainment Interactive; online at its website (www.trivialpursuit.com), and a mobile edition that can be accessed via cell phones. If you are having trouble making dinner conversation on a date—no problem: NTN Entertainment Network has put Trivial Pursuit in about 3000 restaurants.[27]

Marketing Strategies: Introduction Stage and the Pioneer Advantage

Because it takes time to roll out a new product, work out the technical problems, fill dealer pipelines, and gain consumer acceptance, sales growth tends to be slow at this stage.[28] Profits are negative or low and promotional expenditures are at their highest ratio to sales because of the need to (1) inform potential consumers, (2) induce product trial, and (3) secure distribution in retail outlets.[29] Firms focus on those buyers who are the readiest to buy, usually higher-income groups. Prices tend to be high because costs are high.

Companies that plan to introduce a new product must decide when to enter the market. To be first can be rewarding, but risky and expensive. To come in later makes sense if the firm can bring superior technology, quality, or brand strength.

Speeding up innovation time is essential in an age of shortening product life cycles. Being early can pay off. One study found that products that came out six months late—but on budget—earned an average of 33 percent less profit in their first five years; products that came out on time but 50 percent over budget cut their profits by only 4 percent.[30]

Most studies indicate that the market pioneer gains the most advantage.[31] Companies like Campbell, Coca-Cola, Hallmark, and Amazon.com developed sustained market dominance. Carpenter and Nakamoto found that 19 out of 25 companies which were market leaders in 1923 were still the market leaders in 1983, 60 years later.[32] Robinson and Min found that in a sample of industrial-goods businesses, 66 percent of pioneers survived at least ten years, versus 48 percent of the early followers.[33]

What are the sources of the pioneer's advantage?[34] Early users will recall the pioneer's brand name if the product satisfies them. The pioneer's brand also establishes the attributes the product class should possess. The pioneer's brand normally aims at the middle of the market and so captures more users. Customer inertia also plays a role, and there are producer advantages: economies of scale, technological leadership, patents, ownership of scarce assets, and other barriers to entry. Pioneers can have more effective marketing spending and enjoy higher rates of consumer repeat purchases. An alert pioneer can maintain its leadership indefinitely by pursuing various strategies.[35]

The pioneer advantage, however, is not inevitable.[36] Look at the fate of Bowmar (hand calculators), Apple's Newton (personal digital assistant), Netscape (web browser), Reynolds (ballpoint pens), and Osborne (portable computers), market pioneers which were overtaken by later entrants. First movers, like Wikipedia, have to watch out for what some have called "second-mover advantage."

Wikipedia, the Web's first and most popular reader-created encyclopedia, may soon face competition from second-in-the-market Citizendium, a similar site created by Wikipedia's founder.

Wikipedia.org, Citizendium.org

Launched in January 2001, the collaborative Web encyclopedia Wikipedia has ridden its pioneer advantage to become as familiar as eBay and Google. Its five million pages of content are created entirely by volunteers and are available, free of charge, to users in 250 languages. It might seem that no other Web encyclopedia could hope to eclipse Wikipedia's reach and brand equity at this point. Yet, who better than Wikipedia's cofounder, Larry Sanger, to try? Sanger believes his new site, Citizendium, enjoys certain "second mover" advantages that can help it overtake his old site. First, second movers avoid heavy investment in R&D by replicating the first mover's approach. Citizendium will open up as an exact copy of Wikipedia, saving five years of development time. Next, second movers enjoy the advantage of positioning. Because Sanger knows exactly how Wikipedia is perceived, he can use those data to aim Citizendium at what he calls "different social niches." Finally, second movers learn from the pioneer's mistakes. Citizendium is introducing site sponsorship and an editorial team of experts who can prove their expertise in their respective subjects. Wikipedia, watch your back![37]

Steven Schnaars studied 28 industries where the imitators surpassed the innovators.[38] He found several weaknesses among the failing pioneers, including new products that were too crude, were improperly positioned, or appeared before there was strong demand; product-development costs that exhausted the innovator's resources; a lack of resources to compete against larger entering firms; and managerial incompetence or unhealthy complacency. Successful imitators thrived by offering lower prices, improving the product more continuously, or using brute market power to overtake the pioneer. None of the companies that now dominate the manufacture of personal computers—including Dell, Gateway, and Compaq—was a first mover.[39]

Golder and Tellis raise further doubts about the pioneer advantage.[40] They distinguish between an *inventor* (first to develop patents in a new product category), a *product pioneer* (first to develop a working model), and a *market pioneer* (first to sell in the new product category). They also include nonsurviving pioneers in their sample. They conclude that although pioneers may still have an advantage, a larger number of market pioneers fail than has been reported and a larger number of early market leaders (though not pioneers) succeed. Examples of later entrants overtaking market pioneers are IBM over Sperry in mainframe computers, Matsushita over Sony in VCRs, and GE over EMI in CAT-scan equipment.

In a more recent study, Tellis and Golder identify the following five factors as underpinning long-term market leadership: vision of a mass market, persistence, relentless innovation, financial commitment, and asset leverage.[41] Other research has highlighted the importance of the novelty of the product innovation.[42] When a pioneer starts a market with a really new product, as was the case with the Segway Human Transporter, survival can be very challenging. In contrast, when the market is started by an incremental innovation, as was the case with MP3 players with video capabilities, pioneers' survival rates are much higher.

The pioneer should visualize the various product markets it could initially enter, knowing that it cannot enter all of them at once. Suppose market-segmentation analysis reveals the product market segments shown in Figure 10.4. The pioneer should analyze the profit potential of each product market singly and in combination and decide on a market-expansion path. Thus the pioneer in Figure 10.4 plans first to enter product market P_1M_1, then move the product into a second market (P_1M_2), then surprise the competition by developing a second product for the second market (P_2M_2), then take the second product back into the first market (P_2M_1), and then launch a third product for the first market (P_3M_1). If this game plan works, the pioneer firm will own a good part of the first two segments and serve them with two or three products.

Marketing Strategies: Growth Stage

The growth stage is marked by a rapid climb in sales. Early adopters like the product, and additional consumers start buying it. New competitors enter, attracted by the opportunities. They introduce new product features and expand distribution.

Prices remain where they are or fall slightly, depending on how fast demand increases. Companies maintain their promotional expenditures at the same or at a slightly increased level to meet competition and to continue to educate the market. Sales rise much faster than promotional expenditures, causing a welcome decline in the promotion–sales ratio. Profits increase during this stage as promotion costs are spread over a larger volume and unit manufacturing costs fall faster than

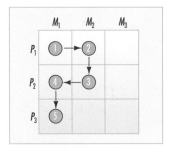

FIGURE 10.4

Long-Range Product-Market Expansion Strategy
(P_1 = Product 1; M_1 = Market 1)

price declines, owing to the producer learning effect. Firms have to watch for a change from an accelerating to a decelerating rate of growth in order to prepare new strategies. See how the launch of Halo 3 helped Microsoft overcome declining sales of its Xbox:

Halo 3

Halo 3, one of the most anticipated titles in video-game history, went on sale on Tuesday, September 25, 2007 in Canada and around the world. Future Shop opened 103 of its 127 stores at midnight as part of the launch. Thousands of eager Canadian fans lined up outside these and 400 other retail stores that opted to open their doors for a midnight sale. To promote the game, Microsoft Canada set up special preview events in Toronto, Vancouver, and Montreal, where passersby could try the game before it went on sale. Visitors could compete head-to-head against one another, or try their luck against a professional gamer from Major League Gaming. Excited consumers responded to the launch and posted their own videos on YouTube. Jason Anderson, who oversaw the launch in Canada, said word-of-mouth buzz was important to draw in gamers, but noted that an extensive promotional campaign was required to reach out to potential customers who weren't hard-core gamers. If new players tried the game, it was hoped they would become part of the Halo franchise once they realized how exciting the game really was. Timing was also important since the team wanted to get Halo 3 onto the Christmas wish lists of non-gamers. The launch was a huge success and Halo 3 became the hottest-selling title in video-game history, generating over US$170 million in first-day sales in North America alone. This beat the $166-million first-day sales record set by the final Harry Potter novel. The game is also credited with increasing sales of Microsoft's Xbox 360 game console. It shipped 1.8 million consoles in the quarter, compared to 900 000 in the same period a year earlier.[43]

During this stage, the firm uses several strategies to sustain rapid market growth:

- It improves product quality and adds new product features and improved styling.
- It adds new models and flanker products (i.e., products of different sizes, flavours, and so forth that protect the main product).
- It enters new market segments.
- It increases its distribution coverage and enters new distribution channels.
- It shifts from product-awareness advertising to product-preference advertising.
- It lowers prices to attract the next layer of price-sensitive buyers.

These market expansion strategies strengthen the firm's competitive position. Consider how Yahoo! and Google have battled for dominance and growth:

Battle of the Brands: Yahoo! versus Google

Founded in 1994 by web-surfing Stanford University grad students, Yahoo! held the number-one place to be on the World Wide Web, until recently. The company grew into more than just a search engine; it became a portal, offering a full-blown package of information and services, from email to online shopping malls. It acquired Overture Services, a competitor of Google's, to help it strengthen its claim as a one-stop shop for advertisers. It went global, putting a strong emphasis on Europe and Asia. But all its efforts at growth and maintaining market share weren't enough, and its "one ad fits all" approach grew stale in the face of Google's more customer-relevant and unobtrusive model, according to one blogger. Google's revenue and profit doubled that of Yahoo! in 2007, and Google surpassed its rival in terms of site visits, according to ComScore Inc. Google's sites had 528 million visitors worldwide in March 2007, a 13-percent gain from the same month a year earlier, while Yahoo! had 476.3 million. The popularity of the Google search engine fueled its growth (it draws 48 percent of the search traffic in North America), but other innovations in its tool-based approach, such as Gmail email service, its online calendar, and its online payment system, have also contributed to Google's surge in popularity.[44]

A firm in the growth stage faces a trade-off between high market share and high current profit. By spending money on product improvement, promotion, and distribution, it can capture a dominant position. It forgoes maximum current profit in the hope of making even greater profits in the next stage.

MARKETING **INSIGHT** | COMPETITIVE CATEGORY DYNAMICS

One of marketing's most astute observers, former U.C. Berkeley professor David Aaker notes that because new categories can represent strategically important threats or opportunities, marketers must be very attentive to the forces that drive their emergence. He cites seven such dynamics that result in new categories.

1. *A new product or service dimension expands the boundaries of an existing category.* In the yogurt business, the "eat-on-the-go" trend led Yoplait to develop Go-Gurt, delivered in a colourful nine-inch tube designed to enhance portability and to appeal to kids. Go-Gurt helped Yoplait forge ahead of Danone's Dannon, a brand it had trailed for decades. A new subcategory had been created in which Dannon was not relevant.

2. *A new product or set of products carves out a fresh niche in an existing category.* The energy-bar market created by PowerBar ultimately fragmented into a variety of subcategories, including those directed at specific segments (such as Luna bars for women) and some possessing specific attributes (such as the protein-associated Balance and the calorie-control bar Pria). Each represented a subcategory for which the original PowerBar was not relevant.

3. *A new competitor devises a way to bundle existing categories into a supercategory.* In the late 1990s, Siebel created Internet-based customer relationship management software by pulling together a host of applications, including customer loyalty programs, customer acquisition, call centres, customer service, customer contact, and sales-force automation. In doing so, Siebel rendered irrelevant, for some customers, the more specialized applications of competitors.

4. *A new competitor repositions existing products or services to create an original category.* In the United Kingdom, Ford positioned its Galaxy minivan in relation to first-class air travel—comfortable enough to be suitable for busy executives. By highlighting attributes far different from those that would appeal to a buyer looking for a family vehicle, the automaker created a new minivan subcategory.

5. *Customer needs propel a new product category or subcategory.* Dual trends—wellness and the use of herbs and natural supplements—have supported a huge new beverage category, healthy-refreshment beverages. It now contains a host of subcategories, including enhanced teas, fruit drinks, soy-based drinks, and specialty waters. The pioneer and category leader is SoBe, which started in 1996 with SoBe Black Tea 3G with ginseng, ginkgo, and guarana, and now has an extensive line of teas, juices, and energy drinks.

6. *A new technology leads to the development of a product category or subcategory.* Asahi reshaped the Japanese beer market by introducing an innovative brewing process that reduced "body" and bitterness while increasing alcohol content. Its new product, Asahi Super Dry, had a taste very different from that of other Japanese lagers and generated a new category, dry beer. As a result, Kirin, for decades the leading brand with a dominant 60-percent share of market, suddenly was not relevant for the many customers attracted to the new category. Asahi's market share— 8 percent when Super Dry was launched in 1986—rose continually until it took share leadership in 1998.

7. *A company exploits changing technologies to invent a new category.* TiVo Inc. created a new category for home-television viewing by combining the personal video player, a computer hard drive, and an electronic program guide, changing the way people watch television. Any new entrant must define itself with respect to TiVo.

Sources: Reprinted from David A. Aaker, "The Relevance of Brand Relevance," *Strategy+Business*, 35 (Summer 2004): 1–10. See also David A. Aaker, *Brand Portfolio Strategy: Creating Relevance, Differentiation, Energy, Leverage, and Clarity* (New York: Free Press, 2004).

Marketing Strategies: Maturity Stage

At some point, the rate of sales growth will slow, and the product will enter a stage of relative maturity. This stage normally lasts longer than the previous stages and poses big challenges to marketing management. Most products are in the maturity stage of the life cycle. The maturity stage has three phases: growth, stable, and decaying maturity. In the first phase, the sales-growth rate starts to decline. There are no new distribution channels to fill. New competitive forces emerge (see "Marketing Insight: Competitive Category Dynamics"). In the second phase, sales flatten on a per-capita basis because of market saturation. Most potential consumers have tried the product, and future sales are governed by population growth and replacement demand. In the third phase, decaying maturity, the absolute level of sales starts to decline, and customers begin switching to other products.

The third phase of maturity poses the most challenges. The sales slowdown creates overcapacity in the industry, which leads to intensified competition. Competitors scramble to find niches. They engage in frequent markdowns. They increase advertising and trade and consumer promotion. They increase R&D budgets to develop product improvements and line extensions. They make deals to supply private brands. A shakeout begins, and weaker competitors withdraw. The industry eventually consists of well-entrenched competitors whose basic drive is to gain or maintain market share.

Dominating the industry are a few giant firms—perhaps a quality leader, a service leader, and a cost leader—that serve the whole market and make their profits mainly through high volume and lower costs. Surrounding these dominant firms is a multitude of market nichers, including market specialists, product specialists, and customizing firms. The issue facing a firm in a mature market is whether to struggle to become one of the "big three" and achieve profits through high volume and low cost or to pursue a niching strategy and achieve profits through low volume and a high margin. Sometimes, however, the market will become polarized between low- and high-end segments, and the firms in the middle see their market share steadily erode. Here's how Swedish appliance manufacturer, Electrolux, has coped with this situation:

Electrolux AB

In 2002, Electrolux began facing a rapidly polarizing appliance market. At one end, low-cost Asian companies such as Haier, LG, and Samsung were applying downward price pressure. At the other end, premium competitors such as Bosch, Sub-Zero, and Viking were continuing to grow at the expense of the middle-of-the-road brands. Electrolux's new CEO, Hans Stråberg, who took over the reins just as the middle was dropping out of the market, decided to escape the middle by rethinking Electrolux's customers' wants and needs. For instance, rather than accept the stratification between low and high, Stråberg segmented the market according to the lifestyle and purchasing patterns of about 20 different types of consumers—"20 product positions" as he calls them. Electrolux now successfully markets its steam ovens to health-oriented consumers, for example, and its compact dishwashers, originally developed for smaller kitchens, to a broader consumer segment interested in washing dishes more often. To companies finding themselves stuck in the middle of a mature market, Stråberg offers these words of advice: "Start with consumers and understand what their latent needs are and what problems they experience . . . then put the puzzle together yourself to discover what people really want to have. Henry Ford is supposed to have said, 'If I had asked people what they really wanted, I would have made faster horses' or something like that. You need to figure out what people really want, although they can't express it."[45]

Some companies abandon weaker products and concentrate on more profitable products and on new products. Yet they may be ignoring the high potential many mature markets and old products still have. Industries widely thought to be mature—autos, motorcycles, television, watches, cameras—were proved otherwise by the Japanese, who found ways to offer new value to customers. Seemingly moribund brands like RCA, Jell-O, and Ovaltine have achieved sales revivals through the exercise of marketing imagination.

Three potentially useful ways to change the course for a brand are market, product, and marketing-program modifications.

MARKET MODIFICATION The company might try to expand the market for its mature brand by working with the two factors that make up sales volume: Volume = number of brand users × usage rate per user, as in Table 10.4.

PRODUCT MODIFICATION Managers also try to stimulate sales by modifying the product's characteristics through quality improvement, feature improvement, or style improvement.

Quality improvement aims at increasing the product's functional performance. A manufacturer can often overtake its competition by launching a "new and improved" product. Grocery manufacturers call this a "plus launch" and promote a new additive or advertise something as "stronger," "bigger," or "better." This strategy is effective to the extent that the quality is improved, buyers accept the claim of improved quality, and a sufficient number of buyers will pay for higher quality. In the case of the canned-coffee industry, manufacturers are using "freshness" to better position their brands in the face of fierce competition from premium rivals, such as store brands whose customers grind their own beans in the store. Kraft's Maxwell House touts coffee sold in its new Fresh Seal packaging and P&G's Folger's ads show how its AromaSeal canisters—plastic, peel-top, resealable, and easy-grip packages—make their ground beans fresher.[46]

TABLE 10.4	ALTERNATIVE WAYS TO INCREASE SALES VOLUME
Expand the Number of Brand Users	**Increase the Usage Rates Among Users**
■ *Convert nonusers.* The key to the growth of air-freight service is the constant search for new users to whom air carriers can demonstrate the benefits of using air freight rather than ground transportation.	■ *Have consumers use the product on more occasions.* Serve Campbell's soup for a snack. Use Heinz vinegar to clean windows. Take Kodak pictures of your pets.
■ *Enter new market segments.* When Goodyear decided to sell its tires via Wal-Mart, Sears, and Discount Tire, it boosted market share from 14 percent to 16 percent in the first year.[47]	■ Have consumers use more of the product on each occasion. Drink a larger glass of orange juice.
■ *Attract competitors' customers.* Marketers of Puffs facial tissues are always wooing Kleenex customers.	■ *Have consumers use the product in new ways.* Use Tums antacid as a calcium supplement.[48]

Feature improvement aims at adding new features (e.g., size, weight, materials, additives, accessories) that expand the product's performance, versatility, safety, or convenience.

This strategy has several advantages. New features build the company's image as an innovator and win the loyalty of market segments that value these features. They provide an opportunity for free publicity and they generate sales force and distributor enthusiasm. The chief disadvantage is that feature improvements are easily imitated; unless there is a permanent gain from being first, the feature improvement might not pay off in the long run.[49]

Style improvement aims at increasing the product's aesthetic appeal. The periodic introduction of new car models is largely about style competition, as is the introduction of new packaging for consumer products. A style strategy might give the product a unique market identity. Yet style competition has problems. First, it is difficult to predict whether people—and which people—will like a new style. Second, a style change usually requires discontinuing the old style, and the company risks losing customers.

Regardless of the type of improvement, marketers must beware a possible backlash. Customers are not always willing to accept an "improved" product, as the now-classic tale of New Coke illustrates.

Coca-Cola

Battered by competition from the sweeter Pepsi-Cola, Coca-Cola decided in 1985 to replace its old formula with a sweeter variation, dubbed New Coke. Coca-Cola spent US$4 million on market research. Blind taste-tests showed that Coke drinkers preferred the new, sweeter formula, but the launch of New Coke provoked a national uproar. Market researchers had measured the taste but had failed to measure the emotional attachment consumers had to Coca-Cola. There were angry letters, formal protests, and even lawsuit threats to force the retention of "The Real Thing." Ten weeks later, the company withdrew New Coke and reintroduced its century-old formula as "Classic Coke," giving the old formula even stronger status in the marketplace.

MARKETING-PROGRAM MODIFICATION Product managers might also try to stimulate sales by modifying other marketing-program elements. They should ask the following questions:

■ *Prices.* Would a price cut attract new buyers? If so, should the list price be lowered, or should prices be lowered through price specials, volume or early-purchase discounts, freight-cost absorption, or easier credit terms? Or would it be better to raise the price to signal higher quality?

■ *Distribution.* Can the company obtain more product support and display in existing outlets? Can more outlets be penetrated? Can the company introduce the product into new distribution channels?

■ *Advertising.* Should advertising expenditures be increased? Should the message or copy be changed? Should the media mix be changed? Should the timing, frequency, or size of ads be changed?

- *Sales promotion.* Should the company step up sales promotion—trade deals, cents-off coupons, rebates, warranties, gifts, and contests?
- *Personal selling.* Should the number or quality of salespeople be increased? Should the basis of sales-force specialization be changed? Should sales territories be revised? Should sales-force incentives be revised? Can sales-call planning be improved?
- *Services.* Can the company speed up delivery? Can it extend more technical assistance to customers? Can it extend more credit?

Marketing Strategies: Decline Stage

Sales decline for a number of reasons, including technological advances, shifts in consumer tastes, and increased domestic and foreign competition. All lead to overcapacity, increased price-cutting, and profit erosion. The decline might be slow, as in the case of sewing machines, or rapid, as in the case of the 5.25" floppy disks. Sales may plunge to zero, or they may petrify at a low level.

As sales and profits decline, some firms withdraw from the market. Those remaining may reduce the number of products they offer. They may withdraw from smaller market segments and weaker trade channels, and they may cut their promotion budgets and reduce prices further. Unfortunately, most companies have not developed a policy for handling aging products.

Unless strong reasons for retention exist, carrying a weak product is very costly to the firm—and not just for the amount of uncovered overhead and profit: There are many hidden costs. Weak products often consume a disproportionate amount of management's time, require frequent price and inventory adjustments, generally involve short production runs in spite of expensive set-up times, require both advertising and sales-force attention that might be better used to make the healthy products more profitable, and can cast a shadow on the company's image. The biggest cost might well lie in the future. Failing to eliminate weak products delays the aggressive search for replacement products. The weak products create a lopsided product mix, long on yesterday's breadwinners and short on tomorrow's.

In handling aging products, a company faces a number of tasks and decisions. The first task is to establish a system for identifying weak products. Many companies appoint a product-review committee with representatives from marketing, R&D, manufacturing, and finance which, based on all available information, makes a recommendation for each product—leave it alone, modify its marketing strategy, or drop it.[50]

Some firms abandon declining markets earlier than others. Much depends on the presence and height of exit barriers in the industry.[51] The lower the exit barriers, the easier it is for firms to leave the industry, and the more tempting it is for the remaining firms to stay and attract the withdrawing firms' customers. For example, Procter & Gamble stayed in the declining liquid-soap business and improved its profits as others withdrew.

The appropriate strategy depends on the industry's relative attractiveness and the company's competitive strength in that industry. A company that is in an unattractive industry but possesses competitive strength should consider shrinking selectively. A company that is in an attractive industry and has competitive strength should consider strengthening its investment. Companies that successfully restage or rejuvenate a mature product often do so by adding value to the original offering.

If the company were choosing between harvesting and divesting, its strategies would be quite different. *Harvesting* calls for gradually reducing a product or business's costs while trying to maintain sales. The first step is to cut R&D costs and plant and equipment investment. The company might also reduce product quality, sales-force size, marginal services, and advertising expenditures. It would try to cut these costs without letting customers, competitors, and employees know what is happening. Harvesting is an ethically questionable strategy, and it is also difficult to execute. Yet many mature products warrant this strategy. Harvesting can substantially increase the company's current cash flow.[52]

When a company decides to drop a product, it faces further decisions. If the product has strong distribution and residual goodwill, the company can probably sell it to another firm. If the company can't find any buyers, it must decide whether to liquidate the brand quickly or slowly. It must also decide on how much inventory and service to maintain for past customers.

Evidence for the Product Life-Cycle Concept

Based on the discussion above, Table 10.5 summarizes the characteristics, marketing objectives, and marketing strategies of the four stages of the PLC. The PLC concept helps marketers interpret product and market dynamics, plan and control, and forecast. One recent research study of 30 product categories unearthed a number of interesting findings concerning the PLC.[53]

TABLE 10.5	SUMMARY OF PRODUCT LIFE-CYCLE CHARACTERISTICS, OBJECTIVES, AND STRATEGIES			
	Introduction	**Growth**	**Maturity**	**Decline**
Characteristics				
Sales	Low sales	Rapidly rising sales	Peak sales	Declining sales
Costs	High cost per customer	Average cost per customer	Low cost per customer	Low cost per customer
Profits	Negative	Rising profits	High profits	Declining profits
Customers	Innovators	Early adopters	Middle majority	Laggards
Competitors	Few	Growing number	Stable number beginning to decline	Declining number
Marketing Objectives				
	Create product awareness and trial	Maximize market share	Maximize profit while defending market share	Reduce expenditure and milk the brand
Strategies				
Product	Offer a basic product	Offer product extensions, service, warranty	Diversify brands and item models	Phase out the weak
Price	Charge cost-plus	Price to penetrate market	Price to match or best competitors'	Cut price
Distribution	Build selective distribution	Build intensive distribution	Build more intensive distribution	Go selective: phase out unprofitable outlets
Advertising	Build product awareness among early adopters and dealers	Build awareness and interest in the mass market	Stress brand differences and benefits	Reduce to level needed to retain hard-core loyals
Sales Promotion	Use heavy sales promotion to entice trial	Reduce to take advantage of heavy consumer demand	Increase to encourage brand switching	Reduce to minimal level

Sources: Chester R. Wasson, *Dynamic Competitive Strategy and Product Life Cycles* (Austin, TX: Austin Press, 1978); John A. Weber, "Planning Corporate Growth with Inverted Product Life Cycles," *Long Range Planning* (October 1976): 12–29; Peter Doyle, "The Realities of the Product Life Cycle," *Quarterly Review of Marketing* (Summer 1976).

New consumer durables show a distinct takeoff, after which sales increase by roughly 45 percent a year, but also show a distinct slowdown, when sales decline by roughly 15 percent a year.

- Slowdown occurs at 34-percent penetration on average, well before the majority of households own a new product.
- The growth stage lasts a little over eight years and does not seem to shorten over time.
- Informational cascades exist, meaning that people are more likely to adopt over time because others already have, instead of because of the making of careful product evaluations. One implication, however, is that product categories with large sales increases at takeoff tend to have larger sales decline at slowdown.

Critique of the Product Life-Cycle Concept

The PLC concept has its share of critics. They claim that life-cycle patterns are too variable in shape and duration. Critics charge that marketers can seldom tell what stage the product is in. A product may appear to be mature when actually it has reached a plateau prior to another upsurge. Critics also charge that, rather than an inevitable course that sales must follow, the PLC pattern is the self-fulfilling result of marketing strategies and that skillful marketing can in fact lead to continued growth.[54] "Marketing Memo: How to Build a Breakaway Brand" provides ten rules for long-term marketing success.

Market Evolution

Because the PLC focuses on what is happening to a particular product or brand rather than on what is happening to the overall market, it yields a product-oriented picture rather than a market-oriented

Arnold Worldwide marketing experts Francis Kelly and Barry Silverstein define a *breakaway brand* as one that stands out, not just in its own product category but from all other brands, and that achieves significant results in the marketplace. Here is a summary of their ten tips for building a breakaway brand:

1. Make a Commitment

Your entire organization, from the top down, needs to make a commitment to build and support a breakaway brand. Get your company behind developing new products that have breakaway attributes.

2. Get a "Chief" Behind It

Few breakaway branding initiatives have a chance of success without the enthusiastic support of your CEO, COO, or CMO. A senior executive at your company must play the role of brand visionary, brand champion, and brand architect.

3. Find Your Brand Truth

Ultimately, the DNA of your breakaway brand is its brand truth. It is what defines and differentiates every breakaway brand. It is the single most important weapon a brand will ever have in the battle for increased awareness, profitability, market share, and even share price.

4. Target a Winning Mind-set

The winning mind-set is the potent, aspirational, shared "view of life" among all core-audience segments. It becomes the filter through which all of your advertising and promotional activities should flow.

5. Create a Category of One

To be a breakaway brand, your brand needs not only to stand apart from others in its own category but also to transcend categories and open a defining gap between itself and its competitors. Then it becomes a category of one.

6. Demand a Great Campaign

Great campaigns are a team sport—they require a partnership between you and your agency to create a campaign that breaks away. Never compromise on a campaign, because without a great campaign, your breakaway brand can fizzle.

7. Tirelessly Integrate

Integration is the name of the game. Depending on the audience you're trying to reach, your campaign might integrate both network and cable TV, print and online advertising, direct mail, email, radio, and nontraditional media—from street marketing to publicity stunts to contests.

8. Take Risks

Today, 80 percent of brands are merely treading water in a sea of grey. Only 20 percent are making waves. You can't afford to have your product sink into the sea (and that may mean taking a calculated risk or two—or three) to ensure that your brand rises above the others.

9. Accelerate New-Product Development

Nothing is more important than differentiating a product in the marketplace—but the only way to rise above me-too branding is to innovate and do something unique with the product. It may mean throwing away an old product brand and reinventing it. Or it may mean starting from scratch.

10. Invest as If Your Brand Depends on It

Building a breakaway brand is serious business, so it takes a serious business investment. Invest in the product, of course— but also in the packaging and a smart integrated marketing campaign. Invest wisely... as if your brand depends on it.

Source: Adapted from Francis J. Kelly III and Barry Silverstein, *The Breakaway Brand* (New York: McGraw-Hill, 2005).

picture. Firms need to visualize a *market's* evolutionary path as it is affected by new needs, competitors, technology, channels, and other developments.[55]

Like products, markets evolve through four stages: emergence, growth, maturity, and decline.

EMERGENCE Before a market materializes, it exists as a latent market. For example, for centuries people have wanted faster means of calculation. The market satisfied this need with abacuses, slide rules, and large adding machines. Suppose an entrepreneur recognizes this need and imagines a technological solution in the form of a small, handheld electronic calculator. He now has to determine the product attributes, including physical size and number of mathematical functions. Because he is market-oriented, he interviews potential buyers and finds that target customers vary greatly in their preferences. Some want a four-function calculator (adding, subtracting, multiplying, and dividing) and others want more functions (calculating percentages, square roots, and logs). Some want a small hand calculator and others want a large one. This type of market, in which buyer preferences scatter evenly, is called a *diffused-preference market.*

The entrepreneur's problem is to design a product optimal for this market. He has three options:

1. The new product can be designed to meet the preferences of one of the corners of the market (*a single-niche strategy*).

2. Two or more products can be simultaneously launched to capture two or more parts of the market (*a multiple-niche strategy*).

3. The new product can be designed for the middle of the market (*a mass-market strategy).*

A small firm does not have the resources for capturing and holding the mass market. A large firm might go after the mass market by designing a product that is medium in size and number of functions. Assume that the pioneering firm is large and designs its product for the mass market. On launching the product, the *emergence* stage begins.[56]

GROWTH If the new product sells well, new firms will enter the market, ushering in a *market-growth stage.* Where will a second firm enter the market, assuming that the first firm established itself in the centre? If the second firm is small, it is likely to avoid head-on competition with the pioneer and to launch its brand in one of the market corners. If the second firm is large, it might launch its brand in the centre against the pioneer. The two firms can easily end up sharing the mass market. Or a large second firm can implement a multiple-niche strategy and surround and box in the pioneer.

MATURITY Eventually, the competitors cover and serve all the major market segments and the market enters the *maturity stage.* In fact, they go further and invade each other's segments, reducing everyone's profits in the process. As market growth slows down, the market splits into finer segments and high *market fragmentation* occurs. This situation is illustrated in Figure 10.5(a), where the letters represent different companies supplying various segments. Note that two segments are unserved because they are too small to yield a profit.

Market fragmentation is often followed by a *market consolidation* caused by the emergence of a new attribute that has strong appeal. This situation is illustrated in Figure 10.5(b) and the expansive size of the X territory.

However, even a consolidated market condition will not last. Other companies will copy a successful brand, and the market will eventually splinter again. Mature markets swing between fragmentation and consolidation. The fragmentation is brought about by competition, and the consolidation is brought about by innovation. Consider the evolution of the paper-towel market:

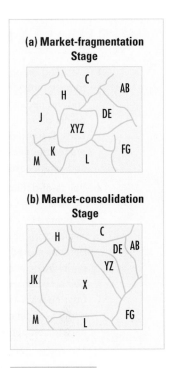

FIGURE 10.5

Market-Fragmentation and Market-Consolidation Strategies

Paper Towels

Originally, homemakers used cotton and linen dishcloths and towels in their kitchens. A paper company, looking for new markets, developed paper towels. This development crystallized a latent market. Other manufacturers entered the market. The number of brands grew and created market fragmentation. Industry overcapacity led manufacturers to search for new features. One manufacturer, hearing consumers complain that paper towels were not absorbent, introduced "absorbent" towels and increased its market share. This market consolidation did not last long because competitors came out with their own versions of absorbent paper towels. The market fragmented again. Then another manufacturer introduced a "super-strength" towel. It was soon copied. Another manufacturer introduced a "lint-free" paper towel, which was subsequently copied. As noted in an earlier example in this chapter, Cascades markets a more environmentally friendly towel made from recycled fibres. Thus, paper towels evolved from a single product to one with various absorbencies, strengths, applications, and environmental benefits. Market evolution was driven by the forces of innovation and competition.

DECLINE Eventually, demand for the present products will begin to decrease, and the market will enter the *decline stage.* Either society's total need-level declines or a new technology replaces the old. For example, shifts in tradition and a trend towards cremation have caused casket makers and funeral homes to reconsider how to conduct their business.[57]

SUMMARY

1. Deciding on positioning requires determination of a frame of reference—by identifying the target market and the nature of the competition—and the ideal points-of-parity and points-of-difference brand associations. Determining the proper competitive frame of reference depends on understanding consumer behaviour and what consumers consider in making brand choices.

2. Points-of-difference are those associations unique to the brand that are also strongly held and favourably evaluated by consumers. Points-of-parity are those associations not necessarily unique to the brand but perhaps shared with other brands. Category point-of-parity associations are associations consumers view as being necessary to a legitimate and credible product offering within a certain category. Competitive point-of-parity associations are those associations designed to negate competitors' points-of-difference.

3. The key to competitive advantage is product differentiation—consumers must find something unique and meaningful about a market offering. These differences may be based directly on the product or service itself or on other considerations such as personnel, channels, and image.

4. Because economic conditions change and competitive activity varies, companies normally find it necessary to reformulate their marketing strategy several times during a product's life cycle. Technologies, product forms, and brands also exhibit life cycles with distinct stages. The general sequence of stages in any life cycle is introduction, growth, maturity, and decline. The majority of products today are in the maturity stage.

5. Each stage of the product life cycle calls for different marketing strategies. The introduction stage is marked by slow growth and minimal profits. If successful, the product enters a growth stage marked by rapid sales growth and increasing profits. There follows a maturity stage in which sales growth slows and profits stabilize. Finally, the product enters a decline stage. The company's task is to identify the truly weak products, develop a strategy for each one, and phase out weak products in a way that minimizes the hardship to company profits, employees, and customers.

6. Like products, markets evolve through four stages: emergence, growth, maturity, and decline.

APPLICATIONS

Marketing Debate: Do Brands Have Finite Lives?

Often, after a brand begins to slip in the marketplace or disappears altogether, commentators observe "all brands have their day." Their rationale is that all brands, in some sense, have a finite life and cannot be expected to be leaders forever. Other experts, however, contend that brands can live forever and their long-term success depends on the skill and insight of the marketers involved.

Take a position: Brands cannot be expected to last forever *versus* There is no reason for a brand to ever become obsolete.

Marketing Discussion

Identify other negatively-correlated attributes and benefits not included in Table 10.3 (page 301). What strategies do firms use to try to position themselves on the basis of pairs of attributes and benefits?

Breakthrough Marketing: UPS

The United Parcel Service was founded by James E. Casey in 1907 to fill a gap in the shipping market: local parcel deliveries. UPS has grown into a US$42.6-billion corporation by clearly focusing on the goal of enabling commerce around the globe. Today, UPS is a global company with one of the most recognized and admired brands in the world. Established in Canada in 1975, it now has over 1040 drop-off boxes, shipping centres, retail stores, and shipping outlets, and employs over 8600 people in Canada. It ships to every address in Canada and is the largest express-carrier and package-delivery company in the world. It is also the leading provider of specialized transportation, logistics, capital, and e-commerce services. But this success didn't come easily.

As the first and largest U.S. national package-delivery company, UPS enjoyed a dominant position until the 1980s when its authority was challenged by upstart Federal Express (as FedEx was then called), which began offering customers a unique "triple play": overnight service, shipment tracking, and volume discounts. UPS launched its next-day service in 1982 and pushed aggressively into this market for the remainder of the decade. In 1987, it expanded its air fleet. By 1990, next-day service accounted for 21 percent of UPS's total business.

Although it attempted to keep pace with FedEx in overnight shipping, UPS sought to differentiate itself by building the largest international shipping network. Between 1988 and 1990, UPS entered 145 countries in Europe and Asia, primarily by buying small local couriers. These acquisitions pushed its share of the foreign shipping market up to 6 percent from 2 percent in 1988. These moves abroad enabled UPS to position itself as the "provider of the broadest range of package-distribution services and solutions in the world." Whereas FedEx offered essentially one service—express air delivery—UPS offered a wider range of shipping options in the air and on the ground, and it shipped to more locations. As a result of its broader scope, by 2000 UPS held a much higher share of on-time package delivery (55 percent) than did FedEx (25 percent).

UPS extended its range of services and solutions in the Internet-enabled world, adding a host of capabilities for e-commerce customers and launching a logistics business that offered manufacturing, warehousing, and supply-chain services. By 2001, UPS was the clear leader in e-commerce shipments, handling 55 percent of all online purchases, compared to 10 percent for FedEx. At the same time, UPS's logistics business was growing 40 percent annually, whereas FedEx was struggling to reverse a decline in its own logistics operations. One of UPS's major wins in this business was designing an online system for Ford that tracked shipments of cars to dealers, which saved Ford an estimated US$1 billion in 2001 by reducing the average number of vehicles in inventory. UPS supported its new suite of shipping and logistics services with the 2002 launch of an approximately US$50-million ad campaign entitled "What Can Brown Do for You?"

UPS expanded its service offering again in 2003, when it rebranded its acquisition Mail Boxes Etc. as The UPS Store. UPS Stores provided one-stop convenience for customers' shipping needs and offered standardized shipping rates that were 20-percent less than the previous average Mail Boxes Etc. rates. In test markets, average UPS shipments from joint-branded stores rose 70 percent annually. FedEx mirrored UPS's move later that year by acquiring Kinko's and establishing FedEx Kinko's joint-branded stores.

In 2006, UPS addressed an area where it was perceived to lag behind FedEx: speed. The resulting campaign, which used the tagline "Covering more ground faster than ever," highlighted UPS's "fast lane" initiative to speed up shipments. To bring home the message to Canadians, UPS sponsored NASCAR driver Dale Jarrett in 2007. Canadians are big NASCAR fans. Research showed that 350 000 Canadian fans have travelled to a race in the U.S., and when race fans are not watching races live, they're watching on TV. To bring home its message of speed, UPS gently mocked itself in its "Race the Truck" TV campaign. In it, UPS executives try to convince an unsure Jarrett to drive their brown delivery truck in a NASCAR race.

DISCUSSION QUESTIONS

1. What are the points-of-parity and the points-of-difference between UPS and FedEx?
2. Which life-cycle pattern best characterizes UPS?
3. What marketing strategies should it use to retain its position in the marketplace?

Sources: www.ups.com/content/ca (viewed March 2008); UPS Annual Report, 2005 and 2002; "Up with Brown," *Brandweek*, January 27, 2003; Charles Haddad, "Ground Wars," *BusinessWeek*, May 21, 2001, p. 64; Brian O'Reilly, "They've Got Mail!" *Fortune*, February 7, 2000, p. 100; Stephen Smith, "Brand Surfin' Safari," *Brandweek*, June 24, 1996, p. 17; Todd Vogel, "Can UPS Deliver the Goods in a New World?" *BusinessWeek*, June 4, 1990, p. 80; Paul Ferriss, "NASCAR, EH?" *Marketing*, February 12, 2007.

IN THIS CHAPTER,
WE WILL ADDRESS
THE FOLLOWING
QUESTIONS:

- How do marketers identify primary competitors?

- How should we analyze competitors' strategies, objectives, strengths, and weaknesses?

- How can market leaders expand the total market and defend market share?

- How should market challengers attack market leaders?

- How can market followers or nichers compete effectively?

PROGRESSIVE®
#1 INSURANCE WEB SITE - 2007 KEYNOTE

1-800-PROGRESSIVE / C

HOME / CAR & VEHICLE INSURANCE / HOME & PROPERTY INSURANCE / INSURANCE BASICS / ARTICLES & BLOGS / VEHICLE RESOURCES / C

» Claims & Concierge

Immediate Response Vehicles
Reporting A Claim
Concierge Service
Claims Offices
Catastrophe Claims
Windshield & Glass
Repair Estimates
Roadside Assistance

Home > Claims & Concierge > **Immediate Response Vehicles**

Immediate Response® Vehicles

ADJUST FONT: A A A

🖨 Print   ✉ Send Page   📋 Link to   🔖 Bookmark

You Could
Save Over $400 on
Your Car Insurance!
Rates & coverage options in about 6 minutes*

Quote & Compare

Buy online and print
your insurance card!

Select:
[Auto ▼]

ZIP Code:
[   ]

QUOTE & COMPARE

RETRIEVE A SAVED QUOTE

Or, shop with a local agent:

[FIND AGENT / GET AGENT QUOTE]

Since 1994, Progressive has used Immediate Response Vehicles (IRVs) — those white SUVs with the Progressive logo on the side — to give your car insurance claim a head start. IRVs transport our claims professionals wherever you need them: to repair shops, tow yards, your house — even the scene of an accident — to help resolve your claim quickly and accurately.

SHARE 🟦🟦🟦🟦🟦🟦

BLOG 🟦🟦🟦🟦🟦

ALSO ON PROGRESSIVE.COM

[UPDATED!]
Auto Tech
Why Can't I Get the Kind of Mileage on the Window Sticke

[NEW!]
Understanding Insurance
What's Covered If Someone Breaks Into Your Car?

[NEW!]
Driving Destinations
Amazing Art Parks in Public Places

CHAPTER 11

DEALING WITH COMPETITION

eleven

Building strong brands requires a keen understanding of competitors, and competition grows more intense every year. New competition is coming from all directions—from global competitors eager to grow sales in new markets, from online competitors seeking cost-efficient ways to expand distribution, from private-label and store brands designed to provide low-priced alternatives, and from brand extensions from strong megabrands leveraging their strengths to move into new categories. One good way to start to deal with competition is through creatively designed and well-executed marketing programs.

When it was still a relatively minor player in the insurance industry, Progressive Insurance specialized in a small niche of the auto insurance business that most other insurers ignored: "nonstandard" insurance typically purchased by motorists whose driving records are marred by accidents and moving-violations. By collecting and analyzing loss data in automobile insurance better than anyone else, Progressive acquired a solid understanding of what it costs to serve various types of customers and how to make a profit serving potentially lucrative but high-risk customers no one else wanted to cover. But Progressive gained its truly sustainable competitive advantage in the mid-1990s when it became one of the first auto insurance companies to sell directly to consumers via the Internet. The company's early adoption of technology enabled it to offer a unique service: In addition to providing free online quotes for its own policies, Progressive also provided quotes from up to three competitors, information that until then had been available only through insurance agents. In addition to saving its customers time, Progressive was able to save them money by showing that, in many cases, its policies were more competitively priced. Once Progressive won new customers' business, it mobilized an army of claims adjusters who speed right to an accident scene—and often cut a cheque right on the spot. It has further enhanced its competitiveness by adding innovative service features such as an "accident concierge" who handles all aspects of the claims and repair process for customers, and online policy management that enables customers to make payments and change coverage at any time. In recent years, Progressive grew an average of 17 percent per year. Today it is the third-largest auto insurer in North America, serving over 12 million customers.

Sources: Louise Lee, "Can Progressive Stay in Gear?" *BusinessWeek*, August 8, 2004, p. 44; Robert J. Dolan and Hermann Simon, "Power Pricers," *Across the Board* (May 1997): 18–19; Carol J. Loomis, "Sex. Reefer? And Auto Insurance," *Fortune*, August 7, 1995, p. 76; www.progressive.com (viewed May 2008).

To effectively devise and implement the best possible brand-positioning strategies, companies must pay keen attention to their competitors. Markets have become too competitive for companies to focus just on the consumer alone. This chapter examines the role competition plays and how marketers can best manage their brands, depending on their market position.[1]

COMPETITIVE FORCES

Michael Porter has identified five forces that determine the intrinsic long-run attractiveness of a market or market segment: industry competitors, potential entrants, substitutes, buyers, and suppliers. His model is shown in Figure 11.1. The threats these forces pose are as follows:

1. *Threat of intense segment rivalry.* A segment is unattractive if it already contains numerous, strong, or aggressive competitors. It is even more unattractive if it is stable or declining, if plant capacity additions are done in large increments, if fixed costs are high, if exit barriers are high, or if competitors have high stakes in staying in the segment. These conditions will lead to frequent price wars, advertising battles, and new-product introductions, and will make it expensive to compete. The cellular phone market has seen fierce competition due to segment rivalry.

2. *Threat of new entrants.* A segment's attractiveness varies with the height of its entry and exit barriers.[2] The most attractive segment is one in which entry barriers are high and exit barriers are low. Few new firms can enter the industry, and poorly performing firms can easily exit. When both entry and exit barriers are high, profit potential is high, but firms face more risk because firms that perform poorly stay in and fight it out. When both entry and exit barriers are low, firms easily enter and leave the industry and the returns are stable and low. The worst case is when entry barriers are low and exit barriers are high: firms enter during good times but find it hard to leave during bad times. The result is chronic overcapacity and depressed earnings for all. The airline industry has low entry barriers but high exit barriers, leaving all the companies struggling during economic downturns.

3. *Threat of substitute products.* A segment is unattractive when there are actual or potential substitutes for the product. Substitutes place a limit on prices and on profits. The company has to monitor price trends closely. If technology advances or competition increases in these substitute industries, prices and profits in the segment are likely to fall. Greyhound buses and Via Rail trains have seen profitability threatened by the rise of air travel.

4. *Threat of buyers' growing bargaining power.* A segment is unattractive if buyers possess strong or growing bargaining power. The rise of retail giants such as Wal-Mart has led some analysts to conclude that the potential profitability of packaged-good companies will become curtailed. Buyers' bargaining power grows when they become more concentrated or organized, when the product represents a significant fraction of the buyers' costs, when the product is undifferentiated, when the buyers' switching costs are low, when buyers are price sensitive because of low profits, or when buyers can integrate upstream. In Canada, grocery retailing is very concentrated in the hands of a few chains such as Loblaws, Sobeys, Canada Safeway, and Metro,

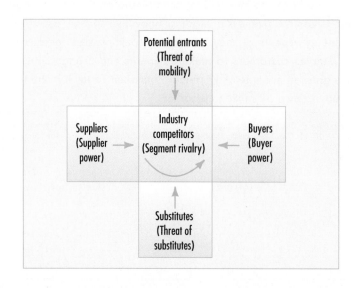

FIGURE 11.1

Five Forces Determining Segment Structural Attractiveness

Source: Reprinted with the permission of the Free Press, an imprint of Simon & Schuster, from Michael E. Porter, *Competitive Advantage: Creating and Sustaining Superior Performance.* Copyright © 1985 by Michael E. Porter.

further curtailing manufacturers' power. To protect themselves, sellers might select buyers which have the least power to negotiate or switch suppliers. A better defence consists of developing superior offers that strong buyers cannot refuse.

5. *Threat of suppliers' growing bargaining power.* A segment is unattractive if the company's suppliers are able to raise prices or reduce quantity supplied. Oil companies such as BP, Chevron-Texaco, ExxonMobil, Imperial Oil, Petro-Canada, and Shell are at the mercy of the amount of oil reserves and the actions of oil-supplying cartels like OPEC. Suppliers tend to be powerful when they are concentrated or organized, when there are few substitutes, when the supplied product is an important input, when the costs of switching suppliers are high, and when the suppliers can integrate downstream. The best defences are to build win–win relationships with suppliers or use multiple supply sources.

IDENTIFYING COMPETITORS

It would seem a simple task for a company to identify its competitors. PepsiCo knows that Coca-Cola's Dasani is the major bottled-water competitor for its Aquafina brand; RBC Financial Group knows that TD Canada Trust is a major banking competitor; and Expedia.ca knows that a major online competitor is Travelocity.ca. However, the range of a company's actual and potential competitors can be much broader. And a company is more likely to be hurt by emerging competitors or new technologies than by current competitors.

In recent years, for instance, a number of new "emerging giants" have arisen from developing countries, and these nimble competitors are not only competing with multinationals on their home turf but also becoming global forces in their own right. They have gained competitive advantage by exploiting their knowledge of local factors of production—capital and talent—and supply chains in order to build world-class businesses.

Indian Software & Services Companies

Tata Consultancy Services, Infosys Technologies, Wipro, and Satyam Computer Services, all of India, have succeeded in catering to the global demand for software and services, even triumphing against multinational software-service providers such as Accenture and EDS. These multinationals have a hard time sorting out talent in a market where the level of people's skills and the quality of educational institutions vary dramatically. Indian companies know their way around the human-resources market and are hiring educated, skilled engineers and technical graduates at salaries much lower than those that similar employees in developed markets earn. Even as the talent in urban centres such as Bangalore and Delhi gets scarce, the Indian companies will keep their competitive advantage by knowing how to find qualified employees in India's second-tier cities.[3]

Inventec

Taiwan-based Inventec has become one of the world's largest manufacturers of notebook computers, PCs, and servers by exploiting its knowledge of local factors of production. It makes products in China and supplies them to giants such as Hewlett-Packard and Toshiba, and also makes cell phones and MP3 players for other multinational customers. Inventec's customers get the low cost of manufacturing products in China without investing in factories there, and they can also use China's talented software and hardware professionals. It won't be long, however, before Inventec begins competing directly with its own customers; it has already started selling computers in Taiwan and China under its own retail brand name.[4]

We can examine competition from both an industry and a marketing point of view.[5]

An **industry** is a group of firms that offer a product or class of products that are close substitutes for one another. Industries are classified according to number of sellers; degree of product differentiation; presence or absence of entry, mobility, and exit barriers; cost structure; degree of vertical integration; and degree of globalization.

Using the **market** approach, we define *competitors* as companies that satisfy the same customer need. For example, a customer who buys a word-processing package really wants "writing ability"—a need that can also be satisfied by pencils, pens, or typewriters. Marketers must overcome "marketing myopia" and stop defining competition in traditional category terms.[6] Coca-Cola, focused on its soft-drink business, missed seeing the market for coffee bars and fresh fruit-juice bars that eventually impinged on its soft-drink business.

The market concept of competition reveals a broader set of actual and potential competitors. Rayport and Jaworski suggest profiling a company's direct and indirect competitors by mapping the buyer's steps in obtaining and using the product. This type of analysis highlights both the opportunities and the challenges a company faces.[7] "Marketing Insight: High Growth Through Value Innovation" describes how firms can tap into new markets that minimize competition from others.

ANALYZING COMPETITORS

Once a company identifies its primary competitors, it must ascertain their strategies, objectives, and strengths and weaknesses.[8]

Strategies

A group of firms following the same strategy in a given target market is called a **strategic group**.[9] Suppose a company wants to enter the major-appliance industry. What is its strategic group? The company develops the chart shown in Figure 11.2 and discovers four strategic groups based on product quality and level of vertical integration. Group A has one competitor (Maytag), group B has three (General Electric, Whirlpool, and Sears), group C has four, and group D has two. Important insights emerge from this exercise. First, the height of the entry barriers differs for each group. Second, if the company successfully enters a group, the members of that group become its key competitors.

Objectives

Once a company has identified its main competitors and their strategies, it must ask: What is each competitor seeking in the marketplace? What drives each competitor's behaviour? Many factors shape a competitor's objectives, including size, history, current management, and financial situation. If the competitor is a division of a larger company, it is important to know whether the parent company is running it for growth, for profits, or milking it.

One useful initial assumption is that competitors strive to maximize profits. However, companies differ in the emphasis they put on short-term versus long-term profits. Many Canadian and U.S. firms have been criticized for operating on a short-run model, largely because current performance is judged by shareholders who might lose confidence, sell their stock, and cause the company's cost of capital to rise. Japanese firms operate largely on a market-share-maximization model. They receive

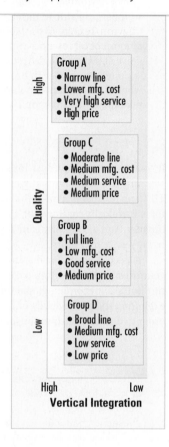

FIGURE 11.2

Strategic Groups in the Major-Appliance Industry

FORMULATION PRINCIPLES

a. Reconstruct market boundaries
  - Look across alternative industries
  - Look across strategic groups within industries
  - Look across chain of buyers
  - Look across complementary product and service offerings
  - Look across functional or emotional appeal to buyers
  - Look across time

b. Focus on the big picture, not the numbers

c. Reach beyond existing demand

d. Get the strategic sequence right
  - Is there buyer utility?
  - Is the price acceptable?
  - Can we attain target cost?
  - What are the adoption challenges?

EXECUTION PRINCIPLES

a. Overcome key organizational hurdles
  - Cognitive hurdle
  - Resource hurdle
  - Motivational hurdle
  - Political hurdle

b. Build execution into strategy

FIGURE 11.3

Key Principles of Blue-Ocean Strategy

Source: W. Chan Kim and Renée Mauborgne, *Blue-Ocean Strategy: How to Create Uncontested Market Space and Make the Competition Irrelevant* (Cambridge, MA: Harvard Business School Press, 2005). Copyright © 2005 by the Harvard Business School Publishing Corporation; all rights reserved.

MARKETING **INSIGHT** | HIGH GROWTH THROUGH VALUE INNOVATION

INSEAD professors W. Chan Kim and Renée Mauborgne believe that too many firms engage in "red-ocean thinking"—seeking bloody, head-to-head battles with competitors based largely on incremental improvements in cost, quality, or both. They advocate engaging instead in "blue-ocean thinking" by creating products and services for which there are no direct competitors. Their belief is that instead of searching within the conventional boundaries of industry competition, managers should look beyond those boundaries to find unoccupied market positions that represent real value innovation.

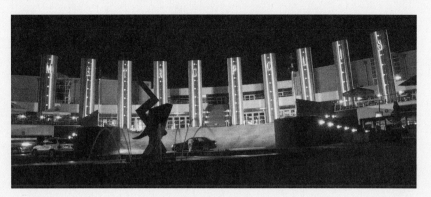

The Belgian Kinepolis movie megaplex exemplifies "blue-ocean thinking": a competitive strategy that focuses on finding unoccupied market positions. Here is an exterior shot of the megaplex in Antwerp, Belgium.

The authors cite as one example Bert Claeys, a Belgian movie-theatre operator, and its introduction of the 25-screen, 7600-seat Kinepolis megaplex. Despite an industry slump, Kineoplis has thrived on a unique combination of features, such as ample, safe, and free parking; large screens and state-of-the-art sound and projection equipment; and roomy, comfortable, oversized seats with unobstructed views. Through smart planning and economies of scale, Bert Claeys creates Kinepolis's unique cinema experience at a lower cost.

This is classic blue-ocean thinking—designing creative business ventures to positively affect both a company's cost structure and its value proposition to consumers. Cost savings result from eliminating and reducing the factors affecting traditional industry competition; value to consumers comes from introducing factors the industry has never before offered. Over time, costs drop even more as superior value leads to higher sales volume, and that generates economies of scale.

Other examples of marketers that exhibit unconventional, blue-ocean thinking include:

- Southwest Airlines created an airline that offers reliable, fun, and convenient service at a low cost.
- Callaway Golf designed "Big Bertha," a golf club with a large head and expanded sweet spot that helped golfers frustrated by the difficulty of hitting a golf ball squarely.
- NetJets figured out how to offer private jet service to a larger group of customers through fractional ownership.
- Cirque du Soleil reinvented circus as a higher form of entertainment by eliminating high-cost elements such as animals and enhancing the theatrical experience instead.

Kim and Mauborgne propose four crucial questions for marketers to ask themselves in guiding blue-ocean thinking and creating value innovation:

1. Which of the factors that our industry takes for granted should we eliminate?
2. Which factors should we reduce well *below* the industry's standard?
3. Which factors should we raise well *above* the industry's standard?
4. Which factors that the industry has never offered should we create?

They maintain that the most successful blue-ocean thinkers took advantage of all three platforms on which value innovation can take place: *physical product*; *service*, including maintenance, customer service, warranties, and training for distributors and retailers; and *delivery*, meaning channels and logistics. Figure 11.3 summarizes key principles driving the successful formulation and execution of blue-ocean strategy.

Sources: W. Chan Kim and Renée Mauborgne, *Blue-Ocean Strategy: How to Create Uncontested Market Space and Make the Competition Irrelevant* (Cambridge, MA: Harvard Business School Press, 2005); W. Chan Kim and Renée Mauborgne, "Creating New Market Space," *Harvard Business Review* (January–February 1999); W. Chan Kim and Renée Mauborgne, "Value Innovation: The Strategic Logic of High Growth," *Harvard Business Review* (January–February 1997).

FIGURE 11.4

A Competitor's Expansion
Plans

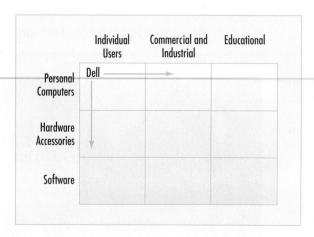

much of their funds from banks at a lower interest rate and in the past have readily accepted lower profits. An alternative assumption is that each competitor pursues some mix of objectives: current profitability, market-share growth, cash flow, technological leadership, or service leadership.[10]

Finally, a company must monitor competitors' expansion plans. Figure 11.4 shows a product-market battlefield map for the personal-computer industry. Dell, which started out as a strong force in selling personal computers to individual users, is now a major force in the commercial and industrial market. Other incumbents may try to set up mobility barriers to Dell's further expansion.

Strengths and Weaknesses

A company needs to gather information on each competitor's strengths and weaknesses. Table 11.1 shows the results of a company survey that asked customers to rate its three competitors, A, B, and C, on five attributes. Competitor A turns out to be well known and respected for producing high-quality products sold by a good sales force. Competitor A is poor at providing product availability and technical assistance. Competitor B is good across the board and excellent in product availability and sales force. Competitor C rates poor to fair on most attributes. This suggests that the company could attack Competitor A on product availability and technical assistance and Competitor C on almost anything, but should not attack B, which has no glaring weaknesses.

In general, a company should monitor three variables when analyzing competitors:

1. *Share of market.* The competitor's share of the target market.
2. *Share of mind.* The percentage of customers who named the competitor in responding to the statement "Name the first company that comes to mind in this industry."
3. *Share of heart.* The percentage of customers who named the competitor in responding to the statement "Name the company from which you would prefer to buy the product."

There is an interesting relationship among these three measures. Table 11.2 shows the numbers for these three measures for the three competitors listed in Table 11.1. Competitor A enjoys the highest market share but is slipping. Its mind share and heart share are also slipping, probably because it is not providing good product availability and technical assistance. Competitor B is steadily gaining market share, probably due to strategies that are increasing its mind share and heart share.

TABLE 11.1	CUSTOMERS' RATINGS OF COMPETITORS ON KEY SUCCESS FACTORS				
	Customer Awareness	Product Quality	Product Availability	Technical Assistance	Selling Staff
Competitor A	E	E	P	P	G
Competitor B	G	G	E	G	E
Competitor C	F	P	G	F	F

Note: E = excellent, G = good, F = fair, P = poor.

| MARKETING MEMO | BENCHMARKING TO IMPROVE COMPETITIVE PERFORMANCE |

Benchmarking is the art of learning from companies that perform certain tasks better than other companies. There can be as much as a tenfold difference in the quality, speed, and cost performance of a world-class company and an average company. The aim of benchmarking is to copy or improve on "best practices," either within an industry or across industries. Benchmarking involves seven steps:

1. Determine which functions to benchmark.
2. Identify the key performance variables to measure.
3. Identify the best-in-class companies.
4. Measure performance of best-in-class companies.
5. Measure the company's performance.
6. Specify programs and actions to close the gap.
7. Implement and monitor results.

How can companies identify best-practice companies? A good starting point is asking customers, suppliers, and distributors whom they rate as doing the best job.

Sources: Robert C. Camp, *Benchmarking: The Search for Industry-Best Practices That Lead to Superior Performance* (White Plains, NY: Quality Resources, 1989); Michael J. Spendolini, *The Benchmarking Book* (New York: Amacom, 1992); Stanley Brown, "Don't Innovate—Imitate!" *Sales & Marketing Management* (January 1995): 24–25; Tom Stemerg, "Spies Like Us," *Inc.* (August 1998): 45–49. See also www.benchmarking.org; Michael Hope, "Contrast and Compare," *Marketing*, August 28, 1997, pp. 11–13; Robert Hiebeler, Thomas B. Kelly, and Charles Ketteman, *Best Practices: Building Your Business with Customer-Focused Solutions* (New York: Arthur Andersen/Simon & Schuster, 1998).

Competitor C seems to be stuck at a low level of market share, mind share, and heart share, probably because of its poor product and marketing attributes. We could generalize as follows: *Companies that make steady gains in mind share and heart share will inevitably make gains in market share and profitability.* Firms such as Fairmont, Timberland, Toyota, and Whole Foods are all reaping the financial benefits of providing emotional, experiential, social, and financial value to satisfy customers and all their constituents.[11]

To improve market share, many companies benchmark their most successful competitors as well as world-class performers.[12] The technique and its benefits are described in "Marketing Memo: Benchmarking to Improve Competitive Performance."

Selecting Competitors

After the company has conducted customer value analysis and examined competitors carefully, it can focus its attack on one of the following classes of competitors: strong versus weak, close versus distant, and "good" versus "bad."

- *Strong versus weak.* Most companies aim their shots at weak competitors, because this requires fewer resources per share-point gained. Yet, the firm should also compete with strong competitors to keep up with the best. Even strong competitors have some weaknesses.

- *Close versus distant.* Most companies compete with competitors who resemble them the most. Chevrolet competes with Ford, not with Ferrari. Yet companies should also recognize distant

| TABLE 11.2 | MARKET SHARE, MIND SHARE, AND HEART SHARE |

	Market Share (%)			Mind Share (%)			Heart Share (%)		
	2007	2008	2009	2007	2008	2009	2007	2008	2009
Competitor A	50	47	44	60	58	54	45	42	39
Competitor B	30	34	37	30	31	35	44	47	53
Competitor C	20	19	19	10	11	11	11	11	8

TABLE 11.3	CUSTOMER-SELECTION GRID	
	Vulnerable	**Not Vulnerable**
Valuable	These customers are profitable but not completely happy with the company. Find out and address their sources of vulnerability to **retain them.**	These customers are loyal and profitable. Don't take them for granted but **maintain margins** and reap the benefits of their satisfaction.
Not Valuable	These customers are likely to defect. Let them go or even **encourage their departure.**	These unprofitable customers are happy. Try to **make them valuable** or vulnerable.

competitors. Coca-Cola states that its number-one competitor is tap water, not Pepsi. Dofasco worries more about plastic and aluminum than about Bethlehem Steel; museums now worry about theme parks and malls.

■ *"Good" versus "bad."* Every industry contains "good" and "bad" competitors.[13] Good competitors play by the industry's rules; they make realistic assumptions about the industry's growth potential; they set prices in reasonable relation to costs; and they favour a healthy industry. Bad competitors try to buy share rather than earn it; they take large risks; they invest in overcapacity; and they upset industrial equilibrium. A company may find it necessary to attack its bad competitors to reduce or end their dysfunctional practices.

Selecting Customers

As part of the competitive analysis, a firm must evaluate its customer base and think about which customers it is willing to lose and which it wants to retain. One way to divide up the customer base is in terms of whether a customer is valuable and vulnerable, creating a grid of four segments as a result; see Table 11.3. Each segment suggests different competitive activities.[14]

Australian telephone company Telstra conducted this type of segment analysis and developed a series of "Flex-Plan" products designed to retain the Valuable/Vulnerables but without losing the margin it realized on the Valuable/Not Vulnerables. The Flex Plans had subscription fees but offered significant net savings. Because Valuable/Vulnerables were highly involved with the category, they were able to see how they could benefit from such plans, but Valuable/Not Vulnerables regarded the plans as unnecessary. As a result, the plans achieved the desired goals.

COMPETITIVE STRATEGIES FOR MARKET LEADERS

We can gain further insight by classifying firms by the roles they play in the target market: leader, challenger, follower, or nicher. Suppose a market is occupied by the firms shown in Figure 11.5. Forty percent of the market is in the hands of a *market leader;* another 30 percent is in the hands of a *market challenger;* another 20 percent is in the hands of a *market follower,* a firm that is willing to maintain its market share and not rock the boat. The remaining 10 percent is in the hands of *market nichers,* firms that serve small market segments not being served by larger firms.

Many industries contain one firm that is the acknowledged market leader. This firm has the largest market share in the relevant product market, and usually leads the other firms in price changes, new-product introductions, distribution coverage, and promotional intensity. Some well-known market leaders are Microsoft (computer software), Intel (microprocessors), Bombardier (aerospace and rail transport), Future Shop and Best Buy (retail electronics), McDonald's (fast food), Gillette (razor blades), RBC Financial Group (financial services), and Visa (credit cards). "Breakthrough Marketing: Accenture" (at the end of this chapter) summarizes how that firm has attained and maintained market leadership.

FIGURE 11.5

Hypothetical Market Structure

The Gap brand has become diluted in an effort to appeal to too broad a market base, and the company plans several strategies to refocus its brand.

Although marketers assume well-known brands are distinctive in consumers' minds, unless a dominant firm enjoys a legal monopoly, it must maintain constant vigilance. A product innovation may come along and hurt the leader; a competitor might unexpectedly find a fresh new marketing angle or commit to a major marketing investment; or the leader might find its cost structure spiralling upwards. One well-known brand and market leader that lost its way is Gap.

Gap

Nowadays when people think about Gap, they don't think of hip, contemporary clothes. They think quite literally of a "gap"—what's missing from the company's 3100 stores located in Canada and around the world. Young people will be quick to tell you that the missing ingredient is a unique style. In an era when small niche fashion brands—Coach, Juicy Couture, Tahari, Laundry—have risen to success, Gap has continued to push timeless, simple, and, some would say, bland casual clothing. The main problem is that Gap doesn't have a target customer but tries to appeal to everyone, from newborn babies to teenagers to senior citizens. "If you stand for everything in fashion today, you stand for nothing," says Paul R. Charron, the former chief executive of Liz Claiborne, who revitalized that ailing clothing company by buying Juicy Couture and Lucky Brand. Since it was not vigilant in responding to (or, better yet, envisioning) the changing retailing scene, Gap has seen sales fall dramatically. Still, the former leading brand is planning a number of strategies to get itself out of the doldrums. Among them are selling other-branded merchandise inside its stores (as it used to sell Levi's and now sells Converse), shrinking the number of stores to cut back on overexposure, and focusing on a narrower group of consumers with clothing tailored to meet their needs.[15]

In many industries, a discount competitor has entered and undercut the leader's prices. "Marketing Insight: When Your Competitor Delivers More for Less" describes how leaders can respond to an aggressive competitive-price discounter.

See what Fairmont Hotels & Resorts is doing to extend its leadership in the North American marketplace worldwide:

Fairmont Hotels & Resorts

Headquartered in Toronto, Fairmont is the largest luxury-hotel management company in North America. It has a worldwide reputation for excellence. Fairmont takes pride in the fact that it earns the loyalty of each guest by exceeding his or her expectations. As it continues to grow globally, it promises that "one thing will remain constant—any hotel under the Fairmont flag will do more than just sell rooms, for we are in the business of creating extraordinary guest experiences in extraordinary places." Fairmont leads in more than just market share—it also has an outstanding reputation for community involvement, innovative social programs, and environmental stewardship.[16]

Remaining number-one calls for action on three fronts. First, the firm must find ways to expand total market demand. Second, the firm must protect its current market share through good defensive and offensive actions. Third, the firm can try to increase its market share, even if market size remains constant.

Expanding the Total Market

The dominant firm normally gains the most when the total market expands. If people increase their consumption of ketchup, Heinz stands to gain the most because it sells the majority of ketchup. If Heinz can convince more people to use ketchup, to use ketchup with more meals, or to use more ketchup on each occasion, Heinz will benefit considerably. In general, the market leader should look for new customers or more usage from existing customers.

NEW CUSTOMERS   Every product class has the potential to attract buyers who are unaware of the product or who are resisting it because of price or lack of certain features. A company can search for new users among three groups: those who might use it but do not *(market-penetration strategy)*, those who have never used it *(new-market-segment strategy)*, or those who live elsewhere *(geographical-expansion strategy)*.

Starbucks Coffee is one of the best-known brands in the world. Starbucks is able to sell a cup of coffee for $3 while the store next door can get only $1. And if you want the popular café latte, it's $4. Starbucks operates in 44 different countries, including Canada. It entered Canada in 1987, and in 1995 it formed an alliance with Chapters, the Canadian bookstore chain. By 2008, Starbucks Coffee Canada had over 400 company-operated stores and 100 licensed-concept stores across the country. In the period 2009 to 2011, Starbucks is projecting a 20-percent growth in revenues with a target of reaching US$14 billion by 2011. Its corporate website (www.starbucks.com) gives a peek into its multi-pronged approach to growth:[17]

> Starbucks purchases and roasts high-quality whole-bean coffees and sells them along with fresh, rich-brewed, Italian-style espresso beverages, a variety of pastries and confections, and coffee-related accessories and equipment—primarily through its company-operated retail stores. In addition, Starbucks sells whole-bean coffees through a specialty sales group and supermarkets. Additionally, Starbucks produces and sells bottled Frappuccino® coffee drink and a line of premium ice creams through its joint venture partnerships and offers a line of innovative premium teas produced by its wholly owned subsidiary, Tazo Tea Company. The company's objective is to establish Starbucks as the most recognized and respected brand in the world. To achieve this goal, the company plans to continue to rapidly expand its retail operations, grow its specialty sales and other operations, and selectively pursue opportunities to leverage the Starbucks brand through the introduction of new products and the development of new distribution channels.

Companies offering the powerful combination of low prices and high quality are capturing the hearts and wallets of consumers in Europe and North America, where more than half of the population now shops weekly at mass merchants like Wal-Mart and Costco, up from 25 percent in 1996. These and similar value players, such as Aldi, Zellers, Dell, E*Trade Financial, WestJet, Dollar Store, and Winners, are transforming the way consumers of nearly every age and income purchase groceries, apparel, airline tickets, financial services, and computers.

The market share gains of value-based players give their higher-priced rivals definite cause for alarm. After years of nearly exclusive sway over all but the most discount-minded consumers, many mainstream companies now face steep cost disadvantages and lack the product and service superiority that once set them apart from low-priced competitors. Today, as value-driven companies in a growing number of industries move from competing solely on price to catching up on attributes such as quality, service, and convenience, traditional players rightly feel threatened.

To compete with value-based rivals, mainstream companies must reconsider the perennial routes to business success: keeping costs in line, finding sources of differentiation, and managing prices effectively. Succeeding in value-based markets requires infusing these timeless strategies with greater intensity and focus and then executing them flawlessly. Differentiation, for example, becomes less about the abstract goal of rising above competitive clutter and more about identifying opportunities left open by the value players' business models. Effective pricing means waging a transaction-by-transaction perception battle to win over consumers predisposed to believe that value-oriented competitors are always cheaper.

Competitive outcomes will be determined, as always, on the ground—in product aisles, merchandising displays, process rethinks, and pricing stickers. When it comes to value-based competition, traditional players can't afford to drop a stitch. Value-driven competitors have changed the expectations of consumers about the trade-off between quality and price. This shift is gathering momentum, placing a new premium on—and adding new twists to—the old imperatives of differentiation and execution.

DIFFERENTIATION

To counter value-based players, it will be necessary to focus on areas where their business models give other companies room to manoeuvre. Instead of trying to compete with Wal-Mart and other value retailers on price, for example, Shoppers Drug Mart (which includes Pharmaprix stores in Quebec) emphasizes convenience, a growing selection of high-end products, and the promise that consumers can trust its expert advice whether they are buying pharmaceutical products or cosmetics. It has expanded rapidly—it now has 925 stores from coast to coast—so that its stores would be ubiquitous. It generally locates in malls with easy parking. It overhauled its in-store layouts by renovating and expanding existing locations and building new-format stores that are as large as 14 000 square feet. It has worked to increase the value it offers customers through its Optimum loyalty program, which it launched in 2000. By the end of 2004, Optimum had become one of the most successful loyalty programs in Canada, boasting over 8 million members. Finally, while pharmacy sales are still Shoppers' mainstay, it is adding many prestige products from giftware to high-end cosmetics and fragrances.

EXECUTION

Value-based markets also place a premium on execution, particularly in prices and costs. Kmart's disastrous experience trying to compete head-on with Wal-Mart highlights the difficulty of challenging value leaders on their own terms. Matching or even beating a value player's prices—as Kmart briefly did—won't necessarily win the battle of consumer perceptions against companies with reputations for the lowest prices. Value players tend to price frequently purchased, easy-to-compare products and services aggressively and to make up for lost margins by charging more for higher-end offerings. Advertising focused on showcase "special buys" and the use of simple, prominent signage enable retailers to get credit for the value they offer and will probably become an ever-more visible feature of the competitive landscape.

Ultimately, of course, the ability to offer even selectively competitive prices depends on keeping costs in line. Continual improvement is necessary, suggesting an increasing role, in a variety of industries, for Toyota's lean-manufacturing methods, which aim to reduce costs and improve quality constantly and simultaneously. In financial services, for example, banks have used lean techniques to speed cheque processing and mortgage approvals and to improve call-centre performance. Lean operations will probably emerge in more industries. Companies have no choice—those that fail to take out costs constantly may perish.

Sources: Robert J. Frank, Jeffrey P. George, and Laxman Narasimhan, "When Your Competitor Delivers More for Less," *McKinsey Quarterly* (Winter 2004): 48–59; Angela Kryhul, "Shoppers' Prestige Play," *Marketing*, January 19, 2004; Chris Daniels, "Vendor Bender," *Marketing*, April 5, 2004; Shoppers Drug Mart website, www.shoppersdrugmart.ca/english/corporate_information/ about_us/index.html (viewed August 24, 2005).

Among Starbucks' expansion efforts has been a new line of premium tea produced by Tazo Tea Company, a Starbucks subsidiary.

MORE USAGE Marketers can try to increase the amount, level, or frequency of consumption. Larger package sizes have been shown to increase the amount of product that consumers use at one time.[18] Usage of "impulse" consumption products such as soft drinks and snacks increases when the product is made more available.

Increasing frequency of use, on the other hand, involves identifying additional opportunities to use the brand in the same basic way or identifying completely new and different ways to use the brand. In some cases, the product may be seen as useful only in certain places and at certain times, especially if it has strong brand associations with particular usage situations or user types.

To generate additional usage opportunities, a marketing program can communicate the appropriateness and advantages of using the brand more frequently in new or existing situations and/or remind consumers to actually use the brand as close as possible to those situations. Clorox has run ads stressing the many benefits of its bleach, such as how it eliminates kitchen odours. Another opportunity arises when consumers' perceptions of their usage differs from the reality. Consumers may fail to replace a short-lived product when they should, because they overestimate how long it stays fresh.[19]

One strategy to speed up product replacement is to tie the act of replacing the product to a certain holiday, event, or time of year. Another strategy might be to provide consumers with better information as to either (1) when the product was first used or would need to be replaced or (2) the current level of product performance. Gillette razor cartridges feature a coloured stripe that slowly fades with repeated use, signalling the user to move on to the next cartridge.

The second approach is to identify completely new and different applications. For example, food product companies have long advertised new recipes that use their branded products in entirely different ways. After discovering that consumers used Arm & Hammer brand baking soda as a refrigerator deodorant, a heavy promotion campaign was launched focusing on this single use. After succeeding in getting a substantial portion of North American homes to place an open box of baking soda in the refrigerator, the brand was then extended into a variety of new product categories, such as toothpaste, antiperspirant, and laundry detergent.

Product development can spur new uses. Chewing-gum manufacturers such as Cadbury Schweppes, maker of Trident, are producing "nutraceutical" products to strengthen or whiten teeth. Aquafresh has successfully launched dental chewing gums with health and cosmetic benefits.[20]

Defending Market Share

While trying to expand total market size, the dominant firm must continuously defend its current business: Boeing against Airbus, Staples against Office Depot, and Google against Yahoo! and Microsoft.[21] The success of online social-network sites MySpace and Facebook has brought challenges from upstarts such as LinkedIn personal business network, Dogster for dog owners, and Eons and Vox for sharing photos, videos, and blog posts for baby boomers and older consumers.[22]

What can a market leader, like Martelli Lavorazioni Tessili, do to defend its terrain? The most constructive response is *continuous innovation*. The leader should lead the industry in developing new product and customer services, distribution effectiveness, and cost cutting. It keeps increasing its competitive strength and value to customers by providing comprehensive solutions.

Martelli Lavorazioni Tessili

Consumers who wonder why it costs $200 or more to buy a pair of designer jeans might feel better about the high price tag if they strolled through a Martelli Lavorazioni Tessili factory in Vedelago, Italy. The market leader in the technology of "distressing" denim, Martelli counts Gucci, Armani, Dolce and Gabbana, and Yves St. Laurent among its clients on the high end and Levi-Strauss, Lee, Wrangler, and Gap on the low end. Martelli is uncontested in Europe; its only competitors are in the United States and Japan. The company stays on top by relentlessly innovating—investing at least US$5 million a year to continually upgrade technology—and by finding cheap but skilled labour to carry out its bizarre but effective techniques. In its main factory with 900 workers, huge washing machines tumble jeans with pumice gravel. Workers wearing face masks put inflated balloons into the legs of jeans which then are moved between sets of plastic brushes that scrub the denim. Some workers do painstaking hand work on individual jeans, applying discolouring chemicals with brushes, applying embroidered designs, or using handheld guns to blast jets of quartz sand. After experimenting with workers from Africa and Romania, Martelli has found that legal Chinese immigrants are the most skilled, patient, and cost effective.[23]

The market leader for "distressing jeans," Italy's Martelli Lavorazioni Tessili counts the eponymous firm of Italian designers Stefano Gabbana and Domenico Dolce, shown here at Milan Fashion Week, as one of its customers.

In satisfying customer needs, a distinction can be drawn among responsive marketing, anticipative marketing, and creative marketing. A *responsive* marketer finds a stated need and fills it. An *anticipative* marketer looks ahead into what needs customers may have in the near future. A *creative* marketer discovers and produces solutions customers did not ask for but to which they enthusiastically respond. Creative marketers are *market-driving firms*, not just market driven. Cascades is one such market-driving firm.

Cascades

Quebec-based Cascades is a pioneer in recycling. From its inception in 1964, it understood sustainable development long before the term became a popular buzzword. Its long history in recycling has enabled it to develop unique expertise long before its competitors ever thought of moving in a similar direction. Today, it is recognized around the world for its ability to recover and re-use discarded containers, packaging, and printed matter. Cascades is also a leader in recycling plastics, which can be used as a substitute for wood in making floors, patios, and furniture. Whether it's producing fine paper, tissue paper, or packaging products, Cascades' concern for the environment is legendary. The company stresses that because it can breathe new life into 2.8 million tonnes of printed paper and cardboard each year, it saves 47 million trees annually.[24]

Market-driving firms become market leaders through superior value delivery of unmet—and maybe even unknown—consumer needs. Think of Sony. In the late 1970s, Akio Morita, the Sony founder, was working on a pet project that would revolutionize the way people listened to music: a portable cassette player he called the Walkman. Engineers at the company insisted there was little demand for such a product, but Morita refused to part with his vision. By the twentieth anniversary of the Walkman, Sony had sold over 250 million in nearly 100 different models.[25]

Even when it does not launch offensives, the market leader must not leave any major flanks exposed. It must consider carefully which terrains are important to defend, even at a loss, and which can be surrendered. The aim of defensive strategy is to reduce the probability of attack, divert attacks

FIGURE 11.6

Six Types of Defence
Strategies

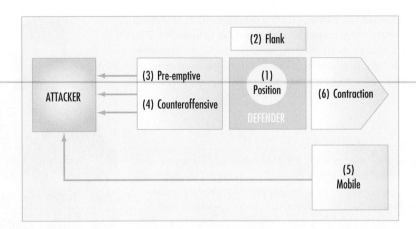

to less threatening areas, and lessen their intensity. The defender's speed of response can make an important difference in the profit consequences. A dominant firm can use the six defence strategies summarized in Figure 11.6.[26]

POSITION DEFENCE   Position defence involves occupying the most desirable market space in the mind of the consumer, making the brand almost impregnable (like Tide laundry detergent with cleaning, Crest toothpaste with cavity prevention, and Pampers diapers with dryness). Porter Air decided to operate out of the Toronto Island airport instead of Pearson International airport (located in north-west Toronto) because of the former's proximity to the downtown core. Many business travellers have switched to the airline because they value the convenience this location offers.

FLANK DEFENCE   Although position defence is important, the market leader should also erect outposts to protect a weak front or possibly serve as an invasion base for counterattack. When Heublein's brand Smirnoff, which had 23 percent of the U.S. vodka market, was attacked by low-priced competitor Wolfschmidt, Heublein actually *raised* the price and put the increased revenue into advertising. At the same time, Heublein introduced another brand, Relska, to compete with Wolfschmidt and still another, Popov, to sell for less than Wolfschmidt. This strategy effectively bracketed Wolfschmidt and protected Smirnoff's flanks.

PRE-EMPTIVE DEFENCE   A more aggressive manoeuvre is to attack *before* the enemy starts its offence. A company can launch a pre-emptive defence in several ways. It can wage guerrilla action across the market—hitting one competitor here, another there—and keep everyone off balance, or it can try to achieve a grand market envelopment. Canada's big five banks with their ubiquitous branches and ATMs provide steep competition to other financial firms and credit unions. They send out market signals to dissuade competitors from attacking.[27]

Marketers can introduce a stream of new products, making sure to precede them with *pre-announcements*—deliberate communications regarding future actions.[28] Pre-announcements can signal to competitors that they will have to fight to gain market share.[29] If Microsoft announces new-product development plans, smaller firms may choose to concentrate their development efforts in other directions to avoid head-to-head competition. Some high-tech firms have even been accused of producing "vaporware"—pre-announced products that miss delivery dates or even are not ever introduced.[30]

COUNTEROFFENSIVE DEFENCE   When attacked, most market leaders will respond with a counter-attack. Counterattacks can take many forms. In a *counteroffensive*, the leader can meet the attacker frontally or hit its flank or launch a pincer movement. An effective counterattack is to invade the attacker's main territory so that it will have to pull back to defend the territory. After FedEx watched UPS successfully invade its airborne-delivery market, FedEx invested heavily in ground-delivery service through a series of acquisitions to challenge UPS on its home turf.[31] When WestJet decided to establish operations at Pearson International Airport in Toronto and attack Air Canada head-on, Air Canada was quick to respond. It first launched its own discount airline and began operations on WestJet's home turf in western Canada. Today, it matches WestJet with its own discount fares on Air Canada flights.

Another common form of counteroffensive is the exercise of economic or political clout. The leader may try to crush a competitor by subsidizing lower prices for the vulnerable product with revenue from its more profitable products, or the leader may prematurely announce that a product upgrade will be available, to prevent customers from buying the competitor's product, or the leader may lobby legislators to take political action to inhibit or cripple the competition.

MOBILE DEFENCE   In mobile defence, the leader stretches its domain over new territories that can serve as future centres for defence and offence through market broadening and market diversification. *Market broadening* involves shifting focus from the current product to the underlying generic need. The company gets involved in R&D across the whole range of technology associated with that need. Thus "petroleum" companies sought to recast themselves as "energy" companies. Implicitly, this change demanded that they dip their research fingers into the oil, coal, nuclear, hydroelectric, and chemical industries.

Market diversification involves shifting into unrelated industries. Canadian company Roots has grown through diversification. Founded in 1973 as a single-product company selling its trademark negative-heel shoe, Roots today is Canada's leading lifestyle brand. It markets an ever-expanding range of products including a range of leather goods (shoes, jackets, bags, and luggage), sportswear, children's clothing, fragrances, timepieces, and a line of goods for the home including furniture, linens, and home accessories.

CONTRACTION DEFENCE   Large companies sometimes recognize that they can no longer defend all of their territory. The best course of action then appears to be *planned contraction* (also called *strategic withdrawal*): giving up weaker territories and reassigning resources to stronger territories. Bombardier did this recently when it made the historic decision to spin off its recreational-products division (maker of the famed Ski-Doo and Sea-Doo products) to focus more closely on aerospace and rail transport.

Expanding Market Share

In many markets, one share point is worth tens of millions of dollars. No wonder competition is fierce in many marketplaces. Gaining increased share in the served market, however, does not automatically produce higher profits—especially for labour-intensive service companies that may not experience many economies of scale. Much depends on the company's strategy.[32]

Because the cost of buying higher market share may far exceed its revenue value, a company should consider four factors before pursuing increased market share:

- *The possibility of provoking antitrust action,* such as recently occurred when Canada's large banks explored the possibilities of merging, and the recent investigations of Microsoft and Intel. Jealous competitors are likely to cry "monopoly" if a dominant firm makes further inroads. This rise in risk would diminish the attractiveness of pushing market-share gains.

Roots has constantly reinvented itself through diversification into different markets. However, its quality and sense of style have been constant.

FIGURE 11.7

The Concept of Optimal Market Share

- *Economic cost.* Figure 11.7 shows that profitability might fall with further market-share gains after some level. In the illustration, the firm's *optimal market share* is 50 percent. The cost of gaining further market share might exceed the value. The "holdout" customers may dislike the company, be loyal to competitive suppliers, have unique needs, or prefer dealing with smaller suppliers. The cost of legal work, public relations, and lobbying rises with market share. Pushing for higher market share is less justified when there are few scale or experience economies, unattractive market segments exist, buyers want multiple sources of supply, and exit barriers are high. Some market leaders have even increased profitability by selectively decreasing market share in weaker areas.[33]

- *Pursuing the wrong marketing-mix strategy.* Companies successfully gaining share typically outperform competitors in three areas: new-product activity, relative product quality, and marketing expenditures.[34] Companies that cut prices more deeply than competitors typically do not achieve significant gains, as enough rivals meet the price cuts and others offer other values so that buyers do not switch. Competitive rivalry and price cutting have been shown to be most intense in industries with high fixed costs, high inventory costs, and stagnant primary demand, such as steel, auto, paper, and chemicals.[35]

- *The effect of increased market share on actual and perceived quality.*[36] Having too many customers can put a strain on the firm's resources, hurting product value and service delivery. America Online experienced growing pains when its customer base expanded, resulting in system outages and access problems. Consumers may also infer that "bigger is not better" and assume that growth will lead to a deterioration of quality. If "exclusivity" is a key brand benefit, existing customers may resent additional new customers.

OTHER COMPETITIVE STRATEGIES

Firms that occupy second, third, and lower ranks in an industry are often called runner-up or trailing firms. Some, such as Colgate, Ford, Avis, and PepsiCo, are quite large in their own right. These firms can adopt one of two postures. They can attack the leader and other competitors in an aggressive bid for further market share (market challengers), or they can sail along and not "rock the boat" (market followers).

Market-Challenger Strategies

Many market challengers have gained ground or even overtaken the leader. Toyota today produces more cars than General Motors, and AMD has been chipping away at Intel's market share.[37] Challengers have high aspirations, leveraging their resources while the market leader often runs its business as usual.[38]

Now let's examine the competitive attack strategies available to market challengers.

DEFINING THE STRATEGIC OBJECTIVE AND OPPONENT(S) A market challenger must first define its strategic objective. Most aim to increase market share. The challenger must decide whom to attack:

- *It can attack the market leader.* This is a high-risk but potentially high-payoff strategy and makes good sense if the leader is not serving the market well. The alternative strategy is to out-innovate the leader across the whole segment. Xerox wrested the copying market from 3M by developing a better copying process. Later, Canon grabbed a large chunk of Xerox's market by introducing desk copiers.

- *It can attack firms of its own size that are not doing the job and are underfinanced.* These firms have aging products, are charging excessive prices, or are not satisfying customers in other ways.

- *It can attack small local and regional firms.* Several credit unions grew to their present size by gobbling up smaller regional banks, or "guppies." Alterna Savings, for example, was born when Toronto's Metro Credit Union merged with Ottawa's CS Co-op to better serve customers in these two cities and outlying regions like Kingston, Pembroke, and North Bay.

CHOOSING A GENERAL ATTACK STRATEGY Given clear opponents and objectives, what attack options are available? We can distinguish among five attack strategies: frontal, flank, encirclement, bypass, and guerrilla attacks.

Frontal Attack In a pure *frontal attack*, the attacker matches its opponent's product, advertising, price, and distribution. The principle of force says that the side with the greater workforce (resources) will win. A modified frontal attack, such as cutting price vis-à-vis the opponent's, can work if the market leader does not retaliate and if the competitor convinces the market that its product is equal to the leader's. Helene Curtis is a master at convincing the market that its brands—such as Suave and Finesse—are equal in quality but a better value than higher-priced brands.

Flank Attack An enemy's weak spots are natural targets. A *flank attack* can be directed along two strategic dimensions—geographic and segmental. In a geographic attack, the challenger spots areas where the opponent is underperforming. Although the Internet has siphoned newspaper readers and advertisers away in many markets, Independent News & Media, a 102-year-old Irish media company, sells a majority of its 175 newspaper and magazine titles in countries where the economy is strong but the Internet is still relatively weak—countries such as Ireland, South Africa, Australia, New Zealand, and India.[39]

Harvey's

Cara Operations, based in Mississauga, Ontario, recently launched a flanking strategy for its Harvey's restaurants, which is a market challenger in the highly competitive fast-food marketplace dominated by big names such as McDonald's, Wendy's, and Burger King. While most of its competitors are jumping on the healthier food bandwagon, adding new salads and other healthy options to their menus, Harvey's wants to occupy a different space. The company believes that healthy food is not what built its business. At the core of Harvey's historical positioning is a better hamburger prepared in a better way. In 2006, it went back to its roots as it reinstated its famous slogan "Harvey's makes your hamburger a beautiful thing." Recent advertising stresses that "there's a burger with your name on it." Harvey's continues to focus on a clear and defined target—"the guys who just want to chow down on a good burger"—by creating new products such as its Angus Burgers. It locates many of its outlets in Home Depot stores to further serve this tightly defined market.[40]

A flanking strategy is another name for identifying shifts in market segments that are causing gaps to develop, and then rushing to fill the gaps and develop them into strong segments. Flanking is in the best tradition of modern marketing, which holds that the purpose of marketing is to discover needs and satisfy them. It is particularly attractive to a challenger, like ChaCha, which will likely have fewer resources than its opponent. A flanking strategy has a greater chance for success than frontal attacks against larger, wealthier opponents.

ChaCha

Given Google's 45-percent share of the Internet search business, it might seem foolhardy for anybody to challenge it. A frontal attack on Google would mean building a better mousetrap—in this case, a better search algorithm. Yet, a handful of smaller search companies are mounting flank attacks on Google, and they're confident they'll be able to swipe some of the search giant's market share. The flank these small companies are attacking is the one element missing in Google's searches: human intelligence and its ability to reason and contextualize. Jim Wales, cofounder of Wikipedia, the collaborative Web encyclopedia, plans to create an open-source search engine called Wikia that uses human deduction as well as a machine-driven algorithm. ChaCha employs a similar strategy and has thrived in Korea, where Google has made few inroads. ChaCha uses its 25 000 part- and full-time employees to offer guided searches in real time. Anyone who has ever "googled" a topic and come up with thousands of webpages, only of a handful of which are truly helpful, can see how guided search might be an attractive offering.[41]

Encirclement Attack The encirclement manoeuvre is an attempt to capture a wide slice of the enemy's territory through a "blitz." It involves launching a grand offensive on several fronts. Encirclement makes sense when the challenger commands superior resources and believes a swift encirclement will break the opponent's will. In making a stand against archrival Microsoft, Sun Microsystems licensed its Java software to hundreds of companies and millions of software developers for all sorts of consumer devices. As consumer-electronics products began to go digital, Java started appearing in a wide range of gadgets.

Bypass Attack The least direct assault strategy is the *bypass*. It calls for bypassing the enemy and attacking easier markets to broaden one's resource base. This strategy offers three lines of approach: diversifying into unrelated products, diversifying into new geographical markets, and leapfrogging into new technologies to supplant existing products. In the past decade, Pepsi has used a bypass strategy against Coke by: (1) aggressively rolling out Aquafina bottled water nationally in 1997 before Coke launched its Dasani brand; (2) purchasing orange-juice giant Tropicana, which owned almost twice the market share of Coca-Cola's Minute Maid, for US$3.3 billion in 1998; and (3) purchasing The Quaker Oats Company, owner of market-leader Gatorade sports drink, for US$14 billion in 2000.[42]

Technological leapfrogging is a bypass strategy practised in high-tech industries. The challenger patiently researches and develops the next technology and launches an attack, shifting the battleground to its territory, where it has an advantage. In July 2008, Apple's much-anticipated iPhone arrived in Canada, home of RIM's BlackBerry. Apple leveraged its competencies in graphic interfaces and Web surfing, music, and video software to attack BlackBerry in its own backyard. Apple's attack was about wresting market share by introducing superior technology and redefining the "competitive space." RIM didn't stand still. Its new products, Bold and Thunder, were designed to thwart Apple's onslaught. Thunder allows users to access corporate email while Bold is the first RIM device with a touch screen.[43]

Guerrilla Warfare Guerrilla warfare consists of waging small, intermittent attacks to harass and demoralize the opponent and eventually secure permanent footholds. The guerrilla challenger uses both conventional and unconventional means of attack. These include selective price cuts, intense promotional blitzes, and occasional legal action. Normally, guerrilla warfare is practised by a smaller firm against a larger one. The smaller firm launches a barrage of attacks in random corners of the larger opponent's market in a manner calculated to weaken the opponent's market power. See how Country Style used such tactics to harass Tim Hortons:

Country Style

In March 2008, right in the middle of Tim Hortons' famous "Roll Up The Rim" promotion, Country Style used guerrilla tactics to win over its rival's customers. In print, radio, Facebook, and in-store materials, Country Style asked "Tired of 'Sorry Try Again'?" Country Style offered to give a free medium coffee to Tim Hortons' customers if they presented a losing coffee tab at any Country Style location across Ontario. Rick Martens, President and Chief Financial Officer of Country Style, explained his reasoning about the campaign as follows: "We've got a great cup of coffee... Our goal is to bring in Tim's customers that wouldn't normally try us." The campaign was also designed to draw attention to Country Style's own contest promotion "Turn Up a Winner." Unlike in the Tim Hortons' promotion, everyone gets some prize when he or she participates in Country Style's contest, and the chain awarded almost six million prizes in 2008.[44]

Military doctrine holds that a continual stream of minor attacks usually creates more cumulative impact, disorganization, and confusion in the enemy than a few major attacks. A guerrilla campaign

Country Style used guerrilla tactics to encourage Tim Hortons' customers to experience the former's own fine coffee.

MARKETING **MEMO** | MAKING SMALLER BETTER

Adam Morgan offers eight suggestions for how small brands can better compete:

1. *Break with your immediate past.* Don't be afraid to ask "dumb" questions to challenge convention and view your brand differently.

2. *Build a "lighthouse identity."* Establish values and communicate who and why you are (e.g., Apple).

3. *Assume thought-leadership of the category.* Break convention in terms of representation (what you say about your-self), where you say it (medium), and experience (what you do beyond talk).

4. *Create symbols of re-evaluation.* A rocket uses half of its fuel in the first kilometre-and-a-half to break loose from Earth's gravitational pull—you may need to polarize people.

5. *Sacrifice.* Focus your target, message, reach and frequency, distribution, and line extensions, and recognize that less can be more.

6. *Overcommit.* Although you may do fewer things, do "big" things when you do them.

7. *Use publicity and advertising to enter popular culture.* Unconventional communications can get people talking.

8. *Be idea-centred, not consumer-centred.* Sustain challenger momentum by not losing sight of what the brand is about and can be, and redefine marketing support and the centre of the company to reflect this vision.

Source: Adam Morgan, *Eating the Big Fish: How Challenger Brands Can Compete Against Brand Leaders* (New York: John Wiley & Sons, 1999).

---

can be expensive, although admittedly less expensive than a frontal, encirclement, or flank attack. Guerrilla warfare is more a preparation for war than a war itself. Ultimately, it must be backed by a stronger attack if the challenger hopes to beat the opponent.

CHOOSING A SPECIFIC ATTACK STRATEGY   The challenger must go beyond the five broad strategies and develop more specific strategies. Any aspect of the marketing program, such as lower-priced or discounted products, new or improved products and services, a wider variety of offerings, and innovative distribution strategies, can serve as the basis for attack. A challenger's success depends on combining several strategies to improve its position over time. "Marketing Memo: Making Smaller Better" provides some additional tips for challenger brands.

Market-Follower Strategies

Some years ago, Theodore Levitt wrote an article entitled "Innovative Imitation" in which he argued that a strategy of *product imitation* might be as profitable as a strategy of *product innovation*.[45] The innovator bears the expense of developing the new product, getting it into distribution, and inform-ing and educating the market. The reward for all this work and risk is normally market leadership. However, another firm can come along and copy or improve on the new product. Although it proba-bly will not overtake the leader, a follower, like S&S Cycle, can achieve high profits because it does not bear the same innovation expense.

S&S Cycle

S&S Cycle is the biggest supplier of complete engines and major motor parts to more than 15 companies that build several thousand Harley-like cruiser bikes each year. These cloners charge as much as $30 000 for their customized creations. S&S has built its name by improv-ing on Harley-Davidson's handiwork. Its customers are often would-be Harley buyers frus-trated by long waiting lines at the dealers. Other customers simply want the incredibly powerful S&S engines. S&S stays abreast of its evolving market by ordering a new Harley bike every year and taking apart the engine to see what it can improve upon.[46]

Many companies prefer to follow rather than challenge the market leader. Patterns of "con-scious parallelism" are common in capital-intensive, homogeneous-product industries, such as

S&S Cycle has become a successful market follower by appealing to would-be Harley owners.

steel, fertilizers, and chemicals. The opportunities for product differentiation and image differentiation are low, service quality is often comparable, and price sensitivity runs high. The mood in these industries is against short-run grabs for market share because that strategy only provokes retaliation. Most firms decide against stealing one another's customers. Instead, they present similar offers to buyers, usually by copying the leader. Market shares show high stability.

This is not to say that market followers lack strategies. A market follower must know how to hold current customers and win a fair share of new customers. Each follower tries to bring distinctive advantages to its target market—location, services, financing. Because the follower is often a major target of attack by challengers, it must keep its manufacturing costs low and its product quality and services high. It must also enter new markets as they open up. The follower has to define a growth path, but one that does not invite competitive retaliation. Four broad strategies can be distinguished:

1. *Counterfeiter.* The counterfeiter duplicates the leader's product and package and sells it on the black market or through disreputable dealers. Music-recording firms, Apple, and Rolex have been plagued with the counterfeiter problem, especially in Asia.

2. *Cloner.* The cloner emulates the leader's products, name, and packaging, with slight variations. For example, Loblaws markets its President's Choice brand of laundry detergent in packaging that closely resembles that of the market leader, Tide. Ralcorp Holding Inc. sells imitations of name-brand cereals in look-alike boxes. Its Tasteeos, Fruit Rings, and Corn Flakes sell for about $1-a-box less than the leading name brands.

3. *Imitator.* The imitator copies some things from the leader but maintains differentiation in terms of packaging, advertising, pricing, or location. The leader does not mind the imitator as long as the imitator does not attack the leader aggressively. Fernandez Pujals grew up in Fort Lauderdale, Florida, and took Domino's home-delivery idea to Spain, where he borrowed US$80 000 to open his first store in Madrid. His TelePizza chain now operates almost 1000 stores in Europe and Latin America.

4. *Adapter.* The adapter takes the leader's products and adapts or improves them. The adapter may choose to sell to different markets, but often the adapter grows into the future challenger, as many Japanese firms have done after adapting and improving products developed elsewhere.

What does a follower earn? Normally, less than the leader. For example, a study of food-processing companies showed the largest firm averaging a 16-percent return on investment; the number-two firm, 6 percent; the number-three firm, –1 percent; and the number-four firm, –6 percent. In this case, only the top-two firms have profits. No wonder Jack Welch, former CEO of GE, told his business units that each must reach the number-one or -two position in its market or else! Followership is often not a rewarding path.

Market-Nicher Strategies

An alternative to being a follower in a large market is to be a leader in a small market, or niche, as we introduced in Chapter 8. Smaller firms normally avoid competing with larger firms by targeting small markets of little or no interest to the larger firms. But even large, profitable firms may choose to use niching strategies for some of their business units or companies. For example, Canada's two mega-brewers—Labatt and Molson—have launched their own specialty beers to take advantage of the double-digit growth in this segment of the marketplace. ITW provides another example of market niching.

ITW (formerly Illinois Tool Works) manufactures thousands of products, including nails, screws, plastic six-pack holders for soda cans, bicycle helmets, backpacks, plastic buckles for pet collars, resealable food packages, and more. Since the late 1980s, each year the company has made between 30 and 40 acquisitions that added new products to the product line. ITW has more than 700 highly autonomous and decentralized business units in 48 countries, including Canada. It employs 50 000 people. When one division commercializes a new product, the company spins off the product and personnel into a new entity.[47]

Firms with low shares of the total market can be highly profitable through smart niching. Such companies tend to offer high value, charge a premium price, achieve lower manufacturing costs, and shape a strong corporate culture and vision. New niche retailers such as the Running Room, headquartered in Edmonton, are following a market-niche strategy to compete against much bigger retailers. The Rocky Mountain Soap Company has made a name for itself despite competition from large global rivals like Colgate-Palmolive and Unilever. It was founded in Canmore, Alberta, in 1995 with a small plant and one retail outlet. Its vision was to impart the scents and healing properties of nature into every product. Today it sells its handmade soaps and skin-care products through its website and eight retail locations, and it has become the largest manufacturer of 100-percent-natural soap and bath products in Canada.[48]

In a study of hundreds of business units, the Strategic Planning Institute found that the return on investment averaged 27 percent in smaller markets, but only 11 percent in larger markets.[49] Why is niching so profitable? The main reason is that the market nicher ends up knowing the target customers so well that it meets their needs better than other firms selling to this niche casually. As a result, the nicher can charge a substantial price over costs. The nicher achieves *high margin*, whereas the mass marketer achieves *high volume.*

Nichers have three tasks: creating niches, expanding niches, and protecting niches. Niching carries a major risk in that the market niche might dry up or be attacked. The company is then stuck with highly specialized resources that may not have high-value alternative uses.

Zippo

With smoking on a steady decline, Zippo Manufacturing is finding the market for its iconic metal cigarette lighter drying up. Zippo marketers now find themselves needing to diversify and to broaden their focus to "selling flame." With a goal of reducing reliance on tobacco-related products to 50 percent of revenue by 2010, the company introduced a long, slender, multipurpose lighter for candles, grills, and fireplaces in 2001, explored licensing arrangements with suppliers of flame-related outdoor products, and diversified its operations by acquiring Case Cutlery, a knife-maker, and D.D.M. Italia, known throughout Europe for fine Italian leather goods.[50]

Small firms like Rocky Mountain Soap Company can be successful by carving out distinct niches in the marketplace.

The key idea in the successful crafting of niches is specialization. Here are some possible niche roles:

- *End-user specialist:* The firm specializes in serving one type of end-use customer. For example, a *value-added reseller (VAR)* customizes the computer hardware and software for specific customer segments and earns a price premium in the process.
- *Vertical-level specialist:* The firm specializes at some vertical level of the production-distribution value chain. A copper firm may concentrate on producing raw copper, copper components, or finished copper products.
- *Customer-size specialist:* The firm concentrates on selling to either small, medium-sized, or large customers. Many nichers specialize in serving small customers neglected by the majors.
- *Specific-customer specialist:* The firm limits its selling to one or a few customers. Many firms sell their entire output to a single company, such as Sears or General Motors.
- *Geographic specialist:* The firm sells only in a certain locality, region, or area of the world.
- *Product or product-line specialist:* The firm carries or produces only one product line or product. A manufacturer may produce only lenses for microscopes. A retailer may carry only ties.
- *Product-feature specialist:* The firm specializes in producing a certain type of product or product feature. Zipcar's car-sharing service targets people who live and work in 13 major cities (in Canada, the U.S., and the U.K.), frequently use public transportation, but still need a car a few times a month.
- *Job-shop specialist:* The firm customizes its products for individual customers.
- *Quality-price specialist:* The firm operates at the low- or high-quality ends of the market. Hewlett-Packard specializes in the high-quality, high-priced end of the handheld-calculator market.
- *Service specialist:* The firm offers one or more services not available from other firms. A bank might take loan requests over the phone and hand-deliver the money to the customer.
- *Channel specialist:* The firm specializes in serving only one channel of distribution. For example, a soft-drink company decides to make a very large-sized serving available only at gas stations.

Because niches can weaken, the firm must continually create new ones. "Marketing Memo: Niche Specialist Roles" outlines some options. The firm should "stick to its niching" but not necessarily to its niche. That is why *multiple niching* is preferable to *single niching*. By developing strength in two or more niches, the company increases its chances for survival.

Firms entering a market should aim initially at a niche rather than the whole market. The cell-phone industry has experienced phenomenal growth but is now experiencing fierce competition as the numbers of new potential users dwindle. An Irish upstart company, Digicel Group, has successfully tapped into one of the few remaining high-growth segments: poor people without cell phones.

Digicel Group

In 2001, Digicel CEO Denis O'Brien heard that the government of Jamaica was opening its local phone market, long monopolized by British telecom giant Cable & Wireless. O'Brien spent nearly US$50 million for a licence, using money from the sale of his first telecom venture, Esat Telecom Group PLC. O'Brien took the plunge because he knew that Jamaicans had to wait over two years for a landline, and only 4 percent of the population had cell phones. Within 100 days, Digicel had signed on 100 000 subscribers, luring them with inexpensive rates and phones and with improved service. Five years later, 70 percent of Jamaica's cell-phone users—now 82 percent of the country's 2.7 million citizens—are Digicel customers. O'Brien has also homed in on the rest of the Caribbean and boasts three million subscribers in 22 countries throughout the Caribbean, Latin America, and even the South Pacific. In an ambitious move, O'Brien now plans to target the United States, specifically U.S. consumers who are young, poor, or immigrants—the kind of customers whom giants such as T-Mobile and Verizon don't court.[51]

BALANCING CUSTOMER AND COMPETITOR ORIENTATIONS

We have stressed the importance of a company's positioning itself competitively as a market leader, challenger, follower, or nicher. Yet a company must not spend all its time focusing on competitors.

Competitor-Centred Companies

A *competitor-centred company* sets its course as follows:

Observed Situation

- Competitor W is going all-out to crush us in Winnipeg.
- Competitor X is improving its distribution coverage in Saskatoon and hurting our sales.
- Competitor Y has cut its price in Montreal, and we lost three share points.
- Competitor Z has introduced a new service feature in Victoria, and we are losing sales.

Reactions

- We will withdraw from the Winnipeg market because we cannot afford to fight this battle.
- We will increase our advertising expenditure in Saskatoon.
- We will meet competitor Y's price cut in Montreal.
- We will increase our sales-promotion budget in Victoria.

This kind of planning has some pluses and minuses. On the positive side, the company develops a fighter orientation. It trains its marketers to be on constant alert, to watch for weaknesses in its competitors' and its own positions. On the negative side, the company is too reactive. Rather than formulating and executing a consistent, customer-oriented strategy, it determines its moves based on its competitors' moves. It does not move towards its own goals. It does not know where it will end up, because so much depends on what its competitors do.

Customer-Centred Companies

A *customer-centred company* focuses more on customer developments in formulating its strategies:

Observed Situation

- The total market is growing at 4-percent annually.
- The quality-sensitive segment is growing at 8-percent annually.
- The deal-prone customer segment is also growing fast, but these customers do not stay with any supplier very long.
- A growing number of customers have expressed an interest in a 24-hour hotline, which no one in the industry offers.

Reactions

- We will focus more effort on reaching and satisfying the quality segment of the market. We will buy better components, improve quality control, and shift our advertising theme to quality.
- We will avoid cutting prices and making deals because we do not want the kind of customer who buys this way.
- We will install a 24-hour hotline if it looks promising.

Clearly, the customer-centred company is in a better position to identify new opportunities and set a course that promises to deliver long-run profits. By monitoring customer needs, it can decide which customer groups and emerging needs are the most important to serve, given its resources and objectives. Jeff Bezos, founder of Amazon.com, strongly favours a customer-centred orientation: "Amazon.com's mantra has been that we were going to obsess over our customer and not our competitors. We watch our competitors, learn from them, see the things that they were doing good for customers and copy those things as much as we can. But we were never going to obsess over them."[52]

SUMMARY

1. To prepare an effective marketing strategy, a company must study competitors as well as actual and potential customers. Companies need to identify competitors' strategies, objectives, strengths, and weaknesses.

2. A company's closest competitors are those seeking to satisfy the same customers and needs and making similar offers. A company should also pay attention to latent competitors, which may offer new or other ways to satisfy the same needs. A company should identify competitors by using both industry and market-based analyses.

3. A market leader has the largest market share in the relevant product market. To remain dominant, the leader looks for ways to expand total market demand, attempts to protect its current market share, and perhaps tries to increase its market share.

4. A market challenger attacks the market leader and other competitors in an aggressive bid for more market share.

Challengers can choose from five types of general attack; challengers must also choose specific attack strategies.

5. A market follower is a runner-up firm that is willing to maintain its market share and not rock the boat. A follower can play the role of counterfeiter, cloner, imitator, or adapter.

6. A market nicher serves small market segments not being served by larger firms. The key to the successful crafting of niches is specialization. Nichers develop offerings to fully meet a certain group of customer's needs, commanding a premium price in the process.

7. As important as a competitive orientation is in today's global markets, companies should not overdo the emphasis on competitors. They should maintain a good balance of consumer and competitor monitoring.

APPLICATIONS

Marketing Debate: How Do You Attack a Category Leader?

Attacking a leader is always difficult. Some strategists recommend attacking a leader head-on by targeting its strengths. Other strategists disagree and recommend flanking and attempting to avoid the leader's strengths.

Take a position: The best way to challenge a leader is to attack its strengths *versus* The best way to attack a leader is to avoid a head-on assault and to adopt a flanking strategy.

Marketing Discussion

Pick an industry. Classify firms according to the four different roles they might play: leader, challenger, follower, or nicher. How would you characterize the nature of competition? Do the firms follow the principles described in the chapter?

Breakthrough Marketing: Accenture

Accenture began in 1942 as Adminstrative Accounting Group, the consulting arm of accounting firm Arthur Andersen. In 1989, it launched as a separate business unit focused on IT consulting and bearing the name Andersen Consulting. At that time, though it was earning US$1 billion annually, Andersen Consulting had low brand awareness among information-technology consultancies and was commonly mistaken for its accounting corporate parent. To build its brand and separate itself from the accounting firm with which it shared a name, Andersen Consulting launched the first large-scale advertising campaign in the professional-services area. By the end of the decade, it was the world's largest management- and technology-consulting organization.

In 2000, following arbitration against its former parent, Andersen Consulting was granted its full independence—but at the price of relinquishing the Andersen name. Andersen Consulting was given three months to find a name that was trademarkable in 49 countries, effective and inoffensive in over 200 languages, and acceptable to employees and clients—and that corresponded with an available URL. The effort that followed was one of the largest—and most successful—rebranding campaigns in corporate history.

As luck would have it, the company's new name came from a consultant at the company's Oslo office, who submitted "Accenture" as part of an internal name-generation initiative dubbed "Brandstorming." The consultant coined the Accenture name because it rhymed with "adventure" and connoted an "accent on the future." The name also retained the "Ac" of the original Andersen Consulting name (echoing the Ac.com website), which would help the firm retain some of its former brand equity. On midnight, December 31, 2000, Andersen Consulting officially adopted the Accenture name and launched a global marketing campaign targeting senior executives at Accenture's clients and prospects, all Accenture partners and employees, the media, leading industry analysts, potential recruits, and academia.

The results of the advertising, marketing, and communications campaigns were quick and impressive. Overall, the number of firms considering purchasing Accenture's services increased by 350 percent. Accenture's brand equity increased 11 percent. Awareness of Accenture's breadth and depth of services achieved 96 percent of its previous level. Globally, awareness of Accenture as a provider of management- and technology-consulting services was 76 percent of the former Andersen Consulting levels. These results enabled Accenture to successfully complete a US$1.7-billion IPO in July 2001.

In 2002, Accenture unveiled a new positioning to reflect its new role as a partner in aiding execution of strategy, summarized succinctly by the tagline "Innovation Delivered." This tagline was supported by the statement "From innovation to execution, Accenture helps accelerate your vision." Accenture surveyed senior executives from different industries and countries and confirmed that they saw inability to execute and deliver on ideas as the number-one barrier to success.

Accenture saw its differentiator as the ability both to provide innovative ideas—ideas grounded in business processes as well as IT—and to execute them. Competitors such as McKinsey were seen as highly specialized at developing strategy, whereas other competitors such as IBM were seen as highly skilled with technological implementation. Accenture wanted to be seen as excelling at both. Ian Watmore, Accenture's U.K. chief, explained the need to have both strategy and execution: "Unless you can provide both

transformational consulting and outsourcing capability, you're not going to win. Clients expect both."

In 2002, the business climate changed. After the dot-com crash and the economic downturn, innovation was no longer enough. Executives wanted bottom-line results. Accenture built upon the "Innovation Delivered" theme when it announced its new "High Performance Delivered" tagline in late 2003, featuring golfer Tiger Woods as the spokesperson. As part of its new commitment to helping clients achieve their business objectives, Accenture introduced a policy whereby many of its contracts contained incentives that it realized only if specific business targets were met. For instance, a contract with British travel agent Thomas Cook was structured such that Accenture's bonus depended on five metrics, including a cost-cutting one. In 2004, 30 percent of the company's contracts contained such incentives. The company's focus on improving its clients' performance proved beneficial to its bottom line: by 2007, Accenture had achieved six consecutive years of record revenues, which grew 13 percent in both 2006 and 2007. In 2007 alone, Accenture added over 900 new employees in Canada.

DISCUSSION QUESTIONS

1. What strategies has Accenture used to become a market leader?
2. Who are Accenture's main competitors?
3. What are Accenture's strengths and weaknesses relative to these competitors?

Sources: www.accenture.com; "Lessons Learned from Top Firms' Marketing Blunders," *Management Consultant International* (December 2003): 1; Sean Callahan, "Tiger Tees Off in New Accenture Campaign," *B to B*, October 13, 2003, p. 3; "Inside Accenture's Biggest UK Client," *Management Consultant International* (October 2003): 1–3; "Accenture's Results Highlight Weakness of Consulting Market," *Management Consultant International* (October 2003): 8–10; "Accenture Re-Branding Wins UK Plaudits," *Management Consultant International* (October 2002): 5.

5

SHAPING THE MARKET OFFERINGS

**IN THIS CHAPTER,
WE WILL ADDRESS
THE FOLLOWING
QUESTIONS:**

- What are the characteristics of products, and how do marketers classify products?

- How can companies differentiate products?

- How can a company build and manage its product mix and product lines?

- How can companies combine products to create strong co-brands or ingredient brands?

- How can companies use packaging, labelling, warranties, and guarantees as marketing tools?

lululemon Ω athletica

guest education centre
1-877-263-930

products   locations   culture   legacies   community   media   investors   about us   talk to us

Friends are more
important than
money. Don't trust
that an old age
pension will be
sufficient.

> Read our manifesto

Lauren Slater
Yoga Instructor
Yoga Tree
Cow Hollow Ambassade

yoga-inspired apparel for healthy living

lululemon athletica makes technical clothing for yoga, dancing, running, and most other sweaty pursuits. We create components for people to live longer, healthier, more fun lives.

Founded in Vancouver BC in 1998, the first lululemon shared its retail space with a yoga studio. We have been growing ever since, and our yoga clothes and apparel are now available at over 80 stores across Canada, the United States and Australia.

Authentic to its West Coast roots, lululemon continues to focus on a healthy, balanced fun-filled way of life.

recent lululemon yoga events

Why did almost 300 people recently gather in front of parliament in Ottawa,

the latest

> **Annapolis - MD**

Annapolis

lululemon is
opening Nov. 14
in Annapolis!

>More Info

> **Austin - TX**

6th & Lamar

Austin, your
new lululemon
opens Nov.
14th!

>More Info

CHAPTER 12

SETTING PRODUCT STRATEGY

twelve

At the heart of a great brand is a great product. Product is a key element in the market offering. Market leaders generally offer products and services of superior quality that provide unsurpassed customer value.

Vancouver-based Lululemon Athletica went public in 2007 and its stock soared. This yoga-inspired athletic-apparel company continues to grow—it expects to operate more than 250 stores worldwide by 2012. Lululemon's success rests in part on its mantra, "product is king," which is apparent in its approach to innovation and customer service. The company's innovative fabric, construction, and fashion are based on customer input. For example, local athletes and fitness instructors test out clothing and provide feedback. Customers are responsible for developing the company's heartbeat bra, which acts as a heart-rate monitor during exercise. A high level of customer service also helps to differentiate the brand. Lululemon's in-store staff are called "educators" and the company invests heavily in employee training. As a result of its efforts, Lululemon has developed a strong and loyal following of customers willing to pay close to $100 for a pair of yoga pants.

Sources: Eve Lazarus, "Stretching its Influence," *Marketing Magazine Online*, www.marketingmag.ca, November 20, 2006; Eve Lazarus, "The Tao of Lululemon," *Marketing Magazine Online*, www.marketingmag.ca, April 14, 2008; Marina Strauss, "Lululemon Links with Descente of Japan," *The Globe and Mail Online*, www.globeandmail.com, October 2, 2006.

FIGURE 12.1

Components of the Marketing
Offering

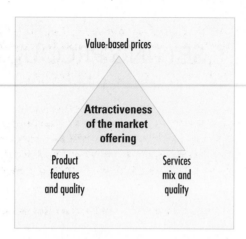

Marketing planning begins with formulating an offering to meet target customers' needs or wants. The customer will judge the offering on three basic elements: product features and quality, services mix and quality, and price (see Figure 12.1). In this chapter, we examine product; in Chapter 13, services; and in Chapter 14, prices. All three elements must be meshed into a competitively attractive offering.

PRODUCT CHARACTERISTICS AND CLASSIFICATIONS

Many people think that a product is a tangible offering, but it can be more than that. A **product** is anything that can be offered to a market to satisfy a want or need. Products that are marketed include physical goods, services, experiences, events, persons, places, properties, organizations, information, and ideas.

Product Levels: The Customer Value Hierarchy

In planning its market offering, the marketer needs to address five product levels (see Figure 12.2).[1] Each level adds more customer value, and the five constitute a **customer value hierarchy**.

- The fundamental level is the **core benefit**: the service or benefit the customer is really buying. A hotel guest is buying "rest and sleep." The purchaser of a drill is buying "holes." Marketers must see themselves as benefit providers.

- At the second level, the marketer has to turn the core benefit into a **basic product**. Thus a hotel room includes a bed, bathroom, towels, desk, dresser, and closet.

- At the third level, the marketer prepares an **expected product**, a set of attributes and conditions buyers normally expect when they purchase this product. Hotel guests expect a clean bed, fresh towels, working lamps, and a relative degree of quiet.

Five Product Levels

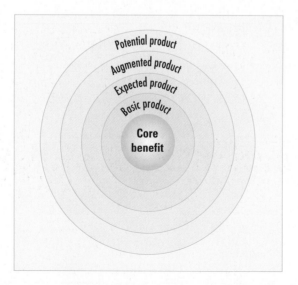

MARKETING **INSIGHT** | METAMARKETS AND METAMEDIARIES

There are some products whose purchase necessitates other purchases. The new-automobile market is a good example of a "metamarket." The consumer chooses an automobile but also must buy insurance from an insurance company and often must get a loan from a bank. A smart auto company or auto dealer would make all three purchases easy for the buyer by partnering with an insurance company and a bank. Such an auto dealer is performing as a "metamediary."

The wedding market is also a metamarket. The wedding couple need bridal gowns and/or tuxedos, a location for the solemnization, a reception hall, a caterer, and possibly a wedding consultant. Here, the wedding-dress seller or the wedding consultant might perform as a wedding metamediary.

Metamarkets are the result of marketers observing the total consumption system and "packaging" a system that simplifies carrying out these related product/service activities. Professor Mohan Sawhney defines a metamarket as "a set of products and services that consumers need to perform a *cognitively related* set of activities. Other metamarkets that are organized around major assets or major life events include:

- Buying a home
- Giving birth to a child
- Getting a divorce
- Planning a vacation

Source: Adapted from Mohan Sawhney, "Rethinking Marketing and Mediation in the Networked Economy," Winning Strategies for E-Commerce Lecture at the Kellogg School of Management, April 7–10, 1999.

- At the fourth level, the marketer prepares an **augmented product** that exceeds customer expectations. In developed countries, brand positioning and competition take place at this level. In developing and emerging markets such as India and Brazil, however, competition takes place mostly at the expected-product level.

- At the fifth level stands the **potential product**, which encompasses all the possible augmentations and transformations the product or offering might undergo in the future. Here is where companies search for new ways to satisfy customers and distinguish their offering.

Differentiation arises and competition increasingly occurs on the basis of product augmentation, which also leads the marketer to look at the user's total **consumption system**: the way the user performs the tasks of getting and using products and related services.[2] Each augmentation adds cost, however, and augmented benefits soon become expected benefits and necessary points-of-parity. Today's hotel guests expect cable or satellite television with a remote control and high-speed Internet access or two phone lines. This means competitors must search for still other features and benefits.

There are some products whose purchase necessitates other purchases. Markets for these products are called *metamarkets*, and these markets are served by *metamediaries*. See "Marketing Insight: Metamarkets and Metamediaries."

As some companies raise the price of their augmented product, others offer a "stripped-down" version at a much lower price. Thus, alongside the growth of fine hotels like Fairmont and Ritz Carlton, we see the emergence of lower-cost hotels and motels like Econo Lodge and Comfort Inn, which cater to clients who simply want the basic product. See how the Jamestown Container Co. augmented its product offerings to meet customer needs:

Jamestown Container Co.

What could be harder to differentiate than corrugated cardboard? Jamestown Container Company, the lead supplier of corrugated products for companies such as 3M, has formed strategic partnerships with area manufacturers to provide every part of the shipping system. It not only provides boxes, but also offers tape, shrink-wrap, and everything else needed either to display or to ship a customer's final product. "It's a combination for survival," says the company's chief operating officer. "More customers want to call one place for everything. We have to keep reinventing ourselves and form these kinds of relationships to remain competitive."[3]

Product Classifications

Marketers have traditionally classified products on the basis of durability, tangibility, and use (consumer or industrial). Each product type has an appropriate marketing-mix strategy.[4]

DURABILITY AND TANGIBILITY   Marketers classify products into three groups according to durability and tangibility:

1. *Nondurable goods* are tangible goods normally consumed in one or a few uses, like beer and soap. Because these goods are consumed quickly and purchased frequently, the appropriate strategy is to make them available in many locations, charge only a small markup, and advertise heavily to induce trial and build preference.

2. *Durable goods* are tangible goods that normally survive many uses: refrigerators, machine tools, and clothing. Durable products normally require more personal selling and service, command a higher margin, and require more seller guarantees.

3. *Services* are intangible, inseparable, variable, and perishable products. As a result, they normally require more quality control, supplier credibility, and adaptability. Examples include haircuts, legal advice, and appliance repairs.

CONSUMER-GOODS CLASSIFICATION   We classify the vast array of goods consumers buy on the basis of shopping habits. We distinguish among convenience, shopping, specialty, and unsought goods.

The consumer usually purchases **convenience goods** frequently, immediately, and with a minimum of effort. Examples include soft drinks, soaps, and newspapers. Convenience goods can be further divided. *Staples* are goods consumers purchase on a regular basis. A buyer might routinely purchase Heinz ketchup, Crest toothpaste, and Ritz crackers. *Impulse goods* are purchased without any planning or search effort. Candy bars and magazines are impulse goods. *Emergency goods* are purchased when a need is urgent—umbrellas during a rainstorm, or boots and shovels during the first winter snowstorm. Manufacturers of impulse and emergency goods will place them in outlets where consumers are likely to experience an urge or compelling need to make a purchase.

Shopping goods are goods that the consumer characteristically compares on such bases as suitability, quality, price, and style. Examples include furniture, clothing, used cars, and major appliances. We further divide this category. *Homogeneous shopping goods* are similar in quality but different enough in price to justify shopping comparisons. *Heterogeneous shopping goods* differ in product features and services that may be more important than price. The seller of heterogeneous shopping goods carries a wide assortment to satisfy individual tastes and must have well-trained salespeople to inform and advise customers.

Specialty goods have unique characteristics or brand identification for which a sufficient number of buyers are willing to make a special purchasing effort. Examples include cars, stereo components, photographic equipment, and men's suits. A Mercedes is a specialty good because interested buyers will travel far to buy one. Specialty goods do not require comparisons; buyers invest time only to reach dealers carrying the wanted products. Dealers do not need convenient locations, although they must let prospective buyers know their locations.

Unsought goods are those the consumer does not know about or does not normally think of buying, like smoke detectors. The classic examples of known but unsought goods are life insurance, cemetery plots, gravestones, and encyclopedias. Unsought goods require advertising and personal-selling support.

INDUSTRIAL-GOODS CLASSIFICATION   Industrial goods can be classified in terms of their relative cost and how they enter the production process: materials and parts, capital items, and supplies and business services. **Materials and parts** are goods that enter the manufacturer's product completely. They fall into two classes: raw materials, and manufactured materials and parts. *Raw materials* fall into two major groups: *farm products* (wheat, cotton, livestock, fruits, vegetables) and *natural products* (fish, lumber, crude petroleum, iron ore). Farm products are supplied by many producers, which turn them over to marketing intermediaries, which provide assembly, grading, storage, transportation, and selling services. Their perishable and seasonal nature gives rise to special marketing practices, whereas their commodity character results in relatively little advertising and promotional activity, with some exceptions. At times, commodity groups will launch campaigns to promote their product—for example, potatoes, cheese, and beef. Some producers brand their product—Dole salads, Mott's apples, and Chiquita bananas.

Natural products are limited in supply. They usually have great bulk and low unit value and must be moved from producer to user. Fewer and larger producers often market them directly to industrial users. Because the users depend on these materials, long-term supply contracts are common. The homogeneity of natural materials limits the amount of demand-creation activity. Price and delivery reliability are the major factors influencing the selection of suppliers.

Manufactured materials and parts fall into two categories: component materials (iron, thread, cement, wires) and component parts (small motors, tires, castings). *Component materials* are usually fabricated further—pig iron is made into steel, and thread is woven into cloth. The standardized nature of component materials usually means that price and supplier reliability are key purchase factors. *Component parts* enter the finished product with no further change in form, as when small motors are put into vacuum cleaners, and tires are put on automobiles. Most manufactured materials and parts are sold directly to industrial users. Price and service are major marketing considerations, and branding and advertising tend to be less important.

Capital items are long-lasting goods that facilitate developing or managing the finished product. They include two groups: installations and equipment. *Installations* consist of buildings (factories, offices) and heavy equipment (generators, drill presses, elevators). Installations are major purchases. They are usually bought directly from the producer, whose sales force includes technical personnel, and a long negotiation period precedes the typical sale. Producers must be willing to design to specification and to supply post-sale services. Advertising is much less important than personal selling.

Equipment includes portable factory equipment and tools (hand tools, lift trucks) and office equipment (personal computers, desks). These types of equipment do not become part of a finished product. They have a shorter life than installations but a longer life than operating supplies. Although some equipment manufacturers sell directly, more often they use intermediaries because the market is geographically dispersed, the buyers are numerous, and the orders are small. Quality, features, price, and service are major considerations. The sales force tends to be more important than advertising, although the latter can be used effectively.

Supplies and business services are short-term goods and services that facilitate developing or managing the finished product. Supplies are of two kinds: *maintenance and repair items* (paint, nails, brooms) and *operating supplies* (lubricants, coal, writing paper, pencils). Together, they go under the name of MRO goods. Supplies are the equivalent of convenience goods; they are usually purchased with minimum effort on a straight rebuy basis. They are normally marketed through intermediaries because of their low unit value and the great number and geographic dispersion of customers. Price and service are important considerations because suppliers are standardized and brand preference is not high.

Business services include *maintenance and repair services* (window cleaning, copier repair) and *business advisory services* (legal, management consulting, advertising). Maintenance and repair services are usually supplied under contract by small producers or are available from the manufacturers of the original equipment. Business advisory services are usually purchased on the basis of the supplier's reputation and staff.

DIFFERENTIATION

To be branded, products must be differentiated. Physical products vary in their potential for differentiation. At one extreme, we find products that allow little variation: chicken, aspirin, and steel. Yet even here, some differentiation is possible: Lilydale chickens, Bayer aspirin, and Ipsco steel have carved out distinct identities in their categories. Procter & Gamble makes Tide, Cheer, and Gain laundry detergents, each with a separate brand identity. At the other extreme are products capable of high differentiation, such as automobiles, commercial buildings, and furniture. Here the seller faces an abundance of design parameters, including form, features, performance quality, conformance quality, durability, reliability, repairability, and style.[5]

Product Differentiation

FORM   Many products can be differentiated in **form**—the size, shape, or physical structure of a product. Consider the many possible forms taken by products such as aspirin. Although aspirin is essentially a commodity, it can be differentiated by dosage size, shape, colour, coating, or action time.

FEATURES   Most products can be offered with varying **features** that supplement their basic function. A company can identify and select appropriate new features by surveying recent buyers and then calculating *customer value* versus *company cost* for each potential feature. The company should also consider how many people want each feature, how long it would take to introduce each feature, and whether competitors could easily copy the feature. To avoid "feature fatigue," the company also must be careful to prioritize those features that are included and find unobtrusive ways to provide information about how consumers can use and benefit from the feature.[6] Companies must also think in terms of feature bundles or packages. Auto companies often manufacture cars at several "trim levels." This lowers manufacturing and inventory costs. Each company must decide whether to offer feature customization at a higher cost or a few standard packages at a lower cost.

CUSTOMIZATION   Marketers can differentiate products by making them customized to an individual. As companies have grown proficient at gathering information about individual customers and business partners (suppliers, distributors, retailers), and as their factories are being designed more flexibly, they have increased their ability to individualize market offerings, messages, and media. Mass customization is the ability of a company to meet each customer's requirements—to prepare on a mass basis individually designed products, services, programs, and communications.[7]

Although Levi's and Lands' End were among the first clothing manufacturers to introduce custom jeans, other players have introduced mass customization into other markets. Procter & Gamble developed OlayForYou.ca to provide customized online skin-care recommendations.[8] Harvey's focuses on personalizing its product by tailoring burgers and garnishes to individual customers. In 2006, Harvey's launched humorous TV advertisements in which customers are shown ordering burgers made to their exact specifications, such as the "Vanessa burger."[9] Lego embraced mass customization from the start.

Lego

In a sense, Lego of Billund, Denmark, has always been mass customized. Every child who has ever had a set of the most basic Legos has built his or her own unique and amazing creations, brick by plastic brick. However, in 2005, Lego set up The Lego Factory, which, as it says on the company website, "lets you design, share, and build your very own custom Lego products." Using Lego's freely downloadable Digital Designer Software, customers can create any structure. The creations can exist—and be shared with other enthusiasts—solely online or, if customers want to build it, the software tabulates the pieces required and sends an order to Lego's Enfield, Connecticut, warehouse. The employees there put all the pieces into a box and send it off. Not only do Lego Factory customers have the pride of building their own creations, but they can also earn royalties if Lego decides the design is good enough to put in its own catalogue. Some of the most creative models include renderings of the Danish parliament building and M.C. Escher's "Another World." In 2006, The Lego Factory initiated a design competition in which eight contestants competed to be profiled on the Lego Factory website along with their creations.[10]

PERFORMANCE QUALITY   Most products are established at one of four performance levels: low, average, high, or superior. **Performance quality** is the level at which the product's primary characteristics operate. Quality is becoming an increasingly important dimension for differentiation as companies adopt a value model and provide higher quality for less money. Firms, however, should not necessarily design the highest possible performance level. The manufacturer must design a performance level appropriate to the target market and competitors' performance levels. A company must also manage performance quality through time. Continuously improving the product can produce high returns and market share; failing to do so can have negative consequences. Lowering quality in an attempt to cut costs often has dire consequences. Schlitz, the number-two beer brand in the United States in the 1960s and 1970s, was driven into the dust because management adopted a financially motivated strategy to increase its short-term profits and curry favour with shareholders. In August of 2007, Mattel Ltd. recalled 21 million toys worldwide because of lead paint and other toy-safety concerns. Canadian toy companies, like Family Pastimes, are responding with safe, Canadian-made toys.

Family Pastimes

Family Pastimes is a 35-year-old company that manufactures board games in a workshop near Perth, Ontario. The company is committed to toy safety and quality—it uses soy-based printing ink, local labour, and recycled materials where possible. Family Pastimes has over 80 board games and it ships 65 000 games to 3500 retailers around the world each year.

While the company's board games may cost more than competing brands, in some cases consumers are willing to pay for differentiated and high-quality products. There are over 200 toy and game manufacturers in Canada.[11] Toronto-based Monster Factory is experiencing a similar success. Its non-toxic and kid-friendly plush toys have been in production since 2003, and by the end of 2007 more than 10 000 monsters had been shipped as far as the U.K., Australia, and New Zealand.[12]

CONFORMANCE QUALITY Buyers expect products to have a high **conformance quality**, which is the degree to which all the produced units are identical and meet the promised specifications. Suppose a Porsche 944 is designed to accelerate to 100 kilometres per hour within 10 seconds. If every Porsche 944 coming off the assembly line does this, the model is said to have high conformance quality. The problem with low conformance quality is that the product will disappoint some buyers.

DURABILITY **Durability**, a measure of the product's expected operating life under natural or stressful conditions, is a valued attribute for certain products. Buyers will generally pay more for vehicles and kitchen appliances that have a reputation for being long lasting. However, this rule is subject to some qualifications. The extra price must not be excessive. Furthermore, the product must not be subject to rapid technological obsolescence, as is the case with personal computers and video cameras.

RELIABILITY Buyers normally will pay a premium for more reliable products. **Reliability** is a measure of the probability that a product will not malfunction or fail within a specified time period. Maytag, which manufactures major home appliances, has an outstanding reputation for creating reliable appliances. "Breakthrough Marketing: Toyota," at the end of this chapter, describes how Toyota has excelled at making and selling high-quality, dependable automobiles.

REPAIRABILITY **Repairability** is a measure of the ease of fixing a product when it malfunctions or fails. Ideal repairability would exist if users could fix the product themselves with little cost in money or time. Some products include a diagnostic feature that allows service people to correct a problem over the telephone or advise the user how to correct it. Many computer hardware and software companies offer technical support over the phone, by fax or email, or by real-time "chat" online.

Monster Factory produces non-toxic, kid-friendly, made-in-Canada toys.

STYLE **Style** describes how the product looks and feels to the buyer. Car buyers pay a premium for Jaguars because of their extraordinary look. Aesthetics plays a key role in such brands as Absolut vodka, Apple computers, Montblanc pens, Godiva chocolates, and Harley-Davidson motorcycles.[13] Style has the advantage of creating distinctiveness that is difficult to copy. On the negative side, strong style does not always mean high performance. A car may look sensational but spend a lot of time in the repair shop.

Design

As competition intensifies, design offers a potent way to differentiate and position a company's products and services.[14] In increasingly fast-paced markets, price and technology are not enough. Design is the factor that will often give a company its competitive edge. **Design** is the totality of features that affect how a product looks and functions in terms of customer requirements.

Design is particularly important in making and marketing retail services, apparel, packaged goods, and durable equipment. The designer must figure out how much to invest in form, feature development, performance, conformance, durability, reliability, repairability, and style. To the company, a well-designed product is one that is easy to manufacture and distribute. To the customer, a well-designed product is one that is pleasant to look at and easy to open, install, use, repair, and dispose of. The designer has to take all these factors into account.

The arguments for good design are particularly compelling for smaller consumer-products companies and start-ups that do not have big advertising dollars. Take the case of Log Homes Canada, a company

that won a BC Export Award in 2003. Winning the award for export and design helped this family-owned business get noticed and grow to become the foremost provider of handcrafted log homes in Canada and abroad. The firm takes tremendous care with design and construction, carefully designing each home and choosing the right-sized logs. Attention to detail is part of its success, and Log Homes Canada insists on the uniformity of its logs. Only hand-peeled logs are used in its homes to ensure quality craftership from beginning to end of the building process. Further, the company buys only from logging companies that practise environmentally friendly logging methods.[15]

Certain countries and companies are winning on design: Italian design in apparel and furniture, Scandinavian design for functionality, aesthetics, and environmental consciousness. Finland's Nokia was the first to introduce user-changeable covers for cell phones, the first to have elliptical-shaped, soft, and friendly forms, and the first with big screens, all contributing to its remarkable ascent. Braun, a German division of Gillette, has elevated design to a high art in its electric shavers, coffee makers, hair dryers, and food processors. The company's design department enjoys status equal to that of engineering and manufacturing. The Danish firm Bang & Olufsen has received much kudos for the design of its stereos, TV equipment, and telephones.

Manufacturers, service providers, and retailers seek new designs to create differentiation and establish a more complete connection with consumers. Holistic marketers recognize the emotional power of design and the importance to consumers of how things look and feel. After seeing some of its brands lose share to competitors with stronger designs and aesthetics, Procter & Gamble appointed a *chief design officer* in 2001 and now hands out an A. G. Lafley Design award each fall. Lafley, P&G's CEO, is credited with pushing for more products to involve design at the front end—not as an afterthought. These products, such as Crest Whitestrips, Olay Daily Facials, and the whole line of Swiffer Quick Clean products, have generated more trials, more repurchases, and more sales.[16]

In an increasingly visually-oriented culture, translating brand meaning and positioning through design is critical. "In a crowded marketplace," writes Virginia Postrel in *The Substance of Style*, "aesthetics is often the only way to make a product stand out." Design can shift consumer perceptions to make brand experiences more rewarding. Consider the lengths Boeing went to in order to make its 777 airplane seem roomier and more comfortable. Raised centre bins, side luggage bins, divider panels, gently arched ceilings, and raised seats make the aircraft interior seem bigger. As one design engineer noted, "If we do our jobs, people don't realize what we have done. They just say they feel more comfortable."

A bad design can also ruin a product's prospects. Sony's e-Villa Internet appliance was intended to allow consumers to have Internet access from their kitchen. But at nearly 15 kilograms and 40 centimetres, the mammoth product was so awkward and heavy that the owner's manual recommended customers use their legs, not their back, to pick it up. The product was withdrawn after three months.

Services Differentiation

When the physical product cannot easily be differentiated, the key to competitive success may lie in adding valued services and improving their quality. Rolls-Royce PLC has ensured its aircraft engines are in high demand by continuously monitoring the health of its 3000 engines for 45 airlines through live satellite feeds. Under its TotalCare program, airlines pay Rolls a fee for every hour an engine is in flight, and Rolls assumes the risks and costs of downtime and repairs in return.[17] Customer service is also an important differentiator. WestJet has introduced a Guest Experience Committee that includes employees from various operational areas to review company processes and suggest service improvements from a customer perspective.[18]

The main service differentiators are ordering ease, delivery, installation, customer training, customer consulting, maintenance and repair, and returns.

ORDERING EASE **Ordering ease** refers to how easy it is for a customer to place an order with the company. Baxter Healthcare has eased the ordering process by supplying hospitals with computer terminals through which they send orders directly to Baxter. Many financial service institutions like TD and RBC offer secure websites to help customers get information and conduct transactions more efficiently.

DELIVERY **Delivery** refers to how well the product or service is brought to the customer. It includes speed, accuracy, and care throughout the delivery process. Today's customers have grown to expect delivery speed: pizza delivered in half an hour, film developed in one hour, eyeglasses made in one hour, cars lubricated in 15 minutes. Levi Strauss, Benetton, and The Limited have adopted computerized *quick response systems* (QRS) that link the information systems of their suppliers, manufacturing plants, distribution centres, and retailing outlets. Cemex, a giant cement company based in Mexico, has transformed the cement business by promising to deliver concrete faster than pizza. Cemex equips every truck with a *global positioning system* (GPS) so that its real-time location is known and full information is available to drivers and dispatchers. Cemex is able to promise that if your load is more than ten minutes late, you get a 20-percent discount.[19]

INSTALLATION   **Installation** refers to the work done to make a product operational in its planned location. Buyers of heavy equipment expect good installation service. Differentiating at this point in the consumption chain is particularly important for companies with complex products. Ease of installation becomes a true selling point, especially when the target market is technology novices.

CUSTOMER TRAINING   **Customer training** refers to training the customer's employees to use the vendor's equipment properly and efficiently. General Electric not only sells and installs expensive X-ray equipment in hospitals; it also gives extensive training to users of this equipment. McDonald's requires its new franchisees to attend Hamburger University in Oak Brook, Illinois, for two weeks, to learn how to manage the franchise properly.

CUSTOMER CONSULTING   **Customer consulting** refers to data, information systems, and advisory services that the seller offers to buyers. See what office furniture company Herman Miller Inc. does for some of its clients:

Herman Miller Inc.'s product strategy consists of more than designing and producing innovative office furniture. The company also helps train office workers in ergonomics (the science of equipment design) to improve efficiency, comfort, and safety.

Herman Miller Inc.

Herman Miller, a large office-furniture company, has partnered with a California firm to show corporate clients how to get the full benefits of its furnishings. The firm, Future Industrial Technologies, specializes in workplace-ergonomics training. Working through Herman Miller's dealership network, customers can arrange two-hour training sessions for small groups of employees. The sessions are run by some of the 1200 physical therapists, occupational therapists, registered nurses, and chiropractors who work under contract to Future Industrial Technologies. Although customer ergonomics training results in only modest revenue gains for Herman Miller, the company feels that teaching healthy work habits creates higher levels of customer satisfaction and sets Herman Miller products apart.[20]

MAINTENANCE AND REPAIR   **Maintenance and repair** describes the service program for helping customers keep purchased products in good working order. Hewlett-Packard offers online technical support, or "e-support," for its customers. In the event of a service problem, customers can use various online tools to find a solution. Those aware of the specific problem can search an online database for fixes; those unaware can use diagnostic software that finds the problem and searches the online database for an automatic fix. Customers can also seek online help from a technician.[21] See how Best Buy worked to resolve the challenges many customers have with their home computer systems:

Best Buy

As consolidation and competitive pricing among electronics retailers continues, companies are increasingly looking for new ways to stand out in the crowd. That's why Best Buy contracted with the Geek Squad, a small residential computer-services company, to revamp the chain's in-store computer-repair services. Best Buy used to send PCs to regional repair facilities, a process that was time consuming and ultimately contributed to a high degree of consumer dissatisfaction. Now about half of all repairs are made in Best Buy stores. But the real differentiator is the Geek Squad's ability to make house calls (at a higher fee). Geek Squad house calls are called a "Beetle Roll" because of the squad's signature fleet of hip VW Beetles.

Geek Squad employees even dress differently for house calls—wearing a distinctive "geek" look as opposed to the traditional Best Buy blue they wear at the in-store service centres. To further differentiate its stores and services, on Earth Day 2008, Best Buy Canada announced its new recycling service (for everything from batteries to CD players), in addition to giving customers handsome discounts when they traded in their old TVs, laptops, and MP3 players.[22]

RETURNS   Although product **returns** are undoubtedly a nuisance to customers, manufacturers, retailers, and distributors alike, they are also an unavoidable reality of doing business, especially with online purchases. Although the average return rate for online sales is roughly 5 percent, return and exchange policies are estimated to serve as a deterrent to one-third to one-half of online buyers. The cost of processing a return can be two to three times that of an outbound shipment, totalling an average of $30–$35 for items bought on the Internet. Offering a superior return policy can help a firm create a competitive advantage, as was the case at Costco.

Costco Wholesale Corp.

Costco guarantees customer satisfaction and backed up this promise with an ultragenerous return policy that was perhaps the cushiest in the retail-electronics business. Until recently, a customer could buy an expensive plasma TV, use it indefinitely, and take it back any time. Then he or she could use the refund to buy a newer model—often at a cheaper price. However, the customer's gain was Costco's loss. The membership warehouse chain ended up losing "tens of millions of dollars" annually with this policy. In early 2007, Costco Canada set stricter limits on returns of desktop and notebook computers to a still-generous six months. Some customers, who had come to rely on the trust and generosity embodied in Costco's return policy, vowed to shop elsewhere. Yet, most realized the good times had to come to a halt. To Costco's credit, it is now offering more technical support for installing and operating the electronics it sells; the company had discovered that most returns were due not so much to problems with the items as to customers' inability to set up today's complicated electronic devices. All other Costco items can still be returned for any reason at any time.[23]

We can think of product returns in two ways:[24]

- *Controllable returns* result from problems, difficulties, or errors of the seller or customer and can be mostly eliminated with proper strategies and programs by the company or its supply-chain partners. Improved handling or storage, better packaging, and improved transportation and forward logistics can eliminate problems before they occur.

- *Uncontrollable returns* can't be eliminated by the company in the short-run through any of these means.

One basic returns strategy that companies can adopt is to attempt to eliminate the root causes of controllable returns while at the same time developing processes for handling uncontrollable product returns. The goal of a product-return strategy is to have fewer products returned and a higher percentage of returns that can go back into the distribution pipeline to be sold again. The Running Room, headquartered in Edmonton, is North America's largest specialty running and walking shoe and sportswear retailer. Operating 92 stores across the country, it trains its salespeople to be as knowledgeable as possible when it comes to recommending the right products, thereby reducing the need for returns.

PRODUCT AND BRAND RELATIONSHIPS

Each product can be related to other products to ensure that a firm is offering and marketing the optimal set of products.

The Product Hierarchy

The product hierarchy stretches from basic needs to particular items that satisfy those needs. We can identify six levels of the product hierarchy, using life insurance as an example:

1. *Need family*—The core need that underlies the existence of a product family. Example: security.

2. *Product family*—All the product classes that can satisfy a core need with reasonable effectiveness. Example: savings and income.

3. *Product class*—A group of products within the product family recognized as having a certain functional coherence. Also known as product category. Example: financial instruments.

4. *Product line*—A group of products within a product class that are closely related because they perform a similar function, are sold to the same customer groups, are marketed through the same outlets or channels, or fall within given price ranges. A product line may be composed of different brands, a single family brand, or an individual brand that has been line extended. Example: life insurance.

5. *Product type*—A group of items within a product line that share one of several possible forms of the product. Example: term life insurance.

6. *Item (also called stock-keeping unit or product variant)*—A distinct unit within a brand or product line distinguishable by size, price, appearance, or some other attribute. Example: Prudential renewable term life insurance.

Product Systems and Mixes

A **product system** is a group of diverse but related items that function in a compatible manner. For example, the PalmOne handheld and smartphone product lines come with attachable products including headsets, cameras, keyboards, presentation projectors, e-books, MP3 players, and voice recorders. A **product mix** (also called a **product assortment**) is the set of all products and items a particular seller offers for sale.

A product mix consists of various product lines. Seagate now makes 29 kinds of drives that are essential to servers, PCs, and consumer-electronic products such as video games, DVRs, and cameras. In General Electric's Consumer Appliance Division, there are product-line managers for refrigerators, stoves, and washing machines. NEC's (Japan) product mix consists of communication products and computer products. Michelin has three product lines: tires, maps, and restaurant-rating services. At Queen's University, there are separate academic deans for the Faculty of Applied Science, the Faculty of Arts and Science, the Faculty of Education, the Faculty of Health Sciences, the Faculty of Law, the School of Business, and the School of Physical and Health Sciences.

A company's product mix has a certain width, length, depth, and consistency. These concepts are illustrated in Table 12.1 for selected Procter & Gamble consumer products.

■ The *width* of a product mix refers to how many different product lines the company carries. Table 12.1 shows a product-mix width of five lines. (In fact, P&G produces many additional lines.)

■ The *length* of a product mix refers to the total number of items in the mix. In Table 12.1, it is 20. We can also talk about the average length of a line. This is obtained by dividing the total length (here 20) by the number of lines (here five), for an average product-line length of four.

■ The *depth* of a product mix refers to how many variants are offered of each product in the line. If Tide comes in two scents (Mountain Spring and Regular), two formulations (liquid and powder), and two additives (with and without bleach), Tide has a depth of eight

To read about French carmaker Renault and its strategy for pursuing international growth, visit www.pearsoned.co.uk/marketingmanagementeurope.

TABLE 12.1	PRODUCT-MIX WIDTH AND PRODUCT-LINE LENGTH FOR PROCTER & GAMBLE PRODUCTS (INCLUDING DATES OF INTRODUCTION)				
	Product-Mix Width				
	Detergents	Toothpaste	Bar Soap	Disposable Diapers	Paper Products
PRODUCT-LINE LENGTH	Ivory Snow (1930)	Gleem (1952)	Ivory (1879)	Pampers (1961)	Charmin (1928)
	Dreft (1933)	Crest (1955)	Camay (1926)	Luvs (1976)	Puffs (1960)
	Tide (1946)		Zest (1952)		Bounty (1965)
	Cheer (1950)		Safeguard (1963)		
	Dash (1954)		Oil of Olay (1993)		
	Bold (1965)				
	Gain (1966)				
	Era (1972)				

because there are eight distinct variants. We can calculate the average depth of P&G's product mix by averaging the number of variants within the brand groups.

- The *consistency* of the product mix refers to how closely related the various product lines are in end use, production requirements, distribution channels, or some other way. P&G's product lines are consistent insofar as they are consumer goods that go through the same distribution channels. The lines are less consistent insofar as they perform different functions for the buyers.

These four product-mix dimensions permit the company to expand its business in four ways. It can add new product lines, thus widening its product mix. It can lengthen each product line. It can add more product variants to each product and deepen its product mix. Finally, a company can pursue more product-line consistency. To make these product and brand decisions, it is useful to conduct product-line analysis.

Product-Line Analysis

In offering a product line, companies normally develop a basic platform and modules that can be added to meet different customer requirements. Car manufacturers build their cars around a basic platform. Homebuilders show a model home to which buyers can add additional features. This modular approach enables the company to offer variety and lower production costs.

Product-line managers need to know the sales and profits of each item in their line in order to determine which items to build, maintain, harvest, or divest.[25] They also need to understand each product line's market profile.

SALES AND PROFITS   Figure 12.3 shows a sales-and-profit report for a five-item product line. The first item accounts for 50 percent of total sales and 30 percent of total profits. The first two items account for 80 percent of total sales and 60 percent of total profits. If these two items were suddenly hurt by a competitor, the line's sales and profitability could collapse. These items must be carefully monitored and protected. At the other end, the last item delivers only 5 percent of the product line's sales and profits. The product-line manager may consider dropping this item unless it has strong growth potential.

Every company's product portfolio contains products with different margins. Supermarkets make almost no margin on bread and milk, reasonable margins on canned and frozen foods, and even better margins on flowers, ethnic-food lines, and freshly baked goods. A local telephone company makes different margins on its core telephone service, call waiting, caller ID, and voice mail.

A company can classify its products into four types that yield different gross margins, depending on sales volume and promotion. To illustrate with personal computers:

- *Core product.* Basic computers that produce high sales volume and are heavily promoted but yield low margins because they are viewed as undifferentiated commodities.

- *Staples.* Items with lower sales volume and no promotion, such as faster CPUs or bigger memories. These yield a somewhat higher margin.

- *Specialties.* Items with lower sales volume but which might be highly promoted (such as digital movie-making equipment) or might generate income from services (such as personal delivery, installation, or on-site training).

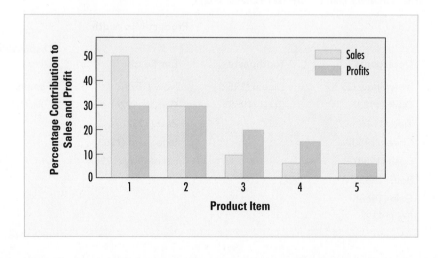

FIGURE 12.3

Product-Item Contributions to a Product Line's Total Sales and Profits

- *Convenience items.* Peripheral items that sell in high volume but receive less promotion, such as carrying cases and accessories, upscale video or sound cards, and software. Consumers tend to buy them where they buy the original equipment because it is more convenient than making further shopping trips. These items can carry higher margins.

The main point is that companies should recognize that these items differ in their potential for being priced higher or advertised more as ways to increase their sales, margins, or both.[26]

MARKET PROFILE The product-line manager must review how the line is positioned against competitors' lines. Consider paper company X with a paper-product line.[27] Two paper attributes are weight and finish quality. Paper is usually offered at standard levels of 90, 120, 150, and 180 weight. Finish quality is offered at low, medium, and high levels. Figure 12.4 shows the location of the various product-line items of company X and four competitors, A, B, C, and D. Competitor A sells two product items in the extra-high weight class ranging from medium to low finish quality. Competitor B sells four items that vary in weight and finish quality. Competitor C sells three items for which the greater the weight, the greater the finish quality. Competitor D sells three items, all lightweight but varying in finish quality. Company X offers three items that vary in weight and finish quality.

The product map shows which competitors' items are competing against company X's items. For example, company X's low-weight, medium-quality paper competes against competitor D's and B's papers, but its high-weight, medium-quality paper has no direct competitor. The map also reveals possible locations for new items. No manufacturer offers a high-weight, low-quality paper. If company X estimates a strong unmet demand and can produce and price this paper at low cost, it could consider adding this item to its line.

Another benefit of product mapping is that it identifies market segments. Figure 12.4 shows the types of paper, by weight and quality, preferred by three industries: general printing, point-of-purchase display, and office supply. The map shows that company X is well positioned to serve the needs of the general printing industry but is less effective in serving the other two industries.

Product-line analysis provides information for two key decision areas—product-line length and product-mix pricing.

Product-Line Length

Company objectives influence product-line length. One objective is to create a product line to induce upselling: thus BMW would like to move customers up from the 3 series to the 5 or 7 series. A different objective is to create a product line that facilitates cross-selling: Hewlett-Packard sells printers as well as computers. Still another objective is to create a product line that protects against economic ups and downs: Electrolux offers refrigerators, dishwashers, and vacuum cleaners under different brand names in the discount, middle market, and premium segments, in part in case the economy moves up or down.[28] Companies seeking high market share and market growth will generally carry longer product lines. Companies that emphasize high profitability will carry shorter lines consisting of carefully chosen items.

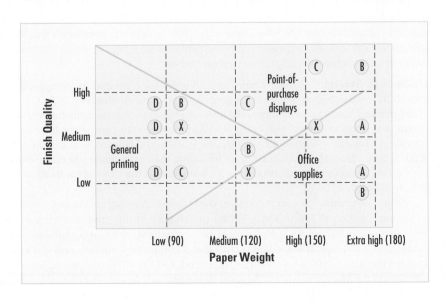

FIGURE 12.4

Product Map for Paper-Product Line

Source: Benson P. Shapiro, *Industrial Product Policy: Managing the Existing Product Line* (Cambridge, MA: Marketing Science Institute Report No. 77–110). Copyright © 2003. Reprinted by permission of Marketing Science Institute and Benson P. Shapiro.

Product lines tend to lengthen over time. Excess manufacturing capacity puts pressure on the product-line manager to develop new items. The sales force and distributors also pressure the company for a more complete product line to satisfy customers. But as items are added, costs rise: there are design and engineering costs, inventory-carrying costs, manufacturing-changeover costs, order-processing costs, transportation costs, and new-item promotional costs. Eventually, someone calls a halt. Top management may stop development because of insufficient funds or manufacturing capacity. The controller may call for a study of money-losing items. A pattern of product-line growth followed by massive pruning may repeat itself many times. Increasingly, consumers are growing weary of dense product lines, over-extended brands, and feature-laden products (see "Marketing Insight: When Less Is More").

A company lengthens its product line in two ways: by line stretching and line filling.

LINE STRETCHING   Every company's product line covers a certain part of the total possible range. For example, BMW automobiles are located in the upper price range of the automobile market. **Line stretching** occurs when a company lengthens its product line beyond its current range. The company can stretch its line down-market, up-market, or both ways.

Down-Market Stretch A company positioned in the middle market may want to introduce a lower-priced line for any of three reasons:

1. The company may notice strong growth opportunities as mass retailers such as Wal-Mart, Best Buy, and others attract a growing number of shoppers who want value-priced goods.

2. The company may wish to tie up lower-end competitors who might otherwise try to move up-market. If the company has been attacked by a low-end competitor, it often decides to counter-attack by entering the low end of the market.

3. The company may find that the middle market is stagnating or declining.

A company faces a number of naming choices in deciding to move down-market. Sony, for example, faced three choices:

1. Use the parent brand name on all its offerings. Sony has used its name on products in a variety of price tiers.

2. Introduce lower-priced offerings using a sub-brand name, such as P&G Charmin Basics, Gillette Good News, and Ramada Limited.

3. Introduce the lower-priced offerings under a different name, such as The Gap's Old Navy brand. This strategy is expensive to implement, and consumers may not accept a new brand that lacks the equity of the parent brand name.

Moving down-market carries risks. Kodak introduced Kodak Funtime film to counter lower-priced brands, but it did not price Kodak Funtime low enough to match the lower-priced film. It also found some of its regular customers buying Funtime, so it was cannibalizing its core brand. It withdrew the product. On the other hand, Mercedes successfully introduced its C-Class cars at US$30 000 without injuring its ability to sell other Mercedes cars for US$100 000. John Deere introduced a lower-priced line of lawn tractors called Sabre from John Deere while still selling its more expensive tractors under the John Deere name. Air Canada has been notorious for doing this with line extensions such as Tango and Zip (which are now no longer operational) to compete with discount airlines such as WestJet, Skyservice, and others.

Up-Market Stretch Companies may wish to enter the high end of the market to achieve more growth, to realize higher margins, or simply to position themselves as full-line manufacturers. Many markets have spawned surprising upscale segments: Starbucks in coffee, Häagen-Dazs in ice cream, and Evian in bottled water. The leading Japanese auto companies have each introduced an upscale automobile—Toyota's Lexus, Nissan's Infiniti, and Honda's Acura. Note that they invented entirely new names rather than using or including their own names, because consumers may not have given the brand "permission" to stretch upward at the time when those different lines were first introduced.

Other companies have included their own name in moving up-market. Gallo introduced Gallo of Sonoma (priced at $10 to $30 a bottle) to compete in the premium-wine segment, using the founder's grandchildren as spokespeople in an intensive push and pull campaign. With a hip, young, and fun image, the line was a critical and commercial success and was rebranded as Gallo Family Vineyards in 2006. General Electric introduced the GE Profile brand for its large-appliance offerings in the upscale market.[29] Some brands have used modifiers to signal a noticeable, although

| MARKETING INSIGHT | WHEN LESS IS MORE |

Although many consumers find appealing the notion of having more choices, the reality is that consumers can sometimes be overwhelmed by the choices involved. With thousands of new products introduced each year, consumers find it harder and harder to successfully navigate through store aisles. One study found that the average shopper spent 40 seconds or more in the supermarket soda aisle, compared to 25 seconds six or seven years ago. Another research study showed that although consumers expressed greater interest in shopping a larger assortment of 24 different jam flavours than a smaller assortment of six, they were ten times more likely to actually make a selection from the smaller assortment.

Although consumers with well-defined preferences may benefit from more differentiated products that offer specific benefits to better suit their needs, too much product choice may be a source of frustration, confusion, and regret

Marketers are learning through sometimes painful experience that product lines can get too long or products can become just too complicated.

for other consumers. Product proliferation has another downside. Exposing the customer to constant product changes and introductions may nudge them into reconsidering their choices, resulting in their switching to a competitor's product.

And not all the new choices may be winners anyway, as Nestlé found out with its KitKat bars, among the best-selling candy bars in the United Kingdom since they were invented there in the 1930s. To increase sales in 2004, the company rolled out a vast array of new flavours. The summer saw the launch of strawberries and cream, passion fruit and mango, and red berry versions; with winter came Christmas pudding, tiramisu (with real wine and mascarpone), and low-carb versions. The new flavours were a disaster—the tastes were too sweet and unusual for many—and even worse, some consumers couldn't find the classic KitKat bars among all the new varieties. An ill-timed switch from the classic slogan, "Have a Break, Have a KitKat," did not help, and sales dropped 18 percent as a result. The new flavours were then discontinued.

Smart marketers are also realizing that it's not just the product lines that are making consumer heads spin—many products themselves are just too complicated for the average consumer. Royal Philips Electronics learned its lesson when the company asked 100 top managers to take various Philips electronic products home one weekend and see whether they could make them work. The number of executives who returned frustrated and angry spoke volumes about the challenges the ordinary consumer faced. A Yankee Group research study in 2004 reinforces this fact: almost a third of all home-networking products sold that year were returned because the consumer couldn't get them to work; almost half of potential digital-camera buyers were delaying their purchase because they thought the products were too complicated; and about a quarter of consumers thought they already owned an HDTV (they didn't). Philips launched an initiative in September 2004 with a goal to make technology simpler, backed by a US$100-million ad campaign: "Sense and Simplicity."

Sources: Deborah Ball, "Flavor Experiment for KitKat Leaves Nestlé with a Bad Taste," *Wall Street Journal*, July 6, 2006; Barry Schwartz, *The Paradox of Choice: Why More Is Less* (New York: Harper Collins Ecco, 2004); Frisco Endt, "It Is Rocket Science," *Newsweek*, October 18, 2004, p. E8; Alexander Chernev, "When More Is Less and Less Is More: The Role of Ideal Point Availability and Assortment in Choice," *Journal of Consumer Research*, 30 (September 2003): 170–83; Sheena S. Iyengar and Mark R. Lepper, "When Choice Is Demotivating: Can One Desire Too Much of a Good Thing?" *Journal of Personality and Social Psychology*, 79, no. 6 (December 2000): 995–1006; Ravi Dhar, "Consumer Preference for a No-Choice Option," *Journal of Consumer Research*, 27 (September 1997): 233–48.

presumably not dramatic, quality improvement, such as Ultra Dry Pampers, Extra Strength Tylenol, and PowerPro Dustbuster Plus.

Two-Way Stretch Companies serving the middle market might decide to stretch their line in both directions. Andrew Peller Limited sells its premium-wine brands, the Andrew Peller Signature Series, for $30 to $90, and it also sells newer brands such as Croc Crossing and XOXO in the $10 to $15 range.[30]

Consider how Purina Dog Food has stretched up and down to create a product line differentiated by benefits to dogs, breadth of varieties, ingredients, and price:

- Pro Plan ($22.49/20-lb bag)—helps dogs live long and healthy lives with high-quality ingredients (real meat, fish, and poultry)

- Purina ONE ($17.99/20-lb bag)—meets dogs' changing and unique nutritional needs and provides super-premium nutrition for good health

- Purina Dog Chow ($11.49/22-lb bag)—provides dogs complete nutrition to build, replenish, and repair at each life stage

- Alpo by Purina ($8.99/17.6-lb bag)—offers beef, liver, and cheese flavour combinations and three meaty varieties

Holiday Inn Worldwide also has performed a two-way stretch of its hotel product line.

Holiday Inn

The Holiday Inn hotel chain broke its domestic hotels into five separate chains to tap into five different benefit segments—the upscale Crowne Plaza, the traditional Holiday Inn, the budget Holiday Inn Express, and the business-oriented Holiday Inn Select and Holiday Inn Suites & Rooms. The differently branded chains received different marketing programs and emphasis. Holiday Inn Express has been advertised with the humorous "Stay Smart" advertising campaign showing the brilliant feats that ordinary people could attempt after staying at the chain. By basing the development of these brands on distinct consumer targets with unique needs, Holiday Inn is able to avoid overlap between brands.

The relative position of a brand and its competitor context will also affect consumer acceptance. Research has shown that a high-end model of a low-end brand is favoured over a low-end model of a high-end brand, even when information about competing categories is made available.[31]

LINE FILLING A firm can lengthen its product line by adding more items within the present range. There are several motives for *line filling*: reaching for incremental profits, trying to satisfy dealers which complain about lost sales because of items missing in the line, trying to utilize excess capacity, trying to be the leading full-line company, and trying to plug holes to keep out competitors.

BMW AG

In four years BMW morphed from a one-brand, five-model carmaker into a three-brand, ten-model powerhouse. Not only has the carmaker expanded BMW's product range downwards with Mini Coopers and its compact 1-series models, but it has also built it upwards with Rolls-Royce while filling the gaps in between with its X3 Sports Activity Vehicle and a 6-series coupe. The company has used line filling successfully to boost its appeal to the rich, the super-rich, and the wannabe-rich, all without departing from its pure premium positioning.[32]

Line filling is overdone if it results in self-cannibalization and customer confusion. The company needs to differentiate each item in the consumer's mind with a *just-noticeable difference*. According to Weber's law, customers are more attuned to relative than to absolute difference.[33] They will perceive the difference between boards 20- and 30-centimetres long and boards 2- and 3-metres long but not between boards 2.9- and 3-metres long. The company should also check that the proposed item meets a market need and is not being added simply to satisfy an internal need. The infamous Edsel automobile, on which Ford lost US$350 million in the late 1950s, met Ford's internal positioning needs for a car between its Ford and Lincoln lines but not the market's needs.

LINE MODERNIZATION, FEATURING, AND PRUNING Product lines need to be modernized. The issue is whether to overhaul the line piecemeal or all at once. A piecemeal approach allows the company to see how customers and dealers take to the new style. It is also less draining on the company's cash flow, but it allows competitors to see changes and to start redesigning their own lines.

In rapidly changing product markets, modernization is continuous. Companies plan improvements to encourage customer migration to higher-valued, higher-priced items. Microprocessor companies such as Intel and AMD, and software companies such as Microsoft and Oracle, continually introduce more advanced versions of their products. A major issue is timing improvements so they do not appear too early (damaging sales of the current line) or too late (after the competition has established a strong reputation for more advanced equipment).

The product-line manager typically selects one or a few items in the line to feature. Sears will announce a special low-priced washing machine to attract customers. At other times, managers will feature a high-end item to lend prestige to the product line. Sometimes a company finds one end of its line selling well and the other end selling poorly. The company may try to boost demand for the slower sellers, especially if they are produced in a factory that is idled by lack of demand; but it could be counter-argued that the company should promote items that sell well rather than try to prop up weak items. Nike's Air Force 1 basketball shoe, introduced in the 1980s, is a billion-dollar brand that is still a consumer and retailer favourite and a moneymaker for the company due to collectable designs and tight supplies.[34]

Product-line managers must periodically review the line for deadwood that is depressing profits.[35] The weak items can be identified through sales and cost analysis. One study found that for a big Dutch retailer, a major assortment reduction led to a short-term drop in category sales, caused mainly by fewer category purchases by former buyers, but it also attracted new category buyers at the same time. These new buyers partially offset the sales losses among former buyers of the delisted items.[36]

In 1999, Unilever announced its "Path to Growth" program designed to get the most value from its brand portfolio by eliminating three-quarters of its 1600 distinct brands by 2003.[37] More than 90 percent of its profits came from just 400 brands, prompting Unilever cochair Niall FitzGerald to liken the brand reduction to weeding a garden, so "the light and air get in to the blooms which are likely to grow the best." The company retained global brands such as Lipton, as well as regional brands and "local jewels" such as Persil, the leading detergent in the United Kingdom.

Multibrand companies all over the world are attempting to optimize their brand portfolios. In many cases, this has led to a greater focus on core-brand growth and to concentrating energy and resources on the biggest and most established brands. Hasbro has designated a set of core toy brands, including GI Joe, Transformers, and My Little Pony, to emphasize in its marketing. Procter & Gamble's "back to basics strategy" concentrated on its brands with over US$1 billion in revenue, such as Tide, Crest, Pampers, and Pringles. Every product in a product line must play a role, as must any brand in the brand portfolio. See how Volkswagen has managed this challenge:

The pruning of slow-selling brands from product lines often benefits the brands that are left, such as Unilever's Lipton (a global bestseller) and Persil (a U.K. bestseller).

Volkswagen

Volkswagen (VW) has four different brands to manage in its European portfolio. Initially, Audi and Seat had a sporty image and VW and Skoda had a family-car image. Audi and VW were in a higher price–quality tier than their respective counterparts. Skoda and Seat, with their basic, spartan interiors and utilitarian engine performance, were clearly differentiated. With the goal of reducing costs, streamlining part/systems designs, and eliminating redundancies, Volkswagen upgraded the Seat and Skoda brands. Once viewed as subpar products by European consumers, Skoda and Seat have captured market share with splashy interiors, a full array of safety systems, and reliable powertrains borrowed from Volkswagen. The danger, of course, is that by borrowing from its upper-echelon Audi and Volkswagen products, Volkswagen may have diluted their cachet. Frugal European automotive consumers may convince themselves that a Seat or Skoda is almost identical to its VW sister, at several thousand euros less.[38]

Product-Mix Pricing

Chapter 14 describes pricing concepts in detail, but let's quickly consider here some basic product-mix pricing issues. Marketers must modify their price-setting logic when the product is part of a product mix. In product-mix pricing, the firm searches for a set of prices that maximizes profits on the total mix. Pricing is difficult because the various products have demand and cost interrelationships and are subject to different degrees of competition. We can distinguish six situations involving product-mix pricing: product-line pricing, optional-feature pricing, captive-product pricing, two-part pricing, byproduct pricing, and product-bundling pricing.

PRODUCT-LINE PRICING   Companies normally develop product lines, rather than single products, and introduce price steps. In many lines of trade, sellers use well-established price points for the products in their line. A men's clothing store might carry men's suits at three price levels: $200, $400, and $600. Customers will associate the three price points with low-, average-, and high-quality suits. The seller's task is to establish perceived quality differences that justify the price differences.

OPTIONAL-FEATURE PRICING   Many companies offer optional products, features, and services along with their main product. The automobile buyer can order power windows, remotely adjustable mirrors, a sunroof, and theft protection. Pricing is a sticky problem, because companies must decide which items to include in the standard price and which to offer as options. For many years, auto companies advertised economy models to pull people into showrooms, but the cars were stripped of so many features that most buyers left the showroom spending thousands more.

Restaurants face a similar pricing problem. Many price their liquor high and their food low. The food revenue covers costs, and the liquor produces the profit. This explains why waiters often press hard to get customers to order drinks. Other restaurants price their liquor low and food high to draw in a drinking crowd.

CAPTIVE-PRODUCT PRICING   Some products require the use of ancillary, or **captive, products**. Manufacturers of razors and cameras often price them low and set high markups on razor blades and film, respectively. Rogers Wireless and Bell Mobility may give a cellular phone free of charge if the person commits to buying two years of phone service.

Hewlett-Packard

In 1996, Hewlett-Packard (HP) began drastically cutting prices on its printers—by as much as 60 percent in some cases. HP could afford to make such dramatic cuts because over the life of the product customers typically spend twice as much on replacement ink cartridges, toner, and specialty paper as on the actual printer. As the price of printers dropped, printer sales rose, as did the number of aftermarket sales. HP now owns about 40 percent of the worldwide printer business. Its inkjet supplies carry 35-percent profit margins and generated US$2.2 billion in operating profits in 2002—over 70 percent of the company's total.[39]

There is a danger in pricing the captive product too high in the aftermarket, however. If parts and service are too expensive, counterfeiting and substitutions can erode sales. Consumers now can buy cartridge refills for their printers from discount suppliers and save 20 to 30 percent of what it would cost them to buy directly from the manufacturers.

TWO-PART PRICING   Service firms often engage in **two-part pricing**, consisting of a fixed fee plus a variable usage fee. Telephone users pay a minimum monthly fee plus charges for calls beyond a certain area. Amusement parks charge an admission fee plus fees for rides over a certain minimum. The service firm faces a problem similar to that of captive-product pricing—namely, how much to charge for the basic service and how much for the variable usage. The fixed fee should be low enough to induce purchase of the service; the profit can then be made on the usage fees.

BYPRODUCT PRICING   The production of certain goods—meats, petroleum products, and other chemicals—often results in byproducts. If the byproducts have value to a customer group, they should be priced on their value. Any income earned on the byproducts will make it easier for the company to charge a lower price on its main product if competition forces it to do so. Formed in 1855, Australia's CSR was originally named Colonial Sugar Refinery and its early reputation was forged as a sugar company. The company began to sell byproducts of its sugar cane: waste sugar-cane fibre was used to manufacture wallboard. Today, through product development and acquisition, the renamed CSR has become one of the top ten companies in Australia selling building and construction materials.

PRODUCT-BUNDLING PRICING   Sellers often bundle products and features. **Pure bundling** occurs when a firm offers its products only as a bundle. Michael Ovitz's company, Artists Management Group, will sign up a "hot" actor if the film company will also accept other talents (directors, writers, scripts) that Ovitz represents. This is a form of *tied-in sales*. In **mixed bundling**, the seller offers goods both individually and in bundles. When offering a mixed bundle, the seller normally charges less for the bundle than if the items were purchased separately. An auto manufacturer might offer an option package at less than the cost of buying all the options separately. A theatre company will price a season's subscription at less than the cost of buying all the performances separately. Because customers may not have planned to buy all the components, the savings on the price bundle must be substantial enough to induce them to buy the bundle.[40]

Some customers will want less than the whole bundle. Suppose a medical-equipment supplier's offer includes free delivery and training. A particular customer might ask to forgo the free delivery and training in exchange for a lower price. The customer is asking the seller to "unbundle" or "rebundle" its offer. If a supplier saves $100 by not supplying delivery and reduces the customer's price by $80, the supplier has kept the customer happy while increasing its profit by $20.

Studies have shown that as promotional activity increases on individual items in the bundle, buyers perceive less saving on the bundle and are less apt to pay for the bundle. This research suggests the following three guidelines for correctly implementing a bundling strategy:[41]

- Do not promote individual products in a package as frequently and cheaply as the bundle. The bundle price should be much lower than the sum of individual products or the consumer will not perceive its attractiveness.

- Limit promotions to a single item in the mix if you still want to promote individual products. Another option: alternate promotions, one after another, in order to avoid conflicting promotions.

- If you decide to offer large rebates on individual products, make them the absolute exception and do it with discretion. Otherwise, the consumer uses the price of individual products as an external reference for the bundle, which then loses value.

Co-Branding and Ingredient Branding

CO-BRANDING Marketers often combine their products with products from other companies in various ways. In co-branding—also called dual branding or brand bundling—two or more well-known brands are combined into a joint product or marketed together in some fashion.[42] One form of co-branding is *same-company co-branding*, as when General Mills advertises Trix and Yoplait yogurt. Still another form is *joint-venture co-branding*, such as General Electric and Hitachi lightbulbs in Japan, and RBC Royal Bank and Starbucks with the Starbucks Duetto Visa card. There is *multiple-sponsor co-branding*, such as Taligent, a one-time technological alliance of Apple, IBM, and Motorola.[43] Finally, there is *retail co-branding* whereby two retail establishments use the same location as a way to optimize both space and profits, such as jointly-owned Tim Hortons and Wendy's fast-food restaurants.

The main advantage of co-branding is that a product may be convincingly positioned by virtue of the multiple brands. Co-branding can generate greater sales from the existing target market as well as open additional opportunities with new consumers and channels. Co-branding also can reduce the cost of product introduction because it combines two well-known images and speeds adoption. And co-branding may be a valuable means to learn about consumers and how other companies approach them. Companies within the automotive industry have reaped all of these benefits of co-branding.

The potential disadvantages of co-branding are the risks and lack of control from becoming aligned with another brand in the minds of consumers. Consumer expectations about the level of involvement and commitment with co-brands are likely to be high, so unsatisfactory performance could have negative repercussions for the brands involved. If one of the brands has entered into a number of co-branding arrangements, overexposure may dilute the transfer of any association. It may also result in a lack of focus on existing brands.

For co-branding to succeed, the two brands must separately have brand equity—adequate brand awareness and a sufficiently positive brand image. The most important requirement is a logical fit between the two brands, such that the combined brand or marketing activity maximizes the advantages of each while minimizing their disadvantages. Research studies show that consumers are more apt to perceive co-brands favourably if the two brands are complementary rather than similar.[44]

Besides these strategic considerations, co-branding ventures require careful entry and execution. There must be the right kind of fit in values, capabilities, and goals, in addition to an appropriate balance of brand equity. There must be detailed plans to legalize contracts, make financial arrangements, and coordinate marketing programs. As one executive at Nabisco put it, "Giving away your brand is a lot like giving away your child—you want to make sure everything is perfect." The financial arrangement between brands may vary, although one common approach is for the brand more deeply involved in the production process to pay a licensing fee and royalty.

An extreme example of self-branding is Westin Hotels' successful marketing of its popular "Heavenly Bed" and related bedding, gift, and bath items.

Brand alliances involve a number of decisions.[45] What capabilities do you not have? What resource constraints are you faced with (people, time, money, etc.)? What are your growth goals or revenue needs? In assessing a joint-branding opportunity, ask whether it is a profitable business venture. How does it help to maintain or strengthen brand equity? Is there any risk of brand equity dilution? Does it offer any extrinsic advantages such as learning opportunities?

INGREDIENT BRANDING **Ingredient branding** is a special case of co-branding. It creates brand equity for materials, components, or parts that are necessarily contained within other branded products. Some popular ingredient-branded products are Lunchables lunch combinations with Taco Bell tacos and Lay's potato chips made with KC Masterpiece barbecue sauce. Ingredient branding is taking off in an area known as "nutraceuticals," food products that have health-increasing properties. For example, there are Danone's Activia yogurt that advertises its trademarked probiotic BL Regularis as promoting healthy digestion, and Burnbrae Farms touting the inclusion of omega-3 fatty acids in its Naturegg Omega 3 eggs.

An interesting take on ingredient branding is "self-branding" in which companies advertise and even trademark their own branded ingredients. For instance, Westin Hotels advertises its "Heavenly Bed" and "Heavenly Shower." The Heavenly Bed has been so successful that Westin now sells the bed, pillows, sheets, and blankets via an online catalogue, along with other "Heavenly" gifts and bath items. If it can be done well, it makes much more sense for companies to use self-brand ingredients because they have more control and can develop the ingredient to suit their purposes.[46]

Ingredient brands attempt to create enough awareness and preference for their product that consumers will not buy a "host" product that does not contain the ingredient. DuPont has achieved success marketing its products as ingredient brands.

DuPont

Over the years, DuPont has introduced a number of innovative products, such as Corian® solid-surface material, for use in markets ranging from apparel to aerospace. Many of these products, such as Lycra® and Stainmaster® fabrics, Teflon® coating, and Kevlar® fibre, became household names as ingredient brands in consumer products manufactured by other companies. Several recent ingredient brands include Supro® isolated soy proteins used in food products and RiboPrinter® genetic fingerprinting technology.[47]

MARKETING MEMO	MAKING INGREDIENT BRANDING WORK

What are the requirements for success for ingredient branding?

1. Consumers must perceive that the ingredient matters to the performance and success of the end product. Ideally, this intrinsic value is easily visible or experienced.

2. Consumers must be convinced that not all ingredient brands are the same and that the ingredient is superior.

3. A distinctive symbol or logo must clearly signal to consumers that the host product contains the ingredient. Ideally, the symbol or logo would function like a "seal" and would be simple and versatile and credibly communicate quality and confidence.

4. A coordinated "pull" and "push" program must help consumers understand the importance and advantages of the branded ingredient. Channel members must offer full support. Often this will involve consumer advertising and promotions and—sometimes in collaboration with manufacturers—retail merchandising and promotion programs.

Sources: Kevin Lane Keller, *Strategic Brand Management,* 3rd ed. (Upper Saddle River, NJ: Prentice Hall, 2008); Philip Kotler and Waldemar Pfoertsch, *B2B Brand Management* (New York: Springer, 2006); Paul F. Nunes, Stephen F. Dull, and Patrick D. Lynch, "When Two Brands Are Better Than One," *Outlook* (January 2003): 14–23.

Many manufacturers make components or materials that enter into final branded products but lose their individual identity. One of the few component branders which have succeeded in building a separate identity is Intel. Intel's consumer-directed brand campaign convinced many personal computer buyers to buy only computer brands with "Intel Inside." As a result, major PC manufacturers—IBM, Dell, Compaq—purchase their chips from Intel at a premium price rather than buy equivalent chips from an unknown supplier. Most component manufacturers, however, would find it difficult to create a successful ingredient brand. "Marketing Memo: Making Ingredient Branding Work" outlines the characteristics of successful ingredient branding.

PACKAGING, LABELLING, WARRANTIES, AND GUARANTEES

Most physical products have to be packaged and labelled. Some packages—such as the Coke bottle and the L'eggs pantyhose container—are world famous. Many marketers have called packaging a fifth P, along with price, product, place, and promotion. Most marketers, however, treat packaging and labelling as an element of product strategy. Warranties and guarantees can also be an important part of the product strategy, and often appear on the package.

Packaging

We define **packaging** as all the activities of designing and producing the container for a product. Packages might include up to three levels of material. Cool Water cologne comes in a bottle (*primary package*) that is in a cardboard box (*secondary package*) that is in a corrugated box (*shipping package*) containing six dozen boxes.

Well-designed packages can build brand equity and drive sales. The package is the buyer's first encounter with the product and is capable of turning the buyer on or off. Packaging also affects consumers' later product experiences. Various factors have contributed to the growing use of packaging as a marketing tool:

- *Self-service.* An increasing number of products are sold on a self-service basis. In an average supermarket, which stocks 15 000 items, the typical shopper passes by some 300 items per minute. Given that 50 to 70 percent of all purchases are made in the store, the effective package must perform many of the sales tasks: attract attention, describe the product's features, create consumer confidence, and make a favourable overall impression.

- *Consumer affluence.* Rising consumer affluence means consumers are willing to pay a little more for the convenience, appearance, dependability, and prestige of better packages.

- *Company and brand image.* Packages contribute to instant recognition of the company or brand. In the store, packages for a brand can create a visible billboard effect, such as Garnier Fructis and its bright green packaging in the hair-care aisle.

- *Innovation opportunity.* Innovative packaging can bring large benefits to consumers and profits to producers. Companies are incorporating unique materials and features such as resealable spouts and openings. Heinz's unique, colourful EZ Squirt ketchup has helped to revitalize the brand's sales.[48]

From the perspective of both the firm and consumers, packaging must achieve a number of objectives:[49]

1. Identify the brand.
2. Convey descriptive and persuasive information.
3. Facilitate product transportation and protection.
4. Assist at-home storage.
5. Aid product consumption.

Increasingly, marketers are adding a sixth criterion to this list: be made of sustainable materials. To recognize innovation in this regard, the Packaging Association of Canada awards manufacturers which have demonstrated commitment to more sustainable packaging. In 2008, Unilever Canada was given the Best of Show award for its Sunlight 3x concentrated liquid laundry detergent. The new 946-mL bottle replaced the regular 2.95-litre bottle (a 54-percent savings in plastic). Moreover, the smaller bottles also mean fewer trucks on the road.[50]

To achieve the marketing objectives for the brand and satisfy the desires of consumers, marketers must correctly choose the aesthetic and functional components of packaging. Aesthetic considerations relate to a package's size and shape, material, colour, text, and graphics. Blue is cool and serene, red is active and lively, yellow is medicinal and weak, pastel colours are feminine, and dark colours are masculine. Functionally, structural design is crucial. For example, innovations with food products over the years have resulted in packages that are resealable, tamper-proof, and more convenient to use (easy-to-hold, easy-to-open, or squeezable). The packaging elements must harmonize with each other and with pricing, advertising, and other parts of the marketing program.

Packaging changes can have an immediate impact on sales. A good example is the book publishing industry, where customers often quite literally choose a book by its cover: The number-one classics publisher, Penguin Books Ltd., repackaged most of its titles and spent $500 000 to promote them under the banner "Classic Books, Fresh Looks." Sales increased 400 percent for Dorothy Parker's *Complete Stories,* 50 percent for a new translation of *Don Quixote,* and 43 percent for *Pride and Prejudice.*[51] Packaging changes can come in all forms. The Liquor Control Board of Ontario (LCBO) challenged wine-makers to develop environmentally friendly alternatives to glass wine bottles. Boisset, a French wine-maker, packaged its French Rabbit brand in recyclable Tetra Pak containers and sales spiked within the first two weeks.[52] A panel of 10 000 Canadian consumers judged CanGro's Del Monte Fruit plastic-jar packaging "award winning" because the product can be seen, resealed, and easily stored.[53]

After the company designs its packaging, it must test it. *Engineering tests* ensure that the package stands up under normal conditions; *visual tests,* that the script is legible and the colours harmonious; *dealer tests,* that dealers find the packages attractive and easy to handle; and *consumer tests,* that buyers will respond favourably.

Although developing effective packaging may cost several hundred thousand dollars and take several months to complete, companies must pay attention to growing environmental and safety concerns and adjust their packaging in light of these issues. Fortunately, many companies have gone "green" and are finding new ways to develop their packaging.

Labelling

The label may be a simple tag attached to the product or an elaborately designed graphic that is part of the package. It might carry only the brand name or a great deal of information. Even if the seller prefers a simple label, the law may require more.

Labels perform several functions. First, the label *identifies* the product or brand—for instance, the name Sunkist stamped on oranges. The label might also *grade* the product; canned peaches are labelled as grade A, B, or C. The label might *describe* the product: who made it, where it was made, when it was made, what it contains, how it is to be used, and how to use it safely. Finally, the label might *promote* the product through attractive graphics. Marketers can use 360-degree shrink-wrapped labels to surround containers with bright graphics and accommodate more on-pack product information, replacing paper labels glued on to cans and bottles.[54]

Labels eventually become outmoded and need freshening. The label on Ivory soap has been redone at least 18 times since the 1890s, with gradual changes in the size and design of the letters. Companies with labels that have become icons need to tread very carefully when initiating a redesign.

Campbell Soup Company

The Campbell Soup Company has estimated that the average shopper sees its familiar red-and-white can 76 times a year, creating the equivalent of millions of dollars worth of advertising. Its label is such an icon that pop artist Andy Warhol immortalized it in one of his silk screens in the 1960s. The original Campbell's Soup label—with its scripted name and signature red-and-white—was designed in 1898, and the company did not redesign it until more than a century later, in 1999. With the goal of making the label more contemporary and making it easier for customers to find individual soups, Campbell made the famous script logo smaller and featured a photo of a steaming bowl of the soup flavour inside. In addition to the new graphic, the company put nutritional information on the packaging, serving suggestions, quick-dinner ideas, and coloured bands identifying the six subgroups of condensed soup—creams, broths, and so on.[55]

There is a long history of legal concerns surrounding labels and packaging. In Canada, it is mandatory that labels have three elements: they must identify the product, give the quantity being sold, and state the producer's name and place of business. There are numerous other regulations affecting labelling practices that vary depending on the type of product being sold. Details can be found on the Government of Canada's Competition Bureau website (www.competitionbureau.gc.ca).

Warranties and Guarantees

All sellers are legally responsible for fulfilling a buyer's normal or reasonable expectations. Warranties are formal statements by the manufacturer of expected product performance. Products under warranty can be returned to the manufacturer or designated repair centre for repair, replacement, or refund. Warranties, whether expressed or implied, are legally enforceable.

Extended warranties can be extremely lucrative for manufacturers and retailers. One consumer organization estimates that, in some cases, warranties have profit margins of up to 50 percent.[56] Sometimes warranties, such as the ones offered by Mitsubishi Motors, are used to signal improved quality.

Mitsubishi Motors North America

To counter consumer perceptions that Mitsubishi lags behind competitors when it comes to quality, the company has begun offering a new ten-year, 160 000-kilometre powertrain warranty. This warranty, which came into effect in 2004, replaced its seven-year, 60 000-mile (97 000-kilometre) warranty. Mitsubishi hopes that the new longer-term warranty will signal to consumers that the company has confidence in the quality and reliability of its vehicles.[57]

Sometimes a warranty can be an incredibly smart marketing strategy. See how Shoes for Crews employs warranties:

Shoes for Crews

Shoes for Crews makes work shoes that are absolutely guaranteed not to slip. No one had ever given much thought to the rather stalwart shoes before the company issued a warranty that most people would consider insane: a US$5000 warranty for a US$50–$75 product. Yet, this was the smartest move the company ever made. A decade after CEO Matthew Smith instituted the warranty, nine of the ten largest restaurant chains in the country either buy the Shoes for Crews brand for their workers or urge them to do so. It works like this: If a restaurant or shop employee does happen to slip on the job while wearing a Shoes for Crews product, it can easily cost an employer US$5000 in worker's comp claims—US$5000 the employer gets back from Shoes for Crews. This kind of warranty is dubbed "risk reversal marketing." The idea behind it is to think about what your customers' biggest fear is when it comes to doing business with you, and then take on some of the risk yourself. Fortunately for Matthew Smith, Shoes for Crews shoes mainly live up to their guarantee. However, when Smith has honored the warranty—ranging from payouts of a few hundred dollars for an ambulance ride to the whole $5K for major surgery, the surprise and gratitude in his customers' voices makes the payout well worth it for him.[58]

Many sellers offer either general guarantees or specific guarantees.[59] A company such as Procter & Gamble promises general or complete satisfaction without being more specific—"If you are not satisfied for any reason, return for replacement, exchange, or refund." Other companies offer specific guarantees and in some cases extraordinary guarantees:

- A. T. Cross guarantees its Cross pens and pencils for life. Customers can mail malfunctioning pens to A. T. Cross (mailing envelopes are provided at stores selling Cross writing instruments) and the pens are repaired or replaced at no charge.

- "Bugs" Burger Bugs Killers (BBBK), a pest extermination company serving the hospitality industry, offers the following guarantee: (1) no payment until all pests are eradicated; (2) if the effort fails, the customer receives a full refund of the next exterminator's charges; (3) if guests on the client's premises spot a pest, BBBK will pay for the guest's room and send an apology letter; and (4) if the client's facility is closed down, BBBK will pay all fines, lost profits, and US$5000.

Guarantees reduce the buyer's perceived risk. They suggest that the product is of high quality and that the company and its service performance are dependable. They can be especially helpful when the company or product is not well known or when the product's quality is superior to competitors.

SUMMARY

1. Product is the first and most important element of the marketing mix. Product strategy calls for making coordinated decisions on product mixes, product lines, brands, and packaging and labelling.

2. In planning its market offering, the marketer needs to think through the five levels of the product: the core benefit, the basic product, the expected product, the augmented product, and the potential product, which encompasses all the augmentations and transformations the product might ultimately undergo.

3. Products can be classified in several ways. In terms of durability and reliability, products can be nondurable goods, durable goods, or services. In the consumer-goods category, products are convenience goods (staples, impulse goods, emergency goods), shopping goods (homogeneous and heterogeneous), specialty goods, or unsought goods. In the industrial-goods class, products fall into one of three categories: materials and parts (raw materials, and manufactured materials and parts), capital items (installations and equipment), or supplies and business services (operating supplies, maintenance and repair items, maintenance and repair services, and business advisory services).

4. Brands can be differentiated on the basis of a number of different product or service dimensions: product form, features, customization, performance, conformance, durability, reliability, repairability, style, and design, as well as such service dimensions as ordering ease, delivery, installation, customer training, customer consulting, and maintenance and repair.

5. Most companies sell more than one product. A product mix can be classified according to width, length, depth, and consistency. These four dimensions are considered when developing the company's marketing strategy and deciding which product lines to grow, maintain, harvest, and divest. To analyze a product line and decide how many resources should be invested in that line, product-line managers need to look at sales and profits and the market profile.

6. A company can change the product component of its marketing mix by lengthening its product via line stretching (down-market, up-market, or both) or line filling, by modernizing its products, by featuring certain products, and by pruning its products to eliminate the least profitable.

7. Brands are often sold or marketed jointly with other brands. Ingredient brands and co-brands can add value, assuming they have equity and are perceived as fitting appropriately.

8. Physical products must be packaged and labelled. Well-designed packages can create convenience value for customers and promotional value for producers. In effect, they can act as "five-second commercials" for the product. Warranties and guarantees can offer further assurance to consumers.

APPLICATIONS

Marketing Debate: With Products, Is It Form or Function?

The "form versus function" debate is relevant in many arenas, including marketing. Some marketers believe that product performance is the end-all and be-all. Other marketers maintain that the looks, feel, and other design elements of products are what really make the difference.

Take a position: Product functionality is the key to brand success *versus* Product design is the key to brand success.

Marketing Discussion

Consider the different means of differentiating products and services. Which have the most impact on your choices? Why?

Can you think of certain brands that excel in a number of these different means of differentiation?

Breakthrough Marketing: Toyota

Toyota may have gotten its start in automaking by being a fast follower, but it is now the innovator. In 1936, Toyota admitted following Chrysler's landmark Airflow and patterning its engine after a 1933 Chevrolet engine. But by 2000, when it introduced the first hybrid electric–gasoline car, the Prius, Toyota was the leader. Worldwide sales of the Prius were 757 600 by 2007, and in Canada 8039 have been sold. Competitors are following suit. For example, in 2006, Ford announced that its Oakville, Ontario auto plant would be the first in Canada to assemble hybrid vehicles. With rising fuel prices in 2008, it may have made a good bet. Ford believes that its EcoBoost engine technology will be available on half a million Ford, Lincoln, and Mercury vehicles annually in North America—far exceeding current hybrid vehicle production capacity.

Toyota offers a full line of cars for the Canadian and U.S. markets, from family sedans to sport utility vehicles, trucks, and minivans. Toyota also has products for different price points, from the lower-cost Yaris to the mid-priced Camry to the luxury Lexus. Designing these different products means listening to different customers, building the cars they want, and then crafting marketing to reinforce each make's image. For example, Toyota spent four years carefully listening to teens before launching the Scion for first-time car buyers in the United States. It learned, for instance, that Scion's target age group of 16- to 21-year-olds wanted personalization. To meet that preference, Toyota builds the car "mono-spec" at the factory with just one well-equipped trim level but lets customers choose at dealerships from over 40 customization elements from stereo components to wheels and even floor mats. Toyota markets the Scion at music events and its showrooms are where "young people feel comfortable hanging out and not a place where they just go stare at a car," said Scion vice president Jim Letz.

In contrast, Toyota's marketing strategy for the Lexus line focuses on perfection. The tagline for the global strategy is "Passionate Pursuit of Perfection." Dealerships offer white-gloved treatment. Toyota markets Lexus globally and understands that each country defines perfection differently. In the United States, for example, perfection and luxury mean comfort, size, and dependability. In Europe, luxury means attention to detail and brand heritage. When the Canadian dollar suddenly reached par with its American counterpart, Toyota Canada notified its "guests" of the value of a Canadian-made Lexus, which may include such features as heated outside mirrors, more robust weather stripping and seats, heavy-duty heaters, and batteries and alternators designed for our more severe climate. Therefore, although the core of Lexus marketing is similar (a consistent Lexus visual vocabulary, logo, font, and overall communication), the advertising varies by country.

A big reason behind Toyota's success is its manufacturing. Toyota's combination of manufacturing speed and flexibility is world class. It is the master of lean manufacturing and continuous improvement. Its plants can make as many as eight different models at the same time, which brings Toyota huge increases in productivity and market responsiveness. Toyota Motor Manufacturing Canada, headquartered in Cambridge, Ontario, employs over 4500 people and is the first site outside of Japan to produce a Lexus—the Lexus RX 350 SUV. The same plant also produces the Toyota Corolla, Matrix, and RAV4. Like all Toyota facilities, it innovates relentlessly. A typical Toyota assembly line makes thousands of operational changes in the course of a single year. Toyota employees see their purpose as threefold: making cars, making cars better, and teaching everyone how to make cars better. The company encourages problem solving, always looking to improve the process by which it improves all other processes.

Toyota is integrating its assembly plants around the world into a single giant network. The plants will customize cars for local markets and be able to shift production quickly to satisfy any surges in demand from markets worldwide. With a manufacturing network, Toyota can build a wide variety of models much less expensively.

That means Toyota will be able to fill market niches as they emerge without building whole new assembly operations. "If there's a market or market segment where they aren't present, they go there," said Tatsuo Yoshida, auto analyst at Deutsche Securities Ltd. And with consumers being increasingly fickle about what they want in a car, such market agility gives Toyota a huge competitive edge.

In 2007, Toyota posted US$54.6 billion in revenue, and its net income surged a whopping 32 percent to US$4.13 billion despite a worldwide decline in demand for vehicles. Capitalizing on the growing demand in Asia, Toyota Motor Corporation took the global-sales lead away from General Motors in the first quarter of 2008. It sold 2.41 million vehicles in the quarter compared to GM's 2.25.

DISCUSSION QUESTIONS

1. How has Toyota used the Customer-Value Hierarchy (see Figure 12.1) to create value for buyers of the Prius?

2. How has Toyota differentiated the Scion?

3. How does Toyota use service differentiation when marketing the Lexus?

Sources: Toyota Canada, "Why a Made-for-Canada Lexus Is More Than Just a Great Vehicle," www.lexus.ca/lexus/experience/en/home/whatsnew/whatsnew_news.jsp#luxury_sedan (viewed April 2008); "Toyota Tops GM in Q1 Sales," *CBCNews.ca*, www.cbc.ca/money/story/2008/04/23/toyotagm.html (viewed April 2008); Kae Inoue and Tersuya Komatsu, "Toyota's Profit Rises on Higher Overseas Sales, Yen," *Bloomberg News*, August 3, 2007, www.bloomberg.com/apps/news?pid=20601087&sid=ahjcb7rUVSsU&refer=home (viewed April 2008); Martin Zimmerman, "Toyota's First Quarter Global Sales Beat GM's Preliminary Numbers," *Los Angeles Times*, April 24, 2007; Charles Fishman, "No Satisfaction at Toyota," *Fast Company* (December 2006–January 2007): 82–90; Stuart F. Brown, "Toyota's Global Body Shop," *Fortune*, February 9, 2004, p. 120; James B. Treece, "Ford Down; Toyota Aims for No. 1," *Automotive News*, February 2, 2004, p.1; Brian Bemner and Chester Dawson, "Can Anything Stop Toyota?" *BusinessWeek*, November 17, 2003, pp. 114–22; www.toyota.com; CBC News, "Sales of Toyota Hybrids Exceed 1 M," *CBC News Online*, www.cbc.ca, June 7, 2007; CBC News, "Ford to Build Hybrid Vehicles in Oakville," *CBC News Online*, www.cbc.ca, February 16, 2006; Greg Keenan, "The little engine that could give Ford its big boost," *Globe and Mail*, July 25, 2008, http://www.theglobeandmail.com/servlet/story/LAC.20080725.FORDSIDEBAR25/TPStory/TPInternational/America/ (viewed September 2008).

IN THIS CHAPTER,
WE WILL ADDRESS
THE FOLLOWING
QUESTIONS:

- How do we define and classify services, and how do they differ from goods?

- How do we market services?

- How can we improve service quality?

- How do services marketers create strong brands?

- How can goods marketers improve customer-support services?

CHAPTER 13

DESIGNING AND MANAGING SERVICES

thirteen

As product companies find it harder and harder to differentiate their physical products, they turn to service differentiation. Many find significant profitability in delivering superior service, whether that means on-time delivery, better and faster answering of inquiries, or quicker resolution of complaints. Service providers know these advantages well. The Stratford Festival is a service that has consistently set new standards in the theatre industry over its fifty-plus years of existence.

The Stratford Festival, inaugurated in 1953, is an entertainment service. Today, because of its unrelenting focus on creating high-quality productions, it is the largest classical-repertory theatre in North America. In fact, it is the second-largest industry in Stratford, a small city in southern Ontario. The Festival has tangible assets in its four theatres and operates over a seven-month season. During the Festival, both classical and contemporary works, ranging from Shakespearean plays to contemporary musical theatre, are staged.

Each summer festival season draws more than ten million visitors. The Festival generates over $40.5 million in revenues, but since its expenses exceeded revenues by approximately $13 million, the Festival has to market itself not only to the ticket-buying public, but also to potential donors, government granting agencies, and corporate sponsors. For example, Bell Canada has been a sponsor since 1954. Bell's sponsorship helps fund the Celebrated Writers Series, and the company promotes the Festival in Bell Phonecentre stores. The sponsorship in turn helps build the Bell Canada Advantage brand name.

The Festival also uses a wide range of other marketing tools including TV commercials, organizing special "festival familiarization days" for media representatives, the Festival website (www.stratfordfestival.ca), special events like its Canada Day affairs, and annual posters. The Festival received a lot of PR when it was featured on CBC's *Mercer Report* TV show in 2006. Festival marketers make extensive use of data mining to segment and reach its target audiences more effectively. The Festival also partners with the City of Stratford to produce and distribute Visitors' Guides to make both the City and the Festival attractive destinations in the minds of potential visitors.

Even though it is a national institution of international renown, in 2007 the Festival decided it was time for a facelift. It hired Karacters Design Group, an offshoot of DDB Canada, to rebrand the

>>>

Festival. Since services are intangible, brand and the associations they create in the minds of their audiences are especially important for service operations. Rachel Hilton, director of marketing at the Stratford Festival, and Antoni Cimolini, general director, wanted to return the Festival to its roots. They gave the agency a lot of freedom to design a bold program that could even include a name change. Rachel Hilton believed it needed "to focus on the differentiators and say why we're different than those theatres in New York or Chicago or Toronto." For Cimolini, the rebranding task meant developing a clearer statement of Stratford's Shakespeare mandate. For years the Festival trumpeted the diversity of its playbill, whereas in the beginning it was more strongly associated with Shakespeare. So while recent advertising campaigns have shouted "Hey, we're more than that," Cimolini now thinks it is time to re-examine the Festival's DNA and return it to things that helped it grow in the beginning. In 1953, he says, "We were surprising, we were innovative, we were world class, and our core was Shakespeare."

Sources: Leonard L. Berry, *On Great Service: A Framework for Action* (New York: Free Press, 2006); Leonard L. Berry, *Discovering the Soul of Service: The Nine Drivers of Sustainable Business Success* (New York: Free Press, 1999); "To Bard or not to Bard?" *Marketing*, May 28, 2007; "NAMMU 2007 Award Winners, Datamining, The Stratford Festival of Canada," www.thekmrgroup.com/awards_2007/2007winners.html; "Stratford Festival in the Community," Newsletter, Summer 2006, www.stratfordfestival.ca/about/newsletters/June06.pdf; "Stratford: The City and the Festival," www.creativecity.ca/resources/project-profiles/Stratford-City-and-Festival.html; Matt Semansky, "Stratford Festival to Rebrand with New Karacters," *Marketing Daily*, May 3, 2007 (all websites viewed May 1, 2008).

Because it is critical to understand the special nature of services and what it means to marketers, in this chapter we systematically analyze services and how to market them most effectively.

THE NATURE OF SERVICES

 To learn how Australia's Royal Automobile Club (RAC) has expanded from motor services to a diverse range of services and benefits to meet the ever-changing needs of its members, visit www.pearsoned.com.au/marketingmanagementaustralia.

One of the megatrends of recent years has been the phenomenal growth of services. In Canada, the services sector accounts for 69 percent of the GDP, while goods-producing industries account for 31 percent. Manufacturing, which is part of the goods-producing sector, accounts for only 15 percent of the GDP. Service industries in Canada grow faster than both goods-producing industries and the economy as a whole. Service industries in Canada grew 3.9 percent between 1997 and 2004, goods-producing industries grew 3.0 percent, and overall GDP grew 3.6 percent. Some service sectors grew even more, such as wholesale trade and information and cultural services, which grew at approximately 6 percent.[1]

Similarly, the services sector is a much larger employer than the goods-producing sector. In 2007, the services sector of the Canadian economy employed almost 13 million Canadians, compared to the four million people working in the goods-producing sector. The retail trade industry employs the most people—1 790 000—of all industries.[2] These numbers and others have led to a growing interest in the special problems of marketing services.[3]

Service Industries Are Everywhere

The *government sector*, with its courts, employment services, hospitals, loan agencies, military services, police and fire departments, postal service, regulatory agencies, and schools, is in the service business. The *private nonprofit sector*, with its museums, charities, churches, universities, colleges, foundations, and hospitals, is in the service business. A good part of the *business sector*, with its airlines, banks, hotels, insurance companies, law firms, management-consulting firms, medical practices, motion-picture companies, plumbing-repair companies, and real estate firms, is in the service business. Many workers in the *manufacturing sector*, such as computer operators, accountants, and legal staff, are really service providers. In fact, they make up a "service factory" providing services to the "goods factory." And those in the *retail sector*, such as cashiers, clerks, sales representatives, and customer-service representatives, are also providing a service.

We define a service as follows: A **service** is any act or performance that one party can offer to another that is essentially intangible and does not result in the ownership of anything. Its production may or may not be tied to a physical product. Increasingly, however, manufacturers (such as those competing in the luxury-automobile segment), distributors, and retailers are providing value-added services, or simply excellent customer service, to differentiate themselves.

Luxury Automobiles

To operate effectively in the lucrative but highly competitive luxury-automobile market, Lexus, Cadillac, and Porsche all are committed to making sure their customers have another car at their disposal if theirs happens to be in the shop. When Lexus had to recall the RX330 in 2006, it gave its inconvenienced customers a free iPod Nano. When customers balked about the price and value of early scheduled maintenance, Lexus implemented a new system that cut the average appointment time in half. For Cadillac, General Motors has put an early-warning system for mechanical problems into its OnStar telematics system, standard in all models. OnStar service helps customers with related tasks including emergency-services dispatch, stolen-vehicle location, roadside assistance, remote diagnostics, and route support. Although the first year of OnStar is free to GM car owners, it now claims renewal rates as high as 80 percent at annual subscription fees ranging from US$200 to more than US$600.[4]

Many services though, include no physical products, and many pure-service firms are now using the Internet to reach customers. Mackenzie Financial Services Inc. won a Digital Marketing Award for its Burn Rate website, which helped Canadians calculate how much money they were "burning" on unnecessary discretionary items like trendy jeans and encouraged Canadians to manage their "burn rate."[5] Some service firms are even purely online. ING Direct Canada, with no physical offices, is able to offer customers higher interest rates on savings accounts and lower service charges. Done right, improvements in customer service can have a big payoff. Figure 13.1 summarizes some high-impact customer-service projects.

	Project	Payoff
Zipcar	Zap busy signals by linking the car-sharing service's phone reservation system to its Web site and client databases. Customers are automatically recognized when they call and their requests are routed efficiently.	Cut in half the number of calls that needed operator assistance and improved service, contributing $3.5 million to 2005's estimated $15 million in sales.
Continental Airlines	Analyze data on the fly to improve customer care. One online system alerts the company when planes arrive late and assesses passengers' needs—delaying departures of other flights or sending carts to make connections easier.	After ranking last in the industry for customer satisfaction in the 1990s, Continental climbed into the top tier—ahead of American, United, and US Air.
Museum of Modern Art	As part of its $425 million rebuilding project, the museum's management pumped up the use of technology to cater better to visitors.	New services include podcast audio tours, on-demand printing of tickets, and a 35-foot flat-panel display featuring art and informational updates on shows and lectures.
Cremation Society of New Hampshire	Buck conventional wisdom by providing information for people researching cremations and letting them order the service online.	Cremations ordered online are expected to account for about 20% of the company's projected $1.8 million in revenues in 2005, up from 11% in 2004.
Enel Telegestore	Install meters for the customers of one of Italy's major electricity utilities and remotely monitor them.	Reaped nearly $600 million annually in savings and benefits by recommending shifts in usage from peak to nonpeak hours and slashing field service costs.
BT Group	Entirely revamp its self-service Web portal used by customers to manage telecom accounts. Link it to the system used by the company's customer-support staff to improve consistency.	Customer-support transactions done via the Web tripled from 2003 to 2006, and half of all new orders for broadband service are made online. Saved tens of millions annually in costs, and boosted customer satisfaction 40%.
Whirlpool	Sign up for Rearden Commerce, an online hub that provides employees at 10 companies with a one-stop shop for services from 130,000 suppliers, including booking travel, shipping packages, and restaurant reservations.	During the first phase of the rollout of the shipping service over a two month period, employees saved 10% and cut the time spent arranging for shipping by 52%.

FIGURE 13.1 High-Impact Online Customer-Service Projects

Source: Catherine Yang, *BusinessWeek*, November 21, 2005, pp. 84–85.

Categories of Service Mix

The service component can be a minor or a major part of the total offering. We distinguish five categories of offerings:

1. *Pure tangible good.* The offering consists primarily of a tangible good such as soap, toothpaste, or salt. No services accompany the product.

2. *Tangible good with accompanying services.* The offering consists of a tangible good accompanied by one or more services. Typically, the more technologically advanced the product, the greater the need for a broad range of high-quality supporting services. Services are often crucial for cars, computers, and cell phones.

3. *Hybrid.* The offering consists of equal parts of goods and services. For example, people patronize restaurants for both food and service.

4. *Major service with accompanying minor goods and services.* The offering consists of a major service along with additional services or supporting goods. For example, though the trip includes a few tangibles such as snacks and drinks, what airline passengers buy is transportation. The service requires a capital-intensive good—an airplane—for its realization, but the primary item is a service.

5. *Pure service.* The offering consists primarily of a service. Examples include baby-sitting, psychotherapy, and massage.

The range of service offerings makes it difficult to generalize without a few further distinctions.

- Services vary as to whether they are *equipment-based* (automated car washes, vending machines) or *people-based* (window washing, accounting services). People-based services vary according to whether unskilled, skilled, or professional workers provide them.

- Service companies can choose among different *processes* to deliver their service. Restaurants have developed cafeteria-style, fast-food, buffet, and candlelight formats.

- Some services need the *client's presence*. Brain surgery involves the client's presence, a car repair does not. If the client must be present, the service provider must be considerate of his or her needs. Thus beauty salon operators will invest in décor, play background music, and engage in light conversation with the client.

- Services may meet a *personal need* (personal services) or a *business need* (business services). Service providers typically develop different marketing programs for personal and business markets.

- Service providers differ in their *objectives* (profit or nonprofit) and *ownership* (private or public). These two characteristics, when crossed, produce four quite different types of organizations. The marketing programs of a private-investor hospital such as the Shouldice Hernia Centre in Thornhill, Ontario, will differ from those of a public hospital such as Ste. Anne's Hospital in Sainte-Anne-de-Bellevue, Quebec.[6]

Customers cannot judge the technical quality of some services even after they have received them. Figure 13.2 shows various products and services according to difficulty of evaluation.[7] At the left are goods high in *search qualities*—that is, characteristics the buyer can evaluate before purchase. In the middle are goods and services high in *experience qualities*—characteristics the buyer can evaluate after purchase. At the right are goods and services high in *credence qualities*—characteristics the buyer normally finds hard to evaluate even after consumption.[8]

Because services are generally high in experience and credence qualities, there is more risk in purchase. This factor has several consequences. First, service consumers generally rely on word of mouth rather than advertising. Second, they rely heavily on price, personnel, and physical cues to judge quality. Third, they are highly loyal to service providers who satisfy them. Fourth, because switching costs are high, consumer inertia can make it challenging to entice a customer away from a competitor.

Distinctive Characteristics of Services

Services have four distinctive characteristics that greatly affect the design of marketing programs: *intangibility, inseparability, variability,* and *perishability.*[9]

INTANGIBILITY Unlike physical products, services cannot be seen, tasted, felt, heard, or smelled before they are bought. The person getting cosmetic surgery cannot see the results before the purchase, and the patient in the psychiatrist's office cannot know the exact outcome of treatment. To

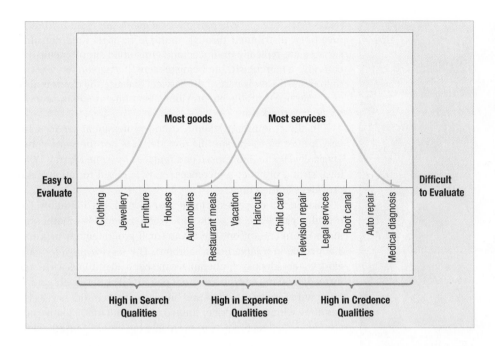

FIGURE 13.2

Continuum of Evaluation for Different Types of Products

Source: Valarie A. Zeithaml, "How Consumer Evaluation Processes Differ between Goods and Services," in *Marketing of Services*, ed. James H. Donnelly and William R. George (Chicago: American Marketing Association, 1981). Reprinted with permission of the American Marketing Association.

reduce uncertainty, buyers will look for evidence of quality by drawing inferences from the place, people, equipment, communication material, symbols, and price. Therefore, the service provider's task is to "manage the evidence," to "tangibilize the intangible."[10]

Service companies can try to demonstrate their service quality through *physical evidence* and *presentation.*[11] A hotel will develop a look and style of dealing with customers that realizes its intended customer value proposition, whether it is cleanliness, speed, or some other benefit. Suppose a bank wants to position itself as the "fast" bank. It could make this positioning strategy tangible through a number of marketing tools:

1. *Place.* The exterior and interior should have clean lines. The layout of the desks and the traffic flow should be planned carefully. Waiting lines should not get overly long.

2. *People.* Personnel should be busy. There should be a sufficient number of employees to manage the workload.

3. *Equipment.* Computers, copying machines, and desks should be and look "state of the art."

4. *Communication material.* Printed materials—text and photos—should suggest efficiency and speed.

5. *Symbols.* The name and symbol should suggest fast service.

6. *Price.* The bank could advertise that it will deposit $5 in the account of any customer who waits in line for more than five minutes.

Service marketers must be able to transform intangible services into concrete benefits and a well-defined experience.[12] The Disney Company is a master at "tangibilizing the intangible" by creating magical fantasies in its theme parks; so are companies such as Nicholas Hoare, McNally Robinson, and Chapters Indigo bookstores in their respective retail stores.[13] Memorial University launched a street campaign to educate Canadians about the tangible benefits of distance education.

Memorial University

Memorial University in St. John's, Newfoundland hit the streets in Toronto to remind potential students—especially Newfoundland expats—that its distance-education programs can be completed at any time, in any place. As part of the street campaign, Memorial alumni rode subways wearing slippers and working on laptops that prominently displayed the Memorial University name. Transit ads directly above the studious alumni stated, "Complete your degree from home or wherever you are" and included an arrow pointing down. Communications Coordinator Kristine Hamlyn explained the goal of the campaign, "We want to show that you can be on the subway or you could be on a train for an hour or two a day, and you can take advantage of this free time and earn an education from a quality institution."[14]

Memorial University's distance-learning program uses a number of techniques (such as this coffee cup) to make its intangible benefits more tangible to its current and prospective students.

Entertainment, like that provided by Measha Brueggergosman, Canada's high-energy soprano with a casual style, exhibits the quality of inseparability. Brueggergosman works to overcome this constraint through recordings and her MySpace page.

INSEPARABILITY Whereas physical goods are manufactured, put into inventory, distributed through multiple resellers, and consumed later, services are typically produced and consumed simultaneously. A barber can't give a haircut without being present. If a person renders the service, then the provider is part of the service. Because the client is also present as the service is produced, provider–client interaction is a special feature of services marketing.

In the case of entertainment and professional services, buyers are very interested in the specific provider. It is not the same concert if the Tragically Hip are indisposed and replaced by Anne Murray. When clients have strong provider preferences, price is raised to ration the preferred provider's limited time.

Several strategies exist for getting around this limitation. The service provider can learn to work with larger groups. Psychotherapists have moved from one-on-one therapy to small-group therapy to groups of over 300 people in a large hotel ballroom. The service provider can learn to work faster—the psychotherapist can spend 30 minutes with each patient instead of 50 minutes to see more patients. The service organization can train more service providers and build up client confidence, as H&R Block has done with its network of trained tax consultants. Creative artists have also developed techniques to overcome the limits of inseparability.

Measha Brueggergosman

Measha Brueggergosman, described as Canada's sassiest, best-known opera star and young diva extraordinaire, has not only a voice that captivates audiences around the world, but also a stage presence and charisma that make listeners fall in love with her. The New Brunswick native is a serious artist—she's commanded some of the best stages in the world, such as Carnegie Hall in New York. Measha is a high-energy soprano with a casual style. At concerts, she has been known to joke with audiences, ask them for help when she forgets words, and even walk barefoot on stage. Her talent and friendly, down-to-earth style result in glowing concert reviews, such as one offered recently in the *Toronto Star*: "She has the voice and technique. She also has that extra ingredient that bumps a performer into the seduction zone." For those who can't see her live performances, she records with Deutsche Grammophon. Measha also uses her website and MySpace Music to allow friends and fans alike to connect with her. When she is not singing, Measha is participating in literacy fundraisers, advertising the World Wildlife Fund's global-warming campaign, or travelling to Kenya with AMREF (African Medical and Research Foundation) Canada.[15]

VARIABILITY Because the quality of services depends on who provides them, when, where, and to whom, services are highly variable. Some doctors have excellent bedside manner; others are less empathetic.

Service buyers are aware of this variability and often talk to others before selecting a service provider. To reassure customers, some firms offer *service guarantees* that may reduce consumer perceptions of risk.[16] Here are three steps service firms can take to increase quality control:

1. *Invest in good hiring and training procedures.* Recruiting the right employees and providing them with excellent training is crucial, regardless of whether employees are highly skilled professionals or low-skilled workers. Better-trained personnel exhibit six characteristics: *competence*—they possess the required skill and knowledge; *courtesy*—they are friendly, respectful, and considerate; *credibility*—they are trustworthy; *reliability*—they perform the service

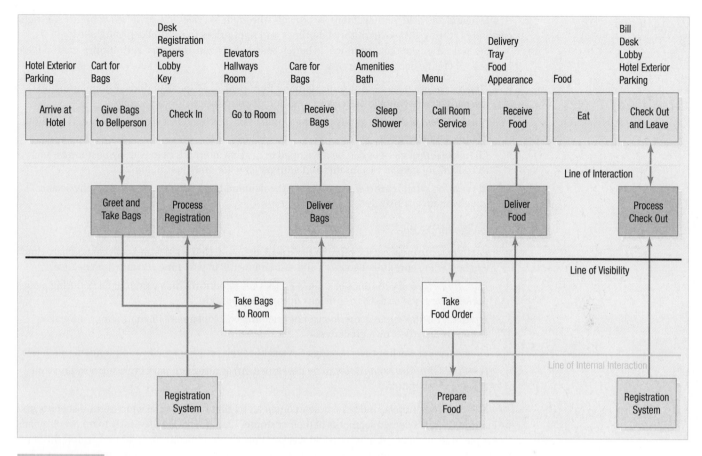

Source: Valarie Zeithaml, Mary Jo Bitner, and Dwayne D. Gremler, *Services Marketing: Integrating Customer Focus across the Firm*, 4th ed. (New York: McGraw-Hill, 2006).

FIGURE 13.3

Blueprint for Overnight Hotel Stay

consistently and accurately; *responsiveness*—they respond quickly to customers' requests and problems; and *communication ability*—they make an effort to understand the customer and communicate clearly.[17] Fairmont Hotels demonstrates its commitment to employees through a variety of training opportunities, ranging from courses on finance to food preparation.[18]

2. *Standardize the service-performance process throughout the organization.* A *service blueprint* can simultaneously map out the service process, the points of customer contact, and the evidence of service from the customer's point of view.[19] Figure 13.3 shows a service blueprint for a guest spending a night at a hotel.[20] The guest's experience includes a series of steps he or she must take before getting to sleep. Behind the scenes, the hotel must skillfully help the guest move from one step to the next. Service blueprints can be helpful in developing new service, supporting a "zero defects" culture, and devising service-recovery strategies.

3. *Monitor customer satisfaction.* Employ suggestion and complaint systems, customer surveys, and comparison shopping. General Electric sends out 700 000 response cards a year asking households to rate its service people's performance. Citibank checks continuously on measures of ART (accuracy, responsiveness, and timeliness). Recognizing how customer needs may vary in different geographical areas can allow firms to develop region-specific programs to improve total customer satisfaction.[21] Firms can also develop customer-information databases and systems to permit more personalized, customized service, especially online.[22]

PERISHABILITY Services cannot be stored so their perishability can be a problem when demand fluctuates. For example, public-transportation companies must own much more equipment because of rush-hour demand than if demand were even throughout the day. Some doctors charge patients for missed appointments because the service value (the doctor's availability) exists only at the time of the appointment.

Demand or yield management is critical—the right services must be available to the right customers at the right places at the right times and right prices to maximize profitability.

Several strategies can produce a better match between demand and supply in a service business.[23] On the demand side:

- *Differential pricing* will shift some demand from peak to off-peak periods. Examples include low early-evening movie prices and weekend discount prices for car rentals.[24]
- *Nonpeak demand* can be cultivated. McDonald's pushes breakfast service, and hotels promote mini-vacation weekends.
- *Complementary* services can be developed to provide alternatives to waiting customers, such as cocktail lounges in restaurants and automated teller machines in banks.
- *Reservation systems* are a way to manage the demand level. Airlines, hotels, and physicians employ them extensively.

On the supply side:

- *Part-time employees* can be hired to serve peak demand. Universities and colleges add part-time teachers when enrollment goes up, and restaurants call in part-time servers when needed.
- *Peak-time efficiency* routines can allow employees to perform only essential tasks during peak periods. Paramedics assist physicians during busy periods.
- *Increased consumer participation* can be encouraged. Consumers fill out their own medical records or bag their own groceries.
- *Shared services* can improve offerings. Several hospitals can share medical-equipment purchases.
- *Facilities for future expansion* can be developed. An amusement park buys surrounding land for later development.

Many airlines, hotels, and resorts send email alerts that offer special short-term discounts and promotions to self-selected segments of their customer base. Club Med uses early to midweek emails to people in its database to pitch unsold weekend packages, typically 30 to 40 percent off the standard package price.[25] After 40 years of making people stand in line at its theme parks, Disney instituted Fastpass, which allows visitors to reserve a spot in line and eliminate the wait. When visitors were polled, it turns out that 95 percent like the change. Disney's Vice-President Dale Stafford told a reporter "We have been teaching people how to stand in line since 1955, and now we are telling them they don't have to. Of all the things we can do and all the marvels we can create with the attractions, this is something that will have a profound effect on the entire industry."[26]

MARKETING STRATEGIES FOR SERVICE FIRMS

At one time, service firms lagged behind manufacturing firms in their use of marketing because they were small, or they were professional businesses that did not use marketing, or they faced large demand or little competition. This has certainly changed. "Marketing Memo: Recommendations for Improving Service Quality" offers a comprehensive set of guidelines to which top service-marketing organizations can adhere.

A Shifting Customer Relationship

Not all companies, however, have invested in providing superior service, at least not to all customers. In many service industries, such as airlines, banks, stores, and hotels, customer satisfaction in North America has actually dropped in recent years.[27] Customers complain about inaccurate information; unresponsive, rude, or poorly trained personnel; and long waiting times. Even worse, many customers find their complaints never actually successfully reach a live human being because of slow or faulty phone or online customer service. When Forrester Research had its analysts contact 16 top companies via their websites, phone agents, interactive voice response (IVR), and email to assess customer service, their experiences were not all positive:[28]

- When analysts called Wal-Mart to track an order and collect additional information, the automated voice system politely told them that their complete satisfaction was a priority, then said "goodbye" and hung up.
- When the researchers called RadioShack for digital-camera recommendations, a sales agent told the caller to call back and request technical support, but the second call was transferred back to the same sales department.

| MARKETING MEMO | RECOMMENDATIONS FOR IMPROVING SERVICE QUALITY |

Pioneers in conducting academic service research, Berry, Parasuraman, and Zeithaml offer ten lessons that they maintain are essential for improving service quality across service industries.

1. *Listening*—Understand what customers really want through continuous learning about the expectations and perceptions of customers and noncustomers (for instance, by means of a service-quality information system).

2. *Reliability*—Reliability is the single most important dimension of service quality and must be a service priority.

3. *Basic service*—Service companies must deliver the basics and do what they are supposed to do—keep promises, use common sense, listen to customers, keep customers informed, and be determined to deliver value to customers.

4. *Service design*—Develop a holistic view of the service while managing its many details.

5. *Recovery*—To satisfy customers who encounter a service problem, service companies should encourage customers to complain (and make it easy for them to do so), respond quickly and personally, and develop a problem-resolution system.

6. *Surprising customers*—Although reliability is the most important dimension in *meeting* customers' service expectations, process dimensions such as assurance, responsiveness, and empathy are most important in *exceeding* customer expectations, for example, by surprising them with uncommon swiftness, grace, courtesy, competence, commitment, and understanding.

7. *Fair play*—Service companies must make special efforts to *be* fair, and to *demonstrate* fairness, to customers and employees.

8. *Teamwork*—Teamwork is what enables large organizations to deliver service with care and attentiveness by improving employee motivation and capabilities.

9. *Employee research*—Marketers should conduct research with employees to reveal why service problems occur and what companies must do to solve problems.

10. *Servant leadership*—Quality service comes from inspired leadership throughout the organization; from excellent service-system design; from the effective use of information and technology; and from a slow-to-change, invisible, all-powerful, internal force called corporate culture.

Sources: Leonard L. Berry, A. Parasuraman, and Valarie A. Zeithaml, "Ten Lessons for Improving Service Quality," *MSI Reports Working Paper Series, No.03-001* (Cambridge, MA: Marketing Science Institute, 2003), pp. 61–82. See also Leonard L. Berry's books, *On Great Service: A Framework for Action* (New York: Free Press, 2006) and *Discovering the Soul of Service* (New York: Free Press, 1999), as well as his articles: Leonard L. Berry, Venkatesh Shankar, Janet Parish, Susan Cadwallader, and Thomas Dotzel, "Creating New Markets through Service Innovation," *Sloan Management Review* (Winter 2006): 56–63; Leonard L. Berry, Stephan H. Haeckel, and Lewis P. Carbone, "How to Lead the Customer Experience," *Marketing Management* (January–February 2003): 18–23; and Leonard L. Berry, Kathleen Seiders, and Dhruv Grewal, "Understanding Service Convenience," *Journal of Marketing* (July 2002): 1–17.

- Cingular's website provided forms for sending email inquiries with a registered account, but the password for the account was sent via text message to a phone that had not been received yet.

It doesn't have to be that way. TD Canada Trust has found many keys to on-going customer satisfaction.

TD Canada Trust

In 2007, for the second year in a row, J.D. Power and Associates (a global marketing-information-services firm famous for its quality and satisfaction rankings) gave TD Canada Trust the top spot in its ranking of customer satisfaction among the "Big Five" Canadian retail banks. Six factors (in order of importance) make up the customer-satisfaction index: quality of transaction experiences, quality of the facility, account setup/product offerings, account statement, fees, and problem resolution. The J.D. Power study also found that convenient services and innovative banking practices differentiate the high-scoring banks like TD Canada Trust. Sixty-one percent of its customers said convenience was "extremely important" in their choice of a bank, compared to 46 percent of customers overall.

TD Canada Trust has focused on this element by extending its hours of operation, and its advertising communicates this clearly to current and potential customers. TD Canada Trust uses other innovative approaches such as programs on Facebook tailored to university students, like the "Split It" application that helps roommates manage how they split bills. It's not surprising that TD Canada Trust's clients perceive the bank as particularly innovative, which contributes to their high level of overall satisfaction.[29]

Hewlett-Packard tries to respond to every email query within an hour, and usually answers within ten minutes. The firm monitors its email centres minute by minute to ensure it meets its service-quality standards. Because of its successful email service centres, HP received 25-percent fewer calls to its call centre between 2005 and 2006. Email volume rose, improving profits because an email response costs HP 60-percent less than a phone call.

Email response must be implemented properly to be effective. One expert believes companies should (1) send an automated reply to tell customers when a more complete answer will arrive (ideally within 24 hours); (2) ensure the subject line always contains the company name; (3) make the message easy to scan for relevant information; and (4) give customers an easy way to respond with follow-up questions.[30]

PROFIT TIERS   Firms have decided to raise fees and lower service to those customers who barely pay their way and to coddle big spenders to retain their patronage as long as possible. Customers in high-profit tiers get special discounts, promotional offers, and lots of special service; customers in lower-profit tiers may get more fees, stripped-down service, and voice messages to process their inquiries.

Charles Schwab's best customers get their calls answered in 15 seconds; other customers can wait longer. Sears sends a repairperson to its best customers within two hours; other customers wait four hours.[31] Companies that provide differentiated levels of service, however, must be careful about claiming superior service—the customers who receive poor treatment will bad-mouth the company and injure its reputation. Delivering services that maximize both customer satisfaction and company profitability can be challenging. "Breakthrough Marketing: Southwest and WestJet Airlines," at the end of this chapter, describes how these spunky airlines took on the big boys and succeeded.

Customer Empowerment   Customers are becoming more sophisticated about buying product support services and are pressing for "services unbundling." They may want separate prices for each service element and the right to select individual elements. Customers also increasingly dislike having to deal with a multitude of service providers handling different types of equipment. Some third-party service organizations now service a greater range of equipment.

Most important, the Internet has empowered customers by letting them vent their rage about bad service—or reward good service—and have their comments beamed around the world with a mouse click.[32] Ninety percent of angry customers reported that they shared their story with a friend. Now, they can share their stories with strangers via the Internet, or "word of mouth on steroids" as some say. With a few clicks on the Planetfeedback.com website, shoppers can send an email complaint, compliment, suggestion, or question directly to a company with the option to post comments publicly at the site as well. David Menzies, a Toronto-based writer, is the last person a call centre might want to frustrate. When reading a *Travel Ontario* brochure, an ad for a cherry-red roller coaster and Coast Hotels beckoned, "Active participation required." David was hooked, and tried to find out just where the fantastic roller coaster and the closest Coast Hotel were located. It seemed an easy task since the ad contained a toll free number, but the Coast Hotel Call Centre was located in North Dakota and didn't seem to have the right information about any of the 60 Ontario cities and towns referred to in the ad. After being put on hold, he was finally given information about the roller coaster—only it was completely wrong. The theme park where the roller coaster was supposed to be located didn't exist and the location of the closest Coast hotel was incorrect. More calls and more requests to "hold please while I check with a supervisor" never produced the needed information. Totally frustrated, Menzies took revenge and published his tale of woe in *Marketing* magazine, which has both print and online versions.[33] Most companies respond quickly, some within an hour. More important than simply responding to a disgruntled customer, however, is preventing dissatisfaction from occurring in the future. That may mean simply taking the time to nurture customer relationships and give customers attention from a real person. Columbia Records spent US$10 million to improve its call centre, and customers who phone the company can now "opt out" of the automated system to reach an operator at any point in their call.

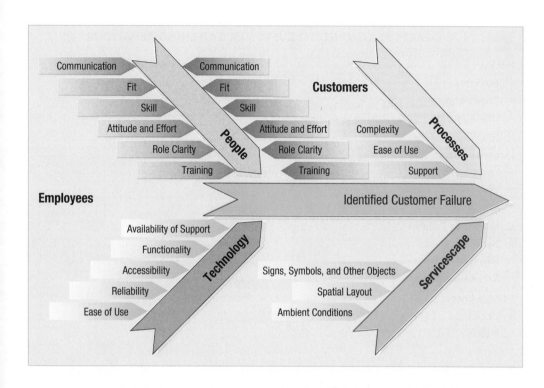

FIGURE 13.4

Root Causes of Customer Failure

Source: Stephen Tax, Mark Colgate, and David Bowen, *MIT Sloan Management Review* (Spring 2006): 30–38.

Coproduction The reality is that customers do not merely purchase and use services, they play an active role in the delivery of that service every step of the way.[34] Their words and actions affect the quality of their service experiences and those of others, and the productivity of frontline employees. One study estimated that one-third of all service problems are caused by the customer.[35] With an increasing shift to self-service technologies, this percentage can be expected to rise.

Preventing service failures from ever happening is crucial, as service recovery is always challenging. One of the biggest problems is attribution—customers will often feel that the firm is at fault or, even if not, that it is still responsible for righting any wrongs. Unfortunately, although many firms have well-designed and well-executed procedures to deal with their own failures, they find that managing customer failures is much more difficult.

Figure 13.4 displays the four broad categories of root causes of customer failures, although there often are multiple causes at work. Solutions come in all forms, as illustrated by some of the following examples:[36]

1. *Redesign processes and redefine customer roles to simplify service encounters*—Canflix Online DVD Rentals allows customers to pay a flat monthly fee in exchange for unlimited movie, TV, and game rentals. Customers across Canada benefit from fast delivery, no late fees, and no due dates—in other words, greater control and flexibility.

2. *Incorporate the right technology to aid employees and customers*—Mountain Equipment Co-op keeps a virtual copy of purchase information in case customers are unable to produce a receipt needed for a return.

3. *Create high-performance customers by enhancing their role clarity, motivation, and ability*—Saturn coaches novice buyers about proper vehicle maintenance. Hewlett-Packard offers Live Coach with the purchase of some digital-camera models sold in Canada. Live Coach kits include a headset and software, and allow customers to receive personalized training via online video-conference in how to use their new camera.[37]

4. *Encourage "customer citizenship" whereby customers help customers*—At golf courses, players can not only follow the rules by playing and behaving appropriately, they can encourage others to do so.

Holistic Marketing for Services

The service outcome, and whether people will remain loyal to a service provider, is influenced by a host of variables. One study identified more than 800 critical behaviours that cause customers to switch services.[38] These behaviours fall into eight categories (see Table 13.1).

TABLE 13.1 | FACTORS LEADING TO CUSTOMER SWITCHING BEHAVIOUR

Pricing
- High price
- Price increases
- Unfair pricing
- Deceptive pricing

Inconvenience
- Location/hours
- Wait for appointment
- Wait for service

Core-Service Failures
- Service mistakes
- Billing errors
- Service catastrophe

Service-Encounter Failures
- Uncaring
- Impolite
- Unresponsive
- Unknowledgeable

Response to Service Failure
- Negative response
- No response
- Reluctant response

Competition
- Found better service

Ethical Problems
- Cheating
- Hard sell
- Unsafe
- Conflict of interest

Involuntary Switching
- Customer moved
- Provider closed

Source: Susan M. Keaveney, "Customer Switching Behavior in Service Industries: An Exploratory Study," *Journal of Marketing* (April 1995): 71–82. Copyright © 1995 American Marketing Association. Used with permission.

Three Types of Marketing in Service Industries

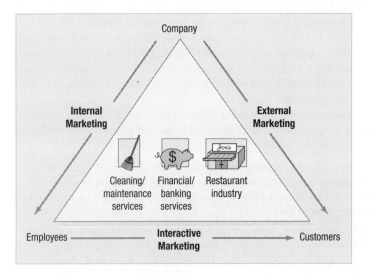

Holistic marketing for services requires external, internal, and interactive marketing (see Figure 13.5).[39] *External marketing* describes the normal work of preparing, pricing, distributing, and promoting the service to customers. *Internal marketing* describes training and motivating employees to serve customers well. The most important contribution the marketing department can make is arguably to be "exceptionally clever in getting everyone else in the organization to practice marketing,"[40] as is the case at Singapore Airlines.

Singapore Airlines (SIA)

Singapore Airlines is consistently recognized as the world's "best" airline—it wins so many awards, it has to update its website monthly to keep up to date—in large part due to its stellar efforts at holistic marketing. SIA continually strives to create a "wow effect" and surpasses customers' expectations. Famous for pampering passengers, it was the first to launch individual video screens at airplane seats. To improve its food, SIA built the first-of-its-kind US$1 million simulator to mimic the air pressure and humidity found inside a plane. Because taste buds change in the air, SIA found that, among other things, it needed to cut back on spices. SIA places a high emphasis on training through its "Transforming Customer Service (TCS)" program, which includes staff in five key operational areas: cabin crew, engineering, ground services, flight operations, and sales support. The TCS culture is embedded in all management training, companywide. TCS also uses a 40-30-30 rule in its holistic approach to people, processes, and products: 40 percent of resources go to training and invigorating staff, 30 percent is spent on reviewing process and procedures, and the last 30 percent on creating new product and service ideas. In 2007, with its innovatively designed Boeing 777-300 ERS and Airbus A380 planes, SIA set new standards for comfort in all classes of service, from eight private minirooms in first class to wider seats, AC power supplies, and USB ports in economy.[41]

Interactive marketing describes employees' skill in serving a client. Clients judge service not only by its *technical quality* (Was the surgery successful?) but also by its *functional quality* (Did the surgeon show concern and inspire confidence?).[42] Teamwork is often key, and delegating authority to frontline employees can allow for greater flexibility and adaptability in service delivery through better problem-solving, closer employee cooperation, and more efficient knowledge transfer.[43]

Technology has great power to make service workers more productive. Many physicians and nurses now carry wireless laptop-like devices in their coat pockets from exam room to exam room. These devices contain all relevant patient information and charts, email correspondence, and suggested treatments for certain diagnoses. They also allow the physicians to write prescriptions, and they store and automatically process all information entered during the patient visit. Workforce automation at Sears Canada is geared at improving service-technician productivity.

Sears Canada

When Sears Canada automated its HomeCentral workforce, it eliminated the burden of paperwork. Real-time, wireless dispatch and mobile workforce automation solution from Mobile Computing Corporation enabled service technicians to connect with company information systems over a secure network. Service technicians have quick access to service information, such as route sheets, and can update information from their handheld units. Sears Canada's goal in implementing automation is to improve productivity, increase customer service, and reduce costs.[44]

Singapore Airlines adopts a holistic approach to its services, dividing its resources among training staff (employees), reviewing its processes (company), and creating new products and services (customers).

However, companies must avoid pushing productivity so hard that they reduce perceived quality. Some methods lead to too much standardization. Service providers must deliver "high touch" as well as "high tech." Fairmont Hotels & Resorts uses its extensive customer database to customize the exceptional service the chain provides to members of its President's Club. This exclusive guest recognition program tailors the guests' experience from the moment they arrive through its express check-in service, and recognition of guest preferences ranging from the type of pillow they want to the size of athletic gear that is provided as one of the benefits of membership.[45]

The Internet is another tool firms use to improve their service offerings and strengthen their relationships with customers by allowing for true interactivity, customer-specific and situational personalization, and real-time adjustments of the firm's offerings.[46] But as companies collect, store, and use more information about customers, concerns have arisen about security and privacy.[47] Companies must incorporate the proper safeguards and reassure customers about their efforts.

MANAGING SERVICE QUALITY

Haier is the preferred brand in China for household appliances—a result of providing its customers with quality service. To learn more about Haier's successful service strategies, visit www.pearsoned-asia.com/marketingmanagementchina.

The service quality of a firm is tested at each service encounter. If service personnel are bored, cannot answer simple questions, or are visiting with each other while customers are waiting, customers will think twice about doing business again with that seller.

Customer Expectations

Customers form service expectations from many sources, such as past experiences, word of mouth, and advertising. In general, customers compare the *perceived service* with the *expected service*.[48] If the perceived service falls below the expected service, customers are disappointed. Successful companies, like Ritz-Carlton hotels, add benefits to their offering that not only *satisfy* customers but also surprise and *delight* them. Delighting customers is a matter of exceeding expectations.[49]

Ritz–Carlton Hotels

Ritz-Carlton Hotels' legendary service starts with 100 hours of training annually for every employee. The goal? To treat every guest like royalty by being warm, friendly, gracious, courteous, and genuinely devoted to making sure every stay is a memorable one. Every manager and frontline employee carries a laminated card with twelve service-values guidelines to help create the brand mystique that lures the luxury traveller, such as "I build strong relationships and create Ritz-Carlton guests for life" (#1) and "I am proud of my professional appearance, language, and behaviour" (#10). Every day at every Ritz-Carlton, employees around the world gather from every department for a 15-minute meeting known as "the line-up." They first review guest experiences, resolve issues, and discuss ways to improve service, before spending the bulk of the time on reinforcing one of the twelve service values. Every meeting each day also shares one "wow story" by a staff person who provided exemplary service by going above and beyond the call of duty. It's perhaps no surprise that Ritz-Carlton, with 60 properties around the world, was the first two-time winner of the Malcolm Baldrige National Quality Award.[50]

The service-quality model in Figure 13.6 highlights the main requirements for delivering high service quality.[51] It identifies five gaps that cause unsuccessful delivery. For example, as Canadian business schools market more and more private or full-fee MBA programs, it is important to understand:

1. *Gap between consumer expectation and management perception.* Management does not always correctly perceive what customers want. MBA-program administrators may think students want more challenging and specialized courses, but students may be more concerned about the responsiveness of professors to their queries.

2. *Gap between management perception and service-quality specification.* Management might correctly perceive customers' wants but not set a performance standard. MBA-program administrators may tell professors to give "fast" responses without specifying a specific time frame, such as "respond to all student queries within 24 hours."

3. *Gap between service-quality specifications and service delivery.* Personnel might be poorly trained, incapable, or unwilling to meet the standard, or they may be held to conflicting standards, such as taking time to listen to students and serving them quickly. Both of these issues

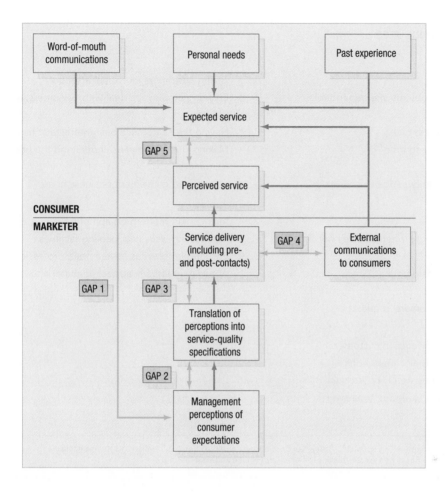

FIGURE 13.6

Service-Quality Model

Sources: A. Parasuraman, Valarie A. Zeithaml, and Leonard L. Berry, "A Conceptual Model of Service Quality and Its Implications for Future Research," *Journal of Marketing* (Fall 1985): 44. Reprinted with permission of the American Marketing Association. The model is more fully discussed in Valarie Zeithaml, Mary Jo Bitner, and Dwayne D. Gremler, *Services Marketing: Integrating Customer Focus across the Firm*, 4th ed. (New York: McGraw-Hill, 2006).

can be a problem for MBA-program administrators as they are forced to hire more and more part-time teaching staff because of budget constraints.

4. *Gap between service delivery and external communications.* Consumer expectations are affected by statements made by organizational representatives and ads. If an MBA-program brochure shows its one and only beautiful, well-equipped classroom, but students arrive and find that most classrooms need refurbishing, external communications have distorted customers' expectations.

5. *Gap between perceived service and expected service.* This gap occurs when the consumer misperceives the service quality. An MBA-program assistant may send potential students exercises to help them pass the GMAT exam as a way to show helpfulness and care, but the students may interpret this as an indication that they are not strong enough candidates for the program.

Based on this service-quality model, researchers identified the following five determinants of service quality, in order of importance.[52]

1. *Reliability*—The ability to perform the promised service dependably and accurately.

2. *Responsiveness*—The willingness to help customers and to provide prompt service.

3. *Assurance*—The knowledge and courtesy of employees and their ability to convey trust and confidence.

4. *Empathy*—The provision of caring, individualized attention to customers.

5. *Tangibles*—The appearance of physical facilities, equipment, personnel, and communication materials.

Based on these five factors, the researchers developed the 21-item SERVQUAL scale (see Table 13.2).[53] They also note that there is a *zone of tolerance* or range where a service dimension would be deemed satisfactory, anchored by the minimum level consumers are willing to accept and the level they believe can and should be delivered. "Marketing Insight: The Role of Expectations in Service-Quality Perceptions" describes important recent research on services marketing. "Marketing Memo: Assessing E-Service Quality" reviews two models of online-service quality.

TABLE 13.2 | **SERVQUAL ATTRIBUTES**

Reliability
- Providing service as promised
- Handling customers' service problems in a dependable manner
- Performing services right the first time
- Providing services at the promised time
- Maintaining error-free records
- Ensuring employees have the knowledge to answer customer questions

Responsiveness
- Keeping customers informed as to when services will be performed
- Providing prompt service to customers
- Being willing to help customers
- Being ready to respond to customers' requests

Assurance
- Ensuring employees instill confidence in customers
- Making customers feel safe in their transactions
- Making sure employees are consistently courteous
- Ensuring employees have the knowledge to answer customer questions

Empathy
- Giving customers individual attention
- Ensuring employees deal with customers in a caring fashion
- Having the customer's best interests at heart
- Making sure employees understand the needs of their customers
- Maintaining convenient business hours

Tangibles
- Maintaining modern equipment
- Maintaining visually appealing facilities
- Ensuring employees have a neat, professional appearance
- Associating visually appealing materials with the service

Source: A. Parasuraman, Valarie A. Zeithaml, and Leonard L. Berry, "A Conceptual Model of Service Quality and Its Implications for Future Research," *Journal of Marketing* (Fall 1985): 41–50. Reprinted by permission of American Marketing Association.

Best Practices of Service-Quality Management

Various studies have shown that well-managed service companies share the following common practices: a strategic concept, a history of top-management commitment to quality, high standards, self-service technologies, systems for monitoring service performance and customer complaints, and an emphasis on employee satisfaction. Manulife Financial embodies many of these practices.

Manulife Financial

One of the most dynamic and progressive financial services companies in the world, Manulife Financial is the only life-insurance company in Canada, and one of only two publicly traded life-insurance companies in the world, to hold Standard and Poor's AAA rating for financial strength. This excellent rating provides its clients with assurance that the company can keep its financial promises now and long into the future. Manulife prides itself on its high-quality customer service. It answers 80 percent of all calls in 30 seconds, and in most cases queries can be answered instantly. It works to have a simple complaint-resolution process and advertises this on its website, stating "we believe that complaint-resolution is important, and it is incumbent upon us to respond to complaints **promptly, accurately,** and with the utmost **courtesy**. We will provide our customers with **accessible means** with which to communicate their complaint, and will employ our best efforts to respond and resolve where possible. All complaints and personal information collected, whether written or oral, must be handled in a **timely, professional,** and **confidential** manner. Our clients are entitled to no less." Customers can quickly resolve most concerns by placing a call to their advisor. In the few cases where this doesn't solve the problem, they are advised to speak to a manager or the Customer Relations Department. In recognition of its quality, Manulife recently received the Certification for Excellence in customer service from the National Quality Institute. Given its attention to service quality, it is not surprising that Manulife has been ranked as Canada's third-most valuable brand.[54]

| MARKETING INSIGHT | THE ROLE OF EXPECTATIONS IN SERVICE-QUALITY PERCEPTIONS |

The service-quality model in Figure 13.6 highlights some of the gaps that cause unsuccessful service delivery. Subsequent research has extended the model to incorporate additional considerations. Boulding, Kalra, Staelin, and Zeithaml have developed a *dynamic process model of service quality*. One dynamic process model of service quality was based on the premise that customer perceptions and expectations of service quality change over time, but at any one point in time are a function of prior expectations of what *will* and what *should* happen during the service encounter, as well as the *actual* service delivered during the last contact. Empirical tests of the model reveal that the two different types of expectations have opposite effects on perceptions of service quality.

1. *Increasing* customer expectations of what the firm *will* deliver can lead to improved perceptions of overall service quality.
2. *Decreasing* customer expectations of what the firm *should* deliver can lead to improved perceptions of overall service quality.

Much work has validated the role of expectations in consumers' interpretations and evaluations of the service encounter and the relationship they adopt with a firm over time. Consumers are often forward-looking with respect to their decision to keep or switch from a service relationship. Any marketing activity that affects current or expected future usage can help to solidify a service relationship.

With continuously provided services, such as public utilities, health care, financial services, computing services, insurance, and other professional, membership, or subscription services, customers have been observed to mentally calculate their *payment equity*—the perceived fairness of the level of economic benefits derived from service usage in relation to the level of economic costs. Payment costs typically consist of some combination of an initial payment such as a membership fee or retainer, a fixed, periodic fee such as a monthly service charge, and a variable fee such as usage-based charges. Payment benefits depend on current payment and usage levels. The perceived fairness of the exchange determines service satisfaction and future usage. In other words, it is as if customers ask themselves "Am I using this service enough, given what I pay for it?"

There can be a dark side to long-term service relationships. For example, with an ad agency, the client may feel that over time, the agency loses objectivity and becomes stale in its thinking or begins to take advantage of the relationship.

Sources: William Boulding, Ajay Kalra, Richard Staelin, and Valarie A. Zeithaml, "A Dynamic Model of Service Quality: From Expectations to Behavioral Intentions," *Journal of Marketing Research*, 30 (February 1993): 7–27; Katherine N. Lemon, Tiffany Barnett White, and Russell S. Winer, "Dynamic Customer Relationship Management: Incorporating Future Considerations into the Service Retention Decision," *Journal of Marketing*, 6 (January 2002): 1–14; Ruth N. Bolton and Katherine N. Lemon, "A Dynamic Model of Customers' Usage of Services: Usage as an Antecedent and Consequence of Satisfaction," *Journal of Marketing*, 36 (May 1999): 171–186; Kent Grayson and Tim Ambler, "The Dark Side of Long-Term Relationships in Marketing Services," *Journal of Marketing Research*, 36 (February 1999): 132–141; Roland T. Rust and Tuck Siong Chung, "Marketing Models of Service and Relationships," *Marketing Science*, 25 (November–December 2006): 560–80.

STRATEGIC CONCEPT Top service companies like Manulife are "customer obsessed." They have a clear sense of their target customers and their needs. They have developed a distinctive strategy for satisfying these needs. At the Four Seasons luxury-hotel chain, employees must pass four interviews before being hired. Each hotel also employs a "guest historian" to track guest preferences.

After surveying more than 200 000 international passengers, the Airports Council International granted the Halifax Stanfield International Airport, which handles 3.4 million passengers annually, the 2007 "airport people award." In fact, it has been ranked as the world's best airport for overall passenger satisfaction in the under-five-million-passengers category for five straight years. To earn this award, the airport—which has been rated by passengers as having the most courteous and helpful airport, airline, and security staff—had to demonstrate that it had developed a strong customer-service culture across the entire airport community. In announcing the award, Tom Ruth, President & CEO, said "Everyone here at HSIA shares in this achievement. We have a terrific group of people at our airport who work together to provide the best passenger-experience possible. These awards are a tribute to the hard work, dedication and exceptional service commitment by the front-line staff from our many partners—airlines, retailers, and service providers—as well as our own HSIA employees and our wonderful volunteer hosts."[55]

| MARKETING MEMO | ASSESSING E-SERVICE QUALITY |

Academic researchers Zeithaml, Parasuraman, and Malhotra define online-service quality as the extent to which a website facilitates efficient and effective shopping, purchasing, and delivery. They identified 11 dimensions of perceived e-service quality: access, ease of navigation, efficiency, flexibility, reliability, personalization, security/privacy, responsiveness, assurance/trust, site aesthetics, and price knowledge. Some of these service-quality dimensions were the same online as offline, but some specific underlying attributes were different. Different dimensions emerged with e-service quality, too. Empathy didn't seem to be as important online, unless there were service problems. Core dimensions of regular service quality were efficiency, fulfillment, reliability, and privacy; core dimensions of service recovery were responsiveness, compensation, and real-time access to help.

Another set of academic researchers, Wolfinbarger and Gilly, developed a reduced scale of online-service quality with four key dimensions: reliability/fulfillment, website design, security/privacy, and customer service. The researchers interpret their study findings to suggest that the most basic building blocks of a "compelling online experience" are reliability and outstanding website functionality in terms of time savings, easy transactions, good selection, in-depth information, and the "right level" of personalization. Their 14-item scale follows.

Reliability/Fulfillment

- The product that came was represented accurately by the website.
- You get what you ordered from this website.
- The product is delivered by the time promised by the company.

Website Design

- This website provides in-depth information.
- The site doesn't waste my time.
- It is quick and easy to complete a transaction at this website.
- The level of personalization at this site is about right, not too much or too little.
- This website has good selection.

Security/Privacy

- I feel that my privacy is protected at this site.
- I feel safe in my transactions with this website.
- This website has adequate security transactions.

Customer Service

- The company is willing and ready to respond to customer needs.
- When you have a problem, the website shows a sincere interest in solving it.
- Inquiries are answered promptly.

Sources: Mary Wolfinbarger and Mary C. Gilly, "E-TailQ: Dimensionalizing, Measuring, and Predicting E-Tail Quality," *Journal of Retailing*, 79 (Fall 2003): 183–98; Valarie A. Zeithaml, A. Parsu Parasuraman, and Arvind Malhotra, "A Conceptual Framework for Understanding e-Service Quality: Implications for Future Research and Managerial Practice," Marketing Science Institute Working Paper, Report No. 00-115, 2000.

TOP-MANAGEMENT COMMITMENT As the above quotation from Tom Ruth of the Halifax airport illustrates, service quality starts with top-management commitment. Companies such as Fairmont, Canadian Tire, and Vancity Credit Union all have a thorough commitment to service quality. Their managements look not only at financial performance on a monthly basis, but also at service performance. Ray Kroc of McDonald's insisted on continually measuring each McDonald's outlet on its conformance to QSCV: quality, service, cleanliness, and value. Some companies insert a reminder along with employees' paycheques: "Brought to you by the customer."

Sam Walton of Wal-Mart required the following employee pledge: "I solemnly swear and declare that every customer that comes within 10 feet of me, I will smile, look them in the eye, and greet them, so help me Sam."

HIGH STANDARDS The best service providers set high service-quality standards. In 1961 the Royal Bank was the first financial institution in Canada to install a computer. Since that time it has leveraged technology to help its people provide superior service anywhere, at any time. The standards must be set *appropriately* high. A 98-percent accuracy standard may sound good, but it would result in 64 000 lost FedEx packages a day; six misspelled words on each page of a book; and unsafe drinking water eight days a year. We can distinguish between companies offering "merely good" service and those offering "breakthrough" service, aimed at being 100-percent defect-free.[56]

A service company can differentiate itself by designing a better and faster delivery system. There are three levels of differentiation.[57] The first is *reliability:* some suppliers are more reliable in their on-time delivery, order completeness, and order-cycle time. The second is *resilience:* some suppliers are better at handling emergencies, product recalls, and answering inquiries. The third is *innovation:* some suppliers create better information systems, introduce bar coding and mixed pallets, and in other ways help the customer. "Marketing Insight: Developing Customer-Interface Systems" discusses how service marketers must reengineer their customer-interface systems for optimal efficiency and effectiveness.

MARKETING INSIGHT | DEVELOPING CUSTOMER-INTERFACE SYSTEMS

Marketing academics and consultants Jeffrey Rayport and Bernie Jaworski define a *customer-service interface* as any place at which a company seeks to manage a relationship with a customer, whether through people, technology, or some combination of the two. They believe that to deliver high levels of customer-perceived value, any interface should excel on four dimensions:

- *Physical presence and appearance:* Be on the scene in sufficient numbers and presentable in appearance. At the Four Seasons Hotel, the frontline staff is differentiated on appearance as uniformed, clean-cut, businesslike, courteous, individual, and authentic.

- *Cognition:* Be able to recognize patterns, draw intelligent conclusions, and communicate articulately. Service personnel at Fairmont Hotels & Resorts, from doorkeepers, to front-desk personnel, to people staffing the gymnasium desk, are skilled at recognizing and rewarding the chain's best customers with appropriate service and attention.

- *Emotion or attitude:* Be respectful and attentive, display brand-consistent personality attributes, and be emotionally calibrated with the customer. WestJet's flight crew's sense of humour and positive dispositions enhance passengers' travel experiences.

- *Connectedness:* Remain well connected to other resources important to the customer's experience. Organizations as diverse as Dalhousie University, Four Seasons, and WestJet all coordinate communications and activities to provide a holistic, positive experience.

Rayport and Jaworski believe companies are facing a crisis in customer interaction and relationship management. Although many companies serve customers through a broad array of interfaces, from retail sales clerks, to websites, to voice-response telephone systems, these more often constitute an interface *collection*, not an actual interface *system*, as the whole set fails to provide superior service and build strong customer relationships. Rising complexity, costs, and customer dissatisfaction can result. Networked technologies, however, such as websites, kiosks, interactive voice-response units, vending machines, and touch screens let managers successfully introduce machines into front-office roles that have long been held by humans. Here are a few examples they note:

- Borders, a book retailer with more than 1100 stores around the world, deployed Title Sleuth self-service kiosks to take the burden of title searches from its employees. The three hundred machines handle up to 1.2 million customer searches per week, and customers using these machines spend 50 percent more per store visit and generate 20 percent more special-order sales.

■ REI, a chain of premier outdoor-gear stores, uses interactive kiosks in its stores to hold information about its 78 000 SKUs—information that would be impossible for even the most intelligent store clerks to store in their heads. Kiosk sales are growing at 30 percent a year, building revenues to the equivalent of an additional 2300-square-feet bricks-and-mortar store.

■ Rite Aid, the third-largest drugstore chain in the United States, is using prescription-dispensing robots and interactive voice-response units to fulfill an anticipated labour shortage—prescriptions filled in the United States are expected to grow by 30 percent over the next two years while the number of pharmacists is projected to expand by only 6 percent. Automation of rote tasks lets Rite Aid pharmacists use their time to personally attend to customers' needs, providing much-needed brand differentiation in a commoditized category of the retail sector.

According to Rayport and Jaworski, successfully integrating technology into the work force requires a comprehensive re-engineering of the front office to identify what people do best, what machines do best, and how to deploy them separately and together. Managers can take the following steps in conducting a service-interface reengineering project:

1. *Understand the experience customers want.* Do customers seek information, advice, social exchange, affirmation, anonymity, discretion, efficiency, or something else? What interactions and relationships will shape those experiences? What are the implications of these experiences for the firm's own goals and objectives?

2. *Understand the potential of technology.* What is the effectiveness and efficiency of possible technology? What new roles can technology assume?

3. *Match the interface type to the task.* Should the interface be people dominant, machine dominant, or a hybrid of the two? What are the associated costs and customer outcomes?

4. *Put work in its right place.* Should services be provided proximally (in stores or on-site) or remotely (through network connections to customers or operations off-site)?

5. *Optimize performance across the system.* Most customers use multiple channels. Is the interface system able to capitalize on the economic potential of each?

Sources: Jeffrey F. Rayport and Bernard J. Jaworski, *Best Face Forward* (Boston: Harvard Business School Press, 2005); Jeffrey F. Rayport and Bernard J. Jaworski, "Best Face Forward," *Harvard Business Review*, 82 (December 2004): 47–58; Jeffrey F. Rayport, Bernard J. Jaworski, and Ellie J. Kyung, "Best Face Forward," *Journal of Interactive Marketing*, 19 (Autumn 2005): 67–80.

SELF-SERVICE TECHNOLOGIES (SSTS) Consumers value convenience in services.[58] Many person-to-person service interactions are being replaced by self-service technologies.[59] To the traditional vending machines we can add automated teller machines (ATMs), self-pumping at gas stations, self-check-out at hotels, and a variety of activities on the Internet, such as ticket purchasing, investment trading, and product customization.

Not all SSTs improve service quality, but they can make service transactions more accurate, convenient, and faster. Obviously they can also reduce costs. IBM saved US$2 billion by shifting 99 million service telephone calls online.[60] Every company needs to think about improving its service using SSTs.

Some companies have found that the biggest obstacle is not the technology itself, but convincing customers to use it, especially for the first time. Customers must have a clear sense of their roles in the SST process, must see a clear benefit to SST, and must feel they have the ability to actually use it.[61] Air Canada simplifies the self check-in process by giving customers the option of entering their booking reference number, entering their Aeroplan or Star Alliance frequent-flyer number or swiping their frequent-flyer card, or swiping their credit card.[62] See how some hotels are handling this challenge:

Hotel Front Desks

After a long journey—from taxi to plane to taxi to hotel—the hotel's front desk can sometimes seem like a barrier to the longed-for respite of the hotel room. In order to reduce lines and get guests to their rooms more quickly, many hotels are trying to streamline the process through self-service check-in kiosks in the hotel lobby. Hilton Hotels already has kiosks in a number of its hotels, including the Hilton at Vancouver's Airport. Travellers can slide in their credit cards and receive their purple key cards. The kiosk is no replacement for the front desk, but it allows front-desk staff to truly serve a concierge function, devoting more time to guests who need attention. Hilton Hotels, then, is using a combination of high tech and high touch to give it a leg up in the fiercely competitive hotel industry.[63]

MONITORING SYSTEMS Top firms audit service performance, both their own and competitors', on a regular basis. They collect *voice of the customer (VOC) measurements* to probe customer satisfiers and dissatisfiers. They use comparison shopping, ghost shopping, customer surveys, suggestion and complaint forms, service-audit teams, and letters to the president.

Mystery shopping—the use of undercover shoppers who are paid to report back to the company—is now big business: US$500 million worldwide. Fast-food chains, big-box stores, gas stations, and even large government agencies are using mystery shoppers to pinpoint and fix customer service problems.

We can judge services on *customer importance* and *company performance*. *Importance-performance analysis* is used to rate the various elements of the service bundle and identify what actions are required. Table 13.3 shows how customers rated 14 service elements (attributes) of an automobile dealer's service department on importance and performance. For example, "Job done right the first time" (attribute 1) received a mean importance rating of 3.83 and a mean performance rating of 2.63, indicating that customers felt it was highly important but not performed well.

The ratings of the 14 elements are displayed in Figure 13.7 and divided into four sections.

▪ Quadrant A shows important service elements that are not being performed at the desired levels; they include elements 1, 2, and 9. The dealer should concentrate on improving the service department's performance on these elements.

▪ Quadrant B shows important service elements that are being performed well; the company needs to maintain the high performance.

TABLE 13.3	CUSTOMER IMPORTANCE AND PERFORMANCE RATINGS FOR AN AUTO DEALERSHIP		
Attribute Number	Attribute Description	Mean Importance Rating[a]	Mean Performance Rating[b]
1	Job done right the first time	3.83	2.63
2	Fast action on complaints	3.63	2.73
3	Prompt warranty work	3.60	3.15
4	Able to do any job needed	3.56	3.00
5	Service available when needed	3.41	3.05
6	Courteous and friendly service	3.41	3.29
7	Car ready when promised	3.38	3.03
8	Perform only necessary work	3.37	3.11
9	Low prices on service	3.29	2.00
10	Clean up after service work	3.27	3.02
11	Convenient to home	2.52	2.25
12	Convenient to work	2.43	2.49
13	Courtesy buses and cars	2.37	2.35
14	Send out maintenance notices	2.05	3.33

[a]Ratings obtained from a four-point scale of "extremely important" (4), "important" (3), "slightly important" (2), and "not important" (1).

[b]Ratings obtained from a four-point scale of "excellent" (4), "good" (3), "fair" (2), and "poor" (1). A "no basis for judgment" category was also provided.

FIGURE 13.7

Importance–Performance
Analysis

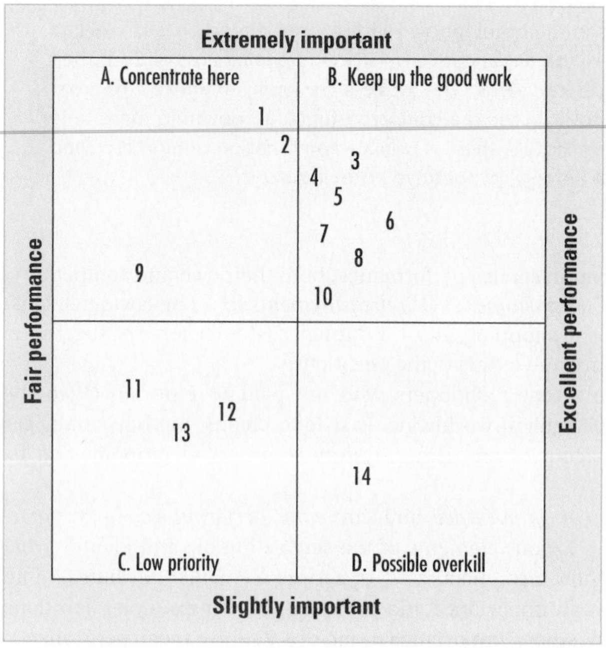

- Quadrant C shows minor service elements that are being delivered in a mediocre way but do not need any attention.
- Quadrant D shows that a minor service element, "Send out maintenance notices," is being performed in an excellent manner.

Perhaps the company should spend less on sending out maintenance notices and use the savings to improve performance on important elements. The analysis can be enhanced by checking on the competitors' performance levels on each element.[64]

SATISFYING CUSTOMER COMPLAINTS   Every complaint is a gift if handled well. Companies that encourage disappointed customers to complain—and also empower employees to remedy the situation on the spot—have been shown to achieve higher revenues and greater profits than companies that do not have a systematic approach to addressing service failures.[65] Pizza Hut prints its toll-free number on all pizza boxes. When a customer complains, Pizza Hut sends voice mail to the store manager, who must call the customer within 48 hours and resolve the complaint. Hyatt Hotels also gets high marks on many of these criteria.

Getting front-line employees to adopt *extra-role behaviours* and to advocate the interests and image of the firm to consumers, as well as take initiative and engage in conscientious behaviour in dealing with customers, can be a critical asset in handling complaints.[66] Research has shown that customers evaluate complaint incidents in terms of the outcomes they receive, the procedures used to arrive at those outcomes, and the nature of the interpersonal treatment during the process.[67] Companies also are increasing the quality of their *call centres* and their *customer-service representatives* (CSRs).

Handling phone calls more efficiently can improve service, reduce complaints, and extend customer longevity. Yet more often than not the problem isn't poor quality but that customers are asked to use an automated voice-response system instead of interacting with a customer-service representative. Although some automated voices are actually popular with customers—the unfailingly polite and chipper voice of Amtrak's "Julie" consistently wins kudos from callers—most just incite frustration and even rage. One savvy entrepreneur took that rage and capitalized on it.

Gethuman.com

Boston-based entrepreneur Paul English got so fed up with automated voice-response systems that he started a web log listing all the ways callers could bypass them. The blog was so popular, he turned it into the gethuman.com website, which now lists over 500 companies and provides keys consumers can use to get around their telephone "trees" to reach a human. If you want to reach a person at Bank of America, for instance, the site directs you to press zero twice after each prompt. The gethuman.com website gets over 10 000 hits a day, proving that this issue has touched a nerve with today's consumers. But English is not devoted only to helping consumers; he also has amassed feedback on how companies can improve their automated-response systems, which he has condensed into the "get human standard." Some of its suggestions are:

- Callers should always be able to press zero, or say "operator," to get to a human.

- The system should always give estimated waiting times and updates every 60 seconds.

- Callers should not be forced to listen to long, verbose prompts.

- When a human is not available, callers should always be offered the option to be called back when one is.

For more suggestions and the get-human core principles, you can go to http://gethuman.com.[68]

SATISFYING EMPLOYEES AS WELL AS CUSTOMERS Excellent service companies know that positive employee attitudes will promote stronger customer loyalty. Instilling a strong customer orientation in employees can also increase their job satisfaction and commitment, especially if they are in service settings that allow for a high degree of customer-contact time. Employees thrive in customer-contact positions when they have an internal drive to (1) pamper customers, (2) accurately read customer needs, (3) develop a personal relationship with customers, and (4) deliver quality service to solve customers' problems.[69]

Consistent with these findings, Sears found a high correlation between customer satisfaction, employee satisfaction, and store profitability. Winners of the 2007 "50 Best Employers in Canada," firms like EllisDon, Sleep Country Canada, and Intuit Canada, understand the crucial role employees play and the importance of employee satisfaction. They have lower turnover among full-time personnel (9.4 percent compared to 12.4 percent for other firms), and receive more job applications for every job posted externally (47 applications compared to 30 applications for other firms). These are important factors in an era when many firms are facing labour shortages. Furthermore, 77 percent of people employed at winning firms report that they are more engaged with their work, compared to 55 percent at other organizations. Engagement captures the emotional and intellectual commitment employees demonstrate to the organization for which they work. High employee engagement also translates into better financial results. For publicly traded companies on the 20 Best Employers list, average annual growth rate in net sales over five years was 12.9 percent, compared with 4.9 percent for those publicly traded companies among the 20 lowest-ranked study participants.[70]

Given the importance of positive employee attitudes, service companies must attract the best employees they can find. They need to market a career rather than just a job. They must design a sound training program and provide support and rewards for good performance. They can use an intranet, internal newsletters, daily reminders, and employee roundtables to reinforce customer-centred attitudes. Finally, they must audit employee job satisfaction regularly.

MANAGING SERVICE BRANDS

Some of the world's strongest brands are services—consider financial service leaders such as the Royal Bank of Canada, Visa, TD Canada Trust, HSBC, and Goldman Sachs. Like any brand, service brands must be skillful at differentiating themselves and developing appropriate brand strategies.

Differentiating Services

Service marketers frequently complain about the difficulty of differentiating their services. The deregulation of several major service industries—communications, transportation, energy, banking—has resulted in intense price competition. To the extent that customers view a service as fairly homogeneous, they care less about the provider than about the price.

Marketers, however, can differentiate service offerings in many ways, through people and processes that add value. The offering can include innovative features. What the customer expects is called the *primary service package*. Vanguard, a major U.S. mutual-fund company, has a unique client ownership structure that lowers costs and permits better fund returns. Strongly differentiated from many competitors, the brand grew through word-of-mouth, PR, and viral marketing.[71]

The provider can add *secondary service features* to the package. In the hotel industry, various chains like the Fairmont have introduced such secondary service features as merchandise for sale, loyalty programs, free breakfast for its gold members, free in-room Internet access and local phone calls, and business centres where guests can book meetings, have their clients greeted by a receptionist, make photocopies, and receive courier packages.

Many companies are using the web to offer secondary service features that were never possible before. Conversely, other service providers, including large drugstore chains, are adding a human element along with advanced technology to combat competition from online businesses. As in-store pharmacies see competition from low-cost online mail-order drugstores, they are playing up the presence of on-site health-care professionals. For instance, Shoppers Drug Mart, Canada's largest retail drug-store group with 1055 stores, makes it known that each store is owned by a pharmacist who is part of the community. This gives the stores local roots along with a person who understands the community and its needs. Shopper's HealthWATCH SYSTEM, a pharmacy computer system designed specifically for Shoppers Drug Mart, maintains medication profiles of individual patients and generates alerts and warnings for possible allergies and drug interactions when a prescription is filled. It enables the Shoppers Drug Mart Pharmacists to work closely with health-care professionals and patients to provide improved health-care services.[72]

Sometimes companies, like Schneider National, achieve differentiation through the sheer range of their service offerings and the success of cross-selling efforts. The major challenge is that most service offerings and innovations are easily copied. Still, the company that regularly introduces innovations will gain a succession of temporary advantages over competitors.

Schneider National

Schneider National is the world's largest long-haul truckload freight carrier, with more than 40 000 bright orange trailers on the roads. Although the core benefit is to move freight from one location to another, Don Schneider is in the *customer solutions* business. His company is expert at providing a cost-minimizing trailer for each load. He offers service guarantees backed by monetary incentives for meeting tight schedules and runs driver-training programs to improve driver performance. Dispatchers are assigned to large customers. Schneider was the first to introduce a computerized tracking system in each truck, and the firm received the single top U.S. national prize in 2006 from The Institute for Operations Research and the Management Sciences for its use of modelling techniques. To actively recruit the best drivers, Schneider advertises on television shows such as Trick My Truck, satellite radio, newspapers, and online; employs webinars and PR; and partners with AARP, local organizations, and veteran groups. Even painting the trucks orange was part of the branding strategy.[73]

Schneider National has differentiated its nationwide trucking business in a number of ways, including computerized tracking for each truck, monetary rewards for drivers who meet tight schedules, and unmistakably orange trucks.

Creativity and innovation are as vital in services as in any industry. There are always ways to improve the customer experience. When a group of hospitality and travel industry experts convened late in 2006 to share their insights into what the ideal 2025 hotel might look like, their visions suggested a totally transformed service experience. One idea, turning hotels into retail showrooms where guests can try out and buy displayed items, was later adopted by chains such as Hyatt and Kimpton. Some of the other ideas have yet to be implemented and may take more time, but they help point out how achieving service excellence is a never-ending process:[74]

1. Kinetic corridors could light up with a blanket of stars and illuminated signs to provide guests with an easy, relaxing entry to their rooms.

2. A multipurpose bed could be flipped over to create more work surfaces or rise all the way up to be a ceiling panel.

3. A multitask chair could be equipped with reading lights, fold-up tray tables, integrated speakers, and a muscle massager.

Developing Brand Strategies for Services

Developing brand strategies for a service brand requires special attention to choosing brand elements, establishing image dimensions, and devising the branding strategy.

CHOOSING BRAND ELEMENTS Because services are intangible, and because service decisions and arrangements are often made away from the actual service location itself (at home or at work), brand recall becomes critically important. In such cases, an easy-to-remember brand name is critical.

Other brand elements—logos, symbols, characters, and slogans—can also "pick up the slack" and complement the brand name to build brand awareness and brand image. These brand elements often attempt to make the service and some of its key benefits more tangible, concrete, and real—for example, the "lion" of RBC.

Because a physical product does not exist, the physical facilities of the service provider—its primary and secondary signage, environmental design and reception area, apparel, collateral material, and so on—are especially important. All aspects of the service-delivery process can be branded, which is why Allied Van Lines is concerned about the appearance of its drivers and labourers; why UPS has developed such strong equity with its brown trucks; and why Tim Hortons takes such care with the design of everything from employee uniforms to the pictures that adorn all of the trucks in its transportation fleet.

ESTABLISHING IMAGE DIMENSIONS Given the human nature of services, it's no surprise that brand personality is an important image dimension of services. Starwood trains its hotel employees and call-centre operators to convey different experiences for the firm's different hotel chains: Sheraton is positioned as warm, comforting, and casual; Westin is positioned in terms of renewal and is a little more formal; Four Points by Sheraton is designed to be all about honest, uncomplicated comfort.[75]

Service firms can also design marketing communication and information programs so that consumers learn more about the brand than the information they get from service encounters alone.

DEVISING BRANDING STRATEGY Finally, services also must consider developing a brand hierarchy and brand portfolio that permits positioning and targeting of different market segments. Marketers can brand classes of service vertically on the basis of price and quality. Vertical extensions often require sub-branding strategies that combine the corporate name with an individual brand name or modifier. In the hotel and airlines industry, brand lines and portfolios have been created by brand extension and introductions. For example, Air Canada brands its business-class service as Executive First Class, its frequent-flier program as Aeroplan, and its in-flight magazine as *enRoute*. Hilton Hotels has a portfolio of brands that includes Hilton Garden Inns, which targets budget-conscious business travellers and competes with the popular Courtyard by Marriott chain, as well as DoubleTree, Embassy Suites, Homewood Suites, and Hampton Inn. Cirque du Soleil has adopted a very disciplined branding strategy.

The RBC Financial Group has one of the best-recognized brand symbols in Canada.

Cirque du Soleil

In its 25-year history, Cirque du Soleil (French for "circus of the sun") has continually broken loose from circus convention. It takes traditional ingredients such as trapeze artists, clowns, muscle men, and contortionists and places them in a nontraditional setting with lavish costumes, contemporary music, and spectacular stage designs. And it eliminates other commonly observed elements—there are no animals. Each production is loosely tied together with a theme such as "a tribute to the nomadic soul" (*Varekai*) or "a phantasmagoria of urban life" (*Saltimbanco*). The group has grown from its Quebec street-performance roots to become a half-billion-dollar enterprise with 3000 employees on four continents, entertaining audiences of millions annually. Part of the success is a company culture that encourages artistic creativity and innovation and carefully safeguards the brand (see Figure 13.8). Each production—roughly one a year—is created in-house and is unique: there are no duplicate touring companies. In addition to using a varied mix of media and local promotion, the company uses an extensive interactive email program to its million-plus-member Cirque Club to create an online community of fans—20 to 30 percent of all ticket sales for touring shows come from club members. The Cirque du Soleil brand has expanded to encompass a record label, a retail operation, and resident productions in Las Vegas (five in all), Orlando, and Tokyo.[76]

FIGURE 13.8

Flying High without a Net: Cirque du Soleil's Formula for Creative Success

Source: Linda Tischler, "Join the Circus," *Fast Company* (July 2005): 53–58. Reprinted by permission of Fast Company via Copyright Clearance Center.

1. **Cast teams for creative conflict.**

   Cirque officials generally make sure there's a mix of nationalities and viewpoints when they draft a creative team. Then they lock creators in a room with the instructions, "Don't come out till you have something great."

2. **Always shoot for the triple somersault.**

   Cirque's founder, Guy Laliberte, is famous for asking his people to stretch beyond the great to the jaw-dropping. "It's a commitment to a degree of sophistication and performance that distinguishes Cirque du Soleil productions from their less demanding peers," says coach Boris Verkhovsky.

3. **Recruit the near-great.**

   Elite athletes who just missed the national team generally have the same work ethic, the same tricks, and nearly the same skills as medal winners. The difference: They still have something to prove, and they're rarely prima donnas.

4. **Push the envelope—at the interview.**

   Cirque scouts routinely ask candidates to do something unexpected at their audition: Climb a rope . . . then sing a song when you get to the top ("Happy Birthday" is forbidden). It's a good way to find talent that's multidimensional and comfortable improvising, not to mention a great character test.

5. **Don't be greedy.**

   Cirque limits its show production to one a year. "If we want to have fun creating shows and pushing the boundaries, one show a year is good enough for us. We don't want to jeopardize quality," Lamarre says. Besides, "if there's not a creative challenge, we're not going to do a deal, regardless of the financial impact."

6. **Protect creative teams from business pressures.**

   Lamarre isolates his creative teams from the Cirque du Soleil "machine." "I want them to eat and breathe their show," he says, "and keeping them away from day-to-day operations is the best thing."

Cirque du Soleil's branding strategy includes spectacular themed performances by circus players with elaborate costumes and contemporary music—and no animals. Each touring production is unique; there are no duplicate casts, which protects the brand from overexposure and easy imitation.

MANAGING PRODUCT SUPPORT SERVICES

No less important than service industries are product-based industries that must provide a service bundle. Manufacturers of equipment—small appliances, office machines, tractors, computers, airplanes—all must provide *product support services*. Product support service is becoming a major battleground for competitive advantage. Chapter 12 described how products could be augmented with key service differentiators—ordering ease, delivery, installation, customer training, customer consulting, and maintenance and repair. Some equipment companies, such as Caterpillar and John Deere, make over 50 percent of their profits from these services. In the global marketplace, companies that make a good product but provide poor local service support are seriously disadvantaged.

Identifying and Satisfying Customer Needs

Customers have three specific worries:[77]

- They worry about reliability and *failure frequency*. A farmer may tolerate a combine that will break down once a year, but not two or three times a year.

- They worry about *downtime*. The longer the downtime, the higher the cost. The customer counts on the seller's *service dependability*—the seller's ability to fix the machine quickly, or at least provide a loaner.[78]

- They worry about *out-of-pocket costs*. How much does the customer have to spend on regular maintenance and repair costs?

A buyer takes all these factors into consideration and tries to estimate the **life-cycle cost**, which is the product's purchase cost plus the discounted cost of maintenance and repair less the discounted salvage value. A one-computer office will need higher product reliability and faster repair service than an office where other computers are available if one breaks down. An airline needs 100-percent reliability in the air. Where reliability is important, manufacturers or service providers can offer guarantees to promote sales.

To provide the best support, a manufacturer must identify the services customers value most and their relative importance. In the case of expensive equipment, manufacturers offer *facilitating services* such as installation, staff training, maintenance and repair services, and financing. They may also add *value-augmenting services* that extend beyond the functioning and performance of the product itself. Johnson Controls introduced services that extended beyond its climate-control equipment and components business to manage integrated facilities by offering products and services that optimize energy use and improve comfort and security.

A manufacturer can offer and charge for product support services in different ways. One specialty organic-chemical company provides a standard offering plus a basic level of services. If the customer wants additional services, it can pay extra or increase its annual purchases to a higher level, in which case additional services are included. Many companies offer *service contracts* (also called *extended warranties*) in which sellers agree to provide maintenance and repair services for a specified period of time at a specified contract price.

Product companies must understand their strategic intent and competitive advantage in developing services. Are service units supposed to support or protect existing product businesses or to grow as an independent platform? Are the sources of competitive advantage based on economies of scale or economies of skill?[79] See Figure 13.9 for examples of different service companies' strategies.

Post-Sale Service Strategy

The quality of customer-service departments varies greatly. At one extreme are departments that simply transfer customer calls to the appropriate person or department for action, with little follow-up. At the other extreme are departments eager to receive customer requests, suggestions, and even complaints and handle them expeditiously. Table 13.4 displays how Canada's top five banks rank on different dimensions of customer service.

CUSTOMER-SERVICE EVOLUTION Manufacturers usually start out by running their own parts-and-service department. They want to stay close to the equipment and know its problems. They also find it expensive and time-consuming to train others, and discover that they can make good money running the parts-and-service business, especially if they are the only supplier of the needed parts

	Strategic Intent	
	Protect or Enhance Product	**Expand Independent Service**
Economies of Scale	■ Apple's iPod music download and transaction management service (iTunes) ■ Otis Elevator's remote monitoring and diagnostics services ■ General Motors' OnStar auto remote diagnostics service ■ Symantec's virus protection and data security services	■ Cardinal Healthcare's hospital inventory-management services ■ IBM's data-center-outsourcing services ■ Johnson Controls' integrated facilities-management services
Economies of Skill	■ Cisco's network integration and maintenance services ■ EMC's storage-management and maintenance services ■ SAP Systems' integration services	■ General Electric's aircraft-engine-maintenance services ■ GE Healthcare's hospital equipment—support and diagnostics services for hospital equipment ■ IBM's systems integration services

(Left axis label: Source of Competitive Advantage)

FIGURE 13.9

Service Strategies for Product Companies

Source: Byron G. Auguste, Eric P. Harmon, and Vivek Pandit, "The Right Service Strategies for Product Companies," *The McKinsey Quarterly*, 1 (2006): 41–51. Reprinted by permission of McKinsey Quarterly.

TABLE 13.4	SYNOVATE BEST BANKING AWARDS 2008 FOR THE TOP FIVE BANKS
Award Category	**Awarded To**
Customer Service Excellence	TD Canada Trust
Value for Money	Scotiabank TD Canada Trust
Recommend to Friends & Family	TD Canada Trust
Values My Business	Scotiabank TD Canada Trust
Products & Services Excellence	TD Canada Trust
Interest Rates & Service Charges	Scotiabank TD Canada Trust
Financial Planning & Advice	BMO Bank of Montreal RBC Royal Bank Scotiabank TD Canada Trust
Branch Service Excellence	RBC Royal Bank TD Canada Trust
ATM Banking Excellence	TD Canada Trust
Online Banking Excellence	TD Canada Trust
Telephone Banking Excellence	TD Canada Trust

Source: Synovate, www.synovate.com/news/article/2008/09/synovate-announces-best-banking-awards-for-2008.html

and can charge a premium price. In fact, many equipment manufacturers price their equipment low and compensate by charging high prices for parts and service.

Over time, manufacturers switch more maintenance and repair services to authorized distributors and dealers. These intermediaries are closer to customers, operate in more locations, and can offer quicker service. Still later, independent service firms emerge and offer a lower price or faster services. A significant percentage of auto-service work is now done outside franchised automobile dealerships by independent garages and chains such as Midas Muffler, Sears, and Canadian Tire. Independent service organizations handle computers, telecommunications equipment, and a variety of other equipment lines.

THE CUSTOMER-SERVICE IMPERATIVE Customer-service choices are increasing rapidly and equipment manufacturers increasingly must figure out how to make money on their equipment, independent of service contracts. Some new cars don't need servicing—beyond oil and filter changes—for 160 000 kilometres. The increase in disposable or never-fail equipment makes customers less inclined to pay from two to ten percent of the purchase price every year for a service. Some large customers handle their own maintenance and repair. A company with several hundred personal computers, printers, and related equipment might find it cheaper to have its own service personnel on-site.

SUMMARY

1. A service is any act or performance that one party can offer to another that is essentially intangible and does not result in the ownership of anything. It may or may not be tied to a physical product.

2. Services are intangible, inseparable, variable, and perishable. Each characteristic poses challenges and requires certain strategies. Marketers must find ways to give tangibility to intangibles; to increase the productivity of service providers; to increase and standardize the quality of the service provided; and to match the supply of services with market demand.

3. In the past, service industries lagged behind manufacturing firms in adopting and using marketing concepts and tools, but this situation has now changed. Service marketing must be done holistically: it calls not only for external marketing but also for internal marketing to motivate employees and interactive marketing to emphasize the importance of both "high-tech" and "high-touch."

4. Customers' expectations play a critical role in their service experiences and evaluations. Companies must manage service quality by understanding the effects of each service encounter.

5. Top service companies excel at the following practices: a strategic concept, a history of top-management commitment to quality, high standards, self-service technologies, systems for monitoring service performance and customer complaints, and an emphasis on employee satisfaction.

6. To brand a service organization effectively, the company must differentiate its brand through primary and secondary service features and develop appropriate brand strategies. Effective branding programs for services often employ multiple brand elements. They also develop brand hierarchies and portfolios and establish image dimensions to reinforce or complement service offerings.

7. Even product-based companies must provide post-purchase service. To provide the best support, a manufacturer must identify the services customers value most and their relative importance. The service mix includes both pre-sale services (facilitating and value-augmenting services) and post-sale services (customer-service departments, repair and maintenance services).

APPLICATIONS

Marketing Debate: Is Service Marketing Different from Product Marketing?

Some services marketers vehemently maintain that services marketing is fundamentally different from product marketing and that different skills are involved. Some traditional product marketers disagree, saying "good marketing is good marketing."

Take a position: Product and services marketing are fundamentally different *versus* Product and services marketing are closely related.

Marketing Discussion

Colleges, universities, and other educational institutions can be classified as service organizations. How can you apply the marketing principles developed in this chapter to your school? Do you have any advice as to how it could become a better service marketer?

Breakthrough Marketing: Southwest Airlines and WestJet

Southwest Airlines entered the airline industry in 1971 with little money, but lots of personality. Marketing itself as the LUV airline, the company featured a bright red heart as its first logo. In the 1970s, flight attendants in red-orange hot pants served Love Bites (peanuts) and Love Potions (drinks). With little money for advertising in the early days, Southwest relied on its outrageous antics to generate word-of-mouth advertising.

Later ads showcased Southwest's low fares, frequent flights, on-time arrivals, and top safety record. Throughout all the advertising, the spirit of fun pervaded. For example, one TV spot showed a small bag of peanuts with the words, "This is what our meals look like at Southwest Airlines . . . It's also what our fares look like." Southwest used ads with humour to poke fun at itself and to convey its personality.

Southwest can offer low fares because it streamlines operations. For example, it flies only Boeing 737s, which saves time and money because training is simplified for pilots, flight attendants, and mechanics, and management can substitute aircraft, reschedule flight crews, and transfer mechanics quickly. Southwest also bucks the traditional hub-and-spoke system and offers only point-to-point service; it chooses to fly to smaller airports that have lower gate fees and less congestion, which speeds aircraft turnaround. Southwest's 15- to 20-minute turnaround time from flight landing to departure is half the industry average, giving it better asset utilization (it flies more flights and more passengers per plane per day).

Southwest grows by entering new markets that are overpriced and underserved by current airlines. The company believes it can bring fares down by one-third to one-half whenever it enters a new market, and it grows the market in every city it serves by making flying affordable to people who previously could not afford to fly. Southwest currently serves 64 cities in 32 American states.

Even though Southwest is a low-cost airline, it has pioneered many additional services and programs such as same-day freight service, seniors' discounts, Fun Fares, and Fun Packs. Despite Southwest's reputation for low fares and no-frills service, the company wins the hearts of customers. It consistently ranks at the top of lists of customer service for airlines, yet the average price of a flight is $105. Southwest has been ranked by *Fortune* magazine as the United States' most admired airline since 1997, as its fifth-most admired corporation in 2007, and as one of the top five best places to work. Southwest's financial results also shine: The company has been profitable for 34 straight years. It has been the only airline to report profits every quarter since September 11, 2001, and one of the few that have had no layoffs amid a travel slump created by the slow economy and the threat of terrorism. Although the hot pants are long gone, the LUVing spirit remains at the heart of Southwest.

Canada's WestJet was founded in 1996 by Clive Beddoe, Mark Hill, Tim Morgan, and Donald Bell, four Calgary entrepreneurs using the Southwest model. Like Southwest, it carved out a successful niche with short-haul flights and low prices, combined with reliable service, and an off-the-wall sense of humour. To offer low prices, WestJet worked to ensure low operating costs. It offers only basic in-

flight service (no meals, no movies) and rapid turnaround at the gates to keep the planes in the air. The "less for less" philosophy is also evident in various service choices: it offers a single class of service, and has ticket offices only at airports. It doesn't offer baggage-transfer services to other airlines. Nonetheless, like Southwest, WestJet's "less service for less money" philosophy is defined as fewer amenities for a lower fare, not less customer service.

Over the years, the company expanded, first bringing more Western cities into WestJet's world and then expanding nationally. Today, it is Canada's second-largest airline. In addition to serving cities across the country, it also offers flights to key destinations in the western and southern United States. Despite one short downturn in profits, it has been consistently profitable. In 2007, its revenues surpassed $2 billion, profits soared to almost $193 million, and employee profit share doubled.

DISCUSSION QUESTIONS

1. Describe how WestJet has managed the five different aspects of service quality to its advantage (see Table 13.2).

2. How has WestJet used self-service technologies to improve customer service and lower prices?

3. With the entry of new Canadian airlines like Porter, what tools can WestJet use to continue to differentiate its services?

Sources: Barney Gimbel, "Southwest's New Flight Plan," *Fortune*, May 16, 2005, pp. 93–98; Melanie Trottman, "Destination: Philadelphia," *Wall Street Journal*, May 4, 2004; Andy Serwer, "Southwest Airlines: The Hottest Thing in the Sky," *Fortune*, March 8, 2004; Colleen Barrett, "Fasten Your Seat Belts," *Adweek*, January 26, 2004, p. 17; "Southwest May Not Be No.1, but It Sure Looks Like the Leader," *Airline Financial News*, November 24, 2003; Eva Kaplan-Leiserson, "Strategic Service," *Training and Development* (November 2003): 14–16; www.southwest.com; Norma Ramage, "WestJet on the Fly," *Marketing*, June 20, 2005;"WestJet profit soars on fourth-quarter boost," *Toronto Star*, February 13, 2008.

**IN THIS CHAPTER,
WE WILL ADDRESS
THE FOLLOWING
QUESTIONS:**

- How do consumers process and evaluate prices?

- How should a company initially set prices for products or services?

- How should a company adapt prices to meet varying circumstances and opportunities?

- When should a company initiate a price change?

- How should a company respond to a competitor's price change?

CHAPTER 14

DEVELOPING PRICING STRATEGIES AND PROGRAMS

fourteen

Ever wondered what you are paying for when you buy an airline ticket? Most customers would think the $479 airfare they paid for a ticket from Toronto to Calgary is for air-travel between the two cities. Is that indeed the case? Not if you are flying Air Canada. The Montreal-based airline has redefined the way airline tickets are priced. Air Canada recognizes that not all customers need or want all the services it offers and so now provides customers an array of pricing options never before seen in the airline industry. Online customers buying an Air Canada ticket can choose which services they wish to purchase and which they don't.

Air Canada, pressured by discount airlines such as WestJet, needed to compete on the basis of price or risk losing market share. Its research showed that many passengers were willing to forgo "extras" such as snacks, advance seat selection, checked baggage, and frequent-flyer miles for a lower-priced ticket. Based on this finding, Air Canada launched *à la carte* pricing on its tickets. When consumers book a seat, they can choose from four price levels: Tango, Tango Plus, Latitude, and Executive Class. Each tier has different frequent-flyer miles awards, booking change fees, and refund policies, besides several other differences. For example, the lowest ticket class, Tango, has the least flexibility and offers the bare minimum for travellers who are interested only in the lowest fares. Latitude is the most expensive economy class and has several frills included. Tango customers can elect to add these extra features for a fee—for example, Tango customers can select a seat in advance for an additional $20, something that is offered complimentarily if one moves up to Tango Plus. Prepaid meal vouchers are available for $6–$8 each way. Those buying a Latitude ticket can purchase Maple Leaf lounge access for an additional $25; lounge access is complimentary for Executive Class passengers. Declining Aeroplan miles saves passengers $6 on the fare. Having no baggage to check reduces the fare by an additional $6. Forgoing the ability to make changes after booking saves $10. Besides giving customers greater ability to design the service they purchase, such opportunities to decrease the price also give customers a sense of being able to discount their ticket.

Through marketing research, Air Canada was able to identify the different levels of price-sensitivity among airline consumers and offer each segment an appropriate product. This pricing strategy not only makes sense from a competitive standpoint, but also appears fair to the customer who is not interested in some of those "extras" that customers of many other airlines are forced to pay for. In other words, Air Canada has "unbundled" the price bundling that the airline industry has traditionally practised.

Since the implementation of this new merchandising strategy in November 2006, Air Canada has seen an increase in the percentage of online bookings, attributed primarily to the more transparent pricing and flexible booking experience for the customer. According to Charles McKee, VP-Marketing of Air Canada, "We are making it easier than ever for customers to choose only the products and services they want with pricing that is transparent and understandable. By coupling our branded fares with an *à la carte* option on our website, we are providing our travellers with an unprecedented ability to find the best value for their individual requirements."

Air Canada's new pricing initiatives don't stop there. In November 2004, Air Canada introduced the Flight Pass, which lets customers buy 10 or 20 tickets in specified zones over a set period. For example, a North America Pass, which connects most Canadian airports with most major US cities, gets you 20 flight credits at the Tango fare for $10 740, as of June 2008. That works out to $537 per flight. This may not sound like a good deal until one considers the fact that this is the fare the customer pays even if the booking is done a day before departure for a flight between any two cities within the specified zone. In addition, it gives the customer the ability to cancel a booking just before flight departure and have the credit restored to the account. The Flight Pass gives business travellers, especially those in small organizations, tremendous flexibility in planning their flight travel. Moreover, organizations can buy several hundred flight credits that can be shared by up to 300 employees. Based on the success of its domestic Flight Pass program, Air Canada has since expanded the program to cover North and Central America, the Caribbean islands, the U.K., and China.

Air Canada's bold and innovative pricing has revolutionized airline merchandising and has its competitors south of the border following suit. Most importantly, these new pricing strategies have protected Air Canada from losing price-conscious consumers to its major domestic competitor: WestJet.

Sources: Air Canada online booking website, www.aircanada.com; Air Canada Flight Pass, http://fp.aircanada.com/wallet/servlet/CTO5RIASearchServlet/booklet_landing; Amadeus Business Release, April 2, 2007, www.amadeus.com/amadeus/x5088.html (all viewed June 14, 2008).

Price is the one element of the marketing mix that produces revenue; the other elements produce costs. Prices are perhaps the easiest element of the marketing program to adjust; product features, channels, and even promotion take more time. Price also communicates to the market the company's intended value positioning of its product or brand. A well-designed and marketed product can command a price premium and reap big profits. Consider Apple's iPod:

Apple iPod

In October 2001, Apple revolutionized the portable music-player market with the release of the iPod, capable of holding up to 1000 CD-quality songs in a 180-gram design. Before the iPod, the market for music players was saturated with a variety of different MP3 and CD players, all with prices relatively lower than the iPod's. When the iPod was introduced, it retailed at US$399—roughly twice the price for MP3 and other hard disk–based players in the market at that time. Although its starting price was much higher than its competition's, the iPod eventually became a market leader in the music-player industry, capturing over 70 percent of the portable music-player market. How did Apple do it? To consumers, the iPod represented innovation and offered unique features that had never been seen in its competitors. It was smaller, lighter, could play more music formats, and could download songs faster than its competitors at the time: Nomad Jukebox, Rio, and various hard-disk and portable CD players. With well in excess of 100 million units sold worldwide, like Apple CEO Steve Jobs said, the iPod truly has become the "the 21st-century Walkman."[1]

Pricing decisions are clearly complex and difficult. Holistic marketers must take into account many factors in making pricing decisions—the company, the customers, the competition, and the marketing environment. Pricing decisions must be consistent with the firm's marketing strategy and its target markets and brand positioning.

In this chapter, we provide concepts and tools to facilitate the setting of initial prices and adjusting prices over time and markets.

UNDERSTANDING PRICING

Price is not just a number on a tag or an item:

> Price is all around us. You pay rent for your apartment, tuition for your education, and a fee to your physician or dentist. The airline, railway, taxi, and bus companies charge you a fare; the local utilities call their price a rate; and the local bank charges you interest for the money you borrow. . . . The company that insures your car charges you a premium. The guest lecturer charges an honorarium. Clubs or societies to which you belong may make a special assessment to pay unusual expenses. Your regular lawyer may ask for a retainer to cover her services. The "price" of an executive is a salary, the price of a salesperson may be a commission, and the price of a worker is a wage. Finally, although economists would disagree, many of us feel that income taxes are the price we pay for the privilege of making money.[2]

Throughout most of history, prices were set by negotiation between buyers and sellers. "Bargaining" is still a sport in some areas. Setting one price for all buyers is a relatively modern idea that arose with the development of large-scale retailing at the end of the nineteenth century. F. W. Woolworth, Tiffany and Co., John Wanamaker, and others advertised a "strictly one-price policy" because they carried so many items and supervised so many employees.

Today the Internet is partially reversing the fixed-pricing trend. Computer technology is making it easier for sellers to use software that monitors customers' movements over the Web and allows them to customize offers and prices. New software applications are also allowing buyers to compare prices instantaneously through online robotic shoppers or "shopbots." As one industry observer noted, "We are moving toward a very sophisticated economy. It's kind of an arms race between merchant technology and consumer technology."[3]

Traditionally, price has operated as the major determinant of buyer choice. This is still the case in poorer nations, among poorer groups, and with commodity-type products. Although nonprice factors have become more important in recent decades, price still remains one of the most important elements determining market share and profitability. Consumers and purchasing agents have more access to price information and price discounters. Consumers put pressure on retailers to lower their prices. Retailers put pressure on manufacturers to lower their prices. The result is a marketplace characterized by heavy discounting and sales promotion.

How Companies Price

Companies do their pricing in a variety of ways. In small companies, prices are often set by the boss. In large companies, pricing is handled by division and product-line managers. Even here, top management sets general pricing objectives and policies and often approves the prices proposed by lower levels of management. In industries where pricing is a key factor (aerospace, railway, oil), companies will often establish a pricing department to set or assist others in determining appropriate prices. This department reports to the marketing department, finance department, or top management. Others who exert an influence on pricing include sales managers, production managers, finance managers, and accountants.

Executives complain that pricing is a big headache—and one that is getting worse by the day. Many companies do not handle pricing well, throwing up their hands with "strategies" like this: "We determine our costs and take our industry's traditional margins." Other common mistakes: price is not revised often enough to capitalize on market changes; price is set independent of the rest of the marketing mix rather than as an intrinsic element of market-positioning strategy; and price is not varied enough for different product items, market segments, distribution channels, and purchase occasions.

Others have a different attitude: they use price as a key strategic tool. Consider what Quiznos Canada is doing:

Quiznos Canada

In 2004, following the market obsession with low-carbohydrate diets, Quiznos decided to launch a new low-carb menu. Calling it the "largest low-carb menu in Canada," Quiznos boasts a line-up of sandwiches made with soy flatbread. However, due to uncertainty about advertising regulations for low-carb food, Quiznos decided to use price as a key strategic tool for getting customers to sample its new offerings, and used a pair of radio spots that advertised a small sandwich for $2.99 (a discount of $2.50) to drive customers to the stores. However, once inside the restaurant, customers were exposed to new point-of-sale displays highlighting the low-carb sandwiches. In addition, Quiznos distributed nationally (excluding Quebec) six million direct mailings featuring a photograph of one of its new low-carb sandwiches and including a coupon offer—"buy one low-carb sandwich, get the second free."[4]

The importance of pricing for profitability was demonstrated in a 1992 study by McKinsey & Company. Examining 2400 companies, McKinsey concluded that a 1-percent improvement in price created an improvement in operating profit of 11.1 percent. By contrast, 1-percent improvements in variable cost, volume, and fixed cost produced profit improvements, respectively, of only 7.8 percent, 3.3 percent, and 2.3 percent.

Effectively designing and implementing pricing strategies requires a thorough understanding of consumer pricing psychology and a systematic approach to setting, adapting, and changing prices.

Consumer Psychology and Pricing

Many economists assume that consumers are "price takers" and accept prices at "face value" or as given. Marketers recognize that consumers often actively process price information, interpreting prices in terms of their knowledge from prior purchasing experience, formal communications (advertising, sales calls, and brochures), informal communications (friends, colleagues, and family members), and point-of-purchase or online resources.[5] Purchase decisions are based on how consumers perceive prices and what they consider to be the current actual price—*not* the marketer's stated price. They may have a lower price threshold below which prices may signal inferior or unacceptable quality, as well as an upper price threshold above which prices are prohibitive and seen as not worth the money.

Understanding how consumers arrive at their perceptions of prices is an important marketing priority. Here we consider three key topics—reference prices, price-quality inferences, and price cues.

REFERENCE PRICES   Prior research has shown that although consumers may have fairly good knowledge of the range of prices involved, surprisingly few can accurately recall specific prices of products.[6] When examining products, however, consumers often employ **reference prices**. In considering an observed price, consumers often compare it to an internal reference price (pricing information from memory) or an external frame of reference (such as a posted "regular retail price").[7]

All types of reference prices are possible (see Table 14.1). Sellers often attempt to manipulate reference prices. For example, a seller can situate its product among expensive products to imply that it belongs in the same class. Department stores will display women's apparel in separate departments differentiated by price; dresses found in the more expensive department are assumed to be of better quality.

Reference-price thinking is also encouraged by stating a high manufacturer's suggested price, as illustrated by the Olympus example, or by indicating that the product was priced much higher originally, or by pointing to a competitor's high price.[8]

Quiznos uses attractive price promotions to get customers to try out its new line of low-carb sandwiches.

TABLE 14.1 | POSSIBLE CONSUMER REFERENCE PRICES

- "Fair price" (what the product should cost)
- Typical price
- Last price paid
- Upper-bound price (reservation price or what most consumers would pay)
- Lower-bound price (lower threshold price or the least consumers would pay)
- Competitor prices
- Expected future price
- Usual discounted price

Source: Russell S. Winer, "Behavioral Perspectives on Pricing: Buyer's Subjective Perceptions of Price Revisited," in Timothy Devinney, ed., *Issues in Pricing: Theory and Research* (Lexington, MA: Lexington Books, 1988), pp. 35–57.

Olympus

On Olympus's website, the manufacturer's suggested retail price often bears no relationship to what you would be charged by a retailer for the same item. For instance, for the SP-550 UZ digital camera, Olympus suggests a retail price of $349.99, but Future Shop was selling it at the same time for $299.99 and "direct from Olympus" versions were being sold on eBay.ca for $225, with the Olympus website itself providing a link to eBay. Compared with other consumer items, from clothing to cars to furniture to toothbrushes, the gap between the prices routinely quoted by manufacturer and retailer in consumer electronics is large. "The simplest thing to say is that we have trained the consumer electronics buyer to think he is getting 20 or 30 or 40 percent off," said Robert Atkins, a vice-president at Mercer Management Consulting. A product manager for Olympus America, known primarily for its cameras, defends the practice by saying that the high manufacturer's suggested retail price is a psychological tool, a reference price that makes people see they are getting something of value for less than top price. Regardless of how inflated—and how perplexing—manufacturers' suggested retail prices are, everyone usually winds up happy. Manufacturers, like Olympus, get their sales, retailers get buyers to think they are getting a bargain, and consumers get gadgets they want at prices they think are good.[9]

Clever marketers try to frame the price to signal the best value possible. For example, a relatively more expensive item can be seen as less expensive by breaking down the price into smaller units. A $500 annual membership may be seen as more expensive than "under $50 a month," even if the totals are the same.[10]

When consumers evoke one or more of these frames of reference, their perceived price can vary from the stated price.[11] Research on reference prices has found that "unpleasant surprises"—when perceived price is lower than the stated price—can have a greater impact on purchase likelihood than pleasant surprises.[12]

PRICE-QUALITY INFERENCES Many consumers use price as an indicator of quality. Image pricing is especially effective with ego-sensitive products such as perfumes and expensive cars. A $100 bottle of perfume might contain $10 worth of scent, but gift givers pay $100 to communicate their high regard for the receiver.

Price and quality perceptions of cars interact.[13] Higher-priced cars are perceived to possess high quality. Higher-quality cars are likewise perceived to be higher priced than they actually are. No matter how good or bad the brand, consumer perceptions of the brand are often better predictors of sales than true quality. Table 14.2 shows consumer perceptions for different car brands. When alternative information about true quality is available, price becomes a less significant indicator of quality. When this information is not available, price acts as a signal of quality. Note how Q-tips is a price–quality leader for a product as simple as a cotton swab. High price is often interpreted to be high quality, and low price is perceived to be low quality. See "Marketing Insight: You Get What You Pay For: A Self-Fulfilling Prophecy?" for an illustration of how low price can lower true quality, not just the perceived quality.

TABLE 14.2 | CONSUMER PERCEPTIONS OF CARS

A December 2007 Auto Pulse survey conducted by Consumer Reports National Research Center examined how consumers perceive and rank car brands in seven crucial areas—safety, quality, value, performance, environmental friendliness, design, and technological innovation. Following are the "winners" and "losers."

Best in Brand Perception: Ranked the highest (base index of 100)

Toyota	189
Honda	146
Ford	112
Chevrolet	110
GMC	102

Worst in Brand Perception: Ranked the lowest (base index of 100)

Acura	8
Audi	14
Mitsubishi	21
Mercury	22
Buick	25

MARKETING INSIGHT | YOU GET WHAT YOU PAY FOR: A SELF-FULFILLING PROPHECY?

Marketers use price discounting to get consumers to buy and to buy more. Although consumers who purchase a product on sale generally think they have gotten the same product at a lower price, marketing researchers Shiv, Cameron, and Ariely posit that this may not always be the case. In three interesting studies, they demonstrate that consumers who pay a discounted price for a product (e.g., an energy drink thought to increase mental acumen) may actually benefit less from consuming the product (e.g., solve fewer puzzles) than consumers who purchase at the regular price. While "placebo effects" are well documented in medicine, Shiv, Cameron, and Ariely have shown that such effects can also appear in relation to price discounts. Although it is common knowledge that consumers perceive lower quality in less-expensive products, their research illustrated that a price discount can affect not only perceived quality, but actual quality as well (i.e., the actual efficacy of a product). These research findings lead to several important public-policy questions, such as:

- Is discounting pharmaceutical drugs detrimental to patients, because they could benefit less from the drug knowing that they bought it at a discount? Should less-expensive generic drugs be discouraged?
- Should products that help overcome addictions (e.g., nicotine patches) be discounted? Buying at a discount could render them less effective.
- If nutritional supplements or exercise products (e.g., a treadmill or gym pass) were discounted, would consumers benefit less from them?
- What happens if tuition fees at educational institutions are lowered? Would it result in students actually learning less?

The placebo effect has important economic implications for marketers as well. If discounting the product results in lower benefit from the product, would that in turn cause customer dissatisfaction and thus lower sales in the long term?

Source: Baba Shiv, Ziv Cameron, and Dan Ariely, "Placebo Effects of Marketing Actions: Consumers May Get What They Pay For," *Journal of Marketing Research* (November 2005), pp. 383–393.

Q-tips

Introduced in 1923, Unilever's Q-tips have become a household name, serving needs ranging from beauty to toolbox. Over the years, Unilever has been able to customize a variety of cotton-swab packages to meet consumer demands ranging from purse packs to whole-family needs. It is this customization, combined with the fact that Q-tips has had a name that has long represented quality and value, that makes consumers accept the product's high price point in comparison to other less-expensive cotton-swab alternatives, like Shoppers Drug Mart's Life brand and SuperStore's Exact brand. Although Unilever has seen much success with its Q-tips brand, in order to remain the cotton-swab market leader, Unilever must focus on its key business strategy: "anticipating the aspirations of its customers and consumers and then providing products that meet their present and emerging needs."[14]

Some brands adopt scarcity as a means to signify quality and justify premium pricing. Some automakers have bucked the massive discounting craze that shook the industry and are producing smaller batches of new models, creating a buzz around them, and using the demand to raise the sticker price.[15] Waiting lists, once reserved for limited-edition cars like Ferraris, are becoming more common for mass-market models, including hybrids and diesel-powered cars.

As the Beanie Baby craze demonstrated, scarcity combined with strong demand can lead to high market prices. Here is another example most Canadians can relate to:

Escalating Gas Prices

One of the most sought-after natural resources in the world is crude oil. With crude oil prices crossing US$130 per barrel in 2008, industry analysts speculate that Canada and the rest of the world will face a period of unprecedented scarcity of oil that will push the price up to US$225 by 2012. This means that Canadian gas prices at the pump will go from a 2008 price of about $1.40 a litre to over $2.25 by 2012. Will this steep increase in gas prices reduce gas consumption? The answer is probably no. Although there have been many developments in the use of biofuels and hybrid and electric vehicles, presently crude oil still takes centre stage when it comes to transportation and activity. Analysts predict that oil production will hardly grow at all while demand will continue to grow. This suggests that oil prices will continue to rise over the next few years, meaning Canadians, who are already in a state of disbelief over soaring gas prices, will have to dig even deeper into their pockets.[16]

PRICE CUES Consumer perceptions of prices are also affected by alternative pricing strategies. Many sellers believe that prices should end in an odd number. Many customers see a stereo amplifier priced at $299 instead of $300 as a price in the $200 range rather than the $300 range. Research has shown that consumers tend to process prices in a "left-to-right" manner rather than by rounding.[17] Price encoding in this fashion is important if there is a mental price break at the higher, rounded price. Another explanation for "9" endings is that they convey the notion of a discount or bargain, suggesting that if a company wants a high-price image, it should avoid the odd-ending tactic.[18] One study even showed that demand actually increased one-third by *raising* the price of a dress from $34 to $39, but demand was unchanged when prices increased from $34 to $44.[19]

Prices that end with "0" and "5" are also common in the marketplace, as they are thought to be easier for consumers to process and retrieve from memory.[20] "Sale" signs next to prices have been shown to spur demand, but only if not overused: total category sales are highest when some, but not all, items in a category have sale signs; past a certain point, use of additional sale signs will cause total category sales to fall.[21]

SETTING THE PRICE

A firm must set a price for the first time when it develops a new product, when it introduces its regular product into a new distribution channel or geographical area, and when it enters bids on new contract work. The firm must decide where to position its product on quality and price.

In some markets, like the auto market, as many as eight *price points* or price tiers and levels can be found:

Segment	Example
Ultimate	Rolls-Royce
Gold Standard	Mercedes-Benz
Luxury	Audi
Special Needs	Volvo
Middle	Buick
Ease/Convenience	Ford Escort
Me Too, but Cheaper	Hyundai
Price Alone	Kia

Most markets have three to five price points or tiers. Marriott Hotels is good at developing different brands for different price points: Marriott Vacation Club–Vacation Villas (highest price), Marriott Marquis (high price), Marriott (high-medium price), Renaissance (medium-high price), Courtyard (medium price), Towne Place Suites (medium-low price), and Fairfield Inn (low price).

Consumers often rank brands according to price tiers in a category.[22] For example, Figure 14.1 shows the three price tiers that resulted from a study of the ice cream market.[23] As the figure shows, there is a relationship between price and quality in the ice cream market, and there is a range of acceptable prices (called *price bands*) within each tier. The price bands provide managers with some indication of the flexibility and breadth they can adopt in pricing their brands within a particular price tier.

The firm has to consider many factors in setting its pricing policy.[24] We will describe a six-step procedure: (1) selecting the pricing objective; (2) determining demand; (3) estimating costs; (4) analyzing competitors' costs, prices, and offers; (5) selecting a pricing method; and (6) selecting the final price.

FIGURE 14.1

Price Tiers in the Ice Cream Market

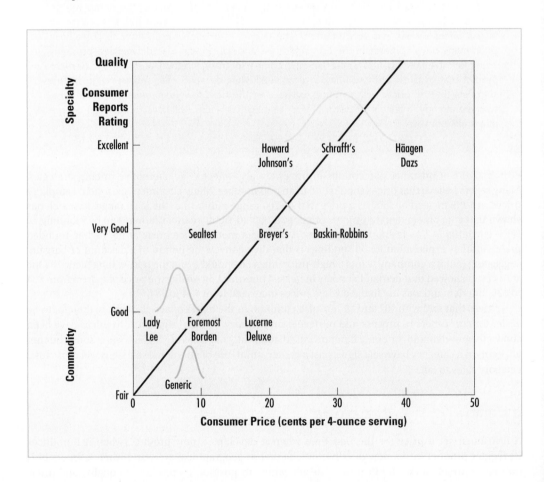

Step 1: Selecting the Pricing Objective

The company first decides where it wants to position its market offering. The clearer a firm's objectives, the easier it is to set price. A company can pursue any of five major objectives through pricing: survival, maximum current profit, maximum market share, maximum market skimming, or product-quality leadership.

SURVIVAL Companies pursue *survival* as their major objective if they are plagued with over-capacity, intense competition, or changing consumer wants. As long as prices cover variable costs and some fixed costs, the company stays in business. Survival is a short-run objective; in the long run, the firm must learn how to add value or face extinction.

MAXIMUM CURRENT PROFIT Many companies try to set a price that will *maximize current profits*. They estimate the demand and costs associated with alternative prices and choose the price that produces maximum current profit, cash flow, or rate of return on investment. This strategy assumes that the firm has knowledge of its demand and cost functions; in reality, these are difficult to estimate. In emphasizing current performance, the company may sacrifice long-run performance by ignoring the effects of other marketing-mix variables, competitors' reactions, and legal restraints on price.

MAXIMUM MARKET SHARE Some companies want to *maximize their market share*. They believe that a higher sales volume will lead to lower unit costs and higher long-run profit. They set the lowest price, assuming the market is price-sensitive. Texas Instruments (TI) has practised this **market-penetration pricing**. TI would build a large plant, set its price as low as possible, win a large market share, experience falling costs, and cut its price further as costs fall.

The following conditions favour setting a low price: (1) The market is highly price-sensitive and a low price stimulates market growth; (2) production and distribution costs fall with accumulated production experience; and (3) a low price discourages actual and potential competition.

MAXIMUM MARKET SKIMMING Companies unveiling a new technology favour setting high prices to *maximize market skimming*. Sony is a frequent practitioner of **market-skimming pricing**, whereby prices start high and are slowly lowered over time. When Sony introduced the world's first high-definition television (HDTV) to the Japanese market in 1990, it was priced at US$43 000. So that Sony could "skim" the maximum amount of revenue from the various segments of the market, the price dropped steadily through the years—a 28-inch HDTV cost just over US$6000 in 1993 and a 40-inch HDTV cost about US$2000 in 2001.[25]

Market skimming makes sense under the following conditions: (1) A sufficient number of buyers have a high current demand; (2) the unit costs of producing a small volume are not so high that they cancel the advantage of charging what the traffic will bear; (3) the high initial price does not attract more competitors to the market; (4) the high price communicates the image of a superior product.

PRODUCT-QUALITY LEADERSHIP A company might aim to be the *product-quality leader* in the market. Many brands strive to be "affordable luxuries"—products or services characterized by high levels of perceived quality, taste, and status, with a price just high enough to not be out of consumer's reach. Brands such as Starbucks coffee, Aveda shampoo, Victoria's Secret lingerie, BMW cars, and Viking ranges are able to position themselves as quality leaders in their respective categories, combining quality, luxury, and premium prices with an intensely loyal customer base.[26] Grey Goose and Absolut carved out a super-premium niche in the essentially odourless, colourless, and tasteless vodka category through clever on-premise and off-premise marketing that made the brands seem hip and exclusive.[27]

OTHER OBJECTIVES Nonprofit and public organizations may have other pricing objectives. A university aims for *partial cost recovery*, knowing that it must rely on private gifts and public grants to cover the remaining costs. A nonprofit theatre company may price its productions to fill the maximum number of theatre seats. A social service agency may set a service price geared to client income.

Whatever the specific objective, businesses that use price as a strategic tool will profit more than those which simply let costs or the market determine their pricing.

To explore how Denmark's Sterling Airlines has successfully competed with Scandinavian Airlines (SAS) as a low-cost alternative, visit www.pearsoned.co.uk/marketingmanagementeurope.

FIGURE 14.2

Inelastic and Elastic Demand

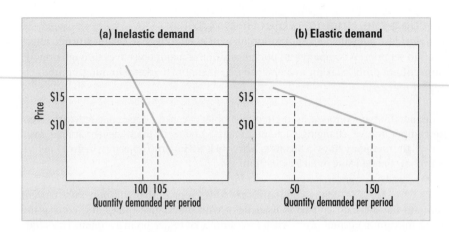

Step 2: Determining Demand

Each price will lead to a different level of demand and therefore have a different impact on a company's marketing objectives. The relationship between alternative prices and the resulting current demand is captured in a demand curve (see Figure 14.2). In the normal case, demand and price are inversely related: the higher the price, the lower the demand. In the case of prestige goods, the demand curve sometimes slopes upward. A perfume company raised its price and sold more perfume rather than less! Some consumers take the higher price to signify a better product. However, if the price is too high, the level of demand may fall.

PRICE SENSITIVITY The demand curve shows the market's probable purchase quantity at alternative prices. It sums the reactions of many individuals who have different price sensitivities. The first step in estimating demand is to understand what affects price sensitivity. Generally speaking, customers are most price-sensitive to products that cost a lot or are bought frequently. They are less price-sensitive to low-cost items or items they buy infrequently. They are also less price-sensitive when price is only a small part of the total cost of obtaining, operating, and servicing the product over its lifetime. A seller can charge a higher price than competitors and still get the business if the company can convince the customer that it offers the lowest *total cost of ownership* (TCO).

Companies, of course, prefer customers who are less price-sensitive. Table 14.3 lists some characteristics that are associated with decreased price sensitivity. On the other hand, the Internet has the potential to increase customers' price sensitivity. In buying a specific book online, for example, a customer can compare the prices offered by over two dozen online bookstores by visiting mySimon.com. These prices can differ by as much as 20 percent.

Although the Internet increases the opportunity for price-sensitive buyers to find and favour lower-price sites, many buyers may not be that price-sensitive. McKinsey conducted a study and found that 89 percent of a sample of Internet customers visited only one book site, 84 percent visited only one toy site, and 81 percent visited only one music site, which indicates that there is less price-comparison shopping taking place on the Internet than is possible.

TABLE 14.3 | FACTORS LEADING TO LESS PRICE SENSITIVITY

- The product is more distinctive.
- Buyers are less aware of substitutes.
- Buyers cannot easily compare the quality of substitutes.
- The expenditure is a smaller part of the buyer's total income.
- The expenditure is small compared to the total cost of the end product.
- Part of the cost is borne by another party.
- The product is used in conjunction with assets previously bought.
- The product is assumed to have more quality, prestige, or exclusiveness.
- Buyers cannot store the product.

Source: Thomas T. Nagle and Reed K. Holden, *The Strategy and Tactics of Pricing*, 3rd ed. (Upper Saddle River, NJ: Prentice Hall, 2001), Chapter 4.

Companies need to understand the price sensitivity of their customers and prospects and the trade-offs people are willing to make between price and product characteristics. Targeting only price-sensitive consumers may in fact be "leaving money on the table."

ESTIMATING DEMAND CURVES   Most companies make some attempt to measure their demand curves using several different methods:

- *Statistical analysis* of past prices, quantities sold, and other factors can reveal their relationships. The data can be longitudinal (over time) or cross-sectional (different locations at the same time). Building the appropriate model and fitting the data with the proper statistical techniques calls for considerable skill.

- *Price experiments* can be conducted. Bennett and Wilkinson systematically varied the prices of several products sold in a discount store and observed the results.[28] An alternative approach is to charge different prices in similar territories to see how sales are affected. Still another approach is to use the Internet. An e-business could test the impact of a 5-percent price increase by quoting a higher price to every fortieth visitor to compare the purchase response. However, it must do this carefully and not alienate customers, as happened when Amazon price-tested discounts of 30 percent, 35 percent, and 40 percent for DVD buyers, only to find that those receiving the 30-percent discount were upset.[29]

- *Surveys* can explore how many units consumers would buy at different proposed prices, although there is always the chance that they might understate their purchase intentions at higher prices to discourage the company from setting higher prices.[30]

In measuring the price–demand relationship, the market researcher must control for various factors that will influence demand. Competitors' responses will make a difference. Also, if the company changes other marketing-mix factors besides price, the effect of the price change itself will be hard to isolate. Nagle presents an excellent summary of the various methods for estimating price sensitivity and demand.[31] See how Monster increased demand for its service through its pricing strategy:

Monster

Monster is a company that connects quality job seekers at all levels with potential employers via its website. Prior to 2002, employers had to pay annual subscription fees of US$10 000 to access its database of resumes. Currently, Monster offers various subscription packages that attract employers which are seeking targeted job-candidate information in a certain location or which want to use the service only for a few weeks or months, rather than an entire year. Developing this pricing strategy has opened the low-end market to Monster without hurting the full-access product that many employers still want.[32]

PRICE ELASTICITY OF DEMAND   Marketers need to know how responsive, or elastic, demand would be to a change in price. Consider the two demand curves in Figure 14.2. With demand curve (a), a price increase from $10 to $15 leads to a relatively small decline in demand from 105 to 100. With demand curve (b), the same price increase leads to a substantial drop in demand from 150 to 50. If demand hardly changes with a small change in price, we say the demand is *inelastic*. If demand changes considerably, demand is *elastic*. The higher the elasticity, the greater the volume growth resulting from a 1-percent price reduction.

Demand is likely to be less elastic under the following conditions: (1) there are few or no substitutes or competitors; (2) buyers do not readily notice the higher price; (3) buyers are slow to change their buying habits; (4) buyers think the higher prices are justified. If demand is elastic, sellers will consider lowering the price. A lower price will produce more total revenue. This makes sense as long as the costs of producing and selling more units do not increase disproportionately.[33]

The effect of not considering the needs of customers for whom demand is most elastic is illustrated by the following:

Public Transit

Understanding different consumer price elasticities should be an important facet of public-transit pricing. To encourage increased use, many transit authorities and companies, like Ottawa-Carleton Transit and Ontario's regional GO Transit, offer riders weekly or monthly passes instead of making them purchase single-ride tickets. These passes strongly appeal to daily commuters who receive a significant benefit from the discounted fare. However, since these people are price inelastic, the transit authorities may be leaving money on the table. In fact, the demand curve of many commuters is perfectly inelastic: no matter what happens to the fare, people without alternative means of transportation must get to work and get back home. Other commuters have a more elastic demand curve. These are people who have cars or who can walk to work. Shoppers and casual users who use transit for special events may be the most price elastic of all. Given these varying price sensitivities, transit authorities could improve their revenues by reversing their pricing strategies. However, this is rarely done, since transit is seen as a public service and a means of reducing pollution by getting cars off the roads.[34]

Price elasticity depends on the magnitude and direction of the contemplated price change. It may be negligible with a small price change and substantial with a large price change. It may differ for a price cut versus a price increase, and there may be a *price indifference band* within which price changes have little or no effect. A McKinsey pricing study estimated that the price indifference band can range as large as 17 percent for mouthwash, 13 percent for batteries, 9 percent for small appliances, and 2 percent for term deposits.

Finally, long-run price elasticity may differ from short-run elasticity. Buyers may continue to buy from a current supplier after a price increase, but they may eventually switch suppliers. Here demand is more elastic in the long run than in the short run, or the reverse may happen: buyers may drop a supplier after being notified of a price increase but return later. The distinction between short-run and long-run elasticity means that sellers will not know the total effect of a price change until time passes.

Step 3: Estimating Costs

Demand sets a ceiling on the price the company can charge for its product. Costs set the floor. The company wants to charge a price that covers its cost of producing, distributing, and selling the product, including a fair return for its effort and risk. Yet, when companies price products to cover full costs, the net result is not always profitability. See "Marketing Memo: Three Myths about Pricing Strategy" for more on common pricing-strategy errors.

TYPES OF COSTS AND LEVELS OF PRODUCTION A company's costs take two forms, fixed and variable. **Fixed costs** (also known as **overhead**) are costs that do not vary with production or sales revenue. A company must pay bills each month for rent, heat, interest, salaries, and so on, regardless of output.

Variable costs vary directly with the level of production. For example, each hand calculator produced by Texas Instruments involves costs for plastic, microprocessor chips, packaging, and the like. These costs tend to be constant per unit produced. They are called variable because their total varies with the number of units produced.

Total costs consist of the sum of the fixed and variable costs for any given level of production. **Average cost** is the cost per unit at that level of production; it is equal to total costs divided by production. Management wants to charge a price that will at least cover the total production costs at a given level of production.

To price intelligently, management needs to know how its costs vary with different levels of production. Take the case in which a company such as Texas Instruments has built a fixed-size plant to produce 1000 hand calculators a day. The cost per unit is high if few units are produced per day. As production approaches 1000 units per day, the average cost falls because the fixed costs are spread over more units. Short-run average cost increases after 1000 units, because the plant becomes inefficient: workers have to line up for machines, machines break down more often, and workers get in each other's way (see Figure 14.3[a]).

If TI believes it can sell 2000 units per day, it should consider building a larger plant. The plant will use more efficient machinery and work arrangements, and the unit cost of producing 2000 units per day will be less than the unit cost of producing 1000 units per day. This is shown in the long-run average cost curve (LRAC) in Figure 14.3(b). In fact, a 3000-capacity plant would be even more efficient according to Figure 14.3(b), but a 4000-capacity production plant would be less efficient because of increasing diseconomies of scale: there are too many workers to manage and paperwork slows things down. Figure 14.3(b) indicates that a 3000-capacity production plant is the optimal size if demand is strong enough to support this level of production.

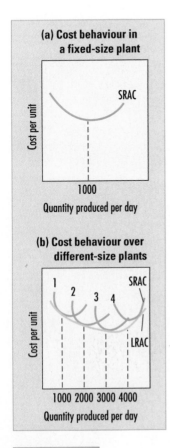

(a) Cost behaviour in a fixed-size plant

Cost per unit

SRAC

1000

Quantity produced per day

(b) Cost behaviour over different-size plants

1 2 3 4

Cost per unit

SRAC

LRAC

1000 2000 3000 4000

Quantity produced per day

FIGURE 14.3

Cost per Unit at Different Levels of Production per Period

MARKETING **MEMO** | THREE MYTHS ABOUT PRICING STRATEGY

According to George E. Cressman Jr., senior pricer at Strategic Pricing Group, marketers nurture three major myths about pricing strategy:

- *Pricing our products to cover full costs will make us profitable.* Marketers often do not realize the value they actually do provide but think in terms of product features. They frequently treat the service elements in a product offering as sales incentives rather than value-enhancing augmentations for which they can charge. Says Cressman, "When we price to cover costs, there is an underlying assumption that customers value us for our costs. Then the logical conclusions would be that we should increase costs so we can increase price, and customers will love us even more!" Marketers should instead determine how many customers will ascribe how much value to their offerings, then ask "Given our cost structure, what volume changes are necessary to make price changes profitable?"

- *Pricing our products to grow market share will make us profitable.* Cressman reminds marketers that share is determined by value delivery at competitive advantage, not just price cuts. Therefore, "The correct question is not 'What level of price will enable us to achieve our sales and market share objectives?' but 'What shares of the market can we most profitably serve?'"

- *Pricing our products to meet customer demands will make us profitable.* Cutting prices to keep customers or beat competitive offers encourages customers to demand price concessions and trains salespeople to offer them. "When you're tempted to ask what customers will pay," says Cressman, "don't ask them. You know you won't like the answer." Instead, marketers should ask, "What prices can we convince customers are supported by the value of our products and services?" and "How can we better segment the market to reflect differences in value delivered to different types of customers?" Create different levels of value and price options for different market segments and their respective value needs. And to finesse a price cut, provide a reduced-priced option. "That makes the demand for a price concession the customer's problem, for it must then choose which benefits to forgo."

Source: Adapted from Bob Donath, "Dispel Major Myths About Pricing," *Marketing News*, February 3, 2003, p. 10.

ACCUMULATED PRODUCTION Suppose TI runs a plant that produces 3000 hand calculators per day. As TI gains experience producing hand calculators, its methods improve. Workers learn shortcuts, materials flow more smoothly, and procurement costs fall. The result, as Figure 14.4 shows, is that average cost falls with accumulated production experience. Thus, the average cost of producing the first 100 000 hand calculators is $10 per calculator. When the company has produced the first 200 000 calculators, the average cost has fallen to $9. After its accumulated production experience doubles again to 400 000, the average cost is $8. This decline in the average cost with accumulated production experience is called the **experience curve** or **learning curve.**

Now suppose three firms compete in this industry, TI, A, and B. TI is the lowest-cost producer at $8, having produced 400 000 units in the past. If all three firms sell the calculator for $10, TI makes $2 profit per unit, A makes $1 per unit, and B breaks even. The smart move for TI would be to lower its price to $9. This will drive B out of the market, and even A may consider leaving. TI will pick up

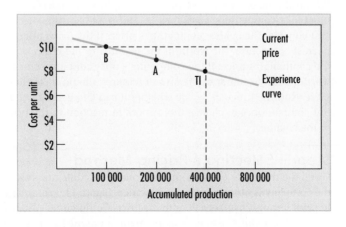

FIGURE 14.4

Cost per Unit as a Function of Accumulated Production: The Experience Curve the business that would have gone to B (and possibly A). Furthermore, price-sensitive customers will enter the market at the lower price. As production increases beyond 400 000 units, TI's costs will drop still further and faster and more than restore its profits, even at a price of $9. TI has used this aggressive pricing strategy repeatedly to gain market share and drive others out of the industry.

Experience-curve pricing nevertheless carries major risks. Aggressive pricing might give the product a cheap image. The strategy also assumes that competitors are weak followers. It can lead the company into building more plants to meet demand, while a competitor innovates a lower-cost technology, leaving the market leader stuck with the old technology. Most experience-curve pricing has focused on manufacturing costs, but all costs, including marketing costs, can be improved upon. If three firms are each investing a large sum of money in telemarketing, the firm that has used it the longest might achieve the lowest costs. This firm can charge a little less for its product and still earn the same return, all other costs being equal.[35]

ACTIVITY-BASED COST ACCOUNTING Today's companies try to adapt their offers and terms to different buyers. A manufacturer, for example, will negotiate different terms with different retail chains. One retailer may want daily delivery (to keep inventory lower) while another may accept twice-a-week delivery in order to get a lower price. The manufacturer's costs will differ with each chain, and so will its profits. To estimate the real profitability of dealing with different retailers, the manufacturer needs to use **activity-based cost (ABC) accounting** instead of standard cost accounting.[36]

ABC accounting tries to identify the real costs associated with serving each customer. It allocates indirect costs like clerical costs, office expenses, supplies, and so on, based on the activities that use them, rather than in some proportion to direct costs. Both variable and overhead costs are tagged back to each customer. Companies that fail to measure their costs correctly are not measuring their profit correctly and are likely to misallocate their marketing effort. The key to effectively employing ABC is to define and judge "activities" properly. One proposed time-based solution calculates the cost of one minute of overhead and then decides how much of this cost each activity uses.[37]

TARGET COSTING Costs change with production scale and experience. They can also change as a result of a concentrated effort by designers, engineers, and purchasing agents to reduce them through **target costing**.[38] Market research is used to establish a new product's desired functions and the price at which the product will sell, given its appeal and competitors' prices. Deducting the desired profit margin from this price leaves the target cost that must be achieved. Each cost element—design, engineering, manufacturing, sales—must be examined, and different ways to bring down costs must be considered. The objective is to bring the final cost projections into the target cost range. If this is not possible, it may be necessary to stop developing the product because it could not sell for the target price and make the target profit.

To hit price and margin targets, marketers of 9 Lives brand of cat food employed target costing to bring their price down to "four cans for a dollar" via a reshaped package and redesigned manufacturing processes. Even with lower prices, profits for the brand doubled. "Marketing Insight: Parking: There's More to It Than Meets the Eye" discusses the variety of factors that are considered while pricing parking spaces.

Step 4: Analyzing Competitors' Costs, Prices, and Offers

Within the range of possible prices determined by market demand and company costs, the firm must take competitors' costs, prices, and possible price reactions into account. The firm should first consider the nearest competitor's price. If the firm's offer contains features not offered by the nearest competitor, the worth of the features to the customer should be evaluated and added to the competitor's price. If the competitor's offer contains some features not offered by the firm, the worth to the customer of the absent features should be evaluated and subtracted from the firm's price. Now the firm can decide whether it can charge more, the same, or less than the competitor. But competitors can change their prices in reaction to the price set by the firm, as we'll see later in the chapter.

Step 5: Selecting a Pricing Method

Given the three Cs—the customers' demand schedule, the cost function, and competitors' prices— the company is now ready to select a price. Figure 14.5 summarizes the three major considerations in price setting. Costs set a floor to the price. Competitors' prices and the price of substitutes provide an orienting point. Customers' assessment of unique features establishes the price ceiling.

High Price
(No possible demand at this price)

Ceiling price

Customers' assessment of unique product features

Orienting point

Competitors' prices and prices of substitutes

Costs

Floor price

Low Price
(No possible profit at this price)

FIGURE 14.5

The Three Cs Model for Price Setting

MARKETING **INSIGHT** | PARKING: THERE'S MORE TO IT THAN MEETS THE EYE

Nobody relishes seeing a parking ticket on his or her windshield. Many people don't think of a parking ticket as the penalty for consuming the product (parking, in this case) without adequately paying for it. Not too many people think of the money they feed a parking meter as the "price" they are paying for parking either.

Parking spaces can be a huge source of revenue for city governments. For example, in 2006, Ottawa raised $11.4 million in parking revenues and an additional $13.5 million from parking tickets. However, revenue generation is not the only reason for providing parking spaces. Parking is provided and parking prices are set by local governments or businesses as part of a traffic-management strategy (to reduce vehicle traffic in an area), a parking-management strategy (to reduce parking problems in a certain location), to recover facility costs, to generate revenues to fund other projects, to make a profit, or a combination of these objectives.

The price of parking is determined by taking several factors into account, such as the costs of the facility, equipment, maintenance, personnel, expected occupancy rates, and the objective of providing parking in an area. A number of pricing options are possible, each leading to a different outcome and benefit for the management. Here are some examples and considerations that go into them:

- Local governments often practise "congestion pricing," setting prices high during peak-traffic periods and low during other times. The high price during peak periods eases traffic with a high turnover of vehicles during that time.

- To encourage use of local transit and reduce vehicle traffic in an area (e.g., downtown), parking prices should be set so as to exceed transit fares. For example, daily parking rates must be more than a round-trip ticket on local transit and monthly parking rates must exceed the cost of a monthly transit pass.

- Commercial parking lots price to maximize revenue. That is, they are priced at the highest amount the market will pay. Parking lots in an area often collectively determine the "going-rate" for parking in that area.

- The average price elasticity of parking demand is relatively inelastic at around –0.3. That is, vehicle parking goes down (up) by 3-percent for a 10-percent increase (decrease) in parking rates.

- Having to pay for parking is not restricted to vehicles on streets. Even aircraft and ships are charged for parking by airports and ports respectively. Interestingly, the parking rate for aircraft is based on weight and that for ships is based on length. For example, Toronto's Pearson Airport charges a daily parking rate of approximately $225 for a Boeing 747-400 that weighs about 250 tons. The Port of Vancouver has a daily "berthage" (parking) fee of about $3000 for a 300-metre cruise ship.

- Determining how many parking spaces to provide at a store or shopping mall requires marginal analysis (i.e., the additional revenue that will be generated by providing one extra space). Parking is usually free for customers at most shopping malls and off-street stores, but downtown malls often charge for parking. Stores and restaurants benefit from customers staying longer, as those who stay longer tend to buy more. Therefore, a high parking price is not in the best interest of the businesses in the mall, because it would make customers leave quickly. As an incentive to buy more, some stores and malls that have paid parking provide it free of charge to those customers who spend a certain amount.

Underpricing parking can lead to inefficient use of parking facilities and excessive demand. Moreover, it can encourage longer-term parking and, therefore, reduce revenue from parking tickets. Overpricing parking can discourage vehicles from visiting the area, thereby adversely affecting nearby businesses served by the parking facility, which in turn will lower the demand for parking in the area. Considerable thought has to go into pricing any product. Determining how much to charge for parking is no different.

Sources: "Parking Pricing: Direct Charges for Using Parking Facilities," *TDM Encyclopedia*, Victoria Transport Policy Institute, September 2007; Erin Vaca and J. Richard Kuzmyak, "Parking Pricing and Fees," *TCRP Report 95*, Chapter 13, www.trb.org/publications/tcrp/tcrp_rpt_95c13.pdf (viewed August 23, 2007); "2007 Airline Rates and Charges," *Greater Toronto Airports Authority*, www.gtaa.com/local/files/en/ RatesAndCharges2007.pdf (viewed August 23, 2007); www.boeing.com/product_list.html (viewed August 23, 2007); "Fee Detail Document," *Vancouver Port Authority*, www.portvancouver.com/trade_shipping/fees.html (viewed August 23, 2007); Glen McGregor, "Driven to Distraction," *Ottawa Citizen*, June 12, 2007.

Companies select a pricing method that includes one or more of these three considerations. We will examine six price-setting methods: markup pricing, target-return pricing, perceived-value pricing, value pricing, going-rate pricing, and auction-type pricing.

MARKUP PRICING The most elementary pricing method is to add a standard **markup** to the product's cost. Construction companies submit job bids by estimating the total project cost and adding a standard markup for profit. Lawyers and accountants typically price by adding a standard markup on their time and costs.

Suppose a toaster manufacturer has the following costs and sales expectations:

Variable cost per unit	$10
Fixed cost	$300 000
Expected unit sales	50 000

The manufacturer's unit cost is given by:

$$\text{Unit cost} = \text{variable cost} + \frac{\text{fixed cost}}{\text{unit sales}} = \$10 + \frac{\$300\,000}{50\,000} = \$16$$

Now assume the manufacturer wants to earn a 20 percent markup on sales. The manufacturer's markup price is given by:

$$\text{Markup price} = \frac{\text{unit cost}}{(1 - \text{desired return on sales})} = \frac{\$16}{1 - 0.2} = \$20$$

The manufacturer would charge dealers $20 per toaster and make a profit of $4 per unit. The dealers in turn will mark up the toaster. If dealers want to earn 50 percent on their selling price, they will mark up the toaster to $40. This is equivalent to a cost markup of 100 percent. Markups are generally higher on seasonal items (to cover the risk of not selling), specialty items, slower-moving items, items with high storage and handling costs, and demand-inelastic items, such as prescription drugs.

Does the use of standard markups make logical sense? Generally, no. Any pricing method that ignores current demand, perceived value, and competition is not likely to lead to the optimal price. Markup pricing works only if the marked-up price actually brings in the expected level of sales.

Companies introducing a new product often price it high, hoping to recover their costs as rapidly as possible. But this strategy could be fatal if a competitor is pricing low. This happened to Philips, the Dutch electronics manufacturer, in pricing its videodisc players. Philips wanted to make a profit on each player. Japanese competitors priced low and succeeded in building their market share rapidly, which in turn pushed down their costs substantially.

Still, markup pricing remains popular. First, sellers can determine costs much more easily than they can estimate demand. By tying the price to cost, sellers simplify the pricing task. Second, where all firms in the industry use this pricing method, prices tend to be similar. Price competition is therefore minimized. Third, many people feel that cost-plus pricing is fairer to both buyers and sellers. Sellers do not take advantage of buyers when the latter's demand becomes acute, and sellers earn a fair return on investment.

TARGET-RETURN PRICING In **target-return pricing**, the firm determines the price that would yield its target rate of return on investment (ROI). Target pricing is used by General Motors, which prices its automobiles to achieve a 15 to 20 percent ROI. This method is also used by public utilities, which need to make a fair return on investment.

Suppose the toaster manufacturer has invested $1 million in the business and wants to set a price to earn a 20-percent ROI, specifically $200 000. The target-return price is given by the following formula:

$$\text{Target-return price} = \text{unit cost} + \frac{\text{desired return} \times \text{invested capital}}{\text{unit sales}}$$

$$= \$16 + \frac{0.20 \times \$1\,000\,000}{50\,000} = \$20$$

The manufacturer will realize this 20 percent ROI provided its costs and estimated sales turn out to be accurate. But what if sales do not reach 50 000 units? The manufacturer can prepare a break-even chart to learn what would happen at other sales levels (see Figure 14.6). Fixed costs are $300 000 regardless of sales volume. Variable costs, not shown in the figure, rise with volume. Total costs equal the sum of fixed costs and variable costs. The total revenue curve starts at zero and rises with each unit sold.

The total revenue and total cost curves cross at 30 000 units. This is the break-even volume. It can be verified by the following formula:

$$\text{Break-even volume} = \frac{\text{fixed cost}}{(\text{price} - \text{variable cost})} = \frac{\$300\,000}{\$20 - \$10} = 30\,000$$

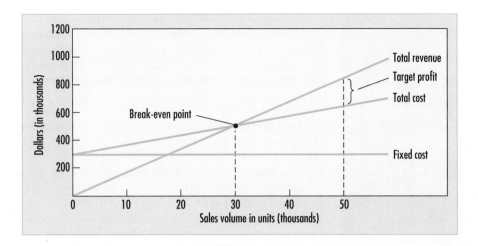

FIGURE 14.6

Break-Even Chart for Determining Target-Return Price and Break-Even Volume

The manufacturer, of course, is hoping that the market will buy 50 000 units at $20, in which case it earns $200 000 on its $1 million investment, but much depends on price elasticity and competitors' prices. Unfortunately, target-return pricing tends to ignore these considerations. The manufacturer needs to consider different prices and estimate their probable impacts on sales volume and profits. The manufacturer should also search for ways to lower its fixed or variable costs, because lower costs will decrease its required break-even volume.

PERCEIVED-VALUE PRICING An increasing number of companies base their price on the customer's **perceived value**. They must deliver the value promised by their value proposition, and the customer must perceive this value. They use the other marketing-mix elements, such as advertising and sales force, to communicate and enhance perceived value in buyers' minds.[39]

Perceived value is made up of several elements, such as the buyer's image of product performance, channel deliverables, warranty quality, customer support, and softer attributes such as the supplier's reputation, trustworthiness, and esteem. Furthermore, each potential customer places different weights on these different elements, with the result that some will be *price buyers*, others will be *value buyers*, and still others will be *loyal buyers*. Companies need different strategies for these three groups. For price buyers, companies need to offer stripped-down products and reduced services. For value buyers, companies must keep innovating new value and aggressively reaffirming their value. For loyal buyers, companies must invest in relationship building and customer intimacy.

Caterpillar uses perceived value to set prices on its construction equipment. It might price its tractor at $100 000, although a similar competitor's tractor might be priced at $90 000. When a prospective customer asks a Caterpillar dealer why he should pay $10 000 more for the Caterpillar tractor, the dealer answers:

$ 90 000	is the tractor's price if it is only equivalent to the competitor's tractor
$ 7 000	is the price premium for Caterpillar's superior durability
$ 6 000	is the price premium for Caterpillar's superior reliability
$ 5 000	is the price premium for Caterpillar's superior service
$ 2 000	is the price premium for Caterpillar's longer warranty on parts
$110 000	is the normal price to cover Caterpillar's superior value
– $ 10 000	discount
$100 000	final price

The Caterpillar dealer is able to indicate why Caterpillar's tractor delivers more value than the competitor's. Although the customer is asked to pay a $10 000 premium, he is actually getting $20 000 in extra value! He chooses the Caterpillar tractor because he is convinced that its lifetime operating costs will be lower.

Yet even when a company claims that its offering delivers more total value, not all customers will respond positively. There is always a segment of buyers who care only about the price. There are other buyers who suspect that the company is exaggerating its product quality and services. One company installed its software system in one or two plants operated by a company. The substantial and well-documented cost savings convinced the customer to buy the software for its other plants.

Shoppers at Wal-Mart get EDLP—everyday low pricing—on major brands.

The key to perceived-value pricing is to deliver more value than the competitor and to demonstrate this to prospective buyers. Basically, a company needs to understand the customer's decision-making process. The company can try to determine the value of its offering in several ways: managerial judgments within the company, value of similar products, focus groups, surveys, experimentation, analysis of historical data, and conjoint analysis.[40]

For example, DuPont educated its customers about the true value of its higher-grade polyethylene resin called Alathon. Instead of claiming only that pipes made from it were 5-percent more durable, DuPont produced a detailed analysis of the comparative costs of installing and maintaining in-ground irrigation pipe. The real savings came from the diminished need to pay the labour and crop-damage costs associated with digging up and replacing underground pipe. DuPont was able to charge 7 percent more and still see its sales double the following year.

VALUE PRICING In recent years, several companies have adopted **value pricing**: they win loyal customers by charging a fairly low price for a high-quality offering. Among the best practitioners of value pricing are IKEA and Southwest Airlines.

In the early 1990s, Procter & Gamble created quite a stir when it reduced prices on supermarket staples such as Pampers and Luvs diapers, liquid Tide detergent, and Folger's coffee to value price them. In the past, a brand-loyal family had to pay what amounted to a US$725 premium for a year's worth of P&G products versus private-label or low-priced brands. To offer value prices, P&G underwent a major overhaul. It redesigned the way it developed, manufactured, distributed, priced, marketed, and sold products to deliver better value at every point in the supply chain.[41]

Value pricing is not a matter of simply setting lower prices; it is a matter of re-engineering the company's operations to become a low-cost producer without sacrificing quality, and lowering prices significantly to attract a large number of value-conscious customers.

An important type of value pricing is **everyday low pricing (EDLP)**, which takes place at the retail level. A retailer which holds to an EDLP pricing policy charges a constant low price with few or no price promotions and special sales. These constant prices eliminate week-to-week price uncertainty and can be contrasted to the "high-low" pricing of promotion-oriented competitors. In **high-low pricing**, the retailer charges higher prices on an everyday basis but then runs frequent promotions in which prices are temporarily lowered below the EDLP level.[42] The two different pricing strategies have been shown to affect consumer price judgments: over time deep discounts (EDLP) can lead to lower perceived prices than do frequent, shallow discounts (high-low)—even if the actual averages are the same.[43]

In recent years, high-low pricing has given way to EDLP at such widely different venues as General Motors' Saturn car dealerships and upscale department stores such as Nordstrom, but the king of EDLP is surely Wal-Mart, which practically defined the term. Except for a few sale items every month, Wal-Mart promises everyday low prices on major brands. "It's not a short-term strategy," says one Wal-Mart executive. "You have to be willing to make a commitment to it, and you have to be able to operate with lower ratios of expense than everybody else."

Some retailers have even based their entire marketing strategy around what could be called *extreme* everyday low pricing. Partly fuelled by an economic downturn, even once unfashionable "dollar stores" are gaining in popularity. Consider the focus on value by Winners:

Winners

Winners, a leading off-price Canadian retailer, operates more than 180 outlets internationally, offering a variety of products such as women's apparel, menswear, children's apparel, lingerie, family footwear, fine jewellery, accessories, toys, and home fashions, among others. At Winners, shoppers can find brand name and designer merchandise for up to 60 percent less than the department store price for the product. Value becomes evident to the customer through the strategy of "compare at" price tagging that details the actual retail price versus the price Winners offers. The goal of Winners, since its conception in 1982, has been to offer brand name apparel and accessories at the lowest possible price, letting customers engage in the "thrill of the find." Their recent slogan *"Winners—Where Else?"* reflects their strategy of offering superior value.[44]

The most important reason retailers adopt EDLP is that constant sales and promotions are costly and have eroded consumer confidence in the credibility of everyday shelf prices. Consumers also have less time and patience for such time-honoured traditions as watching for supermarket specials and clipping coupons. Yet, there is no denying that promotions create excitement and draw shoppers. For this reason, EDLP is not a guarantee of success. As supermarkets face heightened competition from their counterparts and from alternative channels, many find that the key to drawing shoppers is using a combination of high-low and everyday low pricing strategies, with increased advertising and promotions.[45]

GOING-RATE PRICING In **going-rate pricing**, the firm bases its price largely on competitors' prices. The firm might charge the same, more, or less than major competitor(s). In oligopolistic industries that sell a commodity such as steel, paper, or fertilizer, firms normally charge the same price. The smaller firms "follow the leader," changing their prices when the market leader's prices change rather than when their own demand or costs change. Some firms may charge a slight premium or slight discount, but they preserve the amount of difference. Thus minor gasoline retailers usually charge a bit less per litre than the major oil companies, without letting the difference increase or decrease.

Going-rate pricing is quite popular. Where costs are difficult to measure or competitive response is uncertain, firms feel that the going price is a good solution because it is thought to reflect the industry's collective wisdom.

AUCTION-TYPE PRICING Auction-type pricing is growing more popular, especially with the growth of the Internet. There are over 2000 electronic marketplaces selling everything from pigs to used vehicles to cargo to chemicals. One major use of auctions is to dispose of excess inventories or used goods. Companies need to be aware of the three major types of auctions and their separate pricing procedures:

- *English auctions (ascending bids).* One seller and many buyers. On sites such as eBay and WeBidz.com, the seller puts up an item and bidders raise the offer price until the top price is reached. English auctions are being used today for selling antiques, cattle, real estate, and used equipment and vehicles. After seeing ticket brokers and scalpers reap millions by charging what the market would bear, Ticketmaster Corp. began auctioning the best seats to concerts in 2003 through its website, ticketmaster.com.[46]
- *Dutch auctions (descending bids).* One seller and many buyers, or one buyer and many sellers. In the first kind, an auctioneer announces a high price for a product and then slowly decreases the price until a bidder accepts the price. In the other, the buyer announces something that he or she wants to buy and then potential sellers compete to get the sale by offering the lowest price. Each seller sees what the last bid is and decides whether to go lower. FreeMarkets.com helped Royal Mail Group plc, the United Kingdom's public mail-service company, save approximately 2.5 million pounds, in part via an auction whereby 25 airlines bid for its international freight business.[47]
- *Sealed-bid auctions.* Would-be suppliers can submit only one bid and cannot know the other bids. Governments often use this method to procure supplies. A supplier will not bid below its cost but cannot bid too high for fear of losing the job. The net effect of these two pulls can be described in terms of the bid's *expected profit.* Using expected profit for setting price makes sense for the seller that makes many bids. The seller that bids only occasionally or that needs a particular contract badly will not find it advantageous to use expected profit. This criterion does not distinguish between a $1000 profit with a 0.10 probability and a $125 profit with a 0.80 probability. Yet the firm that wants to keep production going would prefer the second contract to the first.

Step 6: Selecting the Final Price

Pricing methods narrow the range from which the company must select its final price. In selecting that price, the company must consider additional factors, including the impact of other marketing activities, company pricing policies, gain-and-risk-sharing pricing, and the impact of price on other parties.

To read about Australia's Internet service provider BigPond and its focus on advertising to drive sales, visit www.pearsoned.com.au/marketingmanagement australia.

IMPACT OF OTHER MARKETING ACTIVITIES   The final price must take into account the brand's quality and advertising relative to the competition. In a classic study, Farris and Reibstein examined the relationships among relative price, relative quality, and relative advertising for 227 consumer businesses and found the following:

- Brands with average relative quality but high relative advertising budgets were able to charge premium prices. Consumers apparently were willing to pay higher prices for known products than for unknown products.
- Brands with high relative quality and high relative advertising obtained the highest prices. Conversely, brands with low quality and low advertising charged the lowest prices.
- The positive relationship between high prices and high advertising held most strongly in the later stages of the product life cycle for market leaders.[48]

These findings suggest that price is not as important as quality and other benefits in the market offering. One study asked consumers to rate the importance of price and other attributes in using online retailing. Only 19 percent cared about price; far more cared about customer support (65 percent), on-time delivery (58 percent), and product shipping and handling (49 percent).[49]

COMPANY PRICING POLICIES   The price must be consistent with company pricing policies. At the same time, companies are not averse to establishing pricing penalties under certain circumstances.[50]

Airlines charge fees to those who change their reservations for discount tickets. Banks charge fees for too many withdrawals in a month or for early withdrawal of a term deposit. Car rental companies charge penalties for no-shows for specialty vehicles. Although these policies are often justifiable, they must be used judiciously so as not to unnecessarily alienate customers. (See "Marketing Insight: Stealth Price Increases.")

Many companies set up a pricing department to develop policies and establish or approve decisions. The aim is to ensure that salespeople quote prices that are reasonable to customers and profitable to the company. Dell has developed some innovative pricing techniques.

Dell

Dell uses a high-tech "cost-forecasting" system that enables it to scale its selling prices[51] based on consumer demand and the company's own costs. The company instituted this flexible pricing model in 2001 to maximize its margins during the economic slowdown. Dell managers get cost information from suppliers, which they then combine with knowledge about profit targets, delivery dates, and competition to set prices for business segments. On any given day, the same computer might sell at different prices depending on whether the purchaser is a government, small business, or home PC buyer. The cost-forecasting system may help to explain why Dell survived the 2001 high-tech meltdown. Dell's innovative pricing strategy and superior customer support have made it a global leader in computer systems, earning it the 34th position on the 2008 Fortune 500 list.[52]

GAIN-AND-RISK-SHARING PRICING   Buyers may resist accepting a seller's proposal because of a perceived high level of risk. The seller has the option of offering to absorb part or all of the risk if he or she does not deliver the full promised value. Baxter Healthcare, for example, offered to develop an information management system that would save a hospital several million dollars over an eight-year period. When the hospital balked, Baxter offered to guarantee the savings. When Queen's School of Business launched its first private MBA program, it guaranteed students their salaries would increase or their tuition would be refunded. An increasing number of companies, especially business marketers which promise great savings with their equipment, may have to stand ready to guarantee the promised savings, and possibly participate in them if the gains are much greater than expected.

IMPACT OF PRICE ON OTHER PARTIES   Management must also consider the reactions of other parties to the contemplated price.[53] How will distributors and dealers feel about it? If they do not make enough profit, they may choose not to bring the product to market. Will the sales force be willing to sell at that price? How will competitors react? Will suppliers raise their prices when they see the company's price? Will the government intervene and prevent this price from being charged?

MARKETING **INSIGHT** | STEALTH PRICE INCREASES

With consumers stubbornly resisting higher prices, companies are trying to figure out how to increase revenue without really raising prices. Increasingly, the solution has been through the addition of fees for what had once been free features. Although some consumers abhor "nickel-and-dime" pricing strategies, small additional charges can add up to a substantial source of revenue for North American firms.

The numbers can be staggering. For instance, fees for consumers who pay bills online, bounce cheques, or use automated teller machines bring Canadian banks an estimated $4 billion annually. In the United States, the number is as high as US$30 billion. Retailers Target and Best Buy charge a 15-percent "restocking fee" for returning electronic products. Credit card late payments—up by 11 percent in 2003—exceed $10 billion in total. The telecommunications industry in general has been aggressive at adding fees for set-up, change of service, service termination, directory assistance, regulatory assessment, number portability, and cable hookup and equipment, costing consumers billions of dollars. By charging its long-distance customers a new 99-cent monthly "regulatory assessment fee," AT&T could bring in as much as US$475 million.

This explosion of fees has a number of implications. Given that list prices stay fixed, they may result in inflation being understated. They also make it harder for consumers to compare competitive offerings. Although various citizen groups have been formed to pressure companies to roll back some of these fees, they don't always get a sympathetic ear from federal, provincial, and municipal governments which have been guilty of levying their own array of fees, fines, and penalties to raise necessary revenue.

Companies justify the extra fees as the only fair and viable way to cover expenses without losing customers. Many argue that it makes sense to charge a premium for added services that cost more to provide, rather than charge all customers the same amount regardless of whether or not they use the extra service. Breaking out charges and fees according to the services involved is seen as a way to keep the basic costs low. Companies also use fees as a means to weed out unprofitable customers or change their behaviour. Air Canada, for example, recently decreased its free baggage allowance. Passengers can now take only two bags weighing up to 50 pounds (23 kg). The previous allowance was 70 pounds (32 kg). If bags are overweight, passengers must pay an excess baggage fee of $35 for travel within North America and $60 for all international travel for bags weighing 50 to 70 pounds (23 to 32 kg).

Ultimately, the viability of extra fees will be decided in the marketplace and by the willingness of consumers to vote with their wallets and pay the fees or vote with their feet and move on.

Source: Adapted from Michael Arndt, "Fees! Fees! Fees!" *BusinessWeek*, September 29, 2003, pp. 99–104; "The Price Is Wrong," *The Economist*, May 25, 2002, pp. 59–60.

As can be seen in the following example, while Loblaw's relentless drive to squeeze out costs and lower prices has benefited consumers, the downward price pressure is taking a big toll on suppliers.

Loblaw

Loblaw Companies Limited is a leading provider of general merchandise products and is Canada's largest food distributor. The company has been experiencing financial difficulties since 2006 and in what appears to be desperation has placed new demands on suppliers. These include a discount of 1.5 percent of sales to the retailer as well as an extended time frame for early-payment discounts. The early-payment discount was 2 percent if paid within 10 days and Loblaw is demanding that it receive the discount if paying within 15 days. These demands are attempts by Loblaw to keep more money in its pockets and take it out of suppliers' pockets. Although small suppliers often comply for fear of losing the account altogether, some of the larger suppliers have chosen to ignore the demands, knowing that Loblaw cannot afford to take their products off the shelves.[54]

Marketers need to know the laws regulating pricing. The Competition Act states that sellers must set prices without talking to competitors: price-fixing is illegal. Many federal and provincial statutes protect consumers against deceptive pricing practices. For example, it is illegal for a company to set artificially high "regular" prices, and then announce a "sale" at prices close to previous everyday prices. "Marketing Memo: Types of Illegal Pricing" discusses pricing strategies that are prohibited by the Competition Act.

| MARKETING MEMO | TYPES OF ILLEGAL PRICING |

In an attempt to increase sales or profits, or simply in order to survive in the marketplace, marketers may be tempted to take their pricing strategies a little too far. According to the Competition Act, here are some pricing tactics considered illegal in Canada:

- Price Fixing—a manufacturer stipulating (rather than just suggesting) what price retailers should sell at, or collaborating with competitors to set prices.
- Predatory Pricing—selling at an unusually low price to eliminate competition.
- False Ordinary Selling Price—promoting product at a sale price with reference to an inflated regular price.
- Bid Rigging—following a call for tenders, collaborating with another bidder on bid amounts or agreeing not to bid.
- Double Ticketing—not selling at the lower of two prices communicated to the customer, displayed in the store or on the product.
- Bait-and-Switch—luring customers into a retail outlet with exceptionally low prices and then switching the customer to a higher priced item, often making the customer believe that the lower-priced product is sold out.

Source: Competition Bureau Canada, Price-related Representations, www.competitionbureau.gc.ca/epic/site/cb-bc.nsf/en/00522e.html (viewed June 15, 2008).

ADAPTING THE PRICE

Companies usually do not set a single price, but rather a pricing structure that reflects variations in geographical demand and costs, market-segment requirements, purchase timing, order levels, delivery frequency, guarantees, service contracts, and other factors. As a result of discounts, allowances, and promotional support, a company rarely realizes the same profit from each unit of a product that it sells. Here we will examine several price-adaptation strategies: geographical pricing, price discounts and allowances, promotional pricing, and differentiated pricing.

Geographical Pricing (Cash, Countertrade, Barter)

Geographical pricing involves the company pricing its products differently for customers in different locations and countries, as shown by the Procter & Gamble example.

Procter & Gamble

China is P&G's second largest market, yet China's population earns less than US$150 per month on average. So in 2003, P&G developed a tiered pricing initiative to help compete against cheaper local brands while still protecting the value of its global brands. P&G introduced a 320-gram bag of Tide Clean White for US$0.23, compared with US$0.33 for 350 grams of Tide Triple Action. The Clean White version doesn't offer such benefits as stain removal and fragrance, but it costs less to make and, according to P&G, outperforms every other brand at that price level.[55]

Should the company charge higher prices to distant customers to cover the higher shipping costs or a lower price to win additional business? How should exchange rates and the strength of different currencies be accounted for? A weakening U.S. dollar over recent years has allowed some U.S. companies to mark up prices and still match more expensive imports.[56]

Another issue is how to get paid. This issue is critical when buyers lack sufficient hard currency to pay for their purchases. Many buyers want to offer other items in payment, a practice known as **countertrade**. Companies are often forced to engage in countertrade if they want the business. Countertrade may account for 15 to 25 percent of world trade and takes several forms:[57] barter, compensation deals, buyback agreements, and offset.

- *Barter.* The direct exchange of goods, with no money and no third party involved. In 1993, Eminence S.A., one of France's major clothing makers, launched a five-year deal to barter

US$25 million worth of underwear and sportswear to customers in eastern Europe, in exchange for a variety of goods and services, including global transportation and advertising space in eastern European magazines.

- *Compensation deal.* The seller receives some percentage of the payment in cash and the rest in products. A British aircraft manufacturer sold planes to Brazil for 70 percent cash and the rest in coffee.

- *Buyback arrangement.* The seller sells a plant, equipment, or technology to another country and agrees to accept as partial payment products manufactured with the supplied equipment. A U.S. chemical company built a plant for an Indian company and accepted partial payment in cash and the remainder in chemicals manufactured at the plant.

- *Offset.* The seller receives full payment in cash but agrees to spend a substantial amount of the money in that country within a stated time period. For example, PepsiCo sells its cola syrup to Russia for rubles and agrees to buy Russian vodka at a certain rate for sale in the United States.

Price Discounts and Allowances

Most companies will adjust their list price and give discounts and allowances for early payment, volume purchases, and off-season buying (see Table 14.4).[58] Companies must do this carefully or find that their profits are much less than planned.[59]

Discount pricing has become the modus operandi of a surprising number of companies offering both products and services. Some product categories tend to self-destruct by always being on sale. Salespeople, in particular, are quick to give discounts in order to close a sale. But word can get around fast that the company's list price is "soft" and discounting becomes the norm. The discounts undermine the value perceptions of the offerings.

Some companies in an overcapacity situation are tempted to give discounts or even begin to supply a retailer with a store-brand version of their product at a deep discount. Because the store brand is priced lower, however, it may start making inroads into the manufacturer's brand. Manufacturers should stop to consider the implications of supplying product at a discount to retailers because they may end up losing long-run profits in an effort to meet short-run volume goals.

Kevin Clancy, chairman of Copernicus, a major marketing research and consulting firm, found that only between 15 and 35 percent of buyers in most categories are price-sensitive. People with higher incomes and higher product involvement willingly pay more for features, customer service, quality, added convenience, and the brand name. So it can be a mistake for a strong, distinctive brand to plunge into price discounting to respond to low-price attacks.[60]

TABLE 14.4	PRICE DISCOUNTS AND ALLOWANCES
Cash Discount:	A price reduction to buyers that pay bills promptly. A typical example is "2/10, net 30," which means that payment is due within 30 days and that the buyer may deduct 2 percent if paying the bill within ten days.
Quantity Discount:	A price reduction to those that buy large volumes. A typical example is "$10 per unit for fewer than 100 units; $9 per unit for 100 or more units." Quantity discounts must be offered equally to all customers and must not exceed the cost savings to the seller. They can be offered on each order placed or on the number of units ordered over a given period.
Functional Discount:	Discount (also called *trade discount*) offered by a manufacturer to trade-channel members if they will perform certain functions, such as selling, storing, and record-keeping. Manufacturers must offer the same functional discounts within each channel.
Seasonal Discount:	A price reduction to those that buy merchandise or services out of season. Hotels, motels, and airlines offer seasonal discounts in slow selling periods.
Allowance:	An extra payment designed to gain reseller participation in special programs. *Trade-in allowances* are granted for turning in an old item when buying a new one. *Promotional allowances* reward dealers for participating in advertising and sales support programs.

At the same time, discounting can be a useful tool if the company can gain concessions in return, such as when the customer agrees to sign a three-year contract, is willing to order electronically (thus saving the company money), or agrees to buy in truckload quantities.

Sales management needs to monitor the proportion of customers who are receiving discounts, the average discount, and the particular salespeople who are overly relying on discounting. Higher levels of management should conduct a **net price analysis** to arrive at the "real price" of their offering. The real price is affected not only by discounts, but by many other expenses (see "Promotional Pricing" below) that reduce the realized price: Suppose the company's list price is $3000. The average discount is $300. The company's promotional spending averages $450 (15 percent of the list price). Co-op advertising money of $150 is given to retailers to back the product. The company's net price is $2100, not $3000.

Promotional Pricing

Companies can use several pricing techniques to stimulate early purchase:

- *Loss-leader pricing.* Supermarkets and department stores often drop the price on well-known brands to stimulate additional store traffic. This pays if the revenue on the additional sales compensates for the lower margins on the loss-leader items. Manufacturers of loss-leader brands typically object because this practice can dilute the brand image and bring complaints from retailers that charge the list price. Manufacturers have tried to restrain intermediaries from loss-leader pricing through lobbying for retail-price-maintenance laws, but these laws have been revoked.

- *Special-event pricing.* Sellers will establish special prices in certain seasons to draw in more customers. Every August, for example, there are back-to-school sales.

- *Cash rebates.* Auto companies and other consumer-goods companies offer cash rebates to encourage purchase of the manufacturers' products within a specified time period. Rebates can help clear inventories without cutting the stated list price.

- *Low-interest financing.* Instead of cutting its price, the company can offer customers low-interest financing. Automakers have even announced no-interest financing to attract customers.

- *Longer payment terms.* Sellers, especially mortgage lenders and auto companies, stretch loans over longer periods and thus lower the monthly payments. Consumers often worry less about the cost (i.e., the interest rate) of a loan and more about whether they can afford the monthly payment.

- *Warranties and service contracts.* Companies can promote sales by adding a free or low-cost warranty or service contract.

- *Psychological discounting.* This strategy involves setting an artificially high price and then offering the product at substantial savings; for example, "Was $359, now $299." Some unscrupulous retailers advertise these types of prices and then try to switch people to higher-priced items by stating the advertised item is sold out. Called "bait and switch," this is illegal under Canada's Competition Act. Retailers must offer rain checks if no stock of the sale item is currently available.

Promotional-pricing strategies are often a zero-sum game. If they work, competitors copy them and they lose their effectiveness. If they do not work, they waste money that could have been put into other marketing tools, such as building up product quality and service or strengthening product image through advertising.

Differentiated Pricing

Companies often adjust their basic price to accommodate differences in customers, products, locations, and so on. **Price discrimination** occurs when a company sells a product or service at two or more prices that do not reflect a proportional difference in costs. In first-degree price discrimination, the seller charges a separate price to each customer depending on the intensity of his or her demand. In second-degree price discrimination, the seller charges less to buyers that buy a larger volume. In third-degree price discrimination, the seller charges different amounts to different classes of buyers, as in the following cases:

- *Customer-segment pricing.* Different customer groups are charged different prices for the same product or service. For example, museums often charge a lower admission fee to students and senior citizens.

- *Product-form pricing.* Different versions of the product are priced differently but not proportionately to their respective costs. Evian prices a 1.5-litre bottle of its mineral water at $2.00. It takes the same water and packages 50 mL in a moisturizer spray for $6.00. Through product-form pricing, Evian manages to charge $6.00 for 50 mL in one form, and about $0.07 for 50 mL in another.

- *Image pricing.* Some companies price the same product at two different levels based on image differences. A perfume manufacturer can put the perfume in one bottle, give it a name and image, and price it at $10 for 10 mL. It can put the same perfume in another bottle with a different name and image and price it at $30 for 10 mL.

- *Channel pricing.* Coca-Cola carries a different price depending on whether it is purchased in a fine restaurant, a fast-food restaurant, or a vending machine.

- *Location pricing.* The same product is priced differently at different locations even though the cost of offering it at each location is the same. A theatre varies its seat prices according to audience preferences for different locations.

- *Time pricing.* Prices are varied by season, day, or hour. Public utilities vary energy rates for commercial users by time of day and weekend versus weekday. Restaurants charge less to "early bird" customers. Hotels charge less on weekends.

In some instances, marketers can have greater success with undifferentiated pricing. Look at how Famous Players cinemas went in the opposite direction, eliminating its differentiated pricing and yet enjoying increased sales:

Famous Players

Over the past decade, the movie-theatre industry has been threatened by competition from movie rentals and pay-per-view TV. In an attempt to draw movie fans back into its theatres, in 2004, Famous Players—now a Cineplex brand of cinemas—slashed movie admission prices by $4 from $13.05 to $9.95 in select cities, instituting a flat-rate price for every day of the week and any time of show. Child and senior admission prices were retained at their $8.50 levels. This flat-rate admission policy meant discounted prices for matinees, "cheap Tuesdays," and student discounts were no longer offered. The strategy resulted in movie attendance at Famous Players theatres rising by 10 to 15 percent. Based on the positive results, Cineplex has since expanded the flat-rate pricing to many of its theatres nationwide.[61]

The airline and hospitality industries use yield management systems and **yield pricing**, by which they offer discounted but limited early purchases, higher-priced late purchases, and the lowest rates on unsold inventory just before it expires.[62] Airlines charge different fares to passengers on the same flight depending on the seating class, the time of day (morning or night economy), the day of the week (workday or weekend), the season, the person's company, past business, or status (youth, military, senior citizen), and so on. That's why on a flight from Toronto to Vancouver you might have paid $300 and be sitting across from someone who has paid $800. Take Continental Airlines: It launches 2000 flights a day and each flight has between 10 and 20 prices. Continental starts booking flights 330 days in advance, and every flying day is different from every other flying day. At any given moment the market has more than 7 million prices. And in a system that tracks the difference in prices and the price of competitors' offerings, airlines change thousands of prices a day! It's a system designed to punish procrastinators by charging them the highest possible prices.

The phenomenon of offering different pricing schedules to different consumers and dynamically adjusting prices is exploding.[63] Most consumers are probably not even aware of the degree to which they are the targets of discriminatory pricing. For instance, catalogue retailers like Victoria's Secret routinely send out catalogues that sell identical goods except at different prices. Consumers who live in a more free-spending region may see only the higher prices. Office-product superstore Staples also sends out office-supply catalogues with different prices.

Some forms of price discrimination (in which sellers offer different price terms to different people within the same trade group) are illegal. However, price discrimination is legal if the seller can prove that its costs are different when selling different volumes or different qualities of the same product to different retailers. Predatory pricing—selling below cost with the intention of destroying competition—is unlawful.[64] Air Canada has been accused of predatory pricing on a number of occasions by competitors such as former airline Canada 3000, CanJet, and WestJet. Even if legal, some differentiated pricing may meet with a hostile reaction. Coca-Cola considered raising its vending machine soda prices on hot days using wireless technology, and lowering the price on cold days. Customers so disliked the idea that Coke abandoned it.

INITIATING AND RESPONDING TO PRICE CHANGES

Companies often face situations where they may need to cut or raise prices.

Initiating Price Cuts

Several circumstances might lead a firm to cut prices. One is excess plant capacity: the firm needs additional business and cannot generate it through increased sales effort, product improvement, or other measures. It may resort to aggressive pricing, but in initiating a price cut, the company may trigger a price war. IKEA Canada is a case in point.

IKEA Canada

IKEA is Canada's third-largest furniture and bedding retailer. In 2006, IKEA drastically slashed its prices, by up to 17 percent on some of its best-selling items. The price cuts were initiated to maintain IKEA's leadership in the competitive home-furnishings sector. According to the president of the Canadian arm of IKEA, the price cuts are part of a business strategy to offer more value to the market, and are not just an aggressive tactic to take over market share. Leon's Furniture and Sears have also had to reduce their prices. The home-furnishings industry could go into a cutthroat price war as big-box retailers such as Wal-Mart and Real Canadian Superstore expand their furnishing offerings, increasing competition in an already competitive industry.[65]

Companies sometimes initiate price cuts in a *drive to dominate the market through lower costs*. Either the company starts with lower costs than its competitors or it initiates price cuts in the hope of gaining market share and lower costs. A price-cutting strategy involves possible traps:

- *Low-quality trap.* Consumers will assume that the product quality is low.
- *Fragile-market-share trap.* A low price buys market share but not market loyalty. The same customers will shift to any lower-priced firm that comes along.
- *Shallow-pockets trap.* The higher-priced competitors may cut their prices and may have longer staying power because of deeper cash reserves.

Initiating Price Increases

A successful price increase can raise profits considerably. For example, if the company's profit margin is 3 percent of sales, a 1-percent price increase will increase profits by 33 percent if sales volume is unaffected. This situation is illustrated in Table 14.5. The assumption is that a company charged $10 and sold 100 units and had costs of $970, leaving a profit of $30, or 3 percent of sales. By raising its price by 10 cents (1-percent price increase), it boosted its profits by 33 percent, assuming the same sales volume.

TABLE 14.5	PROFITS BEFORE AND AFTER A PRICE INCREASE	
	Before	After
Price	$10	$10.10 (a 1-percent price increase)
Units sold	100	100
Revenue	$1000	$1010
Costs	$970	$970
Profit	$30	$40 (a 33.3-percent profit increase)

A major circumstance provoking price increases is *cost inflation*. Rising costs unmatched by productivity gains squeeze profit margins and lead companies to regular rounds of price increases. Companies often raise their prices by more than the cost increase, in anticipation of further inflation or government price controls, in a practice called *anticipatory pricing*.

Another factor leading to price increases is *overdemand*. When a company cannot supply all of its customers, it can raise its prices, ration supplies to customers, or both. The price can be increased in the following ways. Each has a different impact on buyers.

- *Delayed-quotation pricing.* The company does not set a final price until the product is finished or delivered. This pricing is prevalent in industries with long production lead times, such as industrial construction and heavy equipment.

- *Escalator clauses.* The company requires the customer to pay today's price and all or part of any inflation increase that takes place before delivery. An escalator clause bases price increases on some specified price index. Escalator clauses are found in contracts for major industrial projects, like aircraft construction and bridge building.

- *Unbundling.* The company maintains its price but removes or prices separately one or more elements that were part of the former offer, such as free delivery or installation. Car companies sometimes add anti-lock brakes and passenger-side airbags as supplementary extras to their vehicles.

- *Reduction of discounts.* The company instructs its sales force not to offer its normal cash and quantity discounts.

A company needs to decide whether to raise its price sharply on a one-time basis or to raise it by small amounts several times. Generally, consumers prefer small price increases on a regular basis to sudden, sharp increases.

In passing on price increases to customers, the company must avoid looking like a price gouger.[66] Companies also need to think of who will bear the brunt of increased prices. Customer memories are long, and they can turn against companies they perceive as price gougers. Price hikes without corresponding investments in the value of the brand increase vulnerability to lower-priced competition. Consumers may be willing to "trade down" because they can no longer justify to themselves that the higher-priced brand is worth it. This happened to Kraft.

Kraft Foods Inc.

Early in 2003, Kraft responded to increasing commodity costs for coffee and cheese by raising its own prices. The move widened the gap between Kraft's brand-name items and its generic competitors, many of which held the line on price increases. Recession-weary consumers flocked to the cheaper choices. As sales fell, Kraft backpedalled, rolling back many prices and flooding the market with new coupons and promotions. It was a costly misstep. Kraft, which typically spends about US$900 million a year on marketing, spent an extra US$200 million to lure back lost customers. Analysts and other observers questioned whether the company would have been better off boosting margins through additional cost-cutting, including reduced ad spending.[67]

Several techniques help consumers avoid sticker shock and a hostile reaction when prices rise: One is that a sense of fairness must surround any price increase, and customers must be given advance notice so they can do forward buying or shop around. Sharp price increases need to be explained in understandable terms. Making low-visibility price moves first is also a good technique: eliminating discounts, increasing minimum order sizes, and curtailing production of low-margin products are some examples, and contracts or bids for long-term projects should contain escalator clauses based on such factors as increases in recognized national price indexes.[68] "Marketing Memo: Marketing Strategies to Avoid Raising Prices" describes other means by which companies can respond to higher costs or overdemand without raising prices.

Reactions to Price Changes

Any price change can provoke a response from customers, competitors, distributors, suppliers, and even government.

CUSTOMER REACTIONS Customers often question the motivation behind price changes.[69] A price cut can be interpreted in different ways: the item is about to be replaced by a new model; the

---

MARKETING MEMO	MARKETING STRATEGIES TO AVOID RAISING PRICES

Given strong consumer resistance to price hikes, marketers go to great lengths to find alternative approaches that will allow them avoid increasing prices when they otherwise would have done so. Here are a few popular strategies:

- Shrinking the amount of product instead of raising the price. (Hershey Foods maintained its chocolate bar price but trimmed its size. Nestlé maintained its size but raised the price.)
- Substituting less expensive materials or ingredients. (Many candy companies substituted synthetic chocolate for real chocolate to fight price increases in cocoa.)
- Reducing or removing product features. (Sears engineered down a number of its appliances so they could be priced competitively with those sold in discount stores.)
- Removing or reducing product services such as installation and free delivery.
- Using less-expensive packaging material or larger package sizes.
- Reducing the number of sizes and models offered.
- Creating new economy brands. (Jewel food stores introduced 170 generic items selling at 10-percent to 30-percent less than national brands.)

---

item is faulty and is not selling well; the firm is in financial trouble; the price will come down even further; the quality has been reduced. A price increase, which would normally deter sales, may carry some positive meanings to customers: the item is "hot" and represents an unusually good value.

COMPETITOR REACTIONS Competitors are most likely to react when the number of firms is small, the product is homogeneous, and buyers are highly informed. Competitor reactions can be a special problem when they have a strong value proposition. Companies such as Transat A.T. have been combating competition by cutting prices.

Transat A.T.

Transat A.T. Inc., a 3-billion-dollar holiday tour operator based in Montreal, has been facing the challenge of competitor reactions to a booming market. The demand for tours has been healthy and in response new competitors have entered the market to get a piece of the pie. This has resulted in a simultaneous drop in tour prices and increase in market size. The cycle continues as competition continues to drop prices and increase consumer demand. Transat has dropped its prices by 8 percent to stay in the game while the number of travellers has increased by 10 percent, so although profits are still achievable, margins are being squeezed by price reductions.[70]

How can a firm anticipate a competitor's reactions? One way is to assume that the competitor reacts in a set way to price changes. The other is to assume that the competitor treats each price change as a fresh challenge and reacts according to self-interest at the time. A company will need to research its competitors' current financial situations, recent sales, customer loyalty, and corporate objectives. If a competitor has a market-share objective, it is likely to match the price change.[71] If it has a profit-maximization objective, it may react by increasing the advertising budget or improving product quality.

The problem is complicated because a competitor can put different interpretations on a price cut: that the company is trying to steal the market, that the company is doing poorly and trying to boost its sales, or that the company wants the whole industry to reduce prices to stimulate total demand.

Responding to Competitors' Price Changes

How should a firm respond to a price cut initiated by a competitor? In markets characterized by high product homogeneity, the firm should search for ways to enhance its augmented product. If it cannot find any, it will have to meet the price reduction. If the competitor raises its price in a homogeneous-product market, other firms might not match it unless the increase will benefit the industry as a whole. Then the leader will have to roll back the increase.

In nonhomogeneous-product markets, a firm has more latitude. It needs to consider the following issues: (1) Why did the competitor change the price? To steal the market, to utilize excess capacity, to meet changing cost conditions, or to lead an industry-wide price change? (2) Does the competitor plan to make the price change temporary or permanent? (3) What will happen to the company's market share and profits if it does not respond? Are other companies going to respond? (4) What are the competitor's and other firms' responses likely to be to each possible reaction?

Market leaders frequently face aggressive price-cutting by smaller firms trying to build market share. Using price, Fuji attacks Kodak, Schick attacks Gillette, and AMD attacks Intel. Brand leaders also face lower-priced private-store brands. The brand leader can respond in several ways:

- *Maintain price.* The leader might maintain its price and profit margin, believing that (1) it would lose too much profit if it reduced its price, (2) it would not lose much market share, and (3) it could regain market share when necessary. However, the argument against price maintenance is that the attacker gets more confident, the leader's sales force gets demoralized, and the leader loses more share than expected. The leader panics, lowers price to regain share, and finds that regaining its market position is more difficult than expected.

- *Maintain price and add value.* The leader could improve its product, services, and communications. The firm may find it cheaper to maintain price and spend money to improve perceived quality than to cut price and operate at a lower margin.

- *Reduce price.* The leader might drop its price to match a competitor's price. It might do so because (1) its costs fall with volume, (2) it would lose market share because the market is price-sensitive, and (3) it would be hard to rebuild market share once it were lost. This action cuts profits in the short run.

- *Increase price and improve quality.* The leader might raise its price and introduce new brands to bracket the attacking brand.

- *Launch a low-priced fighter line.* It might add lower-priced items to the line or create a separate, lower-priced brand.

The best response varies with the situation. The company has to consider the product's stage in the life cycle, its importance in the company's portfolio, the competitor's intentions and resources, the market's price and quality sensitivity, the behaviour of costs with volume, and the company's alternative opportunities.

An extended analysis of alternatives may not be feasible when the attack occurs. The company may have to react decisively within hours or days. It would make better sense to anticipate possible competitors' price changes and to prepare contingent responses. Figure 14.7 shows a *price-reaction program* to be used if a competitor cuts prices. Reaction programs for meeting price changes find their greatest application in industries where price changes occur with some frequency and where it is important to react quickly—for example, in the meatpacking, lumber, and oil industries.

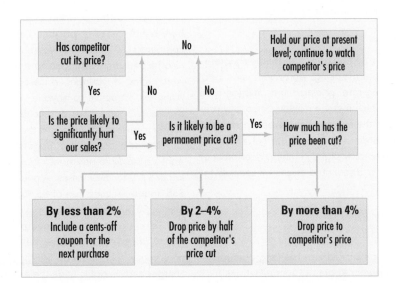

FIGURE 14.7

Price-Reaction Program for Meeting a Competitor's Price Cut

SUMMARY

1. Despite the increased role of nonprice factors in modern marketing, price remains a critical element of the marketing mix. Price is the only one of the four Ps that produces revenue; the others produce costs.

2. In setting pricing policy, a company follows a six-step procedure. It selects its pricing objective. It estimates the demand curve, the probable quantities it will sell at each possible price. It estimates how its costs vary at different levels of output, at different levels of accumulated production experience, and for differentiated marketing offers. It examines competitors' costs, prices, and offers. It selects a pricing method. It selects the final price.

3. Companies do not usually set a single price, but rather a pricing structure that reflects variations in geographical demand and costs, market-segment requirements, purchase timing, order levels, and other factors. Several price-adaptation strategies are available: (1) geographical pricing, (2) price discounts and allowances, (3) promotional pricing, and (4) differentiated pricing.

4. After developing pricing strategies, firms often face situations in which they need to change prices. A price decrease might be brought about by excess plant capacity, declining market share, a desire to dominate the market through lower costs, or economic recession. A price increase might be brought about by cost inflation or overdemand. Companies must carefully manage customer perceptions in raising prices.

5. Companies must anticipate competitor price changes and prepare contingent responses. There are a number of possible responses involving maintaining or changing price or quality.

6. The firm facing a competitor's price change must try to understand the competitor's intent and the likely duration of the change. Strategy often depends on whether a firm is producing homogeneous or nonhomogeneous products. Market leaders attacked by lower-priced competitors can choose to maintain price, raise the perceived quality of their product, reduce price, increase price and improve quality, or launch a low-priced fighter line.

APPLICATIONS

Marketing Debate: Is the Right Price a Fair Price?

Prices are often set to satisfy demand or to reflect the premium that consumers are willing to pay for a product or service. Some critics shudder, however, at the thought of $2 bottles of water, $150 running shoes, and $500 concert tickets.

Take a position: Prices should reflect the value that consumers are willing to pay *versus* Prices should reflect primarily the cost involved in making a product or service.

Marketing Discussion

Think of the various pricing methods described in the chapter—markup pricing, target-return pricing, perceived-value pricing, value pricing, going-rate pricing, and auction-type pricing. As a consumer, which method do you personally prefer to deal with? Why? If the average price were to stay the same, which would you prefer: for firms (1) to set one price and not deviate or (2) to employ slightly higher prices most of the year, but slightly lower discounted prices or specials for certain occasions.

Breakthrough Marketing: Koodo Mobile

The Canadian market for cellular service has long been dominated by three main players: Rogers Communications Inc., Bell Canada Enterprises Inc., and Telus Corporation. Consumers have been roped into long-term contracts and forced to pay high subscription prices by the three service providers, as the wireless plan options in Canada have been rather limited.

This has changed since the rollout of Koodo Mobile, owned by Telus, which launched the brand in March 2008. Kevin Banderk, Koodo's 34-year-old CEO (with the title Chief Koodo Officer), has a vision of the company being a "fat-free" alternative to the crowded mobile market. Koodo's no-frills, bare-bones mobility pricing is its main attraction, but the company's 80's-inspired workout advertising campaign has also helped draw attention to the brand. The market Koodo is targeting is younger, price-conscious consumers, but its plans are attractive to anyone who wants a flexible cellular-service plan and does not need all the extras that cellular-service providers bundle into their calling plans.

Koodo's competitor Rogers has calling plans ranging from $20 to $225 per month for personal use and plans starting at $150 for businesses. A one-time activation fee of about $35, monthly access fee of $6.95, and 911 emergency access fees of $0.50 are added to the plan rate. Rates of Bell Canada and Telus are similar, with their plans also starting at $20 per month, a system access fee between $6.95 and $8.95, and emergency 911 fees of $0.75. These are just the basic charges and do not include the extras such as text messaging, call display, voice mail, conference calling, call waiting, email, and other popular features that many subscribers add to their services. The biggest disadvantage to consumers is that to get the low-rate plans, a user must sign up for a 12-, 24-, or 36-month plan. If the customer chooses to break the contract, a cancellation fee as high as $400 is charged.

Koodo, however, is redefining cellular-service pricing. The company is taking a less complicated approach to wireless service through its lean cellphone plans. There are no fees for system activation, monthly system access, or 911 emergency access, which is relatively new to wireless carriers in Canada. Billing is also done by the second, not rounded up to the minute as is done by most cellular-service providers. A major benefit of going with Koodo is that it does not have any binding contracts and there are no cancellation fees if a customer chooses to leave.

Not only does Koodo offer plans starting from $15 a month, it also has a unique feature, called Tab, which lets subscribers put part or all of the price of their phone (up to $150)

onto a Tab. Each month, 10 percent of their cellular-service bill is put towards the Tab, so the more a user talks, the faster the Tab gets paid off. It can also be used as a credit account towards a new phone if a user so desires. For example, a user's Tab of $100, once paid off, can accumulate monthly contributions (up to $150) to be put towards the next phone purchase.

Koodo phones and talk plans are sold through its website (www.koodomobile.com), its Koodo Shop retail outlets, and major retailers in Canada including Best Buy, Future Shop, The Brick, London Drugs, Wal-Mart, and Zellers.

The Canadian government auctioned off a number of wireless spectrum licences in early 2008, enabling more companies like Koodo to enter the near-oligopolistic market and allow consumers more choice in cellular service. According to the Canadian Wireless Telecommunications Association, nearly 62 percent (or 20.1 million Canadians) subscribe to a wireless network, and these numbers are expected only to grow as more no-frills cellular-service providers like Koodo join the fray.

DISCUSSION QUESTIONS

1. In your opinion, how price-elastic is the demand for personal cellular service in Canada?

2. How would you describe Koodo's new low-price no-frills pricing strategy?

3. What are some challenges that Koodo will face in keeping its prices low?

4. What dangers does Telus face in introducing low-priced Koodo as an independent brand? Would you have retained the Telus brand name instead? Explain why.

Sources: Koodo Mobile website, www.koodomobile.com (viewed June 3, 2008); Bell Canada website, www.bell.ca (viewed June 4, 2008); Rogers Communications Canada website, www.rogers.com (viewed June 4, 2008); LuAnne LaSalle, "Consumers Poised to Become Wireless Winners," *Canadian Press*, May 26, 2008, p. B3; David George-Cosh and Don Mills, "Telus Targets Youth; Koodo Mobile," *National Post*, April 2, 2008, p. FP4; Diana O'Meara, "Koodo Mobility Targets Youth," *Calgary Herald*, March 19, 2008, p. E3; "Koodo Mobile, Canada's Newest Mobile Service Introduces Fat-Free Mobility," *Canada News Wire*, March 31, 2008; Catherine McLean, "Koodo Mobile Aims to Fight 'Bill Bulge,'" *The Globe and Mail*, March 18, 2008, p. B9; Catherine McLean, "Telus May Make Foray Into Discount Wireless Market," *The Globe and Mail*, December 14, 2007, p. B3.

PART
SIX

6

DELIVERING VALUE

CHAPTER 15

DESIGNING AND MANAGING INTEGRATED MARKETING CHANNELS

fifteen

Successful value creation needs successful value delivery. Holistic marketers are increasingly taking a value-network view of their businesses. Instead of limiting their focus to their immediate suppliers, distributors, and customers, they are examining the whole supply chain that links raw materials, components, and manufactured goods and shows how they move toward the final consumers. Companies are looking at their suppliers' suppliers upstream and at their distributors' customers downstream. They are looking at customer segments and considering a wide range of different possible means to sell, distribute, and service their offerings.

Royal Philips Electronics of the Netherlands is one of the world's biggest electronics companies and Europe's largest, with sales of over US$38 billion in 2007. Philips' electronics products are channelled towards the consumer primarily through local and international retailers. The company offers a broad range of products from high to low price/value quartiles, relying on a diverse distribution model that includes mass merchants, retail chains, independents, and small specialty stores. In order to work in the most effective way with these retail channels, Philips has created an organization designed around its retail customers, with dedicated global key account managers serving leading retailers such as Best Buy, Carrefour, Costco, Dixons, Tesco, and Country Ambassadors. Like many modern firms, Philips also sells via the Web through its own online store as well as through a number of other online retailers.

Sources: Kerry Capell, "Thinking Simple at Philips," *BusinessWeek*, December 11, 2006, p. 50; Royal Philips Electronics Annual Report, 2006; "Philips—Unfulfilled," *brandchannel.com*, June 20, 2005; Jennifer L. Schenker, "Fine-Tuning a Fuzzy Image," *TIMEeurope.com* (Spring 2002).

Companies today must build and manage a continuously evolving and increasingly complex channel system and value network. In this chapter, we consider strategic and tactical issues with integrating marketing channels and developing value networks. We will examine marketing-channel issues from the perspective of retailers, wholesalers, and physical distribution agencies in Chapter 16.

To learn how Yum! uses localization strategies to compete in China, visit www.pearsoned-asia.com/ marketingmanagementchina.

MARKETING CHANNELS AND VALUE NETWORKS

Most producers do not sell their goods directly to the final users; between them stands a set of intermediaries performing a variety of functions. These intermediaries constitute a marketing channel (also called a trade channel or distribution channel). Formally, **marketing channels** are sets of interdependent organizations involved in the process of making a product or service available for use or consumption. They are the set of pathways a product or service follows after production, culminating in purchase and use by the final end user.[1]

Some intermediaries—such as wholesalers and retailers—buy, take title to, and resell the merchandise; they are called *merchants*. Others—brokers, manufacturers' representatives, sales agents—search for customers and may negotiate on the producer's behalf but do not take title to the goods; they are called *agents*. Still others—transportation companies, independent warehouses, banks, advertising agencies—assist in the distribution process but neither take title to goods nor negotiate purchases or sales; they are called *facilitators*.

The Importance of Channels

A marketing channel system is the particular set of marketing channels a firm employs, and decisions about it are among the most critical ones management faces. In North America, channel members collectively have earned margins that account for 30 percent to 50 percent of the ultimate selling price. In contrast, advertising typically has accounted for less than 5 percent to 7 percent of the final price.[2] Marketing channels also represent a substantial opportunity cost. One of the chief roles of marketing channels is to convert potential buyers into profitable customers. Marketing channels must not just *serve* markets, they must also *make* markets.[3]

The channels chosen affect all other marketing decisions. The company's pricing depends on whether it uses mass merchandisers or high-quality boutiques. The firm's sales force and advertising decisions depend on how much training and motivation dealers need. In addition, channel decisions include relatively long-term commitments with other firms as well as a set of policies and procedures. When an automaker signs up independent dealers to sell its automobiles, the automaker cannot buy them out the next day and replace them with company-owned outlets. But at the same time, channel choices themselves depend on the company's marketing strategy with respect to segmentation, targeting, and positioning. Holistic marketers ensure that marketing decisions in all these different areas are made to collectively maximize value.

In managing its intermediaries, the firm must decide how much effort to devote to push versus pull marketing. A **push strategy** uses the manufacturer's sales force, trade-promotion money, or other means to induce intermediaries to carry, promote, and sell the product to end users. Push strategy is appropriate when there is low brand loyalty in a category, brand choice is made in the store, the product is an impulse item, and product benefits are well understood. In a **pull strategy** the manufacturer uses advertising, promotion, and other forms of communication to persuade consumers to demand the product from intermediaries, thus inducing the intermediaries to order it. Pull strategy is appropriate when there is high brand loyalty and high involvement in the category, when consumers are able to perceive differences between brands, and when they choose the brand before they go to the store.

Top marketing companies such as Coca-Cola, Intel, and Nike skillfully employ both push and pull strategies. Marketing activities directed towards the channel as part of a push strategy are more effective when accompanied by a well-designed and well-executed pull strategy that activates consumer demand. Some companies have created positions within their firms called Shopper Marketing to integrate these functions.

Shopper Marketing

Companies like Colgate Canada and Unilever Canada have established a new position called shopper marketing. The objective of the position is to get sales departments (that have traditionally focused on retailers) and marketing departments (that have focused on consumers) to think as one. Says Unilever's Lisa Klauser "It means getting everybody aligned around common objectives." Shopper marketers work to understand how and why consumers behave the way they do when they are in a store. They also work with retailers to help them understand shopping behaviour consumers use for particular product categories. Shopper marketers use a lot of data such as information from retailers' frequent-shopper card databases, syndicated data, and custom research including in-store shop-alongs or observation. Krista Cunningham, Shopper Marketing Manager of Oral Care at Colgate-Palmolive Canada, does a lot of in-store research to derive shopper insights that help her better understand the process that takes place between the first thought a consumer has about purchasing toothpaste or a new toothbrush and his or her final purchase. Colgate's research showed that many people stop and browse oral-care products but fail to make purchases because they are overwhelmed by all the choices facing them. To address this issue with regard to toothbrushes, Colgate developed new shelf displays to aid consumer choice. "Shelf talkers" displayed bristles from the different types of brushes, allowing consumers to feel the softness and texture of a brush before purchase. In addition to better product displays, shopper-marketing insight can also lead to the development of new products and better packaging.[4]

Channel Development

A new firm typically starts as a local operation selling in a fairly circumscribed market, using existing intermediaries. The number of such intermediaries is apt to be limited: a few manufacturers' sales agents, a few wholesalers, several established retailers, a few trucking companies, and a few warehouses. Deciding on the best channels might not be a problem; the problem is often to convince the available intermediaries to handle the firm's line.

If the firm is successful, it might branch into new markets and use different channels in different markets. In smaller markets, the firm might sell directly to retailers; in larger markets, it might sell through distributors. In rural areas, it might work with general-goods merchants; in urban areas, with limited-line merchants. In one part of the country, it might grant exclusive franchises; in another, it might sell through all outlets willing to handle the merchandise. In one country, it might use international sales agents; in another, it might partner with a local firm.

International markets pose distinct challenges. Customers' shopping habits can vary by country and many retailers, such as Germany's Aldi, the United Kingdom's Tesco, and Spain's Zara, have redefined themselves to a certain degree when entering a new market to better tailor their image to local needs and wants. Retailers that have largely stuck to the same selling formula regardless of geography, such as Eddie Bauer, Marks & Spencer, and Wal-Mart, have sometimes encountered trouble in entering new markets.[5]

In short, the channel system evolves as a function of local opportunities and conditions, emerging threats and opportunities, company resources and capabilities, and other factors. Consider some of the challenges Dell has encountered in recent years.

Dell

Dell revolutionized the personal computer category by selling products directly to customers via the telephone and later the Internet, rather than through retailers or resellers. Customers could custom design the exact PC they wanted, and rigorous cost cutting allowed for low everyday prices. Sound like a winning formula? It was, for almost two decades. But 2006 saw the company encounter a number of problems that led to a steep stock-price decline. First, reinvigorated competitors such as HP narrowed the gap in productivity and price. Always focused more on the business market, Dell struggled to sell effectively to the consumer market. A shift in consumer preferences to buy in retail stores as opposed to buying direct didn't help, but self-inflicted damage from an ultraefficient supply-chain model that squeezed costs—and quality—out of customer service was perhaps the most painful. Managers evaluated call-centre employees primarily on how long they stayed on each call—a recipe for disaster as scores of customers felt their problems were ignored or not properly handled. A lack of R&D spending that hindered new-product development and led to a lack of differentiation didn't help either. Clearly, Dell was entering a new chapter in its history that would require a fundamental rethinking of its channel strategy and its marketing approach as a whole.[6]

Hybrid Channels

Today's successful companies are also multiplying the number of "go-to-market" or **hybrid channels** in any one market area. In contrast to Dell, HP has used its sales force to sell to large accounts, outbound telemarketing to sell to medium-sized accounts, direct mail with an inbound number to sell to small accounts, retailers to sell to still smaller accounts, and the Internet to sell specialty items. Staples markets through its traditional retail channel, a direct-response Internet site, virtual malls, and thousands of links on affiliated sites.

Companies that manage hybrid channels must make sure these channels work well together and match each target customer's preferred ways of doing business. Customers expect *channel integration*, characterized by features such as:

- the ability to order a product online and pick it up at a convenient retail location
- the ability to return an online-ordered product to a nearby store of the retailer
- the right to receive discounts and promotional offers based on total online and offline purchases

Circuit City estimated in-store pick-ups accounted for more than half its online sales in 2006.[7] Here's a specific example of a company that has carefully managed its multiple channels:

Mountain Equipment Co-op (MEC)

Nothing is more frustrating than buying hiking boots that cripple your feet. At Mountain Equipment Co-op (MEC), a consumer cooperative with 2.6 million active members, outdoor enthusiasts can easily avoid problems. In 11 MEC stores across the country, customers are lighting up gas stoves, pitching tents, and snuggling deep into sleeping bags aided by MEC's knowledgeable staff (who are outdoor enthusiasts themselves). MEC stores are designed to provide an experience, not just sell goods. MEC has been lauded by industry analysts for the seamless integration of its retail store, website, mail-order catalogues, value-priced outlets, and toll-free order number. Whether people shop in-store, online, or through MEC's catalogues, they are provided with a wealth of information to help them make better choices. Knowledgeable staff help customers with everything from choosing the right paddle for a particular type of kayaking to planning and outfitting a family canoe trip. Integrating channels is important since research has shown that dual-channel shoppers spend significantly more than single-channel shoppers, and tri-channel shoppers spend even more.[8]

Understanding Customer Needs

Consumers may choose the channels they prefer based on a number of factors: the price, product assortment, and convenience of a channel option, as well as their own particular shopping goals (economic, social, or experiential).[9] As with products, segmentation exists, and marketers employing

Mountain Equipment Co-op provides its members with a wealth of information no matter which channel they use.

different types of channels must be aware that different consumers have different needs during the purchase process. See what some supermarkets are doing to attract Chinese and South Asian consumers:

T&T Supermarket

Supermarket chains, large and small, are modifying their product assortments to better reach consumers of South Asian and Chinese descent. Together, these consumer groups make up approximately half of all visible minorities in Canada. They account for $5.7 million of grocery spending in Toronto and Vancouver alone and, despite being frugal, spend 23-percent more on groceries per week than the average Canadian household. No wonder they are attractive targets. In 2003, T&T Supermarket of Richmond, B.C., began specializing in foods desired by Chinese Canadians and has recently expanded its product offerings to items like coconut milk and instant noodles with chili to better meet the needs of South Asian consumers as well. Large supermarket chains like No Frills and Food Basics are also starting to change course to lure business from these groups. In addition to offering prices that appeal to these price-conscious consumers, they are stocking more fresh, unpackaged produce and meat, and they are installing tanks for fresh fish and crab.[10]

Researchers Nunes and Cespedes argue that, in many markets, buyers fall into one of four categories:[11]

1. *Habitual shoppers* purchase from the same places in the same manner over time.
2. *High-value deal seekers* know their needs and "channel surf" a great deal before buying at the lowest possible price.
3. *Variety-loving shoppers* gather information in many channels, take advantage of high-touch services, and then buy in their favourite channel, regardless of price.
4. *High-involvement shoppers* gather information in all channels, make their purchase in a low-cost channel, but take advantage of customer support from a high-touch channel.

One study of 40 grocery and clothing retailers in France, Germany, and the United Kingdom found that retailers in those countries served three types of shoppers: (1) *service/quality customers* who cared most about the variety and performance of products in stores as well as the service provided; (2) *price/value customers* who were most concerned about spending their money wisely; and (3) *affinity customers* who sought primarily stores that suited people like themselves or the members of groups they aspired to join. As Figure 15.1 shows, customer profiles for these types of retailers differed across the three markets: in France, shoppers placed more importance on service and quality, in the United Kingdom, affinity, and in Germany, price and value.[12]

Even the same consumer, though, may choose to use different channels for different functions in making a purchase. For instance, someone may choose to browse through a catalogue before visiting a store or take a test-drive at a dealer before ordering a car online. Consumers may also seek different types of channels depending on the particular types of goods involved. Some consumers are willing to "trade up" to retailers offering higher-end goods such as TAG Heuer watches or Callaway golf clubs; these same consumers are also willing to "trade down" to discount retailers to buy private-label paper towels, detergent, or vitamins.[13]

Value Networks

A supply-chain view of a firm sees markets as destination points and amounts to a linear view of the flow. The company should first think of the target market, however, and then design the supply chain backwards from that point. This view has been called **demand chain planning**. Northwestern's Don Schultz says: "A demand chain management approach doesn't just push things through the system. It emphasizes what solutions consumers are looking for, not what products we are trying to sell them." Schultz has suggested that the traditional marketing "four Ps" be replaced by a new acronym, SIVA, which stands for solutions, information, value, and access.[14]

An even broader view sees a company at the centre of a **value network**—a system of partnerships and alliances that a firm creates to source, augment, and deliver its offerings. A value network includes a firm's suppliers and its suppliers' suppliers, and its immediate customers and their end customers. The value network includes valued relations with others such as university researchers and government-approval agencies.

FIGURE 15.1

What Do European Consumers Value?

Source: Peter N. Child, Suzanne Heywood, and Michael Kliger, "Do Retail Brands Travel?" *The McKinsley Quarterly* (January 2002): 11–13. Reprinted by permission.

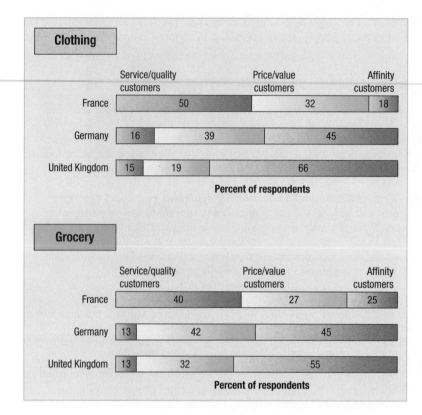

A company needs to orchestrate these parties in order to deliver superior value to the target market. Palm, the leading manufacturer of handheld devices, consists of a whole community of suppliers and assemblers of semiconductor components, plastic cases, LCD displays, and accessories; of offline and online resellers; and of 275 000 developers in the Palm Developer Network who have created over 21 000 software programs and 100 hardware add-ons for the Palm operating systems for handheld computers and smartphones.

Demand-chain planning yields several insights. First, the company can estimate whether more money is made upstream or downstream, in case it might want to integrate backwards or forwards. Second, the company is more aware of disturbances anywhere in the supply chain that might cause costs, prices, or supplies to change suddenly. Third, companies can go online with their business partners to carry on faster and more accurate communications, transactions, and payments to reduce costs, speed up information, and increase accuracy. For example, Ford not only manages numerous supply chains but also sponsors or transacts on many B2B websites and exchanges as needs arise.

Managing this value network has required companies to make increasing investments in information technology (IT) and software. Firms have introduced supply chain management (SCM) software and invited such software firms as SAP and Oracle to design comprehensive enterprise resource planning (ERP) systems to manage cash flow, manufacturing, human resources, purchasing, and other major functions within a unified framework. They hope to break up department silos and carry out core business processes seamlessly. In most cases, however, companies are still a long way from truly comprehensive ERP systems.

Marketers, for their part, have traditionally focused on the side of the value network that looks towards the customer, adopting customer relationship management (CRM) software and practices. In the future, they will increasingly participate in and influence their companies' upstream activities and become network managers, not just product and customer managers.

THE ROLE OF MARKETING CHANNELS

Why would a producer delegate some of the selling job to intermediaries? Delegation means relinquishing some control over how and to whom the products are sold. But producers can often improve effectiveness and efficiency by using intermediaries. Through their contacts, experience,

TABLE 15.1	CHANNEL MEMBER FUNCTIONS

- Gather information about potential and current customers, competitors, and other actors and forces in the marketing environment.
- Develop and disseminate persuasive communications to stimulate purchasing.
- Reach agreements on price and other terms so that transfer of ownership or possession can be effected.
- Place orders with manufacturers.
- Acquire the funds to finance inventories at different levels in the marketing channel.
- Assume risks connected with carrying out channel work.
- Provide for the successive storage and movement of physical products.
- Provide for buyers' payment of their bills through banks and other financial institutions.
- Oversee actual transfer of ownership from one organization or person to another.

specialization, and scale of operation, intermediaries make goods widely available and accessible to target markets, usually offering the firm more than it can achieve on its own.[15]

Many producers lack the financial resources and expertise to sell directly on their own. The William Wrigley Jr. Company would not find it practical to establish small retail gum shops throughout the world or to sell gum by mail order. It would need to sell gum along with many other small products and would end up in the drugstore and grocery store business. Wrigley finds it easier to work through the extensive network of privately owned distribution organizations. Even General Motors would be hard-pressed to replace all the tasks done by its 732 dealer outlets located across Canada.

Channel Functions and Flows

A marketing channel performs the work of moving goods from producers to consumers. It overcomes the time, place, and possession gaps that separate goods and services from those who need or want them. Members of the marketing channel perform a number of key functions (see Table 15.1).

Some functions (physical, title, promotion) constitute a *forward flow* of activity from the company to the customer; other functions (ordering and payment) constitute a *backward flow* from customers to the company. Still others (information, negotiation, finance, and risk taking) occur in both directions. Five flows are illustrated in Figure 15.2 for the marketing of forklift trucks. If these

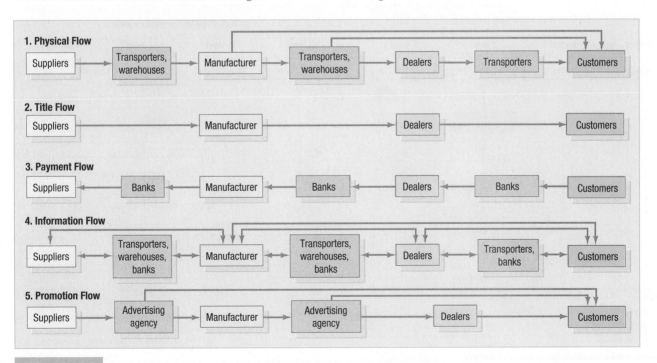

FIGURE 15.2

Five Marketing Flows in the Marketing Channel for Forklift Trucks flows were superimposed in one diagram, the tremendous complexity of even simple marketing channels would be apparent.

A manufacturer selling a physical product and services might require three channels: a *sales channel*, a *delivery channel*, and a *service channel*. To sell its Bowflex fitness equipment, the Nautilus Group historically has emphasized as sales channels direct marketing via television infomercials and ads, inbound/outbound call centres, response mailings, and the Internet; UPS ground service as the delivery channel; and local repair people as the service channel. Reflecting shifting consumer buying habits, Nautilus now also sells Bowflex through commercial, retail, and specialty retail channels.

The question is not *whether* various channel functions need to be performed—they must be—but rather, *who* is to perform them. All channel functions have three things in common: they use up scarce resources; they can often be performed better through specialization; and they can be shifted among channel members. When the manufacturer shifts some functions to intermediaries, the producer's costs and prices are lower, but the intermediary must add a charge to cover its work. If the intermediaries are more efficient than the manufacturer, prices to consumers should be lower. If consumers perform some functions themselves, they should enjoy even lower prices. Changes in channel institutions thus reflect largely the discovery of more efficient ways to combine or separate the economic functions that provide assortments of goods to target customers.

Channel Levels

The producer and the final customer are part of every channel. We will use the number of intermediary levels to designate the length of a channel. Figure 15.3(a) illustrates several consumer-goods marketing channels of different lengths.

A **zero-level channel** (also called a **direct marketing channel**) consists of a manufacturer selling directly to the final customer. The major examples are door-to-door sales, home parties, mail order, telemarketing, TV selling, Internet selling, and manufacturer-owned stores. Avon sales representatives sell cosmetics door-to-door; Tupperware representatives sell kitchen goods through home parties; the Royal Canadian Mint sells coins to collectors through its website; Bell uses the telephone to prospect for new customers or to sell enhanced services to existing customers; Time-Life sells music and video collections through TV commercials or longer "infomercials"; and Apple sells computers and other consumer electronics through its own stores.

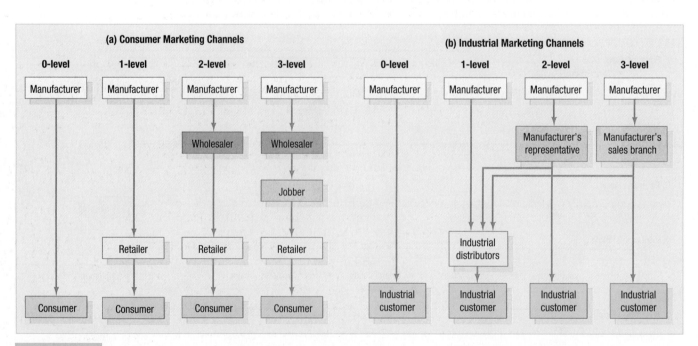

FIGURE 15.3

Consumer and Industrial Marketing Channels

A *one-level channel* contains one selling intermediary, such as a retailer. A *two-level channel* contains two intermediaries. In consumer markets, these are typically a wholesaler and a retailer. A *three-level channel* contains three intermediaries. In the meatpacking industry, wholesalers sell to jobbers, which sell to small retailers. In Japan, food distribution may include as many as six levels. From the producer's point of view, obtaining information about end users and exercising control becomes more difficult as the number of channel levels increases.

Figure 15.3(b) shows channels commonly used in B2B marketing. An industrial-goods manufacturer can use its sales force to sell directly to industrial customers; or it can sell to industrial distributors, which sell to the industrial customers; or it can sell through manufacturer's representatives or its own sales branches directly to industrial customers or indirectly to industrial customers through industrial distributors. Zero-, one-, and two-level marketing channels are quite common.

Channels normally describe a forward movement of products from source to user, but there are also *reverse-flow channels*. These are important in the following cases: (1) to reuse products or containers (such as refillable chemical-carrying drums); (2) to refurbish products (such as circuit boards or computers) for resale; (3) to recycle products (such as paper); and (4) to dispose of products and packaging (waste products). Several intermediaries play a role in reverse-flow channels, including manufacturers' redemption centres, community groups, traditional intermediaries such as soft-drink intermediaries, trash-collection specialists, recycling centres, trash-recycling brokers, and central processing warehousing.[16]

Service Sector Channels

Marketing channels are not limited to the distribution of physical goods. Producers of services and ideas also face the problem of making their output available and accessible to target populations. Schools develop "educational-dissemination systems" and public-health providers develop "health-delivery systems." Institutions like Queen's School of Business must figure out agencies and locations for reaching a population spread out over a large area.

Queen's School of Business

In 1919, Queen's launched the first commerce degree offered in Canada. Today, Queen's reaches a wide variety of business students and executives. It offers undergraduate, MBA, executive MBA, MSc, and doctoral degree programs, as well as nondegree executive-education programs for working professionals. Some programs are delivered through traditional classroom settings, others are offered using video-conferencing facilities, and a third set is given right on the premises of companies that want tailored programs. Those interested in Queen's programs can learn about them online, by attending trade shows like MBA fairs, through information sessions held by the school in cities across the country, or through information presented in brochures tailored to different programs. Queen's School of Business also reaches various channels by publishing case studies and through its monthly newsletter, *The Inquiry*, in both print and online formats.

Marketing channels also keep changing in "person" marketing. Besides live and programmed entertainment, entertainers, musicians, and other artists can reach prospective and existing fans online in many ways—via their own websites, social community sites such as MySpace, and third-party websites. Even legendary former-Beatle Paul McCartney decided to end his 45-year relationship with music conglomerate E.M.I. to launch, in June 2007, his new album, *Memory Almost Full*, as the debut release from Hear Music, a record label cofounded by Starbucks, to be sold at the company's coffee shops, as well as in record stores and on iTunes.[17] Politicians also must choose a mix of channels—mass media, rallies, coffee hours, spot TV ads, direct mail, billboards, faxes, email, blogs, podcasts, websites—for delivering their messages to voters.[18]

As Internet and other technologies advance, service industries such as banking, insurance, travel, and stock buying and selling are operating through new channels. Kodak offers its customers four different ways to print their digital photos—minilabs in retail outlets, home printers, online services with the Kodak-owned Ofoto website, and self-service kiosks. Kodak, the world leader with 80 000 kiosks including 2000 at Wal-Mart stores, makes money both by selling kiosks and by supplying the units with the chemical and paper used to make the prints.[19]

The Queen's School of Business uses multiple channels to deliver its high-quality programs.

CHANNEL-DESIGN DECISIONS

Designing a marketing channel system requires analyzing customer needs, establishing channel objectives, and identifying and evaluating major channel alternatives.

Analyzing Customers' Desired Service-Output Levels

In designing the marketing channel, the marketer must understand the service-output levels its target customers want. Channels produce five service outputs:

1. *Lot size*—The number of units the channel permits a typical customer to purchase on one occasion. In buying cars for its fleet, Hertz prefers a channel from which it can buy a large lot size; a household wants a channel that permits buying a lot size of one.

2. *Waiting and delivery time*—The average time customers wait for receipt of the goods when using a particular channel. Customers increasingly prefer faster and faster delivery channels.

3. *Spatial convenience*—The degree to which the marketing channel makes it easy for customers to purchase the product. Chevrolet, for example, offers greater spatial convenience than Cadillac, because there are more Chevrolet dealers. Chevrolet's greater market decentralization helps customers save on transportation and search costs in buying and repairing an automobile.

4. *Product variety*—The assortment breadth provided by the marketing channel. Normally, customers prefer a greater assortment because more choices increase the chance of finding what they need.

5. *Service backup*—The add-on services (credit, delivery, installation, repairs) provided by the channel. The greater the service backup, the greater the work provided by the channel.[20]

The marketing channel designer knows that providing greater service outputs also means increasing channel costs and raising prices for customers. Different customers have different service needs. The success of discount stores indicates that many consumers are willing to accept smaller service outputs if they can save money.

Establishing Objectives and Constraints

Marketers should state their channel objectives in terms of targeted service-output levels. Under competitive conditions, channel institutions should arrange their functional tasks to minimize total channel costs and still provide desired levels of service outputs.[21] Usually, planners can identify several market segments that want different service levels. Effective planning requires determining which market segments to serve and choosing the best channels for each.

Channel objectives vary with product characteristics. Perishable products require more direct marketing. Bulky products, such as building materials, require channels that minimize the shipping distance and the amount of handling. Nonstandard products, such as custom-built machinery and specialized business forms, are sold directly by company sales representatives. Products requiring installation or maintenance services, such as heating and cooling systems, are usually sold and maintained by the company or by franchised dealers. High-unit-value products such as generators and turbines are often sold through a company sales force rather than intermediaries.

A number of other factors affect channel objectives. In entering new markets, for instance, firms often closely observe what other firms from their home market are doing in those markets. France's Auchan considered the presence of its French rivals Leclerc and Casino in Poland, a key driver for it to also enter that market.[22]

Marketers must adapt their channel objectives to the larger environment. When economic conditions are depressed, producers want to move their goods to market using shorter channels and without services that add to the final price of the goods. Legal regulations and restrictions also affect channel design. The Competition Bureau looks unfavourably on channel arrangements that substantially lessen competition or create a monopoly.

Identifying and Evaluating Major Channel Alternatives

Companies can choose from a wide variety of channels for reaching customers—from sales forces to agents, distributors, dealers, direct mail, telemarketing, and the Internet. Each channel has unique strengths as well as weaknesses. Sales forces can handle complex products and transactions, but they are expensive. The Internet is much less expensive, but it may not be as effective with complex products. Distributors can create sales, but the company loses direct contact with customers. Manufacturers' representatives are able to contact customers at a low cost per customer because several clients share the cost, but the selling effort per customer is less intense than if company sales representatives did the selling.

The problem is further complicated by the fact that most companies now use a mix of channels. The idea is that each channel reaches a different segment of buyers and delivers the right products at the least cost. When this doesn't happen, there is usually channel conflict and excessive cost.

A channel alternative is described by three elements: the types of available business intermediaries, the number of intermediaries needed, and the terms and responsibilities of each channel member.

TYPES OF INTERMEDIARIES A firm needs to identify the types of intermediaries available to carry on its channel work. Table 15.2 lists channel alternatives identified by a consumer-electronics company that produces global positioning systems (GPS).

Companies should search for innovative marketing channels. Medion sold 600 000 PCs in Europe, mostly via major one- or two-week "burst promotions" at Aldi's supermarkets.[23] Columbia House has successfully merchandised music albums through the mail and Internet. Bloomex, which

TABLE 15.2	CHANNEL ALTERNATIVES FOR MANUFACTURER OF AUTOMOBILE GPS SYSTEMS

- The company could sell its GPS systems to automobile manufacturers to be installed as original equipment.
- The company could sell its GPS systems to auto dealers.
- The company could sell its GPS systems to retail automotive-equipment dealers through a direct sales force or through distributors.
- The company could sell its GPS systems to GPS specialist dealers through a direct sales force or dealers.
- The company could sell its GPS systems through mail-order catalogues.
- The company could sell its GPS systems through mass merchandisers such as Best Buy and Future Shop.

bills itself as Canada's national floral company, uses a unique business model so that it can send fresher flowers at lower prices than its competitors'. Since customers order directly through its website, it can provide excellent service and delivery guarantees. (See "Marketing Insight: How CarMax Is Transforming the Auto Business.")

Sometimes a company chooses a new or unconventional channel because of the difficulty, cost, or ineffectiveness of working with the dominant channel. The advantage is that the company will encounter less competition during the initial move into this channel. Years ago, after trying to sell its inexpensive Timex watches through regular jewellery stores, the U.S. Time Company placed them instead in fast-growing mass-merchandise outlets. Frustrated with a printed catalogue it saw as out-of-date and unprofessional, commercial lighting company Display Supply & Lighting developed an interactive online catalogue that drove down costs, sped up the sales process, and increased revenue.[24]

NUMBER OF INTERMEDIARIES Companies must decide on the number of intermediaries to use at each channel level. Three strategies are available: exclusive distribution, selective distribution, and intensive distribution.

Exclusive distribution means severely limiting the number of intermediaries. It's appropriate when the producer wants to maintain control over the service level and outputs offered by the resellers, and it often includes *exclusive dealing* arrangements. By granting exclusive distribution, the producer hopes to obtain more dedicated and knowledgeable selling. Exclusive distribution requires a closer partnership between seller and reseller and is used in the distribution of new automobiles, some major appliances, and some women's apparel brands. Exclusive deals between suppliers and retailers are becoming a mainstay for specialists looking for an edge in a business

By dealing directly with both growers and end consumers, BloomEx can offer fresher flowers and superior customer service at lower prices.

MARKETING **INSIGHT**	HOW CARMAX IS TRANSFORMING THE AUTO BUSINESS

For years, buying a used car was considered a dangerous and risky business; used-car salespeople were stock figures in comedy routines. Then CarMax emerged to change the face of the industry and its standards.

Circuit City, a major U.S. retailer of electronic products, started CarMax, the Auto Superstore, in 1993 in Richmond, Virginia, where its headquarters are located. CarMax is now the U.S.'s leading specialty retailer of used cars; it operates 80 used-car superstores in 19 states and has one Canadian operation in Newfoundland. CarMax also operates a number of new-car franchises that are integrated with its used-car superstores and annually sells a total of over 300 000 cars.

What's so special about CarMax? The company locates its used-car superstores, each carrying around 500 cars, on large lots on the outskirts of a city near a major highway. Customers enter an attractive display room, where a sales associate finds out what kind of car they want and then escorts them to a computer kiosk. Using a touch screen, the associate retrieves a full listing of the cars in stock that meet the customer's criteria. A colour display of each car can be shown, along with the vehicle's features and its fixed selling price. The company has over 25 000 cars in all, nearly every make and model.

There is no price negotiation. The salesperson, paid a commission on the number of cars sold rather than on their value, has no incentive to push higher-priced cars. The customer is informed that CarMax mechanics have carried out a 110-point inspection and made any necessary repairs beforehand. Furthermore, a car buyer receives a five-day money-back guarantee and a 30-day comprehensive warranty. If the buyer wants financing, the CarMax associate can arrange it in 20 minutes. The entire process typically takes less than one hour.

But tight margins mean that CarMax must run a tight ship, buying and selling cars at the right price. Here are some key facts and figures that underlie its business model:

- 25 percent—percentage of sellers who say yes to CarMax's offer
- six—number of days it takes to recondition a car
- $1000—average money spent reconditioning a car
- 30—number of days before a car sells
- 80 percent—percentage of buyers who finance at CarMax
- $1807—average gross profit on a sale

CarMax uses a sophisticated inventory system to keep track of which models sell and when demand shifts. Each car is fitted with an RFID tag to track how long it sits and when a test drive occurs. Eight hundred CarMax buyers draw on the company's voluminous databases to appraise trade-in vehicles at exactly the right price to make sure that any transaction that occurs is profitable to the company. Although the major U.S. auto makers have experienced a decline in sales and profitability in recent years, CarMax has thrived.

Sources: Jonathan Fahey, "Used Cars, New," *Forbes*, March 27, 2006, pp. 98–100; Michael Myser, "The Wal-Mart of Used Cars," *Business 2.0* (September 2006): 58–59; Laura Heller, "Circuit City Restructures, Spins Off CarMax Unit," *DSN Retailing Today*, March 11, 2002, pp. 3–4; Arlena Sawyers, "CarMax Is out of the Red, in the Pink," *Automotive News*, April 16, 2001, p. 28.

world that is increasingly driven by price.[25] When the legendary Italian designer label Gucci found its image severely tarnished by overexposure from licensing and discount stores, it decided to end contracts with third-party suppliers, control its distribution, and open its own stores to bring back some of the lustre.[26]

Selective distribution relies on more than a few but less than all of the intermediaries willing to carry a particular product. It makes sense for established companies and for new companies seeking distributors. The company does not need to worry about too many outlets; it can gain adequate market coverage with more control and less cost than intensive distribution. Lee Valley Tools is a good example of selective distribution.

Lee Valley Tools Ltd.

Lee Valley Tools is a family-owned business headquartered in Ottawa and founded in 1978. It manufactures and sells tools for serious woodworkers and gardeners and has over 5000 products. About one third of its total sales volume comes from products of its own design, sold using the Veritas® brand name. Lee Valley fully guarantees all of the tools it sells, whether they

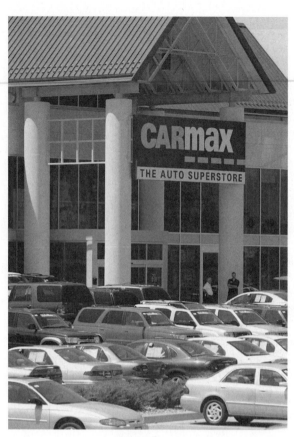

CarMax has streamlined the used-car purchase and revolutionized the business with its unique database of over 25 000 cars.

are manufactured by the company or are sourced from its suppliers located around the world. Lee Valley has only 13 retail outlets located across Canada. It also sells through its website and its catalogues. Lee Valley can use such selective distribution because it treats all its customers like friends. It never uses commissioned sales staff because it believes this leads to sales pressure that is against Lee Valley's philosophy of providing good advice. Providing such advice and never encouraging people to spend more than they can afford not only guarantees high levels of customer satisfaction, it also results in low return rates. Lee Valley believes it is best to get the right tool to the right customer the first time around.[27]

In **intensive distribution**, the manufacturer places the goods or services in as many outlets as possible. This strategy is generally used for items such as snack foods, soft drinks, newspapers, candies, and gum—products that consumers seek to buy frequently or in a variety of locations. Convenience stores such as Mac's, Couche Tarde, 7-Eleven, and gas-station-linked stores have survived by selling items that provide just that—location and time convenience.

Manufacturers are constantly tempted to move from exclusive or selective distribution to more intensive distribution to increase coverage and sales. This strategy may help in the short term, but it can hurt long-term performance. Intensive distribution increases product and service availability but may also encourage retailers to compete aggressively. Price wars can then erode profitability, potentially dampening retailer interest in supporting the product and harming brand equity. Some firms avoid intensive distribution and do not want to be sold everywhere. After Sears department stores acquired discount chain Kmart in 2005, Nike pulled all its products from Sears to make sure that Kmart could not carry the brand.[28]

TERMS AND RESPONSIBILITIES OF CHANNEL MEMBERS   Each channel member must be treated with respect and given the opportunity to be profitable.[29] The main elements in the "trade-relations mix" are price policies, conditions of sale, territorial rights, and specific services to be performed by each party.

- Price policy calls for the producer to establish a price list and schedule of discounts and allowances that intermediaries see as equitable and sufficient.

- Conditions of sale refers to payment terms and producer guarantees. Most producers grant cash discounts to distributors for early payment. Producers might also provide distributors a guarantee against defective merchandise or price declines. A guarantee against price declines gives distributors an incentive to buy larger quantities.

- Distributors' territorial rights define the distributors' territories and the terms under which the producer will enfranchise other distributors. Distributors normally expect to receive full credit for all sales in their territory, whether or not they did the selling.

- Mutual services and responsibilities must be carefully spelled out, especially in franchised and exclusive-agency channels. McDonald's provides franchisees with a building, promotional support, a record-keeping system, training, and general administrative and technical assistance. In turn, franchisees are expected to satisfy company standards for the physical facilities, cooperate with new promotional programs, furnish requested information, and buy supplies from specified vendors.

Evaluating the Major Alternatives

Each channel alternative needs to be evaluated against economic, control, and adaptive criteria.

ECONOMIC CRITERIA   Each channel alternative will produce a different level of sales and costs. Figure 15.4 shows how six different sales channels stack up in terms of the value added per sale and the cost per transaction. For example, in the sale of industrial products costing between $2000 and $5000, the cost per transaction has been estimated at $500 (field sales), $200 (distributors), $50 (telesales), and $10 (Internet). In the sale of retail banking services, a Booz Allen Hamilton study shows the average transaction at a full-service branch costs the bank $4.07, a

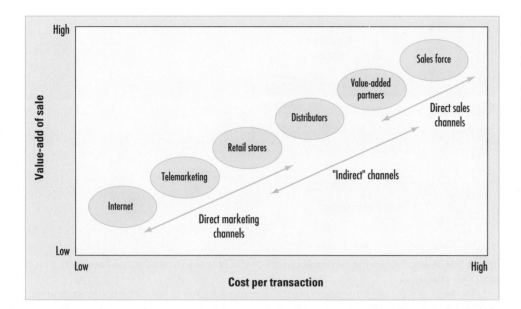

FIGURE 15.4

The Value-Adds versus Costs of Different Channels

Source: Oxford Associates, adapted from Dr. Rowland T. Moriarty, Cubex Corp.

phone transaction costs 54 cents, and an ATM transaction 27 cents, but a typical web-based transaction costs only 1 cent.[30]

Firms will try to align customers and channels to maximize demand at the lowest overall cost. Clearly, sellers try to replace high-cost channels with low-cost channels as long as the value added per sale is sufficient. At Vanguard, an asset management firm, service representatives used the telephone to train customers to use its websites. As a result, Vanguard was able to cut staff in half, an important accomplishment given that a phone call to a representative cost the company $9 versus pennies for a web log-in.[31]

As an example of an economic analysis of channel choices, consider the following situation:

A furniture manufacturer based in Halifax wants to sell its line to retailers on the west coast. The manufacturer is trying to decide between two alternatives: One calls for hiring ten new sales representatives who would operate out of a sales office in Vancouver. They would receive a base salary plus commissions. The other alternative is to use a Vancouver-based manufacturers' sales agency that has extensive contacts with retailers. The agency has 30 sales representatives who would receive a commission based on their sales.

The first step in the analysis is to estimate how many sales are likely to be generated by a company sales force and the sales agency. On one hand, a company sales force will concentrate on the company's products, will be better trained to sell those products, will be more aggressive because each rep's future depends on the company's success, and will be more successful because many customers prefer to deal directly with the company. On the other hand, the sales agency has 30 representatives, not just ten; it may be just as aggressive as a direct sales force, depending on the commission level; it may be better received by customers as more independent; and it may have extensive contacts and marketplace knowledge. The marketer needs to evaluate all these factors in formulating a demand function for the two different channels.

The next step is to estimate the costs of selling different volumes through each channel. The cost schedules are shown in Figure 15.5. The fixed costs of engaging a sales agency are lower than those of establishing a new company sales office, but costs rise faster through an agency because sales agents get a larger commission than company salespeople.

The final step is comparing sales and costs. As Figure 15.5 shows, there is one sales level (S_B) at which selling costs are the same for the two channels. The sales agency is thus the better channel for any sales volume below S_B, and the company sales branch is better at any volume above S_B. Given this information, it is not surprising that sales agents tend to be used by smaller firms or by large firms in smaller territories where the volume is low.

CONTROL AND ADAPTIVE CRITERIA Using a sales agency poses a control problem. A sales agency is an independent firm seeking to maximize its profits. Agents may concentrate on the customers who buy the most, not necessarily on those who buy the manufacturer's goods. Furthermore,

FIGURE 15.5

Break-Even Cost Chart for
the Choice between a
Company Sales Force and a
Manufacturer's Sales Agency

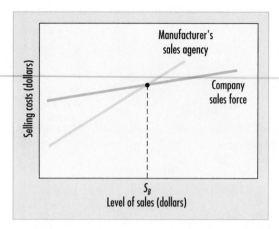

FIGURE 15.5

Break-Even Cost Chart for
the Choice between a
Company Sales Force and a
Manufacturer's Sales Agency

agents might not master the technical details of the company's product or handle its promotion materials effectively.

To develop a channel, members must make some degree of commitment to each other for a specified period of time. Yet these commitments invariably lead to a decrease in the producer's ability to respond to a changing marketplace. In rapidly changing, volatile, or uncertain product markets, the producer needs channel structures and policies that provide high adaptability.

CHANNEL-MANAGEMENT DECISIONS

After a company has chosen a channel system, it must select, train, motivate, and evaluate individual intermediaries for each channel. It must also modify channel design and arrangements over time.

Selecting Channel Members

To customers, the channels are the company. Consider the negative impression customers would get of Rogers, Petro-Canada, or Mercedes-Benz if one or more of their outlets or dealers consistently appeared dirty, inefficient, or unpleasant.

To facilitate channel-member selection, producers should determine which characteristics distinguish the better intermediaries. They should evaluate the number of years in business, other lines carried, growth and profit record, financial strength, cooperativeness, and service reputation. If the intermediaries are sales agents, producers should evaluate the number and character of other lines carried and the size and quality of the sales force. If the intermediaries are department stores that want exclusive distribution, the producer should evaluate locations, future-growth potential, and type of clientele.

Training and Motivating Channel Members

A company needs to view its intermediaries in the same way it views its end users. It needs to determine intermediaries' needs and construct a channel positioning such that its channel offering is tailored to provide superior value to these intermediaries.

Encouraging channel members to perform as well as possible starts with understanding their needs and wants. The company should plan and implement careful training programs, market research programs, and other capability-building programs to improve intermediaries' performance. Microsoft requires third-party service engineers to complete a set of courses and take certification exams. Those who pass are formally recognized as Microsoft Certified Professionals, and they can use this designation to promote their own business. Others use customer surveys rather than exams. The company must constantly communicate its view that the intermediaries are partners in a joint effort to satisfy end users of the product.

Producers vary greatly in their skill in managing distributors. **Channel power** is the ability to alter channel members' behaviour so that they take actions they would not have taken otherwise.[32] Manufacturers can draw on the following types of power to elicit cooperation:

- *Coercive power.* A manufacturer threatens to withdraw a resource or terminate a relationship if intermediaries fail to cooperate. This power can be effective, but its exercise produces resentment and can generate conflict and lead the intermediaries to organize countervailing power.

- *Reward power.* The manufacturer offers intermediaries an extra benefit for performing specific acts or functions. Reward power typically produces better results than coercive power, but it can be overrated. The intermediaries may come to expect a reward every time the manufacturer wants a certain behaviour to occur.

- *Legitimate power.* The manufacturer requests a behaviour that is warranted under the contract. As long as the intermediaries view the manufacturer as a legitimate leader, legitimate power works.

- *Expert power.* The manufacturer has special knowledge the intermediaries value. Once the intermediaries acquire this expertise, however, expert power weakens. The manufacturer must continue to develop new expertise so that the intermediaries will want to continue cooperating.

- *Referent power.* The manufacturer is so highly respected that intermediaries are proud to be associated with it. Companies such as RIM, Caterpillar, and Hewlett-Packard have high referent power.[33]

Coercive and reward power are objectively observable; legitimate, expert, and referent power are more subjective and depend on the ability and willingness of parties to recognize them.

Most producers see gaining intermediaries' cooperation as a huge challenge.[34] They often use positive motivators, such as higher margins, special deals, premiums, cooperative advertising allowances, display allowances, and sales contests. At times they will apply negative sanctions, such as threatening to reduce margins, slow down delivery, or terminate the relationship. The weakness of this approach is that the producer is using crude, stimulus-response thinking.

More sophisticated companies try to forge a long-term partnership with distributors. The manufacturer clearly communicates what it wants from its distributors in the way of market coverage, inventory levels, marketing development, account solicitation, technical advice and services, and marketing information. The manufacturer seeks distributor agreement with these policies and may introduce a compensation plan for adhering to the policies.

To streamline the supply chain and cut costs, many manufacturers and retailers have adopted *efficient consumer response (ECR) practices* to organize their relationships in three areas: (1) *demand-side management,* or collaborative practices to stimulate consumer demand by promoting joint marketing and sales activities, (2) *supply-side management,* or collaborative practices to optimize supply (with a focus on joint logistics and supply-chain activities), and (3) *enablers and integrators*, or collaborative information technology and process-improvement tools to support joint activities that reduce operational problems, allow greater standardization, and so on. Research has shown that although ECR has a positive impact on manufacturers' economic performance and capability development, it may also generate greater perceptions of inequity on the manufacturers' part in that they feel they are inequitably sharing the burdens of ECR adoption and not getting as much as they deserve.[35]

Evaluating Channel Members

Producers must periodically evaluate intermediaries' performance against such standards as sales-quota attainment, average inventory levels, customer delivery time, treatment of damaged and lost goods, and cooperation in promotional and training programs. A producer will occasionally discover that it is paying particular intermediaries too much for what they are actually doing. One manufacturer compensating a distributor for holding inventories found that the inventories were actually held in a public warehouse at its own expense. Producers should set up functional discounts in which they pay specified amounts for the trade channel's performance of each agreed-upon service. Underperformers need to be counselled, retrained, motivated, or terminated.

Modifying Channel Design and Arrangements

A producer must periodically review and modify its channel design and arrangements. It will want to modify them when the distribution channel is not working as planned, consumer buying patterns change, the market expands, new competition arises, innovative distribution channels emerge, and the product moves into later stages in the product life cycle.

No marketing channel will remain effective over the whole product life cycle. Early buyers might be willing to pay for high-value-added channels, but later buyers will switch to lower-cost channels. Small office copiers were first sold by manufacturers' direct sales forces, later through office-equipment dealers, still later through mass merchandisers, and now by mail-order firms and Internet marketers.

To preserve its channel relationships, Apple has justified the opening of hundreds of its own retail stores as a natural extension of its online sales channel. The stores have proved extremely profitable.

In competitive markets with low entry barriers, the optimal channel structure will inevitably change over time. The change could mean adding or dropping individual channel members, adding or dropping particular market channels, or developing a totally new way to sell goods. Consider Apple:

Apple Stores

When Apple stores were launched in 2001, many critics questioned their prospects and *BusinessWeek* published an article entitled "Sorry Steve, Here's Why Apple Stores Won't Work." In 2005, Apple opened its first store in Canada. Fast-forward to 2008, and Apple is celebrating the success of its 209 stores in the U.S., four in Canada, 15 in the UK, seven in Japan, two in Australia, and one in Europe. Annual sales per square foot of US$4032 are much higher than those of other retailers. Just look at the sales per square foot of other well known retailers: Tiffany & Co., US$2666; Best Buy, US$930; and Saks, US$362. Opened because of the company's frustration with its poor retail presentation by others, the stores sell Apple products exclusively and target tech-savvy customers with an in-store concierge dressed in orange who welcomes customers; product presentations and workshops; a full line of Apple products, software, and accessories; and a "Genius Bar" staffed by Apple specialists who provide technical support often free of charge. Although the move upset existing retailers, Apple has worked hard to smooth relationships, in part justifying the decision to add its own stores as a natural evolution of its already existing online sales channel.[36]

Adding or dropping individual channel members requires an incremental analysis. What would the firm's profits look like with and without this intermediary? A producer may drop any intermediary whose sales drop below a certain level. Databases of detailed customer shopping information and sophisticated means to analyze that data can provide guidance in those decisions.[37]

Perhaps the most difficult decision of all is whether to revise the overall channel strategy.[38] Distribution channels clearly become outmoded, and a gap arises between the existing distribution system and the ideal system that would satisfy target customers' needs and desires. Examples abound: Avon's door-to-door system for selling cosmetics was modified as more women entered the workforce. Music retailing in Canada has been turned upside down.

Music World Ltd.

Music World Ltd., the last Canadian-owned national music chain, went bankrupt in 2007—another victim of a rapidly changing landscape for listening to and buying music. The 72-store chain with a presence in almost every province succumbed to the new world of music downloading, online file-swapping services, and digital radio. It also felt pressure from large retailers like Wal-Mart and other big-box stores that sell CDs as loss leaders. With the demise of Music World, British-based HMV will likely be the only remaining national music chain in Canada. HMV is surviving the onslaught of digital downloads by aggressively branching out into non-music products—DVDs and video games—and transforming into an "entertainment" retailer.[39]

In retail banking, despite a belief that technological advances such as automated teller machines, online banking, and telephone call centres would reduce customers' reliance on their neighbourhood branches, banks have found that many people still want "high touch" over "high tech," or at least a choice between the two. Banks are responding by opening more branches and developing more cross-selling and up-selling practices to take advantage of the leverage that face-to-face contact gives them.

CHANNEL INTEGRATION AND SYSTEMS

Distribution channels don't stand still. New wholesaling and retailing institutions emerge, and new channel systems evolve. We'll look at the recent growth of vertical, horizontal, and multi-channel marketing systems; the next section examines how these systems cooperate, conflict, and compete.

Vertical Marketing Systems

One of the most significant recent channel developments is the rise of vertical marketing systems. A conventional marketing channel comprises an independent producer, wholesaler(s), and retailer(s). Each is a separate business seeking to maximize its own profits, even if this goal reduces profit for the system as a whole. No channel member has complete or substantial control over other members.

A **vertical marketing system (VMS)**, by contrast, comprises the producer, wholesaler(s), and retailer(s) acting as a unified system. One channel member, the *channel captain,* owns the others or franchises them or has so much power that they all cooperate. "Marketing Insight: The Importance of Channel Stewards" provides some perspective on how *channel stewards*, a closely related concept, should work.

Vertical marketing systems (VMSs) arose as a result of strong channel members' attempts to control channel behaviour and eliminate the conflict that results when independent members pursue their own objectives. VMSs achieve economies through size, bargaining power, and elimination of duplicated services. Business buyers of complex products and systems have been shown to value the extensive exchange of information they can obtain from a VMS.[40] VMSs have become

As part of its vertical marketing system, Sherwin-Williams both manufactures paint and sells it directly in its own retail outlets.

the dominant mode of distribution in North America, serving between 70 percent and 80 percent of the total market. There are three types of VMS: corporate, administered, and contractual.

CORPORATE VMS   A *corporate VMS* combines successive stages of production and distribution under single ownership. For example, Sears obtains over 50 percent of the goods it sells from companies that it partly or wholly owns. Sherwin-Williams makes paint but also owns and operates over 3000 retail outlets under various banners including Sherwin-Williams, ICI/Glidden, and Benjamin Moore outlets in North America and Latin America. This combination has positioned it as the top-selling paint manufacturer in the U.S. and the third in the world.

ADMINISTERED VMS   An *administered VMS* coordinates successive stages of production and distribution through the size and power of one of the members. Manufacturers of a dominant brand are able to secure strong trade cooperation and support from resellers. Thus Kodak, Gillette, and Campbell Soup are able to command high levels of cooperation from their resellers in connection with displays, shelf space, promotions, and price policies.

The most advanced supplier to distributor arrangement for administered VMSs relies on **distribution programming**, which builds a planned, professionally managed, vertical marketing system that meets the needs of both manufacturer and distributors. The manufacturer establishes a department within the company called *distributor relations planning*. Its job is to identify distributor needs and build up merchandising programs to help each distributor operate as efficiently as possible. This department and the distributors jointly plan merchandising goals, inventory levels, space and visual merchandising plans, sales-training requirements, and advertising and promotion plans. The aim is to convert the distributors from thinking that they make their money primarily on the buying side (through tough negotiation with the manufacturer) to seeing that they make their money on the selling side (by being part of a sophisticated, vertical marketing system).

CONTRACTUAL VMS   A *contractual VMS* consists of independent firms at different levels of production and distribution that integrate their programs on a contractual basis to obtain more economies or sales impact than they could achieve alone. Johnston and Lawrence call them "value-adding partnerships" (VAPs).[41] Contractual VMSs now constitute one of the most significant developments in the economy. They are of three types:

1. *Wholesaler-sponsored voluntary chains*—Wholesalers organize voluntary chains of independent retailers to help them standardize their selling practices and achieve buying economies in order to compete with large chain organizations.

2. *Retailer cooperatives*—Retailers take the initiative and organize a new business entity to carry on wholesaling and possibly some production. Members concentrate their purchases through the retailer co-op and plan their advertising jointly. Profits pass back to members in proportion to their purchases. Nonmember retailers can also buy through the co-op but do not share in the profits.

3. *Franchise organizations*—A channel member called a *franchisor* might link several successive stages in the production-distribution process. Franchising has been the fastest-growing retailing development in recent years.

Although the basic idea is an old one, some forms of franchising are quite new. The traditional system is the *manufacturer-sponsored retailer franchise*. Ford, for example, licenses dealers to sell its cars. The dealers are independent businesspeople who agree to meet specified conditions of sales and services. Another is the *manufacturer-sponsored wholesaler franchise*. For example, in various markets Coca-Cola licenses bottlers (wholesalers) that buy its syrup concentrate and then carbonate, bottle, and sell it to retailers in local markets. A newer system is a retailer franchise which is sponsored by a service firm. A service firm organizes a whole system for bringing its service efficiently to consumers. We find examples in the auto-rental business (Hertz and Avis), fast-food-service business (McDonald's and Harveys), and motel business (Howard Johnson and Ramada Inn). Some franchising is done via a dual-distribution system in which firms use both vertical integration (whereby the franchisor actually owns and runs the units) and market governance (in which the franchisor licenses the units to other franchisees).[42]

THE NEW COMPETITION IN RETAILING   Many independent retailers that have not joined VMSs have developed specialty stores that serve special market segments. The result is a polarization

---

MARKETING **INSIGHT** | THE IMPORTANCE OF CHANNEL STEWARDS

Harvard's V. Kasturi Rangan believes that companies should adopt a new approach to going to market—channel stewardship. He defines **channel stewardship** as the ability of a given participant in a distribution channel—a steward—to create a go-to-market strategy that simultaneously addresses customers' best interests and drives profits for all channel partners. A channel steward might be the maker of the product or service (such as Procter & Gamble or Air Canada), the maker of a key component (such as microchip maker Intel), the supplier or assembler (such as Dell or Nortel), or the distributor (such as Sysco) or retailer (such as The Bay). Within a company, Rangan notes, the stewardship function might reside with the CEO, a top manager, or a team of senior managers.

The concept of channel stewardship is meant to appeal to any organization in the distribution channel that wants to bring a disciplined approach to channel strategy. An effective channel steward considers the channel from the customer's point of view. With that view in mind, the steward then advocates for change among all participants, transforming disparate entities into partners having a common purpose.

Channel stewardship has two important outcomes. One is to expand value for the steward's customers and in the process increase the size of the market or existing customers' purchases through the channel. A second outcome is to create a more tightly woven, and yet adaptable, channel where valuable members are suitably rewarded and the less valuable members are weeded out.

Rangan outlines three key disciplines of channel management:

1. *Mapping* is undertaken at an industry level to gain a sense of what the key determinants of channel strategy are and how they are evolving. It gives an idea of current best practices and gaps, and it projects what the future requirements might be.

2. *Building and editing* is an assessment of the producer's own channels with a view to identifying any deficits in meeting customers' needs and/or competitive best practices.

3. *Aligning and influencing* closes the gaps and works out a compensation package in tune with effort and performance for channel members that add or could add value.

Rangan maintains that the beauty of the channel stewardship discipline is that it works at the level of customer needs and not at the level of channel institutions. As a result, channel managers can evolve and change their fulfillment of customer needs without having to change channel structure all at once. An evolutionary approach to channel change, it requires constant monitoring, learning, and adaptation, but all in the best interests of customers, channel partners, and the channel steward. Rangan also notes that a channel steward need not be a huge company or market leader, citing a number of smaller players, such as Haworth and Atlas Copco, as well as distributors and retailers such as Wal-Mart, Best Buy (consumer electronics), and HEB (supermarkets).

Source: V. Kasturi Rangan, *Transforming Your Go-to-Market Strategy: The Three Disciplines of Channel Management* (Boston: Harvard Business School Press, 2006).

---

in retailing between large vertical marketing organizations and independent specialty stores which creates a problem for manufacturers. They are strongly tied to independent intermediaries but must eventually realign themselves with the high-growth vertical marketing systems on less attractive terms. Furthermore, vertical marketing systems constantly threaten to bypass large manufacturers and set up their own manufacturing. The new competition in retailing is no longer between independent business units but between whole systems of centrally programmed networks (corporate, administered, and contractual) competing against one another to achieve the best cost economies and customer response.

Horizontal Marketing Systems

Another channel development is the **horizontal marketing system**, such as in-store banking, in which two or more unrelated companies put together resources or programs to exploit an emerging marketing opportunity. Each company lacks the capital, know-how, production, or marketing resources to venture alone, or it is afraid of the risk. The companies might work with each other on a temporary or permanent basis or create a joint-venture company.

In-Store Banking

Loblaw Companies Limited joined forces with CIBC to create President's Choice Financial services, complete with the President's Choice Financial® MasterCard® and the PC® points rewards program. Customers are offered a range of financial products, higher interest rates, and lower fees in addition to convenient access to their accounts. They bank online, by telephone, and at President's Choice Financial and CIBC bank machines. When a human face is important, clients can go into an in-store pavilion and talk to a friendly Personal Banking Representative. The partnership has resulted in products and services that won President's Choice Financial services the 2007 J.D. Power and Associates award for "Highest in Customer Satisfaction Among Midsize Retail Banks."[43]

Integrating Multi-Channel Marketing Systems

Most companies today have adopted multi-channel marketing. Disney sells its DVDs through five main channels: movie-rental stores such as Blockbuster; Disney Stores (now owned and run by The Children's Place); retail stores such as Best Buy; online retailers such as Amazon.ca and Disney's own online Disney Stores; and the Disney catalogue and other catalogue sellers. These varied channels afford Disney maximum market coverage and enable the company to offer its videos at a number of price points.[44]

Multi-channel marketing occurs when a single firm uses two or more marketing channels to reach one or more customer segments. An **integrated marketing channel system** is one in which the strategies and tactics of selling through one channel reflect the strategies and tactics of selling through other channels.

By adding more channels, companies can gain three important benefits. The first is increased market coverage. Not only are more customers able to shop for the company's products in more places, but customers who buy in more than one channel are often more profitable than single-channel customers.[45] The second is lower channel cost—selling by phone is cheaper than selling via personal visits to small customers. The third is more customized selling—such as adding a technical sales force to sell more-complex equipment. The gains from adding new channels come at a price, however. New channels typically introduce conflict and problems with control. Two or more channels

The horizontal marketing systems between Loblaw Companies and CIBC allow President's Choice Financial to offer more benefits to consumers than some of its competitors offer.

Demand-Generation Tasks

Marketing Channels and Methods (VENDOR)	Lead Generation	Qualifying Sales	Presales	Close of Sale	Postsales Service	Account Management	
Internet							CUSTOMER
National Account Management							
Direct Sales							
Telemarketing							
Direct Mail							
Retail Stores							
Distributors							
Dealers and Value-Added Resellers							
Advertising							

FIGURE 15.6

The Hybrid Grid

Source: Adapted from Rowland T. Moriarty and Ursula Moran, "Marketing Hybrid Marketing Systems," *Harvard Business Review* (November–December 1990): 150.

may end up competing for the same customers. The new channels may be more independent and make cooperation more difficult. "Marketing Memo: Multi-Channel Shopping Checklist" offers some concrete advice on channel integration of online and offline channels.

Clearly, companies need to think through their channel architecture. They must determine which channels should perform which functions. Figure 15.6 shows a simple grid to help make channel-architecture decisions. The grid consists of major marketing channels (as rows) and the major channel tasks that must be completed (as columns).[46]

The grid illustrates why using only one channel is not efficient. Consider using only a direct sales force. A salesperson would have to find leads, qualify them, presell, close the sale, provide service, and manage account growth. It's more efficient for the company to perform the earlier tasks, leaving the salesperson to invest his or her costly time primarily in closing the sale. The company's marketing department would run a preselling campaign informing prospects about the company's products through advertising, direct mail, and telemarketing; generate leads through telemarketing, direct mail, advertising, and trade shows; and qualify leads into hot, warm, and cool. The salesperson comes to the prospect when the prospect is ready to talk business. This multichannel architecture optimizes coverage, customization, and control while minimizing cost and conflict.

Channels should be designed to work together effectively. Outdoor accessories retailer Smith & Hawken has seen its website sales blossom to 20 percent of total sales while catalogue sales have declined to 15 percent in recent years. But the company would never abandon paper catalogues because it believes they are the most effective way to make an emotional appeal and the best method to convince customers to go online. Catalogues have actually grown in an Internet world as more firms use them as branding devices. Victoria's Secret ships 400 million catalogues a year, and catalogue and online orders account for nearly 28 percent of its overall revenue, growing at double the rate of sales from its stores.[47]

Companies should use different channels for selling to different-sized business customers. A company can use its direct sales force to sell to large customers, telemarketing to sell to midsized customers, and distributors to sell to small customers; but these gains can be compromised by an increased level of conflict over who has account ownership. For example, territory-based sales representatives may want credit for all sales in their territories, regardless of the marketing channel used.

Multi-channel marketers also need to decide how much of their product to offer in each of the channels. Patagonia views the Web as the ideal channel for showing off its entire line of goods, given that its 14 stores and five outlets are limited by space to offering a selection only, and even

| MARKETING MEMO | MULTI-CHANNEL SHOPPING CHECKLIST |

During the 2003 "back-to-school" season, the e-tailing group inc., an e-commerce consulting firm in Chicago, sent mystery shoppers to visit retail locations of 16 e-tailers to test their claims of an integrated shopping experience in the online/retail returns process. Overall, the study found that 44 percent of in-store returns of merchandise purchased online required a store manager to override the retail system in order to accept the return. In response to this and several other inadequacies revealed by the study, the e-tailing group created a "Best of Breed Multi-Channel Shopping Checklist" to help marketers better integrate online and offline channels:

- Train all store associates on processes for online-merchandise returns.
- List your company's 800 number on the website homepage, and be sure your customer-service hours of operation are easily accessible.
- Provide an information centre that is easy to navigate and includes contact information, FAQs, guarantees, return policies, and tips for first-time customers.
- Implement a store-locator feature that includes store locations, hours, and events.
- Make store pickup for purchases an option and include real-time inventory levels, where applicable.
- Post the store's weekly circular online for a more complete multi-channel experience.
- Offer gift certificates that can be redeemed online and offline.
- Send email notifications of the order, shipping, and return credit; in notifications include a reminder of the returns process as well as a link to your store locator.
- Supply all pertinent/compatible information for store return of merchandise on the packing slip or invoice.

Source: Excerpted from Hallie Mummert, "Multichannel Marketers Earn a 'C+' on Returns," *Target Marketing* (October 2003): 158.

its catalogue offers less than 70 percent of its total merchandise. L'Occitane en Provence, a French manufacturer and retailer, has only a limited number of stores in some countries like Canada, where it operates 12 stores. Thus, its website is an important tool for its devoted consumers who may not have easy access to its stores.[48] Other marketers prefer to limit their online offerings on the theory that customers look to websites and catalogues for a "best of" array of merchandise and don't want to have to click through dozens of pages.

L'Occitane operates only 12 stores in Canada, but its website enables all Canadian consumers to purchase the products they love.

CONFLICT, COOPERATION, AND COMPETITION

No matter how well channels are designed and managed, there will be some conflict, if for no other reason than that the interests of independent business entities do not always coincide. **Channel conflict** is generated when one channel member's actions prevent another channel from achieving its goal. Software giant Oracle Corp., plagued by channel conflict between its sales force and its vendor partners, decided to roll out new "All Partner Territories" where all deals except for specific strategic accounts would go through select Oracle partners.[49]

Channel coordination occurs when channel members are brought together to advance the goals of the channel, as opposed to their own potentially incompatible goals.[50] Here we examine three questions: What types of conflict arise in channels? What causes channel conflict? What can marketers do to resolve conflict situations?

Types of Conflict and Competition

Suppose a manufacturer sets up a vertical channel consisting of wholesalers and retailers. The manufacturer hopes for channel cooperation that will produce greater profits for each channel member. Yet vertical, horizontal, and multi-channel conflict can occur.

Vertical channel conflict means conflict between different levels within the same channel. General Motors came into conflict with its dealers in trying to enforce policies on service, pricing, and advertising.

Greater retailer consolidation has led to increased price pressure from, and influence of, retailers. Retail concentration is increasing in Canada, especially in industries like grocery retailing. A recent study reported that 60.7 percent of grocery sales were accounted for by the major chains. Similarly, the ten largest U.S. retailers accounted for 80 percent of the average manufacturer's business in 2005 versus roughly 30 percent a decade earlier.[51] Wal-Mart, for example, is the principal buyer for many manufacturers, including Disney, Procter & Gamble, and Revlon, and is able to command concessions from its suppliers in the form of reduced prices or quantity discounts.[52]

Horizontal channel conflict is conflict between members at the same level within the channel. Some Pizza Inn franchisees complained about other Pizza Inn franchisees cheating on ingredients, providing poor service, and hurting the overall Pizza Inn image.

Multi-channel conflict exists when the manufacturer has established two or more channels that sell to the same market. It's likely to be especially intense when the members of one channel get a lower price (based on larger-volume purchases) or work with a lower margin. When Goodyear began selling its popular tire brands through Sears and Wal-Mart, it angered its independent dealers. It eventually placated them by offering exclusive tire models that would not be sold in other retail outlets. Other strategies to reduce multi-channel conflict are creating and enforcing rules of engagement beforehand (rather than mediating disputes after the fact) and compensating both parties that participate in a sale regardless of which one books the order.[53]

Causes of Channel Conflict

Some causes of channel conflict are easy to resolve, others are not. Conflict may arise from:

- *Goal incompatibility.* For example, the manufacturer may want to achieve rapid market penetration through a low-price policy. Dealers, in contrast, may prefer to work with high margins and pursue short-run profitability.

- *Unclear roles and rights.* HP may sell personal computers to large accounts through its own sales force, but its licensed dealers may also be trying to sell to large accounts. Territory boundaries and credit for sales often produce conflict.

- *Differences in perception.* The manufacturer may be optimistic about the short-term economic outlook and want dealers to carry higher inventory. Dealers may be pessimistic. In the beverage category, it is not uncommon for disputes to arise between manufacturers and their distributors about the optimal advertising strategy.

- *Intermediaries' dependence on the manufacturer.* The fortunes of exclusive dealers, such as auto dealers, are profoundly affected by the manufacturer's product and pricing decisions. This situation creates a high potential for conflict.

Managing Channel Conflict

As companies add channels to grow sales, they run the risk of creating channel conflict. Some channel conflict can be constructive and lead to better adaptation to a changing environment, but too much conflict is dysfunctional.[54] The challenge is not to eliminate conflict but to manage it better. Here's an example of how one B2B company added a potentially conflicting e-commerce channel and still managed to build trust—and not stir up conflict—with its distributors:

AB Dick

Printing-equipment manufacturer AB Dick was on the verge of bypassing an important distributor channel for a direct e-commerce channel. Instead, the company developed a tiered dealer model and formed strategic supply-chain partnerships with influential distributors. AB Dick would deal directly via the Web with all customers in a respective dealer's territory for sales of supplies. The dealer would act as the distribution point, bill and collect from the customer, maintain the relationship in terms of high-end equipment sales, earn incremental margins from the online sales of supplies (even though the transaction would be direct from AB Dick to the end user), and remain the local contact for equipment sales. According to AB Dick's vice-president of technology, the dealers were happy because they picked up margin on business they never had, but they also picked up collections, freight, transportation, and labour. AB Dick benefited from reduced costs per online transaction and incremental sales. It had to balance the efficiencies and convenience of direct online ordering for its end users with the need to maintain its dealers as local points of distribution and customer contact.[55]

There are several mechanisms for effective conflict management (see Table 15.3).[56] One is the adoption of superordinate goals. Channel members come to an agreement on the fundamental goal they are jointly seeking, whether it is survival, market share, high quality, or customer satisfaction. They usually do this when the channel faces an outside threat, such as a more efficient competing channel, an adverse piece of legislation, or a shift in consumer desires.

A useful step is to exchange persons between two or more channel levels. General Motors executives might agree to work for a short time in some dealerships, and some dealership owners might work in GM's dealer-policy department. The hope is that the participants will grow to appreciate each other's point of view.

Similarly, marketers can accomplish much by encouraging joint membership in and between trade associations. For example, there is good cooperation between Food & Consumer Products of Canada, Advertising Standards Canada, and Concerned Children's Advertisers. This affiliation has led to voluntary standards for advertising to children that are praised by many around the world, as well as award-winning social-marketing programs designed to help children deal with media in an informed manner.

Co-optation is an effort by one organization to win the support of the leaders of another organization by including them in advisory councils, boards of directors, and the like. As long as the initiating organization treats the leaders seriously and listens to their opinions, co-optation can reduce conflict, but the initiating organization may need to compromise on its policies and plans to win the leaders' support.

When conflict is chronic or acute, however, the parties may need to resort to diplomacy, mediation, or arbitration. *Diplomacy* takes place when each side sends a person or group to meet with its counterpart to resolve the conflict. *Mediation* means resorting to a neutral third party skilled in conciliating the two parties' interests. *Arbitration* occurs when the two parties agree to present their arguments to one or more arbitrators and accept the arbitration decision.

Finally, when none of these methods proves effective, a company or a channel partner may choose to file a lawsuit. Coca-Cola came into conflict with several of its key bottlers when the

TABLE 15.3	STRATEGIES TO MANAGE CHANNEL CONFLICT
Adoption of superordinate goals	
Exchange of employees	
Joint membership in trade associations	
Co-optation	
Diplomacy, mediation, or arbitration	
Legal recourse	

company decided to distribute Powerade thirst quencher directly to Wal-Mart's regional warehouses. After 60 bottlers complained that the practice would undermine their core direct-store-distribution (DSD) duties and filed a lawsuit, a compromise settlement was reached that allowed for the mutual exploration of new service and distribution systems to supplement the DSD system.[57]

Dilution and Cannibalization

Marketers must also be careful not to dilute their brands through inappropriate channels. This is especially a concern with luxury brands whose images are often built on the basis of exclusivity and personalized service. The images of brands such as Calvin Klein and Tommy Hilfiger took a hit when they sold too many of their products in discount channels. Coach, the manufacturer of high-end leather goods, has worked hard to avoid diluting its image.

Coach

Handbag-maker Coach's sustained double-digit growth was the result of some timely product introductions and well-designed channel expansion. With a global vision in place, Coach is available at over 900 department store locations in the U.S., 140 international department stores, retail store and duty-free shop locations in 21 countries including Canada, 137 department store shop-in-shops, and retail and factory-store locations operated by Coach Japan, Inc. As it turned out, the fastest-growing segment of Coach's business was factory outlets selling discontinued or older styles at 25-percent discounts. The company manages its channels carefully, however, and seeks to keep discount shoppers separate from more upscale and profitable clientele. Coach maintains full price in its regular stores and doesn't discount. Merchandise that doesn't sell is not reduced in price but instead is sent to factory outlets located at least 100 kilometres away. As evidence of the firm's success in distinguishing the two channels, the average full-price shopper (a 35-year-old, college-educated, and single or newly married working woman) is very different from the average factory-outlet shopper (a 45-year-old, college-educated married woman who buys 80 percent of her Coach purchases from outlets).[58]

Coach avoids brand dilution while enjoying multi-channel distribution by keeping its full-price store shoppers separate from its discount shoppers, locating its factory outlets a minimum of 100 kilometres from its retail stores.

To help tap into affluent shoppers who work long hours and have little time to shop, high-end fashion brands such as Dior, Louis Vuitton, and Fendi have unveiled e-commerce sites. These luxury makers also see their websites as a way for customers to research items before walking into a store and as a means to help combat fakes sold over the Internet. Given the emphasis these brands put on pampering their customers in their stores—doorkeepers, glasses of champagne, extravagant surroundings—they have had to work hard to provide a high-quality experience online.[59]

Legal and Ethical Issues in Channel Relations

For the most part, companies are legally free to develop whatever channel arrangements suit them as long as they don't use deceptive, exclusionary, or anti-competitive tactics. Canada's Competition Act regulates many channel practices. The first part of the Act provides the Competition Bureau with civil powers to deal with potentially anti-competitive practices. Thus, the Competition Bureau investigates many proposed mergers to ensure that they don't substantially lessen competition. It is also concerned with other anti-competitive practices like refusal to deal, tied selling, and exclusive dealing. The second part of the Act covers criminal practices such as price fixing and bid rigging and it places particular emphasis on domestic cartels. The Competition Act also places legal restrictions on some specialized distribution practices such as pyramid selling (also called multi-level marketing plans). In particular, it prohibits schemes that have mandatory participation fees, purchase requirements as a condition of participation, inventory loading, or insufficient buy-back guarantees. It also has rules with regard to the nature of competition between wholesalers and retailers,

since they are viewed under the law as direct competitors. New provisions have recently been put in place to govern fraudulent telemarketing practices.[60]

Here we briefly consider the legality of certain practices, including exclusive dealing, exclusive territories, tying agreements, and dealers' rights.

Many producers like to develop exclusive channels for their products. A strategy in which the seller allows only certain outlets to carry its products is called exclusive distribution. When the seller requires that these dealers not handle competitors' products, this is called exclusive dealing. Both parties benefit from exclusive arrangements: the seller obtains more loyal and dependable outlets, and the dealers obtain a steady source of supply of special products and stronger seller support. Exclusive arrangements are legal as long as they do not substantially lessen competition or tend to create a monopoly and as long as both parties enter into the agreement voluntarily.

Exclusive dealing often includes exclusive territorial agreements. The producer may agree not to sell to other dealers in a given area, or the buyer may agree to sell only in its own territory. The first practice increases dealer enthusiasm and commitment. It is also perfectly legal—a seller has no legal obligation to sell through more outlets than it wishes. The second practice, whereby the producer tries to keep a dealer from selling outside its territory, has become a major legal issue.

Producers of a strong brand sometimes sell it to dealers only if they will take some or all of the rest of the line. This practice is called full-line forcing. This practice may be illegal if it substantially lessens competition.

Producers are free to select their dealers, but their right to terminate dealers is somewhat restricted. In general, sellers can drop dealers "for cause," but they cannot drop dealers if, for example, the dealers refuse to cooperate in a doubtful legal arrangement, such as exclusive dealing or tying agreements.

E-COMMERCE MARKETING PRACTICES

E-business describes the use of electronic means and platforms to conduct a company's business. **E-commerce** means that the company or site offers to transact or facilitate the selling of products and services online. E-commerce has given rise in turn to e-purchasing and e-marketing. E-purchasing means companies decide to purchase goods, services, and information from various online suppliers. Smart e-purchasing has already saved companies millions of dollars. **E-marketing** describes company efforts to inform buyers and communicate, promote, and sell its products and services over the Internet.

Online retail sales in Canada have experienced double-digit growth for six consecutive years. By the end of 2007, Internet sales hit an estimated $62.7 billion, up 26 percent from 2006. Despite the continued strong growth, e-commerce still represents a relatively small fraction of total economic activity, representing approximately 2 percent of total operating revenue (up from 1 percent five years earlier). It's easy to see why growth is occurring. Online retailers can predictably provide convenient, informative, and personalized experiences for vastly different types of consumers and businesses. By not having to bear the cost of maintaining retail floor space, staff, and inventory, online retailers can sell low-volume products to niche markets. Online retailers compete among themselves in terms of three key aspects of a transaction: (1) customer interaction with the website, (2) delivery of the product, and (3) ability to address problems when they occur.[61]

We can distinguish between pure e-businesses, those that have launched a website without any previous existence as a firm, and existing companies with physical locations that have added an online site for information or e-commerce.

Pure E-Businesses

There are several kinds of pure e-businesses: search engines, Internet service providers (ISPs), commerce sites, transaction sites, content sites, and enabler sites. Commerce sites sell all types of products and services, notably books, music, toys, insurance, stocks, clothes, and financial services. Commerce sites specialize in order to compete: AutoNation, a leading metamediary of car buying and related services; Hotels.com, the information leader in hotel reservations; Buy.com, the low-price leader; and Winespectator, a single-category specialist. "Breakthrough Marketing: Amazon," at the end of this chapter, describes that quintessential online retailer.

Companies must set up and operate their e-commerce websites carefully. Customer service is critical. Often, online shoppers select an item for purchase but fail to complete the transaction—the conversion rate of Internet shoppers among the top 100 Internet retailers is only about 5 percent, much lower than the norm from similar top firms using traditional channels.[62] Worse, only 1.8 percent of visits to online retailers lead to sales, compared with 5 percent of visits to department stores.

Consumer surveys suggest that the most significant inhibitors of online shopping are the absence of pleasurable experiences, social interaction, and personal consultation with a company representative.[63] Firms are responding. For example, Veseys Seeds of PEI offers customers the ability to chat with a service representative by simply calling a toll-free number.[64] Another benefit of providing live sales assistance is the ability to sell additional items. When a representative is involved in the sale, the average amount per order is typically higher. Online footwear retailer Zappos offers fast turnaround and free returns for a wide selection of shoes and finds that two-thirds of purchases during any one day are from repeat customers.[65] B2B marketers, like Cisco Systems, also need to put a human face on their e-commerce presence, and some are doing so by taking advantage of Web 2.0 technologies such as virtual environments, blogs, online videos, and click-to-chat.

Cisco Systems

Cisco is experimenting with a variety of Web 2.0 applications such as posting videos of its "human network" campaign on YouTube, holding analyst briefings in the virtual world of Second Life, and especially using click-to-chat. "The single biggest home run we've achieved in the last month is click-to-chat," said Michael Metz, Cisco's senior director of web marketing and strategy. When users, who tend to be small-business customers, click on a button in the technical portion of Cisco's website, they are connected to a call-centre representative who helps them solve their problem. Then Cisco added a more sales-oriented click-to-chat feature. If a user comes back to a product page several times to look at a particular item, a chat box comes up saying, "Can we help you with product X?" So-called proactive chat enabled Cisco to improve its lead conversion rate by 50 percent in just the first three months.[66]

To increase the entertainment and information value and the customer satisfaction from web-based shopping experiences, some firms are employing *avatars,* graphical representations of characters that can act as company representatives. Avatars can provide a more interpersonal shopping experience by serving as identification figures, as personal shopping assistants, as website guides, or as conversation partners. Research has shown that avatars can enhance the effectiveness of a web-based sales channel, especially if they are seen as expert or attractive.[67] Unlike human customer-service reps, avatars work 24/7 and never get tired. Still, they're robots, only as smart as their programming. They're unlikely to replace customer-service or sales reps yet, but they do provide a polished, friendly face for e-businesses large and small. See what happened when an editor of *Marketing* magazine took a shopping trip to Second Life:

Second Life

Marketing magazine's editor at large, Angela Kryhul, recently created an avatar and took a tour of Second Life (SL), the online virtual world at www.secondlife.com, to see how brands were interacting with customers. Her first visit was to Sears where she found a spacious, uncluttered, and uncrowded version of its real stores. The store was easier to navigate and it was easier for the company to highlight key product lines like Kenmore appliances. When Angela visited the Telus store she discovered she could buy a Motorola Q-a cell phone specifically designed for avatars. She looked for virtual service reps to show her how to get free stuff, buy things, and in the case of Nissan's SL location, how to test-drive a Sentra. Even through the Telus store was staffed, the avatars were not always available to help. Poor service seems to exist in a virtual world too. Jennifer Morozowich, director of insights at Toronto's Fuse Marketing Group, and an authority on social media, says if retailers go overboard in designing their fantasy stores, their real-life outlets will be seen as under-delivering. She cautions that "Brands entering SL need to stay true to their brand image and provide the user with a positive shopping experience." Not everyone is a fan of the commercialization of virtual spaces and as you navigate the SL world you can see signs of protest like broken trees outside the Sears entrance and broken glass at the American Apparel store, likely the work of angry Second Lifers. "It's the consumer's way of saying 'get out big brands.'"[68]

Ensuring security and privacy online also remains important. Customers must find a website trustworthy, even if it represents an already highly credible offline firm such as Kodak. Investments in website design and processes can help reassure customers sensitive to online risk.[69] Online retailers are also trying new technologies, such as blogs, social networks, and mobile marketing, to attract new shoppers.

Although the popular press has given the most attention to business-to-consumer (B2C) websites, even more activity is being conducted on business-to-business (B2B) sites. These sites are changing the supplier–customer relationship in profound ways. Firms are using B2B auction sites, spot exchanges, online product catalogues, barter sites, and other online resources to obtain better prices. LendingTree brokers millions of loans on behalf of over 200 lenders. Retail loans are an ideal commodity to trade online: they're highly standardized, the lending industry is fragmented, and large volumes of transactions allow small profit margins to add up.[70]

The purpose of B2B sites is to make markets more efficient. In the past, buyers exerted a lot of effort to gather information on worldwide suppliers. With the Internet, buyers have easy access to a great deal of information. They can get information from (1) supplier websites, (2) *infomediaries*, third parties that add value by aggregating information about alternatives, (3) *market makers*, third parties that create markets linking buyers and sellers, and (4) *customer communities*, websites where buyers can swap stories about suppliers' products and services.[71] Ironically, the largest of the B2B market makers, Alibaba, is homegrown in China, a country where businesses have faced decades of Communist antipathy to private enterprise.

Alibaba

The brainchild of 42-year-old Jack Ma, Alibaba has become the world's largest online B2B marketplace, Asia's most popular online auction site, and now, with its acquisition of Yahoo! China, the twelfth-most-popular website in the world. At its heart are two B2B websites, alibaba.com and china.alibaba. The former is a marketplace for companies around the globe to buy and sell in English, and the latter is a domestic Chinese marketplace. Whereas Alibaba's rivals, such as Commerce One, were founded with the goal of slashing procurement costs, the Chinese powerhouse has a more nationalist agenda: to build markets for China's vast number of small- and medium-sized businesses. Alibaba enables them both to trade with each other and to link to global supply chains. Of his focus on SMEs, Jack Ma says "We are interested in catching shrimp, not the whales. When you catch the shrimp, then you will also catch the whales." European importers are particularly drawn to the "shrimp" in Alibaba's B2B net, in large part because Alibaba has set up a system by which businesses can easily establish trust. When membership in Alibaba's B2B exchange was free, members complained "I don't trust this guy!" says Jack Ma, so he set up TrustPass, whereby users pay Alibaba a fee to hire a third party that verifies them. Users must have five people vouch for them and provide a list of all their certificates/business licences. Finally, anyone on Alibaba who has done business with a user is encouraged to comment on the firm, in the same way buyers comment on sellers in Amazon's and eBay's marketplaces. This feature was not very common in the online B2B world, but Alibaba has made it a standard. Businesses are even starting to print "TrustPass" on their business cards, a true sign of Alibaba's B2B credibility.[72]

The net impact of these mechanisms is to make prices more transparent.[73] In the case of undifferentiated products, price pressure will increase. For highly differentiated products, buyers will gain a better picture of the items' true value. Suppliers of superior products will be able to offset price transparency with value transparency; suppliers of undifferentiated products will need to drive down their costs in order to compete.

Traditional Firms with E-Commerce Operations

Many traditional companies debated whether to add an online e-commerce channel for fear that selling their products or services online might produce channel conflict with their offline retailers and agents or their own stores.[74] Most eventually added the Internet as a distribution channel after seeing how much business their online competitors were generating. Canada's large banks have embraced the online channel. In 2008, HubSpot's Website Grader gave the Bank of Montreal (Canada's fifth-largest bank) the highest grade for marketing effectiveness, but Canada's second-largest bank,

TD Canada Trust, has the website that generated the most traffic in HubSpot's rankings.[75] Yet adding an e-commerce channel creates the threat of a backlash from retailers, brokers, agents, and other intermediaries. The question is how to sell both through intermediaries and online. There are at least three strategies for trying to gain acceptance from intermediaries. One, offer different brands or products on the Internet. Two, offer offline partners higher commissions to cushion the negative impact on sales. Three, take orders on the website but have retailers deliver and collect payment. Harley-Davidson treaded carefully before going online.

Harley-Davidson

Given that Harley sells more than $500 million worth of parts and accessories to its loyal followers, an online venture was an obvious next step to generate even more revenue. Harley needed to be careful, however, to avoid the wrath of dealers who benefited from the high margins on those sales. Harley's solution was to send customers seeking to buy accessories online to the company's website. Before they can buy anything, they are prompted to select a participating Harley-Davidson dealer. When the customer places the order, it is transmitted to the selected dealer for fulfillment, ensuring that the dealer still remains the focal point of the customer experience. Dealers, in turn, had to agree to a number of standards, such as checking for orders twice a day and shipping orders promptly. The website now gets more than one million visitors a month.[76]

It's difficult to launch a new brand successfully, so most companies brand their online ventures under their existing brand names. Others go in the opposite direction. Vancity Credit Union wanted to expand its business nationally, but needed a name that would resonate with Canadians across the country. It therefore launched Citizens Bank in 1997. The virtual bank offered a broad range of financial products and innovative services. By 2008, more than 40 percent of the credit union's 33 000 members were from outside B.C. It had $1.9 billion of assets and physical branch offices in Vancouver, Calgary, and Toronto.[77]

M-Commerce

Consumers and businesspeople no longer need to be near a computer to send and receive information. All they need is a cell phone or personal digital assistant (PDA). In 2007, the report *Mobile Commerce: Making It Work for Canadians*, reported that half the world's population uses mobile telephones.[78] While they're on the move, they can connect to the Internet to check stock prices, the weather, and sports scores; send and receive email messages; and place online orders. A whole field called *telematics* places wireless Internet-connected computers in the dashboards of cars and trucks, and makes more home appliances (such as computers) wireless so they can be used anywhere in or near the home. Many see a big future in what is now called *m-commerce* (*m* for mobile). M-commerce began to take off in Canada in 2005 when Bell Mobility, Rogers Wireless, and Telus Mobility announced the launch of Wireless Payment Services, a joint venture designed to facilitate wireless payment transactions.[79]

Considering the fast growth of Internet-connected phones, the potential market opportunities for location-based services are enormous. Imagine some not-too-distant possibilities:

- Getting a Coke by pointing and clicking your phone at a vending machine. The bottle drops down and an appropriate amount is deducted from your bank account.
- Using your phone to search for a nearby restaurant that meets criteria you've entered
- Watching stock prices on your phone while sitting in the restaurant and deciding to place a stock-purchase order
- Clicking your phone to pay the bill for your meal
- Coming home and clicking a combination of keys on your phone to open your door

Some see positive benefits to location-based services, such as locating people making emergency 911 calls and checking on the whereabouts of children late at night. Others worry about privacy issues. What if an employer learns that an employee is being treated for AIDS at a local clinic, or a wife finds her husband is out clubbing? Like so many new technologies, location-based services have potential for good and harm and ultimately will warrant public scrutiny and regulation.

SUMMARY

1. Most producers do not sell their goods directly to final users. Between producers and final users stands one or more marketing channels, a host of marketing intermediaries performing a variety of functions.

2. Marketing-channel decisions are among the most critical decisions facing management. The company's chosen channel(s) profoundly affect all other marketing decisions.

3. Companies use intermediaries when they lack the financial resources to carry out direct marketing, when direct marketing is not feasible, and when they can earn more by doing so. The most important functions performed by intermediaries are information, promotion, negotiation, ordering, financing, risk taking, physical possession, payment, and title.

4. Manufacturers have many alternatives for reaching a market. They can sell direct or use one-, two-, or three-level channels. Deciding which type(s) of channel to use calls for analyzing customer needs, establishing channel objectives, and identifying and evaluating the major alternatives, including the types and numbers of intermediaries involved in the channel.

5. Effective channel management calls for selecting intermediaries and training and motivating them. The goal is to build long-term partnerships that will be profitable for all channel members.

6. Marketing channels are characterized by continuous and sometimes dramatic change. Three of the most important trends are the growth of vertical marketing systems, horizontal marketing systems, and multi-channel marketing systems.

7. All marketing channels have the potential for conflict and competition resulting from such sources as goal incompatibility, poorly defined roles and rights, perceptual differences, and interdependent relationships. Companies can manage conflict by striving for superordinate goals; exchanging people among two or more channel levels; co-opting the support of leaders in different parts of the channel; encouraging joint membership in and between trade associations; employing diplomacy, mediation, or arbitration; or pursuing legal recourse.

8. Channel arrangements are up to the company, but there are certain legal and ethical issues to be considered with regard to practices such as exclusive dealing or territories, tying agreements, and dealers' rights.

9. E-commerce has grown in importance as traditional companies have adopted e-commerce channel systems. Channel integration must recognize the distinctive strengths of online and offline selling and maximize their joint contributions. An emerging new area is m-commerce and marketing through cell phones and PDAs.

APPLICATIONS

Marketing Debate: Does It Matter Where You Are Sold?

Some marketers feel that the image of the particular channel in which they sell their products does not matter—all that matters is that the right customers shop there and the product is displayed in the right way. Others maintain that channel images—such as a retail store—can be critical and must be consistent with the image of the product.

Take a position: Channel images do not really affect the brand images of the products they sell *versus* Channel images must be consistent with the brand image.

Marketing Discussion

Think of your favourite retailers. How have they integrated their channel system? How would you like their channels to be integrated? Do you use multiple channels from them? Why?

Breakthrough Marketing: Amazon

Founded by Jeff Bezos, Amazon.com started as the "world's largest bookstore" in July 1995. It was followed by its Canadian site, Amazon.ca, in 2002. Today, Amazon also has separate websites in the United Kingdom, Germany, Austria, France, China, and Japan. While it lost money initially, it moved into the black in 2003. In 2007, sales increased by 39 percent and revenue exceeded US$14 billion.

A virtual bookstore that physically owned no books, Amazon promised to revolutionize retailing. Although some may debate whether that was accomplished, Bezos clearly blazed an e-commerce trail of innovations that many have studied and followed.

Amazon set out to create personalized storefronts for each customer by providing more useful information and more choices than could be found in the typical neighbourhood bookstore. Readers can review books and evaluate them on a one- to five-star rating system, and browsers can rate which reviews are helpful and which are not. Amazon's personal recommendation service aggregates data on buying patterns to infer who might like which book. The site offers peeks into books' contents with a "search inside the book" feature that lets customers search the entire text of 120 000 books—about as many titles as are in a Chapters bookstore. Amazon's one-click shopping lets buyers make purchases with ease.

Amazon also established itself as an electronic marketplace by enabling merchants of all kinds to sell items on Amazon. It powers and operates retail websites for Target, the NBA, Timex, and Marks & Spencer. Amazon derives about 40 percent of its sales from its million-plus affiliates called "Associates," independent sellers or businesses that receive commissions for referring to the Amazon site customers who then make a purchase.

To overcome the lag between purchase and delivery of product, Amazon has offered fast, inexpensive shipping. Amazon has also diversified its product lines into DVDs, music CDs, computer software, video games, electronics, apparel, furniture, food, toys, and more. One key to Amazon's success in all these different ventures was a willingness to invest in the latest Internet technology to make shopping online faster, easier, and more personally rewarding. The Amazon Web project, launched in 2002, opened up its databases to more than 65 000 programmers and businesses that, in turn, have built moneymaking websites, new

online shopping interfaces, and innovative services for Amazon.com's 800 000 or so active sellers. One application was a service, ScoutPal, that turned cell phones into mobile bar-code scanners.

Amazon.com's next move? The firm is spending heavily on development to allow consumers to download videos, music, and books. As Jeff Bezos wrote in his letter to shareholders in 1997, which he reprinted in Amazon.com's 2005 annual report, "It's all about the long term." The company has been spending heavily on technology and content to fend off attacks by competitors such as Wal-Mart and other well-heeled retailers which are starting to take Internet sales more seriously. Despite the danger from competitors, by 2007 Amazon's margins were improving. Financial analysts like Scorr Devitt are showing renewed confidence in Amazon's stock. In a note to his clients, he wrote "We believe Amazon is a platform company with the capacity to grow significantly, not only within the media category, but in all categories of general merchandise retail and we believe the company retains real option value as a web services and digital media business."

DISCUSSION QUESTIONS

1. What have been the key success factors for Amazon?

2. Where is Amazon vulnerable? What should marketers watch out for?

3. What recommendations would you make to senior marketing executives going forward? What should they be sure to do with the company's marketing?

Sources: "Click to Download," *Economist*, August 19, 2006, pp. 57–58; Robert D. Hof, "Jeff Bezos' Risky Bet," *BusinessWeek*, November 13, 2006; Erick Schonfield, "The Great Giveaway," *Business 2.0* (April 2005): 80–86; Elizabeth West, "Who's Next?" *Potentials* (February 2004): 7–8; Robert D. Hof, "The Wizard of Web Retailing," *BusinessWeek*, December 20, 2004, p. 18; Chris Taylor, "Smart Library," *Time*, November 17, 2003, p. 68; Ben Charny, "Has Amazon.com fixed its profitability problem?" *MarketWatch*, April 27, 2007.

IN THIS CHAPTER,
WE WILL ADDRESS
THE FOLLOWING
QUESTIONS:

- What major types of marketing intermediaries occupy this
  sector?

- What marketing decisions do
  these marketing intermediaries make?

- What are the major trends
  with marketing intermediaries?

CHAPTER 16

MANAGING RETAILING, WHOLESALING, AND LOGISTICS

sixteen

In the previous chapter, we examined marketing intermediaries from the viewpoint of manufacturers which wanted to build and manage marketing channels. In this chapter, we view these intermediaries—retailers, wholesalers, and logistical organizations—as requiring and forging their own marketing strategies. Intermediaries also strive for marketing excellence and can reap the benefits like any other company.

Spain's Zara has become Europe's leading apparel retailer in recent years by adopting a different retail model. After forming a partnership with Montreal-based Reitman's Canada, Zara opened three stores in Canada in 1999, first launching in Vancouver, Toronto, and Montreal. The firm's strategy is to give customers lots of variety at affordable prices. It can make 20 000 different items in a year, about triple what Gap would do. Zara distributes all of its merchandise, regardless of origin, from Spain and is willing to experience occasional shortages to preserve an image of exclusivity. Unlike some other retailers, Zara doesn't spend lavish amounts of money on advertising or on deals with designers and instead invests more in its store locations. Zara places its stores—over 90 percent of which it owns—in heavily trafficked, high-end retail zones. These practices help it to sell more at full price—85 percent of its merchandise—than the industry average of 60 percent. By controlling all aspects of the supply chain, Zara can take an idea and make it a reality on the store floor in about five weeks, compared to the months needed by a typical clothing manufacturer.

But while "fast-forward" retailers such as Zara, Sweden's H&M, Spain's Mango, and Britain's Topshop have thrived in recent years, other former stars like Gap, Home Depot, and Zellers have struggled. Many of the more successful intermediaries use strategic planning, advanced information systems, and sophisticated marketing tools. They measure performance more on a return-on-investment basis than on a profit-margin basis. They segment their markets, improve their market targeting and positioning, and aggressively pursue market expansion and diversification strategies. In this chapter, we consider marketing excellence in retailing, wholesaling, and logistics.

Sources: Kerry Capell, "Fashion Conquistador," *BusinessWeek*, September 4, 2006, pp. 38–39; Rachel Tipaldy, "Zara: Taking the Lead in Fast-Fashion," *BusinessWeek*, April 4, 2006; Kasra Ferdows, Michael A. Lewis, and Jose A. D. Machuca, "Zara's Secret for Fast Fashion," *Harvard Business School Working Knowledge*, February 21, 2005; Vivian Manning-Schaffel, "Zara-Zesty," *brandchannel.com*, August 23, 2004; "Agreement between the Inditex Group and the Canadian Group Reitman's," Inditex press release, July 7, 1999.

RETAILING

Retailing includes all of the activities in selling goods or services directly to final consumers for personal, nonbusiness use. A **retailer** or **retail store** is any business enterprise whose sales volume comes primarily from retailing.

Any organization selling to final consumers—whether it is a manufacturer, wholesaler, or retailer—is doing retailing. It doesn't matter *how* the goods or services are sold (in person, by mail, telephone, vending machine, or on the Internet) or *where* (in a store, on the street, or in the consumer's home).

Types of Retailers

Consumers today can shop for goods and services at store retailers, nonstore retailers, and retail organizations. Perhaps the best-known type of retailer is the department store. While department stores have flourished in some countries, they have struggled in others. Japanese department stores such as Takashimaya and Mitsukoshi attract millions of shoppers each year and feature art galleries, restaurants, cooking classes, fitness clubs, and children's playgrounds. In Canada, department stores have struggled. Famous department stores with long histories like Eaton's and Woodward's have gone out of business. Others, like the Hudson Bay Company have been purchased by U.S. firms. Retail-store types pass through stages of growth and decline that we can think of as the *retail life cycle*.[1] Department stores took 80 years to reach maturity, whereas warehouse retail outlets reached maturity in ten years. The most important retail-store types are described in Table 16.1.

LEVELS OF SERVICE   The *wheel-of-retailing* hypothesis explains one reason that new store types emerge.[2] Conventional retail stores typically increase their services and raise their prices to cover the costs. These higher costs provide an opportunity for new store forms to offer lower prices and less service. New store types meet widely different consumer preferences for service levels and specific services.

Retailers position themselves as offering one of four levels of service:

1. *Self-service*—Self-service is the cornerstone of all discount operations. Many customers are willing to carry out their own locate-compare-select process to save money.

2. *Self-selection*—Customers find their own goods, although they can ask for assistance.

3. *Limited service*—These retailers carry more shopping goods and services such as credit and merchandise-return privileges. Customers need more information and assistance.

4. *Full service*—Salespeople are ready to assist in every phase of the locate-compare-select process. Customers who like to be waited on prefer this type of store. The high staffing cost, along with the higher proportion of specialty goods and slower-moving items and the many services, result in high-cost retailing.

Department stores are the best-known type of retailer. Japan's Takashimaya attracts millions each year with special offerings such as art galleries, playgrounds, and restaurants.

TABLE 16.1	MAJOR RETAILER TYPES

Specialty store: Narrow product line. E.g., Athlete's Foot, The Limited, The Body Shop.

Department store: Several product lines. E.g., Sears, The Bay, Canadian Tire.

Supermarket: Large, low-cost, low-margin, high-volume, self-service store designed to meet total needs for food and household products. E.g., Loblaws, Metro, A&P, Sobeys, Safeway.

Convenience store: Small store in residential area, often open 24/7; limited line of high-turnover convenience products plus takeout. E.g., 7-Eleven, Mac's.

Discount store: Standard or specialty merchandise; low-price, low-margin, high-volume stores. E.g., Wal-Mart, Zellers.

Off-price retailer: Leftover goods, overruns, irregular merchandise sold at less than retail. E.g., Factory outlets, Winners, Dollar Store.

Superstore: Huge selling space, routinely purchased food and household items, plus services (laundry, shoe repair, dry cleaning). E.g., category killers (deep assortment in one category) such as PetSmart, Staples, Home Depot; combination stores such as Jewel-Osco in the U.S.; hypermarkets (huge stores that combine supermarket, discount, and warehouse retailing) such as Carrefour in France and Meijer's in the Netherlands.

By combining these different service levels with different assortment breadths, we can distinguish the four broad positioning strategies available to retailers, as shown in Figure 16.1.

1. *Holt Renfrew*—Stores that feature a broad product assortment and high value-added pay close attention to store design, product quality, service, and image. Their profit margin is high, and if their volume is high enough, they will be very profitable.

2. *Tiffany & Co.*—Stores that feature a narrow product assortment and high value-added cultivate an exclusive image and operate on high margin and low volume.

3. *Sunglass Hut*—Stores that feature a narrow line and low value-added keep costs and prices low by centralizing buying, merchandising, advertising, and distribution.

4. *Zellers*—Stores that feature a broad line and low value-added focus on keeping prices low and have the image of a place for good buys. High volume makes up for low margin.

Although the overwhelming bulk of goods and services—over 97 percent—is sold through stores, *nonstore retailing* has been growing much faster than store retailing. Nonstore retailing falls into four major categories: direct selling, direct marketing (which includes telemarketing and Internet selling), automatic vending, and buying services:

1. *Direct selling, also called multi-level selling and network marketing,* is a multi-billion-dollar industry, with hundreds of companies selling door-to-door or at home sales parties. Well-known

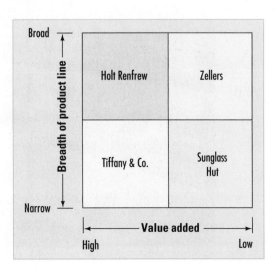

FIGURE 16.1

Retail-Positioning Map

Source: Adapted from William T. Gregor and Eileen M. Friars, *Money Merchandising: Retail Revolution in Consumer Financial Service* (Cambridge, MA: The MAC Group, 1982).

in one-to-one selling are Avon and Electrolux. Tupperware and Mary Kay Cosmetics are sold one-to-many: a salesperson goes to the home of a host who has invited friends; the salesperson demonstrates the products and takes orders. Pioneered by Amway, the multi-level (network) marketing sales system works by recruiting independent business-people who act as distributors. The distributor's compensation includes a percentage of sales made by those he or she recruits, as well as earnings on direct sales to customers. These direct-selling firms, now finding fewer consumers at home, are developing multi-distribution strategies.

2. *Direct marketing* has roots in direct-mail and catalogue marketing (Tilley Endurables, Lands' End, L.L. Bean); it includes *telemarketing* (1-800-FLOWERS), *television direct-response marketing* (The Shopping Channel), and *electronic shopping* (Amazon.ca). As people become more accustomed to shopping on the Internet, they are ordering a greater variety of goods and services from a wider range of websites. Travel, computer equipment and software, automobiles, clothing, and home furnishings tend to be the biggest categories.[3]

    Due to our smaller population, less than a third of Canada's retailers sell online. However, with the rise in the Canadian dollar relative to the U.S. dollar, Canadians are using this new form of cross-border shopping without actually leaving home. Spending by Canadians on American Internet sites has increased. Canada Post noted the volume of shipments through the Canadian postal service's special service for American retailers increased 38 percent between 2006 and 2007.[4]

3. *Automatic vending* offers a variety of merchandise, including impulse goods such as soft drinks, coffee, candy, newspapers, magazines, and other products such as hosiery, cosmetics, hot food, condoms, and paperbacks. Vending machines are found in factories, offices, large retail stores, gasoline stations, hotels, restaurants, and many other places. They offer 24-hour selling, self-service, and merchandise that is always fresh. Japan has the most vending machines per person—Coca-Cola has over 1 million machines there and annual vending sales of $50 billion—twice that in the United States.

4. *Buying service* is a storeless retailer serving a specific clientele—usually employees of large organizations—who are entitled to buy from a list of retailers that have agreed to give discounts in return for membership.

CORPORATE RETAILING   Although many retail stores are independently owned, an increasing number are part of a **corporate retailing** organization. These organizations achieve economies of scale, greater purchasing power, wider brand recognition, and better-trained employees than independent stores can usually gain alone. The major types of corporate retailing—corporate chain stores, voluntary chains, retailer and consumer cooperatives, franchises, and merchandising conglomerates—are described in Table 16.2.

Vending machines are enormously popular retail outlets in Japan, dispensing everything from jeans to expensive food. Coca-Cola alone operates more than a million drink machines there.

TABLE 16.2	MAJOR TYPES OF CORPORATE RETAIL ORGANIZATIONS

Corporate chain store: Two or more outlets owned and controlled, employing central buying and merchandising, and selling similar lines of merchandise. E.g., Gap, Tim Hortons, Swiss Chalet.

Voluntary chain: A wholesaler-sponsored group of independent retailers engaged in bulk buying and common merchandising. E.g., Independent Grocers Alliance (IGA).

Retailer cooperative: Independent retailers using a central buying organization and joint promotion efforts. E.g., Associated Grocers, Home Hardware.

Consumer cooperative: A retail firm owned by its customers. Members contribute money to open their own store, vote on its policies, elect a group to manage it, and receive dividends. E.g., Mountain Equipment Co-op (MEC), Kingston Credit Union.

Franchise organization: Contractual association between a franchisor and franchisees, popular in a number of product and service areas. E.g., McDonald's, East Side Marios, Pizza Hut, HomeWell Senior Care.

Merchandising conglomerate: A corporation that combines several diversified retailing lines and forms under central ownership, with some integration of distribution and management. E.g., Allied Domeq PLC with Dunkin' Donuts and Baskin-Robbins, plus a number of British retailers and a wine and spirits group.

The Canadian Franchise Association estimates that franchise businesses such as Investors Group, Subway, M&M Meat Shops, Oxford Learning Centres, and Mr. Lube account for more than $100 billion in annual sales and roughly 40 percent of all retail transactions.[5] Just see how quickly one new franchise operation was born:

Two Blonds & a Brunette Gift Co.

Two Blonds & a Brunette Gift Co., based in Winnipeg, Manitoba, was founded by Laura McDonald and Seri Blatt (the Blonds) in 2002. Their aim was to bring sophistication, spunk, and style to the corporate and personal gift-giving markets. With only business cards to their name, the two entrepreneurs quickly built a successful and stylish one-location gift company. A new business partner, Anne Kozak (the Brunette), who had a lot of experience with brand management at Unilever, rounded out the team. There was a reason celebrity agents called on Two Blonds & a Brunette Gift Co. when they needed to impress a client. The founders' mandate was simple: No wrapped sausage or processed cheese please! They wanted Vargas Pin-Up Girl Bath Cubes and Brazilian Mango Body Butter, thank you very much! Despite the success of the original venture, McDonald, Blatt, and Kozak quickly realized that there was another market out there—a market of talented, dynamic, driven women and men who were just waiting for the right business to call their own. The idea to franchise the business was born. Publicity, especially a significant editorial mention in a national magazine's Holiday 2005 issue, was instrumental in generating franchise inquiries. Less than six months later, the first two "2B&B" franchise locations opened, in June 2006. Now, two years later, there are over ten franchise locations across North America and the company is growing quickly. Their unique and funky gifts and gift baskets have transformed the once-lowly gift basket into a veritable work of art. When it comes to building a franchise, blonde, brunette, redhead—and all shades in between are welcome![6]

In recent years a franchise explosion has helped saturate the domestic market. To sustain growth, firms are looking overseas and in nontraditional site locations such as airports, sports stadiums, college campuses, hospitals, gambling casinos, theme parks, convention halls, and even riverboats. And franchises that offer a unique product or service can always find customers. The aging population in developed, English-speaking countries is driving the success of an unusual franchise called Comfort Keepers.

Two Blonds & a Brunette Gift Co. is a new franchise that is rapidly expanding. Its unique and funky gifts and gift baskets have transformed the once-lowly gift basket into a veritable work of art and the founders invited others to share in their success.

Comfort Keepers

Comfort Keepers began in 1997 when a registered nurse, Kris Clum, was frustrated that she was allowed to meet only her clients' medical needs. Many of her in-home clients also needed someone to pick up a loaf of bread or drive them to the doctor, to bathe them, or simply to sit and chat. With her husband she founded the Comfort Keepers franchise, which now has 550 franchised offices in the United States, Canada, the United Kingdom, Ireland, Australia, and even Singapore. Comfort Keepers provides a wide range of personal in-home care services to thousands of elderly or home-bound individuals, and visits range from a few hours a week to round-the-clock care. Since 13.4 percent of the Canadian population is aged 65 or older, and since this segment is growing, the future seems bright for Comfort Keepers.[7]

To find out how malls in Malaysia are addressing the challenges of intense competition, visit www.pearsoned-asia.com/ marketingmanagementasia.

In a franchising system, individual *franchisees* are a tightly knit group of enterprises whose systematic operations are planned, directed, and controlled by the operation's innovator, called a *franchisor*. Franchises are distinguished by three characteristics:

1. The franchisor owns a trade or service mark and licenses it to franchisees in return for royalty payments.

2. The franchisee pays for the right to be part of the system. Start-up costs include rental and lease equipment and fixtures, and usually a regular licence fee. McDonald's franchisees may invest as much as $1.6 million in total start-up costs and fees. The franchisee then pays McDonald's a certain percentage of sales plus a monthly rent.

3. The franchisor provides its franchisees with a system for doing business. McDonald's requires franchisees to attend "Hamburger University" or the "Canadian Institute of Hamburgerology" to learn how to manage the business. Franchisees must follow certain procedures in buying materials.

Franchising benefits both franchisor and franchisee. Franchisors gain the motivation and hard work of employees who are entrepreneurs rather than "hired hands," the franchisees' familiarity with local communities and conditions, and the enormous purchasing power of being a franchisor. Franchisees benefit from buying into a business with a well-known and accepted brand name. They find it easier to borrow money for their business from financial institutions, and they receive support in areas ranging from marketing and advertising to site selection and staffing. Franchisees walk a line between being independent and being loyal to the franchisor. Their independence can allow them more flexibility.

The New Retail Environment

In the past, retailers secured customer loyalty by offering convenient locations, special or unique assortments of goods, services greater or better than competitors', and store credit cards. All this has changed. Consumers are less loyal and they are increasingly shopping many different types of retailers—high end one minute and discount retailers the next. Retail-store assortments have grown more alike as national-brand manufacturers place their branded goods in more and more places. Service differentiation also has eroded. Many department stores have trimmed services, and many discounters have increased theirs. Customers have become smarter shoppers. They don't want to pay more for identical brands, especially when service differences have diminished; nor do they need credit from a particular store, because bank credit cards are almost universally accepted.

Retailers must react or risk going out of business. In the face of increased competition from discount houses and specialty stores, department stores are waging a comeback war. In addition to locations in the centres of cities, many have branches in suburban shopping centres, where parking is plentiful and family incomes are higher. To better compete, other department stores update merchandise more frequently, remodel their stores, introduce their own brands, and sell through mail-order catalogues, online websites, and the telephone.[8]

Similarly, supermarkets have opened larger stores, carry a larger number and variety of items, and are upgrading facilities. They've also increased their promotional budgets and moved heavily into private labels. Others, such as Whole Foods, have sought to create stronger differentiation.

Many characteristics of Whole Foods' outlets, such as helpful employees and unique products, exemplify the new retail environment.

Whole Foods Market

As of 2008, 270 Whole Foods Stores operated in North America and the United Kingdom, creating celebrations of food. The markets are bright and well staffed, and food displays are bountiful and seductive. Whole Foods is the largest organic and natural foods grocer in North America, offering more than 1500 items in four lines of private-label products (such as the premium Whole Foods and a line of organic products for children, Whole Kids). Whole Foods offers lots of information about its food. If you want to know, for instance, whether the chicken in the display case lived a happy, free-roaming life, you can get a 16-page booklet and an invitation to visit the farm where it was raised. If you can't find the information you need, you have only to ask a well-trained and knowledgeable employee. Whole Foods' approach is working, especially for consumers who view organic and artisanal food as an affordable luxury. From 2004 to 2008 the company enjoyed double-digit growth in overall and comparable-store, year-to-year sales.[9]

Here are some of the other retail developments that are changing the way consumers buy and manufacturers and retailers sell:

■ *New Retail Forms and Combinations.* Loblaws and CIBC joined forces to offer PC Financial in supermarkets across Canada. Loblaws supermarkets have also added fitness clubs to some of their stores. Chapters and Starbucks formed a partnership. Best Buy Canada Ltd. has struggled to attract young consumers (who love to go to the mall) to their big-box stores located in strip malls. Therefore, in 2008, Best Buy unveiled its new Best Buy Mobile stores that will open in malls to sell phones in this rapidly expanding segment of the electronics marketplace. Shopping malls and bus and train stations have peddlers' carts in their aisles. Retailers are also experimenting with limited-time-only stores called "pop-ups" that let retailers promote brands, reach seasonal shoppers for a few weeks in busy areas, and create buzz. For example, U.S. retailer JCPenney unveiled designer Chris Madden's home, bath, and kitchen line in a 2500-square-foot Rockefeller Center space for one month only. The pop-up offered four PCs for web buying, so that customers were exposed to a wider selection of JCPenney merchandise.[10]

Some stores such as Galeries Lafayette in Paris and Selfridges in London not only sell other companies' brands but get the vendors of those brands to take responsibility for stock, staff, and even the selling space. The vendors then hand over a percentage of the sales to the store's owner. This translates into lower gross margins for the department store, but it also lowers operating costs. The showcase store needs to keep droves of customers coming in, and that means it needs to be an entertainment destination in its own right. Galeries Lafayette's flagship Paris store offered free lessons from professional striptease artists to promote the opening of its huge new lingerie department.[11]

■   *Growth of Intertype Competition.* Department stores can't worry just about other department stores—discount chains such as Wal-Mart and Tesco are expanding into product areas such as clothing, health, beauty, and electrical appliances.[12] Different types of stores—discount stores, specialty retailers, department stores—all compete for the same consumers by carrying the same type of merchandise. The biggest winners: retailers that have helped shoppers to be economically cautious, simplified their increasingly busy and complicated lives, and provided an emotional connection.[13]

■   *Competition between Store-Based and Non-Store-Based Retailing.* Consumers now receive sales offers through direct-mail letters and catalogues, and over television, computers, and telephones. These non-store-based retailers are taking business away from store-based retailers. Although some store-based retailers such as Home Depot initially saw online retailing as a definite threat, they are now finding it advantageous to work with online retailers. Most major retailers such as Canadian Tire, Zellers, and Shoppers Drug Mart have developed their own websites, and some online retailers own or manage physical outlets, either retail stores or warehouses.

■   *Growth of Giant Retailers.* Through their superior information systems, logistical systems, and buying power, giant retailers such as Wal-Mart are able to deliver good service and immense volumes of product at appealing prices to masses of consumers. They are crowding out smaller manufacturers that cannot deliver enough quantity and often dictate to the most powerful manufacturers what to make, how to price and promote, when and how to ship, and even how to improve production and management. Manufacturers need these accounts; otherwise they would lose 10 to 30 percent of the market. Some giant retailers are *category killers* that concentrate on one product category, such as pet supplies (PetSmart), home improvement (Home Depot), or office supplies (Staples). Others are *supercentres* that combine grocery items with a huge selection of nonfood merchandise (Wal-Mart).

■   *Decline of Middle-Market Retailers.* Today we can characterize the retail market as hourglass or dog-bone shaped: Growth seems to be centred at the top (with luxury offerings from retailers such as Holt Renfrew, William Ashley China, Birks) and at the bottom (with discount pricing from retailers such as Dollar Stores and Costco). Opportunities are scarcer in the middle where retailers such as Sears, The Bay, and others have struggled or gone out of business like Eaton's. Supermarkets, department stores, and drugstores are most at risk or on the brink—fewer consumers have shopped these channels weekly in recent years as newer, more relevant places have come to serve their needs. According to market research firm NPD Group, in 2006 traditional department stores in Canada held just a 17-percent share of the $19-billion Canadian apparel market, down from 19.4 percent in 2004.[14] As discount retailers improve their quality and image, consumers have been willing to trade down. Some retailers are fighting back. Kmart has begun selling an extensive line of Joe Boxer underwear and sleepwear.[15] Marks and Spencer in the United Kingdom features in-house brands and has built a strong retail brand image. Although these stores tend to have high operating costs, they command high margins if their in-house brands are both fashionable and popular.[16] See what's happening at Hudson's Bay Co:

Hudson's Bay Co.

Founded in 1670, the Hudson's Bay Co. is Canada's oldest retailer, North America's oldest continuously operating company, and one of Canada's most iconic brands. Despite significant challenges in recent years, the Hudson's Bay Co. (HBC) has begun a revitalization process. It was first taken over by American businessman Jerry Zucker in early 2007. In July 2008, after Zucker's death, HBC was acquired by another American investor who had also turned around the oldest department store in the U.S., the Lord & Taylor chain. HBC has already seen an infusion of experienced retail managers into its senior ranks. Jeffrey Sherman, the new CEO, joined HBC from Polo Ralph Lauren Corp. Canadian consumers can expect to see new brands and service initiatives at The Bay and Zellers locations across the country. In addition, 10 to 15 Lord & Taylor-branded stores are likely to launch throughout Canada in the near future. Before these takeovers, The Bay had an image of being "pedestrian," a "mom store," and an "old department store." It is now working to be more dynamic and responsive to consumer tastes and needs. It has revitalized its advertising and, to compete more effectively with specialty stores, it is moving to a more boutique-style approach. It is also increasing the number of products that are exclusive to The Bay, including Baia ("Bay" in Italian), an exclusive ladies' sportswear collection. The strategy appears to be working. In 2007, HBC experienced the most profitable fourth quarter since 2004 as a result of cost cuts, improved technology, better service, more upscale new brands, and extensive renovations. The new owner still has its hills to climb, however, since sales were flat at HBC's three flagship stores and drawing in more customers continues to be a challenge.[17]

■ *Growing Investment in Technology.* Retailers are using computers to produce better forecasts, control inventory costs, order electronically from suppliers, send email between stores, and even sell to customers within stores. Take the case of Bosley's Pet Food Plus:

Bosley's Pet Food Plus

Bosley's is British Columbia's leading pet specialty store and operates 22 retail outlets. In 2007, operational problems threatened customer service. Communication between the stores was dependent on telephones and fax machines, and since it hadn't computerized any of its systems, sharing information about inventory levels was difficult. It's not surprising that Bosley's head office had no idea what was happening at the store level on a daily basis. With help from Microsoft Canada, Bosley's went from virtually no automation to an advanced Enterprise Resource Planning (ERP) business solution and an automated customer-loyalty program in just over a few months. The new system helped Bosley's better manage its inventory, undertake daily sales reporting, and have real-time business intelligence. Most importantly, Bosley's was able to improve customer service, proving even small firms can benefit from advanced technology.[18]

Other retailers, such as Wendy's International, are borrowing technological tactics from other industries, and with great success.

Wendy's International Inc.

Drive-through business accounts for a sizable percentage of fast-food sales, but the system is dogged by two major profit killers: (1) employee theft (when late-night drive-through employees give food to their friends and pocket the cash) and (2) slowness. No one wants to sit in a hot car waiting for cold french fries to arrive. Now, Wendy's, McDonald's, and a host of fast-food companies are adopting call-centre technology to fill orders even faster. When you pull into one of the drive-through lanes at Wendy's, the voice that takes your order may be coming from a call centre 3000 kilometres away. It's connected to the computer of a call-centre employee using Internet calling technology. The employee needs a mere 40 milliseconds to transfer your order to a screen in the drive-through kitchen. Call centres not only free employees to put orders together faster, they also make orders more accurate and more profitable. Call-centre employees are trained to urge customers to order extras, such as a larger order of fries or a drink with each order. It's a win-win strategy, especially for Wendy's, which differentiates itself on its drive-through speed and has been the industry's speediest server for seven straight years. With call-centre technology, Wendy's expects to complete orders in under 90 seconds.[19]

Retailers are also adopting checkout scanning systems,[20] electronic funds transfer, electronic data interchange,[21] in-store television, store traffic radar systems,[22] and improved merchandise-handling systems. Some employ goggle-like devices that record what test customers see by projecting an infrared beam onto the wearer's retina. One finding was that many shoppers ignored products at eye level—the optimum location was between their waist and chest level.[23]

Retailers are also introducing features to help customers as they shop. Some supermarkets are installing personal shopping "assistants" on shopping carts that help customers locate items in the store, find out about sales and special offers, and even place a deli order.[24]

■   *Global Profile of Major Retailers.* Retailers with unique formats and strong brand positioning are increasingly appearing in other countries.[25] Britain's Marks and Spencer, Italy's Benetton, France's Carrefour hypermarkets, and Sweden's IKEA home-furnishings stores are household names in many countries. U.S. retailers such as The Limited, Gap, and Wal-Mart have become globally prominent. In 2007, Wal-Mart generated 22 percent of its business outside the U.S. and it looked to Canada for growth in the face of sluggish U.S. sales.[26] Dutch retailer Ahold and Belgian retailer Delhaize earn almost 80 percent of their sales in nondomestic markets.

Marketing Decisions

With this new retail environment as a backdrop, we will examine retailers' marketing decisions in the areas of target market, product assortment and procurement, prices, services and store atmosphere, store activities and experiences, communications, and location.

TARGET MARKET   Until it defines and profiles the target market, the retailer cannot make consistent decisions about product assortment, store decor, advertising messages and media, price, and service levels. Ann Taylor has an external client panel of 3000 customers who provide feedback on its merchandise and even its marketing campaigns. The firm also solicits employees' input.[27]

Mistakes in choosing or switching target markets can be costly. Many identify such an error as the cause of Eaton's demise.

To better hit their targets, retailers are slicing the market into finer and finer segments and introducing new lines of stores to provide more relevant sets of offerings to exploit niche markets: Gymboree launched Janie and Jack, selling apparel and gifts for babies and toddlers; Hot Topic introduced Torrid, selling fashions for plus-sized teen girls.

PRODUCT ASSORTMENT   The retailer's product assortment must match the target market's shopping expectations. The retailer must decide on product-assortment *breadth* and *depth*. A restaurant can offer a narrow and shallow assortment (small lunch counters), a narrow and deep assortment (delicatessen), a broad and shallow assortment (cafeteria), or a broad and deep assortment (large restaurant). Table 16.3 provides an illustration of how Chapters could develop category assortment within a section of its stores.

Product assortment can be especially challenging in fast-moving industries such as technology and fashion. Urban Outfitters ran into trouble when it strayed from its "hip, but not too hip" formula, moving to embrace new styles too quickly. Sales fell over 25 percent during 2006.[28] On the other hand, active- and casual-apparel retailer Aéropostale has found success by carefully matching its product assortment to its young teen target market's needs.

When it comes to product assortment, fashion retailers have a particularly hard time staying on top of the right trends. Aéropostale has succeeded by using product tests, focus groups, and online research into its teenaged customers.

TABLE 16.3	RETAIL CATEGORY MANAGEMENT	
Step	**What It Means**	**How Chapters Could Apply It**
1. Define the category.	Decide where you draw the line between product categories. For example, do your customers view alcohol and soft drinks as one beverage category, or should you manage them separately?	Name the cookbook section Food and Cooking because consumers expect to see books on nutrition there as well.
2. Figure out its role.	Determine how the category fits into the whole store. For example, "destination" categories lure folks in, so they get maximum marketing push, whereas "fill-ins" carry a minimal assortment.	Decide to make Food and Cooking a destination category.
3. Assess performance.	Analyze sales data from AC Nielsen, Information Resources Inc., and others. Identify opportunities.	If it's learned that cookbooks sell faster than expected during holidays, respond by creating gift promotions.
4. Set goals.	Agree on the category's objectives, including sales, profit, and average-transaction targets, as well as customer-satisfaction levels.	Aim to grow cookbook sales faster than the store average and to grab market share from competition.
5. Choose the audience.	Sharpen your focus within the category for maximum effect.	Decide to go after repeat buyers. If 30 percent of shoppers buy 70 percent of the cookbooks, this would be a wise move.
6. Figure out tactics.	Decide the best product selection, promotion merchandising, and pricing to achieve the category's goals.	Give more prominent display to books by celebrity chefs such as Jamie Oliver and Rachael Ray. Create a more approachable product selection by reducing the number of titles on certain subjects.
7. Implement the plan.	Set the timetable and execute the tactics.	Introduce changes to cooking sections according to desired schedule.

Source: Adapted from Andrew Raskin, "Who's Minding the Store?" *Business 2.0* (February 2003): 73.

Aéropostale Inc.

Rather than compete head-on with trend-setting Abercrombie & Fitch or American Eagle Outfitters Inc., Aéropostale has chosen to embrace a key reality of its target market: 11-to-18-year-old young men and women, and especially those on the young end, who often want to look like other teens. So while Abercrombie and American Eagle might choose to reduce the number of cargo pants on the sales floor, Aéropostale will keep an ample supply on hand and at an affordable price. Staying on top of the right trends isn't easy, but Aéropostale is among the most diligent of teen retailers when it comes to consumer research. In addition to high-school focus groups and in-store product tests, Aéropostale launched an Internet-based program that seeks online shoppers' input in creating new styles. The company targets 10 000 of its best customers for each of these tests and averages 3500 participants in each of 20 tests a year. Aéropostale has gone from being a lacklustre performer with only 100 stores to a powerhouse with 736 mall stores. Earnings jumped 16.5 percent in fiscal year 2006 alone.[29]

The real challenge begins after defining the store's product assortment, and that is to develop a product-differentiation strategy. Here are some possibilities:

- *Feature exclusive national brands that are not available at competing retailers.* Harry Rosen might get exclusive rights to carry suits of a well-known international designer.

- *Feature mostly private-label merchandise.* Benetton and Gap design most of the clothes carried in their stores. Many supermarket and drug chains like Loblaws and Shoppers Drug Mart feature extensive private-label merchandise.

- *Feature blockbuster distinctive merchandise events.* In 2007, Holt Renfrew's flagship Toronto store on Bloor Street West hosted the launch of Sienna and Savannah Miller's Twenty8Twelve label in Canada. The designers were joined by a bevy of celebrities in town for the Toronto

International Film Festival. The store was decorated with a vintage circus theme, building on Twenty8Twelve's positioning as a contemporary brand combining time-honoured tailoring techniques with a vintage feel.[30]

- *Feature surprise or ever-changing merchandise.* Off-price apparel retailer TJ Maxx offers surprise assortments of distress merchandise (goods the owner must sell immediately because it needs cash), overstocks, and closeouts, totalling 10 000 new items each week.

- *Feature the latest or newest merchandise first.* Hot Topic sells hip clothing and hard-to-find pop-culture merchandise to teens, catching trends in order to launch new products in six to eight weeks, literally months before traditional competitors using off-shore suppliers.[31]

- *Offer merchandise-customizing services.* Harrod's of London will make custom-tailored suits, shirts, and ties for customers, in addition to offering ready-made menswear.

- *Offer a highly targeted assortment.* Lane Bryant carries goods for the larger woman. Brookstone offers unusual tools and gadgets for the person who wants to shop in a "toy store for grown-ups."[32] Merchandise may vary by geographical market. Electronics superstore Best Buy reviewed each of its 25 000 SKUs to adjust its merchandise according to income level and buying habits of shoppers. They will also put different store formats and staffs in different areas—a location with computer sophisticates gets a different store treatment than one with less technically sophisticated computer users.[33] Bed Bath & Beyond allows store managers to pick 70 percent of their own merchandise to ensure that stores cater to local interests.[34]

As Chapter 15 explained, retailers that use multiple selling channels must integrate them effectively. Century-old department store chain Sears Canada has ensured that its online, store, and catalogue businesses are fully intertwined. In 2006, it joined forces with Amazon Enterprise solutions group to re-design its online storefront to provide users with Canada's most extensive online merchandise selection with the latest in e-commerce technology. Just as Sears does in its physical stores, the site makes it easy to compare products and it also features a personalization service designed to make shopping easier and less time consuming. The site is able to recommend merchandise based on a user's past shopping patterns, offer suggestions, and show the customer the more commonly purchased items within a product category. Time-pressed shoppers can transfer items from their shopping basket to the "Save for Later Cart." Others, like brides, can use the "Wish List" feature that enables shoppers to make their desires known to family and friends. These tactics have helped give Sears a younger, more upscale image.[35]

PROCUREMENT　After deciding on the product-assortment strategy, the retailer must establish merchandise sources, policies, and practices. In the corporate headquarters of a supermarket chain, specialist buyers (sometimes called *merchandise managers*) are responsible for developing brand assortments and listening to salespersons' presentations. In some chains, buyers have the authority to accept or reject new items. In other chains, they are limited to screening "obvious rejects" and "obvious accepts"; they bring other items to the buying committee for approval. Even when an item is accepted by a chain-store buying committee, individual stores in the chain may not carry it. About one-third of the items must be stocked, and about two-thirds are stocked at the discretion of each store manager.

Manufacturers face a major challenge trying to get new items onto store shelves. They offer supermarkets between 150 and 250 new items each week, of which store buyers reject over 70 percent. Manufacturers need to know the acceptance criteria used by buyers, buying committees, and store managers. AC Nielsen interviewed store managers and found they are most influenced by (in order of importance) strong evidence of consumer acceptance, a well-designed advertising and sales promotion plan, and generous financial incentives to the trade.

Retailers are rapidly improving their skills in demand forecasting, merchandise selection, stock control, space allocation, and display. They use computers to track inventory, compute economic order quantities, order goods, and analyze dollars spent on vendors and products. Supermarket chains use scanner data to manage their merchandise mix on a store-by-store basis, and soon all stores will probably rely on "smart tags" to track goods, in real time, as they move from factories to supermarkets to shopping baskets. For more on the possible uses—and abuses—of this technology, see "Marketing Insight: Making Labels Smarter."

When retailers do study the economics of buying and selling individual products, they typically find that a third of their square footage is tied up in products that don't make an economic profit for

---

MARKETING **INSIGHT** | MAKING LABELS SMARTER

Radio frequency identification (RFID) systems are made up of "smart" tags—microchips attached to tiny radio antennas—and electronic readers. The smart tags can be embedded in products or stuck on labels, and when the tag is near a reader, it transmits a unique identifying number to the reader's computer database. The use of RFIDs has been exploding. Gartner research reported that sales of the tags generated $1.28 billion in revenues in 2008, up 31 percent from the year before, and forecasts that the market will triple by 2012. Radio-tagging products allow retailers to alert manufacturers before shelves go bare, and consumer-goods manufacturers can further perfect their supply chain so they don't produce or distribute too few or too many goods.

Gillette maintains that retailers and consumer-goods firms lose around $30 billion a year from being out of stock on crucial items. The firm is using smart tags to let store owners know they need to reorder, as well as to provide alerts if a large decrease on a shelf may be the result of shoplifting. Gillette also is using smart tags to improve logistics and shipping from factories. RFID technology enabled Gillette to get the new Fusion razor on store shelves 11 days faster than its normal turnaround time. Gillette forecasts a 25-percent return on its RFID investment over the next ten years, through increased sales and productivity savings.

Gillette isn't alone. Coca-Cola is embedding RFID readers in 200 000 of its one million vending machines in Japan to allow consumers to buy a Coke using wallet phones with RFID chips. Staples Canada uses RFID tags so store associates can accurately tell customers what items it has in stock.

The ability to link product IDs with databases containing the life histories and whereabouts of products makes RFID useful for preventing counterfeiting and even ensuring food and drug safety. A food company could program a system to alert plant managers when cases of meat sit too long unrefrigerated. Regulators have started pushing for the widespread tagging of medicines to keep counterfeit pharmaceuticals from entering the market. Some retailers are using RFID to prevent shoplifting.

Although a potential boon to marketers, smart tags raise issues of consumer privacy. Take tagged medications. Electronic readers in office buildings might detect the type of medication carried by employees—an invasion of privacy. Or what about RFID-enabled customer-loyalty cards that encode all sorts of personal and financial data? Already more than 40 public-interest groups have called for strict public-notification rules, the right to demand deactivation of the tag when people leave stores, and overall limits on the technology's use until privacy concerns have been better addressed. In 2006, the Ontario government issued guidelines on the use of RFID tags to help protect consumers and address such privacy concerns.

Sources: Diane Anderson, "RFID Technology Getting Static in New Hampshire," *Brandweek*, January 23, 2006, p. 13; Mary Catherine O'Conner, "Gillette Fuses RFID with Product Launch," *RFID Journal*, March 27, 2006; "The End of Privacy?" *Consumer Reports* (June 2006): 33–40; Erick Schonfeld, "Tagged for Growth," *Business 2.0* (December 2006): 58–61; "Gartner Says Worldwide RFID Revenue to Surpass $1.2 Billion in 2008," Gartner press release, February 25, 2008, www.gartner.com/it/page.jsp?id=610807 (viewed June 2008); "Canada Issues RFID Privacy Guidelines," *Industry Week*, June 27, 2006, www.industryweek.com/ReadArticle.aspx?ArticleID=12215&SectionID=3 (viewed June 2008); Doreen Carvajal, "EU Looks to Limit Use of Radio ID Tags," *International Herald Tribune*, March 2, 2008.

them (above the cost of capital). Another third is typically allocated to product categories that break even. The final third of the space creates almost 100 percent of the economic profit. Yet, most retailers are unaware of which third of their products generate the profit.[36]

Stores are using **direct product profitability (DPP)** to measure a product's handling costs (receiving, moving to storage, paperwork, selecting, checking, loading, and space cost) from the time it reaches the warehouse until a customer buys it in the retail store. Users learn to their surprise that the gross margin on a product often bears little relation to the direct product profit. Some high-volume products may have such high handling costs that they are less profitable and deserve less shelf space than low-volume products.

To better differentiate themselves and generate consumer interest, some luxury retailers are making their stores and merchandise more varied. Chanel has expanded its "ultralux" goods, including $26 000 alligator bags, while ensuring an ample supply of "must-haves" that are consistently strong sellers.[37] Burberry sells antique cufflinks and made-to-measure Scottish kilts only in London and customized trench coats only in New York.[38]

Rona Inc. is beginning to differentiate itself on two fronts: as a green company and as a lifestyle centre.

Rona Inc.

Knowing that its customers were concerned about climate change, Rona recently began offering a line of green products along with advice on how to build in a sustainable way. It offers a growing line of green products and its website offers information on sustainable architecture that shows prospective builders how to make the best site choices, and use materials, energy, and water efficiently. It's also working to attract younger customers by opening new stores in shopping malls, like its 120 000-square-foot Dix30 outlet in Montreal. Called a "lifestyle centre," it is Rona's newest weapon in the war against rivals Home Depot and Lowe's to win over the hearts and wallets of a younger demographic. Using a concept titled "Rona by Design," home decoration items are presented in a "ready-to-wear" format drawn from the world of fashion where key elements from different departments and product categories are presented in integrated displays that suggest the possibilities for new home renovation projects. Its Spirit assortment, for example, is aimed squarely at Gen Y, with cool, stark lines and bright limes and yellows, as well as slightly lower prices. As you can probably tell, Rona's new stores are anything but the haunt of the macho do-it-yourselfers, and one finds the aisles full of the hard-to-attract 30-and-under crowd.[39]

PRICES Prices are a key positioning factor and must be decided in relation to the target market, the product-and-service assortment mix, and the competition.[40] All retailers would like high *turns* × *earns* (high volumes and high gross margins), but the two don't usually go together. Most retailers fall into the *high-markup, lower-volume* group (fine specialty stores) or the *low-markup, higher-volume* group (mass merchandisers and discount stores). Within each of these groups are further gradations. Harry Rosen's stores price suits starting at $1000 and shoes at $400. At the other end, the highly successful U.S. retailer Target has skillfully combined a hip image with discount prices to offer customers a strong value proposition.

Retailers must also pay attention to pricing tactics. Most retailers will put low prices on some items to serve as traffic builders or loss leaders or to signal their pricing policies.[41] They will run storewide sales. They will plan markdowns on slower-moving merchandise. Shoe retailers, for example, expect to sell 50 percent of their shoes at the normal markup, 25 percent at a 40 percent markup, and the remaining 25 percent at cost.

As Chapter 14 notes, some retailers such as Wal-Mart have abandoned "sales pricing" in favour of everyday low pricing (EDLP). EDLP can lead to lower advertising costs, greater pricing stability, a stronger image of fairness and reliability, and higher retail profits. Research has shown that

Rona's green initiatives and new "lifestyle centres" are its newest weapons in the war against rivals Home Depot and Lowe's to win over the hearts and wallets of a younger demographic.

supermarket chains practising everyday low pricing can be more profitable than those practising high-low sale pricing, but only in certain circumstances.[42]

SERVICES The services mix is a key tool for differentiating one store from another. Retailers must decide on the *services mix* to offer customers:

- Prepurchase services include accepting telephone and mail orders; advertising, window, and interior display; and fitting rooms, shopping hours, fashion shows, and trade-ins.
- Postpurchase services include shipping and delivery, gift wrapping, adjustments and returns, alterations and tailoring, installations, and engraving.
- Ancillary services include general information, cheque cashing, parking, restaurants, repairs, interior decorating, credit, rest rooms, and baby-attendant service.

Retailers also need to consider differentiation based on unerringly reliable customer service, whether it is face-to-face, across telephone lines, or even via a technological innovation. Frontline employees can be a means of differentiating and positioning a retailer's brand. While you might find service staff with visible tattoos and multiple body piercings in clothing stores aimed at a young demographic, you are less likely to see them in stores specializing in clothing for older men and women.

Whatever retailers do to enhance customer service, they must keep women in mind. Approximately 85 percent of everything sold in North America is bought or influenced by a woman, and women are fed up with the decline in customer service. They are finding every possible way to get around the system, from ordering online, to resisting fake sales, or just doing without.[43] And when they do shop, they want well-organized layouts, helpful staff, and speedy checkouts.[44]

STORE ATMOSPHERE *Atmosphere* is another element in the store arsenal. Every store has a look and a physical layout that makes it hard or easy to move around (see "Marketing Memo: Helping Stores to Sell"). One effective design is a floor plan modelled after a racetrack. Designed to convey customers smoothly past all the merchandise in the store, the eight-foot-wide main aisle moves them in a circle around the store. The design also includes a middle aisle that hurried shoppers can use as a shortcut. The racetrack loop yields higher spending levels than many competing layouts.[45] Here's how Safeway increased profits by thoroughly reinventing the look of its stores:[46]

- *Walls.* Replaced plain old white walls with earthy tones to convey freshness and wholesomeness
- *Lighting.* Replaced bright glaring lights with warm accent lights that direct attention to products and departments
- *Signage.* Added big pictures of healthy food, as well as display stations throughout the store to suggest meal ideas for time-starved shoppers
- *Produce department.* Enlarged organic section, moving it from a case against the wall to wooden crates at the centre of the floor, suggesting a farmer's market
- *Floors.* Installed hardwood floors in perishables department to provide a natural feel
- *Bakery.* Knocked down walls to show off bread baking in wood-fired oven; added island in centre of department that offers custom bread slicing

Retailers must consider all the senses in shaping the customer's experience. Supermarkets have found that varying the tempo of music affects average time spent in the store and average expenditures. Retailers are adding fragrances to stimulate certain moods. SonyStyle stores are seasoned with a specially designed subtle vanilla and mandarin-orange fragrance. Every surface in a SonyStyle store is also designed to be touchable, from etched glass with beveled edges on countertops to silk paper to maple panelling. Bloomingdale's uses different essences in different departments: baby powder in the baby store; suntan lotion in the bathing suit area; lilacs in lingerie; and cinnamon and pine scent during the holiday season.[47]

STORE ACTIVITIES AND EXPERIENCES The growth of e-commerce has forced traditional bricks-and-mortar retailers to respond. In addition to their natural advantages, such as products that shoppers can actually see, touch, and test, real-life customer service, and no delivery lag time for small or medium-sized purchases, they also provide a shopping experience as a strong differentiator.[48]

Bricks-and-mortar retailers are adopting practices as simple as calling each shopper a "guest" and as grandiose as building an indoor amusement park. The store atmosphere should match the basic motivations of the shopper—if target consumers are more likely to be in a task-oriented and functional mindset, then a simpler, more restrained in-store environment may be better.[49]

| MARKETING MEMO | HELPING STORES TO SELL |

In the pursuit of higher sales volume, retailers are studying their store environments for ways to improve the shopper experience. Paco Underhill is managing director of the retail consultant Envirosell Inc., whose clients include McDonald's, Starbucks, Estée Lauder, Blockbuster, Citibank, Gap, and Burger King. He offers the following advice for fine-tuning retail space in order to keep shoppers spending:

- *Attract shoppers and keep them in the store.* The amount of time shoppers spend in a store is perhaps the single most important factor in determining how much they will buy. To increase shopping time, give shoppers a sense of community; recognize them in some way, manner, or form; give them ways to deal with their accessories, such as spouses and children; and keep an environment that is both familiar and fresh each time they come in.

- *Honour the "transition zone."* On entering a store, people need to slow down and sort out the stimuli. If they hurry in, they will likely be moving too fast to respond positively to signs, merchandise, or sales clerks in the zone they cross before making that transition. Make sure there are clear sight lines. Create a focal point for information within the store.

- *Don't make them hunt.* Put the most popular products up front to reward busy shoppers and encourage leisurely shoppers to look more. At Staples, ink cartridges are one of the first products shoppers encounter after entering.

- *Make merchandise available to the reach and touch.* It is hard to overemphasize the importance of customers' hands. A store can offer the finest, cheapest, sexiest goods, but if the shopper cannot reach or pick them up, much of their appeal can be lost.

- *Note that men do not ask questions.* Men always move faster than women do through a store's aisles. In many settings, it is hard to get them to look at anything they had not intended to buy. Men also do not like asking where things are. If a man cannot find the section he is looking for, he will wheel about once or twice, then leave the store without ever asking for help.

- *Remember women need space.* A shopper, especially a woman, is far less likely to buy an item if her derriere is brushed, even lightly, by another customer when she is looking at a display. Keeping aisles wide and clear is crucial.

- *Make checkout easy.* Be sure to have the right high-margin goods near cash registers to satisfy impulse shoppers. And people love to buy candy when they check out—so satisfy their sweet tooth.

Some of Paco Underhill's additional words of wisdom for modern retailers include: (1) develop expertise in the mature market, (2) sell both to and through your customer, (3) localize your presence, (4) extend your brand—use your history better, (5) build on the Internet-to-phone-to-store connection, (6) find your customers where they are, (7) refine the details of each point of sale, and (8) go undercover as your reality check.

Sources: Paco Underhill, *Call of the Mall: The Geography of Shopping* (New York: Simon & Schuster, 2004); Paco Underhill, *Why We Buy: The Science of Shopping* (New York: Simon & Schuster, 1999). See also Kenneth Hein, "Shopping Guru Sees Death of Detergent Aisle," *Brandweek*, March 27, 2006, p. 11; "Monday Keynote: Why They Buy," *Loupe Online*, 15 (Fall 2006); Bob Parks, "5 Rules of Great Design," *Business 2.0* (March 2003): 47–49; Keith Hammonds, "How We Sell," *Fast Company* (November 1999): 294; www.envirosell.com.

Consistent with this reasoning, some retailers of experiential products are creating in-store entertainment to attract customers who want fun and excitement:

- REI, seller of outdoor gear and clothing products, allows consumers to test climbing equipment on 25-foot or even 65-foot walls in the store and to try Gore-Tex raincoats under a simulated rain shower.[50]

- Victoria's Secret, retailer of lingerie, other women's clothing, and beauty products, works on the concept of "retail theatre": customers feel they are in a romance novel, with lush music and faint floral scents in the background.

- Bass Pro Shops, a retailer of outdoor sports equipment, features giant aquariums, waterfalls, trout ponds, archery and rifle ranges, putting greens, and classes in everything from ice fishing to conservation—all free.

- The Discovery Zone, a chain of children's play spaces, offers indoor spaces where kids can go wild without breaking anything and stressed-out parents can exchange stories.

COMMUNICATIONS Retailers use a wide range of communication tools to generate traffic and purchases. They place ads, run special sales, issue money-saving coupons, and run frequent-shopper reward programs, in-store food sampling, and coupons on shelves or at checkout points. They will also work with manufacturers to design point-of-sale materials that reflect the retailer's image as well as that of the manufacturer's brand.[51] Fine stores will place tasteful, full-page ads in magazines such as *Vogue, Vanity Fair,* and *Esquire* and carefully train salespeople to greet customers, interpret their needs, and handle complaints. Off-price retailers will arrange their merchandise to promote bargains and savings, while conserving on service and sales assistance.

LOCATION The three keys to retail success are "location, location, and location." Department store chains, oil companies, and fast-food franchisers exercise great care in selecting regions of the country in which to open outlets, then particular cities, and then particular sites. A supermarket chain might decide to operate in Ontario; in the cities of Toronto, Hamilton, Oshawa, Kingston, and Ottawa; and in 14 other locations, mostly suburban, within the Toronto metropolitan area.

REI has responded strongly to the threat of online competition by making its retail outlets exciting destinations full of popular attractions such as play spaces and climbing walls.

Retailers can place their stores in the following locations:

- *Central business districts.* The oldest and most heavily trafficked city areas, often known as "downtown"

- *Regional shopping centres.* Large suburban malls containing 40 to 200 stores, typically featuring one or two nationally known anchor stores, such as Sears or The Bay or a combination of big-box stores such as HomeSense, Circuit City, or Michaels, and a great number of smaller stores, many under franchise operation[52]

- *Community shopping centres.* Smaller malls with one anchor store and between 20 and 39 smaller stores

- *Shopping strips.* A cluster of stores, usually housed in one long building, serving a neighbourhood's needs for groceries, hardware, laundry, shoe repair, and dry cleaning

- *A location within a larger store.* Certain well-known retailers—McDonald's, Starbucks, Nathan's, Dunkin' Donuts—locate new, smaller units as concession space within larger stores or operations, such as airports, schools, and department stores.

In view of the relationship between high traffic and high rents, retailers must decide on the most advantageous locations for their outlets using traffic counts, surveys of consumer shopping habits, and analysis of competitive locations.[53] Several models for site location have also been formulated.[54]

Retailers can assess a particular store's sales effectiveness by looking at four indicators: (1) number of people passing by on an average day, (2) percentage who enter the store, (3) percentage who buy, and (4) average amount per sale.

PRIVATE LABELS

A private-label brand (also called a reseller, store, house, or distributor brand) is a brand that retailers and wholesalers develop. Loblaws, Shoppers Drug Mart, Benetton, The Body Shop, and Marks and Spencer generate a significant proportion of their sales with their own-brand merchandise. In Britain, at the largest food chains, Sainsbury and Tesco, 50 percent and 45 percent of sales (respectively) are store-label goods.

For many manufacturers, retailers can be both collaborators and competitors. Canada has one of the highest penetrations of private-label goods with almost 100 percent of Canadian households buying private-label goods on every shopping trip, especially in the highly concentrated grocery sector where private labels account for 24 percent of all sales. AC Nielsen reports that 72 percent of shoppers said "national brands are not worth the extra cost," whereas 68 percent believed private labels are "an extremely good value."[55]

Private labels are rapidly gaining ascendancy in a way that has many manufacturers of name brands running scared. Consider the following:[56]

- Wal-Mart's Ol'Roy dog food has surpassed Nestlé's venerable Purina brand as the top-selling dog chow.

- One in every two ceiling fans sold is from Home Depot and most of those are its own Hampton Bay brand.

- Loblaws President's Choice products are extremely successful not only in Canada, but also in foreign marketplaces including the U.S. and Latin America.

- Some experts believe, however, that 50 percent is the natural limit for the level of private labels to carry because (1) consumers prefer certain national brands, and (2) many product categories are not feasible or attractive on a private-label basis.[57]

Role of Private Labels

Why do intermediaries bother to sponsor their own brands? First, they can be more profitable. Intermediaries search for manufacturers with excess capacity that will produce the private label at a low cost. Other costs, such as research and development, advertising, sales promotion, and physical distribution are also much lower, so private labels can be sold at a lower price yet generate a higher profit margin. Second, retailers develop exclusive store brands to differentiate themselves from competitors. Many consumers prefer store brands in certain categories, like the President's Choice brand at Loblaws stores.

Loblaws

Since 1984, when its President's Choice line of foods made its debut, the term "private label" has brought Loblaws instantly to mind. Loblaws' Decadent Chocolate Chip Cookie quickly became a Canadian leader and showed how innovative store brands could compete effectively with national brands by matching or even exceeding their quality. A finely tuned brand strategy for its premium President's Choice line and no-frills, yellow-labelled No Name line has helped differentiate its stores and build Loblaws into a powerhouse in Canada and the United States. The President's Choice line of products has become so successful that Loblaws is licensing it to noncompetitive retailers in other countries, thus turning a local store brand into—believe it or not—a global brand.[58]

Some retailers have returned to a "no branding" strategy for certain staple consumer goods and pharmaceuticals. Carrefours, the originator of the French hypermarket, introduced a line of "no

A store brand can become a global one if the product is as good as those from Loblaws' President's Choice line.

brands" or generics in its stores in the early 1970s. Today, a Japanese retailer called Mujirushi Ryohin has taken Carrefours' strategy a step further by successfully defining its stores with the no-brand concept.

Mujirushi Ryohin

Mujirushi Ryohin's full name translates into "no-brand quality products." The Japanese retailer, known simply as "Muji," has become a huge success, with 387 outlets in 15 countries, including 34 in Europe. Until recently, it was unknown in North America, but the no-brand retailer—which carries 7000 products ranging from $4.00 socks to $115 000 prefab homes—is opening a 5000-square-foot store in mid-town Manhattan. Its biggest challenge will be deciding what to charge for its wares. In Japan, low prices are a huge part of Muji's appeal. Another challenge will be to stay true to its no-brand ethos. Muji's intended audience is young 20- to 30-year-olds who are tired of in-your-face logos and designer goods. But its sleek, functional, postindustrial products will probably seem anything but generic to North Americans. Muji's products resonate with the minimalism of Japan's gardens and haiku poetry, and this is how the company will differentiate itself among the competition and—whether it wants to or not—become an identifiable brand.[59]

Generics are unbranded, plainly packaged, less expensive versions of common products such as spaghetti, paper towels, and canned peaches. They offer standard or lower quality at a price that may be as much as 20-percent to 40-percent lower than nationally advertised brands and 10-percent to 20-percent lower than the retailer's private-label brands. The lower price of generics is made possible by lower-quality ingredients, lower-cost labelling and packaging, and minimal advertising. Generic drugs have become big business. Pharma giant Novartis is one of the world's top-five makers of branded drugs, with such successes as Diovan for high blood pressure and Gleevac for cancer, but it is also the world's second-largest maker of generic drugs following its acquisition of Sandoz, Hexal, Eon Labs, and others.[60]

The Private-Label Threat

In the confrontation between manufacturers' and private labels, retailers have many advantages and increasing market power.[61] Because shelf space is scarce, many supermarkets now charge a *slotting fee* for accepting a new brand, to cover the cost of listing and stocking it. Retailers also charge for special display space and in-store advertising space. They typically give more prominent display to their own brands and make sure they are well stocked. Retailers are now building better quality into their store brands and are emphasizing attractive packaging. Some are even advertising aggressively: Loblaws uses its flyers and newsletters to advertise its store brands. In the U.S., Safeway ran a US$100-million integrated communication program in 2005 that featured TV and print ads touting the store brand's quality.[62]

The growing power of store brands is not the only factor weakening national brands. Many consumers are more price sensitive. Competing manufacturers and national retailers copy and duplicate the qualities of the best brands. The continuous barrage of coupons and price specials has trained a generation of shoppers to buy on price. The fact that companies have reduced advertising to 30 percent of their total promotion budget has in some cases weakened their brand equity. A steady stream of brand extensions and line extensions has blurred brand identity at times and led to a confusing amount of product proliferation.

To maintain their power, leading brand marketers are investing significantly in R&D to bring out new brands, line extensions, features, and quality improvements to stay a step ahead of the store brands. They are also investing in strong "pull" advertising programs to maintain high consumer brand recognition and preference and overcome the in-store marketing advantage that private labels can enjoy. Top brand marketers are also seeking ways to partner with major mass distributors in a joint search for logistical economies and competitive strategies that produce savings. Cutting all unnecessary costs allows national brands to command a price premium, although it can't exceed the value perceptions of consumers.[63] "Marketing Memo: How to Compete Against Store Brands" reflects on the severity of the private-label challenge and what leading brand marketers must do in response.[64]

MARKETING **MEMO** | HOW TO COMPETE AGAINST STORE BRANDS

University of North Carolina's Jan-Benedict E. M. Steenkamp and London Business School's Nirmalya Kumar have identified what they feel are the most successful strategies for launching, leveraging, and competing against store brands. Based on extensive research, Kumar and Steenkamp begin their analysis with a number of observations of the sometimes surprising realities of private labels in the marketplace.

- *Private labels are ubiquitous.* Currently, store brands are present in over 95 percent of consumer packaged-goods categories and have made huge inroads in a variety of other industries, from apparel to books, from financial services to pharmaceuticals.

- *Consumers accept private labels.* Two-thirds of consumers around the world believe that "supermarket-owned brands are a good alternative to other brands."

- *Private-label buyers come from all socioeconomic strata.* It is considered "smart" shopping to purchase private-label products of comparable quality for a much lower price, rather than being "ripped off" by high-priced manufacturer brands.

- *Private labels are not a recessionary phenomenon.* Part of private-label growth in a recession is permanent, caused by consumer learning. As consumers learn about the improved quality of private labels in recessions, a significant proportion of them remain loyal to private labels, even after the necessity to save money is over.

- *Consumer loyalty shifts from manufacturers to retailers.* Consumers are becoming first and foremost loyal to a specific retailer.

- *Profits flow from manufacturers to retailers.* Between 1996 and 2003, retailers gained five share points of the combined manufacturer and retailer profit pool and more than 50 percent of the system profit growth.

Kumar and Steenkamp believe manufacturer brands must accept these new private-label realities and respond aggressively. They offer four key sets of strategic recommendations for manufacturers to compete against or collaborate with private labels.

- Fight selectively where manufacturers can win against private labels and add value for consumers, retailers, and shareholders. This is typically where the brand is one or two in the category or occupying a premium niche position.

- Partner effectively by seeking win-win relationships with retailers through strategies that complement the retailer's private labels.

- Innovate brilliantly with new products to help beat private labels. Continuously launching incremental new products keeps the manufacturer brands looking fresh, but this must be punctuated by periodically launching radically new products.

- Create winning value propositions by imbuing brands with symbolic imagery as well as functional quality that beats private labels. Too many manufacturer brands have let private labels equal and sometimes better them on functional quality. In addition, to have a winning value proposition, the pricing needs to be monitored closely to ensure that perceived benefits are equal to the price premium.

Source: Jan-Benedict E. M. Steenkamp and Nirmalya Kumar, *Private Label Strategy: How to Meet the Store-Brand Challenge* (Boston: Harvard Business School Press, 2007).

WHOLESALING

Wholesaling includes all the activities in selling goods or services to those who buy for resale or business use. It excludes manufacturers and farmers because they are engaged primarily in production, and it excludes retailers. The major types of wholesalers are described in Table 16.4.

Wholesalers (also called *distributors*) differ from retailers in a number of ways. First, wholesalers pay less attention to promotion, atmosphere, and location because they are dealing with business customers rather than final consumers. Second, wholesale transactions are usually larger than retail transactions, and wholesalers usually cover a larger trade area than retailers. Why do manufacturers

TABLE 16.4	MAJOR WHOLESALER TYPES

Merchant wholesalers: Independently owned businesses that take title to the merchandise they handle. They are full-service and limited-service jobbers, distributors, and mill supply houses.

Full-service wholesalers: Carry stock, maintain a sales force, offer credit, make deliveries, provide management assistance. Wholesale merchants sell primarily to retailers: some carry several merchandise lines, some carry one or two lines, others carry only part of a line. Industrial distributors sell to manufacturers and also provide services such as credit and delivery.

Limited-service wholesalers: *Cash and carry wholesalers* sell a limited line of fast-moving goods to small retailers for cash. *Truck wholesalers* sell and deliver a limited line of semi-perishable goods to supermarkets, grocery stores, hospitals, restaurants, and hotels. *Drop shippers* serve bulk industries such as coal, lumber, and heavy equipment. They assume title and risk from the time an order is accepted until its delivery. *Rack jobbers* serve grocery retailers in nonfood items. Delivery people set up displays, price goods, and keep inventory records; they retain title to goods and bill retailers only for goods sold to the end of the year. *Producers' cooperatives* assemble farm produce to sell in local markets. *Mail-order wholesalers* send catalogues to retail, industrial, and institutional customers; orders are filled and sent by mail, rail, plane, or truck.

Brokers and agents: Facilitate buying and selling on commission of 2 percent to 6 percent of the selling price. They have limited functions and generally specialize by product line or customer type. *Brokers* bring buyers and sellers together and assist in negotiation, and are paid by the party hiring them (e.g., food brokers, real estate brokers, insurance brokers). *Agents* represent buyers or sellers on a more permanent basis. Most manufacturers' agents are small businesses with a few skilled salespeople: selling agents have contractual authority to sell a manufacturer's entire output; purchasing agents make purchases for buyers and often receive, inspect, warehouse, and ship merchandise; commission merchants take physical possession of products and negotiate sales.

Manufacturers' and retailers' branches and offices: Wholesaling operations conducted by sellers or buyers themselves rather than through independent wholesalers. Separate branches and offices are dedicated to sales or purchasing. Many retailers set up purchasing offices in major market centres.

Specialized wholesalers: Agricultural assemblers (buy the agricultural output of many farms), petroleum bulk plants and terminals (consolidate the output of many wells), and auction companies (auction cars, equipment, etc., to dealers and other businesses).

not sell directly to retailers or final consumers? Why are wholesalers used at all? In general, wholesalers are more efficient in performing one or more of the following functions:

- *Selling and promoting.* Wholesalers' sales forces help manufacturers reach many small business customers at a relatively low cost. They have more contacts, and buyers often trust them more than they trust a distant manufacturer.

- *Buying and assortment building.* Wholesalers are able to select items and build the assortments their customers need, saving them considerable work.

- *Bulk breaking.* Wholesalers achieve savings for their customers by buying large carload lots and breaking the bulk into smaller units.

- *Warehousing.* Wholesalers hold inventories, thereby reducing inventory costs and risks to suppliers and customers.

- *Transportation.* Wholesalers can often provide quicker delivery to buyers because they are closer to the buyers.

- *Financing.* Wholesalers finance customers by granting credit, and finance suppliers by ordering early and paying bills on time.

- *Risk bearing.* Wholesalers absorb some risk by taking title and bearing the cost of theft, damage, spoilage, and obsolescence.

- *Market information.* Wholesalers supply information to suppliers and customers regarding competitors' activities, new products, price developments, and so on.

- *Management services and counselling.* Wholesalers often help retailers improve their operations by training sales clerks, helping with store layouts and displays, and setting up accounting and inventory-control systems. They may help industrial customers by offering training and technical services.

Trends in Wholesaling

Wholesaler-distributors have faced mounting pressures in recent years from new sources of competition, demanding customers, new technologies, and more direct-buying programs by large industrial, institutional, and retail buyers. Manufacturers' major complaints against wholesalers are: they don't aggressively promote the manufacturer's product line, and they act more like order takers; they don't carry enough inventory and therefore fail to fill customers' orders fast enough; they don't supply the manufacturer with up-to-date market, customer, and competitive information; they don't attract high-calibre managers, bringing down their own costs; and they charge too much for their services.

Savvy wholesalers have rallied to the challenge and adapted their services to meet their suppliers' and target customers' changing needs. They recognize that they must add value to the channel.

One major drive by wholesalers, like W. W. Grainger, has been to increase asset productivity by managing inventories and receivables better. They're also reducing operating costs by investing in more advanced materials-handling technology, information systems, and Internet technologies. Finally, they're improving their strategic decisions about target markets, product assortment and services, price, communications, and distribution.

W. W. Grainger

W. W. Grainger Inc. is the leading supplier of facilities maintenance products that help 1.8 million North American businesses and institutions stay up and running. Sales for 2007 were $6.4 billion. To guarantee product availability and quick service, Grainger serves customers through a network of nearly 600 branches in North America and China, 15 distribution centres, numerous catalogues

W.W. Grainger offers its industrial customers an enormous product assortment online, by catalogue, and in hundreds of branches and distribution centres linked by satellite for fast service.

and direct-mail pieces, and four websites. Its 4000-plus-page catalogue features 138 000-plus products, such as motors, lighting, material handlers, fasteners, tools, and safety supplies. It added 45 000 new products to its catalogue in 2007 alone. Customers can purchase over 300 000 products at Grainger.com, which generates over $1 billion in sales annually. The distribution centres are linked by satellite network, which has reduced customer-response time and boosted sales. Helped by more than 1300 suppliers, Grainger offers customers a total of more than 800 000 supplies and repair parts in all.[65]

Narus and Anderson interviewed leading industrial distributors and identified four ways that they strengthened their relationships with manufacturers:

1. They sought a clear agreement with their manufacturers about their expected functions in the marketing channel.

2. They gained insight into the manufacturers' requirements by visiting their plants and attending manufacturer-association conventions and trade shows.

3. They fulfilled their commitments to the manufacturer by meeting the volume targets, paying bills promptly, and feeding customer information back to their manufacturers.

4. They identified and offered value-added services to help their suppliers.[66]

The wholesaling industry remains vulnerable to one of the most enduring trends—fierce resistance to price increases and the winnowing out of suppliers based on cost and quality. The trend toward vertical integration, in which manufacturers try to control or own their intermediaries, is still strong (as exhibited at Arrow Electronics).

Arrow Electronics

Arrow Electronics is a global provider of products, services, and solutions to the electronic-component and computer-product industries. It serves as a supply channel partner for more than 600 suppliers and 140 000 original equipment manufacturers, contract manufacturers, and commercial customers through a global network of 260 locations in 55 countries and territories. With huge contract manufacturers buying more parts directly from suppliers, distributors such as Arrow are being squeezed out. To better compete, Arrow has embraced services, providing financing, on-site inventory management, parts-tracking software, and chip programming. Services helped quadruple Arrow's share price in five years.[67]

MARKET LOGISTICS

Physical distribution starts at the factory. Managers choose a set of warehouses (stocking points) and transportation carriers that will deliver the goods to final destinations in the desired time or at the lowest total cost. Physical distribution has now been expanded into the broader concept of **supply chain management (SCM)**. Supply chain management starts before physical distribution and means strategically procuring the right inputs (raw materials, components, and capital equipment), converting them efficiently into finished products, and dispatching them to their final destinations. An even broader perspective calls for studying how the company's suppliers themselves obtain their inputs. The supply chain perspective can help a company identify superior suppliers and distributors and help them improve productivity, which ultimately brings down the company's costs.

Market logistics includes planning the infrastructure to meet demand, then implementing and controlling the physical flows of materials and final goods from points of origin to points of use, to meet customer requirements at a profit.

Market logistics planning has four steps:[68]

1. Deciding on the company's value proposition to its customers. (What on-time delivery standard should we offer? What levels should we attain in ordering and billing accuracy?)

2. Deciding on the best channel design and network strategy for reaching the customers. (Should the company serve customers directly or through intermediaries? What products should we source from which manufacturing facilities? How many warehouses should we maintain and where should we locate them?)

3. Developing operational excellence in sales forecasting, warehouse management, transportation management, and materials management.

4. Implementing the solution with the best information systems, equipment, policies, and procedures.

Studying market logistics leads managers to find the most efficient way to deliver value. For example, a software company normally sees its challenge as producing and packaging software disks and manuals, then shipping them to wholesalers—which ship them to retailers, which sell them to customers. Customers bring the software package to the home or office and upload the software onto a hard drive. Market logistics would look at two superior delivery systems. The first includes ordering the software to be downloaded directly onto the customer's computer. The second system allows the computer manufacturer to download the software onto its products. Both solutions eliminate the need for printing, packaging, shipping, and stocking millions of disks and manuals. The same solutions are available for distributing music, newspapers, video games, films, and other products that deliver voice, text, data, or images. Even non-profit organizations have to consider logistics. Consider the case of World Vision Canada.

World Vision Canada

World Vision Canada is renowned for its ability to contend with disasters, from famines to civil wars. Mr. Dave Toycen, World Vision Canada's president for more than 28 years, explains that emergency-relief logistics is also one of the most unheralded parts of the logistics sector, and little has been written about it. While emergency-relief logistics involves many of the same components and practices found in private-sector logistics, from procurement and forecasting to transportation, customs clearance, warehousing, insurance, and loss and damage levels, the critical factor is the need for speed versus cost since lives are at stake. Information is another vital element. It is essential that organizations like World Vision learn quickly about the number of people affected, what supplies are required, how they can be delivered, and what cultural issues will affect the delivery of aid. World Vision's logistics procedures have enabled it to deliver pharmaceuticals flawlessly to West Africa despite daunting challenges like temperatures of 52 degrees Celsius. Lisa Moody, World Vision's Senior Co-ordinator, exclaims "Everything is tracked! In remote areas the way we track the delivery of items may be as simple as getting a thumb-imprint of the person receiving aid. But we know where it is, day-by-day, family-by-family. An estimated 99 percent of our shipments are consigned to a local World Vision office and that product will arrive, most times, 100 percent, with no shrinkage, to that consignee, and then it would be divided up to go to hospitals and programs that World Vision is working with." It's a record many for-profit firms envy.[69]

Integrated Logistics Systems

The market logistics task calls for **integrated logistics systems (ILS)**, which include materials management, material flow systems, and physical distribution, aided by information technology (IT). Third-party suppliers, such as FedEx Logistics Services and Metro Canada Logistics (MCL), often manage or participate in designing and managing these systems. MCL, based in Laval, Quebec, was founded in 1974. Its approximately 700 employees located across Canada pride themselves on their ability to provide everything from warehouse management to packaging services to transportation.

Playing a critical role in managing market logistics are information systems, especially computers, point-of-sale terminals, uniform product bar codes, satellite tracking, electronic data interchange (EDI), and electronic funds transfer (EFT). These developments have shortened the order-cycle time, reduced clerical labour, reduced the error rate in documents, and provided improved control of operations. They have enabled companies to make promises such as "the product will be at dock 25 at 10:00 A.M. tomorrow."

Market logistics encompass several activities. The first is sales forecasting, on the basis of which the company schedules distribution, production, and inventory levels. Production plans indicate the materials the purchasing department must order. These materials arrive through inbound transportation, enter the receiving area, and are stored in raw-material inventory. Raw materials are converted into finished goods. Finished-goods inventory is the link between customer orders and manufacturing activity. Customers' orders draw down the finished-goods inventory level, and manufacturing activity builds it up. Finished goods flow off the assembly line and pass through packaging, in-plant warehousing, shipping-room processing, outbound transportation, field warehousing, and customer delivery and servicing.

Management has become concerned about the total cost of market logistics, which can amount for as much as 30 to 40 percent of a product's cost. The grocery industry alone thinks it can decrease its annual operating costs by 10 percent by revamping its market logistics. A box of breakfast cereal can take 104 days to chug through a labyrinth of wholesalers, distributors, brokers, and consolidators from factory to supermarket.

Many experts call market logistics "the last frontier for cost economies," and firms are determined to wring every unnecessary cost out of the system: Logistics costs as a percentage of a company's gross output in Canada varies by industry. The top three industries in terms of logistics costs as a percentage of gross output are the cement and concrete-product industry, where logistics costs 20 percent of gross output, the beverage industry, where it is just under 15 percent, and the dairy product industry, where logistics equals approximately 7 percent of gross output. Compare this to motor vehicle manufacturing, petroleum, or pharmaceutical industries, which spend less than 2 percent of their gross output on logistics costs.[70] Lower market-logistics costs will permit lower prices, yield higher profit margins, or both. Even though the cost of market logistics can be high, a well-planned program can be a potent tool in competitive marketing.

Market-Logistics Objectives

Many companies state their market-logistics objective as "getting the right goods to the right places at the right time for the least cost." Unfortunately, this objective provides little practical guidance. No system can simultaneously maximize customer service and minimize distribution cost. Maximum customer service implies large inventories, premium transportation, and multiple warehouses, all of which raise market-logistics costs.

Nor can a company achieve market-logistics efficiency by asking each market-logistics manager to minimize his or her own logistics costs. Market-logistics costs interact and are often negatively related. For example:

- The traffic manager favours rail shipment over air shipment because rail costs less. However, because the railroads are slower, rail shipment ties up working capital longer, delays customer payment, and might cause customers to buy from competitors which offer faster service.
- The shipping department uses cheap containers to minimize shipping costs. Cheaper containers lead to a higher rate of damaged goods and customer ill will.
- The inventory manager favours low inventories. This increases stockouts, back orders, paperwork, special production runs, and high-cost, fast-freight shipments.

Given that market-logistics activities require strong trade-offs, managers must make decisions on a total-system basis. The starting point is to study what customers require and what competitors are offering. Customers are interested in on-time delivery, supplier willingness to meet emergency needs, careful handling of merchandise, and supplier willingness to take back defective goods and resupply them quickly.

The company must then research the relative importance of these service outputs. For example, service-repair time is very important to buyers of copying equipment. Xerox developed a service delivery standard that "can put a disabled machine anywhere in North America back into operation within three hours after receiving the service request." It then designed a service division of personnel, parts, and locations to deliver on this promise.

The company must also consider competitors' service standards. It will normally want to match or exceed the competitors' service level, but the objective is to maximize profits, not sales. The company must look at the costs of providing higher levels of service. Some companies offer less service and charge a lower price; other companies offer more service and charge a premium price.

The company ultimately must establish some promise it makes to the market. Coca-Cola wants to "put Coke within an arm's length of desire." Lands' End, the giant catalogue-based clothing retailer, aims to respond to every phone call within 20 seconds and to ship every order within 24 hours of receipt. Some companies define standards for each service factor. One appliance manufacturer has established the following service standards: to deliver at least 95 percent of the dealer's orders within seven days of order receipt, to fill the dealer's orders with 99 percent accuracy, to answer dealer inquiries on order status within three hours, and to ensure that damage to merchandise in transit does not exceed 1 percent. Perhaps the king of all logistics is Wal-Mart.

Wal-Mart

Wal-Mart Stores Inc. is the largest retailer in the world, with operations in seven countries other than Canada (Brazil, China, Japan, Mexico, Puerto Rico, the United States, and the United Kingdom). Wal-Mart Canada was founded in March 1994. Wal-Mart employs 70 000 Canadians in its 278 locations. Each location stocks approximately 80 000 different products. Each week, over 100 million customers visit a Wal-Mart store somewhere in the world. Sam Walton founded the company in 1962 with a simple goal: offer low prices to everyone. Wal-Mart keeps prices low through its unrivalled logistics. The company effectively and efficiently coordinates more than 85 000 suppliers, manages billions in inventory in its warehouses, and brings that inventory to its retail shelves. Over 100 million items per day must get to the right store at the right time. To accomplish this goal, Wal-Mart developed several IT systems that work together. Using up-to-the-minute sales information based on point-of-sale (POS) scanner data, Wal-Mart's Inventory Management System calculates the rate of sales, factors in seasonal and promotional elements, and automatically places replenishment orders to distribution centres and vendor partners. Suppliers can use its voluminous POS databases to analyze customers' regional buying habits. Wal-Marts may look the same on the outside, but the company uses its information systems and logistics to customize the offerings inside each store to suit regional demand.[71]

Given the market-logistics objectives, the company must design a system that will minimize the cost of achieving these objectives. Each possible market-logistics system will lead to the following cost:

$$M = T + FW + VW + S$$

where M = total market-logistics cost of proposed system
T = total freight cost of proposed system
FW = total fixed warehouse cost of proposed system
VW = total variable warehouse costs (including inventory) of proposed system
S = total cost of lost sales due to average delivery delay under proposed system

Choosing a market-logistics system calls for examining the total cost *(M)* associated with different proposed systems and selecting the system that minimizes it. If it is hard to measure *S,* the company should aim to minimize $T + FW + VW$ for a target level of customer service.

Market-Logistics Decisions

The firm must make four major decisions about its market logistics: (1) How should we handle orders (order processing)? (2) Where should we locate our stock (warehousing)? (3) How much stock should we hold (inventory)? and (4) How should we ship goods (transportation)?

With its network of IT systems customized for each store, Wal-Mart is the king of logistics and the largest retailer in the world.

ORDER PROCESSING Most companies today are trying to shorten the *order-to-payment cycle*—that is, the elapsed time between an order's receipt, delivery, and payment. This cycle has many steps, including order transmission by the salesperson, order entry and customer credit check, inventory and production scheduling, order and invoice shipment, and receipt of payment. The longer this cycle takes, the lower the customer's satisfaction and the lower the company's profits. General Electric operates an information system that checks the customer's credit standing upon receipt of an order and determines whether and where the items are in stock. The computer issues an order to ship, bills the customer, updates the inventory records, sends a production order for new stock, and relays the message back to the sales representative that the customer's order is on its way—all in less than 15 seconds.

WAREHOUSING Every company must store finished goods until they are sold, because production and consumption cycles rarely match. The storage function helps to smooth discrepancies between production and quantities desired by the market. The company must decide on the number of inventory-stocking locations. Consumer packaged-goods companies have been reducing their number of stocking locations from 10–15 to about 5–7, and pharmaceutical and medical distributors have cut their stocking locations from 90 to about 45. On the one hand, more stocking locations means that goods can be delivered to customers more quickly, but it also means higher warehousing and inventory costs. To reduce warehousing and inventory duplication costs, the company might centralize its inventory in one place and use fast transportation to fill orders.

Some inventory is kept at or near the plant, and the rest is located in warehouses in other locations. The company might own private warehouses and also rent space in public warehouses. *Storage warehouses* store goods for moderate to long periods of time. *Distribution warehouses* receive goods from various company plants and suppliers and move them out as soon as possible. *Automated warehouses* employ advanced materials-handling systems under the control of a central computer. When the Helene Curtis Company replaced its six antiquated warehouses with a new $32-million facility, it cut its distribution costs by 40 percent.[72]

Some warehouses are now taking on activities formerly done in the plant. These include assembly, packaging, and constructing promotional displays. Postponing finalization of the offering can achieve savings in costs and finer matching of offerings to demand.

INVENTORY Inventory levels represent a major cost. Salespeople would like their companies to carry enough stock to fill all customer orders immediately. However, this is not cost-effective. *Inventory cost increases at an accelerating rate as the customer-service level approaches 100 percent.* Management needs to know how much sales and profits would increase as a result of carrying larger inventories and promising faster order fulfillment times, and then make a decision.

Inventory decision making requires knowing when and how much to order. As inventory draws down, management must know at what stock level to place a new order. This stock level is called the *order (or reorder) point.* An order point of 20 means reordering when the stock falls to 20 units. The order point should balance the risks of stockout against the costs of overstock. The other decision is how much to order. The larger the quantity ordered, the less frequently an order needs to be placed. The company needs to balance order-processing costs and inventory-carrying costs. *Order-processing costs* for a manufacturer consist of *setup costs* and *running costs* (operating costs when production is running) for the item. If setup costs are low, the manufacturer can produce the item often, and the average cost per item is stable and equal to the running costs. If setup costs are high, however, the manufacturer can reduce the average cost per unit by producing a long run and carrying more inventory.

Order-processing costs must be compared with *inventory-carrying costs.* The larger the average stock carried, the higher the inventory-carrying costs. These carrying costs include storage charges, cost of capital, taxes and insurance, and depreciation and obsolescence. Carrying costs might run as high as 30 percent of inventory value. This means that marketing managers who want their companies to carry larger inventories need to show that the larger inventories would produce incremental gross profits to exceed incremental carrying costs.

We can determine the optimal order quantity by observing how order-processing costs and inventory-carrying costs sum up at different order levels. Figure 16.2 shows that the order-processing cost per unit decreases with the number of units ordered because the order costs are spread over more units. Inventory-carrying charges per unit increase with the number of units ordered because each unit remains longer in inventory. The two cost curves are summed vertically into a total-cost curve. The lowest point on the total-cost curve is projected down on the horizontal axis to find the optimal order quantity, Q^*.[73]

FIGURE 16.2

Determining Optimal Order
Quantity

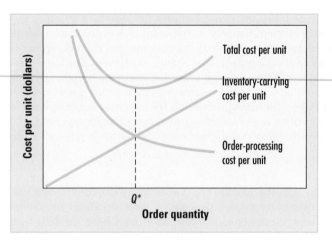

Companies are reducing their inventory costs by treating inventory items differently, position-ing them according to risk and opportunity. They distinguish between bottleneck items (high risk, low opportunity), critical items (high risk, high opportunity), commodities (low risk, high opportuni-ty), and nuisance items (low risk, low opportunity).[74] They are also keeping slowly moving items in a central location and carrying fast-moving items in warehouses closer to customers. All these strate-gies give them more flexibility should anything go wrong, as it often does, be it a dock strike in Montreal, a typhoon in Taiwan, an earthquake in China, or a hurricane in Halifax.[75]

The ultimate answer to carrying *near-zero inventory* is to build for order, not for stock. Sony calls it SOMO, "sell one, make one." Dell, for example, gets the customer to order a computer and pay for it in advance. Then Dell uses the customer's money to pay suppliers to ship the necessary compo-nents. As long as customers do not need the item immediately, everyone can save money. Some retailers are using eBay to unload excess inventory. By cutting out the traditional liquidator mid-dleperson, retailers can make 60 to 80 cents on the dollar as opposed to 10 cents.[76] Some suppliers, like Cameron Hughes, are snapping up excess inventory to create opportunity.

Cameron Hughes

"If a winery has an eight-barrel lot, it may use only five barrels for its customers," says Cameron Hughes, a wine "negociant" who buys the excess juice from wineries and com-bines it to make limited edition, premium blends that taste much more expensive than their price tags. Negociants have been around a long time, first as middlepeople who sold or shipped wine as wholesalers, but the profession has expanded as opportunists such as Hughes became more involved in effectively making their own wines. Hughes doesn't own any grapes, bottling machines, or trucks. He outsources the bottling, and he sells directly and exclusively to Costco, eliminating middlepeople and multiple markups. Hughes never knows which or how many excess lots of wine he will have, but he's turned it to his advan-tage—he creates a new product with every batch. For Costco, this rapid turnover is part of his appeal. The discount store's customers love the idea of finding a rare bargain, and Hughes promotes his wines through in-store wine tastings and insider emails that alert Costco customers to upcoming numbered lots. Because lots sell out quickly, fans subscribe to Cameron's email alerts at chwine.com that tell them when a new lot will be sold.[77]

TRANSPORTATION   Transportation choices will affect product pricing, on-time delivery perform-ance, and the condition of the goods when they arrive, all of which affects customer satisfaction.

In shipping goods to its warehouses, dealers, and customers, the company can choose among five transportation modes: rail, air, truck, waterway, and pipeline. Shippers consider such criteria as speed, frequency, dependability, capability, availability, traceability, and cost. For speed, air, rail, and truck are the prime contenders. If the goal is low cost, then the choice is water or pipeline.

Shippers are increasingly combining two or more transportation modes, thanks to container-ization. Containerization consists of putting the goods in boxes or trailers that are easy to transfer between two transportation modes. *Piggyback* describes the use of rail and trucks; *fishyback*, water and trucks; *trainship*, water and rail; and *airtruck*, air and trucks. Each coordinated mode offers specific advantages. For example, piggyback is cheaper than trucking alone, yet provides flexibility and convenience.

Shippers can choose from private, contract, and common carriers. If the shipper owns its own truck or air fleet, it becomes a *private carrier*. A *contract carrier* is an independent organization selling transportation services to others on a contract basis. A *common carrier* provides services between predetermined points on a scheduled basis and is available to all shippers at standard rates.

To reduce costly handing at arrival, some firms are putting items into shelf-ready packaging so they don't need to be unpacked from a box and placed on a shelf individually. In Europe, Procter & Gamble uses a three-tier logistic system to schedule deliveries of fast-moving and slowly moving goods, bulky items, and small items in the most efficient way.[78]

Organizational Lessons

Market-logistics strategies must be derived from business strategies, rather than solely from cost considerations. The logistics system must be information intensive and establish electronic links among all the significant parties. Finally, the company should set its logistics goals to match or exceed competitors' service standards and should involve members of all relevant teams in the planning process. Getting logistics right can have a big payoff, as the Pepsi Bottling Group has found.

Pepsi Bottling Group

In 2002, Pepsi Bottling Group—Pepsi's largest independent bottler and distributor—was saddled with a creaky supply chain that resulted in many stockouts. It completely overhauled its supply chain, from order taking to truck loading to store deliveries. The new program included technology upgrades, revised work schedules, and a renewed focus on customer service. Warehouse workers, called "pickers," began to wear headsets and barcode scanners on their wrists to create "certified pallets" with close to 100-percent accuracy. By 2006, stockouts had decreased significantly as a result. As one Pepsi Bottling employee said, "It was almost like when I went to bed I was Fred Flintsone and when I woke up I was George Jetson."[79]

Today's stronger demands for logistical support from large customers will increase suppliers' costs. Customers want more frequent deliveries so they don't have to carry as much inventory. They want shorter order-cycle times, which means that suppliers must carry high in-stock availability. Customers often want direct store delivery rather than shipments to distribution centres. They want mixed pallets rather than separate pallets. They want tighter promised delivery times. They may want custom packaging, price tagging, and display building.

Suppliers can't say no to many of these requests, but at least they can set up different logistical programs with different service levels and customer charges. Smart companies will adjust their offerings to each major customer's requirements. The company's trade group will set up *differentiated distribution* by offering different bundled service programs for different customers.

SUMMARY

1. Retailing includes all the activities involved in selling goods or services directly to final consumers for personal, nonbusiness use. Retailers can be understood in terms of store retailing, nonstore retailing, and retail organizations.

2. Like products, retail-store types pass through stages of growth and decline. As existing stores offer more services to remain competitive, costs and prices go up, which opens the door to new retail forms that offer a mix of merchandise and services at lower prices. The major types of retail stores are specialty stores, department stores, supermarkets, convenience stores, discount stores, off-price retailers (factory outlets, independent off-price retailers, and warehouse clubs), and superstores (combination stores and supermarkets).

3. Although most goods and services are sold through stores, nonstore retailing has been growing. The major types of nonstore retailing are direct selling (one-to-one selling, one-to-many party selling, and multi-level network marketing), direct marketing (which includes e-commerce and Internet retailing), automatic vending, and buying services.

4. Although many retail stores are independently owned, an increasing number are falling under some form of corporate retailing. Retail organizations achieve many economies of scale, such as greater purchasing power, wider brand recognition, and better-trained employees. The major types of corporate retailing are corporate chain stores, voluntary chains, retailer cooperatives, consumer cooperatives, franchise organizations, and merchandising conglomerates.

5. Like all marketers, retailers must prepare marketing plans that include decisions on target markets, product assortment and procurement, services and store atmosphere, price, promotion, and location. These decisions must take into account major trends, such as the growth of private labels, new retail forms and combinations, growth of inter-type retail competition, competition between store-based and non-store-based retailing, growth of giant retailers, decline of middle-market retailers, growing investment in technology, and the global presence of major retailers.

6. Wholesaling includes all the activities involved in selling goods or services to those who buy for resale or business use. Wholesalers can perform functions better and more cost-effectively than manufacturers can. These functions include selling and promoting, buying and assortment building, bulk breaking, warehousing, transportation, financing, risk bearing, dissemination of market information, and provision of management services and consulting.

7. There are four types of wholesalers: merchant wholesalers; brokers and agents; manufacturers' and retailers' sales branches, sales offices, and purchasing offices; and miscellaneous wholesalers such as agricultural assemblers and auction companies.

8. Like retailers, wholesalers must decide on target markets, product assortment and services, price, promotion, and location. The most successful wholesalers are those which adapt their services to meet suppliers' and target customers' needs.

9. Producers of physical products and services must decide on market logistics—the best way to store and move goods and services to market destinations—to coordinate the activities of suppliers, purchasing agents, manufacturers, marketers, channel members, and customers. Major gains in logistical efficiency have come from advances in information technology.

APPLICATIONS

Marketing Debate: Should National-Brand Manufacturers Also Supply Private-Label Brands?

One controversial move by some marketers of major brands is to supply private-label makers. For example, Ralston-Purina, Borden, ConAgra, and Heinz have all admitted to supplying products—sometimes lower in quality—to be used for private labels. Other marketers, however, criticize this "if you can't beat them, join them" strategy, maintaining that these actions, if revealed, may create confusion or even reinforce a perception by consumers that all brands in a category are essentially the same.

Take a position: National manufacturers should feel free to sell private labels as a source of revenue *versus* National manufacturers should never get involved with private labels.

Marketing Discussion

Think of your favourite stores. What do they do that encourages your loyalty? What do you like about the in-store experience? What further improvements could they make?

Breakthrough Marketing: Canadian Tire

Canadian Tire is a national institution and it is one of Canada's most recognized and trusted brands. The ubiquitous red and white triangle has been part of the Canadian brand landscape since 1922. Although not part of the initial logo, the maple leaf was incorporated into the brand early in its history to signify that the company is proud to be wholly Canadian owned and operated.[80] A 2007 Ipsos Public Affairs report on corporate reputation rated Canadian Tire's brand as Canada's second most trusted.

The company has a long history of innovation. It was the first retailer in the country to offer a branded MasterCard. Today it is Canada's second-largest MasterCard franchise. Canadian Tire has one of the industry's leading rewards program, its Canadian Tire money, which has achieved iconic status. In 2008, with 473 Canadian Tire retail stores located from coast to coast, 266 gas bars, 259 convenience stores and kiosks, and 74 PartSource automotive-parts specialty stores, it is one of Canada's most successful and trusted retailers. Canadian Tire also acquired Mark's Work Wearhouse in 2002, allowing it to expand its service to the unisex clothing marketplace. There are 360 Mark's stores across Canada including the L'Equipeur stores in Quebec. In addition to serving end consumers, Mark's is the number-one Canadian seller of industrial apparel and footwear. Canadian Tire Financial Services (which includes Canadian Tire MasterCard and the Canadian Tire Bank) rounds out the mix, offering everything from loans to warranties to roadside assistance. In 2007, it launched the innovative One-and-Only™ account that allows Canadians to combine a number of financial services (loans, mortgages, chequing, credit cards, and savings accounts) into one account.

Canadian Tire occupies a unique position in the Canadian retailing landscape. Thanks to its diverse network of businesses and its interrelated and interdependent business model, no other company resembles Canadian Tire. Each business benefits from the strengths of the other. The company has 57 000 employees. In 2007, it generated revenues of $8.6 billion and net earnings of $417.6 million, an increase of 17.8 percent compared to 2006.

Canadian Tire continuously strives to meet the needs of its customers for total value by offering a unique package of location, price, service, and assortment. Canadian Tire stores offer customers a large selection of national and private-label brands through three "stores" under one roof—automotive parts, accessories, and service; sports and leisure products; and home products. Canadiantire.ca, the company's online store, offers more than 24 000 products for sale and also serves as an important communication channel to customers.

Thanks to its dual format, Canadian Tire is Canada's largest hard-goods retailer and most-shopped general merchandise retailer. In fact, nine out of ten adult Canadians shop at Canadian Tire at least twice a year, and 40 percent of Canadians shop at Canadian Tire every week. Its flyer is delivered to 10 million homes every week, making its advertising the highest read in the country. Its retail outlets span the country and 85 percent of the Canadian population lives within a 15-minute drive of a Canadian Tire store.

Throughout its history, Canadian Tire has strived to be the number-one retailer in Canada. When powerful American competitors Wal-Mart and Home Depot entered the market during the 1990s, Canadian Tire had to take a step back from normal day-to-day activities to understand what its customers valued about the business. It was becoming increasingly important for Canadian Tire to show Canadians that it wasn't just the closest store in which to shop, but the best store in which to shop whether they visited a physical location or shopped online. To accomplish this aim, many stores were renovated, new outlets were built, and all operations began to focus on delivering superior customer service.

In melding its online and traditional retail worlds, Canadian Tire has created a powerful new model of retailing—a robust two-tiered system where consumers have the choice of shopping by the method they value most. The model recognizes that, most of the time, customers can visit a local store, but occasionally they will like the convenience and different selection afforded by the Web. Canadian Tire continues to forge ahead by continuously building new stores, creating new retail formats, and integrating its businesses. For example, it has been incorporating its Mark's franchise stores within Canadian Tire stores, and it is expanding its private-label brands and financial service offerings. No matter what it does, it has a singular focus on keeping customers for life, and it is committed to doing the right thing for its employees, customers, shareholders, and business partners.

DISCUSSION QUESTIONS

1. What trends have shaped Canadian Tire's recent history?
2. How has it differentiated itself from its rivals like Wal-Mart?
3. What must Canadian Tire do to continue its success in the Canadian marketplace?

Source: Canadian Tire Corporation Limited, *Annual Report 2007*, http://media.corporate-ir.net/media_files/TOR/CTC.CA/reports/Annual-Report_2007-REVISE.pdf.

COMMUNICATING VALUE

**IN THIS CHAPTER,
WE WILL ADDRESS
THE FOLLOWING
QUESTIONS:**

- What is the role of marketing communications?

- How do marketing communications work?

- What are the major steps in developing effective communications?

- What is the communications mix and how should it be set?

- What is an integrated marketing communications program?

CHAPTER 17

DESIGNING AND MANAGING INTEGRATED MARKETING COMMUNICATIONS

seventeen

Scotiabank has come a long way in its 175 years since inception. Started as a four-person office in Halifax, Nova Scotia, it has grown into an internationally recognized financial institution with over 2100 branches and offices, spread over 50 countries across five continents. Scotiabank is one of the savviest companies in Canada when it comes to marketing, due to its integrated marketing communications strategies. The familiar S-shaped logo has become synonymous with events all over Canada, targeting and reaching those of all ages with its message: it is the financial institution for you.

Scotiabank has realized the benefits advertising and sponsorships have on its bottom line. In 2007, its advertising budget went from $232 million to $311 million, a jump of $79 million, and it paid off. Total income rose from $10.99 billion in 2006 to $12.22 billion in 2007, much due to the increased presence Scotiabank has in the minds of Canadians.

It has not been easy for Scotiabank to achieve these results, and there is a lot of work done to ensure that the relationships it has developed stay beneficial for all involved. In 2007, Scotiabank signed an agreement to extend its national partnership with the Canadian Football League (CFL) for another three years, to the end of the 2009 season. "The CFL is an exceptional organization," says John Doig, senior vice-president of marketing for Scotiabank. "Partnering with the league and local teams ensures we help build richer communities by supporting a Canadian institution that gives people the opportunity to experience football at its best." Scotiabank also became the official bank of the National Hockey League (NHL) in 2007, extending its influence to even more sports fans.

The main message Scotiabank has been putting out to customers is "You're Richer Than You Think." This campaign has become immensely popular, but the impressive thing is how well the message is delivered to different groups. Commercials are run not only on television and radio, but in movie theatres as well. The ads show how everyone has the option to save money, whether it is for retirement, school, a home, renovation, or a vacation. These commercials have managed to reach many new and existing customers, prompting them to do more business with Scotiabank.

In January 2007, Scotiabank made a huge leap forward in attracting young customers when it announced the SCENE program in partnership with Cineplex Entertainment. Through this program, those 14 and older could get a free card that allows them to collect points for each movie they see, as well as receive discounts at the snack counter. Scotiabank also offered its own products, introducing the SCENE debit and VISA cards from its branches. Throughout Canada, the Scotiabank symbol was visible in movie theatres, on screens, and on televisions promoting the new program. The program has become immensely popular on both sides, not only helping revive a slowing movie industry that in 2005 dropped 7.8 percent in total ticket sales, but also getting new, young customers as well as veteran moviegoers hearing the name Scotiabank.

The bank has also sent out a newsletter known as "The Vault" to its clients with tips on how to save, spend, and invest intelligently. One innovative idea that the bank came up with in 2007 was the introduction of "The Money Clip," a monthly podcast filled with financial information for individuals and families. "The podcast was another way to take content that is more conversational and perhaps even more timely, asking experts for their opinion in an interview format. The Money Clip is really an extension of [The Vault] and it allows us to talk to more issues than we have the chance to do in our newsletter," says Michael Seaton, director of digital marketing for Scotiabank. Since the podcast was launched, over a million people have tuned in to hear what Scotiabank has to say when it comes to their finances. It was the first of its kind, and plans are in the works for a business-to-business (B2B) podcast as well, as an extension of the B2B newsletter.

Scotiabank is also heavily involved in community service, sponsoring community events such as Rick Hansen Wheels in Motion and the AIDS Walk 4 Life. These events garner huge community support due to the causes they represent, and Scotiabank is at the helm. In 2007, the bank donated over $43 million to various sponsorships and charities.

So what's next for Scotiabank? Currently, the focus seems to be on continued growth. With revenue having grown over 11 percent in 2007, largely due to intelligent integrated marketing communications, there seems to be little standing in its way. With partnerships secured with widely popular sports leagues CFL and NHL, and movie giant Cineplex, its community involvement, as well as word-of-mouth from satisfied customers and employees, Scotiabank sits in a position envied by many financial institutions worldwide. The marketing tactics used by Scotiabank have since been copied by other banks and companies across Canada, but Scotiabank always seem to stay one step ahead of its competition.

Sources: "175 Years of Success," "Community Development," "Scotiabank 2007 Annual Report," "Scotiabank Scores Historic Partnership with National Hockey League and National Hockey League Players' Association," all from www.scotiabank.ca (viewed June 5, 2008); "Cineplex Entertainment and Scotiabank Launch First-ever Canadian Entertainment Loyalty Rewards Program and Rename Paramount Toronto Theatre to Scotiabank Theatre Toronto," *CNW Group*, January 24, 2007, www.newswire.ca/en/releases/archive/January2007/24/c8473.html (viewed June 4, 2008); Jyotika Malhotra, "How Podcasting is Helping Scotiabank Serve its Customers," *Association of Internet Marketing and Sales*, November 8, 2006, blog.aimscanada.com/aims_canada/2006/11/yesterday_i_tal.html (viewed June 5, 2008); "Motion Picture Theatres," *The Daily*, Statistics Canada, August 3, 2007; "Scotiabank Strengthens Connection With CFL," CFL website, August 15, 2007, www.cfl.ca/article/scotiabank_strengthens_connection_with_cfl (viewed June 5, 2008).

Marketing communications can have a huge payoff. This chapter describes how communications work and what marketing communications can do for a company. It also addresses how holistic marketers combine and integrate marketing communications. Chapter 18 examines the different forms of mass (nonpersonal) communications (advertising, sales promotion, events and experiences, and public relations and publicity); Chapter 19 examines the different forms of personal communications (direct marketing, including e-commerce, and personal selling).

THE ROLE OF MARKETING COMMUNICATIONS

Marketing communications are the means by which firms attempt to inform, persuade, and remind consumers—directly or indirectly—about the products and brands they sell. In a sense, marketing communications represent the "voice" of the brand and are a means by which it can establish a dialogue and build relationships with consumers.

Marketing communications perform many functions for consumers. Consumers can be told or shown how and why a product is used, by what kind of person, and where and when; consumers can learn about who makes the product and what the company and brand stand for; and consumers can be given an incentive or reward for trial or usage. Marketing communications allow companies to link their brands to other people, places, events, brands, experiences, feelings, and things. Marketing communications can contribute to brand equity by establishing the brand in memory and crafting a brand image.

Marketing Communications and Brand Equity

Although advertising is often a central element of a marketing communications program, it is usually not the only one—or even the most important one—in terms of building brand equity. The **marketing communications mix** consists of six major modes of communication:[1]

1. *Advertising.* Any paid form of nonpersonal presentation and promotion of ideas, goods, or services by an identified sponsor.

2. *Sales promotion.* A variety of short-term incentives to encourage trial or purchase of a product or service.

3. *Events and experiences.* Company-sponsored activities and programs designed to create daily or special brand-related interactions.

4. *Public relations and publicity.* A variety of programs designed to promote or protect a company's image or its individual products.

5. *Personal selling.* Face-to-face interaction with one or more prospective purchasers for the purpose of making presentations, answering questions, and procuring orders.

6. *Direct marketing.* Use of mail, telephone, fax, email, or Internet to communicate directly with or solicit response or dialogue from specific customers and prospects.

Consider how Nike used a variety of media to introduce the latest version of its successful line of runners endorsed by basketball star LeBron James:[2]

Nike Air Zoom LeBron IV

Nike's launch of the new version of its shoe line was supported by a wide range of traditional and nontraditional communications that included sponsorship of the first episode of *Sports Center* on ESPN; distribution of 400 000 DVDs about the making of the shoe and the ad campaign; saturation advertising on espn.com, mtv.com, and other sites; a "pop-up retail store" in Manhattan; video clips appearing as short programs on the MTV2 cable network; and a retro-chic neon billboard near Madison Square Garden that showed a continuously dunking Mr. James. The campaign also featured television and print ads, and online video featuring James as "the LeBrons," characters who represent four sides of his personality and who first appeared in ads for the Nike Air Zoom LeBron III shoe the previous year.

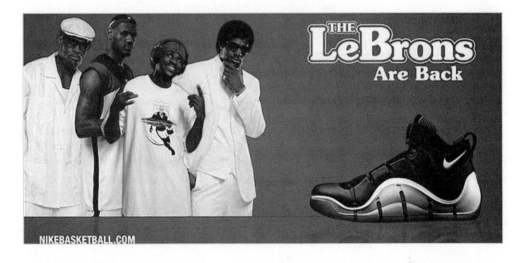

A wide range of marketing activities supported the traditional advertising in Nike's campaign introducing a new line of sneakers endorsed by basketball star LeBron James.

TABLE 17.1	COMMON COMMUNICATION PLATFORMS				

Advertising	Sales Promotion	Events and Experiences	Public Relations and Publicity	Personal Selling	Direct Marketing
Print and broadcast ads	Contests, games, sweepstakes, lotteries	Sports	Press kits	Sales presentations	Catalogues
Packaging–outer	Premiums and gifts	Entertainment	Speeches	Sales meetings	Mailings
Packaging inserts	Sampling	Festivals	Seminars	Incentive programs	Telemarketing
Motion pictures	Fairs and trade shows	Arts	Annual reports	Samples	Electronic shopping
Brochures and booklets	Exhibits	Causes	Charitable donations	Fairs and trade shows	TV shopping
Posters and leaflets	Demonstrations	Factory tours	Publications		Fax mail
Directories	Coupons	Company museums	Community relations		Email
Reprints of ads	Rebates	Street activities	Lobbying		Voice mail
Billboards	Low-interest financing		Identity media		
Display signs	Entertainment		Company magazine		
Point-of-purchase displays	Trade-in allowances				
Audiovisual material	Continuity programs				
Symbols and logos	Tie-ins				
Videotapes					

Table 17.1 lists numerous communication platforms. Company communication goes beyond these specific platforms. The product's styling and price, the package's shape and colour, the salesperson's manner and dress, the store décor, the company's stationery—all communicate something to buyers. Every *brand contact* delivers an impression that can strengthen or weaken a customer's view of the company.

As Figure 17.1 shows, marketing communication activities contribute to brand equity in many ways: by creating awareness of the brand, linking the right associations to the brand image in consumers' memory, eliciting positive brand judgments or feelings, and/or facilitating a stronger consumer-brand connection.

One implication of the concept of brand equity is that the manner in which brand associations are formed does not matter. In other words, a consumer should have an equally strong, favourable, and unique brand association between Subaru and the concepts "outdoors," "active," and "rugged" when exposed to a TV ad showing its cars driving over rugged terrain at different times of the year and when they watch the ski, kayak, and mountain bike events that Subaru sponsors; the impact in terms of brand equity should be identical.

But these marketing communication activities must be integrated to deliver a consistent message and achieve the strategic positioning. The starting point in planning marketing communications is an audit of all the potential interactions that customers in the target market may have with the brand and the company. For example, someone interested in purchasing a new computer might talk to others, see television ads, read articles, look for information on the Internet, and look at computers in a store. Marketers need to assess which experiences and impressions will have the most influence at each stage of the buying process. This understanding will help them allocate communications dollars more efficiently and design and implement the right communication programs.

Armed with these insights, marketers can judge marketing communications according to its ability to build brand equity and drive brand sales. For example, how well does a proposed ad campaign contribute to awareness or to creating, maintaining, or strengthening brand associations? Does a sponsorship cause consumers to have more favourable brand judgments and feelings? To what extent does a promotion encourage consumers to buy more of a product? At what price premium?

From the perspective of building brand equity, marketers should evaluate *all* the different possible communication options according to effectiveness criteria (how well does it work) as well as efficiency considerations (how much does it cost). This broad view of brand-building activities is especially relevant when marketers are considering strategies to improve brand awareness.

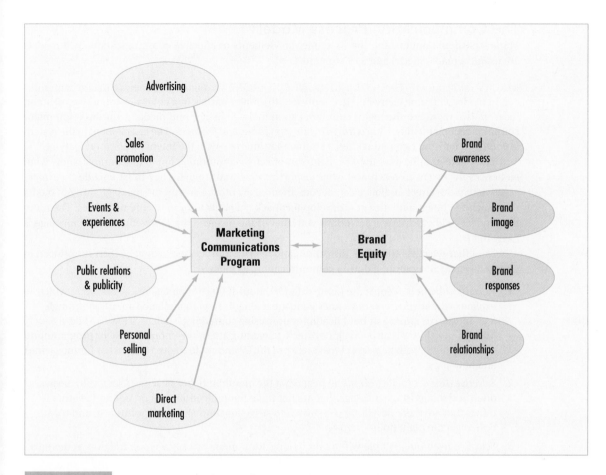

FIGURE 17.1

Integrating Marketing Communications to Build Brand Equity

Brand awareness is a function of the number of brand-related exposures and experiences accumulated by the consumer.[3] *Anything* that causes the consumer to notice and pay attention to the brand can increase brand awareness, at least in terms of brand recognition. The brand visibility typically found with sponsorships suggests that these activities may be especially valuable for enhancing brand recognition. To enhance brand recall, however, more intense and elaborate processing may be necessary so that stronger brand links to the product category or consumer needs are established.

Similarly, because brand associations, responses, and relationships can be created in many different ways, *all* possible marketing communication options should be considered to create the desired brand image and knowledge, as the "Body by Milk" campaign shows.

Body by Milk

In 2006, the California Milk Processor Board (CMPB) was faced with a decline in milk consumption by American teenagers. To counter the decline, the CMPB embarked on a US$20-million advertising campaign—the latest version of the successful 1995 milk mustache campaign—to advocate to young adults that choosing milk will provide them with protein to build muscle and lose weight. The "Body by Milk" campaign featured sports and entertainment celebrities chosen for their athletic physiques including soccer star David Beckham and baseball star Alex Rodriguez. Each full-page ad promoted healthy living by claiming "staying active, eating right, and drinking three glasses a day of low-fat or fat-free milk instead of sugary drinks helps you look your best." The ads ended with the now very familiar slogan "Got milk?" CMPB's original ads had discussed how milk would promote health and was an excellent source of calcium. Although both claims are true, the new body messages are intended to appeal better to teenagers, "because they are very concerned about weight and appearance," according to CMPB.[4]

The Communication Process Models

Marketers should understand the fundamental elements of effective communication. Two models are useful: a macro model and a micro model.

MACRO MODEL OF THE COMMUNICATION PROCESS Figure 17.2 shows a macro communication model with nine elements. Two represent the major parties in a communication—sender and receiver. Two represent the major communication tools—message and media. Four represent major communication functions—*encoding, decoding, response,* and *feedback.* The last element in the system is *noise* (random and competing messages that may interfere with the intended communication).[5]

The model emphasizes the key factors in effective communication. Senders must know what audiences they want to reach and what responses they want to get. They must encode their messages so that the target audience can decode them. They must transmit the message through media that reach the target audience and develop feedback channels to monitor the responses. The more the sender's field of experience overlaps with that of the receiver, the more effective the message is likely to be.

Note that selective attention, distortion, and retention processes—concepts first introduced in Chapter 6—may be operating during communication, as follows:

1. *Selective attention.* People are bombarded by about 1500 commercial messages a day, which explains why advertisers sometimes go to great lengths to grab audience attention through fear, music, sex appeal, or bold headlines promising something, such as "How to Make a Million." Ad clutter is also a major obstacle to gaining attention—noneditorial or programming content ranges from 25 percent to 33 percent for TV and radio to over 50 percent for magazines and newspapers.

2. *Selective distortion.* Receivers will hear what fits into their belief systems. As a result, receivers often add things to the message that are not there (amplification) and do not notice other things that are there (levelling). The task is to strive for simplicity, clarity, interest, and repetition to get the main points across.

3. *Selective retention.* People will retain in long-term memory only a small fraction of the messages that reach them. If the receiver's initial attitude toward the object is positive and he or she rehearses support arguments, the message is likely to be accepted and have high recall. If the initial attitude is negative and the person rehearses counterarguments, the message is likely to be rejected but will stay in long-term memory. Because persuasion requires the receiver's rehearsal of his or her own thoughts, much of what is called persuasion is actually self-persuasion.[6]

MICRO MODEL OF CONSUMER RESPONSES Micro models of marketing communications concentrate on consumers' specific responses to communications. Figure 17.3 summarizes four classic *response hierarchy models.*

All these models assume that the buyer passes through a cognitive, affective, and behavioural stage, in that order. This "learn-feel-do" sequence is appropriate when the audience has high involvement with a product category perceived to have high differentiation, as in purchasing an automobile or house. An alternative sequence, "do-feel-learn," is relevant when the audience has high involvement but perceives little or no differentiation within the product category, as in purchasing an airline ticket or personal computer. A third sequence, "learn-do-feel," is relevant when the audience has low involvement and perceives little differentiation within the product category,

FIGURE 17.2

Elements in the Communication Process

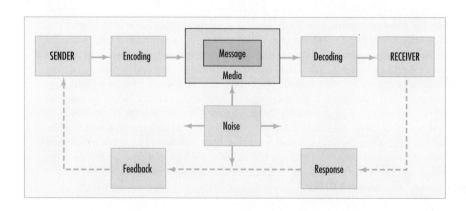

Stages	Models			
	AIDA Model[a]	Hierarchy-of-Effects Model[b]	Innovation-Adoption Model[c]	Communications Model[d]
Cognitive stage	Attention	Awareness ↓ Knowledge	Awareness	Exposure ↓ Reception ↓ Cognitive response
Affective stage	Interest ↓ Desire	Liking ↓ Preference ↓ Conviction	Interest ↓ Evaluation	Attitude ↓ Intention
Behaviour stage	Action	Purchase	Trial ↓ Adoption	Behaviour

FIGURE 17.3

Response Hierarchy Models

Sources: [a]E. K. Strong, *The Psychology of Selling* (New York: McGraw-Hill, 1925), p. 9; [b]Robert J. Lavidge and Gary A. Steiner, "A Model for Predictive Measurements of Advertising Effectiveness," *Journal of Marketing* (October 1961): 61; [c]Everett M. Rogers, *Diffusion of Innovation* (New York: The Free Press, 1962), pp. 79–86; [d]various sources.

as in purchasing salt or batteries. By choosing the right sequence, the marketer can do a better job of planning communications.[7]

Here we will assume that the buyer has high involvement with the product category and perceives high differentiation within the category. We will illustrate the *hierarchy-of-effects model* (in the second column of Figure 17.3) in the context of a marketing communication campaign for a small Saskatchewan university named Assinboia:

- *Awareness.* If most of the target audience is unaware of the object, the communicator's task is to build awareness. Suppose Assinboia seeks applicants from Alberta but has no name recognition there. Suppose there are 30 000 students in grades 11 and 12 in Alberta who may be interested in Assinboia University; the university might set the objective of making 70 percent of these students aware of Assinboia's name within one year.

- *Knowledge.* The target audience might have brand awareness but not know much more. Assinboia may want its target audience to know that it is a private four-year university with excellent programs in English, foreign languages, and history. It needs to learn how many people in the target audience have little, some, or much knowledge about Assinboia. If knowledge is weak, Assinboia may decide to select brand knowledge as its communication objective.

- *Liking.* If target members know the brand, how do they feel about it? If the audience looks unfavourably on Assinboia University, the communicator has to find out why. If the unfavourable view is based on real problems, Assinboia will have to fix its problems and then communicate its renewed quality. Good public relations calls for "good deeds followed by good words."

- *Preference.* The target audience might like the product but not prefer it to others. In this case, the communicator must try to build consumer preference by comparing quality, value, performance, and other features to likely competitors.

- *Conviction.* A target audience might prefer a particular product but not develop a conviction about buying it. The communicator's job is to build conviction and purchase intent among students interested in Assinboia University.

- *Purchase.* Finally, some members of the target audience might have conviction but may not quite get around to making the purchase. The communicator must lead these consumers to take the final step, perhaps by offering the product at a low price, offering a premium, or letting consumers try it out. Assinboia might invite selected high school students to visit the campus and attend some classes, or it might offer partial scholarships to deserving students.

To show how fragile the whole communication process is, assume that the probability of *each* of the six steps being successfully accomplished is 50 percent. The laws of probability suggest that the probability of *all* six steps occurring successfully, assuming they are independent events, would be $0.5 \times 0.5 \times 0.5 \times 0.5 \times 0.5 \times 0.5$, which equals 1.5625 percent. If the probability of each step occurring, on average, were a more moderate 10 percent, then the joint probability of all six events occurring would be 0.0001—in other words, only 1 in 10 000!

To increase the odds for a successful marketing communications campaign, marketers must attempt to increase the likelihood that *each* step occurs. For example, from an advertising standpoint, the ideal ad campaign would ensure that:

1. The right consumer is exposed to the right message at the right place and at the right time.
2. The ad causes the consumer to pay attention to the ad but does not distract from the intended message.
3. The ad properly reflects the consumer's level of understanding about the product and the brand.
4. The ad correctly positions the brand in terms of desirable and deliverable points-of-difference and points-of-parity.
5. The ad motivates consumers to consider purchase of the brand.
6. The ad creates strong brand associations with all of these stored communication effects so that they can have an effect when consumers are considering making a purchase.

DEVELOPING EFFECTIVE COMMUNICATIONS

Figure 17.4 shows the eight steps in developing effective communications. We begin with the basics: identifying the target audience, determining the communications objectives, designing the communications, selecting the channels, and establishing the budget.

Identify the Target Audience

The process must start with a clear target audience in mind: potential buyers of the company's products, current users, deciders, or influencers; individuals, groups, particular publics, or the general public. The target audience is a critical influence on the communicator's decisions as to what to say, how to say it, when to say it, where to say it, and to whom to say it.

The target audience can potentially be profiled in terms of any of the market segments identified in Chapter 8. It is often useful to define target audience in terms of usage and loyalty. Is the target new to the category or a current user? Is the target loyal to the brand, loyal to a competitor, or someone who switches between brands? If the target is a brand user, is he or she a heavy or light user? (See "Marketing Memo: Define Target Market Before Defining Target Audience"). Communication strategy will differ depending on the usage and loyalty involved. *Image analysis* can be conducted to profile the target audience in terms of brand knowledge to provide further insight.

A major part of audience analysis is assessing the current image of the company, its products, and its competitors. **Image** is the set of beliefs, ideas, and impressions a person holds regarding an object. People's attitudes and actions toward an object are highly conditioned by that object's image.

The first step is to measure the target audience's knowledge of the object, using the *familiarity scale:*

Never Heard of	Heard of Only	Know a Little Bit	Know a Fair Amount	Know Very Well

If most respondents circle only the first two categories, the challenge is to build greater awareness.

Respondents who are familiar with the product can be asked how they feel toward it using the *favourability scale:*

Very Unfavourable	Somewhat Unfavourable	Indifferent	Somewhat Favourable	Very Favourable

If most respondents check the first two categories, then the organization must overcome a negative-image problem.

The two scales can be combined to develop insight into the nature of the communication challenge. Suppose area residents are asked about their familiarity with and attitudes toward four

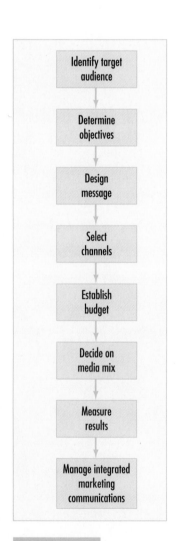

FIGURE 17.4

Steps in Developing Effective Communications

local hospitals, A, B, C, and D. Their responses are averaged and shown in Figure 17.5. Hospital A has the most positive image: most people know it and like it. Hospital B is less familiar to most people, but those who know it like it. Hospital C is viewed negatively by those who know it, but (fortunately for the hospital) not too many people know it. Hospital D is seen as a poor hospital, and everyone knows it!

Each hospital faces a different communication task. Hospital A must work at maintaining its good reputation and high awareness. Hospital B must gain the attention of more people. Hospital C must find out why people dislike it and take steps to improve its quality while keeping a low profile. Hospital D should lower its profile, improve its quality, and then seek public attention.

Images are "sticky"; they persist long after the organization has changed. Image persistence is explained by the fact that once people have a certain image, they perceive what is consistent with that image. It will take highly disconfirming information to raise doubts and open their minds, especially when people do not have continuous or new firsthand experiences with the changed object.

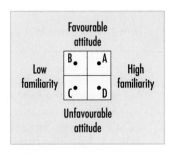

FIGURE 17.5

Familiarity–Favourability Analysis

Boston Pizza

Boston Pizza (BP) has struggled in recent years with developing a focus for its marketing and advertising campaigns. In November 2007, Boston Pizza Inc. moved away from a reliance on using personalities and strange animals in its advertisements to projecting its restaurant as a people-friendly place. Previous campaigns bounced from pitchman Howie Mandel to a giant, hairy beast, Louie the Sasquatch, whose TV spots were too frightening for kids to watch and whose speech was unintelligible. BP realized the error of its ways and hired Lowe Roche as its new advertising firm to recover from failed personalities and animation gimmicks. BP's new focus was to be identified as a place for family as well as a great meeting spot for sports enthusiasts. Its "You're Among Friends" slogan continued, and now took centre stage in its campaign. In addition, to win back customers' respect and trust, BP began highlighting its service to the community with the Boston Pizza Foundation and the support it has provided to neighbourhood schools, local sports teams, and charitable organizations.[8]

Determine the Communication Objectives

As we showed with Assinboia University, communication objectives can be set at any level of the hierarchy-of-effects model. Rossiter and Percy identify four possible objectives, as follows:[9]

1. *Category need.* Establishing a product or service category as necessary to remove or satisfy a perceived discrepancy between a current motivational state and a desired emotional state. A new-to-the-world product such as electric cars would always begin with a communication objective of establishing category need.

2. *Brand awareness.* Ability to identify (recognize or recall) the brand within the category, in sufficient detail to make a purchase. Recognition is easier to achieve than recall—consumers are more likely to recognize Stouffer's distinctive orange packages than recall the brand if asked to think of a brand of frozen entrées. Brand recall is important outside the store; brand recognition is important inside the store. Brand awareness provides a foundation for brand equity.

3. *Brand attitude.* Evaluation of the brand with respect to its perceived ability to meet a currently relevant need. Relevant brand needs may be negatively oriented (problem removal, problem avoidance, incomplete satisfaction, normal depletion) or positively oriented (sensory gratification, intellectual stimulation, or social approval). Household cleaning products often use problem-solution; food products, on the other hand, often use sensory-oriented ads emphasizing appetite appeal.

4. *Brand purchase intention.* Self-instructions to purchase the brand or to take purchase-related action. Promotional offers in the form of coupons or two-for-one deals encourage consumers to make a mental commitment to buy a product. But many consumers do not have an expressed category need and may not be in the market when exposed to an ad, making intentions less likely to be formed. For example, in any given week, only about 20 percent of adults may be planning to buy detergent; only 2 percent may be planning to buy a carpet cleaner; and only 0.25 percent may be planning to buy a car.

The most effective communications often can achieve multiple objectives. For example, Geico advertises that a 15-minute phone call can result in a 15-percent reduction on auto insurance, combining both brand attitude and a call to action to build brand purchase intentions.

| MARKETING MEMO | DEFINE TARGET MARKET BEFORE DEFINING TARGET AUDIENCE |

MARKETING MEMO | DEFINE TARGET MARKET BEFORE DEFINING TARGET AUDIENCE

Some marketers of new products begin thinking about the advertisement even before deciding the target market. This can be putting the cart before the horse. The marketer needs to identify the target market for the product before deciding to whom to target the communications.

Choosing the target market is no easy task either. Once the target market for the product has been identified, it needs to be re-examined. There are three critical questions the marketer should ask to determine if the target is a viable one:

1. Have people in this target shown an interest in my product offering before?
2. Are people in this target already spending money on similar products?
3. Is the target easy to reach?

If any of the above questions are answered with a no, then the target must be altered. The following are some of the many reasons why it is important to spend that extra time and effort re-examining to create the best target possible.

- *Save Money.* The best target ensures that you do not waste money targeting consumers who have no need or desire for what you are offering.
- *Save Time.* Creating a "one-stop-shop message" for your product is a waste of time, money, and resources. Time is better spent targeting consumers who are interested in your product and are good prospects.
- *Create a Better Product.* Once you know exactly to whom you are selling, you are no longer trying to be something to everyone. You can tweak your product to be exactly what your target wants and needs, ultimately fending off competition.
- *Sell Easier.* If a niche is uncovered and you have the perfect solution to serve that niche, you will likely have little competition.
- *Produce a Clear Message.* When you know your target well, you have the ability to get inside consumers' heads and understand their needs and wants. Therefore, you are able to provide them with a tailored solution and satisfy them better.
- *Acquire Referrals.* A clearly targeted message resonates with your audience and enables word-of-mouth communication. Once positive benefits are experienced as a result of your solution, and the message is clear, your business grows faster.
- *Command a Higher Price.* A specialist in an area is usually in a position to charge more. Similarly, a clearly defined target allows you to understand and serve that market better, thereby giving you the ability to dominate your competition and charge a higher price.

Source: Adapted from Jimmy Vee, Travis Miller, and Joel Bauer, *Gravitational Marketing*, 1st ed. (Hoboken, NJ: John Wiley & Sons, Inc., 2008), pp. 54–58.

Design the Communication

Formulating the communication to achieve the desired response will require solving three problems: what to say (message strategy), how to say it (creative strategy), and who should say it (message source).

MESSAGE STRATEGY In determining message strategy, management searches for appeals, themes, or ideas that will tie into the brand positioning and help to establish points-of-parity or points-of-difference. Some of these may be related directly to product or service performance (the quality, economy, or value of the brand) whereas others may be related to more extrinsic considerations (the brand as being contemporary, popular, or traditional).

John Maloney saw buyers as expecting one of four types of reward from a product: rational, sensory, social, or ego satisfaction.[10] Buyers might visualize these rewards from results-of-use experience, product-in-use experience, or incidental-to-use experience. Crossing the four types of rewards with the three types of experience generates 12 types of messages. For example, the appeal "gets clothes cleaner" is a rational-reward promise following results-of-use experience. The phrase "real beer taste in a great light beer" is a sensory-reward promise connected with product-in-use experience.

It is widely believed that industrial buyers are most responsive to performance messages. They are knowledgeable about the product, trained to recognize value, and accountable to others for their

 To read about the troubled advertising campaigns that Toyota and Nike ran in China, visit www.pearsoned-asia.com/ marketingmanagementchina.

choices. Consumers, when they buy certain big-ticket items, also tend to gather information and estimate benefits.

CREATIVE STRATEGY Communication effectiveness depends on how a message is being expressed as well as the content of the message itself. An ineffective communication may mean that the wrong message was used or the right message was just being expressed poorly. *Creative strategies* are how marketers translate their messages into a specific communication. Creative strategies can be broadly classified as involving either "informational" or "transformational" appeals.[11] These two general categories each encompass several different specific creative approaches.

Informational Appeals An *informational appeal* elaborates on product or service attributes or benefits. Examples in advertising are problem-solution ads (Claritin gives you all-day allergy relief without drowsiness), product demonstration ads (Glad Press'n Seal sealable plastic wrap doesn't just cling, it seals), product comparison ads (Rogers offers cheaper Internet and phone services than Bell), and testimonials from unknown or celebrity endorsers (Céline Dion singing for Air Canada). Informational appeals assume very rational processing of the communication on the part of the consumer. Logic and reason rule.

Hovland's research at Yale has shed much light on informational appeals and their relation to such issues as conclusion drawing, one-versus two-sided arguments, and order of argument presentation. Some early experiments supported stating conclusions for the audience. Subsequent research, however, indicates that the best ads ask questions and allow readers and viewers to form their own conclusions.[12] If Honda had hammered away that the Element was for young people, this strong definition might have blocked older age groups from buying it. Some stimulus ambiguity can lead to a broader market definition and more spontaneous purchases.

You would think that one-sided presentations that praise a product would be more effective than two-sided arguments that also mention shortcomings. Yet two-sided messages may be more appropriate, especially when negative associations must be overcome. Heinz ran the message "Heinz Ketchup is slow good" and Listerine ran the message "Listerine tastes bad twice a day."[13] Two-sided messages are more effective with more educated audiences and those who are initially opposed.[14]

Finally, the order in which arguments are presented is important.[15] In the case of a one-sided message, presenting the strongest argument first has the advantage of arousing attention and interest. This is important in media where the audience often does not attend to the whole message. With a captive audience, a climactic presentation might be more effective. In the case of a two-sided message, if the audience is initially opposed, the communicator might start with the other side's argument and conclude with his or her strongest argument.[16]

Transformational Appeals A *transformational appeal* elaborates on a non–product-related benefit or image. It might depict what kind of person uses a brand (VW advertises to active, youthful people with its "Drivers Wanted" campaign) or what kind of experience results from using the brand (The Bay's "More than you came for"). Transformational appeals often attempt to stir up emotions that will motivate purchase. This is the route Clairol took to revive a moribund brand from the 1970s.

Developing creative strategy: This ad for Tilex, a household product, focuses on problem-solution—Tilex is called "The Mold Killer."™

Clairol Herbal Essences

"Yes, Yes, Yes," actresses exclaim as they simulate sexual ecstasy while washing their hair and enjoying what the tagline dubs "A Truly Organic Experience." Some women find the ad's coy double entendre demeaning. Procter & Gamble, which acquired Clairol in 2002, credits the ad with bringing the nearly dead brand back to life. Herbal Essences became one of the fastest-growing brands in the world, climbing in sales from zero to US$700 million in seven years. In explaining the brand's success, the agency creator, the Kaplan Thaler Group, maintains, "Emotion is the lightning rod, the trigger to making a purchase."[17]

Communicators use negative appeals such as fear, guilt, and shame to get people to do things (brush their teeth, have an annual health check-up) or stop doing things (smoking, alcohol abuse, overeating). Fear appeals work best when they are not too strong. Furthermore, fear appeals work better when source credibility is high and when the communication promises to relieve, in a believable and efficient way, the fear it arouses.[18] See "Marketing Insight: Negative Emotional Appeals in Social Marketing" for recommendations on using negative appeals successfully.

Messages are most persuasive when they are moderately discrepant with what the audience believes. Messages that state only what the audience already believes at best only reinforce beliefs, and if the messages are too discrepant, they will be counter-argued and disbelieved. Consider how Campbell Soup Company addressed consumers' health concerns with its V8 product.

Campbell Soup Company

Since 1933, the Campbell Soup Company's V8 brand has been one of the most respected and well-known vegetable juices on the market. However, it has had bland marketing and advertising in the recent past with tag lines such as "Could've had a V8," which failed to generate any real customer interest or increased sales even after it was later changed to "Should've had a V8."

In 2007, the company reacted to the growing public concern with obesity and heart disease and the trend toward healthy eating and drinking. Recognizing this, the company introduced a line of V8 V-Fusion and V8 Splash drinks. It revisited its old and new slogans, but this time around, surrounded them with new and effective ads showing two people, one exercising or eating right and the other doing the opposite and complaining, whereupon the healthy person shames the other with a knock on the head: "Could've had a V8 . . . Use Your Head."[19]

Communicators also use positive emotional appeals such as humour, love, pride, and joy. Motivational or "borrowed interest" devices—such as the presence of cute babies, frisky puppies, popular music, or provocative sex appeals—are often employed to attract consumers' attention and raise their involvement with an ad.

Borrowed-interest techniques are thought to be necessary in the tough new media environment characterized by low-involvement consumer processing and much competing ad and programming clutter. In 2003, British singer Sting, who in the 1980s had refused to allow the song "Don't Stand So Close to Me" to be used in a deodorant ad, made a lucrative deal with Ford Motor Company as part of the company's efforts to reach consumers aged 35 and over. In an ad for Jaguar, he was shown being driven around in the car while his latest single, "Desert Rose," played in the background.[20]

Although these borrowed-interest approaches can attract attention and create more liking and belief in the sponsor, they may also detract from comprehension, wear out their welcome fast, and overshadow the product.[21] Attention-getting tactics are often *too* effective and distract from brand or product claims. Thus, one challenge in arriving at the best creative strategy is figuring out how to "break through the clutter" to attract the attention of consumers—but still be able to deliver the intended message.

The magic to advertising is to bring concepts on a piece of paper to life in the minds of the consumer target. In a print ad, the communicator has to decide on headline, copy, illustration, and colour. For a radio message, the communicator has to choose words, voice qualities, and vocalizations. The "sound" of an announcer promoting a used automobile has to be different from one promoting a new Cadillac. If the message is to be carried on television or in person, all these elements plus body language (nonverbal clues) have to be planned. Presenters have to pay attention to facial expressions, gestures, dress, posture, and hairstyle. If the message is carried by the product or its packaging, the communicator has to pay attention to colour, texture, scent, size, and shape.

Every detail matters. Think how the ad taglines listed on the right were able to bring to life the brand themes listed on the left.

Brand Theme	Ad Tagline
Our hamburgers are bigger.	Where's the Beef? (Wendy's restaurants)
We make good coffee.	Always got time for Tim Hortons (Tim Hortons)
No hard sell, just a good car.	Drivers Wanted (Volkswagen automobiles)
We don't rent as many cars, so we have to do more for our customers.	We Try Harder (Avis auto rental)
Your local, friendly hardware store.	Home of the Handyman (Home Hardware)

| MARKETING INSIGHT | NEGATIVE EMOTIONAL APPEALS IN SOCIAL MARKETING |

The decision to use a positive or negative emotional appeal in a communication message depends greatly on the type of product being sold, the specific message being communicated, and audience characteristics. If the wrong type or degree of appeal is used, consumers may become indifferent to the message, get upset, or get turned off.

Social marketing messages, such as those relating to smoking, drugs, drinking and driving, poverty, hunger, or disease, often require utilizing a negative emotional appeal. When implementing a social marketing program, the ultimate goal often is to cause behavioural change in the targeted audience. Many companies and governments have used negative emotional appeals successfully to promote change, prompting individuals to stop an action such as using drugs or perform one such as giving blood. Negative emotional appeals, however, may not be the best way to influence a change of behaviour. When used in moderation, they can be a very effective way to communicate a message. When used in excess, they cause consumers to disassociate themselves from the message and the intended behaviour.

Innovative campaigns using new forms of persuasion, while still using a degree of negative appeal, may be the direction many social marketers take. The Government of Ontario produced the Stupid.ca multimedia campaign, which used humour and wit to present a smoking-prevention message in a creative way that grabbed the attention of young consumers. The goal of the Ministry of Health and Long-Term Care was to develop a revolutionary campaign that would grab the attention of 12–15-year-olds and encourage them to resist the temptation to smoke. Although the campaign communicated the dangers of smoking, it did so in a fresh way that was radically different from the typical "stop smoking" advertisements adolescents have grown weary of. For example, one version of the campaign showed a teenaged girl holding a long steel pole standing in the middle of a field during a violent thunderstorm with lightning flashing around her. The ad then goes on to say that smoking is more stupid than this teenager's act. The television campaign, designed by youth for youth, received several national and international marketing awards including a silver medal at the 2005 Canadian Marketing Awards.

In a study that explored the development of a new gambling-prevention campaign aimed at adolescents, focus groups were used to uncover the most effective way to motivate change. The participants revealed that real-life stories and emotional appeals portraying the negative consequences associated with gambling problems would be most effective. The study also found that negative appeals, when used in moderation, were approved by both genders and all age groups. The negative effects that participants suggested the campaign show include health, social, family, and financial consequences. Also, the study concluded that this type of campaign should avoid messages that outright discourage the behaviour, as this may encourage a rebellious adolescent to do the opposite. Fear tactics in general were cautioned against, as participants believed that adolescents might reject the message entirely. Similarly, negative emotional appeals do not work well with kids or senior citizens. Kids are easily emotionally disturbed by negative messages. Senior citizens respond better to positive emotional messages and get turned off by negative emotional messages.

Sources: Carmen Messerlian and Jeffrey Derevensky, "Evaluating the Role of Social Marketing Campaigns to Prevent Youth Gambling Problems: A Qualitative Study," *Canadian Journal of Public Health*, 98, no. 2 (March/April 2007): 101; "Government's Stupid.ca Campaign Receives National and International Recognition," *Ontario Ministry of Health and Long-Term Care*, June 12, 2006, www.health.gov.on.ca/english/public/updates/archives/hu_04/tobacco/tobacco_awards.html (viewed June 4, 2008).

MESSAGE SOURCE Many communications do not use a source beyond the company itself. Others use known or unknown people. Messages delivered by attractive or popular sources can potentially achieve higher attention and recall, which is why advertisers often use celebrities as spokespeople. Celebrities are likely to be effective when they personify a key product attribute. Catherine Deneuve's beauty did this for Chanel No. 5 perfume, and Paul Hogan's Aussie ruggedness did this for the Subaru Outback wagon. On the other hand, using James Garner and Cybill Shepherd to sell beef backfired: Garner subsequently had quintuple bypass surgery, and Shepherd proclaimed she was a vegetarian.

What is important is the spokesperson's credibility. What factors underlie source credibility? The three most often identified are expertise, trustworthiness, and likability.[22] *Expertise* is the specialized knowledge the communicator possesses to back the claim. *Trustworthiness* is related to how objective and honest the source is perceived to be. Friends are trusted more than strangers or salespeople, and people who are not paid to endorse a product are viewed as more trustworthy than people who are paid.[23] *Likability* describes the source's attractiveness. Qualities like candour, humour, and naturalness make a source more likable.

The most highly credible source would be a person who scores high on all three dimensions. Pharmaceutical companies want doctors to testify about product benefits because doctors have high credibility. Anti-drug crusaders will use ex–drug addicts because they have higher credibility. Before his death, Dave Thomas, who had folksy appeal and inherent credibility, did over 800 Wendy's commercials in his trademark red tie and short-sleeved shirt. Roots used in its campaigns Canadian Olympic athletes wearing the Roots-designed Olympic uniforms, and the Hudson's Bay Company hopes to win the same accolades now that it has won the Olympic account.

A well-chosen celebrity endorsement can catapult even the most unlikely product to stardom. Consider how Halo, Purely for Pets is trying to do that:

Halo and Ellen DeGeneres

In 1986, pet owner Andi Brown founded Halo, Purely for Pets pet food to provide better nutrition for pets. In 2006, after almost 20 years of moderate sales, Halo was purchased by the private-equity firm Pegasus Capital Advisors LLP. Following the purchase, Pegasus wanted to find a way to make Halo stand out in the multi-billion-dollar pet-food industry dominated by giants such as Nestlé, Mars, Procter & Gamble, and Colgate-Palmolive. In 2008, in order to compete, Pegasus chose celebrity Ellen DeGeneres to promote its brand. Not only is DeGeneres an endorser for Halo, she is also part owner of the company, holding a 15-percent stake in the pet-food label. DeGeneres, who holds distinctions as an Emmy-winning talk-show host, comedienne, movie star, awards-show host, sitcom actress, producer, and writer, is expected to help boost the brand's sales, because she is a celebrity who is also known as an avid pet lover herself.[24]

"Marketing Insight: Who's Left in Sports to Use as Endorser?" discusses how it is becoming increasingly difficult to find good celebrity endorsers.

If a person has a positive attitude toward a source and a message, or a negative attitude toward both, a state of *congruity* is said to exist. What happens if the person holds one attitude toward the source and the opposite toward the message? Suppose a consumer hears a likable celebrity praise a brand that she dislikes? Osgood and Tannenbaum say that "attitude change will take place in the direction of increasing the amount of congruity between the two evaluations."[25] The consumer will end up respecting the celebrity somewhat less or respecting the brand somewhat more. If she encounters the same celebrity praising other disliked brands, she will eventually develop a negative view of the celebrity and maintain her negative attitudes toward the brands. The **principle of congruity** implies that communicators can use their good image to reduce some negative feelings toward a brand but in the process might lose some esteem from the audience.

Multinational companies wrestle with a number of challenges in developing global communications programs: They must decide whether the product is appropriate for a country. They must make sure the market segment they address is both legal and customary. They must decide if the style of the ad is acceptable, and they must decide whether ads should be created at headquarters or locally.[26]

1. *Product.* Many products are restricted or forbidden in certain parts of the world. Beer, wine, and spirits cannot be advertised or sold in Muslim countries. Tobacco products are subject to strict regulation in many countries.

2. *Market segment.* North American toy makers were surprised to learn that in many countries (Norway and Sweden, for example) no TV ads may be directed at children under 12. Sweden lobbied hard to extend that ban to all EU member countries in 2001 but failed. To play it safe, McDonald's advertises itself as a family restaurant in Sweden.

3. *Style.* Comparative ads, while acceptable and even common in Canada and the United States, are less commonly used in the United Kingdom, unacceptable in Japan, and illegal in India and Brazil. PepsiCo had a comparative taste test ad in Japan that was refused by many TV stations and eventually led to a lawsuit.

4. *Location.* Today, more and more multinational companies are attempting to build a global brand image by using the same advertising in all markets. When Daimler AG and Chrysler merged to become the world's fifth-largest automaker, they ran a three-week ad campaign in more than 100 countries consisting of a 12-page magazine insert, nine newspaper spreads, and a 24-page brochure that was sent to business, government, union leaders, and to the news media. The campaign's tagline was "Expect the extraordinary," and it featured people from both companies working together.

Companies that sell their products to different cultures or in different countries must be prepared to vary their messages. In advertising its hair-care products in different countries, Helene Curtis adjusts its messages. Middle-class British women wash their hair frequently, whereas the

---

MARKETING **INSIGHT** | WHO'S LEFT IN SPORTS TO USE AS ENDORSER?

Celebrity endorsements have been known to make or break a product's brand image. The strategy is one that comes with a degree of risk, as it is nearly impossible to predict a celebrity's behaviour following the endorsement. In recent years, several sport celebrities have received negative publicity associated with bad behaviour, making the roster of sport celebrities to choose from rather limited.

Scandals and bad publicity surrounding sport celebrities make it increasingly difficult for marketers. Professional athletes such as Michael Vick, Alex Rodriguez, and Shawne Merriman who have been in the news for all the wrong reasons are being scratched off the list. Sports celebrities clouded by bad publicity in recent years include baseball star Barry Bonds, Olympic multiple-gold-medalist Marion Jones, and discredited 2006 Tour de France winner Floyd Landis. They join a long list of untouchables including Mark McGwire, Mike Tyson, and Rafael Palmeiro.

Athletes such as Kobe Bryant, however, have made reasonable strides in recovering from bad publicity, although he may be more of an exception rather than the rule. A few years after sexual-assault charges against Bryant were dropped, he regained many of his original sponsorships from well-known brands such as Coca-Cola and Nike.

Sports celebrities who have respectable reputations and are therefore highly sought after as endorsers include Tiger Woods, Maria Sharapova, LeBron James, David Beckham, and Dale Earnhardt Jr. However, these popular figures do not come cheap. For example, Nike paid LeBron James US$90 million for a seven-year contract following his graduation from high school, predicting he would become the NBA's next Michael Jordan. Over the years, James has become a billion-dollar athlete. Similarly, McLaren Mercedes paid Lewis Hamilton £70 million and Reebok paid Venus Williams US$40 million for five-year contracts.

Companies not able to pay the huge price for sport-celebrity endorsements are left with few choices such as rookies, Olympians who gain popularity every four years, and retired athletes. Rookies can be a risky choice, Olympians are often forgotten a few months after the event, and retired athletes may not be effective in reaching a younger market.

Nevertheless, new sports celebrities with positive images continue to emerge and are being trusted with major campaigns involving them in strategic aspects of the brand, going as far as product design. Reebok used Yao Ming, an NBA star, as the face for its 2008 Beijing Summer Olympics campaign targeting the Chinese and U.S. markets. The campaign featured two different basketball shoes offered as limited editions designed by Yao Ming himself. This strategy may not always succeed, as evidenced by huge signature shoe flops such as those by Shaquille O'Neal for Reebok and Kobe Bryant for Adidas.

From a financial perspective, marketers consider using celebrity endorsers as an investment in the brand. They hope that the brand image will be sufficiently enhanced by the endorsement to generate enough incremental sales for a healthy return on investment. In recent years, due to the increasing number of prominent sports figures being involved in steroid or drug use, public drunkenness, violence, rape, or even murder, using a sports celebrity has been as speculative as the stock market. But then, anyone who deals with investments knows that big returns often come with big risks. It's no different with sports-celebrity endorsements.

Sources: Barry Janoff, "Sports Marketing in 2007: The Good, the Bad & the Druggies," *Brandweek*, 48, no. 46 (December 2007): 18; Barry Janoff, "Marketing Howard a Slam Dunk; Reebok Has Big Plans for Yao," *Brandweek*, 49, no. 8 (February 2008): 10; Tim Arango, "LEBRON INC.," *Fortune*, 156, no. 12 (December 2007): 100; Bill Saporito, "Kobe rebounds," *Time* (Canadian edition), September 13, 2004, 164, no. 11, pp. 50–51; Edward Gorman, "Lewis Hamilton strikes £70m contract in mutual show of confidence," *The Times*, January 19, 2008, www.timesonline.co.uk/tol/sport/formula_1/article3213065.ece (viewed September 22, 2008).

---

opposite is true of Spanish women. Japanese women avoid overwashing their hair for fear of removing protective oils. Consider how Bell Canada communicated with the Asian community to advertise its satellite television service, Bell ExpressVu:

Bell ExpressVu

Bell ExpressVu launched a print campaign targeted at the large Canadian South Asian community to promote the fact that Bell ExpressVu carries the Asian Television Network, a 24-hour service offering programs in English, Hindi, Punjabi, Tamil, Urdu, and other South Asian languages. The company did not have the budget to launch separate campaigns for all the subtargets in this group. As a result, Toronto-based Vickers & Benson Advertising decided that the solution was to write the copy in English, given that it is spoken throughout the subcontinent. However, they used copywriters who were themselves of Asian descent and employed what is commonly referred to as "Indian English"—the variant of the language typically spoken in South Asian countries. The copy read: "Big big news for all cousin brothers and sisters. We are maha proud to inform you that you are now able to get Asian Television Network full day, full night" and "First dish, then dishum dishum," which meant, "First you buy your satellite dish, then the action begins." Furthermore, they used visual cues that reinforced a connection with Asian countries such as an auto-rickshaw and a piece of sari fabric. Finally, to allay the risk that readers might mistake the ads as mockery, they included the line, "The writers of this advertisement are coming from exactly the same native place as you and, like you, are very homesick also."[27]

Select the Communication Channels

Selecting efficient channels to carry the message becomes more difficult as channels of communication become more fragmented and cluttered. Think of the challenges in the pharmaceutical industry: Sales reps "detail" doctors every day, hoping to get five minutes of a busy doctor's time. Some 40 percent of calls do not even result in seeing the doctor, which makes sales calling extremely expensive. The industry has had to expand its battery of communication channels to include ads in medical journals, direct mail (including audio and videotapes), free samples, and even telemarketing. Pharmaceutical companies sponsor clinical conferences at which they pay physicians to spend a weekend listening to leading physicians extol certain drugs in the morning, followed by an afternoon of golf or tennis.

All of these channels are used in the hope of building physician preference for their branded therapeutic agent. Pharmaceutical companies are also using new technologies to reach doctors through handheld devices, online services, and videoconferencing equipment.[28]

Communication channels may be personal and nonpersonal. Within each are many subchannels.

PERSONAL COMMUNICATION CHANNELS **Personal communication channels** involve two or more persons communicating directly face-to-face, person-to-audience, over the telephone, or through email. Instant messaging and independent sites to collect consumer reviews are another means of growing importance in recent years. Personal communication channels derive their effectiveness through individualized presentation and feedback.

A further distinction can be drawn among advocate, expert, and social communication channels. *Advocate channels* consist of company salespeople contacting buyers in the target market. *Expert channels* consist of independent experts making statements to target buyers. *Social channels* consist of neighbours, friends, family members, and associates talking to target buyers. In a study of 7000 consumers in seven European countries, 60 percent said they were influenced to use a new brand by family and friends.[29]

A study by Burson-Marsteller and Roper Starch Worldwide found that one influential person's word of mouth tends to affect the buying attitudes of two other people, on average. That circle of influence, however, jumps to eight online. There is considerable consumer-to-consumer communication on the web on a whole range of subjects. Online visitors increasingly create product information, not just consume it. They join Internet interest groups to share information, so that "word of web" is joining "word of mouth" as an important buying influence. Words about good companies travel fast; words about bad companies travel even faster. As one marketer noted, "You don't need to reach 2 million people to let them know about a new product—you just need to reach the right 2000 people in the right way and they will help you reach 2 million."[30]

Personal influence carries especially great weight in two situations. One is with products that are expensive, risky, or purchased infrequently. The other is where the product suggests something about the user's status or taste. People often ask others for a recommendation for a doctor, plumber, hotel, lawyer, accountant, architect, insurance agent, interior decorator, or financial consultant. If we have confidence in the recommendation, we normally act on the referral. In such cases, the recommender has potentially benefited the service provider as well as the service seeker. Service providers clearly have a strong interest in building referral sources.

Communication researchers are moving toward a social-structure view of interpersonal communication.[31] They see society as consisting of *cliques*, small groups whose members interact frequently. Clique members are similar, and their closeness facilitates effective communication but also insulates the clique from new ideas. The challenge is to create more openness so that cliques exchange information with others in the society. This openness is helped by people who function as liaisons and bridges. A *liaison* is a person who connects two or more cliques without belonging to either. A *bridge* is a person who belongs to one clique and is linked to a person in another clique.

Many companies are becoming acutely aware of the power of *word of mouth* or *buzz*. Products and brands such as Converse sneakers, Krispy Kreme doughnuts, and the blockbuster movie *The Passion of The Christ* were built through buzz.[32] Companies such as Body Shop, Starbucks, Palm, and Amazon were essentially built by word of mouth, with very little advertising. In some cases, positive word of mouth happens in a natural way and in some cases it is created, as the Global TV example shows.

Global TV

In 2006, Global TV launched two new TV programs, *Brothers and Sisters* and *Shark*. To get the season off to a good start, Global partnered with Agent Wildfire Strategy & Communications to create buzz and get people viewing the new shows. The strategy involved word-of-mouth communication, which can be volatile because of the lack of control a marketer has over the outcomes. To maintain a certain degree of control, the 12-week campaign consisted of recruiting 2000 TV enthusiasts from Vancouver and Toronto to watch the show, discuss it with their friends, and then decide on their own if the shows were worth advocating. The package sent to participants included a DVD and a booklet containing background information on the actors and interesting factoids. Participants were asked to give their feedback to Agent Wildfire and report the conversations they had with their friends. This type of feedback allowed the TV enthusiasts the freedom to express their opinions on the show, and gave Agent Wildfire a chance to respond to negative feedback. Just four weeks into the campaign, thousands of referral conversations had taken place, giving the show high ratings.[33]

In most cases, "buzz" is managed.[34] Agencies have been created solely to help clients create buzz (e.g., Buzz Agent is a company that has assembled an army of volunteers who talk up products in return for samples—and who, to ensure honesty, promote only those they like). Companies can take several steps to stimulate personal influence channels to work on their behalf:

- *Identify influential individuals and companies and devote extra effort to them.* In technology, influencers might be large corporate customers, industry analysts and journalists, selected policy makers, and a sampling of early adopters.[35]

- *Create opinion leaders by supplying certain people with the product on attractive terms.* Pepsi liberally sampled its Mountain Dew spin-off, Code Red, and also encouraged its core 13- to 19-year-old target audience to stumble onto the new flavour in such places as vending machines at malls. As one executive noted, "We allowed these teen influencers to be advocates for the brand. They launched it in their own little world."[36]

- *Work through community influentials such as local disk jockeys, class presidents, and presidents of women's organizations.* When Ford introduced the Focus, it handed out the cars to DJs and trendy people so they would be seen around town in them. Ford also identified 100 influential young consumers in five key marketing regions and gave them cars to drive around.[37]

- *Use influential or believable people in testimonial advertising.* Accenture, American Express, Nike, and Buick use golf mega-star Tiger Woods as an endorser to talk up the virtues of their respective companies and products.

- *Develop advertising that has high "conversation value,"* or better yet, incorporate buzz-worthy features into your product design. Some ads have a slogan that becomes part of the cultural vernacular, such as Molson's "I AM Canadian."

- *Develop word-of-mouth referral channels to build business.* Professionals will often encourage clients to recommend their services. Weight Watchers found that word-of-mouth referrals to those in a relationship with someone in the program had a huge impact on its business.[38]

- *Participate in electronic forums.* Toyota owners who use the Internet can hold online discussions to share experiences. Blogs, regularly updated online journals or diaries, have become an important outlet for word of mouth. Some consumers use blogs and videos as a means for retribution and revenge on companies for bad service and faulty products. Many companies now scan popular blogs for such postings by irate consumers. Blogs can also serve as useful sources of ideas on product improvements and new products.

- *Use viral marketing.* Internet marketers are using **viral marketing** as a form of word of mouth, or word of mouse, to draw attention to their sites.[39] Viral marketing involves passing on company-developed products, services, or information from user to user. As a classic example, Hotmail, an Internet service provider, offered a free email account to anyone who signed up. Each email sent by a Hotmail subscriber included the simple tag at the bottom of each message: "Get your free private email at http://www.hotmail.com." Users were in effect advertising Hotmail to others. Hotmail spent less than US$500 000 on marketing and within 18 months attracted 12 million subscribers.

One team of viral marketing experts caution that while influencers or "alphas" start trends, they are often too introspective and socially alienated to spread them. They advise marketers to cultivate "bees," hyper-devoted customers who are not just satisfied knowing about the next trend but who live to spread the word.[40]

Here's how one company chose rather unconventional methods to spread its name and generate sales:

Killam Properties

Killam Properties, a property-management company owning 8500 units in Atlantic Canada, set out to reduce its vacancy rates with some viral marketing. The campaign introduced Heroic Gatherings where tenants could order food online from fictional character Landlord Lou and have it delivered to their apartment for free. Landlord Lou personally delivered the food, from Boston Pizza and Swiss Chalet, and also gave tenants the option of a themed party. Colour, a marketing agency in Halifax, created three video clips depicting Landlord Lou "coming to the rescue" of young student tenants. Another part of the campaign included hiding thousands of toilet plungers around the city and challenging tenants to find them to earn free rent. Finding 50 plungers would earn a tenant a free month's rent and 500 plungers a free year's rent. All these aspects were aimed at getting people to talk about Killam Properties and think about moving to a Killam-managed apartment. The campaign was a huge success and the costs were considerably lower than regular advertising. As a result of the campaign, Killam achieved a zero vacancy rate in almost all of its buildings.[41]

Killam Properties generates word-of-mouth in rather unusual ways.

Marketers must be careful in reaching out to consumers. Consumers can resent personal communications if unsolicited. A 2003 survey found that roughly 80 percent of the sampled consumers were very annoyed by pop-up ads, spam, and telemarketing.[42]

NONPERSONAL COMMUNICATION CHANNELS
Nonpersonal channels are communications directed to more than one person and include media, sales promotions, events, and publicity and public relations:

- *Media* consist of print media (newspapers and magazines), broadcast media (radio and television), network media (telephone, cable, satellite, wireless), electronic media (audiotape, videotape, videodisk, CD-ROM, webpage), and display media (billboards, signs, posters). Most nonpersonal messages come through paid media. Ownership of media in Canada is converging.

- *Sales promotions* consist of consumer promotions (such as samples, coupons, and premiums); trade promotions (such as advertising and display allowances); and business and sales-force promotions (such as contests for sales reps).

- *Events and experiences* include sports, arts, entertainment, and cause events, as well as less formal activities that create novel brand interactions with consumers.

- *Publicity and public relations* include communications directed internally to employees of the company or externally to consumers, other firms, the government, and media.

Much of the recent growth of nonpersonal channels has been with events and experiences. A company can build its brand image through creating or sponsoring events. Event marketers who once favoured sports events are now using other venues such as art museums, zoos, and ice shows to entertain clients and employees. IBM sponsors Cirque du Soleil performances; Bell Canada is an active sponsor of the Olympics; Harley-Davidson sponsors annual motorcycle rallies; and Perrier sponsors sports and other events.

Companies are searching for better ways to quantify the benefits of sponsorship and are demanding greater accountability from event owners and organizers. Companies can also create events designed to surprise the public and create a buzz. Many amount to guerrilla marketing tactics. Here are some examples:

- *Driver 2*, a new car-chase video game, arranged for a convoy of 20 car wrecks with smoke pouring from their engines to crawl through Manhattan and Los Angeles to attract attention to the new game.
- Ask Jeeves, the Internet search engine, sent 35 actors in British butlers' outfits to guide visitors to their seats and answer tennis trivia questions at the U.S. Open tennis tournament.
- Kibu.com pays hundreds of school girls to do "peer marketing" by hanging around with their peers, handing out free lip gloss, and talking up Kibu's cosmetic site.[43]

The increased use of attention-getting events is a response to the fragmentation of media: consumers can turn to hundreds of cable channels, thousands of magazine titles, and millions of Internet pages. Events can create attention, although whether they have a lasting effect on brand awareness, knowledge, or preference will vary considerably, depending on the quality of the product, the event itself, and its execution. Consider how Canadian Tire increased its popularity through a TV show:

Canadian Tire

Canadian Tire and Debbie Travis collaborated for her TV show *From the Ground Up*. Rather than use typical product placement and 30-second commercial spots, Canadian Tire products were featured throughout the show and became part of the storyline. At the end of each show were vignettes on how to use the featured products and the presentation of the address of the website where the vignettes could be viewed again and e-coupons for the products could be downloaded. According to a survey conducted after the show, the campaign was a success, given that the number of people planning to shop at Canadian Tire had increased 17 percent.[44]

INTEGRATION OF COMMUNICATION CHANNELS Although personal communication is often more effective than mass communication, mass media might be the major means of stimulating personal communication. Mass communications affect personal attitudes and behaviour through a two-step process. Ideas often flow from radio, television, and print to opinion leaders and from these to the less media-involved population groups. This two-step flow has several implications. First, the influence of mass media on public opinion is not as direct, powerful, and automatic as supposed. It is mediated by opinion leaders, people whose opinions are sought or who carry their opinions to others. Second, the two-step flow challenges the notion that consumption styles are primarily influenced by a "trickle-down" or "trickle-up" effect from mass media. People interact primarily within their own social groups and acquire ideas from opinion leaders in their groups. Third, two-step communication suggests that mass communicators should direct messages specifically to opinion leaders and let them carry the message to others.

Finally, any discussion about the effectiveness of mass communication has to take into account the dramatic changes that have eroded the effectiveness of the mass media.

Establish the Total Marketing Communications Budget

One of the most difficult marketing decisions is determining how much to spend on promotion. John Wanamaker, the department-store magnate, once said "I know that half of my advertising is wasted, but I don't know which half."

Industries and companies vary considerably in how much they spend on promotion. Expenditures might be 30 percent to 50 percent of sales in the cosmetics industry and 5 percent to 10 percent in the industrial-equipment industry. Within a given industry, there are low- and high-spending companies.

How do companies decide on the promotion budget? We will describe four common methods: the affordable method, percentage-of-sales method, competitive-parity method, and objective-and-task method.

AFFORDABLE METHOD Many companies set the promotion budget at what they think the company can afford. The affordable method completely ignores the role of promotion as an investment and the immediate impact of promotion on sales volume. It leads to an uncertain annual budget, which makes long-range planning difficult.

PERCENTAGE-OF-SALES METHOD Many companies set promotion expenditures at a specified percentage of sales (either current or anticipated) or of the sales price. Automobile companies typically budget a fixed percentage for promotion based on the planned car price. Oil companies set the appropriation at a fraction of a cent of each litre of gasoline sold under their own label.

Supporters of the percentage-of-sales method see a number of advantages. First, promotion expenditures will vary with what the company can "afford." This satisfies financial managers, who believe that expenses should be closely related to the movement of corporate sales over the business cycle. Second, it encourages management to think of the relationship among promotion cost, selling price, and profit per unit. Third, it encourages stability when competing firms spend approximately the same percentage of their sales on promotion.

In spite of these advantages, the percentage-of-sales method has little to justify it. It views sales as the determiner of promotion rather than as the result. It leads to a budget set by the availability of funds rather than by market opportunities. It discourages experimentation with countercyclical promotion or aggressive spending. Dependence on year-to-year sales fluctuations interferes with long-range planning. There is no logical basis for choosing the specific percentage, except what has been done in the past or what competitors are doing. Finally, it does not encourage building the promotion budget by determining what each product and territory deserves.

COMPETITIVE-PARITY METHOD Some companies set their promotion budget to achieve share-of-voice parity with competitors. Two arguments are made in support of the competitive-parity method. One is that competitors' expenditures represent the collective wisdom of the industry. The other is that maintaining competitive parity prevents promotion wars. Neither argument is valid. There are no grounds for believing that competitors know better. Company reputations, resources, opportunities, and objectives differ so much that promotion budgets are hardly a guide. Furthermore, there is no evidence that budgets based on competitive parity discourage promotional wars.

OBJECTIVE-AND-TASK METHOD The objective-and-task method calls upon marketers to develop promotion budgets by defining specific objectives, determining the tasks that must be performed to achieve these objectives, and estimating the costs of performing these tasks. The sum of these costs is the proposed promotion budget.

For example, suppose Cadbury Schweppes wants to introduce for the casual athlete a new natural energy drink called Sunburst.[45]

1. *Establish the market-share goal.* The company estimates 50 million potential users and sets a target of attracting 8 percent of the market—that is, 4 million users.

2. *Determine the percentage of the market that should be reached by advertising.* The advertiser hopes to reach 80 percent (40 million prospects) with the advertising message.

3. *Determine the percentage of aware prospects who should be persuaded to try the brand.* The advertiser would be pleased if 25 percent of aware prospects (10 million) tried Sunburst. This is because it estimates that 40 percent of all triers, or 4 million people, would become loyal users. This is the market goal.

4. *Determine the number of advertising impressions per 1-percent trial rate.* The advertiser estimates that 40 advertising impressions (exposures) for every 1 percent of the population would bring about a 25-percent trial rate.

5. *Determine the number of gross rating points that would have to be purchased.* A gross rating point is one exposure to 1 percent of the target population. Because the company wants to achieve 40 exposures to 80 percent of the population, it will want to buy 3200 gross rating points.

6. *Determine the necessary advertising budget on the basis of the average cost of buying a gross rating point.* To expose 1 percent of the target population to one impression costs an average of $3277. Therefore, 3200 gross rating points would cost $10 486 400 (= $3277 × 3200) in the introductory year.

The objective-and-task method has the advantage of requiring management to spell out its assumptions about the relationship among dollars spent, exposure levels, trial rates, and regular usage.

A major question is how much weight marketing communications should receive in relation to alternatives such as product improvement, lower prices, and better service. The answer depends on where the company's products are in their life cycles, whether they are commodities or highly differentiable products, whether they are routinely needed or have to be "sold," and other considerations. Marketing communication budgets tend to be higher when there is low channel support, much change in the marketing program over time, many hard-to-reach customers, more complex customer decision making, differentiated products and nonhomogeneous customer needs, and frequent product purchases in small quantities.[46]

In theory, the total communications budget should be established so that the marginal profit from the last communication dollar just equals the marginal profit from the last dollar in the best noncommunication use. Implementing this principle, however, is not easy.

DECIDING ON THE MARKETING COMMUNICATIONS MIX

Companies must allocate the marketing communications budget over the six major modes of communication—advertising, sales promotion, public relations and publicity, events and experiences, sales force, and direct marketing. Within the same industry, companies can differ considerably in their media and channel choices. Avon concentrates its promotional funds on personal selling, whereas Revlon spends heavily on advertising. Electrolux spends heavily on a door-to-door sales force, whereas Hoover relies more on advertising. Consider also some of the unique issues facing the Canadian pharmaceuticals industry:

Novartis

Based in Dorval, Quebec, the pharmaceutical company Novartis has to make some interesting choices about its marketing communications strategy for the company's Diovan drug, which treats high blood pressure. The company's American counterparts employed a campaign consisting of newspaper and television ads, physician communication, and a website (http://healthybp.com). However, because of strict Canadian regulations about direct-to-consumer advertising of prescription pharmaceuticals (ads can feature only information about high blood pressure and the need to treat it; they cannot mention the Diovan brand itself), Novartis has spent the majority of its advertising dollars on reaching out to physicians. The communications budget supports the sponsorship of golf tournaments, guest lectures at medical forums, and having sales reps work with the communications departments at hospitals and medical associations. Novartis aims at offering doctors credible scientific resources to understand the drug. However, the biggest issue with respect to Diovan has been lack of patient understanding. Misperceptions result in patients ceasing use too early to realize the benefits of the drug. To overcome this problem, the company plans to allocate an increasing portion of its budget to empower and educate patients, which will require careful regulatory and ethical considerations.[47]

Companies are always searching for ways to gain efficiency by replacing one promotional tool with others. Many companies are replacing some field sales activity with ads, direct mail, and telemarketing. One auto dealer dismissed his five salespeople and cut his prices, and sales exploded. Companies are shifting advertising funds into sales promotion. The substitutability among promotional tools explains why marketing functions need to be coordinated. For example, a new website and a coordinated TV ad campaign targeting the greater Los Angeles area sparked record sales for Hawaii's Aloha Airlines, selling on one day tickets worth over US$1 million. The TV ads were designed to create awareness of Aloha and drive traffic to the website where the sale would be closed.[48]

Characteristics of the Marketing Communications Mix

Each communication tool has its own unique characteristics and costs.

ADVERTISING Advertising can be used to build up a long-term image for a product (Coca-Cola ads) or trigger quick sales (a Sears ad for a weekend sale). Advertising can efficiently reach geographically dispersed buyers. Certain forms of advertising (TV) can require a large budget, whereas other forms (newspaper) do not. Just the presence of advertising might have an effect on sales: consumers might believe that a heavily advertised brand must offer "good value."[49] Because of the many forms and uses of advertising, it is difficult to make generalizations.[50] Yet the following qualities can be noted:

1. *Pervasiveness.* Advertising permits the seller to repeat a message many times. It also allows the buyer to receive and compare the messages of various competitors. Large-scale advertising says something positive about the seller's size, power, and success.

2. *Amplified expressiveness.* Advertising provides opportunities for dramatizing the company and its products through the artful use of print, sound, and colour.

3. *Impersonality.* The audience does not feel obligated to pay attention or respond to advertising. Advertising is a monologue in front of, not a dialogue with, the audience.

SALES PROMOTION Companies use sales-promotion tools—coupons, contests, premiums, and the like—to draw a stronger and quicker buyer response. Sales promotion can be used for short-run effects such as to highlight product offers and boost sagging sales. Sales-promotion tools offer three distinct benefits:

1. *Communication.* They gain attention and may lead the consumer to the product.

2. *Incentive.* They incorporate some concession, inducement, or contribution that gives value to the consumer.

3. *Invitation.* They include a distinct invitation to engage in the transaction now.

PUBLIC RELATIONS AND PUBLICITY Marketers tend to underuse public relations, yet a well-thought-out program coordinated with the other promotion-mix elements can be extremely effective. Consider how Mountain Equipment Co-op does just that:

Mountain Equipment Co-op

When charged with the task of building a brand, many marketing managers assume that a major investment in advertising is required. But advertising is not necessarily the right or the only solution. In fact, many strong brands like Mountain Equipment Co-op (MEC) have been created through making the right move in the eyes of the public. MEC has been known for its concern for the environment and for the public. For example, MEC removed plastic drinking bottles from its shelves because of the suspected hazardous health effects of bisphenol-A in these bottles. MEC recognized the opportunity to gain some public-relations points and preemptively took the bottles in question off its shelves, before Health Canada even made an official ruling on the chemical. The move gave MEC positive press and in the consumers' eye, MEC was caring for their safety.[51]

The appeal of public relations and publicity is based on three distinctive qualities:

1. *High credibility.* News stories and features are more authentic and credible to readers than ads.

2. *Ability to catch buyers off guard.* Public relations can reach prospects who prefer to avoid salespeople and advertisements.

3. *Dramatization.* Public relations have the potential for dramatizing a company or product.

EVENTS AND EXPERIENCES There are many advantages to events and experiences:

1. *Relevant.* A well-chosen event or experience can be seen as highly relevant as the consumer gets personally involved.

2. *Involving.* Given its live, real-time quality, consumers can find events and experiences more actively engaging.

3. *Implicit.* Events are more of an indirect "soft-sell."

DIRECT MARKETING The many forms of direct marketing—direct mail, telemarketing, Internet marketing—share three distinctive characteristics. Direct marketing is:

1. *Customized.* The message can be prepared to appeal to the addressed individual.

2. *Up to date.* A message can be prepared very quickly.

3. *Interactive.* The message can be changed depending upon the person's response.

PERSONAL SELLING Personal selling is the most effective tool at later stages of the buying process, particularly in building up buyer preference, conviction, and action. Personal selling has three distinctive qualities:

1. *Personal interaction.* Personal selling involves an immediate and interactive relationship between two or more persons. Each party is able to observe the other's reactions.

2. *Cultivation.* Personal selling permits all kinds of relationships to spring up, ranging from a matter-of-fact selling relationship to a deep personal friendship.

3. *Response.* Having listened to the sales talk which is part of personal selling, the buyer feels some obligation to respond favourably.

Factors in Setting the Marketing Communications Mix

Companies must consider several factors in developing their communications mix: type of product market, consumer readiness to make a purchase, and stage in the product life cycle. Also important is the company's market rank.

TYPE OF PRODUCT MARKET Communications mix allocations vary between consumer and business markets. Consumer marketers tend to spend comparatively more on sales promotion and advertising; business marketers tend to spend comparatively more on personal selling. In general, personal selling is used more with complex, expensive, and risky goods and in markets with fewer and larger sellers—these, typically, are business markets.

Although advertising is used less than sales calls in business markets, it still plays a significant role:

- Advertising can provide an introduction to the company and its products.
- Advertising can explain any new features a product has.
- Reminder advertising is more economical than sales calls.
- Advertisements offering brochures that carry the company's phone number are an effective way to generate leads for sales representatives.
- Sales representatives can use tear sheets of the company's ads to legitimize their company and products.
- Advertising can remind customers of how to use the product and reassure them about their purchase.

A number of studies have underscored advertising's role in business markets. Advertising combined with personal selling can increase sales over what would have resulted if there had been no advertising.[52] Corporate advertising can improve a company's reputation and improve the sales force's chances of getting a favourable first hearing and early adoption of the product.[53]

Personal selling can also make a strong contribution in consumer goods marketing. Some consumer marketers use the sales force mainly to collect weekly orders from dealers and to see that sufficient stock is on the shelf. Yet an effectively trained company sales force can make four important contributions:

1. *Increased stock position.* Sales reps can persuade dealers to take more stock and devote more shelf space to the company's brand.

2. *Enthusiasm building.* Sales reps can build dealer enthusiasm by dramatizing planned advertising and sales-promotion backup.

3. *Missionary selling.* Sales reps can sign up more dealers.

4. *Key-account management.* Sales reps can take responsibility for growing business with the most important accounts.

BUYER-READINESS STAGE Communication tools vary in cost-effectiveness at different stages of buyer readiness. Figure 17.6 shows the relative cost-effectiveness of three communication tools. Advertising and publicity play the most important roles in the awareness-building stage. Customer comprehension is affected primarily by advertising and personal selling. Customer conviction is influenced mostly by personal selling. Closing the sale is influenced mostly by personal selling and sales promotion. Reordering is also affected mostly by personal selling and sales promotion, and somewhat by reminder advertising.

PRODUCT LIFE-CYCLE STAGE Communication tools also vary in cost-effectiveness at different stages of the product life cycle. In the introduction stage, advertising and publicity have the highest

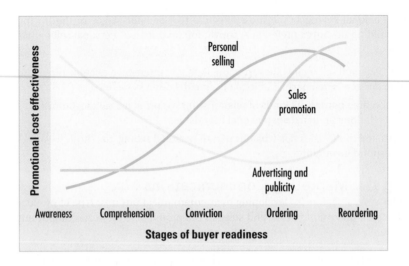

Integrated marketing communications were critical in boosting tourism in Newfoundland and Labrador.

cost-effectiveness, followed by personal selling to gain distribution coverage and sales promotion to induce trial. In the growth stage, demand has its own momentum through word of mouth. In the maturity stage, sales promotion, advertising, and personal selling all grow more important, in that order. In the decline stage, sales promotion continues to be strong, advertising and publicity are reduced, and salespeople give the product only minimal attention. Consider this intriguing example of a promotion mix used in the growth stage of a service life cycle:

Tourism Newfoundland and Labrador

Newfoundland and Labrador tourism marketers know that there is no such thing as an accidental tourist when it comes to someone visiting their province. People must make a deliberate choice to visit there. As a result, the province has been aggressive in promoting the unique benefits of visiting the province. Advertising through a variety of media including its webpage, it demonstrates what is unique and different about Newfoundland culture, history, lifestyle, nature, and scenery. These promotional tools alone aren't enough to guarantee a thriving tourism industry, however. The province also focused on product development, building infrastructure, and improving transportation. These efforts have met with resounding success, and Newfoundland and Labrador has become Canada's fastest-growing tourism destination. An estimated 490 100 visitors came to the province during 2007, spending in excess of $357 million. For the period 2003 to 2007, visitor traffic has increased 15 percent with an average annual growth of 3 percent.[54]

Measuring Communication Results

Senior managers want to know the *outcomes* and *revenues* resulting from their communications investments. Too often, however, their communications directors supply only *outputs* and *expenses:* press clipping counts, numbers of ads placed, media costs. In fairness, the communications directors try to translate outputs into intermediate outputs such as reach and frequency, recall and recognition scores, persuasion changes, and cost-per-thousand calculations. Ultimately, behaviour-change measures capture the real payoff.

After implementing the communication plan, the communications director must measure its impact on the target audience. Members of the target audience are asked whether they recognize or recall the message, how many times they saw it, what points they recall, how they felt about the message, and their previous and current attitudes toward the product and the company. The communicator should also collect behavioural measures of audience response, such as how many people bought the product, liked it, and talked to others about it.

Figure 17.7 provides an example of good feedback measurement. The results for brand A show that 80 percent of the consumers in the total market are aware of it, 60 percent have tried it, and only 20 percent who have tried it are satisfied. This indicates that the communications program is effective in creating awareness, but the product fails to meet consumer expectations. In contrast, only 40 percent of the consumers in the total market are aware of brand B, and only 30 percent have tried it, but 80 percent of those who have tried it are satisfied. In this case, the communications program needs to be strengthened to take advantage of the brand's power.

MANAGING THE INTEGRATED MARKETING COMMUNICATIONS PROCESS

As defined by the American Association of Advertising Agencies, **integrated marketing communications (IMC)** is a concept of marketing-communications planning that recognizes the added value of a comprehensive plan. Such a plan evaluates the strategic roles of a variety of communications disciplines—for example, general advertising, direct response, sales promotion, and public relations—and combines these disciplines to provide clarity, consistency, and maximum impact through the seamless integration of messages.

Unfortunately, many companies still rely on one or two communication tools. This practice persists in spite of the fragmenting of mass markets into a multitude of mini markets, each requiring its own approach, the proliferation of new types of media, and the growing sophistication of consumers. The wide range of communication tools, messages, and audiences makes it imperative that companies move towards integrated marketing communications. Companies must adopt a "360-degree view" of consumers to fully understand all the different ways that communications can affect consumer behaviour in their daily lives.

Here is a successful example of an integrated marketing communication program:

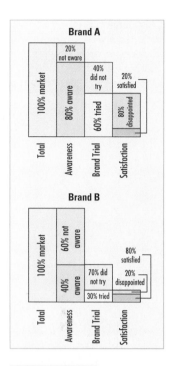

FIGURE 17.7

Current Consumer States for Two Brands

GMC & ESPN

General Motors Corp's GMC unit worked with Disney's ABC and ESPN units to develop a promotion that prompted more than 1.5 million people to enter a competition called "GMC Keys to Victory" during *Monday Night Football*. In addition to a large schedule of traditional commercials on ESPN, the promotion integrated GMC branding and vehicles within the Monday Night Football opening sequence. There was a "Keys to the Game" feature on the *Monday Night Countdown* show and on the episodes of *SportsCenter* that ran just after *Monday Night Football* games. GMC ran a season-long promotion for the competition on ESPN.com, and also ran a large gatefold insert in *ESPN the Magazine*, which included a schedule of the *Monday Night Football* games. As part of the deal, GMC gave away a Sierra pickup weekly for 16 weeks on www.keystovictory.com, linked on both www.GMC.com and www.ESPN.com. GMC marketers noted that the ESPN deal hit a broad spectrum of media that reached the youthful male target of the GMC truck brand.[55]

Coordinating Media

Media coordination can occur across and within media types. Personal and nonpersonal communication channels should be combined to achieve maximum impact. Imagine a marketer using a single tool in a "one-shot" effort to reach and sell a prospect. An example of a *single-vehicle, single-stage campaign* is a one-time mailing offering a cookware item. A *single-vehicle, multiple-stage campaign* would involve successive mailings to the same prospect. Magazine publishers, for example, send about four renewal notices to a household before giving up. A more powerful approach is the *multiple-vehicle, multiple-stage campaign*. Consider the following sequence:

News campaign about a new product → Paid ad with a response mechanism → Direct mail → Outbound telemarketing → Face-to-face sales call → Ongoing communication.

Multiple media deployed within a tightly defined time frame can increase message reach and impact. For a Citibank campaign to market home equity loans, instead of using only "mail plus an 800 number," Citibank used "mail plus coupon plus 800 number plus outbound telemarketing plus print

This Dannon print ad includes a web address and a coupon, to drive readers and customers to the Dannon website as well as to buy the product.

advertising." Although the second campaign was more expensive, it resulted in a 15-percent increase in the number of new accounts compared with direct mail alone.[56]

Research has also shown that promotions can be more effective when combined with advertising.[57] The awareness and attitudes created by advertising campaigns can improve the success of more direct sales pitches. "Marketing Insight: Coordinating Media to Build Brand Equity" describes how to leverage television advertising in other media.

Many companies are coordinating their online and offline communication activities. For example, Microsoft allocated 60 percent of its Microsoft Office advertising budget to online advertising in 2007 and GM spent 25 percent of its media budget on online advertising over the period 2005 to 2008.[58] Listing web addresses in ads (especially print) and on packages allows people to more fully explore a company's products, find store locations, and get more product or service information. Danone makes it a priority to drive traffic to its Dannon Yogurt homepage so that the company can benefit from the twin paybacks of (1) forging direct relationships with customers and (2) building a database of its best customers whose loyalty can be strengthened with more targeted coupon and direct mail promotional efforts.[59]

Pepsi has been highly successful in linking its online and offline efforts. In 2001, Pepsi and Yahoo! joined forces for an online promotion that increased sales 5 percent at a cost of about one-fifth of the previous mail-in promotion. During the promotion, Pepsi displayed the portal's logo on 1.5 billion cans while Yahoo! created a co-branded PepsiStuff.com e-commerce site where visitors could redeem points from bottle caps for prizes ranging from electronic goods to concert tickets.[60] When Dutch financial services firm ING Group launched its brand in North America, TV and print ads were paired with online ads. In one campaign on financial news sites, all the "ings" in the news text turned orange—matching ING's corporate colours.[61]

MARKETING **INSIGHT** | COORDINATING MEDIA TO BUILD BRAND EQUITY

To develop effective integrated marketing communications programs, marketers sometimes must explicitly tie marketing communications together to create or enhance brand equity.

Problem: Weak Brand Links

To build brand equity, communication effects created by advertising must be linked to the brand. Often, such links are difficult to create because of:

- *Competitive clutter.* Competing ads in the product category can create "interference" and consumer confusion as to which ad goes with which brand.[62] When Eveready launched a clever ad campaign for Energizer batteries featuring a pink toy bunny that kept on "going . . . and going . . . and going," 40 percent mistakenly attributed it to Eveready's main competitor, Duracell.

- *Ad content and structure.* Although "borrowed interest" tactics may grab consumers' attention, the resulting processing may *not* create strong brand associations. When the popular actor James Garner was advertising for Polaroid, marketing research surveys routinely noted that interview respondents mistakenly attributed his promotion to Kodak, its chief competitor. Delaying brand identification or providing few brand mentions in an ad may raise processing intensity but result in attention directed away from thinking about the brand, contributing to weak brand links.[63]

- *Consumer involvement.* Consumers may not have any inherent interest in the product or service category or may lack knowledge of the specific brand. The resulting decrease in consumer motivation and ability to process also translates to weaker brand links.[64]

Solution: Strengthening Communication Effects

Advertising may "work" in the sense that communication effects are stored in memory. Yet advertising may "fail" in the sense that these communication effects are *not* accessible when consumers make critical brand-related decisions. To address this problem, one common tactic is to make the brand name and package information prominent in the ad. Unfortunately, although consumers are better able to recall the advertised brand with this tactic, there is less other information about the brand to actually recall. Three potentially more effective strategies are brand signatures, ad retrieval cues, and media interactions:

- *Brand signatures.* The *brand signature* is the manner by which the brand is identified at the conclusion of a TV or radio ad or displayed within a print ad. An effective brand signature provides a seamless connection to the ad as a whole. For example, the famous "Got milk?" campaign always displayed that tagline or slogan in a manner fitting the ad (e.g., in flames for the "yuppie in hell" ad and in primary school print for the "school lunchroom bully" ad).

- *Ad retrieval cues.* An *advertising retrieval cue* is a key visual, a catchy slogan, or any unique advertising element that serves as an effective reminder to consumers. Eveready featured a picture of the pink bunny character on the packages of Energizer batteries to reduce confusion with Duracell. Ad retrieval cues can be placed in the store (on the package or as part of a shelf-talker or some other point-of-purchase device), combined with a promotion (an FSI—Free-Standing Insert—coupon), included as part of a Yellow Pages directory listing, or embedded in any marketing communication option where recall of communication effects can be advantageous.

- *Media interactions.* Print and radio reinforcement of TV ads—whereby the video and audio components of a TV ad serve as the basis for other types of ads—can be an effective means to leverage existing communication effects from TV ad exposure and more strongly link them to the brand. A potentially useful, although rarely employed, media strategy is to run explicitly linked print or radio ads *prior* to the accompanying TV ad. The print and radio ads increase consumer motivation to process the more "complete" TV ad.

Source: Kevin Lane Keller, *Strategic Brand Management*, 2nd edition (Upper Saddle River, NJ: Prentice-Hall, 2003).

Even if consumers do not order online, they can use websites in ways that drive them into stores to buy. Future Shop's website can be seen as a research tool for consumers, as surveys revealed that 40 percent of their customers looked online first before coming into the store.[65]

Implementing IMC

Integrated marketing communications has been slow to take hold for several reasons. To work with their brand managers, large companies often employ several communications specialists who may know comparatively little about other communication tools. Further complicating matters is that many global companies use a large number of ad agencies located in different countries and serving different divisions, resulting in uncoordinated communications and image diffusion.

Today, however, a few large agencies have substantially improved their integrated offerings. To facilitate one-stop shopping, major ad agencies have acquired promotion agencies, public relations firms, package-design consultancies, website developers, and direct-mail houses. Many international clients have opted to put a substantial portion of their communications work through one agency. An example is IBM turning all of its advertising over to Ogilvy to attain uniform branding. The result is integrated and more effective marketing communications and a much lower total communications cost.

MARKETING MEMO | HOW INTEGRATED IS YOUR IMC PROGRAM?

In assessing the collective impact of an IMC program, the overriding goal is to create the most effective and efficient communication program possible. The following six criteria can be used to help determine whether communications are truly integrated:

- *Coverage.* Coverage is the proportion of the audience that is reached by each communication option employed, as well as how much overlap exists among communication options. In other words, to what extent do different communication options reach the designated target market and the same or different consumers making up that market?

- *Contribution.* Contribution is the inherent ability of a marketing communication to create the desired response and communication effects from consumers in the absence of exposure to any other communication option. How much does a communication affect consumer processing and build awareness, enhance image, elicit responses, and induce sales?

- *Commonality.* Commonality is the extent to which *common* associations are reinforced across communication options—that is, the extent to which information conveyed by different communication options share meaning. The consistency and cohesiveness of the brand image is important because it determines how easily existing associations and responses can be recalled and how easily additional associations and responses can become linked to the brand in memory.

- *Complementarity.* Communication options are often more effective when used in tandem. Complementarity relates to the extent to which *different* associations and linkages are emphasized across communication options. Different brand associations may be most effectively established by capitalizing on those marketing communication options best suited to eliciting a particular consumer response or establishing a particular type of brand association. As part of the highly successful "Drivers Wanted" campaign, Volkswagen has used television to introduce a storyline that it continued and embellished on its website.

- *Versatility.* With any integrated communication program, when consumers are exposed to a particular marketing communication, some consumers will have already been exposed to other marketing communications for the brand, whereas other consumers will not have had any prior exposure. Versatility refers to the extent that a marketing communication option is robust and "works" for different groups of consumers. The ability of a marketing communication to work at "two levels"—effectively communicating to consumers who have or have *not* seen other communications—is critically important.

- *Cost.* Evaluations of marketing communications on all of these criteria must be weighed against their cost to arrive at the most effective *and* efficient communications program.

Source: Kevin Lane Keller, *Strategic Brand Management*, 2nd ed. (Upper Saddle River, NJ: Prentice-Hall, 2003).

Integrated marketing communications can produce stronger message consistency and greater sales impact. It forces management to think about every way the customer comes in contact with the company, how the company communicates its positioning, the relative importance of each vehicle, and timing issues. It gives someone the responsibility—where none existed before—to unify the company's brand images and messages as they come through thousands of company activities. IMC should improve the company's ability to reach the right customers with the right messages at the right time and in the right place.[66] "Marketing Memo: How Integrated Is Your IMC Program?" provides some guidelines.

IMC advocates describe it as a way of looking at the whole marketing process instead of focusing on individual parts of it. Companies such as Motorola, Xerox, and Hewlett-Packard are bringing together advertising, direct marketing, public relations, and employee communications experts into "supercouncils" that meet a few times each year for training and improved communications among them. Procter & Gamble recently revised its communications planning by requiring that each new program be formulated jointly, with its ad agency sitting together with P&G's public relations agencies, direct-marketing units, promotion-merchandising firms, and Internet operations.

SUMMARY

1. Modern marketing calls for more than developing a good product, pricing it attractively, and making it accessible to target customers. Companies must also communicate with present and potential stakeholders, and with the general public.

2. The marketing communications mix consists of six major modes of communication: advertising, sales promotion, events and experiences, public relations and publicity, personal selling, and direct marketing.

3. The communication process consists of nine elements: sender, receiver, message, media, encoding, decoding, response, feedback, and noise. To get their messages through, marketers must encode their messages in a way that takes into account how the target audience usually decodes messages. They must also transmit the message through efficient media that reach the target audience and develop feedback channels to monitor response to the message. Consumer response to a communication can often be modelled in terms of a response hierarchy and "learn-feel-do" sequence.

4. Developing effective communications involves eight steps: (1) identify the target audience, (2) determine the communications objectives, (3) design the communication, (4) select the communication channels, (5) establish the total communications budget, (6) decide on the communications mix, (7) measure the communications results, and (8) manage the integrated marketing communications process.

5. In identifying the target audience, the marketer needs to close any gap that exists between current public perception and the image sought. Communications

objectives may involve category need, brand awareness, brand attitude, or brand purchase intention. Formulating the communication requires solving three problems: what to say (message strategy), how to say it (creative strategy), and who should say it (message source). Communications channels may be personal (advocate, expert, and social channels) or nonpersonal (media, atmospheres, and events). The objective-and-task method of setting the promotion budget, which calls upon marketers to develop their budgets by defining specific objectives, is the most desirable.

6. In deciding on the marketing communications mix, marketers must examine the distinct advantages and costs of each communication tool and the company's market rank. They must also consider the type of product market in which they are selling, how ready consumers are to make a purchase, and the product's stage in the product life cycle. Measuring the marketing communications mix's effectiveness involves asking members of the target audience whether they recognize or recall the communication, how many times they saw it, what points they recall, how they felt about the communication, and their previous and current attitudes toward the product and the company.

7. Managing and coordinating the entire communications process calls for integrated marketing communications (IMC): marketing-communications planning that recognizes the added value of a comprehensive plan, evaluates the strategic roles of a variety of communications disciplines, and combines these disciplines to provide clarity, consistency, and maximum impact through the seamless integration of discrete messages.

APPLICATIONS

Marketing Debate: What Is the Biggest Obstacle to Integrating Marketing Communications?

Although integrated marketing communications is a frequently espoused goal, truly integrated programs have been hard to come by. Some critics maintain the problem is an organizational one—the agencies have not done a good job of putting together all the different teams and organizations involved with a communications campaign. Others maintain that the biggest problem is the lack of managerial guidelines for evaluating IMC programs. How does a manager know when his or her IMC program is satisfactorily integrated?

Take a position: The biggest obstacle to effective IMC programs is a lack of agency coordination across communication units *versus* The biggest obstacle to effective IMC programs is a lack of understanding as to how to optimally design and evaluate such programs.

Marketing Discussion

Pick a brand and go to its website. Locate as many forms of communications as you can. Conduct an informal communications audit. What do you notice? How consistent are the different communications?

Breakthrough Marketing: Dove Canada: Campaign for Real Beauty

Evolution. The word is simple, yet it now means so much to young women in Canada. Winner of two Cannes Advertising Awards, Dove's most famous short film called *Evolution* attracted millions of viewers and media attention as it exposed the beauty industry for the impostor it is.

Dove has managed to use multiple forms of marketing to communicate its positive self-esteem message to consumers. The company's innovative and rather unusual Campaign for Real Beauty launched in 2004 with TV spots, print ads, billboards, and press releases in order to get across to its target market the message that every woman and girl is beautiful just the way she is. The campaign matches the brand's mission: "to make more women feel beautiful every day by widening today's stereotypical view of beauty and inspiring women to take great care of themselves." The campaign consists of integrated communications through both personal and impersonal forms such as TV and magazine ads, sales promotions, events, public relations, and direct mail. All of the forms of advertising direct the consumer to visit its website (www.campaignforrealbeauty.ca) to find out more information and to blog with others about the ads, which also helps link all aspects of Dove's marketing communications.

The message Dove is trying to get across through its campaign is that the perception of beauty is distorted because of the unrealistic images the beauty and fashion industry bombards consumers with every day. It wants women of all ages to learn that true beauty is unique. Dove realizes that this message will have to be given in a variety of different forms, all portraying the same message. Ogilvy & Mather, Dove brand's advertising agency, handles the Campaign for Real Beauty which allows it to be more cohesive across all areas.

One form of publicity the company uses is the Dove Self-Esteem Fund, which is designed to promote a wider view of the definition of beauty and prevent self-limiting beauty stereotypes in the next generation of young women. Its goal is to reach 5 million young women by 2010. Its website provides links to articles and resources to help mothers, mentors, and girls discover their true beauty and see the unhealthy, unrealistic images the beauty industry has traditionally been focused on. Partners of the Dove Self-Esteem Fund include the Girl Scouts, National Eating Disorder Information Centre, With Jess, and Step Up Women's Network, among several others. Dove has carefully chosen partners that are consistent with its brand image and help to communicate what the brand stands for.

In June 2008, Dove hosted its first Sleepover for Self-Esteem, whereby it partnered with television stations YTV, The W Network, and CMT to encourage moms and mentors all over Canada to talk to young girls about self-esteem and foster a positive image of themselves. The Sleepover is an event that Dove used to promote itself across Canada by increasing involvement with and awareness of the brand.

Once the younger-market awareness was established with the Campaign for Real Beauty, Dove looked to broaden its offerings to another age group that has long been ignored in advertising. While the majority of companies in the market are pushing their anti-aging products and going along with Canadian society's fixation on staying young, Dove took a new approach and introduced its pro-age line. All forms of advertising for this new line have featured real women over the age of 50 who are not normally portrayed in magazines and TV ads as they are. Other skincare companies, such as Oil of Olay with its Total Effects line which promises to "fight the seven signs of aging," and L'Oréal's Lancôme Rénergie that "lifts, firms, and fights wrinkles," demonstrate the industry's obsession with looking younger and preventing natural aging from occurring.

Dove's newest promotional tool has been its play in Toronto called *Body & Soul* that promotes its pro-age line. The play features 13 real women over the age of 45 telling stories about their life with the help of Canadian director and playwright Judith Thompson, a recipient of the Order of Canada. The play makes no mention of Dove or its products; however, samples of the pro-age products are given out at select showings and pictures of Dove ads are displayed throughout the show.

In 2007, Dove built on the success of its Campaign for Real Beauty and introduced a complementary line of "go fresh" products that are consistent with its image and positioning in the market. The products maintain the message of gaining a fresh perspective on beauty and focus on energy and positive images.

Dove products, manufactured by Unilever, include body washes, beauty bars, face and hair care, antiperspirants/deodorants, and styling aids. Although Dove has many different products, it has stayed consistent with its positioning of all of them. Through integrated communications, consumers have been able to learn what the company is and what it stands for. Campaign for Real Beauty has elicited positive feelings from consumers, helped to build brand equity, and increased repeat purchase. In the first four years of the campaign, sales have grown in the double digits annually, which otherwise is only 2 percent to 3 percent in that category, according to Allison Leung, Dove Canada's marketing manager. With the continued success of its newest lines and campaign, Dove will need to remain innovative with its communications to reach its intended audience and maintain its growth.

DISCUSSION QUESTIONS

1. What have been the key success factors for Dove's Campaign for Real Beauty?

2. What are the risks in engaging in a campaign counter to traditional campaigns as Dove has done?

3. What other forms of communication would you recommend to complement Dove's current campaign?

Sources: Ogilvy website, www.ogilvy.com/press/showpress.php?ID=5843 (viewed June 6, 2008); Dove Canada website, www.dove.ca (viewed June 4, 2008); Hollie Shaw, "Dove's real women fly on stage; Unilever's next step in empowerment marketing," *National Post*, May 8, 2008, p. FP1; "Dove Launches the Dove Digital Channel — Innovative New Media Channel to Transform Dialogue with Consumers," *PR Newswire*, April 10, 2008; Donna Nebenzahl, "Soap firm comes clean by joining 'campaign for real beauty'," *The Gazette*, December 12, 2004, p. D3.

Magic happens when you give smart.

TELUS

MANAGING MASS COMMUNICATIONS: ADVERTISING, SALES PROMOTIONS, EVENTS, AND PUBLIC RELATIONS

eighteen

What do piglets, tropical fish, and geckos have in common? More than one might think, thanks largely to TELUS Corporation. The telecommunications giant has been using spokesanimals as part of its "future friendly" campaign with impressive results. "In the context of the larger campaign, they continue to leverage probably the most integrated and most distinct campaign in Canada," says Randy Stein, partner of Grip Limited, an advertising company that has done work for Acura, Labatt breweries, and GlaxoSmithKline. "Walk into a TELUS Mobility store, or flip through a TELUS brochure, or read a TELUS ad—they all speak in one voice. They all adhere to one style."

The ads are instantly recognizable as being from TELUS, with a cute animal on a white background. The simplicity of the ads is surprising considering how effective they are. In TV commercials and on the TELUS website, the animals' movements are not overly exaggerated or particularly artistic, and the ads with the best consumer responses seem to be those in which the animals are allowed to be just themselves. The cute faces of the animals help to give the company a very cool, hip, down-to-earth feel with consumers. As Rick Seifeddine, previous vice-president of TELUS' corporate marketing and communications department, states, "If you buy a 30-second TV ad, why spend the first 15 seconds telling people who you are? Now they know right away who we are so we can spend more time selling our product."

So how was the idea for this creative campaign generated? Paul Lavoie of Taxi Advertising and Design calls it a "cosmic moment." Taxi was working on advertising for Clearnet in 1996, a company TELUS bought out in 2000, when an ant ran across the table in the boardroom. This led to Clearnet's campaign featuring a family of ants that, among other things, use the shower. The idea to use animals to give technology a more natural, non threatening appeal gave Clearnet a way to connect with customers that was unheard of before this campaign, and it was adopted immediately by TELUS when it took over.

TELUS has come a long way in a short time. It is currently one of the largest telecommunications companies in Canada, second only to Bell Canada Enterprises. Having an easily recognizable brand and a good brand image are necessary in the competitive telecommunications market, which is filled with choices that can easily substitute one another.

The animals' cute faces and vibrant colours have paid off to the tune of $9.1 billion in revenues in 2007—a $2-billion jump since the TELUS animals campaign began. The animals have been there to help usher in the wireless boom and Internet, as well as numerous promotions for the company. They don't seem to be on a path to retirement yet, either. Even though some call the campaign old and tired, it hasn't driven people away from the company. In fact, they have just the opposite effect, with company revenues growing steadily. If you are in the market for a new cellular phone, maybe look by the bunny or the green frog.

Sources: TELUS Corporation, "Investor Fact Sheet Q1 2008," www.telus.ca (viewed June 8, 2008); "Grip Limited— Clients," *Grip Limited*, www.griplimited.com/clients.html (viewed June 8, 2008); Don Mills, "Monkey see, monkey do," *National Post* (National Edition), December 30, 2002, p. FP6; Jason Cella, "TELUS Corporation," *Hoovers*, 2008; Gerry Bellet, "'Cosmic Moment' Inspires TELUS Ad Campaign," *The Vancouver Sun*, December 24, 2002, p. C1.

At an annual Association of Advertising Agencies conference in 1994, Procter & Gamble CEO Ed Atrzt shook up the advertising world by proclaiming that marketers needed to develop and embrace new media. Ten years later, at that same conference, P&G CMO Jim Stengel gave a status report on how well he felt marketers have fared.[1] Stengel pointed out that although new media were now abundant, marketers and agencies were not using or measuring them sufficiently. In 1994, 90 percent of P&G's global ad spending was on TV, but one of its most successful brand launches in history, for Prilosec OTC in 2003, allocated only about one-quarter of its spending to TV. Here is some of what Jim Stengel said:

> There must be—and is—life beyond the 30-second spot. But our systems still revolve around that. Today's marketing world is broken. . . . We are still too dependent on marketing tactics that are not in touch with today's consumers. . . . All marketing should be permission marketing. All marketing should be so appealing that consumers want us in their lives. . . . The traditional marketing model is obsolete. Holistic marketing is driving our business.

Procter & Gamble is not alone. Marketers of all kinds are trying to come to grips with how to best use mass media in the new communication environment. In this chapter, we examine the nature and use of four mass communication tools—advertising, sales promotion, events and experiences, and public relations and publicity.

DEVELOPING AND MANAGING AN ADVERTISING PROGRAM

Advertising is any paid form of nonpersonal presentation and promotion of ideas, goods, or services by an identified sponsor. Ads can be a cost-effective way to disseminate messages, whether to build a brand preference or to educate people.

Organizations handle advertising in different ways. In small companies, advertising is handled by someone in the sales or marketing department who works with an advertising agency. A large company will often set up its own department, whose manager reports to the vice-president of marketing. The department's job is to propose a budget, develop strategy, approve ads and campaigns, and handle direct-mail advertising, dealer displays, and other forms of advertising.

Most companies use an outside agency, such as DDB Canada, to help create advertising campaigns and to select and purchase media. Today, advertising agencies are redefining themselves as *communication companies* that help clients to improve their overall communication effectiveness by offering strategic and practical advice on many forms of communication.[2]

In developing an advertising program, marketing managers must always start by identifying the target market and buyer motives. Then they can make the five major decisions, known as "the five Ms"—*Mission*: What are the advertising objectives? *Money*: How much can be spent? *Message*: What message should be sent? *Media*: What media should be used? *Measurement*: How should the results be evaluated? These decisions are summarized in Figure 18.1 and described in the following sections.

Setting the Objectives

The advertising objectives must flow from prior decisions on target market, brand positioning, and the marketing program.

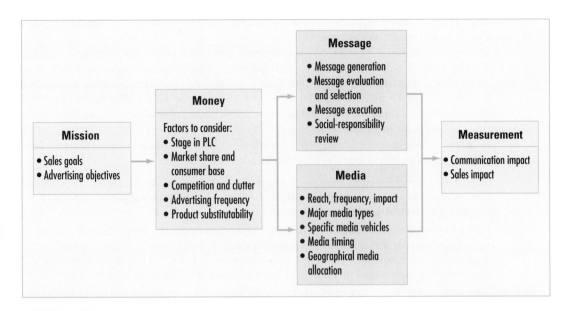

FIGURE 18.1

The Five Ms of Advertising

An **advertising goal** (or **objective**) is a specific communication task and achievement level to be accomplished with a specific audience in a specific period of time:[3]

> To increase among 30 million homemakers who own automatic washers the number who identify brand X as a low-sudsing detergent and who are persuaded that it gets clothes cleaner from 10 percent to 40 percent in one year.

Advertising objectives can be classified according to whether their aim is to inform, persuade, remind, or reinforce. They aim at different stages in the *hierarchy of effects* discussed in Chapter 17.

- *Informative advertising* aims to create brand awareness and knowledge of new products or new features of existing products. One of the all-time most memorable ads starred Australian rugby player Jacko for Energizer batteries. He was shown dressed as a battery, bursting into an early morning subway car, repeatedly shouting out the brand name to the commuters. Unfortunately, people remembered the name—but hated the ad! Brand awareness cannot come at the expense of brand attitudes.

- *Persuasive advertising* aims to create liking, preference, conviction, and purchase of a product or service. Chivas Regal attempts to persuade consumers that it delivers more taste and status than other brands of Scotch whiskey. Some persuasive advertising uses comparative advertising, which makes an explicit comparison of the attributes of two or more brands.[4] For years, VISA has run a successful ad campaign called "It's Everywhere You Want to Be" that showcases desirable locations and events that don't accept the American Express card. Comparative advertising works best when it elicits cognitive and affective motivations simultaneously.[5]

- *Reminder advertising* aims to stimulate repeat purchase of products and services. Expensive, four-colour Coca-Cola ads in magazines are intended to remind people to purchase Coca-Cola.

- *Reinforcement advertising* aims to convince current purchasers that they made the right choice. Automobile ads often depict satisfied customers enjoying special features of their new car.

The advertising objective should emerge from a thorough analysis of the current marketing situation. If the product class is mature, the company is the market leader, and brand usage is low, the proper objective should be to stimulate more usage. If the product class is new, the company is not the market leader, but the brand is superior to the leader, then the proper objective is to convince the market of the brand's superiority.

Deciding on the Advertising Budget

How does a company know if it is spending the right amount? Some critics charge that large consumer packaged-goods firms tend to overspend on advertising as a form of insurance against not spending enough, and that industrial companies underestimate the power of company and product image building and tend to underspend.[6]

Although advertising is treated as a current expense, part of it is really an investment in building brand equity. When $5 million is spent on capital equipment, the equipment may be treated as a five-year depreciable asset and only one-fifth of the cost is written off in the first year. When $5 million is spent on advertising to launch a new product, the entire cost must be written off in the first year. This reduces the company's reported profit and therefore limits the number of new-product launches a company can undertake in any one year.

In Chapter 17, we described some general methods to estimate communication budgets. Here are five specific factors to consider when setting the advertising budget:[7]

1. *Stage in the product life cycle.* New products typically receive large advertising budgets to build awareness and to gain consumer trial. Established brands usually are supported with lower advertising budgets as a ratio to sales.[8]

2. *Market share and consumer base.* High-market-share brands usually require less advertising expenditure as a percentage of sales to maintain share. To build share by increasing market size requires larger expenditures. On a cost-per-impression basis, it is less expensive to reach consumers of a widely used brand than to reach consumers of low-share brands.

3. *Competition and clutter.* In a market with a large number of competitors and high advertising spending, a brand must advertise more heavily to be heard. Even simple clutter from advertisements not directly competitive to the brand creates a need for heavier advertising.

4. *Advertising frequency.* The number of repetitions needed to put across the brand's message to consumers has an important impact on the advertising budget.

5. *Product substitutability.* Brands in less well-differentiated or commodity-like product classes (beer, soft drinks, banks, and airlines) require heavy advertising to establish a differential image. Advertising is also important when a brand can offer unique physical benefits or features.

In one study of budget allocation, Low and Mohr found that managers allocate less to advertising in certain circumstances: As brands move to the more mature phase of the product life cycle, when a brand is well-differentiated from the competition, when managers are rewarded on short-term results, as retailers gain more power, and when managers have less experience with the company.[9]

Developing the Advertising Campaign

In designing and evaluating an ad campaign, it is important to distinguish the *message strategy* or positioning of an ad (what the ad attempts to convey about the brand) from its *creative strategy* (how the ad expresses the brand claims), so designing effective advertising campaigns is both an art and a science. To develop a message strategy, advertisers go through three steps: message generation and evaluation, creative development and execution, and social responsibility review.

MESSAGE GENERATION AND EVALUATION It is important to generate fresh insights and avoid using the same appeals and positions as others. Many of today's automobile ads have a sameness about them—a car driving at high speed on a curved mountain road or across a desert. The result is that only a weak link is established between the brand and the message.

A good ad normally focuses on one or two core selling propositions. As part of refining the brand positioning, the advertiser should conduct market research to determine which appeal works best with its target audience. Once they find an effective appeal, advertisers should prepare a *creative brief*, typically covering one or two pages. This is an elaboration of the *positioning statement* (see Chapter 9) and describes the key message, target audience, communication objectives (to do, to know, to believe), key brand benefits, supports for the brand promise, and media. All the team members working on the campaign need to agree on the creative brief before investing in costly ads.

How many alternative ad themes should the advertiser create before making a choice? The more ads created, the higher the probability of finding an excellent one. Under a commission system, an agency may not like to go to the expense of creating and pretesting many ads. Fortunately, the expense of creating rough ads is rapidly falling due to computers. An ad agency's creative department can compose many alternative ads in a short time by drawing from computer files containing still and video images.

CREATIVE DEVELOPMENT AND EXECUTION   The ad's impact depends not only on what is said, but, often more important, on how it is said. Message execution can be decisive. In preparing an ad campaign, the advertiser can prepare a *copy strategy statement* describing the objective, content, support, and tone of the desired ad. Here is the strategy statement for a Pillsbury product called 1869 Brand Biscuits:

Pillsbury

The advertising *objective* is to convince biscuit users they can buy a canned biscuit that is as good as homemade—Pillsbury's 1869 Brand Biscuits. The *content* consists of emphasizing the following product characteristics: they look like, have the same texture as, and taste like homemade biscuits. *Support* for the "good as homemade" promise will be twofold: (1) 1869 Brand Biscuits are made from a special kind of flour used to make homemade biscuits but never before used in making canned biscuits, and (2) the use of traditional biscuit recipes. The tone of the advertising will be a news announcement, tempered by a warm, reflective mood emanating from a look back at traditional baking quality.

Every advertising medium has specific advantages and disadvantages. Here, we review television, radio, and print advertising media.

Television Ads   Television is generally acknowledged as the most powerful advertising medium and reaches a broad spectrum of consumers. The wide reach translates to low cost per exposure. From a brand-building perspective, TV advertising has two particularly important strengths. First, it can be an effective means of vividly demonstrating product attributes and persuasively explaining their corresponding consumer benefits. Second, TV advertising can be a compelling means for dramatically portraying user and usage imagery, brand personality, and other brand intangibles.

Television advertising also has its drawbacks. Because of the fleeting nature of the message and the potentially distracting creative elements often found in a TV ad, product-related messages and the brand itself can be overlooked. Moreover, the large number of ads and nonprogramming material on television creates clutter that makes it easy for consumers to ignore or forget ads. Another important disadvantage is the high cost of production and placement. Even though the price of TV advertising has skyrocketed, the share of the prime-time audience for the major networks has steadily declined. In fact, a study conducted by the London Business School found that many consumers actively avoid watching TV commercials.[10]

Nevertheless, properly designed and executed TV ads can improve brand equity and affect sales and profits. Over the years, one of the most consistently successful TV advertisers has been Apple. The "1984" ad for the introduction of the Macintosh personal computer—portraying a stark Orwellian future with a feature-film look—ran only once on TV but is one of the best-known ads ever. In the years that followed, Apple advertising successfully created awareness and image for a series of products with its acclaimed "Think Different" campaign. Apple's iPod ads created quite a buzz using ads with bright colours and silhouettes of people dancing to the digital music streaming from their iPod. One spot even included Bono from U2! Apple's latest TV commercials have focused on comparing Macs to PCs and how Macs are superior to PCs in various ways. The "Get a Mac" campaign has been very successful, boosting market share by 42 percent.

Even with the decline in audiences for TV advertising, a well-done TV commercial can still be a powerful marketing tool. However, a poorly done ad can send sales rapidly downhill. The Gap has experienced both ends of the spectrum.

The Gap

In years past, the Gap ran TV ads with happy kids jumping and jiving in khakis. Later ads showed smiling actors dancing to classic popular music. These ads really clicked with consumers who saw the Gap as a "happening" store. Sales and profits rose sharply as a result. In 2007, the Gap swapped the happy, smiling actors with ads featuring black and white images of stern-faced actors. The company wanted these ads to be "emotionally arresting." Unfortunately for the Gap, they were too boring for the average consumer. As a result, barely a few weeks after the new campaign began, sales fell 8 percent compared to the same period the previous year.[11]

Print Ads Print media offers a stark contrast to broadcast media. Because of its self-paced nature, magazines and newspapers can provide detailed product information and can also effectively communicate user and usage imagery. At the same time, the static nature of the visual images in print media makes it difficult to provide dynamic presentations or demonstrations. Another disadvantage is that it can be a fairly passive medium.

In general, the two main print media—magazines and newspapers—have many of the same advantages and disadvantages. Although newspapers are timely and pervasive, magazines are typically more effective at building user and usage imagery. Daily newspapers are read by roughly three-fourths of the population and tend to be used a lot for local—especially retailer—advertising.[12] Although advertisers have some flexibility in designing and placing newspaper ads, poor reproduction quality and short shelf life can diminish their impact.

Format elements such as ad size, colour, and illustration also affect a print ad's impact. A minor rearrangement of mechanical elements can improve attention-getting power. Larger ads gain more attention, though not necessarily by as much as their difference in cost. Four-colour illustrations increase ad effectiveness and ad cost. New electronic eye-movement studies show that consumers can be led through an ad by strategic placement of dominant elements.

Researchers studying print advertisements report that the *picture*, *headline*, and *copy* are important, in that order. The picture must be strong enough to draw attention. Then the headline must reinforce the picture and lead the person to read the copy. The copy itself must be engaging and the advertised brand's name must be sufficiently prominent. Even then, a really outstanding ad will be noted by less than 50 percent of the exposed audience. About 30 percent might recall the headline's main point; about 25 percent might remember the advertiser's name; and less than 10 percent will read most of the body copy. Ordinary ads do not achieve even these results.

Given how consumers process print ads, some clear managerial implications emerge, as summarized in "Marketing Memo: Print Ad Evaluation Criteria." One print ad campaign that successfully carved out a brand image is Gatorade:

Gatorade

Twenty-five years ago, Gatorade was the first in the marketplace with a sports drink that promoted health and energy. Over the years, Gatorade has built substantial brand recognition and an image that is unmatched in the sports-drink category. Its orange lightning logo has become synonymous with sports drinks. Gatorade has exploited this strong brand recognition in its powerful black and white print ads that show athletes sweating bright fluorescent colours representing Gatorade flavours and the tag line "Is it in you?" Proof of Gatorade's brand image is its impressive 82-percent market share in the sports drink market. Compare this to Coca-Cola's Powerade, with a mere 10-percent market share.[13]

Radio Ads Radio is a pervasive medium: Canadians who listen to the radio listen, on average, over 19 hours a week.[14] Perhaps radio's main advantage is flexibility—stations are very targeted, ads are relatively inexpensive to produce and place, and short closings allow for quick response. Radio is a particularly effective medium in the morning; it can also let companies achieve a balance between broad and localized market coverage.

The obvious disadvantages of radio are the lack of visual images and the relatively passive nature of the consumer processing that results.[15] Nevertheless, radio ads can be extremely creative. Some see the lack of visual images as a plus because they feel that clever use of music, sound, and other creative devices can tap into the listener's imagination to create powerfully relevant and liked images. Here is an example:

Motel 6

Motel 6, America's largest budget motel chain, was founded in 1962 when the "6" stood for $6 a night. After its business fortunes hit bottom in 1986 with an occupancy rate of only 66.7 percent, Motel 6 made a number of marketing changes, including the launch of a radio campaign of humorous 60-second ads featuring folksy contractor-turned-writer Tom Bodett delivering the clever tagline "We'll leave the light on for you." The ad campaign is credited with a rise in occupancy and a revitalization of the brand that continues to this day in the United States.[16]

MARKETING **MEMO** | PRINT AD EVALUATION CRITERIA

In judging the effectiveness of a print ad, in addition to considering the communication strategy (target market, communication objectives, and message and creative strategy) the following questions should be answered affirmatively concerning the executional elements:

1. Is the message clear at a glance? Can you quickly tell what the advertisement is all about?
2. Is the benefit in the headline?
3. Does the illustration support the headline?
4. Does the first line of the copy support or explain the headline and illustration?
5. Is the ad easy to read and follow?
6. Is the product easily identified?
7. Is the brand or sponsor clearly identified?

Source: Philip Ward Burton and Scott C. Purvis, *Which Ad Pulled Best*, 9th ed. (Lincolnwood IL: NTC Business Books, 2002).

SOCIAL RESPONSIBILITY REVIEW Advertisers and their agencies must be sure advertising does not overstep social and legal norms. Public-policy makers have developed a substantial body of laws and regulations to govern advertising.

Two bodies oversee Canadian practices: the Canadian Radio-television and Telecommunications Commission (www.crtc.gc.ca), best known as the CRTC, and Advertising Standards Canada (ASC), formerly the Canadian Advertising Foundation (www.adstandards.com). The mission of the CRTC is to find a balance between public- and private-sector interests. It governs ownership of broadcasting outlets, licences, and programming content, and it handles complaints about programming and advertising. It works closely with the ASC, which is a national industry association committed to assuring integrity and viability of advertising through industry self-regulation.

Advertising Standards Canada administers the Canadian Code of Advertising Standards, which was first published in 1963. The Code includes dictates that advertisements must not present inaccurate or deceptive claims, that advertisements must not omit relevant information, and that advertising claims must be supportable. The commercial intent of an advertisement must be obvious to the viewer, listener, or reader. Furthermore, advertisements must not include deceptive price claims or discounts, or unrealistic price comparisons. Advertising to children is subject to a special code, the Broadcast Code for Advertising to Children. (It should also be noted that Quebec prohibits advertising to children.) The ASC carefully considers and responds to all written consumer complaints submitted to it about advertising that does not comply with the Code, and it produces an Advertising Complaints Report.

In addition to the work performed by Canada's two official watchdogs, other groups, such as the Media Awareness Network (www.media-awareness.ca), keep their eye on Canadian advertising practices.

To be socially responsible, advertisers must be careful not to offend the general public or any ethnic groups, racial minorities, or special-interest groups.[17] Ads for Calvin Klein apparel have often been accused of crossing the lines of decency. Ads featuring the waifish model Kate Moss came under attack from Boycott Anorexic Marketing, and ads featuring pubescent models—some reportedly as young as 15—in provocative poses resulted in a massive letter-writing campaign from the American Family Association.[18]

Every year, nonprofit trade group Advertising Women of New York singles out TV and print ads that it feels portray particularly good or bad images of women. In 2007, Pizza Hut won the TV Grand Ugly award for its "Cheesy Bites" ad, which featured a scandalously dressed Jessica Simpson singing to and feeding a young man in a Pizza Hut restaurant. The TV Grand Good ad went to a Dove commercial in which before the audience's eyes a female model's image is transformed to appear picture-perfect for a billboard advertisement.[19]

Men's groups are speaking up too. A Canadian commercial showed a woman eyeing a young male sales clerk as he loaded her groceries into the back of her Ford Focus. She then pushed him in along with the groceries and drove off. Advertising Standards Canada received nine complaints from men's rights groups, asserting that the ad promoted abduction and would not be condoned if the sexes of the characters were reversed. Ford Canada withdrew the commercial.

Some companies and organizations, such as World Wildlife Fund Canada, have begun to build ad campaigns on a platform of social responsibility.

World Wildlife Fund Canada

Created in 1967, World Wildlife Fund Canada, a privately funded conservation organization, is now at the forefront of environmental and ethical issues. Its mission is preventing the degradation of the natural environment to ensure harmony between humans and nature. WWF Canada also focuses on protecting the rights of endangered species; this focus can be seen in the organization's print ads.

To grab people's attention and make them think about endangered animals, WWF Canada undertook a remarkable print-advertising campaign. One print ad featured an African safari scene with animals represented by cardboard cutouts and a group of hunters pointing rifles at them, conveying the message that there will be no real animals around in the future. Another heart-wrenching print ad included a mother leopard and its cub crossing a grasslands field, with 'XL' and 'S' signs respectively displayed on their backs. WWF hopes that these ads will be a powerful means to jolt readers and bring about a global change in people's attitude towards wildlife. In 2007, WWF Canada had over 150 000 supporters and $22 million in annual revenues, most of it going towards preservation of habitats and animals.[20]

DECIDING ON MEDIA AND MEASURING EFFECTIVENESS

After choosing the message, the advertiser's next task is to choose media to carry it. The steps here are deciding on desired reach, frequency, and impact; choosing among major media types; considering alternative advertising options; selecting specific media vehicles; and deciding on media timing. Then the results of these decisions need to be evaluated.

Deciding on Reach, Frequency, and Impact

Media selection is finding the most cost-effective media to deliver the desired number and type of exposures to the target audience. What do we mean by the desired number of exposures? Presumably, the advertiser is seeking a specified advertising objective and response from the target audience—for example, a target level of product trial. The rate of product trial will depend, among other things, on level of brand awareness. Suppose the rate of product trial increases at a diminishing rate with the level of audience awareness, as shown in Figure 18.2(a). If the advertiser seeks a product trial rate of (say) T^*, it will be necessary to achieve a brand awareness level of A^*.

FIGURE 18.2

Relationship Among Trial, Awareness, and the Exposure Function

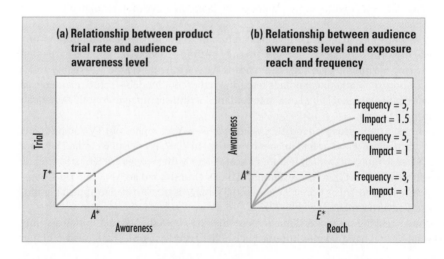

The next task is to find out how many exposures, E^*, will produce a level of audience awareness of A^*. The effect of exposures on audience awareness depends on the exposures' reach, frequency, and impact:

■ *Reach (R).* The number of different persons or households exposed to a particular media schedule at least once during a specified time period.

■ *Frequency (F).* The number of times within the specified time period that an average person or household is exposed to the message.

■ *Impact (I).* The qualitative value of an exposure through a given medium (thus a food ad in *Canadian Living* would have a higher impact than in *Canadian Business*).

Figure 18.2(b) shows the relationship between audience awareness and reach. Audience awareness will be greater the higher the exposures' reach, frequency, and impact. There are important trade-offs among reach, frequency, and impact. Suppose the planner has an advertising budget of $1 000 000 and the cost per thousand exposures of average quality is $5. This means the advertiser can buy 200 000 000 exposures ($1 000 000 ÷ [$5/1000]). If the advertiser seeks an average exposure frequency of 10, then the advertiser can reach 20 000 000 people (200 000 000 ÷ 10) with the given budget. But if the advertiser wants higher-quality media costing $10 per thousand exposures, it will be able to reach only 10 000 000 people unless it is willing to lower the desired exposure frequency.

The relationship between reach, frequency, and impact is captured in the following concepts:

■ *Total number of exposures (E).* This is the reach times the average frequency; that is, $E = R \times F$. This measure is referred to as the gross rating points (GRP). If a given media schedule reaches 80 percent of the homes with an average exposure frequency of 3, the media schedule is said to have a GRP of 240 (80 × 3). If another media schedule has a GRP of 300, it is said to have more weight, but we cannot tell how this weight breaks down into reach and frequency.

■ *Weighted number of exposures (WE):* This is the reach times average frequency times average impact, that is $WE = R \times F \times I$.

The media planner has to figure out the most cost-effective combination of reach, frequency, and impact. Reach is most important when launching new products, flanker brands, extensions of well-known brands, or infrequently purchased brands, or when going after an undefined target market. Frequency is most important where there are strong competitors, a complex story to tell, high consumer resistance, or a frequent-purchase cycle.[21]

Many advertisers believe a target audience needs a large number of exposures for the advertising to work. Others doubt the value of high frequency. They believe that after people see the same ad a few times, they either act on it, get irritated by it, or stop noticing it.[22]

Another factor arguing for repetition is that of forgetting. The job of repetition is partly to put the message back into memory. The higher the forgetting rate associated with a brand, product category, or message, the higher the warranted level of repetition. However, repetition is not enough; ads wear out and viewers tune out. Advertisers should not coast on a tired ad but insist on fresh executions by their advertising agency.

Choosing Among Major Media Types

The media planner has to know the capacity of the major advertising media types to deliver reach, frequency, and impact. The major advertising media along with their costs, advantages, and limitations are profiled in Table 18.1.

Media planners make their choices by considering the following variables:

■ *Target-audience media habits.* Radio and television are the most effective media for reaching teenagers.

■ *Product characteristics.* Media types have different potential for demonstration, visualization, explanation, believability, and colour. Women's dresses are best shown in colour magazines, and vacuum cleaners are best demonstrated on television.

■ *Message characteristics.* Timeliness and information content will influence media choice. A message announcing a major sale tomorrow will require radio, TV, or newspaper. A message containing a great deal of technical data might require specialized magazines or mailings.

■ *Cost.* Television is very expensive, whereas newspaper advertising is relatively inexpensive. What counts is the cost-per-thousand exposures.

TABLE 18.1	PROFILES OF MAJOR MEDIA TYPES	
Medium	**Advantages**	**Limitations**
Newspapers	Flexibility; timeliness; good local-market coverage; broad acceptance; high believability	Short life; poor reproduction quality; small "pass-along" audience
Television	Combines sight, sound, and motion; appealing to the senses; high attention; high reach	High absolute cost; high clutter; fleeting exposure; less audience selectivity
Direct mail	Audience selectivity; flexibility; no ad competition within the same medium; personalization	Relatively high cost; "junk mail" image
Radio	Mass use; high geographic and demographic selectivity; low cost	Audio presentation only; lower attention than television; nonstandardized rate structures; fleeting exposure
Magazines	High geographic and demographic selectivity; credibility and prestige; high-quality reproduction; long life; good pass-along readership	Long ad-purchase lead time; some waste circulation; no guarantee of position
Outdoor	Flexibility; high repeated exposure; low cost; low competition	Limited audience selectivity; creative limitations
Yellow Pages	Excellent local coverage; high believability; wide reach; low cost	High competition; long ad-purchase lead time; creative limitations
Newsletters	Very high selectivity; full control; interactive opportunities; relatively low costs	Costs could run away
Brochures	Flexibility; full control; can dramatize messages	Overproduction could lead to runaway costs
Telephone	Many users; opportunity to give a personal touch	Relatively high cost unless volunteers are used
Internet	High selectivity; interactive possibilities; relatively low cost	Relatively new media with a low number of users in some countries

TABLE 18.2	MARKETING COMMUNICATION REVENUES BY MEDIUM (CANADA, 2007, MILLIONS OF DOLLARS)	
Medium	**$ in 2007**	**$ Projection for 2012**
Newspapers (print)	2560	2610
Newspapers (online)	140	390
TV (conventional)	2000	2400
TV (specialty channels)	847	1100
Radio	1330	2400
Magazines (print)	665	782
Magazines (online)	13	78
Out-of-Home	368	507
Internet	1300	3400
Video Games	104	237

Source: PricewaterhouseCoopers, *Global Entertainment and Media Outlook: 2008–2012*, June 18, 2008; Jesse Kohl, "Canadian Media Revenues Steady 'til 2012: PwC," *Media in Canada: Top Stories*, www.mediaincanada.com/articles/mic/20080619/pwcreport.html (viewed July 16, 2008).

Given the abundance of media, the planner must first decide how to allocate the budget to the major media types (see Table 18.2). In launching a new biscuit, Pillsbury might decide to allocate $3 million to daytime network television, $2 million to women's magazines, $1 million to daily newspapers in 20 major markets, $500 000 to various grassroots cooking events and competitions, and $50 000 to maintaining its homepage on the Internet.

The distribution must be planned with the awareness that people are increasingly time-starved. They are assaulted daily by ads and information from traditional media plus email, voice mail, and instant messages. There is little time for thinking about experiences, let alone for hobbies and other

---

MARKETING **MEMO** | YOU'VE GOT MAIL

More money is spent on direct mail every year than on any other type of marketing. Even the smallest company can put this technique to good use with minimal cost. When done properly, it can provide returns quickly. Below are some guidelines for getting the most out of a direct-mail campaign.

Do:

- *Use sneak-up mail.* Consumers often sort their mail over the garbage. To stop them from immediately disposing of it, simply disguise the mail as something other than junk mail. This can be accomplished by using plain white envelopes, attaching real stamps, addressing by hand or using realistic handwriting fonts, and avoiding the use of a business name in the return address.
- *Use billboard mail.* As an alternative to sneak-up mail, billboard mail presents an attractive offer on the outside of the envelope encouraging the recipient to open it immediately. Billboard mail should use up as much space on the envelope as possible, offer something to the reader for free, and should be related to the reader's demographic group.
- *Send mail in a sequence.* One attempt at mailing does not make a direct-mail campaign. If your last attempt made a profit, then continue mailing until the ROI reaches zero. No mail campaign should be less than three steps in a sequence.

Do not:

- *Be Brief.* There is no reason not to include as much information as possible in the sales letter—the letter should include a powerful headline, a persuasive story, a valuable offer, and a clear and easy way to respond—but, of course, not to the point where the reader gets turned off by the volume of material.
- *Be a Perfectionist.* If you wait around until you perfect every last detail of the letter, it will never get sent.

Source: Adapted from Jimmy Vee, Travis Miller, and Joel Bauer, *Gravitational Marketing*, 1st ed. (Hoboken, NJ: John Wiley & Sons, 2008), pp. 54–58.

---

diversions. Attention is becoming a scarce currency, and advertisers need strong devices to capture people's attention.[23] For tips on how to get your direct mail read, see "Marketing Memo: You've Got Mail." In deciding on the ad budget, marketers must also recognize that consumer response can be S-shaped: an ad threshold effect exists whereby some positive amount of advertising is necessary before any sales impact can be detected, but sales increases eventually flatten out.[24]

Alternative Advertising Options

For a long time, television was the dominant medium. In recent years, researchers have noticed reduced effectiveness due to increased commercial clutter (advertisers beaming shorter and more numerous commercials at the audience), increased "zipping and zapping" of commercials (aided by the arrival of new TV systems such as TiVo and Replay TV), and lower viewing owing to the growth in cable and satellite TV and DVD/VCRs.[25] Furthermore, television advertising costs have risen faster than other media costs. Many marketers are looking for alternative advertising media.[26] Consider how Toyota generated interest for its Yaris model:

Toyota Yaris

With its spring 2006 Toyota Yaris advertising campaign developed by advertising firm Mango Moose Media, Toyota hoped it would create a public buzz around the release of its newest compact car. Mango Moose Media placed a picture of *Uncle Yaris* on pizza boxes of major pizza chains without words or slogans to accompany this new character. This unusual form of advertising was designed to tease curious customers into wondering who Uncle Yaris was, thereby creating recognition and memory for the Yaris brand name. Four different pictures of a Toronto street performer playing Uncle Yaris were featured on each box and the costs were low relative to other forms of advertising; yet, the exposure to the brand name was created effectively.[27]

Using place advertising to increase brand exposure and goodwill: the Oscar Mayer Wienermobile.

PLACE ADVERTISING **Place advertising**, also called out-of-home advertising, is a broadly defined category that captures many different alternative advertising forms. Marketers are using creative and unexpected ad placements to grab consumers' attention. The rationale often given is that marketers are better off reaching people in other environments, such as where they work, play, and, of course, shop. Some of the options available include billboards, public places, product placement, and point-of-purchase.

Billboards Billboards have been transformed over the years and now use colourful, digitally produced graphics, backlighting, sounds, movement, and unusual—even three-dimensional— images.[28] Some ads are even human. Adidas hoisted human billboards in Tokyo and Osaka, Japan. Two soccer players competed for shots during 15-minute matches scheduled five times a day while they and a ball dangled from ropes 12 storeys above ground.[29] Billboards do not even necessarily have to stay in one place. Marketers can buy ad space on billboard-laden trucks that are driven continuously all day in selected areas. Oscar Mayer sends six "Wiener-mobiles" travelling across North America each year to increase brand exposure and goodwill. Software company Oracle used a boat to tow a floating banner bearing the company's logo across San Francisco Bay. CHFX, a radio station in Halifax, also engaged in some creative advertising.

CHFX Country 101.9

To learn how the Gujarat Cooperative Milk Marketing Federation has enhanced its brand image with a successful billboard campaign over the last 40 years in India, visit www.pearsoned.co.in/marketingmanagementindia.

In 2002, Halifax's CHFX Country 101.9 hired the marketing and design firm Extreme Group to spark interest by creating a series of billboards advertising a chance to win $10 000 of plastic surgery. This unique idea came out of a desire to capitalize on the public's obsession with beauty and working towards good looks. CHFX also hoped that the edgy, unique, and slightly controversial billboard ads would increase the station's ratings and expand its listenership to include a younger audience. With such an objective in place, the designers at Extreme Group created a series of attention-grabbing billboard ads that included slogans such as "Don't Hate Me 'Cuz' I'm Purdy," "Want a Bigger Twang?," and "Friends in Low Places," just to name a few. Such provocative ads increased listenership for the station, but also drew undesired attention. The ads created a group of unhappy residents ranging from insulted plastic surgeons to offended parents, who picketed and spoke out against the billboards. Although such controversy may have helped increase the popularity of the radio station, the billboards also angered many of its current and potential listeners.[30]

Public Spaces Advertisers are placing traditional TV and print ads in unconventional places such as movies, airlines, and lounges, as well as classrooms, sports arenas, office and hotel elevators, and other public places. Billboard-type poster ads are showing up everywhere. Transit ads on buses, subways, and commuter trains—around for years—have become a valuable way to reach working women. "Street furniture"—bus shelters, kiosks, and public areas—is another fast-growing option. Coca-Cola, for example, mounted illuminated rectangular displays called "light boxes" on New York subway tunnel walls to advertise its Dasani brand water.

Advertisers can buy space in stadiums and arenas and on garbage cans, bicycle racks, parking meters, airport luggage carousels, gasoline pumps, the bottoms of golf cups, airline snack packages, and supermarket produce in the form of tiny labels on apples and bananas. Advertisers can even buy space in toilet stalls and above urinals, which, according to research studies, office workers visit an average of three to four times a day for roughly four minutes per visit.[31]

PRODUCT PLACEMENT Product placement has expanded from movies to all types of TV shows. Marketers pay fees of $50 000 to $100 000 and even higher so that their products make cameo appearances in movies and on television. The exact sum depends on the amount and nature of the brand exposure. Sometimes placements are the result of a larger network advertising deal, but other times they are the work of small product placement shops that maintain close ties with prop masters, set designers, and production executives.[32] Companies using this strategy to reach a younger market have received criticism in recent years, as discussed in "Marketing Insight: Product Placements in Children's Entertainment."

Product placements can be combined with special promotions to publicize entertainment tie-ins. Aston Martin, 7-UP, Finlandia, VISA, and Omega all initiated major promotional pushes based on product placement tie-ins with the James Bond film *Die Another Day*.[33] With over US$100 million paid for product placement rights, some critics called the film "Buy Another Day."

Some firms get product placement at no cost by supplying their product to the movie company (Nike does not pay to be in movies but often supplies shoes, jackets, bags, etc.).[34] Firms sometimes just get lucky and are included in shows for plot reasons. FedEx, for example, received lots of favourable exposure from the movie *Cast Away*.[35] Some television shows revolve around a central product placement: in 2001, Ford and the WB network created a commercial-free program called *No Boundaries* that featured Ford SUVs.

Marketers are finding other inventive ways to advertise during actual television broadcasts. Sports fans are familiar with the virtual logos networks add digitally to playing fields. Invisible to spectators at the event, these ads look just like painted-on logos to home viewers. Ads also appear in best-selling paperback books and movie videotapes. Written material such as annual reports, data sheets, catalogues, and newsletters increasingly carry ads. **Advertorials** are print ads that offer editorial content that reflects favourably on the brand and is difficult to distinguish from newspaper or magazine content. Many companies include advertising inserts in monthly bills. Some companies mail audiotapes or videotapes to prospects.

Product placement: the Omega–James Bond tie-in ad for *Die Another Day*.

MARKETING INSIGHT	PRODUCT PLACEMENTS IN CHILDREN'S ENTERTAINMENT

There is no question that consumers are constantly bombarded by advertising messages in their daily lives. Children are no exception. Kids are being exposed to a growing number of advertising messages through TV, Internet, video games, in-store advertising, and several other media. For instance, the average North American child watches 38 hours of commercial media each week, being exposed to between 15 and 30 advertisements per hour through TV alone. Advertising spending during children's TV programs is over US$2 billion in the U.S. alone and is increasing year after year. There is an ongoing ethical debate among parents, advertisers, and regulatory agencies about what is okay to promote and sell to kids and what is not.

There is no shortage of marketers' attempts to attract young consumers. Children are strongly influenced by celebrity endorsements of products such as food and toys—an issue that is concerning many parents and the government. The Canadian Radio-television and Telecommunications Commission (CRTC) prohibits celebrity endorsements of products in advertisements targeted towards children. However, marketers are circumventing the law by using product placements in children's TV shows, movies, video games, and other media.

Product placement is showing a character using a particular brand of product, such as James Bond using a Sony Ericsson cell phone in *Casino Royale*. Global spending on this form of indirect advertising is expected to reach nearly US$8 billion by 2010 and is rapidly becoming a preferred alternative to traditional advertising due to its economy and effectiveness. The use of product placements in children's entertainment is becoming increasingly common nowadays. Popular children's movies such as *Charlie and the Chocolate Factory*, *The Chronicles of Narnia*, *Madagascar*, *Shark Tale*, and *Spider-Man 2* integrated numerous product placements. *Madagascar* topped the list, containing ten different product placements from such companies as Coca-Cola, Krispy Kreme, Toys "R" Us, Burger King, Gatorade, and Starbucks.

Product placements used to attract a younger audience are not limited to children's shows or movies. A recent teenage book called *Cathy's Book* includes Cover Girl products produced by Procter & Gamble. Fast food restaurants such as McDonald's hire agencies to surround their brand with song lyrics and music videos to attract young consumers. Video games are following suit in the form of "advergaming," whereby advertisers create games that are designed around a product.

All this attention given to impressionable young consumers is worrisome for many parents. Due to the increase in product placements in children's entertainment there has been a growing demand for more research focusing on the influence of such marketing tactics. This is an important issue to address for two main reasons: children have not yet developed sensitivity to this type of advertising and they are much more vulnerable to product placements than adults. Children find it difficult to distinguish between program content and a promotion. Numerous studies have shown that children under the age of eight are especially vulnerable as they are developmentally unable to understand the intent of advertisements and accept advertising claims as facts.

Parents and numerous organizations are calling on big brand names and governments to make changes. PepsiCo, which includes brands such as Tropicana, Frito-Lay, Gatorade, and Quaker, has pledged not to use product placements in any form of entertainment aimed at children under the age of twelve. Many countries are implementing stricter guidelines regarding advertising to children. Quebec, Norway, and Sweden have completely banned advertising during children's TV programming. The U.K. has banned product placement in TV programs. With increasing concern over marketers' targeting of children, it is expected that many other countries will follow suit and ban product placement in children's entertainment in the coming years.

Sources: Simon Hudson, David Hudson, and John Peloza, "Meet the Parents: A Parents' Perspective on Product Placement in Children's Films," *Journal of Business Ethics* 80, no. 2: 289–304; PepsiCo Inc., "Children's Food and Beverage Advertising Initiative Pledge of PepsiCo, Inc.," www.pepsico.com/PEP_Citizenship/HealthWellness/Philosophy/CARUPEPPLedge.pdf (viewed June 5, 2008); "Product Placement to Triple in Films, TV, Report Says," *CBC News*, August 20, 2006, www.cbc.ca/arts/story/2006/08/20/productplacement-report.html (viewed July 13, 2008); Corinna Hawkes, "Regulating Food Marketing to Young People Worldwide: Trends and Policy Drivers," *American Journal of Public Health*, 97, no.11 (November 1, 2007): 1962–1973.

Other firms are exploring **branded entertainment** such as online mini-films. For its American Express client, Ogilvy and Digitas created a series of three- to five-minute "Webisodes" starring its pitchman Jerry Seinfeld in "The Adventures of Seinfeld and Superman" and also used teaser TV spots.[36] Automakers are promoting cars with exciting online videos with special effects that pack more punch than the typical car ad.

bmwfilms.com

BMW was one of the first automakers to launch a successful video campaign. In 2001, the company hired some of Hollywood's top action-movie directors such as John Woo, Guy Ritchie, and Ang Lee to create short films featuring the company's cars and starring actors such as Mickey Rourke and Madonna. To build traffic to the bmwfilms.com website, BMW used television spots that mirrored movie trailers. According to BMW's ad agency, 55.1 million people viewed "The Hire" series. Mazda followed suit with its "Venus Flytrap" video promoting its RX-8, while Ford's "Evil Twin" video advertises the Sportka. As might be evident from their names, these online videos are designed to cater to 18- to 34-year-old men who are spending less and less time watching television and more and more time online.[37]

POINT-OF-PURCHASE   There are so many ways to communicate with consumers at the **point-of-purchase (P-O-P).** In-store advertising includes ads on shopping carts, cart straps, aisles, and shelves, as well as promotion options such as in-store demonstrations, live sampling, and instant-coupon machines. Some supermarkets are selling floor space for company logos and experimenting with talking shelves. P-O-P radio provides FM-style programming and commercial messages to thousands of food stores and drugstores nationwide. Programming includes a store-selected music format, consumer tips, and commercials. Ads on Wal-Mart TV run in 2500 stores and appear three times an hour. Airtime costs between US$50 000 and US$300 000 for a four-week flight of ads, depending on frequency. The impact can be considerable: according to one research study, more than half of shoppers visit a Wal-Mart at least once a month and one-third go once a week.[38]

The appeal of point-of-purchase advertising lies in the fact that numerous studies show that in many product categories consumers make the bulk of their final brand decisions in the store. One study suggested that 70 percent of all buying decisions are made in the store. In-store advertising is designed to increase the number of spontaneous buying decisions.

EVALUATING ALTERNATIVE MEDIA   Alternative media present some interesting options for marketers. Ads now can appear virtually anywhere consumers have a few spare minutes or even seconds and thus enough time to notice them. The main advantage of nontraditional media is that a very precise and—because of the nature of the setting involved—captive audience often can be reached in a cost-effective manner. The message must be simple and direct. In fact, outdoor advertising is often called the "15-second sell." Strategically, out-of-home advertising is often more effective at enhancing brand awareness or reinforcing brand image than creating new brand associations.

The challenge with nontraditional media is demonstrating its reach and effectiveness through credible, independent research. These new marketing strategies and tactics must be judged ultimately on how they contribute, directly or indirectly, to brand equity. Unique ad placements designed to break through clutter may also be perceived as invasive and obtrusive. There has been some consumer backlash when people see ads in traditionally ad-free spaces, such as in schools, on police cruisers, and in doctors' waiting rooms. U.S. consumer advocate Ralph Nader says "What these people on Madison Avenue don't understand is consumers will reach a saturation point."

But not all North Americans are turned off by the proliferation of advertising. One marketing consultant says "Kids 18 and under aren't thinking twice about it. Branded merchandise is just the landscape of their lives." Perhaps because of the sheer pervasiveness of advertising, consumers seem to be less bothered by nontraditional media now than in the past.

Consumers must be favourably affected in some way to justify the marketing expenditures for nontraditional media. Some firms offering ad placement in supermarket checkout lines, fast food restaurants, physicians' waiting rooms, health clubs, and truck stops have suspended business at least in part because of a lack of consumer interest. The bottom line, however, is that there will always be room for creative means of placing the brand in front of consumers.

Selecting Specific Vehicles

The media planner must search for the most cost-effective vehicles within each chosen media type. The advertiser who decides to buy 30 seconds of advertising on U.S. network television can pay around US$100 000 for a new show, US$780 000 during a popular prime-time show such as *American Idol*, US$400 000 during *Grey's Anatomy*, about $325 000 during *Monday Night Football*, and as high as US$2.7 to $3 million for a 30-second spot during an event like the 2008 Super Bowl.[39] Advertising on Canadian networks is a bargain in comparison. Thirty-second commercials on CBC range from $100 to $52 000 (averaging $6500), while those on Global range from $150 to $48 009 (averaging $7000). On specialty channels, the average rates can be even lower—$450 on Bravo! and $1250 on YTV.[40]

In making choices, the planner has to rely on measurement services that provide estimates of audience size, composition, and media cost. Audience size has several possible measures:

- *Circulation.* The number of physical units carrying the advertising.

- *Audience.* The number of people exposed to the vehicle. (If the vehicle has pass-on readership, then the audience is larger than circulation.)

- *Effective audience.* The number of people with target-audience characteristics exposed to the vehicle.

- *Effective ad-exposed audience.* The number of people with target-audience characteristics who actually see the ad.

Media planners calculate the cost per thousand persons reached by a vehicle. A one-page, four-colour ad in *Maclean's* costs $31 960 and *Maclean's* estimated readership is 3.1 million people (the magazine's circulation is just over 500 000, with an estimated 6.2 readers per copy), so the cost of exposing 1000 persons to the ad is just over $10. The same ad in *Western Living* costs $19 700, but since it reaches only 820 000 persons (210 000 circulation, with an average of 3.9 readers per copy), the cost per thousand is about $24.[41] The media planner ranks each magazine by cost-per-thousand and favours magazines with the lowest cost-per-thousand for reaching target consumers. The magazines themselves often put together a "reader profile" for their advertisers, summarizing the characteristics of the magazine's readers with respect to age, income, residence, marital status, and leisure activities.

Several adjustments have to be applied to the cost-per-thousand measure. First, the measure should be adjusted for *audience quality*. For a baby-lotion ad, a magazine read by 1 million young mothers would have an exposure value of 1 million; if read by 1 million teenagers, it would have almost a zero exposure value. Second, the exposure value should be adjusted for the *audience-attention probability*. Readers of *Flare* may pay more attention to ads than do readers of *Canadian Business*. A "happy" commercial placed within an upbeat television show is more likely to be effective than a downbeat commercial in the same place.[42] Third, the exposure value should be adjusted for the magazine's *editorial quality* (prestige and believability). In addition, people are more likely to believe a TV or radio ad and to become more positively disposed towards the brand when the ad is placed within a program they like.[43] Fourth, the exposure value should be adjusted for the magazine's *ad placement policies and extra services* (such as regional or occupational editions and lead-time requirements).

Media planners are increasingly using more sophisticated measures of effectiveness and employing them in mathematical models to arrive at the best media mix. Many advertising agencies use a computer program to select the initial media and then make further improvements based on subjective factors.[44]

Deciding on Media Timing and Allocation

In choosing media, the advertiser faces both a macro-scheduling and a micro-scheduling problem. The *macro-scheduling problem* involves scheduling the advertising in relation to seasons and the business cycle. Suppose 70 percent of a product's sales occur between June and September. The firm can vary its advertising expenditures to follow the seasonal pattern, to oppose the seasonal pattern, or to be constant throughout the year.

The *micro-scheduling problem* calls for allocating advertising expenditures within a short period to obtain maximum impact. Suppose the firm decides to buy 30 radio spots in the month of September. Figure 18.3 shows several possible patterns. The left side shows that advertising messages for the month can be concentrated ("burst" advertising), dispersed continuously throughout the month, or dispersed intermittently. The top side shows that the advertising messages can be beamed with a level, rising, falling, or alternating frequency.

The most effective pattern depends on the communication objectives in relation to the nature of the product, target customers, distribution channels, and other marketing factors. The timing pattern should consider three factors. *Buyer turnover* expresses the rate at which new buyers enter the market; the higher this rate, the more continuous the advertising should be. *Purchase frequency* is the number of times during the period that the average buyer buys the product; the higher the purchase frequency, the more continuous the advertising should be. The *forgetting rate* is the rate

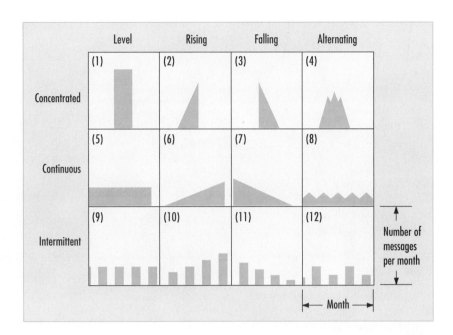

FIGURE 18.3

Classification of Advertising
Timing Patterns

at which the buyer forgets the brand; the higher the forgetting rate, the more continuous the advertising should be.

In launching a new product, the advertiser has to choose among continuity, concentration, flighting, and pulsing:

- *Continuity* is achieved by scheduling exposures evenly throughout a given period. Generally, advertisers use continuous advertising in expanding market situations, with frequently purchased items, and in tightly defined buyer categories.

- *Concentration* calls for spending all the advertising dollars in a single period. This makes sense for products with one selling season or holiday.

- *Flighting* calls for advertising for a period, followed by a period with no advertising, followed by a second period of advertising activity. It is used when funding is limited, the purchase cycle is relatively infrequent, and with seasonal items.

- *Pulsing* is continuous advertising at low-weight levels reinforced periodically by waves of heavier activity. Pulsing draws on the strength of continuous advertising and flights to create a compromise scheduling strategy.[45] Those who favour pulsing feel that the audience will learn the message more thoroughly, and money can be saved.

A company has to decide how to allocate its advertising budget over space as well as over time. The company makes "national buys" when it places ads on national TV networks or in nationally circulated magazines. It makes "spot buys" when it buys TV time in just a few markets or in regional editions of magazines. These markets are called *areas of dominant influence* (ADIs) or *designated marketing areas* (DMAs). Ads reach a market 60 to 100 kilometres from a city centre. The company makes "local buys" when it advertises in local newspapers, radio, or outdoor sites. Consider the example of Pizza Hut:

Pizza Hut

Pizza Hut levies a 4-percent advertising fee on its franchisees. It spends half of its budget on national media and half on regional and local media. Some national advertising is wasted because of low penetration in certain areas. Even though Pizza Hut may have a 30-percent share of the franchised pizza market nationally, this share may vary from 5 percent in some cities to 70 percent in others. The franchisees in the higher market-share cities want much more advertising money spent in their areas, but Pizza Hut does not have enough money to cover the whole nation by region. National advertising offers efficiency but fails to address the different local situations effectively.

Pizza Hut spends only half of its advertising budget on national media.

Evaluating Advertising Effectiveness

Good planning and control of advertising depend on measures of advertising effectiveness. Most advertisers try to measure the communication effect of an ad—that is, its potential effect on awareness, knowledge, or preference. They would also like to measure the ad's sales effect.

COMMUNICATION-EFFECT RESEARCH **Communication-effect research** seeks to determine whether an ad is communicating effectively. Called *copy testing*, it can be done before an ad is put into media and after it is printed or broadcast.

There are three major methods of pretesting. The *consumer feedback method* asks consumers for their reactions to a proposed ad. They respond to questions such as these:

1. What is the main message you get from this ad?
2. What do you think they want you to know, believe, or do?
3. How likely is it that this ad will influence your future actions?
4. What works well in the ad and what works poorly?
5. How does the ad make you feel?
6. Where is the best place to reach you with this message? Where would you be most likely to notice it and pay attention to it? Where are you when you make decisions about this action?

Portfolio tests ask consumers to view or listen to a portfolio of advertisements. Consumers are then asked to recall all the ads and their content, aided or unaided by the interviewer. Recall level indicates an ad's ability to stand out and to have its message understood and remembered.

Laboratory tests use equipment to measure physiological reactions—heartbeat, blood pressure, pupil dilation, galvanic skin response, perspiration—to an ad; or consumers may be asked to turn a knob to indicate their moment-to-moment liking or interest while viewing sequenced material.[46] These tests measure attention-getting power but reveal nothing about impact on beliefs, attitudes, or intentions. Table 18.3 describes some specific advertising research techniques.

Pretest critics maintain that agencies can design ads that test well, but may not necessarily perform well in the marketplace. Proponents of ad pretesting maintain that useful diagnostic information can emerge and that pretests should not be used as the sole decision criterion anyway. Widely acknowledged as being one of the best advertisers around, Nike is notorious for doing very little ad pretesting.

TABLE 18.3 | ADVERTISING RESEARCH TECHNIQUES

For Print Ads. Starch and Gallup & Robinson, Inc., are two widely used print pretesting services. Test ads are placed in magazines, which are then circulated to consumers. These consumers are contacted later and interviewed. Recall and recognition tests are used to determine advertising effectiveness.

For Broadcast Ads. *In-home tests:* A videotape is taken or downloaded into the homes of target consumers, who then view the commercials.

Trailer tests: In a trailer in a shopping centre, shoppers are shown the products and given an opportunity to select a series of brands. They then view commercials and are given coupons to be used in the shopping centre. Redemption rates indicate commercials' influence on purchase behaviour.

Theatre tests: Consumers are invited to a theatre to view a potential new television series along with some commercials. Before the show begins, consumers indicate preferred brands in different categories; after the viewing, consumers again choose preferred brands. Preference changes measure the commercials' persuasive power.

On-air tests: Respondents are recruited to watch a program on a regular TV channel when the test commercial will be shown or are selected based on their having viewed the program. They are asked questions about commercial recall.

Many advertisers use post-tests to assess the overall impact of a completed campaign. If a company hoped to increase brand awareness from 20 percent to 50 percent and succeeded in increasing it to only 30 percent, then the company is not spending enough, its ads are poor, or some other factor has been ignored.

SALES-EFFECT RESEARCH What sales are generated by an ad that increases brand awareness by 20 percent and brand preference by 10 percent? Advertising's sales effect is generally harder to measure than its communication effect. Sales are influenced by many factors, such as features, price, and availability, as well as competitors' actions. The fewer or more controllable these other factors are, the easier it is to measure effect on sales. The sales impact is easiest to measure in direct-marketing situations and hardest to measure in brand or corporate image-building advertising.

Companies are generally interested in finding out whether they are overspending or underspending on advertising. One approach to answering this question is to work with the formulation shown in Figure 18.4.

A company's *share of advertising expenditures* produces a *share of voice* (i.e., proportion of company advertising of that product to all advertising of that product) that earns a *share of consumers' minds and hearts* and, ultimately, a *share of market.*

Researchers try to measure the sales impact by analyzing historical or experimental data. The *historical approach* involves correlating past sales to past advertising expenditures using advanced statistical techniques.[47] Other researchers use an *experimental design* to measure advertising's sales impact. Here is an example:

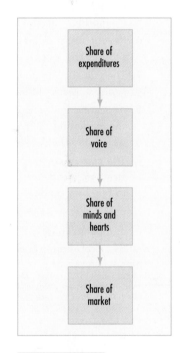

FIGURE 18.4

Formula for Measuring Sales Impact of Advertising

Information Resources, Inc.

Information Resources, Inc. (IRI) offers a service called BehaviorScan that provides marketers in North America with data about advertising effectiveness by tracking consumer purchases tied to specific advertising. Consumers in test markets who sign up to be members of IRI's "Shoppers Hotline" panel agree to have microcomputers record when the TV set is on and to which station it is tuned, while electronic scanners record UPC codes of their household purchases at supermarkets. IRI has the capability to send different commercials to different homes. The company also conducts in-store tests in many North American markets to study the effects of promotions, displays, coupons, store features, and packaging.[48]

"Marketing Insight: Understanding the Effects of Advertising and Promotion" provides a summary of a meta-analysis of IRI research studies.

MARKETING **INSIGHT**	UNDERSTANDING THE EFFECTS OF ADVERTISING AND PROMOTION

Information Resources, Inc. (IRI) has provided a unique, in-depth examination into how advertising works. IRI reviewed the results of 389 research studies conducted over a seven-year period and offered the following general principles concerning advertising and promotion effectiveness:

1. *TV advertising weight alone is not enough.* Only roughly half of TV advertising heavy-up (high concentration of advertising for a short length of time) plans have a measurable effect on sales, although when they do have an effect it is often large. The success rate is higher on new products or line extensions than on established brands.

2. TV advertising is more likely to work when there are changes in copy or media strategy (a new copy strategy or an expanded target market).

3. When advertising is successful in increasing sales, its impact lasts beyond the period of peak spending. Recent evidence shows the long-term positive effects of advertising lasting up to two years after peak spending. Moreover, the long-term incremental sales generated are approximately double the incremental sales observed in the first year of an advertising spending increase.

4. About 20 percent of advertising plans pay out in the short term. However, when the long-term effect of advertising is considered, it is likely that most advertising plans that show a significant effect in a split-cable experiment would pay out.

5. Promotions almost always have a measurable impact on sales. However, the effect is usually purely short term.

6. Payout statistics on promotions are dismal. Roughly 16 percent of trade promotions are profitable. Furthermore, promotions' effects are often purely short term, except for new products.

7. The statistics on advertising and promotion payouts show that many brands are overspending on marketing support. Many classes of spending can be reduced at an increase in profits.

8. Allocating marketing funds involves a continuous search for marketing programs that offer the highest return on the marketing dollar. Trade-offs among advertising, trade, and consumer promotions can be highly profitable when based on reliable evaluation systems measuring this productivity at any point in time.

9. *The current trend towards promotion spending is not sound from a marketing-productivity standpoint.* When the strategic disadvantages of promotions are included—that is, losing control to the trade and training consumers to buy only on deal—the case is compelling for a re-evaluation of current practices and the incentive systems responsible for this trend.

A 2004 IRI study of 23 brands reinforced these findings, finding that advertising often didn't increase sales for mature brands or categories in decline.

Source: Leonard M. Lodish, Magid Abraham, Stuart Kalmenson, Jeanne Livelsberger, Beth Lubetkin, Bruce Richardson, and Mary Ellen Stevens, "How T.V. Advertising Works: A Meta Analysis of 389 Real World Split Cable T.V. Advertising Experiments," *Journal of Marketing Research*, 32 (May 1995): 125–139; Jack Neff, "TV Doesn't Sell Package Goods, *Advertising Age*, May 24, 2004, pp. 1, 30.

A growing number of researchers are striving to measure the sales effect of advertising expenditures instead of settling for communication-effect measures.[49] Millward Brown International has conducted tracking studies in the United Kingdom for many years to provide information to help advertisers decide whether their advertising is benefiting their brand.[50]

SALES PROMOTION

Sales promotion, a key ingredient in marketing campaigns, consists of a collection of incentive tools, mostly short term, designed to stimulate quicker or greater purchase of particular products or services by consumers or the trade.[51]

Whereas advertising offers a *reason* to buy, sales promotion offers an *incentive* to buy. Sales promotion includes tools for *consumer promotion* (samples, coupons, cash-refund offers, prices-off, premiums, prizes, patronage rewards, free trials, warranties, tie-in promotions, cross-promotions, point-of-purchase displays, and demonstrations); *trade promotion* (prices off, advertising and display allowances, and free goods); and *business* and *sales-force promotion* (trade shows and conventions, contests for sales reps, and specialty advertising).

Objectives

Sales-promotion tools vary in their specific objectives. A free sample stimulates consumer trial, whereas a free management-advisory service aims at cementing a long-term relationship with a retailer.

Sellers use incentive-type promotions to attract new triers, to reward loyal customers, and to increase the repurchase rates of occasional users. Sales promotions often attract brand switchers, who are looking primarily for low price, good value, or premiums. Sales promotions generally are unlikely to turn them into loyal users, although they may be induced to make some subsequent purchases.[52] Sales promotions used in markets of high brand similarity can produce a high sales response in the short run but little permanent gain in market share. In markets of high brand dis-similarity, sales promotions may be able to alter market shares permanently. In addition to brand switching, consumers may engage in stockpiling—purchasing earlier than usual (purchase accelera-tion) or purchasing extra quantities.[53] But sales may then hit a post-promotion dip.[54]

A number of sales-promotion benefits flow to manufacturers and consumers.[55] Sales promo-tions enable manufacturers to adjust to short-term variations in supply and demand. They enable manufacturers to test how high a list price they can charge, because they can always discount it. They induce consumers to try new products instead of never straying from current ones. They lead to more varied retail formats, such as the everyday-low-price store and the promotional-pricing store. For retailers, promotions may increase sales of complementary categories (cake mix promotions may help to drive frosting sales) as well as induce some store-switching by consumers. They promote greater consumer awareness of prices. They permit manufacturers to sell more than they would normally sell at the list price. They help the manufacturer adapt programs to different consumer segments. Consumers themselves enjoy some satisfaction from being smart shoppers when they take advantage of price specials.

Service marketers also employ sales promotions to achieve marketing objectives. Some service firms, like Virgin Mobile, use promotions to attract additional sales.

Virgin Mobile

In 2007, a survey conducted by J.D. Power found that Virgin Mobile had the most-satisfied customers. So, Virgin took to the streets to make customers even happier. Branded street teams showed up in Vancouver, Toronto, and Montreal with ice cream–style bicycle carts attending summer hot spots including outdoor concerts, beach volleyball tournaments, Ultimate Frisbee games, and festivals. The teams handed out freezies and flip flops and encouraged people to enter a contest at virginmobile.ca that included a prize to a VIP expe-rience at Virgin Music Festival in Toronto (V Fest). The carts also showed up at retailers such as Future Shop, Best Buy, and Wal-Mart. Toronto-based Wills & Company and Segal Communications designed the campaign in keeping with the brand image, as the carts are flexible, cost effective, and allow contact with Virgin's target market: young adults.[56]

Advertising versus Promotion

A decade ago, the ratio of advertising to sales-promotion was about 60:40. Today, in many con-sumer packaged-goods companies, sales promotion accounts for 75 percent of the combined budget (roughly 50 percent is trade promotion and 25 percent is consumer promotion). Sales-promotion expenditures have been increasing as a percentage of budget expenditure annually for the last two decades. Several factors contribute to this rapid growth, particularly in consumer markets.[57]

Promotion is now more accepted by top management as an effective sales tool, more product managers are qualified to use sales-promotion tools, and product managers are under greater pres-sure to increase current sales. In addition, the number of brands has increased, competitors use pro-motions frequently, many brands are seen as similar, consumers are more price-oriented, the trade has demanded more deals from manufacturers, and advertising efficiency has declined because of rising costs, media clutter, and legal restraints.

There is a danger, however, in letting advertising take too much of a back seat to promotions, because advertising typically builds brand loyalty. The question of whether or not sales promotion weakens brand loyalty is subject to interpretation. Sales promotion, with its incessant prices-off, coupons, deals, and premiums, may devalue the product offering in buyers' minds. However, before jumping to any conclusion, we need to distinguish between price promotions and added-value promotions. Certain types of sales promotion can actually enhance brand image. The rapid growth of sales-promotion media has created clutter similar to advertising clutter. Manufacturers have to find ways to rise above the clutter—for instance, by offering larger coupon-redemption values or using more dramatic point-of-purchase displays or demonstrations.

Usually, when a brand is price promoted too often, the consumer begins to devalue it and buy it mainly when it goes on sale. So there is risk in putting a well-known brand on promotion over 30 percent of the time.[58] Automobile manufacturers turned to 0-percent financing and hefty cash rebates to ignite sales in the soft economy of 2000–2001 but have found it difficult to wean consumers from all the discounts since then: two-thirds of Americans indicated that the timing of their next vehicle purchases will be affected by the level of sales incentives and one-third said they wouldn't buy without them.[59]

Dominant brands offer deals less frequently, because most deals subsidize only current users. Prior research has shown that sales promotions yield faster and more measurable responses in sales than advertising does but do not tend to yield new, long-term buyers in mature markets. Loyal brand buyers tend not to change their buying patterns as a result of competitive promotion. Advertising appears to be more effective at deepening brand loyalty.[60]

There is also evidence that price promotions do not build permanent total-category volume. One study of more than 1000 promotions concluded that only 16 percent paid off.[61] Small-share competitors find it advantageous to use sales promotion because they cannot afford to match the market leaders' large advertising budgets; nor can they obtain shelf space without offering trade allowances or stimulate consumer trial without offering incentives. Price competition is often used by a small brand seeking to enlarge its share, but it is less effective for a category leader whose growth lies in expanding the entire category.[62] The upshot is that many consumer packaged-goods companies feel they are forced to use more sales promotion than they wish. They blame the heavy use of sales promotion for decreasing brand loyalty, increasing consumer price-sensitivity, dilution of the image of brand quality, and a focus on short-run marketing planning.

Major Decisions

In using sales promotion, a company must establish its objectives, select the tools, develop the program, pretest the program, implement and control the program, and evaluate the results.

ESTABLISHING OBJECTIVES Sales-promotion objectives are derived from broader promotion objectives, which are derived from more basic marketing objectives developed for the product. For consumers, companies' objectives include encouraging purchase of larger-sized units, building trial among nonusers, and attracting switchers away from competitors' brands. Ideally, promotions with consumers would have short-run sales impact as well as long-run brand equity effects. For retailers, companies' objectives include persuading retailers to carry new items and higher levels of inventory, encouraging off-season buying, encouraging stocking of related items, offsetting competitive promotions, building brand loyalty, and gaining entry into new retail outlets. For the sales force, companies' objectives include encouraging support of a new product or model, encouraging more prospecting, and stimulating off-season sales.[63]

SELECTING CONSUMER-PROMOTION TOOLS The promotion planner should take into account the type of market, sales-promotion objectives, competitive conditions, and each tool's cost-effectiveness. The main consumer-promotion tools are summarized in Table 18.4. We can distinguish between *manufacturer promotions* and *retailer promotions*. The former are illustrated by the auto industry's frequent use of rebates, gifts to motivate test-drives and purchases, and high-value trade-in credit. The latter include price cuts, feature advertising, retailer coupons, and retailer contests or premiums.

We can also distinguish between sales-promotion tools that are *consumer-franchise building* and reinforce the consumer's brand preference, and those that do not. The former impart a selling message along with the deal, as in the case of free samples, frequency awards, coupons when they

---

TABLE 18.4 | MAJOR CONSUMER-PROMOTION TOOLS

Samples: Offer of a free amount of a product or service delivered door-to-door, sent in the mail, picked up in a store, attached to another product, or featured in an advertising offer.

Coupons: Certificates entitling the bearer to a stated saving on the purchase of a specific product: mailed, enclosed in other products or attached to them, or inserted in magazine and newspaper ads.

Cash Refund Offers (rebates): Provide a price reduction after purchase rather than at the retail shop: consumer sends a specified "proof of purchase" to the manufacturer which "refunds" part of the purchase price by mail.

Price Packs (cents-off deals): Offers to consumers of savings on the regular price of a product, flagged on the label or package. A *reduced-price pack* is a single package sold at a reduced price (such as two for the price of one). A *banded pack* is two related products banded together (such as a toothbrush and toothpaste).

Premiums (gifts): Merchandise offered at a relatively low cost or free as an incentive to purchase a particular product. A *with-pack premium* accompanies the product inside or on the package. A *free in-the-mail premium* is mailed to consumers who send in a proof of purchase, such as a box top or UPC code. A *self-liquidating premium* is sold below its normal retail price to consumers who request it.

Frequency Programs: Programs providing rewards related to the consumer's frequency and intensity in purchasing the company's products or services.

Prizes (contests, sweepstakes, games): *Prizes* are offers of the chance to win cash, trips, or merchandise as a result of purchasing something. A *contest* calls for consumers to submit an entry to be examined by a panel of judges who will select the best entries. A *sweepstakes* asks consumers to submit their names in a drawing. Every time they buy, a *game* presents consumers with something—bingo numbers, missing letters—which might help them win a prize.

Patronage Awards: Values in cash or in other forms that are proportional to patronage of a certain vendor or group of vendors.

Free Trials: Inviting prospective purchasers to try the product without cost in the hope that they will buy.

Product Warranties: Explicit or implicit promises by sellers that the product will perform as specified during a specified period or that the seller will fix it or refund the customer's money.

Tie-in Promotions: Two or more brands or companies team up on coupons, refunds, and contests to increase pulling power.

Cross-Promotions: Using one brand to advertise another noncompeting brand.

Point-of-Purchase (P-O-P) Displays and Demonstrations: P-O-P displays and demonstrations take place at the point-of-purchase or sale.

---

include a selling message, and premiums when they are related to the product. Sales-promotion tools that typically are not brand-building include price-off packs, consumer premiums not related to a product, contests and sweepstakes, consumer refund offers, and trade allowances.

Consumer franchise-building promotions offer the best of both worlds—they build brand equity while moving product. Here's an example of a highly effective consumer franchise-building promotion:

itravel2000.com

itravel2000.com, Canada's largest online travel retailer, served just under half a million customers in 2007. That was in part due to a promotional campaign offered in 2007 called "Let it Snow." The contest stated that if 5 inches [13 cm] of snow fell on January 1, 2008, in either Montreal, Toronto, or Calgary, people who lived in those cities and had booked vacations between the contest dates would get their vacation package, flight, or hotel for free. Customers jumped at the chance and booked vacations so eagerly that the company struggled to keep up with demand. As part of the promotion, itravel2000.com even handed out rulers for measuring snowfall, although official numbers were taken from Environment Canada to determine if any of the cities qualified. To protect themselves, in case it really did snow the required 5 inches [about 13 cm], itravel2000.com took out weather insurance of up to $100 million for the day in question. On January 1, 2008, Montreal did in fact have 5 inches of snowfall. As a result, itravel2000.com issued refund cheques to the many elated winners in Quebec.[64]

Sales promotion seems most effective when used together with advertising. In one study, a price promotion alone produced only a 15-percent increase in sales volume. When combined with feature advertising, sales volume increased 19 percent; when combined with feature advertising and a point-of-purchase display, sales volume increased 24 percent.[65]

Many large companies have a sales-promotion manager whose job is to help brand managers choose the right promotional tool. Some marketers such as Colgate-Palmolive and Hershey Foods are also going online with their coupons, aided by various online coupon sites.

Danone Canada

Danone recently launched a new yogurt probiotic drink called DanActive, first available only in Quebec. To get the word out and promote the new product, Danone chose to distribute free samples to stimulate consumer interest. Over a quarter million samples were handed out on the streets of major cities in Quebec during morning and afternoon rush hour when busy, stressed out commuters were out on the streets at the beginning of the cold season. Those handing out samples wore T-shirts that said "YES to strong natural defences," which aimed to educate consumers about the advantages of probiotic drinks. Along with the free samples, Danone used TV spots, radio ads, and in-store samples.[66]

SELECTING TRADE-PROMOTION TOOLS Manufacturers use a number of trade-promotion tools (Table 18.5). Surprisingly, a higher proportion of the promotion pie is devoted to trade-promotion tools (46.9 percent) than to consumer promotion (27.9 percent). Manufacturers award money to the trade for a variety of reasons: (1) to persuade retailers or wholesalers to carry the brand, (2) to persuade retailers or wholesalers to carry more units than the normal amount, (3) to induce retailers to promote the brand by featuring it with product displays or by giving price reductions, and (4) to stimulate retailers and their sales clerks to push the product.

The growing power of large retailers has increased their ability to demand trade promotion at the expense of consumer promotion and advertising.[67] These retailers depend on promotion money from the manufacturers. No manufacturer could unilaterally stop offering trade allowances without losing retailer support. The company's sales force and its brand managers are often at odds over trade promotion. The sales force says that the local retailers will not keep the company's products on the shelf unless they receive more trade-promotion money, whereas the brand managers want to spend the limited funds on consumer promotion and advertising.

Manufacturers face several challenges in managing trade promotions. First, they often find it difficult to police retailers to make sure they are doing what they agreed to do. Manufacturers are

---

TABLE 18.5 | MAJOR TRADE-PROMOTION TOOLS

Price-Off (off-invoice or off-list): A straight discount on the list price of each case purchased during a stated time period.

Allowance: An amount offered in return for the retailer's agreeing to feature the manufacturer's products in some way. An *advertising allowance* compensates retailers for advertising the manufacturer's product. A *display allowance* compensates them for carrying a special product display.

Free Goods: Offers of extra cases of merchandise to intermediaries which buy a certain quantity or which feature a certain flavour or size.

For more information, see Betsy Spethman, "Trade Promotion Redefined," *Brandweek*, March 13, 1995, pp. 25–32.

increasingly insisting on proof of performance before paying any allowances. Second, more retailers are doing *forward buying*—that is, buying during the deal period a greater quantity than they can sell during the deal period. Retailers might respond to a 10-percent-off case allowance by buying a 12-week or longer supply. The manufacturer then has to schedule more production than planned and bear the costs of extra work shifts and overtime. Third, retailers are diverting more: buying more cases than needed in a region in which the manufacturer offered a deal and shipping the surplus to their stores in nondeal regions. Manufacturers are trying to handle forward buying and diverting by limiting the amount they will sell at a discount or by producing and delivering less than the full order in an effort to smooth production.[68]

All said, manufacturers feel that trade promotion has become a nightmare. It contains layers of deals, is complex to administer, and often leads to lost revenues.

SELECTING BUSINESS- AND SALES-FORCE-PROMOTION TOOLS Companies spend billions of dollars on business- and sales-force-promotion tools (Table 18.6). These tools are used to gather business leads, impress and reward customers, and motivate the sales force to greater effort. Companies typically develop for each business-promotion tool budgets that remain fairly constant from year to year.

DEVELOPING THE PROGRAM In planning sales-promotion programs, marketers are increasingly blending several media into a total campaign concept. Consider how the Canadian Tourism Commission took advantage of this technique:

Canadian Tourism Commission

In 2007, the Canadian Tourism Commission (CTC) used a variety of media to communicate to the world Canada's tourism brand: "Canada. Keep Exploring." In order to differentiate the advertisements, the CTC hired two celebrated artists to articulate the brand in the style of "slam poetry" and had the poems recited at the Canada Day celebrations on Parliament Hill. The CTC also highlighted Canada's healthy vacation opportunities using Canadian health and fitness expert Harley Pasternak; media stories appeared in such publications as *Fitness* and *In Touch Weekly* (with a total estimated circulation of over 4 million). In the U.S., "whispering windows" were set up to grab the attention of consumers on the bustling streets of New York City. Street-level billboards were set up on Manhattan storefronts, allowing the entire surface of the storefront to project sound without any speakers being seen—a technology never before used in North America. The worldwide campaign included billboards in Mexico, a contest at www.canada.travel.com, print ads in the U.K., and e-marketing in South Korea. As a result of these efforts, long-haul arrivals in Canada increased by 2.6 percent in 2007 and travel from nearly every market increased.[69]

TABLE 18.6 | MAJOR BUSINESS- AND SALES-FORCE-PROMOTION TOOLS

Trade Shows and Conventions: Industry associations organize annual trade shows and conventions. Business marketers may spend as much as 35 percent of their annual promotion budget on trade shows. Thousands of trade shows take place every year, drawing millions of attendees. Trade show attendance can range from a few thousand people to over 70 000 for large shows held by the restaurant or hotel–motel industries. Participating vendors expect several benefits, including generating new sales leads, maintaining customer contacts, introducing new products, meeting new customers, selling more to present customers, and educating customers with publications, videos, and other audiovisual materials.

Sales Contests: A sales contest aims at inducing the sales force or dealers to increase their sales results over a stated period, with prizes (money, trips, gifts, or points) going to those who succeed.

Specialty Advertising: Specialty advertising consists of useful, low-cost items that salespeople give to prospects and customers; these items bear the company's name and address, and sometimes an advertising message. Common items are ballpoint pens, calendars, key chains, flashlights, tote bags, and memo pads.

In deciding to use a particular incentive, marketers have several factors to consider. First, they must determine the *size* of the incentive. A certain minimum is necessary if the promotion is to succeed. Second, the marketing manager must establish *conditions* for participation. Incentives might be offered to everyone or to select groups. Third, the marketer has to decide on the *duration* of the promotion. According to one researcher, the optimal frequency is about three weeks per quarter, and optimal duration is the length of the average purchase cycle.[70] Fourth, the marketer must choose a *distribution vehicle*. For example, a 25-cents-off coupon can be distributed in the product package, in stores, by mail, or in advertising.

Fifth, the marketing manager must establish the *timing* of promotion. Finally, the marketer must determine the *total sales-promotion budget*. The cost of a particular promotion consists of the administrative cost (printing, mailing, and promoting the deal) and the incentive cost (cost of premium or cents-off, including redemption costs) multiplied by the expected number of units that will be sold on the deal. In the case of a coupon deal, the cost would take into account the fact that only a fraction of consumers will redeem the coupons.

PRETESTING, IMPLEMENTING, CONTROLLING, AND EVALUATING THE PROGRAM

Although most sales-promotion programs are designed on the basis of experience, pretests can determine if the tools are appropriate, the incentive size optimal, and the presentation method efficient. Consumers can be asked to rate or rank different possible deals, or trial tests can be run in limited geographic areas.

Marketing managers must prepare implementation and control plans for each individual promotion that cover lead time and sell-in time. *Lead time* is the time necessary to prepare the program prior to launching it: initial planning, design, and approval of package modifications or material to be mailed or distributed; preparation of advertising and point-of-sale materials; notification of field sales personnel; establishment of allocations for individual distributors; purchasing and printing of special premiums or packaging materials; production of advance inventories in preparation for release at a specific date; and, finally, the distribution to the retailer.[71] *Sell-in time* begins with the promotional launch and ends when approximately 95 percent of the deal merchandise is in the hands of consumers.

Manufacturers can evaluate the program using three methods: sales data, consumer surveys, and experiments. The first method involves scanner sales data. Marketers can analyze the types of people who took advantage of the promotion, what they bought before the promotion, and how they later behaved towards the brand and other brands. Did the promotion attract new triers and also stimulate more purchasing by existing customers?

In general, sales promotions work best when they attract competitors' customers who then switch. If the company's product is not superior, the brand's share is likely to return to its prepromotion level. *Consumer surveys* can be conducted to learn how many recall the promotion, what they thought of it, how many took advantage of it, and how the promotion affected subsequent brand-choice behaviour.[72] Sales promotions can also be evaluated through *experiments* that vary such attributes as incentive value, duration, and distribution media. For example, coupons can be sent to half of the households in a consumer panel. Scanner data can be used to track whether the coupons led more people to buy the product and when.

There are additional costs beyond the cost of specific promotions. First, promotions might decrease long-run brand loyalty. Second, promotions can be more expensive than they appear. Some are inevitably distributed to the wrong consumers. Third, there are the costs of special production runs, extra sales-force effort, and handling requirements. Finally, certain promotions irritate retailers, which may demand extra trade allowances or refuse to cooperate.[73]

EVENTS AND EXPERIENCES

According to the IEG Sponsorship Report, US$14.93 billion was predicted to be spent on sponsorships in North America during 2007, with 66 percent of this going to sports; another 11 percent to entertainment tours and attractions; 5 percent to festivals, fairs, and annual events; 5 percent to the arts; 3 percent to associations and member organizations; and 10 percent to cause marketing. By becoming part of a special and more personally relevant moment in consumers' lives, companies can broaden and deepen the relationship with the events' target markets.

At the same time, daily encounters with brands may also affect consumers' brand attitudes and beliefs. *Atmospheres* are "packaged environments" that create or reinforce leanings towards product purchase. Law offices decorated with Oriental rugs and oak furniture communicate "stability" and "success."[74] A five-star hotel will use elegant chandeliers, marble columns, and other tangible signs of luxury.

Recognizing that it can now reach only 15 percent of the population with a primetime ad, as compared to 40 percent as recently as the mid-1980s, Coca-Cola has diverted money into new initiatives that allow it to embed itself into the favourite activities of its target audience. The company has created "teen lounges" in major cities where kids can hang out and buy Cokes from see-through vending machines, placed downloadable songs on its myCokeMusic.com website in Britain, and blended its brand into the content of TV shows from the United States to Venezuela.[75]

Coca-Cola is not alone. More firms are creating on-site and off-site product and brand experiences. There is Everything Coca-Cola in Las Vegas, M&M World in Times Square in New York, and General Mills Cereal Adventure in the Mall of America in Minnesota.[76] Small brands, of necessity, are even more likely to take less obvious and less expensive paths in sponsorship and communications. With a limited budget, Yoo-hoo chose to target teens by sponsoring the Warped Tour, an alternative music festival, via free samples and off-the-wall contests. For example, concert-goers could get free products if they were willing to chug the chocolate drink out of a boot (dubbed a "shoe-hoo").[77] Maxwell House Coffee also pursued events as a form of advertising.

Creating a brand experience: Everything Coca-Cola in Las Vegas, with a 30-metre illuminated Coke bottle as part of the front of the building.

Maxwell House Coffee

In the spring of 2008, Maxwell House Coffee began a new campaign called "Brew Some Good," stating that it would donate the bulk of its advertising dollars to charity rather than producing expensive advertisements. The commercial invited consumers to create video nominations of worthwhile charities in their communities and post them online. Six winners received $10 000 each towards the charity of their choice. Another part of the campaign was a Brew Some Good event at RioCan Yonge Eglinton Centre, just outside Toronto's Eglinton subway station. The event was designed to promote random acts of good. Maxwell House gave away 10 000 free subway tickets and provided free coffee to the public. At the event, Canadian singer Chantal Kreviazuk, in collaborative support of Habitat for Humanity, treated the crowd to several songs. Promotions like these connect consumers with the brand and strengthen Maxwell House's image as a company that cares about people.[78]

Events Objectives

Marketers report a number of reasons why they sponsor events:

1. *To identify with a particular target market or lifestyle.* Customers can be targeted geographically, demographically, psychographically, or behaviourally according to events. Events can be chosen based on attendees' attitudes towards and usage of certain products or brands. Advertisers such as Sony, Gillette, and Pepsi have advertised during ESPN's twice-yearly X Games to reach the elusive 12- to 19-year-old audience.[79]

2. *To increase awareness of company or product name.* Sponsorship often offers sustained exposure to a brand, a necessary condition to build brand recognition. By skillfully choosing sponsorship events or activities, identification with a product (and thus brand recall) can also be enhanced, such as Guinness Canada's St. Patrick's Day initiative.

3. *To create or reinforce consumer perceptions of key brand-image associations.* Events themselves have associations that help to create or reinforce brand associations.

Guinness Canada uses event marketing. On Parliament Hill in Ottawa, it held a rally to make St. Patrick's Day a national holiday.

4. *To enhance corporate-image dimensions.* Sponsorship is seen as a means to improve perceptions that the company is likable, prestigious, and so on, so that consumers will credit the company and favour it in later product choices.

5. *To create experiences and evoke feelings.* The feelings engendered by an exciting or rewarding event may also indirectly link to the brand. Marketers can use the Web to provide further event support and additional experiences.

6. *To express commitment to the community or social issues.* Sponsorship that involves corporate tie-ins with nonprofit organizations and charities is often called cause-related marketing. Firms such as Timberland, Home Depot, Starbucks, and American Express have made cause-related marketing an important cornerstone of their marketing programs.

7. *To entertain key clients or reward key employees.* Many events include lavish hospitality tents and other special services or activities that are available only to sponsors and their guests. Involving clients with the event in these and other ways can engender goodwill and establish valuable business contacts. Events can also build employee participation and morale or be used as an employee incentive.

8. *To permit merchandising or promotional opportunities.* Many marketers tie into an event contests or sweepstakes, in-store merchandising, direct response, or other marketing activities. L'Oréal Canada used its sponsorship of the hit TV show *Canadian Idol* in this way.

Despite these potential advantages, there are a number of potential disadvantages to sponsorship. The success of an event can be unpredictable and out of the control of the sponsor. Although

Air Canada agreed to pay $40 million over 20 years to name the Air Canada Centre.

many consumers will credit sponsors for providing the financial assistance to make an event possible, some consumers may still resent the commercialization of events.

Major Decisions

Developing successful sponsored events involves choosing the appropriate events, designing the optimal sponsorship program for the event, and measuring the effects of sponsorship.[80]

CHOOSING EVENT OPPORTUNITIES Because of the huge amount of money involved and the number of event opportunities that exist, many marketers are becoming much more strategic about the events with which they will get involved and the manner in which they will do so.

The marketing objectives and communication strategy that have been defined for the brand must be met by the event. The audience delivered by the event must match the target market of the brand. There must be sufficient awareness of the event, it must possess the desired image, and it must be capable of creating the desired effects with the target market. Consumers must make favourable attributions to the sponsor for its event involvement. An "ideal event" might be one (1) whose audience closely matches the desired target market, (2) that generates much favourable attention, (3) that is unique but not encumbered with many sponsors, (4) that lends itself to ancillary marketing activities, and (5) that reflects or enhances the brand or corporate image of the sponsor.

More and more firms are also using their names to sponsor the arenas, stadiums, and other venues that actually hold events.[81] From 1999 to 2004, over US$2 billion was spent on naming rights to major North American sports facilities. For example, Air Canada agreed to pay Maple Leaf Sports and Entertainment $40 million over 20 years for the right to have the Toronto Raptors' and Maple Leafs' arena named the Air Canada Centre.[82]

DESIGNING SPONSORSHIP PROGRAMS Many marketers believe that it is the marketing program accompanying an event sponsorship that ultimately determines its success. A sponsor can strategically identify itself at an event in a number of ways, including with banners, signs, and programs. For more significant impact, sponsors typically supplement such activities with samples, prizes, advertising, retail promotions, and publicity. At least two to three times the amount of the sponsorship expenditure should be spent on related marketing activities. Jamba Juice augments its running-race sponsorships with bunches of runners in banana costumes. Any runner who finishes the race before a banana gets free smoothies for a year. Jamba Juice banners are displayed all around and smoothies are sampled by race finishers and onlookers.[83]

Event creation is a particularly important skill in publicizing fund-raising drives for nonprofit organizations. Fund-raisers have developed a large repertoire of special events, including anniversary celebrations, art exhibits, auctions, benefit evenings, bingo games, book sales, cake sales, contests, dances, dinners, fairs, fashion shows, parties in unusual places, rummage sales, tours, and walkathons. No sooner is one type of event created, such as a walkathon, than competitors spawn new versions, such as readathons, bikeathons, and jogathons.[84]

MEASURING SPONSORSHIP ACTIVITIES As with public relations, measurement of events is difficult. There are two basic approaches to measuring the effects of sponsorship activities: the *supply-side* method focuses on potential exposure to the brand by assessing the extent of media coverage; and the *demand-side* method focuses on reported exposure from consumers. We examine each in turn.

Supply-side methods attempt to approximate the amount of time or space devoted to media coverage of an event. For example, marketers can estimate the number of seconds that the brand is clearly visible on a television screen or the column inches of press clippings covering an event that mention the brand. This measure of potential "impressions" is then translated into an equivalent "value" in advertising dollars according to the fees associated with actually advertising in the particular media vehicle. Some industry consultants have estimated that 30 seconds of TV logo exposure can be worth 6 to 10 or as much as 25 percent of a 30-second TV ad spot.

Although supply-side exposure methods provide quantifiable measures, their validity can be questioned. The difficulty lies in the fact that equating media coverage with advertising exposure ignores the content of the communications consumers receive. The advertiser uses media space and time to communicate a strategically designed message. Media coverage and telecasts expose only the brand and don't necessarily embellish its meaning in any direct way. Although some public relations professionals maintain that positive editorial coverage can be worth 5 to 10 times the equivalent advertising value, it is rare that sponsorship provides such favourable treatment.[85]

The demand-side method attempts to identify the effects sponsorship has on consumers' brand knowledge. Tracking or customized surveys can explore the ability of the event sponsorship to affect awareness, attitudes, or even sales. Event spectators can be identified and surveyed to measure recall of the sponsor of the event as well as resulting attitudes and intentions towards the sponsor.

PUBLIC RELATIONS

Not only must the company relate constructively to customers, suppliers, and dealers, it must also relate to a large number of interested publics. A **public** is any group that has an actual or potential interest in or impact on a company's ability to achieve its objectives. **Public relations (PR)** involves a variety of programs designed to promote or protect a company's image or its individual products.

A wise company takes concrete steps to manage successful relations with its key publics. Most companies have a public-relations department that monitors the attitudes of the organization's publics and distributes information and communications to build goodwill. The best PR departments spend time counselling top management to adopt positive programs and to eliminate questionable practices so that negative publicity does not arise in the first place. They perform the following five functions:

1. *Press relations.* Presenting news and information about the organization in the most positive light.

2. *Product publicity.* Sponsoring efforts to publicize specific products.

3. *Corporate communication.* Promoting understanding of the organization through internal and external communications.

4. *Lobbying.* Dealing with legislators and government officials to promote or defeat legislation and regulation.

5. *Counselling.* Advising management about public issues and company positions and image during good times and bad.

Marketing Public Relations

Many companies are turning to **marketing public relations (MPR)** to support corporate or product promotion and image making. MPR, like financial PR and community PR, serves a special constituency, the marketing department.[86]

The old name for MPR was **publicity**, which was seen as the task of securing editorial space—as opposed to paid space—in print and broadcast media to promote or "hype" a product, service, idea, place, person, or organization. MPR goes beyond simple publicity and plays an important role in the following tasks:

- *Assisting in the launch of new products.* The amazing commercial success of toys such as Teenage Mutant Ninja Turtles, Mighty Morphin' Power Rangers, Beanie Babies, and Pokémon owes a great deal to clever publicity.

- *Assisting in repositioning a mature product.* New York City had extremely bad press in the 1970s until the "I Love New York" campaign.

- *Building interest in a product category.* Companies and trade associations have used MPR to rebuild interest in declining commodities such as eggs, milk, beef, and potatoes, and to expand consumption of such products as tea, pork, and orange juice.

- *Influencing specific target groups.* The Vancouver Olympic Bid Committee leveraged public relations to build public support for the games and to win the right to hold the Olympics and Paralympics in Vancouver in 2010.

- *Defending products that have encountered public problems.* PR professionals must be adept at managing crises, such as the Coca-Cola incident in Belgium over allegedly contaminated soda, and Firestone's crisis with regard to the tire-tread separation problem.

- *Building the corporate image in a way that reflects favourably on its products.* Bill Gates's speeches and books have helped to create an innovative image for Microsoft Corporation.

As the power of mass advertising weakens, marketing managers are turning to MPR to build awareness and brand knowledge for both new and established products. MPR is also effective in blanketing local communities and reaching specific groups. In several cases, MPR proved more cost-effective than advertising. Nevertheless, it must be planned jointly with advertising.[87] In addition, marketing managers need to acquire more skill in using MPR resources. Gillette is a trendsetter here: each brand manager is required to have a budget line for MPR and to justify not using it. Done right, the impact of MPR can be substantial.

Clearly, creative public relations can affect public awareness at a fraction of the cost of advertising. The company does not pay for the space or time obtained in the media. It pays only for a staff to develop and circulate the stories and manage certain events. If the company develops an interesting story, it could be picked up by the media and be worth millions of dollars in equivalent advertising. Some experts say that consumers are five times more likely to be influenced by editorial copy than by advertising. Here's an example of a powerful PR campaign:

See You in Athens Fund

The not-for-profit organization called the See You in Athens Fund was an organization with a mission to help provide financial support to Canadian amateur athletes prior to the Olympic games in Athens. Its principal objective was to fight the erroneous public perception that athletes are taken care of by government, family, and/or sponsors, when in fact 70 percent of Canada's Olympic contenders actually live below the poverty line. It wasn't until 2003 that the Fund turned to public relations to get its message across. Using a provocative and controversial public service announcement (PSA) created by Taxi of Toronto, the Fund exposed athletes' struggles. The print ads and television commercials that were part of the campaign showed Canadian athletes begging for money (in contrast to the "feel good" podium shots). Using a public-relations campaign to encourage inclusion of the PSA spots resulted in different media picking up the ads and proved to be the key to the campaign's success. Every major newspaper in Canada ran the print ads (at no cost to the organization). The CBC produced a 12-minute documentary on the See You in Athens Fund, which aired several different times on *The National*. Most importantly, corporate partners couldn't wait to sign up. Molson, Beachcomber Hot Tubs, and the Maple Leaf Alumni joined the Fund, and when MasterCard joined the Fund, it made a $500 000 donation! The campaign is still widely regarded as one of the most successful athletic fund-raising efforts in Canadian history.[88]

The See You in Athens Fund used public relations to create one of the most successful athletic fund-raising efforts in Canadian history.

Major Decisions in Marketing PR

In considering when and how to use MPR, management must establish the marketing objectives, choose the PR messages and vehicles, implement the plan carefully, and evaluate the results. The main tools of MPR are described in Table 18.7.[89]

ESTABLISHING OBJECTIVES MPR can build *awareness* by placing stories in the media to bring attention to a product, service, person, organization, or idea. It can build *credibility* by communicating the message in an editorial context. It can help boost sales-force and dealer enthusiasm with stories about a new product before it is launched. It can hold down *promotion cost* because MPR costs less than direct-mail and media advertising.

Whereas PR practitioners reach their target publics through the mass media, MPR is increasingly borrowing the techniques and technology of direct-response marketing to reach target audience members one-on-one.

CHOOSING MESSAGES AND VEHICLES The MPR manager must identify or develop interesting stories about the product. Suppose a relatively unknown university wants more visibility. The MPR practitioner will search for stories. Do any faculty members have unusual backgrounds, or are any working on unusual projects? Are any new and unusual courses being taught? Are any interesting events taking place on campus? If there are no interesting stories, the MPR practitioner should propose newsworthy events the university could sponsor. Here the challenge is to create news. PR ideas include hosting major academic conventions, inviting expert or celebrity speakers, and developing news conferences. Each event is an opportunity to develop a multitude of stories directed at different audiences.

TABLE 18.7	MAJOR TOOLS IN MARKETING PR

Publications: Companies rely extensively on published materials to reach and influence their target markets. These materials include annual reports, brochures, articles, company newsletters and magazines, and audiovisual materials.

Events: Companies can draw attention to new products or company activities by arranging to reach the target publics with special events like news conferences, seminars, outings, trade shows, exhibits, contests and competitions, and anniversaries.

Sponsorships: Companies can promote their brands and corporate name by sponsoring sports and cultural events and highly regarded causes.

News: One of the major tasks of PR professionals is to find or create favourable news about the company, its products, and its people, and get the media to accept press releases and attend press conferences.

Speeches: Increasingly, company executives must field questions from the media or give talks at trade associations or sales meetings, and these appearances can build the company's image.

Public-Service Activities: Companies can build goodwill by contributing money and time to good causes.

Identity Media: Companies need a visual identity that the public immediately recognizes. The visual identity is carried by company logos, stationery, brochures, signs, business forms, business cards, buildings, uniforms, and dress codes.

IMPLEMENTING THE PLAN AND EVALUATING RESULTS MPR's contribution to the bottom line is difficult to measure because it is used along with other promotional tools. The three most commonly used measures of MPR effectiveness are number of exposures; awareness, comprehension, or attitude change; and contribution to sales and profits.

The easiest measure of MPR effectiveness is the number of *exposures* carried by the media. Publicists supply the client with a clippings book showing all the media that carried news about the product and a summary statement such as the following:

> Media coverage included 3500 column inches of news and photographs in 350 publications with a combined circulation of 79.4 million, 2500 minutes of airtime of 290 radio stations and an estimated audience of 65 million, and 660 minutes of air time on 160 television stations with an estimated audience of 91 million. If this time and space had been purchased at advertising rates, it would have cost $1 047 000.[90]

This measure is not very satisfying because it contains no indication of how many people actually read, heard, or recalled the message and what they thought afterwards; nor does it contain information on the net audience reached, because publications overlap in readership. Because publicity's goal is reach, not frequency, it would be more useful to know the number of unduplicated exposures.

A better measure is the change in product awareness, comprehension, or attitude resulting from the MPR campaign (after allowing for the effect of other promotional tools). For example, how many people recall hearing the news item? How many told others about it (a measure of word of mouth)? How many changed their minds after hearing it?

Sales-and-profit impact is the most satisfactory measure. For example, 9 Lives Cat Food sales increased 43 percent by the end of the Morris the Cat PR campaign. However, advertising and sales promotion had also been stepped up. Suppose total sales increase by $1 500 000, and management estimates that MPR contributed 15 percent of the total increase. Then the return on MPR investment is calculated as follows:

Total sales increase	$1 500 000
Estimated sales increase due to PR (15 percent)	225 000
Contribution margin on product sales (10 percent)	22 500
Total direct cost of MPR program	210 000
Contribution margin added by PR investment	$12 500
Return on MPR investment ($12 500/$10 000)	125%

SUMMARY

1. Advertising is any paid form of nonpersonal presentation and promotion of ideas, goods, or services by an identified sponsor. Advertisers include not only business firms but also charitable, nonprofit, and government agencies.

2. Developing an advertising program is a five-step process: (1) set advertising objectives, (2) establish a budget, (3) choose the advertising message and creative strategy, (4) decide on the media, and (5) evaluate communication and sales effects.

3. Sales promotion consists of a diverse collection of incentive tools, mostly short term, designed to stimulate quicker or greater purchase of particular products or services by consumers or the trade. Sales promotion includes tools for consumer promotion, trade promotion, and business and sales-force promotion (trade shows and conventions, contests for sales reps, and specialty advertising). In using sales promotion, a company must establish its objectives, select the tools, develop the program, pretest the program, implement and control the program, and evaluate the results.

4. Events and experiences are a means to become part of special and more personally relevant moments in consumers' lives. Involvement with events can broaden and deepen the relationship of the sponsor with its target market, but only if managed properly.

5. Public relations (PR) involves a variety of programs designed to promote or protect a company's image or its individual products. Many companies today use marketing public relations (MPR) to support the marketing department in corporate or product promotion and image making. MPR can affect public awareness at a fraction of the cost of advertising and is often much more credible. The main tools of PR are publications, events, news, speeches, public-service activities, and identity media.

APPLICATIONS

Marketing Debate: Has TV Advertising Lost Power?

Long deemed the most successful advertising medium, television advertising is increasingly criticized as being too expensive and, even worse, no longer as effective as it once was. Critics maintain that consumers tune out too many ads by zipping and zapping and that it is difficult to make a strong impression. The future, some claim, is with online advertising. Supporters of TV advertising disagree, contending that the multi-sensory impact of TV is unsurpassed and that no other media option offers the same potential impact.

Take a position: TV advertising has faded in importance *versus* TV advertising is still the most powerful advertising medium.

Marketing Discussion

What are some of your favourite TV ads? Why? How effective are the messages and creative strategies? How are they building brand equity?

Breakthrough Marketing: Captivate Network

Consumers are bombarded with over 3000 advertisements a day, making it harder for companies to expose consumers to their messages. With Captivate Network, many companies now have a way to break through the clutter and reach at least part of their audience. Captivate was founded on the principle that downtime is untapped marketing time. Business people take the elevator multiple times a day and the majority of them ride in silence. What better time to reach consumers than when they have nothing else to do but watch a screen right in front of them?

Captivate has placed over 1300 wireless LCD screens in elevators in prominent office towers across Canada. Over 100 million impressions per year are seen by hard-to reach business professionals in Canada. Each impression can last up to two minutes and, according to a study done by Millward Brown, has an average recall rate of 37 percent due to the low-distraction environment. Eighty-five percent of the audience reached is between the ages of 25 and 54 with average household incomes over $100 000. Captivate's screens are a source of breaking news, weather, information, and—of course—advertising.

The Canadian operation, located in Toronto, is a product of Gannett Co. Inc., a leading international news and information company. The company partners with many credible media sources to get the most up-to-date information to its viewers. It currently has its products in Class A office towers in four major demographic market areas: Toronto, Vancouver, Calgary, and Montreal. In July 2007, it joined the Out-of-Home Marketing Association of Canada to help promote the benefits of out-of-home advertising, such as being able to reach consumers on the go in the fast-paced metropolitan cities.

Blue-chip brands help draw attention to the screens and provide credibility. Some current Captivate advertisers in Canada include VISA, Bell Canada, Expedia, BMW, Fidelity,

CanWest, Alliance Atlantis, WestJet, Rogers, McDonald's, Workopolis, Royal Bank, and Microsoft. These major advertisers are able to reach their target market consistently and effectively through Captivate, and other forms of communication, to reinforce their brands and keep them top-of-mind. Besides advertising on elevator screens, another option for Captivate's clients is synchronized sponsorship, which allows them to run a full-motion ad alongside their sponsored program (e.g., weather or news) for maximum impact. Along with their ad campaign run on TV screens, clients have the option of having a booth or promotional display in lobbies, concourses, or courtyards of buildings to build awareness for their product and brand.

The President and General Manager of Captivate Network, Michael DiFranza, realized the importance of reaching audiences at various touch-points when he came up with the idea for Captivate. The company's innovations provide its clients audiences of attentive, hard-to-reach professionals. The company is planning to expand to more suburban-area businesses in the near future. Larger 40-inch screens on pedestals or wall mounts in building lobbies are now becoming a popular Captivate product since they can tie in with the elevator ads and reinforce advertiser brand names. The continuing success of clients which advertise on Captivate's screens allows the company to line up yet more advertisers and has definitely given new meaning to the term "elevator pitch."

DISCUSSION QUESTIONS

1. What differentiates Captivate's channel of advertising from other more traditional channels?

2. How can Captivate advertise itself to build awareness for its product and brand name? Should or shouldn't Captivate use other media?

3. What dangers does Captivate face by selling ad space in elevator TV screens? At what point do you think consumers will react passively to this form of advertising?

Sources: Captivate Network website, www.captivate.ca (viewed June 13, 2008); Gannett website, gannett.com (viewed June 13, 2008); "Captivate Network Joins Out-Of-Home Marketing Association of Canada (OMAC)," *Canada NewsWire*, July 10, 2007, p. 1; "Captivate Hires New Sales and Marketing Executives," *Canada NewsWire*, November 29, 2007, p. 1.

IN THIS CHAPTER, WE WILL ADDRESS THE FOLLOWING QUESTIONS:

- How can companies use integrated direct marketing for competitive advantage?

- How can companies e-market effectively?

- What decisions do companies face in designing a sales force?

- How do companies manage a sales force efficiently?

- How can salespeople improve selling, negotiating, and relationship marketing skills?

CHAPTER 19

MANAGING PERSONAL COMMUNICATIONS: DIRECT MARKETING AND PERSONAL SELLING

nineteen

In this age of electronic communication, some believe that direct-mail marketing is a thing of the past. Try telling that to Canada Post and its customers. In October 2007, Canada Post decided to focus on its ability to offer direct-marketing services to Canadian businesses, with a streamlined approach customized to each customer's specific needs.

Towards this aim, Canada Post decided to offer products tailored to specific situations that businesses find themselves in when they need to connect to customers. For example, businesses that wish to simply make their consumers aware of their products can use the Unaddressed Admail service, whereas those that wish to encourage repeat sales can choose Addressed Admail to target particular households. Marketers can focus their direct mail using the Householder Counts and Maps services which provide detailed information on the households, businesses, and farms in a given area. To get even more "bang" out of their direct-mail bucks, direct marketers can use the GeoPost Plus service to target the best prospects in an area and choose the most appropriate delivery route. These are just some of the many services Canada Post offers businesses to help them get the most out of their direct-mail campaigns. Canada Post even offers scented direct-mail cards to appeal to consumers' sense of smell.

Canadian businesses have responded to these offerings positively, making this a win-win situation for all involved. In 2007, Canada Post realized $1.404 billion in revenues from its direct marketing services, an increase of 7 percent from the previous year. This represented 23.6 percent of Canada Post's total revenue for the year. Many of Canada Post's direct marketing clients are also seeing improved performance after using its services. Bell Canada realized a 250-percent increase in sales following its direct-mail campaign to get Quebec consumers to switch to Bell's communication services. Salisbury House used Canada Post to mail coupons to 266 000 households in Winnipeg and saw an 8-percent increase in sales as a result. Canadian fashion giant Holt Renfrew launched a new menswear book through Canada Post's new system and received a response rate of 29 percent. To put the success of this campaign in perspective, a normal mailer tends to get response rates of 1 to 3 percent. Part of Canada Post's success is that more mail is making it into consumer households instead of being considered "junk" and thrown away even before being read.

>>>

Canada Post's website allows clients to customize their mailers online. The website offers a Direct Marketing Online option, a step-by-step system to help clients get the most out of their mailings. This integrated approach allows companies such as Mountain Equipment Co-op (another Canadian company that has seen impressive results through the program) stay consistent with their environmentally-friendly marketing practices. With much of the work being done online, the Direct Marketing Online system helps save paper, something Canada Post is also looking to do with its Green Marketing plan. "Making environmentally responsible decisions is increasingly important from a social, economic, and ethical perspective," says Laurene Cihosky, senior vice-president of Canada Post's Direct Marketing division. "At Canada Post, we're not only committed to finding ways to protect the environment and minimize our carbon footprint, we are also arming consumers and businesses with the tools to make a real and positive impact."

Canada Post has proved that even with changing technology and consumer habits, there is still a niche for direct marketing . . . and a way to make it financially fruitful if done right.

Sources: "Canada Post Launches Nationwide Green Marketing Program," *Canada Newswire*, May 13, 2008; "Market with Direct Mail–Case Studies and Testimonials" *Canada Post Corporation*, www.canadapost.ca/business/prodserv/mdm/case-e.asp; "Connecting With Customers–Direct Marketing," *Canada Post Corporation Annual Report 2007*, p. 1, www.canadapost.ca/corporate/about/annual_report/cwc-dmarket1-e.html; "Welcome To Direct Marketing Online," *Canada Post Corporation*, www.directmarketingonline.ca/en/home.html; "CMA Marketing FAQs – Direct Mail: Canadian Marketing Association" *Canadian Marketing Association*, www.the-cma.org/?WCE=C=47%7CK=225534 (all viewed June 14, 2008).

Personalizing communications—and saying and doing the right thing to the right person at the right time—is critical. In this chapter, we consider how companies personalize their marketing communications to have more of an impact. We begin by evaluating direct marketing; then we consider personal selling and the sales force.

DIRECT MARKETING

Direct marketing is the use of consumer-direct (CD) channels to reach and deliver goods and services to customers without using marketing intermediaries. These channels include direct mail, catalogues, telemarketing, interactive TV, kiosks, websites, and mobile devices.

Direct marketers seek a measurable response, typically a customer order. This is sometimes called **direct-order marketing**. Today, many direct marketers use direct marketing to build long-term relationships with customers.[1] They send birthday cards, information materials, or small premiums to certain customers. Airlines, hotels, and other businesses build strong customer relationships through frequency award programs and club programs.

Direct marketing is one of the fastest growing avenues for serving customers. More and more business marketers have turned to direct mail and telemarketing in response to the high and increasing costs of reaching business markets through a sales force. Figure 19.1 provides a breakdown of the various types of direct marketing.

One of the most pervasive loyalty marketing programs in Canada is the AIR MILES program run by the Loyalty Group. Over 100 sponsor firms belong to the program, which allows a whopping 70 percent of Canadian households to collect points they can use towards travel and other reward options. Consider how *Chatelaine* magazine used a direct marketing campaign centred on the AIR MILES program to build new relationships and strengthen existing ones:

Chatelaine and the AIR MILES® Reward Program

Using a genie-in-a-bottle concept as the basis of its "What Women Want" contest, *Chatelaine* asked women to make three wishes. Choices included "Buns of steel" and "Room full of orchids." In return for sharing their wishes, women could win prizes as high as 50 000 AIR MILES reward miles—enough for five flights around the world or 2000 movie

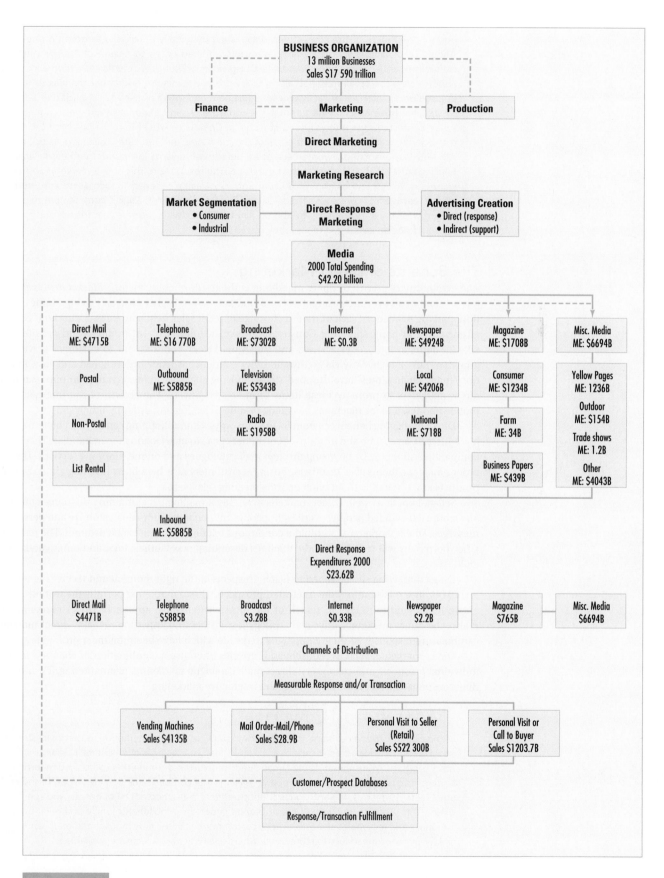

BUSINESS ORGANIZATION
13 million Businesses
Sales $17 590 trillion

Finance --- **Marketing** --- **Production**

Direct Marketing

Marketing Research

Market Segmentation
• Consumer
• Industrial

Direct Response Marketing

Advertising Creation
• Direct (response)
• Indirect (support)

Media
2000 Total Spending
$42.20 billion

| Direct Mail ME: $4715B | Telephone ME: $16 770B | Broadcast ME: $7302B | Internet ME: $0.3B | Newspaper ME: $4924B | Magazine ME: $1708B | Misc. Media ME: $6694B |

Postal — Outbound ME: $5885B — Television ME: $5343B — Local ME: $4206B — Consumer ME: $1234B — Yellow Pages ME: 1236B

Non-Postal — Radio ME: $1958B — National ME: $718B — Farm ME: 34B — Outdoor ME: $154B

List Rental — Business Papers ME: $439B — Trade shows ME: 1.2B

Other ME: $4043B

Inbound ME: $5885B

Direct Response Expenditures 2000 $23.62B

| Direct Mail $4471B | Telephone $5885B | Broadcast $3.28B | Internet $0.33B | Newspaper $2.2B | Magazine $765B | Misc. Media $6694B |

Channels of Distribution

Measurable Response and/or Transaction

| Vending Machines Sales $4135B | Mail Order-Mail/Phone Sales $28.9B | Personal Visit to Seller (Retail) Sales $522 300B | Personal Visit or Call to Buyer Sales $1203.7B |

Customer/Prospect Databases

Response/Transaction Fulfillment

FIGURE 19.1

Direct Marketing Flow Chart

Source: Adapted from *Direct Marketing* magazine, 224 Seventh Street, Garden City, New York, 11530-5771.

passes. Awareness of the contest was established by initially emailing a targeted group of AIR MILES collectors and Chatelaine.com users who had opted to receive online communication from either of the two companies. Using viral marketing, recipients were then encouraged to pass the email message along to friends and family for additional chances to win. In addition to information at www.chatelaine.com and www.airmiles.ca, a magazine ad in *Chatelaine* drove users online to enter the contest and send the email message to a friend. When contestants went to the contest website, *Chatelaine* was able to make a brand statement, show women the different areas of the magazine, and educate consumers as to how AIR MILES sponsors help women achieve a breadth of rewards faster and more easily while fulfilling some of their wishes at the same time. The response to this online marketing effort was huge: 98 000 entries from 65 000 entrants. Chatelaine believed its success resulted from what it learned from previous efforts. Given *Chatelaine*'s and AIR MILES' commitment to privacy, it was very important to "raise it up a notch" and clearly promise that friends and family would not be contacted unless they opted in.[2]

The Benefits of Direct Marketing

The extraordinary growth of direct marketing is the result of many factors. *Market demassification* has resulted in an ever-increasing number of market niches. Higher costs of driving, traffic congestion, parking headaches, lack of time, a shortage of retail sales help, and lines at checkout counters all encourage at-home shopping. Consumers appreciate toll-free phone numbers and websites available 24 hours a day, 7 days a week, and direct marketers' commitment to customer service. The growth of next-day delivery via FedEx and other couriers has made ordering fast and easy. In addition, many chain stores have dropped slower-moving specialty items, creating an opportunity for direct marketers to promote these items to interested buyers. The growth of the Internet, email, mobile phones, and fax machines has made product selection and ordering much simpler.

Direct marketing benefits customers in many ways. Home shopping can be fun, convenient, and hassle-free. It saves time and introduces consumers to a larger selection of merchandise. They can do comparative shopping by browsing through mail catalogues and online shopping services. They can order goods for themselves or others. Business customers also benefit by learning about available products and services without tying up time meeting salespeople.

Sellers benefit as well. Direct marketers can buy a mailing list containing the names of almost any group: left-handed people, overweight people, millionaires. They can customize and personalize messages. Direct marketers can build a continuous relationship with each customer. The parents of a newborn baby will receive periodic mailings describing new clothes, toys, and other goods as the child grows.

Direct marketing can be timed to reach prospects at the right moment and receive higher readership because it is sent to more interested prospects. Direct marketing permits the testing of alternative media and messages in search of the most cost-effective approach. Direct marketing also makes the direct marketer's offer and strategy less visible to competitors. Finally, direct marketers can measure responses to their campaigns to decide which have been the most profitable.

Direct marketers such as Moosehead Breweries often use a combination of channels to reach individual prospects and customers: direct mail, catalogue marketing, telemarketing, TV and other direct-response media, kiosk marketing, and interactive marketing.

Moosehead Breweries

Moosehead Breweries of Saint John, New Brunswick, uses direct marketing as part of its strategy. Having developed an extensive consumer database, as part of an overall customer intimacy program, Moosehead is able to use direct mail and email marketing campaigns to further engage its customers. Consumers receive mailings that contain thank-you messages, birthday and holiday greetings, reward/bonus announcements, advanced notice of events, and special offers. The program involves all major brands under the Moosehead family umbrella, both nationally and regionally, and encourages customers to visit the new Moosehead merchandise site (www.mooseheadcountrystore.com), where a variety of products are available.[3]

Direct Mail

Direct-mail marketing involves sending an offer, announcement, reminder, or other item to a person. Using highly selective mailing lists, direct marketers send out millions of mail pieces each year—letters,

Moosehead Breweries uses direct-mail campaigns both regionally and nationally to engage its customers.

flyers, foldouts, and other "salespeople with wings." Some direct marketers mail audiotapes, videotapes, CDs, and DVDs to prospects and customers.

Direct mail is a popular medium because it permits target market selectivity, can be personalized, is flexible, and allows early testing and response measurement. Although the cost per thousand people reached is higher than with mass media, the people reached are much better prospects. Direct mail may be paper-based and handled by Canada Post, telegraphic services, or for-profit mail carriers such as FedEx, Purolator, and UPS. Alternatively, marketers may employ fax, email, or voice mail to sell directly.

Direct-mail marketing has passed through a number of stages:

- *"Carpet bombing."* Direct mailers gather or buy as many names as possible and send out a mass mailing. Usually the response rate is very low.

- *Database marketing.* Direct marketers mine a database to identify prospects who would have the most interest in an offer.

- *Interactive marketing.* Direct marketers provide recipients a telephone number and web address and sometimes offer the ability to print coupons from a website. Recipients can contact the company with questions. The company uses the interaction as an opportunity to up-sell, cross-sell, and deepen the relationship.

- *Real-time personalized marketing.* Direct marketers know enough about each customer to customize and personalize an offer and message.

- *Lifetime value marketing.* Direct marketers develop a plan for lifetime marketing to each valuable customer, based on knowledge of life events and transitions.

One company long recognized for its strong, beneficial focus on customers is Mountain Equipment Co-op (MEC), which sells outdoor/casual clothing and equipment through mail order, online catalogues, and retail stores. To maximize customer satisfaction, MEC has an unequivocal, 100 percent "rock solid" guarantee for all purchases. MEC goes one step further, however. Unlike most retailers, it also guarantees the product selection advice offered through its catalogue, website, and staff; if an item you've purchased based on this advice turns out to be unsuitable, you can bring it back!

In constructing an effective direct-mail campaign, direct marketers must decide on their objectives, target markets, and prospects; elements of the offer; means of testing the campaign; and measures of campaign success. Consider how Unilever implemented a direct marketing campaign:

Unilever Canada: Knorr Frozen Entrées

To overcome preconceived ideas about the taste of frozen dinners, Knorr decided to adopt a somewhat controversial message to drive home the idea that its dinners are not your typical frozen food. Following their "Not Your Mom's F@#%*N Dinners" television campaign, which bleeped out the word "frozen," Knorr implemented a direct-mail campaign to persuade its target market to try the new product. The target consisted of people who had a positive attitude towards cooking but were unable to cook due to time constraints. Using consumer database information, Knorr targeted tier 1, those closest to the target profile, by offering them a coupon for a free frozen entrée. The next closest matches were mailed less valuable coupons, and the bottom tier was emailed a coupon for $1 off an entrée. To catch the attention of consumers, the front of the direct mail showed a tasty piece of shrimp with fresh basil and the caption "To reveal the full message, put this in your freezer. F_____N delicious." With a 50-percent coupon redemption rate in tier 1, the campaign was so successful that Knorr had to hold back some of its mailings to keep stores from running out of stock.[4]

OBJECTIVES Most direct marketers aim to receive an order from prospects. A campaign's success is judged by its response rate. An order-response rate of 2 percent is normally considered good, although this number varies with product category and price. Direct mail can achieve other communication objectives as well, such as producing prospect leads, strengthening customer relationships, informing and educating customers, reminding customers of offers, and reinforcing recent customer purchase decisions.

TARGET MARKETS AND PROSPECTS Direct marketers need to identify the characteristics of prospects and customers who are most able, willing, and ready to buy. Most direct marketers apply the R-F-M formula (*recency, frequency, monetary amount*) for rating and selecting customers. For any proposed offering, the company selects customers according to how much time has passed since their last purchase, how many times they have purchased, and how much they have spent since becoming a customer. Suppose the company is offering a leather jacket. It might make this offer to customers who made their last purchase between 30 and 60 days ago, who make three to six purchases a year, and who have spent at least $100 since becoming customers. Points are established for varying R-F-M levels, and each customer is scored. The higher the score, the more attractive the customer. The mailing is sent only to the most attractive customers.[5]

Prospects can also be identified on the basis of such variables as age, sex, income, education, and previous mail-order purchases. Occasions provide a good departure point for segmentation. New parents will be in the market for baby clothes and baby toys; students entering university will buy computers and small television sets; newlyweds will be looking for housing, furniture, appliances, and bank loans. Another useful segmentation variable is consumer lifestyle or "passion" groups, such as computer buffs, cooking buffs, and outdoor buffs. For business markets, Dun & Bradstreet operates an information service that provides a wealth of data.

In B2B direct marketing, the prospect is often not an individual but a group of people or a committee that includes both decision makers and multiple decision influencers. See "Marketing Memo: When Your Customer Is a Committee" for tips on crafting a direct-mail campaign aimed at business buyers.

Once the target market is defined, the direct marketer needs to obtain specific names. The company's best prospects are customers who have bought its products in the past. Additional names can be obtained by advertising some free offer. The direct marketer can also buy lists of names from list brokers, but these lists often have problems, including name duplication, incomplete data, and obsolete addresses. The better lists include overlays of demographic and psychographic information. Direct marketers typically buy and test a sample before buying more names from the same list.

OFFER ELEMENTS Nash sees the offer strategy as consisting of five elements—the *product*, the *offer*, the *medium*, the *distribution method*, and the *creative strategy*.[6] Fortunately, all of these elements can be tested.

In addition to these elements, the direct-mail marketer has to decide on five components of the mailing itself: the outside envelope, sales letter, circular, reply form, and reply envelope. Here are some findings:

1. The outside envelope will be more effective if it contains an illustration, preferably in colour, or a catchy reason to open the envelope, such as the announcement of a contest, premium, or benefit. Envelopes are more effective when they contain a colourful commemorative stamp, when the address is hand-typed or handwritten, and when the envelope differs in size or shape from standard envelopes.[7]

2. The sales letter should use a personal salutation and start with a headline in bold type. The letter should be printed on good-quality paper and be brief. A computer-typed letter usually

---

| MARKETING MEMO | WHEN YOUR CUSTOMER IS A COMMITTEE |

One of the many advantages of database marketing and direct mail is that they allow you to tailor format, offer, and sell messages to the target audience(s). Business marketers can create a series of interrelated and reinforced mailings to decision makers and decision influencers. Here are some tips for increasing success in selling to a customer-by-committee:

- When creating lead generation and follow-up mailings, remember that most business mailings are screened once, twice, or even more before reaching your targeted audience.
- Plan and budget for a series of mailings to each of your customer-by-committee members. Timing and multiple exposures are critical in reaching these audiences.
- Whenever possible, mail to individuals by name and title. Using the title helps the in-office mail screener reroute your mailing if the individual addressed has moved on to another job.
- Do not necessarily use the same format and size for reaching all your targeted audiences. A more expensive-looking envelope may reach the president or CEO, but it may be equally effective to use a less expensive, less personal format to reach other decision influencers.
- Tell your customer-by-committee that you are communicating with others in the organization.
- Make your decision influencers feel important. They can be your biggest advocates.
- When communicating with different audiences, make sure you anticipate—and address—their individual buying objectives and objections.
- When your database or mailing lists cannot help you reach all the key people, ask the individual you are addressing to pass along your information.
- When doing a lead-generation mailing, make sure to ask for the names and titles of those who might be interested and involved in the buying decision. Enter this information into your database.
- Even though it may seem like a lot of work (and expense) to write different versions of the same letter and create different offers, there is a big payoff. The final decision maker may be interested in having a payback calculated, but others may be interested in day-to-day benefits such as safety, convenience, and time savings. Tailor your offer to your targets.

Source: Adapted from Pat Friesen, "When Your Customer Is a Committee," *Target Marketing* (August 1998): 40.

---

outperforms a handwritten letter, and the presence of a pithy P.S. increases the response rate, as does the signature of someone whose title is important.

3. In most cases, a colourful circular accompanying the letter will increase the response rate by more than its cost.

4. Direct mailers should feature a toll-free number and web address. Coupons should be available at the website.

5. The inclusion of a postage-free reply envelope will dramatically increase the response rate.

Direct mail should be followed up by an email, which is less expensive and less intrusive than a telemarketing call.

TESTING ELEMENTS One of the great advantages of direct marketing is the ability to test, under real marketplace conditions, different elements of an offer strategy, such as products, product features, copy platform, mailer type, envelope, prices, or mailing lists.

Direct marketers must remember that response rates typically understate a campaign's long-term impact. Suppose only 2 percent of the recipients who receive a direct-mail piece advertising Samsonite luggage place an order. A much larger percentage became aware of the product (direct mail has high readership), and some percentage may have formed an intention to buy at a later date (either by mail or at a retail outlet). Furthermore, some of them may mention Samsonite luggage to others as a result of the direct-mail piece. To derive a more comprehensive estimate of the promotion's impact, some companies are measuring direct marketing's impact on awareness, intention to buy, and word of mouth.

MEASURING CAMPAIGN SUCCESS: LIFETIME VALUE By adding up the planned campaign costs, the direct marketer can figure out in advance the needed break-even response rate. This rate must be net of returned merchandise and bad debts. Returned merchandise can kill an otherwise effective campaign. The direct marketer needs to analyze the main causes of returned merchandise (late shipment, defective merchandise, damage in transit, not as advertised, incorrect order fulfillment).

By carefully analyzing past campaigns, direct marketers can steadily improve performance. Even when a specific campaign fails to break even in the short run, it can still be profitable in the long run if customer lifetime is factored in (see Chapter 5). A customer's ultimate value is not revealed by a purchase response to a particular mailing. Rather, it is the expected profit made on all future purchases net of customer acquisition and maintenance costs. For an average customer, one would calculate the average customer longevity, average customer annual expenditure, and average gross margin, minus the average cost of customer acquisition and maintenance (properly discounted for the opportunity cost of money).[8] However, some marketers such as The Halliburton House Inn may use rather informal and subjective measures of success.

The Halliburton House Inn

The Halliburton House Inn is a relatively small boutique hotel situated in downtown Halifax, Nova Scotia. With 29 individually appointed rooms in three heritage townhouses, the hotel provides a unique experience in accommodations, maintaining a cozy bed and breakfast atmosphere. Managed by a husband and wife team, the hotel has a relatively small promotion budget and relies on direct marketing to promote itself to its customers. Quarterly mailings are sent out to past guests highlighting new promotions and offering special package deals. One of the mail-outs included a Valentine's Day package that included a one-night stay with breakfast and parking, a three-course dinner for two, and tickets to the local theatre, all for $249. Owner Robert Pretty doesn't have a sophisticated tracking system, but he believes that his direct marketing effort does generate a response, based on how much the phone rings during the days after the mailing goes out.[9]

Catalogue Marketing

In catalogue marketing, companies may send full-line merchandise catalogues, specialty consumer catalogues, and business catalogues, usually in print form but also sometimes as CDs, videos, or online. Zellers and Sears send general merchandise catalogues. Victoria's Secret sends specialty clothing catalogues to the upper-middle-class market. Through its catalogues, Avon sells cosmetics and IKEA sells furniture. Many of these direct marketers have found that combining catalogues and websites can be an effective way to sell. Thousands of small businesses also issue specialty catalogues. Large businesses such as Staples, Merck, and others send catalogues to business prospects and customers.

Catalogue marketing has a long history in Canada. In the 1880s, Canadians living in isolated regions waited anxiously for catalogues to arrive. So beloved was the Eaton's catalogue, for example, that it was affectionately known by many nicknames, including the "Bible" and the "Wish Book."[10] In light of rising paper costs and sluggish consumer spending in the United States, many American catalogue marketers such as Williams-Sonoma, L. L. Bean, and Neiman Marcus are trimming down their mailing lists in an attempt to weed out those who will not make purchases.

Williams–Sonoma

The company that produces six catalogues including those of Pottery Barn, Williams-Sonoma, and West Elm pioneered using ZIP codes to better target its customers. In 2007, the company mailed out 393 million catalogues and it aims to cut that circulation by 10 to 15 percent resulting in a cost savings of nearly US$40 million—without hurting sales. Increased costs and slowed consumer spending motivated Williams-Sonoma Inc. to use aggregated data about ZIP codes to develop better mailing lists. Using diverse variables such as housing prices, credit scores, percentage of European automobiles in the area, and the proportion of the population that is four years old or less, Williams-Sonoma analyzes the likelihood that a household will make a purchase and therefore makes the most out of its direct mailing campaigns by not mailing catalogues to those households with a low likelihood of purchase.[11]

Catalogues are a huge business in North America. The Direct Marketing Association estimates that there are currently up to 10 000 mail-order catalogues of all kinds. *Canadian Gardening*, for example, lists over 500 catalogues for its gardening enthusiasts. However, the number of catalogues streaming into consumers' mailboxes is not the only measure of growth in this business. Cataloguers have gotten a big boost from the Internet—about three-quarters of catalogue companies present merchandise and take orders over the Internet. Some catalogue marketers, like Sears, are integrating their print editions with online editions. Others, like Nike Canada, are totally replacing their print catalogues with virtual versions.

Market research conducted by Canada Post suggests, however, that Canadians overwhelmingly prefer hard-copy catalogues to online versions, and would rather receive catalogues through the mail than pick them up from a store.[12] The success of a catalogue business also depends on the company's ability to manage its customer lists carefully so that there is little duplication or bad debts, to control its inventory carefully, to offer quality merchandise so that returns are low, and to project a distinctive image. See how one Canadian company has achieved success with its catalogues:

Awesome Ewe

Launched in 1999, this online mail-order business, which sells fine wool to the knitting community, began simply as a test site for a family of e-commerce software that Len and Marge Stalker developed. The site originally featured 4000 "brand-recognized" products aimed at knitters. Today Awesome Ewe's product line has grown to 18 000 products. Clients can purchase wool and patterns or redeem gift certificates in a couple of clicks. The company's email newsletter has 9000 opt-in subscribers, and the website gets between 500 and 900 unique visitors a day. Stalker's online-survey response rate from opt-in subscribers is 7 to 10 percent. The site was so successful that it was featured as a case study on B.C.'s Ministry of Small Business and Economic Development's eBusiness Connection website.[13]

Global consumers in Asia and Europe are catching on to the catalogue craze. In the 1990s, North American catalogue companies such as L.L. Bean, MEC, Eddie Bauer, and Patagonia began setting up operations in Europe and Japan—and with great success. In just a few years, catalogues have won 5 percent of the US$20 billion Japanese mail-order catalogue market. A full 90 percent of L.L. Bean's international sales come from Japan.

Business marketers are making inroads as well. Sales to overseas (mainly European) markets have driven earnings increases at Viking Office Products and computer and network equipment cataloguer Black Box Corporation. Viking has had success in Europe because it has fewer superstores and is very receptive to mail order. Black Box owes much of its international growth to its customer service policies, which are unmatched in Europe.[14] By putting their entire catalogues online, catalogue companies have better access to global consumers than ever before and save considerable printing and mailing costs in the process. By clicking on the appropriate icon, international shoppers can use the Canadian-based Tilley Endurables website (www.tilley.com) to order products using their own currencies.

Telemarketing

Telemarketing is the use of the telephone and call centres to attract prospects, sell to existing customers, and provide service by taking orders and answering questions. Telemarketing helps companies increase revenue, reduce selling costs, and improve customer satisfaction.

Companies use call centres for *inbound telemarketing* (receiving calls from customers) and *outbound telemarketing* (initiating calls to prospects and customers). In fact, companies carry out four types of telemarketing:

- *Telesales.* Taking orders from catalogues or ads and also doing outbound calling. They can cross-sell the company's other products, upgrade orders, introduce new products, open new accounts, and reactivate former accounts.
- *Telecoverage.* Calling customers to maintain and nurture key account relationships and give more attention to neglected accounts.
- *Teleprospecting.* Generating and qualifying new leads for closure by another sales channel.
- *Customer service and technical support.* Answering service and technical questions.

Telemarketing is increasingly used in business as well as consumer marketing. Raleigh Bicycles uses telemarketing to reduce the amount of personal selling needed for contacting its dealers. In the first year, sales-force travel costs were reduced by 50 percent and sales in a single quarter went up 34 percent. With the increased diffusion of online communication, telemarketing will increasingly replace or supplement more expensive field sales calls. An increasing number of salespeople have made five- and six-figure sales without ever meeting the customer face-to-face. Effective telemarketing depends on choosing the right telemarketers, training them well, and providing performance incentives.

Telemarketing is a major industry in Canada, employing more than 270 000 people across the country. Marketers spend approximately twice as much on telemarketing as they do on advertising, which isn't surprising since it generates approximately $16 billion in sales. Despite its importance as a major direct-marketing tool, it can be intrusive. Many Canadians have run out of patience with some unethical telemarketers which do not follow the code of ethics of the Canadian Marketing Association (CMA). In response, the Canadian Radio-television and Telecommunications Commission (CRTC) developed new regulations in 2004 to help Canadians ward off unwanted telemarketing and faxes. Among the regulations is a requirement that telemarketers give their name and identify their organization before they begin their sales pitch, and give a toll-free telephone number that people can call with questions or complaints. Companies must also maintain lists of people who don't want their numbers called. In September of 2008, the CRTC also implemented a national "Do Not Call" list similar to the one previously established in the United States. Even though the CMA had maintained a voluntary "Do Not Contact" service list since 1988, many agreed that a national list was needed since the CMA's list applied only to member companies and was not legally binding.[15]

Other Media for Direct-Response Marketing

Direct marketers use all the major media to make offers to potential buyers. Newspapers and magazines carry abundant print ads offering books, articles of clothing, appliances, vacations, and other goods and services that individuals can order by dialing a toll-free number. Radio ads present offers to listeners 24 hours a day.

TELEVISION Television is used by direct marketers in several ways:

1. *Direct-response advertising.* Some companies prepare 30- and 60-minute infomercials that attempt to combine the sell of commercials with the draw of educational information and entertainment. *Infomercials* can be seen as a cross between a sales call and a television ad and cost roughly US$250 000 to US$500 000 to make. A number of people (e.g., Tony Robbins, Victoria Principal, and Kathy Smith) have become famous with late-night channel switchers. Increasingly, companies selling products that are complicated, technologically advanced, or simply require a great deal of explanation are turning to infomercials (Callaway Golf, Carnival Cruises, Mercedes, Microsoft, Philips Electronics, Universal Studios, and even the online job search site Monster.com).[16] They share the product's story and benefits with millions of additional prospects at a cost-per-lead or cost-per-order that usually matches or beats that of direct mail or print ads.[17]

2. *At-home shopping channels.* Some television channels are dedicated to selling goods and services. On the Shopping Channel, which broadcasts 24 hours a day, the program's hosts offer bargain prices on such products as clothing, jewellery, lamps, collectible dolls, and power tools. Viewers call in orders on a toll-free number and receive delivery within 48 hours. Millions of adults watch home-shopping programs, and close to half of them buy merchandise.

3. *Videotext and interactive TV.* The consumer's TV set is linked to a seller's catalogue by cable or telephone lines. Consumers can place orders via a special keyboard device connected to the system. Much research is now going on to combine TV, telephones, and computers into interactive TV.

Consider how a hospital has effectively used direct-response marketing:

The Hospital for Sick Children Foundation

The fund-raising arm of Toronto's Hospital for Sick Children uses direct marketing as a cornerstone of its overall marketing strategy. Recently, it began making direct-response television (DRTV) a key part of the foundation's efforts, which typically has fund-raising goals in excess of $50 million. The foundation created a one-hour DRTV program called *Place of*

Miracles: Inside the Hospital for Sick Children in order to boost support and raise funds for its Miracle Club, a monthly donation program. The program, produced by EagleCom in Toronto, used a combination of individual patient stories and appeals from Canadian celebrities to support the hospital. The one-hour program (along with its half-hour version and three two-minute segments) has had considerable success: 61 percent of callers pledged donations, compared to the average for DRTV efforts of 45 percent.[18]

KIOSK MARKETING   A kiosk is a small building or structure that might house a selling or information unit. The name describes newsstands, refreshment stands, and freestanding carts whose vendors sell watches, costume jewellery, and other items. The carts appear in bus and rail stations and along aisles in a mall. The term also covers computer-linked vending machines and "customer-order-placing machines" in stores (as in the Curiosk example, below), airports, and other locations. All of these are direct-selling tools. Some marketers have adapted the self-service feature of kiosks to their businesses. McDonald's found that customers who used its kiosks to order spent 30 percent more per order.[19]

Curiosk Marketing Solutions

In 2007, Curiosk Marketing Solutions Inc. launched its new in-store touch-screen wine kiosk at a downtown Toronto wine store. At the kiosk, consumers can scan the barcode on a bottle of wine to bring up a display of detailed product information. In addition, consumers are given the option to create a personalized greeting card that fits over the neck of the bottle. The card can include information about their wine selection such as tasting information, food pairing suggestions, and cellaring recommendations. The kiosk then allows consumers to print and pay for the card with their credit card. Curiosk expects that the convenience and customization offered by its system at a low cost will allow it to rapidly penetrate the North American retail wine market.[20]

INTERACTIVE MARKETING

The newest channels for direct marketing are electronic.[21] The Internet provides marketers and consumers with opportunities for much greater *interaction* and *individualization*. Companies in the past would send standard media—magazines, newsletters, ads—to everyone. Today, companies such as Sephora can send individualized content and consumers themselves can further individualize the content. Companies can now interact and have dialogue with much larger groups than ever before.

To learn how Stella Artois uses interactive marketing to succeed in Belgium, visit www.pearsoned.co.uk/marketingmanagementeurope.

Sephora and Acxiom

The specialty beauty retailer Sephora teamed up with interactive marketing services company Acxiom Corporation to develop personalized emails for its customers, particularly for the members of its growing loyalty program, Beauty Insider. Operating over 700 stores worldwide, of which nearly 200 are in the United States and Canada, Sephora also retails over 14 000 beauty products through its website, sephora.com. Acxiom's technology has allowed Sephora to combine traditional direct-marketing techniques with online marketing to deliver targeted and relevant content to its vast business and consumer base. A single email campaign will have numerous variations, offering each customer tailored product recommendations and special offers based on previously provided information such as eye and hair colour, skin type, and past purchases.[22]

The exchange process in the age of information, however, has become increasingly customer-initiated and customer-controlled. Marketers and their representatives must wait until customers agree to participate in the exchange. Even after marketers enter the exchange process, customers define the rules of engagement and insulate themselves with the help of agents and intermediaries if they so choose. Customers define what information they need, what offerings they are interested in, and what prices they are willing to pay.[23]

MARKETING MEMO | SEGMENTING TECH USERS

It is easy to exaggerate the pervasiveness of technology, yet not all consumers are plugged in. The Pew Internet and American Life Project published in 2007 found that U.S. adults fall into three groups:

a. 31 percent are heavy technology users
b. 20 percent are moderate technology users
c. 49 percent only occasionally use technology such as the Internet or cell phone

The study also revealed divisions within each group. The high-tech elites, for instance, are almost evenly split into:

1. *Omnivores* (8 percent), who fully embrace technology and express themselves creatively through blogs and personal webpages,
2. *Connectors* (7 percent), who see the Internet and cell phones as effective communications tools,
3. *Productivity Enhancers* (8 percent), who consider technology as a necessary way to efficiently keep up with their jobs and learn new things, and
4. *Lacklustre Veterans* (8 percent), who use the Internet frequently and cell phones much less, but aren't thrilled by either.

The 20 percent of moderate users are evenly divided into *Mobile Centrics*, who primarily use cell phones for voice and text messaging but use the Internet much less, and the *Connected but Hassled*, who have invested significantly in technology but find the connectivity intrusive and the information burdensome.

The 49 percent who rarely use technology are segmented into *Inexperienced Experimenters* (8 percent), those who use technology occasionally but would use it more if they had more experience, *Light but Satisfied* (15 percent), those for whom technology does not play a central role in life, *Indifferents* (11 percent), who find technology annoying, and *Off the Network* (15 percent), those who use neither the Internet nor cell phones and are quite content with older forms of communication.

Sources: Anick Jesdanun, "Survey Defines Split in Technology Use," *Associated Press*, May 6, 2007, www.usatoday.com/tech/webguide/internetlife/2007-05-06-survey-technology_N.htm (viewed August 20, 2008); John B. Horrigan, "A Typology of Information and Communication Technology Users," *Pew Internet & American Life Project*, May 7, 2007.

Electronic marketing is showing explosive growth. According to 24/7 Canada, Internet ad spending is expected to grow the fastest of all advertising media, reaching $306 million in 2008, an increase of 15.5 percent over 2003 figures.[24] More than half of online Canadians have broadband capabilities (a rate that outpaces that of the U.S.) necessary for swift downloading of dense digital video and music files.[25] These new capabilities will spur the growth of rich media ads that combine animation, video, and sound with interactive features. Although this market has grown significantly, online marketers have to recognize that Internet users are not all alike. People have different attitudes towards the Internet and different expectations from it. "Marketing Memo: Segmenting Tech Users" profiles different groups and their usage of technology.

Benefits of Interactive Marketing

Interactive marketing offers many unique benefits.[26] It is highly accountable and its effects can be easily traced. Eddie Bauer cut its marketing cost per sale by 74 percent by concentrating on higher-performing ads.[27] The Web offers the advantage of "contextual placements." Marketers can buy ads from sites that are related to their offerings, as well as place advertising based on contextual keywords from online search outfits like Google. In this way, the Web can reach people when they have actually started the buying process. Light consumers of other media, especially television, can also be reached online, and the Web is especially effective at reaching people during the day. Young, high-income, high-education consumers' total online media consumption exceeds that of TV.[28]

Designing an Attractive Website

Clearly, all companies need to consider and evaluate e-marketing and e-purchasing opportunities. A key challenge is designing a site that is attractive on first viewing and interesting enough to encourage repeat visits.

Rayport and Jaworski have proposed that effective websites feature seven design elements that they call the 7Cs:[29]

- *Context*—Layout and design
- *Content*—Text, pictures, sound, and video the site contains
- *Community*—How the site enables user-to-user communication
- *Customization*—Site's ability to tailor itself to different users or to allow users to personalize the site
- *Communication*—How the site enables site-to-user, user-to-site, or two-way communication
- *Connection*—Degree that the site is linked to other sites
- *Commerce*—Site's capabilities to enable commercial transactions

To encourage repeated visits, companies need to pay special attention to context and content factors and also embrace another "C"—constant change.[30]

Visitors will judge a site's performance on its ease of use and its physical attractiveness. Ease-of-use breaks down into three attributes: (1) the website downloads quickly, (2) the first page is easy to understand, and (3) the visitor finds it easy to navigate to other pages that open quickly. Physical attractiveness is determined by the following factors: (1) the individual pages are clean looking and not overly crammed with content, (2) the typefaces and font sizes are very readable, and (3) the site makes good use of colour (and sound).

Context factors facilitate repeated visits, but they do not ensure that this happens. Returning to a site depends on content. The content must be interesting, useful, and continuously changing. Certain types of content function well to attract first-time visitors and to bring them back again: (1) deep information with links to related sites, (2) changing news of interest, (3) changing free offers to visitors, (4) contests and sweepstakes, (5) humour and jokes, and (6) games.

Placing Ads and Promotion Online

A company has to decide which forms of Internet advertising will be most cost-effective in achieving advertising objectives. **Banner ads** are small rectangular boxes containing text and images. Companies pay to place banner ads on relevant websites. The larger the audience reached, the more the placement will cost. Some banners on websites are not paid for, but instead are accepted on a barter basis. In the early days of the Internet, viewers clicked on roughly 2 to 3 percent of the banner ads they saw, but that percentage quickly plummeted and advertisers began to explore other forms of communication.

Many companies get their name on the Internet by sponsoring special content on websites that carry news, financial information, and so on. **Sponsorships** are best placed in well-targeted sites where they can offer relevant information or service. The sponsor pays for showing the content and in turn receives acknowledgment as the sponsor of that particular service on the website.

A **microsite** is a limited area on the Web managed and paid for by an external advertiser or company. Microsites are particularly relevant for companies selling low-interest products such as insurance. People rarely visit an insurance company's website. However, the insurance company can create a microsite on used-car sites that offers advice for buyers of used cars and at the same time offers a good insurance deal.

Interstitials are advertisements, often with video or animation, that pop up between changes on a website. Ads for Johnson & Johnson's Tylenol headache reliever pop up on brokers' websites whenever the stock market falls by 100 points or more. However, many consumers find pop-up ads intrusive and distracting and install software to block these ads.[31]

The hottest growth area in online promotion has been **search-related ads**.[32] Thirty-five percent of all searches are reportedly for products or services. Search terms are used as a proxy for the consumer's consumption interests and relevant links to product or service offerings are listed alongside the search results from Google, Yahoo!, and MSN. Advertisers pay only if people click on the links. The cost per click depends on how high the link is ranked and the popularity of the keyword searched. Average click-through is about 2 percent, much more than for comparable online ads.[33] At an average of 35 cents, paid search is a lot cheaper than the $1-per-lead for Yellow Pages listings. One Samsung executive estimated that it was 50 times cheaper to reach 1000 people online than on TV. The company now spends 10 percent of its advertising budget online.[34] A newer trend, **content-target advertising**, links ads not to keywords but to the content of webpages.

Companies can set up **alliances** and **affiliate programs**. When one Internet company works with another one, they end up advertising each other. AOL has created many successful alliances with other companies. Amazon has almost 1 million affiliates that post Amazon banners on their websites. Companies can also undertake guerrilla-marketing actions to publicize their site and generate word of mouth. When Yahoo! started its Denmark site, it distributed apples at the busiest train station in Denmark with the message that in the next hours a trip to New York could be won on the Yahoo! site; it also managed to get this mentioned in Danish newspapers. Companies can also offer to push content and ads to targeted audiences who agree to receive them and are presumably more interested in the product or product category.

Web advertising is showing double-digit growth. Costs are reasonable compared with those of other advertising media. For example, ESPN.com (www.espn.com), the number-one Internet sports site, attracts more than 5 million web surfers a week. Based on current advertising rates, running advertising on the site for an entire year may range from US$500 000 to US$1 000 000 (depending on impression levels).[35] Yahoo! employs 100 salespeople who demonstrate how online ads can reach people with particular interests or who live in specific regions.

E-Marketing Guidelines

If a company does an email campaign right, it can not only build customer relationships but also reap additional profits. Email involves only a fraction of the cost of a "d-mail," or direct-mail, campaign. For example, Microsoft used to spend approximately US$70 million a year on paper-driven campaigns. Now, it sends out 20 million pieces of email every month at a significant savings over the cost of paper-based campaigns. When compared to other forms of online marketing, email remains a hands-down winner. Click-through rates for ad banners have dropped to less than 1 percent, whereas click-through rates for email are running around 80 percent.

Here are some important guidelines followed by pioneering email marketers:[36]

- *Give the customer a reason to respond.* Companies should offer surfers powerful incentives for reading email pitches and online ads, like email trivia games, scavenger hunts, and instant-win sweepstakes.

- *Personalize the content of your emails.* IBM's iSource is distributed directly to customers' office email each week, delivering only "the news they choose" in terms of announcements and weekly updates. Customers who agree to receive the newsletter select from topics listed on an interest profile.

- *Offer something the customer could not get via direct mail.* Because email campaigns can be carried out quickly, they can offer time-sensitive information. Travelocity sends frequent emails pitching last-minute cheap airfares. Club Med uses email to pitch unsold, discounted vacation packages to prospects in its database.

- *Make it easy for customers to "unsubscribe."* It is important that online customers have a positive exit experience. According to a Burston-Marsteller and Roper Strach Worldwide study, the top 10 percent of web users who communicate much more often online typically share their views by email with 11 friends when satisfied, but contact 17 friends when they are dissatisfied.[37]

Online merchants face many challenges in expanding the public's use of e-commerce. Customers will have to feel that the information they supply is confidential and not going to be sold to others. Customers will need to trust that online transactions are secure. Companies must encourage communication by inviting prospects and customers to send in questions, suggestions, and even complaints via email. Some sites include a call-me button—the customer clicks on it and his or her phone rings with a customer representative ready to answer a question. Customer-service representatives can in principle respond quickly to these messages. Smart online marketers will answer quickly by sending out newsletters, special product or promotion offers based on purchase histories, reminders of service requirements or warranty renewals, or announcements of special events.

Direct marketing must be integrated with other communication and channel activities.[38] IBM and Ford have used integrated direct marketing to build profitable relations with customers over the years. Retailers such as Sears, IKEA, and Tilley Endurables regularly send catalogues to supplement in-store sales. Veseys, a mail-order and online gardening company based in Prince Edward Island, has been successfully serving Canadians for 65 years. Eddie Bauer made its fortune by establishing a strong brand name in the direct-marketing mail-order and phone-order business before opening its retail stores. Such companies cross-promote their stores, catalogues, and websites, for example, by putting their web addresses on their shopping bags. Consider how Virgin Mobile drove consumers online and increased use of its service:

Virgin Mobile

In a campaign that received a Cannes Lion award, Virgin Mobile created a wireless phone service campaign in Australia to sell 5-cent text messaging that combined TV and outdoor ads and a webpage, all based on Warren, a fictitious, love-hungry character. Outdoor ads with Warren's text address and photo read "Be my text kitten" and "Tell me your favourite text position." During the ten-week campaign, Warren got 600 000 text responses and the website got 3 million hits. Sales increased by over 35 percent month-on-month, with existing users making 15 percent more calls and sending 20 percent more text messages.[39]

DESIGNING THE SALES FORCE

The original and oldest form of direct marketing is the field sales call. Today most industrial companies rely heavily on a professional sales force to locate prospects, develop them into customers, and grow the business, or they hire manufacturers' representatives and agents to carry out the direct-selling task. In addition, many consumer companies use a direct-selling force: insurance agents, stockbrokers, and distributors work for direct-sales organizations such as Amway, Mary Kay, and Tupperware. According to Statistics Canada's 2006 Census data, almost 24 percent of the total workforce works in sales or service occupations.[40] Sales forces are found in nonprofit as well as for-profit organizations. Hospitals and museums, for example, use fund-raisers to contact donors and solicit donations.

No one debates the importance of the sales force in marketing programs. However, companies are sensitive to the high and rising costs (salaries, commissions, bonuses, travel expenses, and benefits) of maintaining a sales force. Because the average cost of a personal sales call ranges from $200 to $300, and closing a sale typically requires four calls, the total cost can range from $800 to $1200.[41] Not surprisingly, companies are trying to increase the productivity of sales forces through better selection, training, supervision, motivation, and compensation.

The term *sales representative* covers a broad range of positions. Six can be distinguished, presented here from the least to the most creative types of selling:[42]

1. *Deliverer*—A salesperson whose major task is the delivery of a product (water, fuel, oil).

2. *Order taker*—A salesperson who acts predominantly as an inside order taker (a salesperson standing behind the counter) or outside order taker (a soap salesperson calling on a supermarket manager).

3. *Missionary*—A salesperson who is not expected or permitted to take an order but whose major task is to build goodwill or to educate the actual or potential user (a medical "detailer" representing an ethical pharmaceutical house).

4. *Technician*—A salesperson with a high level of technical knowledge (an engineering salesperson who is primarily a consultant to client companies).

5. *Demand creator*—A salesperson who relies on creative methods for selling tangible products (vacuum cleaners, cleaning brushes, household products) or intangibles (insurance, advertising services, or education).

6. *Solution vendor*—A salesperson whose expertise is in solving a customer's problem, often with a system of the company's products and services (e.g., computer and communications systems).

Sales personnel serve as a company's personal link to the customers. The sales representative *is* the company to many of its customers. And it is the sales rep who brings much-needed information about the customer back to the company. Therefore, the company needs to carefully consider issues in sales-force design—namely, the development of sales-force objectives, strategy, structure, size, and compensation (see Figure 19.2). Consider how SoBe's sales team affects the brand's success:

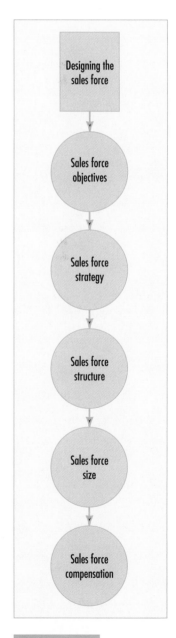

FIGURE 19.2

Designing a Sales Force

SoBe

John Bello, founder of SoBe nutritionally enhanced teas and juices, has given much credit to his sales force for the brand's success. Bello claims that the superior quality and consistent sales effort from the 150 salespeople the company had at its peak was directed towards one simple goal: "SoBe won in the street because our salespeople were there more often and in greater numbers than the competition, and they were more motivated by far." SoBe's sales force operated at every level of the distribution chain: at the distributor level, steady communication gave SoBe disproportionate focus relative to the other brands; at the trade level, with companies such as 7-Eleven, Costco, and Safeway, most senior salespeople had strong personal relationships; and at the individual store level, the SoBe team was always at work setting and restocking shelves, cutting in product, and putting up point-of-sale displays. According to Bello, bottom-line success in any entrepreneurial endeavour depends on sales execution.[43]

Sales-Force Objectives and Strategy

The days when all the sales force would do was "sell, sell, and sell" are long gone. Sales reps need to know how to diagnose a customer's problem and propose a solution. Salespeople show a customer-prospect how their company can help a customer improve profitability.

Companies need to define the specific objectives they want their sales force to achieve. For example, a company might want its sales representatives to spend 80 percent of their time with current customers and 20 percent with prospects, and 85 percent of their time on established products and 15 percent on new products. The specific allocation scheme depends on the kind of products and customers involved, but regardless of the selling context, salespeople will have one or more of the following specific tasks to perform:

- *Prospecting*—Searching for prospects, or leads.
- *Targeting*—Deciding how to allocate time among prospects and customers.
- *Communicating*—Communicating information about the company's products and services.
- *Selling*—Approaching, presenting, answering objections, and closing sales.
- *Servicing*—Providing various services to customers: consulting on problems, rendering technical assistance, arranging financing, expediting delivery.
- *Information gathering*—Conducting market research and doing intelligence work.
- *Allocating*—Deciding which customers will get scarce products during product shortages.

Because of the expense, most companies are moving to the concept of a *leveraged sales force*. A sales force focuses on selling the company's more complex and customized products to large accounts, while low-end selling is done by inside salespeople and web ordering. Tasks such as lead generation, proposal writing, order fulfillment, and post-sale support are turned over to others. Salespeople handle fewer accounts and are rewarded for key account growth. This is far different from expecting salespeople to sell to every possible account, which is usually the weakness of geographically based sales forces.[44]

Companies must deploy sales forces strategically so that they call on the right customers at the right time and in the right way. Today's sales representatives act as "account managers" who arrange fruitful contact between various people in the buying and selling organizations. Selling increasingly calls for teamwork requiring the support of other personnel, such as *top management*, especially when national accounts or major sales are at stake; *technical people*, who supply technical information and service to the customer before, during, or after product purchase; *customer-service representatives*, who provide installation, maintenance, and other services; and an *office staff*, consisting of sales analysts, order expediters, and assistants.

To maintain a market focus, salespeople should know how to analyze sales data, measure market potential, gather market intelligence, and develop marketing strategies and plans. Sales representatives need analytical marketing skills, and these skills become especially important at the higher levels of sales management. Marketers believe that sales forces will be more effective in the long run if they understand marketing as well as selling.

Once the company decides on an approach, it can use a direct or a contractual sales force. A **direct (company) sales force** consists of full- or part-time paid employees who work exclusively for the company. This sales force includes inside sales personnel who conduct business from the office using the telephone and receive visits from prospective buyers, and field sales personnel who travel and visit customers. A **contractual sales force** consists of manufacturers' reps, sales agents, and brokers, who are paid a commission based on sales.

Sales-Force Structure

The sales-force strategy has implications for the sales-force structure. A company that sells one product line to one end-using industry with customers in many locations would use a territorial structure. A company that sells many products to many types of customers might need a product or market structure. Some companies need a more complex structure. Motorola, for example, manages four types of sales forces: (1) a strategic-market sales force composed of technical, applications, and quality engineers and service personnel assigned to major accounts, (2) a geographic sales force calling on thousands of customers in different territories, (3) a distributor sales force calling on and coaching Motorola distributors, and (4) an inside sales force doing telemarketing and taking orders via phone and fax.

Established companies need to revise their sales-force structure as market and economic conditions change. SAS, seller of business intelligence software, reorganized its sales force into industry-specific groups such as banks, brokerages, and insurers, and saw revenue soar by 14 percent.[45]

Sales-Force Size

Once the company clarifies its strategy and structure, it is ready to consider sales-force size. Sales representatives are one of the company's most productive and expensive assets. Increasing their number will increase both sales and costs.

Once the company establishes the number of customers it wants to reach, it can use a *workload approach* to establish sales-force size. This method consists of the following five steps:

1. Customers are grouped into size classes according to annual sales volume.
2. Desirable call frequencies (number of calls on an account per year) are established for each class.
3. The number of accounts in each size class is multiplied by the corresponding call frequency to arrive at the total workload for the country, in sales calls per year.
4. The average number of calls a sales representative can make per year is determined.
5. The number of sales representatives needed is determined by dividing the total annual calls required by the average annual calls made by a sales representative.

Suppose the company estimates that there are 1000 A accounts and 2000 B accounts in the nation. A accounts require 36 calls a year, and B accounts require 12 calls a year. The company needs a sales force that can make 60 000 sales calls a year. Suppose the average rep can make 1000 calls a year. The company would need 60 full-time sales representatives.

Sales-Force Compensation

To attract top-quality sales reps, the company has to develop an attractive compensation package. Sales reps want income regularity, extra reward for above-average performance, and fair payment for experience and longevity. Management wants control, economy, and simplicity. Some of these objectives will conflict. It's no wonder compensation plans exhibit a tremendous variety from industry to industry and even within the same industry.

The company must determine the four components of sales-force compensation—a fixed amount, a variable amount, expense allowances, and benefits. The *fixed amount*, a salary, is intended to satisfy the need for income stability. The *variable amount*, which might be commissions, bonus, or profit sharing, is intended to stimulate and reward effort. *Expense allowances* enable sales reps to meet the expenses involved in travel and entertaining. *Benefits*, such as paid vacations, sickness or accident benefits, pensions, and life insurance, are intended to provide security and job satisfaction.

Fixed compensation receives more emphasis in jobs with a high ratio of nonselling to selling duties and in jobs where the selling task is technically complex and involves teamwork. Variable compensation receives more emphasis in jobs where sales are cyclical or depend on individual initiative. Fixed and variable compensation give rise to three basic types of compensation plans—straight salary, straight commission, and combination salary and commission. Three-quarters of firms use a combination of salary and commission, though the relative proportion varies widely.[46]

Straight-salary plans provide sales reps with a secure income, make them more willing to perform nonselling activities, and give them less incentive to overstock customers. From the company's

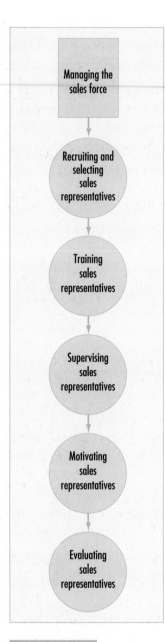

Managing the sales force

FIGURE 19.3

Managing the Sales Force

perspective, they provide administrative simplicity and lower turnover. Straight-commission plans attract higher performers, provide more motivation, require less supervision, and control selling costs. On the negative side, commission plans overemphasize getting a sale rather than building a customer relationship. Combination plans feature the benefits of both plans while reducing their disadvantages.

With compensation plans that combine fixed and variable pay, companies may link the variable portion of a salesperson's pay to a wide variety of strategic goals. Some see a new trend toward de-emphasizing volume measures in favour of factors such as gross profitability, customer satisfaction, and customer retention. For example, IBM now partly rewards salespeople on the basis of customer satisfaction as measured by customer surveys.[47] Other companies are basing the rep's reward partly on a sales team's performance or even companywide performance. This should get reps to work more closely together for the common good.

MANAGING THE SALES FORCE

Once the company has established objectives, strategy, structure, size, and compensation, it has to recruit, select, train, supervise, motivate, and evaluate sales representatives. Various policies and procedures guide these decisions (see Figure 19.3).

Recruiting and Selecting Representatives

At the heart of a successful sales force is the selection of effective representatives. One survey revealed that the top 27 percent of the sales force brought in over 52 percent of the sales. Beyond differences in productivity is the great waste in hiring the wrong people. The average annual turnover rate for all industries is almost 20 percent. Sales force turnover leads to lost sales, costs of finding and training replacements, and often a strain on existing salespeople to pick up the slack.

Selecting sales reps would be simple if one knew what traits to look for. One good starting point is to ask customers what traits they prefer. Most customers say they want the rep to be honest, reliable, knowledgeable, and helpful. A list of desirable characteristics that can be used as a general guide is found in "Marketing Memo: The Top 10 Traits of Effective Salespeople." Finding what traits will actually lead to sales success, however, is challenging. Numerous studies have shown little relationship between sales performance on one hand, and background and experience variables, current status, lifestyle, attitude, personality, and skills on the other hand. More effective predictors have been composite tests and assessment centres where the working environment is simulated and applicants are assessed in an environment similar to the one in which they would work.[48]

After management develops its selection criteria, it must recruit. The human resources department seeks applicants by soliciting names from current sales representatives, using employment agencies, placing job ads, and contacting university and college students. Selection procedures can vary from a single informal interview to prolonged testing and interviewing. Many companies give sales applicants formal tests. Although test scores are only one information element in a set that includes personal characteristics, references, past employment history, and interviewer reactions, they are weighted quite heavily by such companies as IBM, Prudential, and Procter & Gamble. Gillette claims that tests have reduced turnover and correlated well with the subsequent progress of new reps in the sales organization. Some others employers, as illustrated by the following example, have found demographic factors to be an important consideration. However, in the process of using demographic criteria to shortlist candidates, one must be careful not to break any anti-discrimination laws.

1-800-GOT-JUNK?

Today, 1-800-GOT-JUNK? has a presence in four countries, but the company had humble beginnings. It started as a summer job for a university student and became successful enough that he pursued it fulltime and began a franchise business model. The company provides full-service junk removal, picking up almost anything, recycling most of what is picked up, and even cleaning up afterwards. All calls go to a central call centre; the company has discovered that hiring older employees for the call centre is improving customer satisfaction. Therefore, the company makes a concerted effort to hire sales staff over the age of 45 for its call centre.[49]

MARKETING **MEMO** | THE TOP 10 TRAITS OF EFFECTIVE SALESPEOPLE

The following can be used as a foundation to create a customized list of traits to look for when hiring sales representatives. As different industries and managers require unique skills and abilities, the list should be tailored to each situation. This outline could also be used to determine what each member of the sales team may need coaching on and to develop appropriate training programs.

Effective salespeople:

1. Are constantly learning and investing in themselves and their professional development.
2. Are exceptional communicators.
3. Are creative. To practise the art of selling, one must be able to create new solutions and possibilities.
4. Have a positive and healthy attitude.
5. Have a passion for what they do and find joy in delivering unconditional value to their customers.
6. Have the ability to create an environment that allows for the sale to take place.
7. Are proactive, highly adaptable, and flexible rather than reactive and hasty.
8. Personify what their customers want most (they have integrity and are honest, ingenious, solution-driven, reliable, and receptive).
9. Are process-driven. They know what direction to take and how to get to the destination using specific measurable goals and a selling system to manage the selling process.
10. Have mastered time management and organization.

Source: Keith Rosen, *Coaching Sales People into Sales Champions* (Hoboken, NJ: John Wiley & Sons, Inc., 2008).

1-800-GOT-JUNK? has found that older employees provide better customer service.

Training and Supervising Sales Representatives

Today's customers expect salespeople to have deep product knowledge, to add ideas to improve the customer's operations, and to be efficient and reliable. These demands have required companies to make a much larger investment in sales training.

New reps may spend a few weeks to several months in training. The median training period is 28 weeks in industrial-products companies, 12 in service companies, and four in consumer-products companies. Training time varies with the complexity of the selling task and the type of person recruited into the sales organization.

New methods of training are continually emerging, such as role-playing and sensitivity training and the use of training videos, tutorials, simulations, and online training programs. Consider how Xerox and Whirlpool train their sales staff:

Xerox

Xerox found that technology-based training considerably reduces learning time. The company tried out a new method of training using an online interactive website designed by Juggernaut Studios. Using an online training package, Xerox allows its mobile sales force to access the training when it suits them and use it to refresh their knowledge whenever they need to. Juggernaut Studios designed the training module to be entertaining by using animation, video streaming, and games. Participants can even complete against each other for prizes. Although it feels like a game, the sales force is being tested throughout the training process. In addition to increasing learning, the online package also provides the advantage that the quality of the knowledge imparted is the same regardless of the instructor or classroom setting.[50]

Whirlpool

In order to increase its sales reps' understanding of its appliances, Whirlpool rented an eight-bedroom farmhouse near its headquarters in Benton Harbor, Michigan, and outfitted it with Whirlpool dishwashers, microwaves, washers, dryers, and refrigerators. It sent eight new salespeople to live in the house, to cook and do laundry and household chores. When they emerged, they knew a great deal about Whirlpool appliances and gained more confidence than if they had taken the traditional two-week classroom training course.[51]

Companies vary in how closely they supervise sales reps. Reps paid mostly on commission generally receive less supervision. Those who are salaried and who must cover defined accounts are likely to receive substantial supervision. With multilevel selling, used by Avon, Sara Lee, Virgin, AOL Time Warner, and others, independent distributors are also in charge of their own sales force selling company products. These independent contractors or reps are paid a commission not only on their own sales but also on the sales of people they recruit and train.[52]

Sales Rep Productivity

How many calls should a company make on a particular account each year? Some research has suggested that today's sales reps are spending too much time selling to smaller, less profitable accounts when they should be focusing more of their efforts on selling to larger, more profitable accounts.[53]

Whirlpool uses local households to train salespeople and to help its researchers develop intelligent major appliances.

Some firms are employing empathy training to increase sales reps' understanding of customer problems.

NORMS FOR PROSPECT CALLS Companies often specify how much time reps should spend prospecting for new accounts. Spector Freight wants its sales representatives to spend 25 percent of their time prospecting and to stop calling on a prospect after three unsuccessful calls.

Companies set up prospecting standards for a number of reasons. Left to their own devices, many reps will spend most of their time with current customers, who are known quantities. Reps can depend on them for some business, whereas a prospect might never deliver any business. Some companies rely on a missionary sales force to open new accounts.

USING SALES TIME EFFICIENTLY Studies have shown that the best sales reps are those who manage their time effectively.[54] One planning tool is *time-and-duty analysis*, which helps reps understand how they spend their time and how they might increase their productivity. In the course of a day, sales reps spend time planning, travelling, waiting, selling, and in administrative tasks (report writing and billing, attending sales meetings, and talking to others in the company about production, delivery, billing, sales performance, and other matters). With so many duties, it is no wonder that actual face-to-face selling time amounts to as little as 29 percent of total working time![55]

Companies are constantly seeking ways to improve sales-force productivity. Their methods take the form of training sales representatives in the use of "phone power," simplifying record keeping and administrative time, and using the computer and the Internet to develop call and routing plans, supply customer and competitive information, and automate the order-preparation process. Consumer Impact Marketing increases the efficiency of its sales force using computer software.

Consumer Impact Marketing

Toronto-based Consumer Impact Marketing (CIM) provides a variety of services including sales promotion and event, sales, and merchandising management. In particular, CIM has done well in the area of sales-force automation. The company developed sales-force automation software out of its own need to manage its employees and the services they provide to clients. The software, called Field Matrix, is now also sold to its clients. Field Matrix captures and analyzes data in a variety of formats in real time, allowing the sales force to access necessary information in an instant. The software allows sales people to track information, enter sales orders quickly, and generate reports, all of which increase productivity. This software has given CIM the ability to grow and continue to manage its business and client accounts well.[56]

To cut costs, reduce time demands on their outside sales force, and take advantage of computer and telecommunications innovations, many companies have increased the size and responsibilities of their inside sales force.[57]

Inside salespeople are of three types. There are *technical-support people*, who provide technical information and answers to customers' questions. There are *sales assistants*, who provide clerical backup for the outside salespersons: they call ahead and confirm appointments, carry out credit checks, follow up on deliveries, and answer customers' questions. *Telemarketers* use the phone to find new leads, qualify them, and sell to them. Telemarketers can call up to 50 customers a day, compared to the four an outside salesperson can contact.

The inside sales force frees the outside reps to spend more time selling to major accounts, identifying and converting new major prospects, placing electronic ordering systems in customers' facilities, and obtaining more blanket orders and systems contracts. The inside salespeople spend more time checking inventory, following up on orders, and phoning smaller accounts. The outside sales reps are paid largely on an incentive-compensation basis, and the inside reps on a salary or salary-plus-bonus basis.

New technology has also changed the face of inside sales—desktop and laptop computers, PDAs, automatic dialers, email, fax machines, videoconferencing, and online ordering systems have changed the way selling is carried out. Not only is sales and inventory information transferred much faster, but specific computer-based decision support systems have been created for sales managers and sales representatives.

One of the most valuable electronic tools for the sales rep is the company website, and one of its most useful applications is as a prospecting tool. Company websites can help define the firm's relationships with individual accounts and identify those whose business warrants a personal sales call. The website provides an introduction to self-identified potential customers. Depending on the nature of the business, the initial order may even take place online. For more complex transactions, the site provides a way for the buyer to contact the seller. Selling over the Internet supports relationship marketing by solving problems that do not require live intervention and thus allows more time to be spent on issues that are best addressed face-to-face.

Motivating Sales Representatives

The majority of sales representatives require encouragement and special incentives. This is especially true of field selling: Reps usually work alone, their hours are irregular, and they are often away from home. They confront aggressive, competing sales reps; they have an inferior status relative to the buyer; they often do not have the authority to do what is necessary to win an account; and they sometimes lose large orders they have worked hard to obtain.[58] Motivating sales people using an attraction-based strategy will be more effective than motivation by force, as explained in "Marketing Insight: Push versus Pull—Modelling Motivation."

Most marketers believe that the higher the salesperson's motivation, the greater the effort and the resulting performance, rewards, and satisfaction—and thus further motivation. Such thinking is based on certain assumptions:

- Sales managers must be able to convince salespeople that they can sell more by working harder or by being trained to work smarter. But if sales are determined largely by economic conditions or competitive actions, this link is undermined.

- Sales managers must be able to convince salespeople that the rewards for better performance are worth the extra effort. But if the rewards seem to be set arbitrarily or are too small or of the wrong kind, this link is undermined.

To increase motivation, marketers reinforce intrinsic and extrinsic rewards of all types. One research study that measured the importance of different rewards found that the reward with the highest value was pay, followed by promotion, personal growth, and sense of accomplishment.[59] The least-valued rewards were liking and respect, security, and recognition. In other words, salespeople are highly motivated by pay and the chance to get ahead and satisfy their intrinsic needs, and less motivated by compliments and security. However, the researchers also found that the importance of motivators varied with demographic characteristics: Financial rewards were mostly valued by older, longer-tenured people and those who had large families. Higher-order rewards (recognition, liking and respect, sense of accomplishment) were more valued by young salespeople who were unmarried or had small families, and who usually had more formal education.

Many companies set annual sales quotas. Quotas can be set on dollar sales, unit volume, margin, selling effort or activity, and product type. Compensation is often tied to degree of quota fulfillment. Sales quotas are developed from the annual marketing plan. The company first prepares a sales forecast that becomes the basis for planning production, workforce size, and financial requirements.

MARKETING **INSIGHT** | PUSH VERSUS PULL—MODELLING MOTIVATION

There are two types of motivational philosophies according to Keith Rosen, who is called upon by many of the world's leading companies as a sales coach for top managers, sales professionals, and executives. The first philosophy is based on an attraction model and the other is a push structure. The attraction model, or pull model, empowers people, whereas the push structure discourages and eliminates potential. In order for organizations to increase productivity, they must motivate their salespeople in a positive way.

Managers are often obsessed with outcomes and push their sales people into action in order to achieve results. A push structure may include using fear, consequences, or threats to motivate people to reach a certain objective or complete a task. Managers who employ this strategy often feel as if they are pushing an object up a steep hill. They find that when they stop pushing, productivity comes to a halt and all momentum is lost. Ineffective motivational efforts result in poor productivity, high turnover, bad employee relations, and a high likelihood of labour unrest. Instead, managers should find a way to positively encourage sales people so that employees become their own motivators.

An attraction-based strategy motivates people using pleasure, support, and coaching. This alternative motivation strategy taps into the individual salesperson's personal vision or goal, and helps him or her achieve it. Instead of constantly looking over reps' shoulders and pushing them to avoid certain behaviours, the manager should help and encourage sales people to achieve their personal goals.

The attraction model requires much less effort over time and offers long-term benefits. The push strategy, however, is a temporary fix and requires considerable effort. At the end of the day, the goal is to get sales people to become their own motivators, as opposed to being provoked by an external force.

Whether to use a push or pull strategy doesn't have to be the manager's individual decision. Allowing the sales staff to inform management how they want to be motivated will contribute to the formation of an entirely self-managed team. Every member of the sales team will have unique abilities and personal goals. Exceptional managers appreciate employee differences and know not to implement a general selling strategy and incentive program for all team members. Focusing on the individuality of a sales team is critical in making certain that each employee is working at full potential. Once the sales manager is able to tap into the individual characteristics of the sales force, he or she can determine what drives each person and develop customized incentive programs.

Sources: Keith Rosen, *Coaching Sales People into Sales Champions* (Hoboken, NJ: John Wiley & Sons, Inc., 2008); Woodruff Imberman, "Work Harder, Work Smarter to Motivate Workers Effectively," *Foundry Management & Technology*, 135, no. 11 (November 2007): 32–33.

Management then establishes quotas for regions and territories, which typically add up to more than the sales forecast to encourage managers and salespeople to perform at their best levels. If they fail to make their quotas, the company nevertheless might reach its sales forecast.

Each area sales manager divides the area's quota among the area's reps. Sometimes a rep's quotas are set high, to spur extra effort, or, more modestly, to build confidence. One general view is that a salesperson's quota should be at least equal to the person's last year's sales plus some fraction of the difference between territory sales potential and last year's sales. The more favourably the salesperson reacts to pressure, the higher the fraction should be.

Conventional wisdom is that profits are maximized by sales reps focusing on the more important products and more profitable products. Reps are not likely to achieve their quotas for established products when the company is launching several new products at the same time. The company will need to expand its sales force for new product launches.

Setting sales quotas creates problems. If the company underestimates and the sales reps easily achieve their quotas, the company has overpaid its reps. If the company overestimates sales potential, the sales people will find it very hard to reach their quotas and be frustrated or quit. Another downside is that quotas can drive reps to get as much business as possible—often resulting in their ignoring the service side of the business. The company gains short-term results at the cost of long-term customer satisfaction.

Some companies are dropping quotas.[60] Siebel, the leading supplier of sales automation software, judges its sales reps using a number of metrics, such as customer satisfaction, repeated business, and profitable revenues. Almost 40 percent of incentive compensation is based on customers' reported satisfaction with service and product. The company's close scrutiny of the sales process leads to satisfied customers: over 50 percent of Siebel's revenue comes from repeated business.[61]

Nortel and Prudential Insurance also prefer to use a larger set of measures for motivating and rewarding sales reps. Even hard-driving Oracle has changed its approach to sales compensation:

Oracle

Finding sales flagging and customers griping, Oracle, the second-largest software company in the world, overhauled its sales department in 2002. Oracle's rapidly expanding capabilities, with diverse applications such as human resources, supply chain, and CRM, made its account management system difficult. One rep could no longer be responsible for selling all Oracle products to certain customers. Reorganization resulted in reps' specializing in a few particular products. To try to tone down the sales force's reputation as overly aggressive, the commission structure was changed to a flat 4 to 6 percent, as compared to a wider range of 2 to 12 percent depending on how close to the end of the quarter the sale was made.[62]

Evaluating Sales Representatives

We have been describing the *feed-forward* aspects of sales supervision—how management communicates what the sales reps should be doing and motivates them to do it. But good feed-forward requires good *feedback*, which means getting regular information from reps to evaluate performance.

SOURCES OF INFORMATION The most important source of information about reps is sales reports. Additional information comes through personal observation, salesperson self-reports, customer letters and complaints, customer surveys, and conversations with other sales representatives.

Sales reports are divided between *activity plans* and *write-ups of activity results*. The best example of the former is the salesperson's work plan, which reps submit a week or month in advance. The plan describes intended calls and routing. This report forces sales reps to plan and schedule their activities and inform management of their whereabouts. It provides a basis for comparing their plans and accomplishments. Sales reps can be evaluated on their ability to "plan their work and work their plan."

Many companies require representatives to develop an annual territory marketing plan in which they outline their program for developing new accounts and increasing business from existing accounts. This type of report casts sales reps into the role of market managers and profit centres. Sales managers study these plans, make suggestions, and use them to develop sales quotas. Sales reps write up completed activities on *call reports*. Sales representatives also submit expense reports, new-business reports, lost-business reports, and reports on local business and economic conditions.

These reports provide raw data from which sales managers can extract key indicators of sales performance: (1) average number of sales calls per salesperson per day, (2) average sales-call time per contact, (3) average revenue per sales call, (4) average cost per sales call, (5) entertainment cost per sales call, (6) percentage of orders per hundred sales calls, (7) number of new customers per period, (8) number of lost customers per period, and (9) sales-force cost as a percentage of total sales.

FORMAL EVALUATION The sales force's reports along with other observations supply the raw materials for evaluation. There are several approaches to conducting evaluations. One type of evaluation compares current performance to past performance. An example is shown in Table 19.1.

The sales manager can learn many things about a rep from this table. Total sales increased every year (line 3). This does not necessarily mean that the person is doing a better job. The product breakdown shows that he has been able to push the sales of product B further than the sales of product A (lines 1 and 2). According to his quotas for the two products (lines 4 and 5), his success in increasing product B sales could be at the expense of product A sales. According to gross profits (lines 6 and 7), the company earns more selling A than B. The rep might be pushing the higher-volume, lower-margin product at the expense of the more profitable product. Although he increased total sales by $1100 between 2008 and 2009 (line 3), the gross profits on total sales actually decreased by $580 (line 8).

Sales expense (line 9) shows a steady increase, although total expense as a percentage of total sales seems to be under control (line 10). The upward trend in total dollar expense does not seem to be explained by any increase in the number of calls (line 11), although it might be related to success in acquiring new customers (line 14). There is a possibility that in prospecting for new customers, this rep is neglecting present customers, as indicated by an upward trend in the annual number of lost customers (line 15).

The last two lines show the level and trend in sales and gross profits per customer. These figures become more meaningful when they are compared with overall company averages. If this rep's average

TABLE 19.1	FORM FOR EVALUATING SALES REPRESENTATIVE'S PERFORMANCE			
Territory: Midland Sales Representative: John Smith	**2006**	**2007**	**2008**	**2009**
1. Net sales, product A	$251 300	$253 200	$270 000	$263 100
2. Net sales, product B	$423 200	$439 200	$553 900	$561 900
3. Net sales total	$674 500	$692 400	$823 900	$825 000
4. Percentage of quota, product A	95.6	92.0	88.0	84.7
5. Percentage of quota, product B	120.4	122.3	134.9	130.8
6. Gross profits, product A	$50 260	$50 640	$54 000	$52 620
7. Gross profits, product B	$42 320	$43 920	$55 390	$56 190
8. Gross profits, total	$92 580	$94 560	$109 390	$108 810
9. Sales expense	$10 200	$11 100	$11 600	$13 200
10. Sales expense to total sales (%)	1.5	1.6	1.4	1.6
11. Number of calls	1675	1700	1680	1660
12. Cost per call	$6.09	$6.53	$6.90	$7.95
13. Average number of customers	320	324	328	334
14. Number of new customers	13	14	15	20
15. Number of lost customers	8	10	11	14
16. Average sales per customer	$2108	$2137	$2512	$2470
17. Average gross profit per customer	$289	$292	$334	$326

gross profit per customer is lower than the company's average, he could be concentrating on the wrong customers or not spending enough time with each customer. A review of annual number of calls (line 11) shows that he might be making fewer annual calls than the average salesperson. If distances in the territory are similar to other territories, this could mean that he is not putting in a full workday, he is poor at sales planning and routing, or he spends too much time with certain accounts.

The rep might be quite effective in producing sales but not rate high with customers. Perhaps he is slightly better than the competitors' salespeople, or his product is better, or he keeps finding new customers to replace others who do not like to deal with him. Customers' opinion of the salesperson, product, and service can be measured by mail questionnaires or telephone calls.

Evaluations can also assess the salesperson's knowledge of the company, products, customers, competitors, territory, and responsibilities. Personality characteristics can be rated, such as general manner, appearance, speech, and temperament. The sales manager can review any problems in motivation or compliance.[63] Sales reps can provide attributions as to the success or failure of a sales call and how they would propose to improve the odds on subsequent calls. Possible explanations for their performance could be related to internal (effort, ability, and strategy) and external (task and luck) factors.[64]

PRINCIPLES OF PERSONAL SELLING

Personal selling is an ancient art. It has spawned a large literature and many principles. Effective salespersons have more than instinct; they are trained in methods of analysis and customer management. Today's companies spend hundreds of millions of dollars each year to train salespeople in the art of selling. Sales-training approaches try to convert a salesperson from a passive order taker into an active order getter who engages in customer problem solving. An active order getter learns how to listen and question in order to identify customer needs and come up with sound product solutions. This approach assumes that customers have latent needs that constitute opportunities and that they will be loyal to sales reps who can analyze their needs and have their long-term interests at heart. "Marketing Insight: Principles of Customer-Oriented Selling" offers some guidelines.

Most sales-training programs agree on the major steps involved in any effective sales process. We show these steps in Figure 19.4, and discuss next their application to industrial selling.[65]

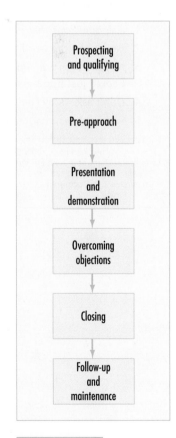

FIGURE 19.4

Major Steps in Effective Selling

| MARKETING INSIGHT | PRINCIPLES OF CUSTOMER-ORIENTED SELLING |

Two vocal proponents of a customer-oriented approach to selling are Neil Rackham and Sharon Drew Morgen. Rackham has developed a method that he calls *SPIN selling* (Situation, Problem, Implication, Need-Payoff). Gone is the script of the slick salesperson, and in its place is the salesperson who knows how to raise good questions and listen and learn. Rackham trains salespeople to raise four types of questions with the prospect:

1. *Situation questions.* These ask about facts or explore the buyer's present situation. For example, "What system are you using to invoice your customers?"

2. *Problem questions.* These deal with problems, difficulties, and dissatisfactions the buyer is experiencing. For example, "What parts of the system create errors?"

3. *Implication questions.* These ask about the consequences or effects of a buyer's problems, difficulties, or dissatisfactions. For example, "How does this problem affect your people's productivity?"

4. *Need-payoff questions.* These ask about the value or usefulness of a proposed solution. For example, "How much would you save if our company could help reduce the errors by 80 percent?"

Rackham suggests that companies, especially those selling complex products or services, should have their salespeople move from *preliminaries*, to *investigating* the prospect's problems and needs, to *demonstrating* the supplier's superior capabilities, and then to *obtaining* a long-term commitment. This approach reflects the growing interest of many companies in moving from pursuing an immediate sale to developing a long-term customer relationship.

Sharon Drew Morgen takes Rackham's approach a step further with what she calls the Buying Facilitation Method. She holds that the job of a salesperson is to help prospects go through a process to decide first whether their company's performance can be improved, and second whether the seller's offering would provide a solution. Prospects buy only when they realize they have a problem, that they lack resources to solve their problem, and that the seller's offering can add value.

Sales guru Tom Hopkins offers some additional tips to help close a deal:

1. *Ask questions that don't leave room for no.* "I could visit you today at 3, or would tomorrow at 9 be better?"

2. *Never use the word "price" or "cost."* Say investment.

3. *Never ask for "an appointment."* It suggests a serious time commitment. Say "I'll be in the area, and I was hoping I could just pop by and visit."

4. *Don't ask, "May I help you?"* They'll reply, "We're just looking." Ask instead what brought them into the store today.

5. *Isolate areas of agreement.* You need a lot of "little yeses" on the way to get a "big yes."

Sources: Neil Rackham, *SPIN Selling* (New York: McGraw-Hill, 1988). See also his *The SPIN Selling Fieldbook* (New York: McGraw-Hill, 1996); Neil Rackham and John De Vincentis, *Rethinking the Sales Force* (New York: McGraw-Hill, 1996); Sharon Drew Morgen, *Selling With Integrity: Reinventing Sales Through Collaboration, Respect, and Serving* (New York: Berkeley Books, 1999); James Lardner, "Selling Salesmenship," *Business 2.0* (December 2002/January 2003): 66.

The Six Steps

PROSPECTING AND QUALIFYING The first step in selling is to identify and qualify prospects. More companies are taking responsibility for finding and qualifying leads so that the salespeople can use their expensive time doing what they can do best: selling. Companies can qualify the leads by contacting them by mail or phone to assess their level of interest and financial capacity. The leads can be categorized, with "hot" prospects turned over to the field sales force and "warm" prospects turned over to the telemarketing unit for follow-up. Even then, it usually takes about four calls on a prospect to consummate a business transaction.

PRE-APPROACH The salesperson needs to learn as much as possible about the prospect company (what it needs, who is involved in the purchase decision) and its buyers (personal characteristics and buying styles). The salesperson should set call objectives: to qualify the prospect, gather information, make an immediate sale. Another task is to decide on the best contact approach, which might be a personal visit, a phone call, or a letter. Finally, the salesperson should plan an overall sales strategy for the account.

PRESENTATION AND DEMONSTRATION The salesperson now tells the product "story" to the buyer, following the AIDA formula of gaining *attention*, holding *interest*, arousing *desire*, and obtaining *action*. The salesperson uses a *features, advantages, benefits,* and *value* approach (FABV). Features describe physical characteristics of a market offering, such as chip processing speeds or memory capacity. Advantages describe why the features provide an advantage to the customer. Benefits describe the economic, technical, service, and social benefits delivered by the offering. Value describes the worth (often in monetary terms) of the offering. Too often, salespeople spend too much time dwelling on product features (a product orientation) and not enough stressing the offering's benefits and value (a customer orientation).

OVERCOMING OBJECTIONS Customers typically pose objections during the presentation or when asked for the order. *Psychological resistance* includes resistance to interference, preference for established supply sources or brands, apathy, reluctance to give up something, unpleasant associations created by the sales rep, predetermined ideas, dislike of making decisions, and a neurotic attitude towards money. *Logical resistance* might consist of objections to the price, delivery schedule, or certain product or company characteristics.

To handle these objections, the salesperson maintains a positive approach, asks the buyer to clarify the objection, questions the buyer in a way that requires the buyer to answer his or her own objection, denies the validity of the objection, or turns the objection into a reason for buying. Handling and overcoming objections is a part of the broader skills of negotiation.

One potential problem is that salespeople give in too often when customers demand a discount. One company recognized this as a problem when its sales revenue went up by 25 percent but its profit had remained flat. The company decided to retrain its salespeople to "sell the price," rather than "sell through price." Salespeople were given richer information about each customer's sales history and behaviour. They received training to recognize value-adding opportunities rather than price-cutting opportunities. As a result, the company's sales revenue climbed and so did its margins.[66]

CLOSING Now the salesperson attempts to close the sale. Salespeople need to know how to recognize closing signs from the buyer, including physical actions, statements or comments, and questions. There are several closing techniques. They can ask for the order, recapitulate the points of agreement, offer to help the secretary write up the order, ask whether the buyer wants A or B, get the buyer to make minor choices such as the colour or size, or indicate what the buyer will lose if the order is not placed now. The salesperson might offer the buyer specific inducements to close, such as a special price, an extra quantity, or a token gift.

FOLLOW-UP AND MAINTENANCE Follow-up and maintenance are necessary if the salesperson wants to ensure customer satisfaction and repeated business. Immediately after closing, the salesperson should cement any necessary details of delivery time, purchase terms, and other matters that are important to the customer. The salesperson should schedule a follow-up call when the initial order is received to make sure there is proper installation, instruction, and servicing. This visit or call will detect any problems, assure the buyer of the salesperson's interest, and reduce any cognitive dissonance that might have arisen. The salesperson should also develop a maintenance and growth plan for the account.

Negotiation

Marketing is concerned with exchange activities and the manner in which the terms of exchange are established. In *routinized exchange*, the terms are established by administered programs of pricing and distribution. In *negotiated exchange*, price and other terms are set via bargaining behaviour, in which two or more parties negotiate long-term binding agreements. Although price is the most frequently negotiated issue, other issues include contract completion time; quality of goods and services offered; purchase volume; responsibility for financing, risk taking, promotion, and title; and product safety.

Marketers who find themselves in bargaining situations need certain traits and skills to be effective. The most important are preparation and planning skill, knowledge of subject matter being negotiated, ability to think clearly and rapidly under pressure and uncertainty, ability to express thoughts verbally, listening skill, judgment and general intelligence, integrity, ability to persuade others, and patience.[67]

Relationship Marketing

The principles of personal selling and negotiation we have described are largely transaction-oriented because their purpose is to close a specific sale. But in many cases the company is not seeking an immediate sale, but rather to build a long-term supplier–customer relationship. The company wants to demonstrate that it has the capabilities to serve the account's needs in a superior way. Today's customers are large and often global. They prefer suppliers which can sell and deliver a coordinated set of products and services to many locations, which can quickly solve problems that arise in different locations, and which can work closely with customer teams to improve products and processes.

Salespeople working with key customers must do more than call when they think customers might be ready to place orders. They should call or visit at other times, take customers to dinner, and make useful suggestions about the business. They should monitor key accounts, know customers' problems, and be ready to serve them in a number of ways, as CIBC tries to do.

CIBC

The Canadian Imperial Bank of Commerce sales force practises relationship marketing regularly. Through mining its data warehouses and tracking leads generated by branch and call-centre staff, the company finds information related to events in its customers' lives, such as marriages or home purchases. For example, CIBC launched an initiative that locates customers with overdrawn accounts. Within 48 hours, CIBC makes contact with the customer to offer him or her overdraft protection. The bank found that customers bought overdraft protection, which protected the customer, created additional revenue, and reduced risk for the bank.[68]

When a relationship management program is properly implemented, the organization will begin to focus as much on managing its customers as on managing its products. At the same time, companies should realize that while there is a strong and warranted move towards relationship marketing, it is not effective in all situations. Ultimately, companies must judge which segments and which specific customers will respond profitably to relationship management.

SUMMARY

1. Direct marketing is an interactive marketing system that uses one or more media to effect a measurable response or transaction at any location. Direct marketing, especially electronic marketing, is showing explosive growth.

2. Direct marketers plan campaigns by deciding on objectives, target markets and prospects, offers, and prices. This is followed by testing and establishing measures to determine the campaign's success.

3. Major channels for direct marketing include face-to-face selling, direct mail, catalogue marketing, telemarketing, interactive TV, kiosks, websites, and mobile devices.

4. Interactive marketing provides marketers with opportunities for much greater interaction and individualization through well-designed websites as well as online ads and promotions.

5. Sales personnel serve as a company's link to its customers. The sales rep *is* the company to many of its customers, and it is the rep who brings much-needed information about the customer back to the company.

6. Designing the sales force requires decisions regarding objectives, strategy, structure, size, and compensation. Objectives may include prospecting, targeting, communicating, selling, servicing, information gathering, and allocating. Determining strategy requires choosing the most effective mix of selling approaches. Choosing the sales-force structure entails dividing territories by geography, product, or market (or some combination of these). Estimating how large the sales force needs to be involves estimating the total workload and how many sales hours (and hence salespeople) will be needed. Compensating the sales force entails determining what types of salaries, commissions, bonuses, expense accounts, and benefits to give, and how much weight customer satisfaction should have in determining total compensation.

7. There are five steps involved in managing the sales force: (1) recruiting and selecting sales representatives, (2) training the representatives in sales techniques and in the company's products, policies, and customer-satisfaction orientation, (3) supervising the sales force and helping reps to use their time efficiently, (4) motivating the sales force, and balancing quotas, monetary rewards, and supplementary motivators, and (5) evaluating individual and group sales performance.

8. Effective salespeople are trained in the methods of analysis and customer management, as well as the art of sales professionalism. No approach works best in all circumstances, but most trainers agree that selling is a six-step process: prospecting and qualifying customers, pre-approach, presentation and demonstration, overcoming objections, closing, and follow-up and maintenance.

APPLICATIONS

Marketing Debate: Are Great Salespeople Born or Made?

One difference of opinion with respect to sales concerns the potential impact of training versus selection in developing an effective sales force. Some observers maintain that the best salespeople are "born" that way and are effective due to their personalities and all the interpersonal skills they have developed over a lifetime. Others contend that application of leading-edge sales techniques can make virtually anyone a sales star.

Take a position: The key to developing an effective sales force is selection *versus* The key to developing an effective sales force is training.

Marketing Discussion

Pick a company and go to its website. How would you evaluate the site? How well does it score on the 7Cs design elements—context, content, community, customization, communication, connection, and commerce?

Breakthrough Marketing: Mobile Marketing

What is the newest medium many marketers are spending money on to reach consumers? It's probably in your pocket. With SMS text-message use growing at a rate of 100 percent each year since 2003, and 97 percent of text messages being read by recipients, many companies have turned to "mobile marketing" through cellular phones to get their promotional messages across.

Approximately 70 percent of North Americans use cell phones today, making SMS marketing a very attractive option for many companies. It has been forecast that in the near future, nearly 90 percent of companies will use mobile marketing to some degree—utilizing from 5 to 25 percent of their marketing budgets. Companies such as Google and Yahoo! already use mobile marketing quite extensively. At the same time, communications companies are upgrading their systems in order to meet expanding messaging demand. The move towards mobile marketing is resulting in a growing marketing opportunity for the brands involved and it is also creating significant revenue for mobile-messaging operators.

Although mobile marketing is here to stay and its use is growing at an exponential rate, some companies are still wary of its use. The main barrier to launching a mobile marketing campaign is uncertainty about what will get the best results. As the field is still in its infancy in North America, companies have little historical data to guide them. However, it is only a matter of time before this changes. Cell phone adoption in European countries is among the highest in the world, and a recent study of Nordic cell phone users reported that almost 40 percent of them are in favour of user-accepted mobile advertising. North Americans are expected to follow suit. With mobile commerce growing in Canada, it won't be long before Canadians get used to the idea of receiving promotional messages on their cell phones. So, the next time you hear a text message alert on your mobile phone, it may be a company reaching out to you in a way it never has before.

DISCUSSION QUESTIONS

1. What risks and challenges do mobile marketers face? What are some factors that can affect the success of a mobile marketing campaign?

2. What are the ethical issues surrounding the use of mobile marketing?

3. For what types of marketing messages would the use of mobile marketing be inappropriate?

Sources: "More: Nordic Survey Shows Steady Increase in Receptiveness to Mobile Marketing," *Business Wire*, June 16, 2008; "89% of Major Brands Planning to Market via Mobile Phones by 2008; Mobile Marketing to Accelerate with More Than Half of Brands Planning to Spend up to 25% of Marketing Budget," *CCNMatthews Newswire*, February 21, 2006; "Company Index," *MobiAD Company Index*, July 4, 2008, www.mobiadnews.com/?cat=19 (viewed July 10, 2008); "Grow Your Business with Kinetix," Kinetix Media Communications, July 3, 2008, www.kinetix.ca/page/mobile-marketing (viewed July 10, 2008).

**IN THIS CHAPTER,
WE WILL ADDRESS
THE FOLLOWING
QUESTIONS:**

- What challenges does a company face in developing new products?

- What organizational structures are used to manage new-product development?

- What are the main stages in developing new products?

- What is the best way to set up the new-product development process?

- What factors affect the rate of diffusion and consumer adoption of river newly launched products?

CHAPTER 20

INTRODUCING NEW MARKET OFFERINGS

twenty

Canadians' growing desire for healthy food has made Canada an attractive market for food manufacturers and retailers. Consuming organic foods is a particularly prominent recent trend. But despite their rising popularity, organic foods still remain a novelty and rather expensive, making them affordable for only a relatively small proportion of Canadians. Shoppers Drug Mart, Canada's largest retail drugstore chain, is trying to change this. It introduced its new, reasonably priced organic food line called Nativa Organics in April 2008. The certified-organic product line features 170 packaged food items and is the company's largest product line launch since it was founded in 1962. The company currently operates over a thousand Shoppers Drug Mart stores (including Pharmaprix stores in Quebec) in prime locations across Canada.

Before launching Nativa, Shoppers Drug Mart conducted extensive market research to find out what consumers were looking for and what products should be included in the line. Shoppers Drug Mart needed a way to differentiate itself from other retailers in the food category, and an organic line was expected to do just that. Before rolling out the new Nativa private-label brand across the country, a few select stores were used to test consumers' reactions and estimate how successful the line would be. With promising results from the test marketing, Nativa Organics was launched in the company's stores coast-to-coast. Products in the line include snacks (such as rice cakes and potato chips), dinner options (such as rice, pasta, and condiments), breakfast items (such as cereal, juice, and coffee), and kids' food (such as ice cream and cookies).

In December 2008, the Canadian Food Inspection Agency began regulating the organic food industry and required its certification label to appear on all recognized organic products. Although there were limited national regulations for organic foods when the Nativa line was created, Shoppers Drug Mart was careful to ensure its suppliers produced credibly organic foods. Each province has its own individual accreditation organization, so Shoppers Drug Mart was sure to use accredited farms and producers when creating its product line.

Shoppers Drug Mart plans to increase its private-label sales to 25 percent of total sales by the end of 2012, including its Nativa and Quo brands. The initial success of Nativa has helped Shoppers Drug Mart to maintain its status as the largest retail drugstore chain in Canada. By expanding its offerings, the company has been able to aggressively combat increasing competition from Loblaws, Safeway, and Wal-Mart, which have all introduced and extended their pharmacy, health, and beauty offerings in the past few years. Loblaws' private-label PC Organics line, with over 300 organic food products, is considered one of Nativa's strongest competitors.

Shoppers Drug Mart continues to perform market reasearch and add new products to its private-label brands. Since organic food is a rapidly growing sector, Shoppers hopes it can grow along with it.

Sources: Shoppers Drug Mart website, www.shoppersdrugmart.ca (viewed June 13, 2008); "New Nativa™ Brand Makes Organic Food More Affordable for Canadians," *Canada NewsWire*, March 11, 2008; Hollie Shaw, "Shoppers Goes Organic in Food Fight with Loblaws," *Star-Phoenix*, March 6, 2008, p. C8; Cheryl Binning, "The Case for Organic," *Winnipeg Free Press*, February 17, 2008, p. B6.

Marketers play a key role in the new-product process by identifying and evaluating new-product ideas and working with R&D and others in every stage of development. This chapter provides a detailed analysis of the new-product development process. Chapter 21 considers how marketers can tap into global markets as another source of long-term growth.

CHALLENGES IN NEW-PRODUCT DEVELOPMENT

To learn how Maple Leaf Sports & Entertainment developed a new product— the Toronto FC—for Major League Soccer, visit www.pearsoned.ca/ marketingmanagementcanada.

A company can add new products through acquisition or development. The acquisition route can take three forms. The company can buy other companies, it can acquire patents from other companies, or it can buy a licence or franchise from another company. Swiss food giant Nestlé increased its presence in North America via its acquisition of such diverse brands as Carnation, Hills Brothers, Stouffer's, and Ralston Purina.[1]

The development route can take two forms. The company can develop new products in its own laboratories, or it can contract with independent researchers or new-product development firms to develop specific new products. We can identify six categories of new products:[2]

1. *New-to-the-world products*—New products that create an entirely new market.

2. *New product lines*—New products that allow a company to enter an established market for the first time.

3. *Additions to existing product lines*—New products that supplement established product lines (with new package sizes, flavours, and so on).

4. *Improvements and revisions of existing products*—New products that provide improved performance or greater perceived value and replace existing products.

5. *Repositionings*—Existing products that are targeted to new markets or market segments.

6. *Cost reductions*—New products that provide similar performance at lower cost.

Less than 10 percent of all new products are truly innovative and new to the world. These products involve the greatest cost and risk because they are new to both the company and the marketplace. W. L. Gore, best known for its durable Gore-Tex outdoor fabric, has innovated breakthrough new products in a number of diverse areas—guitar strings, dental floss, medical devices, and fuel cells. It has adopted several principles to guide its new-product development:[3]

1. *Work with potential customers.* Its thoracic graft designed to combat heart disease was developed in close collaboration with physicians.

2. *Let employees choose projects.* Few actual product leaders and teams are appointed. Gore likes to nurture "passionate champions" who convince others a project is worth their time and commitment. The development of the fuel cell rallied over 100 of the company's 6000 research associates.

3. *Give employees "dabble" time.* All research associates spend 10 percent of their work hours developing their own ideas. Promising ideas are pushed forward and judged

according to a "Real, Win, Worth" exercise. Is the opportunity real? Can we win? Can we make money?

4. *Know when to let go.* Sometimes dead ends in one area can spark an innovation in another. Elixir acoustic guitar strings were a result of a failed venture into bike cables. Even successful ventures may have to move on. Glide shred-resistant dental floss was sold to Procter & Gamble because Gore-Tex knew that retailers would want to deal with a company selling a whole family of health-care products.

Most new-product activity is devoted to improving existing products. At Sony, over 80 percent of new-product activity is actually modifying and improving existing products. Gillette frequently updates its razor systems, launching the new Fusion Power Phenom razor for men and Venus Embrace razor for women in 2008.[4] In many categories, it is becoming increasingly difficult to identify blockbuster products that transform a market. But continually innovating to better satisfy consumer needs can force competitors to play catch-up, as seen in the media storage industry.[5]

Blu-ray

A new media player is expected to forever change how consumers view movies. Blu-ray discs (BDs) are like DVDs in size and shape but can hold 25 GB (gigabytes) on a single-layer disc or 50 GB on a dual-layer disc. Besides being able to store large amounts of data, BDs offer unprecedented video quality surpassing that of high-definition video. The world's first Blu-ray recorder and media became available in Canada in 2006. BDs are distributed through the Blu-ray Disc Association founded with the help of Sony and supported by Apple, HP, Warner Brothers, and 250 other companies. Playable on Blu-ray players, BDs can also be viewed on compatible PCs and on the Sony PlayStation 3. Many major movie producers have already released their movies on Blu-ray discs. With its increasing popularity, BDs are expected to replace DVDs over the next decade.[6]

Launching new products as brand extensions into related product categories is one means of broadening the brand meaning. Nike started as a running shoe manufacturer but now competes in the sports market with all types of athletic shoes, clothing, and equipment. Armstrong World Industries moved from selling floor coverings to ceilings to total interior-surface decoration. Product innovation and effective marketing programs have allowed these firms to expand their "market footprint."

In an economy of rapid change, continuous innovation is necessary. Most companies rarely innovate, some innovate occasionally, and a few innovate continuously. In the last category, McCain, Sony, 3M, Dell Computer, Maple Leaf, Oracle, Maytag, Costco, and Microsoft have been leaders in their respective industries in stock-price gain.[7] These companies have created a positive attitude towards innovation and risk taking, they have routinized the innovation process, they practise teamwork, and they allow their people to experiment and even fail. Table 20.1 lists the 2007 rankings of the world's 25 most innovative firms as determined by a *BusinessWeek*–Boston Consulting Group survey.

Companies that fail to develop new products put themselves at risk. Their existing products are vulnerable to changing customer needs and tastes, new technologies, shortened product life cycles, and increased domestic and foreign competition. New technologies are especially threatening.

Most established companies focus on *incremental innovation.* Newer companies create *disruptive technologies* that are cheaper and more likely to alter the competitive space. Established companies can be slow to react or invest in these disruptive technologies because they threaten their investment. Then they suddenly find themselves facing formidable new competitors, and many fail.[8] To ensure that they don't fall into this trap, incumbent firms must carefully monitor the preferences of both customers and noncustomers over time and uncover evolving, difficult-to-articulate customer needs.[9] Guess Canada has been doing this quite effectively.

Constant innovation is critical in the media-storage industry to avoid the risk of becoming obsolete.

TABLE 20.1	THE WORLD'S TOP 25 MOST INNOVATIVE COMPANIES

2007 Rank	2006 Rank	Company Name	HQ City	HQ Country	HQ Continent	Stock Returns 2001–2006	Revenue Growth 2001–2006	Margin Growth 2001–2006	Patent Citation Index
1	1	APPLE	Cupertino, CA	USA	North America	50.60	29.21	NA	34
2	2	GOOGLE	Mountain View, CA	USA	North America	NA	NA	NA	1
3	4	TOYOTA MOTOR	Toyota	Japan	Asia	20.50	8.30	5.21	361
4	6	GENERAL ELECTRIC	Fairfield, CT	USA	North America	1.11	5.06	1.36	155
5	5	MICROSOFT	Redmond, WA	USA	North America	0.83	11.85	−3.04	174
6	7	PROCTER & GAMBLE	Cincinnati, OH	USA	North America	12.20	11.69	3.70	105
7	3	3M	St. Paul, MN	USA	North America	7.77	7.35	5.49	57
8	43	WALT DISNEY CO	Burbank, CA	USA	North America	11.71	6.29	7.35	8
9	10	IBM	Armonk, NY	USA	North America	−3.48	1.26	4.97	94
10	13	SONY	Tokyo	Japan	Asia	−2.62	0.60	1.14	418
11	20	WAL-MART	Bentonville, AR	USA	North America	−3.35	9.79	3.54	0
12	23	HONDA MOTOR	Tokyo	Japan	Asia	13.61	7.40	0.38	377
13	8	NOKIA	Espoo	Finland	Europe	−9.24	5.68	4.37	287
14	9	STARBUCKS	Seattle, WA	USA	North America	30.04	24.07	1.51	2
15	22	TARGET	Minneapolis, MN	USA	North America	7.55	8.32	4.23	0
16	16	BMW	Munich	Germany	Europe	4.30	4.96	−1.23	84
17	12	SAMSUNG ELECTRONICS	Seoul	South Korea	Asia	36.24	4.60	8.07	1000
18	11	VIRGIN GROUP	London	United Kingdom	Europe	Private	Private	Private	0
19	17	INTEL	Santa Clara, CA	USA	North America	−7.57	5.92	12.55	216
20	21	AMAZON.COM	Seattle, WA	USA	North America	−9.53	27.96	NA	0
21	70	BOEING	Chicago, IL	USA	North America	19.91	1.12	−4.23	59
22	14	DELL	Round Rock, TX	USA	North America	−1.59	12.87	−5.24	16
23	27	GENENTECH	South San Francisco, CA	USA	North America	24.50	34.85	32.40	4
24	18	EBAY	San Jose, CA	USA	North America	12.45	51.47	4.91	1
25	28	CISCO SYSTEMS	San Jose, CA	USA	North America	8.58	5.02	205.04	20

Source: "The World's Fifty Most Innovative Companies," Special Report, *BusinessWeek*, May 9, 2007.

Note: The *BusinessWeek*-Boston Consulting Group 2007 rankings are based on a senior management survey about innovation distributed electronically to executives worldwide in October 2006. Surveys were sent to their top 10 executives in charge of innovation at the 1,500 largest global corporations, determined by market capitalization in U.S. dollars. Surveys were also distributed to senior management members of the *BusinessWeek* Market Advisory Board, an online panel consisting of *BusinessWeek* readers, and via the Knowledge@Wharton e-mail newsletter. Survey participation was voluntary and anonymous, and the survey closed in March 2007. The survey consisted of 20 general questions on innovation and an optional 12 questions focused on innovation metrics. A total of 2,468 executives answered the survey. Of those indicating their location, 77% were from North America, 12% were from Europe, and 9% were from Asia or the Pacific region.

To explore how the Virgin Group with its 'umbrella brand strategy' has become one of the most admired branded companies in the world, visit www.pearsoned.co.uk/marketingmanagementeurope.

Guess Canada

As consumers go "green," more and more companies are doing the same—including Guess Canada. With its new line of eco-friendly products, Guess demonstrates that it cares for the environment and the well being of its customers. Launched in the spring of 2008, the clothing line includes 100-percent-organic cotton tanks for women and T-shirts for men. Also available for both sexes are 100-percent-organic cotton dark-wash jeans that are produced with minimal use of chemicals. A "Guess Green" logo is imprinted on the new eco-friendly line. Ten percent of proceeds from the clothes are donated to the Environmental Media Association, an organization that helps increase public awareness of environmental issues. Through its Green line, Guess has demonstrated that it monitors changes in consumer behaviour and aims to keep up with them.[10]

MARKETING INSIGHT | SUCCESS AND FAILURE OF BRAND EXTENSIONS

For marketers, brand extensions are a natural way to get the most value out of a core brand asset. In order to do this successfully, marketers must be careful in evaluating prospective brand extensions, both in terms of their profitability and the extent to which they are likely to hurt the parent brand. Using a brand extension to build on past successes and show continuity of a brand may be simple in theory, but many companies have struggled to execute the strategy successfully.

Continuous improvement can allow some brands to last for generations. The strategy of constantly changing and innovating in order to keep a business successful is not a new practice by any means. In 1830, James and Cyrus Clark began making sheepskin slippers in Somerset, England, and their company has since grown to 12 700 employees producing and selling 41 million pairs of shoes a year. The Clarks brand has a reputation for quality that has lasted through generations. They chose to stick with what they know best, a philosophy some other companies have not adopted while bringing out brand extensions. For example, Levi Strauss, having a reputation for producing casual clothing, decided to extend the brand into tailored suits. Although Levi's had a positive reputation, its tailored suits failed to take off.

Some marketers chose to enter entirely new industries hoping that the trust that consumers have placed in the brand will rub off on their new, unrelated product. This strategy can have varying degrees of success. Failed brand extensions include Harley-Davidson cologne and a Hooters airline, while extensions such as the Oprah Magazine and Grey Goose Entertainment (a joint-venture of the vodka producer and the Sundance Channel) have had great success.

A study that analyzed the effect of service brand extensions on corporate image found that the final brand image existing after a brand extension is dependent on two factors. The first is the perceived quality of the new offering and the second is the degree of fit consumers perceive between the parent brand and the extension. Even if the brand extension proves profitable, it might erode the parent brand's image. Ultimately, an extension should act as a complementary product that builds on the already valuable image of the core brand.

Sources: "Nike Walk-in Baths Just Wouldn't Wash," 2007, *Strategic Direction*, 22, no. 1: 12–15.; Jose M. Pina, Eva Martinez, Leslie de Chernatony, and Susan Drury, "The Effect of Service Brand Extensions on Corporate Image: An Empirical Model," *European Journal of Marketing*, 40, no. 1/2: 174–197; TippingSprung, "TippingSprung Fields Second Annual Brand-Extension Survey," *brandchannel.com*, www.brandchannel.com/papers_review.asp?sp_id=1222 (viewed June 12, 2008).

At the same time, new-product development can be quite risky. Texas Instruments lost US$660 million before withdrawing from the home computer business, RCA lost US$500 million on its videodisc players, FedEx lost US$340 million on its Zap mail, DuPont lost an estimated US$100 million on a synthetic leather called Corfam, and the British-French Concorde aircraft never recovered its investment.[11] Even companies that have had a very successful brand on the market sometimes fail miserably when they attempt to bring out a brand extension (see "Marketing Insight: Success and Failure of Brand Extensions").

New products designed for consumers and businesses continue to fail at a disturbing rate. Recent studies put the rate at 95 percent in the United States and 90 percent in Europe. In Canada, according to most industry estimates, 80 percent of new consumer products fail, with 20 percent remaining on shelves after two years.[12] New products can fail for many reasons: ignoring or misinterpreting market research; overestimating market size; high development costs; poor design; incorrect positioning, ineffective advertising, or wrong price; insufficient distribution support; and competitors that fight back hard.

Several factors also tend to hinder new-product development:

- *Shortage of important ideas in certain areas.* There may be few ways left to improve some basic products (such as steel and detergents).

- *Fragmented markets.* Companies have to aim their new products at smaller market segments, and this can mean lower sales and profits for each product.

- *Social and governmental constraints.* New products have to satisfy consumer safety and environmental concerns.

- *Cost of development.* A company typically has to generate many ideas to find just one worthy of development, and often faces high R&D, manufacturing, and marketing costs.

- *Capital shortages.* Some companies with good ideas cannot raise the funds needed to research and launch them.

MARKETING MEMO | LESSONS FOR NEW-PRODUCT SUCCESS

Strolling the aisles at Robert McMath's New Product Showcase and Learning Center is like being in some nightmare version of a supermarket. There is Gerber food for adults (pureed sweet-and-sour pork and chicken Madeira), microwaveable ice cream sundaes, parsnip chips, aerosol mustard, Ben-Gay aspirin, and Miller Clear Beer. How about Richard Simmons Dijon Vinaigrette Salad Spray, garlic cake in a jar, and Farrah shampoo?

McMath's unusual showcase represents US$4 billion in product investment. Behind each of the 80 000 products on display are squandered dollars and hopes. From them he has distilled dozens of lessons for an industry that, by its own admission, has a very short memory. McMath, a former marketer for Colgate-Palmolive, has now put his unique insights into a book called *What Were They Thinking?* Here are a few of the marketing lessons McMath offers:

- *The value of a brand is its good name, which it earns over time.* People trust it to deliver a consistent set of attributes. Do not squander this trust by attaching your good name to something totally out of character. Louis Sherry No Sugar Added Gorgonzola Cheese dressing was everything that Louis Sherry, known for its rich candies and ice cream, should not be: sugarless, cheese, and salad dressing.

- *Me-too marketing is the number-one killer of new products.* Pepsi is one of the few survivors among dozens of other brands that have challenged Coke for more than a century. Ever hear of Toca-Cola? Coco-Cola? Yum-Yum Cola? French Wine of Cola? How about King-Cola, "the royal drink"?

- *People usually do not buy products that remind them of their shortcomings.* Gillette's For Oily Hair Only shampoo flopped because people did not want to confess that they had greasy hair, nor do they wish to advertise their faults and foibles to other people by carrying such products in their grocery carts.

- *Some products are too different from the products, services, or experiences consumers normally purchase.* You can tell that some innovative products are doomed as soon as you hear their names: Toaster Eggs, Cucumber Antiperspirant spray, Health-Sea Sea Sausage.

Sources: Paul Lukas, "The Ghastliest Product Launches," *Fortune*, March 16, 1996, p. 44; Jan Alexander, "Failure Inc." *Worldbusiness* (May–June 1996): 46; Ted Anthony, "Where's Farrah Shampoo? Next to the Salsa Ketchup," *Marketing News*, May 6, 1996, p. 13. Bulleted points are adapted from Robert M. McMath and Thom Forbes, *What Were They Thinking? Marketing Lessons I've Learned from Over 80,000 New-Product Innovations and Idiocies* (New York: Times Business, 1998), pp. 22–24, 28, 30–31, and 129–130.

- *Faster required development time.* Companies must learn how to compress development time by using new techniques, strategic partners, early concept tests, and advanced marketing planning.

- *Shorter product life cycles.* When a new product is successful, rivals are quick to copy it. Sony used to enjoy a three-year lead on its new products. Now Matsushita will copy the product within six months, leaving hardly enough time for Sony to recoup its investment.

What can a company do to develop successful new products? Cooper and Kleinschmidt found that the number-one success factor is a unique, superior product. Such products succeed 98 percent of the time, compared to products with a moderate advantage (58 percent success) or minimal advantage (18 percent success). Another key factor is a well-defined product concept. The company carefully defines and assesses its target market, product requirements, and benefits before proceeding. Other success factors are technological and marketing synergy, quality of execution in all stages, and market attractiveness.[13] (See "Marketing Memo: Lessons for New-Product Success.")

Since 2004, *Marketing* magazine had been giving Best New Product awards in several categories. The annual award is given to everyday consumer packaged goods exemplifying the new-product success factors previously described. Ten thousand Canadian consumers vote on a product that is appealing and that they would be willing to purchase again. Consider just two of the 2008 award winners, Quaker Crispy Delights and Ziploc Zip 'n Steam.

Quaker Crispy Delights

These calorie-controlled snacks are meant for people who want a sweet treat but also want to watch their waistlines. More consumers want to eat healthily, and Crispy Delights allows them to have a treat without the calories. The Quaker product comes in convenient packages that allow people to take them anywhere so they can have a healthy snack anytime they are hungry. One consumer described Crispy Delights as "Made with 100% whole grains and comes in handy packages to take to work" while another said "Good for people that have a sweet tooth but don't want the added calories." [14]

Ziploc Zip 'n Steam

This new product was a winner in the Household Care category. With the rise in dual-earner households, couples are finding it increasingly difficult to find time to prepare healthy meals. Ziploc realized that food should be convenient but still taste fresh, even if it is coming from the microwave. Consumers had a lot to say about the easy-to-use product: "Saves lots of time, effort, enables me to get dinner on the table faster at the end of the day" and "They are great! Handy, easy, great taste, easy clean-up and best of all creates a healthy veggie!".

ORGANIZATIONAL ARRANGEMENTS

Once a company has carefully segmented the market, chosen its target customers, identified their needs, and determined its market positioning, it is better able to develop new products. Many companies today use *customer-driven engineering* to design new products. Customer-driven engineering attaches high importance to incorporating customer preferences into the final design.

New-product development requires senior management to define business domains, product categories, and specific criteria. General Motors has a hefty US$400 million benchmark it must apply to new car models—this is what it costs to get a new vehicle into production.[15] One company established the following acceptance criteria:

- The product can be introduced within five years.
- The product has a market potential of at least $50 million and a 15-percent growth rate.
- The product would provide at least 30-percent return on sales and 40 percent on investment.
- The product would achieve technical or market leadership.

Budgeting for New-Product Development

Senior management must decide how much to budget for new-product development. R&D outcomes are so uncertain that it is difficult to use normal investment criteria. Some companies solve this problem by financing as many projects as possible, hoping to achieve a few winners. Other companies apply a conventional percentage of sales figures or spend what the competition spends. Still other companies decide how many successful new products they need and work backwards to estimate the required investment.

Table 20.2 shows how a company might calculate the cost of new-product development. The new-products manager at a large consumer packaged-goods company reviewed the results of

TABLE 20.2	FINDING ONE SUCCESSFUL NEW PRODUCT (STARTING WITH 64 NEW IDEAS)			
Stage	Number of Ideas	Cost per Pass Ratio	Product Idea	Total Cost
1. Idea screening	64	1:4	$ 1000	$ 64 000
2. Concept testing	16	1:2	20 000	320 000
3. Product development	8	1:2	200 000	1 600 000
4. Test marketing	4	1:2	500 000	2 000 000
5. National launch	2	1:2	5 000 000	10 000 000
			$5 721 000	$13 984 000

64 ideas. Only one in four, or 16, passed the screening stage. It cost $1000 to review each idea at this stage. Half of these ideas, or eight, survived the concept-testing stage, at a cost of $20 000 each. Half of these, or four, survived the product-development stage, at a cost of $200 000 each. Half of these, or two, did well in the test market, at a cost of $500 000 each. When these two ideas were launched, at a cost of $5 million each, only one was highly successful. Thus the one successful idea cost the company $5 721 000 to develop.

In the process, 63 other ideas fell by the wayside. The total cost for developing one successful new product was $13 984 000. Unless the company can improve the pass ratios and reduce the costs at each stage, it will have to budget nearly $14 million for each successful new idea it hopes to find. If top management wants four successful new products in the next few years, it will have to budget at least $56 million ($4 \times 14 million) for new-product development.

Organizing New-Product Development

Companies handle the organizational aspect of new-product development in several ways.[16] Many companies assign responsibility for new-product ideas to *product managers*. But product managers are often so busy managing existing lines that they give little thought to new products other than line extensions. They also lack the specific skills and knowledge needed to develop and critique new products. Kraft and Johnson & Johnson have *new-product managers* who report to category managers. Some companies have a *high-level management committee* charged with reviewing and approving proposals. Large companies often establish a *new-product department* headed by a manager who has substantial authority and access to top management. The department's major responsibilities include generating and screening new ideas, working with the R&D department, and carrying out field-testing and commercialization.

3M, Dow, and General Mills often assign new-product development work to *venture teams*. A **venture team** is a cross-functional group charged with developing a specific product or business. These "intrapreneurs" are relieved of their other duties and given a budget, a time frame, and a "skunkworks" setting. *Skunkworks* are informal workplaces, sometimes garages, where intrapreneurial teams attempt to develop new products.

Cross-functional teams can collaborate and use concurrent new-product development to push new products to market.[17] Concurrent product development resembles a rugby match rather than a relay race, with team members passing the new product back and forth as they head towards the goal. Using this system, the Allen-Bradley Corporation (a maker of industrial controls) was able to develop a new electrical control device in just two years, as opposed to six years under its old system.

Cross-functional teams help to ensure that engineers are not driven to create just a "better mousetrap" when potential customers do not really need or want one. Some possible criteria for staffing cross-functional new-product venture teams include:[18]

- *Desired team leadership style and level of expertise.* The more complex the new-product concept, the greater the desired expertise.
- *Team member skills and expertise.* New-venture teams for Aventis, part of a pharmaceutical, agricultural, and chemical conglomerate, contain people with expertise in chemistry, engineering, market research, financial analysis, and manufacturing.
- *Level of interest in the particular new-product concept.* Is there interest or, even better, a high level of ownership and commitment (a "concept champion")?
- *Potential for personal reward.* What motivates individuals to want to participate in this effort?
- *Diversity of team members.* This includes race, gender, nationality, breadth of experience, depth of experience, and personality. The greater the diversity, the greater the range of viewpoints and decision-making potential.

3M, Hewlett-Packard, Lego, and many other companies use the *stage-gate system* to manage the innovation process.[19] The process is divided into stages, and at the end of each stage is a gate or checkpoint. The project leader, working with a cross-functional team, must bring a set of known deliverables to each gate before the project can pass to the next stage. To move from the business-plan stage into product development requires a convincing market research study of consumer needs and interest, a competitive analysis, and a technical appraisal. Senior managers review the criteria at each gate to judge whether the project deserves to move to the next stage. The gatekeepers make one of four decisions: *go, kill, hold,* or *recycle.* Stage-gate systems make the innovation process visible to all involved and clarify the project leader's and team's responsibilities at each stage.[20]

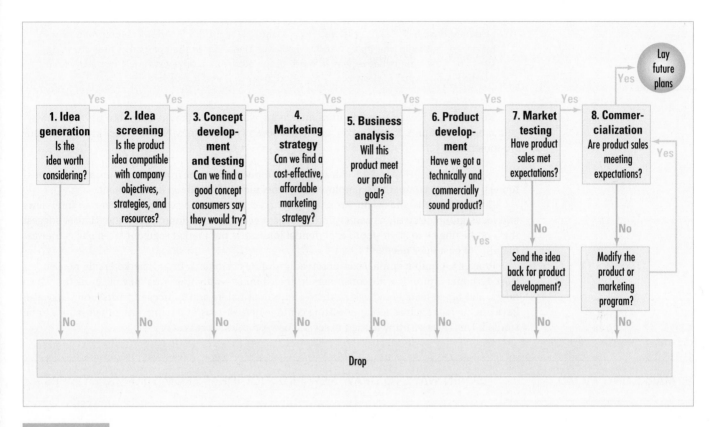

The New-Product Development Decision Process

The stages in the new-product development process are shown in Figure 20.1. Many firms have multiple, parallel sets of projects working through the process, each at a different stage.[21] The process can be depicted as a *funnel:* a large number of initial new-product ideas and concepts are winnowed down to a few high-potential products that are ultimately launched. But the process is not always linear. Many firms use a *spiral development process* that recognizes the value of returning to an earlier stage to make improvements before moving forward.

We now look at the marketing challenges arising during new-product development.

MANAGING THE DEVELOPMENT PROCESS: IDEAS

Idea Generation

The new-product development process starts with the search for ideas. Some marketing experts believe that the greatest opportunities and highest leverage with new products are found by uncovering the best possible set of unmet customer needs or by technological innovation.[22] Adobe uses innovative methods to come up with creative ideas.

Adobe Systems Inc.

A developer of software solutions for graphic designers and publishers, Adobe established a task force in 2004 to identify all the obstacles company innovators faced in trying to develop new products. The team found the corporate hierarchy resisted ideas needing a new sales channel, new business model, or even new packaging, and the company had grown so large that ideas originating in branch offices were not getting a fair shake. The company then established a New Business Initiatives Group that holds quarterly Adobe Idea Champion Showcases. About 20 product managers and other employees (except top executives who are barred from the proceedings) watch as potential employee-entrepreneurs give brief presentations and Q&A sessions. The ideas are vetted by Adobe entrepreneurs-in-residence, but even one that's nixed can still get a hearing on the company's brainstorming site. Since the new initiative was formed, the event has become extremely popular within Adobe—a Canadian Idol–style way for good ideas to come to the fore.[23]

New-product ideas can come from interacting with various groups and from using creativity-generating techniques. (See "Marketing Memo: Seven Ways to Draw New-Product Ideas from Your Customers.")

INTERACTING WITH OTHERS   Ideas for new products can come from many sources, such as customers, scientists, competitors, employees, channel members, and top management.

Customer needs and wants are the logical place to start the search. One-on-one interviews and focus-group discussions can explore product needs and reactions. Griffin and Hauser suggest that conducting 10 to 20 in-depth experiential interviews per market segment often elicits the vast majority of customer needs.[24]

Procter & Gamble emphasizes observations of its customers. Brand marketers there spend at least 12 hours a month with consumers in their homes—watching how they clean dishes, wash floors, and brush teeth—and asking them about their habits and sources of frustration. They also have on-site labs such as a diaper-testing centre where dozens of parents bring their babies to be studied. This close scrutiny has led to several new-product successes.

MARKETING MEMO | SEVEN WAYS TO DRAW NEW-PRODUCT IDEAS FROM YOUR CUSTOMERS

1. *Observe how your customers are using your product.* Medtronic, a medical-device company, has salespeople and market researchers regularly observe spine surgeons who use their products and competitive products to learn how their products can be improved. Similarly, GE has gathered ideas for improving CAT scanners by observing their use by skilled medical personnel.

2. *Ask your customers about their problems with your products.* Komatsu Heavy Equipment sent a group of engineers and designers to the United States for six months to ride with equipment drivers and learn how to make products better. Procter & Gamble, recognizing consumers were frustrated that potato chips would break and were difficult to save after opening the bag, designed Pringles to be uniform in size and encased in a can like a tennis-ball canister so that consumers could open the can, consume a few unbroken chips, and close it again.

3. *Ask your customers about their dream products.* Ask your customers what they want your product to do, even if the ideal sounds impossible. One 70-year-old camera user told Minolta he would like the camera to make his subjects look better and not show their wrinkles and aging. In response, Minolta produced a camera with two lenses, one of which was for rendering softer images of subjects.

4. *Use a customer advisory board to comment on your company's ideas.* Levi Strauss uses youth panels to discuss lifestyles, habits, values, and brand engagements; Cisco runs customer forums to improve its offerings; and Harley-Davidson solicits product ideas from its one million H.O.G. (Harley Owners Group) members.

5. *Form a brand community of enthusiasts who discuss your product.* Harley-Davidson and Apple have strong brand enthusiasts and advocates; Sony engaged in collaborative dialogues with consumers to co-develop Sony's PlayStation 2. LEGO draws on kids and influential adult enthusiasts for feedback on new-product concepts in early stages of development.

6. *Encourage or challenge your customers to change or improve your product.* Salesforce.com wants its users to develop and share new software applications using simple programming tools. International Flavors & Fragrances gives a toolkit to its customers to modify specific flavourings, which IFF then manufactures; LSI Logic Corporation also provides customers with do-it-yourself toolkits so that customers can design their own specialized chips; and BMW posted a toolkit on its website to let customers develop ideas using telematics and in-car online services.

7. *Use websites for new ideas.* Companies can use specialized search engines such as Technorati and Day Pop to find blogs and postings relevant to their businesses. P&G's site has "We're Listening" and "Share Your Thoughts" sections and Advisory Feedback sessions to gain advice and feedback from customers.

Source: Philip Kotler, "Drawing New Ideas from Your Customers," 2007 (unpublished paper).

Procter & Gamble

To develop its Cover Girl Outlast all-day lip colour, P&G tested the product on nearly 30 000 women, inviting 500 of them to come to its labs each morning to apply the lipstick, record their activities, and return eight hours later so it could measure remaining lip colour. The activities, dubbed "torture tests" by P&G, ranged from eating spaghetti to kickboxing to showering. The product comes with a tube of glossy moisturizer that women can reapply on top of their colour—without having to look at a mirror. The blockbuster product quickly became the market leader.[25]

Technical companies can learn a great deal by studying customers who make the most advanced use of the company's products and who recognize the need for improvements before other customers do.[26] Microsoft studied 13- to 24-year-olds—the NetGen—and developed its Threedegrees software product to satisfy their instant-messaging needs.[27] (For the special case of developing high-tech products, see "Marketing Insight: Developing Successful High-Tech Products.")

MARKETING INSIGHT	DEVELOPING SUCCESSFUL HIGH-TECH PRODUCTS

High tech covers a wide range of industries—telecommunications, computers, consumer electronics, biotech, software. Radical innovations carry a high level of risk and typically hurt the company's bottom line at least in the short run. The good news is that success can create a greater sustainable competitive advantage than might come from more ordinary products.

One way to define the scope of high tech is by its common characteristics:

- *High technological uncertainty.* Scientists working on high-tech products are never sure the products will function as promised and be delivered on time.
- *High market uncertainty.* Marketers are not sure what needs the new technology will meet. How will buyers use Interactive TV?
- *High competitive volatility.* Will the strongest competition come from within the industry or from outside? Will competitors rewrite the rules? What products will this new technology replace?
- *High investment cost, low variable cost.* Many high-tech products require a large up-front investment to develop the first unit, but the costs fall rapidly for additional units. The cost of developing a new piece of software is very high, but the cost of distributing it online or on a CD is relatively low.
- *Short life.* Most high-tech products must be constantly upgraded. Competitors will often force the innovator to produce a second-generation product before recouping its investment on the first generation.
- *Finding funding sources for such risky projects is not easy.* Companies must create a strong R&D/marketing partnership to pull it off. Few reliable techniques exist for estimating demand for radical innovations. Focus groups will provide some perspectives on customer interest and need, but high-tech marketers will have to use a probe-and-learn approach based on observing early users and collecting feedback on their experiences.

High-tech marketers also face difficult questions related to the marketing mix:

- *Product.* What features and functions should they build into the new product? Should manufacturing be done in-house or be outsourced?
- *Price.* Should the price be set high? Would a low price be better in order to sell more quickly and go down the experience curve more quickly? Should the product be almost given away to accelerate adoption?
- *Distribution.* Is the product best sold through the company's own sales force or should it be put in the hands of agents, distributors, and dealers? Should the company start with one channel or build multiple sales channels early?
- *Communication.* What are the best messages to convey the basic benefits and features of the new product? What are the best media for communicating these messages? What sales-promotion incentives would drive early interest and purchase?

Source: For further ideas, see Jakki Mohr, *Marketing of High-Technology Products and Innovations*, 2nd ed. (Upper Saddle River, NJ: Prentice Hall, 2005).

Employees throughout a company can be a source of ideas for improving production, products, and services. Toyota claims its employees submit 2 million ideas annually (about 35 suggestions per employee), over 85 percent of which are implemented. Kodak, Milliken, and other firms give monetary, holiday, or recognition awards to employees who submit the best ideas.

Companies can also find good ideas by researching competitors' products and services. They can find out what customers like and dislike about competitors' products. They can buy their competitors' products, take them apart, and build better ones. Company sales representatives and intermediaries are a particularly good source of ideas. These groups have firsthand exposure to customers and are often the first to learn about competitive developments.

Top management can be another major source of ideas. Some company leaders, such as the late Edwin H. Land, former CEO of Polaroid, and Andy Grove of Intel, took personal responsibility for technological innovation in their companies. New-product ideas can also come from inventors, patent lawyers, university and commercial laboratories, industrial consultants, advertising agencies, marketing research firms, and industrial publications. However, although ideas can flow from many sources, their chances of receiving serious attention often depend on someone in the organization taking the role of product champion.

CREATIVITY TECHNIQUES   Here is a sampling of techniques for stimulating creativity in individuals and groups:[28]

- *Attribute listing.* List the attributes of an object, such as a screwdriver. Then modify each attribute, such as replacing the wooden handle with plastic, providing torque power, adding different screw heads, and so on.

- *Forced relationships.* List several ideas and consider each one in relation to each other one. In designing new office furniture, for example, consider a desk, bookcase, and filing cabinet as separate ideas. One can then imagine a desk with a built-in bookcase or a desk with built-in files or a bookcase with built-in files.

- *Morphological analysis.* Start with a problem, such as "getting something from one place to another via a powered vehicle." Now think of dimensions, such as the type of platform (cart, chair, sling, bed), the medium (air, water, oil, rails), and the power source (compressed air, electric motor, magnetic fields). By listing every possible combination, one can generate many new solutions.

- *Reverse assumption analysis.* List all the normal assumptions about an entity and then reverse them. Instead of assuming that a restaurant has menus, charges for food, and serves food, reverse each assumption. The new restaurant may decide to serve only what the chef bought that morning and cooked, may provide some food and charge only for how long the person sits at the table, or may design an exotic atmosphere and rent out the space to people who bring their own food and beverages.

- *New contexts.* Take familiar processes, such as people-helping services, and put them into a new context. Imagine helping dogs and cats instead of people with daycare service, stress reduction, psychotherapy, animal funerals, and so on. As another example, instead of hotel guests going to the front desk to check in, greet them at curbside and use a wireless device to register them.

- *Mind-mapping.* Start with a thought, such as a car, write it on a piece of paper, then think of the next thought that comes up (say Mercedes), link it to car, then think of the next association (Germany), and do this with all associations that come up with each new word. Perhaps a whole new idea will materialize.

Increasingly, new-product ideas arise from *lateral marketing* that combines two product concepts or ideas to create a new offering. Here are some successful examples:

- Gas-station stores = gas stations + food
- Cyber cafés = café + Internet
- Cereal bars = cereal + snacking
- Kinder Surprise = candy + toy
- Multifunction printer = printer + scanner + fax machine

Idea Screening

A company should motivate its employees to submit new ideas to an *idea manager* whose name and phone number are widely circulated. Ideas should be written down and reviewed each week by an *idea committee*. The company then sorts the proposed ideas into three groups: promising ideas, marginal ideas, and rejects. Each promising idea is researched by a committee member, who reports back to the committee. The surviving ideas then move into a full-scale screening process. In screening ideas, the company must avoid two types of errors.

A *drop-error* occurs when the company dismisses an otherwise good idea. It is extremely easy to find fault with other people's ideas (Figure 20.2). Some companies shudder when they look back at ideas they dismissed or breathe sighs of relief when they realize how close they came to dropping what eventually became a huge success.

A *go-error* occurs when the company permits a poor idea to move into development and commercialization, as in the case of the Honda Accord Hybrid. An *absolute product failure* loses money; its sales do not cover variable costs. A *partial product failure* loses money, but its sales cover all its variable costs and some of its fixed costs. A *relative product failure* yields a profit that is less than the company's target rate of return.

Honda Accord Hybrid

Honda, known for its line of top-selling automobiles such as the Civic, Accord, Odyssey, CR-V, and Civic Hybrid, has also had some product failures. In June 2007, the company announced that it was ceasing production of the Accord Hybrid—a car that had been struggling on the market since its launch three years earlier. The Hybrid's fuel economy was no better than that of Honda's four-cylinder, gas-powered model, yet the car cost $9000 more. Honda expected consumers to be impressed by getting four-cylinder fuel economy with six-cylinder horsepower. What Honda failed to recognize was that consumers who bought hybrids were doing so for fuel economy, not for horsepower. Consumers were not willing to pay the price premium to get more of a product feature they didn't care much for. [29]

The purpose of screening is to drop poor ideas as early as possible. The rationale is that product-development costs rise substantially with each successive development stage. Most companies require new-product ideas to be described on a standard form that can be reviewed by a new-product committee. The description states the product idea, the target market, and the competition, and roughly estimates market size, product price, development time and costs, manufacturing costs, and rate of return.

The executive committee then reviews each idea against a set of criteria. Does the product meet a need? Would it offer superior value? Can it be distinctively advertised? Does the company have the necessary know-how and capital? Will the new product deliver the expected sales volume, sales growth, and profit?

The surviving ideas can be rated using a weighted-index method like that in Table 20.3. The first column lists factors required for successful product launches, and the second column assigns importance weights. The third column scores the product idea on a scale from 0 to 1.0, with 1.0 the highest score. The final step multiplies each factor's importance by the product score to obtain an overall rating. In this example, the product idea scores 0.69, which places it in the "good idea" level. The purpose of this basic rating device is to promote systematic evaluation and discussion. It is not supposed to make the decision for management.

TABLE 20.3 | PRODUCT–IDEA RATING DEVICE

Product-Success Requirements	Relative Weight (w)	Product Score (s)	Product Rating (r = w × s)
Unique or superior product	0.40	0.8	0.32
High performance-to-cost ratio	0.30	0.6	0.18
High marketing-dollar support	0.20	0.7	0.14
Lack of strong competition	0.10	0.5	0.05
Total	1.00		0.69[a]

[a]Rating scale: 0.00–0.30 poor; 0.31–0.60 fair; 0.61–0.80 good. Minimum acceptance rate: 0.61.

"I've got a great idea!"

"It won't work here."

"We've tried it before."

"This isn't the right time."

"It can't be done."

"It's not the way we do things."

"We've done all right without it."

"It will cost too much."

"Let's discuss it at our next meeting."

FIGURE 20.2

Forces Fighting New Ideas

Source: With permission of Jerold Panas, Young & Partners, Inc.

As the idea moves through development, the company will constantly need to revise its estimate of the product's overall probability of success using the following formula:

Overall probability of success	=	Probability of technical completion	×	Probability of commercialization given technical completion	×	Probability of economic success given commercialization

For example, if the three probabilities are estimated as 0.50, 0.65, and 0.74, respectively, the overall probability of success is 0.24. The company then has to judge whether this probability is high enough to warrant continued development.

MANAGING THE DEVELOPMENT PROCESS: CONCEPT TO STRATEGY

Attractive ideas must be refined into testable product concepts. A *product idea* is a possible product the company might offer to the market. A *product concept* is an elaborated version of the idea expressed in consumer terms.

Concept Development and Testing

CONCEPT DEVELOPMENT   Let us illustrate concept development with the following situation: a large food-processing company gets the idea of producing a powder to add to milk to improve its nutritional value and taste. This is a product idea, but consumers do not buy product ideas; they buy product concepts.

A product idea can be turned into several concepts. The first question is: Who will use this product? The powder can be aimed at infants, children, teenagers, young or middle-aged adults, or older adults. Second, what primary benefit should this product provide? Taste, nutrition, refreshment, energy? Third, when will people consume this drink? Breakfast, mid-morning, lunch, mid-afternoon, dinner, late evening? By answering these questions, a company can form several concepts:

- *Concept 1.* An instant-breakfast drink for adults who want a quick nutritious breakfast without preparation.
- *Concept 2.* A tasty snack drink for children to drink as a midday refreshment.
- *Concept 3.* A health supplement for older adults to drink in the late evening before they go to bed.

Each concept represents a *category concept* that defines the product's competition. An instant-breakfast drink would compete against bacon and eggs, breakfast cereals, coffee and pastry, and other breakfast alternatives. A tasty snack drink would compete against soft drinks, fruit juices, and other thirst quenchers.

Suppose the concept of an instant-breakfast drink looks best. The next task is to show where this powdered product would stand in relation to other breakfast products. Figure 20.3(a) uses the two dimensions of cost and preparation time to create a *product-positioning map* for the breakfast drink. An instant-breakfast drink offers low cost and quick preparation. Its nearest competitor is cold cereal or breakfast bars; its most distant competitor is bacon and eggs. These contrasts can be utilized in communicating and promoting the concept to the market.

Next, the product concept has to be turned into a *brand concept.* Figure 20.3(b) is a brand-positioning map showing the current positions of three existing brands of instant-breakfast drinks. The company needs to decide how much to charge and how calorific to make its drink. The new brand would be distinctive in the medium-price, medium-calorie market or in the high-price, high-calorie market. The company would not want to position it next to an existing brand, unless that brand is weak or inferior.

CONCEPT TESTING   Concept testing involves presenting the product concept to target consumers and getting their reactions. The concepts can be presented symbolically or physically. The more the tested concepts resemble the final product or experience, the more dependable concept testing is.

In the past, creating physical prototypes was costly and time-consuming, but computer-aided design and manufacturing programs have changed that. Today firms can use *rapid prototyping* to design products (e.g., small appliances or toys) on a computer, and then produce plastic models of each. Potential consumers can view the plastic models and give their reactions.[30] Companies

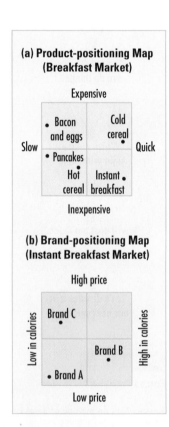

(a) Product-positioning Map (Breakfast Market)

Expensive

Slow — Quick

- Bacon and eggs
- Cold cereal
- Pancakes
- Hot cereal
- Instant breakfast

Inexpensive

(b) Brand-positioning Map (Instant Breakfast Market)

High price

Low in calories — High in calories

- Brand C
- Brand B
- Brand A

Low price

FIGURE 20.3

Product and Brand Positioning

are also using *virtual reality* to test product concepts. Virtual reality programs use computers and sensory devices (such as goggles for a 3-D effect and gloves to touch and feel the product) to simulate reality.

Concept testing entails presenting consumers with an elaborated version of the concept. Here is the elaboration of concept 1 in our milk example:

> Our product is a powdered mixture that is added to milk to make an instant breakfast that gives the person all the needed nutrition along with good taste and high convenience. The product would be offered in three flavours (chocolate, vanilla, and strawberry) and would come in individual packets, six to a box, at $2.49 a box.

After receiving this information, researchers measure product dimensions by having consumers respond to the following questions:

1. *Communicability and believability*—Are the benefits clear to you and believable? If the scores are low, the concept must be refined or revised.

2. *Need level*—Do you see this product solving a problem or filling a need for you? The stronger the need, the higher the expected consumer interest.

3. *Gap level*—Do other products currently meet this need and satisfy you? The greater the gap, the higher the expected consumer interest. The need level can be multiplied by the gap level to produce a *need–gap score*. A high need–gap score means that the consumer sees the product as filling a strong need that is not satisfied by available alternatives.

4. *Perceived value*—Is the price reasonable in relation to the value? The higher the perceived value, the higher the expected consumer interest.

5. *Purchase intention*—Would you (definitely, probably, probably not, definitely not) buy the product? This would be high for consumers who answered the previous three questions positively.

6. *User targets, purchase occasions, purchasing frequency*—Who would use this product, and when and how often will the product be used?

Respondents' answers indicate whether the concept has a broad and strong consumer appeal, what products this new product competes against, and which consumers are the best targets. The need–gap levels and purchase-intention levels can be checked against norms for the product category to see whether the concept appears to be a winner, a long shot, or a loser. One food manufacturer rejects any concept that draws a definitely-would-buy score of less than 40 percent.

CONJOINT ANALYSIS   Consumer preferences for alternative product concepts can be measured through **conjoint analysis**, a method for deriving the utility values that consumers attach to varying levels of a product's attributes.[31] Respondents are shown different hypothetical offers formed by combining varying levels of the attributes, and are then asked to rank the various offers. Management can identify the most appealing offer and the estimated market share and profit the company might realize. Consider how the technique is used at Bell Canada:

Bell Canada

As competition in the $20-billion Canadian telecommunications industry heats up and the major telephone companies such as Telus, Bell Canada, and Rogers expand into each other's territories, the rivals are starting to provide new "bundles" of services. Each company is betting that the key to success is higher-value offers achieved by providing one "bundled" package. Bundling is a marketing strategy that involves combining different products and services into a package at a discount. The trick, of course, is to match these combinations to the right customers. As part of BCE's labyrinth of media companies, Montreal-based Bell Canada has the potential to bundle a wide range of products. For example, "The combination of wireless and the Internet with the ExpressVu satellite system brings a lot of value," says Myrianne Collin, Bell's general manager of integrated offers. Its first bundled offer achieved sales 140 percent above the objectives set for the campaign. The key to Bell's success has been careful market research. Bell uses conjoint analysis to test different bundles of services, and then derives optimal groupings that can be aimed at key market segments. One such bundle is Bell Security Solutions Inc. (BSSI), which provides network and information security for communications networks to Canadian business and government.[32]

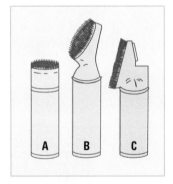

FIGURE 20.4

Samples for Conjoint Analysis

Green and Wind have illustrated the use of this approach in developing a new spot-removing carpet-cleaning agent for home use.[33] Suppose the new-product marketer is considering five design elements:

- Three package designs (A, B, C—see Figure 20.4)
- Three brand names (K2R, Glory, Bissell)
- Three prices ($1.19, $1.39, $1.59)
- A possible *Good Housekeeping* seal (yes, no)
- A possible money-back guarantee (yes, no)

Although the researcher can form 108 possible product concepts ($3 \times 3 \times 3 \times 2 \times 2$), it would be too much to ask consumers to rank 108 concepts. A sample of, say, 18 contrasting product concepts can be chosen, and consumers would rank them from the most to the least preferred.

The marketer now uses a statistical program to derive a consumer's utility functions for each of the five attributes (see Figure 20.5). Utility ranges between zero and one—the higher the utility, the stronger the consumer's preference for that level of the attribute. Looking at packaging, we see that package B is the most favoured, followed by C and then A (A has hardly any utility). The preferred names are Bissell, K2R, and Glory, in that order. The consumer's utility varies inversely with price. A *Good Housekeeping* seal is preferred, but it does not add that much utility and may not be worth the effort to obtain it. A money-back guarantee is strongly preferred.

The consumer's most desired offer would be package design B, with the brand name Bissell, selling at the price of $1.19, with a *Good Housekeeping* seal and a money-back guarantee. We can also determine the relative importance of each attribute to this consumer—the difference between the highest and lowest utility level for that attribute. The greater the difference, the more important the attribute. Clearly, this consumer sees price and package design as the most important attributes, followed by money-back guarantee, brand name, and a *Good Housekeeping* seal.

When preference data are collected from a sufficient sample of target consumers, the data can be used to estimate the market share any specific offer is likely to achieve, given any assumptions about competitive response. However, because of cost considerations the company may not launch

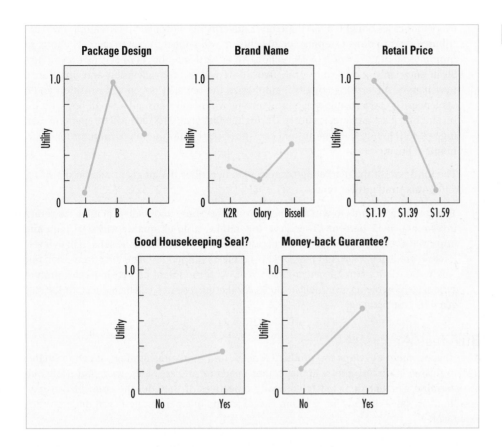

FIGURE 20.5

Utility Functions Based on Conjunct Analysis

the market offer that promises to gain the greatest market share. The offer most appealing to the customer is not always the most profitable offer to make.

Under some conditions, researchers will collect the data not with a full-profile description of each offer, but by presenting two factors at a time. For example, respondents may be shown a table with three price levels and three package types and asked which of the nine combinations they would like most, followed by which one they would prefer next, and so on. They would then be shown a further table consisting of trade-offs between two other variables. The trade-off approach may be easier to use when there are many variables and possible offers. However, it is less realistic in that respondents are focusing on only two variables at a time.

Conjoint analysis has become one of the most popular concept-development and testing tools. Marriott designed its Courtyard hotel concept with the benefit of conjoint analysis. Other applications have included airline travel services, ethical drug design, and credit card features.

Marketing Strategy

Following a successful concept test, the new-product manager will develop a preliminary strategy plan for introducing the new product into the market. The plan consists of three parts. The first part describes the target market's size, structure, and behaviour; the planned product positioning; and the sales, market share, and profit goals sought in the first few years:

> The target market for the instant-breakfast drink is families with children who are receptive to a new, convenient, nutritious, and inexpensive form of breakfast. The company's brand will be positioned at the higher-price, higher-quality end of the instant-breakfast-drink category. The company will aim initially to sell 500 000 cases or 10 percent of the market, with a loss in the first year not exceeding $1.3 million. The second year will aim for 700 000 cases or 14 percent of the market, with a planned profit of $2.2 million.

The second part outlines the planned price, distribution strategy, and marketing budget for the first year:

> The product will be offered in chocolate, vanilla, and strawberry in individual packets of six to a box at a retail price of $2.49 a box. There will be 48 boxes per case, and the case price to distributors will be $24. For the first two months, dealers will be offered one case free for

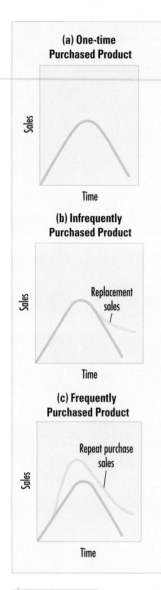

FIGURE 20.6

Sales for Three Types of Products throughout the Product Life Cycle

every four cases bought, plus cooperative-advertising allowances. Free samples will be distributed door to door. Coupons for 20 cents off will appear in newspapers. The total sales-promotional budget will be $2.9 million. An advertising budget of $6 million will be split 50:50 between national and local. Two-thirds will go into television and one-third into newspapers. Advertising copy will emphasize the benefit concepts of nutrition and convenience. The advertising-execution concept will revolve around a small boy who drinks instant breakfast and grows strong. During the first year, $100 000 will be spent on marketing research to buy store audits and consumer-panel information to monitor market reaction and buying rates.

The third part of the marketing-strategy plan describes the long-run sales and profit goals and marketing-mix strategy over time:

The company intends to win a 25-percent market share and realize an after-tax return on investment of 12 percent. To achieve this return, product quality will start high and be improved over time through technical research. Price will initially be set at a high level and lowered gradually to expand the market and meet competition. The total promotion budget will be boosted about 20 percent each year, with the initial advertising–sales promotion split of 65:35 evolving eventually to 50:50. Marketing research will be reduced to $60 000 per year after the first year.

Business Analysis

After management develops the product concept and marketing strategy, it can evaluate the proposal's business attractiveness. Management needs to prepare sales, cost, and profit projections to determine whether they satisfy company objectives. If they do, the concept can move to the development stage. As new information comes in, the business analysis will undergo revision and expansion.

ESTIMATING TOTAL SALES Total estimated sales are the sum of estimated first-time sales, replacement sales, and repeated sales. Sales-estimation methods depend on whether the product is a one-time purchase (such as an engagement ring or retirement home), an infrequently purchased product, or a frequently purchased product. For one-time purchased products, sales rise at the beginning, peak, and later approach zero as the number of potential buyers is exhausted (see Figure 20.6[a]). If new buyers keep entering the market, the curve will not go down to zero.

Infrequently purchased products—such as automobiles, toasters, and industrial equipment—exhibit replacement cycles dictated by physical wearing out or by obsolescence associated with changing styles, features, and performance. Sales forecasting for this product category calls for estimating first-time sales and replacement sales separately (see Figure 20.6[b]).

Frequently purchased products, such as consumer and industrial nondurables, have product life-cycle sales resembling Figure 20.6(c). The number of first-time buyers initially increases and then decreases as fewer buyers are left (assuming a fixed population). Repeated purchases occur soon, providing that the product satisfies some buyers. The sales curve eventually falls to a plateau representing a level of steady repeated-purchase volume; by this time, the product is no longer a new product.

In estimating sales, the manager's first task is to estimate first-time purchases of the new product in each period. To estimate replacement sales, management has to research the product's *survival-age distribution*—that is, the number of units that fail in year one, two, three, and so on. The low end of the distribution indicates when the first replacement sales will take place. The actual timing will be influenced by a variety of factors. Because replacement sales are difficult to estimate before the product is in use, some manufacturers base the decision to launch a new product solely on the estimate of first-time sales.

For a frequently purchased new product, the seller has to estimate repeated sales as well as first-time sales. A high rate of repeated purchasing means that customers are satisfied; sales are likely to stay high even after all first-time purchases take place. The seller should note the percentage of repeated purchases that take place in each repeated-purchase class: those who rebuy once, twice, three times, and so on. Some products and brands are bought a few times and then dropped.[34]

ESTIMATING COSTS AND PROFITS Costs are estimated by the R&D, manufacturing, marketing, and finance departments. Table 20.4 illustrates a five-year projection of sales, costs, and profits for the instant-breakfast drink.

TABLE 20.4	PROJECTED FIVE-YEAR CASH-FLOW STATEMENT (IN THOUSANDS OF DOLLARS)					
	Year 0	Year 1	Year 2	Year 3	Year 4	Year 5
1. Sales revenue	$ 0	$11 889	$15 381	$19 654	$28 253	$32 491
2. Cost of goods sold	0	3981	5150	6581	9461	10 880
3. Gross margin	0	7908	10 231	13 073	18 792	21 611
4. Development costs	−3500	0	0	0	0	0
5. Marketing costs	0	8000	6460	8255	11 866	13 646
6. Allocated overhead	0	1189	1538	1965	2825	3249
7. Gross contribution	−3500	−1281	2233	2853	4101	4716
8. Supplementary contribution	0	0	0	0	0	0
9. Net contribution	−3500	−1281	2233	2853	4101	4716
10. Discounted contribution (15%)	−3500	−1113	1691	1877	2343	2345
11. Cumulative discounted cash flow	−3500	−4613	−2922	−1045	1298	3644

Row 1 shows the projected sales revenue over the five-year period. The company expects to sell $11 889 000 (approximately 500 000 cases at $24 per case) in the first year. Behind this sales projection is a set of assumptions about the rate of market growth, the company's market share, and the factory-realized price. *Row 2* shows the cost of goods sold, which hovers around 33 percent of sales revenue. This cost is found by estimating the average cost of labour, ingredients, and packaging per case. *Row 3* shows the expected gross margin, which is the difference between sales revenue and cost of goods sold.

Row 4 shows anticipated development costs of $3.5 million, including product-development cost, marketing-research costs, and manufacturing-development costs. *Row 5* shows the estimated marketing costs over the five-year period to cover advertising, sales promotion, and marketing research and an amount allocated for sales-force coverage and marketing administration. *Row 6* shows the overhead allocated to this new product to cover its share of the cost of executive salaries, heat, light, and so on.

Row 7, the gross contribution, is found by subtracting the preceding three costs from the gross margin. *Row 8*, supplementary contribution, lists any change in income from other company products caused by the introduction of the new product. It has two components. *Drag-along income* is additional income on other company products resulting from adding this product to the line. *Cannibalized income* is the reduced income on other company products resulting from adding this product to the line.[35] Table 20.4 assumes no supplementary contributions. *Row 9* shows the net contribution, which in this case is the same as the gross contribution. *Row 10* shows the discounted contribution—that is, the present value of each future contribution discounted at 15 percent per annum. For example, the company will not receive $4 716 000 until the fifth year. This amount is worth only about $2 345 000 today if the company can earn 15 percent on its money through other investments.[36]

Finally, *row 11* shows the cumulative discounted cash flow, which is the accumulation of the annual contributions in row 10. Two things are of central interest. The first is the maximum investment exposure, which is the highest loss that the project can create. We see that the company will be in a maximum loss position of $4 613 000 in year 1. The second is the payback period, which is the time when the company recovers all of its investment, including the built-in return of 15 percent. The payback period here is approximately three and a half years. Management therefore has to decide whether to risk a maximum investment loss of $4.6 million and a possible payback period of three and a half years.

Companies use other financial measures to evaluate the merit of a new-product proposal. The simplest is **break-even analysis**, in which management estimates how many units of the product the company would have to sell to break even with the given price and cost structure. Or the estimate may be in terms of how many years it will take to break even. If management believes sales could easily reach the break-even number, it is likely to move the project into product development.

The most complex method of estimating profit is **risk analysis**. Here, three estimates (optimistic, pessimistic, and most likely) are obtained for each uncertain variable affecting profitability under an assumed marketing environment and marketing strategy for the planning period. A computer simulates possible outcomes and computes a rate-of-return probability distribution showing the range of possible rates of returns and their probabilities.[37]

MANAGING THE DEVELOPMENT PROCESS: DEVELOPMENT TO COMMERCIALIZATION

Up to now, the product has existed only as a word description, a drawing, or a prototype. This next step involves a jump in investment that dwarfs the costs incurred in the earlier stages. At this stage the company will determine whether the product idea can be translated into a technically and commercially feasible product. If it cannot, the accumulated project cost will be lost except for any useful information gained in the process.

Product Development

The job of translating target-customer requirements into a working prototype is helped by a set of methods known as *quality function deployment* (QFD). The methodology takes the list of desired *customer attributes* (CAs) generated by market research and turns them into a list of *engineering attributes* (EAs) that the engineers can use. For example, customers of a proposed truck may want a certain acceleration rate (CA). Engineers can turn this into the required horsepower and other engineering equivalents (EAs). The methodology permits measuring the trade-offs and costs of providing the customer requirements. A major contribution of QFD is that it improves communication among marketers, engineers, and manufacturing.[38]

PHYSICAL PROTOTYPES   The R&D department will develop one or more physical versions of the product concept. Its goal is to find a prototype that embodies the key attributes described in the product-concept statement, that performs safely under normal use and conditions, and that can be produced within the budgeted manufacturing costs. Developing and manufacturing a successful prototype can take days, weeks, months, or even years. Sophisticated virtual-reality technology such as that used by the Virtual Reality Applications Center is speeding the process. By designing and testing product designs through simulation, for example, companies achieve the flexibility to respond to new information and to resolve uncertainties by quickly exploring alternatives.

Virtual Reality Applications Center

Iowa State University is home to the Virtual Reality Applications Center (VRAC), which conducts research in virtual reality and visualization technologies for the United States military and corporate business. The centre is home to the C6, a six-sided virtual-reality room that has an incredible 100 million pixels of display space. There are numerous benefits to testing a conceptual design using virtual reality rather than a physical prototype. For example, Frito-Lay tested several different product and packaging designs for its Tostitos product line using VRAC's facilities. This saved Frito-Lay the cost of producing prototypes for each of the multiple Tostitos chips and package designs it tested. VRAC's long line of research projects includes products and services such as farm vehicles, snowplows, snack packaging, cook stoves, eggs, fire-safety training, and education.[39]

With the emergence of the Web, there is a need for more rapid prototyping and more flexible development processes. Michael Schrage, research associate at MIT's media lab, has correctly predicted: "Effective prototyping may be the most valuable 'core competence' an innovative organization can hope to have."[40] This has certainly been true for software companies such as Microsoft, Netscape, and the hundreds of Silicon Valley start-ups. Although Schrage says that specification-driven companies require that every "i" be dotted and "t" be crossed before anything can be shown to the next level of management, prototype-driven companies—such as Yahoo!, Microsoft, and Netscape—cherish quick-and-dirty tests and experiments.

Lab scientists must not only design the product's functional characteristics, but also communicate its psychological aspects through physical cues. How will consumers react to different colours, sizes, and weights? In the case of a mouthwash, a yellow colour supports an "antiseptic" claim

VRAC uses sophisticated virtual-reality technology to test new product ideas.

(Listerine), a red colour supports a "refreshing" claim (Lavoris), and a green or blue colour supports a "cool" claim (Scope). Marketers need to supply lab people with information on what attributes consumers seek and how consumers judge whether these attributes are present.

CUSTOMER TESTS   When the prototypes are ready, they must be put through rigorous functional tests and *customer tests*. *Alpha testing* is the name given to testing the product within the firm to see how it performs in different applications. After refining the prototype further, the company moves to *beta testing* with customers.[41] It enlists a set of customers to use the prototype and give feedback. Table 20.5 shows some of the functional tests products go through before they enter the marketplace.

TABLE 20.5	EXAMPLES OF CUSTOMER-PRODUCT TESTS

Shaw Industries

At Shaw Industries, temps are paid US$5 an hour to pace up and down five long rows of sample carpets for up to eight hours a day, logging an average of 22.5 kilometres each. One regular reads three mysteries a week while pacing and shed 18 kilograms over two years. Shaw Industries counts walkers' steps and figures that 20 000 steps equal several years of average wear.

Apple Computer

Apple Computer assumes the worst of its MacBook customers and submits its computers to a battery of indignities: it drenches the computers in Pepsi and other sodas, smears them with mayonnaise, and bakes them in ovens at temperatures of 60°C or more to simulate conditions in a car trunk.

Gillette

At Gillette, 200 volunteers from various departments come to work unshaven each day, troop to the second floor of the company's South Boston manufacturing and research plant, and enter small booths with a sink and mirror. There they take instructions from technicians on the other side of a small window as to which razor, shaving cream, or aftershave to use, and then they fill out questionnaires. "We bleed so you'll get a good shave at home," says one Gillette employee.

Source: Faye Rice, "Secrets of Product Testing," *Fortune*, November 28, 1994, pp. 172–74; Lawrence Ingrassia, "Taming the Monster: How Big Companies Can Change: Keeping Sharp: Gillette Holds Its Edge by Endlessly Searching for a Better Shave," *Wall Street Journal*, December 10, 1992, p. A1.

Consumer testing can take several forms, from bringing consumers into a laboratory to giving them samples to use in their homes. In-home placement tests are common with products ranging from ice cream flavours to new appliances. When DuPont developed its new synthetic carpeting, it installed free carpeting in several homes in exchange for the homeowners' willingness to report their likes and dislikes about the product.

Consumer preferences can be measured in several ways. Suppose a consumer is shown three items—A, B, and C—such as three cameras, three insurance plans, or three advertisements.

- The *rank-order* method asks the consumer to rank the three items in order of preference. The consumer might respond with A > B > C. Although this method has the advantage of simplicity, it does not reveal how intensely the consumer feels about each item nor whether the consumer likes any item very much. It is also difficult to use this method when there are many objects to be ranked.

- The *paired-comparison* method calls for presenting pairs of items and asking the consumer which one is preferred in each pair. Thus the consumer could be presented with the pairs AB, AC, and BC, and she could say that she prefers A to B, A to C, and B to C. Then we could conclude that A > B > C. People find it easy to state which of two items they prefer, and this method allows the consumer to focus on the two items, noting their differences and similarities.

- The *monadic-rating* method asks the consumer to rate liking of each product on a scale. Suppose a seven-point scale is used, where 1 signifies intense dislike, 4 indifference, and 7 intense like. Suppose the consumer returns the following ratings: A = 6, B = 5, C = 3. We can derive the individual's preference order (i.e., A > B > C), and even know the qualitative levels of the person's preference for each and the rough distance between preferences.

Products must also undergo rigorous testing to ensure their safety, as illustrated by Jaguar.

Jaguar

Jaguar does extensive testing of its vehicles to ensure they measure up to the high standards that consumers have come to expect from the brand. For twenty years, Jaguar has been running cold-weather tests on its vehicles in Timmins, Ontario, where winter lasts at least five months and the temperature drops to –40 degrees Celsius. The cold weather puts electronics, heaters, and lubricants under significant strain and helps the manufacturer troubleshoot any potential problems that are identified. The testing is pretty intense, with the cars putting on over 1000 kilometres a day, from a cold start, on icy roads, and in very cold conditions that cannot not be duplicated in a laboratory. In 2003, the testing facility moved to Thompson, Manitoba, where winter conditions are just as brutal. The testing involves detailed analysis of data and sensor outputs to determine if the parts withstand the less-than-ideal conditions. Jaguar's cold weather testing is a rigorous part of the overall product-safety testing that the vehicles must go through to ensure that they are as safe as can be.[42]

Market Testing

After management is satisfied with functional and psychological performance, the product is ready to be dressed up with a brand name and packaging, and subjected to a market test. The new product is introduced into an authentic setting to learn how large the market is and how consumers and dealers react to handling, using, and repurchasing the product. Even movies, like *Hancock*, are often test-marketed before they are released in theatres.

Columbia Pictures' *Hancock*

The director of the movie *Hancock* went back and forth deleting and changing scenes to please both the Motion Picture Association of America and audiences before the movie's release. *Hancock* was released in the summer of 2008 and centred on an unconventional superhero played by Will Smith. It was twice given an R rating by the MPAA; this rating was changed only when the number of swear words and graphically violent scenes was reduced. One scene in particular raised the eyebrows of the producers themselves, but when the test audience broke out in laughter, they decided they had to keep the scene. Other controversial scenes had to be cut because of minimal reactions from the test audience and will appear on the DVD version only. Even the title of the movie was changed from the original: *Tonight*.[43]

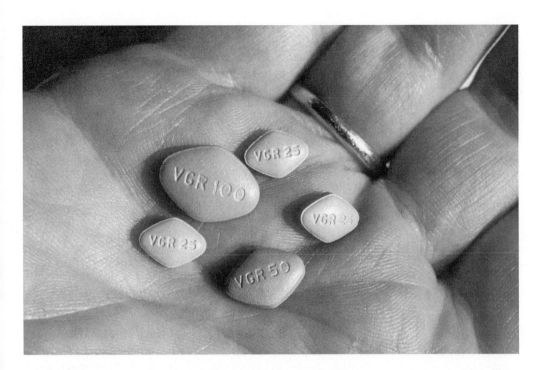

Canada is becoming the "ultimate" test market for many U.S.-based multinationals that also have operations in Canada. Not only are they testing new products, they are testing the marketing campaigns that support the new-product launch. The strategy of such firms is to let Canadian subsidiaries come up with and try out ideas that are more innovative and daring. If an idea works, it can then be rolled out in the United States. Pfizer's New York-based parent and Montreal-based subsidiary have set the pace with their award-winning "Good Morning" and "Champions" ads for Viagra (developed by Taxi Advertising of Toronto) and launches of products such as Listerine PocketPaks and Benylin DM Medicated Freezer Pops for children.[44]

Not all companies undertake market testing. A company officer at Revlon, Inc., stated "In our field—primarily higher-priced cosmetics not geared for mass distribution—it would be unnecessary for us to market test. When we develop a new product, say an improved liquid makeup, we know it's going to sell because we're familiar with the field. And we've got 1500 demonstrators in department stores to promote it." Many companies, however, believe that market testing can yield valuable information about buyers, dealers, marketing program effectiveness, and market potential. The main issues are how much market testing should be done, and what kind(s)?

The amount of market testing is influenced by the investment cost and risk on the one hand, and the time pressure and research cost on the other. High-investment–high-risk products, whose chance of failure is high, must be market tested; the cost of the market tests will be an insignificant percentage of the total project cost. High-risk products—those that create new-product categories (first instant-breakfast drink) or have novel features (first gum-strengthening toothpaste)—warrant more market testing than modified products (another toothpaste brand).

The amount of market testing may be severely reduced if the company is under great time pressure because the season is just starting or because competitors are about to launch their brands. The company may therefore prefer the risk of a product failure to the risk of losing distribution or market penetration of a highly successful product.

CONSUMER-GOODS MARKET TESTING In testing consumer products, the company seeks to estimate four variables: *trial, first repetition, adoption,* and *purchase frequency.* The company hopes to find all these variables at high levels. In some cases, it will find many consumers trying the product but few rebuying it, or it might find high permanent adoption but low purchase frequency (as with gourmet frozen foods).

Here are four major methods of consumer-goods market testing, from the least to the most costly:

Sales-Wave Research In *sales-wave research,* consumers who initially try the product at no cost are reoffered the product, or a competitor's product, at slightly reduced prices. They might be reoffered the product as many as three to five times (sales waves), with the company noting how many customers selected that product again and their reported level of satisfaction. Sales-wave research can also expose consumers to one or more advertising concepts to see the impact of that advertising on repeated purchase.

Sales-wave research can be implemented quickly, conducted with a fair amount of security, and carried out without final packaging and advertising. However, it does not indicate the trial rates that would be achieved with different sales-promotion incentives, because the consumers are preselected to try the product; nor does it indicate the brand's power to gain distribution and favourable shelf position.

Simulated Test Marketing   Simulated test marketing calls for finding 30 to 40 qualified shoppers and questioning them about brand familiarity and preferences in a specific product category. These people are then invited to a brief screening of both well-known and new commercials or print ads. One ad advertises the new product, but it is not singled out for attention. Consumers receive a small amount of money and are invited into a store where they may buy any items. The company notes how many consumers buy the new brand and competing brands. This provides a measure of the ad's relative effectiveness against competing ads in stimulating trial. Consumers are asked the reasons for their purchases or nonpurchases. Those who did not buy the new brand are given a free sample. Some weeks later, they are reinterviewed by phone to determine product attitudes, usage, satisfaction, and repurchase intention and are offered an opportunity to repurchase products.

This method gives fairly accurate results of advertising effectiveness and trial rates (and repeated rates if extended) in a much shorter time and at a fraction of the cost of using real test markets. Pretests often take only three months and may cost US$250 000.[45] The results are incorporated into new-product forecasting models to project ultimate sales levels. Marketing research firms report surprisingly accurate predictions of sales levels of products that are subsequently launched in the market.[46]

Controlled Test Marketing   In this method, a research firm manages a panel of stores that will carry new products for a fee. The company with the new product specifies the number of stores and geographic locations it wants to test. The research firm delivers the product to the participating stores and controls shelf position; number of facings, displays, and point-of-purchase promotions; and pricing. Sales results can be measured through electronic scanners at the checkout. The company can also evaluate the impact of local advertising and promotions.

Controlled test marketing allows the company to test the impact of in-store factors and limited advertising on buying behaviour. A sample of consumers can be interviewed later to give their impressions of the product. The company does not have to use its own sales force, give trade allowances, or "buy" distribution. However, controlled test marketing provides no information on how to sell the trade on carrying the new product. This technique also exposes the product and its features to competitors' scrutiny.

Test Markets   The ultimate way to test a new consumer product is to put it into full-blown test markets. The company chooses a few representative cities, and the sales force tries to sell the trade on carrying the product and giving it good shelf exposure. The company puts on a full advertising and promotion campaign similar to the one it would use in national marketing. Test marketing also permits testing the impact of alternative marketing plans by varying the marketing program in different cities. A full-scale test can cost over US$1 million, depending on the number of test cities, the test duration, and the amount of data the company wants to collect.

Management faces several decisions:

1. *How many test cities?* Most tests use between two and six cities. The greater the maximum possible loss, the greater the number of contending marketing strategies, the greater the regional differences, and the greater the chance of test-market interference by competitors, the greater the number of cities that should be used.

2. *Which cities?* Each company must develop selection criteria such as having good media coverage, cooperative chain stores, and average competitive activity.

3. *Length of test?* Market tests last anywhere from a few months to a year. The longer the average repurchase period, the longer the test period.

4. *What information?* Warehouse shipment data will show gross inventory buying but will not indicate weekly sales at the retail level. Store audits will show retail sales and competitors' market shares but will not reveal buyer characteristics. Consumer panels will indicate which

people are buying which brands and their loyalty and switching rates. Buyer surveys will yield in-depth information about consumer attitudes, usage, and satisfaction.

5. *What action to take?* If the test markets show high trial and repurchase rates, the product should be launched nationally; if they show a high trial rate and a low repurchase rate, the product should be redesigned or dropped; if they show a low trial rate and a high repurchase rate, the product is satisfying but more people have to try it. This means increasing advertising and sales promotion. If trial and repurchase rates are both low, the product should be abandoned.

In spite of its benefits, many companies today skip test marketing and rely on faster and more economical testing methods. General Mills now prefers to launch new products in an area too large for rivals to disrupt. Managers review retail scanner data, which tell them within days how the product is doing and what corrective fine-tuning to do. Colgate-Palmolive often launches a new product in a set of small "lead countries" and keeps rolling it out if it proves successful.

BUSINESS-GOODS MARKET TESTING   Business goods can also benefit from market testing. Expensive industrial goods and new technologies will normally undergo alpha testing (within the company) and beta testing (with outside customers). During beta testing, the vendor's technical people observe how test customers use the product, a practice that often exposes unanticipated problems of safety and servicing and alerts the vendor to customer training and servicing requirements. The vendor can also observe how much value the equipment adds to the customer's operation as a clue to subsequent pricing.

The vendor will ask the test customers to express their purchase intention and other reactions after the test. Vendors must carefully interpret the beta test results because only a small number of test customers are used, they are not randomly drawn, and the tests are somewhat customized to each site. Another risk is that test customers who are unimpressed with the product may leak unfavourable reports about it.

A second common test method for business goods is to introduce the new product at trade shows. The vendor can observe how much interest buyers show in the new product, how they react to various features and terms, and how many express purchase intentions or place orders.

New industrial products can be tested in distributor and dealer display rooms, where they may stand next to the manufacturer's other products and possibly competitors' products. This method yields preference and pricing information in the product's normal selling atmosphere. The disadvantages are that the customers might want to place early orders that cannot be filled, and those customers who come in might not represent the target market.

Industrial manufacturers come close to using full test marketing when they give a limited supply of the product to the sales force to sell in a limited number of areas that receive promotion support and printed catalogue sheets.

Commercialization

If the company goes ahead with commercialization, it will face its largest costs to date. The company will have to contract for manufacture or build or rent a full-scale manufacturing facility. Plant size will be a critical decision. When Quaker Oats launched its Quaker Harvest Crunch breakfast cereal, it built a smaller plant than called for by the sales forecast. The demand so exceeded the forecast that for about a year it could not supply enough product to stores. Although Quaker Oats was gratified with the response, the low forecast cost it a considerable amount of profit.

Another major cost is marketing. To introduce a major new consumer packaged good into the North American market, the company may have to spend from US$25 million to as much as US$100 million in advertising, promotion, and other communications in the first year. In the introduction of new food products, marketing expenditures typically represent 57 percent of sales during the first year. Most new-product campaigns rely on a sequenced mix of market communication tools.

WHEN (TIMING)   In commercializing a new product, market-entry timing is critical. Suppose a company has almost completed the development work on its new product and learns that a competitor is nearing the end of its development work. The company faces three choices:

1. *First entry.* The first firm entering a market usually enjoys the "first mover advantages" of locking up key distributors and customers and gaining leadership. But if the product is rushed to market before it is thoroughly debugged, the first entry can backfire.

2. *Parallel entry.* The firm might time its entry to coincide with the competitor's entry. The market may pay more attention when two companies are advertising the new product.

3. *Late entry.* The firm might delay its launch until after the competitor has entered. The competitor will have borne the cost of educating the market, and its product may reveal faults the late entrant can avoid. The late entrant can also learn the size of the market.

The timing decision involves additional considerations. If a new product replaces an older product, the company might delay the introduction until the old product's stock is drawn down. If the product is seasonal, it might be delayed until the right season arrives;[47] often a product waits for a "killer application" to occur. Complicating new-product launches, many companies are encountering competitive "design-arounds"—rivals are imitating inventions but making their own versions just different enough to avoid patent infringement and the need to pay royalties.

WHERE (GEOGRAPHIC STRATEGY)   The company must decide whether to launch the new product in a single locality, a region, several regions, the national market, or the international market. Most will develop a planned market rollout over time.

Company size is an important factor here. Small companies will select an attractive city and put on a blitz campaign. They will enter other cities one at a time. Large companies will introduce their product into a whole region and then move to the next region. Companies with national distribution networks, such as auto companies, will launch their new models in the national market.

Most companies design new products to sell primarily in the domestic market. If the product does well, the company considers exporting to neighbouring countries or the world market, redesigning the product if necessary. Cooper and Kleinschmidt, in their study of industrial products, found that domestic products designed solely for the domestic market tend to show a high failure rate, low market share, and low growth. In contrast, products designed for the world market—or at least to include neighbouring countries—achieve significantly more profits, both at home and abroad. Yet only 17 percent of the products in Cooper and Kleinschmidt's study were designed with an international orientation.[48] The implication is that companies should adopt an international focus in designing and developing new products.

In choosing rollout markets, the major criteria are market potential, company's local reputation, cost of filling the pipeline, cost of communication media, influence of area on other areas, and competitive penetration. The presence of strong competitors will influence rollout strategy. Suppose McDonald's wants to launch a new chain of fast-food pizza parlours. Pizza Hut, a formidable competitor, is strongly entrenched in the East Coast. Another pizza chain, Boston Pizza, founded in Edmonton in 1964, is entrenched in the West Coast. The Prairies are a battleground between the two other chains. The Ontario market, with its large population, is the most competitive of all with chains large and small competing for market share. McDonald's faces a complex decision in choosing a geographic rollout strategy but could launch in the West given that is where it perceives competition to be the least formidable.

With the Web connecting far-flung parts of the world, competition is more likely to cross national borders. Companies are increasingly rolling out new products simultaneously across the globe, rather than nationally or even regionally. However, masterminding a global launch provides challenges.

Organizations will increasingly use the Web as another advertising medium to launch and describe important new products and services, as the Canadian Parks and Wilderness Society has done.

Canadian Parks and Wilderness Society

The Canadian Parks and Wilderness Society (CPAWS) launched a new campaign in 2008 to preserve Canada's wilderness, with a goal of having 50 percent of Canadian wilderness protected. A number of events were planned to promote the campaign's website (www.bigwild. org). CPAWS partnered with Mountain Equipment Co-op, which placed print ads in the MEC catalogue and sold green shoelaces, an icon for the campaign. A guerilla campaign in which staff members wore backcountry gear to navigate concrete jungles also made the public aware of the website. The site provided a host of information about CPAWS and fundraising and adventure trips, as well as a forum for Canadians to share their wilderness experiences. The website provided the public an interactive way to learn about Canada's unprotected wilderness and helped raise funds to increase wilderness protection.[49]

TO WHOM (TARGET-MARKET PROSPECTS)   Within the rollout markets, the company must target its initial distribution and promotion to the best prospect groups. Presumably, the company has already profiled the prime prospects, who would ideally have the following characteristics: they would be early adopters, heavy users, and opinion leaders, and they could be reached at a low cost.[50] Few groups have all these characteristics. The company should rate the various prospect groups on these characteristics and target the best group. The aim is to generate strong sales as soon as possible to attract further prospects.

HOW (INTRODUCTORY MARKET STRATEGY)   The company must develop an action plan for introducing the new product into the rollout markets. Consider how Cadbury Adams created awareness of its new Trident Splash gum in a rather unusual way:

Trident Splash

Cadbury Adams launched its new Trident Splash gum by sending "Splashman" to hang out and ride transit in Vancouver, Calgary, Montreal, and Toronto wearing only a towel and swimcap and carrying a briefcase. Those brave enough to ask the crazy-looking man what was going on were shown a sign that said "You've just been splashed" and handed a pack of the new gum. The character seen on the streets reinforced the TV spot, in which a man wearing swimming trunks gets splashed waiting at a bus stop. Meeting Splashman gave consumers the chance to connect with the brand personally, rather than just receive a sample. Splashman was seen by about 250 000 Canadians and about 10 000 talked to him and received the package of gum. The word-of-mouth created by the campaign made it a huge success, with Splashman appearing on various TV shows in Toronto and Vancouver.[51]

To coordinate the many activities involved in launching a new product, management can use network-planning techniques such as critical path scheduling. **Critical path scheduling (CPS)** calls for developing a master chart showing the simultaneous and sequential activities that must take place to launch the product. By estimating how much time each activity takes, the planners estimate completion time for the entire project. Any delay in any activity on the critical path will cause the project to be delayed. If the launch must be completed earlier, the planner searches for ways to reduce time along the critical path.[52]

THE CONSUMER-ADOPTION PROCESS

Adoption is an individual's decision to become a regular user of a product. How do potential customers learn about new products, try them, and adopt or reject them? *The consumer-adoption process* is later followed by the *consumer-loyalty process*, which is the concern of the established producer. Years ago, new-product marketers used a *mass-market approach* to launch products. This approach had two main drawbacks: it called for heavy marketing expenditures, and it involved many wasted exposures. These drawbacks led to a second approach, *heavy-user target marketing*. This approach makes sense, provided that heavy users are identifiable and are early adopters. However, even within the heavy-user group, many are loyal to existing brands. New-product marketers now aim at consumers who are early adopters.

The theory of innovation diffusion and consumer adoption helps marketers identify early adopters.

Stages in the Adoption Process

An **innovation** is any good, service, or idea that is *perceived* by someone as new. The idea may have a long history, but it is an innovation to the person who sees it as new. Innovations take time to spread through the social system. Rogers defines the **innovation diffusion process** as "the spread of a new idea from its source of invention or creation to its ultimate users or adopters."[53] The consumer-adoption process focuses on the mental process through which an individual passes from first hearing about an innovation to final adoption.[54]

Adopters of new products have been observed to move through five stages:

1. *Awareness*—The consumer becomes aware of the innovation but lacks information about it.
2. *Interest*—The consumer is stimulated to seek information about the innovation.
3. *Evaluation*—The consumer considers whether to try the innovation.
4. *Trial*—The consumer tries the innovation to improve his or her estimate of its value.
5. *Adoption*—The consumer decides to make full and regular use of the innovation.

The new-product marketer should facilitate movement through these stages. A portable electric-dishwasher manufacturer might discover that many consumers are stuck in the interest stage; they do not buy because of their uncertainty and the large investment cost. But these same consumers would be willing to use an electric dishwasher on a trial basis for a small monthly fee. The manufacturer should consider offering a trial-use plan with option to buy.

Factors Influencing the Adoption Process

Marketers recognize the following characteristics of the adoption process: differences in individual readiness to try new products, the effect of personal influence, differing rates of adoption, and differences in organizations' readiness to try new products.

READINESS TO TRY NEW PRODUCTS AND PERSONAL INFLUENCE   Everett Rogers defines a person's level of innovativeness as "the degree to which an individual is relatively earlier in adopting new ideas than the other members of his social system." In each product area, there are pioneers and early adopters. Some people are the first to adopt new clothing fashions or new appliances, some doctors are the first to prescribe new medicines, and some farmers are the first to adopt new farming methods.[55] People can be classified into the adopter categories shown in Figure 20.7. After a slow start, an increasing number of people adopt the innovation, the number reaches a peak, and then it diminishes as fewer nonadopters remain. The five adopter groups differ in their value orientations and their motives for adopting or resisting the new product.[56]

- *Innovators* are technology enthusiasts and are venturesome and enjoy tinkering with new products and mastering their intricacies. In return for low prices, they are happy to conduct alpha and beta testing and report on early weaknesses.
- *Early adopters* are opinion leaders who carefully search for new technologies that might give them a dramatic competitive advantage. They are less price-sensitive and willing to adopt the product if given personalized solutions and good service support.
- *Early majority* are deliberate pragmatists who adopt the new technology when its benefits are proven and a lot of adoption has already taken place. They make up the mainstream market.

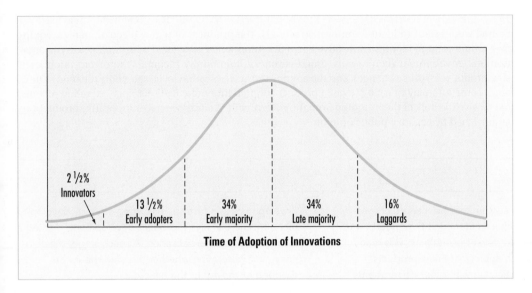

FIGURE 20.7

Adopter Categorization on the Basis of Relative Time of Adoption of Innovations

Source: Redrawn from Everett M. Rogers, *Diffusion of Innovations* (New York: The Free Press, 1983).

■   *Late majority* are skeptical conservatives who are risk averse, technology shy, and price sensitive.

■   *Laggards* are tradition-bound and resist the innovation until they find that the status quo is no longer defensible.

Each of the five groups must be approached with a different type of marketing if the firm wants to move its innovation through the full product life cycle.[57]

Personal influence is the effect one person has on another's attitude or purchase probability. Although personal influence is an important factor, its significance is greater in some situations and for some individuals than for others. Personal influence is more important in the evaluation stage of the adoption process than in the other stages. It has more influence on late adopters than early adopters. It also is more important in risky situations.

Companies often target innovators and early adopters with product rollouts. For Vespa scooters, Piaggio hired models to go to cafés and clubs to talk up the brand.[58] When Nike decided to enter the skateboarding market, it recognized that the anti-establishment attitude and bias against big companies of the teenaged-skater target market could present a sizable challenge. To gain some "street cred," it sold exclusively to independent shops, advertised nowhere but skate magazines, and gained sponsorships from well-admired pro riders by incorporating them into product design.[59]

CHARACTERISTICS OF THE INNOVATION   Some products catch on immediately (inline skates), whereas others take a long time to gain acceptance (diesel-engine autos). Five characteristics influence the rate of adoption of an innovation. We will consider them in relation to the adoption of personal video recorders (PVRs) for home use, as exemplified by TiVo.[60]

The first is *relative advantage*—the degree to which the innovation appears superior to existing products. The greater the perceived relative advantage of using a PVR, say, for easily recording favourite shows, pausing live TV, or skipping commercials, the more quickly PVRs will be adopted. The second is *compatibility*—the degree to which the innovation matches the values and experiences of the individuals. PVRs, for example, are highly compatible with avid television watchers. Third is *complexity*—the degree to which the innovation is relatively difficult to understand or use. PVRs are somewhat complex and will therefore take a slightly longer time to penetrate into home use. Fourth is *divisibility*—the degree to which the innovation can be tried on a limited basis. This provides a sizable challenge for PVRs—sampling can occur only in a retail store or perhaps a friend's house. Fifth is *communicability*—the degree to which the beneficial results of use are observable or describable to others. The fact that PVRs have some clear advantages can help create interest and curiosity.

Other characteristics that influence the rate of adoption are cost, risk and uncertainty, scientific credibility, and social approval. The new-product marketer has to research all these factors and give the key ones maximum attention while designing the new product and its marketing program.[61]

ORGANIZATIONS' READINESS TO ADOPT INNOVATIONS The creator of a new teaching method would want to identify innovative schools. The producer of a new piece of medical equipment would want to identify innovative hospitals. Adoption is associated with variables in the organization's environment (community progressiveness, community income), the organization itself (size, profits, pressure to change), and the administrators (education level, age, sophistication). Other forces come into play in trying to get a product adopted into organizations, such as public schools, that receive the bulk of their funding from the government. A controversial or innovative product can be squelched by negative public opinion.

SUMMARY

1. Once a company has segmented the market, chosen its target customer groups and identified their needs, and determined its desired market positioning, it is ready to develop and launch appropriate new products. Marketing should participate with other departments in every stage of new-product development.

2. Successful new-product development requires the company to establish an effective organization for managing the development process. Companies can choose to use product managers, new-product managers, new-product committees, new-product departments, or new-product venture teams. Increasingly, companies are adopting cross-functional teams and developing multiple product concepts.

3. Eight stages are involved in the new-product development process: idea generation, screening, concept development and testing, marketing-strategy development, business analysis, product development, market testing, and commercialization. At each stage, the company must determine whether the idea should be dropped or moved to the next stage.

4. The consumer-adoption process is the process by which customers learn about new products, try them, and adopt or reject them. Today many marketers are targeting heavy users and early adopters of new products, because both groups can be reached by specific media and tend to be opinion leaders. The consumer-adoption process is influenced by many factors beyond the marketer's control, including consumers' and organizations' willingness to try new products, personal influences, and the characteristics of the new product or innovation.

APPLICATIONS

Marketing Debate: Whom Should You Target with New Products?

Many firms target lead users or innovators with their new products, under the assumption that their adoption will trickle down to influence the broader market. Others disagree with this approach and contend that the most efficient and quickest route is to target the broader or even mass market directly.

Take a position: New products should always target new adopters *versus* New products should target the broadest market possible.

Marketing Discussion

Think about the last new product you bought. How do you think its success will be affected by the five characteristics of an innovation: relative advantage, compatibility, complexity, divisibility, and communicability?

Breakthrough Marketing: Nintendo Wii

Nintendo of Canada Ltd., a subsidiary of Nintendo Co. Ltd. of Japan, manufactures and markets hardware and software for its core brands Wii, Nintendo DS, Game Boy Advance, and GameCube. Many well-known trademarked characters and games, such as Mario, Donkey Kong, Zelda, and Pokemon, have been created by Nintendo. Since its inception, Nintendo has sold over 430 million hardware systems and 2.5 billion video games worldwide.

The first Nintendo video-game console was introduced in 1983 and the company has been a leader in the industry ever since. The Canadian video-game industry is a $1-billion-a-year industry, with Nintendo leading in 2008 with a market share of 29 percent, thanks to its two newest systems—DS and Wii. Nintendo realizes the importance of coming out with new products frequently in order to meet the evolving needs of its customers and to stay ahead of its competition.

Nintendo's latest product, Wii, is an interactive video-game console that is targeted at people of all ages, not just the stereotypical teenaged boy gamer. One game for the system, Wii Fit, is targeted at families (especially moms, since they are the ones buying for the family) according to Matt Ryan, Nintendo Canada spokesperson. Women have been targeted through mall demonstration tours across Canada and with ads in "pink collar" magazines such as *Best Health* to increase awareness that this system is not the typical kid's game but can be an excellent source of activity and fun for the whole family. Nintendo is also reaching out to families via its *getupandplay.ca* website, where it offers games and challenges to try with the Wii system and ideas for hosting a "Wii Party" including activities and food recipes. The website even allows users to send out party e-invitations, design party badges and victory certificates, and, of course, plan party games. Other video games can also be purchased and downloaded from WiiWare, which offers a series of games designed for the console.

According to a study done by the NPD Group, more than 867 000 Wii systems have been sold since they were launched in Canada at the end of 2006. As of April 2008, the Wii had become the top-selling next-generation home console video-game system in Canada. Nintendo DS was the best-selling hand-held video-game system in Canada at the end of 2007. With both these new products under its belt, Nintendo's popularity has grown and sales have climbed 73 percent over the past year; however, the video-game market requires constant innovation to stay on top of the charts. Apple's iPhone and iPod Touch pose a competitive threat to Nintendo DS as they will soon have game software and motion capabilities similar to the Wii. But for the moment, Nintendo is enjoying its top spot in the market: the DS and Wii systems currently outsell all competing systems (including Microsoft's Xbox 360, Sony's PlayStation 2 and 3, and PlayStation Portable) combined.

DISCUSSION QUESTIONS

1. What have been the key success factors for the Nintendo Wii?
2. What can Nintendo do to prevent its competitors from imitating its products and taking market share from it?
3. Besides direct brand competition, what other threats should Nintendo watch out for?
4. What are some natural product extensions you would recommend for Wii Fit?

Sources: Nintendo of Canada Ltd. website, www.nintendo.ca (viewed June 13, 2008); Marta Gold, "Moms Lining Up at Game Stores; Women Can't Wait to Exercise," *The Windsor Star*, June 5, 2008, p. B5; "Nintendo's 'Wii Would Like to Play' Named the Most Effective Marketing Effort at the 40th Annual Effie Awards," *Business Wire*, June 5, 2008; Hollie Shaw, "Mom's New Best Friend," *National Post*, May 16, 2008, p. FP3; "NPD Reports Nintendo's Wii Tops Canadian Sales Charts," *Canada NewsWire*, April 17, 2008.

IN THIS CHAPTER, WE WILL ADDRESS THE FOLLOWING QUESTIONS:

- What factors should a company review before deciding to go abroad?

- How can companies evaluate and select specific foreign markets to enter?

- What are the major ways of entering a foreign market?

- To what extent must the company adapt its products and marketing program to each foreign country?

- How should the company manage and organize its international activities?

CHAPTER 21

TAPPING INTO GLOBAL MARKETS

twenty-one

Bombardier Inc. has come a long way since the 1940s. From humble beginnings as a tracked-vehicle manufacturer, Montreal-based Bombardier is now one of the world's largest manufacturers in the aerospace and transportation industry. The transportation giant has some 60 000 employees worldwide and has established itself as an international force to be reckoned with, generating $17.5 billion in revenues in the 2008 fiscal year. The company owes much of its success to its international business—96 percent of its sales come from outside Canada.

Bombardier's largest market is the United States, with over 31 percent of the company's sales going south of the border. Bombardier also is present in 60 countries across five continents, but its focus is primarily in Europe and North America. The company has manufacturing, engineering, and services facilities in over 21 countries worldwide. "We think we have the experience and know-how to remain the leader in this industry," says Pierre Beaudoin, president of Bombardier Aerospace. "It may mean additional investment," he notes. This massive investment makes it difficult for new competitors to gain a strong foothold in the market, especially when the company continues to upgrade facilities and procedures to keep on top.

Bombardier works hard to keep its reputation as a manufacturer of high-quality aircraft and trains. "When a customer buys into a business aircraft, he or she buys into a brand. Nobody was getting after the emotional side of this. We wanted to determine the emotional triggers that come into action," says Andrew Farrant, general manager for marketing communications and sales support at Bombardier Business Aircraft. The company aired commercials showing employees taking pride in their work, such as an employee taking a picture of a vacationing couple, only to be distracted and take a picture of a Bombardier train instead.

The hard work seems to be paying off, as Bombardier is the world's top passenger-train manufacturer and the third-largest manufacturer of civil aircraft, behind Airbus and Boeing. It has been forecast that global demand for turboprop airplanes over the next 20 years will be nearly 2000 aircraft. Bombardier currently has half of the turboprop market and expects to get a big chunk of the future market as well.

>>> So what's next for Bombardier? The company continues to receive a large number of orders and has a solid backlog of planes. It is looking into an extended version of its most popular turboprop plane, the Q400. New competitors loom, but the company isn't worried. "Bombardier is well-positioned to service [the airline] market now when the airlines need it," says Jacques Kavafian of Research Capital. It is yet to be seen how rising fuel costs will affect the market for planes, but Bombardier is ready to take on the future.

Sources: Bombardier website, www.bombardier.com (viewed August 27, 2008); Ross Marowits, "Bombardier not Worried About Increased Turboprop Competition from China," *Canadian Press*, June 25, 2008; Robert Melnbardis, "Bombardier Profit Soars: Canadian Company Exceeds Expectations with Stellar Fourth Quarter," *Ottawa Citizen*, April 4, 2008, p. E2; John Morris, "Bombardier Undertakes a Rebranding: Learjet, Challenger and Global, Period," *AviationWeek Online*, www.aviationweek.com/shownews/02nbaa/topsto02.htm (viewed June 25, 2008).

With faster communication, transportation, and financial flows, the world is rapidly shrinking. Products developed in one country—Gucci purses, Mont Blanc pens, McDonald's hamburgers, Japanese sushi, Chanel suits, German BMWs—are finding enthusiastic acceptance in others. A German businessman may wear an Armani suit to meet an English friend at a Japanese restaurant, and later return home to drink Russian vodka and watch an American soap on TV. Consider the international success of Starbucks:

Starbucks

Since Starbucks Coffee, Tea and Spices opened its first store in Seattle in 1971, the company, now called Starbucks Coffee Company, has grown to be one of the greatest business success stories of the past two decades. Starbucks now has over 15 000 stores worldwide, with 22 percent of its revenues coming from its overseas operations. Since going international in 1996 with a coffeehouse in Tokyo, the company has now spread to 48 countries, with 4700 of its stores located outside the United States. Starbucks grew by an astronomical 2200 percent over the decade ending in 2001, surpassing growth powerhouses such as Wal-Mart, PepsiCo, and Microsoft. Starbucks' sales have increased an average of 20 percent annually since it went public in 1992. With plans to open about 1000 new foreign stores each year, the company expects its proportion of foreign stores to go up from 29 percent in 2008 to 40 percent within three years.[1]

Although the opportunities for companies to enter and compete in foreign markets are significant, the risks can also be high. Companies selling in global industries, however, really have no choice but to take their operations international. In this chapter, we review the major decisions involved in expanding into global markets.

COMPETING ON A GLOBAL BASIS

Two hundred giant corporations, most of them larger than many national economies, have sales that in total exceed a quarter of the world's economic activity. On that basis, the Altria Group Inc., which is the parent company of Kraft Foods, Philip Morris International, Philip Morris USA, Philip Morris Capital Corporation, and SABMiller (the world's second-largest brewer), is larger than New Zealand's economy and operates in 170 countries.

Trade is Canada's primary engine of economic growth. Our domestic market is relatively small, thus we depend on trade for the creation of jobs and the generation of wealth. As Trade Minister Pettigrew noted in 2001, "Canadians throughout the country profit from the dynamism and success of Canada's export companies." In 2007, the value of Canadian exports rose 2 percent (over 2006 levels) to a record $463.05 billion. Exports represent approximately 38 percent of our gross domestic product (GDP). In comparison, the United States' international sales account for only 25 percent of its GDP, while Japan exports approximately 15 percent of its GDP.[2]

Many companies have conducted international marketing for decades—McCain Foods, Nortel, Nestlé, Shell, Bayer, and Toshiba are familiar to consumers around the world. But global competition is intensifying. Domestic companies which never thought about foreign competitors suddenly find them in their backyards. Newspapers report on the gains of Japanese, German, Swedish, and Korean car imports in the North American market, and the loss of textile and shoe markets to imports from developing countries in Latin America, Eastern Europe, and Asia.

A **global industry** is an industry in which the strategic positions of competitors in major geographic or national markets are fundamentally affected by their overall global positions.[3] A **global firm** is a firm that operates in more than one country and captures R&D, production, logistical, marketing, and financial advantages in its costs and reputation that are not available to purely domestic competitors.

Global firms plan, operate, and coordinate their activities on a worldwide basis. Ford's "world truck" has a European-made cab and a North American–built chassis, is assembled in Brazil, and is imported into the North American market for sale. Otis Elevator gets its door systems from France, small geared parts from Spain, electronics from Germany, and special motor drives from Japan; it uses the United States for systems integration. Consider the international success of the stage-show troupe Cirque du Soleil:

Cirque du Soleil

Its name is a symbol of youth, energy, power, and light and its performers captivate thousands of audiences around the world each year. Headquartered in Montreal, Cirque du Soleil was formed in 1984 by Guy Laliberté and 20 street performers. The company now has a staff of over 3000 from over 40 different countries, making it a very internationally diverse organization. Cirque du Soleil's first international performance was in 1987 at the Los Angeles Festival. It then began a two-year tour of the United States. Since its founding, the group has performed in over 100 cities around the globe and now tours countries all over the world.[4]

A company need not be large, however, to sell globally. Small and medium-sized firms can practise global nichemanship. The Poilane Bakery sells 15 000 loaves of old-style bread each day to 2500 shops and restaurants throughout Paris—2.5 percent of all bread sold in that city—via company-owned delivery trucks. But each day, Poilane-branded bread is also shipped via FedEx to loyal customers in roughly 20 countries around the world.[5]

For a company of any size to go global, it must make a series of decisions (see Figure 21.1). We'll examine each of these decisions here.

DECIDING WHETHER TO GO ABROAD

Most companies would prefer to remain domestic if their domestic market were large enough. Managers would not need to learn other languages and laws, deal with volatile currencies, face political and legal uncertainties, or redesign their products to suit different customer needs and expectations. Business would be easier and safer. Yet several factors are drawing more and more companies into the international arena:

- The company discovers that some foreign markets present higher profit opportunities than the domestic market.

- The company needs a larger customer base to achieve economies of scale.

- The company wants to reduce its dependence on any one market.

- Global firms offering better products or lower prices can attack the company's domestic market. The company might want to counter-attack these competitors in their home markets.

- The company's customers are going abroad and require international servicing.

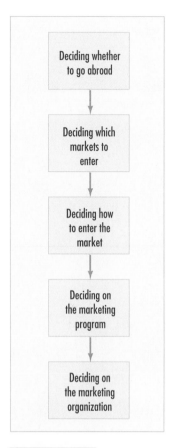

FIGURE 21.1

Major Decisions in International Marketing

Deciding whether to go abroad

↓

Deciding which markets to enter

↓

Deciding how to enter the market

↓

Deciding on the marketing program

↓

Deciding on the marketing organization

The company logo being carved into a loaf of Poilane bread, which is shipped daily via FedEx to loyal customers in countries around the world.

Before making a decision to go abroad, the company must weigh several risks:

- The company might not understand foreign customer preferences and fail to offer a competitively attractive product.
- The company might not understand the foreign country's business culture or know how to deal effectively with foreign nationals.
- The company might underestimate foreign regulations and incur unexpected costs.
- The company might realize that it lacks managers with international experience.
- The foreign country might change its commercial laws, devalue its currency, or undergo a political revolution and expropriate foreign property.

Because of the competing advantages and risks, companies often do not act until some event thrusts them into the international arena. Someone—a domestic exporter, an international importer, a foreign government—solicits the company to sell abroad, or the company is saddled with overcapacity and must find additional markets for its goods.

Most countries lament that too few of their companies participate in international trade. This keeps the country from earning foreign exchange to pay for needed imports. It also raises the spectre of domestic companies eventually being hurt or taken over by foreign multinationals. Many countries sponsor aggressive export-promotion programs to get their companies to export. These programs require a deep understanding of how companies become internationalized. The Canadian government works hard to convince companies to export and provides services and information essential to their success. In 1997, to better coordinate these efforts, Team Canada Inc. was born. The organization was formed from a network of more than 20 federal government departments and agencies working with the provinces, territories, and other partners to provide a single window of access to export information and services. Its aim is to increase the capabilities, preparedness, and international market development success of Canadian businesses.

The internationalization process has four stages:[6]

1. No regular export activities.
2. Export via independent representatives (agents).
3. Establishment of one or more sales subsidiaries.
4. Establishment of production facilities abroad.

The first task is to get companies to move from stage 1 to stage 2. This move is helped by studying how firms make their first export decisions.[7] Most firms work with an independent agent and enter a nearby or similar country. A company then engages further agents to enter additional countries. Later, it establishes an export department to manage its agent relationships. Still later,

The *Canada Business* website provides information on exporting and other topics to help Canadian businesses succeed in world markets.

the company replaces its agents with its own sales subsidiaries in its larger export markets. This increases the company's investment and risk, but also its earning potential.

To manage these subsidiaries, the company replaces the export department with an international department. If certain markets continue to be large and stable, or if the host country insists on local production, the company takes the next step of locating production facilities in those markets. This means a still larger commitment and still larger potential earnings. By this time, the company is operating as a multinational and is engaged in optimizing its global sourcing, financing, manufacturing, and marketing. According to some researchers, top management begins to pay more attention to global opportunities when they find that over 15 percent of revenues comes from foreign markets.[8]

DECIDING WHICH MARKETS TO ENTER

In deciding to go abroad, the company needs to define its marketing objectives and policies. What proportion of foreign to total sales will it seek? Most companies start small when they venture abroad. Some plan to stay small; others have bigger plans. Ayal and Zif have argued that a company should enter fewer countries when:

 To learn about Billabong and how it grew from selling board-shorts in Australia into an international brand offering many more products, visit www.pearsoned.com.au/ marketingmanagementaustralia.

- Market entry and market control costs are high
- Product and communication adaptation costs are high
- Population and income size and growth are high in the initial countries chosen
- Dominant foreign firms can establish high barriers to entry[9]

How Many Markets to Enter

The company must decide how many countries to enter and how fast to expand. Consider Amway's experience:

Amway

Amway Corp., one of the world's largest direct-selling companies, markets its products and services through independent business owners worldwide. Amway expanded from the U.S. into Canada in the 1950s and into Australia in 1971. By 2004, Amway had evolved into a multinational juggernaut with a sales force of more than 3.6 million independent distributors hauling in US$4.5 billion in sales. Established in 1998, Amway India grew to 200 000 active Amway distributors by 2004. Amway currently sells products in 80 countries and territories worldwide. Its corporate goal is to have overseas markets account for 80 percent of its sales. This is not unrealistic or overly ambitious considering that Amway already gains 70 percent of its sales from markets outside North America.[10]

A company's entry strategy typically follows one of two possible approaches: a *waterfall* approach, in which countries are gradually entered sequentially, or a *sprinkler* approach, in which many countries are entered simultaneously within a limited period. Increasingly, companies are *born global* and market to the entire world right from the outset; this is especially true for technology-intensive firms.[11]

Generally speaking, companies such as Matsushita, BMW, and General Electric, and even newer companies such as Dell, Nortel, and The Body Shop, follow the waterfall approach. Expansion can be carefully planned and is less likely to strain human and financial resources. When first-mover advantage is crucial and a high degree of competitive intensity prevails, the sprinkler approach is preferred, as when Microsoft introduces a new form of Windows software. The main risk is the substantial resources involved and the difficulty of planning entry strategies in so many potentially diverse markets.

The company must also decide on the types of countries to consider. Attractiveness is influenced by the product, geography, income and population, political climate, and other factors. Kenichi Ohmae recommends that companies concentrate on selling in the "triad markets"—North America, Western Europe, and the Far East—because these markets account for a large percentage of all international trade.[12]

Developed versus Developing Markets

Although Ohmae's position makes short-run sense, it can spell disaster for the world economy in the long run. The unmet needs of the emerging or developing world represent huge potential markets for

A Russian ad for Nestlé's Nescafé. As consumer spending has risen in Russia, the market for products of major multinationals like Nestlé has boomed.

food, clothing, shelter, consumer electronics, appliances, and other goods. Many market leaders are rushing into Eastern Europe, China, and India. Colgate now draws more personal and household products business from Latin America than North America.[13]

The developed nations and the prosperous parts of developing nations account for less than 15 percent of the world's population. Is there a way for marketers to serve the other 85 percent, which has much less purchasing power? Successfully entering developing markets requires a special set of skills and plans. Consider how the following companies are pioneering ways to serve these consumers:[14]

■ Grameen-Phone markets cell phones to 35 000 villages in Bangladesh by hiring village women as agents who lease phone time to other villagers, one call at a time.

■ Colgate-Palmolive rolls into Indian villages with video vans that show the benefits of brushing one's teeth; it expects to earn over half of its Indian revenue from rural areas by 2003.

■ An Indian–Australian car manufacturer created an affordable rural transport vehicle to compete with bullock carts rather than cars. The vehicle functions well at low speeds and carries up to two tonnes.

■ Fiat developed a "third-world car," the Palio, that far outsells the Ford Fiesta in Brazil and will be launched in other developing nations.

■ Corporacion GEO builds low-income housing in Mexico. The two-bedroom homes are modular and can be expanded. The company is now moving into Chile and southern U.S. communities.

These marketers are able to capitalize on the potential of developing markets by changing their conventional marketing practices to sell their products and services more effectively.[15] It cannot be business as usual when selling into developing markets. Economic and cultural differences abound, a marketing infrastructure may barely exist, and local competition can be surprisingly stiff. In China, PC-maker Legend and mobile phone–provider TCL have thrived despite strong foreign competition. Besides their close grasp of Chinese tastes, they also have vast distribution networks, especially in rural areas.[16]

Smaller packaging and lower sales prices are often critical in markets where incomes are limited. Unilever's 4-cent sachets of detergent and shampoo have been a big hit in rural India, where 70 percent of the country's population still lives. When Coke moved in India to a smaller 200 mL bottle selling for 10 to 12 cents in small shops, bus-stop stalls, and roadside eateries, sales jumped.[17] A Western image can also be helpful, as Coke discovered in China. Part of its success against local cola brand Jianlibao was due to its symbolic values of modernity and affluence.[18]

Recognizing that its cost structure made it difficult to compete effectively in developing markets, Procter & Gamble devised cheaper, clever ways to make the right kinds of products to suit consumer demand. It now uses contract manufacturers in certain markets and gained eight share points in Russia for Always feminine protection pads by responding to consumer wishes for a thicker pad.[19] Due to a boom in consumer spending, Russia has been the fastest-growing market for many major multinationals, including Nestlé, L'Oréal, and IKEA.[20]

The challenge is to think creatively about how marketing can fulfill the dreams of most of the world's population for a better standard of living. And many companies, like General Motors, are betting that they can do just that.

General Motors

After launching Buick in China in 1999, GM poured more than US$2 billion into the region over the next five years, expanding the lineup to 14 models, ranging from the US$8000 Chevrolet Spark mini-car to high-end Cadillacs. Although competition in the world's third-largest car market is fierce, GM was able to secure 11-percent market share in 2004 and reap sizable profits.[21]

Regional Free Trade Zones

Regional economic integration—trading agreements between blocs of countries—has intensified in recent years. This development means that companies are more likely to enter entire regions at one time. Certain countries have formed free trade zones or economic communities—groups of nations organized to work towards common goals in the regulation of international trade. One such community is the European Union (EU).

THE EUROPEAN UNION Formed in 1957, the European Union set out to create a single European market by reducing barriers to the free flow of products, services, finances, and labour among member countries and by developing trade policies with nonmember nations. Today, the European Union is one of the world's single largest markets. The 15 member countries making up the EU increased by 10 in May 2004 with the addition of Cyprus, the Czech Republic, Estonia, Hungary, Latvia, Lithuania, Malta, Poland, Slovakia, and Slovenia. This was followed in 2007 by the addition of Bulgaria and Romania, forming the now 27-member European Union. The EU now contains more than 490 million consumers and accounts for 18 percent of the world's exports. It has a common currency, the euro monetary system.[22]

European unification offers tremendous trade opportunities for non-European firms. However, it also poses threats. European companies will grow bigger and more competitive. Witness the competition in the aircraft industry between Europe's Airbus consortium and Boeing in the United States. Perhaps an even bigger concern, however, is that lower barriers inside Europe will create only thicker outside walls. Some observers envision a "fortress Europe" that heaps favours on firms from EU countries but hinders outsiders by imposing obstacles such as stiffer import quotas, local content requirements, and other nontariff (nontax) barriers.

Also, companies that plan to create "pan-European" marketing campaigns directed to a unified Europe should proceed with caution. Even as the EU standardizes its general trade regulations and currency, creating an economic community will not create a homogeneous market. Companies marketing in Europe face 23 different languages, 2000 years of historical and cultural differences, and a daunting mass of local rules.

NAFTA Closer to home, in North America, the United States and Canada phased out trade barriers in 1989. In January 1994, the North American Free Trade Agreement (NAFTA) established a free trade zone including the United States, Mexico, and Canada.

How effective has the trade agreement been over a decade after its birth? The answer will depend on whom you ask, and the agreement has continued to be controversial. In 2006, 12 years after NAFTA's initiation, trilateral trade among the three countries had more than doubled to $US958 billion annually. The United States is our largest trade partner with total merchandise trade reaching $577 billion in 2006. Our exports to Mexico have tripled since the agreement's launch, and Canada is now Mexico's second-biggest export market, while Mexico is Canada's sixth. The investment landscape has also changed. Canadian investment in Mexico has surged to over $4 billion, 16 times what it was in 1990. Canadian investment in the United States has more than tripled to $223 billion over the same period, while U.S. investment in Canada has soared to $289 billion. The Canadian government reports that the economy has grown by an average of 3.8 percent annually since the agreement came into force, generating 2.1 million jobs. The Canadian Labour Congress, however, doesn't share the government's enthusiasm. It estimates that total employment in manufacturing is now 10 percent below the pre-NAFTA levels while wages in the manufacturing sector have stayed the same or declined. Another critic, the Canadian Auto Workers union, claims that 7000 auto assembly jobs have shifted to Mexico from Canada. The recent softwood lumber dispute with the United States has caused further criticism of the agreement. In late 2004, the "binding" dispute resolution mechanism in NAFTA proved to be anything but binding when a ruling about unfair subsidies went in Canada's favour. The United States refused to agree and did not remove the tariffs on the industry, which accounts for approximately 3 percent of Canada's exports to the United States. Nonetheless, analysts agree that over its history, the agreement has largely been strong and dispute-free.[23]

Since the agreement has been so successful, Canada is taking a leadership role in trying to extend it to countries throughout South America. The envisioned free trade zone extending from Nunavut to Tierra del Fuego would have a combined GDP of more than US$20 trillion, or about 40 percent of the world's economic activity. This would position Canada to compete more effectively with the growing power of the European economic community.

MERCOSUL   Other free trade areas are forming in Latin America. For example, MERCOSUL now links Brazil, Argentina, Paraguay, and Uruguay. Chile and Mexico have also formed a successful free trade zone. It is likely that NAFTA will eventually merge with this and other arrangements to form an all-Americas free trade zone.

It is the European nations that have tapped Latin America's enormous potential. As efforts to extend NAFTA to Latin America have stalled, European countries have moved in with a vengeance. When Latin American countries instituted market reforms and privatized public utilities, European companies rushed in to grab up lucrative contracts for rebuilding Latin America's infrastructure. Spain's Telefonica de Espana spent US$5 billion buying phone companies in Brazil, Chile, Peru, and Argentina. In Brazil, seven of the ten largest private companies are European owned, compared to two controlled by Americans. Among the notable European companies operating in Latin America are automotive giants Volkswagen and Fiat, the French supermarket chain Carrefours, and the Anglo-Dutch personal-care-products group Gessy-Lever.

APEC   Twenty-one Pacific Rim countries, including the NAFTA member states, Japan, and China, form the Asia-Pacific Economic Cooperation forum (APEC). As a founding member, Canada has been involved in the organization since its creation in 1989. Canada's participation is important, given that the Asia-Pacific region represents nearly 50 percent of global trade and 56 percent of world GDP.[24] Unlike the other agreements discussed earlier, APEC is not a free trade agreement. Its mandate is to ease the movement of goods, services, and people across borders. For example, an average trade transaction currently requires 40 documents. To eliminate this time-consuming red tape, APEC is aiming at paperless trading for developing economies by 2010.

Evaluating Potential Markets

Yet, however much nations and regions integrate their trading policies and standards, each nation still has unique features that must be understood. A nation's readiness for different products and services and its attractiveness to foreign firms as a market depend on its economic, political-legal, and cultural environments.

Suppose a company has assembled a list of potential markets to enter. How does it choose among them? Many companies prefer to sell to neighbouring countries because they understand these countries better and can control their costs more effectively. It is not surprising that Canada's largest export market is the United States. As of 2006, 82 percent of our merchandise export trade went south of the border (compare this to our second-largest export market, the European Union, which gets only 3 percent of our merchandise exports).[25]

Psychological proximity also helps determine export-market choice. Many Canadian firms believe the United States is much like Canada, as are England and Australia—thus, they seek these markets rather than markets such as Germany and France; they feel more comfortable with the language, laws, and culture of the former group. Companies should be careful, however, in choosing markets according to cultural distance. Besides the fact that potentially better markets may be overlooked, choosing by cultural distance may result in a superficial analysis of some very real differences among the countries. It may also lead to predictable marketing actions that would be a disadvantage from a competitive standpoint.[26]

Regardless of how chosen, it often makes sense to operate in fewer countries with a deeper commitment and penetration in each. In general, a company prefers to enter countries (1) that rank high on market attractiveness, (2) that are low in market risk, and (3) in which it possesses a competitive advantage. Here is how Bechtel Corporation, the construction giant, goes about evaluating overseas markets:

Bechtel Corporation

Bechtel provides premier technical, management, and directly related services to develop, manage, engineer, build, and operate installations for customers in nearly 60 countries worldwide. Before Bechtel ventures into new markets, the company starts with a detailed strategic market analysis. It looks at its markets and tries to determine where it should be in four or five years' time. A management team conducts a cost-benefit analysis that factors in the position of competitors, infrastructure, regulatory and trade barriers, and the tax situation (both corporate and individual). Ideally, the new market should be a country with an untapped need for its products or services. It should also have a well-qualified skilled-labour pool capable of manufacturing the product and a welcoming environment (both governmental and physical).

Are there countries that meet Bechtel's requirements? Although Singapore has an educated, English-speaking labour force, basks in political stability, and encourages foreign investment, it has a small population. Although many countries in central Europe possess an eager, hungry-to-learn labour pool, their infrastructures create difficulties. The team evaluating a new market must determine whether the company could earn enough on its investment to cover the risk factors or other negatives.[27]

DECIDING HOW TO ENTER THE MARKET

Once a company decides to target a particular country, it has to determine the best mode of entry. Its broad choices are *indirect exporting, direct exporting, licensing, joint ventures,* and *direct investment.* These five market-entry strategies are shown in Figure 21.2. Each succeeding strategy involves more commitment, risk, control, and profit potential.

Indirect and Direct Export

The normal way to get involved in an international market is through export. *Occasional exporting* is a passive level of involvement in which the company exports from time to time, either on its own initiative or in response to unsolicited orders from abroad. *Active exporting* takes place when the company makes a commitment to expand into a particular market. In either case, the company produces its goods in the home country and might or might not adapt them to the international market.

Companies typically start with *indirect exporting*—that is, they work through independent intermediaries. *Domestic-based export merchants* buy the manufacturer's products and then sell them abroad. *Domestic-based export agents* seek and negotiate foreign purchases and are paid a commission. Included in this group are trading companies. *Cooperative organizations* carry on exporting activities on behalf of several producers and are partly under their administrative control. They are often used by producers of primary products such as fruits and nuts. *Export-management companies* agree to manage a company's export activities for a fee.

Indirect export has two advantages. First, it involves less investment: the firm does not have to develop an export department, an overseas sales force, or a set of international contacts. Second, it involves less risk: because international-marketing intermediaries bring know-how and services to the relationship, the seller will normally make fewer mistakes.

Companies eventually may decide to handle their own exports.[28] The investment and risk are somewhat greater, but so is the potential return. A company can carry on direct exporting in several ways:

- *Domestic-based export department or division.* This might evolve into a self-contained export department operating as a profit centre.
- *Overseas sales branch or subsidiary.* The sales branch handles sales and distribution and might handle warehousing and promotion as well. It often serves as a display and customer-service centre.
- *Travelling export sales representatives.* Home-based sales representatives are sent abroad to find business.
- *Foreign-based distributors or agents.* These distributors and agents might be given exclusive rights to represent the company in that country, or only limited rights.

Whether companies decide to export indirectly or directly, many companies use exporting as a way to "test the waters" before building a plant and manufacturing a product overseas. Here's how Australian wine producer Barokes enters foreign markets:

Barokes Wines

A unique Australian invention—wine in a can—is taking off in several countries across five continents. Melbourne-based Barokes Wines spent a decade researching and developing this award-winning, unique product. Globally patented as Vinsafe, the company is seeing increasing demand for its innovative product from around the world. One of its recent export markets is India, particularly the hotel and airline sectors there. The company's canned wine

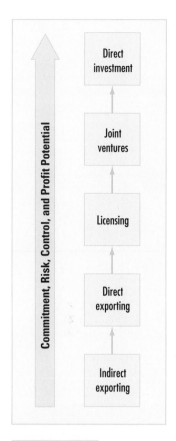

FIGURE 21.2

Five Models of Entry into Foreign Markets

presents several advantages over traditional bottled wine: it is non-breakable, which is attractive to hotels; lighter weight, which is an important consideration for airlines; and stackable, which makes storage easier for any customer. Barokes Wines exports its canned wine to Bommidala Enterprises in India. Bommidala is then responsible for selling the product in the huge Indian market. Vinsafe is currently exported to 23 countries and the company expects to increase that number dramatically over the next few years.[29]

USING A GLOBAL WEB STRATEGY One of the best ways to initiate or extend export activities used to be to exhibit at an overseas trade show. Today, companies can display their products and services on their websites, making trade shows less necessary. Online communication has enabled companies large and small to reach worldwide markets.

Major marketers doing global e-commerce range from automakers (GM) to direct-mail companies (Tilley Endurables) to running-shoe giants (Nike and Reebok) to Amazon.com. Marketers like these are using the Web to reach new customers outside their home countries, to support existing customers who live abroad, to source from international suppliers, and to build global brand awareness. Victoria's Secret has used the Internet to draw attention to the brand and gain consumers worldwide.

Victoria's Secret

When Victoria's Secret launched its highly anticipated online shopping site in 1998, customers from 37 countries placed orders in the first six hours of operation. In 1999, a commercial advertising the first webcast of Victoria's Secret lingerie fashion show drew one million visitors to the company's website. Seventy-two hours after the commercial aired, the world's first fashion-show webcast was viewed by nearly 1.5 million people. With increased competition from well-established brands—such as American Eagle's Aerie—expanding into lingerie, Victoria's Secret continues to heat up its fashion shows to attract consumers. It has also teamed up with celebrities such as the Spice Girls. In its Holiday 2007 campaign, Victoria's Secret offered the Spice Girls' greatest-hits album exclusively in stores and online in order to remain competitive.[30]

Marketers pursing global e-commerce adapt their websites to provide country-specific content and services to their best potential international markets, ideally in the local language. The number of Internet users is rising quickly as access costs decline, local-language content increases, and infrastructure improves. Upscale retailer and cataloguer The Sharper Image now gets more than 25 percent of its online business from overseas customers.[31]

The Internet has become an effective tool for a variety of purposes, including finding free exporting information and guidelines, conducting market research, and offering customers several time zones away a secure process for ordering and paying for products. But "going abroad" on the Internet does pose special challenges. The global marketer may run up against governmental or cultural restrictions. In Germany, a vendor cannot accept payment via credit card until two weeks after an order has been sent. German law also prevents companies from using certain marketing techniques like unconditional lifetime guarantees. On a wider scale, the issue of who pays sales taxes and duties on global e-commerce is murkier still.

Finding free information about trade and exporting has never been easier. Here are some places to start a search:

- The Department of Foreign Affairs and International Trade (www.infoexport.gc.ca)
- Canada Business (www.canadabusiness.ca)
- Export Development Canada (www.edc.ca)
- Industry Canada (www.ic.gc.ca)

In addition, most provincial governments provide information to facilitate international trade (e.g., for Ontario, see the International Trade Branch at www.ontarioexports.com).

Licensing

Licensing is a simple way to become involved in international marketing. The licensor licenses a foreign company to use a manufacturing process, trademark, patent, trade secret, or other item of value for a fee or royalty. The licensor gains entry at little risk; the licensee gains production expertise or a well-known product or brand name. Consider how Coty is introducing its Rimmel brand in new foreign markets:

Coty

Coty Inc., producer of Rimmel cosmetics, made plans in early 2008 to expand the brand into China via a licensing agreement with Tokyo-based Kos Corp. The agreement gives Kos Corp. the right to manufacture and distribute Rimmel's cosmetics, including foundation, mascara, lipstick, and eye shadow, to select department stores and drugstores in China. Rimmel, which was launched in the U.K. in 1834, is now sold in more than 50 countries. Endorsed by model Kate Moss, the brand targets women in their late teens to late 20s. The licensing agreement is part of the company's strategy to grow the Rimmel brand throughout Asia. Kos will develop new products tailored to the Chinese market using Rimmel's hip and edgy positioning to establish the brand as a leader in the beauty products market in China.[32]

Licensing has potential disadvantages. The licensor has less control over the licensee than it does over its own production and sales facilities. Furthermore, if the licensee is very successful, the firm has given up profits, and if and when the contract ends, the company might find that it has created a competitor. To avoid this, the licensor usually supplies some proprietary ingredients or components needed in the product (as Coca-Cola does). But the best strategy is for the licensor to lead in innovation so that the licensee will continue to depend on the licensor.

There are several variations on a licensing arrangement. Companies such as Hyatt and Marriott sell *management contracts* to owners of foreign hotels to manage these businesses for a fee. The management firm may even be given the option to purchase some share in the managed company within a stated period.

In *contract manufacturing*, the firm hires local manufacturers to produce the product. When Sears opened department stores in Mexico and Spain, it found qualified local manufacturers to produce many of its products. Contract manufacturing gives the company less control over the manufacturing process and the loss of potential profits on manufacturing. However, it offers a chance to start more quickly, with less risk, and with the opportunity to form a partnership or buy out the local manufacturer later.

Finally, a company can enter a foreign market through *franchising*, which is a more complete form of licensing. The franchisor offers a complete brand concept and operating system. In return, the franchisee invests in and pays certain fees to the franchisor. McDonald's, KFC, and Avis have entered scores of countries by franchising their retail concepts and making sure their marketing is culturally relevant.

Joint Ventures

Foreign investors may join with local investors to create a **joint venture** company in which they share ownership and control. For instance:[33]

- CAE of Montreal and China Southern Airlines formed a joint venture in January 2003 to provide aviation-training solutions for Asian carriers.

- Vancouver-based Cummins-Westport Inc. is a joint venture between leading diesel-engine manufacturer Cummins Inc. and alternative-fuels engine-technology company Westport Innovations Inc. Cummins-Westport develops and markets the world's widest range of high-performance, low-emission engines for transit and commercial vehicles, as well as advanced alternative fuel system technologies for electrical power generation.

- Coca-Cola and Nestlé joined forces to develop the international market for "ready to drink" tea and coffee, which they currently sell in significant amounts in Japan.

A joint venture may be necessary or desirable for economic or political reasons. The foreign firm might lack the financial, physical, or managerial resources to undertake the venture alone, or the foreign government might require joint ownership as a condition for entry. Even corporate giants need joint ventures to crack the toughest markets. When it wanted to enter China's ice cream market, Unilever joined forces with Sumstar, a state-owned Chinese investment company. The venture's general manager says Sumstar's help with the formidable Chinese bureaucracy was crucial in getting a high-tech ice cream plant up and running in just 12 months.[34]

Joint ownership has certain drawbacks. The partners might disagree over investment, marketing, or other policies. One partner might want to reinvest earnings for growth, and the other partner might want to declare more dividends. Joint ownership can also prevent a multinational company from carrying out specific manufacturing and marketing policies on a worldwide basis.

Direct Investment

The ultimate form of foreign involvement is direct ownership of foreign-based assembly or manufacturing facilities. The foreign company can buy part or full interest in a local company or build its own facilities. General Motors, for example, has invested billions of dollars in auto manufacturers around the world, such as Shanghai GM, Fiat Auto Holdings, Isuzu, Daewoo, Suzuki, Saab, Fuji Heavy Industries, Jinbei GM Automotive Co., and AvtoVAZ.[35]

If the market appears large enough, foreign production facilities offer distinct advantages. First, the firm secures cost economies in the form of cheaper labour or raw materials, foreign-government investment incentives, and freight savings. Second, the firm strengthens its image in the host country because it creates jobs. Third, the firm develops a deeper relationship with government, customers, local suppliers, and distributors, enabling it to better adapt its products to the local environment. Fourth, the firm retains full control over its investment and therefore can develop manufacturing and marketing policies that serve its long-term international objectives. Fifth, the firm assures itself access to the market in case the host country starts insisting that locally purchased goods have domestic content. Previously considered risky or unattractive, countries such as Egypt and Yemen are now good prospects for Canadian exporters.

Egypt and Yemen

Canadian manufacturers, feeling the pressure of the strong Canadian dollar, a skilled-labour shortage at home, and a U.S. economic downturn, have found new promise in markets such as Egypt and Yemen. In 2007, Canadian direct investment in Egypt was $324 million, a 28-percent increase over 2006. Direct investment by Canada in Yemen was $212 million, a 13-percent increase over 2006 levels. As markets in the Americas and Europe get saturated, more and more Canadian marketers hope to increase sales by turning towards countries in Asia and Africa that were previously overlooked or considered unstable.[36]

The main disadvantage of direct investment is that the firm exposes a large investment to risks such as blocked or devalued currencies, worsening markets, and expropriation. The firm will find it expensive to reduce or close down its operations, because the host country might require substantial severance pay to employees. Many Canadian retailers have used direct investment to attack the U.S. marketplace. However, they often find the competition is more intense and changes more rapidly than they expect. Moreover, U.S. retailers often have an advantage in size and name recognition over their Canadian rivals. Until recently, only 20 percent of retailers entering the U.S. market succeeded. Mark's Work Wearhouse, Second Cup Ltd., Canadian Tire, and People's Jewellers have all tested the U.S. waters only to withdraw in defeat. Today, however, the success rate has risen to 50 percent. Retailers like Harry Rosen, Tim Hortons, Club Monaco, and Couche-Tard have led the charge. The more successful entrants have tended to be smaller, specialized retailers that aim at niche markets where they don't have to challenge U.S. competitors head on.[37]

DECIDING ON THE MARKETING PROGRAM

International companies must decide how much to adapt their marketing strategy to local conditions.[38] At one extreme are companies that use a globally *standardized marketing mix* worldwide. Standardization of the product, communication, and distribution channels promises the lowest

TABLE 21.1	GLOBAL MARKETING PROS AND CONS
Advantages	**Disadvantages**
Economies of scale in production and distribution	Differences in consumer needs, wants, and usage patterns for products
Lower marketing costs	Differences in consumer response to marketing-mix elements
Power and scope	Differences in brand and product development and the competitive environment
Consistency in brand image	
Ability to leverage good ideas quickly and efficiently	Differences in the legal environment
Uniformity of marketing practices	Differences in marketing institutions
	Differences in administrative procedures

costs. Table 21.1 summarizes some of the pros and cons of standardizing the marketing program. At the other extreme is an *adapted marketing mix:* the producer adjusts the marketing program to each target market. For a discussion of the main issues, see "Marketing Insight: Global Standardization or Adaptation?"

Between the two extremes, many possibilities exist. Most brands are adapted to some extent to reflect significant differences in consumer behaviour, brand development, competitive forces, and the legal or political environment. Satisfying different consumer needs and wants can require different marketing programs. Cultural differences can often be pronounced across countries. Hofstede identifies four cultural dimensions that can differentiate countries:[39]

1. *Individualism vs. Collectivism.* In collectivist societies, such as Japan, the self-worth of an individual is rooted more in the social system than in individual achievement.
2. *High vs. Low Power Distance.* High power distance cultures tend to be less egalitarian.
3. *Masculine vs. Feminine.* How much the culture is dominated by assertive males versus nurturing females.
4. *Weak vs. Strong Uncertainty Avoidance.* How risk tolerant or aversive people are.

Even global brands, such as Pringles, Always, and Toyota, will undergo some changes in product features, packaging, channels, pricing, or communications in different global markets. (See "Marketing Memo: The Ten Commandments of Global Branding.") Marketers must make sure that their marketing is relevant to consumers in every market, as Western Union has done.

Western Union

As economic migration is booming, so is the remittance money transfer market. Western Union first introduced money transfer back in 1871, but it set up shop outside the United States only in 1990. It is now located in more than 200 countries, with a customer base of economic migrants who send funds home to their families. A key to Western Union's success in the burgeoning global market is its realization that along with money transfers, it is providing a perhaps more important intangible benefit. To Western Union's customers, a money transfer can mean providing for a child's education or an ailing relative's medical treatment. This emotional aspect of its service was emphasized in Western Union's very successful international ad campaign. The company also uses its customer knowledge to build loyalty by supporting popular events such as community festivals and religious celebrations. For instance, it supports its Jamaican customers by sponsoring the Notting Hill Carnival in London and similar events in other Jamaican enclaves of the United Kingdom. Western Union also sponsored the Albanian Football Federation and Africa's football (soccer) competition, the Africa Cup of Nations. With an estimated 185 million global migrants accounting for 6 to 10 percent of the population in European countries, Western Union will likely be doing even more to connect with potential customers.[40]

| MARKETING **INSIGHT** | GLOBAL STANDARDIZATION OR ADAPTATION? |

The question of whether to standardize or adapt in international marketing is an ongoing debate. Supporters of standardization argue that shared consumer traits, economic savings, and the benefits of a global brand make it the better alternative. The expansion of the Internet, the rapid spread of cable and satellite TV around the world, and the global linking of telecommunications networks have led to a convergence of lifestyles, creating global markets for standardized products. Marketers which use the standardization strategy focus on similarities across world markets and achieve economies of scale through standardization of production, distribution, marketing, and management. They often translate their efficiency into greater value for consumers by offering high quality at lower prices.

Those who argue for adaptation, however, cite demographic, cultural, economic, and legal reasons for tailoring the market offering to each country. Varying consumer behaviour across markets, in particular, poses a challenge to standardization. Take beverages for example. One of the highest per-capita consumptions of carbonated soft drinks is the United States' at 203.9 litres; Italy's is among the lowest. Italy has one of the highest per-capita consumptions of bottled water at 164.4 litres, which contrasts with the United Kingdom's at only 20 litres. When it comes to beer, Ireland and the Czech Republic lead the pack at over 150 litres per capita, with France among the lowest at 35.9 litres. Such international variances could mean trouble for a company pursuing a standardization strategy.

Besides other considerations, some products lend themselves to standardization whereas adaptation is the appropriate strategy for some others. Take cosmetics for example. In the beauty-product industry, advertisements use a standardized strategy more often than a localized one. There are many ways in which marketers can standardize an advertising message, whether it is through model selection, language, or message.

Advertising theory suggests that the spokesperson of a product should reflect the attributes of the target audience in order for the product to be well received. However, cross-cultural studies of global brand advertising have shown that models are the easiest and one of the most common elements of an advertising campaign to standardize. A study comparing British and French television ads for the same advertisers revealed that 81 percent of ads contained the same spokesperson. This may be due to practical (economies of scale) or strategic reasons (recognized spokesperson driving a global brand).

If a campaign model is standardized across countries, studies have shown that this typically results in the use of a Western model. An analysis of women's media in Singapore and Taiwan showed that the race of the models used in each culture did not reflect the racial mix of that country's population, with Western models being shown more often than Asian models. International marketers must be mindful of local attitudes towards Westernized advertisements. Some countries such as Brazil and France favour localized products and ads more, and these countries are less likely to appreciate a Western-style advertisement than are Chinese consumers, for example.

The global cosmetic brand Revlon believes that the use of one model can project a universal image of beauty. To accomplish this universal image while still catering to individual attitudes, Revlon studies the preferences of 130 local markets before developing a campaign designed to appeal to all of them. For example, Revlon believes that Japanese women do not have to see a Japanese model in order to identify with the image of beauty. This allows Revlon to use the same model to advertise a product in several countries. The company will make localized changes to a campaign only if it feels the changes will not damage Revlon's global image.

Although cultural differences may pose challenges to a standardization strategy, many companies resolve this by making slight alterations to their product and promotion. Pricing and distribution, however, are relatively more difficult to standardize. Nevertheless, by understanding local preferences across countries, it is possible to achieve a degree of standardization while still catering to local market needs.

Sources: David M. Szymanski, Sundar G. Bharadwaj, and P. Rajan Varadarajan, "Standardization versus Adaptation of International Marketing Strategy: An Empirical Investigation," *Journal of Marketing* (October 1993): 1–17; Theodore Levitt, "The Globalization of Markets," *Harvard Business Review* (May–June 1983): 92–102; "What Makes a Company Great?" *Fortune*, October 26, 1998, pp. 218–226; Victoria Seitz and J. S. Johar, "Advertising Practices for Self-Image Projective Products in the New Europe: A Print Advertising Content Analysis," *Journal of Consumer Marketing*, 10, no. 4 (1993): 15–26; Michelle R. Nelson and Hye-Jin Paek, "A Content Analysis of Advertising in a Global Magazine across Seven Countries: Implications for Global Advertising Strategies," *International Marketing Review*, 24, no. 1 (2007): 64–86.

Product

Some types of products travel better across borders than others—food and beverage marketers have to contend with widely varying tastes.[41] Warren Keegan has distinguished five strategies for adapting products and communications to a foreign market (see Figure 21.3).[42]

MARKETING MEMO | THE TEN COMMANDMENTS OF GLOBAL BRANDING

For many companies, global branding has been both a blessing and a curse. A global branding program can lower marketing costs, realize greater economies of scale in production, and provide a long-term source of growth. If not designed and implemented properly, however, it may ignore important differences in consumer behaviour and/or the competitive environment in the individual countries. These suggestions can help a company retain many of the advantages of global branding while minimizing the potential disadvantages:

1. *Understand similarities and differences in the global branding landscape.* International markets can vary in terms of brand development, consumer behaviour, competitive activity, legal restrictions, and so on.

2. *Do not take shortcuts in brand-building.* Building a brand in new markets should be done from the bottom up, both strategically (building awareness before brand image) and tactically (creating sources of brand equity in new markets).

3. *Establish a marketing infrastructure.* A company must either build marketing infrastructure from scratch or adapt to existing infrastructure in other countries.

4. *Embrace integrated marketing communications.* A company must often use many forms of communication in overseas markets, not just advertising.

5. *Establish brand partnerships.* Most global brands have marketing partners in their international markets that help companies achieve advantages in distribution, profitability, and added value.

6. *Balance standardization and customization.* Some elements of a marketing program can be standardized (packaging, brand name); others typically require greater customization (distribution channels).

7. *Balance global and local control.* Companies must balance global and local control within the organization and distribute decision-making between global and local managers.

8. *Establish operable guidelines.* Brand definition and guidelines must be established, communicated, and properly enforced so that marketers everywhere know what they are expected to do and not do. The goal is to set rules for how the brand should be positioned and marketed.

9. *Implement a global brand-equity measurement system.* A global brand-equity system is a set of research procedures designed to provide timely, accurate, and actionable information for marketers so that they can make the best possible short-run tactical decisions and long-run strategic decisions.

10. *Leverage brand elements.* Proper design and implementation of brand elements (brand name and trademarked brand identifiers) can be an invaluable source of brand equity worldwide.

Source: Adapted from Kevin Lane Keller and Sanjay Sood, "The Ten Commandments of Global Branding," *Asian Journal of Marketing*, 8, no. 2 (2001): 97–108.

	Product		
Communications	Do Not Change Product	Adapt Product	Develop New Product
Do Not Change Communications	Straight extension	Product adaptation	Product invention
Adapt Communications	Communication adaptation	Dual adaptation	Product invention

FIGURE 21.3

Five International Product and Communications Strategies

Source: Based on Warren J. Keegan, *Multinational Marketing Management*, 5th ed. (Upper Saddle River, NJ: Prentice Hall, 1995), pp. 378–381.

Straight extension means introducing the product in the foreign market without any change. Straight extension has been successful with cameras, consumer electronics, and many machine tools. In other cases, it has been a disaster. General Foods introduced its standard powdered Jell-O in the British market only to find that British consumers prefer the solid wafer or cake form. Campbell Soup Company lost an estimated US$30 million in introducing its condensed soups in

England; consumers saw expensive small-sized cans and did not realize that water needed to be added. Straight extension is tempting because it involves no additional R&D expense, manufacturing retooling, or promotional modification; but it can be costly in the long run.

Product adaptation involves altering the product to meet local conditions or preferences. There are several levels of adaptation.

- A company can produce a *regional version* of its product, such as a Western European version. Finnish cellular phone superstar Nokia customized its 6100 series phone for every major market. Developers built in rudimentary voice recognition for Asia, where keyboards are a problem, and raised the ring volume so the phone could be heard on crowded Asian streets.

- A company can produce a *country version* of its product. In Japan, Mister Donut's coffee cup is smaller and lighter to fit the hand of the average Japanese consumer; even the doughnuts are a little smaller. Kraft blends different coffees for the British (who drink their coffee with milk), the French (who drink their coffee black), and Latin Americans (who want a chicory taste).

- A company can produce a *city version* of its product—for instance, a beer to meet Munich tastes or Tokyo tastes.

- A company can produce different *retailer versions* of its product, such as one coffee brew for the Migros chain store and another for the Cooperative chain store, both in Switzerland.

Product invention consists of creating something new. It can take two forms. **Backward invention** is reintroducing earlier product forms that are well adapted to a foreign country's needs. The National Cash Register Company reintroduced its crank-operated cash register at half the price of a modern cash register and sold substantial numbers in Latin America and Africa.

Forward invention is creating a new product to meet a need in another country. There is an enormous need in less-developed countries for low-cost, high-protein foods. Companies such as Quaker Oats, Swift, Monsanto, and Nutriset are researching these countries' nutrition needs by formulating new foods and developing advertising campaigns to gain product trial and acceptance. Toyota produces vehicles specifically designed, with the help of local employees, to suit the tastes of these markets.[43]

Nutriset

Following years of research by nutritionists, Nutriset (a private French company specializing in food for humanitarian relief) developed Plumpy'nut—a peanut-based paste that is saving the lives of children living in Third World countries. Each packet of the high-protein, high-energy Plumpy'nut contains 500 kilocalories and is packaged in a compact, airtight aluminum envelope that protects against light and humidity. It requires no refrigeration and has a 24-month shelf-life. It is inexpensive to transport and enables families to feed their children themselves. A severely malnourished child eating three to four packets a day will gain weight and begin to regain health within a week. For example, Plumpy'nut has been fed to some 30 000 children in Sudan's Darfur region and aid officials claim it has helped cut malnutrition rates in half, with more than 300 tonnes of Plumpy'nut being distributed in Darfur alone.[44]

Product invention is a costly strategy, but the payoffs can be great, particularly if a company can exploit a product innovation in other countries. In globalization's latest twist, North American companies are not only inventing new products for overseas markets, but also lifting products and ideas from their international operations and bringing them home.

In launching products and services globally, certain brand elements may have to be changed. When Clairol introduced into Germany the "Mist Stick," a curling iron, it found that *mist* is slang for manure. Few Germans wanted to purchase a "manure stick." Brand slogans and ad taglines sometimes have to be changed too:[45]

- When Coors put its brand slogan "Turn it loose" into Spanish, it was read by some as "suffer from diarrhea."
- A laundry soap ad claiming to wash "really dirty parts" was translated in French-speaking Quebec to read "a soap for washing private parts."

TABLE 21.2	BLUNDERS IN INTERNATIONAL MARKETING

- Hallmark cards failed when they were introduced in France. The French dislike syrupy sentiment and prefer writing their own cards.
- Philips began to earn a profit in Japan only after it had reduced the size of its coffeemakers to fit into smaller Japanese kitchens and its shavers to fit smaller Japanese hands.
- Coca-Cola had to withdraw its two-litre bottle in Spain after discovering that few Spaniards owned refrigerators with compartments large enough to accommodate it.
- General Foods' Tang initially failed in France because it was positioned as a substitute for orange juice at breakfast. The French drink little orange juice and almost none at breakfast.
- Kellogg's Pop-Tarts failed in Britain because the percentage of British homes with toasters was significantly lower than in North America, and the product was too sweet for British tastes.
- Procter & Gamble's Crest toothpaste initially failed in Mexico when it used the U.S. campaign. Mexicans did not care as much for the decay-prevention benefit, nor did scientifically oriented advertising appeal to them.
- General Foods squandered millions trying to introduce packaged cake mixes to Japanese consumers. The company failed to note that only 3 percent of Japanese homes were equipped with ovens.
- S. C. Johnson's floor polish initially failed in Japan. The wax made floors too slippery, and Johnson had overlooked the fact that Japanese do not wear shoes in their homes.

- Perdue's slogan—"It takes a tough man to make a tender chicken"—was rendered into Spanish as "It takes a sexually excited man to make a chick affectionate."
- Electrolux's British ad line for its vacuum cleaners—"Nothing sucks like an Electrolux"—would certainly not lure customers in North America!

    Table 21.2 lists some other famous blunders in this arena.

Communications

Companies can run the same marketing communications programs as used in the home market or change them for each local market, a process called **communication adaptation**. Strategies for adapting communications are outlined below. If a company adapts both the product and the communication, it engages in **dual adaptation**. Tim Hortons may need to look into adaptation strategies to market its offerings in the United States.

Tim Hortons

Tim Hortons is well-known in Canada for its coffee and doughnuts. The company operates over 2800 restaurants across Canada and nearly 400 in the United States. Although Tim Hortons has been operating south of the border for over 20 years, the success of its U.S. locations has not been as great as in Canada. Tim Hortons holds over 76 percent of the Canadian coffee and pastry fast-food market and has been growing over 6 percent a year in Canada, whereas in the United States the company has only seen around a 3-percent annual growth as it faces strong competition from Starbucks and Dunkin' Donuts. The Canadian market has a soft spot for Tim Hortons and the "double-double" coffee has become an icon in Canada, while the United States has had a different reaction. In order to become as successful as it has been in Canada, Tim Hortons may need to market itself differently in the United States.[46]

First, consider the message. A company can use one message everywhere, varying only the language, name, and colours.[47] Exxon used "Put a tiger in your tank" with minor variations and gained international recognition. Colours can be changed to avoid taboos in some countries.

Purple is associated with death in Burma and some Latin American nations; white is a mourning colour in India; and green is associated with disease in Malaysia.[48]

The second possibility is to use the same theme globally but adapt the copy to each local market. For example, a Camay soap commercial showed a beautiful woman bathing. In Venezuela, a man was seen in the bathroom; in Italy and France, only a man's hand was seen; and in Japan, the man waited outside. The positioning stays the same, but the creative execution reflects local sensibilities.

The third approach consists of developing a global pool of ads, from which each country selects the most appropriate one. Coca-Cola and Goodyear have used this approach. Finally, some companies allow their country managers to create country-specific ads—within guidelines, of course. Kraft uses different ads for Cheez Whiz in different countries, given that household penetration is 95 percent in Puerto Rico, where the cheese is put on everything, and 65 percent in Canada, where it is spread on breakfast toast. In the United States, it is considered a junk food.

The use of media also requires international adaptation because media availability varies from country to country. Norway, Belgium, France, the United States, and Canada do not allow cigarettes to be advertised on TV. Like Quebec, Austria and Italy regulate TV advertising to children. Saudi

A Lands' End ad for Germany. Because Germany has a number of laws preventing or limiting the use of sales-promotion tools, Lands' End cannot advertise its money-back guarantee, though it can accept merchandise returns.

Arabia does not want advertisers to use women in ads. India taxes advertising. Magazines vary in availability and effectiveness; they play a major role in Italy and a minor one in Austria.

Marketers must also adapt sales-promotion techniques to different markets. Several European countries have laws preventing or limiting sales-promotion tools such as discounts, rebates, coupons, games of chance, and premiums. In Germany, Lands' End could not advertise its money-back guarantee, although it does accept returned merchandise. American Express could not award merchandise-redemption points based on charges to its credit cards. A German store could not advertise that it would contribute to the fight against AIDS a small sum for each transaction; a German law limits discounts to 3 percent of list price. However, these restrictions are under attack and are beginning to crumble.

Personal selling tactics may have to change too. The direct, no-nonsense approach favoured by North Americans (characterized by more of a "let's get down to business" stance) may not work as well in Europe, Asia, and other places where a more indirect, subtle approach can be more effective.[49] With younger, more worldly employees, however, such cultural differences may be less pronounced.

Price

Multinationals face several pricing problems when selling abroad. They must deal with price escalation, transfer prices, dumping charges, and grey markets, as Microsoft has experienced.

Microsoft

When Microsoft entered China 15 years ago, the company made its first big blunder by trying to sell its Windows operating system at the same high price it commands in the developed world while pirated copies were available at rock-bottom prices. Microsoft spent the next ten years trying to crack down on piracy in China, suing companies for using its software illegally and always losing in court. The Chinese government grew ever more mistrustful of Microsoft—even suspecting the United States of spying via the software—and put open-source Linux operating systems on all workers' PCs. So how did Microsoft become so respected in China that CEO Bill Gates is now a celebrity? For one thing, by doing a complete turnaround and tolerating piracy. "It's easier for our software to compete with Linux when there's piracy than when there's not," says Gates. Yet, the best move Microsoft made was to collaborate with the Chinese government and open a research centre in Beijing, which today lures the country's top computer scientists. Rather than being known as a company that comes to China to sue people, it's regarded as a company with a long-term vision.[50]

When companies sell their goods abroad, they face a **price escalation** problem. A Gucci handbag may sell for half as much in Italy as in North America. Why? Gucci has to add to its factory price the cost of transportation, tariffs, importer margin, wholesaler margin, and retailer margin. Depending on these added costs, as well as the currency-fluctuation risk, to make the same profit for the manufacturer the product might have to sell for two to five times as much in another country. Because the cost escalation varies from country to country, the question is how to set the prices in different countries. Companies have three choices:

- *Set a uniform price everywhere.* Coca-Cola might want to charge 75 cents for Coke everywhere in the world, but then Coca-Cola would earn quite different profit rates in different countries. Also, this strategy would result in the price being too high in poor countries and not high enough in rich countries.

- *Set a market-based price in each country.* Here Coca-Cola would charge what each country could afford, but this strategy ignores differences in the actual cost from country to country. Also, it could lead to a situation in which intermediaries in low-price countries reship their Coca-Cola to high-price countries.

- *Set a cost-based price in each country.* Here Coca-Cola would use a standard markup of its costs everywhere, but this strategy might price Coca-Cola out of the market in countries where its costs are high.

Another problem arises when a company sets a **transfer price** (the price it charges another unit in the company) for goods that it ships to its foreign subsidiaries. If the company charges too high a price to a subsidiary, it may end up paying higher tariff duties, although it may pay lower income taxes in the foreign country. If the company charges too low a price to its subsidiary, it can be charged with dumping. **Dumping** occurs when a company charges either less than its costs or less than it charges in its home market, in order to enter or win a market. In 2000, Stelco, a Canadian steelmaker, successfully fought dumping of steel products by steelmakers in Brazil, Finland, India, Indonesia, Thailand, and Ukraine. A Canadian tribunal found that cut-price steel imports from these countries caused "material injury to Canadian producers, including Stelco."[51] Various governments are watching for abuses and often force companies to charge the **arm's-length price**— that is, the price charged by other competitors for the same or a similar product.

Many multinationals are plagued by the grey-market problem. The **grey market** consists of branded products diverted from normal or authorized distributions channels in the country of product origin or across international borders. Dealers in the low-price country find ways to sell some of their products in higher-price countries, thus earning more. Industry research suggests that worldwide grey-market activity accounts for over US$40 billion in revenue each year. For example, an estimated 1 million Apple iPhones have already been sold in the grey market in countries such as China and Canada before Apple introduced the product in those countries. Industry analysts estimate the grey market makes up about 60 to 90 percent of Apple product sales in India. This, along with some other problems, has forced Apple to downsize its operations in that country. However, some other companies have been fighting back against grey marketers. In 2008, HP successfully sued Maxicom PC for US$4 million for selling HP hardware on the grey market. Similarly, Sun Microsystems won its lawsuit against Amtec Computer Corporation accused of selling Sun servers on the grey market.[52]

Very often a company finds some enterprising distributors buying more than they can sell in their own country and reshipping the goods to another country to take advantage of price differences. Multinationals try to prevent grey markets by policing distributors, by raising their prices to lower-cost distributors, or by altering the product characteristics or service warranties for different countries. In the European Union, the grey market may disappear altogether with the transition to the euro. Once consumers recognize price differentiation by country, companies will be forced to harmonize prices throughout the countries that have adopted the single currency. Companies and marketers that offer the most innovative, specialized, or necessary products or services will be least affected by price transparency.[53]

The Internet also reduces price differentiation between countries. When companies sell their wares online, price becomes transparent: customers can easily find out for how much products sell in different countries. Take an online training course, for instance. Whereas the price of a classroom-delivered day of training can vary significantly from Canada to France to Thailand, the price of an online-delivered day of training would have to be similar.[54]

Another global pricing challenge that has arisen in recent years occurs when countries with overcapacity, cheap currencies, and the need to export aggressively have pushed prices down and devalued their currencies. For multinational firms this poses challenges: sluggish demand and reluctance to pay higher prices make selling in these emerging markets difficult. Instead of lowering prices and taking a loss, some multinationals, such as General Electric, have found more lucrative and creative means of coping.[55]

General Electric Company

Rather than striving for larger market share, GE's power-systems unit focused on winning a larger percentage of each customer's expenditures. The unit asked its top 100 customers what services were most critical to them and how GE could provide or improve them. The answers prompted the company to cut its response time for replacing old or damaged parts from 12 weeks to six. It began advising customers on the nuances of doing business in the diverse environments of Europe and Asia and providing the maintenance staff for occasional equipment upgrades. By adding value and helping customers reduce their costs and become more efficient, GE was able to avoid a move to commodity pricing and was actually able to generate bigger margins. These margins led to record revenues of US$15 billion in 2000, a 50 percent increase from the previous year.[56]

Distribution Channels

Too many manufacturers think their job is done once the product leaves the factory. They should pay attention to how the product moves within the foreign country and take a whole-channel view of the problem of distributing products to final users. Figure 21.4 shows the three major links between seller and ultimate buyer. In the first link, *seller's international marketing headquarters*, the export department or international division makes decisions on channels and other marketing-mix elements. The second link, *channels between nations*, gets the products to the borders of the foreign nation. The decisions made in this link include the types of intermediaries (agents, trading companies) that will be used, the type of transportation (air, sea), and the financing and risk arrangements. The third link, *channels within foreign nations*, gets the products from their entry point to final buyers and users.

Distribution channels within countries vary considerably. To sell soap in Japan, Procter & Gamble has to work through one of the most complicated distribution systems in the world. It must sell to a general wholesaler, which sells to a product wholesaler, which sells to a product-specialty wholesaler, which sells to a regional wholesaler, which sells to a local wholesaler, which finally sells to retailers. All these distribution levels can mean that the consumer's price ends up double or triple the importer's price. If P&G takes the soap to tropical Africa, the company might sell to an import wholesaler, which sells to several jobbers, which sell to petty traders (mostly women) working in local markets.

Another difference lies in the size and character of retail units abroad. Large-scale retail chains dominate the North American scene, but much foreign retailing is in the hands of small, independent retailers. In India, millions of retailers operate tiny shops or sell in open markets. Their markups are high, but the real price is brought down through haggling. Incomes are low, and people must shop daily for small amounts: they are limited to whatever quantity can be carried home on foot or on a bicycle. Most homes lack storage space and refrigeration. Packaging costs are kept low in order to keep prices low. In India, cigarettes are often bought singly. Breaking bulk remains an important function of intermediaries and helps perpetuate the long channels of distribution, which are a major obstacle to the expansion of large-scale retailing in developing countries.

When multinationals first enter a country, they prefer to work with local distributors which have good local knowledge, but friction often arises later.[57] The multinational might complain that the local distributor does not invest in business growth, does not follow company policy, or does not share enough information. The local distributor might complain of insufficient corporate support, impossible goals, and confusing policies. The multinational must choose the right distributors, invest in them, and set up performance goals to which both parties can agree.[58]

Some companies choose to invest in infrastructure to ensure they benefit from the right channels. Peruvian cola company Kola Real has been able to survive despite competing with Coca-Cola and Pepsi-Cola in Mexico by setting up its own distribution network of 600 leased lorries, 24 distribution centres, and 800 salespeople.[59]

Many retailers are trying to make inroads into global markets. France's Carrefour, Germany's Metro, and the United Kingdom's Tesco have all established global positions. Germany's Aldi follows a simple formula globally. It stocks only about 700 products (compared with more than 20 000 at a traditional grocer such as Royal Ahold's Albert Heijin), almost all under its own exclusive label. Because it sells so few products, Aldi can exert strong control over quality and price and can simplify shipping and handling, leading to large margins. Retail experts expect Aldi to have 1000 stores in the United States by 2010, with as much as 2 percent of the U.S. grocery market. Canadian company IMRIS has learned how to expand internationally and become the global leader in advanced surgical imaging systems.

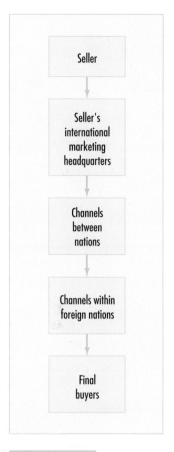

Whole-Channel Concept for International Marketing

IMRIS

IMRIS's products may be state-of-the-art and complex but its goal is simple: to improve patient surgical outcomes and quality of life. For leading neuroscience centres, IMRIS is the supplier of choice for intraoperative imaging systems. IMRIS's flagship product, the IMRIS Neuro, revolutionized the MRI process during surgery and is the only product of its kind in the world. The technology has been sold to 18 hospitals around the world as of June 2008, impressive for a small company based in Winnipeg, Manitoba. David Graves, President and CEO of IMRIS, has been happy to see double-digit annual growth in sales year after year. The company recently added new sales offices in Brussels, Belgium, and Sydney, Australia, due to the increase in demand for its products around the world. Future expansions are planned for hospitals in Beijing, China, and Mumbai, India.[60]

COUNTRY-OF-ORIGIN EFFECTS

In an increasingly connected, highly competitive global marketplace, government officials and marketers are concerned with how attitudes and beliefs about their country affect consumer and business decision making. *Country-of-origin perceptions* are the mental associations and beliefs triggered by a country. Government officials want to strengthen their country's image to help domestic marketers that export and to attract foreign firms and investors. Marketers want to use country-of-origin perceptions in the most advantageous way possible to sell their products and services.

Building Country Images

Governments now recognize that the image of their cities and countries affects more than tourism and has important value in commerce. Attracting foreign business can improve the local economy, which provides jobs and improves infrastructure. City officials in Kobe, Japan, were able to entice multinationals Procter & Gamble, Nestlé, and Eli Lilly to locate their Japanese headquarters in the city through traditional marketing techniques and careful targeting and positioning.[61] Hong Kong officials also developed a symbol—a stylized dragon—to represent their city's core brand values.[62]

Countries all over the world are being marketed like any other brand. In some cases, negative perceptions must be overcome. For example, research by the British Council in 2000 revealed that young opinion leaders in 28 countries saw Britons as weak on creativity and innovation, class-ridden, racist, and cold.[63] Relying partly on the global success of Nokia, Finland launched a campaign to enhance its image as a centre of high-tech innovation.[64] A number of initiatives have been undertaken to improve Canada's image both as prime place for direct investment and as a source of high-quality products.[65]

Branding Canada

In 2001, Investment Partnerships Canada (IPC) commissioned a qualitative research study of American executives' perceptions of Canada as a prime place for investment. Attracting investment is important since one out of every ten jobs in Canada depends directly on foreign investment. The IPC needed a knowledge base to guide Canada's future marketing and branding efforts. The research led to some valuable insights. While Canada was well regarded and reasonably well known by 74 percent of the respondents, it was not high on

Hong Kong's trademark, a stylized dragon with the tagline "Asia's world city."

the radar screens of almost half of the sample (49 percent) as an investment destination. The results suggest a three-part brand proposition that Canada can claim:

- *A thriving marketplace*—Investors can find all the infrastructure and support required to succeed and be profitable.

- *A talented labour pool*—Canada has an abundance of qualified people with the skills to help a company achieve its objectives.

- *An environment almost like home*—Canada's business environment and culture are similar to those of the United States, while it poses lower risks and offers higher returns than other investment options.

In 2004, *Brand Canada* was unveiled at the International Boston Seafood Show as the new logo for Canadian aquaculture. Bob Speller, the minister of agriculture, noted "Exports drive Canada's economy, so it is important that our high-quality products be easily identifiable anywhere in the world. The new *Brand Canada* trade logo appearing on packaging will help promote the overall excellence of Canadian fish and seafood products in the minds of international consumers and commercial buyers." The initiative is part of a long-term strategy designed to differentiate Canada's aquaculture products from those of competitor countries by assuring buyers that Canadian aquaculture products are safe and environmentally sustainable.

Consumer Perceptions of Country-of-Origin

Global marketers know that buyers hold distinct attitudes and beliefs about brands and products from different countries.[66] These country-of-origin perceptions can affect consumer decision making directly and indirectly. The perceptions may be included as an attribute in decision making or influence other attributes in the process ("If it's French, it must be stylish"). The mere fact that a brand is perceived as being successful on a global stage may lend credibility and respect.[67] Several studies have found the following:[68]

- People are often ethnocentric and favourably predisposed to their own country's products, unless they come from a less developed country.

- The more favourable a country's image, the more prominently the "Made in . . . " label should be displayed.

- The impact of country of origin varies with the type of product. Consumers want to know where a car was made but not about the lubricating oil.

- Certain countries enjoy a reputation for certain goods: Japan for automobiles and consumer electronics; the United States for high-tech innovations, soft drinks, toys, cigarettes, and jeans; France for wine, perfume, and luxury goods.

- Sometimes country-of-origin perception can encompass an entire country's products. In one study, Chinese consumers in Hong Kong perceived American products as prestigious, Japanese products as innovative, and Chinese products as cheap.

The favourability of country-of-origin perceptions must be considered both from a domestic and foreign perspective. In the domestic market, country-of-origin perceptions may stir consumers' patriotic notions or remind them of their past. As international trade grows, consumers may view certain brands as symbolically important in their own cultural heritage and identity. Patriotic appeals have been the basis of marketing strategies all over the world. Patriotic appeals, however, can lack uniqueness and even be overused. For example, Molson dropped its famous "I AM CANADIAN" campaign because it was no longer driving sales. "Marketing Insight: Country-of-Origin: To Communicate or Not?" discusses marketers making consumers aware of country-related brand associations.

A company has several options when its products are competitively priced but its place of origin turns off consumers. The company can consider co-production with a foreign company that has a better name: a South Korean firm could make a fine leather jacket that it sends to Italy for finishing, or the firm could adopt a strategy to achieve world-class quality in the local industry, as is the case with Belgian chocolates, Polish ham, and Colombian coffee.

As progress is made, companies can start to build local roots to increase relevance, as exemplified by Toyota, which has made sales in North America a top priority. BMW has been following a similar strategy.[69]

| MARKETING **INSIGHT** | COUNTRY-OF-ORIGIN: TO COMMUNICATE OR NOT? |

A number of studies have shown that positive or negative images of a country influence consumers' evaluations of products associated with that country. This is known as the country-of-origin (COO) effect. In general, brands benefit from positive COO images and are harmed by negative COO images. Although COO effects have been researched extensively, the literature has recently acknowledged that the "Made in . . . " labels on products are no longer good indicators of an item's COO, as most international brands nowadays are not manufactured in their country of origin. Recognizing this, COO researchers have broken the topic down into several pieces—country of design, country of parts, country of manufacture, country of assembly, brand origin, etc.—with several studies examining the impact of each of these factors on consumer attitude towards a brand.

Marketers sometimes explicitly convey country-related information in advertisements, whereas some others try to downplay it. For example, Toyota Canada advertises that its cars are made in Canada and BMW highlights its "German engineering," but LG rarely draws attention to the fact that it is a Korean brand and VW would rather not have consumers know that its Jetta is produced in Mexico. Some companies try to encourage positive national associations when they indeed exist—Foster's advertises itself as "Australian for beer" and many French wines make their origin obvious—but others may try to create false connections to capitalize on the positive images of other countries. Minhas Creek beer cans have created some controversy because they carry a maple leaf, giving the impression that the beer is brewed in Canada, and some Chinese sushi restaurants would like consumers to think they are Japanese to capitalize on the prestige of Japanese cuisine.

One common characteristic of almost all COO-effect studies is that they assume consumers are aware of a product's country of origin. However, some researchers have shown that although most consumers know the country a brand originates in, most consumers are unaware of where a particular product is actually manufactured. For example, most consumers might know that Sony is a Japanese brand but few would know in which country a certain product (such a flat screen TV) was actually manufactured or assembled. Many marketers have found that most well-known brands have acquired such high brand equity that it does not matter where they are produced. For instance, if a Gucci purse is manufactured in China, most consumers will still see the product as Italian and so still regard it as a fashionable product.

Sources: Gary S. Insch, and J. Brad McBride, "The Impact of Country-of-Origin Cues on Consumer Perceptions of Product Quality: A Binational Test of the Decomposed Country-of-Origin Construct," *Journal of Business Research*, 57 (2004): 256–265; George Balabanis, Rene Mueller, and T. C. Melewar, "The Human Values' Lenses of Country of Origin Images," *International Marketing Review*, 19, no. 6 (2002): 582–611; Mrugank Thakor and Anne M. Lavack, "Effect of Perceived Brand Origin Associations on Consumer Perceptions of Quality," *Journal of Product and Brand Management*, 12, no. 6/7 (2003): 394–407; Paul Chao, "The Moderating Effects of Country of Assembly, Country of Parts, and Country of Design on Hybrid Product Evaluation," *Journal of Advertising*, 30, no. 4 (2001): 67–81; Saeed Samiee, "Customer Evaluation of Products in a Global Market," *Journal of International Business Studies*, 25, no. 3 (1994): 579–604.

DECIDING ON THE MARKETING ORGANIZATION

Companies manage their international marketing activities in three ways: through export departments, international divisions, or a global organization.

Export Department

A firm normally gets into international marketing by simply shipping out its goods. If its international sales expand, the company organizes an export department consisting of a sales manager and a few assistants. As sales increase, the export department is expanded to include various marketing services so that the company can go after business more aggressively. If the firm moves into joint ventures or direct investment, the export department will no longer be adequate to manage international operations.

International Division

Many companies become involved in several international markets and ventures. Sooner or later they will create international divisions to handle all of their international activity, as illustrated by the Royal Bank example. The international division is headed by a division president, who sets goals and budgets and is responsible for the company's international growth.

Royal Bank of Canada

In 2008, Royal Bank (RBC) named Jim Westlake the head of international banking and insurance in a move that represented the organization's commitment to growth in its international markets. From 2006 to 2008, international activities accounted for one third of RBC's revenues. RBC currently operates in Canada, the United States, and 36 other countries. With various acquisitions, RBC has recently gained presence in the Caribbean region. Following the completion of its 2008 acquisition in Trinidad and Tobago, RBC will have over US$13.7 billion in assets with 130 branches and more than 6900 employees serving over 1.6 million clients in the Caribbean region alone.[70]

The international division's corporate staff consists of functional specialists who provide services to various operating units. Operating units can be organized in several ways. First, they can be *geographical organizations*. Reporting to the international-division president might be regional vice-presidents for North America, Latin America, Europe, Africa, the Middle East, and the Far East. Reporting to the regional vice-presidents might be country managers responsible for a sales force, sales branches, distributors, and licensees in their respective countries. Or, the operating units may be *world product groups*, each with an international vice-president responsible for worldwide sales of each product group. The vice-presidents may draw on corporate-staff area specialists for expertise on different geographical areas. Finally, operating units may be *international subsidiaries*, each headed by a president. The various subsidiary presidents report to the president of the international division.

Global Organization

Several firms have become truly global organizations. Their top corporate management and staff plan worldwide manufacturing facilities, marketing policies, financial flows, and logistical systems. The global operating units report directly to the chief executive or executive committee, not to the head of an international division. Executives are trained in worldwide operations. Management is recruited from many countries; components and supplies are purchased where they can be obtained at the least cost; and investments are made where the anticipated returns are greatest.

These companies face several organizational complexities. For example, when a company sets the pricing of its high-end computers for sale to a large banking system in Germany, how much influence should the headquarters' product manager have? And the company's market manager for the banking sector? And the company's country manager for Germany?

Bartlett and Ghoshal have proposed circumstances under which different approaches work best. In *Managing Across Borders*, they describe forces that favour "global integration" (capital-intensive production, homogeneous demand) versus "national responsiveness" (local standards and barriers, strong local preferences). They distinguish three organizational strategies:[71]

1. *A global strategy treats the world as a single market.* This strategy is warranted when the forces for global integration are strong and the forces for national responsiveness are weak. This is true of the consumer electronics market, for example, where most buyers will accept a fairly standardized pocket radio, CD player, or TV. Matsushita has performed better than GE and Philips in the consumer electronics market because Matsushita operates in a more globally coordinated and standardized way.

2. *A multinational strategy treats the world as a portfolio of national opportunities.* This strategy is warranted when the forces favouring national responsiveness are strong and the forces favouring global integration are weak. This is the situation in the branded packaged-goods business (food products, cleaning products). Bartlett and Ghoshal cite Unilever as a better performer than Kao and P&G because Unilever grants more decision-making autonomy to its local branches.

3. *A "glocal" strategy standardizes certain core elements and localizes other elements.* This strategy makes sense for an industry (such as telecommunications) in which each nation requires some adaptation of its equipment, but the providing company can also standardize some of the core components. Bartlett and Ghoshal cite Ericsson as balancing these considerations better than NEC (too globally oriented) and ITT (too locally oriented).

Many firms seek a blend of centralized global control from corporate headquarters with input from local and regional marketers. Finding that balance can be tricky. Coca-Cola's "think local, act local" philosophy, which decentralized much of the power and responsibility to design marketing programs and activities, fell apart when many local managers lacked the necessary skills or discipline. Decidedly un-Coke-like ads appeared—such as skinny-dippers streaking down a beach in Italy—and sales stalled. The pendulum swung back, and Coke executives in Atlanta began to play a stronger strategic role again.[72]

SUMMARY

1. Despite the many challenges in the international arena (shifting borders, unstable governments, foreign-exchange problems, corruption, and technological pirating), companies selling in global industries need to internationalize their operations. Companies cannot simply stay domestic and expect to maintain their markets.

2. In deciding to go abroad, a company needs to define its international marketing objectives and policies. The company must determine whether to market in a few countries or many countries. It must decide which countries to consider. In general, the candidate countries should be rated on three criteria: market attractiveness, risk, and competitive advantage. Developing countries offer a unique set of opportunities and risks.

3. Once a company decides on a particular country, it must determine the best mode of entry. Its broad choices are indirect exporting, direct exporting, licensing, joint ventures, and direct investment. Each succeeding strategy involves more commitment, risk, control, and profit potential.

4. In deciding on the marketing program, a company must decide how much to adapt its marketing program—product, communications, distribution, and price—to local conditions. At the product level, firms can pursue a strategy of straight extension, product adaptation, or product invention. At the communication level, firms may choose communication adaptation or dual adaptation. At the price level, firms may encounter price escalation and grey markets. At the distribution level, firms need to take a whole-channel view of the challenge of distributing products to the final users. In creating all elements of the marketing program, firms must be aware of the cultural, social, political, technological, environmental, and legal limitations they face in other countries.

5. Country-of-origin perceptions can affect consumers and businesses alike. Managing those perceptions in the most advantageous way possible is an important marketing priority.

6. Depending on the level of international involvement, companies manage their international marketing activity in three ways: through export departments, international divisions, or a global organization.

APPLICATIONS

Marketing Debate: Is the World Coming Closer Together?

Many social commentators maintain that youth and teens are becoming more and more alike across countries as time goes on. Others, while not disputing that fact, point out that the differences between cultures at even younger ages by far exceed the similarities.

Take a position: People are becoming more and more similar *versus* The differences between people of different cultures far outweigh their similarities.

Marketing Discussion

Think of some of your favourite brands. Do you know where they come from? Where and how they are made or provided? Do their countries of origin affect your perceptions of quality or satisfaction?

Breakthrough Marketing: Elluminate Inc.

Traditionally, companies have established themselves in their home country and then gone international through exporting, licensing, joint ventures, or direct investment. A new trend in going global is via the Web. More and more companies are becoming purely web-based, meaning they have the potential to be a global player right from the start. Such companies often have local production and a website that provides consumers around the world access to their products. Calgary-based Elluminate Inc. is one of these companies, and the way it delivers its products and services internationally is anything but traditional.

Elluminate provides online resources to schools, universities, and businesses. Its products and services include web conferencing, eLearning, advanced moderator tools, meeting rooms, virtual offices, and online tutoring, training, and event hosting. The company's main product, Elluminate Live! provides VoIP technology and interactivity with its trade-marked *No User Left Behind* technology that allows web-conferencing capabilities through any operating system and any Internet connection speed. Elluminate Live! brings students or business people together in virtual seminar settings to collaborate and learn. Elluminate Plan! allows users to organize and script materials online, allowing instructors to automate the delivery of material during a live session. The company's recent Elluminate Publish! Product allows users to create portable, reusable content that can be sent to portable MP3 players or to email accounts.

Elluminate's online services can be accessed by people in different countries at the same time, which reduces costs for businesses and educational institutions and increases productivity. Customers such as Penn State University and University of Calgary offer distance education programs using Elluminate Live! Schools such as New York City's District 75 use the product to host online student debates. Companies such as Sun Microsystems and Interstate Hotels & Resorts offer online training programs to their employees using Elluminate products.

Elluminate has won numerous awards including the 2008 Alberta Business Award of Distinction in the Export category. The company was also in the Visionaries Quadrant of the Gartner Magic Quadrant for Web Conferencing in 2007 and is one of Deloitte's 50 Fastest Growing Technology Companies. Founder and CEO Nashir Samanani was awarded the 2007 Ernst & Young Entrepreneur of The Year Award in the technology category.

Elluminate claims it has served over 300 million web-collaboration minutes to over 3 million people in 185 countries around the world. While most Internet-based companies rely on domestic markets for the majority of their revenues and use the international market as a supplement, Elluminate's exports account for 94 percent of its sales, proving it is a truly international company.

DISCUSSION QUESTIONS

1. What are the unique challenges Elluminate's online market entry presents as compared to traditional market-entry strategies?

2. What risks should Elluminate watch out for?

3. How should Elluminate market its products and services? Should it use the same strategies across all countries/categories? Why or why not?

4. What other market segments could the company expand to? Are there any other services that Elluminate can offer?

Sources: Elluminate Inc. website, www.elluminate.com (viewed August 29, 2008); "New Elluminate Learning Suite Supports Complete Instructional Cycle for Online Learning," *PR Newswire*, June 9, 2008; "UK and Chinese Children to Share Live-Lesson through Interactive Classroom Solutions." *Telecomworldwire*, June 6, 2008; Dina O'Meara, "Calgary Firms Shine at Alberta Business Awards," *Calgary Herald*, March 1, 2008, p. D3; "Elluminate Live! 6.0 Delivers Industry Leading Live Video and Multimedia Capabilities in One Collaborative Solution," *Business Wire*, November 8, 2004, p. 1.

20
07 A new conversation
Social Responsibility Report

CANADA POSTE
POST CANAD

From anywhere... to any

CHAPTER 22

MANAGING A HOLISTIC MARKETING ORGANIZATION

twenty-two

Healthy long-term growth for a brand requires that the marketing organization be managed properly. Holistic marketers must engage in a host of carefully planned, interconnected marketing activities and satisfy an increasingly broad set of constituents. They must also consider a widening range of effects of their actions. Corporate social responsibility and sustainability have become a priority as organizations grapple with the short-term and long-term effects of their marketing. Some firms have embraced this new vision of corporate enlightenment and made it the very core of what they do. Consider Canada Post.

Every business day Canada Post delivers 40 million pieces of mail almost flawlessly across one of the largest geographic expanses on the planet. It provides a vital communications link that enables consumers, businesses, and organizations of every size and type to conduct transactions that promote their economic success. Canada Post also prides itself on being a positive force in every community it serves.

When Moya Greene became the President and CEO of Canada Post in 2004, she focused on achieving two goals: to engage employees and to make customers the focus of all that Canada Post does. The focus on employees is not surprising since people are the heart and soul of the company. Employees must be committed to the delivery of the best products and services to Canadians. Accomplishing these goals was no small challenge since revenues generated by the organization's core product, Lettermail, had been declining. Canada Post had to cut costs and refocus its operations. Beginning in 2005, it aligned its operations into three lines of business: Transaction Mail, Parcels, and Direct Marketing. Through these lines of business and its sales organization, Canada Post listens carefully to end consumers and businesses alike so that it can provide solutions to their specific challenges. These solutions range from addressing core needs, such as improving on-time delivery of Admail, to making it easier to trace parcels, to simplifying products and adding innovative new products like SmartFlow, Canada Post's new multi-channel electronic document management solution. SmartFlow is an important new product that will help Canada Post be a major presence in the Internet arena. Canadians want more choice in delivery options and businesses want higher returns on their mailing-dollar investments. While 85 percent of Canadians say they prefer to receive their bills by

>>>

mail, a growing number of consumers and businesses want the freedom of both physical and secure electronic channels to communicate with each other. SmartFlow will help serve these needs.

With 72 500 employees and a presence in virtually every community across Canada, Canada Post believes it can help effect real change and influence everyday lives. Thus, in 2007 Canada Post declared its commitment to the integration of sustainable practices company-wide. Canada Post has a long history of being actively involved in protecting the environment. Grassroots initiatives including composting, tree planting, and green commuting challenges have complemented corporate environmental programs. Its new Winnipeg plant is being built to "green" building standards and is equipped with environmentally friendly technologies. In 2007, in addition to supporting numerous charities and the United Way, Canada Post made mental health its corporate cause of choice. It is using its wide reach to shine a light on the plight of millions of Canadians who suffer the stigma of mental illness in silence. It raises funds to support awareness, research, and local community treatment for this important cause. In 2008, Canada Post produced its first Corporate Social Responsibility Report outlining its many accomplishments. These efforts position the organization to continue its record of consistent profitability while serving social and environmental interests.

Sources: Keith Fox, Katherine Jocz, and Bernard Jaworski, "A Common Language," *Marketing Management* (May–June 2003): 14–17; Canada Post, *2007 Social Responsibility Report*, and *2007 Annual Report*, www.canadapost.ca (viewed June 2008).

Brands such as Cirque de Soleil, Bullfrog Power (alternative energy), Interface Carpets, HSBC (the first major bank in the world to become carbon neutral), Lululemon, Tembec (a forestry company committed to environmental stewardship), Whole Foods, Patagonia, Timberland, and Body Shop have embraced similar philosophies and practices. Successful holistic marketing requires effective relationship marketing, integrated marketing, internal marketing, and performance marketing. Preceding chapters addressed the first two topics and the strategy and tactics of marketing.[1] In this chapter, we consider the latter two topics and how to conduct marketing responsibly. In our discussion, we look at how firms organize, implement, evaluate, and control marketing activities. We also discuss the increased importance of social responsibility. We begin by examining changes in how companies conduct marketing today.

TRENDS IN MARKETING PRACTICES

Chapters 1 and 3 describe some important changes in the marketing macroenvironment, such as globalization, deregulation, technological advances, customer empowerment, and market fragmentation. In response to this rapidly changing environment, companies have restructured their business and marketing practices in many ways:

- *Reengineering.* Appointing teams to manage the processes of building customer value and to break down walls between departments
- *Outsourcing.* Buying more goods and services from outside domestic or foreign vendors
- *Benchmarking.* Studying "best practice companies" to improve performance
- *Supplier partnering.* Partnering with fewer but better value-adding suppliers
- *Customer partnering.* Working more closely with customers to add value to their operations
- *Merging.* Acquiring or merging with firms in the same or complementary industries to gain economies of scale and scope
- *Globalizing.* Increasing efforts to "think global" and "act local"
- *Flattening.* Reducing the number of organizational levels to get closer to the customer
- *Focusing.* Determining the most profitable businesses and customers and focusing on them

- *Accelerating.* Designing the organization and setting up processes to respond more quickly to changes in the environment
- *Empowering.* Encouraging and empowering personnel to produce more ideas and take more initiative

The role of marketing in the organization is also changing.[2] Traditionally, marketers have played the roles of middlepeople, charged with understanding customer needs and transmitting the voice of the customer to various functional areas in the organization. But in a networked enterprise, *every* functional area can interact directly with customers. Marketing no longer has sole ownership of customer interactions; rather, marketing needs to integrate all the customer-facing processes so customers see a single face and hear a single voice when they interact with the firm.

To learn how the Haier Group implemented the 'market-chain based Business Process Re-Engineering' to transform itself into a top-ranking company in China, visit www.pearsoned-asia.com/ marketingmanagementchina.

INTERNAL MARKETING

Internal marketing requires that everyone in the organization buy into the concepts and goals of marketing and engage in choosing, providing, and communicating customer value. Over the years, marketing has evolved from work done by the sales department into a complex group of activities spread throughout the organization.[3]

Hampton Inn

A unit of Hilton Hotels headquartered in Beverly Hills, California, in 2004 Hampton Inn embarked on a major marketing campaign that included strategic communication, experiential marketing, and a new tagline: "Make It Happen." The campaign was solely an internal one, however, created by Hampton Inn to sell its own general managers on 122 changes it was making to products and services. "We wanted it to be an internal rallying cry that by doing these things, we were making [the customer's stay] unique to Hampton," said the VP of brand management. The 122 changes ranged from serving better breakfasts to installing new shower rods. General managers and franchisees were able to see the improvements for themselves at a 2004 Hampton Inn show via a gigantic model of the hotel. The company walked employees through every change, with the idea that only by experiencing it could they really understand and promote it to guests. With the managers and franchisees on board and enthused, the roll-out to customers lifted Hampton Inn's market share by five percentage points, and the percent of customers who rated Hampton a 9 or 10 for overall satisfaction went up by the same amount.[4]

A company can have an excellent marketing department, however, and fail at marketing. Much depends on how *other* company departments view customers. If they point to the marketing department and say "They do the marketing," the company has not implemented effective marketing. Only when *all* employees realize their job is to create, serve, and satisfy customers does the company become an effective marketer.[5] "Marketing Memo: Characteristics of Company Departments That Are Truly Customer Driven" presents a tool that evaluates which company departments are truly customer driven.[6]

Let's look at how marketing departments are being organized, how they can work effectively with other departments, and how firms can foster a creative marketing culture within the entire organization.

Organizing the Marketing Department

Modern marketing departments can be organized in a number of different, sometimes overlapping ways:[7] functionally, geographically, by product or brand, by market, or in a matrix.

FUNCTIONAL ORGANIZATION   The most common form of marketing organization consists of functional specialists reporting to a marketing vice-president who coordinates their activities. Figure 22.1 shows five specialists. Additional specialists might include a customer service manager, a marketing planning manager, a market logistics manager, a direct marketing manager, and a digital marketing manager.

The main advantage of a functional marketing organization is its administrative simplicity. It can be quite a challenge to develop smooth working relationships, however, within the marketing department.[8] This form also can lose its effectiveness as the number of products and markets

MARKETING MEMO	CHARACTERISTICS OF COMPANY DEPARTMENTS THAT ARE TRULY CUSTOMER-DRIVEN

R&D

____ It spends time meeting customers and listening to their problems.

____ It welcomes the involvement of marketing, manufacturing, and other departments in each new project.

____ It benchmarks competitors' products and seeks "best of class" solutions.

____ It solicits customer reactions and suggestions as a project progresses.

Purchasing

____ It proactively searches for the best suppliers rather than choosing only from those who solicit its business.

____ It builds long-term relations with fewer but more reliable high-quality suppliers.

____ It does not compromise quality for price savings.

Manufacturing

____ It invites customers to visit and tour the plants.

____ Personnel visit customer factories to see how customers use the company's products.

____ Members willingly work overtime when it is important to meet promised delivery schedules.

____ It continuously searches for ways to produce goods faster and/or at lower costs.

____ It continuously improves product quality, aiming for zero defects.

____ It meets customer requirements for "customization" where this can be done profitably.

Marketing

____ It studies customer needs and wants in well-defined market segments.

____ It allocates marketing effort in relation to the long-run profit potential of the targeted segments.

____ It develops winning offerings for each target segment.

____ It measures company image and customer satisfaction on a continuous basis.

____ It continuously gathers and evaluates ideas for new products, product improvements, and services to meet customers' needs.

____ It influences all other company departments and employees to be customer-centred in their thinking and practice.

Sales

____ It has specialized knowledge of the customer's industry.

____ It strives to give the customer "the best solution."

____ It makes only promises it can keep.

____ It provides feedback on customers' needs and ideas to those in charge of product development.

____ It serves the same customers for a long period of time.

Logistics

____ It sets a high standard for service delivery time and it meets this standard consistently.

____ It operates a knowledgeable and friendly customer-service department that can answer questions, handle complaints, and resolve problems in a satisfactory and timely manner.

Accounting

____ It prepares periodic "profitability" reports by product, market segment, geographic area (regions, sales territories), order size, and individual customer.

____ It prepares invoices tailored to customer needs and answers customer queries courteously and quickly.

Finance

____ It understands and supports marketing expenditures (e.g., image advertising) that represent marketing investments that produce long-term customer preference and loyalty.

____ It tailors financial packages to customers' financial requirements.

____ It makes quick decisions on customer creditworthiness.

Public Relations

____ It disseminates favourable news about the company and reacts using "damage control" in the face of unfavourable news.

____ It acts as an internal customer and public advocate for better company policies and practices.

Other Customer-Contact Departments ____ They are competent, courteous, cheerful, credible, reliable, and responsive.

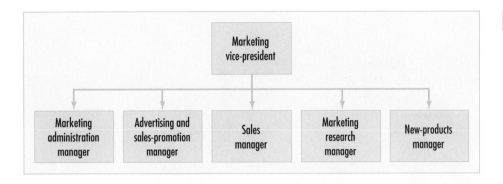

FIGURE 22.1

Functional Organization

increases. A functional organization often leads to inadequate planning for specific products and markets. Then, each functional group competes with others for budget and status. The marketing vice-president constantly weighs the claims of competing functional specialists and faces a difficult coordination problem.

GEOGRAPHIC ORGANIZATION A company selling in a national market often organizes its sales force (and sometimes other functions, including marketing) along geographic lines. The national sales manager may supervise four regional sales managers, who each supervise six zone managers, who in turn supervise eight district sales managers, who each supervise ten salespeople.

Several companies are now adding *area market specialists* (regional or local marketing managers) to support the sales efforts in high-volume markets. One such market might be Vancouver, where almost 10 percent of households are Chinese. The Vancouver specialist would know Vancouver's customer and trade makeup, help marketing managers at headquarters adjust their marketing mix for Vancouver, and prepare local annual and long-range plans for selling all the company's products to Chinese consumers in Vancouver.

One company that has shifted to a greater regional marketing emphasis is McDonald's, which now spends about 50 percent of its total North American advertising budget regionally. Regional marketing is especially important in Canada given the unique language and labelling requirements in Quebec. Some firms, like Labatt, use a separate agency in Quebec to do their media planning. Others, like Telus, use Quebec-based events like "Fire and Ice" (an annual event that combines ice skating and fireworks) to communicate their messages.

PRODUCT- OR BRAND-MANAGEMENT ORGANIZATION Companies producing a variety of products and brands often establish a product- or brand-management organization. The product-management organization does not replace the functional organization, but serves as another layer of management. A product manager supervises product category managers, who in turn supervise specific product and brand managers.

A product-management organization makes sense if the company's products are quite different, or if the sheer number of products is beyond the ability of a functional organization to handle. Kraft has used a product-management organization in its Post division, with separate product category managers in charge of cereals, pet food, and beverages. Within the cereal product group, Kraft has had separate subcategory managers for nutritional cereals, children's pre-sweetened cereals, family cereals, and miscellaneous cereals.

Product and brand management is sometimes characterized as a hub-and-spoke system. The brand or product manager is figuratively at the centre, with spokes emanating to various departments (see Figure 22.2). Some tasks that product or brand managers may perform include:

- Developing a long-range and competitive strategy for the product
- Preparing an annual marketing plan and sales forecast
- Working with advertising and merchandising agencies to develop copy, programs, and campaigns
- Increasing support of the product among the sales force and distributors
- Gathering continuous intelligence on the product's performance, customer and dealer attitudes, and new problems and opportunities
- Initiating product improvements to meet changing market needs

FIGURE 22.2

The Product Manager's
Interactions

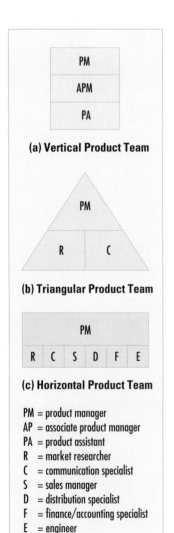

(a) Vertical Product Team

(b) Triangular Product Team

(c) Horizontal Product Team

PM = product manager
AP = associate product manager
PA = product assistant
R = market researcher
C = communication specialist
S = sales manager
D = distribution specialist
F = finance/accounting specialist
E = engineer

FIGURE 22.3

Three Types of Product Teams

The product-management organization lets the product manager concentrate on developing a cost-effective marketing mix and react more quickly to new products in the marketplace; it also gives the company's smaller brands a product advocate. However, this organization has disadvantages too:

- Product and brand managers may lack authority to carry out their responsibilities.
- Product and brand managers become experts in their product area but rarely achieve functional expertise.
- The product-management system often turns out to be costly. One person is appointed to manage each major product or brand, and soon more are appointed to manage even minor products and brands.
- Brand managers normally manage a brand for only a short time. Short-term involvement leads to short-term planning and fails to build long-term strengths.
- The fragmentation of markets makes it harder to develop a national strategy. Brand managers must please regional and local sales groups, transferring power from marketing to sales.
- Product and brand managers focus the company on building market share rather than the customer relationship.

A second alternative in a product-management organization is *product teams*. There are three types of structures: vertical product teams, triangular product teams, and horizontal product teams (see Figure 22.3).

The triangular and horizontal product-team approaches let each major brand be run by a *brand asset management team (BAMT)* consisting of key representatives from functions that affect the brand's performance. The company is made of several BAMTs that periodically report to a BAMT directors committee, which itself reports to a chief branding officer. This is quite different from the way brands have traditionally been handled.

A third alternative for product-management organization is to eliminate product-manager positions for minor products and assign two or more products to each remaining manager. This is feasible where two or more products appeal to a similar set of needs. A cosmetics company doesn't need product managers for each product because cosmetics serve one major need—beauty. A toiletries company needs different managers for headache remedies, toothpaste, soap, and shampoo, because these products differ in use and appeal.

A fourth alternative is to introduce *category management*, in which a company focuses on product categories to manage its brands. Procter & Gamble, pioneers of the brand-management system, and several other top firms have made a significant shift to category management.[9]

P&G cites a number of advantages of category management. By fostering internal competition among brand managers, the traditional brand-management system created strong incentives to excel, but also much internal competition for resources and a lack of coordination. The new scheme was designed to ensure that all categories would be able to receive adequate resources.

Another rationale for category management is the increasing power of the trade. Because the retail trade has tended to think of profitability in terms of product categories, P&G felt it only made sense to deal along similar lines. Retailers and regional grocery chains such as Wal-Mart and Sobeys have embraced category management as a means to define a particular product category's strategic role within the store and to address logistics, the role of private-label products, and the trade-offs between product variety and inefficient duplication.

Category management is not a panacea. It is still a product-driven system. Colgate has moved from brand management (Colgate toothpaste) to category management (toothpaste category) to a new stage called "customer-need management" (mouth care). This last step finally focuses the organization on a basic customer need.[10]

MARKET-MANAGEMENT ORGANIZATION Many companies sell to different markets. Canon sells fax machines to consumer, business, and government markets. Dofasco sells to the railroad, construction, and public-utility industries. When customers fall into different user groups with distinct buying preferences and practices, a **market-management organization** is desirable. Market managers supervise several market-development managers, market specialists, or industry specialists and draw on functional services as needed. Market managers of important markets might even have functional specialists reporting to them.

Market managers are staff (not line) people with duties similar to those of product managers. They develop long-range and annual plans for their markets. Their performance is judged by their market's growth and profitability. This system shares many advantages and disadvantages of product-management systems. Its strongest advantage is organizing marketing activity to meet the needs of distinct customer groups rather than focusing on marketing functions, regions, or products. Many companies are reorganizing along market lines and becoming **market-centred organizations**. Xerox has converted from geographic selling to selling by industry, as have IBM and Hewlett-Packard.

In a **customer-management organization**, companies like Virgin Mobile Canada can organize themselves to understand and deal with individual customers rather than with the mass market or even market segments.[11] When a close relationship is advantageous, such as when customers have diverse and complex requirements and buy an integrated bundle of products and services, customer-management organizations should prevail. IBM's Global Services and General Electric's Power Systems are organized in this fashion because of their need to interact closely with customers. One study showed that companies organized by customer groups reported much higher accountability for the overall quality of relationships and employees' freedom to take actions to satisfy individual customers.[12]

MATRIX-MANAGEMENT ORGANIZATION Companies that produce many products for many markets may adopt a matrix organization. Some provide the context in which a matrix can thrive—flat, lean, team organizations focused on business processes that cut horizontally across functions.[13] DuPont was a pioneer in developing the matrix structure (see Figure 22.4).

FIGURE 22.4

Product/Market-Management Matrix System

DuPont

Before it was spun off, DuPont's textile-fibres department consisted of separate product managers for rayon, acetate, nylon, orlon, and dacron, and separate market managers for menswear, womenswear, home furnishings, and industrial markets. The product managers planned sales and profits for their respective fibres. They asked market managers to estimate how much of their fibre they could sell in each market at a proposed price. Market managers, however, were generally more interested in meeting their market's needs than pushing a particular fibre. In preparing their market plans, they asked each product manager about their fibre's planned prices and availabilities. The final sales forecast of the market managers and the product managers should have added up to the same grand total.

Companies like DuPont can go one step further and view the market managers as the main marketers, and their product managers as suppliers. The menswear market manager, for example, would be empowered to buy textile fibres from DuPont's product managers or, if DuPont's price were too high, from outside suppliers, forcing DuPont product managers to become more efficient. If a DuPont product manager couldn't match the "arm's-length pricing" levels of competitive suppliers, then perhaps DuPont should not produce that fibre.

A matrix organization seems desirable in a multi-product, multi-market company. The rub is that it is costly and often creates conflicts. There're the cost of supporting all the managers and questions about where authority and responsibility for marketing activities should reside—at headquarters or in the division?[14] Some corporate marketing groups assist top management with overall opportunity evaluation, provide divisions with consulting assistance on request, help divisions that have little or no marketing, and promote the marketing concept throughout the company.

Relations with Other Departments

Under the marketing concept, all departments need to "think customer" and work together to satisfy customer needs and expectations. The marketing department must drive this point home. The marketing vice-president, or CMO, has two tasks: (1) to coordinate the company's internal marketing activities and (2) to coordinate marketing with finance, operations, and other company functions to serve the customer.

Yet, there is little agreement on how much influence and authority marketing should have over other departments. Departments define company problems and goals from their viewpoint, so conflicts of interest and communications problems are unavoidable. Typically, the marketing vice-president must work through persuasion rather than authority.

To develop a balanced orientation in which marketing and other functions jointly determine what is in the company's best interests, companies can provide joint seminars to understand each other's viewpoint, joint committees and liaison personnel, personnel-exchange programs, and analytical methods to determine the most profitable course of action.[15]

Many companies, like Jones Lang Lasalle, now focus on key processes rather than departments, because departmental organization can be a barrier to the smooth performance of fundamental business processes. They appoint process leaders who manage cross-disciplinary teams that include marketing and sales people. As a result, marketing personnel may have a solid-line responsibility to their teams and a dotted-line responsibility to the marketing department.

Jones Lang Lasalle (JLL)

A global property and investment management company, Jones Lang Lasalle (JLL) has 150 offices worldwide including two in Toronto and Vancouver. It moved in stages to transform its organizational structure to a customer-centric, rather than a product-management, organization. JLL added an overarching "Corporate Solutions" group, of all three of its service units and an account-management function, run by high-ranking officers with influence on big clients. JLL's revenue from the Corporate Solutions group has been growing at a rate of 50 percent per year, but the service-unit managers didn't like ceding authority to account managers who lacked experience in their service. And single-transaction customers thought the small number of JLL account managers in their local markets was problematic. JLL then made a more dramatic move: it dispensed with service-focused units altogether and organized its business into two groups: Clients and Markets. This restructuring put more employees in the field, where they were closer to and more responsive to clients, and got all internal groups and processes focused on customer needs above all.[16]

Building a Creative Marketing Organization

Many companies realize they're not yet really market and customer driven—they are product and sales driven. Baxter, General Motors, Shell, and JPMorgan are attempting to transform into true market-driven companies. This requires:

1. Developing a company-wide passion for customers
2. Organizing around customer segments instead of products
3. Understanding customers through qualitative and quantitative research

The task is not easy, but the payoffs can be considerable.[17] It won't happen as a result of the CEO making speeches and urging every employee to "think customer." See "Marketing Insight: The Marketing CEO" for actions a CEO can take to improve marketing capabilities.

MARKETING **INSIGHT** | THE MARKETING CEO

What steps can a CEO take to create a market- and customer-focused company?

1. *Convince senior management of the need to become customer focused.* The CEO, like Moya Greene at Canada Post, personally exemplifies strong customer commitment and rewards those in the organization who do likewise. Starbucks is another example. Previous Starbucks CEO Jim Donald visited 10–20 stores a week, always going to the back of the counter to talk to store partners (employees) and customers.
2. *Appoint a senior marketing officer and marketing task force.* The marketing task force should include the CEO; the vice-presidents of sales, R&D, purchasing, manufacturing, finance, and human resources; and other key individuals.
3. *Get outside help and guidance.* Consulting firms have considerable experience in helping companies move towards a marketing orientation.
4. *Change the company's reward measurement system.* As long as purchasing and manufacturing are rewarded for keeping costs low, they will resist accepting some costs required to serve customers better. As long as finance focuses on short-term profit, it will oppose major investments designed to build satisfied, loyal customers.
5. *Hire strong marketing talent.* The company needs a strong marketing vice-president who not only manages the marketing department but also gains respect from and influence with the other vice-presidents. A multi-divisional company will benefit from establishing a strong corporate marketing department.
6. *Develop strong in-house marketing training programs.* The company should design well-crafted marketing training programs for corporate management, divisional general managers, marketing and sales personnel, manufacturing personnel, R&D personnel, and others. Colgate Canada, Deloitte Canada, and Nortel run marketing training programs.
7. *Install a modern marketing planning system.* The planning format will require managers to think about the marketing environment, opportunities, competitive trends, and other forces. These managers then prepare strategies and sales-and-profit forecasts for specific products and segments and are accountable for performance.
8. *Establish an annual marketing-excellence recognition program.* Business units that believe they've developed exemplary marketing plans should submit a description of their plans and results. Winning teams should be rewarded at a special ceremony and the plans disseminated to the other business units as "models of marketing thinking." Accenture, Becton-Dickenson, and DuPont follow this strategy.
9. *Shift from a department focus to a process-outcome focus.* After defining the fundamental business processes that determine its success, the company should appoint process leaders and cross-disciplinary teams to reengineer and implement these processes.
10. *Empower the employees.* Progressive companies encourage and reward their employees for coming up with new ideas and empower them to settle customer complaints to save the customer's business. IBM, for example, lets its frontline employees spend up to $5000 to solve a customer problem on the spot.

MARKETING **MEMO** | FUELLING STRATEGIC INNOVATION

Professor Stephen Brown of Ulster University has challenged a number of fundamental assumptions underlying the marketing concept. He thinks marketers make too much of researching and satisfying consumers, and they risk losing marketing imagination and significant consumer impact. How can companies build a capability for strategic innovation? Here are some approaches he advocates:

- Hire marketers who are unusually creative to counterbalance the majority who do marketing by the textbook. These people may be unconventional, rule breaking, risk taking, and even more argumentative, but their ideas will at least present a challenge.

- Train your employees in the use of creativity techniques, for groups (brainstorming, synectics) and individuals (visualization, attribute listing, forced relationships, morphological analysis, mind mapping).

- Note trends such as longer working hours, single parenting, and new life styles, and tease out their implications for your firm.

- List unmet customer needs and imagine new offerings or solutions: how to help people lose weight, drive vehicles that don't emit carbon, relieve stress, or meet others.

- Run a "best idea" competition once a month. Give a cash reward, extra vacation time, or travel awards to those who come up with the best ideas.

- Have senior managers take small sets of employees out to lunch or dinner once a week to discuss ideas for improving the business. Go to new settings, such as a wrestling match, a drug rehabilitation centre, a poor neighbourhood.

- Set up groups of employees to critique the company's and competitors' products and services. Let them critique the company's cherished beliefs and consider turning them upside down.

- Occasionally hire creative resources from outside the firm. Many large advertising agencies, such as Leo Burnett, run a creativity service for clients.

Sources: For more on Brown's views, see Stephen Brown, *Marketing—The Retro Revolution* (Thousand Oaks, CA: Sage, 2001). For more on creativity, see Pat Fallon and Fred Senn, *Juicing the Orange: How to Turn Creativity into a Powerful Business Advantage* (Boston: Harvard Business School Press, 2006); Bob Schmetterer, *Leap: A Revolution in Creative Business Strategy* (Hoboken, NJ: John Wiley & Sons, 2003); Jean-Marie Dru, *Beyond Disruption: Changing the Rules in the Marketplace* (Hoboken, NJ: John Wiley & Sons, 2002); Michael Michalko, *Cracking Creativity: The Secrets of Creative Genius* (Berkeley, CA: Ten Speed Press, 1998); James M. Higgins, *101 Creative Problem-Solving Techniques* (New York: New Management Publishing, 1994); and all the books by Edward DeBono.

Although it's *necessary* to be customer oriented, it's not *enough*. The organization must also be creative. Companies today copy each others' advantages and strategies with increasing speed. Differentiation gets harder to achieve, let alone maintain, and margins fall when firms become more alike. The only answer is to build a capability in strategic innovation and imagination (see "Marketing Memo: Fuelling Strategic Innovation"). This capability comes from assembling tools, processes, skills, and measures that let the firm generate more and better new ideas than its competitors.[18]

Companies must watch trends and be ready to capitalize on them. Motorola was 18 months late in moving from analogue to digital cellular phones, giving Nokia and Ericsson a big lead. Canadian Tire was late to recognize the importance of having an online store, but it has recovered lost ground. Nestlé was late seeing the trend towards coffeehouses such as Starbucks. Coca-Cola was slow to pick up beverage trends towards fruit-flavoured drinks such as Snapple, energy drinks such as Gatorade, and the move away from designer-water brands. Market leaders tend to miss trends when they are risk averse, obsessed with protecting their existing markets and physical resources, and more interested in efficiency than innovation.[19]

SOCIALLY RESPONSIBLE MARKETING

Effective internal marketing must be matched by a strong sense of ethics, values, and social responsibility.[20] A number of forces are driving companies to practise a higher level of corporate social responsibility: rising customer expectations, evolving employee goals and ambitions, tighter government legislation and pressure, developing investor interest in social criteria, relentless media scrutiny, and changing business procurement practices.[21] According to a recent survey by GlobeScan, 93 percent of Canadians believe that corporate social responsibility should be as important to companies as profit and shareholder value. Most Canadians (92 percent) also state that they are more likely to purchase their products or services from companies they perceive to be socially and environmentally responsible.[22] The commercial success of Al Gore's 2006 documentary *An Inconvenient Truth* shows how the general public has become more concerned about environmental issues.

Virtually all firms have decided to take a more active, strategic role with corporate responsibility. The new focus on corporate social responsibility is typified by Lynn Anderson, vice-president of marketing, Enterprise, HP Canada, who notes "This demonstrates what HP has long understood—the intrinsic link between doing the right thing and being successful."[23] As Wal-Mart CEO Lee Scott said, "We thought we could sit in Bentonville [Arkansas], take care of customers, take care of associates—and the world would leave us alone. It doesn't work that way anymore."[24] Even banana producer Chiquita, which once had a poor reputation for exploiting farm workers, contaminating water, and destroying rain forest, has improved worker conditions; significantly reduced pesticide use, erosion, and chemical runoff; and even implemented a major recycling program on its farms.[25]

There were not always these beliefs in the value of social responsibility. In 1776, Adam Smith proclaimed "I have never known much good done by those who profess to trade for the public good." Legendary economist Milton Friedman famously declared social initiatives "fundamentally subversive" because he felt they undermined the profit-seeking purpose of public companies and wasted shareholders' money. Some critics worry that important business investment in areas such as R&D could suffer as a result of a focus on social responsibility.[26]

But these critics are in the minority. The Conference Board of Canada views corporate social responsibility as the key business issue of the twenty-first century. Many now believe that satisfying customers, employees, and other stakeholders and achieving business success are closely tied to the adoption and implementation of high standards of business and marketing conduct. Firms are finding that one benefit of being seen as a socially responsible company is the ability to attract employees, especially younger people who want to work for companies they feel good about. The Conference Board of Canada found that 79 percent of Canadians want to work for companies they view as socially responsible.[27] The most admired—and increasingly most successful—companies in the world abide by a code of serving people's interests, not only their own.

Firms of Endearment

Researchers Sisodia, Wolfe, and Sheth believe humanistic companies make great companies. They coin the term "firms of endearment" (also the title of their book) which they define as firms that have a culture of caring and serve the interests of their stakeholders. Stakeholders are defined in terms of the acronym SPICE: Society, Partners, Investors, Customers, and Employees. Firms of endearment create a love affair with stakeholders. Their senior managers run an open-door policy, are passionate about customers, and their compensation is modest. They pay more to their employees, relate more closely to a smaller group of excellent suppliers, and give back to the communities in which they work. The researchers assert that firms of endearment actually spend less on marketing as a percentage but yet earn greater profits. It appears that the customers who love the company do most of the marketing. Building on earlier work by Ed Freeman of the University of Virginia's Darden School, the authors of *Firms of Endearment* see the twenty-first-century marketing paradigm as creating value for all stakeholders and becoming a beloved firm.[28]

Table 22.1 displays firms receiving top marks as firms of endearment from a sample of thousands of customers, employees, and suppliers. At the end of this chapter, "Breakthrough Marketing: Starbucks" describes the practices of one high scorer on that list. Molson Canada might be classified as a Canadian example of such a firm, as it has always taken its community responsibilities seriously.

Molson Canada

Molson Canada has a long history of promoting responsible use of its products. In its most recent campaign, it has replaced its more traditional "Don't drink and drive" message with a series of posters featuring the tag line "Here's to responsible choices." The posters are the first phase of a million-dollar campaign that will also use print and radio ads. Ferg Devins, vice-president government and public affairs, explains the change as follows: "The research showed that 'Don't drink and drive' wasn't resonating as well as something more positive might. The majority of people drink responsibly. We felt it was time to highlight and celebrate those that are making responsible choices."[29]

TABLE 22.1	TOP FIRMS OF ENDEARMENT		
Best Buy	BMW	CarMax	Caterpillar
Commerce Bank	Container Store	Costco	eBay
Google	Harley-Davidson	Honda	IDEO
IKEA	JetBlue	Johnson & Johnson	Jordan's Furniture
L.L.Bean	New Balance	Patagonia	Progressive Insurance
REI	Southwest	Starbucks	Timberland
Toyota	Trader Joe's	UPS	Wegmans
Whole Foods			

Source: Raj Sisodia, David B. Wolfe, and Jag Sheth, *Firms of Endearment: How World-Class Companies Profit from Passion and Purpose* (Upper Saddle River, NJ: Wharton School Publishing, 2007).

But many smaller firms excel too. The Rocky Mountain Soap Company of Canmore, Alberta, has customers across the country and around the world who rave about its popular personal-care products. Purdy's Chocolates cares about the conditions of those growing and harvesting cocoa and supports cocoa farmers and their families worldwide through its membership in the World Cocoa Foundation.[30]

Companies are increasingly working with public interest groups to avoid perceptions of "greenwashing"—insincere, phony efforts to appear more environmentally sensitive than they really are. Alliances with environmentalists can achieve more satisfying solutions that both address public concerns and increase the firm's image and profits. When Greenpeace called out Coca-Cola on the eve of the 2000 Sydney Olympics for using a potent greenhouse gas in its nearly 10 million coolers and vending machines, Coke, along with PepsiCo, Unilever, and McDonald's, invested $30 million in a less-damaging system that now displays a "technology approved by Greenpeace" banner.[31] The Royal Bank of Canada took a different approach.

Molson Canada might qualify as a Canadian firm of endearment. Its new campaign is the latest rendition of its longstanding message to drink responsibly.

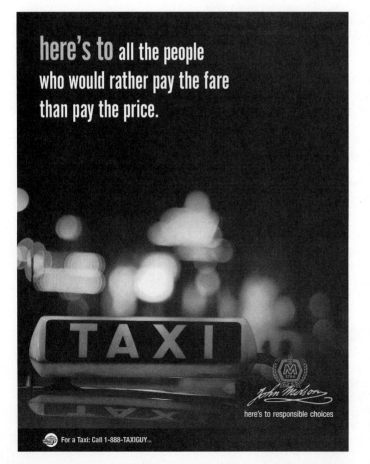

here's **to** all the people who would rather pay the fare than pay the price.

here's to responsible choices

For a Taxi: Call 1-888-TAXIGUY™

Royal Bank of Canada (RBC)'s Blue Water Project

Royal Bank of Canada pledged $50 million over ten years (starting in 2008) to global, regional, and community-based initiatives that tackle water conservation. This is the largest charitable commitment in the bank's long history of philanthropy. Lynn Patterson, RBC's director of corporate responsibility, felt that rather than trying to be all things to all people, RBC could do more good on two key issues: diversity and the environment. "We needed a topic around which our entire company could rally," she said. "Everybody's looking at their paper and energy use right now. We wanted to find something that people aren't thinking about right now." RBC chose water as a foundation for its environmental initiative because Canada has more fresh water than almost any other nation in the world, but we are a water-squandering nation that may soon face a crisis due to overuse of this resource. RBC wanted to be at the forefront of making a difference. It partnered with Unilever Canada, another firm that focuses on water as its central environmental issue, and the Canadian Partnership Initiative of the UN Water for Life Decade to survey Canadians with regard to their concerns about water. The results proved the issue wasn't on the radar screen of most Canadians, so RBC began with an awareness campaign that started with its own employees and then moved to the general public.[32]

Firms are fundamentally changing the way they conduct their business, sometimes even where they work. Business and governments are starting to construct "green" buildings. The Vancouver Island Technology Park was the first project in Canada to achieve a Gold certification under the Leadership in Energy and Environmental Design (LEED) rating system, and the City of Calgary opened The Water Centre near the Stampede grounds. The new structure is 95-percent lit by natural light, uses 59 percent less water, and will result in a 58-percent cost savings in energy consumption each year.

Corporate Social Responsibility

Raising the level of socially responsible marketing calls for making a four-pronged attack that relies on proper legal, ethical, and social responsibility behaviour.

LEGAL BEHAVIOUR Organizations must ensure every employee knows and observes relevant laws. For example, it's illegal for salespeople to lie to consumers or mislead them about the advantages of buying a product. Salespeople's statements legally must match advertising claims. Salespeople may not offer bribes to purchasing agents or others influencing a B2B sale. They may not obtain competitors' technical or trade secrets through bribery or industrial espionage, nor may they use such secrets if obtained illegally. Finally, they must not disparage competitors or their products by suggesting things that are not true. Managers must make sure every sales representative knows the law and acts accordingly.[33]

ETHICAL BEHAVIOUR Business practices come under attack because business situations routinely pose tough ethical dilemmas: It's not easy to draw a clear line between normal marketing practice and unethical behaviour. Some issues sharply divide critics. Though Kraft chose to stop advertising some of its less healthy products such as Oreos and Chips Ahoy! on television programs targeted to children ages 6 to 11, some watch groups felt that was not enough.[34]

At the same time, certain business practices are clearly unethical or illegal. These include bribery, theft of trade secrets, false and deceptive advertising, exclusive dealing and tying agreements, quality and safety defects, false warranties, inaccurate labelling, price-fixing and undue discrimination, and barriers to entry and predatory competition.

Companies must adopt and disseminate a written code of ethics, build a company tradition of ethical behaviour, and hold people fully responsible for observing ethical and legal guidelines.[35] Companies that don't perform ethically or well are at greater risk of being exposed, thanks to the Internet. In the past, a disgruntled customer might bad-mouth a firm to 12 other people; today he or she can reach thousands. Microsoft, for example, has attracted scores of anti-Microsoft sites, including *Hate Microsoft* and *Boycott Microsoft*. The general distrust of companies among consumers around the world is growing, thus companies must increase their vigilance with regard to ethical and responsible conduct.

SOCIAL RESPONSIBILITY BEHAVIOUR Individual marketers must practise a "social conscience" in specific dealings with customers and stakeholders. Increasingly, people want information about a company's record on social and environmental responsibility to help decide which companies to buy from, invest in, and work for.[36] Table 22.2 lists companies receiving high marks for social responsibility.

TABLE 22.2	*CORPORATE KNIGHTS'* TOP-10 BEST CORPORATE CITIZENS IN CANADA 2008
	1. IBM
	2. Petro-Canada
	3. McKesson Canada
	4. Rio Tinto Alcan
	5. Loblaw Companies Limited
	6. Hydro One
	7. BC Hydro and Power Authority
	8. Domtar Corp.
	9. Westport Innovations Inc.
	10. General Electric

Source: "The 2008 Best 50 Corporate Citizens," *Corporate Knights*, http://static.corporateknights.ca/Best50_2008_chart.pdf (viewed July, 2008).

Deciding how to communicate corporate social responsibility can be difficult. Once a firm touts an environmental initiative, it can become a target for criticism. Consider what happened to Lululemon Athletica, the Vancouver-based "yoga-inspired athletic apparel" company in 2007:

Lululemon Athletica

Lululemon has all of the elements of a stellar retail brand with its high prices and flattering, well-made clothing aimed at the yoga segment. It even has celebrity endorsers like Martha Stewart. Sales skyrocketed by 80 percent in 2007 alone. By the end of 2007, the number of stores had grown from 15 to 80 and the company had plans to open another 234 stores in time for the 2010 Vancouver Olympics. Lululemon tops the apparel industry in terms of its sales per square foot ($1400) according to the Toronto-based firm Accountability Research. Its stock price skyrocketed when it went public in July of 2007. Lululemon's initial success was based on its ability to spot trends, like the renewed interest in yoga. It wasn't surprising, therefore, that it also got in early on the wave of eco-products and spirituality marketing.

Disaster struck, however, when the company forgot to check that all its claims were accurate. In November 2007, a shareholder commissioned an independent test of the health claims of the retailer's VitaSea garments. The resulting report stated that VitaSea products actually contain no significant amount of the seaweed which the company claimed gave its products anti-bacterial, stress-reducing, and anti-inflammatory benefits. Even worse, the disenchanted shareholder sent the controversial results to the *New York Times*. The story was rapidly picked up by other media. This was the first time many Americans had even heard of Lululemon, and it was not the kind of press the firm wanted to receive in the face of its plans to expand rapidly in the U.S. marketplace. While the brand stumbled, Eric Peterson, Lululemon's Director of Community Relations, who views himself as the guardian of the brand, believes the firm's long history of grassroots marketing will insulate it from further damage. Petersen has integrated a community focus into Lululemon's corporate fabric. When the firm went public, it even created a huge billboard in Times Square featuring all 1900 employees. With its stock down 50 percent, the firm is hoping he is right.[37]

Corporate philanthropy also can pose problems.[38] Imperial Oil, the Royal Bank, Merck, DuPont, and Wal-Mart have all donated millions to charities in a year. Yet good deeds can be overlooked—even resented—if the company is seen as exploitive or fails to live up to a "good guys" image.[39] Philip Morris Company's $250-million ad campaign touting its charitable activities was met with skepticism because of its negative corporate image.

SUSTAINABILITY *Sustainability*—the importance of meeting humanity's needs without harming future generations—has risen to the top of many corporate agendas. Major corporations now outline in great detail how they are trying to improve the long-term impact of their actions on communities and the environment. As one sustainability consultant put it, "There is a triple bottom line—people, planet, and profit—and the people part of the equation must come first. Sustainability means more than being eco-friendly, it also means you are in it for the long haul."[40]

Many CEOs believe embracing sustainability can avoid the negative consequences of environmental disasters, political protests, and human rights or workplace abuses. Often a target of environmental criticism in the past, DuPont has moved through two phases of sustainability in the past 15 years: first, drastically reducing the emission of greenhouse gases, release of carcinogens, and discharge of hazardous wastes; and second, embracing sustainability as a strategic goal via the introduction of alternative biofuels and energy-saving materials such as its new bio-PDO fibre.[41]

Investors, like Innovest, are also demanding more concrete information about what firms are doing to achieve sustainability. Sustainability ratings exist, although there is little agreement about what the appropriate metrics might be.

Innovest

Founded in 1995, Innovest studies 120 different characteristics of firms, such as energy use, health and safety records, litigation, employee practices, regulatory history, and management systems for dealing with supplier problems. It uses these measures to assign 2200 listed companies grades ranging from AAA to CCC, much like bond ratings. Companies scoring well include Nokia Corp. and Ericsson, which excel at tailoring products to developing nations, and banks such as HSBC Holdings and ABN-AMRO, which study the environmental impact of projects they help finance. Although Hewlett-Packard and Dell both rate AAA, Apple gets a middling BBB rating on the grounds of weaker oversight of offshore factories and lack of a "clear environmental business strategy."[42]

Some feel companies that score well on sustainability factors typically exhibit high levels of management quality in that "they tend to be more strategically nimble and better equipped to compete in the complex, high-velocity, global environment."[43]

Many companies in diverse industries beyond food products are embracing organic offerings that avoid the use of chemicals and pesticides to stress ecological preservation. Apparel and other nonfood items make up the second-fastest growth category of the $3.5-billion organic-product industry. Organic cotton grown by farmers who fight boll weevils with ladybugs, weed their crops by hand, and use manure for fertilizer has become a hot product at retail. Sustainability is becoming more mainstream and consumers are increasingly willing to pay more to support the environment.[44]

Socially Responsible Business Models

The future holds a wealth of opportunities.[45] Technological advances in solar energy, online networks, cable and satellite television, biotechnology, and telecommunications promise to change the world as we know it. At the same time, forces in the socioeconomic, cultural, and natural environments will impose new limits on marketing and business practices. Companies that offer innovative solutions and have socially responsible values are the most likely to succeed.[46]

Many companies such as Molsons, TD Canada Trust, and Sobeys are giving social responsibility a more prominent role. Consider what Aeroplan, the Canadian rewards program, recently did:

Aeroplan and Earth Day

On April 22, 2008, Rupert Duchesne, President and CEO of Aeroplan, sent all members a personalized e-mail message wishing them "Happy Earth Day." His message stated "Earth Day is a particularly special day to me and the staff at Aeroplan. I believe it's important that we recognize and take responsibility for the effects our business has on the environment. Obviously, no one would want to take air travel out of our program, or ask you not to fly. But we are taking steps to mitigate the effects of air travel on the atmosphere and we want to help our members also take action against climate change." The message goes on to note how Aeroplan members can use their points to purchase carbon offsets to help compensate for the environmental damage caused by their air travel and that Aeroplan will match the credits by 25 percent, rather than the usual 20 percent. This may not sound like a big impact, but the letter stressed the power of cumulative effort: "If only 2000 members each redeemed 7500 miles to purchase our carbon offsets reward, along with Aeroplan's match of 25 percent, our impact would be equivalent to taking more than 1300 cars off the road for one year."[47]

Corporate philanthropy as a whole is on the rise, and many wealthy owners of firms, like real estate developers Joseph and Wolf Lebovic, who recently gave $50 million to Toronto's Mount Sinai Hospital, give generously to their favourite causes. Nonetheless, Canadian businesses trail their counterparts in other countries when it comes to giving. Only 3 percent claimed charitable donations on their tax returns in 2003, for a total of $1 billion in donations (representing less than 1 percent of the companies' pre-tax profits), according to Imagine Canada. The figure doesn't include all the charitable work companies do (such as volunteer work by employees on company time), however.[48] Gradually, more firms are coming to the belief that corporate social responsibility in the form of cash donations, in-kind contributions, cause marketing, and employee volunteerism programs is not just the "right thing" but also the "smart thing to do." Microsoft Canada seems to live by this philosophy. It made international headlines for its work with the Toronto police fighting child exploitation on the Internet. "After a Toronto police officer emailed Bill Gates for help, the company stepped in to lend its expertise and build a database for police forces to fight child pornography." Michael Eisen, Chief Legal Officer for Microsoft Canada, explains "We're doing it because it's the right thing to do. But the benefit to Microsoft, and all technology companies, is that the safer the Internet and the greater the trust people have in it, the more people are going to use it."[49] "Marketing Insight: New Views on Corporate Social Responsibility" offers two high-profile perspectives on how to make progress in that area.

Microsoft Canada joined forces with the Toronto Police Service and the RCMP to fight child pornography because it was the right thing to do and it increased public trust in the Internet.

Cause-Related Marketing

Many firms blend corporate social-responsibility initiatives with marketing activities.[50] **Cause-related marketing** links the firm's contributions to a designated cause to customers' engaging directly or indirectly in revenue-producing transactions with the firm.[51] Cause marketing is part of *corporate societal marketing (CSM)*, which Drumwright and Murphy define as marketing efforts "that have at least one noneconomic objective related to social welfare and use the resources of the company and/or of its partners."[52] They also include other activities such as traditional and strategic philanthropy and volunteerism as part of CSM.

Through its on-going cause-related marketing campaign, Tim Hortons has donated over $90 million and has given 13 000 kids from economically disadvantaged homes a fun-filled camp experience that helps them learn positive life skills. Tesco, a leading U.K. retailer, has created a "Computers for Schools" program: customers receive vouchers for every 10 pounds spent, which they can donate to the school of their choice; the school exchanges the vouchers for new computer equipment. Procter & Gamble's Dawn dishwashing liquid introduced a campaign highlighting the fact that the product's grease-cleaning power had an unusual side benefit—it could clean birds caught in oil spills. A web-site launched in 2006, www.DawnSavesWildlife.com, drew 130 000 people who formed virtual groups to encourage friends and others to stop gas and oil leaks from their cars into the environment.[53] British Airways has a particularly successful and highly visible program.

British Airways

British Airways partnered with UNICEF and developed a cause-marketing campaign called Change for Good. Passengers on British Airways flights are encouraged to donate leftover foreign currency from their travels. The scheme is simple: passengers deposit their surplus currency in envelopes provided by British Airways, which collects the deposits and donates them directly to UNICEF. British Airways advertises its program during an in-flight video, on the backs of seat cards, and with in-flight announcements. The company also developed a television ad that featured a child thanking British Airways for its contribution to UNICEF. Because Change for Good can be directly targeted to passengers and can produce immediate results, it does not require extensive advertising or promotion and is highly cost-efficient. Since 1994, it has distributed almost $45 million around the world.[54]

MARKETING INSIGHT | NEW VIEWS ON CORPORATE SOCIAL RESPONSIBILITY

Two of management's most renowned thinkers have turned their attention to corporate social responsibility, offering some unique perspectives that build on their past management research and thinking.

Michael Porter

Harvard's Michael Porter and Mark Kramer, managing director of FSG Social Impact Advisors, believe good corporate citizenship can be a source of opportunity, innovation, and competitive advantage, as long as firms evaluate it using the same frameworks and concepts that guide their core business strategies. They feel corporate social responsibility must mesh with a firm's strengths, capabilities, and positioning. They assert that *strategic corporate social responsibility* results when firms (1) transform value-chain activities to benefit society while reinforcing strategy and (2) engage in strategic philanthropy that leverages capabilities to improve salient areas of competitive context.

According to the authors, firms should select causes that intersect their particular businesses to create shared value for the firm and society. For example, Toyota addressed public concerns about auto emissions by creating a competitively strong and environmentally friendly hybrid vehicle, Prius; Mexican construction company Urbi prospered by using novel financing approaches to build housing for disadvantaged buyers; and French banking giant Crédit Agricole differentiated itself through specialized environmentally friendly financial products.

Porter and Kramer note that "By providing jobs, investing capital, purchasing goods, and doing business every day, corporations have a profound and positive influence on society. The most important thing a corporation can do for society, and for any community, is contribute to a prosperous economy." Although companies can address hundreds of social issues, only a handful offer the opportunity to build focused, proactive, and integrated social initiatives that link with core business strategies to make a real difference to society and create a competitive advantage in the marketplace.

Clayton Christensen

Harvard's Clayton Christensen, along with his research colleagues, advocates *catalytic innovations* to address social sector problems. Like Christensen's disruptive innovations—which challenge industry incumbents by offering simpler, good-enough alternatives to an underserved group of customers—catalytic innovations offer good-enough solutions to inadequately addressed social problems. Catalytic innovators share five qualities:

1. They create systemic social change through scaling and replication.

2. They meet a need that is either overserved (because the existing solution is more complex than many people require) or not served at all.

3. They offer simpler, less costly products and services that may have a lower level of performance but that users consider to be good enough.

4. They generate resources, such as donations, grants, volunteer manpower, or intellectual capital, in ways that are initially unattractive to competitors.

5. They are often ignored, disparaged, or even encouraged by existing players for whom the business model is unprofitable or otherwise unattractive and who therefore avoid or retreat from the market segment.

As support for their approach, the authors note how community colleges have dramatically changed the shape of higher education by providing a low-cost alternative of choice for many undergraduates.

To find organizations that are creating a catalytic innovation for investment or other purposes, Christensen and his colleagues offer some guidelines:

1. *Look for signs of disruption in the process*—Although not necessarily easily observed, preexisting catalytic innovators may already be present in a market.

2. *Identify specific catalytic innovations*—Apply the five criteria listed above.

3. *Assess the business model*—Determine whether the organization can effectively introduce the innovation and scale it up and sustain it.

Sources: Michael F. Porter and Mark R. Kramer, "Strategy & Society," *Harvard Business Review* (December 2006): 78–82; Clayton M. Christensen, Heiner Baumann, Rudy Ruggles, and Thomas M. Stadtler, "Disruption Innovation for Social Change," *Harvard Business Review* (December 2006): 94–101. See also Richard Steckel, Elizabeth Ford, Casey Hilliard, and Traci Sanders, *Cold Cash for Warm Hearts: 101 Best Social Marketing Initiatives* (Homewood, IL: High Tide Press, 2004).

TABLE 22.3	CAUSE ATTITUDES OF THE MILLENNIAL GENERATION
Percentage of 13- to 25-year-olds who say they:	
Feel personally responsible for making a difference in the world	61%
Feel companies should join in the effort to make a difference in the world	75%
Are likely to switch brands (given equal price and quality) to support a cause	89%
Are more likely to pay attention to messages of companies deeply committed to a cause	74%
Consider a company's social commitment when deciding where to shop	69%
Consider a company's social commitment when recommending products	64%

Source: Cone Inc./AMP Insights survey of 1800 13- to 25-year-olds as reported in *BusinessWeek*, November 6, 2006, p. 13.

CAUSE-MARKETING BENEFITS AND COSTS A successful cause-marketing program can improve social welfare, create differentiated brand positioning, build strong consumer bonds, enhance a company's public image with government officials and other decision makers, create a reservoir of goodwill, boost internal morale and galvanize employees, drive sales, and increase the market value of the firm.[55]

Consumers may develop a strong, unique bond with a firm that transcends normal marketplace transactions.[56] Specifically, cause marketing can (1) build brand awareness, (2) enhance brand image, (3) establish brand credibility, (4) evoke brand feelings, (5) create a sense of brand community, and (6) elicit brand engagement.[57] Cause marketing has a particularly interested audience in civic-minded 13- to 25-year-old Millennial consumers (see Table 22.3).

The danger, however, is that a cause-related marketing program could backfire if cynical consumers question the link between the product and the cause and see the firm as self-serving and exploitive. Cadbury Schweppes PLC encountered consumer backlash with its "Sports for Schools" campaign.[58]

Cadbury Schweppes PLC

Cadbury's "Sports for Schools" promotion offered sports and fitness equipment for schools in exchange for tokens. The problem was that the public and media saw a perverse incentive for children to eat more chocolate, a product associated with obesity. As Britain's Food Commission, a nongovernmental organization, said, "Cadbury wants children to eat two million kilograms of fat—to get fit." The commission estimated that to generate the 90 tokens to purchase a £5 netball would require spending £38 on Cadbury candies and consuming more than 20 000 calories and over 1000 grams of fat. The product and the cause seemed to be at war. Cadbury Schweppes quickly discontinued the token program, but it continued its "Get Active" campaign offering teachers tips for sporty games in conjunction with the Youth Sport Trust and sponsored events such as Get Active Day with British sports stars. Putting a positive spin on the bad press, a Cadbury spokesperson insisted "The ensuing debate was very welcome. We have been trying to promote Get Active for two months. I don't think there can be anyone in the country who hasn't heard of it this week."[59]

Nike's alliance with the Lance Armstrong Foundation for cancer research has sold over 70 million yellow LIVE**STRONG** bracelets for $1, but the famed Nike swoosh logo is deliberately nowhere to be seen.[60] One of the more interesting cause programs in recent years is the Project Red campaign.[61]

(RED)

2006 saw the highly publicized launch of (RED), championed by U2 singer and activist Bono and Bobby Shriver, Chairman of DATA. (RED) was created to raise awareness and money for The Global Fund by teaming with some of the world's most iconic branded products—

American Express cards, Apple iPods, Motorola phones, Converse sneakers, Gap T-shirts, and Emporio Armani sunglasses—to produce (PRODUCT)RED branded products. Up to 50 percent of the profits from the sale of (PRODUCT)RED products are given to The Global Fund to help women and children in Africa affected by HIV/AIDS, tuberculosis, and malaria. The parentheses or brackets in the logo were designed to signify "the embrace"—each company that becomes (RED) places its logo in this embrace and is then "elevated to the power of red." Although some critics felt the project was overmarketed, by 2008 it had raised more than $63 million for the The Global Fund.

The knowledge, skills, resources, and experiences of a top firm may be even more important to a nonprofit or community group than funding. Nonprofits must be clear about what their goals are, communicate clearly what they hope to accomplish, and have an organizational structure in place to work with different firms. Developing a productive relationship with a firm can take a long time. As one consultant noted, "What's often a problem between corporations and nonprofits is different expectations and different understanding about the amount of time everything will take."[62]

Firms must make a number of decisions in designing and implementing a cause-marketing program, such as how many and which causes to choose and how to brand the cause program.

CHOOSING A CAUSE Some experts believe the positive impact of cause-related marketing is reduced by sporadic involvement with numerous causes. For example, Cathy Chizauskas, Gillette's director of civic affairs, states: "When you're spreading out your giving in fifty-dollar to one-thousand-dollar increments, no one knows what you are doing. . . . It doesn't make much of a splash."[63]

Many companies choose to focus on one or a few main causes to simplify execution and maximize impact. One such focused marketer is McDonald's. Ronald McDonald Houses in more than 27 countries (including 12 in Canada) offer more than 6000 rooms each night to families needing support while their child is in the hospital. The Ronald McDonald House program has provided a "home away from home" for nearly 10 million family members since its beginning in 1974.

Limiting support to a single cause, however, may limit the pool of consumers or other stakeholders who can transfer positive feelings from the cause to the firm. In addition, many popular causes already have numerous corporate sponsors. Over 300 companies, including Avon, Ford, Estée Lauder, Revlon, Lee Jeans, Polo Ralph Lauren, Yoplait, Saks, BMW, and American Express, have associated themselves with breast cancer as a cause.[64] As a consequence, the brand may find itself "lost in the shuffle," overlooked in a sea of symbolic pink ribbons.

Opportunities may be greater with "orphaned causes"—diseases that afflict fewer than 200 000 people.[65] Another option is overlooked diseases, such as pancreatic cancer, which is the fourth-deadliest form of cancer behind skin, lung, and breast, yet has received little or no corporate support. Even major killers such as prostate cancer for men and heart disease for women have been relatively neglected compared to breast cancer, but a number of firms have begun to fill the void. Recent years have seen a dozen new sponsors, such as Gillette, join longtime supporters Safeway and Major League Baseball in the fight against prostate cancer. The American Heart Association and the Canadian Heart and Stroke Foundation launched the marketing program "Go Red for Women" with a red-dress symbol to heighten awareness of, and attract the interest of corporations and others in, a disease that kills roughly 12 times more women than does breast cancer each year.[66]

Most firms choose causes that fit their corporate or brand image and matter to their employees and shareholders. LensCrafters' Give the Gift of Sight program is a family of charitable vision-care programs that provides free vision screenings, eye exams, and glasses to more than 3 million needy people in North America and developing countries around the world. All stores are empowered to deliver free glasses in their communities. In addition, Give the Gift of Sight sponsors two travelling Vision Vans targeting children in North America, as well as monthly two-week optical missions overseas. "Marketing Memo: Making A Difference" provides some tips from a top cause-marketing firm.

The brainchild of U2's Bono and Bobby Shriver, chairman of DATA, (RED) was a highly publicized effort to raise money for AIDS relief in Africa through partnerships with iconic brands such as Apple, Motorola, American Express, and Gap. Bono and talk-show host Oprah Winfrey are shown here shopping at the (RED) launch in Chicago.

ParticipACTION is a social marketing organization whose goal is to make Canadians the most physically active people on earth.

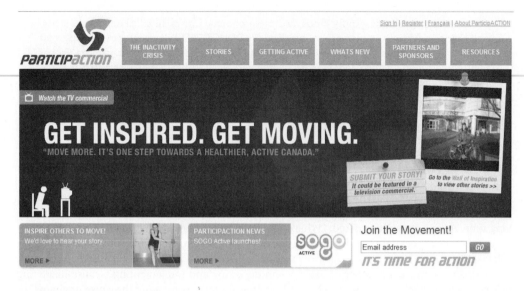

Social Marketing

Cause-related marketing supports a cause. **Social marketing** by nonprofit or government organizations *furthers* a cause. Examples include Health Canada's *ParticipACTION* organization, which aims (along with its partners) to make Canadians the most physically active people on earth, and Concerned Children's Advertisers, headquartered in Toronto, which has focused on producing and delivering social messaging on issues affecting children's lives, such as self-esteem, bullying, media literacy, and child abuse.[67]

Social marketing goes back many years. In the 1950s, India started family-planning campaigns. In the 1970s, Sweden ran social marketing campaigns to turn the country into a nation of nonsmokers and nondrinkers, the Australian government ran "Wear Your Seat Belt" campaigns, and the Canadian government launched campaigns to "Say No to Drugs," "Stop Smoking," and "Exercise for Health." In the 1980s, the World Bank, World Health Organization, and U.S. Centers for Disease

Concerned Children's Advertisers has a long record of effective social marketing with a focus on issues that affect the lives of Canadian children.

One of the most accomplished cause-marketing consulting firms, Cone Inc., offers perspectives on the current state of cause marketing and how it should best be practised:

> With new vigour, consumers, customers, employees, investors, and communities are closely watching how companies behave in relation to them and to society. Influential groups such as Canadian Business for Social Responsibility, Dow Jones Sustainability Index, *Fortune* magazine, and others are judging companies based on a complex series of global standards. Business practices such as governance, philanthropy, sourcing, the environment, employee relations, and community relations have moved from behind the scenes to centre stage. For executives today, appropriately defining, executing, and communicating corporate social responsibility (CSR) and sustainability practices has never been more important.

To help execute and communicate CSR more effectively, Cone offers the following considerations:

- *Define CSR for your company.* Make sure that your senior executives are all talking about the same thing. CSR includes a broad range of complex internal and external business practices. Although they are vital components of the CSR mix, corporate philanthropy and community relations alone don't define CSR.

- *Build a diverse team.* The development and execution of CSR strategies require a collaborative, concerted team effort. Create a decision-making task force that integrates and brings together a range of expertise and resources, including marketing, public affairs, community relations, legal, human resources, manufacturing, and others. Put a formal process in place to approach CSR strategy development, ongoing implementation, and continuous improvement.

- *Analyze your current CSR-related activities and revamp them if necessary.* Do your due diligence at the outset to understand CSR gaps and risks specific to your company. Research industry examples and work to understand best practices from leading case studies. Make sure to consider global trends, as Europe is far in advance of North America when it comes to CSR and sustainability initiatives.

- *Forge and strengthen NGO relationships.* The more than 300 000 nongovernmental organizations (NGOs) around the world are a powerful force acting on corporate policies and behaviour, serving as both advocates and loud critics. Forge sincere partnerships with organizations that can offer you independent, unbiased insight into and evaluation of your CSR activities, provide expertise on social issues and developing global markets, and offer access to key influentials. Becel margarine grew to be the number-one brand in Canada through its partnership with the Heart and Stroke Foundation which helped position the brand as the "best margarine for your heart's health."

- *Develop a cause-branding initiative.* Create a public face for your citizenship activities through a signature cause-branding initiative that integrates philanthropy, community relations, marketing, and human resources assets. ConAgra Foods' award winning Feeding Children Better program, for example, is a multi-year initiative created to feed millions of hungry children through innovative partnerships, grant making, employee volunteerism, education, and awareness.

- *Walk your talk.* Critics often assert that companies exploit CSR as a PR smokescreen to conceal or divert attention from corporate misdeeds and blemishes. Before introducing any new CSR initiative or drawing attention to good corporate behaviour, make sure that your company is addressing stakeholder expectations of CSR at the most basic level.

- *Don't be silent.* Not only do Canadians expect businesses to behave socially, the majority want companies to report their progress against the achievement of their social goals. An overwhelming majority also say they prefer to find out about CSR activities from a third-party source, particularly the media.

- *Beware.* Greater public awareness of your corporate citizenship record can be double-edged. Claims of socially responsible behaviour, even sincere ones, often invite public scrutiny. Be prepared. Even if your company is not ready to proactively communicate about your CSR activities, be ready to respond to public inquiries immediately. Don't let the threat of public scrutiny keep you mute, though. More often than not, silence regarding CSR issues is translated as indifference, or worse, inaction.

Sources: *Cone Buzz* (April 2004). See also Carol L. Cone, Mark A. Feldman, and Alison T. DaSilva, "Cause and Effects," *Harvard Business Review* (July 2003): 95–101.

Control and Prevention started to use the term and promote interest in social marketing. Some notable global social-marketing successes:

- Oral rehydration therapy in Honduras significantly decreased deaths from diarrhea in small children under the age of five.

- Social marketers created booths in marketplaces where Ugandan midwives sold contraceptives at affordable prices.

- Population Communication Services created and promoted two extremely popular songs in Latin America, "Stop" and "When We Are Together," to help young women "say no."

A number of different types of organizations conduct social marketing in Canada. For example, Health Canada uses social marketing as an integrated part of its health-promotion strategies. The Government of Nova Scotia has a social marketing campaign aimed at reducing gambling among those addicted to the practice. The Region of Durham in Ontario uses social marketing to encourage people to reduce their water usage. Literally hundreds of nonprofit organizations conduct social marketing, including the Canadian Red Cross, the World Wildlife Fund, and the Breast Cancer Society of Canada.

Choosing the right goal or objective for a social marketing program is critical. Should a family-planning campaign focus on abstinence or birth control? Should a campaign to fight air pollution focus on ride sharing or mass transit? Social marketing campaigns may have objectives related to changing people's cognitions, values, actions, or behaviours. The following examples illustrate the range of possible objectives.

Cognitive campaigns

- Explain the nutritional value of different foods.
- Explain the importance of conservation.

Action campaigns

- Attract people to mass immunization.
- Motivate people to vote "yes" on a certain issue.
- Motivate people to donate blood.
- Motivate women to have breast exams.

Behavioural campaigns

- Demotivate cigarette smoking.
- Demotivate usage of hard drugs.
- Demotivate excessive consumption of alcohol.

Value campaigns

- Alter ideas about abortion.
- Change attitudes of bigoted people.

Social marketing uses a number of different tactics to achieve its goals.[68] The planning process follows many of the same steps as for traditional products and services (see Table 22.4). Some key factors in developing and implementing a successful social marketing program:

- Study the literature and previous campaigns.
- Choose target markets that are most ready to respond.
- Promote a single, doable behaviour in clear, simple terms.
- Explain the benefits in compelling terms.
- Make it easy to adopt the behaviour.
- Develop attention-grabbing messages and media.
- Consider an education–entertainment approach.

One organization that has accomplished most of these goals via an unusual targeted campaign is the Global Water Foundation.

TABLE 22.4	SOCIAL-MARKETING PLANNING PROCESS

Where Are We?
- Determine program focus
- Identify campaign purpose
- Conduct an analysis of strengths, weaknesses, opportunities, and threats (SWOT)
- Review past and similar efforts

Where Do We Want to Go?
- Select target audiences
- Set objectives and goals
- Analyze target audiences and the competition

How Will We Get There?
- Product: Design the market offering
- Price: Manage costs of behaviour change
- Distribution: Make the product available
- Communications: Create messages and choose media

How Will We Stay on Course?
- Develop a plan for evaluation and monitoring
- Establish budgets and find funding sources
- Complete an implementation plan

Global Water Foundation

The average denizen of Second Life, the web-based virtual world in which residents interact via computer- animated "avatars," is 33, lives in North America or Europe, is tech savvy, and has a relatively high disposable income—a perfect market for the Global Water Foundation (GWF) to launch a campaign. Its Virtual Education Center features streaming video and audio supporting its cause—ensuring clean, drinkable water for the developing world—and photos highlighting its work. Interested visitors click on GWF's website and pick up free virtual GWF T-shirts, enabling their avatars to spread the word. In the first six months after the campaign began on Second Life, GWF logged more than 77 000 web hits. In the next phase, the organization plans to use the growing Second Life economy, based on virtual currency purchased with real-world money, to collect visitor donations that it will reward with virtual premiums such as wristbands and pet dolphins.[69]

Social marketing programs are complex; they take time and may require phased programs or actions. For example, recall the steps in discouraging smoking: cancer reports, labelling of cigarettes, banning cigarette advertising, education about secondary-smoke effects, no smoking in homes, no smoking in restaurants, no smoking on planes, raising taxes on cigarettes to pay for antismoking campaigns, suits against cigarette companies, and the 2008 ban on displaying cigarettes in stores.[70]

Social marketing organizations should evaluate program success in terms of objectives. Criteria might include incidence of adoption, speed of adoption, continuance of adoption, low cost per unit of adoption, and absence of counterproductive consequences.

Once firms have confirmed that they have fully integrated socially responsible marketing into their culture and strategies, they have to turn to issues of implementation.

MARKETING IMPLEMENTATION

Table 22.5 summarizes the characteristics of a great marketing company, great not for "what it is" but for "what it does." **Marketing implementation** is the process that turns marketing plans into action assignments and ensures they accomplish the plans' stated objectives.[71]

A brilliant strategic marketing plan counts for little if not implemented properly. Strategy addresses the *what* and *why* of marketing activities; implementation addresses the *who, where, when,* and *how.* They are closely related: one layer of strategy implies certain tactical implementation

TABLE 22.5	**CHARACTERISTICS OF A GREAT MARKETING COMPANY**

- The company selects target markets in which it enjoys superior advantages and exits or avoids markets where it is intrinsically weak.
- Virtually all of the company's employees and departments are customer- and market-minded.
- There are good working relationships among marketing, R&D, and manufacturing.
- There are good working relationships among marketing, sales, and customer service.
- The company has installed incentives designed to lead to the right behaviours.
- The company continuously builds and tracks customer satisfaction and loyalty.
- The company manages a value-delivery system in partnership with strong suppliers and distributors.
- The company is skilled in building its brand name(s) and image.
- The company is flexible in meeting customers' varying requirements.

assignments at a lower level. For example, top management's strategic decision to "harvest" a product must be translated into specific actions and assignments.

Companies today are striving to make their marketing operations more efficient and their return on marketing investment more measurable (see Chapter 4). Marketing costs can amount to 20 percent to 40 percent of a company's total operating budget. Marketers need better templates for marketing processes, better management of marketing assets, and better allocation of marketing resources. Certain repetitive processes can be automated under such names as *marketing resource management (MRM), marketing investment management (MIM), enterprise marketing management (EMM)*, and *marketing automation systems (MAS)*.[72]

Marketing resource management software provides a set of web-based applications that automate and integrate such activities as project management, campaign management, budget management, asset management, brand management, customer relationship management, and knowledge management. The knowledge management component consists of process templates, how-to wizards, and best practices.

Software packages are web hosted and available to users with passwords. They add up to what some have called *desktop marketing* and give marketers whatever information and decision structures they need on computer dashboards. MRM software lets marketers improve spending and investment decisions, bring new products to market more quickly, and reduce decision time and costs. Rydex Investments benefited greatly from a well-implemented MRM system.

Rydex Investments

In one year, the marketing department of Rydex Investments, a Maryland fund-management company, had over 800 projects in the works, ranging from simple updates of marketing pieces to full-scale campaign launches. It was getting harder to complete projects on time because 30 to 35 people needed to approve them. Paper folders went through the marketing group, design department, communications, and then the legal department. As Rydex doubled its staff over two years, it was clear it had outgrown this cumbersome manual process, so it adopted a web-based marketing resource management system (MRS) from MarketingCentral of Georgia. The system lets Rydex create a centralized space for marketing projects, organized by folders, that managers in all departments can collaborate on. It lets them create schedules and track approvals to make sure all regulatory steps are taken, and it even gives participants a chance to comment on the projects as they're being finished. Since adopting the MRS, Rydex has seen the time it takes to get a message to market shrink by 20 percent.[73]

EVALUATION AND CONTROL

In spite of the need to monitor and control marketing activities, many companies have inadequate control procedures. Table 22.6 lists four types of needed marketing control: annual-plan control, profitability control, efficiency control, and strategic control. We consider each.

TABLE 22.6	TYPES OF MARKETING CONTROL		
Type of Control	**Prime Responsibility**	**Purpose of Control**	**Approaches**
I. Annual-plan control	Top management Middle management	To examine whether the planned results are being achieved	▪ Sales analysis ▪ Market-share analysis ▪ Sales-to-expense ratios ▪ Financial analysis ▪ Market-based scorecard analysis
II. Profitability control	Marketing controller	To examine where the company is making and losing money	Profitability by: ▪ product ▪ territory ▪ customer ▪ segment ▪ trade channel ▪ order size
III. Efficiency control	Line and staff management Marketing controller	To evaluate and improve the spending efficiency and impact of marketing expenditures	Efficiency of: ▪ sales force ▪ advertising ▪ sales promotion ▪ distribution
IV. Strategic control	Top management Marketing auditor	To examine whether the company is pursuing its best opportunities with respect to markets, products, and channels	▪ Marketing-effectiveness rating instrument ▪ Marketing audit ▪ Marketing excellence review ▪ Company ethical and social responsibility review

Annual-Plan Control

Annual-plan control ensures the company achieves the sales, profits, and other goals established in its annual plan. At its heart is management by objectives. There are four steps (see Figure 22.5). First, management sets monthly or quarterly goals. Second, management monitors its performance in the marketplace. Third, management determines the causes of serious performance deviations. Fourth, management takes corrective action to close gaps between goals and performance.

This control model applies to all levels of the organization. Top management sets annual sales and profit goals; each product manager, regional district manager, sales manager, and sales rep is committed to attaining specified levels of sales and costs. Each period, top management reviews and interprets the results.

Marketers today have better marketing metrics for measuring the performance of marketing plans (see Table 22.7 for some samples).[74] They can use four tools to check on plan performance: sales analysis, market-share analysis, marketing expense-to-sales analysis, and financial analysis.

Profitability Control

Companies can benefit from deeper financial analysis and should measure the profitability of their products, territories, customer groups, segments, trade channels, and order sizes. This information can help management determine whether to expand, reduce, or eliminate any products or marketing activities.

Efficiency Control

Suppose a profitability analysis reveals the company is earning poor profits in certain products, territories, or markets. Are there more efficient ways to manage the sales force, advertising, sales promotion, and distribution in connection with these marketing entities?

Some companies have established a *marketing controller* position to work out of the controller's office but specialize in improving marketing efficiency. At companies such as General Foods, DuPont, and Johnson & Johnson, they perform a sophisticated financial analysis of marketing expenditures and results. They examine adherence to profit plans, help prepare brand managers' budgets, measure the efficiency of promotions, analyze media production costs, evaluate customer and geographic profitability, and educate marketing personnel on the financial implications of marketing decisions.[75] They can examine the efficiency of the channel, sales force, advertising, and any other form of marketing communication.

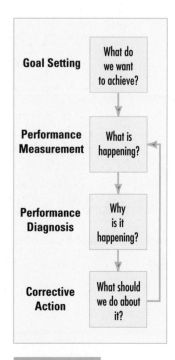

FIGURE 22.5

The Control Process

TABLE 22.7	MARKETING METRICS	
Sales Metrics		**Distribution Metrics**
■ Sales growth		■ Number of outlets
■ Market share		■ Share in shops handling
■ Sales from new products		■ Weighted distribution
Customer Readiness-to-Buy Metrics		■ Distribution gains
■ Awareness		■ Average stocks volume (value)
■ Preference		■ Stocks cover in days
■ Purchase intention		■ Out-of-stock frequency
■ Trial rate		■ Share of shelf
■ Repurchase rate		■ Average sales per point of sale
Customer Metrics		**Communication Metrics**
■ Customer complaints		■ Spontaneous (unaided) brand awareness
■ Customer satisfaction		■ Top-of-mind brand awareness
■ Number of promoters to detractors		■ Prompted (aided) brand awareness
■ Customer-acquisition costs		■ Spontaneous (unaided) advertising awareness
■ New-customer gains		
■ Customer losses		■ Prompted (aided) advertising awareness
■ Customer churn		■ Effective reach
■ Retention rate		■ Effective frequency
■ Customer lifetime value		■ Gross rating points (GRP)
■ Customer equity		■ Response rate
■ Customer profitability		
■ Return on customer		

For example, in assessing channel efficiency, management needs to search for distribution economies in inventory control, warehouse locations, and transportation modes. It should track such measures as:

■ Logistics costs as a percentage of sales

■ Percentage of orders filled correctly

■ Percentage of on-time deliveries

■ Number of billing errors

Management should strive to reduce inventory while at the same time speeding up the order-to-delivery cycle. Dell Computer shows how to do both simultaneously.

A customer-customized computer ordered from Dell's website at 9:00 A.M. on Wednesday can be on the delivery truck by 9:00 P.M. Thursday. In that short period, Dell electronically orders the computer components from its suppliers' warehouses. Equally impressive, Dell gets paid electronically within 24 hours, whereas Compaq, supplying its computers to retailers, receives payment days later.

Strategic Control

Each company should periodically reassess its strategic approach to the marketplace with a good marketing audit. Companies can also perform marketing excellence reviews and ethical/social responsibility reviews.

THE MARKETING AUDIT The average North American corporation loses half its customers in five years, half its employees in four years, and half its investors in less than one year. Clearly, this points to some weaknesses. Companies that discover weaknesses should undertake a thorough study known as a marketing audit.[76] A **marketing audit** is a comprehensive, systematic, independent, and periodic examination of a company's or business unit's marketing environment, objectives, strategies, and activities, with a view to determining problem areas and opportunities and recommending a plan of action to improve the company's marketing performance.

Let's examine the marketing audit's four characteristics:

1. *Comprehensive*—The marketing audit covers all the major marketing activities of a business, not just a few trouble spots. It would be called a functional audit if it covered only the sales force, pricing, or some other marketing activity. Although functional audits are useful, they sometimes mislead management. Excessive sales-force turnover, for example, could be a symptom not of poor sales-force training or compensation but of weak company products and promotion. A comprehensive marketing audit usually is more effective in locating the real source of problems.

2. *Systematic*—The marketing audit is an orderly examination of the organization's macro- and micromarketing environments, marketing objectives and strategies, marketing systems, and specific activities. The audit indicates the most-needed improvements, incorporating them into a corrective-action plan with short- and long-run steps to improve overall effectiveness.

3. *Independent*—Marketers can conduct a marketing audit in six ways: self-audit, audit from across, audit from above, company auditing office, company task-force audit, and outsider audit. Self-audits, in which managers use a checklist to rate their own operations, lack objectivity and independence.[77] The 3M Company has made good use of a corporate auditing office, which provides marketing-audit services to divisions on request.[78] Generally speaking, however, the best audits come from outside consultants who have the necessary objectivity, broad experience in a number of industries, some familiarity with the industry being audited, and undivided time and attention.

4. *Periodic*—Typically, firms initiate marketing audits only after sales have turned down, sales-force morale has fallen, and other problems have occurred. Companies are thrown into a crisis partly because they failed to review their marketing operations during good times. A periodic marketing audit can benefit companies in good health as well as those in trouble.

A marketing audit starts with a meeting between the company officer(s) and the marketing auditor(s) to work out an agreement on the audit's objectives, coverage, depth, data sources, report format, and time frame. It includes a detailed plan of who is to be interviewed, the questions to be asked, and where and when to minimize time and cost. The cardinal rule in marketing auditing: don't rely solely on company managers for data and opinions. Ask customers, dealers, and other outside groups. Many companies don't really know how their customers and dealers see them, nor do they fully understand customer needs.

The marketing audit examines six major components of a company's marketing situation. Table 22.8 lists the major questions.

THE MARKETING EXCELLENCE REVIEW   The three columns in Table 22.9 distinguish among poor, good, and excellent business and marketing practices. Management can place a checkmark to indicate its perception of where the business stands. The profile that results from this marketing excellence review exposes weaknesses and strengths, highlighting where the company might make changes to become a truly outstanding player in the marketplace.

TABLE 22.8	COMPONENTS OF A MARKETING AUDIT
Part I. Marketing Environment Audit	
Macroenvironment	
A. Demographic	What major demographic developments and trends pose opportunities for or threats to this company? What actions has the company taken in response to these developments and trends?
B. Economic	What major developments in income, prices, savings, and credit will affect the company? What actions has the company been taking in response to these developments?
C. Environmental	What is the outlook for the cost, availability, and sustainability of natural resources and energy needed by the company? What concerns have been expressed about the company's role in pollution and conservation, and what steps has the company taken?
D. Technological	What major changes are occurring in product and process technology? What is the company's position in these technologies? What major generic substitutes might replace this product?
E. Political	What changes in laws and regulations might affect marketing strategy and tactics? What is happening in the area of pollution control?
F. Cultural	What is the public's attitude towards business and towards the company's products? What changes in customer lifestyles and values might affect the company?

TABLE 22.8 | (*continued*)

Task Environment

A. Markets	What is happening to market size, growth, geographical distribution, and profits? What are the major market segments?
B. Customers	What are the customers' needs and buying processes? How do customers and prospects rate the company and its competitors on reputation, product quality, service, sales force, and price? How do different customer segments make their buying decisions?
C. Competitors	Who are the major competitors? What are their objectives, strategies, strengths, weaknesses, sizes, and market shares? What trends will affect future competition and substitutes for the company's products?
D. Distribution and Dealers	What are the main trade channels for bringing products to customers? What are the efficiency levels and growth potentials of the different trade channels?
E. Suppliers	What is the outlook for the availability of key resources used in production? What trends are occurring among suppliers? Are suppliers following ethical and sustainable practices?
F. Facilitators and Marketing Firms	What is the cost and availability outlook for transportation services, warehousing facilities, and financial resources? How effective are the company's advertising agencies and marketing research firms?
G. Publics	Which publics represent particular opportunities or problems for the company? What steps has the company taken to deal effectively with each public?

Part II. Marketing Strategy Audit

A. Business Mission	Is the business mission clearly stated in market-oriented terms? Is it feasible?
B. Marketing Objectives and Goals	Are the company's marketing objectives and goals stated clearly enough to guide marketing planning and performance measurement? Are the marketing objectives appropriate, given the company's competitive position, resources, and opportunities?
C. Strategy	Has the management articulated a clear marketing strategy for achieving its marketing objectives? Is the strategy convincing? Is the strategy appropriate to the stage of the product life cycle, competitors' strategies, and the state of the economy? Is the company using the best basis for market segmentation? Does it have clear criteria for rating the segments and choosing the best ones? Has it developed accurate profiles of each target segment? Has the company developed an effective positioning and marketing mix for each target segment? Are marketing resources allocated optimally to the major elements of the marketing mix? Are enough resources or too many resources budgeted to accomplish the marketing objectives?

Part III. Marketing Organization Audit

A. Formal Structure	Does the marketing vice-president have adequate authority and responsibility for company activities that affect customers' satisfaction? Are the marketing activities optimally structured along functional, product, segment, end user, and geographical lines?
B. Functional Efficiency	Are there good communication and working relations between marketing and sales? Is the product-management system working effectively? Are product managers able to plan profits or only sales volume? Are there any groups in marketing that need more training, motivation, supervision, or evaluation?
C. Interface Efficiency	Are there any problems between marketing and manufacturing, R&D, purchasing, finance, accounting, and/or legal that need attention?

Part IV. Marketing Systems Audit

A. Marketing Information System	Is the marketing intelligence system producing accurate, sufficient, and timely information about marketplace developments with respect to customers, prospects, distributors and dealers, competitors, suppliers, and various publics? Are company decision makers asking for enough marketing research, and are they using the results? Is the company employing the best methods for market measurement and sales forecasting?
B. Marketing Planning System	Is the marketing planning system well conceived and effectively used? Do marketers have decision support systems available? Does the planning system result in acceptable sales targets and quotas?
C. Marketing Control System	Are the control procedures adequate to ensure that the annual-plan objectives are being achieved? Does management periodically analyze the profitability of products, markets, territories, and channels of distribution? Are marketing costs and productivity periodically examined?
D. New-Product Development System	Is the company well organized to gather, generate, and screen new-product ideas? Does the company conduct adequate concept research and business analysis before investing in new ideas? Does the company carry out adequate product and market testing before launching new products?

TABLE 22.8	*(continued)*

Part V. Marketing Productivity Audit

A. Profitability Analysis	What is the profitability of the company's different products, markets, territories, and channels of distribution? Should the company enter, expand, contract, or withdraw from any business segments?
B. Cost-Effectiveness Analysis	Do any marketing activities seem to have excessive costs? Can cost-reducing steps be taken?

Part VI. Marketing Function Audits

A. Products	What are the company's product-line objectives? Are they sound? Is the current product line meeting the objectives? Should the product line be stretched or contracted upwards, downwards, or both ways? Which products should be phased out? Which products should be added? What are buyers' knowledge and attitudes towards the company's and competitors' product quality, features, styling, brand names, and so on? What areas of product and brand strategy need improvement?
B. Price	What are the company's pricing objectives, policies, strategies, and procedures? To what extent are prices set on cost, demand, and competitive criteria? Do customers see the company's prices as being in line with the value of its offer? What does management know about the price elasticity of demand, experience-curve effects, and competitors' prices and pricing policies? To what extent are price policies compatible with the needs of distributors and dealers, suppliers, and government regulation?
C. Distribution	What are the company's distribution objectives and strategies? Is there adequate market coverage and service? How effective are distributors, dealers, manufacturers' representatives, brokers, agents, and others? Should the company consider changing its distribution channels?
D. Marketing Communications	What are the organization's advertising objectives? Are they sound? Is the right amount being spent on advertising? Are the ad themes and copy effective? What do customers and the public think about the advertising? Are the advertising media well chosen? Is the internal advertising staff adequate? Is the sales promotion budget adequate? Is there effective and sufficient use of sales promotion tools such as samples, coupons, displays, and sales contests? Is the public relations staff competent and creative? Is the company making enough use of direct, online, and database marketing?
E. Sales Force	What are the sales force's objectives? Is the sales force large enough to accomplish the company's objectives? Is the sales force organized along the proper principles of specialization (territory, market, product)? Are there enough (or too many) sales managers to guide the field sales representatives? Do the sales compensation level and structure provide adequate incentive and reward? Does the sales force show high morale, ability, and effort? Are the procedures adequate for setting quotas and evaluating performance? How does the company's sales force compare to competitors' sales forces?

TABLE 22.9	THE MARKETING EXCELLENCE REVIEW: BEST PRACTICES

Poor	Good	Excellent
Product driven	Market driven	Market driving
Mass-market oriented	Segment oriented	Niche oriented and customer oriented
Product offer	Augmented product offer	Customer solutions offer
Average product quality	Better than average	Legendary
Average service quality	Better than average	Legendary
End-product oriented	Core-product oriented	Core-competency oriented
Function oriented	Process oriented	Outcome oriented
Reacting to competitors	Benchmarking competitors	Leapfrogging competitors
Supplier exploitation	Supplier preference	Supplier partnership
Dealer exploitation	Dealer support	Dealer partnership
Price driven	Quality driven	Value driven
Average speed	Better than average	Legendary
Hierarchy	Network	Teamwork
Vertically integrated	Flattened organization	Strategic alliances
Shareholder driven	Stakeholder driven	Societally driven

THE FUTURE OF MARKETING

Top management recognizes that past marketing has been highly wasteful and demands more accountability. "Marketing Memo: Major Marketing Weaknesses" summarizes companies' major deficiencies in marketing and how to find and correct them.

Going forward, marketing must be "holistic" and less departmental. Marketers must achieve larger influence in the company if they are to be the main architects of business strategy. They must continuously create new ideas if the company is to prosper in a hypercompetitive economy faced with environmental issues. They must strive for customer insight and treat customers differently but appropriately. Marketers must build their brands through performance more than through promotion. They must consider the sustainability of inputs into products as well as their reusability. Marketers must go electronic and win through building superior information and communication systems.

In these ways, modern marketing will continue to evolve and confront new challenges and opportunities. As a result, the coming years will see the following:

■   The demise of the marketing department and the rise of holistic marketing
■   The demise of free-spending marketing and the rise of ROI marketing
■   The demise of marketing intuition and the rise of marketing science
■   The demise of manual marketing and the rise of automated marketing
■   The demise of mass marketing and the rise of precision marketing

To accomplish these changes and become truly holistic, marketers need a new set of skills and competencies in areas such as:

■   Customer relationship management (CRM)
■   Partner relationship management (PRM)
■   Database marketing and datamining
■   Contact-centre management and telemarketing
■   Management of environmental impacts of products and services
■   Public relations marketing (including event and sponsorship marketing)
■   Brand-building and brand-asset management
■   Experiential marketing
■   Integrated marketing communications
■   Profitability analysis by segment, customer, and channel

It is an exciting time for marketing. In the relentless pursuit of marketing superiority and dominance, new rules and practices are emerging. The benefits of successful twenty-first-century marketing are many but will come only with hard work, insight, and inspiration.

MARKETING **MEMO**	MAJOR MARKETING WEAKNESSES

A number of "deadly sins" signal that a marketing program is in trouble. Here are ten deadly sins, the signs, and some solutions.

Deadly Sin: The company is not sufficiently market focused and customer driven.

Signs: There is evidence of poor identification of market segments, poor prioritization of market segments, no market segment managers, employees who think it is the job of marketing and sales to serve customers, no training program to create a customer culture, and no incentives to treat the customer especially well.

Solutions: Use more advanced segmentation techniques, prioritize segments, specialize the sales force, develop a clear hierarchy of company values, foster more "customer consciousness" in employees and company agents, make it easy for customers to reach the company, and respond quickly to any communication.

Deadly Sin: The company does not fully understand its target customers.

Signs: The latest study of customers is three years old, customers are not buying the product like they once did, competitors' products are selling better, and there is a high level of customer returns and complaints.

Solutions: Conduct more sophisticated consumer research, use more analytical techniques, establish customer and dealer panels, use customer relationship software, and conduct datamining.

Deadly Sin: The company needs to better define and monitor its competitors.

Signs: The company focuses on near competitors, misses distant competitors and disruptive technologies, and has no system for gathering and distributing competitive intelligence.

Solutions: Establish an office for competitive intelligence, hire competitors' people, watch for technology that might affect the company, and prepare offerings like those of competitors.

Deadly Sin: The company does not properly manage relationships with stakeholders.

Signs: Employees, dealers, and investors are not happy, and good suppliers do not come. Activists are attacking the company.

Solutions: Move from zero-sum thinking to positive-sum thinking and do a better job of creating value for employees, suppliers, distributors, dealers, investors, and communities.

Deadly Sin: The company is not good at finding new opportunities.

Signs: The company has not identified any exciting new opportunities for years, and the new ideas the company has launched have largely failed.

Solutions: Set up a system for stimulating the flow of new ideas.

Deadly Sin: The company's marketing planning process is deficient.

Signs: The marketing plan format does not have the right components, there is no way to estimate the financial implications of different strategies, and there is no contingency planning.

Solutions: Establish a standard format including situational analysis, SWOT, major issues, objectives, strategy, tactics, budgets, and controls; ask marketers what changes they would make if they were given 20 percent more or less budget; and run an annual marketing awards program with prizes for the best plans and performance.

Deadly Sin: Product and service policies need tightening.

Signs: There are too many products and many are losing money, the company is giving away too many services, and the company is poor at cross-selling products and services.

Solutions: Establish a system to track weak products and fix or drop them, offer and price services at different levels, and improve processes for cross-selling and up-selling.

Deadly Sin: The company's brand-building and communications skills are weak.

Signs: The target market does not know much about the company, the brand is not seen as distinctive, the company allocates its budget to the same marketing tools in about the same proportion each year, and there is little evaluation of the ROI impact of promotions.

Solutions: Improve brand-building strategies and measurement of results, shift money into effective marketing instruments, and require marketers to estimate the ROI impact in advance of funding requests.

Deadly Sin: The company is not organized for effective and efficient marketing.

Signs: Staff lacks twenty-first-century marketing skills, and there are bad vibes between marketing/sales and other departments.

Solutions: Appoint a strong leader to build new skills in the marketing department and improve relationships between marketing and other departments.

Deadly Sin: The company has not made maximum use of technology.

Signs: There is evidence of minimal use of the Internet, an outdated sales automation system, no market automation, no decision-support models, and no marketing dashboards.

Solutions: Use the Internet more, improve the sales automation system, apply market automation to routine decisions, and develop formal marketing decision models and marketing dashboards.

Source: Philip Kotler, *Ten Deadly Marketing Sins: Signs and Solutions* (Hoboken, NJ: John Wiley & Sons, 2004).

SUMMARY

1. The modern marketing department has evolved through the years from a simple sales department to an organizational structure where marketing personnel work mainly on cross-disciplinary teams.

2. Modern marketing departments can be organized in a number of ways. Some companies are organized by functional specialization, whereas others focus on geography and regionalization. Still others emphasize product and brand management or market-segment management. Some companies establish a matrix organization consisting of both product and market managers. Finally, some companies have strong corporate marketing, others have limited corporate marketing, and still others place marketing only in the divisions.

3. Effective modern marketing organizations are marked by a strong customer focus in, and strong cooperation among, the company's departments: marketing, R&D, engineering, purchasing, manufacturing, operations, finance, accounting, and credit.

4. Companies must practise social responsibility through their legal, ethical, and social words and actions. Cause marketing can be a means for companies to productively link social responsibility to consumer marketing programs. Social marketing is done by a nonprofit or government organization to directly address a social problem or cause.

5. A brilliant strategic marketing plan counts for little if it is not implemented properly. Implementing marketing plans calls for skills in recognizing and diagnosing a problem, assessing the company level where the problem exists, and evaluating results.

6. The marketing department must monitor and control marketing activities continuously. Efficiency control focuses on finding ways to increase the efficiency of the sales force, advertising, sales promotion, and distribution. Strategic control entails a periodic reassessment of the company and its strategic approach to the marketplace using the tools of the marketing effectiveness and marketing excellence reviews, as well as the marketing audit.

7. Achieving marketing excellence in the future will require meeting new challenges and opportunities. The resulting marketing imperatives will require a new set of skills and competencies.

APPLICATIONS

Marketing Debate: Is Marketing Management an Art or a Science?

Some marketing observers maintain that good marketing is something that is more of an art and does not lend itself to rigorous analysis and deliberation. Others strongly disagree and contend that marketing management is a highly disciplined enterprise that shares much in common with other business disciplines.

Take a position: Marketing management is largely an artistic exercise and therefore highly subjective *versus* Marketing management is largely a scientific exercise with well-established guidelines and criteria.

Marketing Discussion

How does cause or corporate societal marketing affect your personal consumer behaviour? Do you ever buy or not buy any products or services from a company because of its environmental policies or programs? Why or why not?

Breakthrough Marketing: Starbucks

Starbucks opened in Seattle in 1971 at a time when coffee consumption in the United States had been declining for a decade and rival coffee brands used cheaper coffee beans to compete on price. Starbucks' founders decided to experiment with a new concept: a store that would sell only the finest imported coffee beans and coffee-brewing equipment. The original store didn't sell coffee by the cup, only beans.

Howard Schultz came to Starbucks in 1982. While in Milan on business, he had walked into an Italian coffee bar and had an epiphany with his espresso. "There was nothing like this in America. It was an extension of people's front porch. It was an emotional experience," he said. He knew right away that he wanted to bring this concept to the United States. Schultz set about creating an environment for Starbucks coffeehouses that would meld Italian elegance with U.S. informality. He envisioned Starbucks as a "personal treat" for its customers, a "Third Place"—a comfortable, sociable gathering spot bridging the workplace and the home.

From its launch in Seattle, Starbucks' expansion throughout the United States was carefully planned. The management team agreed that all stores would be owned and operated by the company, ensuring complete control in order to cultivate an unparalleled image of quality. Starbucks employed a "hub" expansion strategy, in which coffeehouses entered a new market in a clustered group. Although this deliberate saturation often cannibalized 30 percent of one store's sales by introducing a store nearby, any drop in revenue was offset by efficiencies in marketing and distribution costs, and the enhanced image of convenience. A typical customer would stop by Starbucks 18 times a month. No U.S. retailer has had a higher frequency of customer visits.

Part of the success of Starbucks undoubtedly lies in its products and services, and its relentless commitment to providing customers with the richest possible sensory experiences. But another key is the enlightened sense of responsibility that manifests itself in a number of different ways.

Schultz believes that to exceed the expectations of customers, it is first necessary to exceed the expectations of employees. As far back as 1990, Starbucks provided comprehensive health care to all employees, including part-timers. Health insurance now costs Starbucks more each year than coffee. The firm also introduced a stock option plan called "Bean Stock," which allows Starbucks' employees to participate in the company's financial success.

The company donates millions of dollars to charities via The Starbucks Foundation, created in 1997 with proceeds from the sale of Schultz's book. The mission of the foundation is to "create hope, discovery, and opportunity in communities where Starbucks partners [employees] live and work." The primary focus of the foundation has been on improving young peoples' lives by supporting literacy programs for children and families. By 2007, the foundation had provided over $12 million to more than 700 youth-focused organizations in the United States and Canada.

Starbucks also has donated 5 cents of every sale of its Ethos bottled water to improving the quality of water in poor countries as part of a five-year, US$10-million pledge.

Starbucks also promotes "fair-trade" export practices with Third World coffee bean producers—no other retailer in North America sells more fair-trade coffee—and pays its producers in those countries an average of 23 percent above market price. It took the company ten years of development to create the world's first recycled beverage cup made from ten percent postconsumer fibre, conserving 5 million pounds of paper or approximately 78 000 trees a year. The company has 87 urban locations co-owned by Earvin "Magic" Johnson.

Starbucks currently has over 12 400 stores worldwide, with 115 000 employees and almost US$8 billion in revenue. The company hopes to expand to 40 000 outlets, cafés, and kiosks worldwide, half of them outside the United States. By mid-2008, Starbucks Canada had over 1000 company-owned and licensed stores across Canada.[79] Starbucks is enjoying rapid growth and is opening new stores in Canada at the rate of approximately five per month. This expansion helped drive significant increases in brand awareness and company market share over the past few years. But no matter what the growth trajectory, Schultz believes that Starbucks must retain a passion for coffee and a sense of humanity, must remain small even as it gets big, and must always treat workers as individuals.

DISCUSSION QUESTIONS

1. Opening campus stores presents a growth opportunity for Starbucks Canada. What challenges might Starbucks face when pursuing this opportunity?

2. Will its record of social responsibility be a help or a hindrance if it decides to pursue this market opportunity?

3. What advice would you give to Starbucks' managers when considering this opportunity?

Sources: Howard Schultz, "Dare to Be a Social Entrepreneur," *Business 2.0* (December 2006): 87; Edward Iwata, "Owner of Small Coffee Shop Takes On Java Titan Starbucks," *USA Today*, December 20, 2006; "Staying Pure: Howard Schultz's Formula for Starbucks," *Economist*, February 25, 2006, p. 72; Diane Anderson, "Evolution of the Eco Cup," *Business 2.0* (June 2006): 50; Bruce Horovitz, "Starbucks Nation," *USA Today*, May 19, 2006; Theresa Howard, "Starbucks Takes Up Cause for Safe Drinking Water," *USA Today*, August 2, 2005; Howard Schultz and Dori Jones Yang, *Pour Your Heart into It: How Starbucks Built a Company One Cup at a Time* (New York: Hyperion, 1997); www.starbucks.com.

NOTES

Chapter 1

1. "Sears Canada Appoints Chief Marketing Officer," Sears Canada Press Release, March 22, 2007, www.newswire.ca/en/releases/archive/March2007/22/c5748.html (viewed March 2008).

2. The Conference Board, "The CEO Challenge 2006—Top Ten Challenges," Research Report R-1380-05-RR, 2006.

3. Norma Ramage, "Big Rock Brewery Campaign Looks Back to Go Forward," *Marketing*, July 7, 2005, Big Rock Press Releases 2007, www.bigrockbeer.com/bigrockpress-releases.htm (viewed March 2008).

4. "AMA Adopts New Definition of Marketing," *Marketing News*, www.marketingpower.com/Community/ARC/Pages/Additional/Definition/default.aspx, September 15, 2004 (viewed November 11, 2008).

5. Peter Drucker, *Management: Tasks, Responsibilities, Practices* (New York: Harper and Row, 1973), pp. 64–65.

6. Statistics Canada, "Gross Domestic Product at Basic Prices, Primary Industries," January 31, 2008, www40.statcan.ca/l01/cst01/prim03.htm (viewed March 2008); Statistics Canada, "Gross Domestic Product at Basic Prices, Manufacturing and Construction Industries," January 31, 2008, www40.statcan.ca/l01/cst01/manuf10.htm (viewed March 2008).

7. "Smart Ass Intimates Launches Sassy New Signature Sayings for Spring," company press release, January 2008, www.smartassgals.com/pressreleases.htm?AdID=69 (viewed March 2008).

8. "Opening Doors to the World: Canada's International Market Access Priorities 2006," *Foreign Affairs and International Trade Canada*, November 19, 2007, www.international.gc.ca/trade-agreements-accords-commerciaux/cimar-rcami/2006/2006_3_06.aspx?lang=en (viewed March 2008).

9. "An overview of the service sector," A guide to the BC Economy and Labour Market, http://www.guidetobceconomy.org/major_industries/service_sector.htm; "Business, consumer and property services," Statistics Canada, September 7, 2007, http://www41.statcan.ca/2007/0163/ceb0163_000_e.htm (viewed June 2008).

10. B. Joseph Pine II and James Gilmore, *The Experience Economy* (Boston: Harvard Business School Press, 1999); Bernd Schmitt, *Experience Marketing* (New York: Free Press, 1999); Philip Kotler, "Dream Vacations: The Booming Market for Designed Experiences," *The Futurist* (October 1984): 7–13.

11. Irving J. Rein, Philip Kotler, Michael Hamlin, and Martin Stoller, *High Visibility*, 3rd ed. (New York: McGraw-Hill, 2006).

12. "Nova Scotia maps out online tourism strategy," *Marketing Daily*, April 25, 2007.

13. Kerry Capell, "Thinking Simple at Philips," *BusinessWeek*, December 11, 2006, p. 50; www.philips.com.

14. Carl Shapiro and Hal R. Varian, "Versioning: The Smart Way to Sell Information," *Harvard Business Review* (November–December 1998): 106–14.

15. John R. Brandt, "Dare to Be Different," *Chief Executive*, May 2003, pp. 34–38.

16. Geoffrey York and Bertrand Marotte, "Fasten your seatbelts," *The Globe and Mail*, September 15, 2007.

17. "Government Business Enterprises: Finances: 2005 and 2006," *The Daily*, November 15, 2007, www.statcan.ca/Daily/English/071115/d071115c.htm (viewed March 2008).

18. Jeffrey Rayport and John Sviokla, "Exploring the Virtual Value Chain," *Harvard Business Review* (November–December 1995): 75–85. See also their "Managing in the Marketspace," *Harvard Business Review* (November–December 1994): 141–150.

19. Mohan Sawhney, *Seven Steps to Nirvana* (New York: McGraw-Hill, 2001).

20. Constantine von Hoffman, "Armed With Intelligence," *Brandweek*, May 29, 2006, pp. 17–20.

21. Ibid., p. 19.

22. Richard Rawlinson, "Beyond Brand Management," *Strategy + Business*, Summer 2006.

23. Gail McGovern and John A. Quelch, "The Fall and Rise of the CMO," *Strategy + Business*, Winter 2004.

24. Matt Semansky, "Mom races against the clock in M&M campaign," *Marketing Daily*, April 20, 2007; Canadian Marketing Association, "Demystifying Business Intelligence—How M&M Meat Shops Chops Through Data to Gain Market and Consumer Insight," *Next: 2008 Education Sessions*, www.the-cma.org/convention/Convention.asp?WCE=C=47%7CK=226297 (viewed March 2008).

25. Adam Lashinsky, "Shoutout in Gadget Land," *Fortune*, November 10, 2003, pp. 77–86.

26. Yankelovich Partners Inc., "2005 Marketing Receptivity Survey," April 18, 2005.

27. Danielle Sacks, "MAC Cosmetics Inc.," *Fast Company*, September 2006, p. 62.

28. David Kiley, "Advertisers, Start Your Engines," *BusinessWeek*, March 6, 2006, p. 26.

29. Anya Kamenetz, "The Network Unbound," *Fast Company*, June 2006, pp. 69–73.

30. "The Blogs in the Corporate Machine," *Economist*, February 11, 2006, pp. 55–56.

31. Bruce Einhorn, "Mad as Hell in China's Blogosphere," *BusinessWeek*, August 14, 2006, p. 39.

32. Annette Bourdeau, "Oxfam's Intimidation Tactics Score Great Work," *Strategy Magazine*, March 2008, p. 14.

33. Brian Morrissey, "Banking on the Internet for Better Brand Building," *Adweek*, February 3, 2006.

34. Laura Mazur, "Personal Touch Is Now Crucial to Growing Profits," *Marketing*, November 27, 2003, p. 18.

35. Kenneth Hein, "Marketers Map Out Their GPS Ad Plans," *Brandweek*, April 24, 2006, p. 4.

36. Suzanne Vranica, "Marketers Aim New Ads at Video iPod Users," *Wall Street Journal*, January 31, 2006.

37. Li Yuan and Brian Steinberg, "Sales Call: More Ads Hit Cell Phone Screens," *Wall Street Journal*, February 2, 2006.

38. Bruce Horovitz, "In Trend Toward Vanity Food, It's Getting Personal," *USA Today*, August 9, 2006.

39. Stanley Holmes, "Into the Wild Blog Yonder," *BusinessWeek*, May 22, 2006, pp. 84–85.

40. Gerry Khermouch, "Breaking into the Name Game," *BusinessWeek*, April 7, 2003, p. 54; "China's Challenge," *Marketing Week*, October 2, 2003, pp. 22–24.

41. Bruce I. Newman, ed., *Handbook of Political Marketing* (Thousand Oaks, CA: Sage Publications, 1999); and Bruce I. Newman, *The Mass Marketing of Politics* (Thousand Oaks, CA: Sage Publications, 1999).

42. Robert J. Keith, "The Marketing Revolution," *Journal of Marketing* (January 1960): 35–38; John B. McKitterick, "What Is the Marketing Management Concept?" in Frank M. Bass, ed. *The Frontiers of Marketing Thought and Action* (Chicago: American Marketing Association, 1957), pp. 71–82; Fred J. Borch, "The Marketing Philosophy as a Way of Business Life," *The Marketing Concept: Its Meaning to Management* (Marketing series, no. 99; New York: American Management Association, 1957), pp. 3–5.

43. Theodore Levitt, "Marketing Myopia," *Harvard Business Review* (July–August 1960): 50.

44. Rohit Deshpande and John U. Farley, "Measuring Market Orientation: Generalization and Synthesis," *Journal of Market-Focused Management, 2* (1998): 213–32; Ajay K. Kohli and Bernard J. Jaworski, "Market Orientation: The Construct, Research Propositions, and Managerial Implications," *Journal of Marketing* (April 1990): 1–18; John C. Narver and Stanley F. Slater, "The Effect of a Market Orientation on Business Profitability," *Journal of Marketing* (October 1990): 20–35.

45. John C. Narver, Stanley F. Slater, and Douglas L. MacLachlan, "Responsive and Proactive Market Orientation and New-Product Success," *Journal of Product Innovation Management, 21*, no. 5 (September 2004): 334–47. See also, Ken Matsuno and John T. Mentzer, "The Effects of Strategy Type on the Market Orientation–Performance Relationship," *Journal on Marketing* (October 2000): 1–16.

46. Evert Gummesson, *Total Relationship Marketing* (Boston: Butterworth-Heinemann, 1999); Regis McKenna, *Relationship Marketing* (Reading, MA: Addison-Wesley, 1991); Martin Christopher, Adrian Payne, and David Ballantyne, *Relationship Marketing: Bringing Quality, Customer Service, and Marketing Together* (Oxford, UK: Butterworth-Heinemann, 1991).

47. James C. Anderson, Hakan Hakansson, and Jan Johanson, "Dyadic Business Relationships within a Business Network Context," *Journal of Marketing* (October 15, 1994): 1–15.

48. Larry Selden and Yoko S. Selden, "Profitable Customer: The Key to Great Brands," *Advertising Age* (July 10, 2006): S7.

49. Jeff Buckstein, "Navigating the outsourcing minefield," *The Globe and Mail*, November 7, 2007.

50. For another framework, see George S. Day, "The Capabilities of Market-Driven Organizations," *Journal of Marketing, 58*, no. 4 (October 1994): 37–52; Neil H. Borden, "The Concept of the Marketing Mix," *Journal of Advertising Research, 4* (June 1964): 2–7.

51. E. Jerome McCarthy and William D. Perreault, *Basic Marketing: A Global-Managerial Approach,* 14th ed. (Homewood, IL: McGraw-Hill Irwin, 2002).

52. Chekitan S. Dev and Don E. Schultz, "A Customer-Focused Approach Can Bring the Current Marketing Mix into the 21st Century," *Marketing Management, 14* (January/February 2005).

53. Allison Fass, "Theirspace.com," *Forbes*, May 8, 2006, pp. 122–24.

54. Christian Homburg, John P. Workman Jr., and Harley Krohmen, "Marketing's Influence within the Firm," *Journal of Marketing* (January 1999): 1–15.

55. Samar Farah, "Future Tense," Editorial, *CMO Magazine*, May 2005.

56. Robert Shaw and David Merrick, *Marketing Payback: Is Your Marketing Profitable?* (London, UK: Pearson Education, 2005).

57. Rajendra Sisodia, David Wolfe, and Jagdish Sheth, *Firms of Endearment: How World-Class Companies Profit from Passion* (Upper Saddle River, NJ: Wharton School Publishing, 2007).

58. *Point*, June 2005, p. 4.

59. John Ehernfield, "Feeding the Beast," *Fast Company* (December 2006/January 2007): 41–43.

60. If choosing to develop a strategic corporate social-responsibility program, see Michael E. Porter and Mark R. Kramer, "Strategy and Society: The Link between Competitive Advantage and Corporate Social Responsibility," *Harvard Business Review* (December 2006): 78–92.

61. Jeffrey Hollender and Stephen Fenichell, *What Matters Most* (New York: Basic Books, 2004), p. 168.

62. Jonathan Glancey, "The Private World of the Walkman," *Guardian*, October 11, 1999.

63. Joann Muller, "Ford: Why It's Worse Than You Think," *BusinessWeek*, June 25, 2001; Ford *1999 Annual Report*; Greg Keenan, "Six Degrees of Perfection," *The Globe and Mail*, December 20, 2000.

Chapter 2

1. Nirmalya Kumar, *Marketing as Strategy: The CEO's Agenda for Driving Growth and Innovation* (Boston: Harvard Business School Press, 2004).

2. Frederick E. Webster, Jr., "The Future Role of Marketing in the Organization," in *Reflections on the Futures of Marketing*, edited by Donald R. Lehmann and Katherine Jocz (Cambridge, MA: Marketing Science Institute, 1997), pp. 39–66.

3. Michael E. Porter, *Competitive Advantage: Creating and Sustaining Superior Performance* (New York: The Free Press, 1985).

4. Robert Hiebeler, Thomas B. Kelly, and Charles Ketteman, *Best Practices: Building Your Business with Customer-Focused Solutions* (New York: Simon and Schuster, 1998).

5. James Carbone, "At Today's Cisco Systems, the Fewer Suppliers the Better," *Purchasing*, April 20, 2006, pp. 18–21.

6. Michael Hammer and James Champy, *Reengineering the Corporation* (New York: HarperBusiness, 1993).

7. Jon R. Katzenbach and Douglas K. Smith, *The Wisdom of Teams: Creating the High-Performance Organization* (Boston: Harvard Business School Press, 1993); Hammer and Champy, *Reengineering the Corporation.*

8. Michael Johnsen, "Profiting from a First-Place Focus," *Drug Store News*, January 20, 2003, p. 26.

9. Myron Magnet, "The New Golden Rule of Business," *Fortune*, November 28, 1994, pp. 60–64.

10. Marina Strauss, "Lululemon stretched by demand," *The Globe and Mail*, September 10, 2007.

11. C. K. Prahalad and Gary Hamel, "The Core Competence of the Corporation," *Harvard Business Review*, (May–June 1990): 79–91.

12. John Menary, "Institutional Report Form Questions (for the Year April 2002–March 2003)," Canada Foundation for Innovation website, www.innovation.ca (viewed July 7, 2004); Hospital for Sick Children website, www.sickkids.on.ca (viewed July 7, 2004).

13. George S. Day, "The Capabilities of Market-Driven Organizations," *Journal of Marketing* (October 1994): 38.

14. "Kodak Plans to Cut Up to 5,000 More Jobs," *Bloomberg News*, February 8, 2007; Leon Lazaroff, "Kodak's Big Picture Focusing on Image Change," *Chicago Tribune*, January 29, 2006.

15. *Pew Internet and American Life Project Survey*, November–December 2000.

16. Kasuaki Ushikubo, "A Method of Structure Analysis for Developing Product Concepts and Its Applications," *European Research, 14*, no. 4, 1986, 174–175.

17. Yoram J. Wind and Vijay Mahajan with Robert E. Gunther, *Convergence Marketing: Strategies for Reaching the New Hybrid Consumer* (Upper Saddle River, NJ: Prentice Hall PTR, 2002).

18. Peter Drucker, *Management: Tasks, Responsibilities and Practices* (New York: Harper and Row, 1973), Ch. 7.

19. Ralph A. Oliva, "Nowhere to Hide," *Marketing Management*, July/August 2001, pp. 44–46.

20. "Bioniche Recognized as One of the Top 10 Life Science Companies in Canada," Bioniche news release, December 4, 2007.

21. "DRAXIS Granted U.S. Patent for Bifunctional Compounds," DRAXIS news release, October 1, 2003, www.draxis.com/news/2003/news01102003.asp.

22. *Pew Internet and American Life Project Survey*, November–December 2000.

23. *The Economist: Business Miscellany* (London: Profile Books Ltd., 2005), pp. 32–33.

24. Chuck Martin, *Net Future* (New York: McGraw-Hill, 1999).

25. Jeffrey F. Rayport and Bernard J. Jaworski, *e-commerce* (New York: McGraw-Hill, 2001), p. 116.

26. This section is based on Chapter 16 of Robert M. Grant's, *Contemporary Strategy Analysis*, 5th ed., (Malden, MA: Blackwell Publishing, 2005).

27. The same matrix can be expanded into nine cells by adding modified products and modified markets. See S. J. Johnson and Conrad Jones, "How to Organize for New Products," *Harvard Business Review* (May–June 1957): 49–62.

28. www.starbucks.com; Howard Schultz, *Pour Your Heart into It* (New York: Hyperion, 1997); Andy Serwer, "Hot Starbucks to Go," *Fortune*, January 26, 2004, pp. 60–74.

29. Tim Goodman, "NBC Everywhere?" *San Francisco Chronicle*, September 4, 2003, p. E. 1.

30. Bobby White, "Expanding into Consumer Electronics, Cisco Aims to Jazz Up its Stodgy Image," *Wall Street Journal*, September 6, 2006.

31. "The Consumer-Centric Marketer as Guru of Exponential Growth: Kelly Styring," *KNOW*, Spring/Summer 2006; www.knowledgenetworks.com.

32. Jena McGregor, "The World's Most Innovative Companies," *BusinessWeek*, April 24, 2006, pp. 63–74.

33. E. Jerome McCarthy, *Basic Marketing: A Managerial Approach*, 12th ed. (Homewood, IL: Irwin, 1996).

34. Dev Patnaik, "Insight," *In* (June 2006): 32.

35. Paul J. H. Shoemaker, "Scenario Plannning: A Tool for Strategic Thinking," *Sloan Management Review* (Winter 1995): 25–40.

36. Philip Kotler, *Kotler on Marketing* (New York: Free Press, 1999).

37. Ibid.

38. Dominic Dodd and Ken Favaro, "Managing the Right Tension," *Harvard Business Review* (December 2006): 62–74.

39. Ram Charan and Noel M. Tichy, *Every Business Is a Growth Business: How Your Company Can Prosper Year after Year* (New York: Times Business, Random House, 1998).

40. Michael E. Porter, *Competitive Strategy: Techniques for Analyzing Industries and Competitors* (New York: The Free Press, 1980), Ch. 2.

41. Stephen C. Miller, "It Protects Electronic Devices from Power Surges and Gives Dust Bunnies No Place to Hide," *New York Times*, September 14, 2006; www.belkin.com/pressrom/releases/uploads/08_15_06Concealed_CompactSurge.html.

42. Michael E. Porter, "What Is Strategy?" *Harvard Business Review* (November–December 1996): 61–78.

43. "Michelin Begins Grand Prix Promotion," *Adnews On-Line Daily*, May 21, 2002.

44. For some readings on strategic alliances, see Peter Lorange and Johan Roos, *Strategic Alliances: Formation, Implementation and Evolution* (Cambridge, MA: Blackwell, 1992); Jordan D. Lewis, *Partnerships for Profit: Structuring and Managing Strategic Alliances* (New York: The Free Press, 1990); John R. Harbison and Peter Pekar Jr., *Smart Alliances: A Practical Guide to Repeatable Success* (San Francisco, CA: Jossey-Bass, 1998); *Harvard Business Review on Strategic Alliances* (Cambridge, MA: Harvard Business School Press, 2002).

45. Anonymous, "Trends Report: Looking for the Pharmaceutical-Biotechnology Alliance Creates a Win-Win," *Health and Medicine Week*, December 29, 2003, p. 726.

46. Robin Cooper and Robert S. Kaplan, "Profit Priorities from Activity-Based Costing," *Harvard Business Review* (May–June 1991): 130–135.

47. Robert S. Kaplan and David P. Norton, *The Balanced Scorecard: Translating Strategy into Action* (Boston: Harvard Business School Press, 1996), as a tool for monitoring stakeholder satisfaction.

48. Thomas J. Peters and Robert H. Waterman Jr., *In Search of Excellence: Lessons from America's Best-Run Companies* (New York: Harper and Row, 1982), pp. 9–12.

49. Terrence E. Deal and Allan A. Kennedy, *Corporate Cultures: The Rites and Rituals of Corporate Life* (Reading, MA: Addison-Wesley, 1982); "Corporate Culture," *BusinessWeek*, October 27, 1980, pp. 148–160; Stanley M. Davis, *Managing Corporate Culture* (Cambridge, MA: Ballinger, 1984); John P. Kotter and James L. Heskett, *Corporate Culture and Performance* (New York: The Free Press, 1992).

50. Nitin Nohria, William Joyce, and Bruce Roberson, "What Really Works," *Harvard Business Review, 81*, no. 7 (2003): 42–53.

51. Marian Burk Wood, *The Marketing Plan: A Handbook* (Upper Saddle River, NJ: Prentice Hall, 2003).

52. Donald R. Lehmann and Russell S. Winer, *Product Management*, 3rd ed (Boston, MA: McGraw-Hill/Irwin, 2001).

Chapter 3

1. Susan Warren, "Pillow Talk: Stackers Outnumber Plumpers; Don't Mention Drool," *Wall Street Journal*, January 8, 1998, p. B1.

2. Steve Weinstein, "Realistic Partnering: How to Do Business Better," *Progressive Grocer, 71* (February 1992): 80–85; Charles Fishman, "The Wal-Mart You Don't Know," *Fast Company* (December 2003): 68–80.

3. "Clarica receives national recognition for innovative e-Business achievements: Web-enabled sales force," www.insurance-canada.ca/distribution/canada/Clarica200106.php, May 23, 2001 (viewed September 16, 2008).

4. Julie Forster, "You Deserve a Better Break Today," *BusinessWeek*, September 30, 2002, p. 42.

5. Kevin Helliker, "Smile: That Cranky Shopper May Be a Store Spy," *Wall Street Journal*, November 30, 1994, pp. B1, B6; Edward F. McQuarrie, *Customer Visits: Building a Better Market Focus*, 2nd ed. (Newbury Park, CA: Sage Press, 1998).

6. Kim Girard, "Strategies to Turn Stealth Into Wealth," *Business 2.0*, May 2003, p. 66.

7. Andy Serwer, "P&G's Covert Operation," *Fortune*, September 17, 2001, pp. 42–44.

8. Biz360 website, www.biz360.com/partner/contentpartners.aspx (viewed September 16, 2008).

9. Robin T. Peterson and Zhilin Yang, "Web Product Reviews Help Strategy," *Marketing News*, April 7, 2004, p. 18.

10. Peter Hadekel, "Data mining company arms geologists with the right tools to strike gold," *The Gazette*, February 15, 2008, p. B1.

11. See www.badfads.com for examples of fads and collectibles through the years.

12. Matt Andrejczak, "Safeway to Expand Organic Food Sales," *Market Watch*, December 13, 2007, www.marketwatch.com/news/story/safeway-expand-organic-food-sales/story.aspx?guid=%7B6FEA631B-AB3B-48F3-B467-74CFC0CFF044%7D (viewed February 20, 2008); Birchall, Jonathan, "Safeway and Carrefour Form Organic Link," *Financial Times*, January 8, 2008, p. 21.

13. John Naisbitt and Patricia Aburdene, *Megatrends 2000* (New York: Avon Books, 1990).

14. U. S. Census Bureau, www.census.gov/ipc/www/idb/worldpopinfo.html (viewed March 17, 2008).

15. Statistics Canada, "Canada's Population Estimates," *The Daily*, December 19, 2007, www.statcan.ca/Daily/English/071219/d071219b.htm (viewed March 17, 2008).

16. Statistics Canada, "A Profile of the Canadian Population: Where We Live," 2001 Census-Release 1, March 12, 2002, www.geodepot.statscan.ca/Diss/Highlights/Highlights_e.cfm (viewed June 5, 2002); and *The Daily*, "Latest Indicators: Population Estimate (as of July 2004)," www.statcan.ca/start.html (viewed November 1, 2004).

17. Although over 10-years old, this breakdown provides useful perspective. See Donella H. Meadows, Dennis L. Meadows, and Jorgen Randers, *Beyond Limits* (Chelsea Green Publishing Company, 1993), for some commentary.

18. U. S. Census Bureau, IDB Aggregation Data, "Vital Rates and Events," www.census.gov/cgi-bin/ipc/agggen (viewed April 6, 2008).

19. Sally D. Goll, "Marketing: China (Only) Children Get the Royal Treatment," *Wall Street Journal*, February 8, 1995, p. B1.

20. U. S. Census Bureau, IDB Aggregation Data, "Mid-year Population by Age and Sex," www.census.gov/cgi-bin/ipc/idbagg (viewed April 6, 2008).

21. "Survey: Forever Young," *The Economist*, March 27, 2004, pp. 53–54.

22. Statistics Canada, "Age Groups and Sex for the Population," in *2006 Census*, www.statcan.ca (viewed June 20, 2008).

23. Chris Daniels, "Canada Post's Second Life," *Marketing Magazine*, December 10, 2007, pp. 40–42.

24. "Further Along the X Axis," *American Demographics* (May 2004): 21–24.

25. "Pepsi-Cola Canada Ltd.–Making Out During Super Bowl XLI," *CNW* Group, January 29, 2007, www.canadanewswire.ca/en/media/details.cgi?EventID=216 (viewed February 18, 2008); "Diet Pepsi to Bring 90 Seconds of Laugh-Out-Loud Humour to the Super Bowl," *Smart Money*, February 2, 2008, www.smartmoney.com/news/pr/index.cfm?story=PR-20080202-000185-0828 (viewed February 18, 2008).

26. David Leonhardt, "Hey Kids, Buy This," *BusinessWeek*, June 30, 1997, pp. 62–67; Don Tapscott, "*Growing Up Digital; The Rise of the Net Generation* (New York: McGraw Hill, 1997); Statistics Canada, "Canadian Statistics: Population by Age and Sex (as of July 1, 2004)," www.statcan.ca/english/Pgdb/demo10a.htm.

27. Data for this section were drawn from Statistics Canada 2006 Census, "Ethnic Origin and Visible Minorities," www12.statcan.ca/english/census06/release/ethnicorigin.cfm (viewed April 2, 2008).

28. Bobby Siu, "Ethnic Marketing: Demographic Wave Well Worth Riding," *Strategy: The Canadian Marketing Report*, July 6, 1998, p. 15; and David Todd, "Special Report: Multicultural Marketing: Nike Takes It to the Streets," *Strategy: The Canadian Marketing Report*, August 17, 1998, p. 26.

29. Siu, "Ethnic Marketing: Demographic Wave Well Worth Riding"; Todd, "Special Report: Multicultural Marketing: Nike Takes It to the Streets."

30. Statistics Canada 2006 Census, "Population by Mother Tongue and Age Groups," www12.statcan.ca/english/census06/data/highlights/Language/Index.cfm (viewed April 6, 2008).

31. Statistics Canada, "Canadians with Disabilities," Canadian Centre for Justice Statistics Profile Series, June 2001, www.statscan.ca/english/freepub/850033MIE01002.pdf (viewed May 26, 2002).

32. ABC Canada, "Adult Literacy Canada," www.abc-canada.org/literacy_facts/ (viewed January 27, 2005); Statistics Canada, "Canadians with Literacy Problems," Canadian Centre for Justice Statistics Profile Series, June 2001, www.statscan.ca/english/freepub/85F0033MIE/85F0033MIE01003.pdf (viewed May 26, 2002); Statistics Canada, "Population 15 Years and Over by Highest Level of Schooling, by Provinces and Territories (2001 Census)," www.statscan.ca/english/Pgdb/educ43a.htm (viewed November 1, 2004); Statistics Canada, "Population 15 Years and Over by Highest Degree, Certificate or Diploma, by Provinces and Territories (2001 Census)," www.statscan.ca/english/Pgdb/educ41a.htm (viewed November 1, 2004).

33. Angela Phillips, "Friends Are the New Family," *The Guardian*, December 12, 2003, p. 1.

34. Michelle Halpren, "In Your Face," *Marketing Magazine*, July 16, 2007, pp. 45–47; Facebook.com Statistics, www.facebook.com/press/info.php?statistics (viewed March 20, 2008).

35. "Study: Healthcare use among gay, lesbian, and bisexual Canadians," *The Daily*, Statistics Canada, March 19, 2008, www.statcan.ca/Daily/English/080319/d080319b.htm (viewed April 8, 2008).

36. Rebecca Gardyn, "A Market Kept in the Closet," *American Demographics* (November 2001): 37–43.

37. Hollie Shaw, "Pink Money Talks," *Financial Post*, April 18, 2008, www.financialpost.com/news/story.html?id=455619 (viewed June 15, 2008).

38. Statistics Canada, "Population and dwelling counts, for Canada, provinces and territories, 2006 and 2001 censuses," www12.statcan.ca/english/census06/data/popdwell/Table.cfm?T=101&SR=1&S=5&O=D (viewed April 10, 2008).

39. Statistics Canada, "A Profile of the Canadian Population: Where We Live," 2001 Census-Release 1, March 12, 2002, www.geodepot.statcan.ca/Diss/Highlights/Highlights_e.cfm (viewed June 5, 2002); Statistics Canada and Ross Finnie, "The Effects of Inter-Provincial Mobility on Individuals' Earnings: Panel Model Estimated for Canada," Analytical Studies Branch Research Paper Series, Report 163, Catalogue No. 11F0019MIE200163, October 2001, www.collection.nlc-bnc.ca/100/20/301/statscan/research_paper_analytical _11f0019-e/no163/11Foo19MIE011163.pdf (viewed September 22, 2002).

40. Lauri J. Flynn, "Not Just a Copy Shop Any Longer, Kinko's Pushes Its Computer Services," *New York Times*, July 6, 1998, p. D1; www.kinkos.com; "FedEx Kinko's Escalates Expansion Efforts," *Business Wire*, August 6, 2007, findarticles.com/p/articles/mi_m0EIN/is_2007_August_6/ai_n19395817 (viewed February 20, 2008).

41. Ian Rowley, "My Other Car is a Tata," *BusinessWeek*, January 14, 2008, pp. 33–34.

42. Statistics Canada, "Earnings and Incomes of Canadians Over the Past Quarter Century, 2006 Census: Highlights," www12.statcan.ca/english/census06/analysis/income/highlights.cfm#earnings2 (viewed June 14, 2008).

43. Chris Daniels, "Almost Rich," *Marketing Magazine Online*, www.marketingmag.ca, April 26, 2004 (viewed November 3, 2004).

44. Statistics Canada, "Recent Trends in Household Net Worth," Latest Developments in the Canadian Economic Accounts, June 24, 2004, www.statcan.ca/english/freepub/13-605-XIE/2003001/chronology/2004networth/index.htm (viewed November 3, 2004); "Credit Card Statistics," October 2003, Canadian Bankers Association, www.cba.ca/en/ViewDocument.asp?fl=6&sl=110&tl=&docid=421 (viewed November 3, 2004).

45. Stephen Baker and Manjeet Kripalani, "Software: Will Outsourcing Hurt America's Supremacy?" *BusinessWeek*, March 1, 2004, pp. 84–94; Jennifer Reingold, "Into Thin Air," *Fast Company* (April 2004): 76–82.

46. "Love Hurts when Wars Paid for by Gem Trade," *Toronto Star*, February 15, 2007, p. R8.

47. Pamela Paul, "Corporate Responsibility," *American Demographics* (May 2002): 24–25.

48. Paul Wenske, "You Too Could Lose $19,000!" *Kansas City Star*, October 31, 1999; "Clearing House Suit Chronology," Associated Press, January 26, 2001.

49. www.madd.ca/english/redribbon/index.html (viewed February 20, 2008).

50. Michael Adams, *Fire and Ice: The United States, Canada and the Myth of Converging Values* (Toronto: Penguin Canada, 2003).

51. David MacDonald and Michael Adams, "We Are What We Drive," *Marketing Magazine*, March 15, 2004; Lynn Fletcher, "UNDER SIEGE, but Still Upbeat," *Marketing Magazine Online*, www.marketingmag.ca, October 27, 2003 (viewed November 3, 2004).

52. Laura Zinn, "Teens: Here Comes the Biggest Wave Yet," *BusinessWeek*, April 11, 2004, pp. 76–86.

53. Rebecca Gardyn, "Eco-Friend or Foe," *American Demographics*, October 2003, pp. 12–13. See also Rebecca Gardyn, "Being Green," *American Demographics*, September 2002, pp. 10–11.

54. OPEC website, www.opec.org/home/basket.aspx (viewed July 17, 2008).

55. Environment Canada, www.ec.gc.ca/EnviroRegs/eng/ ceparegs.cfm (viewed November 3, 2004).

56. Keith McArthur, "Canadians Put the Environment First," *The Globe and Mail*, June 23, 1997, p. A4.

57. Phil Hahn, "iPhone Hysteria Reaches Epic Proportions," *CTV.ca*, June 27, 2007, www.ctv.ca/servlet/ArticleNews/story/CTVNews/20070627/iPhone_hype_070627/20070627?hub=Specials (viewed February 17, 2008); Kris Abel, "Apple Unveils iPhone," CTV.ca, January 9, 2007, krisabel.ctv.ca/blog/_archives/2007/1/9/2635773.html (viewed Feb. 17, 2008); "Global Cellphone Penetration Reaches 50 pct," Reuters UK, November 29, 2007, investing.reuters.co.uk/news/articleinvesting.aspx?type=media&storyID=nL29172095 (viewed February 17, 2008).

58. Statistics Canada, *The Daily*, "Are There High-Tech Industries or Only High-Tech Firms?" December 10, 1998, www.statcan.ca/English/981210/d981210.htm (viewed September 22, 2002); Statistics Canada, "Abstract: Canadian agriculture at a glance," www.statcan.ca:8096/bsolc/english/bsolc?catno=96-325-X20010006959 (viewed November 3, 2004).

59. Cathy Ellis, "Banff upgrades bus fare boxes," *Calgary Herald*, Calgary, AB: Jan 8, 2008. p. B7.

60. National Research Council of Canada, "GERD as a % of GDP for Selected OECD Countries 2001," September 2, 2004, www.nserc.gc.ca/about/stats/2002-2003/en/slides/slide82.htm (viewed January 27, 2005).

61. Research Info Source, "Canada's Top 100 Corporate R&D Spenders 2002," www.researchinfosource.com/2002-top100.pdf (viewed January 27, 2005).

62. See Dorothy Cohen, *Legal Issues on Marketing Decision Making* (Cincinnati: South-Western, 1995).

63. Rebecca Gardyn, "Swap Meet," *American Demographics* (July 2001): 51–55.

64. Pamela Paul, "Mixed Signals," *American Demographics* (July 2001): 45–49.

Chapter 4

1. Thomas Kinnear and Ann Root, eds., *1994 Survey of Market Research* (Chicago: American Marketing Association, 1994).

2. "True Believers," *BusinessWeek*, Winter 2006, www.businessweek.com/magazine/content/06_52/b4015401.htm (viewed March 1, 2008); Emily Sweeney, "Karmaloop Shapes Urban Fashion by Spotting Trends Where They Start," *Boston Globe*, July 8, 2004, p. D3.

3. Kevin J. Clancy and Robert S. Shulman, *Marketing Myths That Are Killing Business* (New York: McGraw-Hill, 1994), p. 58; Phaedra Hise, "Comprehensive CompuServe," *Inc.* (June 1994): 109; "Business Bulletin: Studying the Competition," *Wall Street Journal*, pp. A1–5.

4. Kate Maddox, "The ROI of Research," *B to B*, April 5, 2004, pp. 25, 28.

5. For some background information on in-flight Internet service, see "In-Flight Dogfight," *Business2.Com*, January 9, 2001, pp. 84–91; John Blau, "In-Flight Internet Service Ready for Takeoff," *IDG News Service*, June 14, 2002; "Boeing In-Flight Internet Plan Goes Airborne," *The Associated Press*, April 18, 2004.

6. For a discussion of the decision-theory approach to the value of research, see Donald R. Lehmann, Sunil Gupta, and Joel Steckel, *Market Research* (Reading, MA: Addison-Wesley, 1997).

7. Allison Stein Wellner, "Look Who's Watching," *Continental* (April 2003): 39–41; Linda Tischler, "Every Move You Make," *Fast Company* (April 2004): 73–75.

8. Scott Christie, "Burger King Branches Out With Healthful Fresh-Cut Option," *Fresh Cut*, www.freshcut.com/pages/arts.php?ns=741 (viewed March 1, 2008).

9. www.homedepotopinion.com (viewed March 1, 2008).

10. Dennis W. Rook, "Loss of Vision: Focus Groups Fail to Connect Theory, Current Practice," *Marketing News*, September 15, 2003, p. 40.

11. Bruce Nussbaum, "The Power of Design," *BusinessWeek*, May 17, 2004, pp. 86–94.

12. Roger D. Blackwell, James S. Hensel, Michael B. Phillips, and Brian Sternthal, *Laboratory Equipment for Marketing Research* (Dubuque, IA: Kendall/Hunt, 1970); Wally Wood, "The Race to Replace Memory," *Marketing and Media Decisions* (July 1986): 166–167. See also Gerald Zaltman, "Rethinking Market Research: Putting People Back In," *Journal of Marketing Research, 34*, no. 4 (November 1997): 424–437; Andy Raskin, "A Face Any Business Can Trust," *Business 2.0*, December 2003, pp. 58–60; Louise Witt, "Inside Intent," *American Demographics* (March 2004): 34–39.

13. www.asientertainment.com.

14. Adam Froman, "Real Time Research," *Marketing Magazine Online*, www.marketingmag.ca, June 7, 2004 (viewed November 5, 2004).

15. Rajiv Grover and Marco Vriens, *The Handbook of Marketing Research; Uses, Misuses, and Future Advances* (Thousand Oaks, CA: Sage Publications, 2006), p. 112; Cam Davis, "2007 Online Research Forum Net Gain: Best Practices and Innovations, MRIA's First Online Research Forum Conference: Setting the New Standards," 2007.

16. www.ideastorm.com (viewed February 24, 2008), "Marketing 2.0," *Marketing*, April 30, 2007, www.marketingmag.ca/magazine/current/feature/article.jsp?content=20070430_69539_69539 (viewed February 25, 2008).

17. Peter Fuller, "A Two-Way Conversation," *Brandweek*, February 25, 2002, pp. 21–27.

18. www.ipsos.ca (viewed February 24, 2008); Ipsos-Reid Canada, www.ipsos-reid.com/ca/index.cfm (viewed May 22, 2002); Terry Poulton, "Givin' It Away," *Strategy: The Canadian Marketing Report*, January 28, 2002, p. 24.

19. Canadian Radio-television and Telecommunications Commission, "Facts about September 2008 launch of the National Do Not Call List," July 3, 2007, www.crtc.gc.ca/eng/INFO_SHT/t1026.htm (viewed April 18, 2008).

20. Muriel Draaisma, "Do-not-call list," *CBC News*, February 27, 2008, www.cbc.ca/news/background/telemarketing (viewed February 29, 2008); "Majority don't want telemarketers' calls: Survey," *Edmonton Journal*, October 31, 2007, pg. A7.

21. Joe Dysart, "Cutting Market Research Costs with On-Site Surveys," *The Secured Lender*, March/April 2004, pp. 64–67.

22. Suzy Bashford, "The Opinion Formers," *Revolution*, May 2004, pp. 42–46.

23. Bob Lamons, "Eureka! Future of B-to-B Research Is Online," *Marketing News*, September 24, 2001, pp. 9–10.

24. Lisa D'Innocenzo, "Focus Groups for a New Age?" *Strategy Magazine Online*, www.strategymag.com, August 23, 2004 (viewed November 5, 2004).

25. Kevin J. Clancy and Peter C. Krieg, *Counterintuitive Marketing: How Great Results Come from Uncommon Sense* (New York: The Free Press, 2000).

26. John D. C. Little, "Decision Support Systems for Marketing Managers," *Journal of Marketing* (Summer 1979): 11. See "Special Issue on Managerial Decision Making," *Marketing Science, 18*, no. 3 (1999) for some contemporary perspectives.

27. Leonard M. Lodish, "CALLPLAN: An Interactive Salesman's Call Planning System," *Management Science* (December 1971): 25–40.

28. Christine Moorman, Gerald Zaltman, and Rohit Deshpandé, "Relationships Between Providers and Users of Market Research: The Dynamics of Trust Within and Between Organizations," *Journal of Marketing Research, 29* (August 1992): 314–328.

29. Stephanie Bentley and John Vidal, "Big Mac Under Attack," *Marketing Week*, June 26, 1997, *20*, no. 13, pp. 38–41.

30. John McManus, "Stumbling Into Intelligence," *American Demographics* (April 2004): 22–25.

31. John Gaffney, "The Buzz Must Go On," *Business 2.0* (February 2002): 49–50.

32. Tim Ambler, *Marketing and the Bottom Line: The New Metrics of Corporate Wealth* (London: FT Prentice-Hall, 2000).

33. Bob Donath, "Employ Marketing Metrics with a Track Record," *Marketing News*, September 15, 2003, p. 12.

34. Kusum L. Ailawadi, Donald R. Lehmann, and Scott A. Neslin, "Revenue Premium as an Outcome Measure of Brand Equity," *Journal of Marketing, 67* (October 2003): 1–17.

35. Tim Ambler, *Marketing and the Bottom Line: The New Metrics of Corporate Wealth* (London: FT Prentice-Hall, 2000); Tim Ambler, "What Does Marketing Success Look Like?," *Marketing Management* (Spring 2001): 13–18.

36. Fred Vogelstein, "Mighty Amazon," *Fortune*, May 26, 2003, pp. 60–74.

37. Samson Okalow, "What's in Your Wallet?" *Strategy Magazine Online*, www.strategymag.com, September 17, 2004 (viewed November 5, 2004).

38. Robert S. Kaplan and David P Norton, *The Balanced Scorecard* (Boston: Harvard Business School Press, 1996).

39. Marion Debruyne and Katrina Hubbard, "Marketing Metrics," working paper series, Conference Summary, Marketing Science Institute, Report No. 00-119, 2000.

40. Alfred R. Oxenfeldt, "How to Use Market-Share Measurement," *Harvard Business Review* (January–February 1969): 59–68.

41. There is a one-half chance that a successive observation will be higher or lower. Therefore, the probability of finding six successively higher values is given by (1/2) to the sixth, or 1/64.

42. Alternatively, companies need to focus on factors affecting shareholder value. The goal of marketing planning is to increase shareholder value, which is the present value of the future income stream created by the company's present actions. Rate-of-return analysis usually focuses on only one year's results. See Alfred Rapport, *Creating Shareholder Value*, rev. ed. (New York: The Free Press, 1997).

43. For additional reading on financial analysis, see Peter L. Mullins, *Measuring Customer and Product Line Profitability* (Washington, DC: Distribution Research and Education Foundation, 1984).

44. The MAC Group, *Distribution: A Competitive Weapon* (Cambridge, MA: MAC Group, 1985), p. 20.

45. Robin Cooper and Robert S. Kaplan, "Profit Priorities from Activity-Based Costing," *Harvard Business Review* (May–June 1991): 130–135.

46. Jack Neff, "P&G, Clorox Rediscover Modeling," *Advertising Age*, March 29, 2004, p. 10.

47. Laura Q. Hughes, "Econometrics Take Root," *Advertising Age*, August 5, 2002, p. S4.

48. Burt Helm, "Energy Drinks Build Their Buzz," *BusinessWeek*, January 5, 2005, www.businessweek.com/smallbiz/content/jan2005/sb2005015_8196_sb017.htm (viewed February 26, 2008).

49. Rebecca Harris, "Heir Apparent," *Marketing*, August 13, 2007, www.marketingmag.ca/magazine/current/feature/article.jsp?content=20070813_70048_70048 (viewed February 25, 2008); Loblaw Companies Ltd., "Financial Highlights," *Loblaw Companies Limited: 2007 Annual Report*, pp. 1–2.

50. For a good discussion and illustration, see Roger J. Best, *Market-Based Management*, 2nd ed. (Upper Saddle River, NJ: Prentice Hall, 2000), pp. 71–75.

51. Ipsos Reid, "Almost 70 Per Cent of Canadian Home Owners Opt for Conservative Fixed Rate Mortgage Strategy According to New BMO Bank of Montreal Survey," www.ipsos-na.com/news/pressrelease.cfm?id=2434, October 29, 2004 (viewed November 6, 2004).

52. For further discussion, see Gary L. Lilien, Philip Kotler, and K. Sridhar Moorthy, *Marketing Models* (Upper Saddle River, NJ: Prentice Hall, 1992).

53. www.naics.com; www.census.gov/epcd/naics02.

54. Brian Sternthal and Alice M. Tybout, "Segmentation and Targeting," in *Kellogg on Marketing*, Dawn Iacobucci, ed. (New York: John Wiley & Sons, 2001), pp. 3–30.

55. Norman Dalkey and Olaf Helmer, "An Experimental Application of the Delphi Method to the Use of Experts," *Management Science* (April 1963): 458–467. See also Roger J. Best, "An Experiment in Delphi Estimation in Marketing Decision Making," *Journal of Marketing Research* (November 1974): 447–452. For an excellent overview of market forecasting, see Scott Armstrong, ed., *Principles of Forecasting: A Handbook for Researchers and Practitioners* (Norwell, MA: Kluwer Academic Publishers, 2001) and his website: http://fourps.wharton.upenn.edu/forecast/handbook.html.

Chapter 5

1. From eBay Media Centre: eBay Marketplace Fast Facts, news.ebay.com/fastfacts_ebay_marketplace.cfm (viewed May 20, 2008).

2. Glen L. Urban, "The Emerging Era of Customer Advocacy," *MIT Sloan Management Review* (Winter 2004): 77–82; Robert D. Hof, "The eBay Economy," *BusinessWeek*, August 25, 2003, pp. 125–128; http://pages.ebay.ca/community/aboutebay/index.html?ssPageName=STRK:STMP:245 (viewed September 30, 2004).

3. Glen L. Urban, "The Emerging Era of Customer Advocacy," *MIT Sloan Management Review*, Winter 2004, 45, no. 2, p. 77.

4. Irwin P. Levin and Richard D. Johnson, "Estimating Price-Quality Tradeoffs Using Comparative Judgments," *Journal of Consumer Research* (June 11, 1984): 593–600. Customer perceived value can be measured as a difference or as a ratio. If total customer value is $20 000 and total customer cost is $16 000, then the customer perceived value is $4000 (measured as a difference) or 1.25 (measured as a ratio). Ratios that are used to compare offers are often called *value-price ratios*.

5. For more on customer perceived value, see David C. Swaddling and Charles Miller, *Customer Power* (Dublin, OH: The Wellington Press, 2001).

6. Richard L. Oliver, "*Satisfaction: A Behavioral Perspective on the Consumer*," 1997, Irwin-McGrawHill, New York, NY.

7. Michael J. Lanning, *Delivering Profitable Value* (Oxford, UK: Capstone, 1998).

8. Larry Selden and Geoffrey Colvin, "What Customers Want," *Fortune*, July 7, 2003, pp. 122–127.

9. Simon Knox and Stan Maklan, *Competing on Value: Bridging the Gap Between Brand and Customer Value* (London, UK: Financial Times, 1998). See also Richard A. Spreng, Scott B. MacKenzie, and Richard W. Olshawskiy, "A Reexamination of the Determinants of Consumer Satisfaction," *Journal of Marketing*, 3 (July 1996): 15–32.

10. WestJet website, www.westjet.com (viewed May 20, 2008).

11. For some provocative analysis, see Susan Fournier and David Glenmick, "Rediscovering Satisfaction," *Journal of Marketing* (October 1999): pp. 5–23.

12. For an interesting analysis of the effects of different types of expectations, see William Boulding, Ajay Kalra, and Richard Staelin, "The Quality Double Whammy," *Marketing Service, 18*, no. 4 (1999): 463–484.

13. www.saturn.com; "Saturn Illustrates Value of Customer Loyalty," *Louisville Courier-Journal*, September 5, 1999.

14. Enterprise Rent-A-Car website, aboutus.enterprise.com/who_we_are/customer_service.html (viewed March 12, 2008).

15. Lesley Young, "Taking Marketing to the Bank," *Marketing*, February 11, 2002, pp. 4–7; Bernadette Johnson, "Bankers' Online Offerings Reflect Today's Savvy Consumers," *Strategy: The Canadian Marketing Report*, February 25, 2002, p. D2.

16. Thomas O. Jones and W. Earl Sasser, Jr., "Why Satisfied Customers Defect," *Harvard Business Review* (November–December 1995): 88–99.

17. Companies should also note that managers and salespeople can manipulate customer-satisfaction ratings. They can be especially nice to customers just before the survey. They can also try to exclude unhappy customers. Another danger is that if customers know the company will go out of its way to please customers, some may express high dissatisfaction in order to receive more concessions.

18. Anne Chen, "Customer Feedback Key for Theme Park; Inquisite Lets Visitors Sound Off," *eWeek*, December 15, 2003, p. 58.

19. Frederick K. Reichheld, "The One Number You Need to Grow," *Harvard Business Review* (December 2003): 46–54.

20. Alex Taylor III, "Mercedes Hits a Pothole," *Fortune*, October 27, 2003, pp. 140–146.

21. Andy Holloway, "I'm Down Here, Guys," *Canadian Business Online*, www.canadianbusiness.com, October 28, 2002 (viewed July 8, 2004).

22. "The Gurus of Quality: American Companies Are Heeding the Quality Gospel Preached by Deming, Juran, Crosby, and Taguchi," *Traffic Management* (July 1990): 35–39.

23. Cyndee Miller, "U.S. Firms Lag in Meeting Global Quality Standards," *Marketing News*, February 15, 1993.

24. J. Daniel Beckham, "Expect the Unexpected in Health Care Marketing Future," *The Academy Bulletin* (July 1992): 3.

25. "Quality: The U.S. Drives to Catch Up," *Business Week*, November 1982, pp. 66–80. For a more recent assessment of progress, see "Quality Programs Show Shoddy Results," *Wall Street Journal*, May 14, 1992, p. B1. See also Roland R. Rust, Anthony J. Zahorik, and Timothy L. Keiningham, "Return on Quality (ROQ): Making Service Quality Financially Accountable," *Journal of Marketing*, 59, no. 2 (April 1995): 58–70.

26. Robert D. Buzzell and Bradley T. Gale, *The PIMS Principles: Linking Strategy to Performance* (New York: The Free Press, 1987), ch. 6. (PIMS stands for Profit Impact of Market Strategy.)

27. David Greising, "Quality: How to Make It Pay," *BusinessWeek*, August 8, 1994, pp. 54–59; Roland R. Rust, Anthony J. Zahorik, and Timothy L. Keiningham, "Return on Quality (ROQ): Making Service Quality Financially Accountable," *Journal of Marketing*, 59, no. 2 (April 1995): 58–70.

28. Roland T. Rust, Christine Moorman, and Peter R. Dickson, "Getting Return on Quality: Revenue Expansion, Cost Reduction, or Both," *Journal of Marketing*, 65 (October 2002): 7–24.

29. Quoted in Don Peppers and Martha Rogers, *The One-to-One Future: Building Relationships One Customer at a Time* (New York: Currency Doubleday, 1993), p. 108.

30. William A. Sherden, *Market Ownership: The Art and Science of Becoming #1* (New York: Amacom, 1994), p. 77.

31. Robert J. Bowman, "Good Things, Smaller Packages," *World Trade*, 6, no. 9 (October 1993): 106–110.

32. Werner J. Reinartz and V. Kumar, "The Impact of Customer Relationship Characteristics on Profitable Lifetime Duration," *Journal of Marketing*, 67 (January 2003): 77–99; Werner J. Reinartz and V. Kumar, "On the Profitability of Long-Life Customers in a Noncontractual Setting: An Empirical Investigation and Implications for Marketing," *Journal of Marketing*, 64 (October 2000): 17–35.

33. Rakesh Niraj, Mahendra Gupta, and Chakravarthi Narasimhan, "Customer Profitability in a Supply Chain," *Journal of Marketing* (July 2001): 1–16.

34. Sara Minogue, "Customer Profitability Management," *Strategy Magazine Online*, www.strategymag.com, February 9, 2004 (viewed July 8, 2004).

35. Ravi Dhar and Rashi Glazer, "Hedging Customers," *Harvard Business Review* (May 2003): 86–92.

36. Michael E. Porter, *Competitive Strategy: Techniques for Analyzing Industries and Competitors* (New York: Free Press, 1980).

37. Carl Sewell and Paul Brown, *Customers for Life* (New York: Pocket Books, 1990), p. 162.

38. Greg Farrel, "Marketers Put a Price on Your Life." *USA Today*, July 7, 1999.

39. Stephan A. Butscher, "Welcome to the Club: Building Customer Loyalty," *Marketing News*, September 9, 1996, p. 9.

40. Cited in Don Peppers and Martha Rogers, *The One-to-One Future* (New York: Currency, 1993), pp. 37–38.

41. Ian Gordon, *Relationship Marketing* (Toronto: John Wiley & Sons Canada Ltd., 1998), p. 9.

42. Robert C. Blattberg and John Deighton, "Manage Marketing by the Customer Equity Test," *Harvard Business Review* (July–August 1996): 136–144.

43. Roland T. Rust, Valerie A. Zeithaml, and Katherine A. Lemon, *Driving Customer Equity* (New York: Free Press 2000).

44. Mohan Sawhney, "Beyond CRM: Managing Relational Equity," from a talk given at "Managing Customer Relationships in the Network Economy," September 20, 2000. For a broad discussion of the term "equity," see Roderick J. Brodie, Mark S. Glynn, and Joel Van Durme, "Towards a Theory of Marketplace Equity," *Marketing Theory*, 2, no. 1 (2000): 5–28.

45. Nicole E. Coviello, Roderick J. Brodie, Peter J. Danaher, and Wesley J. Johnston, "How Firms Relate to Their Markets: An Empirical Examination of Contemporary Marketing Practices," *Journal of Marketing*, 66 (July 2002): pp. 33–46.

46. Michael J. Lanning, *Delivering Profitable Value* (Oxford, UK: Capstone, 1998).

47. Peter Gumbel, "BMW Drives Germany," *Time*, 170, no. 3 (July 16, 2007).

48. Nora A. Aufreiter, David Elzinga, and Jonathan W. Gordon, "Better Branding," *The McKinsey Quarterly*, 4 (2003): 29–39.

49. Michael J. Lanning, *Delivering Profitable Value* (Oxford, UK: Capstone, 1998).

50. Vawn Himmelsbach, "Harry Rosen tailors customer service with made-to-measure CRM," *ITbusiness.ca*, June 8, 2006, www.itbusiness.ca/it/client/en/home/News.asp?id=39722 (viewed March 11, 2008); "Harry Rosen, Inc. Expands Customer Service Capabilities and Profits by Implementing Web-based Sage CRM SalesLogix," *BNet Business Network, Market Wire*, May 2006, findarticles.com/p/articles/mi_pwwi/is_200605/ai_n16430432 (viewed March 12,2008); www.harryrosen.com.

51. Don Peppers and Martha Rogers, *The One to One Future: Building Relationships One Customer at a Time,*" (New York: Doubleday 1993); Don Peppers and Martha Rogers, *Enterprise One to One: Tools for Competing in the Interactive Age* (New York: Currency, 1997); Don Peppers and Martha Rogers, *The One-to-One Manager: Real-World Lessons in Customer Relationship Management* (New York: Doubleday 1999); Don Peppers, Martha Rogers, and Bob Dorf, *The One-to-One Fieldbook: The Complete Toolkit for Implementing a 1 to 1 Marketing Program* (New York: Bantam, 1999); Don Peppers and Martha Rogers, *One-to-One B2B: Customer Development Strategies for the Business-to-Business World* (New York: Doubleday, 2001).

52. Katherine O'Brien, "Differentiation Begins with Customer Knowledge," *American Printer* (July 2003): p. 8.

53. Alan W. H. Grant and Leonard A. Schlesinger, "Realize Your Customer's Full Profit Potential," *Harvard Business Review* (September–October 1995): 59–72; Art Friedman, "Harley-Davidson Motorcycles Posts Record Revenue, Earnings for 2003," *Motorcycle Cruiser*, www.motorcyclecruiser.com/newsandupdates/hd4q03/ (viewed September 30, 2004).

54. Jeffrey Gitomer, *Customer Satisfaction Is Worthless; Customer Loyalty Is Priceless: How to Make Customers Love You, Keep Them Coming Back and Tell Everyone They Know* (Austin, TX: Bard Press, 1998).

55. Technical Assistance Research Programs (TARP), U.S Office of Consumer Affairs Study on Complaint Handling in America, 1986.

56. Karl Albrecht and Ron Zemke, *Service America!* (Homewood Il: Dow Jones-Irwin, 1985), pp. 6–7; Roland T. Rust, Bala Subramanian, and Mark Wells, "Making Complaints a Management Tool," *Marketing Management*, 1, no. 3 (1992): 40–45; Ruth Bolton and Tina M. Bronkhorst, "The Relationship Between Customer Complaints to the Firm and Subsequent Exit Behavior," *Advances in Consumer Research*, 22 (Provo, Utah: Association for Consumer Research, 1995); Stephen S. Tax and Stephen W. Brown, "Recovering and Learning from Service Failure," *Sloan Management Review*, 40, no. 1 (1998): 75–88.

57. Maryfran Johnson, "Colliding with Customers," *Computerworld*, December 15, 2003, p. 20; Bob Brewin, "User Complaints Push Dell to Return PC Support to U.S.," *Computerworld*, December 1, 2003, p. 6.

58. Frederick F. Reichheld, *The Loyalty Effect* (Boston: Harvard Business School Press, 1996).

59. Robert Blattberg, Byung-Do Kim, and Scott Neslin, *Database Marketing: Theory and Practice* (in press).

60. www.onstar.com.

61. Michael Totty, "E-Commerce (A Special Report); Business Solutions," *Wall Street Journal*, October 20, 2003, p. R4.

62. Jeffrey Pfeffer, "The Face of Your Business," *Business 2.0* (December 2002–January 2003): 58.

63. Frederick F. Reichheld, "Learning from Customer Defections," *Harvard Business Review* (March–April 1996): 56–69.

64. Frederick Reichheld, "Learning from Customer Defections," *Harvard Business Review*, Mar/Apr 1996, 74, no. 2; pp. 56–67.

65. Leonard L. Berry and A. Parasuraman, *Marketing Services: Computing through Quality* (New York: The Free Press, 1991), pp. 136–142. See also Richard Cross and Janet Smith, *Customer Bonding: Pathways to Lasting Customer Loyalty* (Lincolnwood, IL: NTC Business Books, 1995).

66. For a review, see Grahame R. Dowling and Mark Uncles, "Do Customer Loyalty Programs Really Work?" *Sloan Management Review, 38* (1997): 71–82.

67. Samson Okalow, "Auditing Loyalty," *Strategy Magazine Online*, www.strategymag.com, April 21, 2003 (viewed July 8, 2004).

68. www.etsy.com (viewed March 12, 2008).

69. www.hallmark.com; www.goldcrowncard.com/HTDocs/Hlk-phase1/welcome_incl.cfm (viewed March 12, 2008).

70. James H. Donnelly Jr., Leonard L. Berry, and Thomas W. Thompson, *Marketing Financial Services—A Strategic Vision* (Homewood, IL: Dow Jones–Irwin, 1985), p. 113.

71. Susan Stellin, "For Many Online Companies, Customer Service Is Hardly a Priority," *New York Times*, February 19, 2001; Michelle Johnson, "Getting Ready for the Onslaught," *Boston Globe*, November 4, 1999.

72. Akamai, "Akamai and JupiterResearch Identify '4 Seconds' as the New Threshold of Acceptability for Retail Web Page Response Times," Press Release, November 6, 2006, www.akamai.com/html/about/press/releases/2006/press_110606.html (viewed May 21, 2008).

73. "A Great User Experience Is The Most Cost-Effective Way To Win Online," Forrester Research Press Release, May 31, 2001.

74. www.veseys.com/sub.cfm (viewed September 30, 2004).

75. From a privately circulated paper: Lester Wunderman, "The Most Elusive Word in Marketing," June 2000. See also Lester Wunderman, *Being Direct* (NewYork: Random House 1996).

76. Andrea Haman "Suzy Shier Fashions Extensive Database Initiatives," *Strategy Magazine*, July 16, 2001, p. D-10.; www.suzyshier.com (viewed March 13, 2008).

77. Ian Mount, "Marketing," *Business 2.0* (August/September 2001): 84.

78. Peter R. Peacock, "Data Mining in Marketing: Part 1," *Marketing Management* (Winter 1998): 9–18, and "Data Mining in Marketing: Part 2," *Marketing Management* (Spring 1998): 15–25; Ginger Conlon, "What the !@#!*?!! Is a Data Warehouse?" *Sales & Marketing Management* (April 1997): 41–48; Skip Press, "Fool's Gold? As Companies Rush to Mine Data, They May Dig Up Real Gems—Or False Trends," *Sales & Marketing Management* (April 1997): 58, 60, 62; John Verity, "A Trillion-Byte Weapon," *BusinessWeek*, July 31, 1995, pp. 80–81.

79. James Lattin, Doug Carroll, and Paul Green, *Analyzing Multivariate Data* (Florence, KY: Thomson Brooks/Cole, 2003); Simon Haykin, *Neural Networks: A Comprehensive Foundation*, 2nd edition (Upper Saddle River, NJ: Prentice-Hall, 1998); Michael J. A. Berry and Gordon Linoff, *Data Mining Techniques: For Marketing, Sales, and Customer Support* (New York: John Wiley & Sons, 1997).

80. Werner Reinartz and V. Kumar, "The Mismanagement of Customer Loyalty," *Harvard Business Review* (July 2002): 86–94; Susan M. Fournier, Susan Dobscha, and David Glen Mick, "Preventing the Premature Death of Relationship Marketing," *Harvard Business Review* (January–February 1998): 42–51.

81. Jon Swartz, "Ebay Faithful Expect Loyalty in Return," *USA TODAY*, July 1, 2002, pp. B1–B2.

82. "Justifying CRM Costs and Boosting Return on Invesment," *Reaping Business Rewards from CRM*, Gartner Group, 2004, p. 2 and p. 11.

83. George S. Day, "Creating a Superior Customer-Relating Capability," *Sloan Management Review, 44*, (2003): 77–82.

84. Darrell K. Rigby, Frederick F. Reichheld, and Phil Schefter, "Avoid the Four Perils of CRM," *Harvard Business Review* (February 2002): 101–109.

Chapter 6

1. "Real Men Get Waxed," *The Economist*, July 5, 2003, p. 57; Robyn Meredith and Melanie Wells, "Today's Man," *Forbes*, September 1, 2003, p. 52.

2. For discussions of Canadian values, see Reginald W. Bibby, *The Bibby Report: Social Trends Canadian Style* (Toronto: Stoddart, 1995) and Michael Adams, *Sex in the Snow: Canadian Social Values at the End of the Millennium* (Toronto: Viking, 1997). See also Leon G. Schiffman and Leslie Lazar Kanuk, *Consumer Behavior*, 6th ed. (Upper Saddle River, NJ: Prentice Hall, 1997).

3. Shawna Steinberg, "Oh Canada in the Spotlight," *Marketing Magazine*, November 2, 1998, pp. 10–11.

4. Awais Jaffery, "Anokhi and Alia Khan launch FUSIA," *DesiVibe.ca*, desivibe.ca/index.php?option=com_content&task=view&id=321&Itemid=2 (viewed March 24, 2008); "Multicultural Marketing," *CBC News Toronto*, March 2008, www.cbc.ca/toronto/features/diversity/ (viewed March 24, 2008).

5. The Centre for Canadian Studies, *The Political Voice of Canadian Regional Identities*, 2001, www.mta.ca/faculty/arts/canadian_studies/english/about/study_guide/regional/index.html (viewed October 16, 2004).

6. Leon Schiffman and Leslie Kanuk, *Consumer Behavior*, 9th edition, 2006, Pearson Education, NJ.

7. The Influencers website, www.theinfluencers.ca (viewed March 28, 2008).

8. Norihiko Shirouzu, "Japan's High School Girls Excel in Art of Setting Trends," *Wall Street Journal*, April 27, 1998, pp. B1–B6.

9. Rosann L. Spiro, "Persuasion in Family Decision Making," *Journal of Consumer Research* (March 1983): 393–402; David J. Burns, "Husband–Wife Innovative Consumer Decision Making: Exploring the Effect of Family Power," *Psychology & Marketing* (May–June 1992): 175–189; Robert Boutilier, "Pulling the Family's Strings," *American Demographics* (August 1993): 44–48; Elizabeth S. Moore, William L. Wilkie, and Richard J. Lutz, "Passing the Torch: Intergenerational Influences as a Source of Brand Equity," *Journal of Marketing* (April 2002): 17–37. For cross-cultural comparisons of husband–wife buying roles, see John B. Ford, Michael S. LaTour, and Tony L. Henthorne, "Perception of Marital Roles in Purchase-Decision Processes: A Cross-Cultural Study," *Journal of the Academy of Marketing Science* (Spring 1995): 120–131.

10. Kay M. Palan and Robert E. Wilkes," Adolescent–Parent Interaction in Family Decision Making," *Journal of Consumer Research, 24*, no. 2 (1997): 159–169; Sharon E. Beatty and Salil Talpade, "Adolescent Influence in Family Decision Making: A Replication with Extension," *Journal of Consumer Research, 21* (1994): 332–341.

11. Lyle V. Harris, "Men Rule the Aisles," *Globe and Mail*, May 6, 1999, p. C5.

12. Marilyn Lavin, "Husband-Dominant, Wife-Dominant, Joint: A Shopping Typology for Baby Boom Couples?" *Journal of Consumer Marketing, 10*, no. 3 (1993): 33–42.

13. Jim Hopkins, "Financial Firms Cater to Powerful Women," *USA TODAY*, June 18, 2002, p. 3B.

14. "Retailers Learn That Electronics Shopping Isn't Just a Guy Thing," *Wall Street Journal*, January 15, 2004, p. D3.

15. Hillary Chura, "Failing to Connect: Marketing Messages for Women Fall Short," *Advertising Age* (September 23, 2002): pp. 13–14.

16. Kristin Goff, "Canadian Tire Gets Makeover to Get in Touch with Feminine Side," *Edmonton Journal*, August 24, 2005, p. G1; www.canadiantire.ca (viewed June 7, 2008).

17. James U. McNeal, "Tapping the Three Kids' Markets," *American Demographics* (April 1998): 37–41.

18. Chris Powell, "Under the Influence," *Marketing*, February 16, 2004; Media Awareness Network, "How Marketers Target Kids," www.media-awareness.ca/english/parents/marketing/marketers_target_kids.cfm.

19. Jennifer Bayot, "The Teenage Market; Young, Hip and Looking for a Bargain," *New York Times*, December 1, 2003, p. C8.

20. Hummer Kids website, www.hummerkids.com (viewed March 23, 2008).

21. YTV website, www.ytv.com/about/ (viewed March 24, 2008); Corus Entertainment, www.corusent.com/tv/ytv/index.asp (viewed October 16, 2004).

22. Courtney Kane, "TV and Movie Characters Sell Children's Snacks," *New York Times*, December 8, 2003, p. C7.

23. Doreen Carvajal, "Cell Phone Industry Increasing Marketing to Children," *The Ledger.com*. March 12, 2008, www.theledger.com/article/20080312/NEWS/803120549/1021/news&tc=yahoo (viewed March 23, 2008); Laura Petrecca, "Cell Phone Marketers Calling All Preteens." *USA Today*, September 5, 2005.

24. See Frederick Herzberg, *Work and the Nature of Man* (Cleveland: William Collins, 1966); Henk Thierry and Agnes M. Koopman-Iwerna, "Motivation and Satisfaction," in P. J. Drenth (ed.), *Handbook of Work and Organizational Psychology* (New York: John Wiley, 1984), pp. 141–142.

25. Harold H. Kassarjian and Mary Jane Sheffet, "Personality and Consumer Behavior: An Update," in Harold H. Kassarjian and Thomas S. Robertson (eds.), *Perspectives in Consumer Behavior* (Glenview, IL: Scott, Foresman, 1981), pp. 160–180.

26. Jennifer Aaker, "Dimensions of Measuring Brand Personality," *Journal of Marketing Research, 34* (August 1997): 347–356.

27. M. Joseph Sirgy, "Self Concept in Consumer Behavior: A Critical Review," *Journal of Consumer Research, 9* (December 1982), pp. 287–300.

28. Timothy R. Graeff, "Consumption Situations and the Effects of Brand Image on Consumers' Brand Evaluations," *Psychology & Marketing*, 1997, *14*, no. 1: 49–70; Timothy R. Graeff, "Image Congruence Effects on Product Evaluations: The Role of Self-Monitoring and Public/Private Consumption," *Psychology & Marketing, 13*, no. 5 (1996): 481–499.

29. Jennifer L. Aaker, "The Malleable Self: The Role of Self-Expression in Persuasion," *Journal of Marketing Research, 36*, no. 2 (1999): 45–57.

30. LOHAS website, www.lohas.com/about.html (viewed March 20, 2008); Amy Cortese, "They Care About the World (and They Shop Too)," *New York Times*, July 20, 2003, pp. 3–4.

31. Anthony Banco and Wendy Zellner, "Is Wal-Mart Too Powerful?" *BusinessWeek*, October 6, 2003, p. 100.

32. Toby Weber, "All Three? Gee," *Wireless Review* (May 2003): 12–14.

33. Kraft Canada website, www.kraftcanada.com/en/ProductsPromotions/J-L/KraftDinnerBrandPage.htm (viewed March 20, 2008).

34. Thomas J. Reynolds and Jonathan Gutman, "Laddering Theory, Method, Analysis, and Interpretation," *Journal of Advertising Research* (February–March 1988): 11–34.

35. Ernest Dichter, *Handbook of Consumer Motivations* (New York: McGraw-Hill, 1964).

36. Jan Callebaut, et al., *The Naked Consumer: The Secret of Motivational Research in Global Marketing* (Antwerp, Belgium: Censydiam Institute, 1994).

37. Melanie Wells, "Mind Games," *Forbes*, September 1, 2003, p. 70.

38. Abraham Maslow, *Motivation and Personality* (New York: Harper and Row, 1954), pp. 80–106.

39. See Frederick Herzberg, *Work and the Nature of Man* (Cleveland: William Collins, 1966); Henk Thierry and Agnes M. Koopman-Iwerna, "Motivation and Satisfaction," in P. J. Drenth (ed.), *Handbook of Work and Organizational Psychology* (New York: John Wiley, 1984), pp. 141–142.

40. Bernard Berelson and Gary A. Steiner, *Human Behavior: An Inventory of Scientific Findings* (New York: Harcourt, Brace Jovanovich, 1964), p. 88.

41. J. Edward Russo, Margaret G. Meloy, T.J. Wilks, "The Distortion of Product Information During Brand Choice," *Journal of Marketing Research, 35* (1998): 438–452.

42. Leslie de Chernatony and Simon Knox, "How an Appreciation of Consumer Behavior Can Help in Product Testing," *Journal of Market Research Society*, (July 1990): 333. See also Chris Janiszewski and Stiju M. J. Osselar, "A Connectionist Model of Brand-Quality Association," *Journal of Marketing Research*, August 2000, pp. 331–351.

43. Florida's Chris Janiszewski has developed a fascinating research program looking at preconscious-processing effects. See Chris Janiszewski, "Preattentive Mere Exposure Effects," *Journal of Consumer Research, 20* (December 1993): 376–392, as well as some of his earlier and subsequent research.

44. See Timothy E. Moore, "Subliminal Advertising: What You See Is What You Get," *Journal of Marketing, 46* (1982): pp. 38–47, for an early classic and Andrew B. Aylesworth, Ronald C. Goodstein, and Ajay Kalra, "Effect of Archetypal Embeds on Feelings: An Indirect Route to Affecting Attitudes?" *Journal of Advertising, 28*, no. 3 (1999): 73–81 for a more current treatment.

45. John R. Anderson, *The Architecture of Cognition* (Cambridge, MA: Harvard University Press, 1983); Robert S. Wyer Jr. and Thomas K. Srull, "Person Memory and Judgment," *Psychological Review, 96*, no. 1 (1989): 58–83.

46. "MasterCard Worldwide," *America's Greatest Brands: Volume IV*, 2007, pp. 68–69.

47. For additional discussion, see John G. Lynch Jr. and Thomas K. Srull, "Memory and Attentional Factors in Consumer Choice: Concepts and Research Methods," *Journal of Consumer Research, 9* (June 1982): 18–36, and Joseph W. Alba, J. Wesley Hutchinson, and John G. Lynch Jr., "Memory and Decision Making," in *Handbook of Consumer Theory and Research*, Harold H. Kassarjian and Thomas S. Robertson (eds.) (Englewood Cliffs, NJ: Prentice-Hall, Inc., 1992), pp. 1–49.

48. Fergus I. M. Craik and Robert S. Lockhart, "Levels of Processing: A Framework for Memory Research," *Journal of Verbal Learning and Verbal Behavior, 11* (1972): 671–684; Fergus I. M. Craik and Endel Tulving, "Depth of Processing and the Retention of Words in Episodic Memory," *Journal of Experimental Psychology, 104*, no. 3 (1975): 268–294; Robert S. Lockhart, Fergus I. M. Craik, and Larry Jacoby, "Depth of Processing, Recognition, and Recall," in *Recall and Recognition*, John Brown, ed. (New York: John Wiley & Sons, Inc., 1976).

49. Leonard M. Lodish, Magid Abraham, Stuart Kalmenson, Jeanne Livelsberger, Beth Lubetkin, Bruce Richardson, and Mary Ellen Stevens, "How T.V. Advertising Works: A Meta Analysis of 389 Real World Split Cable T.V. Advertising Experiments," *Journal of Marketing Research, 32* (May 1995): 125–139.

50. Elizabeth F. Loftus and Gregory R. Loftus, "On the Permanence of Stored Information in the Human Brain," *American Psychologist, 35* (May 1980): 409–420.

51. Benson Shapiro, V. Kasturi Rangan, and John Sviokla, "Staple Yourself to an Order," *Harvard Business Review* (July–August 1992): 113–122. See also Carrie M. Heilman, Douglas Bowman, and Gordon P. Wright, "The Evolution of Brand Preferences and Choice Behaviors of Consumers New to a Market," *Journal of Marketing Research* (May 2000): 139–155.

52. Alison Stein Wellner, "Research on a Shoestring," *American Demographics* (April 2001): 38–39.

53. Marketing scholars have developed several models of the consumer buying process. See John A. Howard and Jagdish N. Sheth, *The Theory of Buyer Behavior* (New York: Wiley, 1969); James F. Engel, Roger D. Blackwell, and Paul W. Miniard, *Consumer Behavior*, 8th ed. (Fort Worth, TX: Dryden, 1994); Mary Frances Luce, James R. Bettman, and John W. Payne, *Emotional Decisions: Tradeoff Difficulty and Coping in Consumer Choice*, (Chicago, IL: University of Chicago Press, 2001).

54. William P. Putsis Jr. and Narasimhan Srinivasan, "Buying or Just Browsing? The Duration of Purchase Deliberation," *Journal of Marketing Research* (August 1994): 393–402.

55. Earle Eldridge, "Many Car Shoppers First Stop Is 'Consumer Reports,'" *USA Today*, September 16, 2003, pp. 1B–2B.

56. Adrienne Sanders, "Yankee Imperialism," *Forbes*, December 13, 1999, p. 56.

57. Maclean's website, www.macleans.ca/about/index.jsp (viewed March 25, 2008).

58. Chem L. Narayana and Rom J. Markin, "Consumer Behavior and Product Performance: An Alternative Conceptualization," *Journal of Marketing* (October 1975): 1–6. See also Wayne S. DeSarbo and Kamel Jedidi, "The Spatial Representation of Heterogeneous Consideration Sets," *Marketing Science,14*, no. 3, pt. 2 (1995): 326–342; Lee G. Cooper and Akihiro Inoue, "Building Market Structures from Consumer Preferences," *Journal of Marketing Research, 33,* no. 3 (August 1996): 293–306.

59. Virginia Postrel, "The Lessons of the Grocery Shelf Also Have Something to Say About Affirmative Action," *New York Times*, January 30, 2003, p. C2.

60. David Krech, Richard S. Crutchfield, and Egerton L. Ballachey, *Individual in Society* (New York: McGraw-Hill, 1962), ch. 2.

61. "Biotech Council Breaks Toronto Transit Shelter Campaign," *Adnews On-Line Daily*, June 10, 2002.

62. See Paul E. Green and Yoram Wind, *Multiattribute Decisions in Marketing: A Measurement Approach* (Hinsdale, IL: Dryden, 1973), ch. 2; Leigh McAlister, "Choosing Multiple Items from a Product Class," *Journal of Consumer Research* (December 1979): 213–224; Richard J. Lutz, "The Role of Attitude Theory in Marketing," in Kassarjian and Robertson (eds.) *Perspectives in Consumer Behavior*, 317–339.

63. This expectancy-value model was originally developed by Martin Fishbein, "Attitudes and Prediction of Behavior," in Martin Fishbein (ed.), *Readings in Attitude Theory and Measurement* (New York: John Wiley, 1967), pp. 477–492. For a critical review, see Paul W. Miniard and Joel B. Cohen, "An Examination of the Fishbein-Ajzen Behavioral-Intentions Model's Concepts and Measures," *Journal of Experimental Social Psychology* (May 1981): 309–339.

64. Michael R. Solomon, *Consumer Behavior: Buying, Having and Being* (Upper Saddle River, NJ: Prentice-Hall, 2001).

65. James R. Bettman, Eric J. Johnson, and John W. Payne, "Consumer Decision Making," in *Handbook of Consumer Theory and Research*, Harold H. Kassarjian and Thomas S. Robertson (eds.) (Englewood Cliffs, NJ: Prentice-Hall, Inc., 1992), pp. 50–84.

66. Jagdish N. Sheth, "An Investigation of Relationships among Evaluative Beliefs, Affect, Behavioral Intention, and Behavior," in John U. Farley, John A. Howard, and L. Winston Ring (eds.), *Consumer Behavior: Theory and Application* (Boston: Allyn & Bacon, 1974), pp. 89–114.

67. Fishbein, "Attitudes and Prediction of Behavior."

68. Raymond A. Bauer, "Consumer Behavior as Risk Taking," in Donald F. Cox (ed.), *Risk Taking and Information Handling in Consumer Behavior* (Boston: Division of Research, Harvard Business School, 1967); James W. Taylor, "The Role of Risk in Consumer Behavior," *Journal of Marketing* (April 1974): 54–60.

69. Priscilla A. La Barbera and David Mazursky, "A Longitudinal Assessment of Consumer Satisfaction/Dissatisfaction: The Dynamic Aspect of the Cognitive Process," *Journal of Marketing Research* (November 1983): 393–404.

70. Ralph L. Day, "Modeling Choices among Alternative Responses to Dissatisfaction," *Advances in Consumer Research, 11* (1984): 496–499. Also see Philip Kotler and Murali K. Mantrala, "Flawed Products: Consumer Responses and Marketer Strategies," *Journal of Consumer Marketing* (Summer 1985): 27–36.

71. Barry L. Bayus, "Word of Mouth: The Indirect Effects of Marketing Efforts," *Journal of Advertising Research* (June–July 1985): 31–39.

72. Albert O. Hirschman, *Exit, Voice, and Loyalty* (Cambridge, MA: Harvard University Press, 1970).

73. Mary C. Gilly and Richard W. Hansen, "Consumer Complaint Handling as a Strategic Marketing Tool," *Journal of Consumer Marketing* (Fall 1985): 5–16.

74. James H. Donnelly Jr. and John M. Ivancevich, "Post-Purchase Reinforcement and Back-Out Behavior," *Journal of Marketing Research* (August 1970): 399–400.

75. John D. Cripps, "Heuristics and Biases in Timing the Replacement of Durable Products," *Journal of Consumer Research, 21* (September 1994): 304–318.

76. Richard E. Petty and John T. Cacioppo, *Attitudes and Persuasion: Classic and Contemporary Approaches* (New York: McGraw-Hill, 1981); Richard E. Petty, *Communication and Persuasion: Central and Peripheral Routes to Attitude Change* (New York: Springer-Verlag, 1986).

77. Herbert E. Krugman, "The Impact of Television Advertising: Learning without Involvement," *Public Opinion Quarterly* (Fall 1965): 349–356.

78. Frank R. Kardes, *Consumer Behavior and Managerial Decision-Making*, 2nd ed. (Upper Saddle River, NJ: Prentice-Hall, 2003).

79. See Richard Thaler, "Mental Accounting and Consumer Choice," *Marketing Science, 4*, no. 3 (1985): 199–214 for a seminal piece, and Richard Thaler, "Mental Accounting Matters," *Journal of Behavioral Decision-Making, 12*, no. 3 (1999): 183–206 for more contemporary perspectives.

80. Gary L. Gastineau and Mark P. Kritzman, *Dictionary of Financial Risk Management*, 3rd ed. (New York: John Wiley & Sons, 1999).

81. Example adapted from Daniel Kahneman, and Amos Tversky, "Prospect Theory: An Analysis of Decision Under Risk," *Econometrica, 47* (March 1979): pp. 263–291.

82. Harper W. Boyd Jr. and Sidney Levy, "New Dimensions in Consumer Analysis," *Harvard Business Review,163* (November–December): 129–140.

83. Sandra Vandermerwe, *Customer Capitalism: Increasing Returns in New Market Spaces* (London: Nicholas Brealey Publishing), ch. 11.

84. Patricia B. Seybold, "Get Inside the Lives of Your Customers," *Harvard Business Review* (May 2001): 81–89.

Chapter 7

1. Accenture website, www.accenture.com/Global/About_Accenture/Company_Overview/CompanyDescription.htm (viewed May 3, 2008).

2. James C. Anderson and James A. Narus, *Business Market Management: Understanding, Creating and Delivering Value* (Upper Saddle River, NJ: Prentice Hall, 1998).

3. Frederick E. Webster Jr. and Yoram Wind, *Organizational Buying Behavior* (Upper Saddle River, NJ: Prentice Hall, 1972), p. 2.

4. Jennifer Gilbert, "Small but Mighty," *Sales & Marketing Management* (January 2004): pp. 30–35.

5. Michael Collins, "Breaking into the Big Leagues," *American Demographics* (January 1996): 24.

6. Industry Canada, *Report on "Key Small Business Statistics,"* www.strategis.ic.gc.ca, April 2004 (viewed July 19, 2004).

7. Patrick J. Robinson, Charles W. Faris, and Yoram Wind, *Industrial Buying and Creative Marketing* (Boston: Allyn & Bacon, 1967).

8. Daniel H. McQuiston, "Novelty, Complexity, and Importance as Causal Determinants of Industrial Buyer Behavior," *Journal of Marketing* (April 1989): 66–79; Peter Doyle, Arch G. Woodside,

and Paul Mitchell, "Organizational Buying in New Task and Rebuy Situations," *Industrial Marketing Management* (February 1979): 7–11.

9. Urban B. Ozanne and Gilbert A. Churchill Jr., "Five Dimensions of the Industrial Adoption Process," *Journal of Marketing Research* (August 1971): 322–328.

10. Magna International Inc. website, www.magna.com (viewed May 3, 2008); Magna International *2003 Annual Report* (viewed July 19, 2004).

11. Sun Microsystems website, www.sun.com/aboutsun/company/index.jsp and www.sun.com/customers/overview.html (viewed April 30, 2008).

12. Donald W. Jackson Jr., Janet E. Keith, and Richard K. Burdick, "Purchasing Agents' Perceptions of Industrial Buying Center Influence: A Situational Approach," *Journal of Marketing* (Fall 1984): 75–83.

13. Webster and Wind, *Organizational Buying Behavior*, p. 6.

14. Webster and Wind, *Organizational Buying Behavior*, p. 6.

15. Frederick E. Webster Jr. and Yoram Wind, "A General Model for Understanding Organizational Buying Behavior," *Journal of Marketing*, 36 (April 1972): 12–19; Webster and Wind, *Organizational Buying Behavior*.

16. David Welch, "Renault-Nissan: Say Hello to Bo," *BusinessWeek* (July 31, 2006), p. 56.

17. Frederick E. Webster Jr. and Kevin Lane Keller, "A Roadmap for Branding in Industrial Markets," working paper, Amos Tuck School of Business, Dartmouth College.

18. Scott Ward and Frederick E. Webster Jr., "Organizational Buying Behavior" in *Handbook of Consumer Behavior*, edited by Tom Robertson and Hal Kassarjian (Upper Saddle River, NJ: Prentice-Hall, 1991), pp. 419–458.

19. Webster and Wind, *Organizational Buying Behavior*, p. 6.

20. CN Web site, "CN Announces New Sales and Marketing Structure to Improve Customer Service," CN News Release, April 14, 2004 (viewed July 23, 2004).

21. Nirmalya Kumar, *Marketing as Strategy: Understanding the CEO's Agenda for Driving Growth and Innovation* (Boston: Harvard Business School Press, 2004).

22. Kumar, *Marketing as Strategy*.

23. Sara Lorge, "Purchasing Power," *Sales & Marketing Management* (June 1998): 43–46.

24. Quality Foods website, www.qualityfoods.com/aboutQF/history.html (viewed May 10, 2008); GS1 Canada, "Winner of 2006 GS1 Canada Supply Chain Efficiency Award Announced," Press Release, October 24, 2006, www.gs1ca.org/Page.asp?intNodeID=6&intPageID=847 (viewed May 10, 2008).

25. Anderson and Narus, *Business Market Management: Understanding, Creating and Delivering Value*.

26. Adapted from Peter Kraljic, "Purchasing Must Become Supply Management," *Harvard Business Review* (September–October 1993): 109–117.

27. Tim Minahan, "OEM Buying Survey—Part 2: Buyers Get New Roles but Keep Old Tasks," *Purchasing*, July 16, 1998, pp. 208–209.

28. Robinson, Faris, and Wind, *Industrial Buying and Creative Marketing*.

29. Ceridian Canada, "New Branding Campaign from Ceridian Canada Offers Businesses 'The Freedom to Succeed,'" News Release, February 12, 2002, www.ceridian.ca (viewed June 8, 2002).

30. Industry Canada, "The Digital Economy in Canada: Canadian e-Commerce Statistics," www.ic.gc.ca/epic/site/ecic-ceac.nsf/en/gv00163e.html (viewed July 24, 2008).

31. Royal Bank website, www.rbc.com/sourcing/eproc_8.html (viewed June 4, 2008).

32. Karen J. Bannan, "10 Great Web Sites," *BtoB*, 90, no. 11 (September 12, 2005): pp. 36–42; Staples website, www.staples.com/sbd/content/about/media/fastfacts.html (viewed May 3, 2008).

33. "Xerox Multinational Supplier Quality Survey," *Purchasing*, January 12, 1995, p. 112.

34. Daniel J. Flint, Robert B. Woodruff, and Sarah Fisher Gardial, "Exploring the Phenomenon of Customers' Desired Value Change in a Business-to-Business Context," *Journal of Marketing*, 66 (October 2002): 102–117.

35. Donald R. Lehmann and John O'Shaughnessy, "Differences in Attribute Importance for Different Industrial Products," *Journal of Marketing* (April 1974): 36–42.

36. Procter & Gamble website, www.pg.com/company/who_we_are/diversity/supplier/success.jhtml (viewed May 10, 2008); "P&G: Supplier Diversity Development," pg.com/images/company/who_we_are/diversity/supplier/PG_Sup_Div_Rpt.pdf (viewed May 10, 2008).

37. Minahan, "OEM Buying Survey–Part 2: Buyers Get New Roles but Keep Old Tasks."

38. Ariba website, www.ariba.com (viewed May 1, 2008).

39. Arnt Buvik and George John, "When Does Vertical Coordination Improve Industrial Purchasing Relationships?" *Journal of Marketing*, 64 (October 2000): 52–64.

40. Shankar Ganesan, "Determinants of Long-Term Orientation in Buyer–Seller Relationships," *Journal of Marketing*, 58 (April 1994): 1–19; Patricia M. Doney and Joseph P. Cannon, "An Examination of the Nature of Trust in Buyer–Seller Relationships," *Journal of Marketing*, 61 (April 1997): 35–51.

41. John H. Sheridan, "An Alliance Built on Trust," *Industry Week*, March 17, 1997, pp. 66–70.

42. William W. Keep, Stanley C. Hollander, and Roger Dickinson, "Forces Impinging on Long-Term Business-to-Business Relationships in the United States: An Historical Perspective," *Journal of Marketing*, 62 (April 1998): 31–45.

43. Joseph P. Cannon and William D. Perreault Jr., "Buyer–Seller Relationships in Business Markets," *Journal of Marketing Research*, 36 (November 1999): 439–460.

44. Joseph P. Cannon and William D. Perreault Jr., "Buyer–Seller Relationships in Business Markets, *Journal of Marketing Research*, 36 (November 1999): 439–460.

45. Thomas G. Noordewier, George John, and John R. Nevin, "Performance Outcomes of Purchasing Arrangements in Industrial Buyer–Vendor Arrangements," *Journal of Marketing*, 54 (October), 80–93; Arnt Buvik and George John, "When Does Vertical Coordination Improve Industrial Purchasing Relationships?" *Journal of Marketing*, 64 (October 2000): 52–64.

46. Akesel I. Rokkan, Jan B. Heide, and Kenneth H. Wathne, "Specific Investment in Marketing Relationships: Expropriation and Bonding Effects," *Journal of Marketing Research*, 40 (May 2003): 210–224.

47. Mrinal Ghosh and George John, "Governance Value Analysis and Marketing Strategy," *Journal of Marketing*, 63 (Special Issue, 1999): 131–145.

48. Sandy Jap, "Pie Expansion Effects: Collaboration Processes in Buyer–Seller Relationships," *Journal of Marketing Research*, 36 (November 1999): 461–475.

49. Arnt Buvik and George John, "When Does Vertical Coordination Improve Industrial Purchasing Relationships?" *Journal of Marketing*, 64 (October 2000): 52–64.

50. Kenneth H. Wathne and Jan B. Heide, "Opportunism in Interfirm Relationships: Forms, Outcomes, and Solutions," *Journal of Marketing*, 64 (October 2000): 36–51.

51. Mary Walton, "When Your Partner Fails You," *Fortune*, 135, no. 10, pp. 87–89.

52. Mark B. Houston and Shane A. Johnson, "Buyer–Supplier Contracts Versus Joint Ventures: Determinants and Consequences of Transaction Structure," *Journal of Marketing Research*, 37 (February 2000): 1–15.

53. Akesel I. Rokkan, Jan B. Heide, and Kenneth H. Wathne, "Specific Investment in Marketing Relationships: Expropriation and Bonding Effects," *Journal of Marketing Research*, 40 (May 2003): 210–224.

54. Contracts Canada, "The Basics of Selling to Government," www.contractscanada.gc.ca (viewed July 19, 2004).

55. Microsoft, "Microsoft Case Studies: Government of Alberta," www.microsoft.com/casestudies/casestudy.aspx?casestudyid= 4000001308 (viewed May 1, 2008); Microsoft, "Windows Server 2008 Customer Solutions Case Study: Government Enhances IT Security, Increases Productivity with Operating System," January 2008.

Chapter 8

1. James C. Anderson and James A. Narus, "Capturing the Value of Supplementary Services," *Harvard Business Review* (January–February 1995): 75–83.

2. Brent Jang, "The Twin Otter Flies Again," *The Globe and Mail*, March 10, 2008, pp. 1, 3.

3. Tevfik Dalgic and Maarten Leeuw, "Niche Marketing Revisited: Concept, Applications, and Some European Cases," *European Journal of Marketing*, 28, no. 4 (1994): 39–55.

4. Robert D. Hof, "There's Not Enough 'Me' in MySpace," *Business Week*, December 4, 2006, p. 40; Abbey Klaassen, "Niche-Targeted Social Networks Find Audiences," *Advertising Age*, 77, no. 4 (November 6, 2006): p. 15.

5. Brunico Communications website, www.brunico.com (viewed March 2008).

6. Robert Blattberg and John Deighton, "Interactive Marketing: Exploiting the Age of Addressibility," *Sloan Management Review*, 33, no. 1 (1991): 5–14.

7. Brian Morrissey, "Dan Myrick on the Spot," *Adweek*, May 8, 2006, p. 28.

8. Don Peppers and Martha Rogers, *The One-to-One Future: Building Relationships One Customer at a Time* (New York: Currency/ Doubleday, 1993).

9. Jerry Wind and A. Rangaswamy, "Customerization: The Second Revolution in Mass Customization," Wharton School Working Paper, June 1999.

10. James C. Anderson and James A. Narus, "Capturing the Value of Supplementary Services," *Harvard Business Review* (January–February 1995): 75–83.

11. Joann Muller, "Kmart Con Salsa: Will It Be Enough?" *Business Week*, September 9, 2002.

12. Steve Friedman, "You Paid How Much for That Bike?" *New York Times*, November 9, 2006; Camilla Cornell, "The Amazing Race: Cervélo Cycles," *Profit*, May 2006, www.canadianbusiness.com/ entrepreneur/managing/article.jsp?content=20060404_153018_ 5420 (viewed March 10, 2008); Zena Olijnyk, "Beat China On Quality: Cervélo Cycles Bets on Premium Design to Win," *Canadian Business*, November 7–20, 2005, www.canadianbusiness. com/managing/strategy/article.jsp?content=20060109_ 154920_3740 (viewed March 10, 2008).

13. Nanette Byrnes, "What's Beyond for Bed Bath and Beyond?" *Business Week*, January 19, 2004; Andrea Lillo, "Bed Bath Sees More Room for Growth," *Home Textiles Today*, July 7, 2003, p. 2; Kate Kane, "It's a Small World," *Working Woman*, October 1997, p. 22.

14. Matt Semansky, "Alberta Business Mag Targets Young Up-and-Comers," *Marketing Daily*, September 13, 2007; *Unlimited* website, www.unlimitedmagazine.com (viewed March 2008). Other leading suppliers of geodemographic data are ClusterPlus (by Donnelly Marketing Information Services) and Acord (C.A.C.I., Inc.).

15. See "Environics Analytics PRIZM CE & Links," www. environicsanalytics.ca/prizmce_links.aspx (viewed March 2008).

16. "PRIZM_{CE} Snapshots," www.tetrad.com/pub/documents/ prizmcesnapshots.pdf (viewed March 2008).

17. Michael J. Weiss, *The Clustering of America* (New York: Harper and Row, 1988); *Breaking Up Is Hard to Do: The Clustered World* (Boston: Little, Brown & Co., 2000).

18. Michael J. Weiss, "To Be about to Be," *American Demographics*, September 2003, pp. 29–36.

19. Gina Chon, "Car Makers Talk 'Bout G-G-Generations," *Wall Street Journal*, May 9, 2006.

20. Trevor Cole, "A Day to Remember," *The Globe and Mail*, May 23, 2007; "Planning for Marriage, Not Just a Wedding," *Presbyterian Record*, February 1, 2006.

21. For some consumer behaviour perspectives on gender, see "What Women Want," *Brand Strategy*, December 2006–January 2007, pp. 40–41; Robert J. Fisher and Laurette Dube, "Gender Differences in Responses to Emotional Advertising: a Social Desirability Perspective," *Journal of Consumer Research*, 31 (March 2005): pp. 850–858; Joan Meyers-Levy and Brian Sternthal, "Gender Differences in the Use of Message Cues and Judgments," *Journal of Marketing Research*, 28 (February 1991): pp. 84–96.

22. Tom Lowry, "Young Man, Your Couch is Calling," *BusinessWeek*, July 28, 2003, pp. 68–69.

23. Constantine von Hoffman, "So Long Unisex, Make it His or Hers," *Brandweek*, 47, no. 25 (June 19, 2006): p. S50.

24. Jessica Hopper, "The Dove Campaign: Conforming or Transforming," *National Now Times*, 38, no. 3, p. 16.

25. Dawn Klingensmith, "Marketing Gurus Try to Read Women's Minds," *Chicago Tribune*, April 19, 2006; Matt Semansky, "Yahoo Targets Women with New Website," *Marketing Daily*, June 4, 2007.

26. Marti Barietta, "Who's Really Buying That Car? Ask Her," *Brandweek*, September 4, 2006, p. 20; Robert Craven, Kiki Maurey and John Davis, "What Women Really Want," *Critical Eye*, 15 (July 2006): pp. 50–53.

27. Pamela Sebastian Ridge, "Tool Sellers Tap Their Feminine Side," *Wall Street Journal*, June 16, 2002.

28. Louise Lee, "She's Not an Also Ran," *BusinessWeek*, June 12, 2006, p. 79.

29. Constantine Van Hoffman, "For Some Marketers, Low Income is Hot," *Brandweek*, September 11, 2006, p. 6.

30. Samson Okalow, "BMO InvestorLine Hits the Links for RSP Season," *Strategy Magazine*, May 3, 2004, p. 13.

31. Ian Zack, "Out of the Tube," *Forbes*, November 26, 2001, p. 200.

32. Gregory L. White and Shirley Leung, "Middle Market Shrinks as Americans Migrate toward the Higher End," *Wall Street Journal*, March 29, 2002, pp. A1, A8.

33. Linda Tischler, "The Price Is Right," *Fast Company*, November 2003, pp. 83–91; Statistics Canada 2001 Census, "Income of Families, Individuals and Households," www.statscan.ca (viewed August 3, 2004).

34. Christopher Noxon, "Toyification Nation," *Brandweek*, October 9, 2006; Rod O'Connor, "Adulthood: Are We There Yet? If You're Still Watching Cartoons or Playing Kickball, Then You, Kiddo, Just Might Be a 'Rejevenile,'" *Chicago Tribune*, August 6, 2006.

35. Andrew E. Serwer, "42,496 Secrets Bared," *Fortune*, January 24, 1994, pp. 13–14; Kenneth Labich, "Class in America," *Fortune*, February 7, 1994, pp. 114–126.

36. www.sric-bi.com (viewed March 2008).

37. Harold Thorkilsen, "Manager's Journal: Lessons of the Great Cranberry Crisis," *Wall Street Journal*, December 21, 1987, p. 20.

38. Pam Danziger, "Getting More for V-Day," *Brandweek*, February 9, 2004, p. 19.

39. Andrew Kaplan, "A Fruitful Mix," *Beverage World*, May 2006, pp. 28–36.

40. Rebecca Harris, "Gotta Be Good," *Marketing*, February 27, 2007; Rebecca Harris, "Buzz Boosts Brands," *Marketing*, February 27, 2007.

41. This classification was adapted from George H. Brown, "Brand Loyalty: Fact or Fiction?" *Advertising Age*, June 1952–January 1953, a series. See also Peter E. Rossi, R. McCulloch, and G. Allenby, "The Value of Purchase History Data in Target Marketing," *Marketing Science*, 15, no. 4 (1996): 321–340.

42. Chip Walker, "How Strong Is Your Brand," *Marketing Tools* (January/February 1995): pp. 46–53.

43. www.conversionmodel.com (viewed March 2008).

44. Daniel Yankelovich and David Meer, "Rediscovering Market Segmentation," *Harvard Business Review* (February 2006), pp. 122–131.

45. Industry Canada, "Key Small Business Statistics—April 2004," www.strategis.ic.gc.ca (viewed August 8, 2004).

46. Lisa D'Innocenzo, "Big Box Goes Downtown," *Strategy Magazine Online*, www.Strategymag.com, December 1, 2003 (viewed August 8, 2004).

47. For a review of many of the methodological issues in developing segmentation schemes, see William R. Dillon and Soumen Mukherjee, "A Guide to the Design and Execution of Segmentation Studies," in *Handbook of Marketing Research*, ed. Rajiv Grover and Marco Vriens (Thousand Oaks, CA: Sage, 2006); and Michael Wedel and Wagner A. Kamakura, *Market Segmentation: Conceptual and Methodological Foundations* (Boston: Kluwer, 1997).

48. Wendell R. Smith, "Product Differentiation and Market Segmentation as Alternative Marketing Strategies," *Journal of Marketing* (July 1956): p. 4.

49. www.esteelauder.com (viewed March 2008).

50. Christopher Hosford, "A Transformative Experience," *Sales and Marketing Management*, 158, no. 5 (June 2006): pp. 32–36.

51. Bart Macchiette and Roy Abhijit, "Sensitive Groups and Social Issues," *Journal of Consumer Marketing*, 11, no. 4 (1994): 55–64.

52. Jeff Gray, "Limit Junk-Food Ads, Report Urges," *The Globe and Mail*, February 26, 2008.

53. Kristin Laird, "Royal Bank Sponsors Cricket Program," *Marketing Daily*, February 29, 2008.

Chapter 9

1. For foundational work on branding, see Jean-Noel Kapferer, *Strategic Brand Management*, 2nd ed. (New York: Free Press, 2005); David A. Aaker and Erich Joachimsthaler, *Brand Leadership* (New York: Free Press, 2000); David A. Aaker, *Building Strong Brands* (New York: Free Press, 1996); David A. Aaker, *Managing Brand Equity* (New York: Free Press, 1991).

2. Interbrand Group, *World's Greatest Brands: An International Review* (New York: John Wiley, 1992). See also Karl Moore and Susan E. Reid, "The Birth of a Brand," Working paper, Desautels Faculty of Management, McGill University, 2006.

3. Rajneesh Suri and Kent B. Monroe, "The Effects of Time Pressure on Consumers' Judgments of Prices and Products," *Journal of Consumer Research*, 30 (June 2003): 92–104.

4. Rita Clifton and John Simmons, eds., *The Economist on Branding* (New York: Bloomberg Press, 2004); Rik Riezebos, *Brand Management: A Theoretical and Practical Approach* (Essex, England: Pearson Education, 2003); and Paul Temporal, *Advanced Brand Management: From Vision to Valuation* (Singapore: John Wiley & Sons, 2002).

5. Constance E. Bagley, *Managers and the Legal Environment: Strategies for the 21st Century*, 3rd ed. (Cincinnati, OH: Southwestern College/West Publishing, 2005). For a marketing academic's point of view of some important legal issues, see Judith Zaichkowsky, *The Psychology behind Trademark Infringement and Counterfeiting* (Mahwah, NJ: LEA Publishing, 2006) and Maureen Morrin and Jacob Jacoby, "Trademark Dilution: Empirical Measures for an Elusive Concept," *Journal of Public Policy & Marketing*, 19, no. 2 (May 2000): 265–76.

6. Tulin Erdem, "Brand Equity as a Signaling Phenomenon," *Journal of Consumer Psychology*, 7, no. 2 (1998): 131–57.

7. Scott Davis, *Brand Asset Management: Driving Profitable Growth through Your Brands* (San Francisco: Jossey-Bass, 2000); Mary W. Sullivan, "How Brand Names Affect the Demand for Twin Automobiles," *Journal of Marketing Research*, 35 (May 1998): 154–65; D. C. Bello and M. B. Holbrook, "Does an Absence of Brand Equity Generalize across Product Classes?" *Journal of Business Research*, 34 (October 1996): 125–31; Adrian J. Slywotzky and Benson P. Shapiro, "Leveraging to Beat the Odds: The New Marketing Mindset," *Harvard Business Review* (September–October 1993): 97–107.

8. The power of branding is not without its critics, however, some of whom reject the commercialism associated with branding activities. See Naomi Klein, *No Logo: Taking Aim at the Brand Bullies* (New York: Picador, 2000).

9. Natalie Mizik and Robert Jacobson, "Talk about Brand Strategy," *Harvard Business Review* (October 2005): 1; Baruch Lev, *Intangibles: Management, Measurement, and Reporting* (Washington, DC: Brookings Institute, 2001).

10. For an academic discussion of how consumers become so strongly attached to people as brands, see Matthew Thomson, "Human Brands: Investigating Antecedents to Consumers' Stronger Attachments to Celebrities," *Journal of Marketing*, 70 (July 2006): 104–19. For some practical branding tips from the world of rock and roll, see Roger Blackwell and Tina Stephan, *Brands That Rock*, (Hoboken, NJ: John Wiley & Sons, 2004), and from the world of sports, see Irving Rein, Philip Kotler, and Ben Shields, *The Elusive Fan: Reinventing Sports in a Crowded Marketplace*, (New York: McGraw-Hill, 2006).

11. Kristin Laird, "Becel promotes healthy hearts," *Marketing Daily*, February 25, 2008.

12. Other approaches are based on economic principles of signaling (e.g., Tulin Erdem, "Brand Equity as a Signaling Phenomenon," *Journal of Consumer Psychology*, 7, no. 2 [1998]: 131–57), or more of a sociological, anthropological, or biological perspective (e.g., Grant McCracken, *Culture and Consumption II: Markets, Meaning, and Brand Management* [Bloomington: Indiana University Press, 2005], or Susan Fournier, "Consumers and Their Brands: Developing Relationship Theory in Consumer Research," *Journal of Consumer Research*, 24 [September 1998]: 343–73).

13. Kevin Lane Keller, *Strategic Brand Management*, 3rd ed. (Upper Saddle River, NJ: Prentice Hall, 2008); David A. Aaker and Erich Joachimsthaler, *Brand Leadership* (New York: Free Press 2000); David A. Aaker, *Building Strong Brands* (New York: Free Press, 1996); David A. Aaker, *Managing Brand Equity* (New York: Free Press, 1991).

14. Jennifer L. Aaker, "Dimensions of Brand Personality," *Journal of Marketing Research* (August 1997): 347–56; Jean-Noel Kapferer, *Strategic Brand Management: New Approaches to Creating and Evaluating Brand Equity* (London: Kogan Page, 1992), p. 38; Davis, *Brand Asset Management*. For an overview of academic research on branding, see Kevin Lane Keller, "Branding and Brand Equity," in *Handbook of Marketing*, ed. Bart Weitz and Robin Wensley (London: Sage Publications, 2002), pp. 151–78.

15. Keller, *Strategic Brand Management*.

16. Theodore Levitt, "Marketing Success through Differentiation—of Anything," *Harvard Business Review* (January–February 1980): 83–91.

17. Kusum Ailawadi, Donald R. Lehmann, and Scott Neslin, "Revenue Premium as an Outcome Measure of Brand Equity," *Journal of Marketing*, 67 (October 2003): 1–17.

18. Alice Z. Cuneo, "Apple Transcends as Lifestyle Brand," *Advertising Age*, June 15, 2003, pp. S2, S6; "Apple and the Environment: US and Canada," www.apple.com/environment/recycling/nationalservices/japan.html (viewed March 2008).

19. Jon Miller and David Muir, *The Business of Brands* (West Sussex, England: John Wiley & Sons, 2004).

20. Douglas Holt, *How Brands Become Icons: The Principle of Cultural Branding* (Cambridge, MA: Harvard Business School Press, 2004); Douglas Holt, "Branding as Cultural Activism," zibs.com (viewed March 2008); Douglas Holt, "What Becomes an Icon Most," *Harvard Business Review*, 81 (March 2003): 43–49.

21. Stuart Elliott, "Letting Consumers Control Marketing: Priceless," *New York Times*, October 9, 2006; Elizabeth Holmes, "On MySpace, Millions of Users Make 'Friends' with Ads," *Wall Street Journal*, August 7, 2006.

22. Ted Matthews, "Staples Branding's Boost to the Bottom Line," *Instinct*, August 8, 2007; "About Staples," www.staples.ca/ENG/Static/static_pages.asp?pagename=corp%5Fabout (viewed March 2008).

23. David A. Aaker and Erich Joachimsthaler, *Brand Leadership* (New York: Free Press, 2000).

24. David A. Aaker, *Building Strong Brands* (New York: Free Press, 1996).

25. Kevin Lane Keller, "Building Customer-Based Brand Equity: A Blueprint for Creating Strong Brands," *Marketing Management,* 10 (July–August 2001): 15–19.

26. For some academic insights, see Matthew Thomson, Deborah J. MacInnis, and C. W. Park, "The Ties That Bind: Measuring the Strength of Consumers' Emotional Attachments to Brands," *Journal of Consumer Psychology,* 15, no. 1 (2005): 77–91, and Jennifer Edson Escalas, "Narrative Processing: Building Consumer Connections to Brands," *Journal of Consumer Psychology,* 14, nos. 1 & 2 (1996): 168–79. For some managerial guidelines, see Kevin Roberts, *Lovemarks: The Future beyond Brands* (New York: Powerhouse Books, 2004), and Douglas Atkins, *The Culting of Brands* (New York: Penguin Books, 2004).

27. Kristin Laird, "Harley-Davidson Plays Numbers Game," *Marketing Daily,* March 14, 2008.

28. Daphne Gordon, "Killing Mold – The Natural Way," *Toronto Star,* January 6, 2006; www.concrobium.com/home.html (viewed March 2008).

29. Rachel Dodes, "From Tracksuits to Fast Track," *Wall Street Journal,* September 13, 2006.

30. "42 Below," www.betterbydesign.org.nz (viewed September 14, 2007).

31. Alina Wheeler, *Designing Brand Identity* (Hoboken, NJ: John Wiley & Sons, 2003).

32. Pat Fallon and Fred Senn, *Juicing the Orange: How to Turn Creativity into a Powerful Business Advantage* (Cambridge, MA: Harvard Business School Press, 2006).

33. Robert Salerno, "We Try Harder: An Ad Creates a Brand," *Brandweek,* September 8, 2003, pp. 32–33.

34. John R. Doyle and Paul A. Bottomly, "Dressed for the Occasion: Font–Product Congruity in the Perception of Logotype," *Journal of Consumer Psychology*, 16, no. 2 (2006): 112–23; Kevin Lane Keller, Susan Heckler, and Michael J. Houston, "The Effects of Brand Name Suggestiveness on Advertising Recall," *Journal of Marketing,* 62 (January 1998): 48–57. For an in-depth examination of how brand names get developed, see Alex Frankel, *Wordcraft: The Art of Turning Little Words into Big Business* (New York: Crown Publishers, 2004).

35. Don Schultz and Heidi Schultz, *IMC: The Next Generation* (New York: McGraw-Hill, 2003); Don E. Schultz, Stanley I. Tannenbaum, and Robert F. Lauterborn, *Integrated Marketing Communications* (Lincolnwood, IL: NTC Business Books, 1993).

36. Mohanbir Sawhney, "Don't Harmonize, Synchronize," *Harvard Business Review* (July–August 2001): 101–8.

37. David C. Court, John E. Forsyth, Greg C. Kelly, and Mark A. Loch, "The New Rules of Branding: Building Strong Brands Faster," *McKinsey White Paper Fall 1999;* Scott Bedbury, *A New Brand World* (New York: Viking Press, 2002).

38. Ted Matthews, "Tutus, chain saws and emotional connections, *Instinct,* August 1, 2007.

39. Christopher Locke, Rick Levine, Doc Searls, and David Weinberger, *The Cluetrain Manifesto: The End of Business as Usual* (Cambridge, MA: Perseus Press, 2000).

40. Seth Godin, *Permission Marketing: Turning Strangers into Friends, and Friends into Customers* (New York: Simon & Schuster, 1999). See also Susan Fournier, Susan Dobscha, and David Mick, "Preventing the Premature Death of Relationship Marketing," *Harvard Business Review* (January–February 1998): 42–51.

41. Dawn Iacobucci and Bobby Calder, eds., *Kellogg on Integrated Marketing* (New York: John Wiley & Sons, 2003).

42. Kristin Laird, "CCM gets under the skin in new ads," *Marketing Daily,* March 10, 2008.

43. Pete Engardio, "Taking a Brand Name Higher," *BusinessWeek,* July 31, 2006, p. 48; Rob Walker, "Haier Goals," *New York Times Magazine,* November 20, 2005.

44. Michael Dunn and Scott Davis, "Building Brands from the Inside," *Marketing Management* (May–June 2003): 32–37; Scott Davis and Michael Dunn, *Building the Brand-Driven Business* (New York: John Wiley & Sons, 2002).

45. Stan Maklan and Simon Knox, *Competing on Value* (Upper Saddle River, NJ: Financial Times, Prentice Hall, 2000).

46. Coeli Carr, "Seeking to Attract Top Prospects, Employers Brush Up on Brands," *New York Times,* September 10, 2006.

47. Sherrie Bossung and Mark Pocharski, "Building a Communication Strategy: Marketing the Brand to Employees," presentation at Marketing Science Institute Conference, *Brand Orchestration,* Orlando, Florida, December 4, 2003.

48. The principles and examples from this passage are based on Colin Mitchell, "Selling the Brand Inside," *Harvard Business Review* (January 2002): 99–105. For an in-depth discussion of how two organizations, QuikTrip and Wawa, have developed stellar internal branding programs, see Neeli Bendapudi and Venkat Bendapudi, "Creating the Living Brand," *Harvard Business Review* (May 2005): 124–32.

49. Norma Ramage, "Bronco branding," *Marketing Magazine,* July 3, 2006.

50. Deborah Roeddder John, Barbara Loken, Kyeong-Heui Kim, and Alokparna Basu Monga, "Brand Concept Maps: A Methodology for Identifying Brand Association Networks," *Journal of Marketing Research,* 43 (November 2006): 549–63.

51. For related empirical insights, see Manoj K. Agrawal and Vithala Rao "An Empirical Comparison of Consumer-Based Measures of Brand Equity," *Marketing Letters,* 7, no. 3 (July 1996): 237–47, and Walfried Lassar, Banwari Mittal, and Arun Sharma, "Measuring Customer-Based Brand Equity," *Journal of Consumer Marketing,* 12, no. 4 (1995): 11–19.

52. "The Best Global Brands," *BusinessWeek,* August 6, 2007. The article ranks and critiques the 100 best global brands using the valuation method developed by Interbrand. For more discussion on some brand winners and losers, see Matt Haig, *Brand Royalty: How the Top 100 Brands Thrive and Survive* (London: Kogan Page, 2004), and Matt Haig, *Brand Failures: The Truth about the 100 Biggest Branding Mistakes of All Time* (London: Kogan Page, 2003). For an academic discussion of valuing brand equity, see V. Srinivasan, Chan Su Park, and Dae Ryun Chang, "An Approach to the Measurement, Analysis, and Prediction of Brand Equity and Its Sources," *Management Science,* 51 (September 2005): 1433–48.

53. Mark Sherrington, *Added Value: The Alchemy of Brand-Led Growth* (Hampshire, UK: Palgrave Macmillan, 2003).

54. For an up-to-date discussion of what factors determine long-term branding success, see Allen P. Adamson, *Brand Simple* (New York: Palgrave Macmillan, 2006).

55. David Kiley, "To Boost Sales, Volvo Returns to Its Roots: Safety," *USA Today,* August 26, 2002.

56. Natalie Mizik and Robert Jacobson, "Trading Off between Value Creation and Value Appropriation: The Financial Implications of Shifts in Strategic Emphasis," *Journal of Marketing,* 67 (January 2003): 63–76.

57. Mark Speece, "Marketer's Malady: Fear of Change," *Brandweek,* August 19, 2002, p. 34.

58. Joseph Weber, "Harley Just Keeps on Cruisin'," *BusinessWeek,* November 6, 2006, pp. 71–72.

59. Keith Naughton, "Fixing Cadillac," *Newsweek,* May 28, 2001, pp. 36–37.

60. Peter Farquhar, "Managing Brand Equity," *Marketing Research,* 1 (September 1989): 24–33.

61. Steven M. Shugan, "Branded Variants," 1989 AMA Educators' Proceedings (Chicago: American Marketing Association, 1989), pp. 33–38; M. Bergen, S. Dutta, and S. M. Shugan, "Branded

Variants: A Retail Perspective," *Journal of Marketing Research*, 33 (February 1996): 9–21.

62. Adam Bass, "Licensed Extension – Stretching to Communicate," *Journal of Brand Management*, 12 (September 2004): 31–38. See also Aaker, *Building Strong Brands*.

63. Jean Halliday, "Troubled Automakers' Golden Goose," *AutoWeek*, August 14, 2006; Becky Ebenkamp, "The Creative License," *Brandweek*, June 9, 2003, pp. 36–40.

64. William J. Holstein, "The Incalculable Value of Building Brands," *Chief Executive* (April–May 2006): 52+.

65. For comprehensive corporate branding guidelines, see James R. Gregory, *The Best of Branding: Best Practices in Corporate Branding* (New York: McGraw-Hill, 2004). For some international perspectives, see *The Expressive Organization: Linking Identity, Reputation, and Corporate Brand*, ed. Majken Schultz, Mary Jo Hatch, and Mogens Holten Larsen (Oxford, UK: Oxford University Press, 2000), and *Corporate Branding: Purpose, People, and Process*, ed. Majken Schultz, Yun Mi Antorini, and Fabian F. Csaba (Denmark: Copenhagen Business School Press, 2005).

66. Guido Berens, Cees B. M. van Riel, and Gerrit H. van Bruggen, "Corporate Associations and Consumer Product Responses: The Moderating Role of Corporate Brand Dominance," *Journal of Marketing*, 69 (July 2005): 35–48; Zeynep Gürhan-Canli and Rajeev Batra, "When Corporate Image Affects Product Evaluations: The Moderating Role of Perceived Risk," *Journal of Marketing Research*, 41 (May 2004): 197–205; Kevin Lane Keller and David A. Aaker, "Corporate-Level Marketing: The Impact of Credibility on a Company's Brand Extensions," *Corporate Reputation Review* 1 (August 1998): 356–78; Thomas J. Brown and Peter Dacin, "The Company and the Product: Corporate Associations and Consumer Product Responses," *Journal of Marketing*, 61 (January 1997): 68–84.

67. Vithala R. Rao, Manoj K. Agarwal, and Denise Dalhoff, "How Is Manifest Branding Strategy Related to the Intangible Value of a Corporation?" *Journal of Marketing*, 68 (October 2004): 126–41. For an examination of the financial impact of brand portfolio decisions, see Neil A. Morgan and Lopo L. Rego, "The Marketing and Financial Performance Consequences of Firms' Brand Portfolio Strategy," Working paper, Kelley School of Business, Indiana University, 2006.

68. Rebecca Harris, "Top of the Food Chain, *Marketing Magazine*, February 25, 2008.

69. Byung-Do Kim and Mary W. Sullivan, "The Effect of Parent Brand Experience on Line Extension Trial and Repeat Purchase," *Marketing Letters*, 9 (April 1998): 181–93.

70. John Milewicz and Paul Herbig, "Evaluating the Brand Extension Decision Using a Model of Reputation Building," *Journal of Product & Brand Management*, 3, no. 1 (January 1994): 39–47; Kevin Lane Keller and David A. Aaker, "The Effects of Sequential Introduction of Brand Extensions," *Journal of Marketing Research*, 29 (February 1992): 35–50.

71. Valarie A. Taylor and William O. Bearden, "Ad Spending on Brand Extensions: Does Similarity Matter?" *Journal of Brand Management*, 11 (September 2003): 63–74; Sheri Bridges, Kevin Lane Keller, and Sanjay Sood, "Communication Strategies for Brand Extensions: Enhancing Perceived Fit by Establishing Explanatory Links," *Journal of Advertising*, 29 (Winter 2000): 1–11; Daniel C. Smith, "Brand Extension and Advertising Efficiency: What Can and Cannot Be Expected," *Journal of Advertising Research* (November–December 1992): 11–20; Daniel C. Smith and C. Whan Park, "The Effects of Brand Extensions on Market Share and Advertising Efficiency," *Journal of Marketing Research*, 29 (August 1992): 296–313.

72. Bruce Meyer, "Rubber Firms Extend Brands to Gain Customers, Revenue," *B to B*, 90, no. 12, October 10, 2005, p. 6.

73. Subramanian Balachander and Sanjoy Ghose, "Reciprocal Spillover Effects: A Strategic Benefit of Brand Extensions," *Journal of Marketing*, 67, no. 1 (January 2003): 4–13.

74. Bharat N. Anand and Ron Shachar, "Brands as Beacons: A New Source of Loyalty to Multiproduct Firms," *Journal of Marketing Research*, 41 (May 2004): 135–50.

75. Kevin Lane Keller and David A. Aaker, "The Effects of Sequential Introduction of Brand Extensions," *Journal of Marketing Research*, 29 (February 1992): 35–50. For consumer processing implications, see Huifung Mao and H. Shanker Krishnan, "Effects of Prototype and Exemplar Fit on Brand Extension Evaluations: A Two-Process Contingency Model," *Journal of Consumer Research*, 33 (June 2006): 41–49.

76. Maureen Morrin, "The Impact of Brand Extensions on Parent Brand Memory Structures and Retrieval Processes," *Journal of Marketing Research*, 36, no. 4 (November 1999): 517–25; John A. Quelch and David Kenny, "Extend Profits, Not Product Lines," *Harvard Business Review* (September–October 1994): 153–60; Perspectives from the Editors, "The Logic of Product-Line Extensions," *Harvard Business Review* (November–December 1994): 53–62;

77. Al Ries and Jack Trout, *Positioning: The Battle for Your Mind, 20th Anniversary Edition* (New York: McGraw-Hill, 2000).

78. David A. Aaker, *Brand Portfolio Strategy: Creating Relevance, Differentiation, Energy, Leverage, and Clarity* (New York: Free Press, 2004).

79. "Lego's Turnaround: Picking Up the Pieces," *The Economist*, October 28, 2006, p. 76.

80. Mary W. Sullivan, "Measuring Image Spillovers in Umbrella-Branded Products," *Journal of Business*, 63, no. 3 (July 1990): 309–29.

81. Deborah Roedder John, Barbara Loken, and Christopher Joiner, "The Negative Impact of Extensions: Can Flagship Products Be Diluted?" *Journal of Marketing* (January 1998): 19–32; Susan M. Broniarcyzk and Joseph W. Alba, "The Importance of the Brand in Brand Extension," *Journal of Marketing Research* (May 1994): 214–28 (this entire issue of *JMR* is devoted to brands and brand equity); Barbara Loken and Deborah Roedder John, "Diluting Brand Beliefs: When Do Brand Extensions Have a Negative Impact?" *Journal of Marketing* (July 1993): 71–84. See also Chris Pullig, Carolyn Simmons, and Richard G. Netemeyer, "Brand Dilution: When Do New Brands Hurt Existing Brands?" *Journal of Marketing*, 70 (April 2006): 52–66; R. Ahluwalia and Z. Gürhan-Canli, "The Effects of Extensions on the Family Brand Name: An Accessibility-Diagnosticity Perspective," *Journal of Consumer Research*, 27 (December 2000): 371–81; Z. Gürhan-Canli and M. Durairaj, "The Effects of Extensions on Brand Name Dilution and Enhancement," *Journal of Marketing Research*, 35 (November 1998): 464–73; S. J. Milberg, C. W. Park, and M. S. McCarthy, "Managing Negative Feedback Effects Associated with Brand Extensions: The Impact of Alternative Branding Strategies," *Journal of Consumer Psychology*, 6 (1997): 119–40.

82. See also Franziska Völckner and Henrik Sattler, "Drivers of Brand Extension Success," *Journal of Marketing*, 70 (April 2006): 1–17.

83. Andrea Rothman, "France's Bic Bets U.S. Consumers Will Go for Perfume on the Cheap," *Wall Street Journal*, January 12, 1989.

84. Philip Kotler, Marketing Management, 11th ed. (Upper Saddle River, NJ: Prentice-Hall, 203); Patrick Barwise and Thomas Robertson, "Brand Portfolios," *European Management Journal*, 10, no. 3 (September 1992): 277–285.

85. David A. Aaker, *Brand Portfolio Strategy: Creating Relevance, Differentiation, Energy, Leverage, and Clarity* (New York: Free Press, 2004).

86. Jack Trout, *Differentiate or Die: Survival in Our Era of Killer Competition* (New York: John Wiley, 2000).

87. Nirmalya Kumar, "Kill a Brand, Keep a Customer," *Harvard Business Review* (December 2003): 87–95. For a methodological approach for assessing the extent and nature of cannibalization, see Charlotte H. Mason and George R. Milne, "An Approach for Identifying Cannibalization within Product Line Extensions and MultiBrand Strategies," *Journal of Business Research*, 31 (October–November 1994): 163–70.

88. Paul W. Farris, "The Chevrolet Corvette," Case UVA-M-320, The Darden Graduate Business School Foundation, University of Virginia, Charlottesville.

89. Roland T. Rust, Valerie A. Zeithaml, and Katherine A. Lemon, "Measuring Customer Equity and Calculating Marketing ROI," in *Handbook of Marketing Research*, ed. Rajiv Grover and Marco Vriens (Thousand Oaks, CA: Sage Publications, 2006), pp. 588–601; Roland T. Rust, Valerie A. Zeithaml, and Katherine A. Lemon, *Driving Customer Equity* (New York: Free Press, 2000).

90. Robert C. Blattberg and John Deighton, "Manage Marketing by the Customer Equity Test," *Harvard Business Review* (July–August 1996): 136–44.

91. Robert C. Blattberg and Jacquelyn S. Thomas, "Valuing, Analyzing, and Managing the Marketing Function using Customer Equity Principles," in *Kellogg on Marketing*, ed. Dawn Iacobucci (New York: John Wiley & Sons, 2002); Robert C. Blattberg, Gary Getz, and Jacquelyn S. Thomas, *Customer Equity: Building and Managing Relationships as Valuable Assets* (Boston: Harvard Business School Press, 2001).

92. Much of this section is based on Robert Leone, Vithala Rao, Kevin Lane Keller, Man Luo, Leigh McAlister, and Rajendra Srivatstava, "Linking Brand Equity to Customer Equity," *Journal of Service Research*, 9 (November 2006): 125–38. This special issue is devoted to customer equity and has a number of thought-provoking articles.

93. Niraj Dawar, "What Are Brands Good For?" *MIT Sloan Management Review* (Fall 2004): 31–37.

Chapter 10

1. Darrell Dunn, "Aligned at Last," *InformationWeek*, March 15, 2004; Kortney Stringer, "Hard Lesson Learned: Premium and No-Frills Don't Mix," *Wall Street Journal*, November 3, 2003.

2. Al Ries and Jack Trout, *Positioning: The Battle for Your Mind*, 20th Anniversary Edition (New York: McGraw-Hill, 2000).

3. Eve Lazarus, "Victoria's secret," *Marketing Daily*, March 26, 2007.

4. Theresa Howard, "DiGiorno's Campaign Delivers Major Sales," *USA Today*, April 1, 2002; Alice M. Tybout and Brian Sternthal, "Brand Positioning," in *Kellogg on Marketing*, ed. Dawn Iacobucci (New York: John Wiley & Sons, 2001), p. 35.

5. Bob Weber, "Firms with 'Eco-Friendly' Claims Need to Come Clean: Study," *Canadian Press*, November 19, 2007; Cascades Fine Papers Group website, http://www.environmentalbychoice.com; "Cascades Inc.: Company Snapshot," *Gloveinvestor.com*, http://investdb.theglobeandmail.com/invest/investSQL/gx.company_prof?company_id=181649 (viewed March 2008).

6. Kevin Lane Keller, Brian Stenthal, and Alice Tybout, "Three Questions You Need to Ask about Your Brand," *Harvard Business Review*, 80 (September 2002): 80–89.

7. Lisa D'Innocenzo, "Moores: For Guys Who Hate to Shop," *Strategy*, May 3, 2004; Moores Clothing for Men website, www.mooresclothing.com/english/moores.htm (viewed March 2008).

8. Patrick Tickle, Kevin Lane Keller, and Keith Richey, "Branding in High-Technology Markets," *Market Leader*, 22 (Autumn 2003): 21–26.

9. Jim Hopkins, "When the Devil Is in the Design," *USA Today*, December 31, 2001.

10. Keith Naughton, "Ford's 'Perfect Storm'," *Newsweek*, September 17, 2001, pp. 48–50.

11. Dale Buss, "Sweet Success," *Brandweek*, May 12, 2003, pp. 22–23.

12. Susan M. Broniarczyk and Andrew D. Gershoff, "The Reciprocal Effects of Brand Equity and Trivial Attributes," *Journal of Marketing Research*, 40 (May 2003): 161–75; Gregory S. Carpenter, Rashi Glazer, and Kent Nakamoto, "Meaningful Brands from Meaningless Differentiation: The Dependence on Irrelevant Attributes," *Journal of Marketing Research*, 31 (August 1994): 339–50.

13. Cecilie Rohwedder, "Playing Down the Plaid," *Wall Street Journal*, July 7, 2006, http://online.wsj.com/article_print/SB115222828906800109.html.

14. Michael Applebaum, "Comfy to Cool: A Brand Swivel," *Brandweek*, May 2, 2005, pp. 18–19.

15. Porter website, www.flyporter.com/ (viewed June 2008); Matt Semansky, "Will the Racoon Fly," *Marketing*, August 14, 2006.

16. Michael E. Porter, *Competitive Strategy: Techniques for Analyzing Industries and Competitors* (New York: Free Press, 1980).

17. Willow Duttge, "Counting Sleep," *Advertising Age*, June 5, 2006, pp. 4, 50.

18. Patrick Barwise, *Simply Better: Winning and Keeping Customers by Delivering What Matters Most* (Cambridge, MA: Harvard Business School Press, 2004).

19. "The 25 Best Sales Forces," *Sales & Marketing Management* (July 1998): 32–50.

20. Some authors distinguished additional stages. Wasson suggested a stage of competitive turbulence between growth and maturity. See Chester R. Wasson, *Dynamic Competitive Strategy and Product Life Cycles* (Austin, TX: Austin Press, 1978). Maturity describes a stage of sales growth slowdown and saturation, a stage of flat sales after sales have peaked.

21. John E. Swan and David R. Rink, "Fitting Market Strategy to Varying Product Life Cycles," *Business Horizons* (January–February 1982): 72–76; Gerald J. Tellis and C. Merle Crawford, "An Evolutionary Approach to Product Growth Theory," *Journal of Marketing* (Fall 1981): 125–34.

22. William E. Cox Jr., "Product Life Cycles as Marketing Models," *Journal of Business* (October 1967): 375–84.

23. Jordan P. Yale, "The Strategy of Nylon's Growth," *Modern Textiles Magazine* (February 1964): 32. See also Theodore Levitt, "Exploit the Product Life Cycle," *Harvard Business Review* (November–December 1965): 81–94.

24. Chester R. Wasson, "How Predictable Are Fashion and Other Product Life Cycles?" *Journal of Marketing* (July 1968): 36–43.

25. Wasson, "How Predictable Are Fashion and Other Product Life Cycles?"

26. William H. Reynolds, "Cars and Clothing: Understanding Fashion Trends," *Journal of Marketing* (July 1968): 44–49.

27. Bryan Curtis, "Trivial Pursuit," *Slate.com*, April 13, 2005; Patrick Butters, "What Biggest-Selling Adult Game Still Cranks Out Vexing Questions?" *Insight on the News*, January 26, 1998, p. 39.

28. Robert D. Buzzell, "Competitive Behavior and Product Life Cycles," in *New Ideas for Successful Marketing*, ed. John S. Wright and Jack Goldstucker (Chicago: American Marketing Association, 1956), p. 51.

29. Rajesh J. Chandy, Gerard J. Tellis, Deborah J. MacInnis, and Pattana Thaivanich, "What to Say When: Advertising Appeals in Evolving Markets," *Journal of Marketing Research*, 38 (November 2001): 399–414.

30. As reported in Joseph T. Vesey, "The New Competitors: They Think in Terms of Speed to Market." *Academy of Management Executive* 5, no. 2 (May 1991): 23–33, and Brian Dumaine, "How Managers Can Succeed through Speed," *Fortune*, February 13, 1989, pp. 54–59.

31. Glen L. Urban et al., "Market Share Rewards to Pioneering Brands: An Empirical Analysis and Strategic Implications," *Management Science* (June 1986): 645–59; William T. Robinson and Claes Fornell, "Sources of Market Pioneer Advantages in Consumer Goods Industries," *Journal of Marketing Research* (August 1985): 305–17.

32. Gregory S. Carpenter and Kent Nakamoto, "Consumer Preference Formation and Pioneering Advantage," *Journal of Marketing Research* (August 1989): 285–98.

33. William T. Robinson and Sungwook Min, "Is the First to Market the First to Fail? Empirical Evidence for Industrial Goods Businesses," *Journal of Marketing Research*, 39 (February 2002): 120–28.

34. Frank R. Kardes, Gurumurthy Kalyanaram, Murali Chankdrashekaran, and Ronald J. Dornoff, "Brand Retrieval, Consideration Set Composition, Consumer Choice, and the Pioneering Advantage," *Journal of Consumer Research* (June 1993): 62–75. See also Frank H. Alpert and Michael A. Kamins, "Pioneer Brand Advantage and Consumer Behavior: A Conceptual Framework and Propositional Inventory," *Journal of the Academy of Marketing Science* (Summer 1994): 244–53.

35. Thomas S. Robertson and Hubert Gatignon, "How Innovators Thwart New Entrants into Their Market," *Planning Review* (September–October 1991): 4–11, 48; Douglas Bowman and Hubert Gatignon, "Order of Entry as a Moderator of the Effect of Marketing Mix on Market Share," *Marketing Science,* 15, no. 3 (Summer 1996): 222–42.

36. Venkatesh Shankar, Gregory S. Carpenter, and Lakshman Krishnamurthi, "Late Mover Advantage: How Innovative Late Entrants Outsell Pioneers," *Journal of Marketing Research,* 35 (February 1998): 54–70.

37. Mark Ritson, "It Sometimes Pays to Come Second," *Marketing,* October 25, 2006, p. 23; Richard Waters, "Wikipedia Founder Plans Rival 'Citizendium' Aims to Introduce Order to Chaos of Web Encyclopedias; Editors Will Control the Posting of Articles," *Financial Times,* October 17, 2006, p. 19.

38. Steven P. Schnaars, *Managing Imitation Strategies* (New York: Free Press, 1994). See also Jin K. Han, Namwoon Kim, and Hony-Bom Kin, "Entry Barriers: A Dull-, One-, or Two-Edged Sword for Incumbents? Unraveling the Paradox from a Contingency Perspective," *Journal of Marketing* (January 2001): 1–14.

39. Victor Kegan, "Second Sight: Second Movers Take All," *The Guardian,* October 10, 2002.

40. Peter N. Golder, "Historical Method in Marketing Research with New Evidence on Long-Term Market Share Stability," *Journal of Marketing Research,* 37 (May 2000): 156–72; Peter N. Golder and Gerald J. Tellis, "Pioneer Advantage: Marketing Logic or Marketing Legend?" *Journal of Marketing Research* (May 1992): 34–46. See also Shi Zhang and Arthur B. Markman, "Overcoming the Early Advantage: The Role of Alignable and Nonalignable Differences," *Journal of Marketing Research* (November 1998): 1–15.

41. Gerald Tellis and Peter Golder, *Will and Vision: How Latecomers Can Grow to Dominate Markets* (New York: McGraw-Hill, 2001); Rajesh K. Chandy and Gerald J. Tellis, "The Incumbent's Curse? Incumbency, Size, and Radical Product Innovation," *Journal of Marketing Research* (July 2000): 1–17.

42. Sungwook Min, Manohar U. Kalwani, and William T. Robinson, "Market Pioneer and Early Follower Survival Risks: A Contingency Analysis of Really New Versus Incrementally New Product-Markets," *Journal of Marketing,* 70 (January 2006): 15–35. See also Raji Srinivasan, Gary L. Lilien, and Arvind Rangaswamy, "First In, First Out? The Effects of Network Externalities on Pioneer Survival," *Journal of Marketing,* 68 (January 2004): 41–58.

43. Jeromy Lloyd, "The Halo Effect for Microsoft," *Marketing Daily,* September 26, 2007.

44. Ben Elgin, "Yahoo!'s Boulevard of Broken Dreams," *BusinessWeek,* March 13, 2006, pp. 76–77; Fred Vogelstein, Yahoo!'s Brilliant Solution," *Fortune,* August 8, 2005, pp. 42–56; "Yahoo!'s Personality Crisis," *The Economist,* August 13, 2005, pp. 49–50; Ben Elgin, "The Search War Is About to Get Bloody," *BusinessWeek,* July 28, 2003, pp. 72–73; Amy Thomson and Crayton Harrison, "Yahoo! Shares Jump on Renewed Takeover Buzz," *The Globe and Mail,* July 3, 2007; Eric Auchard, "Google CEO Maps Out Company Strategy," *The Globe and Mail,* June 12, 2008; Miguel Helft, "Yahoo! Profits Steady, Revenue Up 8%," *New York Times,* July 18, 2007.

45. Trond Riiber Knudsen, "Escaping the Middle-Market Trap: An Interview with CEO of Electrolux," *McKinsey Quarterly* (December 2006): 72–79.

46. Stephanie Thompson, "Coffee Brands Think Outside of the Can," *Advertising Age,* July 28, 2003, p. 26.

47. Allen J. McGrath, "Growth Strategies with a '90s Twist," *Across the Board* (March 1995): 43–46.

48. Brian Wansink and Michael L. Ray, "Advertising Strategies to Increase Usage Frequency," *Journal of Marketing* (January 1996): 31–46. See also Brian Wansink, "Expansion Advertising," in *How Advertising Works,* ed. John Philip Jones (Thousand Oaks, CA: Sage Publications), pp. 95–103.

49. Stephen M. Nowlis and Itamar Simonson, "The Effect of New Product Features on Brand Choice," *Journal of Marketing Research* (February 1996): 36–46.

50. Rajan Varadarajan, Mark P. DeFanti, and Paul S. Busch, "Brand Portfolio, Corporate Image, and Reputation: Managing Brand Deletions," *Journal of the Academy of Marketing Science,* 34 (Spring 2006): 195–205; Stephen J. Carlotti Jr., Mary Ellen Coe, and Jesko Perrey, "Making Brand Portfolios Work," *McKinsey Quarterly,* 4 (2004): 24–36; Nirmalya Kumar, "Kill a Brand, Keep a Customer," *Harvard Business Review,* 81 (December 2003): 86–95; George J. Avlonitis, "Product Elimination Decision Making: Does Formality Matter?" *Journal of Marketing* (Winter 1985): 41–52; Philip Kotler, "Phasing Out Weak Products," *Harvard Business Review* (March–April 1965): 107–18.

51. Kathryn Rudie Harrigan, "The Effect of Exit Barriers upon Strategic Flexibility," *Strategic Management Journal,* 1 (February 1980): 165–76.

52. Laurence P. Feldman and Albert L. Page, "Harvesting: The Misunderstood Market Exit Strategy," *Journal of Business Strategy* (Spring 1985): 79–85; Philip Kotler, "Harvesting Strategies for Weak Products," *Business Horizons* (August 1978): 15–22.

53. Peter N. Golder and Gerard J. Tellis, "Growing, Growing, Gone: Cascades, Diffusion, and Turning Points in the Product Life Cycle," *Marketing Science,* 23 (Spring 2004): 207–18.

54. Youngme Moon, "Break Free from the Product Life Cycle," *Harvard Business Review* (May 2005): 87–94.

55. Hubert Gatignon and David Soberman, "Competitive Response and Market Evolution," in *Handbook of Marketing,* ed. Barton A. Weitz and Robin Wensley (London, UK: Sage Publications, 2002), pp. 126–47; Robert D. Buzzell, "Market Functions and Market Evolution," *Journal of Marketing,* 63 (Special Issue 1999): 61–63.

56. For a discussion of the evolution of the minivan market between 1982 and 1998, see Jose Antonio Rosa, Joseph F. Porac, Jelena Runser-Spanjol, and Michael S. Saxon, "Sociocognitive Dynamics in a Product Market," *Journal of Marketing,* 63 (Special Issue 1999): 64–77.

57. Daniel Fisher, "Six Feet Under," *Forbes,* July 7, 2003, pp. 66–68.

Chapter 11

1. For a detailed academic treatment of a number of issues on competition, see the Special Issue on Competitive Responsiveness, *Marketing Science,* 24 (Winter 2005).

2. Michael E. Porter, *Competitive Strategy* (New York: Free Press, 1980), pp. 22–23.

3. Tarun Khanna and Krishna G. Palepu, "Emerging Giants," *Harvard Business Review,* 84, no. 10 (October 2006): 60–69.

4. Ibid.

5. Allan D. Shocker, "Determining the Structure of Product-Markets: Practices, Issues, and Suggestions," in *Handbook of Marketing,* ed. Barton A. Weitz and Robin Wensley (London: Sage, 2002), pp. 106–25. See also Bruce H. Clark and David B. Montgomery, "Managerial Identification of Competitors," *Journal of Marketing,* 63 (July 1999): 67–83.

6. "What Business Are You In? Classic Advice from Theodore Levitt," *Harvard Business Review* (October 2006): 127–37. See also Theodore Levitt's seminal article, "Marketing Myopia," *Harvard Business Review* (July–August 1960): 45–56.

7. Jeffrey F. Rayport and Bernard J. Jaworski, *e-Commerce* (New York: McGraw-Hill, 2001), p. 53.

8. Richard A. D'Aveni, "Competitive Pressure Systems: Mapping and Managing Multimarket Contact," *MIT Sloan Management Review* (Fall 2002): 39–49.

9. Porter, *Competitive Strategy,* Chapter 7.

10. For discussion of some of the long-term implications of marketing activities, see Koen Pauwels, "How Dynamic Consumer Response, Competitor Response, Company Support, and Company Inertia Shape Long-Term Marketing Effectiveness," *Marketing Science,* 23 (Fall 2004): 596–610; Koen Pauwels, Dominique M. Hanssens, and S. Siddarth, "The Long-Term Effects of Price Promotions on Category Incidence, Brand Choice, and Purchase Quantity," *Journal of Marketing Research,* 34 (November 2002): 421–39; and Marnik Dekimpe and Dominique Hanssens, "Sustained Spending and Persistent Response: A New Look at Long-term Marketing Profitability," *Journal of Marketing Research,* 36 (November 1999): 397–412.

11. Rajendra S. Sisodia, David B. Wolfe, and Jagdish N. Sheth, *Firms of Endearment: How World-Class Companies Benefit Profit from Passion & Purpose* (Upper Saddle River, NJ: Wharton School Publishing, 2007).

12. For an academic treatment of benchmarking, see Douglas W. Vorhies and Neil A. Morgan, "Benchmarking Marketing Capabilities for Sustained Competitive Advantage," *Journal of Marketing,* 69, no. 1 (January 2005): 80–94.

13. Michael E. Porter, *Competitive Strategy* (New York: Free Press, 1980), Chapter 7.

14. This taxonomy and the Telstra example come from the writings of Australian marketing academic John H. Roberts: John H. Roberts, "Defensive Marketing: How a Strong Incumbent Can Protect Its Position," *Harvard Business Review* (November 2005): 150–57; John Roberts, Charlie Nelson, and Pamela Morrison, "Defending the Beachhead: Telstra vs. Optus," *Business Strategy Review,* 12 (Spring 2001): 19–24.

15. Michael Barbaro and Hillary Chura, "The Gap Is in Need of a Niche," *New York Times,* January 27, 2007 p. C1 Copyright © 2007 *The New York Times.* Reprinted by permission.

16. Fairmont Hotels & Resorts website, www.fairmont.com (viewed August 26, 2004); Paul Fengler and Garric Ng, "Green Consumer Guide," *Corporate Knights,* 1, no. 2 (Fall 2002): 25–27.

17. www.starbucks.com/aboutus/overview.asp, viewed March 7, 2007.

18. Brian Wansink, "Can Package Size Accelerate Usage Volume?" *Journal of Marketing,* 60 (July 1996): 1–14. See also Priya Raghubir and Eric A. Greenleaf, "Ratios in Proportion: What Should the Shape of the Package Be?" *Journal of Marketing,* 70 (April 2006): 95–107, and Valerie Folkes and Shashi Matta, "The Effect of Package Shape on Consumers' Judgments of Product Volume: Attention as a Mental Contaminant," *Journal of Consumer Research,* 31 (September 2004): 390–401.

19. John D. Cripps, "Heuristics and Biases in Timing the Replacement of Durable Products," *Journal of Consumer Research,* 21 (September 1994): 304–18.

20. "Business Bubbles," *The Economist,* October 12, 2002.

21. George Stalk Jr. and Rob Lachanauer, "Hardball: Five Killer Strategies for Trouncing the Competition," *Harvard Business Review,* 82 (April 2004): 62–71; Richard D'Aveni, "The Empire Strikes Back: Counterrevolutionary Strategies for Industry Leaders," *Harvard Business Review* (November 2002): 66–74.

22. Robert D. Hof, "There's Not Enough 'Me' in MySpace," *Business-Week,* December 4, 2006, p. 40; Patricia Sellers, "MySpace Cowboys," *Fortune,* September 4, 2006, pp. 66–74; Aaron Pressman, "MySpace for Baby Boomers," *BusinessWeek,* October 16, 2006, pp. 120–22.

23. John Tagliabue, "Yeah, They Torture Jeans. But It's All for the Sake of Fashion," *New York Times,* July 12, 2006, p. C1. Copyright © 2006 *The New York Times.* Reprinted by permission.

24. Cascades website, www.cascades.com (viewed March 2008).

25. Jonathan Glancey, "The Private World of the Walkman," *Guardian,* October 11, 1999.

26. These six defence strategies, as well as the five attack strategies, are taken from Philip Kotler and Ravi Singh, "Marketing Warfare in the 1980s," *Journal of Business Strategy* (Winter 1981): 30–41.

27. Porter, *Competitive Strategy,* Chapter 4; Jaideep Prabhu and David W. Stewart, "Signaling Strategies in Competitive Interaction: Building Reputations and Hiding the Truth," *Journal of Marketing Research,* 38 (February 2001): 62–72.

28. Roger J. Calantone and Kim E. Schatzel, "Strategic Foretelling: Communication-Based Antecedents of a Firm's Propensity to Preannounce," *Journal of Marketing,* 64 (January 2000): 17–30; Jehoshua Eliashberg and Thomas S. Robertson, "New Product Preannouncing Behavior: A Market Signaling Study," *Journal of Marketing Research,* 25 (August 1988): 282–92.

29. Thomas S. Robertson, Jehoshua Eliashberg, and Talia Rymon, "New-Product Announcement Signals and Incumbent Reactions," *Journal of Marketing,* 59 (July 1995): 1–15.

30. Yuhong Wu, Sridhar Balasubramanian, and Vijay Mahajan, "When Is a Preannounced New Product Likely to Be Delayed?" *Journal of Marketing,* 68 (April 2004): 101–13; Barry L. Bayus, Sanjay Jain, and Ambar G. Rao, "Truth or Consequences: An Analysis of Vaporware and New-Product Announcements," *Journal of Marketing Research,* 38 (February 2001): 3–13.

31. Kevin Kelleher, "Why FedEx Is Gaining Ground," *Business 2.0* (October 2003): 56–57; Charles Haddad, "FedEx: Gaining on Ground," *BusinessWeek,* December 16, 2002, pp. 126–28.

32. J. Scott Armstrong and Kesten C. Green, "Competitor-Oriented Objectives: The Myth of Market Share," *International Journal of Business,* 12, no. 1 (Winter 2007): 115–34; Stuart E. Jackson, *Where Value Hides: A New Way to Uncover Profitable Growth for Your Business* (New York: John Wiley & Sons, 2006).

33. Nirmalya Kumar, *Marketing as Strategy* (Cambridge, MA: Harvard Business School Press, 2004); Philip Kotler and Paul N. Bloom, "Strategies for High-Market-Share Companies," *Harvard Business Review* (November–December 1975): 63–72.

34. Robert D. Buzzell and Frederick D. Wiersema, "Successful Share-Building Strategies," *Harvard Business Review* (January–February 1981): 135–44.

35. Robert J. Dolan, "Models of Competition: A Review of Theory and Empirical Evidence," in *Review of Marketing,* ed. Ben M. Enis and Kenneth J. Roering (Chicago: American Marketing Association, 1981), pp. 224–34.

36. Linda Hellofs and Robert Jacobson, "Market Share and Customer's Perceptions of Quality: When Can Firms Grow Their Way to Higher versus Lower Quality?" *Journal of Marketing,* 63 (January 1999): 16–25.

37. Jon Birger, "Second-Mover Advantage," *Fortune,* March 20, 2006, pp. 20–21.

38. Venkatesh Shankar, Gregory Carpenter, and Lakshman Krishnamurthi, "Late-Mover Advantage: How Innovative Late Entrants Outsell Pioneers," *Journal of Marketing Research,* 35 (February 1998): 54–70; Gregory S. Carpenter and Kent Nakamoto, "The Impact of Consumer Preference Formation on Marketing Objectives and Competitive Second-Mover Strategies," *Journal of Consumer Psychology,* 5, no. 4 (1996): 325–58; Gregory S. Carpenter and Kent Nakamoto, "Competitive Strategies for Late Entry into a Market with a Dominant Brand," *Management Science* (October 1990): 1268–78.

39. Megan Johnston, "The Ketchup Strategy," *Forbes,* November 13, 2006, p. 185.

40. Harvey's web site www.harveys.ca (viewed August 26, 2004); Lisa D'Innocenzo, "Triumph of the Underdog," *Strategy Magazine Online,* October 20, 2003.

41. Abby Klassen, "Search Davids Take Aim at Goliath Google," *Advertising Age,* January 8, 2007, p. 1+; "Cha-Cha—Ceo Interview," *CEO Wire,* January 9, 2007.

42. Katrina Booker, "The Pepsi Machine," *Fortune,* February 6, 2006, pp. 68–72.

43. "iPhone Debuts Big in BlackBerry Country," *Sify,* July 12, 2008, http://sify.com/finance/fullstory.php?id=14714465&cid=20742.

44. Kristin Laird, "Country Style lures those let down by Tim Hortons," *Marketing Daily*, February 28, 2008.

45. Theodore Levitt, "Innovative Imitation," *Harvard Business Review* (September–October 1966): 63. See also Steven P. Schnaars, *Managing Imitation Strategies: How Later Entrants Seize Markets from Pioneers* (New York: Free Press, 1994).

46. Stuart F. Brown, "The Company That Out-Harleys Harley," *Fortune*, September 28, 1998, pp. 56–57; www.sscycle.com.

47. Melita Marie Garza, "Illinois Tool Works Stock Continues to Suffer Since Acquisition of Firm," *Chicago Tribune*, November 16, 2000; www.itw.com/about_home.html.

48. Rocky Mountain Soap Company website, http://www.rockymountainsoap.com/webpage/1000787/1000144 (viewed June 2008).

49. Reported in E. R. Linneman and L. J. Stanton, *Making Niche Marketing Work* (New York: McGraw-Hill, 1991).

50. Thomas A. Fogarty, "Keeping Zippo's Flame Eternal," *USA Today*, June 24, 2003; www.zippo.com.

51. Kathleen Kingsbury, "The Cell Islands," *Time*, 168, no. 21, November 20, 2006, p. G20.

52. Robert Spector, *Amazon.com: Get Big Fast* (New York: HarperBusiness, 2000), p. 151.

Chapter 12

1. This discussion is adapted from Theodore Levitt, "Marketing Success through Differentiation: Of Anything," *Harvard Business Review* (January–February 1980): 83–91. The first level, core benefit, has been added to Levitt's discussion.

2. Harper W. Boyd Jr. and Sidney Levy, "New Dimensions in Consumer Analysis," *Harvard Business Review* (November–December 1963): 129–140.

3. Joe Iannarelli, "Jamestown Container Thinks Outside the Box," *Business First*, October 3, 2003, p. 4.

4. For some definitions, see Peter D. Bennett, ed., *Dictionary of Marketing Terms* (Chicago: American Marketing Association, 1995). See also Patrick E. Murphy and Ben M. Enis, "Classifying Products Strategically," *Journal of Marketing* (July 1986): 24–42.

5. Some of these bases are discussed in David A. Garvin, "Competing on the Eight Dimensions of Quality," *Harvard Business Review* (November–December 1987): 101–109.

6. Paul Kedrosky, "Simple Minds," *Business 2.0* (April 2006): 38; Debora Viana Thompson, Rebecca W. Hamilton, and Roland Rust, "Feature Fatigue: When Product Capabilities Become Too Much of a Good Thing," *Journal of Marketing Research*, 42 (November 2005): 431–42.

7. James H. Gilmore and B. Joseph Pine, *Markets of One: Creating Customer-Unique Value through Mass Customization* (Boston: Harvard Business School Press, 2000).

8. Kristin Laird, "P&G Offers Skin Care Help from Olay," *Marketing Magazine Online*, www.marketingmag.ca, February 1, 2008.

9. Sarah Dobson, "Harvey's Shifts from Grill to Garnishes," *Marketing Magazine Online*, www.marketingmag.ca, June 8, 2006.

10. Paul Grimaldi, "Consumers Design Products Their Way." *Knight Ridder Tribune Business News*, November 25, 2006; Michael A. Prospero, *Fast Company* (September 2005): 35.

11. Michelle Grimes, "Toy Makers Tout Made in Canada Label," *The Globe and Mail Online*, www.globeandmail.com, October 23, 2007.

12. Nathalie Atkinson, "Lovable Little Devils," *National Post Online*, www.nationalpost.com, November 10, 2007.

13. Bernd Schmitt and Alex Simonson, *Marketing Aesthetics: The Strategic Management of Brand, Identity, and Image* (New York: The Free Press, 1997).

14. Bruce Nussbaum, "The Power of Design," *BusinessWeek*, May 17, 2004, pp. 88–94; "Masters of Design," *Fast Company*, June 2004: 61–75. See also Philip Kotler, "Design: A Powerful but

14. (cont.) Neglected Strategic Tool," *Journal of Business Strategy* (Fall 1984): 16–21.

15. "New Exporter Winner: Chilliwack Mountain Log Homes Ltd.," 2008 BC Export Awards, Previous Winners 2003, www.bcexportawards.com/template_bc.asp?p=25 (viewed April 2008).

16. A. G. Lafley, "Delivering Delight," *Fast Company* (June 2004): 51; Frank Nuovo, "A Call for Fashion," *Fast Company* (June 2004): 52; Bobbie Gossage, "Strategies: Designing Success," *Inc.* (May 2004): 27–29; Jerome Kathman, "Building Leadership Brands by Design," *Brandweek*, December 1, 2003, p. 20; Bob Parks, "Deconstructing Cute," *Business 2.0* (December 2002–January 2003): 47–50; J. Lynn Lunsford and Daniel Michaels, "Masters of Illusion," *Wall Street Journal*, November 25, 2002; Jim Hopkins, "When the Devil Is in the Design," *USA Today*, December 31, 2001.

17. Stanley Reed, "Rolls Royce at Your Service," *BusinessWeek*, November 15, 2005, pp. 92–93.

18. Norma Ramage, "Be Our Guest," *Marketing Magazine Online*, www.marketingmag.ca, September 10, 2007.

19. For a comprehensive discussion of Cemex, see Adrian J. Slywotzky and David J. Morrison, *How Digital Is Your Business* (New York: Crown Business, 2000), Chapter 5.

20. Mark Sanchez, "Herman Miller Offers Training to Its Furniture Users," *Grand Rapids Business Journal*, December 2, 2002, p. 23.

21. Linda Knapp, "A Sick Computer?" *Seattle Times*, January 28, 2001, p. D8.

22. Matthew Boyle, "Best Buy's Giant Gamble," *Fortune*, April 3, 2006, pp. 69–75; Geoffrey Colvin, "Talking Shop," *Fortune*, August 21, 2006, pp. 73–80; "Best Buy Turns on the Geek Appeal," *DSN Retailing Today*, February 24, 2003, p. 22; Kristin Laird, "Best Buy Runs Earth-friendly Trade-in Program," *Marketing Daily*, April 21, 2008.

23. Leslie Earnest and Adrian G. Uribarri, "Costco Halts Liberal Electronics Return Policy; Refunds Were Costing the Warehouse Store Chain 'Tens of Millions of Dollars' a Year," *Los Angeles Times*, February 28, 2007, p. C1. Reprinted by permission.

24. This section is based on a comprehensive treatment of product returns, James Stock and Thomas Speh, "Managing Product Returns for Competitive Advantage," *MIT Sloan Management Review* (Fall 2006): 57–62.

25. Robert Bordley, "Determining the Appropriate Depth and Breadth of a Firm's Product Portfolio, *Journal of Marketing Research*, 40 (February 2003): 39–53; Peter Boatwright and Joseph C. Nunes, "Reducing Assortment: An Attribute-Based Approach, *Journal of Marketing*, 65 (July 2001): 50–63.

26. Adapted from a Hamilton Consultants White Paper, December 1, 2000.

27. This illustration is found in Benson P. Shapiro, *Industrial Product Policy: Managing the Existing Product Line* (Cambridge, MA: Marketing Science Institute, 1977), pp. 3–5, 98–101.

28. "Brand Challenge," *The Economist*, April 6, 2002, p. 68.

29. Amna Kirmani, Sanjay Sood, and Sheri Bridges, "The Ownership Effect in Consumer Responses to Brand-Line Stretches," *Journal of Marketing*, 63 (January 1999): 88–101; T. Randall, K. Ulrich, and D. Reibstein, "Brand Equity and Vertical Product-Line Extent," *Marketing Science*, 17 (Fall 1998): 356–79; David A. Aaker, "Should You Take Your Brand to Where the Action Is?" *Harvard Business Review* (September–October 1997): 135–43.

30. Paul-Mark Rendon, "Bottling Success," *Marketing Magazine Online*, www.marketingmag.ca, November 20, 2006.

31. France Leclerc, Christopher K. Hsee, and Joseph C. Nunes, "Narrow Focusing: Why the Relative Position of a Good in Its Category Matters More Than It Should," *Marketing Science*, 24 (Spring 2005): 194–205.

32. Neal E. Boudette, "BMW's Push to Broaden Line Hits Some Bumps in the Road," *Wall Street Journal*, January 25, 2005; Alex Taylor III, "The Ultimate Fairly Inexpensive Driving Machine," *Fortune*, November 1, 2004, pp. 130–40.

33. Steuart Henderson Britt, "How Weber's Law Can Be Applied to Marketing," *Business Horizons* (February 1975): 21–29.

34. Stanley Holmes, "All the Rage Since Reagan," *BusinessWeek*, July 25, 2005, p. 68.

35. Nirmalya Kumar, "Kill a Brand, Keep a Customer," *Harvard Business Review* (December 2003): 86–95; Brad Stone, "Back to Basics," *Newsweek*, August 4, 2003, pp. 42–44.

36. Laurens M. Sloot, Dennis Fok, and Peter Verhoef, "The Short- and Long-Term Impact of an Assortment Reduction on Category Sales," *Journal of Marketing Research*, 43 (November 2006): 536–48.

37. Patricia O'Connell, "A Chat with Unilever's Niall FitzGerald," *BusinessWeek Online*, August 2, 2001; John Willman, "Leaner, Cleaner, and Healthier Is the Stated Aim," *Financial Times*, February 23, 2000; "Unilever's Goal: 'Power Brands'," *Advertising Age*, January 3, 2000.

38. George Rädler, Jan Kubes, and Bohdan Wojnar, "Skoda Auto: From 'No-Class' to World-Class in One Decade," *Critical EYE*, 15 (July 2006); Scott D. Upham, "Beneath the Brand," *Automotive Manufacturing & Production* (June 2001).

39. Ben Elgin, "Can HP's Printer Biz Keep Printing Money?" *BusinessWeek*, July 14, 2003, pp. 68–70; Simon Avery, "H-P Sees Room for Growth in Printer Market," *Wall Street Journal*, June 28, 2001; Lee Gomes, "Computer-Printer Price Drop Isn't Starving Makers," *Wall Street Journal*, August 16, 1996.

40. See Gerald J. Tellis, "Beyond the Many Faces of Price: An Integration of Pricing Strategies," *Journal of Marketing* (October 1986): 155. See also Dilip Soman and John T. Gourville, "Transaction Decoupling: How Price Bundling Affects the Decision to Consume," *Journal of Marketing Research*, 38 (February 2001): 30–44.

41. Adapted from George Wuebker, "Bundles Effectiveness Often Undermined," *Marketing News*, March 18, 2002, pp. 9–12. See Stefan Stremersch and Gerard J. Tellis, "Strategic Bundling of Products and Prices," *Journal of Marketing*, 66 (January 2002): 55–72.

42. Akshay R. Rao, Lu Qu, and Robert W. Ruekert, "Signaling Unobservable Quality through a Brand Ally," *Journal of Marketing Research*, 36, no. 2 (May 1999): 258–68; Akshay R. Rao and Robert W. Ruekert, "Brand Alliances as Signals of Product Quality," *Sloan Management Review* (Fall 1994): 87–97.

43. Bernard L. Simonin and Julie A. Ruth, "Is a Company Known by the Company It Keeps? Assessing the Spillover Effects of Brand Alliances on Consumer Brand Attitudes," *Journal of Marketing Research* (February 1998): 30–42; see also C. W. Park, S. Y. Jun, and A. D. Shocker, "Composite Branding Alliances: An Investigation of Extension and Feedback Effects," *Journal of Marketing Research*, 33 (November 1996): 453–66.

44. C. W. Park, S. Y. Jun, and A. D. Shocker, "Composite Branding Alliances: An Investigation of Extension and Feedback Effects," *Journal of Marketing Research*, 33 (1996): 453–466; Lance Leuthesser, Chiranjier Kohli, and Rajneesh Suri, "2 + 2 = 5? A Framework for Using Co-branding to Leverage a Brand," *Journal of Brand Management*, 2, no. 1 (September 2003): 35–47.

45. Based in part on a talk by Nancy Bailey: "Using Licensing to Build the Brand," Brand Masters conference, December 7, 2000.

46. Kalpesh Kaushik Desai and Kevin Lane Keller, "The Effects of Brand Expansions and Ingredient Branding Strategies on Host Brand Extendibility," *Journal of Marketing*, 66 (January 2002): 73–93; D. C. Denison, "Ingredient Branding Puts Big Names in the Mix," *Boston Globe*, May 26, 2002, p. E2.

47. www.dupont.com.

48. Seth Goldin, "In Praise of Purple Cows," *Fast Company* (February 2003): 74–85.

49. Susan B. Bassin, "Value-Added Packaging Cuts Through Store Clutter," *Marketing News*, September 26, 1988, p. 21.

50. "Unilever Canada Ltd. Sunlight Small & Mighty," Best of Show 2008, The Packaging Association of Canada Sustainable Packaging Leadership Awards, www.pac.ca/events/events_npc2.html (viewed April 2008).

51. Karen Springen, "Nancy's Still Nice," *Newsweek*, February 16, 2004, p. 9; Judith Rosen, "Classics Strategies; Classics Sale," *Publishers Weekly*, October 6, 2003, pp. 16–18.

52. Annette Bourdeau, "Brilliant Package Design," *Strategy Magazine Online*, www.strategymag.com, September 2005, p. 8.

53. Rebecca Harris, "Top of the Food Chain," *Marketing Magazine Online*, www.marketingmag.ca, February 25, 2008.

54. Kate Fitzgerald, "Packaging Is the Capper," *Advertising Age*, May 5, 2003, p. 22.

55. Kate Novack, "Tomato Soup with a Side of Pop Art," *Time*, May 10, 2004; "Campbell Soup Co. Changes the Look of Its Famous Cans," *Wall Street Journal*, August 26, 1999.

56. "Skip Extended Warranties, Consumers Union Urges," *CBC News Online*, www.cbc.ca, November 15, 2006.

57. Jason Stein, "10-year Mitsubishi Warranty Is Small Part of a Larger Plan," *Automotive News*, January 12, 2004, p. 16.

58. Dee Gill, ". . . Or Your Money Back," *Inc.*, 27, no. 9 (September 2005): 46. Reprinted by permission of *Inc.* via Copyright Clearance Center.

59. Barbara Ettore, "Phenomenal Promises Mean Business," *Management Review* (March 1994): 18–23; "More Firms Pledge Guaranteed Service," *Wall Street Journal*, July 17, 1991. Also see Sridhar Moorthy and Kannan Srinivasan, "Signaling Quality with a Money-Back Guarantee: The Role of Transaction Costs," *Marketing Science*, 14, no. 4 (Fall 1995): 442–46; Christopher W. L. Hart, *Extraordinary Guarantees* (New York: Amacom, 1993).

Chapter 13

1. Statistics Canada, "Gross Domestic Product at Basic Prices, By Industry (2007 data)," www40.statcan.ca/l01/cst01/econ41.htm; Statistics Canada, "Gross Domestic Product (GDP) Service Producing Industries (NAICS 41 to NAICS 91)," www.strategis.ic.gc.ca/sc_ecnmy/sio/cis41-91gdpe.html, May 2008.

2. Statistics Canada, "Employment by Industry," www40.statcan.ca/l01/cst01/econ40.htm; Statistics Canada "Employment, Payroll Employment, By Industry" www40.statcan.ca/l01/cst01/labr71a.htm, May 2008.

3. Benjamin Scheider and David E. Bowen, *Winning the Service Game* (Boston: Harvard Business School Press, 1995); Leonard L. Berry, "Services Marketing Is Different," *Business* (May–June 1980): 24–30. For a thorough review of academic research into services, see Roland T. Rust and Tuck Siong Chung, "Marketing Models of Service and Relationships," *Marketing Science* 25 (November–December 2006): 560–80.

4. Jena McGregor, "Customer Service Champs," *BusinessWeek*, March 5, 2007, pp. 52–64; Mohanbir Sawhney, Sridhar Balasubramanian, and Vish V. Krishnan, "Creating Growth with Services," *MIT Sloan Management Review* (Winter 2004): 34–43.

5. "2006 Digital Marketing Awards, Website: Services," *Marketing Magazine Online*, www.marketingmag.ca, November 6, 2006.

6. Further classifications of services are described in Christopher H. Lovelock, *Services Marketing*, 3rd ed. (Upper Saddle River, NJ: Prentice Hall, 1996). See also John E. Bateson, *Managing Services Marketing: Text and Readings*, 3rd ed. (Hinsdale, IL: Dryden, 1995).

7. Valarie A. Zeithaml, "How Consumer Evaluation Processes Differ between Goods and Services," in *Marketing of Services*, ed. J. Donnelly and W. R. George (Chicago: American Marketing Association, 1981), pp. 186–90.

8. Amy Ostrom and Dawn Iacobucci, "Consumer Trade-Offs and the Evaluation of Services," *Journal of Marketing* (January 1995): 17–28.

9. For discussion of how the blurring of the line distinguishing products and services changes the meaning of this taxonomy, see Christopher Lovelock and Evert Gummesson, "Whither Services Marketing? In Search of a New Paradigm and Fresh Perspectives," *Journal of Service Research* 7 (August 2004): 20–41, and Stephen L. Vargo and Robert F. Lusch, "Evolving to a New Dominant Logic for Marketing," *Journal of Marketing* 68 (January 2004): 1–17.

10. Theodore Levitt, "Marketing Intangible Products and Product Intangibles," *Harvard Business Review* (May–June 1981): 94–102; Berry, "Services Marketing Is Different," *Business* (May–June 1980): 24–30.

11. B. H. Booms and M. J. Bitner, "Marketing Strategies and Organizational Structures for Service Firms," in *Marketing of Services,* ed. J. Donnelly and W. R. George (Chicago: American Marketing Association, 1981), pp. 47–51.

12. Lewis P. Carbone and Stephan H. Haeckel, "Engineering Customer Experiences," *Marketing Management,* 3 (Winter 1994): 17.

13. Bernd H. Schmitt, *Customer Experience Management* (New York: John Wiley & Sons, 2003).

14. Rob Gerlsbeck, "Memorial University Targets Toronto Commuters," *Marketing Magazine Online,* www.marketingmag.ca, August 30, 2007.

15. "A Barefooted Anti-Diva for the Opera Stage," *Maclean's,* 115, no. 13, p. 1–2; Danielle Groen, "My, My, Measha," *Chatelaine Magazine Online,* www.chatelaine.com, January 2008; Sabine Kortals, "Soprano, N.Y. Philharmonic at Peaks in Vail," *Denver Post Online,* www.denverpost.com, July 25, 2007; John Terauds, "An Hour in the Life of a Diva," *Toronto Star,* November 22, 2007, p. E3; John Terauds, "Love Affair with Measha Brueggergosman Has Only Just Begun," *Toronto Star,* November 26, 2007, p. L5; www.measha.com, May 2008.

16. Gila E. Fruchter and Eitan Gerstner, "Selling with 'Satisfaction Guaranteed,'" *Journal of Service Research,* 1, no. 4 (May 1999): 313–23. See also Rebecca J. Slotegraaf and J. Jeffrey Inman, "Longitudinal Shifts in the Drivers of Satisfaction with Product Quality: The Role of Attribute Resolvability," *Journal of Marketing Research,* 41 (August 2004): 269–80.

17. For a similar list, see Leonard L. Berry and A. Parasuraman, *Marketing Services: Competing through Quality* (New York: Free Press, 1991), p. 16.

18. "The Financial Post's Ten Best Companies to Work For: Fairmont Hotels & Resorts (Profile)," *Canada.com Network,* working.canada.com, September 27, 2007.

19. The material in this paragraph is based in part on Valarie Zeithaml, Mary Jo Bitner, and Dwayne D. Gremler, *Services Marketing: Integrating Customer Focus across the Firm,* 4th ed. (New York: McGraw-Hill, 2006), chapter 9.

20. G. Lynn Shostack, "Service Positioning through Structural Change," *Journal of Marketing* (January 1987): 34–43.

21. Vikas Mittal, Wagner A. Kamakura, and Rahul Govind, "Geographical Patterns in Customer Service and Satisfaction: An Empirical Investigation," *Journal of Marketing,* 68 (July 2004): 48–62.

22. Asim Ansari and Carl F. Mela, "E-Customization," *Journal of Marketing Research,* 40 (May 2003): 131–45; Jeffrey F. Rayport, Bernard J. Jaworski, and Ellie J. Kyung, "Best Face Forward: Improving Companies' Service Interface with Customers," *Journal of Interactive Marketing,* 19 (Autumn 2005): 67–80.

23. W. Earl Sasser, "Match Supply and Demand in Service Industries," *Harvard Business Review* (November–December 1976): 133–40.

24. Eyal Biyalogorsky and Eitan Gerstner, "Contingent Pricing to Reduce Price Risks," *Marketing Science,* 23, no. 1 (Winter 2003): 146–55; Steven M. Shugan and Jinhong Xie, "Advance Pricing of Services and Other Implications of Separating Purchase and Consumption," *Journal of Service Research,* 2, no. 3 (February 2000): 227–39; Steven M. Shugan and Jinhong Xie, "Advance Selling for Services," *California Management Review,* 46, no. 3 (Spring 2004): 37–54.

25. Carol Krol, "Case Study: Club Med Uses E-Mail to Pitch Unsold, Discounted Packages," *Advertising Age,* December 14, 1998, p. 40; www.clubmed.com.

26. Seth Godin, "If It's Broke, Fix It," *Fast Company* (October 2003): 131.

27. Diane Brady, "Why Service Stinks," *BusinessWeek,* October 23, 2000, pp. 119–28.

28. Kenneth Hein, "Communications Breakdown: Why Brands Can't Connect," *Brandweek,* February 19, 2007, p. 10.

29. "President's Choice Financial and TD Canada Trust Rank Highest in Customer Satisfaction with Retail Banks in Canada," Press Release, J.D. Power and Associates, August 30, 2007, www.jdpower.com/corporate/news/releases/pdf/2007157.pdf; William Azaroff, "TD Canada Trust Launches "Split It" on Facebook," August 16, 2007, www.netbanker.com/2007/08/td_canada_trust_launches_split_it_on_facebook.html (both sites viewed May 2008).

30. Hannah Clark, "Customer Service Hell," *Forbes,* March 30, 2006.

31. Horovitz, "Whatever Happened to Customer Service? Automated Answering, Long Waits Irk Consumers," *USA Today,* September 26, 2003.

32. Richard Halicks, "You Can Count on Customer Disservice," *Atlanta Journal Constitution,* June 29, 2003; Bruce Horovitz, "Whatever Happened to Customer Service?" *USA Today,* September 26, 2003; Judi Ketteler, "Grumbling Groundswell," *Cincinnati Business Courier,* September 8, 2003; Michelle Slatella, "Toll-Free Apology Soothes Savage Beast," *New York Times,* February 12, 2004; Jane Spencer, "Cases of Customer Rage Mount as Bad Service Prompts Venting," *Wall Street Journal,* September 17, 2003.

33. David Menzies, "Tourist trap," *Marketing,* July 16, 2007.

34. Matthew L. Meuter, Amy L. Ostrom, Robert I. Roundtree, and Mary Jo Bitner, "Self-Service Technologies: Understanding Customer Satisfaction with Technology-Based Service Encounters," *Journal of Marketing,* 64, no. 3 (July 2000): 50–64; Stephen S. Tax, Mark Colgate, and David Bowen, "How to Prevent Your Customers from Failing," *MIT Sloan Management Review* (Spring 2006): 30–38; Mei Xue and Patrick T. Harker, "Customer Efficiency: Concept and Its Impact on E-Business Management," *Journal of Service Research,* 4, no. 4 (May 2002): 253–67.

35. Valarie Zeithaml, Mary Jo Bitner, and Dwayne D. Gremler, *Services Marketing: Integrating Customer Focus across the Firm,* 4th ed. (New York: McGraw-Hill, 2006).

36. Stephen S. Tax, Mark Colgate, and David Bowen, "How to Prevent Your Customers from Failing," *MIT Sloan Management Review* (Spring 2006): 30–38.

37. Terrence Belford, "On-line Coaches Rescue Baffled Buyers," *The Globe and Mail,* Thursday, July 7, 2005, p. B9.

38. Susan M. Keaveney, "Customer Switching Behavior in Service Industries: An Exploratory Study," *Journal of Marketing* (April 1995): 71–82. See also Jaishankar Ganesh, Mark J. Arnold, and Kristy E. Reynolds, "Understanding the Customer Base of Service Providers: An Examination of the Differences between Switchers and Stayers," *Journal of Marketing,* 64 (July 2000): 65–87; Michael D. Hartline and O. C. Ferrell, "The Management of Customer-Contact Service Employees: An Empirical Investigation," *Journal of Marketing* (October 1996): 52–70; Linda L. Price, Eric J. Arnould, and Patrick Tierney, "Going to Extremes: Managing Service Encounters and Assessing Provider Performance," *Journal of Marketing* (April 1995): 83–97; Lois A. Mohr, Mary Jo Bitner, and Bernard H. Booms, "Critical Service Encounters: The Employee's Viewpoint," *Journal of Marketing* (October 1994): 95–106.

39. Christian Gronroos, "A Service-Quality Model and Its Marketing Implications," *European Journal of Marketing,* 18, no. 4 (1984): 36–44.

40. Leonard Berry, "Big Ideas in Services Marketing," *Journal of Consumer Marketing* (Spring 1986): 47–51. See also Jagdip Singh, "Performance Productivity and Quality of Frontline Employees in Service Organizations," *Journal of Marketing,* 64 (April 2000): 15–34; Walter E. Greene, Gary D. Walls, and Larry J. Schrest, "Internal Marketing: The Key to External Marketing Success," *Journal of Services Marketing,* 8, no. 4 (1994): 5–13; John R. Hauser, Duncan I. Simester, and Birger Wernerfelt, "Internal

Customers and Internal Suppliers," *Journal of Marketing Research* (August 1996): 268–80.

41. "What Makes Singapore a Service Champion?" *Strategic Direction* (April 2003): 26–28; Justin Doebele, "The Engineer," *Forbes*, January 9, 2006, pp. 122–24; Stanley Holmes, "Creature Comforts at 30,000 Feet," *BusinessWeek*, December 18, 2006, p. 138.

42. Christian Gronroos, "A Service-Quality Model," pp. 38–39; Michael D. Hartline, James G. Maxham III, and Daryl O. McKee, "Corridors of Influence in the Dissemination of Customer-Oriented Strategy to Customer-Contact Service Employees," *Journal of Marketing* (April 2000): 35–50.

43. Michael D. Hartline and O. C. Ferrell, "The Management of Customer-Contact Service Employees: An Empirical Investigation," *Journal of Marketing*, 60 (October 1996): 52–70; Ad de Jong, Ko de Ruyter, and Jos Lemmink, "Antecedents and Consequences of the Service Climate in Boundary-Spanning Self-Managing Service Teams," *Journal of Marketing*, 68 (April 2004): 18–35.

44. "Sears Canada Mobilizes Service Repair Network with Enterprise Wireless Dispatch System from Mobile Computing Corporation," *Canada NewsWire*, May 17, 2005, p. 1.

45. "Fairmont President's Club," www.fairmont.com/fpc/ (viewed May 2008).

46. Roland T. Rust and Katherine N. Lemon, "E-Service and the Consumer," *International Journal of Electronic Commerce*, 5, no. 3 (Spring 2001): 83–99. See also B. P. S. Murthi and Sumit Sarkar, "The Role of the Management Sciences in Research on Personalization," *Management Science* 49, no. 10 (October 2003): 1344–62 and Balaji Padmanabhan and Alexander Tuzhilin, "On the Use of Optimization for Data Mining: Theoretical Interactions and ECRM opportunities," *Management Science*, 49, no. 10 (October 2003): 1327–43.

47. Roland T. Rust, P. K. Kannan, and Na Peng, "The Customer Economics of Internet Privacy," *Journal of the Academy of Marketing Science* 30, no. 4 (2002): 455–64.

48. Glenn B. Voss, A. Parasuraman, and Dhruv Grewal, "The Role of Price, Performance, and Expectations in Determining Satisfaction in Service Exchanges," *Journal of Marketing* 62 (October 1998): 46–61.

49. Roland T. Rust and Richard L. Oliver, "Should We Delight the Customer?" *Journal of the Academy of Marketing Science* 28, no. 1 (Fall 2002): 86–94.

50. www.ritzcarlton.com; Roger Crockett, "Keeping Ritz-Carlton at the Top of Its Game," *BusinessWeek*, May 29, 2006; Carmine Gallo, "How Ritz-Carlton Maintains Its Mystique," *BusinessWeek*, February 13, 2007; Special Issue on Service Excellence, *Expert Magazine* 3, no. 6 (2006).

51. A. Parasuraman, Valarie A. Zeithaml, and Leonard L. Berry, "A Conceptual Model of Service Quality and Its Implications for Future Research," *Journal of Marketing* (Fall 1985): 41–50. See also Michael K. Brady and J. Joseph Cronin Jr., "Some New Thoughts on Conceptualizing Perceived Service Quality," *Journal of Marketing*, 65 (July 2001): 34–49; Susan J. Devlin and H. K. Dong, "Service Quality from the Customer's Perspective," *Marketing Research* (Winter 1994): 4–13.

52. Leonard L. Berry and A. Parasuraman, *Marketing Services: Competing through Quality* (New York: Free Press, 1991), p. 16.

53. Parasuraman, Zeithaml, and Berry, "A Conceptual Model of Service Quality and Its Implications for Future Research," pp. 41–50.

54. Manulife's Customer Satisfaction and Complaint Resolution website, www.manulife.ca/canada/Canada1.msf/Public/complaintresolution (viewed May 2008).

55. "Airport Service Quality Awards 2007," Press Release, Airports Council International, Geneva, February 25, 2008, www.airports.org/cda/aci_common/display/main/aci_content07_c.jsp?zn=aci&cp=1-7-46%5E21375_666_2__; "Airport Celebrates Ranking as 'World's Best,'" Halifax Stanfield International Airport Press Release, Halifax, April 10, 2008 (viewed May 2008).

56. James L. Heskett, W. Earl Sasser Jr., and Christopher W. L. Hart, *Service Breakthroughs* (New York: Free Press, 1990).

57. William C. Copacino, *Supply Chain Management* (Boca Raton, FL: St. Lucie Press, 1997).

58. Leonard L. Berry, Kathleen Seiders, and Dhruv Grewal, "Understanding Service Convenience," *Journal of Marketing*, 66 (July 2002): 1–17.

59. Mary Jo Bitner, "Self-Service Technologies: What Do Customers Expect?" *Marketing Management* (Spring 2001): 10–11; Matthew L. Meuter, Amy L. Ostrom, Robert J. Roundtree, and Mary Jo Bitner, "Self-Service Technologies: Understanding Customer Satisfaction with Technology-Based Service Encounters," *Journal of Marketing*, 64 (July 2000): 50–64.

60. Peter Burrows, "The Era of Efficiency," *BusinessWeek*, June 18, 2001, pp. 94–98.

61. Matthew L. Meuter, Mary Jo Bitner, Amy L. Ostrom, and Stephen W. Brown, "Choosing among Alternative Service Delivery Modes: An Investigation of Customer Trial of Self-Service Technologies," *Journal of Marketing*, 69 (April 2005): 61–83.

62. Air Canada, "News Release: Air Canada Expands Web Check-in World Wide; Uses Technology to Further Simplify the Travel Experience," March 8, 2005.

63. Michelle Higgins, "Go Directly to Your Room Key! Pass the Desk!" *New York Times*, August 20, 2006, pp. 5–6. Copyright © 2006 The New York Times. Reprinted by permission.

64. John A. Martilla and John C. James, "Importance–Performance Analysis," *Journal of Marketing* (January 1977): 77–79.

65. Jeffrey G. Blodgett and Ronald D. Anderson, "A Bayesian Network Model of the Customer Complaint Process," *Journal of Service Research*, 2, no. 4 (May 2000): 321–38; Claes Fornell and Birger Wernerfelt, "A Model for Customer Complaint Management," *Marketing Science*, 7 (Summer 1988): 271–86; Stephen S. Tax and Stephen W. Brown, "Recovering and Learning from Service Failures," *Sloan Management Review* (Fall 1998): 75–88.

66. Barry J. Rabin and James S. Boles, "Employee Behavior in a Service Environment: A Model and Test of Potential Differences between Men and Women," *Journal of Marketing*, 62 (April 1998): 77–91; James G. Maxham III and Richard G. Netemeyer, "Firms Reap What They Sow: The Effects of Shared Values and Perceived Organizational Justice on Customers' Evaluations of Complaint Handling," *Journal of Marketing*, 67 (January 2003): 46–62; Singh, "Performance Productivity and Quality of Frontline Employees in Service Organizations," pp. 15–34.

67. Stephen S. Tax, Stephen W. Brown, and Murali Chandrashekaran, "Customer Evaluations of Service Complaint Experiences: Implications for Relationship Marketing," pp. 60–76; Tax and Brown, "Recovering and Learning from Service Failures," pp. 75–88.

68. Tania Padgett, "Some Automated Voice Systems Are More Human Than Others," *Chicago Tribune*, January 28, 2007; http://gethuman.com.

69. D. Todd Donovan, Tom J. Brown, and John C. Mowen, "Internal Benefits of Service Worker Customer Orientation: Job Satisfaction, Commitment, and Organizational Citizenship Behaviors," *Journal of Marketing*, 68 (January 2004): 128–46.

70. Dale Buss, "Success from the Ground Up," *Brandweek*, June 16, 2003, pp. 21–22; Melanie Joy Douglas, "50 Best Employers in Canada 2007," Monster.ca, undated, http://content.monster.ca/12021_en-CA_p1.asp; Best Employers website at www.hewitt.com/bestemployerscanada, (viewed May 2008).

71. Amy Barrett, "Vanguard Gets Personal," *BusinessWeek*, October 3, 2005, pp. 115–18; Carolyn Marconi and Donna MacFarland, "Growth by Marketing under the Radar," Presentation made at Marketing Science Institute Board of Trustees Meeting: Pathways to Growth, Tucson, AZ, November 7, 2002.

72. Shoppers Drug Mart website, www.shoppersdrugmart.ca (viewed May 2008).

73. www.schneider.com; www.informs.org; Todd Raphael, "Facing 'Fierce Competition,' Schneider National Struggles to Fill Trucking Jobs," *Inside Recruiting*, May 32, 2006.

74. Susanna Hamner, "Checking In at the Hotel of Tomorrow," *Business 2.0* (November 2006): 38–40.

75. Mike Beirne and Javier Benito, "Starwood Uses Personnel to Personalize Marketing," *Brandweek*, April 24, 2006, p. 9.

76. Robin D. Rusch, "Cirque du Soleil—Contorts," *brandchannel. com*, December 1, 2003; Linda Tischler, "Join the Circus," *Fast Company* (July 2005): 53–58; "Cirque du Soliel," *America's Greatest Brands* 3 (2004); Geoff Keighley, "The Phantasmagoria Factory," *Business 2.0* (February 2004): 102.

77. Milind M. Lele and Uday S. Karmarkar, "Good Product Support Is Smart Marketing," *Harvard Business Review,* 61 (November–December 1983): 124–32; Mark Vandenbosch and Niraj Dawar, "Beyond Better Products: Capturing Value in Customer Interactions," *MIT Sloan Management Review,* 43 (Summer 2002): 35–42.

78. For recent research on the effects of delays in service on service evaluations, see Michael K. Hui and David K. Tse, "What to Tell Consumers in Waits of Different Lengths: An Integrative Model of Service Evaluation," *Journal of Marketing* (April 1996): 81–90; Shirley Taylor, "Waiting for Service: The Relationship between Delays and Evaluations of Service," *Journal of Marketing* (April 1994): 56–69.

79. Byron G. Auguste, Eric P. Harmon, and Vivek Pandit, "The Right Service Strategies for Product Companies," *McKinsey Quarterly,* 1 (2006): 41–51.

Chapter 14

1. Walter S. Mossberg, "Apple Brings Its Flair for Smart Designs to Digital Music Player," *Wall Street Journal* (Eastern Edition), November 1, 2001, p. B1; Jonathan Seff, "Apple iPod," *Macworld,* 19, no. 1 (January 2002), pp. 29; Betsy Morris, "What Makes Apple Golden," *Fortune,* 157, no. 5 (March 17, 2008), p. 68; Brent Schlender. "Apple's 21st century Walkman," *Fortune,* 144, no. 9 (November 12, 2001), pp. 213–220.

2. David J. Schwartz, *Marketing Today: A Basic Approach*, 3rd ed. (New York: Harcourt Brace Jovanovich, 1981), p. 271.

3. Michael Menduno, "Priced to Perfection," *Business 2.0*, March 6, 2001, pp. 40–42.

4. Lisa D'Innocenzo, "Quiznos Slashes Price, Touts 20 New Low-Carb Subs," *Strategy Magazine Online*, www.strategymag.com, April 19, 2004 (viewed October 4, 2004).

5. For a thorough, up-to-date review of pricing research, see Chezy Ofir and Russell S. Winer, "Pricing: Economic and Behavioral Models," in *Handbook of Marketing*, edited by Bart Weitz and Robin Wensley (New York: Sage Publications, 2002), pp. 267–281.

6. Peter R. Dickson and Alan G. Sawyer, "The Price Knowledge and Search of Supermarket Shoppers," *Journal of Marketing* (July 1990): 42–53. For a methodological qualification, however, see Hooman Estalami, Alfred Holden, and Donald R. Lehmann, "Macro-Economic Determinants of Consumer Price Knowledge: A Meta-Analysis of Four Decades of Research," *International Journal of Research in Marketing*, 18 (December 2001): 341–355.

7. For a different point of view, see Chris Janiszewski and Donald R. Lichtenstein, "A Range Theory Account of Price Perception," *Journal of Consumer Research* (March 1999): 353–368.

8. K. N. Rajendran and Gerard J. Tellis, "Contextual and Temporal Components of Reference Price," *Journal of Marketing* (January 1994): 22–34; Goromurthy Kalyanaram and Rossell S. Winer, "Empirical Generalizations from Reference Price Research," *Marketing Science*, 14, no. 3 (1995): G161–G169.

9. Olympus Canada website, www.olympuscanada.com/cpg_section/product.asp?product=1289; Future Shop website, www.futureshop.ca; eBay website, www.ebay.ca (all viewed June 5, 2008); Robert Strauss, "Prices You Just Can't Believe," *New York Times*, January 17, 2002, p. G1.

10. John T. Gourville, "Pennies-a-Day: The Effect of Temporal Reframing on Transaction Evaluation," *Journal of Consumer Research* (March 1998): 395–408.

11. Gurumurthy Kalyanaram and Russell S. Winer, "Empirical Generalizations from Reference Research," *Marketing Science* (Fall 1995): 161–169.

12. Glenn E. Mayhew and Russell S. Winer, "An Empirical Analysis of Internal and External Reference Price Effects Using Scanner Data," *Journal of Consumer Research* (June 1992): 62–70.

13. Gary M. Erickson and Johny K. Johansson, "The Role of Price in Multi-Attribute Product-Evaluations," *Journal of Consumer Research* (September 1985): 195–199.

14. Unilever Canada website, "Our Brands: Q-tips," www.unilever.ca/ourbrands/personalcare/qtips.asp; Our History, www.unilever.ca/ourcompany/aboutunilever/ourhistory/default.asp (all viewed June 5, 2008).

15. Jonathan Welsh, "A New Status Symbol: Overpaying for Your Minivan Despite Discounts, More Cars Sell Above the Sticker Price," *Wall Street Journal*, July 23, 2003, p. D1.

16. Claudia Cattaneo, "Oil 'Scarcity' on Horizon: Gasoline Prices May Hit $2.25 a Litre by 2012: Economist," *National Post,* April 25, 2008, p. FP1.

17. Mark Stiving and Russell S. Winer, "An Empirical Analysis of Price Endings with Scanner Data," *Journal of Consumer Research* (June 1997): 57–68.

18. Eric Anderson and Duncan Simester, "The Role of Price Endings: Why Stores May Sell More at $49 Than at $44," an unpublished conference paper, April 2001.

19. Eric Anderson and Duncan Simester, "Mind Your Pricing Cues," *Harvard Business Review* (September 2003): 96–103.

20. Robert M. Schindler and Patrick N. Kirby, "Patterns of Rightmost Digits Used in Advertised Prices: Implications for Nine-Ending Effects," *Journal of Consumer Research* (September 1997): 192–201.

21. Eric Anderson and Duncan Simester, "Mind Your Pricing Cues," *Harvard Business Review* (September 2003): 96–103.

22. Robert C. Blattberg and Kenneth Wisniewski, "Price-Induced Patterns of Competition," *Marketing Science*, 8 (Fall 1989): 291–309.

23. Elliot B. Ross, "Making Money with Proactive Pricing," *Harvard Business Review* (November–December 1984): 145–155.

24. Shantanu Dutta, Mark J. Zbaracki, and Mark Bergen, "Pricing Process as a Capability: A Resource Based Perspective," *Strategic Management Journal*, no. 7 (2000): 615–630.

25. Kara Swisher, "Electronics 2001: The Essential Guide," *Wall Street Journal*, January 5, 2001.

26. Michael Silverstein and Neil Fiske, *Trading Up: The New American Luxury* (New York: Portfolio, 2003).

27. Christopher Lawton, "A Liquor Maverick Shakes Up Industry with Pricey Brands," *Wall Street Journal*, May 21, 2003, pp. A1, A9.

28. Sidney Bennett and J. B. Wilkinson, "Price-Quantity Relationships and Price Elasticity under In-Store Experimentation," *Journal of Business Research* (January 1974): 30–34.

29. Walter Baker, Mike Marn, and Craig Zawada, "Price Smarter on the Net," *Harvard Business Review* (February 2001): 122–127.

30. John R. Nevin, "Laboratory Experiments for Estimating Consumer Demand: A Validation Study," *Journal of Marketing Research* (August 1974): 261–268; Jonathan Weiner, "Forecasting Demand: Consumer Electronics Marketer Uses a Conjoint Approach to Configure Its New Product and Set the Right Price," *Marketing Research: A Magazine of Management & Applications* (Summer 1994): 6–11.

31. Thomas T. Nagle and Reed K. Holden, *The Strategy and Tactics of Pricing*, 3rd ed. (Upper Saddle River, NJ: Prentice-Hall, 2002).

32. Monster Canada website, hiring.monster.com (viewed June 9, 2008); George Mannes, "The Urge to Unbundle," *Fast Company*, 91 (February 2005) p. 23.

33. For a summary of elasticity studies, see Dominique M. Hanssens, Leonard J. Parsons, and Randall L. Schultz, *Market Response Models: Econometric and Time Series Analysis* (Boston: Kluwer Academic Publishers, 1990), pp. 187–191.

34. Gene Epstein, "Economic Beat: Stretching Things," *Barron's*, December 15, 1997, p. 65.

35. William W. Alberts, "The Experience Curve Doctrine Reconsidered," *Journal of Marketing* (July 1989): 36–49.

36. Robin Cooper and Robert S. Kaplan, "Profit Priorities from Activity-Based Costing," *Harvard Business Review* (May–June 1991): 130–135. For more on ABC, see Chapter 24.

37. "Easier Than ABC," *The Economist*, October 25, 2003, p. 56.

38. "Japan's Smart Secret Weapon," *Fortune*, August 12, 1991, p. 75.

39. Tung-Zong Chang and Albert R. Wildt, "Price, Product Information, and Purchase Intention: An Empirical Study," *Journal of the Academy of Marketing Science* (Winter 1994): 16–27. See also G. Dean Kortge and Patrick A. Okonkwo, "Perceived Value Approach to Pricing," *Industrial Marketing Management* (May 1993): 133–140.

40. James C. Anderson, Dipak C. Jain, and Pradeep K. Chintagunta, "Customer Value Assessment in Business Markets: A State-of-Practice Study," *Journal of Business-to-Business Marketing*, 1, no. 1 (1993): 3–29.

41. Bill Saporito, "Behind the Tumult at P&G," *Fortune*, March 7, 1994, pp. 74–82. For empirical analysis of its effects, see Kusim L. Ailawadi, Donald R. Lehmann, and Scott A. Neslin, "Market Response to a Major Policy Change in the Marketing Mix: Learning from Procter & Gamble's Value Pricing Strategy," *Journal of Marketing*, 65 (January 2001): 44–61.

42. Stephen J. Hoch, Xavier Dreze, and Mary J. Purk, "EDLP, Hi-Lo, and Margin Arithmetic," *Journal of Marketing* (October 1994): 16–27; Rajiv Lal and R. Rao, "Supermarket Competition: The Case of Everyday Low Pricing," *Marketing Science*, 16, no. 1 (1997): 60–80.

43. Joseph W. Alba, Carl F. Mela, Terence A. Shimp, and Joel E. Urbany, "The Effect of Discount Frequency and Depth on Consumer Price Judgments," *Journal of Consumer Research* (September 1999): 99–114.

44. Winners website, www.winners.ca/en/about_us.asp; The TJX Companies Inc. website, *2006 Annual Report*, p. 4, www.tjx.com/ir/ar.html (both viewed June 4, 2008).

45. Becky Bull, "No Consensus on Pricing," *Progressive Grocer* (November 1998): 87–90.

46. Chris Nelson, "Ticketmaster Auction Will Let Highest Bidder Set Concert Prices," *New York Times*, September 1, 2003, p. C6.

47. "Royal Mail Drives Major Cost Savings Through Free Markets," Free Markets press release, December 15, 2003.

48. Paul W. Farris and David J. Reibstein, "How Prices, Expenditures, and Profits Are Linked," *Harvard Business Review* (November–December 1979): 173–184. See also Makoto Abe, "Price and Advertising Strategy of a National Brand against Its Private-Label Clone: A Signaling Game Approach," *Journal of Business Research* (July 1995): 241–250.

49. J. P. Morgan Report, "eTailing and the Five C's," March 2000.

50. Eugene H. Fram and Michael S. McCarthy, "The True Price of Penalties," *Marketing Management* (October 1999): 49–56.

51. Kissan Joseph, "On the Optimality of Delegating Pricing Authority to the Sales Force," *Journal of Marketing*, 65 (January 2001): 62–70.

52. Gary McWilliams, "How Dell Fine-Tunes Its PC Pricing to Gain Edge in a Slow Market," *Wall Street Journal*, June 8, 2001, p. A1; "Dell," http://company.monster.ca/dellca/ (viewed March 11, 2005); http://money.cnn.com/magazines/fortune/fortune500/2008/snapshots/1053.html (viewed September 17, 2008).

53. Joel E. Urbany, "Justifying Profitable Pricing," *Journal of Product and Brand Management*, 10, no. 3 (2001): 141–157.

54. George H. Condon, "Loblaw Wrong to Demand More Supplier Dollars," *Canadian Grocer* 121, no. 10 (December 2007/January 2008), p. 84; Loblaw Companies Limited, "About Us: Company Profile," www.loblaw.ca/en/abt_corprof.html (viewed on June 9, 2008).

55. Normandy Madden, "P&G Adapts Attitude Toward Local Markets," *Advertising Age*, February 23, 2004, pp. 28–29.

56. James Mehring, "Let the Markups Begin," *BusinessWeek*, May 19, 2003, p. 100.

57. Michael Rowe, *Countertrade* (London: Euromoney Books, 1989); P. N. Agarwala, *Countertrade: A Global Perspective* (New Delhi: Vikas Publishing House, 1991); Christopher M. Korth, ed., *International Countertrade* (New York: Quorum Books, 1987).

58. For an interesting discussion of a quantity surcharge, see David E. Sprott, Kenneth C. Manning, and Anthony Miyazaki, "Grocery Price Settings and Quantity Surcharges, *Journal of Marketing*, 67 (July 2003): 34–46.

59. Michael V. Marn and Robert L. Rosiello, "Managing Price, Gaining Profit," *Harvard Business Review* (September–October 1992): 84–94. See also Gerard J. Tellis, "Tackling the Retailer Decision Maze: Which Brands to Discount, How Much, When, and Why?" *Marketing Science,* 14, no. 3, pt. 2 (1995): 271–299; Kusom L. Ailawadi, Scott A. Neslin, and Karen Gedeak, "Pursuing the Value-Conscious Consumer: Store Brands Versus National Brand Promotions," *Journal of Marketing*, 65 (January 2001): 71–89.

60. Kevin J. Clancy, "At What Profit Price?" *Brandweek*, June 23, 1997.

61. "Famous Players Opts for Flat-rate Pricing in B.C., Calgary," *CBC Arts*, April 1, 2004, www.cbc.ca/story/arts/national/2004/04/01/Arts/tickets20040401.html (viewed June 14, 2008); "Famous Players Lowers Ticket Prices in Ontario," *Canadian Press*, January 26, 2005; Leonard Klady, "In Praise of Popcorn," *Movie City News*, April 9, 2005.

62. Ramarao Deesiraju and Steven M. Shugan, "Strategic Service Pricing and Yield Management," *Journal of Marketing*, 63 (January 1999): 44–56; Robert E. Weigand, "Yield Management: Filling Buckets, Papering the House," *Business Horizons* (September–October 1999): 55–64.

63. Charles Fishman, "Which Price Is Right?" *Fast Company* (March 2003): 92–102; John Sviokla, "Value Poaching," *Across the Board* (March/April 2003): 11–12.

64. Mike France, "Does Predatory Pricing Make Microsoft a Predator?" *BusinessWeek*, November 23, 1998, pp. 130–132. See also Joseph P. Guiltinan and Gregory T. Gundlack, "Aggressive and Predatory Pricing: A Framework for Analysis," *Journal of Advertising* (July 1996): 87–102.

65. Michael J. Knell. "Ikea Canada Cuts Prices," *Furniture Today*, 29, no. 50 (August 29, 2005), pp. 1–2.

66. Margaret C. Campbell, "Perceptions of Pricing Unfairness: Antecedents and Consequences," *Journal of Marketing Research*, 36 (May 1999): 187–199.

67. Delroy Alexander, "Products, Profits Put Kraft, Leader in Pinch," *Chicago Tribune*, November 2, 2003, p. 5.

68. Eric Mitchell, "How Not to Raise Prices," *Small Business Reports* (November 1990): 64–67.

69. For a classic review, see Kent B. Monroe, "Buyers' Subjective Perceptions of Price," *Journal of Marketing Research* (February 1973): 70–80. See also Z. John Zhang, Fred Feinberg, Aradhna Krishna,"Do We Care What Others Get? A Behaviorist Approach to Targeted Promotions," *Journal of Marketing Research*, 39 (August 2002): 277–291.

70. Transat A.T. Inc., "First Quarter 2008 Results: Strong Demand Drive Revenues Up, Excess Supply Puts Pressure on Margins," Transat Press Release, March 5, 2008, www.transat.com (viewed June 10, 2008); Ross Marowits, "Canadians Paid Less For Winter Holidays as Overcapacity Hits Transat's Profits," *Canadian Press News Wire*, Toronto, March 12, 2008.

71. Kusim L. Ailawadi, Donald R. Lehmann, and Scott A. Neslin, "Market Response to a Major Policy Change in the Marketing Mix: Learning from Procter & Gamble's Value Pricing Strategy," *Journal of Marketing*, 65 (January 2001): 44–61.

Chapter 15

1. Anne T. Coughlan, Erin Anderson, Louis W. Stern, and Adel I. El-Ansary, *Marketing Channels*, 6th ed. (Upper Saddle River, NJ: Prentice Hall, 2001).

2. Louis W. Stern and Barton A. Weitz, "The Revolution in Distribution: Challenges and Opportunities," *Long Range Planning*, 30, no. 6 (December 1997): 823–29.

3. For an insightful summary of academic research, see Erin Anderson and Anne T. Coughlan, "Channel Management: Structure, Governance, and Relationship Management," in *Handbook of Marketing*, ed. Bart Weitz and Robin Wensley (London: Sage, 2001), pp. 223–47. See also Gary L. Frazier, "Organizing and Managing Channels of Distribution," *Journal of the Academy of Marketing Sciences*, 27, no. 2 (Spring 1999): 226–40.

4. "Team Unilever," *The Hub*, May/June 2008, pp. 26–30; personal interview with Krista Cunningham by Peggy Cunningham.

5. Peter Child, Suzanne Heywood, and Michael Kilger, "Do Retail Brands Travel?" *McKinsey Quarterly* (January 2002): 11–13.

6. David Whitford, "Uh . . . Maybe Should I Drive," *Fortune*, April 30, 2007, pp. 125–28; Louise Lee, "It's Dell vs. the Dell Way," *BusinessWeek*, March 6, 2006, pp. 61–62; David Kirkpatrick, "Dell in the Penalty Box," *Fortune*, September 18, 2006, pp. 70–78; Nanette Byrnes, Peter Burrows, and Louise Lee, "Dark Days at Dell," *BusinessWeek*, September 4, 2006, pp. 27–30; Elizabeth Corcoran, "A Bad Spell for Dell," *Forbes*, June 19, 2006, pp. 44–46.

7. "Click to Download," *The Economist*, August 19, 2006, pp. 57–58.

8. Martin Wildberger, "Multichannel Business Basics for Successful E-Commerce," *Electronic Commerce News*, September 16, 2002, p. 1; Matthew Haeberle, "REI Overhauls Its E-Commerce," *Chain Store Age* (January 2003): 64; Mountain Equipment Co-op website www.mec.ca (viewed June 2008).

9. Asim Ansari, Carl F. Mela, and Scott A. Neslin, "Customer Channel Migration," *Journal of Marketing Research*, 45 (February 2008); Jacquelyn S. Thomas and Ursula Y. Sullivan, "Managing Marketing Communications," *Journal of Marketing*, 69 (October 2005): 239–51; Sridhar Balasubramanian, Rajagopal Raghunathan, and Vijay Mahajan, "Consumers in a Multichannel Environment: Product Utility, Process Utility, and Channel Choice," *Journal of Interactive Marketing*, 19, no. 2 (Spring 2005): 12–30; Edward J. Fox, Alan L. Montgomery, and Leonard M. Lodish, "Consumer Shopping and Spending across Retail Formats," *The Journal of Business*, 77, no. 2 (April 2004): S25–S60.

10. Marina Strauss, "Grocers target big-spending South Asian, Chinese shoppers," *The Globe and Mail*, May 19, 2008.

11. Paul F. Nunes and Frank V. Cespedes, "The Customer Has Escaped," *Harvard Business Review* (November 2003): 96–105.

12. Peter Child, Suzanne Heywood, and Michael Kilger, "Do Retail Brands Travel?" *McKinsey Quarterly* (January 2002): 11–13.

13. John Helyar, "The Only Company Wal-Mart Fears," *Fortune*, November 24, 2003, pp. 158–66. See also Michael Silverstein and Neil Fiske, *Trading Up: The New American Luxury* (New York: Portfolio, 2003).

14. Chekitan S. Dev and Don E. Schultz, "In the Mix: A Customer-Focused Approach Can Bring the Current Marketing Mix into the 21st Century," *Marketing Management*, 14 (January–February 2005).

15. Coughlan, Anderson, Stern, and El-Ansary, *Marketing Channels*, pp. 5–6.

16. For additional information on backward channels, see Marianne Jahre, "Household Waste Collection as a Reverse Channel: A Theoretical Perspective," *International Journal of Physical Distribution and Logistics*, 25, no. 2 (1995): 39–55; Terrance L. Pohlen and M. Theodore Farris II, "Reverse Logistics in Plastics Recycling," *International Journal of Physical Distribution and Logistics*, 22, no. 7 (1992): 35–37.

17. John Colapinto, "When I'm Sixty-Four," *New Yorker*, June 4, 2007.

18. Irving Rein, Philip Kotler, and Martin Stoller, *High Visibility* (New York: Dodd, Mead, 1987).

19. William M. Bulkeley, "Kodak Revamps Wal-Mart Kiosks," *Wall Street Journal*, September 6, 2006; Faith Keenan, "Big Yellow's Digital Dilemma," *BusinessWeek*, March 24, 2003, pp. 80–81.

20. Coughlan, Anderson, Stern, and El-Ansary, *Marketing Channels*.

21. Louis P. Bucklin, *A Theory of Distribution Channel Structure* (Berkeley: Institute of Business and Economic Research, University of California, 1966).

22. Katrijn Gielens and Marnik G. Dekimpe, "The Entry Strategies of Retail Firms into Transition Economies," *Journal of Marketing*, 71 (April 2007): 196–212.

23. Bridget Finn, "A Quart of Milk, a Dozen Eggs, and a 2.6-GHz Laptop," *Business 2.0* (October 2003): 58.

24. Allison Enright, "Shed New Light," *Marketing News*, May 1, 2006, pp. 9–10.

25. "Exclusives Becoming a Common Practice," *DSN Retailing Today*, February 9, 2004, pp. 38, 44.

26. "Trouser Suit," *Economist*, November 24, 2001, p. 56.

27. Lee Valley website, www.leevalley.com (viewed June 2008).

28. "Nike Says No to Blue-Light Specials," *Fortune*, May 4, 2005.

29. For more on relationship marketing and the governance of marketing channels, see Jan B. Heide, "Interorganizational Governance in Marketing Channels," *Journal of Marketing* (January 1994): 71–85.

30. Robert K. Heady, "Online Bank Offers Best Rates," *South Florida Sun-Sentinel*, November 22, 2004.

31. Duff McDonald, "Customer, Support Thyself," *Business 2.0* (April 2004): 56.

32. Anderson and Coughlan, "Channel Management: Structure, Governance, and Relationship Management," pp. 223–47.

33. These bases of power were identified in John R. P. French and Bertram Raven, "The Bases of Social Power," in *Studies in Social Power*, ed. Dorwin Cartwright (Ann Arbor: University of Michigan Press, 1959), pp. 150–67.

34. Bert Rosenbloom, *Marketing Channels: A Management View*, 5th ed. (Hinsdale, IL: Dryden, 1995).

35. Daniel Corsten and Nirmalya Kumar, "Do Suppliers Benefit from Collaborative Relationships with Large Retailers? An Empirical Investigation of Efficient Consumer Response Adoption," *Journal of Marketing*, 69 (July 2005): 80–94.

36. Jerry Useem, "Simply Irresistible," *Fortune*, March 19, 2007, pp. 107–12; Nick Wingfield, "How Apple's Store Strategy Beat the Odds," *Wall Street Journal*, May 17, 2006; Tobi Elkin, "Apple Gambles with Retail Plan," *Advertising Age*, June 24, 2001; Apple Store (Retail), http://en.wikipedia.org/wiki/Apple_Store_(retail) (viewed June 2008).

37. Thomas H. Davenport and Jeanne G. Harris, *Competing on Analytics: The New Science of Winning* (Boston: Harvard Business School Press, 2007).

38. Junhong Chu, Pradeep K. Chintagunta, and Naufel J. Vilcassim, "Assessing the Economic Value of Distribution Channels: An Application to the Personal Computer Industry," *Journal of Marketing Research*, 44 (February 2007): 29–41.

39. Marina Strauss, "Music World to Close Stores," *The Globe and Mail*, November 11, 2007.

40. Stefan Wuyts, Stefan Stremersch, Christophe Van Den Bulte, and Philip Hans Franses, "Vertical Marketing Systems for Complex Products: A Triadic Perspective," *Journal of Marketing Research*, 41 (November 2004): 479–87.

41. Russell Johnston and Paul R. Lawrence, "Beyond Vertical Integration: The Rise of the Value-Adding Partnership," *Harvard Business Review* (July–August 1988): 94–101. See also Arnt Bovik and George John, "When Does Vertical Coordination Improve Industrial Purchasing Relationships?" *Journal of Marketing*, 64 (October 2000): 52–64; Judy A. Siguaw, Penny M. Simpson, and Thomas L. Baker, "Effects of Supplier Market Orientation on Distributor

Market Orientation and the Channel Relationship: The Distribution Perspective," *Journal of Marketing* (July 1998): 99–111; Narakesari Narayandas and Manohar U. Kalwani, "Long-Term Manufacturer–Supplier Relationships: Do They Pay Off for Supplier Firms?" *Journal of Marketing* (January 1995): 1–16.

42. Raji Srinivasan, "Dual Distribution and Intangible Firm Value: Franchising in Restaurant Chains," *Journal of Marketing*, 70 (July 2006): 120–35.

43. "About Us," www.banking.pcfinancial.ca/a/aboutus/aboutUs.page?referid=topNav_aboutus (viewed May 2008).

44. www.disney.com/; Edward Helmore, "Media: Why House of Mouse Is Haunted by Failures," *Observer*, February 11, 2001, p. 10.

45. Rajkumar Venkatesan, V. Kumar, and Nalini Ravishanker, "Multichannel Shopping: Causes and Consequences," *Journal of Marketing*, 71 (April 2007): 114–32.

46. Based on Rowland T. Moriarty and Ursula Moran, "Marketing Hybrid Marketing Systems," *Harvard Business Review* (November–December 1990): 146–55.

47. Louise Lee, "Catalogs, Catalogs, Everywhere," *BusinessWeek*, December 4, 2006, pp. 32–34.

48. Susan Casey, "Eminence Green," *Fortune*, April 2, 2007, pp. 64–70; L'Occitane website: www.loccitane.ca (viewed May 2008).

49. Barbara Darow, "Oracle's New Partner Path," *CRN*, August 21, 2006, p. 4.

50. Anne T. Coughlan and Louis W. Stern, "Marketing Channel Design and Management," *Kellogg on Marketing* (New York: Wiley, 2001), pp. 247–69.

51. Matthew Boyle, "Brand Killers," *Fortune*, August 11, 2003, pp. 51–56; for an opposing view, see Anthony J. Dukes, Esther Gal-Or, and Kannan Srinivasan, "Channel Bargaining with Retailer Asymmetry," *Journal of Marketing Research*, 43 (February 2006): 84–97; George K. Criner, Remy E. Lambert, and Yannick P. Rancourt, "An Analysis of Canadian Food Industry Concentration," www.ivry.inra.fr/loria/eaaefichiers/ProgCom_fichiers/Criner.pdf (viewed May 2008).

52. Jerry Useem, Julie Schlosser, and Helen Kim, "One Nation under Wal-Mart," *Fortune* (Europe), March 3, 2003.

53. Alberto Sa Vinhas and Erin Anderson, "How Potential Conflict Drives Channel Structure: Concurrent (Direct and Indirect) Channels," *Journal of Marketing Research*, 42 (November 2005): 507–15.

54. For an example of when conflict can be viewed as helpful, see Anil Arya and Brian Mittendorf, "Benefits of Channel Discord in the Sale of Durable Goods," *Marketing Science*, 25 (January–February 2006): 91–96, and Nirmalya Kumar, "Living with Channel Conflict," *CMO Magazine* (October 2004).

55. Fareena Sultan and Andrew J. Rohm, "The Evolving Role of the Internet in Marketing Strategy: An Exploratory Study," *Journal of Interactive Marketing* (Spring 2004): 6–19.

56. This section draws on Stern and El-Ansary, *Marketing Channels*, Chapter 6. See also Jonathan D. Hibbard, Nirmalya Kumar, and Louis W. Stern, "Examining the Impact of Destructive Acts in Marketing Channel Relationships," *Journal of Marketing Research*, 38 (February 2001): 45–61; Kersi D. Antia and Gary L. Frazier, "The Severity of Contract Enforcement in Interfirm Channel Relationships," *Journal of Marketing*, 65 (October 2001): 67–81; James R. Brown, Chekitan S. Dev, and Dong-Jin Lee, "Managing Marketing Channel Opportunism: The Efficiency of Alternative Governance Mechanisms," *Journal of Marketing*, 64 (April 2001): 51–65.

57. Andrew Kaplan, "All Together Now?" *Beverage World* (March 2007): 14–16.

58. Allison Fass, "Trading Up," *Forbes*, January 29, 2007, pp. 48–49; Diane Brady, "Coach's Split Personality," *BusinessWeek*, November 7, 2005, pp. 60–62.

59. Christina Passriello, "Fashionably Late? Designer Brands Are Starting to Embrace E-Commerce," *Wall Street Journal*, May 19, 2006.

60. Competition Bureau website, www.competitionbureau.gc.ca/epic/site/cb-bc.nsf/en/02542e.html; in particular, see the "Speaking Notes for Sheridan Scott Commissioner of Competition," December 13, 2007.

61. Joel C. Collier and Carol C. Bienstock, "How Do Customers Judge Quality in an E-Tailer," *MIT Sloan Management Review* (Fall 2006): 35–40; "Electronic Commerce and Technology," *The Daily*, April 24, 2008, www.statcan.ca/Daily/English/080424/d080424a.htm, (viewed May 2008).

62. Nielsen/NetRatings, "Online Retail Report Card," press release, April 7, 2005.

63. Alexis K. J. Barlow, Noreen Q. Siddiqui, and Mike Mannion, "Development in Information and Communication Technologies for Retail Marketing Channels," *International Journal of Retail and Distribution Management*, 32 (March 2004): 157–63; G&J Electronic Media Services, *7th Wave of the GfK-Online-Monitor* (Hamburg: GfK Press, 2001).

64. Heather Green, "Lessons of the Cyber Survivors," *BusinessWeek*, April 22, 2002, p. 42.

65. Sidra Durst, "Shoe In," *Business 2.0* (December 2006): 54.

66. Kate Maddox, "Online Marketing Summit Probes New Technologies," *BtoB*, 92, no. 3, March 12, 2007, pp. 3, 39. Reprinted by permission.

67. Martin Holzwarth, Chris Janiszewski, and Marcus M. Newmann, "The Influence of Avatars on Online Consumer Shopping Behavior," *Journal of Marketing*, 70 (October 2006): 19–36.

68. Pepys Fadoodle (the avatar of Angela Kryhul, editor at large) "Life, or something like it," *Marketing*, February 12, 2007; "Your Friendly Local Avatar," *Marketplace*, May 23, 2007, http://marketplace.publicradio.org/shows/2007/05/23/AM200705232.

69. Ann E. Schlosser, Tiffany Barnett White, and Susan M. Lloyd, "Converting Web Site Visitors into Buyers: How Web Site Investment Increases Consumer Trusting Beliefs and Online Purchase Intentions," *Journal of Marketing*, 70 (April 2006): 133–48.

70. Steve Bodow, "The Care and Feeding of a Killer App," *Business 2.0* (August 2002): 76–78.

71. Ronald Abler, John S. Adams, and Peter Gould, *Spatial Organizations: The Geographer's View of the World* (Upper Saddle River, NJ: Prentice Hall, 1971), pp. 531–32.

72. "China's Pied Piper," *The Economist*, September 23, 2006, p. 80; www.alibaba.com.

73. For an in-depth academic examination, see John G. Lynch Jr. and Dan Ariely, "Wine Online: Search Costs and Competition on Price, Quality, and Distribution," *Marketing Science*, 19 (Winter 2000): 83–103.

74. Described in *Inside 1-to-1*, Peppers and Rogers Group newsletter, May 14, 2001.

75. Daniel Workman, "Top Canadian Bank Websites," *Suite101.com*, April 23, 2008, http://e-commerce-marketing.suite101.com/article.cfm/top_canadian_bank_websites (viewed May 2008).

76. Bob Tedeshi, "How Harley Revved Online Sales," *Business 2.0* (December 2002–January 2003): 44.

77. "About Us," *Citizens Bank of Canada*, www.citizensbank.ca/Personal/AboutUs(viewed may 2008).

78. Public Interest Advocacy Centre, *Mobile Commerce: Making It Work for Canadians*, November 12, 2007, www.piac.ca/telecom/mobile_commerce_making_it_work_for_canadians_1/(viewed May 2008).

79. Marc Weingarten, "The Medium Is the Instant Message," *Business 2.0* (February 2002): 98–99; Douglas Lamont, *Conquering the Wireless World: The Age of M-Commerce* (New York: Wiley, 2001).

Chapter 16

1. William R. Davidson, Albert D. Bates, and Stephen J. Bass, "Retail Life Cycle," *Harvard Business Review* (November–December 1976): 89–96.

2. Stanley C. Hollander, "The Wheel of Retailing," *Journal of Marketing* (July 1960): 37–42.

3. "Click to Download," *Economist*, August 19, 2006, pp. 57–58.

4. Ian Austen, "Canadian Dollar Aiding Online Retailers," *The New York Times*, September 28, 2007.

5. Talbot Boggs, "Would You Like Franchise With That?" *Canadian Retailer*, January–February 2007, pp. 17–19.

6. Courtesy of Anne Kozak, Two Blonds & a Brunette Gift Co.

7. Robert Curran, "Comfort Keepers Fills Vital Niche for 'Boomers,'" *Northeaset Pennsylvania Business Journal*, January 1, 2007, p. 20; www.comfortkeepers.com.

8. Amy Merrick, Jeffrey Trachtenberg, and Ann Zimmerman, "Department Stores Fight to Preserve Role That May Be Outdated," *Wall Street Journal*, March 12, 2002; Ann Zimmerman, "Dillard's Counts on House Brands to Recapture Reputation," *Wall Street Journal*, March 2001.

9. Charles Fishman, "The Anarchist's Cookbook," *Fast Company* (July 2004): 70–78.

10. Marina Strauss, "Big-box Best Buy goes to the mall," *The Globe and Mail*, June 7, 2008, p. B1; Theresa Howard, "Retail Stores Pop Up for Limited Time Only," *USA Today*, May 28, 2004.

11. "Reinventing the Store—the Future of Retailing," *Economist*, November 22, 2003, pp. 65–68.

12. "Storm Clouds over the Mall," *Economist*, October 8, 2005, pp. 71–72.

13. Wendy Liebmann, "Consumers Push Back," *Brandweek*, February 23, 2004, pp. 19–20.

14. Chris Daniels, "The Dawn of a New Bay," *Marketing*, April 30, 2007; Liebmann, "Consumers Push Back," pp. 19–20.

15. Teri Agins, "Todd Does Target," *Wall Street Journal*, April 11, 2002.

16. "Reinventing the Store—the Future of Retailing," *Economist*, November 22, 2003, pp. 65–68.

17. Chris Daniels, "The Dawn of a New Bay," *Marketing*, April 30, 2007; Hollie Shaw, "Owner of U.S. Retail Chain Acquired Hudson's Bay," *Calgary Herald*, July 17, 2008; Hollie Shaw, "U.S. Chain Lord & Taylor Seeks HBC Takeover: Sources," *Canwest News Service*, July 10, 2008; Christine Persaud, "Iconic Canadian Retailer Hudson's Bay Sold to Lord & Taylor," *MarketNews*, July 17, 2008; "Hudson's Bay Co. Names New CEO," *The Star*, July 17, 2008.

18. "Bosley's Pet Food Plus," Microsoft Canada case study, August 8, 2007, www.microsoft.com/canada/casestudies/Bosley.mspx (viewed May 2008).

19. Jenn Abelson, "Miles Away, 'I'll Have a Burger,'" *Knight Ridder Tribune Business News*, November 5, 2006, p. 1.

20. Catherine Yang, "Maybe They Should Call Them Scammers," *BusinessWeek*, January 16, 1995, pp. 32–33; Ronald C. Goodstein, "UPC Scanner Pricing Systems: Are They Accurate?" *Journal of Marketing* (April 1994): 20–30.

21. For a listing of the key factors involved in success with an EDI system, see R. P. Vlosky, D. T. Wilson, and P. M. Smith, "Electronic Data Interchange Implementation Strategies: A Case Study," *Journal of Business & Industrial Marketing*, 9, no. 4 (1994): 5–18.

22. "Business Bulletin: Shopper Scanner," *Wall Street Journal*, February 18, 1995.

23. Michael Freedman, "The Eyes Have It," *Forbes*, September 4, 2006, p. 70.

24. Matthew Boyle, "IBM Goes Shopping," *Fortune*, November 27, 2006, pp. 77–78.

25. For further discussion of retail trends, see Anne T. Coughlan, Erin Anderson, Louis W. Stern, and Adel I. El-Ansary, *Marketing Channels*, 6th ed. (Upper Saddle River, NJ: Prentice Hall, 2001).

26. Carla Rapoport with Justin Martin, "Retailers Go Global," *Fortune*, February 20, 1995, pp. 102–8; Shelley Donald Coolidge, "Facing Saturated Home Markets, Retailers Look to Rest of World," *Christian Science Monitor*, February 14, 1994, p. 7; "Wal-Mart looks to Canada for growth," *CBCNews.ca*, March 21, 2007, www.cbc.ca/money/story/2007/03/21/walmart.html (viewed May 2008).

27. Amy Merrick, "Asking 'What Would Ann Do?'" *Wall Street Journal*, September 15, 2006.

28. Jessi Hempel, "Urban Outfitters, Fashion Victim," *BusinessWeek*, July 17, 2006, p. 60.

29. Robert Berner, "To Lure Teenager Mall Rats, You Need the Right Cheese," *BusinessWeek*, June 7, 2004, pp. 96–101.

30. Steve Levenstein, "Holt Renfrew Hosts Brand Launch Under Big Top," *BizBash*, September 21, 2007, www.bizbash.com/toronto/content/editorial/e8805.php (viewed may 2008).

31. Kimberly L. Allers, "Retail's Rebel Yell," *Fortune*, November 10, 2003, pp. 137–42.

32. Laurence H. Wortzel, "Retailing Strategies for Today's Marketplace," *Journal of Business Strategy* (Spring 1987): 45–56.

33. Mark Tatge, "Fun & Games," *Forbes*, January 12, 2004, pp. 138–44.

34. Nanette Byrnes, "What's Beyond for Bed Bath & Beyond," *BusinessWeek*, January 19, 2004, pp. 48–50.

35. "Sears Canada launches the newly re-designed sears.ca: Canada's leading-edge, interactive online shopping destination," Sears press release, June 6, 2006, www.e-consultancy.com/news-blog/361208/sears-canada-launches-the-newly-re--designed-sears-ca-canada-s-leading--edge-interactive-online-shopping-destination.html (viewed June 2008).

36. Uta Werner, John McDermott, and Greg Rotz, "Retailers at the Crossroads: How to Develop Profitable New Growth Strategies," *Journal of Business Strategy*, 25, no. 2 (2004): 10–17.

37. Robert Berner, "Chanel's American in Paris," *BusinessWeek*, January 29, 2007, pp. 70–71.

38. Cecilie Rohwedder, "Viva la Differenza," *Wall Street Journal*, January 29, 2003.

39. Bertrand Marotte, "Home renovation goes 'ready-to-wear,'" *The Globe and Mail*, April 26, 2008.

40. Venkatesh Shankar and Ruth N. Bolton, "An Empirical Analysis of Determinants of Retailer Pricing Strategy," *Marketing Science*, 23 (Winter 2004): 28–49.

41. Duncan Simester, "Signaling Price Image Using Advertised Prices," *Marketing Science*, 14 (Summer 1995): 166–88. See also Jiwoong Shin, "The Role of Selling Costs in Signaling Price Image," *Journal of Marketing Research*, 42 (August 2005): 305–12.

42. Frank Feather, *The Future Consumer* (Toronto: Warwick Publishing, 1994), p. 171. See also David R. Bell and James M. Lattin, "Shopping Behavior and Consumer Preference for Retail Price Format: Why 'Large Basket' Shoppers Prefer EDLP," *Marketing Science*, 17 (Spring 1998): 66–68; Stephen J. Hoch, Xavier Dreeze, and Mary E. Purk, "EDLP, Hi-Lo, and Margin Arithmetic," *Journal of Marketing* (October 1994): 1–15.

43. Constance L. Hays, "Retailers Seeking to Lure Customers with Service," *New York Times*, December 1, 2003.

44. Amy Gillentine, "Marketing Groups Ignore Women at Their Own Peril," *Colorado Springs Business Journal*, January 20, 2006; Mary Lou Quinlan, "Women Aren't Buying It," *Brandweek*, June 2, 2003, pp. 20–22.

45. Cametta Coleman, "Kohl's Retail Racetrack," *Wall Street Journal*, March 1, 2000.

46. Justin Hibbard, "Put Your Money Where Your Mouth Is," *BusinessWeek*, September 18, 2006, pp. 61–63.

47. Mindy Fetterman and Jayne O'Donnell, "Just Browsing at the Mall? That's What *You* Think," *USA Today*, September 1, 2006.

48. "Reinventing the Store," *Economist*, November 22, 2003, pp. 65–68; Moira Cotlier, "Census Releases First E-Commerce Report," *Catalog Age*, May 1, 2001; Associated Press, "Online Sales Boomed at End of 2000," *Star-Tribune of Twin Cities*, February 17, 2001; Kenneth T. Rosen and Amanda L. Howard, "E-Tail: Gold Rush or Fool's Gold?" *California Management Review*, April 1, 2000, pp. 72–100.

49. Velitchka D. Kaltcheva and Barton Weitz, "When Should a Retailer Create an Exciting Store Environment?" *Journal of Marketing*, 70 (January 2006): 107–18.

50. For more discussion, see Philip Kotler, "Atmospherics as a Marketing Tool," *Journal of Retailing* (Winter 1973–1974): 48–64. See also B. Joseph Pine II and James H. Gilmore, *The Experience Economy* (Boston: Harvard Business School Press, 1999).

51. Jeff Cioletti, "Super Marketing," *Beverage World* (November 2006): 60–61.

52. Carol Tice, "Anchors Away: Department Stores Lose Role at Malls," *Puget Sound Business Journal,* February 13, 2004, p. 1.

53. R. L. Davies and D. S. Rogers, eds., *Store Location and Store Assessment Research* (New York: John Wiley, 1984).

54. Sara L. McLafferty, *Location Strategies for Retail and Service Firms* (Lexington, MA: Lexington Books, 1987).

55. Kevin Grier, "Private Label Moves to the Next Level in Canada," *Grocery Trade Review*, January 2003, http://ageconsearch.umn.edu/bitstream/18133/1/sr03gr01.pdf (viewed June 2008); Sonia Reyes, "Saving Private Labels," *Brandweek*, May 8, 2006, pp. 30–34.

56. Matthew Boyle, "Brand Killers," *Fortune*, August 11, 2003, pp. 88–100.

57. Kusum Ailawadi and Bari Harlam, "An Empirical Analysis of the Determinants of Retail Margins: The Role of Store-Brand Share," *Journal of Marketing,* 68 (January 2004): 147–65.

58. Boyle, "Brand Killers," pp. 88–100; William C. Copacino, *Supply Chain Management* (Boca Raton, FL: St. Lucie Press, 1997).

59. Kenji Hall, "Zen and the Art of Selling Minimalism," *Business-Week*, April 9, 2007, p. 45; Rob Walker, "Museum Quality," *New York Times Magazine*, January 9, 2005, p. 25.

60. Jeanne Whalen, "Betting $10 Billion on Generics, Novartis Seeks to Inject Growth," *Wall Street Journal*, May 4, 2006.

61. Michael Felding, "No Longer Plain, Simple," *Marketing News*, May 15, 2006, pp. 11–13; Rob Walker, "Shelf Improvement," *New York Times*, May 7, 2006.

62. Sonia Reyes, "Saving Private Labels," *Brandweek*, May 8, 2006, pp. 30–34.

63. James A. Narus and James C. Anderson, "Contributing as a Distributor to Partnerships with Manufacturers," *Business Horizons* (September–October 1987). See also James D. Hlavecek and Tommy J. McCuistion, "Industrial Distributors—When, Who, and How," *Harvard Business Review* (March–April 1983): 96–101.

64. Nirmalya Kumar and Jan-Benedict E. M. Steenkamp, *Private Label Strategy: How to Meet the Store-Brand Challenge* (Boston: Harvard Business School Press, 2007).

65. Grainger website, www.grainger.com.

66. Narus and Anderson, "Contributing as a Distributor to Partnerships with Manufacturers." See also Hlavecek and McCuistion, "Industrial Distributors—When, Who, and How," pp. 96–101.

67. Brett Nelson, "Stuck in the Middle," *Forbes*, August 15, 2005, p. 88.

68. Copacino, *Supply Chain Management.*

69. Fred Moody, "Emegency Relief Logistics—A Faster Way Across the Global Divide," (undated), www.ataoc.ca/default.asp?V_DOC_ID=883 (viewed June 2008).

70. Industry Canada, "Logistics: Canada/United States Manufacturing Perspective," January 22, 2008, www.ic.gc.ca/epic/site/dsib-logi.nsf/en/pj00228e.html (viewed June 2008).

71. Anthony Bianco, "Wal-Mart's Midlife Crisis," *BusinessWeek*, April 30, 2007, pp. 46–56; Matthew Maier, "How to Beat Wal-Mart," *Business 2.0* (May 2005); Jerry Useem, "Should We Admire Wal-Mart?" *Fortune*, March 8, 2004, pp. 118–21; www.walmart.com; www.walmart.ca.

72. Rita Koselka, "Distribution Revolution," *Forbes*, May 25, 1992, pp. 54–62.

73. The optimal order quantity is given by the formula $Q* = 2DS/IC$, where D = annual demand, S = cost to place one order, and I = annual carrying cost per unit. Known as the economic-order quantity formula, it assumes a constant ordering cost, a constant cost of carrying an additional unit in inventory, a known demand,

and no quantity discounts. For further reading on this subject, see Richard J. Tersine, *Principles of Inventory and Materials Management*, 4th ed. (Upper Saddle River, NJ: Prentice Hall, 1994).

74. Copacino, *Supply Chain Management*, pp. 122–23.

75. "Shining Examples," *Economist: A Survey of Logistics*, June 17, 2006, pp. 4–6.

76. Renee DeGross, "Retailers Try eBay Overstocks, Returns for Sale Online," *Atlanta Journal-Constitution*, April 10, 2004.

77. Chuck Salter, "Savvy, with Hints of Guile and Resourcefulness," *Fast Company,* 112 (February 2007): 50; Heather Mcpherson, "Lots to Like about This Concept: As a Wine Negociant, Cameron Hughes Can Offer Premium Wines at Affordable Prices," *Knight Ridder Tribune Business News*, February 21, 2007, p. 1.

78. "Manufacturing Complexity," *Economist: A Survey of Logistics*, June 17, 2006, pp. 6–9.

79. Chad Terhune, "Pepsi's Supply Chain Fix," *Wall Street Journal*, June 6, 2006.

80. http://www.ctcid.ca/english/en_history.php.html (viewed September 26, 2008).

Chapter 17

1. Some of these definitions are adapted from Peter D. Bennett, ed., *Dictionary of Marketing Terms* (Chicago: American Marketing Association, 1995).

2. Stuart Elliott, "Nike Reaches Deeper into New Media to Find Young Buyers," *Wall Street Journal*, October 31, 2006.

3. Joseph W. Alba and J. Wesley Hutchinson, "Dimensions of Consumer Expertise," *Journal of Consumer Research*, 13 (March 1987): 411–453.

4. Jane L. Levere, "Body by Milk: More Than Just a White Mustache," *New York Times (Late Edition [East Coast])*, August 30, 2006, p. C3.

5. For an alternative communication model developed specifically for advertising communications, see Barbara B. Stern, "A Revised Communication Model for Advertising: Multiple Dimensions of the Source, the Message, and the Recipient," *Journal of Advertising* (June 1994): 5–15. For some additional perspectives, see Tom Duncan and Sandra E. Moriarity, "A Communication-Based Marketing Model for Managing Relationships," *Journal of Marketing* (April 1998): 1–13.

6. Brian Sternthal and C. Samuel Craig, *Consumer Behavior: An Information Processing Perspective* (Upper Saddle River, NJ: Prentice Hall, 1982), pp. 97–102.

7. Demetrios Vakratsas and Tim Ambler, "How Advertising Works: What Do We Really Know," *Journal of Marketing*, 63, no. 1 (January 1999): 26–43.

8. Jeromy Lloyd, "Lowe's In, Louie's Out," *Marketing*, February 25, 2008, pp 14-15; "Boston Pizza's New Ad Campaign Features Real Canadian Stories," *Canada Newswire*, March 31, 2008.

9. This section is based on the excellent text, John R. Rossiter and Larry Percy, *Advertising and Promotion Management*, 2nd ed. (New York: McGraw-Hill, 1997).

10. James F. Engel, Roger D. Blackwell, and Paul W. Minard, *Consumer Behavior*, 9th ed. (Fort Worth, TX: Dryden, 2001).

11. Rossiter and Percy, *Advertising and Promotion Management*.

12. Engel, Blackwell, and Minard, *Consumer Behavior*.

13. Ayn E. Crowley and Wayne D. Hoyer, "An Integrative Framework for Understanding Two-Sided Persuasion," *Journal of Consumer Research* (March 1994): 561–574.

14. C. I. Hovland, A. A. Lumsdaine, and F. D. Sheffield, *Experiments on Mass Communication*, vol. 3 (Princeton, NJ: Princeton University Press, 1948), ch. 8; Crowley and Hoyer, "An Integrative Framework for Understanding Two-Sided Persuasion." For an alternative viewpoint, see George E. Belch, "The Effects of Message Modality on One- and Two-Sided Advertising Messages," *Advances in Consumer Research*, edited by Richard P. Bagozzi and Alice M. Tybout (Ann Arbor, MI: Association for Consumer Research, 1983), pp. 21–26.

15. Curtis P. Haugtvedt and Duane T. Wegener, "Message Order Effects in Persuasion: An Attitude Strength Perspective," *Journal of Consumer Research* (June 1994): 205–218; H. Rao Unnava, Robert E. Burnkrant, and Sunil Erevelles, "Effects of Presentation Order and Communication Modality on Recall and Attitude," *Journal of Consumer Research* (December 1994): 481–490.

16. Sternthal and Craig, *Consumer Behavior*, pp. 282–284.

17. Stuart Elliott, "Why a Duck? Because It Sells Insurance," *The New York Times*, June 24, 2002, p. C11.

18. Michael R. Solomon, *Consumer Behavior*, 6th ed. (Upper Saddle River, NJ: Prentice Hall, 2004).

19. Sarah Theodore, "A Modern Classic," *Beverage Industry*, May 1, 2008, www.bevindustry.com/CDA/Articles/Cover_Story/BNP_GUID_9-5-2006_A_10000000000000335605 (viewed June 9, 2008).

20. "The Death of the Jingle," *The Economist*, February 8, 2003, p. 61.

21. Kevin Goldman, "Advertising: Knock, Knock. Who's There? The Same Old Funny Ad Again," *Wall Street Journal*, November 2, 1993, p. B10. See also Marc G. Weinberger, Harlan Spotts, Leland Campbell, and Amy L. Parsons, "The Use and Effect of Humor in Different Advertising Media," *Journal of Advertising Research* (May–June 1995): 44–55.

22. Herbert C. Kelman and Carl I. Hovland, "Reinstatement of the Communication in Delayed Measurement of Opinion Change," *Journal of Abnormal and Social Psychology,* 48 (1953): 327–335.

23. David J. Moore, John C. Mowen, and Richard Reardon, "Multiple Sources in Advertising Appeals: When Product Endorsers Are Paid by the Advertising Sponsor," *Journal of the Academy of Marketing Science* (Summer 1994): 234–243.

24. Suzanne Vranica, "New Breed of Celebrity Endorsements," *Wall Street Journal* (Eastern Edition), February 29, 2008, pp. B3; Jen Muccia, "Ellen DeGeneres Has a New 'Halo,'" Halo Press Release, March 18, 2008, www.halopets.com/news/ellen-degeneres-has-a-new-halo.html (viewed June 20, 2008).

25. C. E. Osgood and P. H. Tannenbaum, "The Principles of Congruity in the Prediction of Attitude Change," *Psychological Review,* 62 (1955): 42–55.

26. Richard C. Morais, "Mobile Mayhem," *Forbes*, July, 6 1998, p. 138; "Working in Harmony," *Soap Perfumery & Cosmetics*, July 1, 1998, p. 27; Rodger Harrabin, "A Commercial Break for Parents," *Independent*, September 8, 1998, p. 19; Naveen Donthu, "A Cross Country Investigation of Recall of and Attitude toward Comparative Advertising," *Journal of Advertising*, 27 (June 22, 1998): 111; "EU to Try Again on Tobacco Advertising Ban," *Associated Press*, May 9, 2001.

27. David Todd, "Multicultural Marketing: Bell ExpressVu Promises a Dose of 'Dishum Dishum,'" *Marketing Magazine Online*, www.marketingmag.ca, February 15, 1999 (viewed October 21, 2004).

28. "Rebirth of a Salesman," *The Economist*, April 14, 2001, 359, no. 8217, p. 62.

29. Michael Kiely, "Word-of-Mouth Marketing," *Marketing* (September 1993): 6. See also Aric Rindfleisch and Christine Moorman, "The Acquisition and Utilization of Information in New Product Alliances: A Strength-of-Ties Perspective," *Journal of Marketing* (April 2001): 1–18.

30. Ian Mount, "Marketing," *Business 2.0* (August/September 2001): 84.

31. J. Johnson Brown and P. Reingen, "Social Ties and Word-of-Mouth Referral Behavior," *Journal of Consumer Research*, 14 (1987): 350–362; Jacqueline Johnson Brown, Peter M. Reingen, and Everett M. Rogers, *Diffusion of Innovations*, 4th ed. (New York: The Free Press, 1995).

32. Elizabeth Wellington, "Freebies and Chitchat Are Hot Marketing Tools," *Philadelphia Inquirer*, December 31, 2003; Bob Sperber, "Krispy Kreme Word-of-Mouth Tactics Continue to Go Against the Grain," *Brandweek*, October 21, 2002, p. 9.

33. Patti Summerfield, "Everyone Wants their 15 Megs of Fame: What's a Brand to Do? CGM Strategies: Move from a Planning Mind-set of Control to one of Hopeful Influence," *Strategy* (November 2006): 26.

34. Renée Dye, "The Buzz on Buzz," *Harvard Business Review* (November/December 2000): 139–146.

35. John Batelle, "The Net of Influence," *Business 2.0* (March 2004): 70.

36. Kenneth Hein, "Run Red Run," *Brandweek*, February 25, 2002, pp. 14–15.

37. Malcolm Macalister Hall, "Selling by Stealth," *Business Life* (November 2001): 51–55.

38. Ann Meyer, "Word-of-Mouth Marketing Speaks Well for Small Business," *Chicago Tribune*, July 28, 2003.

39. Emanuel Rosen, *The Anatomy of Buzz* (New York: Currency, 2000), Ch. 12; "Viral Marketing," *Sales & Marketing Automation* (November 1999): 12–14; George Silverman, *The Secrets of Word-of-Mouth Marketing* (New York: Amacom, 2001).

40. Marian Salzman, Ira Matathia, and Ann O'Reilly, *Buzz: Harness the Power of Influence and Create Demand* (New York: Wiley, 2003).

41. Annette Bourdeau, "Free Food, Rent Fuel Viral Buzz," *Strategy* (January 2008): 9.

42. Jack Neff, "Spam Research Reveals Disgust with Pop-Up Ads," *Advertising Age*, August 25, 2003, pp. 1, 21.

43. Thomson H. Davenport and John C. Beck, *The Attention Economy: Understanding the New Current of Business* (Boston: Harvard Business School Press, 2000).

44. Natalia Williams, "Bronze case study: Canadian Tire," *Strategy* (October 2006): 44.

45. Adapted from G. Maxwell Ule, "A Media Plan for 'Sputnik' Cigarettes," *How to Plan Media Strategy* (American Association of Advertising Agencies, 1957 Regional Convention), pp. 41–52.

46. Thomas C. Kinnear and Kenneth L. Bernhardt, *Principles of Marketing*, 2nd ed. (Glenview, IL: Scott Foresman and Co., 1986).

47. Andrea Zoe Aster, "The Patient Princess," *Marketing Magazine Online*, www.marketingmag.ca, September 13, 2004 (viewed October 22, 2004).

48. Terrence Sing, "Integrated Marketing More Than Just an Internet Brochure," *Pacific Business News*, February 18, 2004, p. 23.

49. Amna Kirmani, "The Effect of Perceived Advertising Costs on Brand Perceptions," *Journal of Consumer Research*, 17 (September 1990): 160–171; Amna Kirmani and Peter Wright, "Money Talks: Perceived Advertising Expense and Expected Product Quality," *Journal of Consumer Research*, 16 (December 1989): 344–353.

50. Vakratsas and Ambler, "How Advertising Works: What Do We Really Know," 26–43.

51. "Polycarbonate Water Bottles," MEC notice, www.mec.ca (viewed June 12, 2008); Wing Sze Tang, "Message in a Bottle," *Marketing*, 113, no. 8 (May 2008): 12; Maria Babbage, "Mountain Equipment Co-op Drops Products with Bisphenol A, Waits for Fed Study," *Canadian Business Online*, www.canadianbusiness.com/markets/headline_news/article.jsp?content=b1207100A (viewed June 22, 2008).

52. *How Advertising Works in Today's Marketplace: The Morrill Study* (New York: McGraw-Hill, 1971), p. 4.

53. Theodore Levitt, *Industrial Purchasing Behavior: A Study in Communication Effects* (Boston: Division of Research, Harvard Business School, 1965).

54. Tourism Newfoundland and Labrador website, www.gov.nf.ca/tourism (viewed October 28, 2002).

55. Janet Stilson, "Wide-Ranging Deals Help ESPN Score with Marketers," *Advertising Age*, March 12, 2007, p. S2.

56. Ernan Roman, *Integrated Direct Marketing: The Cutting Edge Strategy for Synchronizing Advertising, Direct Mail, Telemarketing, and Field Sales* (Lincolnwood, IL: NTC Business Books, 1995).

57. William T. Moran, "Insights from Pricing Research," in E. B. Bailey, ed., *Pricing Practices and Strategies* (New York: The Conference Board, 1978), pp. 7–13.

58. Kate Maddox, "Microsoft Puts Emphasis Online," *B2B*, May 7, 2007, 92, no. 6, p. 14.; Jean Halliday, "At GM, 25% of Marketing Dollars Doled out to Digital," *Advertising Age*, July 28, 2008, 79, no. 29, pp. 4–5.

59. Gerry Khermouch, "The Top 5 Rules of the Ad Game," *Business-Week*, January 20, 2003, pp. 72–73.

60. Dale Buss, "On Again, Off Again," *Brand Marketing*, February 2001, p. 51; Kenneth Hein, "Pepsi: This Time It's All About the Dew,'" *Brandweek*, January 19, 2004, p. 4.

61. Heather Green, "Online Ads Take Off Again," *BusinessWeek*, May 5, 2003, p. 75.

62. Raymond R. Burke and Thomas K. Srull, "Competitive Interference and Consumer Memory for Advertising," *Journal of Consumer Research*, 15 (June 1988): 55–68; Kevin Lane Keller, "Memory Factors in Advertising: The Effect of Advertising Retrieval Cues on Brand Evaluations," *Journal of Consumer Research*, 14 (December 1987): 316–333; Kevin Lane Keller, "Memory and Evaluations in Competitive Advertising Environments," *Journal of Consumer Research*, 17 (March 1991): 463–476; Robert J. Kent and Chris T. Allen, "Competitive Interference Effects in Consumer Memory for Advertising: The Role of Brand Familiarity," *Journal of Marketing*, 58 (July 1994): 97–105.

63. David Walker and Michael J. von Gonten, "Explaining Related Recall Outcomes: New Answers from a Better Model," *Journal of Advertising Research*, 29 (1989): 11–21.

64. Kevin Lane Keller, Susan Heckler, and Michael J. Houston, "The Effects of Brand Name Suggestiveness on Advertising Recall," *Journal of Marketing*, 62 (January 1998): 48–57.

65. Maria Puente, "Online Experience Is Now a Much Better Fit," *USA Today*, December 4, 2002, p. 2E.

66. Don E. Shultz, Stanley I. Tannenbaum, and Robert F. Lauterborn, *Integrated Marketing Communications: Putting It Together and Making It Work* (Lincolnwood, IL: NTC Business Books, 1992); Don E. Schultz and Heidi Schultz, *IMC, The Next Generation: Five Steps for Delivering Value and Measuring Financial Returns* (New York: McGraw-Hill, 2003).

Chapter 18

1. Jack Neff and Lisa Sanders, "It's Broken," *Advertising Age*, February 16, 2004, pp. 1, 30.

2. Ellen Neuborne, "Ads That Actually Sell Stuff," *Business 2.0* (June 2004): 78.

3. Russell H. Colley, *Defining Advertising Goals for Measured Advertising Results* (New York: Association of National Advertisers, 1961).

4. William L. Wilkie and Paul W. Farris, "Comparison Advertising: Problem and Potential," *Journal of Marketing* (October 1975): 7–15.

5. Randall L. Rose, Paul W. Miniard, Michael J. Barone, Kenneth C. Manning, and Brian D. Till, "When Persuasion Goes Undetected: The Case of Comparative Advertising," *Journal of Marketing Research* (August 1993): 315–330; Sanjay Putrevu and Kenneth R. Lord, "Comparative and Noncomparative Advertising: Attitudinal Effects under Cognitive and Affective Involvement Conditions," *Journal of Advertising* (June 1994): 77–91; Dhruv Grewal, Sukumar Kavanoor, and James Barnes, "Comparative versus Noncomparative Advertising: A Meta-Analysis," *Journal of Marketing* (October 1997): 1–15; Dhruv Grewal, Kent B. Monroe, and P. Krishnan, "The Effects of Price-Comparison Advertising on Buyers' Perceptions of Acquisition Value, Transaction Value, and Behavioral Intentions," *Journal of Marketing* (April 1998): 46–59.

6. For a good discussion, see David A. Aaker and James M. Carman, "Are You Overadvertising?" *Journal of Advertising Research* (August–September 1982): 57–70.

7. Donald E. Schultz, Dennis Martin, and William P. Brown, *Strategic Advertising Campaigns* (Chicago: Crain Books, 1984), pp. 192–197.

8. Rajesh Chandy, Gerard J. Tellis, Debbie MacInnis, and Pattana Thaivanich, "What to Say When: Advertising Appeals in Evolving Markets," *Journal of Marketing Research*, 38, no. 4 (November 2001); Gerard J. Tellis, Rajesh Chandy, and Pattana Thaivanich, "Decomposing the Effects of Direct Advertising: Which Brand Works, When, Where, and How Long?" *Journal of Marketing Research*, 37 (February 2000): 32–46.

9. See George S. Low and Jakki J. Mohr, "Brand Managers' Perceptions of the Marketing Communications Budget Allocation Process" (Cambridge, MA: Marketing Science Institute, Report No. 98-105, March 1998), and their "The Advertising Sales Promotion Trade-Off: Theory and Practice" (Cambridge, MA: Marketing Science Institute, Report No. 92-127, October 1992). See also Gabriel J. Beihal and Daniel A. Sheinen, "Managing the Brand in a Corporate Advertising Environment: A Decision-Making Framework for Brand Managers," *Journal of Advertising*, 17 (June 22, 1998): 99.

10. Mark Ritson, "Are you paying attention? A new study shows that people spend most of their time avoiding TV ads," *Financial Times*, May 14, 2002, p. 2.

11. "Gap Inc. Reports May Sales Down 8 Percent; Comparable Store Sales Down 14 Percent," *Business Wire*, 48, no. 30 (June 5, 2008); Eric Newman, "Holy Gap, These Ads are Really Boring," *Brandweek* (August 20–August 27, 2007): 46.

12. "2007 Readership Highlights," *NADbank Study*, www.nadbank. com/en/study/readership (viewed September 24, 2008).

13. Natalie Zmuda, "Why Gatorade is Losing its Zip," *Advertising Age* (Midwest region edition) 79, no. 16, p. 3; Brad Cook, "Gatorade Endures," May 6, 2002, www.brandchannel.com/ features_profile.asp?pr_id=68 (viewed June 12, 2008).

14. Statistics Canada, "Radio Listening," *The Daily*, July 28, 2004, www.statcan.ca/Daily/English/040728/d040728b.htm, (viewed November 25, 2004).

15. David Ogilvy, *Ogilvy on Advertising* (New York: Vintage Books, 1983).

16. "Motel 6 Only Lodging Chain to be Named One of the Top 100 Ad Campaigns of Century," *Business Wire*, New York, April 19, 1999, p. 1.

17. Kim Bartel Sheehan, *Controversies in Contemporary Advertising* (Thousand Oaks, CA: Sage Publications, 2003); Advertising Standards Canada, "CO2001 Ad Complaints Report," www. adstandards.com/en/standards.report.asp (PDF document, p. 15). For further reading, see Dorothy Cohen, *Legal Issues in Marketing Decision Making* (Cincinnati, OH; South-Western, 1995).

18. "Calvin Klein: A Case Study," Media Awareness Network, Ottawa, Ontario.

19. Advertising Educational Foundation, *The Good, Bad & Ugly Advertising Awards*, www.aef.com/exhibits/awards/gbu/2007 (viewed July 2, 2008).

20. World Wildlife Fund Canada, "2007 Annual Report," *WWF Canada*, www.wwf.ca/annualreport; World Wildlife Fund Canada, "Where The Money Goes," *WWF Canada*, www.wwf.ca/ AboutWWF/WhoWeAre/Financial.asp?lang=EN (both viewed June 11, 2008).

21. Schultz, et al., *Strategic Advertising Campaigns*, p. 340.

22. Herbert E. Krugman, "What Makes Advertising Effective?" *Harvard Business Review* (March–April 1975): 98.

23. Thomas H. Davenport and John C. Beck, *The Attention Economy: Understanding the New Currency of Business* (Boston: Harvard Business School Press, 2000).

24. Demetrios Vakratsas, Fred M. Feinberg, Frank M. Bass, Gurumurthy Kalyanaram, "The Shape of Advertising Response Functions Revisited: A Model of Dynamic Probabilistic Thresholds," *Marketing Science*, 23, no. 1 (Winter 2004): 109–119.

25. Susan Thea Posnock, "It Can Control Madison Avenue," *American Demographics* (February 2004): 29–33.

26. James Betzold, "Jaded Riders Are Ever-Tougher Sell," *Advertising Age*, July 9, 2001; Michael McCarthy, "Ads Are Here, There,

Everywhere," *USA Today,* June 19, 2001; Kipp Cheng, "Captivating Audiences," *Brandweek,* November 29, 1999; Michael McCarthy, "Critics Target 'Omnipresent' Ads," *USA Today,* April 16, 2001.

27. Sasha Nagy, "Cheesy Advertising," *The Globe and Mail Report on Business,* March 30, 2006, www.theglobeandmail.com/servlet/story/RTGAM.20060330.wcheese30/BNStory (viewed July 14, 2008).

28. Sam Jaffe, "Easy Riders," *American Demographics* (March 2004): 20–23.

29. Theresa Howard, "Ads Seek Greatness," *USA Today,* June 23, 2004, p. 4B.

30. Jennifer Henderson, "Radio Contest Offers Listeners Free Plastic Surgery – Surgeons Say it Trivializes their Work," *Manitoban,* September 18, 2002, www.themanitoban.com/2002-2003/0918/news_6.shtml (viewed June 13, 2008); Extreme Group website, www.extremegroup.com/work/20 (viewed June 13, 2008); "Archives: Country 101's New Contrast to Draw Pickets," *HalifaxLive.com,* www.halifaxlive.com/Archives.htm (viewed June 13, 2008).

31. Jeff Pelline, "New Commercial Twist in Corporate Restrooms," *San Francisco Chronicle,* October 6, 1986.

32. Brian Steinberg and Suzanne Vranica, "Prime-Time TV's New Guest Stars: Products," *Wall Street Journal,* January 13, 2004, pp. B1, B4.

33. Jane Weaver, "A License to Shill," November 17, 2002, MSNBC News.

34. Joanne Lipman, "Product Placement Can Be Free Lunch," *Wall Street Journal,* November 25, 1991, p. B6; John Lippman and Rick Brooks, "Hot Holiday Flick Pairs FedEx, Hanks," *Wall Street Journal,* December 11, 2000, pp. B1, B6.

35. Warren Berger, "That's Advertainment," *Business 2.0* (March 2003): 91–95.

36. Catherine P. Taylor, "Digitas," *Brandweek IQ Quarterly,* February 23, 2004, pp. 24–25.

37. Jean Halliday, "Mazda Goes Viral to Tout New Cars," *Automotive News,* November 24, 2003, p. 42B.

38. Matthew Boyle, "Hey Shoppers: Ads on Aisle 7!" *Fortune,* November 24, 2003.

39. "Fox Makes Out Like Bandit with 'Idol' and Bowl," *Advertising Age,* 78, no. 50 (December 17, 2007): pp.1–2; "Frequently Asked Questions About Television Advertising," *TelevisionAdvertising.com,* http://televisionadvertising.com/faq.htm (viewed August 31, 2008).

40. Canadian Media Directors' Council, *2002-2003 Media Digest* (Toronto: Marketing Magazine, 2002), p. 19.

41. Canadian Media Directors' Council, p. 43.

42. Michael A. Kamins, Lawrence J. Marks, and Deborah Skinner, "Television Commercial Evaluation in the Context of Program Induced Mood: Congruency versus Consistency Effects," *Journal of Advertising* (June 1991): 1–14.

43. Kenneth R. Lord and Robert E. Burnkrant, "Attention versus Distraction: The Interactive Effect of Program Involvement and Attentional Devices on Commercial Processing," *Journal of Advertising* (March 1993): 47–60; Kenneth R. Lord, Myung-Soo Lee, and Paul L. Sauer, "Program Context Antecedents of Attitude Toward Radio Commercials," *Journal of the Academy of Marketing Science* (Winter 1994): 3–15.

44. Roland T. Rust, *Advertising Media Models: A Practical Guide* (Lexington, MA: Lexington Books, 1986).

45. Hani I. Mesak, "An Aggregate Advertising Pulsing Model with Wearout Effects," *Marketing Science* (Summer 1992): 310–326; Fred M. Feinberg, "Pulsing Policies for Aggregate Advertising Models," *Marketing Science* (Summer 1992): 221–234.

46. Josephine L.C.M. Woltman Elpers, Michel Wedel, and Rik G.M. Pieters, "Why Do Consumers Stop Viewing Television Commercials? Two Experiments on the Influence of Moment-to-Moment Entertainment and Information Value," *Journal of Marketing Research,* 40 (November), 2003, pp. 437–453.

47. Kristian S. Palda, *The Measurement of Cumulative Advertising Effect* (Upper Saddle River, NJ: Prentice Hall, 1964), p. 87; David

B. Montgomery and Alvin J. Silk, "Estimating Dynamic Effects of Market Communications Expenditures," *Management Science* (June 1972): 485–501.

48. www.infores.com; Leonard M. Lodish, Magid Abraham, Stuart Kalmenson, Jeanne Livelsberger, Beth Lubetkin, Bruce Richardson, and Mary Ellen Stevens, "How T.V. Advertising Works: A Meta-Analysis of 389 Real World Split Cable T.V. Advertising Experiments," *Journal of Marketing Research,* 32 (May 1995): pp. 125–139.

49. In addition to the sources cited below, see David Walker and Tony M. Dubitsky, "Why Liking Matters," *Journal of Advertising Research* (May–June 1994): 9–18; Abhilasha Mehta, "How Advertising Response Modeling (ARM) Can Increase Ad Effectiveness," *Journal of Advertising Research* (May–June 1994): 62–74; Karin Holstius, "Sales Response to Advertising," *International Journal of Advertising,* 9, no. 1 (1990): 38–56; John Deighton, Caroline Henderson, and Scott Neslin, "The Effects of Advertising on Brand Switching and Repeat Purchasing," *Journal of Marketing Research* (February 1994): 28–43; Anil Kaul and Dick R. Wittink, "Empirical Generalizations about the Impact of Advertising on Price Sensitivity and Price," *Marketing Science,* 14, no. 3, pt. 1 (1995): G151–160; Ajay Kalra and Ronald C. Goodstein, "The Impact of Advertising Positioning Strategies on Consumer Price Sensitivity," *Journal of Marketing Research* (May 1998): 210–224; Gerard J. Tellis, Rajesh K. Chandy, and Pattana Thaivanich, "Which Ad Works, When, Where, and How Often? Modeling the Effects of Direct Television Advertising," *Journal of Marketing Research,* 37 (February 2000): 32–46.

50. Nigel Hollis, "The Link between TV Ad Awareness and Sales: New Evidence from Sales Response Modelling," *Journal of the Market Research Society* (January 1994): 41–55.

51. From Robert C. Blattberg and Scott A. Neslin, *Sales Promotion: Concepts, Methods, and Strategies* (Upper Saddle River, NJ: Prentice Hall, 1990). This text provides the most comprehensive and analytical treatment of sales promotion to date. An extremely up-to-date and comprehensive review of academic work on sales promotions can be found in Scott Neslin, "Sales Promotion," in *Handbook of Marketing,* edited by Bart Weitz and Robin Wensley (London: Sage Publications, 2002), pp. 310–338.

52. Kusum Ailawadi, Karen Gedenk, and Scott A. Neslin, "Heterogeneity and Purchase Event Feedback in Choice Models: An Empirical Analysis with Implications for Model Building," *International Journal of Research in Marketing,* 16 (1999): 177–198. See also Eric T. Anderson and Duncan Simester, "The Long-Run Effects of Promotion Depth on New Versus Established Customers: Three Field Studies," *Marketing Science,* 23, no. 1 (Winter 2004): 4–20.

53. Carl Mela, Kamel Jedidi, and Douglas Bowman, "The Long Term Impact of Promotions on Consumer Stockpiling," *Journal of Marketing Research,* 35, no. 2 (May 1998): 250–262.

54. Harald J. Van Heerde, Peter S. H. Leeflang, and Dick Wittink, "The Estimation of Pre- and Postpromotion Dips with Store-Level Scanner Data," *Journal of Marketing Research,* 37, no. 3 (August 2000): 383–395.

55. Paul W. Farris and John A. Quelch, "In Defense of Price Promotion," *Sloan Management Review* (Fall 1987): 63–69.

56. Patti Summerfield, "Virgin does Happy with Freezie-Cart-as-Media Road Trip," *Strategy,* August 2007, p. 40.

57. Roger A. Strang, "Sales Promotion: Fast Growth, Faulty Management," *Harvard Business Review* (July–August 1976): 116–119.

58. For a good summary of the research on whether promotion erodes the consumer franchise of leading brands, see Blattberg and Neslin, *Sales Promotion.*

59. AutoVIBES, *AutoBeat Daily,* March 3, 2004; Karen Lundegaard and Sholnn Freeman, "Detroit's Challenge: Weaning Buyers from Years of Deals," *Wall Street Journal,* January 6, 2004, pp. A1, A2.

60. Robert George Brown, "Sales Response to Promotions and Advertising," *Journal of Advertising Research* (August 1974): 36–37. See also Carl F. Mela, Sunil Gupta, and Donald R. Lehmann,

"The Long-Term Impact of Promotion and Advertising on Consumer Brand Choice," *Journal of Marketing Research* (May 1997): 248–261; Purushottam Papatla and Lakshman Krishnamurti, "Measuring the Dynamic Effects of Promotions on Brand Choice," *Journal of Marketing Research* (February 1996): 20–35; Kamel Jedidi, Carl F. Mela, and Sunil Gupta, "Managing Advertising and Promotion for Long-Run Profitability," *Marketing Science,* 18, no. 1 (1999): 1–22.

61. Magid M. Abraham and Leonard M. Lodish, "Getting the Most Out of Advertising and Promotion," *Harvard Business Review* (May–June 1990): 50–60. See also Shuba Srinivasan, Koen Pauwels, Dominique Hanssens, and Marnik Dekimpe, "Do Promotions Benefit Manufacturers, Retailers, or Both?" *Management Science,* 2004.

62. F. Kent Mitchel, "Advertising/Promotion Budgets: How Did We Get Here, and What Do We Do Now?" *Journal of Consumer Marketing* (Fall 1985): 405–447.

63. For a model for setting sales-promotions objectives, see David B. Jones, "Setting Promotional Goals: A Communications Relationship Model," *Journal of Consumer Marketing,* 11, no. 1 (1994): 38–49.

64. Pat Hewitt, "Thousands of Quebec Travellers Win Free Vacation Contest to Begin New Year," *Canadian Press NewsWire,* January 2, 2008; "itravel2000 Extends 'Let it Snow' Offer Due to Overwhelming Demand! Last Chance for Consumers to Get in on The Largest Travel Promotion in Canadian History!" *marketwire,* September 4, 2007, www.marketwire.com/mw/release.do?id=765973 (viewed June 16, 2008).

65. See John C. Totten and Martin P. Block, *Analyzing Sales Promotion: Text and Cases,* 2nd ed. (Chicago: Dartnell, 1994), pp. 69–70.

66. Carey Toane, "Danone Hits the Cold Streets," *Strategy,* February, 2008, p. 9.

67. Paul W. Farris and Kusum L. Ailawadi, "Retail Power: Monster or Mouse?" *Journal of Retailing* (Winter 1992): 351–369.

68. "Retailers Buy Far in Advance to Exploit Trade Promotions," *Wall Street Journal,* October 9, 1986, p. 35; Rajiv Lal, J. Little, and J. M. Vilas-Boas, "A Theory of Forward Buying, Merchandising, and Trade Deals," *Marketing Science,* 15, no. 1 (1996): 21–37.

69. "2007 Annual Report: Leveraging Canada's Tourism Brand," *Canada Tourism Commission,* www.corporate.canada.travel/docs/about_ctc/2007_Annual_Report_en.pdf (viewed June 17, 2008).

70. Arthur Stern, "Measuring the Effectiveness of Package Goods Promotion Strategies" (paper presented to the Association of National Advertisers, Glen Cove, NY, February 1978).

71. Kurt H. Schaffir and H. George Trenten, *Marketing Information Systems* (New York: Amacom, 1973), p. 81.

72. Joe A. Dodson, Alice M. Tybout, and Brian Sternthal, "Impact of Deals and Deal Retraction on Brand Switching," *Journal of Marketing Research* (February 1978): 72–81.

73. Books on sales promotion include Totten and Block, *Analyzing Sales Promotion: Text and Cases;* Don E. Schultz, William A. Robinson, and Lisa A. Petrison, *Sales Promotion Essentials,* 2nd ed. (Lincolnwood, IL: NTC Business Books, 1994); John Wilmshurst, *Below-the-Line Promotion* (Oxford, England: Butterworth/Heinemann, 1993); Blattberg and Neslin, *Sales Promotion: Concepts, Methods, and Strategies.* For an expert systems approach to sales promotion, see John W. Keon and Judy Bayer, "An Expert Approach to Sales Promotion Management," *Journal of Advertising Research* (June–July 1986): 19–26.

74. Philip Kotler, "Atmospherics as a Marketing Tool," *Journal of Retailing* (Winter 1973–1974): 48–64.

75. Dean Foust, "Coke: Wooing the TiVo Generation," *Business Week,* March 1, 2004, pp. 77–78.

76. Kathleen Kerwin, "When the Factory Is a Theme Park," *BusinessWeek,* May 3, 2004, p. 94; Vanessa O'Connell, "'You-Are-There' Advertising," *Wall Street Journal,* August 5, 2002, pp. B1, B3.

77. Kenneth Hein, "The Age of Reason," *Brandweek,* October 27, 2003, pp. 24–28.

78. David Weinstein, "Maxwell House Declares Wednesday, March 26, 2008, a Day to Brew Some Good," *Canada NewsWire,* March 26, 2008; Terry Poulton, "Maxwell House launches "Brew Some Good," *Media in Canada,* www.mediaincanada.com/articles/mic/20080327/maxwellhouse.html (viewed June 13, 2008); Garin Tcholakian, "Empower: Maxwell House Brews Some Good," *Strategy,* June 2008, p. 30.

79. Monte Burke, "X-treme Economics," *Forbes,* February 2, 2004, pp. 42–44.

80. The Association of National Advertisers has a useful source, *Event Marketing: A Management Guide,* which is available at www.ana.net/bookstore.

81. Ian Mount, "Exploding the Myths of Stadium Naming," *Business 2.0* (April 2004): 82.

82. "Air Canada Centre Name Likely to Stay," *Marketing Magazine Daily,* www.marketingmag.ca, April 4, 2003 (viewed November 29, 2004).

83. Kelley Gates, "Wild in the Streets," *Brand Marketing* (February 2001): 54.

84. Dwight W. Catherwood and Richard L. Van Kirk, *The Complete Guide to Special Event Management* (New York: John Wiley, 1992).

85. William L. Shankin and John Kuzma, "Buying That Sporting Image," *Marketing Management* (Spring 1992): 65.

86. For an excellent account, see Thomas L. Harris, *The Marketer's Guide to Public Relations* (New York: John Wiley, 1991). See also Harris, *Value-Added Public Relations* (Chicago: NTC Business Books, 1998).

87. Tom Duncan, *A Study of How Manufacturers and Service Companies Perceive and Use Marketing Public Relations* (Muncie, IN: Ball State University, December 1985). For more on how to contrast the effectiveness of advertising with the effectiveness of PR, see Kenneth R. Lord and Sanjay Putrevu, "Advertising and Publicity: An Information Processing Perspective," *Journal of Economic Psychology* (March 1993): 57–84.

88. Julie Rusciolelli, "PR Discovers Metrics," *Marketing Magazine Online,* www.marketingmag.ca, March 29, 2004 (viewed November 29, 2004); Taxi Canada website, www.taxi.ca (viewed November 29, 2004); See You In Torino website, www.seeyouintorino.com (viewed November 29, 2004).

89. For further reading on marketing PR, see P. Rajan Varadarajan and Anil Menon, "Cause-Related Marketing: A Co-Alignment of Marketing Strategy and Corporate Philanthropy," *Journal of Marketing* (July 1988): 58–74.

90. Arthur M. Merims, "Marketing's Stepchild: Product Publicity," *Harvard Business Review* (November–December 1972): 111–112. See also Katherine D. Paine, "There Is a Method for Measuring PR," *Marketing News,* November 6, 1987, p. 5.

Chapter 19

1. The terms *direct-order marketing* and *direct-relationship marketing* were suggested as subsets of direct marketing by Stan Rapp and Tom Collins in *The Great Marketing Turnaround* (Upper Saddle River, NJ: Prentice Hall, 1990).

2. Sarah Smith, "Women Want More Air Miles Reward Miles," *Marketing Magazine Online,* www.marketingmag.ca, February 18, 2002.

3. Michael J. McGovern, "The Precise Art of Direct Marketing," *Marketing Magazine Online,* www.marketingmag.ca, March 22, 2004 (viewed December 1, 2004).

4. "Not Your Mom's F@#%*N Dinners," *Canadian Business,* 81, no. 2 (February 2008): S5-S7.

5. Bob Stone, *Successful Direct Marketing Methods,* 6th ed. (Lincolnwood, IL: NTC Business Books, 1996). See also David Shepard Associates, *The New Direct Marketing,* 2nd ed. (Chicago: Irwin, 1995); Amiya K. Basu, Atasi Basu, and Rajeev Batra, "Modeling the Response Pattern to Direct Marketing

Campaigns," *Journal of Marketing Research* (May 1995): 204–212.

6. Edward L. Nash, *Direct Marketing: Strategy, Planning, Execution,* 3rd ed. (New York: McGraw-Hill, 1995).

7. Rachel McLaughlin, "Get the Envelope Opened!" *Target Marketing* (September 1998): 37–39.

8. The *average customer longevity* (N) is related to the *customer retention rate* (CR). Suppose the company retains 80 percent of its customers each year. Then the average customer longevity is given by: $N = 1 / (1 – CR) = 1 / 0.2 = 5$.

9. Chris Daniels, "Thinking Big," *Marketing,* 111, no. 21 (June 12, 2006): 14-15; www.thehalliburton.com (viewed June 18, 2008).

10. "Canadian Mail Order Catalogues," Library and Archives Canada, www.collectionscanada.ca/mailorder/index-e.html.

11. Jennifer Saranow, "A ZIP-Code Screen for Catalog Customers," *Wall Street Journal* (Eastern Edition), June 24, 2008, p. B1.

12. "Catalogue Mail: Frequently Asked Questions," *Canada Post,* www.canadapost.ca/business/offerings/catalogue_mail/can/about_faqs-e.asp.

13. "Case Study: Awesome Ewe," www.e-bc.ca/casestudies_details.asp?id=2 (viewed March 23, 2005).

14. Mari Yamaguchi, "Japanese Consumers Shun Local Catalogs to Buy American," *Marketing News,* December 2, 1996, p. 12; Cacilie Rohwedder, "U.S. Mail-Order Firms Shake Up Europe—Better Service, Specialized Catalogs Find Eager Shoppers," *Wall Street Journal,* January 6, 1998; Kathleen Kiley, "B-to-B Marketers High on Overseas Sales," *Catalog Age* (January 1997): 8.

15. "Do Not Call: CRTC Rules," *CBC News Online,* www.cbc.ca/news/background/telemarketing/ (viewed December 13, 2004); "Ottawa Leans to DNC Registry as Flak Rises over CRTC Rules," *Direct Marketing News,* October 2004, www.dmn.ca/Articles/Articles/2004/Nov/dnc1104.htm; Telecom Decision CRTC 2004-63, Application by the Canadian Marketing Association to Stay Decision 2004-35, Reference: 8662-C131-200408543, Ottawa, 28 September 2004; Telecom Decision CRTC 2004-35, Review of Telemarketing Rules, Reference: 8665-C12-13/0, Ottawa, 21 May 2004.

16. Jim Edwards, "The Art of the Infomercial," *Brandweek,* September 3, 2001, pp. 14–19.

17. "Infomercial Offers Multiple Uses," *Direct Marketing* (September 1998): 11; Tim Hawthorne, When and Why to Consider Infomercials," *Target Marketing* (February 1998): 52–53.

18. Michelle Warren, "Sick Kids' Direct Drama," *Marketing Magazine Online,* www.marketingmag.ca, February 10, 2003 (viewed December 1, 2004).

19. Charles Fishman, "The Tool of a New Machine," *Fast Company,* May 2004, 92–95.

20. "Shopping For Wine? Information and Greeting Card Kiosk Enhances the Experience," *Canada NewsWire,* September 10, 2007, p. 1.

21. Tony Case, "Growing Up," *Interactive Quarterly,* April 19, 2004, pp. 32–34.

22. "Acxiom Corporation; Sephora Extends Contract with Acxiom for Integrated Digital Marketing Campaigns," *Business & Finance Week,* June 16, 2008, p. 94.

23. Asim Ansari and Carl F. Mela (2003), "E-Customization," *Journal of Marketing Research,* 40, no. 2 (May 2003): 131–145.

24. "Internet Ad Market Heating Up: Report," *The Banner,* August 2004, www.247canada.com/en/newsletter/newsletter-0408.html#article08.

25. Marketing Magazine Digital Marketing Report, "Logging On," *Marketing Magazine Online,* April 21, 2003 (viewed December 1, 2004).

26. David L. Smith and Karen McFee, "Media Mix 101: Online Media for Traditional Marketers," September 2003, http://advantage.msn.com/articles/MediaMix101_2.asp.

27. Paul C. Judge, "Will Online Ads Ever Click?" *Fast Company* (March 2001): 181–192.

28. Online Publishers Association, "OPA Media Consumption Study," January 2002.

29. Jeffrey F. Rayport and Bernard J. Jaworski, *e-commerce* (New York: McGraw-Hill, 2001), p. 116.

30. Bob Tedeschi, "E-Commerce Report," *The New York Times,* June 24, 2002, p. C8.

31. Stephen Baker, "Pop-Up Ads Had Better Start Pleasing," *BusinessWeek,* December 8, 2003, p. 40.

32. "Prime Clicking Time," *The Economist,* May 31, 2003, p. 65; Ben Elgin, "Search Engines Are Picking Up Steam," *BusinessWeek,* March 24, 2003, pp. 86–87.

33. Ned Desmond, "Google's Next Runaway Success," *Business 2.0,* November 2002, p. 73.

34. Heather Green, "Online Ads Take Off Again," *BusinessWeek,* May 5, 2003, p. 75.

35. These numbers reflect average 2008 figures based on a study of CPM by the Interactive Advertising Bureau and Bain & Company of seven well-known media companies for an online display ad of US$15 (although most major advertisers may not have to pay this price).

36. Seth Godin, *Permission Marketing: Turning Strangers into Friends and Friends into Customers* (New York: Simon & Schuster, 1999).

37. Chana R. Schoenberger, "Web? What Web?" *Forbes,* June 10, 2002, p. 132.

38. Rapp and Collins, *Maximarketing* (New York: McGraw-Hill, 1987).

39. Theresa Howard, "Ad Winners Able to Implement 'Total Communications Strategy,'" *USA Today,* June 22, 2004, www.usatoday.com/money/advertising/2004-06-22-cannes-first-awards_x.htm (viewed September 25, 2008).

40. Statistics Canada, "Occupation – National Occupational Classification for Statistics 2006, Class of Worker and Sex for the Labour Force 15 Years and Over of Canada, Provinces, Territories, Census Metropolitan Areas and Census Agglomerations, 2006 Census – 20% Sample Data," Catalogue no. 97-559-XCB2006011.

41. William Keenan Jr., "Cost-per-call Data Deserve Scrutiny," *Industry Week,* January 10, 2000, 249, no. 1, p. 14.

42. Adapted from Robert N. McMurry, "The Mystique of Super-Salesmanship," *Harvard Business Review* (March–April 1961): 114. See also William C. Moncrief III, "Selling Activity and Sales Position Taxonomies for Industrial Salesforces," *Journal of Marketing Research* (August 1986): 261–270.

43. Jon Bello, "Sell Like Your Outfit Is at Stake. It Is," *BusinessWeek Online,* February 5, 2004.

44. Lawrence G. Friedman and Timothy R. Furey, *The Channel Advantage: Going to Marketing with Multiple Sales Channels* (Oxford, UK: Butterworth-Heinemann, 1999).

45. Michael Copeland, "Hits and Misses," *Business 2.0* (April 2004): 142.

46. Luis R. Gomez-Mejia, David B. Balkin, and Robert L. Cardy, *Managing Human Resources* (Upper Saddle River, NJ: Prentice Hall, 1995), pp. 416–418.

47. "What Salespeople Are Paid," *Sales & Marketing Management* (February 1995): 30–31; Christopher Power, Lisa Driscoll, and Earl Bohn, "Smart Selling: How Companies are Winning Over Today's Tougher Customer," *Business Week,* August 3, 1992, p. 46; William Keenan Jr., ed., *The Sales & Marketing Management Guide to Sales Compensation Planning: Commissions, Bonuses & Beyond* (Chicago: Probus Publishing, 1994).

48. Sonke Albers, "Salesforce Management—Compensation, Motivation, Selection, and Training," in *Handbook of Marketing,* edited by Bart Weitz and Robin Wensley (London: Sage Publications, 2002), pp. 248–266.

49. Betsy Cummings, "Wanted: Older Workers," *Sales and Marketing Management*, 158, no. 7: 12; 1-800-GOT-JUNK website, www.1800gotjunk.com (viewed June 19, 2008).

50. Geoffrey Downey, "Xerox Looks Outside for E-learning Tutor," *Computing Canada*, 28, no. 18 (September 13, 2002): p. 29.

51. "Welcome to the Real Whirled: How Whirlpool Training Forced Salespeople to Live with the Brand," *Sales & Marketing Management* (February 2001): 87–88.

52. Nanette Byrnes, "Avon Calling—Lots of New Reps," *Business-Week*, June 2, 2003, pp. 53–54.

53. Michael R. W. Bommer, Brian F. O'Neil, and Beheruz N. Sethna, "A Methodology for Optimizing Selling Time of Salespersons," *Journal of Marketing Theory and Practice* (Spring 1994): 61–75. See also Lissan Joseph, "On the Optimality of Delegating Pricing Authority to the Sales Force," *Journal of Marketing*, 65 (January 2001): 62–70.

54. Thomas Blackshear and Richard E. Plank, "The Impact of Adaptive Selling on Sales Effectiveness within the Pharmaceutical Industry," *Journal of Marketing Theory and Practice* (Summer 1994): 106–125.

55. Dartnell Corporation, 30th Sales Force Compensation Survey. Other breakdowns show that 12.7 percent is spent in service calls, 16 percent in administrative tasks, 25.1 percent in telephone selling, and 17.4 percent in waiting/travelling.

56. Robert Colman, "Smarter, Faster, and Tech Savvy," *CMA Management*, 77, no. 5 (August/September 2003): 22–25.

57. James A. Narus and James C. Anderson, "Industrial Distributor Selling: The Roles of Outside and Inside Sales," *Industrial Marketing Management,* 15 (1986): 55–62.

58. Willem Verbeke and Richard P. Bagozzi, "Sales Call Anxiety: Exploring What It Means When Fear Rules a Sales Encounter," *Journal of Marketing*, 64 (July 2000): 88–101.

59. Gilbert A. Churchill Jr., Neil M. Ford, and Orville C. Walker Jr., *Sales Force Management: Planning, Implementation and Control*, 4th ed. (Homewood, IL: Irwin, 1993). See also Jhinuk Chowdhury, "The Motivational Impact of Sales Quotas on Effort," *Journal of Marketing Research* (February 1993): 28–41; Murali K. Mantrala, Prabhakant Sinha, and Andris A. Zoltners, "Structuring a Multiproduct Sales Quota-Bonus Plan for a Heterogeneous Sales Force: A Practical Model-Based Approach," *Marketing Science* 13, no. 2 (1994): 121–144; Wujin Chu, Eitan Gerstner, and James D. Hess, "Costs and Benefits of Hard-Sell," *Journal of Marketing Research* (February 1995): 97–102; Manfred Krafft, "In Empirical Investigation of the Antecedents of Sales Force Control Systems," *Journal of Marketing*, 63 (July 1999): 120–134.

60. Eilene Zimmerman, "Quota Busters," *Sales & Marketing Management* (January 2001): pp. 59–63.

61. Melanie Warner, "Confessions of a Control Freak," *Fortune*, September 4, 2000, p. 30; Peter Burrows, "The Era of Efficiency," *BusinessWeek*, June 18, 2001, p. 92.

62. Ian Mount, "Out of Control," *Business 2.0* (August 2002): 38–44.

63. Philip M. Posdakoff and Scott B. MacKenzie, "Organizational Citizenship Behaviors and Sales Unit Effectiveness," *Journal of Marketing Research* (August 1994): 351–363. See also Andrea L. Dixon, Rosann L. Spiro, and Magbul Jamil, "Successful and Unsuccessful Sales Calls: Measuring Salesperson Attributions and Behavioral Intentions," *Journal of Marketing*, 65 (July 2001): 64–78; Willem Verbeke and Richard P. Bagozzi, "Sales Call Anxiety: Exploring What It Means When Fear Rules a Sales Encounter," *Journal of Marketing*, 64 (July 2000): 88–101.

64. Andrea L. Dixon, Rosann L. Spiro, and Maqbul Jamil, "Successful and Unsuccessful Sales Calls: Measuring Salesperson Attributions and Behavioral Intentions," *Journal of Marketing*, 65 (July 2001): 64–78.

65. Some of the following discussion is based on W. J. E. Crissy, William H. Cunningham, and Isabella C. M. Cunningham, *Selling: The Personal Force in Marketing* (New York: John Wiley, 1977), pp. 119–129.

66. Joel E. Urbany, "Justifying Profitable Pricing," Working Paper Series, Marketing Science Institute, Report No. 00-117, 2000, pp. 17–18.

67. For additional reading, see Howard Raiffa, *The Art and Science of Negotiation* (Cambridge, MA: Harvard University Press, 1982); Max H. Bazerman and Margaret A. Neale, *Negotiating Rationally* (New York: The Free Press, 1992); James C. Freund, *Smart Negotiating* (New York: Simon & Schuster, 1992); Frank L. Acuff, *How to Negotiate Anything with Anyone Anywhere Around the World* (New York: American Management Association, 1993); Jehoshua Eliashberg, Gary L. Lilien, and Nam Kim, "Searching for Generalizations in Business Marketing Negotiations," *Marketing Science*, 14, no. 3, pt. 1 (1995): G47–G60.

68. Kristen Vinakmens, "Timing Is Everything: Top Marketers Experiment with Systems That React to Customer Behaviour with Just the Right Offer at Just the Right Time," *Marketing Magazine Online*, www.marketingmag.ca, September 8, 2003 (viewed December 2, 2004).

Chapter 20

1. Deborah Ball and Sarah Ellison, "Nestlé's Appetite for Acquisitions Quickens," *Wall Street Journal*, August 7, 2002, p. B3.

2. Booz, Allen & Hamilton, *New Products Management for the 1980s* (New York: Booz, Allen & Hamilton, 1982).

3. Ann Harrington, "Who's Afraid of a New Product," *Fortune*, November 10, 2003, pp. 189–192; Brad Weiners, "Gore-Tex Tackles the Great Indoors," *Business 2.0* (April 2004): 32.

4. William Symonds, "Can Gillette Regain Its Edge," *BusinessWeek*, January 26, 2004, p. 46; Gillette website, www.gillette.com; Gillette Venus website, www.gillettevenus.com/ca/.

5. "Don't Laugh at Gilded Butterflies," *The Economist*, April 24, 2004, pp. 71–73.

6. Blu-ray website, www.blu-ray.com (viewed June 23, 2008); "Sony Delivers Full HD 1080p Quality with Blu-ray Disc™," *Canada NewsWire*, May 18, 2006. p.1.

7. For details, see Thomas Kuczmarski, Arthur Middlebrooks, and Jeffrey Swaddling, *Innovating the Corporation: Creating Value for Customers and Shareholders* (Lincolnwood, IL: NTC, 2000).

8. Clayton M. Christensen, *The Innovator's Dilemma: When New Technologies Cause Great Firms to Fail* (Boston, MA: Harvard University Press, 1997).

9. Ely Dahan and John R. Hauser, "Product Development: Managing a Dispersed Process," in *Handbook of Marketing*, edited by Bart Weitz and Robin Wensley (London: Sage Publications), pp. 179–222.

10. Guess Canada website, www.guess.ca (viewed June 23, 2008); Khanh T. L. Tran, "Guess Joins Green Scene for Spring," *Women's Wear Daily*, 195, no. 54 (March 13, 2008): 8.

11. Christopher Power, "Flops," *BusinessWeek*, August 16, 1993, pp. 76–82.

12. Andrea Zoe Aster, "Consumer Research Goes Online," *Marketing Magazine*, June 7, 2004; Deloitte and Touche, "Vision in Manufacturing Study," Deloitte Consultng and Kenan-Flagler Business School, March 6, 1998; A. C. Nielsen, "New Product Introduction—Successful Innovation/Failure: Fragile Boundary," A. C. Nielsen BASES and Ernst & Young Global Client Consulting, June 24, 1999.

13. Robert G. Cooper and Elko J. Kleinschmidt, *New Products: The Key Factors in Success* (Chicago: American Marketing Association, 1990).

14. "2008 Best New Product Awards' Winners Announced: Over 10,000 Canadian Consumers Weigh in with their Top Choices for Best New Products," *Marketwire*, February 7, 2008, p. 1.

15. David Welch, "Can Stodgy GM Turn Stylish?" *BusinessWeek*, November 11, 2002, pp. 111–112.

16. David S. Hopkins, *Options in New-Product Organization* (New York: Conference Board, 1974); Doug Ayers, Robert Dahlstrom, and Steven J. Skinner, "An Exploratory Investigation of

Organizational Antecedents to New Product Success," *Journal of Marketing Research* (February 1997): 107–116.

17. Rajesh Sethi, Daniel C. Smith, and C. Whan Park, "Cross Functional Product Development Teams, Creativity, and the Innovativeness of New Consumer Products," *Journal of Marketing Research*, 38 (February 2001): 73–85.

18. Don H. Lester, "Critical Success Factors for New Product Development," *Research Technology Management* (January–February 1998): 36–43.

19. Robert G. Cooper, "Stage-Gate Systems: A New Tool for Managing New Products," *Business Horizons* (May–June 1990): 44–54. See also "The New Prod System: The Industry Experience," *Journal of Product Innovation Management*, 9 (1992): 113–127.

20. Robert Cooper, *Product Leadership: Creating and Launching Superior New Products* (New York: Perseus Books, 1998).

21. Ely Dahan and John R. Hauser, "Product Development: Managing a Dispersed Process," in *Handbook of Marketing*, edited by Bart Weitz and Robin Wensley (London: Sage Publications), pp. 179–222.

22. John Hauser, Gerard J. Tellis, and Abbie J. Griffin, "Research on Innovation: A Review and Agenda for Marketing," *Marketing Science*, 25, no. 6 (Nov/Dec 2006): 687–720.

23. Danielle Sacks, Chuck Salter, Alan Deutschman, and Scott Kirsner, "Innovation Scouts," *Fast Company* (May 2007): 90–94.

24. Abbie J. Griffin and John Hauser, "The Voice of the Customer," *Marketing Science* (Winter 1993): 1–27.

25. Emily Nelson, "Stuck on You," *Wall Street Journal*, May 9, 2002, pp. B1, B4.

26. Eric von Hippel, "Lead Users: A Source of Novel Product Concepts," *Management Science* (July 1986): 791–805. See also *The Sources of Innovation* (New York: Oxford University Press, 1988); "Learning from Lead Users," in *Marketing in an Electronic Age*, edited by Robert D. Buzzell (Cambridge, MA: Harvard Business School Press, 1985), pp. 308–317.

27. Steven Levy, "Microsoft Gets a Clue from its Kiddie Corps," *Newsweek*, February 24, 2003, pp. 56–57.

28. Michael Michalko, *Cracking Creativity: The Secrets of Creative Genius* (Berkeley, CA: Ten Speed Press, 1998); James M. Higgins, *101 Creative Problem Solving Techniques* (New York: New Management Publishing Company, 1994); Darren W. Dahl and Page Moreau, "The Influence and Value of Analogical Thinking During New Product Ideation," *Journal of Marketing Research*, 39 (February 2002): 47–60.

29. David Kiley, "Failure of Accord Hybrid is a Marketing Fiasco," *BusinessWeek*, www.businessweek.com/the_thread/brandnewday/archives/2007/06/failure_of_acco.html (viewed July 20, 2008); Martin Zimmerman, "Honda Decides to Stop Making Accord Hybrid Sedan," *The Ottawa Citizen*, June 8, 2007, p. C4.

30. "The Ultimate Widget: 3-D 'Printing' May Revolutionize Product Design and Manufacturing," *U.S. News & World Report*, July 20, 1992, p. 55.

31. For additional information, see also Paul E. Green and V. Srinivasan, "Conjoint Analysis in Marketing: New Developments with Implications for Research and Practice," *Journal of Marketing* (October 1990): 3–19; Dick R. Wittnick, Marco Vriens, and Wim Burhenne, "Commercial Uses of Conjoint Analysis in Europe: Results and Critical Reflections," *International Journal of Research in Marketing* (January 1994): 41–52; Jordan J. Louviere, David A. Hensher, and Joffre D. Swait, *Stated Choice Models: Analysis and Applications* (New York: Cambridge University Press, 2000).

32. Lesley Young, "Peddling Telecom Bundles," *Marketing Magazine*, May 7, 2001, www.marketingmag.ca/magazine/current/feature/article.jsp?content=20010507_17481#; "Bell Canada Launches Bell Security Solutions Inc.," Bell Canada Press Release, (Ottawa), February 15, 2005, http://enterprise.bell.ca/en/default.asp?sid=256&did=807.

33. The full-profile example was taken from Paul E. Green and Yoram Wind, "New Ways to Measure Consumers' Judgments," *Harvard Business Review* (July–August 1975): 107–117.

34. Robert Blattberg and John Golany, "Tracker: An Early Test Market Forecasting and Diagnostic Model for New Product Planning," *Journal of Marketing Research* (May 1978): 192–202; Glen L. Urban, Bruce D. Weinberg, and John R. Hauser, "Premarket Forecasting of Really New Products," *Journal of Marketing* (January 1996): 47–60; Peter N. Golder and Gerald J. Tellis, "Will It Ever Fly? Modeling the Takeoff of Really New Consumer Durables," *Marketing Science*, 16, no. 3 (1997): 256–270.

35. Roger A. Kerin, Michael G. Harvey, and James T. Rothe, "Cannibalism and New Product Development," *Business Horizons* (October 1978): 25–31.

36. The present value (V) of a future sum (S) to be received t years from today and discounted at the interest rate (r) is given by $V = S/(1 + r)t$. Thus $4\ 761\ 000/(1 + 0.15)5 = \$2\ 344\ 685.48$.

37. David B. Hertz, "Risk Analysis in Capital Investment," *Harvard Business Review* (January–February 1964): 96–106.

38. John Hauser, "House of Quality," *Harvard Business Review* (May–June 1988): 63–73. See also "quality function deployment." See Lawrence R. Guinta and Nancy C. Praizler, *The QFD Book: The Team Approach to Solving Problems and Satisfying Customers through Quality Function Deployment* (New York: AMACOM, 1993); V. Srinivasan, William S. Lovejoy, and David Beach, "Integrated Product Design for Marketability and Manufacturing," *Journal of Marketing Research* (February 1997): 154–163.

39. Beth Stackpole, "Virtual Reality Gets Real," *Design News*, 63, no. 1 (January 2008): 85; "Research," *Virtual Reality Applications Center*, www.vrac.iastate.edu/c6.php (viewed July 31, 2008).

40. Tom Peters, *The Circle of Innovation* (New York: Alfred A. Knopf, 1997), p. 96. For more general discussion, see also Rajesh Sethi, "New Product Quality and Product Development Teams," *Journal of Marketing* (April 2000): 1–14; Christine Moorman and Anne S. Miner, "The Convergence of Planning and Execution Improvisation in New Product Development," *Journal of Marketing* (July 1998): 1–20; Ravinchoanath MacChavan and Rajiv Graver, "From Embedded Knowledge to Embodied Knowledge: New Product Development as Knowledge Management," *Journal of Marketing* (October 1998): 1–12.

41. Michael J. Prasse, "Achieving Better Systems Development Through Usability Testing," *Journal of Systems Management*, September 1991, 42, no. 9, pp. 10-12.

42. "Jaguar Testers Leave the North," *Sudbury Star,* March 30, 2003, p. A2; Jeremy Hart, "An Ice-cold Buzz in Timmins," *Financial Times*, January 27, 2001, p. 17.

43. Michael Cieply, "A Man of Steel with Feet of Clay," *New York Times*, May 4, 2008, www.nytimes.com/2008/05/04/movies/moviesspecial/04ciep.html (viewed September 25, 2008); "Survey's and Market Research in Action," *Survey Bounty*, www.surveybounty.com/articles/surveyfacts.html (viewed July 7, 2008).

44. Jim McElgunn, "The Ultimate Test Market," *Marketing Magazine*, February 10, 2003, www.marketingmag.ca/magazine/current/editorial/article.jsp?content=20030210_24163.

45. Christopher Power, "Will It Sell in Podunk? Hard to Say," *Business Week*, August 10, 1992, pp. 46–47.

46. Kevin J. Clancy, Robert S. Shulman, and Marianne Wolf, *Simulated Test Marketing: Technology for Launching Successful New Products* (New York: Lexington Books, 1994); V. Mahajan and Jerry Wind, "New Product Models: Practice, Shortcomings, and Desired Improvements," *Journal of Product Innovation Management*, 9 (1992): 129–139; Glen L. Urban, John R. Hauser, and Roberta A. Chicos, "Information Acceleration: Validation and Lessons from the Field," *Journal of Marketing Research* (February 1997): 143–153.

47. For further discussion, see Robert J. Thomas, "Timing: The Key to Market Entry," *Journal of Consumer Marketing* (Summer 1985): 77–87; Thomas S. Robertson, Jehoshua Eliashberg, and Talia

Rymon, "New Product Announcement Signals and Incumbent Reactions," *Journal of Marketing* (July 1995): 1–15; Frank H. Alpert and Michael A. Kamins, "Pioneer Brand Advantages and Consumer Behavior: A Conceptual Framework and Propositional Inventory," *Journal of the Academy of Marketing Science* (Summer 1994): 244–236; Barry L. Bayos, Sanjay Jain, and Ambar Rao, "Consequences: An Analysis of Truth or Vaporware and New Product Announcements," *Journal of Marketing Research* (February 2001): 3–13.

48. Cooper and Kleinschmidt, *New Products*, pp. 35–38.

49. Jonathan Paul, "MEC Goes Wild with Online Hub," *Strategy*, June 2008, p. 8.

50. Philip Kotler and Gerald Zaltman, "Targeting Prospects for a New Product," *Journal of Advertising Research* (February 1976): 7–20.

51. "Spotting Splashman Trident's Latest Campaign Makes, Ahem, Waves," *Strategy*, September 2005, p. 62.

52. For details, see Keith G. Lockyer, *Critical Path Analysis and Other Project Network Techniques* (London: Pitman, 1984). See also Arvind Rangaswamy and Gary L. Lilien, "Software Tools for New Product Development," *Journal of Marketing Research* (February 1997): 177–184.

53. The following discussion leans heavily on Everett M. Rogers, *Diffusion of Innovations* (New York: The Free Press, 1962). See also his third edition, published in 1983.

54. C. Page Moreau, Donald R. Lehmann, and Arthur B. Markman, "Entrenched Knowledge Structures and Consumer Response to New Products," *Journal of Marketing Research*, 38 (February 2001): 14–29.

55. Steve Hoeffler, "Measuring Preferences for Really New Products," *Journal of Marketing Research*, 40 (November 2003): 406–420.

56. Rogers, *Diffusion of Innovations*, p. 192; Geoffrey A. Moore, *Crossing the Chasm: Marketing and Selling High-Tech Products to Mainstream Customers* (New York: HarperBusiness, 1999).

57. A. Parasuraman and Charles L. Colby, *Techno-Ready Marketing* (New York: The Free Press, 2001); Jakki Mohr, *Marketing of High-Technology Products and Innovations* (Upper Saddle River, NJ: Prentice Hall, 2001).

58. Malcolm Macalister Hall, "Selling by Stealth," *Business Life* (November 2001): 51–55.

59. Jordan Robertson, "How Nike Got Street Cred," *Business 2.0* (May 2004): 43–46.

60. Cliff Edwards, "Is TiVo's Signal Still Fading?" *BusinessWeek*, September 10, 2001, pp. 72–74; Cliff Edwards, "Will Souping Up TiVo Save It?" *BusinessWeek*, May 17, 2004, pp. 63–64.

61. Hubert Gatignon and Thomas S. Robertson, "A Propositional Inventory for New Diffusion Research," *Journal of Consumer Research* (March 1985): 849–867; Vijay Mahajan, Eitan Muller, and Frank M. Bass, "Diffusion of New Products: Empirical Generalizations and Managerial Uses," *Marketing Science*, 14, no. 3, part 2 (1995): G79–G89; Fareena Sultan, John U. Farley, and Donald R. Lehman, "Reflection on 'A Meta-Analysis of Applications of Diffusion Models,'" *Journal of Marketing Research* (May 1996): 247–249; Minhi Hahn, Sehoon Park, and Andris A. Zoltners, "Analysis of New Product Diffusion Using a Four-segment Trial-repeat Model," *Marketing Science*, 13, no. 3 (1994): 224–247.

Chapter 21

1. "Starbucks Corporation: Fiscal 2007 Year in Review," www.starbucks.com (viewed June 30, 2008); Carol Matlack, "Will Global Growth Help Starbucks?" *BusinessWeek Online*, July 3, 2008, www.businessweek.com/globalbiz/content/jul2008/gb2008072_462789.htm (viewed August 26, 2008); Marc de Swaan Arons, "What It Takes to Really Win Globally," *Advertising Age*, May 19, 2008, p. 22.

2. Statistics Canada, "Exports of Goods on a Balance-of-Payments Basis, by Product," www40.statcan.ca/l01/cst01/gblec04.htm?bcsi_scan_15D00938B02C633E=0&bcsi_scan_filename=gblec04.htm; Statistics Canada, "Canada: Economic and financial data,"

www40.statcan.ca/l01/cst01/dsbbcan.htm (both viewed June 18, 2008).

3. Michael E. Porter, *Competitive Strategy* (New York: The Free Press, 1980), p. 275.

4. Cirque du Soleil website, www.cirquedusoleil.com (viewed July 22, 2008); "Clear Channel Entertainment and Cirque du Soleil Announce New Partnership to Launch a Major North American Tour of Cirque du Soleil in Concert," *PR Newswire*, January 25, 2005, p. 1.

5. Ron Lieber, "Give Us This Day Our Global Bread," *Fast Company* (March 2001): 158.

6. Jan Johanson and Finn Wiedersheim-Paul, "The Internationalization of the Firm," *Journal of Management Studies* (October 1975): 305–322.

7. Stan Reid, "The Decision Maker and Export Entry and Expansion," *Journal of International Business Studies* (Fall 1981): 101–112; Igal Ayal, "Industry Export Performance: Assessment and Prediction," *Journal of Marketing* (Summer 1982): 54–61; Somkid Jatusripitak, *The Exporting Behavior of Manufacturing Firms* (Ann Arbor: University of Michigan Press, 1986).

8. Michael R. Czinkota and Ilkka A. Ronkainen, *International Marketing*, 5th ed. (New York: Harcourt Brace Jovanovich, 1999).

9. Igal Ayal and Jehiel Zif, "Market Expansion Strategies in Multinational Marketing," *Journal of Marketing* (Spring 1979): 84–94.

10. Yumiro Ono, "On a Mission: Amway Grows Abroad, Sending 'Ambassadors' to Spread the Word," *Wall Street Journal*, May 14, 1997, p. A1; www.amway.com.

11. For a timely and thorough review of academic research on global marketing, see Johny K. Johansson, "Global Marketing: Research on Foreign Entry, Local Marketing, Global Management," in *Handbook of Marketing*, edited by Bart Weitz and Robin Wensley (London: 2002 Sage Publications), pp. 457–483. See also Johny K. Johansson, *Global Marketing*, 2nd ed. (New York: McGraw-Hill, 2003). For some global marketing research issues, see Susan Douglas and Samuel R. Craig, *International Marketing Research*, 2nd ed. (Upper Saddle River, NJ: Prentice Hall, 2000).

12. Kenichi Ohmae, *Triad Power* (New York: The Free Press, 1985); Philip Kotler and Nikhilesh Dholakia, "Ending Global Stagnation: Linking the Fortunes of the Industrial and Developing Countries," *Business in the Contemporary World* (Spring 1989): 86–97.

13. Jack Neff, "Submerged," *Advertising Age*, March 4, 2002, p. 14.

14. Adapted from Vijay Mahajan, Marcos V. Pratini De Moraes, and Jerry Wind, "The Invisible Global Market," *Marketing Management* (Winter 2000): 31–35.

15. Niraj Dawar and Amitava Chattopadhyay, "Rethinking Marketing Programs for Emerging Markets," *Long Range Planning*, 35, no. 5 (October 2002).

16. Gabriel Kahn, "Local Brands Outgun Foreigners in China's Advertising Market," *Wall Street Journal*, October 8, 2003, p. B6A; "The Local Touch," *The Economist*, March 8, 2003, p. 58.

17. Manjeet Kripalani, "Finally, Coke Gets It Right," *BusinessWeek*, February 10, 2003, p. 47; Manjeet Kripalani, "Battling for Pennies in India's Villages," *BusinessWeek*, June 10, 2002, p. 22E7.

18. "Not So Fizzy," *The Economist*, February 23, 2002, pp. 66–67; Rajeev Batra, Venkatram Ramaswamy, Dana L. Alden, Jan-Benedict E. M. Steenkamp, and S. Ramachander, "Effects of Brand Local and Nonlocal Origin on Consumer Attitudes in Developing Countries," *Journal of Consumer Psychology*, 9, no. 2 (2000): 83–95.

19. Patricia Sellers, "P & G: Teaching an Old Dog New Tricks," *Fortune*, May 31, 2004, pp. 167–180.

20. Catherine Belton, "To Russia, With Love: The Multinationals Song," *BusinessWeek*, September 16, 2002, pp. 44–46.

21. David Welch, "GM: Gunning It in China," *BusinessWeek*, June 21, 2004, pp. 112–115; Joann Muller, "Thanks, Now Move Over," *Forbes*, July 26, 2004, pp. 76–78.

22. European Commission, "Key Facts and Figures about Europe and the Europeans," europa.eu/abc/keyfigures/index_en.htm (viewed June 18, 2008).

23. Government of Canada, "Fast Facts: North American Free Trade Agreement," Foreign Affairs and International Trade Canada, May 2007; US Department of State, "Background Note: Canada," www.state.gov/r/pa/ei/bgn/2089.htm (both viewed June 18, 2008); "NAFTA—10 Years Later," *CBC News Online*, January 7, 2004, www.cbc.ca/news/background/summitofamericas/nafta.html; Rob Portman, "Washington Speaks: Good Neighbours Must Talk," *The Globe and Mail*, September 3, 2005, p. A23; Norman Spector, "Old Fights, New Rounds, Same Politicization," *The Globe and Mail*, September 5, 2005, p. A15.

24. New Zealand Ministry of Foreign Affairs and Trade, "APEC," www.mfat.govt.nz/Trade-and-Economic-Relations/APEC/index.php (viewed June 18, 2008).

25. Government of Canada, "Canada's Exports Diversify Away from the U.S.," *Foreign Affairs and International Trade Canada*, June 20, 2007, www.mfat.govt.nz/Trade-and-Economic-Relations/APEC/index.php (viewed June 18, 2008).

26. Johny K. Johansson, "Global Marketing: Research on Foreign Entry, Local Marketing, Global Management," in *Handbook of Marketing*, edited by Bart Weitz and Robin Wensley (London: Sage Publications, 2002), pp. 457–483.

27. Charlene Marmer Solomon, "Don't Get Burned by Hot Markets," *Workforce* (January 1998): 12–22.

28. For an academic review, see Leonidas C. Leonidou, Constantine S. Katsikeas, and Nigel F. Piercy, "Identifying Managerial Influences on Exporting: Past Research and Future Directions," *Journal of International Marketing*, 6, no. 2 (1998): 74–102.

29. Barokes Wines website, www.wineinacan.com; "India Takes to Australian 'Wine in a Can'," *Australian Trade Commission, Case Studies*, www.austrade.gov.au/India-takes-to-Australian-wine-in-a-can-/default.aspx (both viewed August 26, 2008).

30. Lauren Sherman, "Pushing Up Results at Victoria's Secret," *Forbes*, December 6, 2007, www.forbes.com/2007/12/06/victorias-secret-marketing-markets-equity-cx_ls_1206markets1.html (viewed June 24, 2008); Kelly Mooney and Nita Rollins, "The Open Brand: When Push Comes to Pull in a Web-Made World," (Berkeley, CA: AIGA Design Press, 2008).

31. Brandon Mitchener, "E-Commerce: Border Crossings," *Wall Street Journal*, November 22, 1999, p. R41.

32. Michelle Edgar, Ellen Groves, Marcy Medina, "Coty Set to Bring Rimmel Brand into China," *WWD*, 195, no. 39 (February 2008): 9.

33. Laura Mazur and Annik Hogg, *The Marketing Challenge* (Wokingham, England: Addison-Wesley, 1993), pp. 42–44; Jan Willem Karel, "Brand Strategy Positions Products Worldwide," *Journal of Business Strategy*, 12, no. 3 (May–June 1991): 16–19; Canadian Embassy Beijing Newsletter, February 2004, www.beijing.gc.ca/beijing/en/navmain/media/partnerships/1059.htm.

34. Paula Dwyer, "Tearing Up Today's Organization Chart," *Business Week*, November 18, 1994, pp. 80–90.

35. Joann Muller, "Global Motors," *Forbes*, January 12, 2004, pp. 62–68.

36. "Foreign Direct Investment Statistics," *Foreign Affairs and International Trade Canada*, www.international.gc.ca/eet/foreign-statements-en.asp (viewed August 27, 2008).

37. Paul Brent, "It's Tough to Make It South of the Border," *Financial Post*, March 10, 1999, C6; Zena Olijnyk, "Plan to Quit U.S. Lifts Future Shop Stock 24%," *Financial Post*, March 10, 1999, p. C6.

38. Shaoming Zou and S. Tamer Cavusgil, "The GMS: A Broad Conceptualtization of Global Marketing Strategy and Its Effect on Firm Performance," *Journal of Marketing*, 66 (October 2002): 40–56.

39. Geert Hofstede, *Culture's Consequences* (Beverley Hills, CA: Sage, 1980).

40. "Brand Strategy Briefing: Remittance Goes Global," *Brand Strategy*, November 2, 2005, p. 50.

41. Arundhati Parmar, "Dependent Variables: Sounds Global Strategies Rely on Certain Factors," *Marketing News*, September 16, 2002, p. 4.

42. Warren J. Keegan, *Multinational Marketing Management*, 5th ed. (Upper Saddle River, NJ: Prentice Hall, 1995), pp. 378–381.

43. "What Makes a Company Great?" *Fortune*, October 26, 1998, pp. 218–226.

44. Roger Thurow, "In Battling Hunger, A New Advance: Peanut-Butter Paste," *Wall Street Journal*, April 12, 2005, p. A1; Susan Semenak, "From a Hula Hoop to a House," *The Gazette*, December 8, 2007, p. B4.

45. Richard P. Carpenter and the Globe Staff, "What They Meant to Say Was . . .," *Boston Globe*, August 2, 1998, p. M6.

46. "U.S. Competition Hits Tim Hortons," *Calgary Herald*, Calgary, June 28, 2008, p. E1; Michael Urlocker, "Tim's Needs a Splash to Make Waves in U.S.," *National Post*, March 25, 2006, p. FP3.

47. For an interesting distinction based on the concept of global consumer culture positioning, see Dana L. Alden, Jan-Benedict E. M. Steenkamp, and Rajeev Batra, "Brand Positioning Through Advertising in Asia, North America, and Europe: The Role of Global Consumer Culture," *Journal of Marketing*, 63 (January 1999): 75–87.

48. Thomas J. Madden, Kelly Hewett, and Martin S. Roth, "Managing Images in Different Cultures: A Cross-National Study of Color Meanings and Preferences," *Journal of International Marketing*, 8, no. 4 (2000): 90–107; Zeynep Gürhan-Canli and Durairaj Maheswaran, "Cultural Variations in Country of Origin Effects," *Journal of Marketing Research*, 37 (August 2000): 309–317.

49. John L. Graham, Alma T. Mintu, and Waymond Rogers, "Explorations of Negotiations Behaviors in Ten Foreign Cultures Using a Model Developed in the United States," *Management Science*, 40 (January 1994): 72–95.

50. David Kirpatrick, "How Microsoft Conquered China," *Fortune*, 156, no. 2 (July 23, 2007): 78–84.

51. Tony Van Alphen, "Some U.S. Makers Dumping Steel in Canada," *Toronto Star*, May 2, 2001, p. E01.

52. Peter Burrows, "Inside the iPhone Gray Market," *BusinessWeek* (Online), February 12, 2008, www.businessweek.com/technology/content/feb2008/tc20080211_152894.htm; Scott Carney, "iPod Gray Market Booms in India," *Wired*, August 23, 2006, www.wired.com/gadgets/mac/news/2006/08/71639; Shaun Nichols, "HP Agrees Settlement with Maxicom PC: Assault on 'Grey-Market' Sales Channels Continues," *Computing*, www.computing.co.uk/vnunet/news/2211779/hp-settles-gray-market-case; Sara Yirrell, "Amtec Settles with Sun," *CRN*, February 15, 2007, www.channelweb.co.uk/crn/news/2183436/amtec-settles-sun (all viewed September 26, 2008).

53. Maricris G. Briones, "The Euro Starts Here," *Marketing News*, July 20, 1998, pp. 1, 39.

54. Elliott Masie, "Global Pricing in an Internet World," *Computer Reseller News*, May 11, 1998, pp. 55, 58.

55. Ram Charan, "The Rules Have Changed," *Fortune*, March 16, 1998, pp. 159–162.

56. www.ge.com.

57. David Arnold, "Seven Rules of International Distribution," *Harvard Business Review* (November–December 2000): 131–137.

58. Arnold, "Seven Rules of International Distribution," 131–137.

59. "Cola Down Mexico Way," *The Economist*, October 11, 2003, pp. 69–70.

60. IMRIS website, www.imris.com (viewed July 22, 2008); "Business Watch," *Winnipeg Free Press*, June 17, 2008, p. B6; "IMRIS Reports Continued Growth in Sales and Order Backlog," *Canada NewsWire*, May 14, 2008.

61. "From Head & Shoulders to Kobe," *The Economist*, March 27, 2004, p. 64.

62. "A Dragon with Core Values," *The Economist*, March 30, 2002, 362, no. 8266, p. 20.

63. "The Shock of Old," *The Economist*, July 13, 2002, p. 49.

64. Jim Rendon, "When Nations Need a Little Marketing," *New York Times*, November 23, 2003, p. 3.

65. "Regan Unveils New Brand Canada Aquaculture Logo," Fisheries and Oceans Canada, News Release, March 15, 2004, www.dfo-mpo.gc.ca/media/newsrel/2004/hq-ac19_e.htm; "Branding Canada," Canadian Embassy Washington, DC, News Release, March 2001, www.canadianembassy.org/invest/branding-en.asp.

66. Zeynep Gurhan-Canli and Durairaj Maheswaran, "Cultural Variations in Country of Origin Effects," *Journal of Marketing Research*, 37 (August 2000): 309–317.

67. Jan-Benedict, E. M. Steenkamp, Rajeev Batra, and Dana L. Alden, "How Perceived Brand Globalness Creates Brand Value," *Journal of International Business Studies*, 34 (2003): 53–65.

68. Johny K. Johansson, "Global Marketing: Research on Foreign Entry, Local Marketing, Global Management," pp. 457–483; Johny K. Johansson, "Determinants and Effects of the Use of 'Made In' Labels," *International Marketing Review (UK)*, 6, no. 1 (1989): 47–58; Warren J. Bilkey and Erik Nes, "Country-of-Origin Effects on Product Evaluations," *Journal of International Business Studies* (Spring–Summer 1982): 89–99; "Old Wine in New Bottles," *The Economist*, February 21, 1998, p. 45; Zeynep Gürhan-Canli and Durairaj Maheswaran, "Cultural Variations in Country of Origin Effects," pp. 309–317.

69. Alex Taylor III, "BMW Turns More American Than Ever," *Fortune*, February 23, 2004, p. 42.

70. "RBC Announces Changes to Banking Businesses to Drive Growth Potential Outside Canada." *PR Newswire*, April 11, 2008.

71. Christopher A. Bartlett and Sumantra Ghoshal, *Managing Across Borders* (Cambridge, MA: Harvard Business School Press, 1989).

72. Betsy McKay, "Coke Hunts for Talent to Re-establish Its Marketing Might," *Wall Street Journal*, March 6, 2002, p. B4.

Chapter 22

1. For additional updates on the latest academic thinking on marketing strategy and tactics, see *Kellogg on Integrated Marketing*, ed. Dawn Iacobucci and Bobby Calder (New York: Wiley, 2003) and *Kellogg on Marketing*, ed. Dawn Iacobucci (New York: Wiley, 2001).

2. Frederick E. Webster Jr., Alan J. Malter, and Shankar Ganesan, "Can Marketing Regain Its Seat at the Table?" *Marketing Science Institute Report No. 03-113* (Cambridge, MA: Marketing Science Institute, 2003).

3. For a broad historical treatment of marketing thought, see D. G. Brian Jones and Eric H. Shaw, "A History of Marketing Thought," in *Handbook of Marketing*, ed. Barton A. Weitz and Robin Wensley (London: Sage, 2002), pp. 39–65.

4. Julia Chang, "From the Inside Out," *Sales and Marketing Management*, 157, no. 8 (August 2005): 14.

5. Hamish Pringle and William Gordon, *Beyond Manners: How to Create the Self-Confident Organisation to Live the Brand* (West Sussex, England: John Wiley & Sons, 2001); Frederick E. Webster Jr., "The Changing Role of Marketing in the Corporation," *Journal of Marketing* (October 1992): 1–17. See also John P. Workman Jr., Christian Homburg, and Kjell Gruner, "Marketing Organization: An Integrative Framework of Dimensions and Determinants," *Journal of Marketing* (July 1998): 21–41; Ravi S. Achrol, "Evolution of the Marketing Organization: New Forms for Turbulent Environment," *Journal of Marketing* (October 1991): 77–93. For some contemporary perspectives, see Special Issue 1999 of *Journal of Marketing Fundamental Issues and Directions for Marketing*.

6. For an excellent account of how to convert a company into a market-driven organization, see George Day, *The Market-Driven Organization: Aligning Culture, Capabilities, and Configuration to the Market* (New York: Free Press, 1989).

7. Frederick E. Webster Jr., "The Role of Marketing and the Firm," in *Handbook of Marketing*, ed. Barton A. Weitz and Robin Wensley (London: Sage, 2002), pp. 39–65.

8. Frank V. Cespedes, *Managing Marketing Linkages: Text, Cases, and Readings* (Upper Saddle River, NJ: Prentice Hall, 1996); Frank V. Cespedes, *Concurrent Marketing: Integrating Product, Sales, and Service* (Boston: Harvard Business School Press, 1995).

9. Laurie Freeman, "P&G Widens Power Base: Adds Category Managers," *Advertising Age*; Michael J. Zenor, "The Profit Benefits of Category Management," *Journal of Marketing Research*, 31 (May 1994): 202–13; Gerry Khermouch, "Brands Overboard," *Brandweek*, August 22, 1994, pp. 25–39; Zachary Schiller, "The Marketing Revolution at Procter & Gamble," *BusinessWeek*, July 25, 1988, pp. 72–76.

10. For further reading, see Robert Dewar and Don Shultz, "The Product Manager, an Idea Whose Time Has Gone," *Marketing Communications* (May 1998): 28–35; George S. Low and Ronald A. Fullerton, "Brands, Brand Management, and the Brand Manager System: A Critical Historical Evaluation," *Journal of Marketing Research* (May 1994): 173–90; Michael J. Zanor, "The Profit Benefits of Category Management," *Journal of Marketing Research* (May 1994): 202–13.

11. Larry Selden and Geoffrey Colvin, *Angel Customers & Demon Customers* (New York: Portfolio [Penguin], 2003).

12. For an in-depth discussion of issues around implementing a customer-based organization on which much of this paragraph is based, see George S. Day, "Aligning the Organization with the Market," *MIT Sloan Management Review* (Fall 2006): 41–49.

13. Richard E. Anderson, "Matrix Redux," *Business Horizons* (November–December 1994): 6–10.

14. Frederick E. Webster Jr., "The Role of Marketing and the Firm," in *Handbook of Marketing*, ed. Barton A. Weitz and Robin Wensley (London: Sage, 2002), pp. 39–65.

15. Benson P. Shapiro, "Can Marketing and Manufacturing Coexist?" *Harvard Business Review* (September–October 1977): 104–14. See also Robert W. Ruekert and Orville C. Walker Jr., "Marketing's Interaction with Other Functional Units: A Conceptual Framework with Other Empirical Evidence," *Journal of Marketing* (January 1987): 1–19.

16. Ranjay Gulati, "Silo Busting: How to Execute on the Promise of Customer Focus," *Harvard Business Review*, 85, no. 5, May 1, 2007, pp. 98+.

17. Erik Brynjolfsson and Lorin Hitt, "The Customer Counts," *InformationWeek*, September 9, 1996.

18. Gary Hamel, *Leading the Revolution* (Boston: Harvard Business School Press, 2000).

19. Jagdish N. Sheth, *The Self-Destructive Habits of Good Companies . . . And How to Break Them* (Upper Saddle River, NJ: Wharton School Publishing, 2007).

20. William L. Wilkie and Elizabeth S. Moore, "Marketing's Relationship to Society," in *Handbook of Marketing*, ed. Barton A. Weitz and Robin Wensley (London: Sage, 2002), pp. 1–38.

21. "Special Report: Corporate Social Responsibility," *Economist*, December 14, 2002, pp. 62–63.

22. "Expectations for Corporate Social Responsibility Rising With Clear Consequences for Not Measuring Up," Hewlett Packard Press Release, April 20, 2006, http://h41131.www4.hp.com/ca/en/pr/04202006a.html (viewed June 2008).

23. "Expectations for Corporate Social Responsibility Rising With Clear Consequences for Not Measuring Up," Hewlett Packard press release, April 20, 2006, http://h41131.www4.hp.com/ca/en/pr/04202006a.html (viewed June 2008).

24. Brian Grow, "The Debate over Doing Good," *BusinessWeek*, August 15, 2005, pp. 76–78.

25. Jennifer Alsever, "Chiquita Cleans Up Its Act," *Business 2.0* (August 2006): 56–58.

26. Brian Grow, "The Debate over Doing Good," *BusinessWeek*, August 15, 2005, pp. 76–78.

27. Susan Flynn, "Winning with Integrity: The Business Case for Corporate Social Responsibility," undated, www.cbsr.ca/files/

ReportsandPapers/WinningwithIntegrityAMpdf.pdf (viewed June 2008).

28. Raj Sisodia, David B. Wolfe, and Jag Sheth, *Firms of Endearment: How World-Class Companies Profit from Passion and Purpose* (Upper Saddle River, NJ: Wharton School Publishing, 2007).

29. Kathleen Martin, "Molson celebrates moderation," *Marketing Daily*, July 11, 2007.

30. Jeff Nachtigal, "It's Easy and Cheap Being Green," *Fortune*, October 16, 2006, p. 53.

31. John Carey, "Hugging the Tree Huggers," *BusinessWeek*, March 12, 2007, pp. 66–68.

32. Carey Toane, "Water, water everywhere," *Strategy Magazine*, May 2008, p. 16.

33. For further reading, see Dorothy Cohen, *Legal Issues in Marketing Decision Making* (Cincinnati, OH: South-Western College Publishing, 1995).

34. Sarah Ellison, "Kraft Limits on Kids' Ads May Cheese Off Rivals," *Wall Street Journal*, January 13, 2005.

35. Shelby D. Hunt and Scott Vitell, "The General Theory of Marketing Ethics: A Retrospective and Revision," in *Ethics in Marketing*, ed. John Quelch and Craig Smith (Chicago: Irwin, 1992).

36. Majken Schultz, Yun Mi Antorini, and Fabian F. Csaba, *Corporate Branding: Purpose, People, and Process* (Køge, Denmark: Copenhagen Business School Press, 2005); Ronald J. Alsop, *The 18 Immutable Laws of Corporate Reputation: Creating, Protecting, and Repairing Your Most Valuable Asset* (New York: Free Press, 2004); Marc Gunther, "Tree Huggers, Soy Lovers, and Profits," *Fortune*, June 23, 2003, pp. 98–104; Ronald J. Alsop, "Perils of Corporate Philanthropy," *Wall Street Journal*, January 16, 2002.

37. Carey Toane, "Cult brand growing pains," *Strategy*, December 2007, p. 26; Lianne George, "How Lululemon lost its balance," *Macleans*, February 6, 2008, www.macleans.ca/business/companies/article.jsp?content=20080206_87890_87890 (viewed June 2008).

38. Michael E. Porter and Mark R. Kramer, "The Competitive Advantage of Corporate Philanthropy," *Harvard Business Review* (December 2002): 5–16.

39. Dwane Hal Deane, "Associating the Corporation with a Charitable Event through Sponsorship: Measuring the Effects on Corporate Community Relations," *Journal of Advertising* (Winter 2002): 77–87.

40. Sandra O'Loughlin, "The Wearin' o' the Green," *Brandweek*, April 23, 2007, pp. 26–27. For a critical response, see also John R. Ehrenfield, "Feeding the Beast," *Fast Company* (December 2006–January 2007): 42–43.

41. Nicholas Varchaver, "Chemical Reaction," *Fortune*, April 2, 2007, pp. 53–58.

42. Pete Engardio, "Beyond the Green Corporation," *BusinessWeek*, January 29, 2007, pp. 50–64.

43. Engardio, "Beyond the Green Corporation."

44. Kenneth Hein, "The World on a Platter," *Brandweek*, April 23, 2007, pp. 27–28; Megan Johnston, "Hard Sell for a Soft Fabric," *Forbes*, October 30, 2006, pp. 73–80.

45. See Philip Kotler and Nancy Lee, *Corporate Social Responsibility: Doing the Most Good for Your Company and Your Cause* (New York: John Wiley, 2005).

46. Lynn Upshaw, *Truth: The New Rules for Marketing in a Skeptical World* (New York: Amacon, 2007); Cheryl Dahle, "A More Powerful Path," *Fast Company* (December 2006–January 2007): 68–81.

47. Adapted from an e-mail letter sent to Peggy Cunningham by Rupert Duchesne, President and CEO of Aeroplan on April 22, 2008.

48. Colin Campbell, "Canadian Companies Need Some Lessons in How to Be Charitable," *Macleans*, February 19, 2007, www.macleans.ca/article.jsp?content=20070219_140886_140886 (viewed June 2008).

49. Robert Berner, "Smarter Corporate Giving," *BusinessWeek*, November 28, 2005, pp. 68–76; Craig N. Smith, "Corporate Social Responsibility: Whether or How?" *California Management Review*, 45, no. 4 (Summer 2003): 52–76.

50. Larry Chiagouris and Ipshita Ray, "Saving the World with Cause-Related Marketing," *Marketing Management* (July–August 2007): 48–51; Hamish Pringle and Marjorie Thompson, *Brand Spirit: How Cause-Related Marketing Builds Brands* (New York: John Wiley & Sons, 1999); Sue Adkins, *Cause-Related Marketing: Who Cares Wins* (Oxford, England: Butterworth-Heineman, 1999); "Marketing, Corporate Social Initiatives, and the Bottom Line," Marketing Science Institute Conference Summary, *MSI Report No. 01-106*, 2001.

51. Rajan Varadarajan and Anil Menon, "Cause-Related Marketing: A Co-Alignment of Marketing Strategy and Corporate Philanthropy," *Journal of Marketing*, 52 (July 1988): 58–74.

52. Minette Drumwright and Patrick E. Murphy, "Corporate Societal Marketing," in *Handbook of Marketing and Society*, ed. Paul N. Bloom and Gregory T. Gundlach (Thousand Oaks, CA: Sage, 2001), pp. 162–83. See also Minette Drumwright, "Company Advertising with a Social Dimension: The Role of Noneconomic Criteria," *Journal of Marketing*, 60 (October 1996): 71–87.

53. Jack Neff and Stephanie Thompson, "Eco-Marketing Has Staying Power This Time Around," *Advertising Age*, April 30, 2007, p. 55.

54. British Airways website, www.britishairways.com.

55. Xueming Luo and C. B. Bhattacharya, "Corporate Social Responsibility, Customer Satisfaction, and Market Value," *Journal of Marketing*, 70 (October 2006): 1–18; Pat Auger, Paul Burke, Timothy Devinney, and Jordan J. Louviere, "What Will Consumers Pay for Social Product Features?" *Journal of Business Ethics*, 42 (February 2003): 281–304.

56. Dennis B. Arnett, Steve D. German, and Shelby D. Hunt, "The Identity Salience Model of Relationship Marketing Success: The Case of Nonprofit Marketing," *Journal of Marketing*, 67 (April 2003): 89–105; C. B. Bhattacharya and Sankar Sen, "Consumer–Company Identification: A Framework for Understanding Consumers' Relationships with Companies," *Journal of Marketing*, 67 (April 2003): 76–88; Sankar Sen and C. B. Bhattacharya, "Does Doing Good Always Lead to Doing Better? Consumer Reactions to Corporate Social Responsibility," *Journal of Marketing Research*, 38, no. 2 (May 2001): 225–44.

57. Paul N. Bloom, Steve Hoeffler, Kevin Lane Keller, and Carlos E. Basurto, "How Social-Cause Marketing Affects Consumer Perceptions," *MIT Sloan Management Review* (Winter 2006): 49–55; Carolyn J. Simmons and Karen L. Becker-Olsen, "Achieving Marketing Objectives through Social Sponsorships," *Journal of Marketing*, 70 (October 2006): 154–69; Guido Berens, Cees B. M. van Riel, and Gerrit H. van Bruggen, "Corporate Associations and Consumer Product Responses: The Moderating Role of Corporate Brand Dominance," *Journal of Marketing*, 69 (July 2005): 35–48; Donald R. Lichtenstein, Minette E. Drumwright, and Bridgette M. Braig, "The Effect of Social Responsibility on Customer Donations to Corporate-Supported Nonprofits," *Journal of Marketing*, 68 (October 2004): 16–32; Stephen Hoeffler and Kevin Lane Keller, "Building Brand Equity through Corporate Societal Marketing," *Journal of Public Policy and Marketing*, 21, no. 1 (Spring 2002): 78–89. See also Special Issue: Corporate Responsibility, *Journal of Brand Management*, 10, nos. 4–5 (May 2003).

58. Mark R. Forehand and Sonya Grier, "When Is Honesty the Best Policy? The Effect of Stated Company Intent on Consumer Skepticism," *Journal of Consumer Psychology*, 13, no. 3 (2003): 349–56; Dwane Hal Dean, "Associating the Corporation with a Charitable Event through Sponsorship: Measuring the Effects on Corporate Community Relations," *Journal of Advertising*, 31, no. 4 (Winter 2002): 77–87.

59. N. Craig Smith, "Out of Left Field," *Business Strategy Review*, 18, no. 2 (Summer 2007): 55–59; Adam Jones, "Choc Horror over Cadbury Tokens," *Financial Times*, May 3, 2003, p. 14.

60. Lauren Gard, "We're Good Guys, Buy from Us," *BusinessWeek*, November 22, 2004, pp. 72–74.

61. Mya Frazier, "Costly Red Campaign Reaps Meager $18 Million," *Advertising Age*, March 5, 2007; Viewpoint: Bobby Shriver, "CEO:

Red's Raised Lots of Green," *Advertising Age*, March 12, 2007; Michelle Conlin, "Shop (in the Name of Love)," *BusinessWeek*, October 2, 2006, p. 9.

62. Todd Cohen, "Corporations Aim for Strategic Engagement," *Philanthropy Journal*, September 20, 2006; John A. Quelch and Nathalie Laidler-Kylander, *The New Global Brands: Managing Non-Governmental Organizations in the 21st Century* (Cincinnati, OH: South-Western College Publishing, 2005).

63. Alsop, *The 18 Immutable Laws of Corporate Reputation: Creating, Protecting, and Repairing Your Most Valuable Asset*, p. 125.

64. Susan Orenstein, "The Selling of Breast Cancer," *Business 2.0* (February 2003): 88–94; H. Meyer, "When the Cause Is Just," *Journal of Business Strategy* (November–December 1999): 27–31.

65. Christine Bittar, "Seeking Cause and Effect," *Brandweek*, November 11, 2002, pp. 18–24.

66. Paula Andruss, "'Think Pink' Awareness Much Higher Than Threat," *Marketing News*, February 15, 2006, pp. 14–16; Jessi Hempel, "Selling a Cause, Better Make It Pop," *BusinessWeek*, February 13, 2006, p. 75; Elizabeth Woyke, "Prostate Cancer's Higher Profile," *BusinessWeek*, October 9, 2006, p. 14.

67. Philip Kotler, Ned Roberto, and Nancy Lee, *Social Marketing: Improving the Quality of Life* (Thousand Oaks, CA: Sage, 2002); Michael L. Rothschild, "Carrots, Sticks, and Promises: A Conceptual Framework for the Management of Public Health and Social Issue Behaviors," *Journal of Marketing*, 63 (October 1999): 24–37.

68. See Rothschild, "Carrots, Sticks, and Promises: A Conceptual Framework for the Management of Public Health and Social Issue Behaviors," pp. 24–37.

69. Amy Syracuse, "Social Marketing for a Cause," *Target Marketing*, 30, no. 7 (July 2007): 13.

70. Carly Weeks, "Cigarette display rules spark controversy," *The Globe and Mail*, May 30, 2008, http://www.theglobeandmail.com/servlet/story/RTGAM.20080530.wlsmoke30/BNStory/specialScienceandHealth/ (accessed June 2008).

71. For more on developing and implementing marketing plans, see H. W. Goetsch, *Developing, Implementing, and Managing an Effective Marketing Plan* (Chicago: NTC Business Books, 1993). See also Thomas V. Bonoma, *The Marketing Edge: Making Strategies Work* (New York: Free Press, 1985). Much of this section is based on Bonoma's work.

72. C. Marcus, "Marketing Resource Management: Key Components," *Gartner Research Note*, August 22, 2001.

73. Julia Chang, "Cover Your Tracks," *Sales and Marketing Management* (June 2007): 12.

74. For other examples, see Paul W. Farris, Neil T. Bendle, Phillip E. Pfeifer, and David J. Reibstein, *Marketing Metrics: 50+ Metrics Every Executive Should Master* (Upper Saddle River, NJ: Wharton School Publishing, 2006); Marion Debruyne and Katrina Hubbard, "Marketing Metrics," working paper series, Conference Summary, Marketing Science Institute, Report No. 00-119, 2000.

75. Sam R. Goodman, *Increasing Corporate Profitability* (New York: Ronald Press, 1982), chapter 1. See also Bernard J. Jaworski, Vlasis Stathakopoulos, and H. Shanker Krishnan, "Control Combinations in Marketing: Conceptual Framework and Empirical Evidence," *Journal of Marketing* (January 1993): 57–69.

76. Philip Kotler, William Gregor, and William Rodgers, "The Marketing Audit Comes of Age," *Sloan Management Review* (Winter 1989): 49–62. Frederick Reichheld, *The Loyalty Effect* (Boston: Harvard Business School Press, 1996) discusses attrition of the figures.

77. Useful checklists for a marketing self-audit can be found in Aubrey Wilson, *Aubrey Wilson's Marketing Audit Checklists* (London: McGraw-Hill, 1982) and Mike Wilson, *The Management of Marketing* (Westmead, England: Gower Publishing, 1980). A marketing-audit software program is described in Ben M. Enis and Stephen J. Garfein, "The Computer-Driven Marketing Audit," *Journal of Management Inquiry* (December 1992): 306–18.

78. Kotler, Gregor, and Rodgers, "The Marketing Audit Comes of Age," pp. 49–62.

79. Starbucks Customer Call Centre, 1-800-23-LATTE, August 2008.

GLOSSARY

activity-based cost (ABC) accounting procedures that can quantify the true profitability of different activities by identifying their actual costs.

adoption an individual's decision to become a regular user of a product.

advertising any paid form of nonpersonal presentation and promotion of ideas, goods, or services by an identified sponsor.

advertising goal (objective) a specific communication task and achievement level to be accomplished with a specific audience in a specific period of time.

advertorials print ads that offer editorial content that reflects favourably on the brand and resemble newspaper or magazine content.

alliances (or affiliate programs) situation where a company agrees to cooperate with another firm to accomplish a particular objective. For example, one Internet company works with another one to advertise each other's products or services.

anchoring and adjustment heuristic when consumers arrive at an initial judgment and then make adjustments of their first impressions based on additional information.

arm's-length price the price charged by other competitors for the same or a similar product.

aspirational groups groups a person hopes or would like to join.

associative network memory model a conceptual representation that views memory as consisting of a set of nodes and interconnecting links where nodes represent stored information or concepts and links represent the strength of association between different pieces of information or concepts.

attitude a person's enduring favourable or unfavourable evaluation, emotional feeling, and action tendencies toward some object or idea.

augmented product a product that includes features that go beyond consumer expectations and differentiate the product from competitors.

availability heuristic when consumers base their predictions on the quickness and ease with which a particular example of an outcome comes to mind.

available market the set of consumers who have interest, income, and access to a particular offer.

average cost the cost per unit at a given level of production; it is equal to total costs divided by production quantity.

backward invention reintroducing earlier product forms that can be well adapted to a foreign country's needs.

banner ads (Internet) small, rectangular boxes containing text and images to promote a brand or product.

basic product what, specifically, the actual product is.

belief a descriptive thought that a person holds about something.

brand a name, term, sign, symbol, or design, or a combination of these, intended to identify the goods or services of one seller or group of sellers and to differentiate them from those of competitors.

brand associations all brand-related thoughts, feelings, perceptions, images, experiences, beliefs, attitudes, and so on that become linked to the brand in a person's memory.

brand audit a consumer-focused exercise that involves a series of procedures to assess the health of the brand, uncover its sources of brand equity, and suggest ways to improve and leverage its equity.

brand awareness consumers' ability to identify the brand under different conditions, as reflected by their brand recognition or recall performance.

brand contact any information-bearing experience a customer or prospect has with a brand, product category, or the market that relates to a marketer's product or service.

brand development index (BDI) the index of brand sales to category sales.

brand dilution when consumers no longer associate a brand with a specific product or highly similar products or start thinking less favourably about the brand.

brand elements those trademarkable devices that serve to identify and differentiate a brand, such as a brand name, logo, or character.

brand equity the added value endowed to products and services.

brand extension a company's use of an established brand to introduce a new product.

brand image the perceptions and beliefs held by consumers, as reflected in the associations held in consumer memory.

brand knowledge all the thoughts, feelings, images, experiences, beliefs, and so on that become associated with a brand.

brand line all products, original as well as line and category extensions, sold under a particular brand name.

brand mix the set of all brand lines that a particular seller makes available to buyers.

brand personality the specific mix of human traits that may be attributed to a particular brand.

brand portfolio the set of all brands and brand lines a particular firm offers for sale to buyers in a particular category.

brand promise the marketer's vision of what a brand must be and do for consumers.

brand-tracking studies studies that collect quantitative data from consumers on a routine basis over time to provide marketers with consistent, baseline information about how their brands and marketing programs are performing on key dimensions.

brand valuation an estimate of the total financial value of a brand.

brand value chain a structured approach to assessing the sources and outcomes of brand equity and the manner in which marketing activities create brand value.

branded entertainment using sports, music, arts, or other entertainment activities to build brand equity.

branded variants specific brand lines uniquely supplied to different retailers or distribution channels.

branding endowing products and services with the power of a brand.

branding strategy the number and nature of common and distinctive brand elements applied to the different products sold by a firm.

break-even analysis a means by which management estimates how many units of a product the company would have to sell to break even with the given price and cost structure.

brick-and-click existing companies that have added an online site for information and/or e-commerce.

business database complete information about business customers' past purchases; past volumes, prices, and profits; buyer team-member names and information; status of current contracts; an estimate of the supplier's share of the customer's business; competitive suppliers; assessment of competitive strengths and weaknesses in selling and servicing the account; and relevant buying practices, patterns, and policies

business market all the organizations that acquire goods and services used in the production of other products or services that are sold, rented, or supplied to others.

capital items long-lasting goods that facilitate developing or managing a finished product.

captive products products that are necessary to the use of other products, such as razor blades or film.

category extension using a parent brand to brand a new product outside the product category currently served by the parent brand.

category membership the products or sets of products with which a brand competes and which function as close substitutes.

cause-related marketing marketing that links a firm's contributions to a designated cause to customers' engaging directly or indirectly in revenue-producing transactions with the firm.

channel advantage when a company successfully switches its customers to lower-cost channels, while assuming no loss of sales or deterioration in service quality.

channel conflict when one channel member's actions prevent the channel from achieving its goal.

channel coordination when channel members are brought together to advance the goals of the channel, as opposed to their own potentially incompatible goals.

channel power the ability to alter channel members' behaviour so that they take actions they would not otherwise take.

clustered preferences a situation where different groups (or clusters) of people with shared preferences populate a particular market segment.

co-branding situation in which two or more well-known existing brands are combined into a joint product and/or marketed together in some fashion.

communication adaptation changing marketing communications programs for each local market.

communication-effect research determining whether an ad is communicating effectively.

company demand a company's estimated share of market demand at alternative levels of company marketing effort in a given time period.

company sales forecast the expected level of company sales based on a chosen marketing plan and an assumed marketing environment.

competitive advantage a company's ability to perform in one or more ways that competitors cannot or will not match.

conformance quality the degree to which all produced units of a product are identical and meet promised specifications.

conjoint analysis a method for deriving the utility values that consumers attach to varying levels of a product's attributes.

conjunctive heuristic the consumer sets a minimum acceptable cutoff level for each attribute and chooses the first alternative that meets the minimum standard for all attributes.

consumer behaviour the study of how individuals, groups, and organizations select, buy, use, and dispose of goods, services, ideas, or experiences to satisfy their needs and wants.

consumer involvement the level of engagement and active processing undertaken by the consumer in responding to a marketing stimulus.

consumerist movement an organized movement of citizens and government to strengthen the rights and powers of buyers in relation to sellers.

consumption system the way a user performs the tasks of getting and using products and related services.

content-target advertising links ads to the content of a webpage rather than keywords.

contractual sales force manufacturers' reps, sales agents, and brokers, who are paid a commission based on sales.

convenience goods goods a consumer purchases frequently, immediately, and with minimal effort.

conventional marketing channel an independent producer, wholesaler(s), and retailer(s).

core benefit the service or benefit the customer is really buying.

core competency attribute that (1) is a source of competitive advantage in that it makes a significant contribution to perceived customer benefits, (2) has applications in a wide variety of markets, (3) is difficult for competitors to imitate.

core values the belief systems that underlie consumer attitudes and behaviour, and that determine people's choices and desires over the long term.

corporate culture the shared experiences, stories, beliefs, and norms that characterize an organization.

corporate retailing corporately owned retailing outlets that achieve economies of scale, greater purchasing power, wider brand recognition, and better-trained employees.

countertrade offering products, services, or other benefits instead of (or in combination with) money to make a purchase. It may take the form of barter, compensation deals, buyback agreements, and offset arrangements.

critical path scheduling (CPS) developing a master chart showing the simultaneous and sequential activities that must take place to launch a product.

cues stimuli that determine when, where, and how a person responds.

culture the fundamental determinant of a person's wants and behaviour.

customer-based brand equity the differential effect that brand knowledge has on a consumer response to the marketing of that brand.

customer churn high customer defection.

customer consulting data, information systems, and advice services that a seller offers to buyers.

customer database an organized collection of comprehensive information about individual customers or prospects that is current, accessible, and actionable for marketing purposes.

customer equity the total of the discounted lifetime values of all of a firm's customers.

customer lifetime value (CLV) the net present value of the stream of future profits expected over a customer's lifetime purchases.

customer mailing list a set of names, addresses, and telephone numbers.

customer perceived value (CPV) the difference between the prospective customer's evaluation of all the benefits and all the costs of an offering and the perceived alternatives.

customer-performance scorecard how well the company is doing year after year on particular customer-based measures.

customer-profitability analysis (CPA) a means of assessing and ranking customer profitability through accounting techniques such as activity-based costing (ABC).

customer relationship management (CRM) the process of managing detailed information about individual customers and carefully managing all customer "touch points" to maximize customer loyalty.

customer training training a customer's employees to use a vendor's equipment properly and efficiently.

customer value analysis report of the company's strengths and weaknesses relative to various competitors.

customer value hierarchy five product levels that must be addressed by marketers in planning a market offering.

customerization combination of operationally driven mass customization with customized marketing in a way that empowers consumers to design a product and service offering of their choice.

data warehouse a collection of current data captured, organized, and stored in a company's contact centre.

database marketing the process of building, maintaining, and using customer databases and other databases for the purpose of contacting, transacting, and building customer relationships.

datamining the extracting of useful information about individuals, trends, and segments from a mass of data.

delivery how well a product or service is delivered to a customer.

demand chain planning the process of designing the supply chain based on adopting a target market perspective and working backward.

design the totality of features that affect how a product looks and functions in terms of customer requirements.

diffused preferences a situation where members of a particular market segment have diffused or widely varying preferences.

direct marketing the use of consumer-direct (CD) channels to reach and deliver goods and services to customers without using marketing intermediaries.

direct-marketing channel channel in which the manufacturer sells directly to the final customer.

direct-order marketing marketing in which direct marketers seek a measurable response, typically a customer order.

direct product profitability (DDP) a way of measuring a product's handling costs from the time it reaches a warehouse until a customer buys it in a retail store.

direct (company) sales force full- or part-time paid sales employees who work exclusively for the company.

discrimination the process of recognizing differences in sets of similar stimuli and adjusting responses accordingly.

dissociative groups those groups whose values or behaviour an individual rejects.

distribution programming building a planned, professionally managed, vertical marketing system that meets the needs of both manufacturer and distributors.

drive a strong internal stimulus impelling action.

dual adaptation adapting both a product and communications to a local market.

dumping situation in which a company charges either less than its costs or less than it charges in its home market, in order to enter or win a market.

durability a measure of a product's expected operating life under natural or stressful conditions.

e-business the use of electronic means and platforms to conduct a company's business.

e-commerce a company or site offers to transact or facilitate the selling of products and services online.

e-marketing company efforts to inform buyers and communicate, promote, and sell its products and services over the Internet.

e-procurement purchase of goods, services, and information from various online suppliers.

elimination-by-aspects heuristic a situation in which a consumer compares brands on an attribute selected probabilistically, and brands are eliminated if they do not meet minimum acceptable cutoff levels.

environmental threat a challenge posed by an unfavourable trend or development that would lead to lower sales or profit.

everyday low pricing (EDLP) in retailing, a constant low price with few or no price promotions and special sales.

exchange the process of obtaining a desired product from someone by offering something in return.

exclusive distribution severely limiting the number of intermediaries, in order to maintain control over the service level and outputs offered by resellers.

expectancy-value model consumers evaluate products and services by combining their brand beliefs—positive and negative—according to their weighted importance.

expected product a set of attributes and conditions buyers normally expect when they purchase a product.

experience curve (learning curve) a decline in the average cost with accumulated production experience.

fad a craze that is unpredictable, short-lived, and without social, economic, and political significance.

family brand situation in which the parent brand is already associated with multiple products through brand extensions.

family of orientation a person's parents and siblings.

family of procreation a person's spouse and children.

features things that enhance the basic function of a product.

fixed costs (overhead) costs that do not vary with production or sales revenue.

flexible market offering an offering that includes (1) a naked solution containing the product and service elements that all segment members value, and (2) discretionary options that some segment members value.

focus group a gathering of six to ten people who are carefully selected based on certain demographic, psychographic, or other considerations and brought together to discuss various topics of interest.

forecasting the art of anticipating what buyers are likely to do under a given set of conditions.

form the size, shape, or physical structure of a product.

forward invention creating a new product to meet a need in another country.

frequency programs (FPs) designed to provide rewards to customers who buy frequently and in substantial amounts.

generics unbranded, plainly packaged, less expensive versions of common products.

global firm a firm that operates in more than one country and captures R&D, production, logistical, marketing, and financial advantages in its costs and reputation that are not available to purely domestic competitors.

global industry an industry in which the strategic positions of competitors in major geographic or national markets are fundamentally affected by their overall global positions.

goal formulation the process of developing specific goals for a planning period.

going-rate pricing basing product prices largely on competitors' prices.

grey market branded products diverted from normal or authorized distribution channels in the country of product origin or across international borders.

heuristics rules of thumb or mental shortcuts in a decision process.

high-low pricing charging higher prices on an everyday basis but then running frequent promotions and special sales.

holistic marketing a concept based on the development, design, and implementation of marketing programs, processes, and activities that recognizes their breadth and interdependencies.

homogeneous preferences a situation when all customers in a particular market segment have the same preferences.

horizontal marketing system two or more unrelated companies put together resources or create programs to exploit an emerging market opportunity.

hybrid channels use of multiple channels of distribution to reach customers in a defined market.

image the set of beliefs, ideas, and impressions a person holds regarding an object.

industry a group of firms that offer a product or class of products that are close substitutes for one another.

ingredient branding a special case of co-branding that involves creating brand equity for materials, components, or parts that are necessarily contained within other branded products.

innovation diffusion process the spread of a new idea from its source of invention or creation to its ultimate users or adopters.

innovation any good, service, or idea that is perceived by someone as new.

installation the work required to make a product operational in its planned location.

institutional market schools, hospitals, nursing homes, prisons, and other institutions that must provide goods and services to people in their care.

integrated logistics systems (ILS) materials management, material flow systems, and physical distribution, abetted by information technology (IT).

integrated marketing communications (IMC) a concept of marketing communications planning that recognizes the added value of a comprehensive plan.

integrated marketing mixing and matching marketing activities to maximize their individual and collective efforts.

integrated marketing channel system a system in which the strategies and tactics of selling through one channel reflect the strategies and tactics of selling through other channels.

intensive distribution a manufacturer placing goods or services in as many outlets as possible.

internal branding activities and processes that help to inform and inspire employees.

interstitials advertisements, often with video or animation, that pop up between changes on a website.

joint venture a company in which multiple investors share ownership and control.

learning changes in an individual's behaviour arising from experience.

lexicographic heuristic consumer choosing the best brand on the basis of its perceived most important attribute.

licensed product one whose brand name has been licensed to other manufacturers who actually make the product.

life-cycle cost the product's purchase cost plus the discounted cost of maintenance and repair less the discounted salvage value.

life stage part of the life cycle; defines a person's major concerns, such as going through a divorce or taking care of an older parent.

lifestyle a person's pattern of living in the world as expressed in activities, interests, and opinions.

line extension a parent brand is used to brand a new product that targets a new market segment within a product category currently served by the parent brand.

line stretching when a company lengthens its product line beyond its current range.

long-term memory (LTM) a permanent repository of information.

loyalty a commitment to rebuy or repatronize a preferred product or service.

maintenance and repair a service program for helping customers keep purchased products in good working order.

market approach (to competition) defines competitors as firms that satisfy the same customer need.

market-buildup method method in which a firm identifies all the potential buyers in each market and estimates their potential purchases.

market demand the total volume of a product that would be bought by a defined customer group in a defined geographical area in a defined time period in a defined marketing environment under a defined marketing program.

market forecast the market demand corresponding to the level of industry marketing expenditure.

market logistics planning the infrastructure to meet demand, then implementing and controlling the physical flows or materials and final goods from points of origin to points of use, to meet customer requirements at a profit.

market opportunity analysis (MOA) a system used to determine the attractiveness and probability of success in a market.

market penetration index a comparison of the current level of market demand to the potential demand level.

market potential the upper limit to market demand whereby increased marketing expenditures would not be expected to stimulate further demand.

market share a company's share of a total market expressed as a percentage of the revenues the firm earns as a portion of total market revenues or the volume it sells as a portion of the total volume sold in the marketplace.

marketer someone who seeks a response (attention, a purchase, a vote, a donation) from another party, called the prospect.

marketing process of planning and executing the conception, pricing, promotion, and distribution of ideas, goods, and services to create exchanges that satisfy individual and organizational goals.

marketing audit a comprehensive, systematic, independent, and periodic examination of a company's or business unit's marketing environment, objectives, strategies, and activities.

marketing channel system the particular set of marketing channels employed by a firm.

marketing channels sets of interdependent organizations involved in the process of making a product or service available for use or consumption.

marketing communications the means by which firms attempt to inform, persuade, and remind consumers—directly or indirectly—about products and brands that they sell.

marketing communications mix advertising, sales promotion, events and experiences, public relations and publicity, direct marketing, and personal selling.

marketing decision-support system (MDSS) a coordinated collection of data, systems, tools, and techniques with supporting software and hardware by which an organization gathers and interprets relevant information from business and the environment and turns it into a basis for marketing action.

marketing implementation the process that turns marketing plans into action assignments and ensures that such assignments are executed in a manner that accomplishes the plan's stated objectives.

marketing information system (MIS) the people, equipment, and procedures used to gather, sort, analyze, evaluate, and distribute information to marketing decision makers.

marketing intelligence system a set of procedures and sources managers use to obtain everyday information about developments in the marketing environment.

marketing management the art and science of choosing target markets and getting, keeping, and growing customers through creating, delivering, and communicating superior customer value.

marketing metrics the set of measures that helps firms to quantify, compare, and interpret their marketing performance.

marketing network a company and its supporting stakeholders, with whom it has built mutually profitable business relationships.

marketing opportunity an area of buyer need and interest in which there is a high probability that a company can profitably satisfy that need.

marketing plan written document that summarizes what a marketer has learned about the marketplace, indicates how the firm plans to reach its marketing objectives, and helps direct and coordinate the marketing effort.

marketing public relations (MPR) publicity and other activities that build corporate or product image to facilitate marketing goals.

marketing research the systematic design, collection, analysis, and reporting of data and findings relevant to a specific marketing situation facing a company.

market-penetration pricing pricing strategy where prices start low to drive higher sales volume from price-sensitive customers and produce productivity gains.

market-skimming pricing pricing strategy where prices start high and are slowly lowered over time to maximize profits from less price-sensitive customers.

markup pricing an item by adding a standard increase to the product's cost.

mass customization the ability of a company to meet each customer's requirements—to prepare on a mass basis individually designed products, services, programs, and communications.

mass marketing situation in which a seller engages in mass production, mass distribution, and mass promotion of one product for all buyers.

materials and parts goods that enter a manufacturer's product completely.

media selection finding the most cost-effective media to deliver the desired number and type of exposures to a target audience.

megamarketing the strategic coordination of economic, psychological, political, and public relations skills to gain the cooperation of a number of parties in order to enter or operate in a given market.

megatrends large social, economic, political, and technological changes that are slow to form, and once in place have an influence for seven to ten years or longer.

membership groups groups having a direct influence on a person.

memory encoding how and where information is stored in memory.

memory retrieval how and from where information is retrieved from memory.

mental accounting the manner by which consumers code, categorize, and evaluate financial outcomes of choices.

microsales analysis examination of specific products and territories that fail to produce expected sales.

microsite a limited area on the web managed and paid for by an external advertiser/company.

mission statements statements of purpose that organizations develop to share with managers, employees, and (in many cases) customers.

mixed bundling a seller offers goods both individually and in bundles.

motive a need that is sufficiently pressing to drive a person to act.

multi-channel marketing a single firm uses two or more marketing channels to reach one or more customer segments.

multitasking doing two or more things at the same time.

N

net price analysis analysis that encompasses company list price, average discount, promotional spending, and co-op advertising to arrive at net price.

noncompensatory models in consumer choice, when consumers do not simultaneously consider all positive and negative attribute considerations in making a decision.

O

opinion leader the person in informal, product-related communications who offers advice or information about a specific product or product category.

ordering ease how easy it is for a customer to place an order with a company.

organization a company's structures, policies, and corporate culture.

organizational buying the decision-making process by which formal organizations establish a need for purchased products and services and identify, evaluate, and choose among alternative brands and suppliers.

overall market share the company's sales expressed as a percentage of total market sales.

overhead costs that do not vary with production or sales revenue.

P

packaging all the activities of designing and producing the container for a product.

parent brand an existing brand that gives birth to a brand extension.

partner relationship management (PRM) activities a firm undertakes to build mutually satisfying long-term relations with key partners such as suppliers, distributors, ad agencies, and marketing research suppliers.

penetrated market the set of consumers who are buying a company's product.

perceived value the value promised by the company's value proposition and perceived by the customer.

perception the process by which an individual selects, organizes, and interprets information inputs to create a meaningful picture of the world.

performance quality the level at which a product's primary characteristics operate.

personal communication channels two or more persons communicating directly face-to-face, person-to-audience, over the telephone, or through e-mail.

personal influence the effect one person has on another's attitude or purchase probability.

personality a set of distinguishing human psychological traits that lead to relatively consistent responses to environmental stimuli.

place advertising (also out-of-home advertising) ads that appear outside of the home and where consumers work and play.

point-of-purchase (P-O-P) the location where a purchase is made, typically thought of in terms of a retail setting.

positioning the act of designing a company's offering and image to occupy a distinctive place in the mind of the target market.

potential market the set of consumers who profess a sufficient level of interest in a market offer.

price discrimination a company sells a product or service at two or more prices that do not reflect a proportional difference in costs.

price escalation an increase in the price of a product due to added costs of selling it in different countries.

primary groups groups with which a person interacts continuously and informally, such as family, friends, neighbours, and co-workers.

principle of congruity psychological mechanism that states that consumers like to see seemingly related objects as being as similar as possible in their favourability.

private label brands brands that retailers and wholesalers develop and market.

product anything that can be offered to a market to satisfy a want or need.

product adaptation altering a product to meet local conditions or preferences.

product assortment the set of all products and items a particular seller offers for sale.

product invention creating something new via product development or other means.

product mix see product assortment.

product penetration percentage the percentage of ownership or use of a product or service in a population.

product system a group of diverse but related items that function in a compatible manner.

profitable customer a person, household, or company that over time yields a revenue stream that exceeds by an acceptable amount the company's cost stream of attracting, selling, and servicing that customer.

prospect person or group from whom a marketer is seeking a response (e.g., attention, a purchase, a vote, a donation).

prospect theory when consumers frame decision alternatives in terms of gains and losses according to a value function.

psychographics the science of using psychology and demographics to better understand consumers.

public any group that has an actual or potential interest in or impact on a company's ability to achieve its objectives.

public relations (PR) a variety of programs designed to promote or protect a company's image or its individual products.

publicity the task of securing editorial space—as opposed to paid space—in print and broadcast media to promote something.

pull strategy when a manufacturer uses advertising and promotion to persuade consumers to ask intermediaries for the product, thus inducing the intermediaries to order it.

purchase probability scale a scale to measure the probability of a buyer making a particular purchase.

pure bundling a firm only offers its products as a bundle.

pure-online companies that have launched a website without any previous existence as a firm.

push strategy when a manufacturer uses its sales force and trade promotion money to induce intermediaries to carry, promote, and sell the product to end users.

Q

quality the totality of features and characteristics of a product or service that bear on its ability to satisfy stated or implied needs.

R

reference groups all the groups that have a direct or indirect influence on a person's attitudes or behaviour.

reference prices pricing information a consumer retains in memory that is used to interpret and evaluate a new price.

relational equity the cumulative value of a firm's network of relationships with its customers, partners, suppliers, employees, and investors.

relationship marketing building mutually satisfying long-term relationships with key parties in order to earn and retain their business.

relative market share market share in relation to a company's largest competitor.

reliability a measure of the probability that a product will not malfunction or fail within a specified time period.

reparability a measure of the ease of fixing a product when it malfunctions or fails.

representativeness heuristic when consumers base their predictions on how representative or similar an outcome is to other examples.

retailer (or retail store) any business enterprise whose sales volume comes primarily from retailing.

retailing all the activities involved in selling goods or services directly to final consumers for personal, nonbusiness use.

returns products that consumers return to a seller for a refund.

risk analysis a method by which possible rates of returns and their probabilities are calculated by obtaining estimates for uncertain variables affecting profitability.

role the activities a person is expected to perform.

S

sales analysis measuring and evaluating actual sales in relation to goals.

sales budget a conservative estimate of the expected volume of sales, used for making current purchasing, production, and cash flow decisions.

sales promotion a collection of incentive tools, mostly short term, designed to stimulate quicker or greater purchase of particular products or services by consumers or the trade.

sales quota the sales goal set for a product line, company division, or sales representative.

sales-variance analysis a measure of the relative contribution of different factors to a gap in sales performance.

satisfaction a person's feelings of pleasure or disappointment resulting from comparing a product's perceived performance or outcome in relation to his or her expectations.

search-related ads ads in which search terms are used as a proxy for the consumer's consumption interests and relevant links to product or service offerings are listed alongside the search results.

secondary groups groups that tend to be more formal and require less interaction than primary groups, such as religious, professional, and trade-union groups.

selective attention the mental process of screening out certain stimuli while noticing others.

selective distortion the tendency to interpret product information in a way that fits consumer perceptions.

selective distribution the use of more than a few but less than all of the intermediaries who are willing to carry a particular product.

selective retention good points about a product that consumers like are remembered and good points about competing products are forgotten.

served market all the buyers who are able and willing to buy a company's product.

served market share a company's sales expressed as a percentage of the total sales to its served market.

service any act or performance that one party can offer to another that is essentially intangible and does not result in the ownership of anything.

share penetration index a comparison of a company's current market share to its potential market share.

shopping goods goods that a consumer, in the process of selection and purchase, characteristically compares on such bases as suitability, quality, price, and style.

short-term memory (STM) a temporary repository of information.

social classes homogeneous and enduring divisions in a society that are hierarchically ordered and whose members share similar values, interests, and behaviour.

social marketing marketing done by a nonprofit or government organization to further a cause, such as "say no to drugs."

specialty goods goods that have unique characteristics or brand identification for which a sufficient number of buyers are willing to make a special purchasing effort.

sponsorship financial support of an event or activity in return for recognition and acknowledgment as the sponsor.

stakeholder-performance scorecard a measure to track the satisfaction of various constituencies who have a critical interest in and impact on a company's performance.

status a person's position within their own hierarchy or culture.

straight extension introducing a product in a foreign market without any change in the product.

strategic brand management the design and implementation of marketing activities and programs to build, measure, and manage brands to maximize their value.

strategic business units (SBUs) a single business or collection of related businesses that can be planned separately from the rest of the company, with its own set of competitors and a manager who is responsible for strategic planning and profit performance.

strategic group firms pursuing the same strategy directed to the same target market.

strategic marketing plan laying out the target markets and the value proposition that will be offered, based on analysis of the best market opportunities.

strategy a company's game plan for achieving its goals.

style a product's look and feel to a buyer.

sub-brand a new brand combined with an existing brand.

subcultures subdivisions of a culture that provide more specific identification and socialization, such as nationalities, religions, racial groups, and geographical regions.

subliminal perception receiving and processing subconscious messages that affect behaviour.

super-segment a set of segments sharing some exploitable similarity.

supplies and business services short-term goods and services that facilitate developing or managing a finished product.

supply chain see value-delivery network.

supply chain management (SCM) procuring the right inputs (raw materials, components, and capital equipment); converting them efficiently into finished products; and dispatching them to the final destinations.

T

tactical marketing plan marketing tactics, including product features, promotion, merchandising, pricing, sales channels, and service.

target costing deducting the desired profit margin from the price at which a product will sell, given its appeal and competitors' prices.

target market the part of the qualified available market a company decides to pursue.

target-return pricing determining the price that would yield the firm's target rate of return on investment (ROI).

telemarketing the use of telephone and call centres to attract prospects, sell to existing customers, and provide service by taking orders and answering questions.

total costs the sum of the fixed and variable costs for any given level of production.

total customer cost the bundle of costs customers expect to incur in evaluating, obtaining, using, and disposing of a given market offering, including monetary, time, energy, and psychic costs.

total customer value the perceived monetary value of the bundle of economic, functional, and psychological benefits customers expect from a given market offering.

total quality management (TQM) an organization-wide approach to continuously improving the quality of all the organization's processes, products, and services.

tracking studies collecting information from consumers on a routine basis over time.

transfer price the price a company charges another unit in the company for goods it ships to foreign subsidiaries.

trend a direction or sequence of events that has some momentum and durability.

two-part pricing selling a product for a fixed fee plus a variable usage fee.

tying agreements agreements in which producers of strong brands sell their products to dealers only if dealers purchase related products or services, such as other products in the brand line.

unsought goods goods consumers do not know about or do not normally think of buying, like smoke detectors.

value chain a tool for identifying ways to create more customer value; identifies strategically relevant activities that create value and cost in a specific business.

value-delivery network (or supply chain) a company's supply chain and how it partners with specific suppliers and distributors to make products and bring them to markets.

value-delivery system all the expectancies the customer will have on the way to obtaining and using an offering.

value network a system of partnerships and alliances that a firm creates to source, augment, and deliver its offerings.

value pricing winning loyal customers by charging a fairly low price for a high-quality offering.

value proposition the whole cluster of benefits a company promises to deliver.

variable costs costs that vary directly with the level of production.

venture team a cross-functional group charged with developing a specific product or business.

vertical integration situation in which manufacturers try to control or own their suppliers, distributors, or other intermediaries.

vertical marketing system (VMS) producer, wholesaler(s), and retailer(s) acting as a unified system.

viral marketing using the Internet to create word of mouth effects to support marketing efforts and goals.

wholesaling all the activities involved in selling goods or services to those who buy for resale or business use.

yield pricing situation in which companies offer (1) discounted but limited early purchases, (2) higher-priced late purchases, and (3) the lowest rates on unsold inventory just before it expires.

zero-level channel (direct-marketing channel) a manufacturer selling directly to the final customer.

NAME INDEX

Note: *f* denotes a figure, *t* denotes a table, *n* denotes sourcelines.

COMPANY/BRAND INDEX

SUBJECT INDEX

CREDITS